CROSS-TALK IN COMP THEORY

CROSS-TALK IN COMP THEORY

A Reader

Fourth Edition

Edited by

Kristin L. Arola
Michigan State University

Victor Villanueva
Washington State University, Retired

National Council of Teachers of English
340 N. Neil St., Suite #104, Champaign, Illinois 61820

Staff Editor: Cynthia Gomez
Interior Design: Precision Graphics
Typesetting: Barbara Frazier
Cover Design: Pat Mayer
Cover Image: iStock.com/hqrloveq

ISBN (print): 978-0-8141-0158-2; ISBN (epub): 978-0-8141-0159-9; ISBN (PDF): 978-0-8141-0160-5
©2023 by the National Council of Teachers of English.

It is the policy of NCTE in its journals and other publications to provide a forum for the open discussion of ideas concerning the content and the teaching of English and the language arts. Publicity accorded to any particular point of view does not imply endorsement by the Executive Committee, the Board of Directors, or the membership at large, except in announcements of policy, where such endorsement is clearly specified.

NCTE provides equal employment opportunity (EEO) to all staff members and applicants for employment without regard to race, color, religion, sex, national origin, age, physical, mental or perceived handicap/disability, sexual orientation including gender identity or expression, ancestry, genetic information, marital status, military status, unfavorable discharge from military service, pregnancy, citizenship status, personal appearance, matriculation or political affiliation, or any other protected status under applicable federal, state, and local laws.

Every effort has been made to provide current URLs and email addresses, but because of the rapidly changing nature of the web, some sites and addresses may no longer be accessible.

Library of Congress Control Number: 2023944354

To the teachers who inspire me,
the students who challenge me,
the relations who keep me honest,
and to Jeff and Cecil for helping me imagine new worlds.
—Kristin L. Arola

For the students over the decades,
Those who went out into the world,
And those who are now Professors of Rhetoric and Writing Studies.
To my Babies and their Babies
The joys of being a father and of being a grandfather.
And Rochelle, more than a mate; no greater a friend.
—Victor Villanueva

Contents

Contents

Preface to the Fourth Edition

Cross-Talk in Comp Theory is a collection of pivotal texts that mark the rebirth of a field, composition, that began with the rise of the process movement. And along the way, the collection has been thrice revised to account for shortfalls and/or changing conversations. The second edition gave increased attention to the significance of gender, the rise in voices of people of color, and the move toward technology. The third edition deepened the conversation as it included technology and multimodal composing while keeping most of what had been important in prior editions of the collection. In the fourth edition, we recognize that discussions of discourse have become commonplace. Meanwhile, issues of social justice—who we teach, how we teach, who "we" are—have become much more prevalent. Additionally, as technology changes, so too do our discussions of the role of technology and multimodality in our classrooms. And so, here we arrive at a fourth edition.

FROM VICTOR

A friend reminded me that retirement in Spanish is *la jubilación*, not withdrawal or seclusion (the root for the word *retire*), not a kind of isolation, but jubilation, the joy of a new phase in life that doesn't necessitate leaving one's earlier phases.

In this new phase, I take joy in learning more of my ancestry, the story of the forever colony that has always been a part of my identity, even as I became English dominant and moved further and further away from the homelands I have nevertheless always claimed: Puerto Rico and the Puerto Ricans of New York. And the teacher in me (four decades, making for more than a "phase") has me compelled to pass on this new learning (even if what I learn is known to those raised on the Island), tapping into whatever skills I might claim as a writer, never ever removed from rhetoric and from writing, the learning that has filled my life for those forty years and more.

But even as I realized that *Cross-Talk* would never be complete, no more than there is such a thing as a truly final draft (only a submission draft), I was nagged by the exclusions that students and other writers would have me face, not as criticisms of *Cross-Talk* but in their own dedications to other otherings. Would Kristin join me—even take the lead—in one more edition, as the profession discusses the should-never-have-been-forgotten and discusses the new discoveries brought about by technology? She would. She has. And this is it: one more nudge at the complexities of learning about writing and the teaching of writing, and all the technologies that arise from the fully human drive of rhetoric.

FROM KRISTIN

Time is a circle, or so my Ojibwe friends and family tell me. To come from reading the first edition of *Cross-Talk* as a wide-eyed MA student in Flagstaff to having my mentor ask me—a young, nervous, pre-tenured scholar—to join him in composing the third edition to now watching him retire as I imagine what this anthology might look like in future editions, and who I might ask to join me, is bittersweet, and full of beginnings, and endings, and around we go.

As Victor and I thought through this new edition, we wanted to keep the big conversations of where comp has been while also making sure to add the newer conversations of where it should go, particularly when it comes to issues of inclusivity. You'll see some of our biggest changes in Section 4 with the addition of queer composition (Alexander and Rhodes), rhetorical sovereignty (Lyons), translingualism (Matsuda and Gilyard), antiracist pedagogy (Inoue), and (dis)ability (Kerschbaum). While it is impossible to account for all conversations in an anthology as capacious as *Cross-Talk*, we believe these additions speak more robustly about where we are in our discipline currently. Specifically, these essays call to question issues of standards, assimilation, agency, and power.

Revisiting the final section, "Virtual Talk," the section that Victor originally brought me on to add, was again a reminder of the squishiness of time. The third edition section break, which I remember working on for weeks in a Pullman, Washington, coffeeshop, reads like a version of myself caught between my graduate student self and the young scholar I was becoming. My words in that section break are so carefully chosen, citations plucked to boost my ethos, and articles chosen that had shaped me as a computer and writing scholar. Yet now, some ten plus years after the third edition was written, the conversations continue to change, as they do, and I have continued to find my footing. I hope this version captures where we've been and where we might be headed.

While I feel much more grounded as a mid-career scholar than I did as the pre-tenure, uncertain, mess-of-nerves I was ten years ago, I am forever grateful for the amazing graduate students I get to work with who push and challenge me. This next generation of students, including folks like Everardo Cuevas, Roland Dumavor, and Nissele Contreras, who I have the great pleasure of learning from and with, are much bolder and unapologetic in their calls for justice than I ever was. Their voices sit on my shoulders as I write, reminding me of the generations yet to come, of the work we have left to do, and of the ways time is, in fact, a circle.

Preface to the Third Edition

FROM VICTOR

My father was a mechanic for the army during World War II. And he used to state proudly that he had attended a school for auto mechanics under the GI Bill (essentially, his ninth-grade education). So he would tell me about cars, and as a good son, I would listen. I got the basics of the internal combustion engine. So I know that that squeaky sound under the hood means a belt needs tightening and that the jerkiness of the chassis means time for new plugs or distributor (and usually both). I listen to Click and Clack on NPR on Sundays and usually guess right before Tom and Ray finish chortling. But for all of that, I can't say that I know anything really about cars, apart from being glad to own one (fossil fuel issues notwithstanding).

My relation with cars is somewhat analogous to my relation with computers. I worked as a computer operator when I was eighteen years old, the Honeywell H200, one of the seven competitors to IBM. And even as I worked for an IBM competitor, I started to learn FORTRAN (but dropped out) and began to learn (well, for a few weeks) what would become Pascal, even took a night course on programming (which I never finished). I wrote my dissertation on the first Apple model. Did DOS a few years later, and friends across the nation and I tried to figure out how to make email work in 1992. Returned to Apple in 1995, even as a friend who worked for Microsoft told me that there would be no Apple in a couple of years. And now when things explode (remember the little Mac bomb?), I tend to figure my way around. I don't shout obscenities at the machine; I go "hmm." Yet my interest in computers, apart from my "driving" them, was never piqued. So while there has been a conversation going on in composition studies for as long as I've been in this profession, I have been willfully deaf.

But I have students who force me to think about computer gaming or the new ways ideologies are represented in digital media, hypertextually. Just two examples: Chris Ritter had me consider how racial stereotypes are morphed into racialized stereotypes in the avatars of *World of Warcraft*, and Paul Muhlhauser looked to all kinds of representations in the human gamete industry. Patty Ericsson makes my head spin as she tells of discussions she assumes I know about—but don't. And through her students I learn of the rhetorics of bureaucracy in a digitized world. Jason Farman had me look at "mobile interface theory." Kristin Arola makes me think of Web design and identity. I read, discuss, and learn.

The discussions concerning computers and composition studies are rich, and have been for some time. So we offer one more edition of *Cross-Talk*, to include a glimpse at the conversation concerning the digital paradigm. But since I can't really compensate for a quarter-century of ignorance, I have asked a colleague, Kristin Arola, to help me out. She did more than help, however. She constructed the new Section Six of the collection— "Virtual Talk." In keeping with the basic premise of this book, this section is not comprehensive, but is, rather, fuel with which to prime the pump: some talk and some cross-talk, the utopic and the dystopic, maybe.

Otherwise, the collection remains pretty much the same, some additions and some deletions to reflect current conversations (and to satisfy publisher-imposed page limits). My hope—our hope, Kristin's and mine—is that this collection will continue to serve the needs of those coming into the conversations in our community of theorists of the teaching of writing.

FROM KRISTIN

Cross-Talk has always been with me: in the hallways of Northern Arizona University as a wide-eyed first-year master's student; at my family holiday dinners when I tried to explain what it was that I was actually *doing* in graduate school; and as I wrote my dissertation at Michigan Tech, when I tried to place my work within a larger narrative of composition studies. Yet I often found myself holding the history of composition in one hand and the history of computers and writing in the other. We all come from similar training, and we all are concerned with how to best teach first-year composition, but at times I found it difficult to pull these two strands together.

Truthfully, for me, coming of age in the digital era and going to graduate school when you couldn't swing a dead cat without hitting a PhD student whose research focused on digital-or-visual-something-or-other, I found it easy to stick with the computers and writing canon. I knew that Composition (capital C) and Computers and Writing (capital CW) were inextricable, yet the latter felt like the sexy choice. Even today, I feel this pull when I choose one conference over another, or read one journal over the other. Yet I think there's a lot to be learned when we place folks like Donald Murray alongside Cindy Selfe, or James Berlin alongside Richard Ohmann. They might not be talking directly to each other, but if we listen closely enough we'll hear the resonances and the dissonances, and perhaps be able to see how the digital is not, and should not be, relegated to its own corner of the field.

As Victor has (repeatedly) reminded me, it is nearly impossible to encapsulate thirty years of conversation in six essays. Yet I hope the essays that constitute Section Six create a cross-talk not only with one another, but also with the other pieces in the collection. We need to be talking with one another and finding connections, because even if we don't research the digital, it informs, and is, the stuff with which we work every day.

Preface to the Second Edition

Second editions are like movie sequels. And I don't figure I've got a Part II to *The Godfather* or *Aliens*. But the profession has continued to move ahead, so the sequel to *Cross-Talk* seems like a good idea. One of the editors kept referring to it as "Son of Cross-Talk."

The acorn hasn't landed far from the tree, though. The book isn't all that different from the first edition. It's still divided into the same categories. My biases remain my biases, though as in the first edition, I try to remain true to the profession by giving preference to essays that are most frequently cited. And as in the first edition, there are a lot of interesting things going on in composition studies that don't get addressed, things like empirical research, assessment, or linguistics.

But some things have happened since I conducted the research for the first edition in 1992 to 1994. The most remarkable has been the technological explosion, with new software packages that affect our work coming out weekly, or so it seems, and with the pervasiveness of the Internet and its World Wide Web. The Net changed the way I conducted the research for this volume, a two-year process reduced to a few weeks on computerized databases and journal archives on the Web—often with whole texts available at the stroke of a few keys. Yet for all that, it doesn't appear as if technology has made its way into our theoretical discussions. Despite the great work of Cynthia Selfe and Gail Hawisher, not much has emerged in our journals that can stand the test of time—not because of any shortcoming in our scholars but because of the speed with which the things written about become archaic, this morning's innovation becoming this evening's anachronism. Technology has been included in this version, but not significantly, surely not as significantly as its presence in our lives would suggest.

In a very real sense, *Cross-Talk* is intended as a historical artifact, a way of tracking theoretical discussions in a field that continues to find itself forming its theoretical foundations. Even the givens of comp—writing as process—are contending with cross-talk, like post-process theory. It's hard to track the history we're in.

The other big change in composition studies—at least in our journals—has been the increased presence of writers of color and the greater acceptance of critical pedagogy. As I point out in the final essay to this volume, writers of color are still not present in this profession in the kinds of numbers that would affect our discussions on racism in truly meaningful ways, but something did happen in the second half of the 1990s: the beginnings of rich discussion on racism clearly centered on the concerns of this profession (a somewhat different set of discussions on racism from those which took place in journals like *College English* at the beginning of the second half of the twentieth century).

Readers of the first edition will likely miss the discussion between Peter Elbow and David Bartholomae. It was, I recognize, an interesting discussion centering on academic discourse versus other kinds of writing. It's gone because the discussion has taken a different turn—the personal versus the academic. That discussion has its representatives here, through Gesa Kirsch and Joy Ritchie, through Jacqueline Jones Royster, and in some sense through Richard Miller. Joy Ritchie and Kathleen Boardman broaden the discussion on feminism. And service learning is introduced, a relatively new entry into the conversation on composition.

Composition studies has moved on. New students are learning of our field, a field still in flux, still growing. It was time to account for the 1990s in the conversation, in the talk and cross-talk. Something gets lost with a sequel, I know, even a good sequel. Robert De Niro might have been great, but I missed Brando. Some of the Brandos will be missed in Son of Cross-Talk, but I trust this sequel will continue to serve, to initiate graduate students and more experienced teachers into the theories that inform composition studies.

Preface to the First Edition

I wanted to prepare a healthier pancake for the children. The whole-wheat recipe in the healthier cookbook hadn't quite gone over. But my adjustments made for pretty pancakes that came out, time and again, uncooked at the center. I figured I'd better add another egg to the batter next time around. And that worked. That egg added just the touch more leavening the batter needed, the touch more air to cook the batter through. If I had wanted to go just a bit healthier, I could have substituted that egg with two egg whites, beaten to a froth, since the fat of the yolk wouldn't have been necessary to the batter, as it would have been for, say, a custard. I made healthy pancakes that the kids would (and did and do) eat.

The point is this: I could adjust, take control of the process, because I had an understanding of how eggs work in cooking. I understood the theory.

But then, theories of leavening have been pretty well worked out. Theories of written composition have not. And operating from the gut, what feels right, what sounds right, what might be fun for the students, can too easily lead to theoretical contradictions. And students know. I don't know how they know, but they seem to sense or maybe outwardly recognize theoretical inconsistencies, reacting too often with passive compliance, never arriving at the full benefits possible in engaging—really engaging—in written discourse.

What those benefits of literacy might be aren't exactly clear, though. Plato tells of the god Thoth claiming that writing would be the key to remembrance. And writing was, we are told, used as a memory aid, a mnemonic device. In recent times, as we will find in the articles to follow, writing has been credited with learning, cognitive development, social cohesion, political power. What writing can provide has never been altogether clear.

So composition studies has divided itself, either to find out what writing is, or how to teach it better, or to discern the degree to which it either removes or bestows power. Composition studies finds its historicists (with some compositionists as revisionist historicists), current-traditionalists, cognitivists, expressionists, social-constructionists (who tend also to be epistemicists), empiricists, anti-foundationalists, and leftists, among others. Academic books on composition studies tend to historicize, theorize, polemicize, or synthesize, as well as proselytize. Composition is complex and diverse.

But with the greater diversity and sophistication has come greater confusion. I have seen teachers come to accept writing as a process, a common-enough notion nowadays, without recognizing the theoretical bases to different approaches to process. I have heard a new compositionist on the job market betray his confusion, claiming a Marxist bent, yet aligning himself with Kenneth Bruffee and Peter Elbow—highly respected compositionists, but hardly representatives of the political left. Another candidate clearly knew research on composition (for which there are several good collections) but seemed not to know of the philosophical objections to classical-empirical research. The overwhelming majority of candidates—even those fortunate enough to study with prestigious compositionists—seem unable to navigate their ways through composition's currents.

What follows, then, is an aid for you—the teacher of graduate composition theory, the graduate student of composition, the veteran teacher of composition back in the graduate comp course. What follows is a book of readings whose objective is to introduce you to some of the concepts and methods available to writing teachers today and to have you regard some of the controversy. This is a reader of previously published works, mainly by those who tend to be mentioned in the works of others. The book's further objective is to have you begin to consider your own predispositions toward language, discourse, writing, and writing instruction, predispositions which can then be considered critically and discussed knowledgeably. The list of suggested readings adds book-length considerations. With the books I have suggested, the books and articles cited in the essays that pique your interest, and the essays themselves, you should be able to come up with quite the pancake recipe, something you can swallow.

I mention the readings and the works the essays themselves cite because, though this book is comprehensive, it is not complete. It is not intended to establish a canon of comp. It's an overview, manageable within an academic quarter or semester. So the readings contained herein do not encompass all there is to composition studies. There are gaps. Writing across the curriculum is absent. Linguistics is minimally represented, which means there is little here on research on those who come into the classroom speaking a nonstandard dialect or those whose primary language is other than English (which includes sociolinguistic and applied linguistic studies of the hundreds of American Indian languages still spoken in the United States today). There is little on grammar, and the current discussions on multiculturalism and the comp classroom aren't explicitly represented. But all of these concerns really are here, in large terms, in the theoretical discussions concerning those who have been traditionally excluded or underrepresented in the academy.

Nor is evaluation explicitly represented. I know that the teacher is always concerned with evaluation and assessment. And how a teacher decides to respond, evaluate, and grade essays should be a reflection of the philosophy or theory of writing that the classroom curriculum embodies. But the subject of evaluation is large, almost another theoretical sphere, more concerned with what you do with writing in the classroom than with what writing is or even what writing instruction might be. I've relegated evaluation to the list of suggested readings. In other words, to learn more you'll still have to read those more complete academic books on composition contained in the list of readings or mentioned in the collection. But after going through this book, you will have a sense of who you might want to read. This book is intended as a primer, drops to activate the pump.

Selection suggests a selector, one with particular biases. But though my own biases in selecting the readings will no doubt come through, no single viewpoint is presented. The readings are presented in such a way as to establish a dialectic—a way for you to come to your own conclusions by considering opposing viewpoints. The process approach espoused in the first section receives a critical assessment in the "Mulligan Stew" article. Walter Ong provides a necessary reconsideration of product. The cognitive explanations of basic writers' problems advanced by Andrea Lunsford and by Frank D'Angelo are countered by Mike Rose's article on cognitive development. Cognitive explanations generally are countered by social-construction's explanations, with Patricia Bizzell explicitly drawing the comparison, offering the critique; both the cognitivist and the social-constructionist become subject to ideological critiques. Points find counterpoints throughout the book—talk and cross-talk.

Some articles will address matters of race or ethnicity, gender, the poor or working class. Considerations of race and the like have had a great deal to do with establishing the theoretical controversies. One compositionist of note, at least, Maxine Hairston, has argued that our changing theories of composition are in part the result of the introduction into our college classrooms of those we have come to call basic writers, those who come to college not quite prepared to undertake college writing, most often people of color and the poor. There are always a few in every composition classroom, at every level, from first-year college students to seniors. To ponder how composition might affect the more troublesome, those basic writers, would inform our approach to the less troublesome.

Although the book's layout is principally concerned with establishing a dialectic, presenting varying views, there is something of a chronology to the ordering, a near chronology of the profession's changes—process to cohesion to cognition to social construction to ideology. The first two sections present the views that seem to have lasted: writing-as-process, writing as a means of learning, James Kinneavy's aims of discourse, some basic research. Yet even these sections contain some controversial matters: the generalizability of case studies, Frank D'Angelo's ontogeny recapitulating phylogeny (terms you'll come to understand through the reading). The third section looks to the cognitive sciences and developmental psychology, pretty popular till recently. The fourth section addresses that which has compromised cognition's popularity: social construction. It introduces Kenneth Bruffee and something of a counter in John Trimbur; there is also Charles Schuster's reading of Mikhail Bakhtin as informing social construction. Section five looks to the debate over whether freshman composition courses should concern themselves with narration or with academic discourse, with the discourses about and by those traditionally excluded from the academy—women, people of color. Then an important set of postscripts. And so the profession stands, kind of, for the moment.

The Givens in Our Conversations

The Writing Process

- "Teach Writing as a Process Not Product" Donald M. Murray
- "Writing as a Mode of Learning" Janet Emig
- "The Composing Processes of Unskilled College Writers" Sondra Perl
- "Revision Strategies of Student Writers and Experienced Adult Writers" Nancy Sommers
- "The Writer's Audience Is Always a Fiction" Walter J. Ong, S.J.
- "Audience Addressed/Audience Invoked: The Role of Audience in Composition Theory and Pedagogy" Lisa Ede and Andrea Lunsford
- "Post-Process 'Pedagogy': A Philosophical Exercise" Lee-Ann M. Kastman Breuch
- "Contemporary Composition: The Major Pedagogical Theories" James A. Berlin

That writing is a process sounds pretty obvious. We know that texts don't appear magically on pages as whole products. There is a process in getting from mind to page. As obvious as that might be, however, there remains a tendency among teachers of writing to look at texts as finished products based on models. Students in composition classes are enjoined to look at texts, analyze and discuss what happens in those texts, and then produce something of their own that followed the patterns they found in those texts. Ideas were to be provided by the text, the form provided by the text, with evaluation based on how well the student paper emulated the ideal text. The process was rather like having students watch and discuss a video of a prima ballerina then having the students attempt the same dance, with the students evaluated based on how well they approximated the ballerina's performance—without knowing how the ballerina came to master those steps. No attention was given to the process of arriving at the product.

In 1959 the National Academy of Sciences sponsored the Woods Hole Conference. Its director was a cognitive psychologist with a keen interest in education and language, Jerome Bruner. The result of the conference was a shift in emphasis for all schooling to the process of cognitive development. *Process* became the new catchword. Then in 1966, about fifty teachers of English from England and from the United States met to discuss common problems. What the Americans discovered was that the British did not teach writing as discipline-specific. The British, rather than teach writing to serve some external purpose or genre, taught writing as a process of individual development, a matter of self-discovery. This was the Dartmouth Conference. Its discoveries fit well with the Woods Hole discoveries.

Woods Hole and Dartmouth made for a new attention to the whole concept of process. Writers and teachers like Donald Murray, Ken Macrorie, and Peter Elbow turned to what they knew as writers and as teachers to shed light on what writers do when they write. At about the same time, researchers in composition were heeding the call provided by Richard Braddock, Richard Lloyd-Jones, and Lowell Schoer's *Research in Written Composition*, a collection of research on composing to 1963. Their call? More research on writing itself (as opposed to products or pedagogy). Janet Emig's *The Composing Processes of Twelfth Graders* was the first significant answer to the call. Others presented here looked to what professional writers do when they revise, comparing that with what students in writing classes don't do, and what basic writers—students not quite ready for the tasks of college literacy—do when they write.

So, writing is a process. But that doesn't mean that at the end of the process there won't be a product. The idea is to place greater emphasis on the process than on the product. Rhetorician Walter Ong reminds us, in a classic article that combines matters of literary criticism with rhetoric and the teaching of writing, that there are consequences to the writing produced, that what is written affects and is affected by audiences, by readers. Lisa Ede and Andrea Lunsford broaden the picture on audience. Then comes the question as to whether "process" has overshadowed other concerns with writing. This comes to be called "post-process theory," a reconsideration of the givens of our conversation. Lee-Ann M. Kastman Breuch tells us about post-process.

James Berlin has us look at underlying epistemological assumptions that can affect our teaching of writing as process. In other words, Berlin outlines what he sees as the underlying assumptions about the relations among words, thoughts, and the things represented in those words and thoughts that are implicit in various approaches to teaching composition. His categories become the terms with which we discuss ideological and epistemological assumptions about discourse and writing instruction. In so doing, writing is reconnected to rhetoric.

2

Teach Writing as a Process Not Product

Donald M. Murray

Most of us are trained as English teachers by studying a product: writing. Our critical skills are honed by examining literature, which is finished writing; language as it has been used by authors. And then, fully trained in the autopsy, we go out and are assigned to teach our students to write, to make language live.

Naturally we try to use our training. It's an investment and so we teach writing as a product, focusing our critical attentions on what our students have done, as if they had passed literature in to us. It isn't literature, of course, and we use our skills, with which we can dissect and sometimes almost destroy Shakespeare or Robert Lowell to prove it.

Our students knew it wasn't literature when they passed it in, and our attack usually does little more than confirm their lack of self-respect for their work and for themselves; we are as frustrated as our students, for conscientious, doggedly responsible, repetitive autopsying doesn't give birth to live writing. The product doesn't improve, and so, blaming the student—who else?—we pass him along to the next teacher, who is trained, too often, the same way we were. Year after year the student shudders under a barrage of criticism, much of it brilliant, some of it stupid, and all of it irrelevant. No matter how careful our criticisms, they do not help the student since when we teach composition we are not teaching a product, we are teaching a process.

And once you can look at your composition program with the realization you are teaching a process, you may be able to design a curriculum which works. Not overnight, for writing is a demanding, intellectual process;

Pulitzer Prize–winning journalist Donald M. Murray presented this paper at the 1972 convention of the New England Association of Teachers of English; it appeared in their journal, *The Leaflet*, in November 1972. Reprinted with permission.

but sooner than you think, for the process can be put to work to produce a product which may be worth your reading.

What is the process we should teach? It is the process of discovery through language. It is the process of exploration of what we know and what we feel about what we know through language. It is the process of using language to learn about our world, to evaluate what we learn about our world, to communicate what we learn about our world.

Instead of teaching finished writing, we should teach unfinished writing, and glory in its unfinishedness. We work with language in action. We share with our students the continual excitement of choosing one word instead of another, of searching for the one true word.

This is not a question of correct or incorrect, of etiquette or custom. This is a matter of far higher importance. The writer, as he writes, is making ethical decisions. He doesn't test his words by a rule book, but by life. He uses language to reveal the truth to himself so that he can tell it to others. It is an exciting, eventful, evolving process.

This process of discovery through language we call writing can be introduced to your classroom as soon as you have a very simple understanding of that process, and as soon as you accept the full implications of teaching process, not product.

The writing process itself can be divided into three stages: *prewriting, writing,* and *rewriting.* The amount of time a writer spends in each stage depends on his personality, his work habits, his maturity as a craftsman, and the challenge of what he is trying to say. It is not a rigid lock-step process, but most writers most of the time pass through these three stages.

Prewriting is everything that takes place before the first draft. Prewriting usually takes about 85% of the writer's time. It includes the awareness of his world from which his subject is born. In prewriting, the writer focuses on that subject, spots an audience, chooses a form which may carry his subject to his audience. Prewriting may include research and daydreaming, note-making and outlining, title-writing and lead-writing.

Writing is the act of producing a first draft. It is the fastest part of the process, and the most frightening, for it is a commitment. When you complete a draft you know how much, and how little, you know. And the writing of this first draft—rough, searching, unfinished—may take as little as one percent of the writer's time.

Rewriting is reconsideration of subject, form, and audience. It is researching, rethinking, redesigning, rewriting—and finally, line-by-line editing, the demanding, satisfying process of making each word right. It may take many times the hours required for a first draft, perhaps the remaining fourteen percent of the time the writer spends on the project.

4

How do you motivate your student to pass through this process, perhaps even pass through it again and again on the same piece of writing?

First by shutting up. When you are talking he isn't writing. And you don't learn a process by talking about it, but by doing it. Next by placing the opportunity for discovery in your student's hands. When you give him an assignment you tell him what to say and how to say it, and thereby cheat your student of the opportunity to learn the process of discovery we call writing.

To be a teacher of a process such as this takes qualities too few of us have, but which most of us can develop. We have to be quiet, to listen, to respond. We are not the initiator or the motivator; we are the reader, the recipient.

We have to be patient and wait, and wait, and wait. The suspense in the beginning of a writing course is agonizing for the teacher, but if we break first, if we do the prewriting for our students they will not learn the largest part of the writing process.

We have to respect the student, not for his product, not for the paper we call literature by giving it a grade, but for the search for truth in which he is engaged. We must listen carefully for those words that may reveal a truth, that may reveal a voice. We must respect our student for his potential truth and for his potential voice. We are coaches, encouragers, developers, creators of environments in which our students can experience the writing process for themselves.

Let us see what some of the implications of teaching process, not product, are for the composition curriculum.

Implication No. 1. The text of the writing course is the student's own writing. Students examine their own evolving writing and that of their classmates, so that they study writing while it is still a matter of choice, word by word.

Implication No. 2. The student finds his own subject. It is not the job of the teacher to legislate the student's truth. It is the responsibility of the student to explore his own world with his own language, to discover his own meaning. The teacher supports but does not direct this expedition to the student's own truth.

Implication No. 3. The student uses his own language. Too often, as writer and teacher Thomas Williams points out, we teach English to our students as if it were a foreign language. Actually, most of our students have learned a great deal of language before they come to us, and they are quite willing to exploit that language if they are allowed to embark on a serious search for their own truth.

Implication No. 4. The student should have the opportunity to write all the drafts necessary for him to discover what he has to say on this particular subject. Each new draft, of course, is counted as equal to a new paper. You are not teaching a product, you are teaching a process.

Implication No. 5. The student is encouraged to attempt any form of writing which may help him discover and communicate what he has to say. The process which produces "creative" and "functional" writing is the same. You are not teaching products such as business letters and poetry, narrative and exposition. You are teaching a product your students can use—now and in the future—to produce whatever product his subject and his audience demand.

Implication No. 6. Mechanics come last. It is important to the writer, once he has discovered what he has to say, that nothing get between him and his reader. He must break only those traditions of written communication which would obscure his meaning.

Implication No. 7. There must be time for the writing process to take place and time for it to end. The writer must work within the stimulating tension of unpressured time to think and dream and stare out windows, and pressured time—the deadline—to which the writer must deliver.

Implication No. 8. Papers are examined to see what other choices the writer might make. The primary responsibility for seeing the choices is the student. He is learning a process. His papers are always unfinished, evolving, until the end of the marking period. A grade finishes a paper, the way publication usually does. The student writer is not graded on drafts any more than a concert pianist is judged on his practice sessions rather than on his performance. The student writer is graded on what he has produced at the end of the writing process.

Implication No. 9. The students are individuals who must explore the writing process in their own way, some fast, some slow, whatever it takes for them, within the limits of the course deadlines, to find their own way to their own truth.

Implication No. 10. There are no rules, no absolutes, just alternatives. What works one time may not another. All writing is experimental.

None of these implications require a special schedule, exotic training, extensive new materials or gadgetry, new classrooms, or an increase in federal, state, or local funds. They do not even require a reduced teaching load. What they do require is a teacher who will respect and respond to his students, not for what they have done, but for what they may do; not for what they have produced, but for what they may produce, if they are given an opportunity to see writing as a process, not a product.

Writing as a Mode of Learning

JANET EMIG

Writing represents a unique mode of learning—not merely valuable, not merely special, but unique. That will be my contention in this paper. The thesis is straightforward. Writing serves learning uniquely because writing as process-and-product possesses a cluster of attributes that correspond uniquely to certain powerful learning strategies.

Although the notion is clearly debatable, it is scarcely a private belief. Some of the most distinguished contemporary psychologists have at least implied such a role for writing as heuristic. Lev Vygotsky, A. R. Luria, and Jerome Bruner, for example, have all pointed out that higher cognitive functions, such as analysis and synthesis, seem to develop most fully only with the support system of verbal language—particularly, it seems, of written language.[1] Some of their arguments and evidence will be incorporated here.

Here I have a prior purpose: to describe as tellingly as possible *how* writing uniquely corresponds to certain powerful learning strategies. Making such a case for the uniqueness of writing should logically and theoretically involve establishing many contrasts, distinctions between (1) writing and all other verbal languaging processes—listening, reading, and especially talking; (2) writing and all other forms of composing, such as composing a painting, a symphony, a dance, a film, a building; and (3) composing in words and composing in the two other major graphic symbol systems of mathematical equations and scientific formulae. For the purposes of this paper, the task is simpler, since most students are not permitted by most curricula to discover the values of composing, say, in dance, or even in film; and most students are not sophisticated enough to create, to originate formulations, using the highly abstruse symbol system of equations and formulae. Verbal language

Reprinted from *College Composition and Communication* 28.2 (May 1977): 122–28. Copyright © 1977 by Janet Emig. Used with permission.

represents the most *available* medium for composing; in fact, the significance of sheer availability in its selection as a mode for learning can probably not be overstressed. But the uniqueness of writing among the verbal languaging processes does need to be established and supported if only because so many curricula and courses in English still consist almost exclusively of reading and listening.

WRITING AS A UNIQUE LANGUAGING PROCESS

Traditionally, the four languaging processes of listening, talking, reading, and writing are paired in either of two ways. The more informative seems to be the division many linguists make between first-order and second-order processes, with talking and listening characterized as first-order processes; reading and writing, as second-order. First-order processes are acquired without formal or systematic instruction; the second-order processes of reading and writing tend to be learned initially only with the aid of formal and systematic instruction.

The less useful distinction is that between listening and reading as receptive functions and talking and writing as productive functions. Critics of these terms like Louise Rosenblatt rightfully point out that the connotation of passivity too often accompanies the notion of receptivity when reading, like listening, is a vital, construing act.

An additional distinction, so simple it may have been previously overlooked, resides in two criteria: the matters of origination and of graphic recording. Writing is originating and creating a unique verbal construct that is graphically recorded. Reading is creating or re-creating *but not* originating a verbal construct that is graphically recorded. Listening is creating or re-creating but not originating a verbal construct that is *not* graphically recorded. Talking is creating *and* originating a verbal construct that is *not* graphically recorded (except for the circuitous routing of a transcribed tape). Note that a distinction is being made between creating and originating, separable processes.

For talking, the nearest languaging process, additional distinctions should probably be made. (What follows is not a denigration of talk as a valuable mode of learning.) A silent classroom or one filled only with the teacher's voice is anathema to learning. For evidence of the cognitive value of talk, one can look to some of the persuasive monographs coming from the London Schools Council project on writing: *From Information to Understanding* by Nancy Martin or *From Talking to Writing* by Peter Medway.[2] We also know that for some of us, talking is a valuable, even necessary, form of pre-writing. In his curriculum, James Moffett makes the value of such talk quite explicit.

But to say that talking is a valuable form of pre-writing is not to say that writing is talk recorded, an inaccuracy appearing in far too many composition texts. Rather, a number of contemporary trans-disciplinary sources suggest that talking and writing may emanate from different organic sources and represent quite different, possibly distinct, language functions. In *Thought and Language*, Vygotsky notes that "written speech is a separate linguistic function, differing from oral speech in both structure and mode of functioning."[3] The sociolinguist Dell Hymes, in a valuable issue of *Daedalus*, "Language as a Human Problem," makes a comparable point: "That speech and writing are not simply interchangeable, and have developed historically in ways at least partly autonomous, is obvious."[4] At the first session of the Buffalo Conference on Researching Composition (4–5 October 1975), the first point of unanimity among the participant-speakers with interests in developmental psychology, media, dreams and aphasia was that talking and writing were markedly different functions.[5] Some of us who work rather steadily with writing research agree. We also believe that there are hazards, conceptually and pedagogically, in creating too complete an analogy between talking and writing, in blurring the very real differences between the two.

What Are These Differences?

1. Writing is learned behavior; talking is natural, even irrepressible, behavior.

2. Writing then is an artificial process; talking is not.

3. Writing is a technological device — not the wheel, but early enough to qualify as primary technology; talking is organic, natural, earlier.

4. Most writing is slower than most talking.

5. Writing is stark, barren, even naked as a medium; talking is rich, luxuriant, inherently redundant.

6. Talk leans on the environment; writing must provide its own context.

7. With writing, the audience is usually absent; with talking, the listener is usually present.

8. Writing usually results in a visible graphic product; talking usually does not.

9. Perhaps because there is a product involved, writing tends to be a more responsible and committed act than talking.

10. It can even be said that throughout history, an aura, an ambience, a mystique has usually encircled the written word; the spoken word

has for the most part proved ephemeral and treated mundanely (ignore, please, our recent national history).

11. Because writing is often our representation of the world made visible, embodying both process and product, writing is more readily a form and source of learning than talking.

UNIQUE CORRESPONDENCES BETWEEN LEARNING AND WRITING

What then are some *unique* correspondences between learning and writing? To begin with some definitions: Learning can be defined in many ways, according to one's predilections and training, with all statements about learning of course hypothetical. Definitions range from the chemo-physiological ("Learning is changed patterns of protein synthesis in relevant portions of the cortex")[6] to transactive views drawn from both philosophy and psychology (John Dewey, Jean Piaget) that learning is the re-organization or confirmation of a cognitive scheme in light of an experience.[7] What the speculations seem to share is consensus about certain features and strategies that characterize successful learning. These include the importance of the classic attributes of re-inforcement and feedback. In most hypotheses, successful learning is also connective and selective. Additionally, it makes use of propositions, hypotheses, and other elegant summarizers. Finally, it is active, engaged, personal—more specifically, self-rhythmed—in nature.

Jerome Bruner, like Jean Piaget, through a comparable set of categories, posits three major ways in which we represent and deal with actuality: (1) enactive—we learn "by doing"; (2) iconic—we learn "by depiction in an image"; and (3) representational or symbolic—we learn "by restatement in words."[8] To overstate the matter, in enactive learning, the hand predominates; in iconic, the eye; and in symbolic, the brain.

What is striking about writing as a process is that, by its very nature, all three ways of dealing with actuality are simultaneously or almost simultaneously deployed. That is, the symbolic transformation of experience through the specific symbol system of verbal language is shaped into an icon (the graphic product) by the enactive hand. If the most efficacious learning occurs when learning is re-inforced, then writing through its inherent re-inforcing cycle involving hand, eye, and brain marks a uniquely powerful multi-representational mode for learning.

Writing is also integrative in perhaps the most basic possible sense: the organic, the functional. Writing involves the fullest possible functioning of the brain, which entails the active participation in the process of both the left and the right hemispheres. Writing is markedly bispheral, although in some popular accounts, writing is inaccurately presented as a chiefly left-hemisphere activity, perhaps because the linear written product is somehow regarded as analogue for the process that created it; and the left hemisphere seems to process material linearly.

The right hemisphere, however, seems to make at least three, perhaps four, major contributions to the writing process—probably, to the creative process generically. First, several researchers, such as Geschwind and Snyder of Harvard and Zaidal of Cal Tech, through markedly different experiments, have very tentatively suggested that the right hemisphere is the sphere, even the *seat*, of emotions.[9] Second—or perhaps as an illustration of the first—Howard Gardner, in his important study of the brain-damaged, notes that our sense of emotional appropriateness in discourse may reside in the right sphere:

> Emotional appropriateness, in sum—being related not only to *what* is said, but to how it is said and to what is *not* said, as well—is crucially dependent on right hemisphere intactness.[10]

Third, the right hemisphere seems to be the source of intuition, of sudden gestalts, of flashes of images, of abstractions occurring as visual or spatial wholes, as the initiating metaphors in the creative process. A familiar example: William Faulkner noted in his *Paris Review* interview that *The Sound and the Fury* began as the image of a little girl's muddy drawers as she sat in a tree watching her grandmother's funeral.[11]

Also, a unique form of feedback, as well as reinforcement, exists with writing, because information from the *process* is immediately and visibly available as that portion of the *product* already written. The importance for learning of a product in a familiar and available medium for immediate, literal (that is, visual) re-scanning and review cannot perhaps be overstated. In his remarkable study of purportedly blind sculptors, Géza Révész found that without sight, persons cannot move beyond a literal transcription of elements into any manner of symbolic transformation—by definition, the central requirement for reformulation and re-interpretation, i.e., revision, that most aptly named process.[12]

As noted in the second paragraph, Vygotsky and Luria, like Bruner, have written importantly about the connections between learning and writing. In his essay "The Psychobiology of Psychology," Bruner lists as one of six axioms regarding learning: "We are connective."[13] Another correspondence then between learning and writing: in *Thought and Language*, Vygotsky notes that writing makes a unique demand in that the writer must engage in "deliberate semantics" — in Vygotsky's elegant phrase, "deliberate structuring of the web of meaning."[14] Such structuring is required because, for Vygotsky, writing centrally represents an expansion of inner speech, that mode whereby we talk to ourselves, which is "maximally compact" and "almost entirely predicative"; written speech is a mode which is "maximally detailed" and which requires explicitly supplied subjects and topics. The medium then of written verbal language requires the establishment of systematic connections and relationships. Clear writing by definition is that writing which signals without ambiguity the nature of conceptual relationships, whether they be coordinate, subordinate, superordinate, causal, or something other.

Successful learning is also engaged, committed, personal learning. Indeed, impersonal learning may be an anomalous concept, like the very notion of objectivism itself. As Michael Polanyi states simply at the beginning of *Personal Knowledge*: "the ideal of strict objectivism is absurd." (How many courses and curricula in English, science, and all else does that one sentence reduce to rubble?) Indeed, the theme of *Personal Knowledge* is that

> into every act of knowing there enters a passionate contribution of the person knowing what is being known, ... this coefficient is no mere imperfection but a vital component of his knowledge.[15]

In *Zen and the Art of Motorcycle Maintenance*, Robert Pirsig states a comparable theme:

> The Quality which creates the world emerges as *a relationship* between man and his experience. He is a *participant* in the creation of all things.[16]

Finally, the psychologist George Kelly has as the central notion in his subtle and compelling theory of personal constructs man as a scientist steadily and actively engaged in making and re-making his hypotheses about the nature of the universe.[17]

We are acquiring as well some empirical confirmation about the importance of engagement in, as well as self-selection of, a subject for the student learning to write and writing to learn. The recent Sanders and Littlefield study, reported in *Research in the Teaching of English*, is persuasive evidence on this point, as well as being a model for a certain type of research.[18]

As Luria implies in the quotation above, writing is self-rhythmed. One writes best as one learns best, at one's own pace. Or to connect the two processes, writing can sponsor learning because it can match its pace. Support

12

for the importance of self-pacing to learning can be found in Benjamin Bloom's important study "Time and Learning."[19] Evidence for the significance of self-pacing to writing can be found in the reason Jean-Paul Sartre gave last summer for not using the tape-recorder when he announced that blindness in his second eye had forced him to give up writing:

> I think there is an enormous difference between speaking and writing. One rereads what one rewrites. But one can read slowly or quickly: in other words, you do not know how long you will have to take deliberating over a sentence. . . . If I listen to a tape recorder, the listening speed is determined by the speed at which the tape turns and not by my own needs. Therefore I will always be either lagging behind or running ahead of the machine.[20]

Writing is connective as a process in a more subtle and perhaps more significant way, as Luria points out in what may be the most powerful paragraph of rationale ever supplied for writing as heuristic:

> Written speech is bound up with the inhibition of immediate synpractical connections. It assumes a much slower, repeated mediating process of analysis and synthesis, which makes it possible not only to develop the required thought, but even to revert to its earlier stages, thus transforming the sequential chain of connections in a simultaneous, self-reviewing structure. Written speech thus represents a new and powerful instrument of thought.[21]

But first to explicate: writing inhibits "immediate synpractical connections." Luria defines *synpraxis* as "concrete-active" situations in which language does not exist independently but as a "fragment" of an ongoing action "outside of which it is incomprehensible."[22] In *Language and Learning*, James Britton defines it succinctly as "speech-cum-action."[23] Writing, unlike talking, restrains dependence upon the actual situation. Writing as a mode is inherently more self-reliant than speaking. Moreover, as Bruner states in explicating Vygotsky, "Writing virtually forces a remoteness of reference on the language user."[24]

Luria notes what has already been noted above: that writing, typically, is a "much slower" process than talking. But then he points out the relation of this slower pace to learning: this slower pace allows for—indeed, encourages—the shuttling among past, present, and future. Writing, in other words, connects the three major tenses of our experience to make meaning. And the two major modes by which these three aspects are united are the processes of analysis and synthesis: analysis, the breaking of entities into their constituent parts; and synthesis, combining or fusing these, often into fresh arrangements or amalgams.

Finally, writing is epigenetic, with the complex evolutionary development of thought steadily and graphically visible and available throughout as a record of the journey, from jottings and notes to full discursive formulations.

For a summary of the correspondences stressed here between certain learning strategies and certain attributes of writing see Figure 1.

This essay represents a first effort to make a certain kind of case for writing—specifically, to show its unique value for learning. It is at once over-elaborate and under specific. Too much of the formulation is in the off-putting jargon of the learning theorist, when my own predilection would have been to emulate George Kelly and to avoid terms like *reinforcement* and *feedback* since their use implies that I live inside a certain paradigm about learning I don't truly inhabit. Yet I hope that the essay will start a crucial line of inquiry; for unless the losses to learners of not writing are compellingly described and substantiated by experimental and speculative research, writing itself as a central academic process may not long endure.

Figure 1   Unique cluster of correspondences between certain learning strategies and certain attributes of writing.

Selected Characteristics of Successful Learning Strategies	Selected Attributes of Writing Process and Product
1. Profits from multi-representational and integrative re-inforcement	1. Represents process uniquely multi-representational and integrative
2. Seeks self-provided feedback:	2. Represents powerful instance of self-provided feedback:
a. immediate	a. provides product uniquely available for *immediate* feedback (review and re-evaluation)
b. long-term	b. provides record of evolution of thought since writing is epigenetic as process-and-product
3. Is connective:	3. Provides connections:
a. makes generative conceptual groupings, synthetic and analytic	a. establishes explicit and systematic conceptual groupings through lexical, syntactic, and rhetorical devices
b. proceeds from propositions, hypotheses, and other elegant summarizers	b. represents most available means (verbal language) for economic recording of abstract formulations
4. Is active, engaged, personal—notably, self-rhythmed	4. Is active, engaged, personal—notably, self-rhythmed

NOTES

1. Lev S. Vygotsky, *Thought and Language*, trans. Eugenia Hanfmann and Gertrude Vakar (Cambridge: The M.I.T. Press, 1962); A. R. Luria and F. la. Yudovich, *Speech and the Development of Mental Processes in the Child*, ed. Joan Simon (Baltimore: Penguin, 1971); Jerome S. Bruner, *The Relevance of Education* (New York: W. W. Norton and Co., 1971).

2. Nancy Martin, *From Information to Understanding* (London: Schools Council Project Writing Across the Curriculum, 11–13, 1973); Peter Medway, *From Talking to Writing* (London: Schools Council Project Writing Across the Curriculum, 11–13, 1973).

3. Vygotsky, p. 98.

4. Dell Hymes, "On the Origins and Foundations of Inequality Among Speakers," *Daedalus*, 102 (Summer, 1973), 69.

5. Participant-speakers were Loren Barrett, University of Michigan; Gerald O'Grady, SUNY/Buffalo; Hollis Frampton, SUNY/Buffalo; and Janet Emig, Rutgers.

6. George Steiner, *After Babel: Aspects of Language and Translation* (New York: Oxford University Press, 1975), p. 287.

7. John Dewey, *Experience and Education* (New York: Macmillan, 1938); Jean Piaget, *Biology and Knowledge: An Essay on the Relations between Organic Regulations and Cognitive Processes* (Chicago: University of Chicago Press, 1971).

8. Bruner, pp. 7–8.

9. Boyce Rensberger, "Language Ability Found in Right Side of Brain," *New York Times*, 1 August 1975, p. 14.

10. Howard Gardner, *The Shattered Mind: The Person After Brain Damage* (New York: Alfred A. Knopf, 1975), p. 372.

11. William Faulkner, *Writers at Work: The Paris Review Interviews*, ed. Malcolm Cowley (New York: The Viking Press, 1959), p. 130.

12. Géza Révész, *Psychology and Art of the Blind*, trans. H. A. Wolff (London: Longmans-Green, 1950).

13. Bruner, p. 126.

14. Vygotsky, p. 100.

15. Michael Polanyi, *Personal Knowledge: Toward a Post-Critical Philosophy* (Chicago: University of Chicago Press, 1958), p. viii.

16. Robert Pirsig, *Zen and the Art of Motorcycle Maintenance* (New York: William Morrow and Co., Inc., 1974), p. 212.

17. George Kelly, *A Theory of Personality: The Psychology of Personal Constructs* (New York: W. W. Norton and Co., 1963).

18. Sara E. Sanders and John H. Littlefield, "Perhaps Test Essays Can Reflect Significant Improvement in Freshman Composition: Report on a Successful Attempt," *RTE*, 9 (Fall, 1975), 145–153.

19. Benjamin Bloom, "Time and Learning," *American Psychologist*, 29 (September 1974), 682–688.

20. Jean-Paul Sartre, "Sartre at Seventy: An Interview," with Michel Contat, *New York Review of Books*, 7 August 1975.

21. Luria, p. 118.

22. Luria, p. 50.

23. James Britton, *Language and Learning* (Baltimore: Penguin, 1971), pp. 10–11.

24. Bruner, p. 47.

The Composing Processes
of Unskilled College Writers

SONDRA PERL

This paper presents the pertinent findings from a study of the composing processes of five unskilled college writers (Perl, 1978). The first part summarizes the goals of the original study, the kinds of data collected, and the research methods employed. The second part is a synopsis of the study of Tony, one of the original five case studies. The third part presents a condensed version of the findings on the composing process and discusses these findings in light of current pedagogical practice and research design.

GOALS OF THE STUDY

This research addressed three major questions: (1) How do unskilled writers write? (2) Can their writing processes be analyzed in a systematic, replicable manner? and (3) What does an increased understanding of their processes suggest about the nature of composing in general and the manner in which writing is taught in the schools?

In recent years, interest in the composing process has grown (Britton, 1975; Burton, 1973; Cooper, 1974; Emig, 1967, 1971). In 1963, Braddock, Lloyd-Jones, and Schoer, writing on the state of research in written composition, included the need for "direct observation" and case study procedures in their suggestions for future research (pp. 24, 31–32). In a section entitled "Unexplored Territory," they listed basic unanswered questions such as, "What is involved in the act of writing?" and "Of what does skill in writing actually consist?" (p. 51). Fifteen years later, Cooper and Odell (1978)

Reprinted from *Research in the Teaching of English* 13.4 (December 1979): 317–36. Used with permission.

edited a volume similar in scope, only this one was devoted entirely to issues and questions related to research on composing. This volume in particular signals a shift in emphasis in writing research. Alongside the traditional, large scale experimental studies, there is now widespread recognition of the need for works of a more modest, probing nature, works that attempt to elucidate basic processes. The studies on composing that have been completed to date are precisely of this kind; they are small-scale studies, based on the systematic observation of writers engaged in the process of writing (Emig, 1971; Graves, 1973; Mischel, 1974; Pianko, 1977; Stallard, 1974).

For all of its promise, this body of research has yet to produce work that would insure wide recognition for the value of process studies of composing. One limitation of work done to date is methodological. Narrative descriptions of composing processes do not provide sufficiently graphic evidence for the perception of underlying regularities and patterns. Without such evidence, it is difficult to generate well-defined hypotheses and to move from exploratory research to more controlled experimental studies. A second limitation pertains to the subjects studied. To date no examination of composing processes has dealt primarily with unskilled writers. As long as "average" or skilled writers are the focus, it remains unclear as to how process research will provide teachers with a firmer understanding of the needs of students with serious writing problems.

The present study is intended to carry process research forward by addressing both of these limitations. One prominent feature of the research design involves the development and use of a meaningful and replicable method for rendering the composing process as a sequence of observable and scorable behaviors. A second aspect of the design is the focus on students whose writing problems baffle the teachers charged with their education.

DESIGN OF THE STUDY

This study took place during the 1975–76 fall semester at Eugenio Maria de Hostos Community College of the City University of New York. Students were selected for the study on the basis of two criteria: writing samples that qualified them as unskilled writers and willingness to participate. Each student met with the researcher for five 90-minute sessions (see Table 1). Four sessions were devoted to writing with the students directed to compose aloud, to externalize their thinking processes as much as possible, during each session. In one additional session, a writing profile on the students' perceptions and memories of writing was developed through the use of an open-ended interview. All of the sessions took place in a soundproof room in the

Table 1   Design of the study.

	Session 1 (S1)	Session 2 (S2)	Session 3 (S3)	Session 4 (S4)	Session 5 (S5)
Mode	Extensive	Reflexive		Extensive	Reflexive
Topic	Society & Culture	Society & Culture	Interview: Writing Profile	Capitalism	Capitalism
Directions	Students told to compose aloud; no other directions given	Students told to compose aloud; no other directions given		Students told to compose aloud; also directed to talk out ideas before writing	Students told to compose aloud; also directed to talk out ideas before writing

college library. Throughout each session, the researcher assumed a noninterfering role.

The topics for writing were developed in an introductory social science course in which the five students were enrolled. The "content" material they were studying was divided into two modes: extensive, in which the writer was directed to approach the material in an objective, impersonal fashion, and reflexive, in which the writer was directed to approach similar material in an affective, personalized fashion. Contrary to Emig's (1971) definitions, in this study it was assumed that the teacher was always the audience.

DATA ANALYSIS

Three kinds of data were collected in this study: the students' written products, their composing tapes, and their responses to the interview. Each of these was studied carefully and then discussed in detail in each of the five case study presentations. Due to limitations of space, this paper will review only two of the data sets generated in the study.

Coding the Composing Process

One of the goals of this research was to devise a tool for describing the movements that occur during composing. In the past such descriptions have taken the form of narratives which detail, with relative precision and insight, observable composing behaviors; however, these narratives provide no way of ascertaining the frequency, relative importance, and place of each behavior within an individual's composing process. As such, they are cumbersome and difficult to replicate. Furthermore, lengthy, idiosyncratic narratives run the risk of leaving underlying patterns and regularities obscure. In contrast, the method created in this research provides a means of viewing the composing process that is:

1. Standardized — it introduces a coding system for observing the composing process that can be replicated;
2. Categorical — it labels specific, observable behaviors so that types of composing movements are revealed;
3. Concise — it presents the entire sequence of composing movements on one or two pages;
4. Structural — it provides a way of determining how parts of the process relate to the whole; and
5. Diachronic — it presents the sequences of movements that occur during composing as they unfold in time.

In total, the method allows the researcher to apprehend a process as it unfolds. It lays out the movements or behavior sequences in such a way that if patterns within a student's process or among a group of students exist, they become apparent.

The Code

The method consists of coding each composing behavior exhibited by the student and charting each behavior on a continuum. During this study, the coding occurred after the student had finished composing and was done by working from the student's written product and the audiotape of the session. It was possible to do this since the tape captured both what the student was saying and the literal sound of the pen moving across the page. As a result, it was possible to determine when students were talking, when they were writing, when both occurred simultaneously, and when neither occurred.

The major categorical divisions in this coding system are talking, writing, and reading; however, it was clear that there are various kinds of talk and various kinds of writing and reading operations, and that a coding system would need to distinguish among these various types. In this study the following operations were distinguished:

1. General planning [PL]—organizing one's thoughts for writing, discussing how one will proceed.
2. Local planning [PLL]—talking out what idea will come next.
3. Global planning [PLG]—discussing changes in drafts.
4. Commenting [C]—sighing, making a comment or judgment about the topic.
5. Interpreting [I]—rephrasing the topic to get a "handle" on it.
6. Assessing [A(+); A(−)]—making a judgment about one's writing; may be positive or negative.
7. Questioning [Q]—asking a question.
8. Talking leading to writing [T→W]—voicing ideas on the topic, tentatively finding one's way, but not necessarily being committed to or using all one is saying.
9. Talking and writing at the same time [TW]—composing aloud in such a way that what one is saying is actually being written at the same time.
10. Repeating [re]—repeating written or unwritten phrases a number of times.
11. Reading related to the topic:
    a. Reading the directions [R_D]
    b. Reading the question [R_Q]
    c. Reading the statement [R_S]
12. Reading related to one's own written product:
    a. Reading one sentence or a few words [R^a]
    b. Reading a number of sentences together [R^{a-b}]
    c. Reading the entire draft through [R^{Wl}]
13. Writing silently [W].
14. Writing aloud [TW].
15. Editing [E]:
    a. Adding syntactic markers, words, phrases, or clauses [Eadd]
    b. Deleting syntactic markers, words, phrases, or clauses [Edel]
    c. Indicating concern for a grammatical rule [Egr]
    d. Adding, deleting, or considering the use of punctuation [Epunc]

   e. Considering or changing spelling [Esp]

   f. Changing the sentence structure through embedding, coordination or subordination [Ess]

   g. Indicating concern for appropriate vocabulary (word choice) [Ewc]

   h. Considering or changing verb form [Evc]

16. Periods of silence [s].

By taking specific observable behaviors that occur during composing and supplying labels for them, this system thus far provides a way of analyzing the process that is categorical and capable of replication. In order to view the frequency and the duration of composing behaviors and the relation between one particular behavior and the whole process, these behaviors need to be depicted graphically to show their duration and sequence.

The Continuum

The second component of this system is the construction of a time line and a numbering system. In this study, blank charts with lines like the following were designed:

10	20	30	40	50	60	70

A ten-digit interval corresponds to one minute and is keyed to a counter on a tape recorder. By listening to the tape and watching the counter, it is possible to determine the nature and duration of each operation. As each behavior is heard on the tape, it is coded and then noted on the chart with the counter used as a time marker. For example, if a student during prewriting reads the directions and the question twice and then begins to plan exactly what she is going to say, all within the first minute, it would be coded like this:

Prewriting

RDRQRDRQPLL

10

If at this point the student spends two minutes writing the first sentence, during which time she pauses, rereads the question, continues writing, and then edits for spelling before continuing on, it would be coded like this:

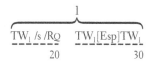

At this point two types of brackets and numbering systems have appeared. The initial sublevel number linked with the TW code indicates which draft the student is working on. TW_1 indicates the writing of the first draft; TW_2 and TW_3 indicate the writing of the second and third drafts. Brackets such as [Esp] separate these operations from writing and indicate the amount of time the operation takes. The upper-level number above the horizontal bracket indicates which sentence in the written product is being written and the length of the bracket indicates the amount of time spent on the writing of each sentence. All horizontal brackets refer to sentences, and from the charts it is possible to see when sentences are grouped together and written in a chunk (adjacent brackets) or when each sentence is produced in isolation (gaps between brackets). (See Appendix for sample chart.)

The charts can be read by moving along the time line, noting which behaviors occur and in what sequence. Three types of comments are also included in the charts. In bold-face type, the beginning and end of each draft are indicated; in lighter type-face, comments on the actual composing movements are provided; and in the lightest type-face, specific statements made by students or specific words they found particularly troublesome are noted.

From the charts, the following information can be determined:

1. the amount of time spent during prewriting;
2. the strategies used during prewriting;
3. the amount of time spent writing each sentence;
4. the behaviors that occur while each sentence is being written;
5. when sentences are written in groups or "chunks" (fluent writing);
6. when sentences are written in isolation (choppy or sporadic writing);
7. the amount of time spent between sentences;
8. the behaviors that occur between sentences;
9. when editing occurs (during the writing of sentences, between sentences, in the time between drafts);
10. the frequency of editing behavior;

11. the nature of the editing operations; and

12. where and in what frequency pauses or periods of silence occur in the process.

The charts, or *composing style sheets* as they are called, do not explain what students wrote but rather *how* they wrote. They indicate, on one page, the sequences of behavior that occur from the beginning of the process to the end. From them it is possible to determine where and how these behaviors fall into patterns and whether these patterns vary according to the mode of discourse.

It should be noted that although the coding system is presented before the analysis of the data, it was derived from the data and then used as the basis for generalizing about the patterns and behavioral sequences found within each student's process. These individual patterns were reported in each of the five case studies. Thus, initially, a style sheet was constructed for each writing session on each student. When there were four style sheets for each student, it was possible to determine if composing patterns existed among the group. The summary of results reported here is based on the patterns revealed by these charts.

Analyzing Miscues in the Writing Process

Miscue analysis is based on Goodman's model of the reading process. Created in 1962, it has become a widespread tool for studying what students do when they read and is based on the premise that reading is a psycholinguistic process which "uses language, in written form, to get to the meaning" (Goodman, 1973, p. 4). Miscue analysis "involves its user in examining the observed behavior of oral readers as an interaction between language and thought, as a process of constructing meaning from a graphic display" (Goodman, 1973, p. 4). Methodologically, the observer analyzes the mismatch that occurs when readers make responses during oral reading that differ from the text. This mismatch or miscueing is then analyzed from Goodman's "meaning-getting" model, based on the assumption that "the reader's preoccupation with meaning will show in his miscues, because they will tend to result in language that still makes sense" (Goodman, 1973, p. 9).

In the present study, miscue analysis was adapted from Goodman's model in order to provide insight into the writing process. Since students composed aloud, two types of oral behaviors were available for study: encoding processes or what students spoke while they were writing and decoding processes or what students "read"[1] after they had finished writing. When a discrepancy existed between encoding or decoding and what was on the paper, it was referred to as miscue.

24

For encoding, the miscue analysis was carried out in the following manner:

1. The students' written products were typed, preserving the original style and spelling.
2. What students said while composing aloud was checked against the written products; discrepancies were noted on the paper wherever they occurred.
3. The discrepancies were categorized and counted.

Three miscue categories were derived for encoding:

1. Speaking complete ideas but omitting certain words during writing.
2. Pronouncing words with plural markers or other suffixes completely but omitting these endings during writing.
3. Pronouncing the desired word but writing a homonym, an approximation of the word or a personal abbreviation of the word on paper.

For decoding, similar procedures were used, this time comparing the words of the written product with what the student "read" orally. When a discrepancy occurred, it was noted. The discrepancies were then categorized and counted.

Four miscue categories were derived for decoding:

1. "Reading in" missing words or word endings;
2. Deleting words or word endings;
3. "Reading" the desired word rather than the word on the page;
4. "Reading" abbreviations and misspellings as though they were written correctly.

A brief summary of the results of this analysis appears in the findings.

SYNOPSIS OF A CASE STUDY

Tony was a 20-year-old ex-Marine born and raised in the Bronx, New York. Like many Puerto Ricans born in the United States, he was able to speak Spanish, but he considered English his native tongue. In the eleventh grade, Tony left high school, returning three years later to take the New York State

high school equivalency exam. As a freshman in college, he was also working part-time to support a child and a wife from whom he was separated.

Behaviors

The composing style sheets provide an overview of the observable behaviors
exhibited by Tony during the composing process. (See Appendix for samples
of Tony's writing and the accompanying composing style sheet.) The most
salient feature of Tony's composing process was its recursiveness. Tony rarely
produced a sentence without stopping to reread either a part or the whole.
This repetition set up a particular kind of composing rhythm, one that was
cumulative in nature and that set ideas in motion by its very repetitiveness.
Thus, as can be seen from any of the style sheets, talking led to writing
which led to reading which led to planning which again led to writing.

The style sheets indicated a difference in the composing rhythms exhibited in the extensive and reflexive modes. On the extensive topics there was
not only more repetition within each sentence but also many more pauses
and repetitions between sentences, with intervals often lasting as long as two
minutes. On the reflexive topics, sentences were often written in groups,
with fewer rereadings and only minimal time intervals separating the creation of one sentence from another.

Editing occurred consistently in all sessions. From the moment Tony
began writing, he indicated a concern for correct form that actually inhib-
ited the development of ideas. In none of the writing sessions did he ever
write more than two sentences before he began to edit. While editing fit into
his overall recursive pattern, it simultaneously interrupted the composing
rhythm he had just initiated.

During the intervals between drafts, Tony read his written work, assessed
his writing, planned new phrasings, transitions or endings, read the directions and the question over, and edited once again.

Tony performed these operations in both the extensive and reflexive
modes and was remarkably consistent in all of his composing operations.
The style sheets attest both to this consistency and to the densely packed,
tight quality of Tony's composing process—indeed, if the notations on these
sheets were any indication at all, it was clear that Tony's composing process
was so full that there was little room left for invention or change.

Fluency

Table 2 provides a numerical analysis of Tony's writing performance. Here
it is possible to compare not only the amount of time spent on the various

Table 2 Tony: Summary of four writing sessions (time in minutes).

			S1 TW_1			S4 T→W	
		Drafts	Words	Time	Drafts	Words	Time
Extensive Mode				Prewriting: 7.8			Prewriting: 8.0
		W1	132	18.8	W1	182	29.0
		W2	170	51.0	W2	174	33.9
		Total	302	Total composing: 91.2*	Total	356	Total composing: 82.0*
				S2 TW_1			S5 T→W
		Drafts	Words	Time	Drafts	Words	Time
Reflexive Mode				Prewriting: 3.5			Prewriting: 5.7
		W1	165	14.5	W1	208	24.0
		W2	169	25.0	W2	190	38.3
		W3	178	24.2	W3	152	20.8
		Total	512	Total composing: 76.0*	Total	550	Total composing: 96.0*

* Total composing includes time spent on editing and rereading, as well as actual writing.

composing operations but also the relative fluency. For Sessions 1 and 2 the data indicate that while Tony spent more time prewriting and writing in the extensive mode, he actually produced fewer words. For Sessions 4 and 5, a similar pattern can be detected. In the extensive mode, Tony again spent more time prewriting and produced fewer words. Although writing time was increased in the reflexive mode, the additional 20 minutes spent writing did not sufficiently account for an increase of 194 words. Rather, the data indicate that Tony produced more words with less planning and generally in less time in the reflexive mode, suggesting that his greater fluency lay in this mode.

Strategies

Tony exhibited a number of strategies that served him as a writer whether the mode was extensive or reflexive. Given my topic, the first operation he performed was to focus in and narrow down the topic. He did this by rephrasing the topic until either a word or an idea in the topic linked up with something in his own experience (an attitude, an opinion, an event). In this way he established a connection between the field of discourse and himself and at this point he felt ready to write.

Level of Language Use

Once writing, Tony employed a pattern of classifying or dividing the topic into manageable pieces and then using one or both of the divisions as the basis for narration. In the four writing sessions, his classifications were made on the basis of economic, racial, and political differences. However, all of his writing reflected a low level of generality. No formal principles were used to organize the narratives nor were the implications of ideas present in the essay developed.

In his writing, Tony was able to maintain the extensive/reflexive distinction. He recognized when he was being asked directly for an opinion and when he was being asked to discuss concepts or ideas that were not directly linked to his experience. However, the more distance between the topic and himself, the more difficulty he experienced, and the more repetitive his process became. Conversely, when the topic was close to his own experience, the smoother and more fluent the process became. More writing was produced, pauses were fewer, and positive assessment occurred more often. However, Tony made more assumptions on the part of the audience in the reflexive mode. When writing about himself, Tony often did not stop to explain the context from which he was writing; rather, the reader's understanding of the context was taken for granted.

Editing

Tony spent a great deal of his composing time editing. However, most of this time was spent proofreading rather than changing, rephrasing, adding, or evaluating the substantive parts of the discourse. Of a total of 234 changes made in all of the sessions, only 24 were related to changes of content and included the following categories:

1. Elaborations of ideas through the use of specification and detail;
2. Additions of modals that shift the mood of a sentence;
3. Deletions that narrow the focus of a paper;
4. Clause reductions or embeddings that tighten the structure of a paper;
5. Vocabulary choices that reflect a sensitivity to language;

6. Reordering of elements in a narrative;

7. Strengthening transitions between paragraphs;

8. Pronoun changes that signal an increased sensitivity to audience.

The 210 changes in form included the following:

Additions	19	Verb changes	4
Deletions	44	Spelling	95
Word choice	13	Punctuation	35
Unresolved problems	89		

The area that Tony changed most often was spelling, although, even after completing three drafts of a paper, Tony still had many words misspelled.

Miscue Analysis

Despite continual proofreading, Tony's completed drafts often retained a look of incompleteness. Words remained misspelled, syntax was uncorrected or overcorrected, suffixes, plural markers, and verb endings were missing, and often words or complete phrases were omitted.

The composing aloud behavior and the miscue analysis derived from it provide one of the first demonstrable ways of understanding how such seemingly incomplete texts can be considered "finished" by the student. (See Table 3 for a summary of Tony's miscues.) Tony consistently voiced complete sentences when composing aloud but only transcribed partial sentences. The same behavior occurred in relation to words with plural or marked endings. However, during rereading and even during editing, Tony supplied the missing endings, words, or phrases and did not seem to "see" what was missing from the text. Thus, when reading his paper, Tony "read in" the meaning he expected to be there which turned him into a reader of content rather than form. However, a difference can be observed between the extensive and reflexive modes, and in the area of correctness Tony's greater strength lay in the reflexive mode. In this mode, not only were more words produced in less time (1,062 vs. 658), but fewer decoding miscues occurred (38 vs. 46), and fewer unresolved problems remained in the text (34 vs. 55).

When Tony did choose to read for form, he was handicapped in another way. Through his years of schooling, Tony learned that there were sets of rules to be applied to one's writing, and he attempted to apply these rules of form to his prose. Often, though, the structures he produced were far more

Table 3   Tony—Miscue analysis.

	ENCODING			
	Speaking complete ideas but omitting certain words during writing	Pronouncing words with plural markers or other suffixes completely but omitting these endings during writing	Pronouncing the desired word but writing a homonym, an approximation of the word or a personal abbreviation of the word on paper	Total
S1	1	4	11	16
S2	8	0	14	22
S4	4	0	16	20
S5	3	1	15	19
	16	5	56	77

	DECODING			
	Reading in missing words or word endings	Deleting words or word endings	Reading the desired word rather than the word on the page	Reading abbreviations and misspellings as though they were written correctly	Total
S1	10	1	1	15	27
S2	5	1	2	10	18
S4	3	3	0	13	19
S5	7	1	2	10	20
	25	6	5	48	84

complicated than the simple set of proofreading rules he had at his disposal. He was therefore faced with applying the rule partially, discarding it, or attempting corrections through sound. None of these systems was completely helpful to Tony, and as often as a correction was made that improved the discourse, another was made that obscured it.

Summary

Finally, when Tony completed the writing process, he refrained from commenting on or contemplating his total written product. When he initiated writing, he immediately established distance between himself as writer and his discourse. He knew his preliminary draft might have errors and might need revision. At the end of each session, the distance had decreased if not entirely disappeared. Tony "read in" missing or omitted features, rarely perceived syntactic errors, and did not untangle overly embedded sentences. It was as if the semantic model in his head predominated, and the distance with which he entered the writing process had dissolved. Thus, even with his concern for revision and for correctness, even with the enormous amount of time he invested in rereading and repetition, Tony concluded the composing process with unresolved stylistic and syntactic problems. The conclusion here is not that Tony can't write, or that Tony doesn't know how to write, or that Tony needs to learn more rules: Tony is a writer with a highly consistent and deeply embedded recursive process. What he needs are teachers who can interpret that process for him, who can see through the tangles in the process just as he sees meaning beneath the tangles in his prose, and who can intervene in such a way that untangling his composing process leads him to create better prose.

SUMMARY OF THE FINDINGS

A major finding of this study is that, like Tony, all of the students studied displayed consistent composing processes; that is, the behavioral subsequences prewriting, writing, and editing appeared in sequential patterns that were recognizable across writing sessions and across students.

This consistency suggests a much greater internalization of process than has ever before been suspected. Since the written products of basic writers often look arbitrary, observers commonly assume that the students' approach is also arbitrary. However, just as Shaughnessy (1977) points out that there is "very little that is random . . . in what they have written" (p. 5), so, on close observation, very little appears random in *how* they write. The students observed had stable composing processes which they used whenever they were presented with a writing task. While this consistency argues against seeing these students as beginning writers, it ought not necessarily imply that they are proficient writers. Indeed, their lack of proficiency may be attributable to the way in which premature and rigid attempts to correct and edit their work truncate the flow of composing without substantially improving the form of what they have written. More detailed findings will be reviewed in the following subsections which treat the three major aspects of composing: prewriting, writing, and editing.

31

Prewriting

When not given specific prewriting instructions, the students in this study began writing within the first few minutes. The average time they spent on prewriting in sessions 1 and 2 was four minutes (see Table 4), and the planning strategies they used fell into three principal types:

1. Rephrasing the topic until a particular word or idea connected with the student's experience. The student then had "an event" in mind before writing began.

2. Turning the large conceptual issue in the topic (e.g., equality) into two manageable pieces for writing (e.g., rich vs. poor; black vs. white).

3. Initiating a string of associations to a word in the topic and then developing one or more of the associations during writing.

When students planned in any of these ways, they began to write with an articulated sense of where they wanted their discourse to go. However, frequently students read the topic and directions a few times and indicated that they had "no idea" what to write. On these occasions, they began writing without any secure sense of where they were heading, acknowledging only that they would "figure it out" as they went along. Often their first sentence was a rephrasing of the question in the topic which, now that it was in their own handwriting and down on paper in front of them, seemed to enable them to plan what ought to come next. In these instances, writing led to planning which led to clarifying which led to more writing. This sequence of planning and writing, clarifying and discarding, was repeated frequently in all of the sessions, even when students began writing with a secure sense of direction.

Although one might be tempted to conclude that these students began writing prematurely and that planning precisely what they were going to write ought to have occurred before they put pen to paper, the data here suggest:

1. that certain strategies, such as creating an association to a key word, focusing in and narrowing down the topic, dichotomizing and classifying, can and do take place in a relatively brief span of time; and

2. that the developing and clarifying of ideas is facilitated once students translate some of those ideas into written form. In other words, seeing ideas on paper enables students to reflect upon, change and develop those ideas further.

32

Table 4 Overview of all writing sessions.

	Prewriting time*				Total words / Total composing time				Editing changes		Unresolved problems	Miscues during reading
	S1	S2	S4	S5	S1	S2	S4	S5	Content	Form		
Tony	7.8	3.5	8.0	5.7	302 / 91.2	512 / 76.0	356 / 82.0	550 / 96.0	24	210	89	84
Dee	2.5	2.9	5.0	5.0	409 / 55.5	559 / 65.0	91 / 24.5	212 / 29.0	7	24	40	32
Stan	3.5	4.3	14.8	14.7	419 / 62.0	553 / 73.1	365 / 73.0	303 / 68.0	13	49	45	55
Lueller	2.0	1.5	4.0	13.0	518 / 90.8	588 / 96.8	3.5 / 95.0	363 / 77.8	2	167	143	147
Beverly	5.5	7.0	32.0	20.0	519 / 79.0	536 / 80.3	348 / 97.4	776 / 120.0	21	100	55	30

* Due to a change in the prewriting directions, only Sessions 1 and 2 are used to calculate the average time spent in prewriting.

Writing

Careful study revealed that students wrote by shuttling from the sense of what they wanted to say forward to the words on the page and back from the words on the page to their intended meaning. This "back and forth" movement appeared to be a recursive feature: at one moment students were writing, moving their ideas and their discourse forward; at the next they were backtracking, rereading, and digesting what had been written.

Recursive movements appeared at many points during the writing process. Occasionally sentences were written in groups and then reread as a "piece" of discourse; at other times sentences and phrases were written alone, repeated until the writer was satisfied or worn down, or rehearsed until the act of rehearsal led to the creation of a new sentence. In the midst of writing, editing occurred as students considered the surface features of language. Often planning of a global nature took place: in the midst of producing a first draft, students stopped and began planning how the second draft would differ from the first. Often in the midst of writing, students stopped and referred to the topic in order to check if they had remained faithful to the original intent, and occasionally, though infrequently, they identified a sentence or a phrase that seemed, to them, to produce a satisfactory ending. In all these behaviors, they were shuttling back and forth, projecting what would come next and doubling back to be sure of the ground they had covered.

A number of conclusions can be drawn from the observations of these students composing and from the comments they made: although they produced inadequate or flawed products, they nevertheless seemed to understand and perform some of the crucial operations involved in composing with skill. While it cannot be stated with certainty that the patterns they displayed are shared by other writers, some of the operations they performed appear sufficiently sound to serve as prototypes for constructing two major hypotheses on the nature of their composing processes. Whether the following hypotheses are borne out in studies of different types of writers remains an open question:

1. Composing does not occur in a straightforward, linear fashion. The process is one of accumulating discrete bits down on the paper and then working from those bits to reflect upon, structure, and then further develop what one means to say. It can be thought of as a kind of "retrospective structuring"; movement forward occurs only after one has reached back, which in turn occurs only after one has some sense of where one wants to go. Both aspects, the reaching back and the sensing forward, have a clarifying effect.

2. Composing always involves some measure of both construction and discovery. Writers construct their discourse inasmuch as they begin with a sense of what they want to write. This sense, as long as it remains implicit, is not equivalent to the explicit form it gives rise to. Thus, a process of constructing meaning is required. Rereading or backward movements become a way of assessing whether or not the words on the page adequately capture the original sense intended. Constructing simultaneously affords discovery. Writers know more fully what they mean only after having written it. In this way the explicit written form serves as a window on the implicit sense with which one began.

Editing

Editing played a major role in the composing processes of the students in this study (see Table 5). Soon after students began writing their first drafts, they began to edit, and they continued to do so during the intervals between drafts, during the writing of their second drafts and during the final reading of papers.

While editing, the students were concerned with a variety of items: the lexicon (i.e., spelling, word choice, and the context of words); the syntax (i.e., grammar, punctuation, and sentence structure); and the discourse as a whole (i.e., organization, coherence, and audience). However, despite the students' considered attempts to proofread their work, serious syntactic and stylistic problems remained in their finished drafts. The persistence of these

Table 5   Editing changes.

	Tony	Dee	Stan	Lueller	Beverly	Totals
Total number of words produced	1720	1271	1640	1754	2179	8564
Total form	210	24	49	167	100	550
Additions	19	2	10	21	11	63
Deletions	44	9	18	41	38	150
Word choice	13	4	1	27	6	51
Verb changes	4	1	2	7	12	26
Spelling	95	4	13	60	19	191
Punctuation	35	4	5	11	14	69
Total content	24	7	13	2	21	67

errors may, in part, be understood by looking briefly at some of the problems that arose for these students during editing.

Rule Confusion

(1) All of the students observed asked themselves, "Is this sentence [or feature] correct?" but the simple set of editing rules at their disposal was often inappropriate for the types of complicated structures they produced. As a result, they misapplied what they knew and either created a hypercorrection or impaired the meaning they had originally intended to clarify; (2) The students observed attempted to write with terms they heard in lectures or class discussions, but since they were not yet familiar with the syntactic or semantic constraints one word placed upon another, their experiments with academic language resulted in what Shaughnessy (1977, p. 49) calls, "lexical transplants" or "syntactic dissonances"; (3) The students tried to rely on their intuitions about language, in particular the sound of words. Often, however, they had been taught to mistrust what "sounded" right to them, and they were unaware of the particular feature in their speech codes that might need to be changed in writing to match the standard code. As a result, when they attempted corrections by sound, they became confused, and they began to have difficulty differentiating between what sounded right in speech and what needed to be marked on the paper.

Selective Perception

These students habitually reread their papers from internal semantic or meaning models. They extracted the meaning they wanted from the minimal cues on the page, and they did not recognize that outside readers would find those cues insufficient for meaning.

A study of Table 6 indicates that the number of problems remaining in the students' written products approximates the number of miscues produced during reading. This proximity, itself, suggests that many of these errors persisted because the students were so certain of the words they wanted to have on the page that they "read in" these words even when they were absent; in other words, they reduced uncertainty by operating as though what was in their heads was already on the page. The problem of selective perception, then, cannot be reduced solely to mechanical decoding; the semantic model from which students read needs to be acknowledged and taken into account in any study that attempts to explain how students write and why their completed written products end up looking so incomplete.

Table 6 The talk-write paradigm.
Miscues—Decoding behaviors

	Tony	Dee	Stan	Lueller	Beverly	Totals
Unresolved problems	89	40	45	143	55	372
"Reading in" missing words or word endings	25	13	11	44	11	104
Deleting words or word endings	6	2	4	14	9	35
"Reading" the desired word rather than the word on the page	5	6	18	15	8	52
"Reading" abbreviations and misspellings as though they were written correctly	48	11	22	74	2	157
	84	32	55	147	30	348

Egocentricity

The students in this study wrote from an egocentric point of view. While they occasionally indicated a concern for their readers, they more often took the reader's understanding for granted. They did not see the necessity of making their referents explicit, of making the connections among their ideas apparent, of carefully and explicitly relating one phenomenon to another, or of placing narratives or generalizations within an orienting, conceptual framework.

On the basis of these observations one may be led to conclude that these writers did not know how to edit their work. Such a conclusion must, however, be drawn with care. Efforts to improve their editing need to be based on an informed view of the role that editing already plays in their composing processes. Two conclusions in this regard are appropriate here:

1. Editing intrudes so often and to such a degree that it breaks down the rhythms generated by thinking and writing. When this happens the students are forced to go back and recapture the strands of their thinking once the editing operation has been completed. Thus, editing occurs prematurely, before students have generated enough discourse to approximate the ideas they have, and it often results in their losing track of their ideas.

2. Editing is primarily an exercise in error-hunting. The students are prematurely concerned with the "look" of their writing; thus, as soon as a few words are written on the paper, detection and correction of errors replaces writing and revising. Even when they begin writing with a tentative, flexible frame of mind, they soon become locked into whatever is on the page. What they seem to lack as much as any rule is a conception of editing that includes flexibility, suspended judgment, the weighing of possibilities, and the reworking of ideas.

IMPLICATIONS FOR TEACHING AND RESEARCH

One major implication of this study pertains to teachers' conceptions of unskilled writers. Traditionally, these students have been labeled "remedial," which usually implies that teaching ought to remedy what is "wrong" in their written products. Since the surface features in the writing of unskilled writers seriously interfere with the extraction of meaning from the page, much class time is devoted to examining the rules of the standard code. The pedagogical soundness of this procedure has been questioned frequently,[2] but in spite of the debate, the practice continues, and it results in a further complication, namely that students begin to conceive of writing as a "cosmetic" process where concern for correct form supersedes development of ideas. As a result, the excitement of composing, of constructing and discovering meaning, is cut off almost before it has begun.

More recently, unskilled writers have been referred to as "beginners," implying that teachers can start anew. They need not "punish" students for making mistakes, and they need not assume that their students have already been taught how to write. Yet this view ignores the highly elaborated, deeply embedded processes the students bring with them. These unskilled college writers are not beginners in a *tabula rasa* sense, and teachers err in assuming they are. The results of this study suggest that teachers may first need to identify which characteristic components of each student's process facilitate writing and which inhibit it before further teaching takes place. If they do not, teachers of unskilled writers may continue to place themselves in a defeating position: imposing another method of writing instruction upon the students' already internalized processes without first helping students to extricate themselves from the knots and tangles in those processes.

A second implication of this study is that the composing process is now amenable to a replicable and graphic mode of representation as a sequence of codable behaviors. The composing style sheets provide researchers and teachers with the first demonstrable way of documenting how individual students write. Such a tool may have diagnostic as well as research benefits. It may be used to record writing behaviors in large groups, prior to and after instruction, as well as in individuals. Certainly it lends itself to the longitudinal study of the writing process and may help to elucidate what it is that changes in the process as writers become more skilled.

A third implication relates to case studies and to the theories derived from them. This study is an illustration of the way in which a theoretical model of the composing process can be grounded in observations of the individual's experience of composing. It is precisely the complexity of this experience that the case study brings to light. However, by viewing a series of cases, the researcher can discern patterns and themes that suggest regularities in composing behavior across individuals. These common features lead to hypotheses and theoretical formulations which have some basis in shared experience. How far this shared experience extends is, of course, a question that can only be answered through further research.

A final implication derives from the preponderance of recursive behaviors in the composing processes studied here, and from the theoretical notion derived from these observations: retrospective structuring, or the going back to the sense of one's meaning in order to go forward and discover more of what one has to say. Seen in this light, composing becomes the carrying forward of an implicit sense into explicit form. Teaching composing, then, means paying attention not only to the forms or products but also to the explicative process through which they arise.

APPENDIX

Composing Style Sheet

Name: __Tony__   Mode: __Extensive TW1__   Date: __October 31, 1975__

Session: __1__   Topic: __Society & Culture__   Time: __11:00 AM – 12:30 PM__

Prewriting

								1	
RDRQAPL	QWCRIQPLRQ	PLRQPLRQRI	PLRQPLRQPLRQ	TA(-)QRIP L	RIRI RQ T	QDQTPLRQPLG	RQ	TW1 AR¹[Eₐₚ] R¹	PL RQPLG T
10	20	rephrasing 30 question	40	50	60	70	80	90	100

				2			3		
RW1RQTQRW1 To PL	RW1RW1RQRQ	RQ TPL	TW1[E(-)]	RW1→TW1	R²T	RW1 RW1 E RW1	TW1 PLL R1-3	TW1 PLL TW1	
10	developing 20 ideas	30	40	not a good way to 50 start a sentence	developing 60 narrative	70	80	90	200

4	5	6	7		8+9				
R3T→TW1 TW1	TW1T→TW1	PLT TW1[re]	TW1 T RQ	PL R²	TW1 [re] TW1 PLG RQ	RW1 [PL→E]	RW1 TE	RW1 [Eadd] PL	
10	20	ending 30	effects 40 of crisis	ending 50	60 End of W1 70	80	read for 90 content first	300	

							1		
RW1 A(-) TPL	RW1 A(+) RW1	[Eₐₛ] T	RW1	PLW2	TW2 [Egᵣ] TW2[Egᵣ]TW2 PL				
go into 10 more depth	20	30	40	elaborating 50 lay-offs—jobs	60	70 Begin W2 80	90	400	

2					3				
R2A(+) TW2	[R2]A(+) TW2	[Eₐₚ]	R² R³ PL	T[Eₐₛ gᵣ]PL	A(+)TW2 [PL→ E] TW2 [Eₐ_del^add] TW2[Egᵣ] TW2 PLR³ PL-R³			Tadd	
10	20	30	40	there is 50 there are	60	70	80	90	500

4					5				
TW2—[EPL	]TW2	PL RW2 [E PL]RW2[EWC]RIQ	RW1 [EWC^add]	A(+) TW2 [re] TW2 T	TW2[re]RW1 T PL RW1 T [re] TW2 [re]				
10	20	30	40	50	60	70 elaborating 80	90	600	

6									
[re][re]TW2 [re]	TW2 [re] TW2		PLRW1	RW2 [re] RW2	A(+) RW2 TE	PL RW1		RW2	PL
10	20	30	40	50	explaining 60 changes	70	80	90	700

			7						
RW1 T PI	RW2 T R⁴ T	R⁴TW2	[re]	TW2 [re] TW2		R^6-7 [Eadd] R^6-7 [re]	PL R^5-7 A(+)PIRW1		
10	20 elaborating 30 new sentence	40	50	60	70	80	90	800	

	8	9		10					
TS→PL	RQ PL	T RW1→TW2[re]	R⁸ TW2	Tadd RQ A(-) RW1 A(+) R⁹ TW2			PL	RQ RW2	
should 10 I add more?	20	30	40	elaborating 50	changes 60 mind	ending 70 End of W2 80	90	900	

RW2	WS to 960								
10	Total 20 composing finished	30	40	50	60	70	80	90	1000

Writing Sample
TONY
Session 1
W1

All men can't be consider equal in a America base on financial situation.[1] Because their
are men born in rich families that will never have to worry about any financial difficulties.[2]

    are

And then theyre / ~~the~~ another type of Americans that is born to a poor family and al-

  may

way / have some kind of fina—difficulty.[3] Espeicaly nowadays in New York city With

    and all If he is able

the budgit Crisis /   .[4] ~~He may~~ be able To get a job.[5] But are now he lose the job just
as easy as he got it.[6] So when he loses his job he'll have to try to get some fina—assistance.[7]

        here

~~A~~ Then he'll probley have even more fin—diffuicuty.[8] So right / you can't see that In
Amerian, all men are not create equal in the fin—sense.[9]

Writing Sample
TONY
Session 1
W2

All men can not be consider equal in America base on financial situation.[1] Because
their are men born in rich families that will never have to worry about any financial ~~diffuci~~

    the

diffuliculties.[2] And then they're are / another type of ameraicans that are born to a poor

    may

famitly.[3] And This is the type of Americans that ~~will~~ / alway have some kind of finanical
diffuliculty.[4] Espeical today ~~today thei~~n new york The way the city has fallen ~~has fallen~~

    working

into fin—debt.[5] It has become such a big crisis for the ~~people~~ people, in the [6] If the

    with the   the is

working man is able to find a job, espeicaly ~~for~~ / ~~city a~~ city The way ~~the way~~ city / fin—
sitionu is set up now, ~~h~~He'll probley lose the job a whole lot faster than what he got it.[7]
When he loses his job he'll ~~p~~ have even more fin—difficulty.[8] And then he'll be force to
go~~t~~ to the city for some fini—assi—.[9] So right here you can see that all men in America
are not create equal in the fin—sense.[10]

NOTES

1. The word "read" is used in a particular manner here. In the traditional sense, reading
refers to accurate decoding of written symbols. Here it refers to students' verbalizing words or
endings even when the symbols for those words are missing or only minimally present.
Whenever the term "reading" is used in this way, it will be in quotation marks.

2. For discussions on the controversy over the effects of grammar instruction on writing ability, see the following: Richard Braddock, Richard Lloyd-Jones, and Lowell Schoer, *Research in Written Composition* (Urbana, Ill.: National Council of Teachers of English, 1963); Frank O'Hare, *Sentence Combining* (NCTE Research Report No. 15, Urbana, Ill.: National Council of Teachers of English, 1973); Elizabeth F. Haynes, "Using Research in Preparing to Teach Writing," *English Journal*, 1978, 67, 82–89.

REFERENCES

Braddock, R., Lloyd-Jones, R., & Schoer, L. *Research in written composition.* Urbana, Ill.: National Council of Teachers of English, 1963.

Britton, J., Burgess, T., Martin, N., McLeod, A., & Rosen, H. *The development of writing abilities (11–18).* London: Macmillan Education Ltd., 1975.

Burton, D. L. Research in the teaching of English: The troubled dream. *Research in the Teaching of English*, 1973, 1, 160–187.

Cooper, C. R. Doing research/reading research. *English Journal*, 1974, 63, 94–99.

Cooper, C. R., & Odell, L. (Eds.) *Research on composing: Points of departure.* Urbana, Ill.: National Council of Teachers of English, 1978.

Emig, J. A. *The composing processes of twelfth graders.* Urbana, Ill.: National Council of Teachers of English, 1971. (Research Report No. 13) (Ed. D. Dissertation, Harvard University, 1969).

Emig, J. A. On teaching composition: Some hypotheses as definitions. *Research in the Teaching of English*, 1967, 1, 127–135.

Goodman, K. S. (Ed.) *Miscue analysis: Applications to reading instruction.* Urbana, Ill.: NCTE and ERIC, 1973.

Graves, D. H. Children's writing: Research directions and hypotheses based upon an examination of the writing process of seven year old children (Doctoral dissertation, State University of New York at Buffalo, 1973). *Dissertation Abstracts International*, 1974, 34, 6255A.

Haynes, E. F. Using research in preparing to teach writing. *English Journal*, 1978, 67, 82–89.

Mischel, T. A case study of a twelfth-grade writer. *Research in the Teaching of English*, 1974, 8, 303–314.

O'Hare, F. *Sentence-combining: Improving student writing without formal grammar instruction.* Urbana, Ill.: National Council of Teachers of English, 1973. (Research Report No. 15)

Perl, S. *Five writers writing: Case studies of the composing processes of unskilled college writers.* Unpublished doctoral dissertation, New York University, 1978.

Pianko, S. *The composing acts of college freshmen writers.* Unpublished Ed.D. dissertation, Rutgers University, 1977.

Shaughnessy, M. P. *Errors and expectations: A guide for the teacher of basic writing.* New York: Oxford University Press, 1977.

Stallard, C. K. An analysis of the writing behavior of good student writers. *Research in the Teaching of English*, 1974, 8, 206–218.

Revision Strategies of Student Writers and Experienced Adult Writers

Nancy Sommers

Although various aspects of the writing process have been studied extensively of late, research on revision has been notably absent. The reason for this, I suspect, is that current models of the writing process have directed attention away from revision. With few exceptions, these models are linear; they separate the writing process into discrete stages. Two representative models are Gordon Rohman's suggestion that the composing process moves from prewriting to writing to rewriting and James Britton's model of the writing process as a series of stages described in metaphors of linear growth, conception—incubation—production.[1] What is striking about these theories of writing is that they model themselves on speech: Rohman defines the writer in a way that cannot distinguish him from a speaker ("A writer is a man who . . . puts [his] experience into words in his own mind"—p. 15); and Britton bases his theory of writing on what he calls (following Jakobson) the "expressiveness" of speech.[2] Moreover, Britton's study itself follows the "linear model" of the relation of thought and language in speech proposed by Vygotsky, a relationship embodied in the linear movement "from the motive which engenders a thought to the shaping of the thought, *first* in inner speech, *then* in meanings of words, and *finally* in words" (quoted in Britton, p. 40). What this movement fails to take into account in its linear structure—"first . . . then . . . finally"—is the recursive shaping of thought by language; what it fails to take into account is *revision*. In these linear

Reprinted from *College Composition and Communication* 31.4 (December 1980): 378–88.
Used with permission.

conceptions of the writing process revision is understood as a separate stage at the end of the process—a stage that comes after the completion of a first or second draft and one that is temporally distinct from the prewriting and writing stages of the process.[3]

The linear model bases itself on speech in two specific ways. First of all, it is based on traditional rhetorical models, models that were created to serve the spoken art of oratory. In whatever ways the parts of classical rhetoric are described, they offer "stages" of composition that are repeated in contemporary models of the writing process. Edward Corbett, for instance, describes the "five parts of a discourse"—*inventio, dispositio, elocutio, memoria, pronuntiatio*—and, disregarding the last two parts since "after rhetoric came to be concerned mainly with written discourse, there was no further need to deal with them,"[4] he produces a model very close to Britton's conception [*inventio*], incubation [*dispositio*], production [*elocutio*]. Other rhetorics also follow this procedure, and they do so not simply because of historical accident. Rather, the process represented in the linear model is based on the irreversibility of speech. Speech, Roland Barthes says, "is irreversible":

> "A word cannot be retracted, except precisely by saying that one retracts it. To cross out here is to add: if I want to erase what I have just said, I cannot do it without showing the eraser itself (I must say: '*or rather. . .*' '*I expressed myself badly. . .*'); paradoxically, it is ephemeral speech which is indelible, not monumental writing. All that one can do in the case of a spoken utterance is to tack on another utterance."[5]

What is impossible in speech is *revision*: like the example Barthes gives, revision in speech is an afterthought. In the same way, each stage of the linear model must be exclusive (distinct from the other stages) or else it becomes trivial and counterproductive to refer to these junctures as "stages."

By staging revision after enunciation, the linear models reduce revision in writing, as in speech, to no more than an afterthought. In this way such models make the study of revision impossible. Revision, in Rohman's model, is simply the repetition of writing; or to pursue Britton's organic metaphor, revision is simply the further growth of what is already there, the "preconceived" product. The absence of research on revision, then, is a function of a theory of writing which makes revision both superfluous and redundant, a theory which does not distinguish between writing and speech.

What the linear models do produce is a parody of writing. Isolating revision and then disregarding it plays havoc with the experiences composition teachers have of the actual writing and rewriting of experienced writers. Why should the linear model be preferred? Why should revision be forgotten,

44

superfluous? Why do teachers offer the linear model and students accept it? One reason, Barthes suggests, is that "there is a fundamental tie between teaching and speech," while "writing begins at the point where speech becomes *impossible.*"[6] The spoken word cannot be revised. The possibility of revision distinguishes the written text from speech. In fact, according to Barthes, this is the essential difference between writing and speaking. When we must revise, when the very idea is subject to recursive shaping by language, then speech becomes inadequate. This is a matter to which I will return, but first we should examine, theoretically, a detailed exploration of what student writers as distinguished from experienced adult writers *do* when they write and rewrite their work. Dissatisfied with both the linear model of writing and the lack of attention to the process of revision, I conducted a series of studies over the past three years which examined the revision processes of student writers and experienced writers to see what role revision played in their writing processes. In the course of my work the revision process was redefined as *a sequence of changes in a composition—changes which are initiated by cues and occur continually throughout the writing of a work.*

METHODOLOGY

I used a case study approach. The student writers were twenty freshmen at Boston University and the University of Oklahoma with SAT verbal scores ranging from 450–600 in their first semester of composition. The twenty experienced adult writers from Boston and Oklahoma City included journalists, editors, and academics. To refer to the two groups, I use the terms *student writers* and *experienced writers* because the principal difference between these two groups is the amount of experience they have had in writing.

Each writer wrote three essays, expressive, explanatory, and persuasive, and rewrote each essay twice, producing nine written products in draft and final form. Each writer was interviewed three times after the final revision of each essay. And each writer suggested revisions for a composition written by an anonymous author. Thus extensive written and spoken documents were obtained from each writer.

The essays were analyzed by counting and categorizing the changes made. Four revision operations were identified: deletion, substitution, addition, and reordering. And four levels of changes were identified: word, phrase, sentence, theme (the extended statement of one idea). A coding system was developed for identifying the frequency of revision by level and operation. In addition, transcripts of the interviews in which the writers interpreted their revisions were used to develop what was called a *scale of concerns* for each writer. This scale enabled me to codify what were the writer's primary concerns, secondary concerns, tertiary concerns, and whether the writers used the same scale of concerns when revising the second or third drafts as they used in revising the first draft.

REVISION STRATEGIES OF STUDENT WRITERS

Most of the students I studied did not use the terms *revision* or *rewriting*. In fact, they did not seem comfortable using the word *revision* and explained that revision was not a word they used, but the word their teachers used. Instead, most of the students had developed various functional terms to describe the type of changes they made. The following are samples of these definitions:

> *Scratch Out and Do Over Again*: "I say scratch out and do over, and that means what it says. Scratching out and cutting out. I read what I have written and I cross out a word and put another word in; a more decent word or a better word. Then if there is somewhere to use a sentence that I have crossed out, I will put it there."
>
> *Reviewing*: "Reviewing means just using better words and eliminating words that are not needed. I go over and change words around."
>
> *Reviewing*: "I just review every word and make sure that everything is worded right. I see if I am rambling; I see if I can put a better word in or leave one out. Usually when I read what I have written, I say to myself, 'that word is so bland or so trite,' and then I go and get my thesaurus."
>
> *Redoing*: "Redoing means cleaning up the paper and crossing out. It is looking at something and saying, no that has to go, or no, that is not right."
>
> *Marking Out*: "I don't use the word rewriting because I only write one draft and the changes that I make are made on top of the draft. The changes that I make are usually just marking out words and putting different ones in."
>
> *Slashing and Throwing Out*: "I throw things out and say they are not good. I like to write like Fitzgerald did by inspiration, and if I feel inspired then I don't need to slash and throw much out."

The predominant concern in these definitions is vocabulary. The students understand the revision process as a rewording activity. They do so because they perceive words as the unit of written discourse. That is, they concentrate on particular words apart from their role in the text. Thus one student quoted above thinks in terms of dictionaries, and, following the

46

eighteenth century theory of words parodied in *Gulliver's Travels*, he imagines a load of things carried about to be exchanged. Lexical changes are the major revision activities of the students because economy is their goal. They are governed, like the linear model itself, by the Law of Occam's Razor that prohibits logically needless repetition: redundancy and superfluity. Nothing governs speech more than such superfluities; speech constantly repeats itself precisely because spoken words, as Barthes writes, are expendable in the cause of communication. The aim of revision according to the students' own description is therefore to clean up speech; the redundancy of speech is unnecessary in writing, their logic suggests, because writing, unlike speech, can be reread. Thus one student said, "Redoing means cleaning up the paper and crossing out." The remarkable contradiction of cleaning by marking might, indeed, stand for student revision as I have encountered it.

The students place a symbolic importance on their selection and rejection of words as the determiners of success or failure for their compositions. When revising, they primarily ask themselves: can I find a better word or phrase? A more impressive, not so cliched, or less hum-drum word? Am I repeating the same word or phrase too often? They approach the revision process with what could be labeled as a "thesaurus philosophy of writing"; the students consider the thesaurus a harvest of lexical substitutions and believe that most problems in their essays can be solved by rewording. What is revealed in the students' use of the thesaurus is a governing attitude toward their writing: that the meaning to be communicated is already there, already finished, already produced, ready to be communicated, and all that is necessary is a better word "rightly worded." One student defined revision as "redoing"; "redoing" meant "just using better words and eliminating words that are not needed." For the students, writing is translating: the thought to the page, the language of speech to the more formal language of prose, the word to its synonym. Whatever is translated, an original text already exists for students, one which need not be discovered or acted upon, but simply communicated.[7]

The students list repetition as one of the elements they most worry about. This cue signals to them that they need to eliminate the repetition either by substituting or deleting words or phrases. Repetition occurs, in large part, because student writing imitates—transcribes—speech: attention to repetitious words is a manner of cleaning speech. Without a sense of the developmental possibilities of revision (and writing in general) students seek, on the authority of many textbooks, simply to clean up their language and prepare to type. What is curious, however, is that students are aware of lexical repetition, but not conceptual repetition. They only notice the repetition if they can "hear" it; they do not diagnose lexical repetition as symptomatic of problems on a deeper level. By rewording their sentences to avoid the lexical repetition, the students solve the immediate problem, but blind themselves to problems on a textual level; although they are using different words, they are sometimes merely restating the same idea with different words. Such blindness, as I discovered with student writers, is the inability to "see" revision as a process: the inability to "re-view" their work again, as it were, with different eyes, and to start over.

The revision strategies described above are consistent with the students' understanding of the revision process as requiring lexical changes but not semantic changes. For the students, the extent to which they revise is a function of their level of inspiration. In fact, they use the word *inspiration* to describe the ease or difficulty with which their essay is written, and the extent to which the essay needs to be revised. If students feel inspired, if the writing comes easily, and if they don't get stuck on individual words or phrases, then they say that they cannot see any reason to revise. Because students do not see revision as an activity in which they modify and develop perspectives and ideas, they feel that if they know what they want to say, then there is little reason for making revisions.

The only modification of ideas in the students' essays occurred when they tried out two or three introductory paragraphs. This results, in part, because the students have been taught in another version of the linear model of composing to use a thesis statement as a controlling device in their introductory paragraphs. Since they write their introductions and their thesis statements even before they have really discovered what they want to say, their early close attention to the thesis statement, and more generally the linear model, function to restrict and circumscribe not only the development of their ideas, but also their ability to change the direction of these ideas.

Too often as composition teachers we conclude that students do not willingly revise. The evidence from my research suggests that it is not that students are unwilling to revise, but rather that they do what they have been taught to do in a consistently narrow and predictable way. On every occasion when I asked students why they hadn't made any more changes, they essentially replied, "I knew something larger was wrong, but I didn't think it would help to move words around." The students have strategies for handling words and phrases and their strategies helped them on a word or sentence level. What they lack, however, is a set of strategies to help them identify the "something larger" that they sensed was wrong and work from there. The students do not have strategies for handling the whole essay. They lack procedures or heuristics to help them reorder lines of reasoning or ask questions about their purposes and readers. The students view their compositions in a linear way as a series of parts. Even such potentially useful concepts as "unity" or "form" are reduced to the rule that a composition, if it is to have form, must have an introduction, a body, and a conclusion, or the sum total of the necessary parts.

The students decide to stop revising when they decide that they have not violated any of the rules for revising. These rules, such as "Never begin a sentence with a conjunction" or "Never end a sentence with a preposition," are lexically cued and rigidly applied. In general, students will subordinate the demands of the specific problems of their text to the demands of the rules. Changes are made in compliance with abstract rules about the product, rules that quite often do not apply to the specific problems in the text. These revision strategies are teacher-based, directed towards a teacher-reader who expects compliance with rules—with pre-existing "conceptions"—and who will only examine parts of the composition (writing comments about those parts in the margins of their essays) and will cite any violations of rules in those parts. At best the students see their writing altogether passively through the eyes of former teachers or their surrogates, the textbooks, and are bound to the rules which they have been taught.

REVISION STRATEGIES OF EXPERIENCED WRITERS

One aim of my research has been to contrast how student writers define revision with how a group of experienced writers define their revision processes. Here is a sampling of the definitions from the experienced writers:

> *Rewriting*: "It is a matter of looking at the kernel of what I have written, the content, and then thinking about it, responding to it, making decisions, and actually restructuring it."

> *Rewriting*: "I rewrite as I write. It is hard to tell what is a first draft because it is not determined by time. In one draft, I might cross out three pages, write two, cross out a fourth, rewrite it, and call it a draft. I am constantly writing and rewriting. I can only conceptualize so much in my first draft—only so much information can be held in my head at one time; my rewriting efforts are a reflection of how much information I can encompass at one time. There are levels and agenda which I have to attend to in each draft."

> *Rewriting*: "Rewriting means on one level, finding the argument, and on another level, language changes to make the argument more effective. Most of the time I feel as if I can go on rewriting forever. There is always one part of a piece that I could keep working on. It is always difficult to know at what point to abandon a piece of writing. I like this idea that a piece of writing is never finished, just abandoned."

Rewriting: "My first draft is usually very scattered. In rewriting, I find the line of argument. After the argument is resolved, I am much more interested in word choice and phrasing."

Revising: "My cardinal rule in revising is never to fall in love with what I have written in a first or second draft. An idea, sentence, or even a phrase that looks catchy, I don't trust. Part of this idea is to wait a while. I am much more in love with something after I have written it than I am a day or two later. It is much easier to change anything with time."

Revising: "It means taking apart what I have written and putting it back together again. I ask major theoretical questions of my ideas, respond to those questions, and think of proportion and structure, and try to find a controlling metaphor. I find out which ideas can be developed and which should be dropped. I am constantly chiseling and changing as I revise."

The experienced writers describe their primary objective when revising as finding the form or shape of their argument. Although the metaphors vary, the experienced writers often use structural expressions such as "finding a framework," "a pattern," or "a design" for their argument. When questioned about this emphasis, the experienced writers responded that since their first drafts are usually scattered attempts to define their territory, their objective in the second draft is to begin observing general patterns of development and deciding what should be included and what excluded. One writer explained, "I have learned from experience that I need to keep writing a first draft until I figure out what I want to say. Then in a second draft, I begin to see the structure of an argument and how all the various sub-arguments which are buried beneath the surface of all those sentences are related." What is described here is a process in which the writer is both agent and vehicle. "Writing," says Barthes, unlike speech, "develops like a seed, not a line,"[8] and like a seed it confuses beginning and end, conception and production. Thus, the experienced writers say their drafts are "not determined by time," that rewriting is a "constant process," that they feel as if (they) "can go on forever." Revising confuses the beginning and end, the agent and vehicle; it confuses, *in order to find*, the line of argument.

After a concern for form, the experienced writers have a second objective: a concern for their readership. In this way, "production" precedes "conception." The experienced writers imagine a reader (reading their product) whose existence and whose expectations influence their revision process. They have abstracted the standards of a reader and this reader seems to be partially a reflection of themselves and functions as a critical and productive collaborator—a collaborator who has yet to love their work. The anticipation of a reader's judgment causes a feeling of dissonance when the writer recognizes incongruities between intention and execution, and requires these writers to make revisions on all levels. Such a reader gives them just what the students lacked: new eyes to "re-view" their work. The experienced writers believe that they have learned the causes and conditions, the product, which will influence their reader, and their revision strategies are geared towards creating these causes and conditions. They demonstrate a complex understanding of which examples, sentences, or phrases should be included or excluded. For example, one experienced writer decided to delete public examples and add private examples when writing about the energy crisis because "private examples would be less controversial and thus more persuasive." Another writer revised his transitional sentences because "some kinds of transitions are more easily recognized as transitions than others." These examples represent the type of strategic attempts these experienced writers use to manipulate the conventions of discourse in order to communicate to their reader.

But these revision strategies are a process of more than communication; they are part of the process of *discovering meaning* altogether. Here we can see the importance of dissonance; at the heart of revision is the process by which writers recognize and resolve the dissonance they sense in their writing. Ferdinand de Saussure has argued that meaning is differential or "diacritical," based on differences between terms rather than "essential" or inherent qualities of terms. "Phonemes," he said, "are characterized not, as one might think, by their own positive quality but simply by the fact that they are distinct."[9] In fact, Saussure bases his entire *Course in General Linguistics* on these differences, and such differences are dissonant; like musical dissonances which gain their significance from their relationship to the "key" of the composition which itself is determined by the whole language, specific language (parole) gains its meaning from the system of language (langue) of which it is a manifestation and part. The musical composition— a "composition" of parts—creates its "key" as in an over-all structure which determines the value (meaning) of its parts. The analogy with music is readily seen in the compositions of experienced writers: both sorts of composition are based precisely on those structures experienced writers seek in their writing. It is this complicated relationship between the parts and the whole in the work of experienced writers which destroys the linear model; writing cannot develop "like a line" because each addition or deletion is a reordering of the whole. Explicating Saussure, Jonathan Culler asserts that "meaning depends on difference of meaning."[10] But student writers constantly struggle to bring their essays into congruence with a predefined meaning. The experienced writers do the opposite: they seek to discover (to create) meaning in the engagement with their writing, in revision. They seek to emphasize and exploit the lack of clarity, the differences of meaning, the dissonance, that writing as opposed to speech allows in the possibility of revision. Writing has spatial and temporal features not apparent in speech—words are recorded in space and fixed in time—which is why writing is susceptible to reordering and later addition. Such features make possible the dissonance that both provokes revision and promises, from itself, new meaning.

For the experienced writers the heaviest concentration of changes is on the sentence level, and the changes are predominantly by addition and deletion. But, unlike the students, experienced writers make changes on all levels and use all revision operations. Moreover, the operations the students fail to use—reordering and addition—seem to require a theory of the revision process as a totality—a theory which, in fact, encompasses the *whole* of the composition. Unlike the students, the experienced writers possess a nonlinear theory in which a sense of the whole writing both precedes and grows out of an examination of the parts. As we saw, one writer said he needed "a first draft to figure out what to say," and "a second draft to see the structure of an argument buried beneath the surface." Such a "theory" is both theoretical and strategical; once again, strategy and theory are conflated in ways that are literally impossible for the linear model. Writing appears to be more like a seed than a line.

Two elements of the experienced writers' theory of the revision process are the adoption of a holistic perspective and the perception that revision is a recursive process. The writers ask: what does my essay as a *whole* need for form, balance, rhythm, or communication. Details are added, dropped, substituted, or reordered according to their sense of what the essay needs for emphasis and proportion. This sense, however, is constantly in flux as ideas are developed and modified; it is constantly "re-viewed" in relation to the parts. As their ideas change, revision becomes an attempt to make their writing consonant with that changing vision.

The experienced writers see their revision process as a recursive process—a process with significant recurring activities—with different levels of attention and different agenda for each cycle. During the first revision cycle their attention is primarily directed towards narrowing the topic and delimiting their ideas. At this point, they are not as concerned as they are later about vocabulary and style. The experienced writers explained that they get closer to their meaning by not limiting themselves too early to lexical concerns. As one writer commented to explain her revision process, a comment inspired by the summer 1977 New York power failure: "I feel like Con Edison cutting off certain states to keep the generators going. In first and second drafts, I try to cut off as much as I can of my editing generator, and in a third draft, I

52

try to cut off some of my idea generators, so I can make sure that I will actually finish the essay." Although the experienced writers describe their revision process as a series of different levels or cycles, it is inaccurate to assume that they have only one objective for each cycle and that each cycle can be defined by a different objective. The same objectives and sub-processes are present in each cycle, but in different proportions. Even though these experienced writers place the predominant weight upon finding the form of their argument during the first cycle, other concerns exist as well. Conversely, during the later cycles, when the experienced writers' primary attention is focused upon stylistic concerns, they are still attuned, although in a reduced way, to the form of the argument. Since writers are limited in what they can attend to during each cycle (understandings are temporal), revision strategies help balance competing demands on attention. Thus, writers can concentrate on more than one objective at a time by developing strategies to sort out and organize their different concerns in successive cycles of revision.

It is a sense of writing as discovery—a repeated process of beginning over again, starting out new—that the students failed to have. I have used the notion of dissonance because such dissonance, the incongruities between intention and execution, governs both writing and meaning. Students do not see the incongruities. They need to rely on their own internalized sense of good writing and to see their writing with their "own" eyes. Seeing in revision—seeing beyond hearing—is at the root of the word *revision* and the process itself; current dicta on revising blind our students to what is actually involved in revision. In fact, they blind them to what constitutes good writing altogether. Good writing disturbs: it creates dissonance. Students need to seek the dissonance of discovery, utilizing in their writing, as the experienced writers do, the very difference between writing and speech—the possibility of revision.

NOTES

1. D. Gordon Rohman and Albert O. Wlecke, "Pre-writing: The Construction and Application of Models for Concept Formation in Writing," Cooperative Research Project No. 2174, U.S. Office of Education, Department of Health, Education, and Welfare; James Britton, Anthony Burgess, Nancy Martin, Alex McLeod, Harold Rosen, *The Development of Writing Abilities (11–18)* (London: Macmillan Education, 1975).

2. Britton is following Roman Jakobson, "Linguistics and Poetics," in T. A. Sebeok, *Style in Language* (Cambridge, Mass: MIT Press, 1960).

3. For an extended discussion of this issue see Nancy Sommers, "The Need for Theory in Composition Research," *College Composition and Communication,* 30 (February, 1979), 46–49.

4. *Classical Rhetoric for the Modern Student* (New York: Oxford University Press, 1965), p. 27.

5. Roland Barthes, "Writers, Intellectuals, Teachers," in *Image-Music-Text*, trans. Stephen Heath (New York: Hill and Wang, 1977), pp. 190–191.

6. "Writers, Intellectuals, Teachers," p. 190.

7. Nancy Sommers and Ronald Schleifer, "Means and Ends: Some Assumptions of Student Writers," *Composition and Teaching*, II (in press).

8. *Writing Degree Zero* in *Writing Degree Zero and Elements of Semiology*, trans. Annette Lavers and Colin Smith (New York: Hill and Wang, 1968), p. 20.

9. *Course in General Linguistics*, trans. Wade Baskin (New York, 1966), p. 119.

10. Jonathan Culler, *Saussure* (Penguin Modern Masters Series; London: Penguin Books, 1976), p. 70.

Acknowledgment: The author wishes to express her gratitude to Professor William Smith, University of Pittsburgh, for his vital assistance with the research reported in this article and to Patrick Hays, her husband, for extensive discussions and critical editorial help.

The Writer's Audience
Is Always a Fiction

WALTER J. ONG, S.J.

Epistola . . . non erubescit.
　　—Cicero, Epistolae ad familiares *v. 12.1.*

Ubi nihil erit quae scribas, id ipsum scribes.
　　—Cicero, Epistolae ad Atticum *iv.8.4.*

I

Although there is a large and growing literature on the differences between oral and written verbalization, many aspects of the differences have not been looked into at all, and many others, although well known, have not been examined in their full implications. Among these latter is the relationship, of the so-called "audience" to writing as such, to the situation that inscribed communication establishes and to the roles that readers as readers are consequently called on to play. Some studies in literary history and criticism at times touch near this subject, but none, it appears, take it up in any detail.

The standard locus in Western intellectual tradition for study of audience responses has been rhetoric. But rhetoric originally concerned oral communication, as is indicated by its name, which comes from the Greek word for public speaking. Over two millennia, rhetoric has been gradually extended to include writing more and more, until today, in highly technological cultures, this is its principal concern. But the extension has come

Reprinted by permission of the Modern Language Association of America from *PMLA* 90.1 (January 1975): 9–21. Copyright © 1975 by the Modern Language Association of America.

gradually and has advanced pari passu with the slow and largely unnoticed emergence of markedly chirographic and typographic styles out of those originating in oral performance, with the result that the differentiation between speech and writing has never become a matter of urgent concern for the rhetoric of any given age: when orality was in the ascendancy, rhetoric was oral-focused; as orality yielded to writing, the focus of rhetoric was slowly shifted, unreflectively for the most part, and without notice.

Histories of the relationship between literature and culture have something to say about the status and behavior of readers, before and after reading given materials, as do mass media studies, readership surveys, liberation programs for minorities or various other classes of persons, books on reading skills, works of literary criticism, and works on linguistics, especially those addressing differences between hearing and reading. But most of these studies, except perhaps literary criticism and linguistic studies, treat only perfunctorily, if at all, the roles imposed on the reader by a written or printed text not imposed by spoken utterance. Formalist or structuralist critics, including French theorists such as Paul Ricoeur as well as Roland Barthes, Jacques Derrida, Michel Foucault, Philippe Sollers, and Tzvetan Todorov, variously advert to the immediacy of the oral as against writing and print and occasionally study differences between speech and writing, as Louis Lavelle did much earlier in *La Parole et l'écriture* (1942). In treating of masks and "shadows" in his *Sociologie du théâtre* (1965), Jean Duvignaud brilliantly discusses the projections of a kind of collective consciousness on the part of theater audiences. But none of these appear to broach directly the question of readers' roles called for by a written text, either synchronically as such roles stand at present or diachronically as they have developed through history. Linguistic theorists such as John R. Searle and John L. Austin treat "illocutionary acts" (denoted by "warn," "command," "state," etc.), but these regard the speaker's or writer's need in certain instances to secure a special hold on those he addresses,[1] not any special role imposed by writing.

Wayne Booth in *The Rhetoric of Fiction* and Walker Gibson, whom Booth quotes, come quite close to the concerns of the present study in their treatment of the "mock reader," as does Henry James, whom Booth also cites, in his discussion of the way an author makes "his reader very much as he makes his character."[2] But this hint of James is not developed—there is no reason why it should be—and neither Booth nor Gibson discusses in any detail the history of the ways in which readers have been called on to relate to texts before them. Neither do Robert Scholes and Robert Kellogg in their invaluable work, *The Nature of Narrative*: they skirt the subject in their chapter on "The Oral Heritage of Written Narrative,"[3] but remain chiefly concerned with the oral performer, the writer, and techniques, rather than with the recipient of the message. Yet a great many of the studies noted here as well as many others, among which might be mentioned Norman N. Holland's *The Dynamics of Literary Response* (1968), suggest the time is ripe for a study of the history of readers and their enforced roles, for they show that we have ample phenomenological and literary sophistication to manage many of the complications involved.

So long as verbal communication is reduced to a simplistic mechanistic model which supposedly moves corpuscular units of something labeled "information" back and forth along tracks between two termini, there is of course no special problem with those who assimilate the written or printed word. For the speaker, the audience is in front of him. For the writer, the audience is simply further away, in time or space or both. A surface inscribed with information can neutralize time by preserving the information and conquer space by moving the information to its recipient over distances that sound cannot traverse. If, however, we put aside this alluring but deceptively neat and mechanistic mock-up and look at verbal communication in its human actuality, noting that words consist not of corpuscular units but of evanescent sound and that, as Maurice Merleau-Ponty has pointed out,[4] words are never fully determined in their abstract signification but have meaning only with relation to man's body and to its interaction with its surroundings, problems with the writer's audience begin to show themselves. Writing calls for difficult, and often quite mysterious, skills. Except for a small corps of highly trained writers, most persons could get into written form few if any of the complicated and nuanced meanings they regularly convey orally. One reason is evident: the spoken word is part of present actuality and has its meaning established by the total situation in which it comes into being. Context for the spoken word is simply present, centered in the person speaking and the one or ones to whom he addresses himself and to whom he is related existentially in terms of the circumambient actuality.[5] But the meaning caught in writing comes provided with no such present circumambient actuality, at least normally. (One might except special cases of written exchanges between persons present to one another physically but with oral channels blocked: two deaf persons, for example, or two persons who use different variants of Chinese and are orally incomprehensible to one another but can communicate through the same written characters, which carry virtually the same meanings though they are sounded differently in the different varieties of Chinese.)

Such special cases apart, the person to whom the writer addresses himself normally is not present at all. Moreover, with certain special exceptions such as those just suggested, he must not be present. I am writing a book which will be read by thousands, or, I modestly hope, by tens of thousands. So, please, get out of the room. I want to be alone. Writing normally calls for some kind of withdrawal.

How does the writer give body to the audience for whom he writes? It would be fatuous to think that the writer addressing a so-called general audience tries to imagine his readers individually. A well-known novelist friend of mine only laughed when I asked him if, as he was writing a novel, he imagined his real readers—the woman on the subway deep in his book, the student in his room, the businessman on a vacation, the scholar in his study. There is no need for a novelist to feel his "audience" this way at all. It may be, of course, that at one time or another he imagines himself addressing one or another real person. But not all his readers in their particularities. Practically speaking, of course, and under the insistent urging of editors and publishers, he does have to take into consideration the real social, economic, and psychological state of possible readers. He has to write a book that real persons will buy and read. But I am speaking—or writing—here of the "audience" that fires the writer's imagination. If it consists of the real persons who he hopes will buy his book, they are not these persons in an untransmuted state.[6]

Although I have thus far followed the common practice in using the term "audience," it is really quite misleading to think of a writer as dealing with an "audience," even though certain considerations may at times oblige us to think this way. More properly, a writer addresses readers—only, he does not quite "address" them either: he writes to or for them. The orator has before him an audience which is a true audience, a collectivity. "Audience" is a collective noun. There is no such collective noun for readers, nor, so far as I am able to puzzle out, can there be. "Readers" is a plural. Readers do not form a collectivity, acting here and now on one another and on the speaker as members of an audience do. We can devise a singularized concept for them, it is true, such as "readership." We can say that the *Reader's Digest* has a readership of I don't know how many millions—more than it is comfortable to think about, at any rate. But "readership" is not a collective noun. It is an abstraction in a way that "audience" is not.

The contrast between hearing and reading (running the eye over signals that encode sound) can be caught if we imagine a speaker addressing an audience equipped with texts. At one point, the speaker asks the members of the audience all to read silently a paragraph out of the text. The audience immediately fragments. It is no longer a unit. Each individual retires into his own microcosm. When the readers look up again, the speaker has to gather them into a collectivity once more. This is true even if he is the author of the text they are reading.

To sense more fully the writer's problem with his so-called audience let us envision a class of students asked to write on the subject to which schoolteachers, jaded by summer, return compulsively every autumn: "How I Spent My Summer Vacation." The teacher makes the easy assumption, inviting and plausible but false, that the chief problem of a boy and a girl in writing is finding a subject actually part of his or her real life. In-close subject matter is supposed to solve the problem of invention. Of course it does not. The problem is not simply what to say but also whom to say it to. Say? The student is not talking. He is writing. No one is listening. There is no feedback. Where does he find his "audience"? He has to make his readers up, fictionalize them.

If the student knew what he was up against better than the teacher giving the assignment seemingly does, he might ask, "Who wants to know?" The answer is not easy. Grandmother? He never tells grandmother. His father or mother? There's a lot he would not want to tell them, that's sure. His classmates? Imagine the reception if he suggested they sit down and listen quietly while he told them how he spent his summer vacation. The teacher? There is no conceivable setting in which he could imagine telling his teacher how he spent his summer vacation other than in writing this paper, so that writing for the teacher does not solve his problems but only restates them. In fact, most young people do not tell anybody how they spent their summer vacation, much less write down how they spent it. The subject may be in-close; the use it is to be put to remains unfamiliar, strained, bizarre.

How does the student solve the problem? In many cases, in a way somewhat like the following. He has read, let us say, *The Adventures of Tom Sawyer*. He knows what this book felt like, how the voice in it addressed its readers, how the narrator hinted to his readers that they were related to him and he to them, whoever they may actually have been or may be. Why not pick up that voice and, with it, its audience? Why not make like Samuel Clemens and write for whomever Samuel Clemens was writing for? This even makes it possible to write for his teacher—itself likely to be a productive ploy—whom he certainly has never been quite able to figure out. But he knows his teacher has read *Tom Sawyer*, has heard the voice in the book, and could therefore obviously make like a *Tom Sawyer* reader. His problem is solved, and he goes ahead. The subject matter now makes little difference, provided that it is something like Mark Twain's and that it interests him on some grounds or other. Material in-close to his real life is not essential, though, of course, it might be welcome now that he has a way to process it.

If the writer succeeds in writing, it is generally because he can fictionalize in his imagination an audience he has learned to know not from daily life but from earlier writers who were fictionalizing in their imagination audiences they had learned to know in still earlier writers, and so on back to the dawn of written narrative. If and when he becomes truly adept, an "original writer," he can do more than project the earlier audience, he can alter it. Thus it was that Samuel Clemens in *Life on the Mississippi* could not merely project the audience that the many journalistic writers about the Midwestern rivers had brought into being, but could also shape it to his own demands. If you had read Isaiah Sellers, you could read Mark Twain, but with a difference. You had to assume a part in a less owlish, more boisterous setting, in which Clemens' caustic humor masks the uncertainty of his seriousness. Mark Twain's reader is asked to take a special kind of hold on himself and on life.

II

These reflections suggest, or are meant to suggest, that there exists a tradition in fictionalizing audiences that is a component part of literary tradition in the sense in which literary tradition is discussed in T. S. Eliot's "Tradition and the Individual Talent." A history of the ways audiences have been called on to fictionalize themselves would be a correlative of the history of literary genres and literary works, and indeed of culture itself.

What do we mean by saying the audience is a fiction? Two things at least. First, that the writer must construct in his imagination, clearly or vaguely, an audience cast in some sort of role—entertainment seekers, reflective sharers of experience (as those who listen to Conrad's Marlow), inhabitants of a lost and remembered world of prepubertal latency (readers of Tolkien's hobbit stories), and so on. Second, we mean that the audience must correspondingly fictionalize itself. A reader has to play the role in which the author has cast him, which seldom coincides with his role in the rest of actual life. An office worker on a bus reading a novel of Thomas Hardy is listening to a voice which is not that of any real person in the real setting around him. He is playing the role demanded of him by this person speaking in a quite special way from the book, which is not the subway and is not quite "Wessex" either, though it speaks of Wessex. Readers over the ages have had to learn this game of literacy, how to conform themselves to the projections of the writers they read, or at least how to operate in terms of these projections. They have to know how to play the game of being a member of an audience that "really" does not exist. And they have to adjust when the rules change, even though no rules thus far have ever been published and even though the changes in the unpublished rules are themselves for the most part only implied.

A history of literature could be written in terms of the ways in which audiences have successively been fictionalized from the time when writing broke away from oral performance, for, just as each genre grows out of what went before it, so each new role that readers are made to assume is related to previous roles. Putting aside for the moment the question of what fictionalizing may be called for in the case of the audience for oral performance, we can note that when script first came on the scene, the fictionalizing of readers was relatively simple. Written narrative at first was merely a transcription of oral narrative, or what was imagined as oral narrative, and it assumed some kind of oral singer's audience, even when being read. The transcribers of the *Iliad* and the *Odyssey* presumably imagined an audience of real listeners in attendance on an oral singer, and readers of those works to this day do well if they can imagine themselves hearing a singer of tales.[7] How these texts and other oral performances were in fact originally set down in writing remains puzzling, but the transcribers certainly were not composing in writing, but rather recording with minimal alteration what a singer was singing or was imagined to be singing.

Even so, a scribe had to fictionalize in a way a singer did not, for a real audience was not really present before the scribe, so it would seem, although it is just possible that at times one may have been (Lord, pp. 125–28). But, as transcription of oral performance or imagined oral performance gave way gradually to composition in writing, the situation changed. No reader today imagines *Second Skin* as a work that John Hawkes is reciting extempore to a group of auditors, even though passages from it may be impressive when read aloud.

III

We have noted that the roles readers are called on to play evolve without any explicit rules or directives. How readers pick up the implicit signals and how writers change the rules can be illustrated by examining a passage from a specialist in unpublished directives for readers, Ernest Hemingway. The passage is the opening of *A Farewell to Arms*. At the start of my comment on the passage, it will be clear that I am borrowing a good deal from Walker Gibson's highly discerning book on modern American prose styles, *Tough, Sweet, and Stuffy*.[8] The Hemingway passage follows:

> In the late summer of that year we lived in a house in a village that looked across the river and the plain to the mountains. In the bed of the river there were pebbles and boulders, dry and white in the sun, and the water was clear and swiftly moving and blue in the channels.

Hemingway's style is often characterized as straightforward, unadorned, terse, lacking in qualifiers, close-lipped; and it is all these things. But none of them were peculiar to Hemingway when his writing began to command attention. A feature more distinctive of Hemingway here and elsewhere is the way he fictionalizes the reader, and this fictionalizing is often signaled largely by his use of the definite article as a special kind of qualifier or of the demonstrative pronoun "that," of which the definite article is simply an attenuation.

"The late summer of that year," the reader begins. What year? The reader gathers that there is no need to say. "Across the river." What river? The reader apparently is supposed to know. "And the plain." What plain? "*The* plain"—remember? "To the mountains." What mountains? Do I have to tell you? Of course not. *The* mountains—*those* mountains we know. We have somehow been there together. Who? You, my reader, and I. The reader—every reader—is being cast in the role of a close companion of the writer. This is the game he must play here with Hemingway, not always exclusively or totally, but generally, to a greater or lesser extent. It is one reason why the writer is tight-lipped. Description as such would bore a boon companion. What description there is comes in the guise of pointing, in verbal gestures, recalling humdrum, familiar details. "In the bed of the river there were pebbles and boulders, dry and white in the sun." The known world, accepted and accepting. Not presentation, but recall. The writer needs only to point, for what he wants to tell you about is not the scene at all but his feelings. These, too, he treats as something you really had somehow shared, though you might not have been quite aware of it at the time. He can tell you what was going on inside him and count on sympathy, for you were there. You *know*. The reader here has a well-marked role assigned him. He is a companion-in-arms, somewhat later become a confidant. It is a flattering role. Hemingway readers are encouraged to cultivate high self-esteem.

The effect of the definite article in Hemingway here is quite standard and readily explicable. Normally, in English, we are likely to make an initial reference to an individual object by means of the indefinite article and to bring in the definite only subsequently. "Yesterday on the street *a* man came up to me, and when I stopped in my stride *the* man said. . . ." "A" is a modified form of the term "one," a kind of singular of "some." "A man" means "one man" (of many real or possible men). The indefinite article tacitly acknowledges the existence or possibility of a number of individuals beyond the immediate range of reference and indicates that from among them one is selected. Once we have indicated that we are concerned not with all but with one-out-of-many, we train the definite article or pointer article on the object of our attention.[9] The definite article thus commonly signals some previous, less definite acquaintanceship. Hemingway's exclusion of indefinite in favor of definite articles signals the reader that he is from the first on familiar ground. He shares the author's familiarity with the subject matter. The reader must pretend he has known much of it before.

Hemingway's concomitant use of the demonstrative distancing pronoun "that" parallels his use of "the." For "the" is only an attenuated "that." It is a modified form of the demonstrative pronoun that replaced the original Old English definite article "seo." Both hold their referents at a distance, "that" typically at a somewhat greater distance than "the." *That* mountain you see ten miles away is indicated there on *the* map on *the* wall. If we wish to think of the map as close, we would say, "*This* map on this wall." In distancing their objects, both "that" and "the" can tend to bring together the speaker and the one spoken to. "That" commonly means that-over-there at a distance from you-and-me here, and "the" commonly means much the same. These terms thus can easily implement the Hemingway relationship: you-and-me.

This you-and-me effect of the distancing demonstrative pronoun and the definite article can be seen perhaps more spectacularly in romance etymology. The words for "the" in the romance languages come from the Latin word *ille, illa, illud*, which yields in various romance tongues *il, le, la, el, lo*, and their cognates. *Ille* is a distancing demonstrative in Latin: it means "that-over-there-away-from-you-and-me" and stands in contrastive opposition to another Latin demonstrative which has no counterpart in English, *iste, ista, istud*, which means "that-over-there-by-you" (and thus can readily become pejorative—"that-little-no-account-thing-of-yours"). *Ille* brings together the speaker and the one spoken to by contrast with the distanced object; *iste* distances from the speaker the one spoken to as well as the object. *Ille* yields the romance definite articles, which correspond quite closely in function to the English "the," and thus advertises the close tie between "the" and "that."

Could readers of an earlier age have managed the Hemingway relationship, the you-and-me relationship, marked by tight-lipped empathy based on shared experience? Certainly from antiquity the reader or hearer of an epic was plunged in medias res. But this does not mean he was cast as the author's boon companion. It means rather that he was plunged into the middle of a narrative sequence and told about antecedent events only later. A feeling of camaraderie between companions-in-arms is conveyed in epics, but the companions-in-arms are fictional characters; they are not the reader or hearer and the narrator. *"Forsan et haec olim meminisse iuvabit"* —these words in the *Aeneid*, "perhaps some day it will help to recall these very things," are spoken by Aeneas to his companions when they are undergoing a period of hardships. They are one character's words to other characters, not Virgil's words to his hearer or reader. One might urge further that, like Hemingway's reader, the reader or hearer of an epic—most typically, of an oral folk epic—was hearing stories with which he was already acquainted, that he was thus on familiar ground. He was, but not in the sense that he was forced to pretend he had somehow lived as an alter ego of the narrator. His familiarity with the material was not a pretense at all, not a role, but a simple fact. Typically, the epic audience had heard the story, or something very much like it, before.

The role in which Hemingway casts the reader is somewhat different not only from anything these situations in early literature demand but also from anything in the time immediately before Hemingway. This is what makes Hemingway's writing interesting to literary historians. But Hemingway's demands on the reader are by no means entirely without antecedents. The existence of antecedents is indicated by the fact that Hemingway was assimilated by relatively unskilled readers with very little fuss. He does not recast the reader in a disturbingly novel role. By contrast, the role in which Faulkner casts the reader is a far greater departure from preceding roles than is Hemingway's. Faulkner demands more skilled and daring readers, and consequently had far fewer at first, and has relatively fewer even today when the Faulkner role for readers is actually taught in school. (Perhaps we should say the Faulkner roles.)

No one, so far as I know, has worked up a history of the readers' roles that prepared for that prescribed by Hemingway. But one can discern significantly similar demands on readers beginning as early as Addison and Steele, who assume a new fashionable intimacy among readers themselves and between all readers and the writer, achieved largely by casting readers as well as writer in the role of coffeehouse habitués. Defoe develops in his own way comparable author-reader intimacy. The roots of these eighteenth-century intimacies are journalistic, and from earlier journalism they push out later in Hemingway's own day into the world of sportswriters and war correspondents, of whom Hemingway himself was one. With the help of print and the near instantaneousness implemented by electronic media (the telegraph first, later radio teletype and electronic transmission of photography), the newspaper writer could bring his reader into his own on-the-spot experience, availing himself in both sports and war of the male's strong sense of camaraderie based on shared hardships. Virgil's *forsan et haec olim meminisse iuvabit* once more. But Virgil was telling a story of the days of old and, as has been seen, the camaraderie was among characters in the story, Aeneas and his men. Sports and war journalism are about the here and now, and, if the story can be got to the reader quickly, the camaraderie can be easily projected between the narrator and the reader. The reader is close enough temporally and photographically to the event for him to feel like a vicarious participant. In journalism Hemingway had an established foundation on which to build, if not one highly esteemed in snobbish literary circles. And he in turn has been built upon by those who have come later. Gibson has shown how much the style of *Time* magazine is an adaptation of Hemingway (pp. 48–54). To Hemingway's writer-reader camaraderie *Time* adds omniscience, solemnly "reporting," for example, in eyewitness style, the behavior and feelings of a chief of state in his own bedroom as he answers an emergency night telephone call and afterward returns to sleep. Hemingway encouraged his readers in high self-esteem. *Time* provides its readers, on a regular weekly basis, companionship with the all-knowing gods.

When we look the other way down the corridors of time to the period before the coffeehouses and the beginnings of intimate journalism, we find that readers have had to be trained gradually to play the game Hemingway engages them in. What if, *per impossibile*, a Hemingway story projecting the reader's role we have attended to here had turned up in Elizabethan England? It would probably have been laughed out of court by readers totally unable to adapt to its demands upon them. It would certainly have collided with representative literary theory, as propounded for example by Sir Philip Sidney in *The Defense of Poesie*. For Sidney and most of his age, poetry—that is to say, literature generally—had as its aim to please, but even more basically to teach, at least in the sense that it gave the reader to know what he did not know before. The Hemingway convention that the reader had somehow been through it all before with the writer would have been to Sidney's age at best confusing and at worst wrongheaded. One could argue that the Hemingway narrator would be telling the reader at least something he did not know before—that is, largely, the feelings of the narrator. But even this revelation, as we have seen, implies in Hemingway a covert awareness on the part of the reader, a deep sympathy or empathy of a basically romantic, nonpublic sort, grounded in intimacy. Sidney would have sent Hemingway back to his writing table to find something newer to write about, or to find a way of casting his material in a fresher-sounding form.

Another, and related, feature of the Hemingway style would have repelled sixteenth-century readers: the addiction to the "the" and "that" to the calculated exclusion of most descriptive qualifiers. There is a deep irony here. For in the rhetorical world that persisted from prehistoric times to the age of romanticism, descriptive qualifiers were commonly epithetic, expected qualifiers. The first chapter of Sidney's *Arcadia* (1590) presents the reader with "the hopeless shepheard," the "friendly rival," "the necessary food," "natural rest," "flowery fields," "the extreme heat of summer," and countless other souvenirs of a country every rhetorician had trod many times before. Is this not making the reader a recaller of shared experience much as Hemingway's use of "the" and "that" does? Not at all in the same way. The sixteenth-century reader recalls the familiar accouterments of literature, which are the familiar accouterments or commonplaces also of sculpture, painting, and all art. These are matters of shared public acquaintanceship, not of private experience. The sixteenth-century reader is walking through land all educated men know. He is not made to pretend he knows these familiar objects because he once shared their presence with this particular author, as a Hemingway reader is made to pretend. In Sidney, there is none of the you-and-I-know-even-if-others-don't ploy.

IV

To say that earlier readers would have been nonplussed at Hemingway's demands on them is not to say that earlier readers did not have special roles to play or that authors did not have their own problems in devising and signaling what the roles were. A few cases might be instanced here.

First of all, it is only honest to admit that even an oral narrator calls on his audience to fictionalize itself to some extent. The invocation to the Muse is a signal to the audience to put on the epic-listener's cap. No Greek, after all, ever talked the kind of language that Homer sang, although Homer's contemporaries could understand it well enough. Even today we do not talk in other contexts quite the kind of language in which we tell fairy stories to children. "Once upon a time," we begin. The phrase lifts you out of the real world. Homer's language is "once upon a time" language. It establishes a fictional world. But the fictionalizing in oral epic is directly limited by live interaction, as real conversation is. A real audience controls the narrator's behavior immediately. Students of mine from Ghana and from western Ireland have reported to me what I have read and heard from many other sources: a given story may take a skilled or "professional" storyteller anywhere from ten minutes to an hour and a half, depending on how he finds the audience relates to him on a given occasion. "You always knew ahead of time what he was going to say, but you never knew how long it would take him to say it," my Irish informant reported. The teller reacts directly to audience response. Oral storytelling is a two-way street.

Written or printed narrative is not two-way, at least in the short run. Readers' reactions are remote and initially conjectural, however great their ultimate effects on sales. We should think more about the problems that the need to fictionalize audiences creates for writers. Chaucer, for example, had a problem with the conjectural readers of the *Canterbury Tales*. There was no established tradition in English for many of the stories, and certainly none at all for a collection of such stories. What does Chaucer do? He sets the stories in what, from a literary-structural point of view, is styled a frame. A group of pilgrims going to Canterbury tell stories to one another: the pilgrimage frames the individual narratives. In terms of signals to his readers, we could put it another way: Chaucer simply tells his readers how they are to fictionalize themselves. He starts by telling them that there is a group of pilgrims doing what real people do, going to a real place, Canterbury. The reader is to imagine himself in their company and join the fun. Of course this means fictionalizing himself as a member of a nonexistent group. But the fictionalizing is facilitated by Chaucer's clear frame-story directives. And to minimize the fiction by maximizing real life, Chaucer installs himself, the narrator, as one of the pilgrims. His reader-role problem is effectively solved. Of course, he got the idea pretty much from antecedent writers faced with similar problems, notably Boccaccio. But he naturalizes the frame in the geography of southeast England.

The frame story was in fact quite common around Europe at this period. Audience readjustment was a major feature of mature medieval culture, a culture more focused on reading than any earlier culture had been. Would it not be helpful to discuss the frame device as a contrivance all but demanded by the literary economy of the time rather than to expatiate on it as a singular stroke of genius? For this it certainly was not, unless we define genius as the ability to make the most of an awkward situation. The frame is really a rather clumsy gambit, although a good narrator can bring it off pretty well when he has to. It hardly has widespread immediate appeal for ordinary readers today.

In the next period of major audience readjustment, John Lyly's *Euphues* and even more Thomas Nashe's *The Unfortunate Traveler* can be viewed as attempts to work out a credible role in which Elizabethan readers could cast themselves for the new medium of print. Script culture had preserved a heavy oral residue signaled by its continued fascination with rhetoric, which had always been orally grounded, a fascination that script culture passed on to early print culture. But the new medium was changing the noetic economy, and, while rhetoric remained strong in the curriculum, strain was developing. Lyly reacts by hyperrhetoricizing his text, tongue-in-cheek, drowning the audience and himself in the highly controlled gush being purveyed by the schools. The signals to the reader are unmistakable, if unconsciously conveyed: play the role of the rhetorician's listener for all you are worth (*Euphues* is mostly speeches), remembering that the response the rhetorician commands is a serious and difficult one—it takes hard work to assimilate the baroque complexity of Lyly's text—but also that there is something awry in all the isocola, apophonemata, and antisagogai, now that the reader is so very much more a reader than a listener. Such aural iconographic equipment had been functional in oral management of knowledge, implementing storage and recall, but with print it was becoming incidental—which is, paradoxically, why it could be so fantastically elaborated.

Nashe shows the same uneasiness, and more, regarding the reader's role. For in the phantasmagoria of styles in *The Unfortunate Traveler* he tries out his reader in every role he can think of: whoever takes on Nashe's story must become a listener bending his ear to political orations, a participant in scholastic disputations, a hanger-on at goliardic Woodstocks, a camp follower fascinated by merry tales, a simpering reader of Italian revenge stories and sixteenth-century true confessions, a fellow conspirator in a world of picaresque cheats, and much more.

Nashe gives a foretaste of other trial-and-error procedures by which recipes were to be developed for the reader of the narrative prose works we now call novels. Such recipes were being worked out in other languages, too: in French notably by Rabelais, whose calls for strenuous shifts in the reader's stance Nashe emulated, and in Spanish by Cervantes, who explores all sorts of ironic possibilities in the reader's relationship to the text, incorporating into the second part of *Don Quixote* the purported reactions of readers and of the tale's characters to the first part of the work. Picaresque travels, well known at least since Apuleius' *Golden Ass*, multiplied, with major audience adjustments, in English down through *Tom Jones*: the unsettled role of the reader was mirrored and made acceptable by keeping the hero himself on the move. Samuel Richardson has his readers pretend they have access to other persons' letters, out of which a story emerges. Journals and diaries also multiplied as narrative devices: the reader becoming a snooper or a collector of seeming trivia that turn out not to be trivia at all. Ultimately, Laurence Sterne is able to involve his reader not only in the procreation of his hero Tristram Shandy but also in the hero's writing of his autobiography, in which pages are left blank for the reader to put his "own fancy in." The audience-speaker interaction of oral narrative here shows the reader in a new ironic guise—somewhat destructive of the printed book, toward which, as an object obtruding in the person-to-person world of human communication, the eighteenth century was feeling some ambiguous hostilities, as Swift's work also shows.

The problem of reader adjustment in prose narrative was in great part due to the difficulty that narrators long had in feeling themselves as other than oral performers. It is significant that, although the drama had been tightly plotted from classical antiquity (the drama is the first genre controlled by writing, and by the same token, paradoxically, the first to make deliberate use of colloquial speech), until the late eighteenth century there is in the whole Western world (and I suspect in the East as well) no sizable prose narrative, so far as I know, with a tidy structure comparable to that known for two millennia in the drama, moving through closely controlled tensions to a climax, with reversal and denouement. This is not to say that until the modern novel emerged narrative was not organized, or that earlier narrators were trying to write modern novels but regularly fell short of their aims. (Scholes and Kellogg have warned in *The Nature of Narrative* against this retroactive analysis of literary history.) But it is to say that narrative had not fully accommodated itself to print or, for that matter, to writing, which drama had long before learned to exploit. *Tom Jones* is highly programed, but in plot it is still episodic, as all prose narrative had been all the way back through the Hellenic romances. With Jane Austen we are over the hurdle: but Jane Austen was a woman, and women were not normally trained in the Latin-based academic, rhetorical, oral tradition. They were not trained speechmakers who had turned belatedly to chirography and print.

Even by Jane Austen's time, however, the problem of the reader's role in prose narrative was by no means entirely solved. Nervousness regarding the role of the reader registers everywhere in the "dear reader" regularly invoked in fiction well through the nineteenth century. The reader had to be reminded (and the narrator, too) that the recipient of the story was indeed a reader—not a listener, not one of the crowd, but an individual isolated with a text. The relationship of audience-fictionalizing to modern narrative prose is very mysterious, and I do not pretend to explain it all here, but only to point to some of the strange problems often so largely overlooked in the relationship. Tightly plotted prose narrative is the correlative of the audiences fictionalized for the first time with the aid of print, and the demands of such narrative on readers were new.

V

The present reflections have focused on written fictional narrative as a kind of paradigm for the fictionalizing of writers' "audiences" or readers. But what has been said about fictional narrative applies ceteris paribus to all writing. With the possible[10] exception noted above of persons in the presence of one another communicating by writing because of inability to communicate orally, the writer's audience is always a fiction. The historian, the scholar or scientist, and the simple letter writer all fictionalize their audiences, casting them in a made-up role and calling on them to play the role assigned.

Because history is always a selection and interpretation of those incidents the individual historian believes will account better than other incidents for some explanation of a totality, history partakes quite evidently of the nature of poetry. It is a making. The historian does not make the elements out of which he constructs history, in the sense that he must build with events that have come about independently of him, but his selection of events and his way of verbalizing them so that they can be dealt with as "facts," and consequently the overall pattern he reports, are all his own creation, a making. No two historians say exactly the same thing about the same given events, even though they are both telling the truth. There is no *one* thing to say about anything; there are many things that can be said.

The oral "historian" captures events in terms of themes (the challenge, the duel, the arming of the hero, the battle, and so on), and formulas (the brave soldier, the faithful wife, the courageous people, the suffering people), which are provided to him by tradition and are the only ways he knows to talk about what is going on among men. Processed through these conventions, events become assimilable by his auditors and "interesting" to them. The writer of history is less reliant on formulas (or it may be he has such a variety of them that it is hard to tell that is what they are). But he comes to his material laden with themes in much vaster quantity than can be available to any oral culture. Without themes, there would be no way to deal with events. It is impossible to tell everything that went on in the Pentagon even in one day: how many stenographers dropped how many sheets of paper into how many wastebaskets when and where, what they all said to each other, and so on ad infinitum. These are not the themes historians normally use to write what really "happened." They write about material by exploiting it in terms of themes that are "significant" or "interesting." But what is "significant" depends on what kind of history you are writing—national political history, military history, social history, economic history, personal biography, global history. What is significant and, perhaps even more, what is "interesting" also depends on the readers and their interaction with the historian. This interaction in turn depends on the role in which the historian casts his readers. Although so far as I know we have no history of readers of history, we do know enough about historiography to be aware that one could well be worked out. The open-faced way the reader figures in Samuel Eliot Morison's writings is different from the more conspiratorial way he figures in Perry Miller's and both are quite different from the way the reader figures in Herodotus.

Scholarly works show comparable evolution in the roles they enforce on their readers. Aristotle's works, as has often been pointed out, are an agglomerate of texts whose relationship to his own holographs, to his students' notes, and to the work of later editors will remain always more or less a puzzle. Much of Aristotle consists of school logia or sayings, comparable to the logia or sayings of Jesus to his followers of which the Gospels chiefly consist. Aristotle's logia were addressed to specific individuals whom he knew, rather than simply to the wide world. Even his more patently written compositions retain a personal orientation: his work on ethics is the *Nicomachean Ethics*, named for his son. This means that the reader of Aristotle, if he wants to understand his text, will do well to cast himself in the role of one of Aristotle's actual listeners.

The practice of orienting a work, and thereby its readers, by writing it at least purportedly for a specific person or persons continues well through the Renaissance. The first edition of Peter Ramus' *Dialectic* was the French *Dialectique de Pierre de la Ramée à Charles de Lorraine Cardinal, son Mécène* (Paris, 1555), and the first edition of the far more widely used Latin version preserved the same personal address: *Dialectici Libri Duo . . . ad Carolum Lotharingum Cardinalem* (Paris, 1556). Sidney's famous romance or epic is *The Countess of Pembroke's Arcadia*. Often in Renaissance printed editions a galaxy of prefaces and dedicatory epistles and poems establishes a whole cosmos of discourse which, among other things, signals the reader what roles he is to assume. Sidney's, Spenser's, and Milton's works, for example, are heavily laden with introductory material — whole books have been devoted to the study of Sidney's introductory matter alone.

Until recent times the rhetorical tradition, which, with the allied dialectical or logical tradition, dominated most written as well as oral expression, helped in the fictionalizing of the audience of learned works in a generic but quite real way. Rhetoric fixed knowledge in agonistic structures.

For this reason, the roles of the reader of learned works until fairly recent times were regularly more polemic than those demanded of the reader today. Until the age of romanticism reconstituted psychological structures, academic teaching of all subjects had been more or less polemic, dominated by the ubiquitous rhetorical culture, and proceeding typically by proposing and attacking theses in highly partisan fashion. (The academic world today preserves much of the nomenclature, such as "thesis" and "defense" of theses, but less of the programed fighting spirit, which its members let loose on the social order more than on their subject matter or colleagues.) From Augustine through St. Thomas Aquinas and Christian Wolff, writers of treatises generally proceeded in adversary fashion, their readers being cast as participants in rhetorical contests or in dialectical scholastic disputations.

Today the academic reader's role is harder to describe. Some of its complexities can be hinted at by attending to certain fictions which writers of learned articles and books generally observe and which have to do with reader status. There are some things the writer must assume that every reader knows because virtually every reader does. It would be intolerable to write, "Shakespeare, a well-known Elizabethan playwright," not only in a study on Renaissance drama but even in one on marine ecology. Otherwise the reader's role would be confused. There are other things that established fiction holds all readers must know, even though everyone is sure all readers do not know them: these are handled by writing, "as everyone knows," and then inserting what it is that not quite everyone really does know. Other things the reader can safely be assumed not to know without threatening the role he is playing. These gradations of admissible ignorance vary from one level of scholarly writing to another, and since individual readers vary in knowledge and competence, the degree to which they must fictionalize themselves to match the level of this or that reading will vary. Knowledge of the degrees of admissible ignorance for readers is absolutely essential if one is to publish successfully. This knowledge is one of the things that separates the beginning graduate student or even the brilliant undergraduate from the mature scholar. It takes time to get a feel for the roles that readers can be expected comfortably to play in the modern academic world.

Other kinds of writing without end could be examined in our reflections here on the fictionalizing of readers' roles. For want of time and, frankly, for want of wider reflection, I shall mention only two others. These are genres that do not seem to fall under the rule that the writer's audience is always a fiction since the "audience" appears to be simply one clearly determined person, who hardly need fictionalize himself. The first of the genres is the familiar letter and the second the diary.

The case of the letter reader is really simple enough. Although by writing a letter you are somehow pretending the reader is present while you are writing, you cannot address him as you do in oral speech. You must fictionalize him, make him into a special construct. Whoever saluted a friend on the street with "Dear John"? And if you try the informal horrors, "Hi!" or "Greetings!" or whatever else, the effect is not less but more artificial. You are reminding him that you wish you were not writing him a letter, but, then, why are you? There is no way out. The writer has to set up another relationship to the reader and has to set the reader in a relationship to the writer different from that of nonchirographical personal contact.

The dimensions of fiction in a letter are many. First, you have no way of adjusting to the friend's real mood as you would be able to adjust in oral conversation. You have to conjecture or confect a mood that he is likely to be in or can assume when the letter comes. And, when it does come, he has to put on the mood that you have fictionalized for him. Some of this sort of adjustment goes on in oral communication, too, but it develops in a series of exchanges: a tentative guess at another's mood, a reaction from him, another from yourself, another from him, and you know about where you are. Letters do not have this normal give-and-take: they are one-way movements. Moreover, the precise relationships of writer to reader in letters vary tremendously from age to age even in intensively role-playing correspondence. No one today can capture exactly the fiction in Swift's *Journal to Stella*, though it is informative to try to reconstruct it as fully as possible, for the relationships of children to oldsters and even of man to woman have subtly altered, as have also a vast mesh of other social relationships which the *Journal to Stella* involves.

The epistolary situation is made tolerable by conventions, and learning to write letters is largely a matter of learning what the writer-reader conventions are. The paradoxes they involve were well caught some years ago in a Marx Brothers movie—if I recall correctly where the incident occurred. Letters start with "Dear Sir." An owlish, bemused businessman calls his secretary in. "Take this letter to Joseph Smithers," he directs. "You know his address. 'Dear Sir: You dirty rat. . . .'" The fiction of the exordium designed to create the *lector benevolens* is first honored and then immediately wiped out.

The audience of the diarist is even more encased in fictions. What is easier, one might argue, than addressing oneself? As those who first begin a diary often find out, a great many things are easier. The reasons why are not hard to unearth. First of all, we do not normally talk to ourselves—certainly not in long, involved sentences and paragraphs. Second, the diarist pretending to be talking to himself has also, since he is writing, to pretend he is somehow not there. And to what self is he talking? To the self he imagines he is? Or would like to be? Or really thinks he is? Or thinks other people think he is? To himself as he is now? Or as he will probably or ideally be twenty years hence? If he addresses not himself but "Dear Diary," who in the world is "Dear Diary"? What role does this imply? And why do more women than men keep diaries? Or if they don't (they really do—or did), why do people think they do? When did the diary start? The history of diaries, I believe, has yet to be written. Possibly more than the history of any other genre, it will have to be a history of the fictionalizing of readers.

The case of the diary, which at first blush would seem to fictionalize the reader least but in many ways probably fictionalizes him or her most, brings into full view the fundamental deep paradox of the activity we call writing, at least when writing moves from its initial account-keeping purposes to other more elaborate concerns more directly and complexly involving human persons in their manifold dealings with one another. We are familiar enough today with talk about masks—in literary criticism, psychology, phenomenology, and elsewhere. Personae, earlier generally thought of as applying to characters in a play or other fiction (dramatis personae), are imputed with full justification to narrators and, since all discourse has roots in narrative, to everyone who uses language. Often in the complexities of present-day fiction, with its "unreliable narrator" encased in layer after layer of persiflage and irony, the masks within masks defy complete identification. This is a game fiction writers play, harder now than ever.

But the masks of the narrator are matched, if not one-for-one, in equally complex fashion by the masks that readers must learn to wear. To whom is *Finnegans Wake* addressed? Who is the reader supposed to be? We hesitate to say—certainly I hesitate to say—because we have thought so little about the reader's role as such, about his masks, which are as manifold in their own way as those of the writer.

Masks are inevitable in all human communication, even oral. Role playing is both different from actuality and an entry into actuality: play and actuality (the world of "work") are dialectically related to one another. From the very beginning, an infant becomes an actual speaker by playing at being a speaker, much as a person who cannot swim, after developing some ancillary skills, one day plays at swimming and finds that he is swimming in truth. But oral communication, which is built into existential actuality more directly than written, has within it a momentum that works for the removal of masks. Lovers try to strip off all masks. And in all communication, insofar as it is related to actual experience, there must be a movement of love. Those who have loved over many years may reach a point where almost all masks are gone. But never all. The lover's plight is tied to the fact that every one of us puts on a mask to address himself, too. Such masks to relate ourselves to ourselves we also try to put aside, and with wisdom and grace we to some extent succeed in casting them off. When the last mask comes off, sainthood is achieved, and the vision of God. But this can only be with death.

No matter what pitch of frankness, directness, or authenticity he may strive for, the writer's mask and the reader's are less removable than those of the oral communicator and his hearer. For writing is itself an indirection. Direct communication by script is impossible. This makes writing not less but more interesting, although perhaps less noble than speech. For man lives largely by indirection, and only beneath the indirections that sustain him is his true nature to be found. Writing, alone, however, will never bring us truly beneath to the actuality. Present-day confessional writing—and it is characteristic of our present age that virtually all serious writing tends to the confessional, even drama—likes to make an issue of stripping off all masks. Observant literary critics and psychiatrists, however, do not need to be told that confessional literature is likely to wear the most masks of all. It is hard to bare your soul in any literary genre. And it is hard to write outside a genre. T. S. Eliot has made the point that so far as he knows, great love poetry is never written solely for the ear of the beloved (p. 97), although what a lover speaks with his lips is often indeed for the ear of the beloved and of no other. The point is well made, even though it was made in writing.

NOTES

1. See, e.g., J. R. Searle, *The Philosophy of Language* (London: Oxford Univ. Press, 1971), pp. 24–28, where Austin is cited, and Searle's bibliography, pp. 146–48.

2. *The Rhetoric of Fiction* (Chicago: Univ. of Chicago Press, 1961), pp. 49–52, 138, 363–64.

3. *The Nature of Narrative* (New York: Oxford Univ. Press, 1966), pp. 17–56. Among recent short studies exhibiting concerns tangent to but not the same as those of the present article might be mentioned three from *New Literary History*: Georges Poulet, "Phenomenology of Reading," 1 (1969–70), 53–68; Geoffrey H. Hartman, "History-Writing as Answerable Style," 2 (1970–71), 73–84; and J. Hillis Miller, "The Still Heart: Poetic Form in Wordsworth," 2 (1970–71), 297–310, esp. p. 310; as well as Gerald Prince, "Introduction à l'étude du narrataire," *Poétique*, No. 14 (1973), pp 178–96, which is concerned with the "narrataire" only in novels ("narratee" in a related English-language study by the same author as noted by him here) and with literary taxonomy more than history. See also Paul Ricoeur, "What Is a Text? Explanation and Interpretation," Appendix, pp. 135–50, in David Rasmussen, *Mythic-Symbolic Language and Philosophical Anthropology: A Constructive Interpretation of the Thought of Paul Ricoeur* (The Hague: Martinus Nijhoff, 1971).

4. *Phenomenology of Perception*, trans. Colin Smith (London: Routledge, 1962), pp. 181–84.

5. See my *The Presence of the Word* (New Haven and London: Yale Univ. Press, 1967), pp. 116–17.

6. T. S. Eliot suggests some of the complexities of the writer-and-audience problem in his essay on "The Three Voices of Poetry," by which he means (1) "the voice of the poet talking to himself—or to nobody," (2) "the voice of the poet addressing an audience," and (3) "the voice of the poet when he attempts to create a dramatic character speaking" (*On Poetry and Poets*, New York: Noonday Press, 1961, p. 96). Eliot, in the same work, states that these voices often mingle and indeed, for him, "are most often found together" (p. 108). The approach I am here taking cuts across Eliot's way of enunciating the problem and, I believe, brings out some of the built-in relationships among the three voices which help account for their intermingling. The "audience" addressed by Eliot's second voice not only is elusively constituted but also, even in its elusiveness, can determine the voice of the poet talking to himself or to nobody (Eliot's first sense of "voice"), because in talking to oneself one has to objectify oneself, and one does so in ways learned from addressing others. A practiced writer talking "to himself" in a poem has a quite different feeling for "himself" than does a complete illiterate.

7. See Albert B. Lord, *The Singer of Tales*, Harvard Studies in Comparative Literature, No. 24 (Cambridge, Mass.: Harvard Univ. Press, 1964), pp. 124–38.

8. *Tough, Sweet, and Stuffy* (Bloomington and London: Indiana Univ. Press, 1966), pp. 28–54. In these pages, Gibson gets very close to the concern of the present article with readers' roles.

9. The present inclination to begin a story without the initial indefinite article, which tacitly acknowledges a range of existence beyond that of the immediate reference, and to substitute for the indefinite article a demonstrative pronoun of proximity, "this," is one of many indications of the tendency of present-day man to feel his lifeworld—which is now more than ever the whole world—as in-close to him, and to mute any references to distance. It is not uncommon to hear a conversation begin, "Yesterday on the street this man came up to me, and. . . ." A few decades ago, the equivalent would very likely have been, "Yesterday on the street a man came up to me, and. . . ." This widespread preference, which Hemingway probably influenced little if at all, does show that Hemingway's imposition of fellowship on the reader was an indication, perhaps moderately precocious, of a sweeping trend.

10. "Possible," because there is probably a trace of fictionalizing even when notes are being exchanged by persons in one another's presence. It appears unlikely that what is written in such script "conversations" is exactly the same as what it would be were voices used. The interlocutors are, after all, to some extent pretending to be talking, when in fact they are not talking but writing.

Audience Addressed/ Audience Invoked

The Role of Audience in Composition Theory and Pedagogy

LISA EDE AND ANDREA LUNSFORD

One important controversy currently engaging scholars and teachers of writing involves the role of audience in composition theory and pedagogy. How can we best define the audience of a written discourse? What does it mean to address an audience? To what degree should teachers stress audience in their assignments and discussions? What *is* the best way to help students recognize the significance of this critical element in any rhetorical situation?

Teachers of writing may find recent efforts to answer these questions more confusing than illuminating. Should they agree with Ruth Mitchell and Mary Taylor, who so emphasize the significance of the audience that they argue for abandoning conventional composition courses and instituting a "cooperative effort by writing and subject instructors in adjunct courses. The cooperation and courses take two main forms. Either writing instructors can be attached to subject courses where writing is required, an organization which disperses the instructors throughout the departments participating; or the composition courses can teach students how to write the papers assigned in other concurrent courses, thus centralizing instruction but diversifying topics."[1] Or should teachers side with Russell Long, who asserts that those advocating greater attention to audience overemphasize the role of "observable physical or occupational characteristics" while

Reprinted from *College Composition and Communication* 35.2 (May 1984): 155–71. Used with permission.

ignoring the fact that most writers actually create their audiences. Long argues against the usefulness of such methods as developing hypothetical rhetorical situations as writing assignments, urging instead a more traditional emphasis on "the analysis of texts in the classroom with a very detailed examination given to the signals provided by the writer for his audience."[2]

To many teachers, the choice seems limited to a single option—to be for or against an emphasis on audience in composition courses. In the following essay, we wish to expand our understanding of the role audience plays in composition theory and pedagogy by demonstrating that the arguments advocated by each side of the current debate oversimplify the act of making meaning through written discourse. Each side, we will argue, has failed adequately to recognize (1) the fluid, dynamic character of rhetorical situations; and (2) the integrated, interdependent nature of reading and writing. After discussing the strengths and weaknesses of the two central perspectives on audience in composition—which we group under the rubrics of *audience addressed* and *audience invoked*[3]—we will propose an alternative formulation, one which we believe more accurately reflects the richness of "audience" as a concept.*

AUDIENCE ADDRESSED

Those who envision audience as addressed emphasize the concrete reality of the writer's audience; they also share the assumption that knowledge of this audience's attitudes, beliefs, and expectations is not only possible (via observation and analysis) but essential. Questions concerning the degree to which this audience is "real" or imagined, and the ways it differs from the speaker's audience, are generally either ignored or subordinated to a sense of the audience's powerfulness. In their discussion of "A Heuristic Model for Creating a Writer's Audience," for example, Fred Pfister and Joanne Petrik attempt to recognize the ontological complexity of the writer-audience relationship by noting that "students, like all writers, must fictionalize their audience."[4] Even so, by encouraging students to "construct in their

---

*A number of terms might be used to characterize the two approaches to audience which dominate current theory and practice. Such pairs as identified/envisaged, "real"/fictional, or analyzed/created all point to the same general distinction as do our terms. We chose "addressed/invoked" because these terms most precisely represent our intended meaning. Our discussion will, we hope, clarify their significance; for the present, the following definitions must serve. The "addressed" audience refers to those actual or real-life people who read a discourse, while the "invoked" audience refers to the audience called up or imagined by the writer.

imagination an audience that is as nearly a replica as is possible of *those many readers who actually exist in the world of reality,*" Pfister and Petrik implicitly privilege the concept of audience as addressed.[5]

Many of those who envision audience as addressed have been influenced by the strong tradition of audience analysis in speech communication and by current research in cognitive psychology on the composing process.[6] They often see themselves as reacting against the current-traditional paradigm of composition, with its a-rhetorical, product-oriented emphasis.[7] And they also frequently encourage what is called "real-world" writing.[8]

Our purpose here is not to draw up a list of those who share this view of audience but to suggest the general outline of what most readers will recognize as a central tendency in the teaching of writing today. We would, however, like to focus on one particularly ambitious attempt to formulate a theory and pedagogy for composition based on the concept of audience as addressed: Ruth Mitchell and Mary Taylor's "The Integrating Perspective: An Audience-Response Model for Writing." We choose Mitchell and Taylor's work because of its theoretical richness and practical specificity. Despite these strengths, we wish to note several potentially significant limitations in their approach, limitations which obtain to varying degrees in much of the current work of those who envision audience as addressed.

In their article, Mitchell and Taylor analyze what they consider to be the two major existing composition models: one focusing on the writer and the other on the written product. Their evaluation of these two models seems essentially accurate. The "writer" model is limited because it defines writing as either self-expression or "fidelity to fact" (p. 255)—epistemologically naive assumptions which result in troubling pedagogical inconsistencies. And the "written product" model, which is characterized by an emphasis on "certain intrinsic features [such as a] lack of comma splices and fragments" (p. 258), is challenged by the continued inability of teachers of writing (not to mention those in other professions) to agree upon the precise intrinsic features which characterize "good" writing.

Most interesting, however, is what Mitchell and Taylor *omit* in their criticism of these models. Neither the writer model nor the written product model pays serious attention to invention, the term used to describe those methods designed to aid in retrieving information, forming concepts, analyzing complex events, and solving certain kinds of problems."[9] Mitchell and Taylor's lapse in not noting this omission is understandable, however, for the same can be said of their own model. When these authors discuss the writing process, they stress that "our first priority for writing instruction at every level ought to be certain major tactics for structuring material because these structures are the most important in guiding the reader's comprehension and memory" (p. 271). They do not concern themselves with where "the material" comes from—its sophistication, complexity, accuracy, or rigor.

Mitchell and Taylor also fail to note another omission, one which might be best described in reference to their own model (Figure 1). This model has four components. Mitchell and Taylor use two of these, "writer" and "written product," as labels for the models they condemn. The third and fourth components, "audience" and "response," provide the title for their own "audience-response model for writing" (p. 249).

Mitchell and Taylor stress that the components in their model interact. Yet, despite their emphasis on interaction, it never seems to occur to them to note that the two other models may fail in large part because they overemphasize and isolate one of the four elements—wrenching it too greatly from its context and thus inevitably distorting the composing process. Mitchell and Taylor do not consider this possibility, we suggest, because their own model has the same weakness.

Mitchell and Taylor argue that a major limitation of the "writer" model is its emphasis on the self, the person writing, as the only potential judge of effective discourse. Ironically, however, their own emphasis on audience leads to a similar distortion. In their model, the audience has the sole power of evaluating writing, the success of which "will be judged by the audience's reaction: 'good' translates into 'effective,' 'bad' into 'ineffective.'" Mitchell and Taylor go on to note that "the audience not only judges writing; it also motivates it" (p. 250),[10] thus suggesting that the writer has less control than the audience over both evaluation and motivation.

Despite the fact that Mitchell and Taylor describe writing as "an interaction, a dynamic relationship" (p. 250), their model puts far more emphasis on the role of the audience than on that of the writer. One way to pinpoint

Figure 1 Mitchell and Taylor's "general model of writing" (p. 250).

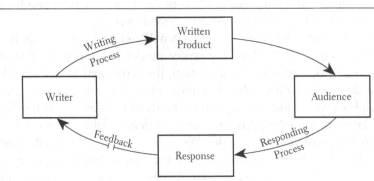

the source of imbalance in Mitchell and Taylor's formulation is to note that they are right in emphasizing the creative role of readers who, they observe, "actively contribute to the meaning of what they read and will respond according to a complex set of expectations, preconceptions, and provocations" (p. 251), but wrong in failing to recognize the equally essential role writers play throughout the composing process not only as creators but also as *readers* of their own writing.

As Susan Wall observes in "In the Writer's Eye: Learning to Teach the Rereading/Revising Process," when writers read their own writing, as they do continuously while they compose, "there are really not one but two contexts for rereading: there is the writer-as-reader's sense of what the established text is actually saying, as of this reading; and there is the reader-as-writer's judgment of what the text might say or should say. . . ."[11] What is missing from Mitchell and Taylor's model, and from much work done from the perspective of audience as addressed, is a recognition of the crucial importance of this internal dialogue, through which writers analyze inventional problems and conceptualize patterns of discourse. Also missing is an adequate awareness that, no matter how much feedback writers may receive after they have written something (or in breaks while they write), as they compose writers must rely in large part upon their own vision of the reader, which they create, as readers do their vision of writers, according to their own experiences and expectations.

Another major problem with Mitchell and Taylor's analysis is their apparent lack of concern for the ethics of language use. At one point, the authors ask the following important question: "Have we painted ourselves into a corner, so that the audience-response model must defend sociologese and its related styles?" (p. 265). Note first the ambiguity of their answer, which seems to us to say no and yes at the same time, and the way they try to deflect its impact:

> No. We defend only the right of audiences to set their own standards and we repudiate the ambitions of English departments to monopolize that standard-setting. If bureaucrats and scientists are happy with the way they write, then no one should interfere.
> But evidence is accumulating that they are not happy. (p. 265)

Here Mitchell and Taylor surely underestimate the relationship between style and substance. As those concerned with Doublespeak can attest, for example, the problem with sociologese is not simply its (to our ears) awkward, convoluted, highly nominalized style, but the way writers have in certain instances used this style to make statements otherwise unacceptable to lay persons, to "gloss over" potentially controversial facts about programs and their consequences, and thus violate the ethics of language use. Hence, although we support Mitchell and Taylor when they insist that we must better understand and respect the linguistic traditions of other disciplines and professions, we object to their assumption that style is somehow value free.

As we noted earlier, an analysis of Mitchell and Taylor's discussion clarifies weaknesses inherent in much of the theoretical and pedagogical research based on the concept of audience as addressed. One major weakness of this research lies in its narrow focus on helping students learn how to "continually modify their work with reference to their audience" (p. 251). Such a focus, which in its extreme form becomes pandering to the crowd, tends to undervalue the responsibility a writer has to a subject and to what Wayne Booth in *Modern Dogma and the Rhetoric of Assent* calls "the art of discovering good reasons."[12] The resulting imbalance has clear ethical consequences, for rhetoric has traditionally been concerned not only with the effectiveness of a discourse, but with truthfulness as well. Much of our difficulty with the language of advertising, for example, arises out of the ad writer's powerful concept of audience as addressed divorced from a corollary ethical concept. The toothpaste ad that promises improved personality, for instance, knows too well how to address the audience. But such ads ignore ethical questions completely.

Another weakness in research done by those who envision audience as addressed suggests an oversimplified view of language. As Paul Kameen observes in "Rewording the Rhetoric of Composition," "discourse is not grounded in forms or experience or audience; it engages all of these elements simultaneously."[13] Ann Berthoff has persistently criticized our obsession with one or another of the elements of discourse, insisting that meaning arises out of their synthesis. Writing is more, then, than "a means of acting upon a receiver" (Mitchell and Taylor, p. 250); it is a means of making meaning for writer *and* reader.[14] Without such a unifying, balanced understanding of language use, it is easy to overemphasize one aspect of discourse, such as audience. It is also easy to forget, as Anthony Petrosky cautions us, that "reading, responding, and composing are aspects of understanding, and theories that attempt to account for them outside of their interaction with each other run the serious risk of building reductive models of human understanding."[15]

AUDIENCE INVOKED

Those who envision audience as invoked stress that the audience of a written discourse is a construction of the writer, a "created fiction" (Long,

p. 225). They do not, of course, deny the physical reality of readers, but they argue that writers simply cannot know this reality in the way that speakers can. The central task of the writer, then, is not to analyze an audience and adapt discourse to meet its needs. Rather, the writer uses the semantic and syntactic resources of language to provide cues for the reader — cues which help to define the role or roles the writer wishes the reader to adopt in responding to the text. Little scholarship in composition takes this perspective; only Russell Long's article and Walter Ong's "The Writer's Audience Is Always a Fiction" focus centrally on this issue.[16] If recent conferences are any indication, however, a growing number of teachers and scholars are becoming concerned with what they see as the possible distortions and oversimplifications of the approach typified by Mitchell and Taylor's model.[17]

Russell Long's response to current efforts to teach students analysis of audience and adaptation of text to audience is typical: "I have become increasingly disturbed not only about the superficiality of the advice itself, but about the philosophy which seems to lie beneath it" (p. 221). Rather than detailing Long's argument, we wish to turn to Walter Ong's well-known study. Published in *PMLA* in 1975, "The Writer's Audience Is Always a Fiction" has had a significant impact on composition studies, despite the fact that its major emphasis is on fictional narrative rather than expository writing. An analysis of Ong's argument suggests that teachers of writing may err if they uncritically accept Ong's statement that "what has been said about fictional narrative applies ceteris paribus to all writing" (p. 17).

Ong's thesis includes two central assertions: "What do we mean by saying the audience is a fiction? Two things at least. First, that the writer must construct in his imagination, clearly or vaguely, an audience cast in some sort of role. . . . Second, we mean that the audience must correspondingly fictionalize itself" (p. 12). Ong emphasizes the creative power of the adept writer, who can both project and alter audiences, as well as the complexity of the reader's role. Readers, Ong observes, must learn or "know how to play the game of being a member of an audience that 'really' does not exist" (p. 12).

On the most abstract and general level, Ong is accurate. For a writer, the audience is not *there* in the sense that the speaker's audience, whether a single person or a large group, is present. But Ong's representative situations — the orator addressing a mass audience versus a writer alone in a room — oversimplify the potential range and diversity of both oral and written communication situations.

Ong's model of the paradigmatic act of speech communication derives from traditional rhetoric. In distinguishing the terms audience and reader, he notes that "the orator has before him an audience which is a true audience, a collectivity. . . . Readers do not form a collectivity, acting here and

now on one another and on the speaker as members of an audience do",
(p. 11). As this quotation indicates, Ong also stresses the potential for interaction among members of an audience, and between an audience and a
speaker.

But how many audiences are actually collectives, with ample opportunity
for interaction? In *Persuasion: Understanding, Practice, and Analysis,* Herbert
Simons establishes a continuum of audiences based on opportunities for interaction.[18] Simons contrasts commercial mass media publics, which "have little
or no contact with each other and certainly have no reciprocal awareness of
each other as members of the same audience" with "face-to-face work groups
that meet and interact continuously over an extended period of time." He goes
on to note that: "Between these two extremes are such groups as the following:
(1) the *pedestrian audience,* persons who happen to pass a soap box orator . . . ;
(2) the *passive, occasional audience,* persons who come to hear a noted lecturer in a large auditorium . . . ; (3) the *active, occasional audience,* persons
who meet only on specific occasions but actively interact when they do meet"
(pp. 97–98).

Simons' discussion, in effect, questions the rigidity of Ong's distinctions
between a speaker's and a writer's audience. Indeed, when one surveys a
broad range of situations inviting oral communication, Ong's paradigmatic
situation, in which the speaker's audience constitutes a "collectivity, acting
here and now on one another and on the speaker" (p. 11), seems somewhat
atypical. It is certainly possible, at any rate, to think of a number of instances
where speakers confront a problem very similar to that of writers: lacking
intimate knowledge of their audience, which comprises not a collectivity
but a disparate, and possibly even divided, group of individuals, speakers,
like writers, must construct in their imaginations "an audience cast in some
sort of role."[19] When President Carter announced to Americans during a
speech broadcast on television, for instance, that his program against infla-
tion was "the moral equivalent of warfare," he was doing more than merely
characterizing his economic policies. He was providing an important cue to
his audience concerning the role he wished them to adopt as listeners—that
of a people braced for a painful but necessary and justifiable battle. Were we
to examine his speech in detail, we would find other more subtle, but
equally important, semantic and syntactic signals to the audience.

We do not wish here to collapse all distinctions between oral and written
communication, but rather to emphasize that speaking and writing are, after
all, both rhetorical acts. There are important differences between speech
and writing. And the broad distinction between speech and writing that Ong
makes is both commonsensical and particularly relevant to his subject, fictional narrative. As our illustration demonstrates, however, when one turns

to precise, concrete situations, the relationship between speech and writing can become far more complex than even Ong represents.

Just as Ong's distinction between speech and writing is accurate on a highly general level but breaks down (or at least becomes less clear-cut) when examined closely, so too does his dictum about writers and their audiences. Every writer must indeed create a role for the reader, but the constraints on the writer and the potential sources of and possibilities for the reader's role are both more complex and diverse than Ong suggests. Ong stresses the importance of literary tradition in the creation of audience: "If the writer succeeds in writing, it is generally because he can fictionalize in his imagination an audience he has learned to know not from daily life but from earlier writers who were fictionalizing in their imagination audiences they had learned to know in still earlier writers, and so on back to the dawn of written narrative" (p. 11). And he cites a particularly (for us) germane example, a student "asked to write on the subject to which schoolteachers, jaded by summer, return compulsively every autumn: 'How I Spent My Summer Vacation'" (p. 11). In order to negotiate such an assignment successfully, the student must turn his real audience, the teacher, into someone else. He or she must, for instance, "make like Samuel Clemens and write for whomever Samuel Clemens was writing for" (p. 11).

Ong's example is, for his purposes, well-chosen. For such an assignment does indeed require the successful student to "fictionalize" his or her audience. But why is the student's decision to turn to a literary model in this instance particularly appropriate? Could one reason be that the student knows (consciously or unconsciously) that his English teacher, who is still the literal audience of his essay, appreciates literature and hence would be entertained (and here the student may intuit the assignment's actual aim as well) by such a strategy? In Ong's example the audience—the "jaded" schoolteacher—is not only willing to accept another role but, perhaps, actually yearns for it. How else to escape the tedium of reading 25, 50, 75 student papers on the same topic? As Walter Minot notes, however, not all readers are so malleable:

> In reading a work of fiction or poetry, a reader is far more willing to suspend his beliefs and values than in a rhetorical work dealing with some current social, moral, or economic issue. The effectiveness of the created audience in a rhetorical situation is likely to depend on such constraints as the actual identity of the reader, the subject of the discourse, the identity and purpose of the writer, and many other factors in the real world.[20]

An example might help make Minot's point concrete.

Imagine another composition student faced, like Ong's, with an assignment. This student, who has been given considerably more latitude in her choice of a topic, has decided to write on an issue of concern to her at the moment, the possibility that a home for mentally-retarded adults will be built in her neighborhood. She is alarmed by the strongly negative, highly emotional reaction of most of her neighbors and wishes in her essay to persuade them that such a residence might not be the disaster they anticipate.

This student faces a different task from that described by Ong. If she is to succeed, she must think seriously about her actual readers, the neighbors to whom she wishes to send her letter. She knows the obvious demographic factors—age, race, class—so well that she probably hardly needs to consider them consciously. But other issues are more complex. How much do her neighbors know about mental retardation, intellectually or experientially? What is their image of a retarded adult? What fears does this project raise in them? What civic and religious values do they most respect? Based on this analysis—and the process may be much less sequential than we describe here—she must, of course, define a role for her audience, one congruent with her persona, arguments, the facts as she knows them, etc. She must, as Minot argues, *both* analyze and invent an audience.[21] In this instance, after detailed analysis of her audience and her arguments, the student decided to begin her essay by emphasizing what she felt to be the genuinely admirable qualities of her neighbors, particularly their kindness, understanding, and concern for others. In so doing, she invited her audience to see themselves as *she* saw them: as thoughtful, intelligent people who, if they were adequately informed, would certainly not act in a harsh manner to those less fortunate than they. In accepting this role, her readers did not have to "play the game of being a member of an audience that 'really' does not exist" (Ong, "The Writer's Audience," p. 12). But they did have to recognize in themselves the strengths the student described and to accept her implicit linking of these strengths to what she hoped would be their response to the proposed "home."

When this student enters her history class to write an examination she faces a different set of constraints. Unlike the historian who does indeed have a broad range of options in establishing the reader's role, our student has much less freedom. This is because her reader's role has already been established and formalized in a series of related academic conventions. If she is a successful student, she has so effectively internalized these conventions that she can subordinate a concern for her complex and multiple audiences to focus on the material on which she is being tested and on the single audience, the teacher, who will respond to her performance on the test.[22]

We could multiply examples. In each instance the student writing—to friend, employer, neighbor, teacher, fellow readers of her daily newspaper—would need, as one of the many conscious and unconscious decisions required in composing, to envision and define a role for the reader. But *how* she defines that role—whether she relies mainly upon academic or technical writing conventions, literary models, intimate knowledge of friends or neighbors, analysis of a particular group, or some combination thereof—will vary tremendously. At times the reader may establish a role for the reader which indeed does not "coincide[s] with his role in the rest of actual life" (Ong, p. 12). At other times, however, one of the writer's primary tasks may be that of analyzing the "real life" audience and adapting the discourse to it. One of the factors that makes writing so difficult, as we know, is that we have no recipes: each rhetorical situation is unique and thus requires the writer, catalyzed and guided by a strong sense of purpose, to reanalyze and reinvent solutions.

Despite their helpful corrective approach, then, theories which assert that the audience of a written discourse is a construction of the writer present their own dangers.[23] One of these is the tendency to overemphasize the distinction between speech and writing while undervaluing the insights of discourse theorists, such as James Moffett and James Britton, who remind us of the importance of such additional factors as distance between speaker or writer and audience and levels of abstraction in the subject. In *Teaching the Universe of Discourse*, Moffett establishes the following spectrum of discourse: recording ("the drama of what is happening"), reporting ("the narrative of what happened"), generalizing ("the exposition of what happens"), and theorizing ("the argumentation of what will, may happen").[24] In an extended example, Moffett demonstrates the important points of connection between communication acts at any one level of the spectrum, whether oral or written:

> Suppose next that I tell the cafeteria experience to a friend some time later in conversation. . . . Of course, instead of recounting the cafeteria scene to my friend in person I could write it in a letter to an audience more removed in time and space. Informal writing is usually still rather spontaneous, directed at an audience known to the writer, and reflects the transient mood and circumstances in which the writing occurs. Feedback and audience influence, however, are delayed and weakened. . . . *Compare in turn now the changes that must occur all down the line when I write about this cafeteria experience in a discourse destined for publication and distribution to a mass, anonymous audience of present and perhaps unborn people.* I cannot allude to things and ideas that only my friends know about. I must use a vocabulary, style, logic, and rhetoric that anybody in that mass audience can understand and respond to. I must name and organize what happened during those moments in the cafeteria that day in such a way that

this mythical average reader can relate what I say to some primary moments of experience of his own. (pp. 37–38; our emphasis)

Though Moffett does not say so, many of these same constraints would obtain if he decided to describe his experience in a speech to a mass audience—the viewers of a television show, for example, or the members of a graduating class. As Moffett's example illustrates, the distinction between speech and writing is important; it is, however, only one of several constraints influencing any particular discourse.

Another weakness of research based on the concept of audience as invoked is that it distorts the processes of writing and reading by overemphasizing the power of the writer and undervaluing that of the reader. Unlike Mitchell and Taylor, Ong recognizes the creative role the writer plays as reader of his or her own writing, the way the writer uses language to provide cues for the reader and tests the effectiveness of these cues during his or her own rereading of the text. But Ong fails adequately to recognize the constraints placed on the writer, in certain situations, by the audience. He fails, in other words, to acknowledge that readers' own experiences, expectations, and beliefs do play a central role in their reading of a text, and that the writer who does not consider the needs and interests of his audience risks losing that audience. To argue that the audience is a "created fiction" (Long, p. 225), to stress that the reader's role "seldom coincides with his role in the rest of actual life" (Ong, p. 12), is just as much an oversimplification, then, as to insist, as Mitchell and Taylor do, that "the audience not only judges writing, it also motivates it" (p. 250). The former view overemphasizes the writer's independence and power; the latter, that of the reader.

RHETORIC AND ITS SITUATIONS[25]

If the perspectives we have described as audience addressed and audience invoked represent incomplete conceptions of the role of audience in written discourse, do we have an alternative? How can we most accurately conceive of this essential rhetorical element? In what follows we will sketch a tentative model and present several defining or constraining statements about this apparently slippery concept, "audience." The result will, we hope, move us closer to a full understanding of the role audience plays in written discourse.

Figure 2 represents our attempt to indicate the complex series of obligations, resources, needs, and constraints embodied in the writer's concept of audience. (We emphasize that our goal here is *not* to depict the writing process as a whole—a much more complex task—but to focus on the writer's

Figure 2   The concept of audience.

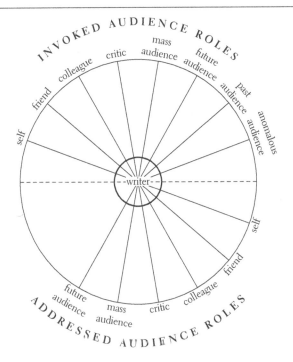

relation to audience.) As our model indicates, we do not see the two perspectives on audience described earlier as necessarily dichotomous or contradictory. Except for past and anomalous audiences, special cases which we describe paragraphs hence, all of the audience roles we specify—self, friend, colleague, critic, mass audience, and future audience—may be invoked or addressed.[26] It is the writer who, as writer and reader of his or her own text, one guided by a sense of purpose and by the particularities of a specific rhetorical situation, establishes the range of potential roles an audience may play. (Readers may, of course, accept or reject the role or roles the writer wishes them to adopt in responding to a text.)

Writers who wish to be read must often adapt their discourse to meet the needs and expectations of an addressed audience. They may rely on past experience in addressing audiences to guide their writing, or they may engage a representative of that audience in the writing process. The latter occurs, for instance, when we ask a colleague to read an article intended for scholarly publication. Writers may also be required to respond to the intervention of others—a teacher's comments on an essay, a supervisor's suggestions for improving a report, or the insistent, catalyzing questions of an editor. Such intervention may in certain cases represent a powerful stimulus to the writer, but it is the writer who interprets the suggestions—or even commands—of others, choosing what to accept or reject. Even the conscious decision to accede to the expectations of a particular addressed audience may not always be carried out; unconscious psychological resistance, incomplete understanding, or inadequately developed ability may prevent the writer from following through with the decision—a reality confirmed by composition teachers with each new set of essays.

The addressed audience, the actual or intended readers of a discourse, exists outside of the text. Writers may analyze these readers' needs, anticipate their biases, even defer to their wishes. But it is only through the text, through language, that writers embody or give life to their conception of the reader. In so doing, they do not so much create a role for the reader—a phrase which implies that the writer somehow creates a mold to which the reader adapts—as invoke it. Rather than relying on incantations, however, writers conjure their vision—a vision which they hope readers will actively come to share as they read the text—by using all the resources of language available to them to establish a broad, and ideally coherent, range of cues for the reader. Technical writing conventions, for instance, quickly formalize any of several writer-reader relationships, such as colleague to colleague or expert to lay reader. But even comparatively local semantic decisions may play an equally essential role. In "The Writer's Audience Is Always a Fiction," Ong demonstrates how Hemingway's use of definite articles in *A Farewell to Arms* subtly cues readers that their role is to be that of a "companion in arms . . . a confidant" (p. 13).

Any of the roles of the addressed audience cited in our model may be invoked via the text. Writers may also invoke a past audience, as did, for instance, Ong's student writing to those Mark Twain would have been writing for. And writers can also invoke anomalous audiences, such as a fictional character—Hercule Poirot perhaps. Our model, then, confirms Douglas Park's observation that the meanings of audience, though multiple and complex, "tend to diverge in two general directions: one toward actual people external to a text, the audience whom the writer must accommodate; the other toward the text itself and the audience implied there: a set of suggested or evoked attitudes, interests, reactions, conditions of knowledge which may or may not fit with the qualities of actual readers or listeners."[27] The most complete understanding of audience thus involves a synthesis of the perspectives we have termed audience addressed, with its focus on the reader, and audience invoked, with its focus on the writer.

One illustration of this constantly shifting complex of meanings for "audience" lies in our own experiences writing this essay. One of us became interested in the concept of audience during an NEH Seminar, and her first audience was a small, close-knit seminar group to whom she addressed her work. The other came to contemplate a multiplicity of audiences while working on a textbook; the first audience in this case was herself, as she debated the ideas she was struggling to present to a group of invoked students. Following a lengthy series of conversations, our interests began to merge: we shared notes and discussed articles written by others on audience, and eventually one of us began a draft. Our long distance telephone bills and the miles we travelled up and down I-5 from Oregon to British Columbia attest most concretely to the power of a co-author's expectations and criticisms and also illustrate that one person can take on the role of several different audiences: friend, colleague, and critic.

As we began to write and re-write the essay, now for a particular scholarly journal, the change in purpose and medium (no longer a seminar paper or a textbook) led us to new audiences. For us, the major "invoked audience" during this period was Richard Larson, editor of this journal, whose questions and criticisms we imagined and tried to anticipate. (Once this essay was accepted by *CCC*, Richard Larson became for us an addressed audience: he responded in writing with questions, criticisms, and suggestions, some of which we had, of course, failed to anticipate.) We also thought of the readers of *CCC* and those who attend the annual CCCC, most often picturing you as members of our own departments, a diverse group of individuals with widely varying degrees of interest in and knowledge of composition. Because of the generic constraints of academic writing, which limit the range of roles we may define for our readers, the audience represented by the readers of *CCC* seemed most vivid to us in two situations: (1) when we were concerned about the degree to which we needed to explain concepts or terms; and (2) when we considered central organizational decisions, such as the most effective way to introduce a discussion. Another, and for us extremely potent, audience was the authors—Mitchell and Taylor, Long, Ong, Park, and others—with whom we have seen ourselves in silent dialogue. As we read and reread their analyses and developed our responses to them, we felt a responsibility to try to understand their formulations as fully as possible, to play fair with their ideas, to make our own efforts continue to meet their high standards.

Our experience provides just one example, and even it is far from complete. (Once we finished a rough draft, one particular colleague became a potent but demanding addressed audience, listening to revision upon revision and challenging us with harder and harder questions. And after this essay is published, we may revise our understanding of audiences we thought we knew or recognize the existence of an entirely new audience.

The latter would happen, for instance, if teachers of speech communication for some reason found our discussion useful.) But even this single case demonstrates that the term *audience* refers not just to the intended, actual, or eventual readers of a discourse, but to *all* those whose image, ideas, or actions influence a writer during the process of composition. One way to conceive of "audience," then, is as an overdetermined or unusually rich concept, one which may perhaps be best specified through the analysis of precise, concrete situations.

We hope that this partial example of our own experience will illustrate how the elements represented in Figure 2 will shift and merge, depending on the particular rhetorical situation, the writer's aim, and the genre chosen. Such an understanding is critical: because of the complex reality to which the term audience refers and because of its fluid, shifting role in the composing process, any discussion of audience which isolates it from the rest of the rhetorical situation or which radically overemphasizes or underemphasizes its function in relation to other rhetorical constraints is likely to oversimplify. Note the unilateral direction of Mitchell and Taylor's model (p. 5 [p. 80]), which is unable to represent the diverse and complex role(s) audience(s) can play in the actual writing process—in the creation of meaning. In contrast, consider the model used by Edward P. J. Corbett in his *Little Rhetoric and Handbook*[28] (see Figure 3). This representation, which allows for interaction among all the elements of rhetoric, may at first appear less elegant and predictive than Mitchell and Taylor's. But it is finally more useful since it accurately represents the diverse range of potential interrelationships in any written discourse.

We hope that our model also suggests the integrated, interdependent nature of reading and writing. Two assertions emerge from this relationship. One involves the writer as reader of his or her own work. As Donald Murray notes in "Teaching the Other Self: The Writer's First Reader," this role is

Figure 3   Corbett's model of "The Rhetorical Interrelationships" (p. 5).

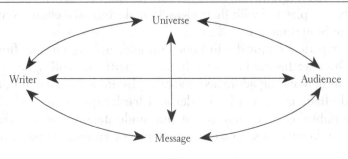

critical, for "the reading writer—the map-maker and map-reader—reads the word, the line, the sentence, the paragraph, the page, the entire text. This constant back-and-forth reading monitors the multiple complex relationships between all the elements in writing."[29] To ignore or devalue such a central function is to risk distorting the writing process as a whole. But unless the writer is composing a diary or journal entry, intended only for the writer's own eyes, the writing process is not complete unless another person, someone other than the writer, reads the text also. The second assertion thus emphasizes the creative, dynamic duality of the process of reading and writing, whereby writers create readers and readers create writers. In the meeting of these two lies meaning, lies communication.

A fully elaborated view of audience, then, must balance the creativity of the writer with the different, but equally important, creativity of the reader. It must account for a wide and shifting range of roles for both addressed and invoked audiences. And, finally, it must relate the matrix created by the intricate relationship of writer and audience to all elements in the rhetorical situation. Such an enriched conception of audience can help us better understand the complex act we call composing.

NOTES

1. Ruth Mitchell and Mary Taylor, "The Integrating Perspective: An Audience-Response Model for Writing," *CE*, 41 (November, 1979), 267. Subsequent references to this article will be cited in the text.

2. Russell C. Long, "Writer-Audience Relationships: Analysis or Invention," *CCC*, 31 (May, 1980), 223 and 225. Subsequent references to this article will be cited in the text.

3. For these terms we are indebted to Henry W. Johnstone, Jr., who refers to them in his analysis of Chaim Perelman's universal audience in *Validity and Rhetoric in Philosophical Argument: An Outlook in Transition* (University Park, PA: The Dialogue Press of Man & World, 1978), p. 105.

4. Fred R. Pfister and Joanne F. Petrik, "A Heuristic Model for Creating a Writer's Audience," *CCC*, 31 (May, 1980), 213.

5. Pfister and Petrik, 214; our emphasis.

6. See, for example, Lisa S. Ede, "On Audience and Composition," *CCC*, 30 (October, 1979), 291–295.

7. See, for example, David Tedlock, "The Case Approach to Composition," *CCC*, 32 (October, 1981), 253–261.

8. See, for example, Linda Flower's *Problem-Solving Strategies for Writers* (New York: Harcourt Brace Jovanovich, 1981) and John P. Field and Robert H. Weiss' *Cases for Composition* (Boston: Little Brown, 1979).

9. Richard E. Young, "Paradigms and Problems: Needed Research in Rhetorical Invention," in *Research on Composing: Points of Departure*, ed. Charles R. Cooper and Lee Odell (Urbana, IL: National Council of Teachers of English, 1978), p. 32 (footnote #3).

10. Mitchell and Taylor do recognize that internal psychological needs ("unconscious challenges") may play a role in the writing process, but they cite such instances as an "extreme

case (often that of the creative writer)" (p. 251). For a discussion of the importance of self-evaluation in the composing process see Susan Miller, "How Writers Evaluate Their Own Writing," *CCC*, 33 (May, 1982), 176–183.

11. Susan Wall, "In the Writer's Eye: Learning to Teach the Rereading/Revising Process," *English Education*, 14 (February, 1982), 12.

12. Wayne Booth, *Modern Dogma and the Rhetoric of Assent* (Chicago: The University of Chicago Press, 1974), p. xiv.

13. Paul Kameen, "Rewording the Rhetoric of Composition," *Pre/Text*, 1 (Spring-Fall, 1980), 82.

14. Mitchell and Taylor's arguments in favor of adjunct classes seem to indicate that they see writing instruction, wherever it occurs, as a skills course, one instructing students in the proper use of a tool.

15. Anthony R. Petrosky, "From Story to Essay: Reading and Writing," *CCC*, 33 (February, 1982), 20.

16. Walter J. Ong, S. J., "The Writer's Audience Is Always a Fiction," *PMLA*, 90 (January, 1975), 9–21. Subsequent references to this article will be cited in the text.

17. See, for example, William Irmscher, "Sense of Audience: An Intuitive Concept," unpublished paper delivered at the CCCC in 1981; Douglas B. Park, "The Meanings of Audience: Pedagogical Implications," unpublished paper delivered at the CCCC in 1981; and Luke M. Reinsma, "Writing to an Audience: Scheme or Strategy?" unpublished paper delivered at the CCCC in 1982.

18. Herbert W. Simons, *Persuasion: Understanding, Practice, and Analysis* (Reading, MA: Addison-Wesley, 1976).

19. Ong, p. 12. Ong recognizes that oral communication also involves role-playing, but he stresses that it "has within it a momentum that works for the removal of masks" (p. 20). This may be true in certain instances, such as dialogue, but does not, we believe, obtain broadly.

20. Walter S. Minot, "Response to Russell C. Long," *CCC*, 32 (October, 1981), 337.

21. We are aware that the student actually has two audiences, her neighbors and her teacher, and that this situation poses an extra constraint for the writer. Not all students can manage such a complex series of audience constraints, but it is important to note that writers in a variety of situations often write for more than a single audience.

22. In their paper on "Student and Professional Syntax in Four Disciplines" (unpublished paper delivered at the CCCC in 1981), Ian Pringle and Aviva Freedman provide a good example of what can happen when a student creates an aberrant role for an academic reader. They cite an excerpt from a third year history assignment, the tone of which "is essentially the tone of the opening of a television travelogue commentary" and which thus asks the reader, a history professor, to assume the role of the viewer of such a show. The result is as might be expected: "Although the content of the paper does not seem significantly more abysmal than other papers in the same set, this one was awarded a disproportionately low grade" (p. 2).

23. One danger which should be noted is a tendency to foster a questionable image of classical rhetoric. The agonistic speaker-audience relationship which Long cites as an essential characteristic of classical rhetoric is actually a central point of debate among those involved in historical and theoretical research in rhetoric. For further discussion, see: Lisa Ede and Andrea Lunsford, "On Distinctions Between Classical and Modern Rhetoric," in *Classical Rhetoric and Modern Discourse: Essays in Honor of Edward P. J. Corbett*, ed. Robert Connors, Lisa Ede, and Andrea Lunsford (Carbondale, IL: Southern Illinois University Press, 1984).

24. James Moffett, *Teaching the Universe of Discourse* (Boston: Houghton Mifflin, 1968), p. 47. Subsequent references will be mentioned in the text.

25. We have taken the title of this section from Scott Consigny's article of the same title, *Philosophy and Rhetoric*, 7 (Summer, 1974), 175–186. Consigny's effort to mediate between two opposing views of rhetoric provided a stimulating model for our own efforts.

26. Although we believe that the range of audience roles cited in our model covers the general spectrum of options, we do not claim to have specified all possibilities. This is particularly the case since, in certain instances, these roles may merge and blend — shifting subtly in character. We might also note that other terms for the same roles might be used. In a business setting, for instance, colleague might be better termed co-worker; critic, supervisor.

27. Douglas B. Park, "The Meanings of 'Audience,' " *CE*, 44 (March, 1982), 249.

28. Edward P. J. Corbett, *The Little Rhetoric & Handbook*, 2nd edition (Glenview, IL: Scott, Foresman, 1982), p. 5.

29. Donald M. Murray, "Teaching the Other Self: The Writer's First Reader," *CCC*, 33 (May, 1982), 142.

Post-Process "Pedagogy"

A Philosophical Exercise

LEE-ANN M. KASTMAN BREUCH

Recently, "post-process" theories of composition instruction have suggested that process (prewriting, writing, rewriting) is no longer an adequate explanation of the writing act. Many post-process scholars, largely influenced by postmodernist and anti-foundationalist perspectives, suggest that the process paradigm has reduced the writing act to a series of codified phases that can be taught. These critics suggest that process pedagogy simply offers us another foundational explanation of writing.[1] Indeed, the dominant contention of post-process scholars is that process has come to represent Theory with a capital "T."[2] Gary Olson explains, for example, that the process approach is problematic because it attempts to generalize the writing act:

> The problem with process theory, then, is not so much that scholars are attempting to theorize various aspects of composing as it is that they are endeavoring (consciously or not) to construct a model of the composing process, thereby constructing a Theory of Writing, a series of generalizations about writing that supposedly hold true all or most of the time. (8)

This generalization can be especially problematic if teachers of writing present the writing process as one universal process rather than as plural processes (see Russell 80).

The suggestion that process is no longer a viable explanation for the writing act has spurred further discussion about the nature of the writing

First published in JAC 22.1 (Winter 2002): 119–50. Reprinted with permission.

process. For example, while some scholars suggest that the process approach may attempt to represent the act of writing universally, others find this characterization of process inaccurate. Bruce McComiskey notes his disagreement with this characterization: "Invention and revision strategies, as I understand and teach them, do not assume a stable and predictable linguistic system for generating universal meaning; their function is, instead, to harness the polyphonic character of language in communities, to develop rather than constrict a writer's sense of purpose" (39–40). David Russell also argues that the idea of a universal process—"*the* process," as he puts it—is less accurate than the idea of plural processes. He argues for a "progressively wider understanding of writing processes as they are played out in a range of activity systems in our culture(s)" (88). Joseph Petraglia suggests that we should not abandon or reject process, but simply move past it:

> Of course, the fundamental observation that an individual produces text by means of a writing process has not been discarded. Instead, it has dissolved and shifted from figure to ground. . . . We now have the theoretical and empirical sophistication to consider the mantra "writing is a process" as the right answer to a really boring question. We have better questions now, and the notion of process no longer counts as much of an insight. (53)

Because process is so often the topic of discussion in post-process scholarship, post-process has come to mean a critique of the process movement in composition studies. In response, I argue that post-process scholarship is shortchanged by the continued emphasis on process in that the broader implications of post-process theory have very little to do with process. Furthermore, I suggest that the only importance process has to post-process theory is in the form of an illustration—and a poor one at that. That is, "process" as it is cast by post-process scholarship is the scapegoat in an argument to forward postmodern and anti-foundationalist perspectives that are critical to post-process theory.

In this article, I attempt to clarify what I believe post-process theory can contribute to composition pedagogy. In accordance with Sidney Dobrin, who suggests that post-process theory should not fall into the "pedagogical imperative," I suggest that there is no identifiable post-process pedagogy that we can concretely apply to writing classrooms; however, I believe post-process theory offers many insights for the profession of teaching that we all should consider (*Constructing* 63). Specifically, I argue that post-process theory encourages us to reexamine our definition of writing as an activity rather than a body of knowledge, our methods of teaching as indeterminate activities rather than exercises of mastery, and our communicative interactions with students as dialogic rather than monologic. My mission to highlight these insights is driven by what I perceive to be a lack of clarity in post-process theory, fueled by a diversion into discussions of process and by arguments that seemingly resist pedagogical application. When we look past arguments that dominate current scholarship in post-process theory and instead uncover the assumptions that guide post-process theory, we may find helpful and even profound contributions that inform our pedagogical prac- tice—if not in specific pedagogical agendas, then in philosophical princi- ples that guide our practice.

In the next section, I explain how post-process theory may seemingly defy pedagogical application. I specifically review central arguments made by Thomas Kent, a prominent post-process scholar, and I offer a critique of current scholarship on post-process theory.

POST-PROCESS RESISTANCE

On the surface, post-process theory seems to resist pedagogical application because of post-process claims that writing cannot be taught, vague peda- gogical agendas, and divergent depictions of post-process pedagogy. If one were to casually explore post-process theory, these three characterizations might leave the impression that teaching writing is a hopeless endeavor. I argue that the wrong arguments are highlighted in this scholarship—argu- ments that focus on the negatives of process pedagogy rather than on the possibilities of post-process theory. In this section, I explore these argu- ments further to uncover central assumptions that inform the post-process perspective.

Pedagogical resistance is perhaps most apparent in the claim that writ- ing cannot be taught, which stems from the argument forwarded by Kent that writing is a situated, interpretive, and indeterminate act. In *Paralogic Rhetoric*, Kent suggests that accepting a post-process perspective (at least in a paralogic sense) means rejecting process as the ultimate explanation for the writing act and instead recognizing the role of interpretation and inde- terminacy in the writing act. Consequently, if we consider writing as an indeterminate and interpretive activity, he asserts, then "writing and reading— conceived broadly as processes or bodies of knowledge—cannot be taught, for nothing exists to teach" (161). This statement is critical to the post-pro- cess perspective for its rejection of process as both an explanation of the writ- ing act and a method of teaching writing. Indeed, this claim seems to have spurred discussions about what Petraglia has called "life after process," so it is necessary to examine it more closely.

Certainly, the claim that writing cannot be taught—and that writing process is inadequate to explain the writing act—on the surface indicates resistance to pedagogical application. However, when investigating more closely, we see that Kent does not completely abandon writing pedagogy, as the following passage from *Paralogic Rhetoric* about his "externalist pedagogy" reveals:

> Stated baldly, an externalist pedagogy endorses the following claims: (1) writing and reading are kinds of communicative interaction; (2) communicative interaction requires triangulation; (3) triangulation requires us to make hermeneutic guesses about how others will interpret our utterances; (4) the process we employ to make our hermeneutic guesses cannot be codified; (5) consequently, no system or framework theory can predict in advance how our utterances will be interpreted; (6) therefore, neither writing nor reading can be reduced to a systemic process or to a codifiable set of conventions, although clearly some of the background knowledge useful for writing—like grammar, sentence structure, paragraph cohesion, and so forth—can be codified and reduced to a system. However, we should remember that knowing a framework or process is necessary but not sufficient for communicative interaction; knowing a grammar, for example, only prepares us to write or to read. (161)

I argue that this passage demonstrates not a total resistance to pedagogy, but rather a careful pedagogical position, for Kent's stance on teaching writing depends on the definition of *writing* that he has outlined in this passage. Kent distinguishes background knowledge—grammar systems and so forth—from the writing act, which he says is indeterminate and dynamic and defies systems. That is, while grammar and rules about cohesion or sentence structure can be easily codified and transmitted to students, these systems should not be confused with the writing act—an act that he describes as uncertain and indeterminate: "Certain background skills, such as an understanding of grammar, can be taught, but the acquisition of these skills never guarantees that a student will be able to communicate effectively; no framework theory of any kind can help a student predict in advance the interpretation that someone else may give to an utterance" (161).

It is important to note that Kent does not reject the instruction of system-based content such as grammar; rather, he suggests that these skills do not in themselves comprise the writing act and that we cannot reduce the writing act to a system that can then be taught. These statements help us to understand that in saying "nothing exists to teach," Kent is not rejecting pedagogical application altogether, but rather the specific pedagogical application of process pedagogy, which he claims attempts to reduce the writing act (not background knowledge) into content that can be taught to students:

So, any composition or literature pedagogy that presupposes such a frame-work assumes that writing and reading consists of a well-defined process that, once mastered, allows us to engage unproblematically in communicative interaction. These process-oriented pedagogies generally assume that discourse production and reception are cognitive activities that may be reduced either to frameworks that describe the mental processes writers and readers employ or to social activities that describe the conventions or conceptual schemes that hold together a discourse community. (161–62)

Let's take this claim for what it's worth. Kent suggests that writing is not a system or process and therefore cannot be taught as such. Consequently, he does not suggest that teaching writing is impossible; he suggests that teaching writing *as a system* is impossible. Thus, while some may take the claim that "nothing exists to teach" to mean that writing pedagogy is an impossible project, I argue that the claim exists to attack process pedagogy specifically.

While Kent's project here seems to be to dismantle process pedagogy, he does provide suggestions for reconceptualizing pedagogy based on the theoretical framework he has outlined. Yet these, too, demonstrate resistance to pedagogical application. As some scholars have pointed out, Kent's discussions of pedagogy are "vague," "cautious," and "less developed" than his theoretical framework (Dobrin, *Constructing* 89; Ward 158). Nonetheless, in order to illustrate the ways in which Kent moves away from process pedagogy, it is important to review the pedagogical insights he does offer. Kent's reconceptualization of pedagogy begins with the suggestion that we use a new vocabulary to discuss writing in relation to communicative interaction:

As strong externalists, we would stop talking about writing and reading as processes and start talking about these activities as determinate social acts. This shift from an internalist conception of communicative interaction—the notion that communication is a product of the internal workings of the mind or the workings of the discourse communities in which we live—to an externalist conception that I have outlined here would challenge us to drop our current process-oriented vocabulary and to begin talking about our social and public uses of language. (169)

What results from this proposal is an increased emphasis on communicative interaction between teachers and students. Kent discusses at length how this emphasis would affect teacher-student roles in writing classrooms:

Instead of dialecticians who initiate students into new knowledge, mentors who endorse a paralogic rhetoric become co-workers who actively collaborate with their students to help them through different communicative situations both within and outside the university. As co-workers, these men-tors—by relinquishing their roles as high priests—engender a new rela-tionship with their students in that they actively collaborate with their students and become, in a sense, students themselves. (166)

Kent's (re)vision of writing pedagogy, then, pushes past process and toward a dialogic understanding of meaning-making. This dialogic pedagogy requires two-way rather than one-way communication, suggesting that teachers move away from a transmission model of education and toward a transformative model that includes active participation from both teachers and students as collaborators.

While Kent's comments about pedagogy do provide direction beyond process, some scholars have been quick to point out that his comments are not specific enough to outline any pedagogy that could be labeled "post-process," thus increasing the resistance to applying post-process theory to pedagogy. Indeed, the vagueness of Kent's proposed pedagogy has indicated to some that post-process theory should remain a theoretical enterprise. Dobrin in particular supports this viewpoint: "Perhaps Kent's own glossing of classroom application should serve as an indication that these theories, while informative about the nature of discourse, are not necessarily practice-oriented theories, a recognition which, of course, puts us at an awkward crossroads" (*Constructing* 86). Dobrin argues that post-process theory is not yet developed enough for pedagogical application: "Even those who see the classroom potential of post-process theory have too hastily fallen into the pedagogical imperative and seek to create pedagogies from theories we are just beginning to discuss" (64). Warning of the "pedagogical imperative," or the idea that a theory must have direct classroom application, Dobrin says that rushing to outline pedagogical application is "frivolous" (86).

Further resistance to pedagogical application of post-process theory exists in the inevitable trap of trying to specify a pedagogy that upholds anti-foundationalist and postmodern beliefs. That is, post-process theory as out-lined by Kent upholds the anti-foundationalist view that knowledge is situated, indeterminate, and thoroughly hermeneutic. Thus, in advocating a pedagogy based on anti-foundationalism, one must wrestle with the paradox of any pedagogical agenda it forwards. David Wallace explains:

> If we recognize that structural understandings of language and rhetoric are not *objective* and have no intrinsic basis in *reality*, then we must also recog-nize that any act of pedagogy that requires (or encourages) conformity to convention is ultimately a power move. . . . Thus *any* pedagogical act must be seen as socially and culturally implicated because asking students to move in any direction—whether that be toward mastery of the conventions

of standard written English or toward a critical awareness of the social and political consequences of acts of literacy—is to ask them to change not just what they know but who they are. (110–11)

Wallace claims that any pedagogy—postmodern or anti-foundationalist—adopts a stance and therefore cannot be considered indeterminate or ambiguous. Note that Wallace suggests that *any* pedagogical act is an act of power, thus reinforcing the paradox of any anti-foundationalist pedagogy.

What results from this inherent paradox of pedagogical application is confusion about any pedagogical insights post-process theory might offer; in addition, the resistance to a single pedagogical agenda encourages pluralism. For example, in recent years, various "post-process pedagogies" have emerged that bear no resemblance to one another. One example of post-process pedagogy is offered by McComiskey, who openly rejects what he calls Kent's "anti-process" and builds a post-process pedagogy on the idea of "social-process rhetorical inquiry," which he defines as "a method of invention that usually manifests itself in composition classes as a set of heuristic questions based on the cycle of cultural production, contextual distribution, and critical consumption" (40, 42). Raúl Sánchez, who stays closer to Kent's arguments and advocates pedagogy as a one-to-one mentored relationship between teacher and student, articulates another pedagogy that claims to be post-process. In this proposed pedagogy, Sánchez suggests that writing courses no longer focus on process as content, but rather use class time to engage in discourse about writing (see Dobrin, *Constructing* 84). Irene Ward also builds on Kent's ideas to articulate a "functional dialogism" for writing pedagogy, which includes the following forms of dialogue in the writing classroom:

♦ internal dialogues between a self and an internalized audience

♦ dialogue between teacher and student

♦ dialogue between students and other larger social institutions, including but not limited to the educational institution or some other social institution within any one or more of the student's immediate communities

♦ dialogues among students about the formal matters of the composition or the ideas or subject of the discourse

♦ composing using dialogic forms in order to understand an issue or group of issues from various points of view and gain insight into one's relationship to those ideas and into multiple perspectives represented by many voices that have already entered into public dialogue. (171)

Still others articulate different visions for how post-process theory might apply to pedagogy. For example, Barbara Couture suggests that pedagogy must move beyond modeling a process and toward the development of agency in students:

> Our current scholarship on diverse ways of knowing, meaning, and communicating strongly suggests that modeling specific conventions and procedures will not ensure that writers learn all they need to know in order to communicate effectively to others. . . . Writers need to become subjective agents, making willful judgments effected in concrete actions that convey them successfully to others. (42)

Russell takes a different approach and does not advocate rejecting process outright but, rather, extending the notion of process—or, as he puts it, "to extend the activity system of the discipline of composition studies, to offer to teachers and students more and more refined tools for helping people in and entering various activity systems to write and learn to write and transform their activity through writing" (91).

Lest we become confused by these divergent attempts to apply post-process theory to pedagogy, Petraglia reminds us that given the increase in scholarship about writing in the past two decades, both qualitative and quantitative, it is "natural" for post-process theory to exhibit such complexity (53). Yet, this does not help us understand with any clarity just what post-process theory can offer. Kent admits to the hybrid nature of scholarship about post-process theory in the introduction to his edited collection about post-process theory: "Although the authors appearing in these pages may disagree about the nature of the 'post' in 'post-process' theory, all of them agree that change is in the air" (5). Further, he describes three assumptions that he claims most post-process scholars share: writing is public; writing is interpretive; and writing is situated (1). Perhaps these assumptions clarify to some degree how we might understand post-process theory, and I return to them later in this essay.

In sum, there are good reasons to believe that post-process theory resists pedagogical application: the declaration that writing cannot be taught, the lack of a clear pedagogical agenda, and the divergent applications thus far of post-process theory. With respect to Dobrin's insistence that we too easily fall into the "pedagogical imperative," I suggest that there are implications for pedagogy but that they are not highlighted in a productive way. The first implication is the recognition that writing is more than a body of knowledge to be mastered, which I address in the next section.

POST-PROCESS REJECTION OF MASTERY

While it is unclear what post-process theory offers in the way of concrete assignments or classroom environment, post-process theory does make an important pedagogical contribution through its rejection of mastery. Not coincidentally, many post-process scholars associate the process movement with mastery, suggesting (as Kent does) that process represents a system of writing that can be learned and perfected.[3] Couture explains: "We pay a price . . . by reducing those acts that make us uniquely human—speaking and writing—to a device or technology to be mastered, ignoring their more central role in shaping the way we are and live" (39). In this section, I explain in further detail the assumptions of mastery that post-process scholars have articulated (and rejected) about process pedagogy. I argue that whether or not we agree with the depiction of process as mastery, the post-process rejection of mastery is an important recognition for writing scholars and teachers.

One way post-process theorists depict process as mastery is by suggesting that writing process is a "thing"—a system, body of knowledge, or model—that can be skillfully practiced and conquered. When we reexamine Kent's claim about writing pedagogy, this language becomes apparent: "Writing and reading—conceived broadly as processes or bodies of knowledge—cannot be taught, for nothing exists to teach" (161). Helen Ewald observes that Kent's claim "seems based on the assumption that the ability to teach a subject rests on its having a codified body of knowledge that can be transmitted" (122). Of course, Kent ultimately rejects the idea that writing can be described as a body of knowledge, but in doing so process becomes the scapegoat, representing little more than a body of knowledge. Dobrin, also speaking from a post-process perspective, makes this point clear: "Certainly, process pedagogy is convenient; process pedagogy makes it easy to define texts and to write texts. We can unproblematically, clearly present a body of knowledge and evaluate students' abilities to absorb and rehash that body of knowledge, that process" ("Paralogic" 139). According to these and other post-process scholars, process means little more than content—a body of knowledge.

This depiction of process as a body of knowledge often leads to what Erika Lindemann calls "what-centered" teaching approaches, in which teachers emphasize subject matter above all else. It is helpful to examine process pedagogy in this light to better understand the post-process critique that process leads to mastery. According to Lindemann, a what-centered writing course might emphasize subject matter such as literature, films, linguistic systems (grammar and sentence structure), or even modes of writing. In contrast, "how-centered" approaches emphasize activities that occur in a writing class (Lindemann includes process pedagogy here) such as prewriting, writing, and rewriting, in addition to activities such as listening to and discussing the writing of students in class (251, 252). She suggests that "what-centered" courses emphasize nouns (content), while "how-centered" courses emphasize verbs (activities).

The distinction between what-centered and how-centered approaches is particularly important where process pedagogy is concerned. If process pedagogy is considered an approach that reduces writing to a thing—a body of knowledge that can be transmitted to students—then process pedagogy would certainly be considered a what-centered approach to teaching writing. However, Lindemann notes (and I agree) that process pedagogy as it was originally introduced in composition represents a *how-centered* approach because of its emphasis on the activities involved in process approaches to writing (prewriting, writing, rewriting). Indeed, process pedagogy and the research of Janet Emig, Ken Macrorie, and Peter Elbow in many ways encouraged a shift away from content-based approaches, such as current-traditional pedagogy, which emphasized grammatical structures. But viewed through post-process lenses, process seems to have lost its luster. Indeed, post-process scholarship has ignored process as how-centered and has curiously assumed that process is content-based.

Thinking about process or writing as "what-centered" facilitates mastery, as Lindemann explains: "We turn process-centered courses into what-centered courses every time we're tempted to interrupt students engaged in writing with an explanation of some subject matter. Or, if we 'explain' pre-writing strategies during the first few weeks and never refer to them again, we've made prewriting a subject matter, a body of information to learn about rather than an activity to practice" (252). Lindemann argues that this turn is not productive and that teachers should be conscious of their efforts to uphold process as how-centered. However, post-process theory seems to be certain that this turn toward content has in fact occurred. Couture explains that instructors have emphasized process as content as a result of a historical habit of modeling writing in the classroom: "How did the emphasis upon process, like so many ideas about writing that are derived from scholarship and research, lose so much when applied en masse in our classrooms? At least one reason can be traced back to how we traditionally have approached composition instruction, teaching students to model technique rather than to emulate expression" (30). As Couture explains, our tendency to perceive process as mastery is historically consistent with past pedagogy, such as current-traditional approaches:

> Teaching the writing process as the modeling of technique certainly is consistent with a tradition of composition pedagogy extending from the practice of imitating good writing by good writers; through the practice of perfecting the argumentative strategies of deduction, induction, comparing, contrasting, and defining; to following the basic pattern of the five-paragraph theme, mastered by most of us in high school English and freshman composition classes. And, too, emphasis on process as model has reflected an overt desire of many composition instructors to identify methods for improving writing instruction so as to "right" their students' writing. . . . (33)

Couture explains well how we—both students and teachers—might interpret process as mastery of writing techniques. From a student's perspective, process could be presented as a technique that could be mastered to improve student writing. From a teacher's perspective, process could be viewed as a pedagogical method that could be mastered in the classroom. Either way, the argument presented here suggests that process has been treated as a thing to master in writing pedagogy. Yet, this characterization of process as mastery seems too simple. Lisa Ede reminds us, for example, that research on writing process has displayed enormous complexity. To illustrate this complexity, she reviews the work of several process scholars such as Emig, Elbow, Donald Murray, Linda Flower, and John Hayes, and she reminds us of their divergent approaches to process. But, as Ede articulates, process became "co-opted and commodified—by textbooks that oversimplified and rigidified a complex phenomenon, by overzealous language arts coordinators and writing program administrators who assumed that the process approach to teaching could be 'taught' in one or two in-service sessions" (35–36; see also Russell 84).

I review these arguments to problematize the assumption that process is "what-centered," based solely on content or a body of knowledge. While it may be true that process has been "co-opted," as Ede suggests, I argue that this commodification of process should be considered as a slip and not as a fact. As Lindemann reminds us, the characterization of process as how-centered is more true to the origins of the process movement. Simply stated, before accepting post-process arguments about the failure of process, we need to examine the assumptions informing them. When we do, we can find value in the post-process insistence that we reexamine the way we think of process in the writing classroom, as well as our approaches to mastery. That is, post-process scholars seem most concerned about writing being characterized as a thing, whether that thing is process, grammatical systems, discourse conventions, and so on. When considering these arguments, the value in post-process scholarship appears not to be the rejection of process, but the rejection of mastery—the rejection of the belief that writing can be categorized as a thing to be mastered.

Post-process opposition to mastery is also apparent in arguments that characterize process as Theory—or process as having universal explanatory power. And, as in the "what-centered" characterization of process, process as a Theory is rejected by post-process scholars, as Olson reminds us:

> The problem with process theory, then, is not so much that scholars are attempting to theorize various aspects of composing as it is that they are endeavoring (consciously or not) to construct a model of the composing process, thereby constructing a Theory of Writing, a series of generalizations about writing that supposedly hold true all or most of the time. (8)

Couture's observation that process is a way to teach writing the "right" way also supports the argument that process presents a Theory. Like the rejection of mastery, these arguments illustrate the postmodern and anti-foundationalist influences on post-process theory. As Olson explains, "The postmodern critique of theory serves as a useful corrective in that it alerts us to the dangers of creating master narratives and then adhering to these explanations as if we have obtained truth" (8). Postmodern critique is especially helpful in deconstructing what Pullman describes as the "rhetorical narrative" of process pedagogy, a "motivated selection and sequencing of events that sacrifices one truth in order to more clearly represent another" (16; see also Foster 149). Indeed, the postmodern influences on post-process theory denounce the search for universal truth. Kent reminds us of the "master narrative of objectivity," the idea that truth resides outside of language and that knowledge is systematic rather than interpretive (*Paralogic* 63). At the root of the post-process critique of process pedagogy is the idea that process is a systematic method for learning writing—one that is objective rather than subjective.

Again, considering the post-process opposition to mastery, we must reexamine the claim that process represents a Theory or a grand narrative. I suggest that given the postmodern and anti-foundationalist influences on post-process theory, post-process scholars are more concerned with the rejection of universal theories in general than the rejection of process pedagogy in particular. Process appears to be merely a convenient illustration of the post-process perspective. For example, because process scholarship has been the dominant perspective in writing pedagogy, it is easy to paint it as an illustration of a master narrative, a Theory, or a model to be imitated. It is tempting to wonder if the purpose of post-process scholarship is to simply knock process off of its pedestal. Similar moves have been made in the past regarding the current-traditional movement in composition studies. Pullman describes the rush to associate the term *current-traditional* with a movement, theory, or label about teaching writing effectively:

> We forget that [this] expression did not refer to a theory but was instead a shorthand and off-the-cuff way of alluding to the way the tradition of rhetoric was currently being purveyed in the Freshman Composition textbooks of [the] day. Because we forget this, we tend to think that current-traditional rhetoric was a bogus theory based on prejudice and misunderstanding, a kind of mindless application of traditional folklore or naive interpretations of Aristotle's *Rhetoric* when in fact it did not exist as a theory except to the extent one could extrapolate a theory from the textbooks current at the time. (22)

Pullman asserts that the rush to define current-traditional rhetoric forwarded the process movement: "The writing process was not, in other words, so much discovered as created . . ." (23). Further, he suggests that this "creation" of process gave scholars reason to reject current-traditional rhetoric: "In a sense, the reified expression *current-traditional rhetoric* does little more than create a daemon for the sake of expelling it" (23).

In describing the building and rejecting of current-traditional rhetoric, Pullman illustrates his perception of the rhetorical narrative of process. Ede makes a similar observation of this rhetorical move, suggesting that advocates of the process movement depicted current-traditional rhetoric negatively. She claims that the process movement "in effect constituted itself through a denial of origins that involves creating that which it wishes to oppose and then erasing the shared ground that made the original construction of the other possible. In an important sense current-traditional rhetoric did not exist until advocates of writing as a process created it" (37). Ede calls this strategy "a characteristic move of the western intellectual project," and the point I wish to make is that this same move may be apparent in post-process scholarship (37). Here, process is described as a master narrative, a Theory, a content- and what-centered approach. Process is first described as a thing and is then promptly rejected. Petraglia articulates this move: "As I understand it, 'post-process' signifies a rejection of the generally formulaic framework for understanding writing that process suggested" (53). It could easily be argued that post-process scholars have created their own rhetorical narrative of process as content-based, thus casting process as the scapegoat.

As I suggested previously, I disagree with the depiction of process as a formula, model, or "thing," but I do agree with Petraglia's assertion that post-process scholarship signifies a rejection of generally formulaic frameworks for explaining writing. This broader understanding of post-process scholarship—focused not on process, but on the rejection of formulaic explanations of writing—is a key contribution to the reconceptualization of writing. Petraglia explains this well: "This reconceptualization requires that the discipline let go of its current pedagogical shape (i.e., its focus on supplying students with productive rhetorical skills that can be exercised through writing) and instead deploy its efforts to inculcate *receptive* skills" (61–62). Thus, I argue that rather than the rejection of process, the post-process critique contributes to our discipline through the rejection of mastery—the description of writing as a "thing," and the description of a master narrative or theory of writing. In giving up the search for a way to teach writing, post-process theory advocates, in the words of Petraglia, the "letting go" of the discipline. As I explain in the next section, post-process theory can be more fully explained by reviewing key assumptions critical to the theory, assumptions that are informed by postmodern and anti-foundationalist perspectives.

POST-PROCESS ASSUMPTIONS ABOUT WRITING

In moving away from writing as a "thing," post-process theory encourages us to examine writing again as an activity—an indeterminate activity. By "indeterminate" I mean that the writing act cannot be predicted in terms of how students will write (through certain formulas or content) or how students will learn (through certain approaches). The shift from writing as content to writing as activity can be more fully explained by assumptions that are central to the post-process perspective. These are, according to Kent, the following: "(1) writing is public; (2) writing is interpretive; and (3) writing is situated" (Introduction 1). As I suggest in this section, because so much post-process scholarship has focused on the rejection of process, we need further explanation about assumptions that support a post-process view of writing. In my attempt to provide more background and explanation of these assumptions, I refer to the work of Donald Davidson, Richard Rorty, Thomas Kuhn, Stanley Fish, and scholars in composition who have discussed these assumptions.

Writing Is Public

The assumption that writing is public grows out of the post-process perspective that meaning making is a product of our communicative interaction with others rather than a product of an individual.[4] Acknowledging the public nature of writing means acknowledging a reading audience—people to whom the writing matters—whether that audience is oneself, another person, a group of people, or any other reader. Emphasizing the public nature of writing reminds us that beyond writing correctly, writers must work toward communicating their message to an audience. It is this goal—being understood—that Kent suggests cannot be "guaranteed"; therefore, we cannot know with certainty if students are successful, nor can we know how to teach students to be successful in communicative interaction. However, we *can* encourage students to become more aware of their interactions with others.

We can further understand the assumption that writing is public by examining the Davidsonian perspective of "language-in-use," a concept that has influenced some post-process scholars, particularly Kent. Davidson explains in "A Nice Derangement of Epitaphs" that language-in-use does not rely on some sort of foundational structure (like Noam Chomsky's deep structure) or even conventions of language. His description of language-in-use has radical implications for the idea that language is contextually or "convention" bound:

> There is no such thing as a language, not if a language is anything like what many philosophers and linguists have supposed. There is therefore no such thing to be learned, mastered, or born with. We must give up the idea of a clearly defined shared structure which language-users acquire and then apply to cases. And we should try again to say how convention in any important sense is involved in language; or, as I think, we should give up the attempt to illuminate how we communicate by appeal to conventions. (446)[5]

Davidson's version of communicative interaction suggests that meaning is not relative to a community or to discourse conventions but is a product of language-in-use, and language-in-use, as Reed Way Dasenbrock explains, is always public and accessible to other language users:

> Networks of meaning, thus, are both inner and outer, including ourselves and others in a web. It is not that we have something unique to say stemming from our personal experience before we negotiate the public structures of meaning, but what we have to say forms as a response to that public structure, to what has come before us and what is being said and done around us. (29)

Davidson terms this public interaction "triangulation," which he understands as the connection between language users and the world.[6] In explaining triangulation, Davidson writes that the "basic idea is that our concept of objectivity—our idea that our thoughts may or may not correspond to the truth—is an idea that we would not have if it weren't for interpersonal relations. In other words, the source of objectivity is intersubjectivity: the triangle consists of two people and the world" (Kent, "Language" 7–8). Triangulation is a key concept for explaining how meanings are located within our communicative interactions with others, and it suggests that we can't know things without knowing others.

The public aspect of writing, which incorporates Davidson's depiction of language-in-use, is already apparent in some writing pedagogies; however, these pedagogies are often described as "dialogic" instead of "post-process" because they emphasize communicative interaction in the teaching of writing. Sánchez outlines a writing pedagogy, for example, as a one-to-one mentored relationship between teacher and student that emphasizes communicative interaction. In this proposed pedagogy, writing instruction is no longer focused on process as content, but rather on class time used to engage students in discourse about writing (see Dobrin, *Constructing* 83–85). Similarly, Ewald suggests that a pedagogy emphasizing communicative interaction would "enjoy an intimate connection between instructional subjects and methods. Writing instruction could be organized around discourse moves" (128).

Other pedagogies that emphasize dialogue employ concepts from Bakhtin—particularly the concepts of heteroglossia and addressivity. Ward explains how these concepts relate to writing pedagogy: "The self in a dialogic pedagogy is not autonomous and solitary but multiple, composed of all the voices or texts one has ever heard or read and therefore capable of playing an infinite number of roles in service of the internal dialogic interaction" (172–73). Using Bakhtinian concepts of dialogue, Ward describes a "functional dialogism," a pedagogy that encourages students to interact with others, thus reinforcing the public aspect of writing:

> Because learning takes place best in communicative interaction, a functional dialogic pedagogy will have to employ a great deal of public writing—that is, writing directed to others capable of and interested in responding—if we are to produce students who are able to generate not only correct, readable prose, but also prose that can elicit a response from others, thereby enabling students to become active participants in communities beyond the classroom. (170)

Dialogue is even more prominent in Kay Halasek's *A Pedagogy of Possibility*, in which she argues that "dialogue has replaced writing as a process as a defining metaphor for the discipline" (3–4). Halasek's decidedly post-process pedagogy emphasizes Bakhtinian scholarship, which she conceptualizes as "a world that recognizes the viability and necessity of existing social, economic, and national languages. Through the concept of dialogism, Bakhtin establishes the critical need to sustain dialogue in the unending quest to maintain difference and diversity, hallmarks of intellectual growth and health . . ." (8). Emphasizing the importance of communicative interaction, Halasek suggests that heteroglossia—reflexivity and response— ought to characterize writing pedagogy.

The assumption that writing is public, therefore, incorporates the idea that meaning is made through our interactions. Terms used to describe this emphasis include language-in-use, communicative interaction, and dialogue, but they all point to the idea that writing is an activity—an interaction with others—rather than content to be mastered.

Writing Is Interpretive

A second assumption of the post-process perspective is that writing is interpretive. That is, the production—not just the reception—of discourse is thoroughly interpretive (or what Rorty calls "interpretation all the way down").[7] This assumption supports the belief that writing is indeterminate, for saying writing is interpretive suggests that meaning is not stable. We can better understand this assumption by reviewing what has been called the "interpretive turn" in philosophy, the claim that what we know is shaped by our interpretations. The interpretive turn, as described by James Bohman, David Hiley, and Richard Shusterman, follows previous philosophical movements such as the "epistemological turn" of the eighteenth century (where knowledge was equated with rational thought, especially the kind of rational thought exemplified by the scientific method) and the "linguistic turn" early in this century, where emphasis was placed on the structure of language and the meanings generated through language systems. According to Bohman, Hiley, and Shusterman, the interpretive turn breaks with these previous traditions by giving up the notion that the essence or the foundations of knowledge and meaning can be discovered: "The views about the foundations of knowledge and the knowing subject that were the basis for the epistemological turn have been called into question, and it has seemed to many philosophers that language and meaning cannot bear the kind of weight the linguistic turn required" (1). When we give up our search for the foundations of knowledge, and when we relinquish our attempts to reduce knowledge and meaning to foundational categories of linguistic or mental states, we encounter the interpretive turn—the acknowledgment that meaning is shaped by our interpretive acts.

Critical to the assumption that writing is interpretive is the degree to which interpretation penetrates. That is, are there some things, ideas, concepts, that are not subject to interpretation? The post-process assumption is that writing is thoroughly interpretive, or what Rorty calls "interpretation all the way down." Bohman, Hiley, and Shusterman explain that the move toward interpretation can take one of two forms: either "hermeneutic universalism" or "hermeneutic contextualism" (7). Hermeneutic universalism holds that interpretation never stops—that communication itself constitutes an interpretive act. Hermeneutic contextualism holds that interpretation takes place within some context, community, or background (7). In short, contextualism suggests that there are limits to interpretation, while universalism does not.

These competing conceptions of interpretation characterize a recurring debate within current hermeneutic theory, and clear examples of this debate are found in the writings of Kuhn and Rorty. For example, in "The Natural and the Human Sciences," Kuhn, a hermeneutic contextualist, notes that both the natural and the human sciences rely on interpretation, but the human sciences rely on interpretation more completely: "The natural sciences, therefore, though they may require what I have called a hermeneutic base, are not themselves hermeneutic enterprises. The human sciences, on the other hand, often are, and they may have no alternative." Kuhn endorses the idea that the natural sciences are more objective, and, finally, more "truthful" than the human sciences because the natural sciences "are not themselves hermeneutic enterprises" (23).

In contrast, Rorty, a hermeneutic universalist, argues that interpretation goes "all the way down": "My fantasy is of a culture so deeply anti-essentialist that it makes only a sociological distinction between sociologists and physicists, not a methodological or philosophical one" (71). In "Inquiry as Recontextualization," Rorty asserts that our minds are "webs of beliefs and desires, of sentential attitudes—webs that continually reweave themselves so as to accommodate new sentential attitudes" (59). For Rorty, both the human sciences and the natural sciences are thoroughly hermeneutic enterprises, and he argues that what we know or could ever know about the world derives from the webs of beliefs and desires that we continually reweave or "recontextualize":

> As one moves along the spectrum from habit to inquiry—from instinctive revision of intentions through routine calculation toward revolutionary science or politics—the number of beliefs added to or subtracted from the web increases. At a certain point in this process it becomes useful to speak of "recontextualization." The more widespread the changes, the more use

we have for the notion of "a new context." This new context can be a new explanatory theory, a new comparison class, a new descriptive vocabulary, a new private or political purpose, the latest book one has read, the last person one talked to; the possibilities are endless. (60–61)

According to Rorty, interpretation—what he calls "reinterpretation" and "recontextualization"—never ceases, for every interpretation is based on a previous interpretation. The different views about the power of interpretation held by Rorty and Kuhn exemplify the current debate concerning hermeneutic universalism and hermeneutic contextualization that we encounter in studies of both the reception and the production of discourse.

To understand writing as a thoroughly interpretive activity (in the spirit of hermeneutic universalism) means accepting that no foundational knowledge is the basis for writing as a discipline. Given this assumption, we can better understand the post-process rejection of mastery and its depiction and consequent rejection of process as a foundational body of knowledge. In addition, when we understand writing as thoroughly interpretive, we must also accept the indeterminate nature of the writing activity. Writing becomes an activity that requires an understanding of context, interaction with others, and our attempts to communicate a message. Understanding interpretation as universal helps illuminate the third post-process assumption: that writing is situated.

Writing Is Situated

The assumption that writing is situated also illustrates the indeterminacy of the writing act, as writing must correspond to specific contexts that naturally vary. Of all three post-process assumptions, the assumption that writing is situated has been discussed most frequently by scholars interested in postmodern or anti-foundationalist perspectives. For example, James Sosnoski asserts that postmodern classrooms "do not have to follow a single blueprint and should change according to the situation" (210). Also endorsing situatedness, Thomas Barker and Fred Kemp explain that postmodernism is "a self-conscious acknowledgment of the immediate present and an attempt to respond to it in new ways" (1). James Berlin draws on postmodern thought and social-epistemic rhetoric to suggest that pedagogy becomes enforced through "dialectical interaction, working out a rhetoric more adequate to the historical moment and the actual conditions of teacher and students" (25). Situatedness, for these postmodern scholars, refers to the ability to respond to specific situations rather than rely on foundational principles or rules.

Situatedness has been discussed similarly in the anti-foundationalist perspective. For example, Patricia Bizzell asserts that "an anti-foundationalist understanding of discourse would see the student's way of thinking and interacting with the world, the student's very self, as fundamentally altered by participation in any new discourse" (43). She includes situatedness in her definition of rhetoric: "Rhetoric is the study of the personal, social and historical elements in human discourse—how to recognize them, interpret them, and act on them, in terms both of situational context and of verbal style" (52). Likewise, Susan Wells suggests that technical writing pedagogy should help students enter into communicative action and to help them understand their situatedness (264). Further, in "Teaching Professional Writing as Social Praxis," Thomas Miller suggests that we need to teach technical writing not as *techné* (or cognitive skills) but as *praxis*, which means that writers must understand the situations and contexts that surround them: "We can foster such 'practical wisdom' by developing a pedagogy that contributes to our students' ability to locate themselves and their professional communities in the larger public context" (68).

While situatedness has been addressed more explicitly in these passages, we can see traces of all three post-process assumptions in this scholarship. They are evident in assertions that writing should *change with the situation*, that students *interact with the world* through *dialectical interaction*, and that rhetoric involves *interpretation of social and historical elements of human discourse*. Given these similarities, we see that post-process scholarship is not advocating new directions, but rather endorsing anti-foundationalist and postmodern approaches that have already been articulated. To see writing in terms of post-process assumptions—as public, interpretive, and situated—encourages us to think of writing as an indeterminate activity rather than a body of knowledge to be mastered. These post-process assumptions (strongly influenced by postmodern and anti-foundationalist perspectives) finally shed light on how post-process theory might inform teaching.

POST-PROCESS PEDAGOGY?

My purpose thus far has been to reveal the post-process rejection of mastery and to outline the anti-foundationalist assumptions informing post-process theory. In doing so, I have suggested that post-process theory rejects system-based explanations of writing and embraces indeterminacy in the writing act. Given this understanding of post-process theory, in this final section I assert that post-process theory resists pedagogical agendas that are comprised of content, but that it offers valuable pedagogical principles about the activity of teaching. I discuss implications of these principles, which include mentoring and tutorial approaches to writing instruction.

Understanding the anti-foundationalist nature of post-process theory places us, as Dobrin suggests, "at an awkward crossroads" (*Constructing* 86). To articulate any kind of pedagogy based on anti-foundationalism would be to support the claim that knowledge can be rooted in a particular approach or system and, therefore, would no longer be anti-foundational. It is for this reason that I do not advocate a specific pedagogical agenda that espouses post-process theory, for I believe doing so presents an inherent paradox. Fish more clearly explains that we ought not to place too much pedagogical stock in anti-foundationalist assumptions such as situatedness:

> To put the matter in a nutshell, the knowledge that one is in a situation has no particular payoff for any situation you happen to be in, because the constraints of that situation will not be relaxed by that knowledge. It follows, then, that teaching our students the lesson of anti-foundationalism, while it will put them in possession of a new philosophical perspective, will not give them a tool for operating in the world they already inhabit. Being told that you are in a situation will help you neither to dwell in it more perfectly nor to *write* within it more successfully. (351)

Similarly, if we accept the post-process perspective that writing is indeterminate, public, interpretive, and situated, there is little we can do with this knowledge.

When it comes to pedagogy, however, the temptation is to turn our revelations into content to be delivered in the classroom, thereby falling prey to what Dobrin calls the "pedagogical imperative." While we may want to translate the post-process assumptions (writing is public, interpretive, and situated) into content to have our students learn, what good does this do? I completely agree with Dobrin that the force of the "pedagogical imperative" is alive and well and also that it is premature in relation to post-process theory. Dobrin suggests that post-process theory is too new to generate pedagogical insights—that its discussions should be theoretical at this point (*Constructing* 64). While I agree with Dobrin, I suggest that because of the anti-foundationalist influence on post-process theory, it is unlikely that we will *ever* see a "post-process pedagogy," complete with neat, bulleted points about applying a specific approach to the writing classroom. Fish is again insightful here, for he argues a similar point in declaring that the project to develop a postmodern or anti-foundationalist pedagogy should be abandoned—not simply because the project would be difficult, but because it is impossible. According to Fish, anti-foundationalism only helps us understand *that* we are situated. He argues that we can do nothing with this knowledge, and we certainly can't put it to use. In the conclusion of "Anti-Foundationalism, Theory Hope, and the Teaching of Composition," Fish offers a kind of apology for this view: "Perhaps I should apologize for taking up so much of your time in return for so small a yield; but the smallness of the yield has been my point. It is also the point of anti-foundationalism, which offers you nothing but the assurance that what it is unable to give you—knowledge, goals, purposes, strategies—is what you already have" (355). Similarly, I offer a kind of apology that I have no specific pedagogical agenda to offer that I could claim would be "post-process pedagogy," for I don't believe such an agenda is compatible with the theory.

More to the point, Fish's viewpoint actualizes, in my opinion, the "letting go" of the discipline that Petraglia spoke of in terms of post-process theory. Petraglia suggests that instructors of writing need to let go of the idea that writing is built on a foundational body of knowledge and accept the idea that we need to focus on situational response. Likewise, we must resist the temptation to turn our understanding of post-process assumptions into content to be delivered and mastered by students. Accepting post-process assumptions truly implies a "letting go" of the desire to find a right way to learn and teach writing.

While post-process theory does not offer concrete pedagogical agendas based on content, I believe that it offers valuable pedagogical principles that guide our practice as teachers. I see two main principles that post-process theory can offer pedagogy: the rejection of mastery and the engagement in dialogue rather than monologue with students. I have already illustrated these principles in my explanation of post-process assumptions (writing is public, interpretive, and situated), so I won't explain them again here. It is worth noting, however, that these principles have been present in previous scholarship about composition pedagogy, alternative pedagogies, and pragmatic theories dating back to John Dewey. We need to recognize that these post-process principles are not out in left field but, rather, that they support excellent scholarship in education. It is worth briefly reviewing these principles, most notably in the scholarship of Dewey and Paulo Freire.

We find traces of the rejection of mastery and engagement in dialogue in Dewey's declaration that education is a social process instead of subject matter (230). In "My Pedagogic Creed," Dewey suggests that "the only true education comes through the stimulation of the child's powers by the demands of the social situations in which he finds himself," that education is a lifelong process, and that school "must represent present life—life as real and vital to the child as that which he carries on in the home, in the neighborhood, or on the playground" (229, 230–31). In declaring these beliefs, he rejects the idea that education is a fixed body of knowledge to be transmitted passively to the student: "I believe, therefore, that the true centre of correlation of the school subjects is not science, nor literature, nor history, nor geography, but the child's own social activities" (232). The idea is that the rote learning of subject matter, without understanding its relevance to one's situation and the world, does not improve one's education. Dewey's ideas resonate with the post-process rejection of system-based writing approaches and its emphasis on language-in-use.

In some regards, an even more striking resemblance exists between post-process principles and the work of Freire, particularly his notion of the "banking concept." In *Pedagogy of the Oppressed*, Freire describes the banking concept as "an act of depositing, in which the students are the depositories and the teacher is the depositor. Instead of communicating, the teacher issues communiques and makes deposits which the students patiently receive, memorize, and repeat" (67). Freire considers the banking method of teaching to be a dehumanizing practice that ultimately reinforces teachers as oppressors, controlling knowledge, and students as the oppressed, incapable of response (68). In place of the banking concept of education, Freire advocates a "problem-posing" concept of education, which would require students to play active rather than passive roles:

> Those truly committed to liberation must reject the banking concept in its entirety, adopting instead a concept of women and men as conscious beings and consciousness intent upon the world. They must abandon the educational goal of deposit-making and replace it with the posing of the problems of human beings in their relationship with the world. (74)

By suggesting that critical consciousness requires that students must communicate with the world, not just be in the world, Freire illustrates the post-process emphasis on writing as public interaction with others and the world. And he emphasizes the social aspect of education when he asserts that human life can only have meaning through communication (72). He encourages the teacher-student relationship to be a "partnership" in which teacher and student engage in two-way dialogue. To do so requires a dialogic relationship between students and teacher in which roles of the traditional banking concept of education no longer exist and in which "the students—no longer docile listeners—are now critical co-investigators in dialogue with the teacher" (70, 75). Although Freire's pedagogy is thoroughly ideological—a premise Dewey's pedagogy does not share to the same degree—both principles of rejection of mastery and engagement of dialogue can be seen in this scholarship.

In composition studies, we have also heard these principles before. As I outlined earlier in this essay, postmodern and anti-foundationalist "pedagogies" have advocated writing as situated, interpretive, and public rather than based on foundational knowledge, and several "dialogic" pedagogies have also been discussed in composition scholarship. Although the principles of rejection of mastery and engagement in dialogue have been discussed in previous scholarship, what is different about post-process theory is the combination of these principles in one theoretical perspective, as well as its sharp criticism of the dominant paradigm in composition studies. These features of post-process theory push the discipline forward in a most pronounced way, as its very name suggests.

Although I am unable to produce specific content-based pedagogical agendas that can be immediately transferred to the classroom, I do suggest that the rejection of mastery and engagement in dialogue lead to an important implication for how we teach writing: such a stance helps us reconsider teaching as an act of mentoring rather than a job in which we deliver content. To think of teaching as mentoring means spending time and energy on our interactions with students—listening to them, discussing ideas with them, letting them make mistakes, and pointing them in the right direction. This type of teacher-student relationship demonstrates instruction that is collaborative and dialogic, and it in fact reflects Kent's suggestions for pedagogy in *Paralogic Rhetoric*: "By working in partnership with their students, mentors would no longer stand outside their students' writing and reading experiences. Instead, they would become an integral part of their students' learning experiences . . ." (166). This type of mentoring suggests a release of the idea of mastery and the embrace of indeterminacy in teaching situations. Indeed, the connection could be made that like the post-process description of writing, the act of *teaching* is also public, interpretive, and situated—another type of indeterminate activity.

Given this emphasis on mentoring, I believe the strongest application of post-process theory is in the practice of one-to-one instruction that manifests itself in teacher-student interactions. Kent, Sánchez, Ward, and Halasek have come to similar conclusions, drawing attention to dialogue between teacher-student and to student-student interactions in the classroom. I support the kind of one-to-one, dialogic instruction these scholars have advocated; however, their descriptions of one-to-one interactions tend to be broad and abstract, leaving readers with little concrete sense of how post-process theory might apply to one-to-one instruction. For purposes of illustration, a more immediate and tangible application of post-process theory might exist in tutorial interactions between tutors and students in writing centers. Writing centers provide a concrete context for post-process theory because one-to-one interactions are the primary practice of writing center tutors, as well as the subject of writing center research. For example,

Christina Murphy and Steve Sherwood suggest that the essence of tutoring is *conversation*, or language-in-use (2). Similarly, Eric Hobson suggests that writing center scholarship often derives its credibility from practice, or "lore." In addition, illustrations of one-to-one teaching interactions abound in writing center literature; many scholars have addressed the dynamics of teaching interactions, teacher-student roles, and methods involved in one-to-one writing instruction.[8] Given that post-process theory emphasizes dialogue in writing instruction, as well as the importance of mentoring, and given that such dialogue in writing instruction is the core of writing center work, the connection between post-process theory and writing center pedagogy is easy to support.

Post-process theory, then, could find immediate application in writing center work and could benefit from writing center scholarship about one-to-one teaching. Alternatively, writing centers could benefit from post-process theory in exploring theoretical avenues to support writing center practice. There exists a wonderful irony in this connection because of the sometimes perceived gap in prestige between post-process theory and writing center practice. That is, post-process theory, at least in the terms Dobrin describes, appears on the surface to be an ivory-tower endeavor. Writing centers, on the other hand, because of their focus on practice, have historically been marginalized and have consequently struggled to legitimize scholarship based on tutorial practice. The connection between the two might result in a happy marriage. For instance, anti-foundationalist and postmodernist perspectives are appearing more frequently in writing center scholarship.[9] Traces of the public, situated, and interpretive aspects of post-process theory in writing centers exist in Joan Mullin's suggestion that writing centers "provide spaces where the personal and public, the individual and other, struggle to honor the singular voice, to recognize different language communities" (xiii). In addition, claims such as that expressed by Hobson ("no single theory can dictate writing center instruction") are reminiscent of the post-process rejection of a grand theory or narrative to describe communicative practice (8). The union of post-process theory and writing center practice could potentially demonstrate how theory and practice could live in harmony, providing both illustration and explanation of one-to-one writing instruction. Of course, while there are some interesting overlaps between post-process theory and writing center work, asserting a strong connection would require another lengthy and careful discussion, which I do not have time to develop here. But I do see this connection as a fruitful area for future research, and I see writing centers as an immediate illustration of the kind of instructional dialogue post-process theory endorses.

For the purposes of my discussion here, however, I wish to suggest that post-process theory is, at its very core, concerned with pedagogical practice.

In asserting this claim, I disagree with those scholars who suggest post-process theory should remain a theoretical enterprise, and I suggest that post-process theory is most decidedly connected to a *how-centered* approach to teaching. Critiques that deny any pedagogical relevance of post-process theory are, I believe, based on the expectation that pedagogy is what-centered and needs to produce a concrete pedagogical agenda based on content. The real pedagogical thrust of post-process theory has to do not with content or subject matter, but rather with *what we do with content*. As such, post-process theory has much to offer teachers in any discipline, whether they teach writing, math, physics, women's studies, history, or occupational therapy, for the pedagogical thrust of post-process theory is in its reminder that teaching does not equal mastery of content but rather how teachers and students can interact with one another *about* content. Thus, in addition to posing the question "what does it mean to write?" post-process theory also poses the question "what does it mean to teach?"

LETTING GO

As discerning scholars, we must not take post-process theory at face value, associating it only with a critique of process. If, as many post-process scholars articulate, post-process theory means accepting an anti-foundationalist perspective and adopting language-in-use, then its relevance to pedagogy is to encourage us to reexamine the "foundations" from which we may have been operating, as well as our communicative practices with students. Even if this examination does not make anti-foundationalists out of us, it reminds us to think carefully about our teaching practices, to avoid co-opting or reducing complex research in composition studies, and to become more aware of our interactions with students in the classroom.

"Letting go" in the case of post-process theory does not mean an avoidance of the teaching of writing; it does not mean becoming irresponsible teachers. It means, quite frankly, the opposite. It means becoming teachers who are more in tune to the pedagogical needs of students, more willing to discuss ideas, more willing to listen, more willing to be moved by moments of mutual understanding. It means, in sum, to be more conscientious in our attempts to meet the needs of students in their educational journeys. Post-process theory does not prescribe a pedagogy and ask us to adopt it blindly. Rather, it enhances our sensitivity as teachers, our knowledge and expertise, and the way we communicate with students to help them learn. In short, post-process theory asks us to take a close look at ourselves as teachers. Thinking through the principles of rejection of mastery and engagement in dialogue provides all teachers with a valuable philosophical exercise.[10]

NOTES

1. See, for example, Olson; Pullman; Kent, "Introduction."

2. See Petraglia; Dobrin, "Constructing"; Kent, "Introduction"; Pullman.

3. See, for example, Pullman, Olson, Couture.

4. In his *Paralogic Rhetoric*, Kent identifies this assumption with "externalism."

5. We can note similarities between Davidson's argument that "there is no such thing as language" and Kent's argument that "we cannot teach writing . . . for nothing exists to teach." Both arguments reject the idea that language and writing are comprised of foundational systems.

6. The term "triangulation" that Davidson uses is not to be confused with the term "triangulation" that denotes qualitative research methodology in which data are compiled from three or more perspectives to establish a more verifiable analysis.

7. While much has been discussed about interpretation in the reception of discourse—for example, Stanley Fish's concept of interpretive communities and how meaning is received—little has been discussed about the interpretive nature of writing or speaking.

8. See, for example, Murphy and Sherwood; Hobson; Harris; Black; Clark; Mullin and Wallace.

9. See Nancy Grimm's fine book, *Good Intentions: Writing Center Work for Postmodern Times*, as well as scholarship by Hobson and Abascal-Hildebrand.

10. I wish to thank colleagues who reviewed this article and provided comments that contributed to substantive improvements: Peter T. Breuch, Thomas Kent, Mary Lay, John Logie, David Beard, and James Thomas Zebroski.

WORKS CITED

Abascal-Hildebrand, Mary. "Tutor and Student Relations: Applying Gadamer's Notions of Translation." Mullin and Wallace 172–83.

Barker, Thomas T., and Fred O. Kemp. "Network Theory: A Postmodern Pedagogy for the Writing Classroom." *Computers and Community: Teaching Composition in the Twenty-First Century*. Ed. Carolyn Handa. Portsmouth: Boynton, 1990. 1–27.

Berlin, James A. "Poststructuralism, Cultural Studies, and the Composition Classroom: Postmodern Theory in Practice." *Rhetoric Review* 11 (1992): 16–33.

Bizzell, Patricia A. "Foundationalism and Anti-Foundationalism in Composition Studies." *Pre/Text* 7.1–2 (1986): 37–56.

Black, Laurel Johnson. *Between Talk and Teaching: Reconsidering the Writing Conference*. Logan: Utah State UP, 1998.

Bohman, James F., David R. Hiley, and Richard Shusterman. "Introduction: The Interpretive Turn." Hiley, Bohman, and Shusterman 1–14.

Clark, Gregory. *Dialogue, Dialectic, and Conversation: A Social Perspective on the Function of Writing*. Carbondale: Southern Illinois UP, 1990.

Couture, Barbara. "Modeling and Emulating: Rethinking Agency in the Writing Process." Kent, *Post-Process* 30–48.

Dasenbrock, Reed Way. "Do We Write the Text We Read?" *Literary Theory After Davidson*. Ed. Reed Way Dasenbrock. University Press: Pennsylvania State UP, 1993. 18–36.

_____. "The Myths of the Subjective and of the Subject in Composition Studies." *Journal of Advanced Composition* 13 (1993): 21–32.

Davidson, Donald. "A Nice Derangement of Epitaphs." *Inquiries into Truth and Interpretation: Perspectives on the Philosophy of Donald Davidson.* Ed. Ernst LePore. New York: Oxford UP, 1984. 433–46.

Dewey, John. "My Pedagogic Creed." 1897. *The Essential Dewey: Pragmatism, Education, Democracy.* Ed. Larry A. Hickman and Thomas M. Alexander. Vol. 1. Bloomington: Indiana UP, 1998. 229–35.

Dobrin, Sidney I. *Constructing Knowledges: The Politics of Theory-Building and Pedagogy in Composition.* Albany: State U of New York P, 1997.

_____. "Paralogic Hermeneutic Theories, Power, and the Possibility for Liberating Pedagogies." Kent, *Post-Process* 132–48.

Ede, Lisa. "Reading the Writing Process." *Taking Stock: The Writing Process Movement in the '90s.* Ed. Lad Tobin and Thomas Newkirk. Portsmouth: Boynton, 1994. 31–43.

Elbow, Peter. *Writing without Teachers.* New York: Oxford UP, 1973.

Emig, Janet. *The Composing Processes of Twelfth Graders.* Urbana, IL: NCTE, 1971.

Ewald, Helen Rothschild. "A Tangled Web of Discourses: On Post-Process Pedagogy and Communicative Interaction." Kent, *Post-Process* 116–31.

Fish, Stanley. "Anti-Foundationalism, Theory Hope, and the Teaching of Composition." *Doing What Comes Naturally: Change, Rhetoric, and the Practice of Theory in Literary and Legal Studies.* Durham: Duke UP, 1989. 315–41.

_____. "Consequences." *Doing What Comes Naturally: Change, Rhetoric, and the Practice of Theory in Literary and Legal Studies.* Durham: Duke UP, 1989. 342–55.

Flower, Linda, and John Hayes. "Identifying the Organization of the Writing Processes." *Cognitive Processes in Writing.* Ed. Lee W. Gregg and Erwin R. Steinberg. Hillsdale: Erlbaum, 1980. 3–30.

Foster, David. "The Challenge of Contingency: Process and the Turn to the Social in Composition." Kent, *Post-Process* 149–62.

Freire, Paulo. *Pedagogy of the Oppressed.* Rpt. in *The Paulo Freire Reader.* Ed. Ana Maria Araujo Freire and Donaldo Macedo. New York: Continuum, 1998.

Grimm, Nancy Maloney. *Good Intentions: Writing Center Work for Postmodern Times.* Portsmouth: Boynton, 1999.

Halasek, Kay. *A Pedagogy of Possibility: Bakhtinian Perspectives on Composition Studies.* Carbondale: Southern Illinois UP, 1999.

Harris, Muriel. *Teaching One to One: The Writing Conference.* Urbana, IL: NCTE: 55–75, 1986.

Hiley, David R., James F. Bohman, and Richard Shusterman, eds. *The Interpretive Turn: Philosophy, Science, Culture.* Ithaca: Cornell UP, 1991.

Hobson, Eric H. "Writing Center Practice Often Counters Its Theory. So What?" Mullin and Wallace 1–10.

Kent, Thomas. Introduction. Kent, *Post-Process* 1–6.

_____. "Language Philosophy, Writing, and Reading: A Conversation with Donald Davidson." *Journal of Advanced Composition* 13 (1993): 1–20.

_____. *Paralogic Rhetoric: A Theory of Communicative Interaction.* Lewisburg: Bucknell UP, 1993.

_____, ed. *Post-Process Theory: Beyond the Writing-Process Paradigm.* Carbondale: Southern Illinois UP, 1999.

Kuhn, Thomas S. "The Natural and the Human Sciences." Hiley, Bohman, and Shusterman 17–24.

Lindemann, Erika. *A Rhetoric for Writing Teachers.* 3rd ed. New York: Oxford UP, 1995.

Macrorie, Ken. *Writing to Be Read.* Rochelle Park, NJ: Hayden, 1976.

McComiskey, Bruce. "The Post-Process Movement in Composition Studies." *Reforming College Composition: Writing the Wrongs.* Ed. Ray Wallace, Alan Jackson, and Susan Lewis Wallace. London: Greenwood, 2000. 37–53.

Miller, Thomas P. "Treating Professional Writing as Social *Praxis.*" *Journal of Advanced Composition* 11 (1991): 57–72.

Mullin, Joan A. "Introduction: The Theory Behind the Centers." Mullin and Wallace vii–xiii.

Mullin, Joan A., and Ray Wallace, eds. *Intersections: Theory-Practice in the Writing Center.* Urbana, IL: NCTE, 1994.

Murphy, Christina, and Steve Sherwood. "The Tutoring Process: Exploring Paradigms and Practices." *The St. Martin's Sourcebook for Writing Tutors.* New York: St. Martin's, 1995. 1–18.

Murray, Donald M. *A Writer Teaches Writing.* Boston: Houghton, 1968.

Olson, Gary A. "Toward a Post-Process Composition: Abandoning the Rhetoric of Assertion." Kent, *Post-Process* 7–15.

Petraglia, Joseph. "Is There Life after Process? The Role of Social Scientism in a Changing Discipline." Kent, *Post-Process* 49–64.

Pullman, George. "Stepping Yet Again into the Same Current." Kent, *Post-Process* 16–29.

Rorty, Richard. "Inquiry as Recontextualization: An Anti-Dualist Account of Interpretation." Hiley, Bohman, and Shusterman 59–80.

Russell, David. "Activity Theory and Process Approaches: Writing in School and Society." Kent, *Post-Process* 80–95.

Sosnoski, James J. "Postmodern Teachers in Their Postmodern Classrooms: Socrates Begone!" *Contending with Words: Composition and Rhetoric in a Postmodern Age.* Ed. Patricia Harkin and John Schilb. New York: MLA, 1991. 198–219.

Wallace, David. "Reconsidering Behaviorist Composition Pedagogies: Positivism, Empiricism, and the Paradox of Postmodernism." *Journal of Advanced Composition* 6 (1996): 103–17.

Ward, Irene. *Literacy, Ideology, and Dialogue: Towards a Dialogic Pedagogy.* Albany: State U of New York P, 1994.

Wells, Susan. "Jürgen Habermas, Communicative Competence, and the Teaching of Technical Discourse." *Theory in the Classroom.* Ed. Cary Nelson. Urbana: U of Illinois P, 1986. 245–69.

Young, Richard E. "Paradigms and Problems: Needed Research in Rhetorical Invention." *Research on Composing: Points of Departure.* Ed. Charles R. Cooper and Lee Odell. Urbana: NCTE, 1978. 29–47.

Contemporary Composition

The Major Pedagogical Theories

JAMES A. BERLIN

A number of articles attempting to make sense of the various approaches to teaching composition have recently appeared. While all are worth considering, some promote a common assumption that I am convinced is erroneous.[1] Since all pedagogical approaches, it is argued, share a concern for the elements of the composing process—that is, for writer, reality, reader, and language—their only area of disagreement must involve the element or elements that ought to be given the most attention. From this point of view, the composing process is always and everywhere the same because writer, reality, reader, and language are always and everywhere the same. Differences in teaching theories, then, are mere cavils about which of these features to emphasize in the classroom.

I would like to say at the start that I have no quarrel with the elements that these investigators isolate as forming the composing process, and I plan to use them myself. While it is established practice today to speak of the composing process as a recursive activity involving prewriting, writing, and rewriting, it is not difficult to see the writer-reality-audience-language relationship as underlying, at a deeper structural level, each of these three stages. In fact, as I will later show, this deeper structure determines the shape that instruction in prewriting, writing, and rewriting assumes—or does not assume, as is sometimes the case.

I do, however, strongly disagree with the contention that the differences in approaches to teaching writing can be explained by attending to the degree of emphasis given to universally defined elements of a universally defined

Reprinted from *College English* 44.8 (December 1982): 765–77. Used with permission.

composing process. The differences in these teaching approaches should instead be located in diverging definitions of the composing process itself—that is, in the way the elements that make up the process—writer, reality, audience, and language—are envisioned. Pedagogical theories in writing courses are grounded in rhetorical theories, and rhetorical theories do not differ in the simple undue emphasis of writer or audience or reality or language or some combination of these. Rhetorical theories differ from each other in the way writer, reality, audience, and language are conceived—both as separate units and in the way the units relate to each other. In the case of distinct pedagogical approaches, these four elements are likewise defined and related so as to describe a different composing process, which is to say a different world with different rules about what can be known, how it can be known, and how it can be communicated. To teach writing is to argue for a version of reality, and the best way of knowing and communicating it—to deal, as Paul Kameen has pointed out, in the metarhetorical realm of epistemology and linguistics.[2] And all composition teachers are ineluctably operating in this realm, whether or not they consciously choose to do so.

Considering pedagogical theories along these lines has led me to see groupings sometimes similar, sometimes at variance, with the schemes of others. The terms chosen for these categories are intended to prevent confusion and to be self-explanatory. The four dominant groups I will discuss are the Neo-Aristotelians or Classicists, the Positivists or Current-Traditionalists, the Neo-Platonists or Expressionists, and the New Rhetoricians. As I have said, I will be concerned in each case with the way that writer, reality, audience, and language have been defined and related so as to form a distinct world construct with distinct rules for discovering and communicating knowledge. I will then show how this epistemic complex makes for specific directives about invention, arrangement, and style (or prewriting, writing, and rewriting). Finally, as the names for the groups suggest, I will briefly trace the historical precedents of each, pointing to their roots in order to better understand their modern manifestations.

My reasons for presenting this analysis are not altogether disinterested. I am convinced that the pedagogical approach of the New Rhetoricians is the most intelligent and most practical alternative available, serving in every way the best interests of our students. I am also concerned, however, that writing teachers become more aware of the full significance of their pedagogical strategies. Not doing so can have disastrous consequences, ranging from momentarily confusing students to sending them away with faulty and even harmful information. The dismay students display about writing is, I am convinced, at least occasionally the result of teachers unconsciously offering contradictory advice about composing—guidance grounded in assumptions that simply do not square with each other. More important, as I have already indicated and as I plan to explain in detail later on, in teaching writing we are tacitly teaching a version of reality and the student's place and mode of operation in it. Yet many teachers (and I suspect most) look upon their vocations as the imparting of a largely mechanical skill, important only because it serves students in getting them through school and in advancing them in their professions. This essay will argue that writing teachers are perforce given a responsibility that far exceeds this merely instrumental task.[3]

I begin with revivals of Aristotelian rhetoric not because they are a dominant force today—far from it. My main purpose in starting with them is to show that many who say that they are followers of Aristotle are in truth opposed to his system in every sense. There is also the consideration that Aristotle has provided the technical language most often used in discussing rhetoric—so much so that it is all but impossible to talk intelligently about the subject without knowing him.

In the Aristotelian scheme of things, the material world exists independently of the observer and is knowable through sense impressions. Since sense impressions in themselves reveal nothing, however, to arrive at true knowledge it is necessary for the mind to perform an operation upon sense data. This operation is a function of reason and amounts to the appropriate use of syllogistic reasoning, the system of logic that Aristotle himself developed and refined. Providing the method for analyzing the material of any discipline, this logic offers, as Marjorie Grene explains, "a set of general rules for scientists (as Aristotle understood science) working each in his appropriate material. The rules are rules of validity, not psychological rules" (*A Portrait of Aristotle* [London: Faber and Faber, 1963], p. 69). Truth exists in conformance with the rules of logic, and logic is so thoroughly deductive that even induction is regarded as an imperfect form of the syllogism. The strictures imposed by logic, moreover, naturally arise out of the very structure of the mind and of the universe. In other words, there is a happy correspondence between the mind and the universe, so that, to cite Grene once again, "As the world is, finally, so is the mind that knows it" (p. 234).

Reality for Aristotle can thus be known and communicated, with language serving as the unproblematic medium of discourse. There is an uncomplicated correspondence between the sign and the thing, and—once again emphasizing the rational—the process whereby sign and thing are united is considered a mental act: words are not a part of the external world, but both word and thing are a part of thought.[4]

Rhetoric is of course central to Aristotle's system. Like dialectic—the method of discovering and communicating truth in learned discourse—rhetoric deals with the realm of the probable, with truth as discovered in the areas of law, politics, and what might be called public virtue. Unlike scientific discoveries, truth in these realms can never be stated with absolute certainty. Still, approximations to truth are possible. The business of rhetoric then is to enable the speaker—Aristotle's rhetoric is preeminently oral—to find the means necessary to persuade the audience of the truth. Thus rhetoric is primarily concerned with the provision of inventional devices whereby the speaker may discover his or her argument, with these devices naturally falling into three categories: the rational, the emotional, and the ethical. Since truth is rational, the first is paramount and is derived from the rules of logic, albeit applied in the relaxed form of the enthymeme and example. Realizing that individuals are not always ruled by reason, however, Aristotle provides advice on appealing to the emotions of the audience and on presenting one's own character in the most favorable light, each considered with special regard for the audience and the occasion of the speech.

Aristotle's emphasis on invention leads to the neglect of commentary on arrangement and style. The treatment of arrangement is at best sketchy, but it does display Aristotle's reliance on the logical in its commitment to rational development. The section on style is more extensive and deserves special mention because it highlights Aristotle's rationalistic view of language, a view no longer considered defensible. As R. H. Robins explains:

> The word for Aristotle is thus the minimal meaningful unit. He further distinguishes the meaning of a word as an isolate from the meaning of a sentence; a word by itself "stands for" or "indicates" . . . something, but a sentence affirms or denies a predicate of its subject, or says that its subject exists or does not exist. One cannot now defend this doctrine of meaning. It is based on the formal logic that Aristotle codified and, we might say, sterilized for generations. The notion that words have meaning just by standing for or indicating something, whether in the world at large or in the human mind (both views are stated or suggested by Aristotle), leads to difficulties that have worried philosophers in many ages, and seriously distorts linguistic and grammatical studies.[5]

It should be noted, however, that despite this unfavorable estimate, Robins goes on to praise Aristotle as in some ways anticipating later developments in linguistics.

Examples of Aristotelian rhetoric in the textbooks of today are few indeed. Edward P. J. Corbett's *Classical Rhetoric for the Modern Student* (1971) and Richard Hughes and Albert Duhamel's *Principles of Rhetoric* (1967) revive the tradition. Most textbooks that claim to be Aristotelian are operating within the paradigm of what has come to be known as Current-Traditional Rhetoric, a category that might also be called the Positivist.

The Positivist or Current-Traditional group clearly dominates thinking about writing instruction today. The evidence is the staggering number of textbooks that yearly espouse its principles. The origins of Current-Traditional Rhetoric, as Albert Kitzhaber showed in his dissertation (University of Washington, 1953) on "Rhetoric in American Colleges," can be found in the late nineteenth-century rhetoric texts of A. S. Hill, Barett Wendell, and John F. Genung. But its epistemological stance can be found in eighteenth-century Scottish Common Sense Realism as expressed in the philosophy of Thomas Reid and James Beattie, and in the rhetorical treatises of George Campbell, Hugh Blair, and to a lesser extent, Richard Whately.

For Common Sense Realism, the certain existence of the material world is indisputable. All knowledge is founded on the simple correspondence between sense impressions and the faculties of the mind. This so far sounds like the Aristotelian world view, but is in fact a conscious departure from it. Common Sense Realism denies the value of the deductive method — syllogistic reasoning — in arriving at knowledge. Truth is instead discovered through induction alone. It is the individual sense impression that provides the basis on which all knowledge can be built. Thus the new scientific logic of Locke replaces the old deductive logic of Aristotle as the method for understanding experience. The world is still rational, but its system is to be discovered through the experimental method, not through logical categories grounded in a mental faculty. The state of affairs characterizing the emergence of the new epistemology is succinctly summarized by Wilbur Samuel Howell:

> The old science, as the disciples of Aristotle conceived of it at the end of the seventeenth century, had considered its function to be that of subjecting traditional truths to syllogistic examination, and of accepting as new truth only what could be proved to be consistent with the old. Under that kind of arrangement, traditional logic had taught the methods of deductive analysis, had perfected itself in the machinery of testing propositions for consistency, and had served at the same time as the instrument by which truths could be arranged so as to become intelligible and convincing to other learned men. . . . The new science, as envisioned by its founder, Francis Bacon, considered its function to be that of subjecting physical and human facts to observation and experiment, and of accepting as new truth only what could be shown to conform to the realities behind it.[6]

The rhetoric based on the new logic can be seen most clearly in George Campbell's *Philosophy of Rhetoric* (1776) and Hugh Blair's *Lectures on*

Rhetoric and Belles Lettres (1783). The old distinction between dialectic as the discipline of learned discourse and rhetoric as the discipline of popular discourse is destroyed. Rhetoric becomes the study of all forms of communication: scientific, philosophical, historical, political, legal, and even poetic. An equally significant departure in this new rhetoric is that it contains no inventional system. Truth is to be discovered outside the rhetorical enterprise—through the method, usually the scientific method, of the appropriate discipline, or, as in poetry and oratory, through genius.

The aim of rhetoric is to teach how to adapt the discourse to its hearers—and here the uncomplicated correspondence of the faculties and the world is emphasized. When the individual is freed from the biases of language, society, or history, the senses provide the mental faculties with a clear and distinct image of the world. The world readily surrenders its meaning to anyone who observes it properly, and no operation of the mind—logical or otherwise—is needed to arrive at truth. To communicate, the speaker or writer—both now included—need only provide the language which corresponds either to the objects in the external world or to the ideas in his or her own mind—both are essentially the same—in such a way that it reproduces the objects and the experience of them in the minds of the hearers (Cohen, pp. 38–42). As Campbell explains, "Thus language and thought, like body and soul, are made to correspond, and the qualities of the one exactly to co-operate with those of the other."[7] The emphasis in this rhetoric is on adapting what has been discovered outside the rhetorical enterprise to the minds of the hearers. The study of rhetoric thus focuses on developing skill in arrangement and style.

Given this epistemological field in a rhetoric that takes all communication as its province, discourse tends to be organized according to the faculties to which it appeals. A scheme that is at once relevant to current composition theory and typical in its emulation of Campbell, Blair, and Whately can be found in John Francis Genung's *The Practical Elements of Rhetoric* (1886).[8] For Genung the branches of discourse fall into four categories. The most "fundamental" mode appeals to understanding and is concerned with transmitting truth, examples of which are "history, biography, fiction, essays, treatises, criticism." The second and third groups are description and narration, appealing again to the understanding, but leading the reader to "feel the thought as well as think it." For Genung "the purest outcome" of this kind of writing is poetry. The fourth kind of discourse, "the most complex literary type," is oratory. This kind is concerned with persuasion and makes its special appeal to the will, but in so doing involves all the faculties. Genung goes on to create a further distinction that contributed to the departmentalization of English and Speech and the division of English into literature and composition. Persuasion is restricted to considerations of experts in the spoken language and poetry to discussions of literature teachers, now first appearing. College writing courses, on the other hand, are to focus on discourse that appeals to the understanding—exposition, narration, description, and argumentation (distinct now from persuasion). It is significant, moreover, that college rhetoric is to be concerned solely with the communication of truth that is certain and empirically verifiable—in other words, not probabilistic.

Genung, along with his contemporaries A. S. Hill and Barrett Wendell, sets the pattern for most modern composition textbooks, and their works show striking similarities to the vast majority of texts published today.[9] It is discouraging that generations after Freud and Einstein, college students are encouraged to embrace a view of reality based on a mechanistic physics and a naive faculty psychology—and all in the name of a convenient pedagogy.

The next theory of composition instruction to be considered arose as a reaction to current-traditional rhetoric. Its clearest statements are located in the work of Ken Macrorie, William Coles, Jr., James E. Miller and Stephen Judy, and the so-called "Pre-Writing School" of D. Gordon Rohman, Albert O. Wlecke, Clinton S. Burhans, and Donald Stewart (see Harrington, et al., pp. 645–647). Frequent assertions of this view, however, have appeared in American public schools in the twentieth century under the veil of including "creative expression" in the English curriculum.[10] The roots of this view of rhetoric in America can be traced to Emerson and the Transcendentalists, and its ultimate source is to be found in Plato.

In the Platonic scheme, truth is not based on sensory experience since the material world is always in flux and thus unreliable. Truth is instead discovered through an internal apprehension, a private vision of a world that transcends the physical. As Robert Cushman explains in *Therepeia* (Chapel Hill: University of North Carolina Press, 1958), "The central theme of Platonism regarding knowledge is that truth is not brought to man, but man to the truth" (p. 213). A striking corollary of this view is that ultimate truth can be discovered by the individual, but cannot be communicated. Truth can be learned but not taught. The purpose of rhetoric then becomes not the transmission of truth, but the correction of error, the removal of that which obstructs the personal apprehension of the truth. And the method is dialectic, the interaction of two interlocutors of good will intent on arriving at knowledge. Because the respondents are encouraged to break out of their ordinary perceptual set, to become free of the material world and of past error, the dialectic is often disruptive, requiring the abandonment of long held conventions and opinions. Preparing the soul to discover truth is often painful.

Plato's epistemology leads to a unique view of language. Because ultimate truths cannot be communicated, language can only deal with the
realm of error, the world of flux, and act, as Gerald L. Bruns explains, as "a
preliminary exercise which must engage the soul before the encounter with
'the knowable and truly real being' is possible" (p. 16). Truth is finally inex-
pressible, is beyond the resources of language. Yet Plato allows for the possibility that language may be used to communicate essential realities. In the
Republic he speaks of using analogy to express ultimate truth, and in the
Phaedrus, even as rhetoric is called into question, he employs an analogical
method in his discussion of the soul and love. Language, it would appear,
can be of some use in trying to communicate the absolute, or at least to
approximate the experience of it.

The major tenets of this Platonic rhetoric form the center of what are
commonly called "Expressionist" textbooks. Truth is conceived as the result
of a private vision that must be constantly consulted in writing. These textbooks thus emphasize writing as a "personal" activity, as an expression of
one's unique voice. In *Writing and Reality* (New York: Harper and Row,
1978), James Miller and Stephen Judy argue that "all good writing is *personal*, whether it be an abstract essay or a private letter," and that an important justification for writing is "to sound the depths, to explore, and to
discover." The reason is simple: "Form in language grows from content—
something the writer has to say—and that something, in turn, comes directly
from the self" (pp. 12, 15). Ken Macrorie constantly emphasizes "Telling
Truths," by which he means a writer must be "true to the feeling of his experience." His thrust throughout is on speaking in "an authentic voice" (also in
Donald Stewart's *The Authentic Voice: A Pre-Writing Approach to Student
Writing*, based on the work of Rohman and Wlecke), indicating by this the
writer's private sense of things.[11] This placement of the self at the center of
communication is also, of course, everywhere present in Coles' *The Plural I*
(New York: Holt, Rinehart, and Winston, 1978).

One obvious objection to my reading of these expressionist theories is
that their conception of truth can in no way be seen as comparable to Plato's
transcendent world of ideas. While this cannot be questioned, it should also
be noted that no member of this school is a relativist intent on denying the
possibility of any certain truth whatever. All believe in the existence of verifiable truths and find them, as does Plato, in private experience, divorced
from the impersonal data of sense experience. All also urge the interaction
between writer and reader, a feature that leads to another point of similarity
with Platonic rhetoric—the dialectic.

Most expressionist theories rely on classroom procedures that encourage
the writer to interact in dialogue with the members of the class. The purpose

is to get rid of what is untrue to the private vision of the writer, what is, in a word, inauthentic. Coles, for example, conceives of writing as an unteachable act, a kind of behavior that can be learned but not taught. (See especially the preface to *The Plural I*.) His response to this denial of his pedagogical role is to provide a classroom environment in which the student learns to write—although he or she is not taught to write—through dialectic. *The Plural I*, in fact, reveals Coles and his students engaging in a dialogue designed to lead both teacher and class—Coles admits that he always learns in his courses—to the discovery of what can be known but not communicated. This view of truth as it applies to writing is the basis of Coles' classroom activity. Dialogue can remove error, but it is up to the individual to discover ultimate knowledge. The same emphasis on dialectic can also be found in the texts of Macrorie and of Miller and Judy. Despite their insistence on the self as the source of all content, for example, Miller and Judy include "making connections with others in dialogue and discussion" (p. 5), and Macrorie makes the discussion of student papers the central activity of his classroom.

This emphasis on dialectic, it should be noted, is not an attempt to adjust the message to the audience, since doing so would clearly constitute a violation of the self. Instead the writer is trying to use others to get rid of what is false to the self, what is insincere and untrue to the individual's own sense of things, as evidenced by the use of language—the theory of which constitutes the final point of concurrence between modern Expressionist and Platonic rhetorics.

Most Expressionist textbooks emphasize the use of metaphor either directly or by implication. Coles, for example, sees the major task of the writer to be avoiding the imitation of conventional expressions because they limit what the writer can say. The fresh, personal vision demands an original use of language. Rohman and Wlecke, as well as the textbook by Donald Stewart based on their research, are more explicit. They specifically recommend the cultivation of the ability to make analogies (along with meditation and journal writing) as an inventional device. Macrorie makes metaphor one of the prime features of "good writing" (p. 21) and in one form or another takes it up again and again in *Telling Writing*. The reason for this emphasis is not hard to discover. In communicating, language does not have as its referent the object in the external world or an idea of this object in the mind. Instead, to present truth language must rely on original metaphors in order to capture what is unique in each personal vision. The private apprehension of the real relies on the metaphoric appeal from the known to the unknown, from the public and accessible world of the senses to the inner and privileged immaterial realm, in order to be made available to others. As in Plato, the analogical method offers the only avenue to expressing the true.

135

The clearest pedagogical expression of the New Rhetoric—or what might be called Epistemic Rhetoric—is found in Ann E. Berthoff's *Forming/Thinking/Writing: The Composing Imagination* (Rochelle Park, N.J.: Hayden, 1978) and Richard E. Young, Alton L. Becker, and Kenneth L. Pike's *Rhetoric: Discovery and Change* (New York: Harcourt Brace Jovanovich, 1970). These books have behind them the rhetorics of such figures as I. A. Richards and Kenneth Burke and the philosophical statements of Susan Langer, Ernst Cassirer, and John Dewey. Closely related to the work of Berthoff and Young, Becker, and Pike are the cognitive-developmental approaches of such figures as James Moffett, Linda Flower, Andrea Lunsford, and Barry Kroll. While their roots are different—located in the realm of cognitive psychology and empirical linguistics—their methods are strikingly similar. In this discussion, however, I intend to call exclusively upon the textbooks of Berthoff and of Young, Becker, and Pike to make my case, acknowledging at the start that there are others that could serve as well. Despite differences, their approaches most comprehensively display a view of rhetoric as epistemic, as a means of arriving at truth.

Classical Rhetoric considers truth to be located in the rational operation of the mind, Positivist Rhetoric in the correct perception of sense impressions, and Neo-Platonic Rhetoric within the individual, attainable only through an internal apprehension. In each case knowledge is a commodity situated in a permanent location, a repository to which the individual goes to be enlightened.

For the New Rhetoric, knowledge is not simply a static entity available for retrieval. Truth is dynamic and dialectical, the result of a process involving the interaction of opposing elements. It is a relation that is created, not pre-existent and waiting to be discovered. The basic elements of the dialectic are the elements that make up the communication process—writer (speaker), audience, reality, language. Communication is always basic to the epistemology underlying the New Rhetoric because truth is always truth for someone standing in relation to others in a linguistically circumscribed situation. The elements of the communication process thus do not simply provide a convenient way of talking about rhetoric. They form the elements that go into the very shaping of knowledge.

It is this dialectical notion of rhetoric—and of rhetoric as the determiner of reality—that underlies the textbooks of Berthoff and of Young, Becker, and Pike. In demonstrating this thesis I will consider the elements of the dialectic alone or in pairs, simply because they are more easily handled this way in discussion. It should not be forgotten, however, that in operation they are always simultaneously in a relationship of one to all, constantly modifying their values in response to each other.

The New Rhetoric denies that truth is discoverable in sense impression since this data must always be interpreted—structured and organized—in order to have meaning. The perceiver is of course the interpreter, but she is likewise unable by herself to provide truth since meaning cannot be made apart from the data of experience. Thus Berthoff cites Kant's "Percepts without concepts are empty; concepts without percepts are blind" (p. 13). Later she explains: "The brain puts things together, composing the percepts by which we can make sense of the world. We don't just 'have' a visual experience and then by thinking 'have' a mental experience; the mutual dependence of seeing and knowing is what a modern psychologist has in mind when he speaks of 'the intelligent eye'" (p. 44). Young, Becker, and Pike state the same notion:

> Constantly changing, bafflingly complex, the external world is not a neat, well-ordered place replete with meaning, but an enigma requiring interpretation. This interpretation is the result of a transaction between events in the external world and the mind of the individual—between the world "out there" and the individual's previous experience, knowledge, values, attitudes, and desires. Thus the mirrored world is not just the sum total of eardrum rattles, retinal excitations, and so on; it is a creation that reflects the peculiarities of the perceiver as well as the peculiarities of what is perceived. (p. 25)

Language is at the center of this dialectical interplay between the individual and the world. For Neo-Aristotelians, Positivists, and Neo-Platonists, truth exists prior to language so that the difficulty of the writer or speaker is to find the appropriate words to communicate knowledge. For the New Rhetoric truth is impossible without language since it is language that embodies and generates truth. Young, Becker, and Pike explain:

> Language provides a way of unitizing experience: a set of symbols that label recurring chunks of experience. . . . Language depends on our seeing certain experiences as constant or repeatable. And seeing the world as repeatable depends, in part at least, on language. A language is, in a sense, a theory of the universe, a way of selecting and grouping experience in a fairly consistent and predictable way. (p. 27)

Berthoff agrees: "The relationship between thought and language is dialectical: ideas are conceived by language; language is generated by thought" (p. 47). Rather than truth being prior to language, language is prior to truth and determines what shapes truth can take. Language does not correspond to the "real world." It creates the "real world" by organizing it, by determining what will be perceived and not perceived, by indicating what has meaning and what is meaningless.

The audience of course enters into this play of language. Current-Traditional Rhetoric demands that the audience be as "objective" as the writer; both shed personal and social concerns in the interests of the unobstructed perception of empirical reality. For Neo-Platonic Rhetoric the audience is a check to the false note of the inauthentic and helps to detect error, but it is not involved in the actual discovery of truth—a purely personal matter. Neo-Aristotelians take the audience seriously as a force to be considered in shaping the message. Still, for all its discussion of the emotional and ethical appeals, Classical Rhetoric emphasizes rational structures, and the concern for the audience is only a concession to the imperfection of human nature. In the New Rhetoric the message arises out of the interaction of the writer, language, reality, and the audience. Truths are operative only within a given universe of discourse, and this universe is shaped by all of these elements, including the audience. As Young, Becker, and Pike explain:

> The writer must first understand the nature of his own interpretation and how it differs from the interpretations of others. Since each man segments experience into discrete, repeatable units, the writer can begin by asking how his way of segmenting and ordering experience differs from his reader's. How do units of time, space, the visible world, social organization, and so on differ? . . .
>
> Human differences are the raw material of writing—differences in experiences and ways of segmenting them, differences in values, purposes, and goals. They are our reason for wishing to communicate. Through communication we create community, the basic value underlying rhetoric. To do so, we must overcome the barriers to communication that are, paradoxically, the motive for communication. (p. 30)

Ann E. Berthoff also includes this idea in her emphasis on meaning as a function of relationship.

> *Meanings are relationships.* Seeing means "seeing relationships," whether we're talking about seeing as *perception* or seeing as *understanding.* "I see what you mean" means "I understand how you put that together so that it makes sense." The way we make sense of the world is to see something *with respect to, in terms of, in relation to* something else. We can't make sense of one thing by itself; it must be seen as being *like* another thing; or *next to, across from, coming after* another thing; or as a repetition of another thing. *Something* makes sense—is meaningful—only if it is taken with *something else.* (p. 44)

The dialectical view of reality, language, and the audience redefines the writer. In Current-Traditional Rhetoric the writer must efface himself; stated differently, the writer must focus on experience in a way that makes possible the discovery of certain kinds of information—the empirical and rational—and the neglect of others—psychological and social concerns. In Neo-Platonic Rhetoric the writer is at the center of the rhetorical act, but is finally isolated, cut off from community, and left to the lonely business of discovering truth alone. Neo-Aristotelian Rhetoric exalts the writer, but circumscribes her effort by its emphasis on the rational—the enthymeme and example. The New Rhetoric sees the writer as a creator of meaning, a shaper of reality, rather than a passive receptor of the immutably given. "When you write," explains Berthoff, "you don't follow somebody else's scheme; you design your own. As a writer, you learn to make words behave the way you want them to. . . . Learning to write is not a matter of learning the rules that govern the use of the semicolon or the names of sentence structures, nor is it a matter of manipulating words; it is a matter of making meanings, and that is the work of the active mind" (p. 11). Young, Becker, and Pike concur: "We have sought to develop a rhetoric that implies that we are all citizens of an extraordinarily diverse and disturbed world, that the 'truths' we live by are tentative and subject to change, that we must be discoverers of new truths as well as preservers and transmitter of old, and that enlightened cooperation is the preeminent ethical goal of communication" (p. 9).

This version of the composing process leads to a view of what can be taught in the writing class that rivals Aristotelian rhetoric in its comprehensiveness. Current-Traditional and Neo-Platonic Rhetoric deny the place of invention in rhetoric because for both truth is considered external and self-evident, accessible to anyone who seeks it in the proper spirit. Like Neo-Aristotelian Rhetoric, the New Rhetoric sees truth as probabilistic, and it provides students with techniques—heuristics—for discovering it, or what might more accurately be called creating it. This does not mean, however, that arrangement and style are regarded as unimportant, as in Neo-Platonic Rhetoric. In fact, the attention paid to these matters in the New Rhetoric rivals that paid in Current-Traditional Rhetoric, but not because they are the only teachable part of the process. Structure and language are a part of the formation of meaning, are at the center of the discovery of truth, not simply the dress of thought. From the point of view of pedagogy, New Rhetoric thus treats in depth all the offices of classical rhetoric that apply to written language—invention, arrangement, and style—and does so by calling upon the best that has been thought and said about them by contemporary observers.

In talking and writing about the matters that form the substance of this essay, at my back I always hear the nagging (albeit legitimate) query of the overworked writing teacher: But what does all this have to do with the teaching of freshman composition? My answer is that it is more relevant than most of us are prepared to admit. In teaching writing, we are not simply offering training in a useful technical skill that is meant as a simple complement to the more important studies of other areas. We are teaching a way of experiencing the world, a way of ordering and making sense of it. As I have shown, subtly informing our statements about invention, arrangement, and even style are assumptions about the nature of reality. If the textbooks that sell the most copies tell us anything, they make abundantly clear that most writing teachers accept the assumptions of Current-Traditional Rhetoric, the view that arose contemporaneously with the positivistic position of modern science. Yet most of those who use these texts would readily admit that the scientific world view has demonstrated its inability to solve the problems that most concern us, problems that are often themselves the result of scientific "breakthroughs." And even many scientists concur with them in this view—Oppenheimer and Einstein, for example. In our writing classrooms, however, we continue to offer a view of composing that insists on a version of reality that is sure to place students at a disadvantage in addressing the problems that will confront them in both their professional and private experience.

Neo-Platonic, Neo-Aristotelian, and what I have called New Rhetoric are reactions to the inadequacy of Current-Traditional Rhetoric to teach students a notion of the composing process that will enable them to become effective persons as they become effective writers. While my sympathies are obviously with the last of these reactions, the three can be considered as one in their efforts to establish new directions for a modern rhetoric. Viewed in this way, the difference between them and Current-Traditional Rhetoric is analogous to the difference Richard Rorty has found in what he calls, in *Philosophy and the Mirror of Nature* (Princeton, N.J.: Princeton University Press, 1979), hermeneutic and epistemological philosophy. The hermeneutic approach to rhetoric bases the discipline on establishing an open dialogue in the hopes of reaching agreement about the truth of the matter at hand. Current-Traditional Rhetoric views the rhetorical situation as an arena where the truth is incontrovertibly established by a speaker or writer more enlightened than her audience. For the hermeneuticist truth is never fixed finally on unshakable grounds. Instead it emerges only after false starts and failures, and it can only represent a tentative point of rest in a continuing conversation. Whatever truth is arrived at, moreover, is always the product of individuals calling on the full range of their humanity, with esthetic and moral considerations given at least as much importance as any others. For Current-Traditional Rhetoric truth is empirically based and can only be achieved through subverting a part of the human response to experience. Truth then stands forever, a tribute to its method, triumphant over what most of us consider important in life, successful through subserving writer, audience, and language to the myth of an objective reality.

One conclusion should now be incontestable. The numerous recommendations of the "process"-centered approaches to writing instruction as superior to the "product"-centered approaches are not very useful. Everyone teaches the process of writing, but everyone does not teach the *same* process. The test of one's competence as a composition instructor, it seems to me, resides in being able to recognize and justify the version of the process being taught, complete with all of its significance for the student.

NOTES

1. I have in mind Richard Fulkerson, "Four Philosophies of Composition," *College Composition and Communication*, 30 (1979), 343–348; David V. Harrington, et al., "A Critical Survey of Resources for Teaching Rhetorical Invention," *College English*, 40 (1979), 641–661; William F. Woods, "Composition Textbooks and Pedagogical Theory 1960–80," *CE*, 43 (1981), 393–409.

2. "Rewording the Rhetoric of Composition," *PRE/TEXT*, 1 (1980), 39. I am indebted to Professor Kameen's classification of pedagogical theories for the suggestiveness of his method; my conclusions, however, are substantially different.

3. There is still another reason for pursuing the method I recommend, one that explains why rhetorical principles are now at the center of discussions in so many different disciplines. When taken together, writer, reality, audience, and language identify an epistemic field—the basic conditions that determine what knowledge will be knowable, what not knowable, and how the knowable will be communicated. This epistemic field is the point of departure for numerous studies, although the language used to describe it varies from thinker to thinker. Examples are readily available. In *Science and the Modern World* (New York: Macmillan, 1926), A. N. Whitehead sees this field as a product of the "fundamental assumptions which adherents of all variant systems within the epoch unconsciously presuppose" (p. 71). Susanne Langer, in *Philosophy in a New Key* (Cambridge, Mass.: Harvard University Press, 1979), calls it the "tacit, fundamental way of seeing things" (p. 6). Michael Polanyi uses the terms "tacit knowledge" in *Personal Knowledge* (Chicago: University of Chicago Press, 1962). Michel Foucault, in *The Order of Things* (1971; rpt. New York: Vintage Books, 1973), speaks of the "episteme," and Thomas Kuhn, in *Structure of Scientific Revolutions* (Chicago: University of Chicago Press, 1970), discusses at length the "paradigm" that underlies a scientific discipline. The historian Hayden White, in *Metahistory: The Historical Imagination in Nineteenth-Century Europe* (Baltimore: Johns Hopkins University Press, 1973), has translated the elements of the composing process into terms appropriate to the writing of history, seeing the historical field as being made up of the historian, the historical record, the historical accounts, and an audience. One compelling reason for studying composition theory is that it so readily reveals its epistemic field, thus indicating, for example, a great deal about the way a particular historical period defines itself—a fact convincingly demonstrated in Murray Cohen's *Sensible Words: Linguistic Practice in England 1640–1785* (Baltimore: Johns Hopkins University Press, 1977), a detailed study of English grammars.

4. See Gerald L. Bruns, *Modern Poetry and the Idea of Language* (New Haven, Ct.: Yale University Press, 1974), p. 34.

5. *Ancient and Mediaeval Grammatical Theory in Europe* (London: G. Bell and Sons, 1951), pp. 20–21.

6. *Eighteenth-Century British Logic and Rhetoric* (Princeton, N.J.: Princeton University Press, 1971), pp. 5–6.

7. *The Philosophy of Rhetoric*, ed. Lloyd F. Bitzer (Carbondale: Southern Illinois University Press, 1963), p. 215.

8. For a more detailed discussion of Genung see my "John Genung and Contemporary Composition Theory: The Triumph of the Eighteenth Century," *Rhetoric Society Quarterly*, 11 (1981), 74–84.

9. For an analysis of modern composition textbooks, see James A. Berlin and Robert P. Inkster, "Current-Traditional Rhetoric: Paradigm and Practice," *Freshman English News*, 8 (1980), 1–4, 13–14.

10. Kenneth J. Kantor, "Creative Expression in the English Curriculum: A Historical Perspective," *Research in the Teaching of English*, 9 (1975), 5–29.

11. *Telling Writing* (Rochelle Park, N.J.: Hayden Book Company, 1978), p. 13.

SECTION TWO

Scientific Talk

Developmental Schemes

- "A Cognitive Process Theory of Writing" Linda Flower and John R. Hayes
- "Cognitive Development and the Basic Writer" Andrea A. Lunsford
- "Diving In: An Introduction to Basic Writing" Mina P. Shaughnessy
- "William Perry and Liberal Education" Patricia Bizzell
- "Is Teaching Still Possible? Writing, Meaning, and Higher Order Reasoning" Ann E. Berthoff
- "Narrowing the Mind and Page: Remedial Writers and Cognitive Reductionism" Mike Rose
- "Cognition, Convention, and Certainty: What We Need to Know about Writing" Patricia Bizzell

Among James Berlin's epistemological categories in "Contemporary Composition" there is positivism. The assumptions that are carried by positivism remain the most pervasive for our society and for composition studies (though not without some sharp criticism). Implicit in the term (and the concept) is that knowledge is scaffolded, building upon itself, always ascending. So given rhetoric's and thereby composition's concern with mind, and given the cognitive emphasis of Woods Hole (as described in the Section One preface), the positivistic schemes that composition found most attractive were those concerning cognitive development.

The stages of development were determined by Jean Piaget's developmental scheme, and the approach to tapping into the "natural" process of cognitive development was inductive reasoning, a process of discovery. In 1968, James

Moffett published *Teaching the Universe of Discourse*, a developmental scheme for teaching discourse that spanned from the elementary grades to the secondary. The curricular stages he developed—from the egocentric to the public, from interior dialogue to conversation to correspondence to public narrative—followed the cognitive stages of development offered by Piaget. Piaget's interpretation of the mind as structuring knowledge systematically, his genetic epistemology, continues to hold sway with the education community. And since language plays a crucial role in his developmental scheme, his scheme holds a particular attraction for compositionists. This attraction becomes magnified in the work of Lev Vygotsky, a contemporary of Piaget's. For Vygotsky, language doesn't simply play a role; language is central, that which provides for our conceptions of reality. Vygotsky's concept of "inner speech," in which Piaget's egocentric speech doesn't disappear but becomes internalized and removed from the sounds of discourse, causes Piaget to revise his theories.

So intriguing and suggestive are the language and thought connections provided by Piaget and Vygotsky that composition becomes obsessed with recognizing those stages, fostering their development, believing in their lack when expectations for student writing are not met. Other developmental schemes, like William Perry's scheme of ethical and intellectual development in college, gain new attention. Mina Shaughnessy—who first coins the term "basic writer" to describe college writers otherwise termed "developmental" or "remedial"—creates a parody of developmental schemes to discuss how teachers come to consider basic writers when first confronted with them. Linda Flower and John R. Hayes turn to the cognitive sciences, the research method of protocol analysis developed by Carl Jung, to build a model of the composing process. Mike Rose, Ann Berthoff, and Patricia Bizzell provide the cross-talk: Rose using his own understanding of cognitive psychology to question some of the assertions arising within composition studies' cognitivists, Berthoff looking to other schemes, and Bizzell calling the whole turn to cognition into question.

A Cognitive Process Theory
of Writing

LINDA FLOWER AND JOHN R. HAYES

There is a venerable tradition in rhetoric and composition which sees the composing process as a series of decisions and choices.[1] However, it is no longer easy simply to assert this position, unless you are prepared to answer a number of questions, the most pressing of which probably is: "What then are the criteria which govern that choice?" Or we could put it another way: "What guides the decisions writers make as they write?" In a recent survey of composition research, Odell, Cooper, and Courts noticed that some of the most thoughtful people in the field are giving us two reasonable but somewhat different answers:

> How do writers actually go about choosing diction, syntactic and organizational patterns, and context? Kinneavy claims that one's purpose—informing, persuading, expressing, or manipulating language for its own sake—guides these choices. Moffett and Gibson contend that these choices are determined by one's sense of the relation of speaker, subject, and audience. Is either of these two claims borne out by the actual practice of writers engaged in drafting or revising? Does either premise account adequately for the choices writers make?[2]

Rhetoricians such as Lloyd Bitzer and Richard Vatz have energetically debated this question in still other terms. Lloyd Bitzer argues that speech always occurs as a response to a rhetorical situation, which he succinctly defines as containing an exigency (which demands a response), an audience,

Reprinted from *College Composition and Communication* 32.4 (December 1981): 365–87. Used with permission.

and a set of constraints.[3] In response to this "situation-driven" view, Vatz claims that the speaker's response, and even the rhetorical situation itself, are determined by the imagination and art of the speaker.[4]

Finally, James Britton has asked the same question and offered a linguist's answer, namely, that syntactic and lexical choices guide the process.

> It is tempting to think of writing as a process of making linguistic choices from one's repertoire of syntactic structures and lexical items. This would suggest that there is a meaning, or something to be expressed, in the writer's mind, and that he proceeds to choose, from the words and structures he has at his disposal, the ones that best match his meaning. But is that really how it happens?[5]

To most of us it may seem reasonable to suppose that all of these forces—"purposes," "relationships," "exigencies," "language"—have a hand in guiding the writer's process, but it is not at all clear how they do so or how they interact. Do they, for example, work in elegant and graceful coordination, or as competitive forces constantly vying for control? We think that the best way to answer these questions—to really understand the nature of rhetorical choices in good and poor writers—is to follow James Britton's lead and turn our attention to the writing process itself: to ask, "but is that really how it happens?"

This paper will introduce a theory of the cognitive processes involved in composing in an effort to lay groundwork for more detailed study of thinking processes in writing. This theory is based on our work with protocol analysis over the past five years and has, we feel, a good deal of evidence to support it. Nevertheless, it is for us a working hypothesis and springboard for further research, and we hope that insofar as it suggests testable hypotheses it will be the same for others. Our cognitive process theory rests on four key points, which this paper will develop:

1. The process of writing is best understood as a set of distinctive thinking processes which writers orchestrate or organize during the act of composing.

2. These processes have a hierarchical, highly embedded organization in which any given process can be embedded within any other.

3. The act of composing itself is a goal-directed thinking process, guided by the writer's own growing network of goals.

4. Writers create their own goals in two key ways: by generating both high-level goals and supporting sub-goals which embody the writer's developing sense of purpose, and then, at times, by changing major

goals or even establishing entirely new ones based on what has been learned in the act of writing.

1. Writing is best understood as a set of distinctive thinking processes which writers orchestrate or organize during the act of composing.

To many this point may seem self-evident, and yet it is in marked contrast to our current paradigm for composing—the stage process model. This familiar metaphor or model describes the composing process as a linear series of stages, separated in time, and characterized by the gradual development of the written product. The best examples of stage models are the Pre-Write/Write/Re-Write model of Gordon Rohman[6] and The Conception/Incubation/Production model of Britton et al.[7]

STAGE MODELS OF WRITING

Without doubt, the wide acceptance of Pre-Writing has helped improve the teaching of composition by calling attention to planning and discovery as legitimate parts of the writing process. Yet many question whether this linear stage model is really an accurate or useful description of the composing process itself. The problem with stage descriptions of writing is that they model the growth of the written product, not the inner process of the person producing it. "Pre-Writing" is the stage before words emerge on paper; "Writing" is the stage in which a product is being produced; and "Re-Writing" is a final reworking of that product. Yet both common sense and research tell us that writers are constantly planning (pre-writing) and revising (re-writing) as they compose (write), not in clean-cut stages.[8] Furthermore, the sharp distinctions stage models make between the operations of planning, writing, and revising may seriously distort how these activities work. For example, Nancy Sommers has shown that revision, as it is carried out by skilled writers, is not an end-of-the-line repair process, but is a constant process of "revision" or re-seeing that goes on while they are composing.[9] A more accurate model of the composing process would need to recognize those basic thinking processes which unite planning and revision. Because stage models take the final product as their reference point, they offer an inadequate account of the more intimate, moment-by-moment intellectual process of composing. How, for example, is the output of one stage, such as pre-writing or incubation, transferred to the next? As every writer knows, having good ideas doesn't automatically produce good prose. Such models are typically silent on the inner processes of decision and choice.

A COGNITIVE PROCESS MODEL

A cognitive process theory of writing, such as the one presented here, represents a major departure from the traditional paradigm of stages in this way: in a stage model the major units of analysis are *stages* of completion which reflect the growth of a written product, and these stages are organized in a *linear* sequence or structure. In a process model, the major units of analysis are elementary mental *processes*, such as the process of generating ideas. And these processes have a *hierarchical* structure (see p. 288, below) such that idea generation, for example, is a sub-process of Planning. Furthermore, each of these mental acts may occur at any time in the composing process. One major advantage of identifying these basic cognitive processes or thinking skills writers use is that we can then compare the composing strategies of good and poor writers. And we can look at writing in a much more detailed way.

In psychology and linguistics, one traditional way of looking carefully at a process is to build a model of what you see. A model is a metaphor for a process: a way to describe something, such as the composing process, which refuses to sit still for a portrait. As a hypothesis about a dynamic system, it attempts to describe the parts of the system and how they work together. Modeling a process starts as a problem in design. For example, imagine that you have been asked to start from scratch and design an imaginary, working "Writer." In order to build a "Writer" or a theoretical system that would reflect the process of a real writer, you would want to do at least three things:

1. First, you would need to define the major elements or sub-processes that make up the larger process of writing. Such sub-processes would include planning, retrieving information from long-term memory, reviewing, and so on.

2. Second, you would want to show how these various elements of the process interact in the total process of writing. For example, how is "knowledge" about the audience actually integrated into the moment-to-moment act of composing?

3. And finally, since a model is primarily a tool for thinking with, you would want your model to speak to critical questions in the discipline. It should help you see things you didn't see before.

Obviously, the best way to model the writing process is to study a writer in action, and there are many ways to do this. However, people's after-the-fact, *introspective analysis* of what they did while writing is notoriously inaccurate and likely to be influenced by their notions of what they should have done. Therefore we turned to *protocol analysis,* which has been successfully used to study other cognitive processes.[10] Unlike introspective reports, thinking aloud protocols capture a detailed record of what is going on in the writer's mind during the act of composing itself. To collect a protocol, we give writers a problem, such as "Write an article on your job for the readers of *Seventeen* magazine," and then ask them to compose out loud near an unobtrusive tape recorder. We ask them to work on the task as they normally would—thinking, jotting notes, and writing—except that they must think out loud. They are asked to verbalize everything that goes through their minds as they write, including stray notions, false starts, and incomplete or fragmentary thought. The writers are *not* asked to engage in any kind of introspection or self-analysis while writing, but simply to think out loud while working like a person talking to herself.

The transcript of this session, which may amount to 20 pages for an hour session, is called a protocol. As a research tool, a protocol is extraordinarily rich in data and, together with the writer's notes and manuscript, it gives us a very detailed picture of the writer's composing process. It lets us see not only the development of the written product but many of the intellectual processes which produced it. The model of the writing process presented in Figure 1 attempts to account for the major thinking processes and constraints we saw at work in these protocols. But note that it does *not* specify the order in which they are invoked.

The act of writing involves three major elements which are reflected in the three units of the model: **the task environment, the writer's long-term memory, and the writing processes.** The task environment includes all of those things outside the writer's skin, starting with the rhetorical problem or assignment and eventually including the growing text itself. The second element is the writer's long-term memory in which the writer has stored knowledge, not only of the topic, but of the audience and of various writing plans. The third element in our model contains writing processes themselves, specifically the basic processes of **Planning, Translating, and Reviewing,** which are under the control of a Monitor.

This model attempts to account for the processes we saw in the composing protocols. It is also a guide to research, which asks us to explore each of these elements and their interaction more fully. Since this model is described in detail elsewhere,[11] let us focus here on some ways each element contributes to the overall process.

Figure 1 Structure of the writing model. (For an explanation of how to read a process model, please see endnote 11.)

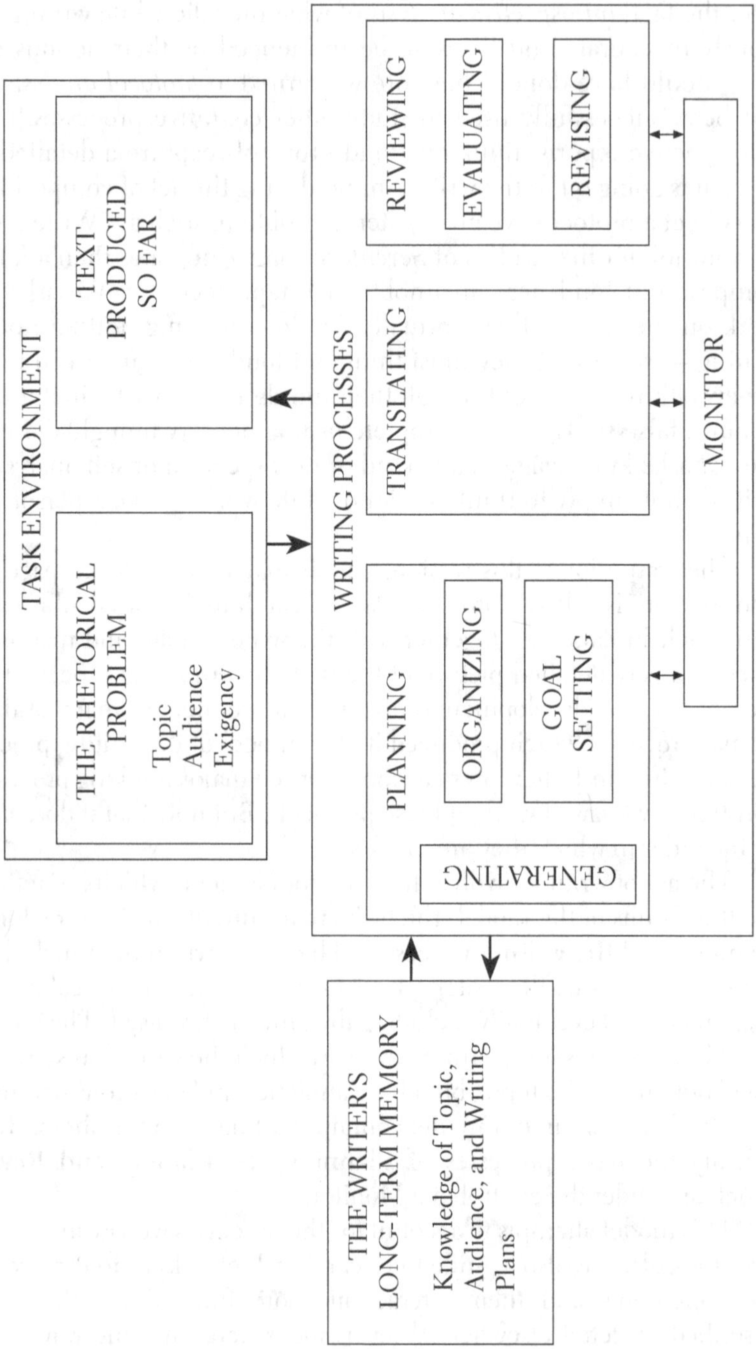

TASK ENVIRONMENT

THE RHETORICAL PROBLEM

Topic
Audience
Exigency

TEXT PRODUCED SO FAR

WRITING PROCESSES

PLANNING

GENERATING

ORGANIZING

GOAL SETTING

TRANSLATING

REVIEWING

EVALUATING

REVISING

MONITOR

THE WRITER'S LONG-TERM MEMORY

Knowledge of Topic, Audience, and Writing Plans

OVERVIEW OF THE MODEL

The Rhetorical Problem

At the beginning of composing, the most important element is obviously the **rhetorical problem** itself. A school assignment is a simplified version of such a problem, describing the writer's topic, audience, and (implicitly) her role as student to teacher. Insofar as writing is a rhetorical act, not a mere artifact, writers attempt to "solve" or respond to this rhetorical problem by writing something.

In theory this problem is a very complex thing: it includes not only the rhetorical situation and audience which prompts one to write, it also includes the writer's own goals in writing.[12] A good writer is a person who can juggle all of these demands. But in practice we have observed, as did Britton,[13] that writers frequently reduce this large set of constraints to a radically simplified problem, such as "write another theme for English class." Redefining the problem in this way is obviously an economical strategy as long as the new representation fits reality. But when it doesn't, there is a catch: people only solve the problems they define for themselves. If a writer's representation of her rhetorical problem is inaccurate or simply underdeveloped, then she is unlikely to "solve" or attend to the missing aspects of the problem. To sum up, defining the rhetorical problem is a major, immutable part of the writing process. But the way in which people choose to define a rhetorical problem to themselves can vary greatly from writer to writer. An important goal for research then will be to discover how this process of representing the problem works and how it affects the writer's performance.

The Written Text

As composing proceeds, a new element enters the task environment which places even more constraints upon what the writer can say. Just as a title constrains the content of a paper and a topic sentence shapes the options of a paragraph, each word in the growing text determines and limits the choices of what can come next. However, the influence that the growing text exerts on the composing process can vary greatly. When writing is incoherent, the text may have exerted too little influence; the writer may have failed to consolidate new ideas with earlier statements. On the other hand, one of the earmarks of a basic writer is a dogged concern with extending the previous sentence[14] and a reluctance to jump from local, text-bound planning to more global decisions, such as "what do I want to cover here?"

151

As we will see, the growing text makes large demands on the writer's time and attention during composing. But in doing so, it is competing with two other forces which could and also should direct the composing process; namely, the writer's knowledge stored in long-term memory and the writer's plans for dealing with the rhetorical problem. It is easy, for example, to imagine a conflict between what you know about a topic and what you might actually want to say to a given reader, or between a graceful phrase that completes a sentence and the more awkward point you actually wanted to make. Part of the drama of writing is seeing how writers juggle and integrate the multiple constraints of their knowledge, their plans, and their text into the production of each new sentence.[15]

The Long-Term Memory

The writer's long-term memory, which can exist in the mind as well as in outside resources such as books, is a storehouse of knowledge about the topic and audience, as well as knowledge of writing plans and problem representations. Sometimes a single cue in an assignment, such as "write a persuasive . . . ," can let a writer tap a stored representation of a problem and bring a whole raft of writing plans into play.

Unlike short-term memory, which is our active processing capacity or conscious attention, long-term memory is a relatively stable entity and has its own internal organization of information. The problem with long-term memory is, first of all, getting things out of it—that is, finding the cue that will let you retrieve a network of useful knowledge. The second problem for a writer is usually reorganizing or adapting that information to fit the demands of the rhetorical problem. The phenomena of "writer-based" prose nicely demonstrates the results of writing strategy based solely on retrieval. The organization of a piece of writer-based prose faithfully reflects the writer's own discovery process and the structure of the remembered information itself, but it often fails to transform or reorganize the knowledge to meet the different needs of a reader.[16]

Planning

People often think of planning as the act of figuring out how to get from here to there, i.e., making a detailed plan. But our model uses the term in its much broader sense. In the **planning** process writers form an internal *representation* of the knowledge that will be used in writing. This internal representation is likely to be more abstract than the writer's prose representation will eventually be. For example, a whole network of ideas might be represented by a single key word. Furthermore, this representation of one's knowledge will not necessarily be made in language, but could be held as a visual or perceptual code, e.g., as a fleeting image the writer must then capture in words.

Planning, or the act of building this internal representation, involves a number of sub-processes. The most obvious is the act of **generating ideas**, which includes retrieving relevant information from long-term memory. Sometimes this information is so well developed and organized *in memory* that the writer is essentially generating standard written English. At other times one may generate only fragmentary, unconnected, even contradictory thoughts, like the pieces of a poem that hasn't yet taken shape.

When the structure of ideas already in the writer's memory is not adequately adapted to the current rhetorical task, the sub-process of **organizing** takes on the job of helping the writer make meaning, that is, give a meaningful structure to his or her ideas. The process of **organizing** appears to play an important part in creative thinking and discovery since it is capable of grouping ideas and forming new concepts. More specifically, the organizing process allows the writer to identify categories, to search for subordinate ideas which develop a current topic, and to search for superordinate ideas which include or subsume the current topic. At another level the process of organizing also attends to more strictly textual decisions about the presentation and ordering of the text. That is, writers identify first or last topics, important ideas, and presentation patterns. However, organizing is much more than merely ordering points. And it seems clear that all rhetorical decisions and plans for reaching the audience affect the process of organizing ideas at all levels, because it is often guided by major goals established during the powerful process of **goal-setting**.

Goal-setting is indeed a third, little-studied but major, aspect of the **planning** process. The goals writers give themselves are both procedural (e.g., "Now let's see—a—I want to start out with 'energy'") and substantive, often both at the same time (e.g., "I have to relate this [engineering project] to the economics [of energy] to show why I'm improving it and why the steam turbine needs to be more efficient" or "I want to suggest that—that—um—the reader should sort of—what—what should one say—the reader should look at what she is interested in and look at the things that give her pleasure . . . ").

The most important thing about writing goals is the fact that they are *created* by the writer. Although some well-learned plans and goals may be drawn intact from long-term memory, most of the writer's goals are generated, developed, and revised by the same processes that generate and organize new ideas. And this process goes on throughout composing. Just as goals lead a writer to generate ideas, those ideas lead to new, more complex goals which can then integrate content and purpose.

Our own studies on goal setting to date suggest that the act of defining one's own rhetorical problem and setting goals is an important part of "being creative" and can account for some important differences between good and poor writers.[17] As we will argue in the final section of this paper, the act of developing and refining one's own goals is not limited to a "pre-writing stage" in the composing process, but is intimately bound up with the ongoing, moment-to-moment process of composing.

Translating

This is essentially the process of putting ideas into visible language. We have chosen the term **translate** for this process over other terms such as "transcribe" or "write" in order to emphasize the peculiar qualities of the task. The information generated in **planning** may be represented in a variety of symbol systems other than language, such as imagery or kinetic sensations. Trying to capture the movement of a deer on ice in language is clearly a kind of translation. Even when the **planning** process represents one's thought in words, that representation is unlikely to be in the elaborate syntax of written English. So the writer's task is to translate a meaning, which may be embodied in key words (what Vygotsky calls words "saturated with sense") and organized in a complex network of relationships, into a linear piece of written English.

The process of **translating** requires the writer to juggle all the special demands of written English, which Ellen Nold has described as lying on a spectrum from generic and formal demands through syntactic and lexical ones down to the motor tasks of forming letters. For children and inexperienced writers, this extra burden may overwhelm the limited capacity of short-term memory.[18] If the writer must devote conscious attention to demands such as spelling and grammar, the task of translating can interfere with the more global process of planning what one wants to say. Or one can simply ignore some of the constraints of written English. One path produces poor or local planning, the other produces errors, and both, as Mina Shaughnessy showed, lead to frustration for the writer.[19]

In some of the most exciting and extensive research in this area, Marlene Scardamalia and Carl Bereiter have looked at the ways children cope with the cognitive demands of writing. Well-learned skills, such as sentence construction, tend to become automatic and lost to consciousness. Because so little of the writing process is automatic for children, they must devote conscious attention to a variety of individual thinking tasks which adults perform quickly and automatically. Such studies, which trace the development of a given skill over several age groups, can show us the hidden components of an adult process as well as show us how children learn. For example, these studies have been able to distinguish children's ability to handle idea complexity from their ability to handle syntactic complexity; that is, they demonstrate the difference between seeing complex relationships and translating them into appropriate language. In another series of studies Bereiter and Scardamalia showed how children learn to handle the translation process by adapting, then eventually abandoning, the discourse conventions of conversation.[20]

Reviewing

As you can see in Figure 1, **reviewing** depends on two sub-processes: **evaluating** and **revising**. Reviewing, itself, may be a conscious process in which writers choose to read what they have written either as a springboard to further translating or with an eye to systematically evaluating and/or revising the text. These periods of planned reviewing frequently lead to new cycles of planning and translating. However, the reviewing process can also occur as an unplanned action triggered by an evaluation of either the text or one's own planning (that is, people revise written as well as unwritten thoughts or statements). The sub-processes of revising and evaluating, along with generating, share the special distinction of being able to interrupt any other process and occur at any time in the act of writing.

The Monitor

As writers compose, they also monitor their current process and progress. The **monitor** functions as a writing strategist which determines when the writer moves from one process to the next. For example, it determines how long a writer will continue generating ideas before attempting to write prose. Our observations suggest that this choice is determined both by the writer's goals and by individual writing habits or styles. As an example of varied composing styles, writers appear to range from people who try to move to polished prose as quickly as possible to people who choose to plan the entire discourse in detail before writing a word. Bereiter and Scardamalia have shown that much of a child's difficulty and lack of fluency lies in their lack of an "executive routine" which would promote switching between processes or encourage the sustained generation of ideas.[21] Children for example, possess the skills necessary to generate ideas, but lack the kind of monitor which tells them to "keep using" that skill and generate a little more.

IMPLICATIONS OF A COGNITIVE PROCESS MODEL

A model such as the one presented here is first and foremost a tool for researchers to think with. By giving a testable shape and definition to our observations, we have tried to pose new questions to be answered. For example, the model identifies three major processes (**plan, translate, and review**) and a number of sub-processes available to the writer. And yet the first assertion of this cognitive process theory is that people do not march through these processes in a simple 1, 2, 3 order. Although writers may spend more time in planning at the beginning of a composing session, planning is not a unitary stage, but a distinctive thinking process which writers use over and over during composing. Furthermore, it is used at all levels, whether the writer is making a global plan for the whole text or a local representation of the meaning of the next sentence. This then raises a question: if the process of writing is not a sequence of stages but a set of optional actions, how are these thinking processes in our repertory actually orchestrated or organized as we write? The second point of our cognitive process theory offers one answer to this question.

2. The processes of writing are hierarchically organized, with component processes embedded within other components.

A hierarchical system is one in which a large working system such as composing can subsume other less inclusive systems, such as generating ideas, which in turn contain still other systems, and so on. Unlike those in a linear organization, the events in a hierarchical process are not fixed in a rigid order. A given process may be called upon at any time and embedded within another process or even within another instance of itself, in much the same way we embed a subject clause within a larger clause or a picture within a picture.

For instance, a writer trying to construct a sentence (that is, a writer in the act of **translating**) may run into a problem and call in a condensed version of the entire writing process to help her out (e.g., she might generate and organize a new set of ideas, express them in standard written English, and review this new alternative, all in order to further her current goal of translating). This particular kind of embedding, in which an entire process is embedded within a larger instance of itself, is known technically in linguistics as recursion. However, it is much more common for writers to simply embed individual processes as needed—to call upon them as sub-routines to help carry out the task at hand.

Writing processes may be viewed as the writer's tool kit. In using the tools, the writer is not constrained to use them in a fixed order or in stages. And using any tool may create the need to use another. Generating ideas may require evaluation, as may writing sentences. And evaluation may force the writer to think up new ideas.

Figure 2 demonstrates the embedded processes of a writer trying to compose (translate) the first sentence of a paper. After producing and reviewing two trial versions of the sentence, he invokes a brief sequence of planning, translating, and reviewing—all in the service of that vexing sentence. In our example the writer is trying to translate some sketchily represented meaning about "the first day of class" into prose, and a hierarchical process allows him to embed a variety of processes as sub-routines within his overall attempt to translate.

A process that is hierarchical and admits many embedded sub-processes is powerful because it is flexible: it lets a writer do a great deal with only a few relatively simple processes—the basic ones being **plan**, **translate**, and **review**. This means, for instance, that we do not need to define "revision" as a unique stage in composing, but as a thinking process that can occur at any time a writer chooses to evaluate or revise his text or his plans. As an important part of writing, it constantly leads to new planning or a "re-vision" of what one wanted to say.

Embedding is a basic, omni-present feature of the writing process even though we may not be fully conscious of doing it. However, a theory of composing that only recognized embedding wouldn't describe the real complexity of writing. It wouldn't explain *why* writers choose to invoke the processes

---

Figure 2   An example of embedding.

(**Plan**)   Ok, first day of class. . . . . just jot down a possibility.

(**Translate**)   *Can you imagine what your first day of a college English class will be like?*

(**Review**)   I don't like that sentence, it's lousy—sounds like theme talk.

(**Review**)   Oh Lord—I get closer to it and I get closer—

(**Plan**)   Could play up the sex thing a little bit

(**Translate**)   *When you walk into an English class the first day you'll be interested, you'll be thinking about boys, tasks, and professor—*

(**Review**)   That's banal—that's awful.

157

they do or how they know when they've done enough. To return to Lee Odell's question, what guides the writers' decisions and choices and gives an overall purposeful structure to composing? The third point of the theory is an attempt to answer this question.

3. Writing is a goal-directed process. In the act of composing, writers create a hierarchical network of goals and these in turn guide the writing process.

This proposition is the keystone of the cognitive process theory we are proposing—and yet it may also seem somewhat counter-intuitive. According to many writers, including our subjects, writing often seems a serendipitous experience, as act of discovery. People start out writing without knowing exactly where they will end up; yet they agree that writing is a purposeful act. For example, our subjects often report that their writing process seemed quite disorganized, even chaotic, as they worked, and yet their protocols reveal a coherent underlying structure. How, then, does the writing process manage to seem so unstructured, open-minded, and exploratory ("I don't know what I mean until I see what I say") and at the same time possess its own underlying coherence, direction, or purpose?

One answer to this question lies in the fact that people rapidly forget many of their own local working goals once those goals have been satisfied. This is why thinking aloud protocols tell us things retrospection doesn't.[22] A second answer lies in the nature of the goals themselves, which fall into two distinctive categories: process goals and content goals. Process goals are essentially the instructions people give themselves about how to carry out the process of writing (e.g., "Let's doodle a little bit." "So . . . , write an introduction." "I'll go back to that later."). Good writers often give themselves many such instructions and seem to have greater conscious control over their own process than the poorer writers we have studied. Content goals and plans, on the other hand, specify all things the writer wants to say or to do to an audience. Some goals, usually ones having to do with organization, can specify both content and process, as in, "I want to open with a statement about political views." In this discussion we will focus primarily on the writer's content goals.

The most striking thing about a writer's content goals is that they grow into an increasingly elaborate network of goals and sub-goals as the writer composes. Figure 3 shows the network one writer had created during four minutes of composing. Notice how the writer moves from a very abstract goal of "appealing to a broad range in intellect" to a more operational definition of that goal, i.e., "explain things simply." The eventual plan to "write an

Figure 3   Beginning of a network of goals.

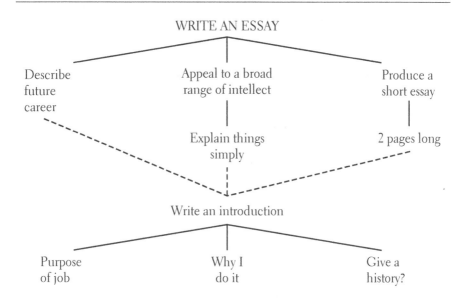

introduction" is a reasonable, if conventional, response to all three top-level goals. And it too is developed with a set of alternative sub-goals. Notice also how this network is hierarchical in the sense that new goals operate as a functional part of the more inclusive goals above them.

These networks have three important features:

1. They are created as people compose, throughout the entire process. This means that they do not emerge full-blown as the result of "pre-writing." Rather, as we will show, they are created in close interaction with ongoing exploration and the growing text.

2. The goal-directed thinking that produces these networks takes many forms. That is, goal-setting is not simply the act of stating a well-defined end point such as "I want to write a two-page essay." Goal-directed thinking often involves describing one's starting point ("They're not going to be disposed to hear what I'm saying"), or laying out a plan for reaching a goal ("I'd better explain things simply"), or evaluating one's success ("That's banal—that's awful"). Such statements are often setting implicit goals, e.g., "Don't be banal." In order to understand a writer's goals, then, we must be sensitive to the broad range of plans, goals, and criteria that grow out of goal-directed thinking.

Goal-directed thinking is intimately connected with discovery. Consider for example, the discovery process of two famous explorers—Cortez, silent on his peak in Darien, and that bear who went over the mountain. Both, indeed, discovered the unexpected. However, we should note that both chose to climb a long hill to do so. And it is this sort of goal-directed search for the unexpected that we often see in writers as they attempt to explore and consolidate their knowledge. Furthermore, this search for insight leads to new, more adequate goals, which in turn guide further writing.

The beginning of an answer to Odell's question, "What guides composing?" lies here. The writer's own set of self-made goals guide composing, but these goals can be inclusive and exploratory or narrow, sensitive to the audience or chained to the topic, based on rhetorical savvy or focused on producing correct prose. All those forces which might "guide" composing, such as the rhetorical situation, one's knowledge, the genre, etc., are mediated through the goals, plans, and criteria for evaluation of discourse actually set up by the writer.

This does not mean that a writer's goals are necessarily elaborate, logical, or conscious. For example, a simple-minded goal such as "Write down what I can remember" may be perfectly adequate for writing a list. And experienced writers, such as journalists, can often draw on elaborate networks of goals which are so well learned as to be automatic. Or the rules of a genre, such as those of the limerick, may be so specific as to leave little room or necessity for elaborate rhetorical planning. Nevertheless, whether one's goals are abstract or detailed, simple or sophisticated, they provide the "logic" that moves the composing process forward.

3. Finally writers not only create a hierarchical network of guiding goals, but, as they compose, they continually return or "pop" back up to their higher-level goals. And these higher-level goals give direction and coherence to their next move. Our understanding of this network and how writers use it is still quite limited, but we can make a prediction about an important difference one might find between good and poor writers. Poor writers will frequently depend on very abstract, undeveloped top-level goals, such as "appeal to a broad range of intellect," even though such goals are much harder to work with than a more operational goal such as "give a brief history of my job." Sondra Perl has seen this phenomenon in the basic writers who kept returning to reread the assignment, searching, it would seem, for ready-made goals, instead of forming their own. Alternatively, poor writers will depend on only very low-level goals, such as finishing a sentence or correctly spelling a word. They will be, as Nancy Sommers' student revisers were, locked in by the myopia in their own goals and criteria.

Therefore, one might predict that an important difference between good and poor writers will be in both the quantity and quality of the middle range of goals they create. These middle-range goals, which lie between intention and actual prose (cf., "give a brief history" in Figure 3), give sub-stance and direction to more abstract goals (such as "appealing to the audi-ence") and they give breadth and coherence to local decisions about what to say next.

GOALS, TOPIC, AND TEXT

We have been suggesting that the logic which moves composing forward grows out of the goals which writers create as they compose. However, com-mon sense and the folklore of writing offer an alternative explanation which we should consider, namely, that one's own knowledge of the topic (memo-ries, associations, etc.) or the text itself can take control of this process as fre-quently as one's goals do. One could easily imagine these three forces constituting a sort of eternal triangle in which the writer's goals, knowledge, and current text struggle for influence. For example, the writer's initial plan-ning for a given paragraph might have set up a goal or abstract representa-tion of a paragraph that would discuss three equally important, parallel points on the topic of climate. However, in trying to write, the writer finds that some of his knowledge about climate is really organized around a strong cause-and-effect relationship between points 1 and 2, while he has almost nothing to say about point 3. Or perhaps the text itself attempts to take con-trol, e.g., for the sake of a dramatic opening, the writer's first sentence sets up a vivid example of an effect produced by climate. The syntactic and seman-tic structure of that sentence now demand that a cause be stated in the next, although this would violate the writer's initial (and still appropriate) plan for a three-point paragraph.

Viewed this way, the writer's abstract plan (representation) of his goals, his knowledge of the topic, and his current text are all actively competing for the writer's attention. Each wants to govern the choices and decisions made next. This competitive model certainly captures that experience of seeing the text run away with you, or the feeling of being led by the nose by an idea. How then do these experiences occur within a "goal-driven process"? First, as our model of the writing process describes, the processes of **generate** and **evaluate** appear to have the power to interrupt the writer's process at any point—and they frequently do. This means that new knowledge and/or some feature of the current text can interrupt the process at any time through the processes of **generate** and **evaluate**. This allows a flexible col-laboration among goals, knowledge, and text. Yet this collaboration often culminates in a revision of previous goals. The persistence and functional importance of initially established goals is reflected by a number of signs:

the frequency with which writers refer back to their goals; the fact that writers behave consistently with goals they have already stated; and the fact that they evaluate text in response to the criteria specified in their goals.

Second, some kinds of goals steer the writing process in yet another basic way. In the writers we have studied, the overall composing process is clearly under the direction of global and local *process* goals. Behind the most free-wheeling act of "discovery" is a writer who has recognized the heuristic value of free exploration or "just writing it out" and has chosen to do so. Process goals such as these, or "I'll edit it later," are the earmarks of sophisticated writers with a repertory of flexible process goals which let them use writing for discovery. But what about poorer writers who seem simply to free associate on paper or to be obsessed with perfecting the current text? We would argue that often they too are working under a set of implicit process goals which say "write it as it comes," or "make everything perfect and correct as you go." The problem then is not that knowledge or the text have taken over, so much as that the writer's own goals and/or images of the composing process put these strategies in control.[23]

To sum up, the third point of our theory—focused on the role of the writer's own goals—helps us account for purposefulness in writing. But can we account for the dynamics of discovery? Richard Young, Janet Emig, and others argue that writing is uniquely adapted to the task of fostering insight and developing new knowledge.[24] But how does this happen in a goal-directed process?

We think that the remarkable combination of purposefulness and openness which writing offers is based in part on a beautifully simple, but extremely powerful principle, which is this: *In the act of writing, people regenerate or recreate their own goals in the light of what they learn.* This principle then creates the fourth point of our cognitive process theory.

4. Writers create their own goals in two key ways: by generating goals and supporting sub-goals which embody a purpose; and, at times, by changing or regenerating their own top-level goals in light of what they have learned by writing.

We are used, of course, to thinking of writing as a process in which our *knowledge* develops as we write. The structure of knowledge for some topic becomes more conscious and assertive as we keep tapping memory for related ideas. That structure, or "schema," may even grow and change as a result of library research or the addition of our own fresh inferences. However, writers must also generate (i.e., create or retrieve) the unique goals which guide their process.

In this paper we focus on the goals writers create for a particular paper, but we should not forget that many writing goals are well-learned, standard ones stored in memory. For example, we would expect many writers to draw automatically on those goals associated with writing in general, such as, "interest the reader," or "start with an introduction," or on goals associated with a given genre, such as making a jingle rhyme. These goals will often be so basic that they won't even be consciously considered or expressed. And the more experienced the writer the greater this repertory of semi-automatic plans and goals will be.

Writers also develop an elaborate network of working "sub-goals" as they compose. As we have seen, these sub-goals give concrete meaning and direction to their more abstract top-level goals, such as "interest the reader," or "describe my job." And then on occasion writers show a remarkable ability to regenerate or change the very goals which had been directing their writing and planning: that is, they replace or revise major goals in light of what they learned through writing. It is these two creative processes we wish to consider now.

We can see these two basic processes — creating sub-goals and regenerating goals — at work in the following protocol, which has been broken down into episodes. As you will see, writers organize these two basic processes in different ways. We will look here at three typical patterns of goals which we have labeled **"Explore and Consolidate," "State and Develop," "Write and Regenerate."**

EXPLORE AND CONSOLIDATE

This pattern often occurs at the beginning of a composing session, but it could appear anywhere. The writers frequently appear to be working under a high-level goal or plan to explore: that is, to think the topic over, to jot ideas down, or just start writing to see what they have to say. At other times the plan to explore is subordinate to a very specific goal, such as to find out "what on earth can I say that would make a 15-year-old girl interested in my job?" Under such a plan, the writer might explore her own knowledge, following out associations or using more structured discovery procedures such as tagmemics or the classical topics. But however the writer chooses to explore, the next step is the critical one. The writer pops back up to her top-level goal and from that vantage point reviews the information she has generated. She then consolidates it, producing a more complex idea than she began with by drawing inferences and creating new concepts.

Even the poor writers we have studied often seem adept at the exploration part of this process, even to the point of generating long narrative trains of association—sometimes on paper as a final draft. The distinctive thing about good writers is their tendency to return to that higher-level goal and to review and consolidate what has just been learned through exploring. In the act of consolidating, the writer sets up a *new goal* which replaces the goal of explore and directs the subsequent episode in composing. If the writer's topic is unfamiliar or the task demands creative thinking, the writer's ability to explore, to consolidate the results, and to regenerate his or her goals will be a critical skill.

The following protocol excerpt, which is divided into episodes and sub-episodes, illustrates this pattern of **explore and consolidate**.

Episode 1 a, b

In the first episode, the writer merely reviews the assignment and plays with some associations as he attempts to define his rhetorical situation. It ends with a simple process goal—"On to the task at hand"—and a reiteration of the assignment.

> (la) Okay - Um . . . Open the envelope - just like a quiz show on TV - My job for a young thirteen to fourteen teenage female audience - Magazine - *Seventeen.* My job for a young teenage female audience - Magazine - *Seventeen.* I never have read *Seventeen,* but I've referred to it in class and other students have. (1b) This is like being thrown the topic in a situation - you know - in an expository writing class and asked to write on it on the board and I've done that and had a lot of fun with it - so on to the task at hand. My job for a young teenage female audience - Magazine - *Seventeen.*

Episode 2 a, b, c, d

The writer starts with a plan to explore his own "job," which he initially defines as being a teacher and not a professor. In the process of exploring he develops a variety of sub-goals which include plans to: make new meaning by exploring a contrast; present himself or his persona as a teacher; and affect his audience by making them reconsider one of their previous notions. The extended audience analysis of teen-age girls (sub-episode 2c) is in response to his goal of affecting them.

At the end of episode 2c, the writer reaches tentative closure with the statement, "By God, I can change that notion for them." There are significantly long pauses on both sides of this statement, which appears to consolidate much of the writer's previous exploration. In doing this, he dramatically extends his earlier, rather vague plan to merely "compare teachers and professors"—he has regenerated and elaborated his top-level goals. This consolidation leaves the writer with a new, relatively complex, rhetorically sophisticated working goal, one which encompasses plans for a topic, a persona, and the audience. In essence the writer is learning through planning and his goals are the creative bridge between his exploration and the prose he will write.

Perhaps the writer thought his early closure at this point was too good to be true, so he returns at 2d to his initial top-level or most inclusive goal (write about my job) and explores alternative definitions of his job. The episode ends with the reaffirmation of his topic, his persona, and, by implication, the consolidated goal established in Episode 2c.

(2a) Okay lets see - lets doodle a little bit - Job - English teacher rather than professor - I'm doodling this on a scratch sheet as I say it. -ah- (2b) In fact that might be a useful thing to focus on - how a professor differs from - how a teacher differs from a professor and I see myself as a teacher - that might help them - my audience to reconsider their notion of what an English teacher does. (2c) -ah- English teacher - young teen-age female audience - they will all have had English - audience - they're in school - they're taking English - for many of them English may be a favorite subject   doodling still - under audience, but for the wrong reasons - some of them will have wrong reasons in that English is good because its tidy - can be a neat tidy little girl - others turned off of it because it seems too prim. By God I can change that notion for them. (2d) My job for a young teenage female audience - Magazine - *Seventeen*. -ah- Job - English teacher - guess that's what I'll have to go - yeah - hell - go with that - that's a challenge - rather than - riding a bicycle across England that's too easy and not on the topic - right, or would work in a garden or something like that - none of those are really my jobs - as a profession - My job for a young teenage female audience - Magazine - *Seventeen*. All right - I'm an English teacher.

STATE AND DEVELOP

This second pattern accounts for much of the straightforward work of composing, and is well illustrated in our protocol. In it the writer begins with a relatively general high-level goal which he then proceeds to develop or flesh out with sub-goals. As his goals become more fully specified, they form a bridge from his initial rather fuzzy intentions to actual text. Figure 4 is a

Figure 4   Writer developing a set of sub-goals.

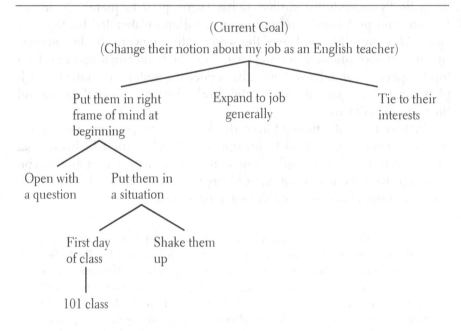

schematic representation of the goals and sub-goals which the writer eventually creates.

Episode 3 a, b, c

The episode starts with a sub-goal directly subordinate to the goal established in Episode 2 (change their notion of English teachers). It takes the pattern of a search in which the writer tries to find ways to carry out his current goal of "get [the audience?] at the beginning." In the process he generates yet another level of sub-goals (i.e., open with a question and draw them into a familiar situation). (A note on our terminology: in order to focus on the overall structure of goals and sub-goals in a writer's thinking, we have treated the writer's plans and strategies all as sub-goals or operational definitions of the larger goal.)

Notice how the content or ideas of the essay are still relatively unspecified. The relationship between creating goals and finding ideas is clearly reciprocal: it was an initial exploration of the writer's ideas which produced these goals. But the writing process was then moved forward by his attempt to flesh out a network of goals and sub-goals, not just by a mere "pre-writing" survey of what he knew about the topic. Episode 3c ends in an effort to test one of his new goals against his own experience with students.

(3a) All right - I'm an English teacher. I want to get at the beginning - I know that they're not going to be disposed - to hear what I'm saying - partly for that reason and partly to put them in the right, the kind of frame of mind I want - I want to open with an implied question or a direct one and put them in the middle of some situation - then expand from there to talk about my job more generally . . . and try to tie it in with their interest. (3b) So one question is where to begin - what kind of situation to start in the middle of - probably the first day of class. . . . They'd be interested - they'd probably clue into that easily because they would identify with first days of school and my first days are raucous affairs - it would immediately shake-em up and get them to thinking a different context. (3c) Okay - so - First day of class - lets see. - Maybe the first 101 class with that crazy skit I put on - that's probably better than 305 because 101 is freshmen and that's nearer their level and that skit really was crazy and it worked beautifully.

WRITE AND REGENERATE

This pattern is clearly analogous to the explore and consolidate pattern, except that instead of planning, the writer is producing prose. A miniature example of it can be seen in Figure 2, in which the writer, whose planning we have just seen, attempts to compose the first sentence of his article for *Seventeen*. Although he had done a good deal of explicit planning before this point, the prose itself worked as another, more detailed representation of what he wanted to say. In writing the sentence, he not only saw that it was inadequate, but that his goals themselves could be expanded. The reciprocity between writing and planning enabled him to learn even from a failure and to produce a new goal, "play up sex." Yet it is instructive to note that once this new plan was represented in language — subjected to the acid test of prose — it too failed to pass, because it violated some of his tacit goals or criteria for an acceptable prose style.

The examples we cite here are, for the purposes of illustration, small and rather local ones. Yet this process of setting and developing sub-goals, and — at times — regenerating those goals is a powerful creative process. Writers and teachers of writing have long argued that one learns through the act of writing itself, but it has been difficult to support the claim in other ways. However, if one studies the process by which a writer uses a goal to generate ideas, then consolidates those ideas and uses them to revise or

167

regenerate new, more complex goals, one can see this learning process in action. Furthermore, one sees why the process of revising and clarifying goals has such a broad effect, since it is through setting these new goals that the fruits of discovery come back to inform the continuing process of writing. In this instance, some of our most complex and imaginative acts can depend on the elegant simplicity of a few powerful thinking processes. We feel that a cognitive process explanation of discovery, toward which this theory is only a start, will have another special strength. By placing emphasis on the inventive power of the writer, who is able to explore ideas, to develop, act on, test, and regenerate his or her own goals, we are putting an important part of creativity where it belongs — in the hands of the working, thinking writer.

NOTES

1. Aristotle, *The Rhetoric*, trans. Lane Cooper (New York: Appleton-Century-Crofts, 1932); Richard Lloyd-Jones, "A Perspective on Rhetoric," in *Writing: The Nature, Development and Teaching of Written Communication*, ed. C. Frederiksen, M. Whiteman, and J. Dominic (Hillsdale, NJ: Lawrence Erlbaum Associates, in press.)

2. Lee Odell, Charles R. Cooper, and Cynthia Courts, "Discourse Theory: Implications for Research in Composing," in *Research on Composing: Points of Departure*, ed. Charles Cooper and Lee Odell (Urbana, IL: National Council of Teachers of English, 1978), p. 6.

3. Lloyd Bitzer, "The Rhetorical Situation," *Philosophy and Rhetoric*, 1 (January, 1968), 1–14.

4. Richard E. Vatz, "The Myth of the Rhetorical Situation," in *Philosophy and Rhetoric*, 6 (Summer, 1973), 154–161.

5. James Britton et al., *The Development of Writing Abilities, 11–18* (London: Macmillan, 1975), p. 39.

6. Gordon Rohman, "Pre-Writing: The Stage of Discovery in the Writing Process," CCC, 16 (May, 1965), 106–112.

7. See Britton et al., *The Development of Writing Abilities*, pp. 19–49.

8. Nancy Sommers, "Response to Sharon Crowley, 'Components of the Process,'" CCC, 29 (May, 1978), 209–211.

9. Nancy Sommers, "Revision Strategies of Student Writers and Experienced Writers," CCC, 31 (December, 1980), 378–388.

10. John R. Hayes, *Cognitive Psychology: Thinking and Creating* (Homewood, IL: Dorsey Press, 1978); Herbert A. Simon and John R. Hayes, "Understanding Complex Task Instruction," in *Cognition and Instruction*, ed. D. Klahr (Hillsdale, NJ: Lawrence Erlbaum Associates, 1976), pp. 269–285.

11. John R. Hayes and Linda S. Flower, "Identifying the Organization of Writing Processes," in *Cognitive Processes in Writing: An Interdisciplinary Approach*, ed. Lee Gregg and Erwin Steinberg (Hillsdale, NJ: Lawrence Erlbaum Associates, 1980), pp. 3–30. Although diagrams of the sort in Figure 1 help distinguish the various processes we wish our model to describe, these schematic representations of processes and elements are often misleading. The arrows indicate that *information* flows from one box or process to another; that is, knowledge about the writing assignment or knowledge from memory can be transferred or used in

the **planning** process, and information from **planning** can flow back the other way. What the arrows *do not mean* is that such information flows in a predictable left to right circuit, from one box to another as if the diagram were a one-way flow chart. This distinction is crucial because such a flow chart implies the very kind of stage model against which we wish to argue. One of the central premises of the cognitive process theory presented here is that writers are constantly, instant by instant, orchestrating a battery of cognitive processes as they integrate planning, remembering, writing, and rereading. The multiple arrows, which are conventions in diagramming this sort of model, are unfortunately only weak indications of the complex and active organization of thinking processes which our work attempts to model.

12. Linda S. Flower and John R. Hayes, "The Cognition of Discovery: Defining a Rhetorical Problem," *CCC*, 31 (February, 1980), 21–32.

13. Britton et al., *The Development of Writing Abilities*, pp. 61–65.

14. Sondra Perl, "Five Writers Writing: Case Studies of the Composing Process of Unskilled College Writers," Diss. New York University, 1978.

15. Linda S. Flower and John R. Hayes, "The Dynamics of Composing: Making Plans and Juggling Constraints," in *Cognitive Processes in Writing: An Interdisciplinary Approach*, ed. Lee Gregg and Erwin Steinberg (Hillsdale, NJ: Lawrence Erlbaum Associates, 1980), pp. 31–50.

16. Linda S. Flower, "Writer-Based Prose: A Cognitive Basis for Problems in Writing," *College English*, 41 (September, 1979), 19–37.

17. Flower, "The Cognition of Discovery," pp. 21–32.

18. Ellen Nold, "Revising," in *Writing: The Nature, Development, and Teaching of Written Communication*, ed. C. Frederiksen et al. (Hillsdale, NJ: Lawrence Erlbaum Associates, in press).

19. Mina Shaughnessy, *Errors and Expectations* (New York: Oxford University Press, 1977).

20. Marlene Scardamalia, "How Children Cope with the Cognitive Demands of Writing," in *Writing: The Nature, Development and Teaching of Written Communication*, ed. C. Frederiksen et al. (Hillsdale, NJ: Lawrence Erlbaum Associates, in press). Carl Bereiter and Marlene Scardamalia, "From Conversation to Composition: The Role of Instruction in a Developmental Process," in *Advances in Instructional Psychology*, Volume 2, ed. R. Glaser (Hillsdale, NJ: Lawrence Erlbaum Associates, in press).

21. Bereiter and Scardamalia, "From Conversation to Composition."

22. John R. Hayes and Linda Flower, "Uncovering Cognitive Processes in Writing: An Introduction to Protocol Analysis," in *Methodological Approaches to Writing Research*, ed. P. Mosenthal, L. Tamor, and S. Walmsley (in press).

23. Cf. a recent study by Mike Rose on the power of ineffective process plans, "Rigid Rules, Inflexible Plans, and the Stifling of Language: A Cognitivist's Analysis of Writer's Block," *CCC*, 31 (December, 1980), 389–400.

24. Janet Emig, "Writing as a Mode of Learning," *CCC*, 28 (May, 1977), 122–128; Richard E. Young, "Why Write? A Reconsideration," unpublished paper delivered at the convention of the Modern Language Association, San Francisco, California, 28 December 1979.

Cognitive Development and the Basic Writer

Andrea A. Lunsford

In her article, "Writing as a Mode of Learning," Janet Emig argues that

> Writing . . . connects the three major tenses of our experience to make meaning. And the two major modes by which these three aspects are united are the processes of analysis and synthesis: analysis, the breaking of entities into their constituent parts; and synthesis, combining or fusing these, often into fresh arrangements or amalgams [1]

I agree with Professor Emig, and her work as well as that of Mina Shaughnessy has led me to ponder the relationship of writing and the processes of analysis and synthesis to the teaching of basic writers. In general, my study of basic writers—their strategies, processes, and products[2]—leads me to believe that they have not attained that level of cognitive development which would allow them to form abstractions or conceptions. That is, they are most often unable to practice analysis and synthesis and to apply successfully the principles thus derived to college tasks. In short, our students might well perform a given task in a specific situation, but they have great difficulty abstracting from it or replicating it in another context.

Let me offer one concrete example to illustrate this point. Asked to read ten consecutive issues of a comic strip, choose one of the major characters, and infer the basic values of that character from the information provided in the ten issues, typical basic writing students find it almost impossible to articulate anything about the values of characters unlike themselves. In short, they have problems drawing inferences or forming concepts based on what they have read. Instead, they tend either to describe the characters or,

Reprinted from *College English* 41.1 (September 1979): 449–59. Used with permission.

more typically, to drop the comic strip character after a few sentences and shift to what they see as their own values. When I first began teaching basic writers, their response to this type of assignment gave me the first hint of how their difficulties were related to cognitive development.

In *Thought and Language*, the Russian psychologist Lev Vygotsky identifies three basic phases in the ascent to concept formation: the initial syncretic stage, in which "word meaning denotes nothing more to the child than a vague syncretic conglomeration of individual objects that have . . . coalesced into an image"; the "thinking in complexes" stage during which "thought . . . is already coherent and objective . . . , although it does not reflect objective relationships in the same way as conceptual thinking"; and, finally, the true-concept formation stage.[3] Vygotsky cautions, however, that

> even after the adolescent has learned to produce concepts, . . . he does not abandon elementary forms; they continue for a long time to operate, indeed to predominate, in many areas of his thinking. . . . The transitional character of adolescent thinking becomes especially evident when we observe the actual functioning of the newly acquired concepts. Experiments specially devised to study the adolescent's operations bring out. . . a striking discrepancy between his ability to form concepts and his ability to define them. (p. 79)

Vygotsky goes on to distinguish between "spontaneous" concepts, those which are formed as a result of ordinary, day-to-day experiences, and "scientific" concepts, which are formed largely in conjunction with instruction. The student described above by Vygotsky is like my basic writing students confronted with the comic strips in that they all are able to formulate spontaneous concepts, but not able to remove themselves from such concepts, to abstract from them, or to define them into the scientific concepts necessary for successful college work. In my experience, basic writing students most often work at what Vygotsky calls the "thinking in complexes" stage and the spontaneous-concept stage rather than at the true-concept formation stage. While these writers may have little difficulty in dealing with familiar everyday problems requiring abstract thought based on concepts, they are *not aware of the processes they are using*. Thus they often lack the ability to infer principles from their own experience. They are not forming the "scientific concepts" which are basic to mastery of almost all college material.

Jean Piaget categorizes mental development basically into four stages: the sensori-motor stage; the pre-operational stage; the concrete-operations stage; and the formal-operations stage characterized by the ability to abstract, synthesize, and form coherent logical relationships.[4] At the stage of concrete operations, the child's thought is still closely linked to concrete data; completely representational, hypothetical, or verbal thought still eludes him. As the child moves through the stages of cognitive development, he goes through what Piaget calls the process of "de-centering," a process further defined by Lee Odell as "getting outside one's own frame of reference, understanding the thoughts, values, feelings of another person; . . . projecting oneself into unfamiliar circumstances, whether factual or hypothetical; . . . learning to understand why one reacts as he does to experience."[5] Although children first begin to "de-center" as early as the pre-operational stage, egocentricity is still strong in the concrete stage, and, indeed, we apparently continue the process of "de-centering" throughout our lives.

The relationship of Piaget's concrete stage to Vygotsky's "thinking in complexes" stage and "spontaneous-concept formation" stage is, I believe, clear. Furthermore, the work of both Piaget and Vygotsky strongly indicates that cognitive development moves first from doing, to doing consciously, and only then to formal conceptualization. As Eleanor Duckworth says in an essay in *Piaget in the Classroom*, "thoughts are our way of connecting things up for ourselves. If somebody else tells us about the connections he has made, we can only understand him to the extent that we do the work of making those connections ourselves."[6] This notion is directly related to the highly influential work of Gilbert Ryle. In *The Concept of Mind* (New York: Barnes and Noble, 1949), Ryle makes his crucial distinction between knowing *how* and knowing *that*.

> Learning *how* or improving in ability is not like learning *that* or acquiring information. Truths can be imparted, procedures can only be inculcated, and while inculcation is a gradual process, imparting is relatively sudden. It makes sense to ask at what moment someone became apprised of a truth, but not to ask at what moment someone acquired a skill. "Part-trained" is a significant phrase, "part-informed" is not. Training is the art of setting tasks which the pupils have not yet accomplished but are not any longer quite incapable of accomplishing. . . . Misunderstanding is a by-product of knowing how. Only a person who is at least a partial master of the Russian tongue can make the wrong sense of a Russian expression. Mistakes are exercises of competences. (pp. 59–60)

Chomsky's distinction between "competence" and "performance" has similar implications. Chomsky's views as expressed in *Aspects of the Theory of Syntax* (Cambridge, Mass.: MIT Press, 1965) can be used to argue against the notion that "language is essentially an adventitious construct, taught by 'conditioning' . . . or by a drill and explicit explanation" (p. 51). In other words, students learn by doing and *then* by extrapolating principles from their activities. This theory informs an educational model proposed by James Britton in a recent lecture at Ohio State University (and based on his 1970 *Language and Learning*). Essentially, this paradigm incorporates learning by doing as opposed to learning solely by the study of abstract principles or precepts.

Britton's model is closely related to that articulated in Michael Polanyi's discussion of skills in *Personal Knowledge* (New York: Harper and Row, 1964). Polanyi begins his discussion by citing "the well-known fact that the *aim of a skillful performance is achieved by the observance of a set of rules which are not known as such to the person following them*" (p. 49). Polanyi uses examples of the person who rides a bicycle, keeps afloat in the water, or plays a musical instrument without at all comprehending the underlying rules. "Rules of art can be useful," Polanyi says, "but they do not determine the practice of an art; they are maxims, which can serve as a guide to an art only if they can be integrated into the practical knowledge" (p. 50). Polanyi goes on to discuss the importance of apprenticeship in acquiring a skill or an art, by which he means that we learn by doing *with* a recognized "master" or "connoisseur" better than by studying or reading about abstract principles. Vygotsky puts it quite succinctly: "What a child can do in cooperation today he can do alone tomorrow. Therefore the only good kind of instruction is that which marches ahead of development and leads it; it must be aimed not so much at the ripe as at the ripening functions" (*Thought and Language*, p. 104).

I have attempted this very cursory theoretical review partially in support of the premise asserted at the beginning of my essay: that most of our basic writing students are operating well below the formal-operations or true-concept formation stage of cognitive development, and hence they have great difficulty in "de-centering" and performing tasks which require analysis and synthesis. But once we are convinced that our basic writing students are most often characterized by the inability to analyze and synthesize, what then? How can we, as classroom teachers, use what we know about theory and about our students' levels of cognitive development to guide the ways in which we organize our basic writing classes and create effective assignments?

The theory reviewed above offers, I believe, a number of implications which will help us answer these questions. First, basic writing classes should never be teacher-centered; set lectures should always be avoided. Instead, the classes should comprise small workshop groups in which all members are active participants, apprentice-writers who are "exercising their competence" as they learn *how* to write well. Class time should be spent writing, reading what has been written aloud to the group/audience, and talking about that writing. Such sessions require an atmosphere of trust, and they demand careful diagnosis and preparation by the teacher. But these suggestions offer only a very general guide. Exactly *what* preparation should the basic writing teacher do?

The best way to move students into conceptualization and analytic and synthetic modes of thought is to create assignments and activities which allow students to practice or exercise themselves in these modes continuously. While an entire course plan would take more space than is available here, I can offer a series of examples, from activities focusing on grammatical categories and sentence-building to essay assignments, each of which is designed to foster conceptualization and analytic thinking.

One reason drill exercises have so often failed to transfer a skill into a student's own writing is that the student is operating below the cognitive level at which he or she could abstract and generalize a principle from the drill and then apply that principle to enormously varied writing situations. Memorizing precepts has been equally ineffective. Instead of either one, why not present students with a set of data, from their own writing or from that of someone else, and help them approach it inductively? Following is an exercise on verb recognition which attempts to engage students in inferential reasoning.

RECOGNIZING VERBS

Read the following sentences, filling in the missing word(s) in each one:

a. The cow _____ over the moon.

b. The farmer _____ a wife.

c. Jack Sprat _____ _____ no fat; his wife _____ _____ no lean.

d. Jack Horner _____ in a corner.

e. Jack _____ over the candlestick.

f. Don't _____ on my blue suede shoes.

g. The cat _____ away with the spoon.

h. Sunshine on my shoulder _____ me happy.

i. Little Miss Muffett _____ on a tuffet.

j. He _____ for his pipe, and he _____ for his fiddlers three.

k. The three little kittens _____ their mittens.

l. Little Boy Blue, come _____ your horn.

m. They all _____ in a yellow submarine.

n. The three little pigs _____ to market.

o. Jack and Jill _____ up the hill.

p. One _____ over the cuckoo's nest.

q. Everywhere that Mary _____ the lamb was sure to _____

Whether or not you recognize the songs and rhymes these sentences come from, you will have filled in the blanks with VERBS. Look back over the verbs you have used, and then list five other lines from songs or rhymes and underline the verbs in them.

1.
2.
3.
4.
5.

Now try your hand at formulating the rest of the following definition: Verbs are words which _____

_____

You may have noted in your definition that verbs *do something;* or you may have remembered learning a traditional definition of verbs. No matter what definition we come up with, though, verbs are essential to our communication: they complete or comment on the subjects of our sentences. Now revise your definition so that it includes the major *function* which verbs have in sentences:

_____

_____

CHARACTERISTICS OF VERBS

In this assignment, your job is to discover some major characteristics of verbs. To find the first one, begin studying the following lists of verbs. Then try to determine what characterizes each group. How do the groups differ?

Group One	Group Two	Group Three
break	prayed	will go
sweep	climbed	will run
strikes	altered	will fall
say	passed	will listen
heeds	dug	will look
catch	failed	will move
engages	wrote	will organize
operates	chose	will win
arrests	swore	will answer
play	questioned	will ride
reads	promised	will act
study	gave	will sing

Can you state what characterizes each group? _____

_____

_____

If you are having difficulty answering this question, try answering the next three questions first.

The action named by the verbs in Group One takes place at what time?

_____

The action named by the verbs in Group Two takes place at what time?

_____

The action named by the verbs in Group Three takes place at what time?

_____

Now go back and fill in an answer to the first question about what characterizes each group.

By now, you will have been able to identify the TENSE of the verbs in the three groups. Tense, or relation to time, is one of the major characteristics of verbs; it distinguishes them from other kinds of words such as nouns. Do you know the names of the three tenses represented in Group One, Group Two, and Group Three?

This same inductive or analytic approach can be applied to any grammatical concept or convention we wish our students to become familiar with. Rather than asking students to memorize the functions of the semi-colon, for instance, workshop groups can be presented with a passage or short essay which uses semi-colons frequently. The students' task is to isolate those sentences which use semi-colons and then draw some conclusions based on their data: they might be asked to group sentences which use semi-colons in the same way, to define the semi-colon, etc. Whatever the task, the group will be engaged in inferential problem-solving rather than in isolated drill or memorization. In Vygotsky's terms, analytic thinking is the "ripening function" we are attempting to foster.

In spite of their general effectiveness, sentence-combining drills will often fail to transfer new patterns into the basic writer's own writing—unless the sentence-combining work helps build inferential bridges. The sequential sentence-combining exercise below is designed to give students practice in inferring and analyzing. It is based primarily on the ancient practice of *imitatio*, which we would do well to introduce in all of our basic writing classes.

Pattern Sentence: The General Motors assembly line grinds out cars swiftly, smoothly, and almost effortlessly.

A. After studying the sentence pattern, combine each of the following sets of sentences into a sentence which imitates the pattern.

1. The cat eyed its prey.
2. The cat was scruffy.
3. The cat was yellow.
4. The prey was imaginary.
5. The cat eyed it craftily.
6. It eyed it tauntingly.
7. It even eyed it murderously.

---

1. Oil massages you.
2. The oil is bath oil.
3. It is Beauty's oil.
4. The massaging is gentle.
5. The massaging is soothing.
6. The massaging is almost loving.

---

1. We tend to use technologies.
2. The technologies are new.
3. Our use of them is profuse.
4. Our use is unwise.
5. Our use is even harmful.

---

1. H. L. Mencken criticized foibles.
2. The foibles belonged to society.
3. The society was American.
4. The criticism was witty.
5. It was sarcastic.
6. It was often unmerciful.

---

1. The lecturer droned.
2. The lecturer was nondescript.
3. The lecturer was balding.
4. The droning went on and on.
5. The droning was mechanical.
6. It was monotonous.
7. It was interminable.

B. Now fill in appropriate words to complete the following sentence, again being careful to imitate the pattern sentence.

The _____ _____ wins _____
_____ly, _____ly, and almost _____ly.

C. Now write a series of seven sentences and then combine them into one sentence which imitates the pattern sentence. Then write at least one more sentence which imitates the pattern.

Such exercises are not difficult to create; they can easily be adapted to specialized interests of any particular group or class. And they can lead to the kind of paragraph- and theme-length sentence-combining exercises recommended recently by Donald Daiker, Andrew Kerek, and Max Morenberg of Miami of Ohio.[7] Furthermore, such exercises can be supplemented by visual stimuli, pictures or video tapes, which can be used as raw material from which to generate new sentences in imitation of the pattern. But to be maximally effective, sentence-combining exercises must be designed to lead basic writing students to bridge the cognitive gap between imitating and generating.

I have yet to offer any sample essay assignments, but I do not thereby mean to imply that writing whole essays should only occur at or toward the end of a basic writing course. On the contrary, basic writers should begin composing whole paragraphs and essays, practicing the entire process of writing, from the very onset of the course. A pitcher does not practice by articulating one mini-movement at a time but by engaging in an entire, continuous process, from warm-up and mental preparation, to the wind-up, the release, and the follow-through: an analogy, to be sure, but one which I hope is not overly-strained. In addition to having students write paragraphs and essays early in the course, I would like especially to emphasize the importance of working with analytic modes in basic writing classes. Basic writers often fall back on narrative and descriptive modes because these modes are more adaptable to their own experience, or to what Linda Flower has described as "writer-based prose."[8] Yet the work of Ed White in California and of James Britton and his colleagues in England has shown us that little correlation exists in student performance between the spatial and temporal modes of narration and description and the logical and analytic modes of exposition and argumentation. Therefore, the basic writing course that works exclusively on narration and description will probably fail to build the cognitive skills its students will need to perform well in other college courses.

The comic-strip assignment I described earlier in this essay helped me learn that my students needed practice in using and assimilating analytic modes; it also helped me see that I had made several crucial mistakes in giving that assignment. First, I assigned it when the students had had little or no formal practice in inferential reasoning; second, I asked students to do the assignment at home rather than in workshop groups. In short, I ignored one of the lessons both Polanyi and Vygotsky have taught us: that often we learn best by working at a task in cooperation with a "master" or "connoisseur." I have since profited from these mistakes, and that same assignment, properly prepared for by workshop discussion and practice, has proven considerably more effective. Following are two other assignments, one calling for a brief response, the other for a longer essay, which are designed to help students gain control of analytic modes.

WRITING ASSIGNMENT A

Study the following set of data:

1. New York City lost 600,000 jobs between 1969–76.
2. In 1975, twenty buildings in prime Manhattan areas were empty.
3. Between 1970–75, ten major corporations moved their headquarters from New York City to the Sunbelt.
4. In 1976, New York City was on the brink of bankruptcy.
5. Between February, 1977, and February, 1978, New York City gained 9,000 jobs.
6. Since January, 1978, one million square feet of Manhattan floor space has been newly rented.
7. AT&T has just built a $110 million headquarters in New York.
8. IBM has just built an $80 million building at 55th and Madison in New York.
9. Co-op prices and rents have increased since 1977.
10. Even $1 million luxury penthouses are sold out.
11. There is currently an apartment shortage in Manhattan.
12. The President recently signed a bill authorizing $1.65 billion in federal loan guarantees for New York City.

After reading and thinking about the information listed above, how would you describe the current economic trend in New York City? Using your answer to that question as an opening sentence, write a paragraph in which you explain and offer support for your conclusion by using the information provided in the original set of data.

An assignment like the one above, which gives students practice in analyzing, generalizing, and abstracting, can be readily adapted to workshop groups in which discussion, criticism, and revision can take place.

WRITING ASSIGNMENT B

Preparing: Choose a person (but NOT someone you know well) whom you can observe on at least 5–7 occasions. You might choose someone who rides the same bus as you do, or one of your instructors, or someone who is in one of your classes. Be sure that you are on no closer than "how are you today?" terms with the person you choose.

Gathering Data: Arrange the times you can observe your person so that you can make notes during or immediately after the observation. Note down anything that seems important to you. For a start, answer these questions after each observation.

1. What is X wearing? (Be detailed; include colors, types of fabric, etc.)
2. How is X's hair fixed? (What kind of hair-cut, length of hair, style, etc.)
3. What, if anything, does X have with him or her? (Bag, knapsack, purse, books, etc.)
4. What is X doing? (Be as detailed as possible.)
5. What does X say? (Get exact wording whenever you can.)
6. Who does X associate with?
7. What seems to be X's mood?

Grouping Data: Study all your notes. Then group them under the following headings: APPEARANCE, ACTIONS, WORDS.

Analyzing Data: Now study all the information you have categorized. Based on that information, what would you say is X's lifestyle? What does your observation suggest about X's top priorities? What is most important to X?

Writing About your Data: Write a short essay which begins by answering the questions asked under "Analyzing Data." Use the data you have grouped in your notes to explain and support your analysis of the lifestyle and priorities of X.

This assignment begins with workshop discussion; the results of each stage are discussed by the group. Revision, sorting, and excluding are thus continuous, with the teacher helping students move more and more surely from *describing* their subjects to *analyzing* them. To save space, I have omitted the revising stages, which involve group response to and criticism of the essays and which vary, of course, with the particular difficulties encountered by each group.

Writing projects based on inference-drawing and conceptualization are easily adapted to almost any topic. I have used excerpts from the *Foxfire* books as the basis for essays in which students draw conclusions and generalize about the people interviewed. David Bartholomae, of the University of Pittsburgh, recommends Studs Terkel's *Working* as the basis for similar assignments building conceptual skills. Role-playing exercises and persona paraphrases offer other effective means of helping students "de-center" and hence gain the distance necessary to effective analysis and synthesis. In fact, it is possible and, I would urge, highly profitable, to build an entire basic writing course on exercises like the ones described above, assignments which "march ahead of development and lead it." If we can do so successfully, and if we can find valid ways to substantiate our success, certainly we will have put all our theory to the best practical use. And as a bonus, we will help to establish what Janet Emig argues is the unique value of writing to the entire learning process.

NOTES

1. "Writing as a Mode of Learning," *CCC*, 28 (1977), 127.
2. "The Ohio State University Remedial English Pilot Project: Final Report and Follow-Up Study," Ohio State University, 1977, and "An Historical, Descriptive, and Evaluative Study of Remedial English in American Colleges and Universities," Diss. Ohio State University, 1977.
3. Lev Semenovich Vygotsky, *Thought and Language*, trans. Eugenia Hanfmann and Gertrude Vakar (Cambridge, Mass.: MIT Press, 1962), pp. 59–61.
4. *Six Psychological Studies* (New York: Random House, 1967).
5. "Teaching Reading: An Alternative Approach," *English Journal*, 22 (1973), 455.
6. "Language and Thought," in *Piaget in the Classroom*, ed. Milton Schwebel and Jane Raph (New York: Basic Books, 1973), p. 148.
7. *The Writer's Options: College Sentence Combining* (New York: Harper and Row, 1979).
8. Linda Flower and John R. Hayes, "Problem Solving Strategies and the Writing Process," *College English*, 39 (1977), 449–461.

Diving In

An Introduction to Basic Writing

MINA P. SHAUGHNESSY

Basic writing, alias remedial, developmental, pre-baccalaureate, or even handicapped English, is commonly thought of as a writing course for young men and women who have many things wrong with them. Not only do medical metaphors dominate the pedagogy (*remedial, clinic, lab, diagnosis,* and so on), but teachers and administrators tend to discuss basic-writing students much as doctors tend to discuss their patients, without being tinged by mortality themselves and with certainly no expectations that questions will be raised about the state of *their* health.

Yet such is the nature of instruction in writing that teachers and students cannot easily escape one another's maladies. Unlike other courses, where exchanges between teacher and student can be reduced to as little as one or two objective tests a semester, the writing course requires students to write things down regularly, usually once a week, and requires teachers to read what is written and then write things back and every so often even talk directly with individual students about the way they write.

This system of exchange between teacher and student has so far yielded much more information about what is wrong with students than about what is wrong with teachers, reinforcing the notion that students, not teachers, are the people in education who must do the changing. The phrase "catching up," so often used to describe the progress of BW students, is illuminating here, suggesting as it does that the only person who must move in the teaching situation is the student. As a result of this view, we are much more likely

Reprinted from *College Composition and Communication* 27.3 (October 1976): 234–39. Used with permission.

in talking about teaching to talk about students, to theorize about *their* needs and attitudes or to chart *their* development and ignore the possibility that teachers also change in response to students, that there may in fact be important connections between the changes teachers undergo and the progress of their students.

I would like, at any rate, to suggest that this is so, and since it is common these days to "place" students on developmental scales, saying they are eighth-graders or fifth-graders when they read and even younger when they write or that they are stalled some place on Piaget's scale without formal propositions, I would further like to propose a developmental scale for teachers, admittedly an impressionistic one, but one that fits the observations I have made over the years as I have watched traditionally prepared English teachers, including myself, learning to teach in the open-admissions classroom.

My scale has four stages, each of which I will name with a familiar metaphor intended to suggest what lies at the center of the teacher's emotional energy during that stage. Thus I have chosen to name the first stage of my developmental scale GUARDING THE TOWER, because during this stage the teacher is in one way or another concentrating on protecting the academy (including himself) from the outsiders, those who do not seem to belong in the community of learners. The grounds for exclusion are various. The mores of the times inhibit anyone's openly ascribing the exclusion to genetic inferiority, but a few teachers doubtless still hold to this view.

More often, however, the teacher comes to the basic-writing class with every intention of preparing his students to write for college courses, only to discover, with the first batch of essays, that the students are so alarmingly and incredibly behind any students he has taught before that the idea of their ever learning to write acceptably for college, let alone learning to do so in one or two semesters, seems utterly pretentious. Whatever the sources of their incompetence—whether rooted in the limits they were born with or those that were imposed upon them by the world they grew up in—the fact seems stunningly, depressingly obvious: they will never "make it" in college unless someone radically lowers the standards.

The first pedagogical question the teacher asks at this stage is therefore not "How do I teach these students?" but "What are the consequences of flunking an entire class?" It is a question that threatens to turn the class into a contest, a peculiar and demoralizing contest for both student and teacher, since neither expects to win. The student, already conditioned to the idea that there is something wrong with his English and that writing is a device for magnifying and exposing this deficiency, risks as little as possible on the page, often straining with what he does write to approximate the academic style and producing in the process what might better be called "written Anguish" rather than English—sentences whose subjects are crowded out by such phrases as "it is my conviction that" or "on the contrary to my opinion," inflections that belong to no variety of English, standard or nonstandard, but grow out of the writer's attempt to be correct, or words whose idiosyncratic spellings reveal not simply an increase in the number of conventional misspellings but new orders of difficulty with the correspondences between spoken and written English. Meanwhile, the teacher assumes that he must not only hold out for the same product he held out for in the past but teach unflinchingly in the same way as before, as if any pedagogical adjustment to the needs of students were a kind of cheating. Obliged because of the exigencies brought on by open admissions to serve his time in the defense of the academy, he does if not his best, at least his duty, setting forth the material to be mastered, as if he expected students to learn it, but feeling grateful when a national holiday happens to fall on a basic-writing day and looking always for ways of evading conscription next semester.

But gradually, student and teacher are drawn into closer range. They are obliged, like emissaries from opposing camps, to send messages back and forth. They meet to consider each other's words and separate to study them in private. Slowly, the teacher's preconceptions of his students begin to give way here and there. It now appears that, in some instances at least, their writing, with its rudimentary errors and labored style has belied their intelligence and individuality. Examined at a closer range, the class now appears to have at least some members in it who might, with hard work, eventually "catch up." And it is the intent of reaching these students that moves the teacher into the second stage of development—which I will name CONVERTING THE NATIVES.

As the image suggests, the teacher has now admitted at least some to the community of the educable. These learners are perceived, however, as empty vessels, ready to be filled with new knowledge. Learning is thought of not so much as a constant and often troubling reformulation of the world so as to encompass new knowledge but as a steady flow of truth into a void. Whether the truth is delivered in lectures or modules, cassettes or computers, circles or squares, the teacher's purpose is the same: to carry the technology of advanced literacy to the inhabitants of an underdeveloped country. And so confident is he of the reasonableness and allure of what he is presenting, it does not occur to him to consider the competing logics and values and habits that may be influencing his students, often in ways that they themselves are unaware of.

Sensing no need to relate what he is teaching to what his students know, to stop to explore the contexts within which the conventions of academic discourse have developed, and to view these conventions in patterns large enough to encompass what students do know about language already, the teacher becomes a mechanic of the sentence, the paragraph, and the essay. Drawing usually upon the rules and formulas that were part of his training in composition, he conscientiously presents to his students flawless schemes for achieving order and grammaticality and anatomizes model passages of English prose to uncover, beneath brilliant, unique surfaces, the skeletons of ordinary paragraphs.

Yet too often the schemes, however well meant, do not seem to work. Like other simplistic prescriptions, they illuminate for the moment and then disappear in the melee of real situations, where paradigms frequently break down and thoughts will not be regimented. S's keep reappearing or disappearing in the wrong places; regular verbs shed their inflections and irregular verbs acquire them; tenses collide; sentences derail; and whole essays idle at one level of generalization.

Baffled, the teacher asks, "How is it that these young men and women whom I have personally admitted to the community of learners cannot learn these simple things?" Until one day, it occurs to him that perhaps these simple things—so transparent and compelling to him—are not in fact simple at all, that they only appear simple to those who already know them, that the grammar and rhetoric of formal written English have been shaped by the irrationalities of history and habit and by the peculiar restrictions and rituals that come from putting words on paper instead of into the air, that the sense and nonsense of written English must often collide with the spoken English that has been serving students in their negotiations with the world for many years. The insight leads our teacher to the third stage of his development, which I will name SOUNDING THE DEPTHS, for he turns now to the careful observation not only of his students and their writing but of himself as writer and teacher, seeking a deeper understanding of the behavior called writing and of the special difficulties his students have in mastering the skill. Let us imagine, for the sake of illustration, that the teacher now begins to look more carefully at two common problems among basic writers—the problem of grammatical errors and the problem of undeveloped paragraphs.

Should he begin in his exploration of error not only to count and name errors but to search for patterns and pose hypotheses that might explain them, he will begin to see that while his lessons in the past may have been "simple," the sources of the error he was trying to correct were often complex. The insight leads not inevitably or finally to a rejection of all rules and standards, but to a more careful look at error, to the formulation of what might be called a "logic" of errors that serves to mark a pedagogical path for teacher and student to follow.

Let us consider in this connection the "simple" *s* inflection on the verb, the source of a variety of grammatical errors in BW papers. It is, first, an alien form to many students whose mother tongues inflect the verb differently or not at all. Uniformly called for, however, in all verbs in the third person singular present indicative of standard English, it would seem to be a highly predictable or stable form and therefore one easily remembered. But note the grammatical concepts the student must grasp before he can apply the rule: the concepts of person, tense, number, and mood. Note that the *s* inflection is an atypical inflection within the modern English verb system. Note too how often it must seem to the student that he hears the stem form of the verb after third person singular subjects in what sounds like the present, as he does for example whenever he hears questions like "Does *she want* to go?" or "Can the *subway stop?*" In such sentences, the standard language itself reinforces the student's own resistance to the inflection.

And then, beyond these apparent unpredictabilities within the standard system, there is the influence of the student's own language or dialect, which urges him to ignore a troublesome form that brings no commensurate increase in meaning. Indeed, the very *s* he struggles with here may shift in a moment to signify plurality simply by being attached to a noun instead of a verb. No wonder then that students of formal English throughout the world find this inflection difficult, not because they lack intelligence or care but because they think analogically and are linguistically efficient. The issue is not the capacity of students finally to master this and the many other forms of written English that go against the grain of their instincts and experience but the priority this kind of problem ought to have in the larger scheme of learning to write and the willingness of students to mobilize themselves to master such forms at the initial stages of instruction.

Somewhere between the folly of pretending that errors don't matter and the rigidity of insisting that they matter more than anything, the teacher must find his answer, searching always under pressure for short cuts that will not ultimately restrict the intellectual power of his students. But as yet, we lack models for the maturation of the writing skill among young, native-born adults and can only theorize about the adaptability of other models for these students. We cannot say with certainty just what progress in writing ought to look like for basic-writing students, and more particularly how the elimination of error is related to their over-all improvement.

Should the teacher then turn from problems of error to his students' difficulties with the paragraphs of academic essays, new complexities emerge. Why, he wonders, do they reach such instant closure on their ideas, seldom moving into even one subordinate level of qualification but either moving on to a new topic sentence or drifting off into reverie and anecdote until the point of the essay has been dissolved? Where is that attitude of "suspended conclusion" that Dewey called thinking, and what can one infer about their intellectual competence from such behavior?

Before consigning his students to some earlier stage of mental development, the teacher at this stage begins to look more closely at the task he is asking students to perform. Are they aware, for example, after years of right/wrong testing, after the ACT's and the GED's and the OAT's, after straining to memorize what they read but never learning to doubt it, after "psyching out" answers rather than discovering them, are they aware that the rules have changed and that the rewards now go to those who can sustain a play of mind upon ideas—teasing out the contradictions and ambiguities and frailties of statements?

Or again, are the students sensitive to the ways in which the conventions of talk differ from those of academic discourse? Committed to extending the boundaries of what is known, the scholar proposes generalizations that cover the greatest possible number of instances and then sets about supporting his case according to the rules of evidence and sound reasoning that govern his subject. The spoken language, looping back and forth between speakers, offering chances for groping and backing up and even hiding, leaving room for the language of hands and faces, of pitch and pauses, is by comparison generous and inviting. The speaker is not responsible for the advancement of formal learning. He is free to assert opinions without a display of evidence or recount experiences without explaining what they "mean." His movements from one level of generality to another are more often brought on by shifts in the winds of conversation rather than by some decision of his to be more specific or to sum things up. For him the injunction to "be more specific" is difficult to carry out because the conditions that lead to specificity are usually missing. He may not have acquired the habit of questioning his propositions, as a listener might, in order to locate the points that require amplification or evidence. Or he may be marooned with a proposition he cannot defend for lack of information or for want of practice in retrieving the history of an idea as it developed in his own mind.

Similarly, the query "What is your point?" may be difficult to answer because the conditions under which the student is writing have not allowed for the slow generation of an orienting conviction, that underlying sense of the direction he wants his thinking to take. Yet without this conviction, he cannot judge the relevance of what comes to his mind, as one sentence branches out into another or one idea engenders another, gradually crowding from his memory the direction he initially set for himself.

Or finally, the writer may lack the vocabulary that would enable him to move more easily up the ladder of abstraction and must instead forge out of a nonanalytical vocabulary a way of discussing thoughts about thoughts, a task so formidable as to discourage him, as travelers in a foreign land are discouraged, from venturing far beyond bread-and-butter matters.

From such soundings, our teacher begins to see that teaching at the remedial level is not a matter of being simpler but of being more profound, of not only starting from "scratch" but also determining where "scratch" is. The experience of studenthood is the experience of being just so far over one's head that it is both realistic and essential to work at surviving. But by underestimating the sophistication of our students and by ignoring the complexity of the tasks we set before them, we have failed to locate in precise ways where to begin and what follows what.

But I have created a fourth stage in my developmental scheme, which I am calling DIVING IN in order to suggest that the teacher who has come this far must now make a decision that demands professional courage—the decision to remediate himself, to become a student of new disciplines and of his students themselves in order to perceive both their difficulties and their incipient excellence. "Always assume," wrote Leo Strauss, to the teacher, "that there is one silent student in your class who is by far superior to you in head and in heart." This assumption, as I have been trying to suggest, does not come easily or naturally when the teacher is a college teacher and the young men and women in his class are labeled remedial. But as we come to know these students better, we begin to see that the greatest barrier to our work with them is our ignorance of them and of the very subject we have contracted to teach. We see that we must grope our ways into the turbulent disciplines of semantics and linguistics for fuller, more accurate data about words and sentences; we must pursue more rigorously the design of developmental models, basing our schemes less upon loose comparisons with children and more upon case studies and developmental research of the sort that produced William Perry's impressive study of the intellectual development of Harvard students; we need finally to examine more closely the nature of speaking and writing and divine the subtle ways in which these forms of language both support and undo each other.

The work is waiting for us. And so irrevocable now is the tide that brings the new students into the nation's college classrooms that it is no longer within our power, as perhaps it once was, to refuse to accept them into the community of the educable. They are here. DIVING IN is simply deciding that teaching them to write well is not only suitable but challenging work for those who would be teachers and scholars in a democracy.

William Perry
and Liberal Education

Patricia Bizzell

The work of psychologist William G. Perry, Jr. has attracted much attention recently from college writing teachers who seek a developmental model to inform composition courses and writing-across-the-curriculum programs. To assess Perry's usefulness to writing instruction, I would like first to summarize his work, giving his own interpretation of its significance, and then to say how I think we should, and should not, use it.

After taking a BA in psychology at Harvard College, Perry began his academic career teaching English literature at Williams College. In 1947 he returned to Harvard to head the Bureau of Study Counsel, and there he performed the research that led to the publication of his influential book, *Forms of Intellectual and Ethical Development in the College Years: A Scheme* (New York: Holt, Rinehart, and Winston, 1968). Perry describes how college students pass from childhood to adulthood by moving through nine developmental positions. The shape of this process and the nature of the positions were defined through a series of interviews with Harvard undergraduate men in each of their four years in college.

Perry's nine-position scheme chronicles movement through three world views, "Dualism," "Relativism," and "Commitment in Relativism." The young person typically passes through them in this order, sometimes pausing or backtracking. Each world view shapes value judgments on religion, politics, family relations, and so on. Drawing on the student interviews, Perry depicts each world view primarily in terms of the young person's attitude toward schoolwork.

Reprinted from *College English* 46.5 (September 1984): 447–54. Used with permission.

The first world view, "Dualism," is characterized by the belief that every-thing in the world can be ordered in one of two categories—right or wrong. These categories are defined by axiomatic statements or "Absolutes," which are possessed by "Authority," adults who have perfect knowledge of the Abso-lutes. The proper task of Authority is to convey the Absolutes to the ignorant. For the dualist, knowing the world means memorizing the Absolutes and applying them to individual instances. For the student Dualist, education is a process of finding right answers (correct applications of Absolutes), with the help of the teacher (Authority). The student Dualist resists exploring academic problems that have no one right solution, and prefers teachers who supply answers and disciplines in which answers can be securely quantified.

In the second world view, "Relativism," Absolutes either are unknow-able or no longer exist. Without them Authority can no longer empower one to categorize the world as right or wrong. In place of these generally appli-cable standards, selfish interest becomes the basis for each individual's deci-sions. For the Relativist, knowing the world means devising an individual strategy for survival. For the student Relativist, education is a process of devising persuasive answers, since right answers no longer exist. The teacher judges persuasiveness according to idiosyncratic criteria, not Absolute stan-dards. As the student Relativist learns how to satisfy teachers' demands, he or she enjoys exploring problematic questions and prefers disciplines in which they abound. This student also prefers teachers who do not stand on the (now unfounded) authority of their office but relate personally to the student.

In the third world view, "Commitment in Relativism," the world is still without Absolutes and Authority. Nevertheless, it is not without order, and decisions need not be based on solitary self-interest. For the Committed Rela-tivist, knowing the world means understanding what has been rendered important by one's family, friends, religious and ethnic traditions, and intel-lectual interests. These priorities derived from social surroundings guide choices about the values that will order one's life, choices that Perry calls "Commitments." As one's Commitments develop, one can make confident judgments of what is better or worse relative to them, while still realizing that other people who have sufficiently examined their values may employ differ-ent but valid standards of judgment. For the student Committed Relativist, education is a process of achieving the knowledge necessary for making Commitments. Once Committed to a field of study, this student does not seek right or glib answers; rather he or she tries to start working productively in the chosen field. The teacher is neither Authority nor personal friend dur-ing this process, but rather a more experienced fellow worker, or mentor.

Perry does not clearly explain what his developmental scheme describes. Is it a process through which all normal 18- to 21-year-olds can be expected to pass, a process that is automatic, genetically determined? If so, Perry's scheme would extend the developmental scheme put forward for younger children by Jean Piaget. Piaget sees children moving through a series of stages of cognitive activity, from sensori-motor on to formal-operational; this process unfolds independent of a child's particular cultural context. Most researchers in the development of adolescents seek to complete Piaget's scheme, that is, to describe the stages children pass through after puberty; and Perry, too, nods in the direction of Piaget. He suggests that he follows Piaget in the notion that developmental processes repeat themselves on different levels—in other words, that we can expect to find some process in the adolescent analogous to the movement through cognitive stages in the young child.

Perry differentiates his study from Piaget's, however, when he says that *Forms of Intellectual and Ethical Development* focuses on "the level at which a person undertakes the development of his 'philosophical assumptions' about his world" (p. 29). I see two distinctions from Piaget here. First, Perry describes this development as something a person "undertakes"; in other words, it is a process of which the person is conscious and which he or she can guide to some extent. In contrast, Piaget describes cognitive development as unfolding naturally, with only occasional awareness on the child's part that changes are occurring, and without much possibility of anyone, child or observing adult, altering the course of the development. The second distinction follows from this self-conscious aspect of the development Perry describes: what are developed are "philosophical assumptions," not cognitive stages. Philosophical assumptions, I take it, can be examined, revised, and consciously affirmed by their possessor, unlike cognitive stages. Perry puts the phrase in quotation marks to indicate that he does not see the typical undergraduate as a systematic thinker; nevertheless, he wants to use such language because it suggests that the scheme focuses on beliefs consciously held in the mind. The process of developing philosophical assumptions may be analogous to that of developing mature cognitive abilities, but it is not the same kind of process.

But if Perry derives from Piaget only the concept of a developmental process, then what kind of process does Perry's scheme describe? Perry's answer to this question is not clear. I think, however, that in spite of Perry's nod to Piaget, his developmental scheme describes something that does not necessarily happen to all cognitively normal 18- to 21-year-olds. Perry drops many hints that what he is describing is what happens to young people when they receive an education. Furthermore, he suggests that an education-induced developmental process should not be regarded as value-neutral, as we would presumably have to regard a process that unfolded according to some genetic necessity, such as that described by Piaget. Education initiates one into the traditions, habits, and values of a community. Perry's scheme focuses particularly on liberal arts education and the world view it inculcates. Obviously, then, it is possible to pass through the ages of 18 to 21 quite "normally" from the psychological point of view without undergoing this kind of development.

Perry aims in his book to convince us that undergraduates in a liberal arts college do pass through the developmental process he describes, but he also does something more. He tries, I think, to persuade us that this development, although not necessary for normal cognition, is desirable. There is, of course, an implicit argument for the desirability of a developmental process in any work that claims simply to describe such a process. If the process is developmental, then by definition, movement through it must be good and arrest at an early stage bad. The researcher is not supposed to assign such values to the stages being described and therefore is not expected to defend the implicit values. Perry, however, has openly assigned values to his developmental stages: successful completion of a liberal arts education requires moving eventually into the world view of Committed Relativism. Perry must either defend the values or be charged with bias in his research.

Consequently Perry openly states: "The values built into our scheme are those we assume to be commonly held in significant areas of our culture, finding their most concentrated expression in such institutions as colleges of liberal arts, mental health movements, and the like" (p. 45). He understands that these values are "statements of opinion," with which others may differ (p. 45), and that framing these values in a developmental scheme implicitly argues for them by implying that the closer one adheres to them, the more one "grows" (p. 44). But he is unembarrassed at arguing for these values because he believes that they lead ultimately to the truest world view, or as he puts it, "an optimally congruent and responsible address to the present state of man's predicament" (p. 45). Ultimately Perry sees the achievement of this world view as having spiritual significance; he refers several times to his scheme's being a sort of modern-day *Pilgrim's Progress*, and he stresses the courage it takes for young people to win through to the end (see pp. 37, 44).

Perry's scheme, then, charts the creation of, not just any intellectually and ethically mature adult, but precisely "the liberally educated man," a man (or woman) "who has learned to think about even his own thoughts, to examine the way he orders his data and the assumptions he is making, and to compare these with other thoughts that other men might have" (p. 39). Perry characterizes the adult who cannot be self-reflective in this way as "anti-intellectual," even if he or she is otherwise intelligent (p. 39). To develop this kind of self-reflective intellectual maturity, Perry explicitly recommends a pedagogy of pluralism, which forces students to confront opposing views on an issue, forcing them out of the Dualist world view on into Relativism and beyond. Persuasively arguing for this pedagogy, Perry cites Socrates as its first practitioner and finds an American supporter for it in Henry Adams (p. 35). Pluralism is also the pedagogy of Harvard College. Perry recognizes that its pervasiveness at Harvard has conditioned his research results, but he does not seek to claim universality for his results. Rather, he argues for this particular education-induced development. Let other colleges, Perry implies, follow Harvard, as they have done in the past, in defining "the very heart of liberal education" (pp. 35–36).

Perry does not discuss the place of writing in the development for which he argues. He does not say, for example, that a Dualist student will write a particular kind of essay. Indeed, to determine a student's position in the scheme, Perry looks at nothing other than what the student tells the interviewer about his experiences. From the transcript of the interview Perry derives the student's attitudes toward schoolwork, which serve to characterize the positions in the scheme, as I explain above.

These general attitudes toward schoolwork presumably do inform particular kinds of academic performance, however. In a much anthologized essay Perry has distinguished between the attitudes that produce "cow" writing, or data unorganized by theory, and "bull" writing, or theory unsupported by data.[1] He does not use the descriptive terms from his scheme to characterize "cow" and "bull" writers, but he does connect students' papers with their understanding of academic ways of thinking.

With this indirect encouragement from Perry, many writing teachers have found it easy to match typical kinds of student essays with positions in the scheme. For example, a familiar sort of undergraduate essay is the one without an organizing thesis, the essay that is simply a collocation of facts strung together like beads with connectives such as "another" or "next." Typically, too, this kind of essay is either hypercorrect or fraught with errors that seem to have kept the student's attention fixed on the sentence level, so underdeveloped are the ideas in the whole paper. In place of generalizations from data this paper relies on maxims used so uncritically as to strike us as dreadful clicheés. Mina Shaughnessy has found these characteristics in the writing of students at the most "basic" level of approximation to academic discourse (*Errors and Expectations* [New York: Oxford University Press, 1977], pp. 198–202). Building on Shaughnessy's work, Andrea Lunsford finds similar characteristics in the essays of some of her Basic Writers.[2] It seems easy to identify such writing as the work of what Perry calls Dualist students, with their belief in unquestionable Absolutes and their view of education as the collecting of right answers.

Much more research is needed, however, before we can use Perry's scheme to classify kinds of student writing. No doubt there are common kinds of undergraduate essays other than that described above, which seems to fit the scheme so neatly; we do not know whether Perry's scheme can provide an exhaustive explanation of variation in student writing. We should remember that Perry's scheme was based on the experiences of students who were highly successful academically and who were attending one of the most selective liberal arts colleges in the country. Although Shaughnessy and Lunsford, working with students somewhat different from Perry's, found signs in student writing of a development similar to the one he describes (neither of them refers to Perry), we do not know to what extent Perry's scheme can extend its explanatory power across a variety of student abilities, academic preparation, and college experiences. We should also note that Perry provides no timetable for progress through his scheme; nowhere does he suggest that all freshmen can be expected to be Dualists, who then as sophomores and juniors traverse Relativism and achieve Committed Relativism as seniors. The existence of these gaps in our knowledge of the scheme's application to student writing argues against using the scheme to classify student writing in any detailed way.

Furthermore, I would argue that we should not use Perry's scheme as a blueprint for writing curricula. Mechanical applications of Perry's scheme will tend to trivialize it while producing curricula that really tell us nothing new. For example, one freshman composition curriculum based on Perry uses his analysis of Relativism to justify the already familiar recommendation to ask students to read several essays that take opposing views on a controversial issue and then to develop their own argumentative positions.[3] The method is so familiar as already to have been embodied in numberless freshman composition anthologies. Furthermore, because students require prolonged exposure to pluralistic methods in many disciplines, and time to reduce the domain of Dualism, this curriculum does not do justice to the rather elaborate process whereby a student achieves the Relativist world view, according to Perry. Some research has suggested that Dualists make more progress if teachers initially take a nurturing, rather than a challenging, stance with them.[4] Moreover, students who have already achieved Relativism may not be greatly benefited by lessons in recognizing and arguing from opposing views on a controversial issue. Such practice may only entrench them in intransigently held personal views, a mind-set which, according to Perry, often retards students' progress through Relativism to Commitment.

If we agree with Perry that students pass through certain positions on their way to the kind of intellectual maturity valued in liberal arts colleges, it does not necessarily follow that we can get them to progress faster by forcing them to imitate more advanced positions until their brains kick on and hold these positions on their own. We should not, in other words, commit a version of what has come to be known as the "American heresy" with respect to the work of Piaget, that is, the attempt to find ways of moving children faster through the Piagetian levels. Perry's scheme describes the effects of a certain liberal arts curriculum, to be sure—Harvard's—but this does not mean that we can turn the effects into a model of causes for a new curriculum that will perform the same changes more efficiently. To try would be to neglect the emphasis Perry himself places on the function of education as acculturation, not training; inculcation of values, not practice in techniques.

Of what use, then, is Perry's work to college writing teachers? I think his scheme can help us to understand why the differences occur in student writing, even if we cannot apply his classification scheme rigidly. Shaughnessy and Lunsford do not agree on why such differences occur. Shaughnessy suggests that they arise from students' unequal ability to meet the expectations of the academic discourse community. Lunsford argues that the students are at different levels of cognitive development in the Piagetian sense—Basic Writers are "egocentric" (p. 284). Perry's scheme forges a link between these social and cognitive explanations because, as I argued above, he is describing a developmental process that is only analogous to but not identical with Piaget's. Perry's analysis describes the changes in student thinking that result from their socialization into the academic community. The great strength of his scheme is its focus on one important constant in the struggles of all college writers: the intellectual demands of liberal education.

Perry's work should make us realize that as we bring our students through the process of liberal education, we are not simply teaching them to think or to grow up, as we sometimes like to say that we are. Rather, we are teaching them to think in a certain way, to become adults with a certain set of intellectual habits and ethical predilections. We are asking them to accept a certain kind of relation to their culture, from among the range of relations that are possible.

Thus Perry's greatest use to writing teachers is to provide us with a sort of philosophical map of the changes liberal education seeks to induce in our students. Such a map can help us understand that certain typical problems students have with writing in college should be regarded as problems with accepting the academic community's preferred world view, and not necessarily as problems with achieving "normal" cognition. This is supported by the rough match between Perry's scheme and the characteristics Shaughnessy and Lunsford note in the writing of students who are different from those in Perry's research sample.

In short, Perry provides us with a useful picture of the kind of "cultural literacy" required in a liberal arts college. The term "cultural literacy" refers to the objects of knowledge and the ways of thinking that one must master in order to participate in a particular community.[5] Following Perry we come to realize that the academic community requires students to know, for example, not only what Genesis says about the creation of the earth but also what geologists, biologists, and other scientists say about it. A community of religious fundamentalists might require only knowledge of Genesis. Furthermore, the academic community requires students to know how to evaluate competing ideas according to criteria of logical structure, adequate evidence, and so on; this academic way of thinking might not be valued, for instance, in a fundamentalist community in which tradition or the judgment of a revered authority is sufficient to validate arguments.

Literacy in the more usual sense of the ability to read and write is also highly valued in the academic community. Clearly, literacy is not required for participation in every sort of community. Some communities, too, value reading over writing—when there is a sacred text to be chanted, for example. But the academic community places a high value on writing, and Perry can help us see why. The whole thrust of his developmental scheme is toward an increasing distance on the beliefs of one's childhood. These beliefs can no longer be accepted uncritically as Absolutes, once we realize that well-intentioned people may hold beliefs different from our own. As the pedagogical pluralism which Perry recommends widens the students' perspectives, it also fosters relativism by casting their beliefs into comparative relations with those of others.

Many theorists in composition studies have argued that writing is a unique mode of learning precisely because it fosters this kind of distancing.[6] One's ideas can be more easily examined, critiqued in comparison with other views, and reformulated as they are worked out in written form. Learning to write, then, can be seen as a process of learning to think about one's own thinking, a process which may well be unfamiliar to students in their home communities.

Furthermore, Perry's quasi-spiritual tone should remind us that we tend to invest teaching with moral fervor. I submit that most teachers will recognize in themselves a sort of moral repugnance about bad writing, a feeling that students "ought" to be able to organize and develop their ideas better, even while recognizing that this feeling partakes of the irrational blaming of the victim. Given that we do have this moral investment in the objects of knowledge and the ways of thinking that we teach, it seems hypocritical to pretend that academic activity is value-neutral, that we are merely teaching "thinking," not thinking in a certain way. And it seems more respectful to our students to see what we are doing when we teach as attempting to persuade them to accept our values, not simply inculcating our values.

Is this development desirable? The nature of Perry's scheme makes this question inevitable, fortunately. As in all discussions of cultural literacy the issue is, whose culture will be empowered to set the terms of literacy? Writing teachers are already acquainted with one such discussion in the debate over students' right to their own language. Personally, I believe that the kind of cultural literacy whose development is both chronicled and advocated in Perry's scheme is desirable for all students. But I do not want to begin here the lengthy argument that would be needed to defend that view.

Here I would simply like to make the point that our assumptions about the ends of education are strongly culture-bound, as Perry helps us see. Furthermore, Perry gives us a perspective on all college teachers as, in effect, rhetors. To a high degree we persuade students to our values through our use of language, in lectures, textbooks, informal discussions, and writing assignments. Writing-across-the-curriculum programs do not so much create important roles for writing in all disciplines as they render us self-conscious about the role writing already plays. Some college teachers may not be comfortable with the view of themselves as rhetors, preferring to see themselves as investigators, reporters, value-neutral conveyors of truth. Perry's most important contribution to writing instruction may well be the critique he implies of this positivistic view of the teacher's role.

NOTES

1. "Examsmanship and the Liberal Arts," in *Examining at Harvard College*, ed. L. Bramson (Cambridge, Mass.: Faculty of the Arts and Sciences, Harvard University, 1963).

2. "The Content of Basic Writers' Essays," *College Composition and Communication*, 31 (1980), 279–283, 285.

3. This new, experimental composition program was described in a paper presented by Professor Gene Krupa of the University of Iowa at the 1983 Conference on College Composition and Communication. Professor Krupa did not want to draw any conclusions yet about its worth.

4. See, for example, Kiyo Morimoto, "Notes on the Context for Learning," *Harvard Educational Review*, 43 (1973), 245–257.

5. For a definition of the term, and an argument in favor of a cultural literacy similar to that in Perry's scheme, see Richard Hoggart, "The Importance of Literacy," *Journal of Basic Writing*, 3 (1980), 74–87.

6. See, for example, Janet Emig, "Writing as a Mode of Learning," *College Composition and Communication*, 28 (1977), 122–128; and Linda Flower, "Writer-Based Prose: A Cognitive Basis for Problems in Writing," *College English*, 41 (1979), 19–37.

Is Teaching Still Possible?

Writing, Meaning, and Higher Order Reasoning

ANN E. BERTHOFF

In the memorable disquisition with which he begins *Permanence and Change* (Indianapolis, Ind.: Bobbs Merrill, 1954), Kenneth Burke explains how thinking which does not include thinking about thinking is merely problem-solving, an activity carried out very well by trouts.

> Though all organisms are critics in the sense that they interpret the signs about them, the experimental speculative technique made available by speech would seem to single out the human species as the only one possessing an equipment for going beyond the criticism of experience to a criticism of criticism. We not only interpret the characters of events. . . . We may also interpret our interpretations. (pp. 5–6)

That species-specific capacity for thinking about thinking, for interpreting interpretations, for knowing our knowledge, is, I think, the chief resource for any teacher and the ground of hope in the enterprise of teaching reading and writing.

I plan to be cheerful but there is a certain amount of setting aside which needs to be done before I can confidently claim that teaching is still possible. About half my time will go to nay-saying: I want first to assess the hazards of developmental models and the positivist views of language which underwrite them. I will turn then to a consideration of how alternative views of language and learning can help us invent a pedagogy that views reading and writing as interpretation and the making of meaning.

Reprinted from *College English* 46.8 (December 1984): 743–55. Used with permission.

What we have these days is properly described, I think, as a pedagogy of exhortation: "Feel comfortable. . . . Wake up! . . . Find something you're interested in. . . . Get your thesis statement. . . . Say what you really think. . . . Go over your paper and take out all unnecessary words." But exhortation, whether left-wing or right-wing, is not instructive. (No writer ever puts in words which he or she thinks are unnecessary; learning to discover that some *are* is one of the chief challenges in learning to write.) What must supplant the pedagogy of exhortation is a "pedagogy of knowing." The phrase is Paulo Freire's, and he means by it what Socrates, Montessori, Jane Addams, I. A. Richards, Roger Ascham, or other great teachers would have meant, namely, that unless and until the mind of the learner is engaged, no meaning will be made, no knowledge can be won.

What chiefly forestalls our moving from a pedagogy of exhortation to a pedagogy of knowing is a dependence on a view of language which cannot account *for* meaning nor give an account *of* meanings. A positivist conception of language as a "communication medium," as a set of muffin tins into which the batter of thought is poured, leads to question-begging representations and models of the composing process. Understanding what a pedagogy of knowing would involve is prevented by an unhealthy confusion about what development means and a damaging dependence on the stage models which cognitive psychologists have elaborated, supposedly for the benefit of rhetoricians as well as for guidance counsellors, therapists, curriculum designers, and the publishers of values clarification kits.

Let me begin with a passage from an article by a rhetorician who is discussing cross-disciplinary programs.

> Since the early 1970s evidence has been accumulating which suggests that up to fifty percent of the adolescent population in this country fail to make the transition from the concrete operational stage to formal operations by the time they have reached late high school or college age. Judging from this empirical research, it would appear that as many as half of our students from junior high on into adulthood are unable to think abstractly, to process and produce logical propositions.[1]

Three points are notable: First, the Piagetian model, which is of course intended to represent the stages of development of the language and thought of the child, is here applied to the reasoning of young adults; second, "empirical research" is taken as providing evidence in support of certain claims about learning; third, the failure to reach the stage of formal operations is made equivalent to an inability to "think abstractly," which, in turn, is identified as processing and producing logical propositions. These are all misconceptions. The attempt to apply the Piagetian stage model to non-children is futile; the claim that empirical research supports the efficacy of doing so is false; the identification of abstract thought with processing propositions begs the question of what constitutes that process.

What the child does or does not do may look like what the incompetent or deficient or uneducated adult does or does not do, but it does not follow that the two instances are alike so far as motivation or function are concerned. Just so, the savage is not a child; the lunatic is not a poet; the chimp who has been taught sign language cannot be said to be using it as either the hearing or deaf human being does. To see the similarities without noting the differences is to settle for pseudo-concepts, in Vygotsky's phrase.

If we do form a concept of language as not just a medium of communication but a means of making meaning, we preclude a dependence on empirical research to find out what is happening in our classrooms, to see what writers do when they compose. If you start with a working concept of language as a means of making meaning, you are recognizing that language can only be studied by means of language. Understood in such terms as *context, purpose, intention, import, reference, significance, ambiguity, representation,* and so on, linguistic structures or texts or speech acts can only be studied by interpreting the interdependencies of meanings—and by interpreting our interpretations. But if these conceptions are central, what is there for empirical researchers to investigate? Empiricists do not generally recognize that all method, including scientific method, entails interpretation; they do not generally recognize that there are no raw data; there are no self-sufficient facts; there is no context-free evaluation. Their method is not to recognize the fact that all knowledge is mediated and that facts must be formulated, but to proceed as if interpretation were supererogatory. Empirical researchers leave out of account meaning because they have no means of accounting for it. I. A. Richards observed of this kind of investigator that he "does not know how to respect the language."

> He does not yet have a conception of the language which would make it respectable. He thinks of it as a code and has not yet learned that it is an organ—the supreme organ of the mind's self-ordering growth. Despite all his claims to be expert in collecting, reporting, comparing, and systematizing linguistic facts, he has not yet apprehended the greatest of them all: that language is an instrument for controlling our becoming.[2]

Some of the human sciences have seen the folly of denying the very subject which should be at the heart of the study of the language animal, the *animal symbolicum.* The anthropologist Clifford Geertz, in a wonderful essay called "Thick Description," shows just what it means to ask questions about what human beings are doing.[3] He undertakes to explain how context and perspective function in interpretation by subjecting an example of Gilbert Ryle's to analysis: A boy is seen to wink; another boy has a tic which involves his eyelid; a third boy is seen practicing an imitation of the boy with the tic. Try describing these "behaviors," as the empirical researcher would call them, and watch two of them become human acts, motivated and meaningful—and subject to interpretation.

If meaning is set aside in the search for "data," the findings will not then be applicable to the making of meaning. But composition specialists who follow psycholinguistic principles of analysis want to have it both ways: their empirical research requires that meaning be left out of account, but they also want to claim that their findings are relevant to pedagogy. What writers do is thus confused with what psycholinguists want to study. This methodological pitfall is impossible to avoid when the investigator is guided by a conception of language as a code.[4]

The empiricist needs something to measure, and cohesive devices can be counted, once there is a taxonomy. They are a feature of discourse analysis, which is not, as one might have thought, a matter of studying the dialectic of what-is-said and what-is-meant; it is not the analysis of intention and recalcitrant linguistic structures in dialectic, the relationship that makes the representation of meaning possible; it is by no means simply a fancy name for "critical reading": discourse analysis is the study of "information management," "thematic structure," "sentence rules," and, preeminently, of "cohesion." Now the "cohesiveness" of a text is not the same thing as "coherence." Coherence is mentalistic; it isn't there on the page; it cannot be measured and graphed; it can only be interpreted in terms of the emergent meanings of the writer. But for the psycholinguistic investigator, it is not writers who produce texts; texts are created by cohesive devices.

At a recent conference I heard a psycholinguist explain how, in order to foreground the cohesive devices, he had to reduce the role of meaning. The first problem in the design of his experiment was to find a passage or a stretch of discourse in which meaning was not important so that it would be easier to measure the responsiveness of college students to cohesive devices. He spent some time in preparing the text, but I wondered why he didn't simply excise something from any textbook in any discipline published in any year, since they are generally written so that readers will not be irritated or distracted by the need to interpret what is being said in an attempt to understand what was intended.

This kind of empirical research institutionalizes the pedagogy of exhortation: "Does your paper flow? If not, check your transitions. Can your reader follow you? Be sure to give him clues." Thus we get papers full of roadsigns pointing in the wrong direction—*however*, when there is no *however* relationship; *on the other hand*, introducing a faulty parallel; redundancy (the uninstructed writer's only means of emphasis); end linkages—which I call Nixonian Syntactic Ligature—with the beginning of each sentence picking up the exact wording of the end of the preceding sentence. Research on cohesive devices easily seeps into composition theory because it sounds scientific and because anything that lets us count will seem helpful in evaluating what we think we are teaching. But the fact that cohesive ties may be identified and classified can easily distract us from the problem of learning how to help writers discover, in the very act of realizing their intentions, the discursive power of language itself, what Edward Sapir meant by calling language heuristic. Empirical research into "discourse acquisition" is likely, I think, to mislead us—to lead us away from thinking about thinking, to keep us from studying the process whereby writers discover the resources of language and learn to control them in the making of meaning.[5]

The challenge to experimental design should be not to reduce meaning or to try to eliminate it; this is a primitive conception of what disembedding involves. The challenge to experimental design is not to dispense with meaning but to control language so that there are not too many meanings at a time; so that the learners can discern, in I. A. Richards' words, "the partially parallel task" (*Speculative Instruments*, p. 96) when they confront it; so that the teacher, by means of a careful sequence of lessons or assignments, can assure that the students are conscious of their minds in action, can develop their language by means of exercising deliberate choice. Positivists see no virtue whatsoever in consciousness of consciousness since they model conceptualization on motor skills—and everybody knows that there consciousness becomes self-consciousness: you'll fall off the bicycle if you think hard about what you're doing. What is forgotten is that wherever language is concerned we are dealing with symbolic acts. Consciousness there is not that "self" consciousness which is so destructive but Freire's "conscientization" or Burke's "interpretation of our interpretations" or Richards' "comprehending our comprehensions more comprehensively" or Coleridge's "knowing our knowledge" or Cassirer's "confrontation of an act of awareness" and so on. Consciousness of consciousness is entailed in our activity as language animals.

If psychologists would read Susanne K. Langer's *Mind: An Essay on Human Feeling*, they would have a clearer idea of what they are about. Or they could read a little phenomenology, but psychology is usually about a generation behind. Thus psychologists have recently taken up structuralism, just as it's being laid to rest elsewhere. And before that it was operationalism, which fed itself on hard data. Robert Oppenheimer, in a brilliant talk to the American Psychological Association in 1955, urged the members not to mimic a determinist physics "which is not there any more" ("Analogy in Science," reprinted in *Reclaiming the Imagination*, pp. 189–202). He suggested, rather, that they listen to a man named Jean Piaget. Nowadays, when psychology is awash in Piagetian concepts, it is hard to imagine that this warning was necessary, but Oppenheimer realized that those in charge were the successors to those whom William James had called "brass instrument psychologists." Oppenheimer said: "I make this plea not to treat too harshly those who tell you a story, having observed carefully without having established that they are sure that the story is the whole story and the general story" (p. 201).

The story Piaget had to tell was certainly interesting, but it isn't the whole story or the general story, and some psychologists, by examining Piaget's experimental designs very carefully, have shown how and where he went wrong. I call your attention to an excellent little book, *Children's Minds*, by Margaret Donaldson (New York: Norton, 1979). (She is neither polemical about Piaget nor worshipful of some anti-Piaget.) Dozens of experiments are described which offer alternative explanations of children's responses to certain questions and situations designed to test their cognitive skills. They clearly establish that Piaget's findings, in instance after instance, are the artifacts of his procedures. The alleged incapacity to "decenter" is seen to be a matter of difficulty in locomotion and movement and not in a lack of "object concept" or an incapacity to entertain other points of view. It seems clear that children who made "egocentric" responses in various experiments of Piaget did not fully understand what they were supposed to do.

Margaret Donaldson writes in one of the summaries:

> Children are not at any stage as egocentric as Piaget has claimed . . . [they] are not so limited in ability to reason deductively as Piaget—and others— have claimed. . . . There is no reason to suppose that [the child] is born with an 'acquisitive device' which enables him to structure and make sense of the language he hears while failing to structure and make sense of the other features of his environment. (pp. 55–56)

The recent corrective experiments she discusses are fascinating, but there are precedents. What Margaret Donaldson's psychologists have done for the semantics and syntax of Piagetian questions, Rudolf Arnheim did for visual representation in Piagetian problems. Ever alert to the powers of visual thinking, Arnheim illustrates what he calls "visual illiteracy" with a pair of drawings in cross section of a water tap in open and closed position, schematic representations used in one of Piaget's perceptual problems. In a series of devastating questions in *Visual Thinking* (Berkeley: University of California Press, 1969) he points out the ambiguities and concludes as follows:

> I am not denying that a person, immunized and warned by years of exposure to mediocre textbook illustrations, mail order catalogues, and similar products of visual ineptness, can figure out the meaning of these drawings, especially if helped by verbal explanation. But surely, if a child passes the test he does so in spite of the drawing, not with the help of it; and if he fails, he has not shown that he does not understand the working of a tap. He may simply be unable to extricate himself from a visual pitfall. (p. 312)

But of course the centrally important critique of Piaget's work came from Lev Vygotsky as early as 1932. Vygotsky's strictures concern not only the relationship of language and thought but also that of learning and instruction.[6] All study of language and thought, Vygotsky argued, must begin with the "unit of meaning," since neither language as element nor thought as element can be apprehended in its real character without the context provided by the other. Speech is not articulated sound plus intention; it is not speech until and unless it is meaningful. Neither language nor thought is meaningful outside a social context—which is to say that purpose and intention are from the first constrained not by a need for "communication" but by a need for representation, which of course invites and demands interpretation. Language is symbolic activity and from the first establishes itself in a social setting. The crucial difference between Vygotsky's procedures and Piaget's is that language is built into Vygotsky's test design and the tester is actively involved in exchanges with the subject. Piaget, Vygotsky thought, did not appreciate the complex dialectic of the learning curve and the role of instruction. The explanation for the misleading questions and the ambiguous directions is to be sought in the fact that Piaget thought that the only way to test cognitive skills was to isolate them as far as possible from language-dependent settings. The failure to understand the interdependence of language and thought is consonant with the misconception of the role of instruction which, like test design, is considered by Piaget in mechanistic terms.

Why should we care about Piaget and his critics? Don't we have enough to do, taking care of course design and teacher training and writing across the curriculum and trying to assure the survival of departments of English and to assuage deans who are counting FTE's—don't we have enough to do without worrying over arguments which may or may not be intelligible or important? The answer is that if we don't understand the grounds for a critical appraisal of theories of cognitive development, if we let our practice be guided by whatever we are told has been validated by empirical research, we will get what we have got: a conception of learning as contingent on development in a straightforward, linear fashion; of development as a pre-set program which is autonomous and does not require instruction; of language as words used as labels; of meaning as a one-directional, one-dimensional attribute; of the human mind as an adaptive mechanism. Thus are we wrecked on the rocks of teaching seen as intervention; of the so-called student-centered classroom; of single-skill correction; of discourse analysis, in which the chief function of discourse is disregarded; of reading instruction in which language is considered solely as a graphic code; of writing seen as the assignment of topics sequenced according to the commonplaces of classical rhetoric, as interpreted by associationist psychology: narrative before description, compare-contrast separate from definition, expression way before exposition; an affective English 101 (Turn off your mind and float downstream) and a cognitive English 102 (Get your thesis statement! Generalize! Be brief! Don't generalize!).

Developmental models uncritically deployed lead to the kind of judgment exemplified in the final sentence of the text I took as my point of departure, the one stating that students can't think abstractly, that they can't "produce or process logical propositions." We should not be surprised that this writer goes on to say that "It is fairly obvious from work done in psychology that we cannot accelerate the transition from concrete to formal operations." What is surprising is the rest of the sentence: "but we may be able to promote its natural development by creating a more natural classroom environment" (Freisinger, p. 163). Why would we aim to promote its "natural development" if we don't think we can "accelerate the transition" to a stage now long overdue? Yet I am cheered by this absurd contradiction, cheered according to the same logic by which Gide was led to praise hypocrisy as a step in the right direction. I think the writer is a better teacher than the theory he explicitly depends on lets him be; so he discards it! He finds another which allows him to speak of promoting natural development in a natural environment. That sounds like somebody who believes that teaching is still possible!

I am now ready to be cheerful. The first piece of good news is that what college students find difficult—what everybody finds difficult, what diplomats and doctors, of medicine and of philosophy, find difficult, is not *abstraction* but *generalization*. These acts of mind are conflated by positivists, but they are not the same. Abstraction is not generalization. This is not a quibble; if it were, our enterprise would be futile and the very idea of education fatuous.

Abstraction is natural, normal: it is the way we make sense of the world in perception, in dreaming, in all expressive acts, in works of art, in all imagining. Abstraction is the work of the active mind; it is what the mind does as it forms. The name for this power of mind used to be imagination. We do not have to teach it: it is the work of our Creator. It is a God-given power or, if you prefer, it is a specific power the *animal symbolicum* has in lieu of a repertory of instincts which obviate the necessity of interpreting interpretations. We do not have to teach abstraction. What we do have to do is to show students how to reclaim their imaginations so that "the prime agent of all human perception" can be for them a living model of what they do when they write. What we must learn to do, if we are to move from the pedagogy of exhortation to a pedagogy of knowing, is to show our students how to use what they already do so cleverly in order to learn how to generalize—how to move from abstraction in the non-discursive mode to discursive abstraction, to generalization. We must strive to "raise implicit recognitions to explicit differentiations": that phrase comes from a book called *The Philosophy of Rhetoric*, published nearly fifty years ago by I. A. Richards. We do not yet have a philosophy of rhetoric, for the very good reason that we, teachers of reading and writing and those responsible for literacy at all levels, have not "taken charge of the criticism of our own assumptions," as Richards urged. The second piece of good news is that there is a semiotics which can guide that enterprise.

It starts from a triadic rather than a dyadic conception of the sign and you can represent it rather easily by drawing two triangles. Draw first an equilateral triangle, pointing upward. At the southwest corner write "Writer or encoder"; at the southeast, write "Audience or decoder" and at the top, write "Message." This constitutes what positivist rhetoricians call the triangle of discourse: It is worthless. As you can easily see, it leaves out purpose, meaning, and intention; it confuses message with signal. Now draw another equilateral triangle and make the base a dotted line. Label the southwest angle "representamen or symbol"; the southeast angle, "object or referent"; at the apex, write "interpretant or reference." You can get from the symbol to what it represents only by means of a meaning, a mediating idea. This curious triangle represents the triadicity central to C. S. Peirce's *semeiotics* and it appears in *The Meaning of Meaning* (New York: Harcourt, Brace, 1944) by Ogden and Richards, a work first published in 1922. I know of no evidence that Vygotsky had read either Peirce or Ogden and Richards, but the triangle with the dotted line appears in an excellent paper of his on symbolization as mediated activity, first published in 1930 ("Mind in Society," reprinted in *Reclaiming the Imagination*, pp. 61–72).

Triadicity is an idea whose time has surely come. It can help us take charge of the criticism of our assumptions about teaching because in the triadic conception of the sign, the symbol-user, the knower, the learner is integral to the process of making meaning. The curious triangle, by thus representing the mediating function of interpretation, can serve as an emblem for a pedagogy of knowing. Indeed, my third piece of good news is that triadicity can help us reclaim imagination and the idea of language as "the supreme organ of the mind's self-ordering growth." I will conclude now with a sketch of this view of language and how it can lead us towards an authentic pedagogy of knowing.

Language seen as a means of making meaning has two aspects, the hypostatic and the discursive. By naming the world, we hold images in mind; we remember; we can return to our experience and reflect on it. In reflecting, we can change, we can transform, we can envisage. Language thus becomes the very type of social activity by which we might move towards changing our lives. The hypostatic power of language to fix and stabilize frees us from the prison of the moment. Language recreates us as historical beings. In its discursive aspect language runs along and brings thought with it, as Cassirer puts it. Discourse grows from inner dialogue (and the differing accounts by Piaget and Vygotsky of that development make a fascinating study). From this earliest activity of the mind, language gradually takes on the discursive forms which serve the communicative function. Because of this tendency to syntax, we can articulate our thoughts; we can think about thinking and thus interpret our interpretations.

Seeing language in this perspective encourages the recognition that meaning comes first; that it is complex from the start; that its articulation is contingent on the mind's activity in a human world. The chief hazard of the developmental model is that it sanctions the genetic fallacy—that what comes first is simple, not complex, and that what comes after is a bigger version of a little beginning. Thus we have the idea that there is first one word and then another, another, another, until there is enough to fill out the awaiting syntactic structures. But this isn't the way it happens. The hypostatic word, the single uttered syllable, is a protosentence; syntax is deeply implicated, we might say, in every human cry. Children let a single word do the work of the sentence until the discursive power of language can draw out and articulate the meaning. The conception of a semantic component added to a syntactic structure is a mechanistic conception which must be supplanted. I suggest as an image of the growth and development of language one of those little wooden flowers which the Japanese used to make— before they turned to silicon chips—a tiny compacted form which, placed in a dish of water, opens and expands, blossoming in the shape of a fully articulated flower. Please note the dialectic: it is the water which acts to release the form. In my extended metaphor, the water is our social life, the essential context for the making of meaning. Cognitive psychologists who deliberately ignore it have not advanced over those early kings whose hobby it was to try to discover which language is oldest. They sequestered newborn twins in castle keep or cottage, in the care of a mute nurse, and breathlessly awaited news of what language it would be, when the babies came to speak. And you can safely bet that the court astrologer — that proto-psycholinguist — saw to it that the first reported syllables were construed as Swedish or Hebrew or whatever language it was that the monarch — that proto-funding agency — expected.

In my opinion the ambiguities of the determinism suggested by any account of natural, normal development can serve as the hinges of our thinking about thinking in the interest of discovering the laws of growth, the interdependency of nature and nurture, seed and soil. Language and learning, like syntax and semantics, are in a dialectical relationship which we must learn to construe and represent so that it is accessible to our students. Just so, we must guide their consciousness of consciousness so that it can become the means of freeing the self from itself: as a pleasant way of resolving that paradox, I recommend Walker Percy's new book, *Lost in the Cosmos: The Last Self-Help Book*. After a startling and instructive analysis of twenty versions of the lost self, we have a chapter on triadicity, the means of reclaiming the self. Dr. Percy is an artist, a scientist, and a philosopher for whom triadicity provides the means of conceiving that symbolic activity which defines the mind.

Because they make interpretation central, triadic models of the composing process are the trustworthy ones we need in developing a pedagogy of knowing. The two I consider most useful are perception and dialogue. Every course I teach begins with observation — with looking and looking again. It is my strong conviction that what is looked at should include organic objects, themselves compositions. But of course we must also "problematize the existential situation," as Freire rather infelicitously puts it. I bring seaweed and crab legs to class, the seed pods of sedges and five kinds of pine cones, but I also ask students to problematize the soda cans and milk cartons left from the last class.[7] (I haven't dared to undertake the archeology of the waste basket: God knows what we might find!) We use my version of the journalist's heuristic, *HDWDWW?* — deliberately constructed to resist becoming an acronym: *How does who do what and why?* How does that come to be on your desk? Who left it there? Why do you leave this junk around? What are these things in evidence of? What is the meaning of this litter? Looking and looking again helps students learn to transform things into questions; they learn to see names as "titles for situations," as Kenneth Burke puts it. In looking and naming, looking again and re-naming, they develop perspectives and contexts, discovering how each controls the other. They are composing; they are forming; they are abstracting.

Perception is non-discursive abstraction; the questioning of perceptions is the beginning of generalization, of discursive abstraction. Perception as a model of the composing process lets us capitalize on the hypostatic function of language. Students can discover that they are already thinking; by raising implicit recognitions to explicit differentiations, they can, as it were, *feel* the activity of their minds. By beginning with meaning, with complexity, we assure that minds will, indeed, be active. As I've been arguing, that complexity must be controlled by the way we use language or it will overwhelm, but the complexity entailed in making meaning should never be put off: *elements of what we want to end with must be present in some form from the first or we will never get to them.* That, I take it, is the chief law of growth.

Dialogue is the other triadic model. The "natural environment" necessary to the growth and development of the discursive power of language requires dialogue. Looking again starts that questioning which is the beginning of dialectic and it should be practiced in dialogue in class, of course, but also in what I call a "dialectical notebook," the facing pages offering a structure which enables the student to talk to herself. Dialogue is essential not only because it provides practice in those other uses of language—speaking and listening—but because it can model that constant movement from the particular to the general and back again which for Vygotsky is the defining characteristic of concept formation. But let me be explicit about this natural environment: it is a *prepared* environment, in the sense in which Montessori spoke of her classroom as a prepared environment. This dialectic of particularizing and generalizing, this conceptualizing, this thinking, though it is a power natural by reason of language itself, though it is natural to the human mind, must be put into practice. Like speech itself, it requires a social context in which purposes can be arrived at, intentions discovered and formulated and represented in different modes of discourse.

If college students find generalizing difficult, it's because nobody has ever taught them how to go about it, and abstraction which proceeds by means of generalizing—*concept formation*, as it is often called—must be deliberately learned and should therefore be deliberately taught. But few methods for doing so have been developed and those which have are, generally speaking, of the type Freire calls the banking model: the teacher deposits valuable information. Developmental models are most dangerous when they distract teachers from recognizing the deficiencies of their pedagogy. When we are told, as we are by almost everybody reporting research, that students are good at narrative but fall apart when faced with exposition, it is not necessary to hypothesize that students have come bang up against a developmental fence. The first step of the analysis should be to look at the character of the assignments, at the sequence of "tasks." In an interesting variation on this theme of "narrative good, exposition terrible," one researcher contrasts how well students do with persuasion and how poorly they do with argument.[8] She reports how intelligently students have jumped through the hoops of compare-contrast, "explain a process," "describe an incident," etc., etc.—all in the interest of composing in the persuasive mode—only to fall flat on their faces with the argumentation paper. And guess where it came from? Not from exploration or dialogue or observation or a close reading of texts. No: it came from an assigned topic on euthanasia. Why is anybody surprised when they get terrible writing from a terrible assignment? "Who is to get the kidney machine?" is no advance at all over "Which is greater, fire or water?" "Provocative" topics stimulate cant and cliché; they breed Engfish; they lead to debate, which is by no means dialectic. Nobody learns from debate because, as Richards often observed, the disputant is commonly too busy making a point to trouble to see what it is.

Assigning topics—the essential strategy of the pedagogy of exhortation—is no substitute for instruction. But the deeper reason for the failure in the argumentation paper is the same as for the proclaimed success in the persuasion paper. Persuasion is the air we breathe; it is the mode of advertisement. But where do our students hear argument? Mine do not have the faintest idea of the conventions of an editorial—and when have they ever heard an authentic, dialectical exchange on television information shows? The discourse we find familiar to the point of being able to reproduce it has nothing to do with developmental stages, once childhood is passed—or maybe even before. You may be sure that prepubescent Presbyterians in the eighteenth century were capable of composing arguments on natural depravity, while pre-pubescent Baptists were writing on grace abounding unto the chief of sinners, and little Methodists were writing on topics like "Must the drunkard be an unhappy man?" My advanced composition students find almost intolerably difficult Huxley's "On a Piece of Chalk," a public lecture which a century ago famously enthralled workers with no secondary education—but Huxley's audience had heard two or three sermons every week of their lives! Argument was the air you breathed, a hundred years ago. I am not, of course, claiming authenticity or moral superiority for those who can argue. I mean only that the capacity to manage disputation is a culture-bound skill and that its dependence on neurobiological development is a necessary but not a sufficient condition.

Ironically, it is sometimes students themselves who misconceive the developmental model. Especially older students fear that they must return to Square One. They have to make it all up, they think. When we ask them, like everybody else, to look and look again, we must, by a careful choice of reading—on the model of malt whiskey, not diet soda—lead them to discover that scientists and lawyers and poets look and look again. Of course we must begin with where they are—as meaning makers. We must, in I. A. Richards' phrase, offer them "assisted invitations" to look carefully at what they are doing—observing a weed or drawing up a shopping list—in order to discover *how* to do it.[9] Our job is to devise sequences of assignments which encourage conscientization, the discovery of the mind in action. That will not be accomplished by setting topics, no matter how nicely matched to the "appropriate" developmental stage they might be.

Rather, in our pedagogy of knowing, we will encourage the discovery of mind by assuring that language is seen not as a set of slots, not as an inert code to be mastered by drill, but as a means of *naming* the world; of holding the images by whose means we human beings recognize the forms of our experience; of reflecting on those images, as we do on other words. We teachers will assure that language is continually exercised to name and establish likes and differents so that by sorting and gathering, students will learn to define: they will learn to abstract in the discursive mode; they will learn to generalize. They will thus be able to "think abstractly" because they will be learning how meanings make further meanings possible, how form finds further form. And we will, in our pedagogy of knowing, be giving our students back their language so that they can reclaim it as an instrument for controlling their becoming.

NOTES

1. Randall Freisinger, "Cross-Disciplinary Writing Workshops: Theory and Practice," *College English*, 42 (1980), 163.

2. *Speculative Instruments* (New York: Harcourt Brace, 1955), p. 9. It is the lack of a philosophy of language that could properly account for meaning which invalidates the procedures so frequently recommended for students of the composing process. George Hillocks, for instance, suggests that inquiry procedures are well-modelled by ethology. (See his article "Inquiry and the Composing Process: Theory and Research," *College English*, 44 [1982], 659–673.) But as Susanne K. Langer has shown in the second volume of *Mind: An Essay on Human Feeling* (Baltimore, Md.: Johns Hopkins University Press, 1972), Frisch, Tinbergen, et al. are unaware of the role metaphor plays in their descriptions; of presuppositions which remain entirely unexamined; of distortions resulting from a failure to differentiate animal and human acts. Ethological interpretations are shown to be pseudoconcepts, generalizations about particular cases, not authentic concepts.

3. *The Interpretation of Cultures* (New York: Basic Books, 1973), pp. 3–30. Reprinted in my *Reclaiming the Imagination*, (Upper Montclair, N.J.: Boynton/Cook, 1984), pp. 226–248.

4. Max Black in an essay on Whorf entitled "Linguistic Relativity" notes "the linguist's fallacy of imputing his own sophisticated attitudes to the speakers he is studying" (*Models and Metaphors* [Ithaca, N.Y.: Cornell University Press, 1962], p. 247).

5. I do not deny the value of analyzing cohesive devices in the context of discourse; this, I take it, is precisely what Richards had in mind when he called rhetoric "the study of how words work." But "discourse analysis," as presently practiced, does not always take into account the interdependence of linguistic and rhetorical functions. It begs the question of the relationship of language and thought, because the positivist conception of language by which it is guided does not provide the means for accounting for meaning. Discourse analysts separate thinking from writing, which they conceive of as the manipulation of *devices*. When Charles R. Cooper tells us in "Procedures for Describing Written Texts" (in *Research on Writing*, ed. Peter Mosenthal and Shaun Walmsley [New York: Longman, 1983]) that the "thinking process leads the writer to choose appropriate strategies and forms for presenting the outcomes of thought *as written text*" (p. 291), he has not been alert to those hazards Vygotsky urges us to avoid by beginning with the unit of meaning. For Professor Cooper it is clearly not part of the procedure for describing, much less for producing, "texts" to take into account the heuristic powers of language or the interplay of feedback and what Richards calls "feedforward." Yet "shaping at the point of utterance" is not exclusively an oral phenomenon.

It should be noted that for Halliday and Hasan, whose taxonomy is widely used, the working concept of a text is as a semantic unit. For an excellent discussion of the interdependence of meaning and grammatical, logical, and rhetorical forms, see Jeanne Fahnestock, "Semantic and Lexical Coherence," *College Composition and Communication*, 34 (1983), 400–416. And see anything Josephine Miles has ever written.

6. See especially "Development of Scientifc Concepts in Childhood" in *Thought and Language*, trans. and ed. Eugenia Hanfman and Gertrude Vakar (Cambridge, Mass.: MIT Press, 1962). Vygotsky analyzes the theories of the relationship of learning and development held by Piaget, William James, and the Gestaltists and then goes on to outline his own theory, the central feature of which is "the zone of proximal development." The interdependence of "scientihc" and "spontaneous" concepts is exactly analogous to that of discursive and mythic forms of thought in Cassirer's philosophy of symbolic forms and Susanne K. Langer's philosophy of mind. The idea of development "upward" in spontaneous conceptualization and "downward" in the formation of scientific concepts is fundamental to Vygotsky's dialectical conception of learning and development as set forth in *Mind in Society: The Development of Higher Psychological Processes*, ed. Michael Cole, Vera John-Steiner, Sylvia Scribner, and Ellen Souberman (Cambridge, Mass.: Harvard University Press, 1978). See especially pp. 78–91.

7. For excellent examples and interesting procedures, see Ira Shor, *Critical Teaching and Everyday Life* (Boston: South End Press, 1980), pp. 155–194.

8. Susan Miller, "Rhetorical Maturity: Definition and Development," in *Reinventing the Rhetorical Tradition*, ed. Aviva Freedman and Ian Pringle (Conway, Ark.: L & S Books, 1980), pp. 119–127.

9. I have borrowed the phrase "assisted invitations" for the exercises in *Forming/Thinking/Writing: The Composing Imagination* (Upper Montclair, N.J.: Boynton/Cook, 1982). Richards returns continually to the importance of the conscious and deliberate auditing of meaning as a means of making further meaning. See Ann E. Berthoff, "I. A. Richards and the Audit of Meaning," *New Literary History*, 14 (1982), 64–79.

Narrowing the Mind and Page

Remedial Writers and Cognitive Reductionism

MIKE ROSE

There has been a strong tendency in American education—one that took modern shape with the I.Q. movement—to seek singular, unitary cognitive explanations for broad ranges of poor school performance. And though this trend—I'll call it cognitive reductionism—has been challenged on many fronts (social and political as well as psychological and psychometric), it is surprisingly resilient. It re-emerges. We see it in our field in those discussions of basic and remedial writers that suggest that unsuccessful writers think in fundamentally different ways from successful writers. Writing that is limited to the concrete, that doesn't evidence abstraction or analysis, that seems illogical is seen, in this framework, as revealing basic differences in perception, reasoning, or language.[1] This speculation has been generated, shaped, and supported by one or more theories from psychology, neurology, and literary studies.

Studies of cognitive style suggest that people who can be characterized as "field-dependent" (vs. those who are "field-independent") might have trouble with analytical tasks. *Popular articles on brain research* claim a neuro-physiological base for some humans to be verbal, logical, analytical thinkers and for others to be spatial, holistic, non-verbal thinkers. *Jean Piaget's work on the development of logical thought* seems pertinent as well: some students might not have completed their developmental ascent from concrete to abstract reasoning. And *orality-literacy theorists* make connections between literacy and logic and suggest that the thinking of some minority groups

Reprinted from *College Composition and Communication* 39.3 (October 1988): 267–98. Used with permission.

might be affected by the degree to which their culture has moved from oral to literate modes of behavior.

The applications of these theories to poor writers appear in composition journals and papers at English, composition, and remedial education conferences. This is by no means the only way people interested in college-age remedial writers talk about thinking-writing connections, but the posing of generalized differences in cognition and the invoking of Piaget, field dependence and the rest has developed into a way of talking about remediation. And though this approach has occasionally been challenged in journals, it maintains a popular currency and encourages a series of bold assertions: poor writers can't form abstractions; they are incapable of analysis; they perceive the world as an undifferentiated whole; the speech patterns they've acquired in their communities seriously limit their critical capacity.

I think we need to look closely at these claims and at the theories used to support them, for both the theories and the claims lead to social distinctions that have important consequences, political as well as educational. This is not to deny that the theories themselves have contributed in significant ways to our understanding of mental processes (and Piaget, of course, shaped an entire field of research), but their richness should not keep us from careful consideration of their limits, internal contradictions, and attendant critical discussions and counterstatements. Consideration of the theories leads us naturally to consideration of their applicability to areas beyond their original domain. Such application often overgeneralizes the theory: Ong's brilliant work on orality and literacy, for example, moves beyond its history-of-consciousness domain and becomes a diagnostic framework. A further problem—sometimes inherent in the theories themselves, sometimes a result of reductive application—is the tendency to diminish cognitive complexity and rely on simplified cognitive oppositions: independent vs. dependent, literate vs. oral, verbal vs. spatial, concrete vs. logical. These oppositions are textbook-neat, but, as much recent cognitive research demonstrates, they are narrow and misleading. Yet another problem is this: these distinctions are usually used in a way meant to be value-free (that is, they highlight differences rather than deficits in thinking), but, given our culture, they are anything but neutral. Social and political hierarchies end up encoded in sweeping cognitive dichotomies.

In this article I would like to reflect on the problems with and limitations of this particular discourse about remediation. To do this, I'll need to provide a summary of the critical discussion surrounding each of the theories in its own field, for that complexity is too often lost in discussions of thought and writing. As we move through the essay, I'll point out the problems in applying these theories to the thought processes of poor writers. And, finally, I'll conclude with some thoughts on studying cognition and writing in less reductive ways.

COGNITIVE STYLE:
FIELD DEPENDENCE-INDEPENDENCE

Cognitive style, broadly defined, is an "individual's characteristic and consistent manner of processing and organizing what he [or she] sees and thinks about" (Harré and Lamb 98). In theory, cognitive style is separate from verbal, quantitative, or visual intelligence; it is not a measure of how much people know or how well they mentally perform a task, but the manner in which they perform, their way of going about solving a problem, their style. Cognitive style research emerges out of the study of individual differences, and there have been a number of theories of cognitive style proposed in American and British psychology since the late 40's. Varied though they are, all the theories discuss style in terms of a continuum existing between two polar opposites: for example, reflectivity vs. impulsivity, analytic vs. global, complexity vs. simplicity, levelling vs. sharpening, risk-taking vs. cautiousness, field-dependence vs. field-independence. Field dependence-independence, first described by Herman A. Witkin in 1949, is, by far, the most researched of the cognitive styles, and it is the style that seems to be most discussed in composition circles.

The origins of the construct are, as Witkin, Moore, Goodenough, and Cox note, central to its understanding. Witkin's first curiosity concerned the degree to which people use their surrounding visual environment to make judgments about the vertical position of objects in a field. Witkin devised several devices to study this issue, the best known being the Rod and Frame Test. A square frame on a dark background provides the surrounding visual field, and a rod that rotates within it is the (potentially) vertical object. Both the frame and the rod can separately be rotated clockwise or counter-clockwise, and "[t]he subject's task is to adjust the rod to a position where he perceives it as upright, while the frame around it remains in its initial position of tilt" ("Field-Dependent" 3). Witkin, et al.'s early findings revealed some interesting individual differences:

> For some, in order for the rod to be apprehended as properly upright, it must be fully aligned with the surrounding frame, whatever the position of the frame. If the frame is tilted 30 [degrees] to the right, for example, they will tilt the rod 30 [degrees] to the right, and say the rod is perfectly straight in that position. At the opposite extreme of the continuous performance

range are people who adjust the rod more or less close to the upright in making it straight, regardless of the position of the surrounding frame. They evidently apprehend the rod as an entity discrete from the prevailing visual frame of reference and determine the uprightness of the rod according to the felt position of the body rather than according to the visual frame immediately surrounding it. ("Field-Dependent" 3–4)

A subject's score is simply the number of degrees of actual tilt of the rod when the subject claims it is straight.

Witkin and his associates later developed another measure—one that was much less cumbersome and could be given to many people at once—The Embedded Figures Test.[2] Witkin, et al. considered the Embedded Figures Test to be similar to the Rod and Frame Test in its "essential perceptual structure." The subject must locate a simple geometric design in a complex figure, and "once more what is at issue is the extent to which the surrounding visual framework dominates perception of the item within it" (6). A subject's score on the test is the number of such items he or she can disembed in a set time.

The "common denominator" between the two tests is "the extent to which the person perceives part of the field as discrete from the surrounding field as a whole, rather than embedded in the field; or the extent to which the organization of the prevailing field determines perception of its components" (7). Put simply, how strong is our cognitive predisposition to let surrounding context influence what we see? Witkin soon began to talk of the differences between field dependence vs. independence as differences between articulated (or analytic) vs. global perception:

> At one extreme there is a consistent tendency for experience to be global and diffuse; the organization of the field as a whole dictates the manner in which its parts are experienced. At the other extreme there is a tendency for experience to be delineated and structured; parts of a field are experienced as discrete and the field as a whole organized. To these opposite poles of the cognitive styles we may apply the labels "global and articulated." ("Psychological Differentiation" 319)

Witkin's tests were tapping interesting individual differences in perception and cognition, but the really tantalizing findings emerged as Witkin and his colleagues began pursuing a wide-ranging research agenda that, essentially, sought correlations between performance on field dependence-independence tests and performance on a variety of other cognitive, behavioral, and personality tests, measures, and activities. Hundreds of these studies followed, ranging from the insightful (correlating cognitive style with the way teachers structure social science concepts) to the curious (correlating cognitive style with the shortness of women's skirts). Some of the studies yielded low correlations, and some were inconclusive or were contradictory—but, in general, the results, as summarized by educational psychologist Merlin Wittrock, resulted in the following two profiles:

♦ To the degree that people score high on field independence they tend to be: "relatively impersonal, individualistic, insensitive to others and their reinforcements, interested in abstract subject matter, and intrinsically motivated. They have internalized frames of reference, and experience themselves as separate or differentiated from others and the environment. They tend to use previously learned principles and rules to guide their behavior" (93).

♦ To the degree that people score low on field independence they are, by default, field-dependent, and they tend to be: "more socially oriented, more aware of social cues, better able to discern feelings of others from their facial expressions, more responsive to a myriad of information, more dependent on others for reinforcement and for defining their own beliefs and sentiments, and more in need of extrinsic motivation and externally defined objectives" (93).

The tendency of the field-independent person to perceive particular shapes and orientations despite context, and the tendency of the field-dependent person to let "the organization of the field as a whole dictate the manner in which its parts are experienced" seemed to be manifesting themselves in motivation, cognition, and personality. A few relatively simple tests were revealing wide-ranging differences in the way people think and interact.

The psychometric neatness of this work seems a little too good to be true, and, in fact, problems have been emerging for some time. My discussion of them will be oriented toward writing.

You'll recall that it is central to the theory that cognitive style is not a measure of ability, of how well people perform a task, but a measure of their manner of performance, their style. If we applied this notion to writing, then, we would theoretically expect to find interesting differences in the way discourse is produced, in the way a rhetorical act is conceived and executed: maybe the discourse of field independents would be more analytical and impersonal while field-dependent discourse would be richer in social detail. But these differences should not, theoretically, lead to gross differences in quality. By some general measure, papers written by field-dependent and field-independent students should have equal possibility of being acceptable discourse. They would just be different. However, the most detailed and comprehensive cognitive style study of college-level writers I've yet seen yields this: papers written by field-dependent students are simply poor papers, and along most dimensions—spelling, grammar, development (Williams). This doesn't fit. Conclusions emerge, but they don't jibe with what the theory predicts.

Such conceptual and testing perplexities are rooted, I believe, in the field dependence-independence work itself. My review of the psychological literature revealed seven problems with the construct, and they range from the technical to the conceptual level.

For cognitive style to be a legitimate construct, it has to be distinct from general intelligence or verbal ability or visual acuity, because cognitive style is not intended to be a measure of how "smart" someone is, but of the manner in which she or he engages in an intellectual task. Unfortunately, there are a number of studies which suggest that field dependence-independence significantly overlaps with measures of intelligence, which are, themselves, complex and controversial. As early as 1960, Lee J. Cronbach wrote in his authoritative *Essentials of Psychological Testing*: "General reasoning or spatial ability accounts for much of Embedded Figures performance as does difficulty in handling perceptual interference" (549). In 1972, Philip Vernon, also a prominent researcher of individual differences, reviewed studies that investigated relations between scores on field dependence-independence and various measures of "visual intelligence." He concluded that "the strong positive correlation with such a wide range of spatial tests is almost embarrassing" (368). And after conducting his own study, Vernon declaimed that Embedded Figures Tests "do not define a factor distinct from general intelligence . . . and spatial ability or visualization" (386). Things become more complicated. Vernon, and other researchers (see, for example, Linn and Kyllonen), present factor-analytic data that suggest that determining the position of the rod within the frame and disembedding the hidden figures tap *different* mental constructs, not the unitary construct Witkin had initially postulated.[3] It is possible, of course, that different aspects of field dependence-independence are being tapped by the different tests and that two of them should be administered together—as Witkin, in fact, recommended. But even if researchers used multiple measures (as few have—most use only the Embedded Figures Test because of its utility), the problem of overlap with measures of intelligence would remain. In short, it's not certain just what the field dependence-independence tests are measuring, and it's very possible that they are primarily tapping general or spatial intelligence.

There is a further testing problem. In theory, each pole of a cognitive style continuum "has adaptive value in certain circumstances . . . neither end of [a] cognitive style dimension is uniformly more adaptive . . . adaptiveness depends upon the nature of the situation and upon the cognitive requirements of the task at hand" (Messick 9). Now, there have been studies which show that field-dependent people seem to attend more readily than field-independent people to social cues (though the effects of these studies tend to be small or inconsistent—see McKenna), but it is important to note that Witkin and his colleagues have never been able to develop a test that *positively* demonstrates field dependence. The Rod and Frame Test, the Embedded Figures Test—and all the other tests of field dependence-independence—assess how well a person displays field *in*dependence. Field dependence is essentially determined by default—the more a person fails at determining the true position of the rod or the slower he is at disembedding the figure, the more field dependent he is. This assessment-by-default would not be a problem if one were testing some level of skill or intellectual ability, say, mechanical aptitude. But where a bipolar and "value-free" continuum is being assessed—where one is not "deficient" or "maladaptive" regardless of score, but only different, where both field-independent and field-dependent people allegedly manifest cognitive strengths as well as limitations—then it becomes a problem if you can't devise a test on which field-dependent subjects would score well. Witkin, et al. admit that the development of such a test is "an urgent task" (16). It has not yet been developed.

But even if a successful test of field dependence could be created, problems with assessment would not be over. All existing tests of field dependence-independence are, as Paul L. Wachtel points out:

> in certain respects poorly suited for exploration of the very problem [they were] designed to deal with—that of style. It is difficult to organize ideas about different directions of development upon a framework which includes only one dimension, and only the possibility of "more" or "less." (186)

Consider the notion of style. It would seem that style is best assessed by the observation and recording of a range of behaviors over time. Yet the Rod and Frame and Embedded Figures Tests don't allow for the revelation of the cognitive processes in play as the person tries to figure them out. That is, there is no provision made for the subject to speak aloud her mental processes or offer a retrospective account of them or explain—as in Piagetian method—why she's doing what she's doing. We have here what Michael Cole and Barbara Means refer to as the problem of drawing process inferences from differences in task performance (65). It would be unfair to lay this criticism on Witkin's doorstep alone, for it is a general limitation with psychometric approaches to cognition. (See, for example, Hunt.) But Witkin's work, since it purports to measure style, is especially vulnerable to it.

Let us now rethink those composite profiles of field-independent vs. field-dependent people. You'll recall that the correlations of all sorts of measures suggest that field-dependent people are more socially oriented, more responsive to a myriad of information, etc., while field-independent people tend to be individualistic, interested in abstract subject matter, and so on. These profiles can be pretty daunting; they're built on hundreds of studies, and they complement our folk wisdom about certain kinds of personalities. But we must keep in mind that the correlations between tests of field independence and personality or cognitive measures are commonly .25 to .3 or .4; occasionally, correlations as high as .5 or .6 are recorded, but they are unusual. That means that, typically, 84% to 94% of the variance between one measure and the other remains to be accounted for by factors other than those posited by the cognitive style theorist. Such studies accrue, and eventually the theorist lays them all side by side, notes the seeming commonalities, and profiles emerge. You could consider these profiles telling and veridical, but you could also consider them webs of thin connection.

We in the West are drawn to the idea of consistency in personality (from Renaissance humors to Jungian types), and that attraction, I think, compels us to seek out similar, interrelated consistencies in cognition. Certainly there are regularities in the way human beings approach problems; we don't go at our cognitive tasks willy-nilly. But when cognitive researchers try to chart those consistencies by studying individual people solving multiple problems they uncover a good deal of variation, variation that is potentially efficient and adaptive. William F. Battig, for example, found in his studies of adult verbal learning that most subjects employed different strategies at different times, even when working on a single problem. At least in the cognitive dimension, then, it has proven difficult to demonstrate that people approach different problems, in different settings, over time in consistent ways. This difficulty, it seems to me, presents a challenge to the profiles provided by cognitive style theorists.

There are, finally, troubling conceptual-linguistic problems with field dependence-independence theory, and they emerge most dramatically for me when I try to rephrase some of Witkin's discussions of the two styles. Here is one example:

Persons with a global style are more likely to go along with the field "as is," without using such mediational processes as analyzing and structuring. In many situations field-independent people tend to behave as if governed by general principles which they have actively abstracted from their experiences. . . . In contrast, for field-dependent people information processing systems seem to make less use of such mediators. (Witkin, et al. 21)

Statements like this are common in Witkin, and they flow along and make sense in the discussion he offers us—but you stop cold if you consider for a minute what it might mean for people to have a tendency to operate in the world "without using such mediational processes as analyzing and structuring" or, by implication, to not "behave as if governed by general principles which they have actively abstracted from their experiences." These seem like pretty extreme claims, given the nature and limitations of tests of cognitive style. All current theories of cognition that I'm familiar with posit that human beings bring coherence to behavior by abstracting general principles from experiences, by interpreting and structuring what they see and do. When people can't do this sort of thing, or can only do it minimally, we assume that something is seriously wrong with them.

Witkin and his colleagues faced the dilemma that all theory builders face: how to find a language with which to express complex, abstract ideas. (For a Wittgensteinian analysis of Witkin's language, see Kurtz.) And given the nature of language, such expression is always slippery. I think, though, that Witkin and company get themselves into more than their fair share of trouble. The language they finally choose is often broad and general: it is hard to operationalize, and, at times, it seems applicable post hoc to explain almost any result (see Wachtel 184–85). It is metaphoric in troubling ways. And it implies things about cognition that, upon scrutiny, seem problematic. I would suggest that if we're going to apply Witkin's notions to the assessment of writing and cognition we'll need more focussed, less problematic definitions. Now, Witkin does, in fact, occasionally provide such definitions, but they raise problems of a different order. And here again we see the complications involved in connecting Witkin's theory to composing.

In an admirably precise statement, Witkin, et al. note:

The individual who, in perception, cannot keep an item separate from the surrounding field—in other words, who is relatively field-dependent—is likely to have difficulty with that class of problems, and, we must emphasize, *only* with that class of problems, where the solution depends on taking some critical element out of the context in which it is presented and restructuring the problem material so that the item is now used in a different context. (9)

Consider rhetoric and the production of written language. For Witkin's formulation to apply, we would have to define rhetorical activity and written language production as *essentially* involving the disembedding of elements from contexts and concomitant restructuring of those contexts. It seems to me that such application doesn't hold. Even if there were a rhetorical-linguistic test of cognitive style—and there isn't; the tests are visual, perceptual-orientational—I think most of us would say that while we could think of linguistic-rhetorical problems that might fit Witkin's description, it would be hard to claim that it characterizes rhetorical activity and linguistic production in any broad and inclusive way.

Second of all, it's important to remember that Witkin is talking about a *general* disembedding skill, a skill that would be effective in a wide range of contexts: engineering, literature, social relations. A number of contemporary students of cognition, however, question the existence of such general cognitive skills and argue for more domain-specific strategies, skills, and abilities (see, for example, Carey; Fodor; Gardner, *Frames*; Glaser; Perkins). Given our experience in particular domains, we may be more or less proficient at disembedding and restructuring problem areas in literature but not in engineering. Our ability to disembed the hidden geometric figures in Witkin's test may be more related to our experience with such visual puzzles than to some broad cognitive skill at disembedding. If a student can't structure an essay or take a story apart in the way we've been trained to do, current trends in cognitive research would suggest that her difficulties have more to do with limited opportunity to build up a rich network of discourse knowledge and strategy than with some general difference or deficit in her ability to structure or analyze experience.

HEMISPHERICITY

The French physician Paul Broca announced in 1865 that "we speak with the left hemisphere"; neurologists have had clinical evidence for some time that damage to certain areas of the left side of the brain could result in disruptions in production or comprehension of speech-aphasia—and that damage to certain areas of the right could result in space and body orientation problems; laboratory experiments with healthy people over the last 25 or so years have demonstrated that particular linguistic or spatial capacities seem to require the function of regions in the left or right brain respectively (though it is also becoming clear that there is some degree of right hemisphere involvement in language production and comprehension and left hemispheric involvement in spatial tasks); and radical neurosurgery on a dozen or so patients with intractable epilepsy—a severing of the complex band of neural fibers (the commissures) that connect the left and right cerebral hemispheres—has provided dramatic, if highly unusual, illustration of the anatomical specialization of the hemispheres. It is pretty much beyond question, then, that different areas of the brain contribute to different aspects of human cognition. As with any biological structure there is variation, but in 98% of right handers and 70% of "non-right" handers, certain areas of the left hemisphere are critical for the processing of phonology and syntax and for the execution of fine motor control, and certain areas of the right hemisphere are involved in various kinds of visual and spatial cognition.

These conclusions evolve from either clinical observation or experimental studies. Most studies fit the following paradigm: a set of tasks is presented to a subject, and the tasks are either isomorphic with the process under investigation (e.g., distinguishing nonsense syllables like "pa," "ta," "ka," "ba" as a test of phonetic discrimination) or can be assumed, in a common sense way, to tap the activity under investigation (e.g., mentally adding a list of numbers as a test of serial processing). The subject's speed or accuracy is recorded and, in some studies, other measures are taken that are hypothesized to be related to the mental processes being studied (e.g., recording the brain wave patterns or blood flow or glucose metabolism of the cerebral hemispheres while the subject performs the experimental task).

Studies of this type have enabled researchers to gain some remarkable insight into the fine neuropsychological processes involved in understanding language and, to a lesser degree, in making spatial-orientational discriminations. But it is also true that, ingenious as the work has been, the field is still at a relatively primitive state: many studies are difficult to duplicate (a disturbing number of them yield conflicting results), and the literature is filled with methodological quarrels, competing theories, and conceptual tangles. (For a recent, and very sympathetic, overview see Benson and Zaidel.)

In spite of the conflicts, there are various points of convergence in the data, and, in the yearning for parsimony that characterizes science, the areas of agreement have led some neuroscientists to seek simple and wide-ranging characterizations of brain function. They suggest that beneath all the particular findings about syntax and phonetics and spatial discrimination lie *fundamental* functional differences in the left and right cerebral hemispheres: each is best suited to process certain kinds of stimuli and/or each processes stimuli in distinct ways. A smaller number of neuroscientists—and many popularizers—go a step further and suggest that people tend toward reliance on one hemisphere or the other when they process information. This theory is commonly referred to as "hemisphericity" (Bogen, DeZure, TenHouton, and Marsh). And a few sociologically oriented theorists take another, truly giant, step and suggest that entire dominant and subdominant groups of people can be characterized by a reliance on left or right hemispheric processing (TenHouten). We have, then, the emergence of a number of cognitive dichotomies: the left hemisphere is characterized as being analytic while the right is holistic (or global or synthetic); the left is verbal, the right non-verbal (or spatial); the left a serial processor, the right a parallel processor—and the list continues: focal vs. diffuse, logical vs. intuitive, propositional vs. appositional, and so on.

The positing of hemispheric dichotomies is understandable. Human beings are theory-makers, and parsimony is a fundamental criterion by which we judge the value of a theory: can it account for diverse data with a simple explanation? But, given the current state of brain research, such generalizations, to borrow Howard Gardner's phrase, leapfrog from the facts ("What We Know" 114). Gardner is by no means alone in his criticism. My reading of the neuroscientific literature reveals that the notion of dichotomous hemispheric function is very controversial, and the further notion of hemisphericity is downright dismissed by a broad range of neuroscientists, psychologists, psycholinguists, and research psychiatrists:

> [T]he concepts [analytic/synthetic, temporal/spatial, etc.] are currently so slippery that it sometimes proves impossible to maintain consistency throughout one paper. (John C. Marshall in Bradshaw and Nettleton 72)

> [M]uch of perception (certainly of visual perception) is very difficult to split up this way. The alleged dichotomy [between temporal-analytic and spatial-holistic] is, if it exists at all, more a feature of laboratory experiments than of the real world. (M.J. Morgan in Bradshaw and Nettleton 74)

> [T]he idea of hemisphericity lacks adequate foundation and. . . because of the assumptions implicit in the idea of hemisphericity, it will never be possible to provide such a foundation. The idea is a misleading one which should be abandoned. (Beaumont, Young, and McManus 191)

The above objections rise from concerns about method, subjects, and conceptualization. Let me survey each of these concerns.

A significant amount of the data used to support hemisphericity—and certainly the most dramatic—is obtained from people in whom accident or pathology has highlighted what particular sections of the brain can or can't do. The most unusual group among these (and they are much-studied) is the handful of people who have had severe and life-threatening epilepsy alleviated through a radical severing of the neural fibers that connect the right and left hemispheres. Such populations, however, present a range of problems: tumors and wounds can cause disruptions in other areas of the brain; stroke victims could have had previous "silent strokes" and could, as well, be arteriosclerotic; long disease histories (certainly a characteristic of the severe epileptics who underwent split-brain surgery) can lead to compensatory change in brain function (Bogen, "The Dual Brain"; Whitaker and Ojemann). Furthermore, extrapathological factors, such as education and motivation, can, as Bradshaw and Nettleton put it, also "mask or accentuate the apparent consequences of brain injury" (51). And, as a final caution, there is this: the whole enterprise of localizing linguistic function through pathological performance is not without its critics (see Caplan).

Studies with healthy subjects—and there are increasing numbers of these—remove one major difficulty with hemisphericity research, though here methodological problems of a different sort arise. Concern not with subjects but with instruments and measures now comes into focus. Space as well as my own technological shortcomings prohibit a full review of tools and methods, but it might prove valuable to briefly survey the problems with a representative research approach: electroencephalographic methods. (Readers interested in critical reviews of procedures other than the one I cover can consult the following: Regional Cerebral Blood Flow: Beaumont; Lateral Eye Movements: Ehrlichman and Weinberger; Tachistoscopic Methods: Young; Dichotic-Listening Tests: Efron.)

If you hypothesize that certain kinds of tasks (like discriminating between syllables or adding a list of numbers) are primarily left-brain tasks and that others (like mentally rotating blocks or recognizing faces) are primarily right-brain tasks, then neuroelectric activity in the target hemisphere should vary in predictable ways when the subject performs the respective tasks. And, in fact, such variation in brain wave activity has been empirically demonstrated for some time. Originally, such studies relied on the electroencephalogram (EEG)—the ongoing record of brain wave activity—but now it is possible to gain a more sophisticated record of what are called event-related potentials (ERP). ERP methods use the electroencephalographic machinery, but rely on computer averaging and formalization to more precisely relate brain wave activity to repeated presentations of specific stimuli (thus the waves are "event-related"). The advantage of EEG and ERP methods is that they offer a direct electrophysiological measurement of brain activity and, especially in the case of ERP, "can track rapid fluctuation in brain electrical fields related to cognitive processing . . ." (Brown, Marsh, and Ponsford 166). Such tracking is important to hemisphericity theorists, for it can lend precision to their claims.

There are problems, however. EEG/ERP methods are among the most technically demanding procedures in psychology, and that technical complexity gives rise to a number of difficulties involving variation in cortical anatomy, electrode placement, and data analysis (Beaumont; Gevins, Zeitlin, Doyle, Schaffer, and Callaway). And, when it comes to the study of language processing—certainly an area of concern to writing researchers—ERP procedures give rise to problems other than the technical. Most ERP studies must, for purposes of computer averaging, present each stimulus as many as 50 times, and such repetition creates highly artificial linguistic processing conditions. Even relatively natural language processing studies have trouble determining which perceptual, linguistic, or cognitive factors are responsible for results (see, e.g., Hillyard and Woods). So, though hemispheric differences in brain wave patterns can be demonstrated, the exceptional technical and procedural difficulties inherent in the EEG/ERP studies of language processing make it hard to interpret data with much precision. Cognitive psychophysiologists Emanuel Donchin, Gregory McCarthy and Marta Kutas summarize this state of affairs:

> [A]lthough a substantial amount of clinical data support the theory of left hemisphere superiority in language reception and production, the ERP data regarding this functional asymmetry are far from consistent. The methodological and statistical shortcomings which exist in some of the studies cited [in their review article] along with inconsistencies in the others render any decision about the efficacy of ERP's as indices of linguistic processing inconclusive. (239. For similar, more recent, assessments, see Rugg; Beaumont, Young, and McManus.)

In considering the claims of the hemisphericity theorists, we have reviewed problems with subjects, techniques, and procedures. There is yet a further challenge to the notion of hemisphericity. Some hemisphericity theorists believe that since people can be characterized by a tendency to rely on one hemisphere or the other, then such reliance should manifest itself in the way people lead their lives: in the way they solve problems, in the jobs they choose, and so on. Yet the few studies that have investigated this dimension of the theory yielded negative results. Hemisphericity advocates Robert Ornstein and David Galin failed to find overall systematic EEG differences between lawyers (assumed to be left hemispheric) and sculptors and ceramicists (assumed to be right hemispheric). In a similar study, Dumas and Morgan failed to find EEG differences between engineers and artists, leading the researchers to conclude that "the conjecture that there are 'left hemispheric' people and 'right hemispheric' people seems to be an oversimplification" (227). In a more ambitious study, Arndt and Berger gave graduate students in law, psychology, and sculpture batteries of tests to assess verbal analytic ability (for example, a vocabulary test) and spatial ability (for example, a figure recognition test), and, as well, tests to assess hemisphericity (letter and facial recognition tachistoscopic tasks). While they found—as one would expect—a significant correlation between verbal or spatial ability and occupation (e.g., sculptors scored better than lawyers on the spatial tests), they *did not* find significant correlations between the verbal or spatial tests and the hemisphericity task; nor did they find significant correlation between the hemisphericity task and occupation.

A postscript on the above. Failures to find hemispheric differences between individuals of various occupational groups—along with the methodological difficulties mentioned earlier—throw into serious doubt the neurosociological claim that entire *groups* of people can be characterized as being left or right hemispheric. The neurosociological literature makes some remarkable speculative leaps from the existence of left-right dualities in cultural myth and symbol to asymmetries in left-right brain function, and relies, for empirical support, on the results of individual verbal and spatial tests (like the sub-tests in I.Q. assessments)—precisely the kinds of tests that a number of psychologists and neurologists have shown to be limited in assessing left or right hemispheric performance (see, e.g., DeRenzi).

Let me try to draw a few conclusions for rhetoric and composition studies.

It is important to keep in mind that the experimental studies that do support hemispheric specialization suggest small differences in performance capacities, and the differences tend to be of degree more than kind: in the range of 6–12%. Researchers have to expose subjects to many trials to achieve these differences. (One hundred and fifty to two hundred is common; one facial recognition study ran subjects through 700 trials.) And the experiments deal with extremely specific—even atomistic—functions. (Researchers consider the distinguishing of homonyms in a sentence— "bear" vs. "bare"—to be a "complex verbal task.") It is difficult to generalize from results of this type and magnitude to broad statements about one hemisphere being the seat of logic and the other of metaphor. What happens, it seems, is that theorists bring to very particular (though, admittedly, very important) findings about phonology or syntax or pattern recognition a whole array of cultural beliefs about analytic vs. synthetic thinking and logic vs. creativity and apply them in blanket fashion. There is a related problem here, and it concerns the hemisphericity theorists' assumption that, say, distinguishing phonemes is an analytical or serial or propositional task while, say, facial recognition is synthetic or holistic or appositional. These assumptions are sensible, but they are not proven. In fact, *one could argue the other way around*: e.g., that recognizing faces, for example, is not a holistic but a features analysis task. Unfortunately, neuroscientists don't know enough to resolve this very important issue. They work with indirect measures of information processing: differences in reaction time or variations in electrophysiological measures. They would need more direct access than they now have to the way information is being represented and problems are being solved.

Because the accounts of cerebral asymmetry can be so dramatic — particularly those from split-brain studies — it is easy to dwell on differences. But, in fact, there is wide-ranging similarity, overlap, and cooperation in the function of the right and left hemispheres:

> Complex psychological processes are not 'localized' in any one hemisphere but are the result of integration between hemispheres. (Alexander Luria cited in LeDoux 210)

If Luria's dictum applied anywhere, it would certainly be to the "complex psychological processes" involved in reading and writing. Under highly controlled laboratory conditions researchers can show that phoneme discrimination or word recognition can be relatively localizable to one hemisphere or the other. But attempts to comprehend or generate writing — what is perceived or produced as logical or metaphoric or coherent or textured — involve a stunning range of competencies: from letter recognition to syntactic fluency to an understanding of discourse structure and genre (see, e.g., Gardner and Winner 376–80). And such a range, according to everything we know, involves the whole brain in ways that defy the broad claims of the hemisphericity theorists. When students have trouble structuring an argument or providing imagistic detail, there is little neurophysiological evidence to support contentions that their difficulties originate in organic predisposition or social conditioning to rely on one hemisphere or the other.

JEAN PIAGET AND STAGES OF COGNITIVE DEVELOPMENT

Piaget's theory of cognitive development is generally held to be, even by its revisors and detractors, the modern West's most wide-ranging and significant account of the way children think. The theory, which Piaget began to articulate over 50 years ago, covers infancy to adolescence and addresses the development of scientific and mathematical reasoning, language, drawing, morality, and social perception; it has shaped the direction of inquiry into childhood cognition; and it has led to an incredible number of studies, a good many of which have been cross-cultural. In holding to the focus of this article, then, there's a lot I'll have to ignore—I'll be limiting myself to those aspects of Piaget's theory that have been most widely discussed in reference to college-age writers.

Though Piaget and his colleagues adjusted their theory to account for the wealth of data being generated by researchers around the world, there are several critical features that remain central to the theory. Piaget's theory is a stage theory. He posits four general stages (some with substages), and all children pass through them in the same order. A child's reasoning at each stage is *qualitatively* different from that at earlier or later stages, though the knowledge and strategies of earlier stages are incorporated into later ones. During any given stage, the child reasons in *similar* ways regardless of the kinds of problems she or he faces, and Piaget tended to rule out the possibility that, during a given stage, a child could be trained to reason in much more sophisticated ways. Passage, evolution really, from one stage to the next occurs over time, an interaction of genetic processes and engagement with the world. The child continually assimilates new information which both reshapes and is reshaped by the knowledge structures the child currently has—and, as the child continues to interact with the world, she or he experiences discontinuities between the known and the new, and these discontinuities lead to further development of knowledge of how things work. Thinking, then, gradually evolves to ever more complex levels, represented by each of the stages.

It is important to keep in mind that Piaget's perspective on cognition is fundamentally logical and mathematical. Late in his life he observed that he did not wish "to appear only as a child psychologist":

> My efforts, directed toward the psychogenesis of thought, were for me only a link between two dominant preoccupations: the search for the mechanisms of biological adaptation and the analysis of that higher form of adaptation which is scientific thought, the epistemological interpretation of which has always been my central aim. (in Gruber and Vonèche xi)

With this perspective in mind, let us very briefly consider the stages of Piaget's theory that are appropriated to discussions of college-age remedial writers.

♦ *Concrete Operational* (6–7 to 11–12 years). The cognitive milestone here is that children are freed from immediate perception and enter the realm of logical—if concrete—operations. They can use logic to solve everyday problems, can take other points of view, can simultaneously take into account more than one perspective. In many ways, though, the child's reasoning is still linked to the environment, to tasks that are concrete and well-specified: "Tasks that demand very abstract reasoning, long chains of deduction, or the recognition that the available evidence is insufficient to reach any conclusion are thought to be beyond the reach" of children at the concrete operational stage (Siegler 89). Children have trouble separating out and recombining variables, performing sophisticated conservation tasks, and solving proportionality problems. They also have trouble planning systematic experiments and understanding "purely hypothetical questions that are completely divorced from anything in their experience" (Siegler 90).

♦ *Formal Operational* (11–15 years). During this stage, children develop into sophisticated logical thinkers—Piaget compared them to scientists—and can solve problems that throw concrete-operational children: like the pendulum task described below. Flavell summarizes the ability of the formal-operational child this way: "His thinking is *hypothetico-deductive* rather than *empirico-inductive*, because he creates hypotheses and then deduces the empirical states of affairs that should occur if his hypotheses are correct . . . The older individual's thinking can . . . be totally abstract, totally formal-logical in nature." (145. For a critical discussion of the notion of stages, see Brainerd.)

Piaget and his colleagues developed a number of tasks to distinguish concrete from formal operational thinking. The pendulum task is representative:

Children observed strings with metal balls at their ends swinging from a metal frame. The strings varied in length and the metal balls varied in how much they weighed; the task was to identify the factor or combination of factors that determined the pendulum's period. Plausible hypotheses included the weight of the metal balls, the length of the strings, the height from which the strings were dropped, and the force with which they were pushed. Although the length of the string is in fact the only relevant factor . . . 10- and 11-year olds almost always concluded that the metal ball's weight played a key role, either as the sole determining factor or in combination with the string's length. Thus the children failed to dis-entangle the influence of the different variables to determine which one caused the effect. (Siegler 89–90)

In the 1970's a number of studies appeared reporting that up to 50% of American college freshmen could not solve formal-operational problems like the pendulum task. The conclusion was that an alarming number of our 18-year-olds were locked at the level of concrete operations, a stage Piaget contends they should have begun evolving beyond by early and cer-tainly by mid-adolescence. These data quickly found their way to a more general readership, and some people in composition understandably saw relevance in them and began to use them to explain the problems with the writing of remedial students. With support of the data, they wrote that up to 50% of college freshmen were locked into the level of the concrete, couldn't think abstractly, couldn't produce logical propositions, couldn't conceptual-ize—and, borrowing further from Piagetian terminology, they speculated that these students couldn't decenter, couldn't take another's point of view, were cognitively egocentric. The last two stages of the Piagetian framework became in application a kind of cognitive dichotomy unto themselves. If students couldn't produce coherent abstractions in writing, if they wrote about what was in front of them and couldn't express themselves on the con-ceptual level, if they described something in writing as though their reader shared their knowledge of it—then those limits in written expression sug-gested something broad and general about the state of their thinking: they might be unable to form abstractions . . . any abstractions; they couldn't decenter . . . at all. There are problems with this line of reasoning, however, and they have to do with the application of the framework as well as with the framework itself.

As any developmental psychologist will point out, there are major con-ceptual problems involved in applying a *developmental* model to adults. Piaget's theory was derived from the close observation of infants, children, and early- to mid-adolescents; it was intended as a description of the way thinking evolves in the growing human being. Applying it to college-age stu-dents and, particularly, to adult learners is to generalize it to a population other than the one that yielded it. There are more specific problems to con-sider as well, and they have to do with testing.

It is important to underscore the fact that Piaget implies broad limita-tions in cognition from specific inadequacies on a circumscribed set of tasks. This is not an unreasonable induction—all sorts of general theories are built on the performance of specific tasks—but it must be pointed out that we are dealing with an inference of major consequence. As developmental psychologist Rochelle Gelman put it: "The child is said to lack cognitive principles of broad significance simply because he fails a particular task involving those principles" (326). It is, then, an inferential leap of some magnitude to say that because college students fail to separate out variables and formally test hypotheses in a few tasks typical of the physics lab, they cannot conceptualize or abstract or tease out variables in any other sphere of their lives. Piaget himself said as much in one of his late articles:

> In our investigation of formal structures we used rather specific types of experimental situations which were of a physical and logical-mathematical nature because these seemed to be understood by the school children we sampled. However, it is possible to question whether these situations are, fundamentally, very general and therefore applicable to any school or professional environment. . . . It is highly likely that [people like apprentice carpenters, locksmiths, or mechanics] will know how to reason in a hypothetical manner in their speciality, that is to say, dissociating the variables involved, relating terms in a combinatorial manner and reasoning with propositions involving negations and reciprocities. (10)

Piaget's tests are clever and complex. To assist in replication, Piaget and his colleagues provided explicit instructions on how to set up the tests, what to say, and how to assess performance. This clarity contributed to the welter of Piagetian studies conducted over the years, many of which supported the theory. A significant body of recent research, however, has raised serious questions about the social conditions created when these tests are given. Most of this research has been done with younger children, and probably the best summary of it is Donaldson's. The thrust of this work is contained in one of Donaldson's chapter titles; when a child performs poorly on a Piagetian task, is it because of a "failure to reason or a failure to understand"? The tasks might be unfamiliar; the child might misunderstand the instructions; because psychological experiments are new to her, she might confuse the experimenter's intentions and "not see the experiment as the experimenter hopes [she] will" (Gelman 324). (See also philosopher Jonathan Adler's Grician critique of Piagetian testing.) What psychologists like Donaldson have done is keep the formal requirements of Piagetian tasks but change the particular elements to make them more familiar (e.g., substituting a toy policeman and a wall for a doll and a mountain), provide a chance for children to get familiar with the tasks, and rephrase instructions to make sure children understand what is being asked. Children in these conditions end up performing remarkably better on the tasks; significantly higher percentages of them can, for example, adopt other points of view, conserve quantity and number, and so on. What limited some children on Piaget's tasks, then, seems to be more related to experimental conditions rather than some absolute restriction in their ability to reason.

A somewhat related set of findings has do with training—one of the more controversial issues in Piagetian theory. This is not the place to recap the controversy; suffice it to say that a large number of studies has demonstrated that brief training sessions can have dramatic results on performance. One such study has direct bearing on our discussion. Kuhn, Ho, and Adams provided training to college freshman who failed at formal-operational tasks. After training, the students were once again presented with the tests, and "most of the college subjects showed immediate and substantial formal reasoning." The authors go on to speculate that the absence of formal-operational performance "may to a large extent reflect cognitive processing difficulties in dealing with the problem formats, rather than absence of underlying reasoning competencies" (1128).

I will conclude this brief critique by considering, once again, the mathematico-logical base of Piaget's theory. There is a tradition in the 20th century West—shaped by Russell, Whitehead, Carnap, and others—to study human reasoning within the framework of formal, mathematical logic, to see logic not only as a powerful tool, but as a representation of how people actually reason—at least when they're reasoning effectively. This tradition had a strong influence on Piaget's theory. In Toulmin's words, Piaget's "overall intellectual goal" was to:

> discover how growing children "come to *recognize the necessity* of" conforming to the intellectual structures of logic, Euclidean geometry, and the other basic Kantian forms. (256)

And as Inhelder and Piaget themselves said: "[R]easoning is nothing more than the propositional calculus itself" (305).

Mathematical logic is so privileged that we tend to forget that this assumption about logic being isomorphic with reasoning is highly controversial; it lies at the center of a number of current debates in cognitive psychology, artificial intelligence, and philosophy. Here is one of many counterstatements:

> Considerations of pure logic . . . may be useful for certain kinds of information under certain circumstances by certain individuals. But logic cannot serve as a valid model of how most individuals solve most problems most of the time. (Gardner, *Mind's New Science* 370)

Formal logic essentially strips away all specific connections to human affairs and things of the world; it allows us to represent relations and interactions within a wholly abstract system. Our elevation of this procedure blinds us to the overwhelming degree to which powerful and effective reasoning can be practical, non-formal, and concrete. As psychologist Barbara Rogoff puts it, "thinking is intricately interwoven with the context of the problem to be solved" (2). She continues:

> Evidence suggests that our ability to control and orchestrate cognitive skills is not an abstract context-free competence which may be easily transferred across widely diverse problem domains but consists rather of cognitive activity tied specifically to context. (3)

Much problem-solving and, I suspect, the reasoning involved in the production of most kinds of writing rely not only on abstract logical operations, but, as well, on the rich interplay of visual, auditory, and kinesthetic associations, feeling, metaphor, social perception, the matching of mental representations of past experience with new experience, and so on. And writing, as the whole span of rhetorical theory makes clear, is deeply embedded in the particulars of the human situation. It is a context-dependent activity that calls on many abilities. We may well need to engage in formal-logical reasoning when writing certain kinds of scientific or philosophical papers or when analyzing certain kinds of hypotheses and arguments, but we cannot assume that the ability or inability to demonstrate formal-operational thought on one or two Piagetian tasks has a necessary connection to our students' ability or inability to produce coherent, effective discourse.

ORALITY-LITERACY

Orality-literacy theory draws on the studies of epic poetry by Milman Parry and Albert Lord, the classical-philological investigations of Eric Havelock, the wide-ranging theoretical work of Walter Ong, and, to a lesser degree, on the compelling, though dated, cross-cultural investigations of thought in primitive, non-literate cultures. The work is broad, rich, and diverse—ranging from studies of the structure of the epic line to the classification schemes of unlettered rural farmers—but as it comes to those of us in composition, its focus is on the interrelation of language and cognition. Various scholars say it in various ways, but the essential notion is that the introduction of literacy into a society affects the way the members of the society think. There seem to be strong and weak versions of this theory.

The strong version states that the acquisition of literacy brings with it not only changes in linguistic possibilities—e.g., subordinative and discursive rather than additive and repetitive styles, less reliance on epithets and maxims and other easily remembered expressions—but *necessarily* results in a wide variety of changes in thinking: only after the advent of literacy do humans possess the ability to engage in abstraction, generalization, systematic thinking, defining, logos rather than mythos, puzzlement over words as words, speculation on the features of language. And these abilities, depending on who you read, lead to even wider changes in culture, summarized, not without exasperation, by social historian Harvey Graff:

> These characteristics include, in typical formulations or listings, attitudes ranging *from* empathy, innovativeness, achievement orientation, "cosmopoliteness," information and media awareness, national identification, technological acceptance, rationality, and commitment to democracy, *to* opportunism, linearity of thought and behavior, or urban residence. ("Reflections" 307)

The operative verb here is "transformed." Writing *transforms* human cognition.

The weak version of the oral-literate construct acknowledges the role literacy plays in developing modes of inquiry, building knowledge, etc., but tends to rely on verbs like "facilitate," "favor," "enable," "extend"—the potential of human cognition is extended more than transformed. Here's Jack Goody, an anthropologist who is often lumped in with those holding to the "strong version," but who, at least in his late work, takes issue with the oral-literate dichotomy. In discussing various differences between literate and oral expression, for example, he warns that such differences "do not relate primarily to differences of 'thought' or 'mind' (though there are consequences for these) but to differences in the nature of communicative acts" (26). So though Goody grants that writing "made it possible to scrutinize discourse in a different kind of way" and "increased the potentiality for cumulative knowledge" and freed participants from "the problem of memory storage" dominating "intellectual life," (37), he also insists that:

> Even in non-literate societies there is no evidence that individuals were prisoners of pre-ordained schemes, of primitive classifications, of the structures of myth. Constrained, yes; imprisoned, no. Certain, at least, among them could and did use language in a generative way, elaborating metaphor, inventing songs and "myths", creating gods, looking for new solutions to recurring puzzles and problems, changing the conceptual universe. (33)

The theory is a sensible one: literacy must bring with it tremendous repercussions for the intellect. The problem is that when the theory, particularly the strong version, is applied to composition studies, it yields some troubling consequences. Late twentieth-century American inner-city adolescents and adults are thought to bear cognitive resemblance to (ethnocentric notions of) primitive tribesmen in remote third-world cultures (or these adolescents and adults think like children, and children think like primitives): they don't practice analytic thinking; they are embedded in the context of their lives and cannot analyze it; they see things only as wholes; they think that printed words are concrete things; they cannot think abstractly.

A little reflection on this application of orality-literacy theory—given its origins—reveals a serious problem of method. The theory emerges from anthropological work with primitive populations, from historical-philological study of Homeric texts, from folkloric investigations of non-literate taletellers, and from brilliant, though speculative, literary-theoretical reflection on what might have happened to the human mind as it appropriated the alphabet. It is, then, a tremendous conceptual leap to apply this theory to urban-industrial Americans entering school in the penultimate decade of the twentieth century. We have here a problem of generalizability.

Now one could admit these problems yet still see some analogic value in applying the oral-literate construct with a hedge—for it at least, as opposed to the other theories we've been exploring, is directly concerned with written language. Fair enough. Yet my reading has led me to doubt the strength and utility of the theory on its own terms. (My concern rests primarily with the strong version. The weak version makes less dramatic claims about cognition, though some of what I found would qualify weak versions as well.) There are problems with what the theory implies about the way written language emerges in society and the role it plays in determining how people lead their linguistic lives and conduct their cognitive affairs. This is not to deny the profound effects literacy can have on society; it is to question the strength of the orality-literacy construct in characterizing those effects. Let me briefly survey some of the difficulties.

Literacy and Society

The historical record suggests that the technology and conventions of literacy work their way slowly through a society and have gradual—and not necessarily linearly progressive—influence on commerce, politics, bureaucracy, law, religion, education, the arts. (See, e.g., Marrou; Clanchy; Cressy.) Furthermore, it is hard to maintain, as the strong version does, that literacy is the primum mobile in social-cultural change. What emerges, instead, is a complex interaction of economic, political, and religious forces of which literacy is a part—and not necessarily the strongest element. Though there is no doubt that literacy shapes the way commerce, government, and religion are conducted, it, as John Oxenham puts it: "would have followed, not preceded, the formation of certain kinds of society" (59). And Harvey Graff, pointing out all the "discontinuities" and "contradictions" in linear, evolutionary assumptions about the spread of literacy, emphasizes that "[n]either writing [n]or printing alone is an 'agent of change'; their impacts are determined by the manner in which human agency exploits them in a specific setting" ("Reflections" 307).[4]

Another way to view the problems with the transformational claims about literacy is to consider the fact that a number of societies have appropriated literacy to traditional, conservative purposes. In such societies literacy did not trigger various cultural-cognitive changes—changes in mores, attitudes, etc.—but reinforced patterns already in place. Again, John Oxenham:

> We have always to bear in mind that there have been literate social groups, who so far from being inventive and trusting, have been content merely to copy their ancient scriptures and pass them on virtually unaltered. It may be, then, that literate people can respond more readily to leadership for change in culture, technology, social mores, but that literacy by itself does not induce appetites for change, improvement or exploration. (52)

There are a number of illustrations of this; one specific case-study is provided by Kenneth Lockridge, whose inquiry into the social context of literacy in Colonial New England leads him to conclude:

> [T]here is no evidence that literacy ever entailed new attitudes among men, even in the decades when male literacy was spreading rapidly toward universality, and there is positive evidence that the world view of literate New Englanders remained as traditional as that of their illiterate neighbors. (4)

It is even difficult to demonstrate causal links between reading and writing and changes in the economic sphere—an area that "modernization theorists" generally thought to be particularly sensitive to gains in literacy. Harvey Graff's study of social mobility in three mid-19th century towns revealed that "systematic patterns of inequality and stratification . . . were deep and pervasive and relatively unaltered by the influence of literacy." He continues:

> Class, ethnicity, and sex were the major barriers of social inequality. The majority of Irish Catholic adults, for example, were literate . . . but they

stood lowest in wealth and occupation, as did laborers and servants. Women and blacks faired little better, regardless of literacy . . . social realities contradicted the promoted promises of literacy. (*The Literacy Myth* 320–21)

Similar assertions are made closer to home by Carman St. John Hunter and David Harmon, whose overview of the research on contemporary adult illiteracy leads to this conclusion:

> For most persons who lack literacy skills, illiteracy is simply one factor interacting with many others—class, race and sex discrimination, welfare dependency, unemployment, poor housing, and a general sense of powerlessness. The acquisition of reading and writing skills would eliminate conventional illiteracy among many but would have no appreciable effect on the other factors that perpetuate the poverty of their lives. (9–12. See also Ogbu.)

The oral-literate distinction can help us see differences in the communicative technologies available to the members of a society, to get a sense of formats, means, and forums through which communication occurs (Enos and Ackerman). But it appears to be historically, culturally, and economically reductive—and politically naive—to view literacy as embodying an automatic transformational power. What is called for is a contextual view of literacy: the ability to read or to write is a technology or a method or a behavior, a set of conventions that interact in complex ways with a variety of social forces to shape society and culture. It is, to use Harvey Graff's phrasing, a "myth" to assume that literacy necessarily sparks social change.

Literacy and Cognition

Let us move now from the social-cultural realm to some of the claims made about cognition. These come from two highly diverse sources: classical philological studies of epic poetry and anthropological studies of thought and language. There are problems with both.

The key work in the classicist vein is Eric Havelock's investigation of Greek culture before and after the advent of the alphabet. In books ranging from *Preface to Plato* (published in 1963) to *The Muse Learns to Write* (1986) Havelock has made the strong claim that pre-alphabetic Greeks, ingenious as they were, were barred from philosophical thought because oral discourse could not generate abstract, propositional language or self-conscious reflection on language as language. To be sure, there are times when Havelock's claims are less extreme, but even in *The Muse Learns to*

Write, a tempered book, one finds questions and statements like these: "May not all logical thinking as commonly understood be a product of Greek alphabetic literacy?" (39) and "it is only as language is written down that it becomes possible to think about it" (112). And such theorizing quickly leads to a troublesome alphabetic determinism.

Havelock's work is compelling, but we must remember that when it comes to cognition, he is operating very much in the realm of speculation. That is, he infers things about cognitive processes and the limits of reasoning ability from the study of ancient texts, some of which represent genres that one would not expect to give rise to philosophic inquiry. Furthermore, even if we accepted his method, we could find powerful counterstatements to his thesis—and some of these are contained in a festschrift issued by the Monist Press. Examining the same texts from which Havelock built his case, University of Chicago classicist Arthur W. H. Adkins provides evidence of abstraction, verbal self-consciousness, and the linguistic resources to engage in systematic thinking. He concludes that:

> Havelock has not as yet demonstrated any *necessary* link between literacy and abstract thought . . . he has not as yet demonstrated that *in fact* the stimulus to abstract thought in early Greece was the invention of writing; [and] some features denied by Havelock to be available in oral speech are found in the Homeric poems. (220. See also Margolis.)

The other line of argument about literacy and cognition comes from twentieth-century anthropological studies of the reasoning of rural farmers and primitive tribesmen. These studies tend not to be of literacy-orality per se, but are appropriated by some orality-literacy theorists. A good deal of this cross-cultural research has involved classification tasks: a set of objects (or a set of pictures of the objects) is given to a tribesman, and the investigator asks the tribesman to group the objects/pictures. The key issue is the scheme by which the tribesman completes the grouping: does he, for example, place a hoe with a potato and offer the *concrete* reason that they go together because you need one to get the other, or does he place the hoe with a knife because he reasons *abstractly* that they are both tools? The Western anthropologist considers concrete reasoning to be less advanced than abstract reasoning, and orality-literacy theorists like to pose literacy as the crucial variable fostering abstract reasoning. It is because the tribesman lacks letters that he is locked into the concrete. This is an appealing conjecture, but, as I hope the previous discussion suggests, literacy is too intertwined with schooling and urbanization, with economics, politics, and religion to be able to isolate it and make such a claim. There are other problems too, not just with the causal linking of literacy and abstraction, but with traditional comparative research itself. Cole and Means put it this way:

> [D]epartures from the typical performance patterns of American adults are not necessarily deficits, but may indeed be excellent adaptations to the life circumstances of the people involved. . . . Which type of classification is preferable will depend upon the context, that is, the number of different types of objects to be grouped and the way in which the materials are going to be used . . . preference for one type of grouping over another is really no more than that—just a matter of preference. (161–62)

In line with the above, it must be kept in mind that because "primitive" subjects tend to classify objects in ways we label concrete does not necessarily mean that they can think in no other way. Consider, as we close this section, a wonderful anecdote from anthropologist Joseph Glick, as retold by Jacqueline Goodenow:

> The investigators had gathered a set of 20 objects, 5 each from 4 categories: food, clothing, tools, and cooking utensils. . . . [W]hen asked to put together the objects that belonged together, [many of the tribesmen produced] not 4 groups of 5 but 10 groups of 2. Moreover, the type of grouping and the type of reason given were frequently of the type we regard as extremely concrete, e.g., "the knife goes with the orange because it cuts it." Glick . . . notes, however, that subjects at times volunteered "'that a wise man would do things in the way this was done.' When an exasperated experimenter asked finally, 'How would a fool do it?' he was given back groupings of the type . . . initially expected—four neat piles with foods in one, tools in another." (170–71. For fuller cross-cultural discussions of concrete vs. abstract reasoning see Ginsburg; Lave; and Tulkin and Konner.)

Literacy and Language

It is problematic, then, to claim that literacy necessarily causes a transformation of culture, society, or mind or that societies without high levels of literacy are barred from the mental activities that some theorists have come to associate with literacy: verbal self-consciousness, abstraction, etc. Perhaps, though, the orality-literacy construct does have value if one strips away the cultural-cognitive baggage; its real benefit might be its ability to help us understand the nature of the language experiences students received in their homes and communities and further help to distinguish between the oral and literate features in their writing. But even here there are problems, for the reality of speaking-writing relationships seems to be more complex than the oral-literate distinction suggests.

Certainly, there are bioanatomical and perceptual differences between speech and writing—differences in the way each is acquired, produced, and comprehended. And if you examine very different types of language (e.g., dinner-table conversation vs. academic prose), you will find significant grammatical and stylistic differences as well. (See, for example, Chafe.) But the oral-literate construct leads us to focus attention too narrowly on the channel, the mode of communication, in a way that can (a) imply a distinctive uniformity to oral modes vs. written modes and (b) downplay the complex interaction among human motive, language production, and social setting. Linguists currently working with oral narratives and written texts suggest that the notion of an oral narrative itself is problematic, for oral traditions can differ in major ways (Scollon and Scollon); that the narrative variations we see may have less to do with literateness than with cultural predispositions (Tannen, "A Comparative Analysis"); that features often defined as literate are frequently found in oral discourse and vice versa (Polanyi; Tannen, "Relative Focus"); that characteristics identified by some as a mark of preliterate discourse—e.g., formulaic expressions—are woven throughout the language of literate people (Fillmore); that while spoken sentences can be shown to differ from written sentences, they are not necessarily less complex grammatically (Halliday); and so on. Finally, it seems that many of the differences we can find between stretches of speech and writing might, as Karen Beamon suggests, depend on factors such as genre, context, register, topic, level of formality, and purpose as much as whether the passage is spoken or written.

These closer examinations of a wide variety of texts and utterances should make us wary of neat, bipolar characterizations—whether dichotomies or simple continua—of oral vs. written language. And it seems to me that this caution about the linguistic reality of the oral-literate distinction could lead to reservations about its contemporary social reality—that is, can we accurately and sensitively define, in late twentieth-century America, entire communities and subcultures as being oral and others as being literate? By what criteria, finally, will we be able to make such a distinction? In asking these questions, I am not trying to downplay the obvious: children enter school with widely different degrees of exposure to literacy activities and with significantly different experiences as to how those activities are woven into their lives. And these differences clearly have consequences for schooling.

What I do want to raise, though, is the possibility that the oral-literate continuum does not adequately characterize these differences. The continuum, because it moves primarily along the single dimension of speech-print, slights history and politics—remember, it weights literacy as *the* primary force in cognitive development and social change—and it encourages, because of its bipolarity, a dichotomizing of modes where complex interweaving seems to exist. Finally, the orality-literacy construct tends to reduce the very social-linguistic richness it is meant to describe. Here is Shirley Brice Heath on the language behaviors of two working-class communities in the Carolinas:

> The residents of each community are able to read printed and written materials in their daily lives and, on occasion, they produce written messages as part of the total pattern of communication in the community. In both communities, the residents turn from spoken to written uses of language and vice versa as the occasion demands, and the two modes of expression serve to supplement and reinforce each other. Yet, in terms of the usual distinctions made between oral and literate traditions, neither community may be simply classified as either "oral" or "literate." (*Ways with Words* 203)

Work like Heath's challenges the sociological and linguistic utility of the orality-literacy construct; in fact, elsewhere Heath directly criticizes "current tendencies to classify communities as being at one or another point along a hypothetical [oral-literate] continuum which has no societal reality" ("Protean Shapes" 116).

What is most troubling on this score is the way the orality-literacy construct is sometimes used to represent language use in the urban ghetto. What emerges is a stereotypic characterization of linguistic homogeneity—all the residents learn from the sermon but not the newspaper; they run the dozens but are ignorant of print. The literacy backgrounds of people who end up in remedial, developmental, or adult education classes are more complex than that: they represent varying degrees of distance from or involvement with printed material, various attitudes toward it and skill with it, various degrees of embracement of or complicated rejection of traditions connected with their speech. Important here is what Mina Shaughnessy and Glynda Hull so carefully demonstrate: some of the most vexing problems writing teachers face are rooted in the past attempts of educationally marginalized people *to make sense of the uses of print.* Print is splattered across the inner city, and, in effective and ineffective ways, people incorporate it into their lives.

There is a related problem. Some theorists link Piagetian notions of cognitive egocentrism with generalizations about orality and conclude that without the language of high literacy, people will be limited in their ability to "decenter," to recognize the need to "decontextualize" what they are communicating, to perceive and respond to the social and informational needs of the other. Certainly, people with poor educations will have a great deal of trouble doing such things in writing, but one must be very cautious about leaping from stunted and limited texts to inferences about deficits in social cognition or linguistic flexibility. Developmentally and sociologically oriented linguists have demonstrated for some time that human beings are not locked into one way of speaking, one register, and develop, at quite a young age, the recognition that different settings call for different kinds of speech (Hudson). Poor writers are not as a population cognitively egocentric; they are aware of the other, of "audience"—some disenfranchised people acutely so. What they lack are the opportunities to develop both oral and written communicative facility in a range of settings. Or they may resist developing that facility out of anger or fear or as an act of identity. They may prefer one way of speaking, most of us do, and thus haven't developed a fluency of voices. But rather than being cognitively locked out of other registers, other linguistic roles, other points of view, they are more likely emotionally and politically barred from them.

It is obvious that literacy enables us to do a great deal. It provides a powerful solution to what Walter Ong calls "the problem of retaining and retrieving carefully articulated thought" (34). It enables us to record discourse, scan and scrutinize it, store it—and this has an effect on the way we educate, do business, and run the courts. And as we further pursue intellectual work, reading and writing become integral parts of inquiry, enable us to push certain kinds of analysis to very sophisticated levels. In fact, as investigations of academic and research settings like Latour and Woolgar's *Laboratory Life* suggest, it becomes virtually impossible to tease writing and reading out of the conduct and progress of Western humanistic *or* scientific inquiry. One of the values of the orality-literacy construct is that it makes us aware of how central literacy is to such inquiry. But, finally, the bipolarity of the construct (as with the others we've examined) urges a way of thinking about language, social change, and cognition that easily becomes dichotomous and reductive. "The tyranny of conceptual dichotomies," Graff calls it ("Reflections" 313). If writing is thought to possess a given characteristic—say, decontextualization or abstraction—then the dichotomy requires you to place the opposite characteristic—contextualization, concreteness—in the non-writing category (cf. Elbow). We end up splitting cognition along linguistic separations that exist more in theory than in social practice.

CONCLUSION

Witkin uncovered interesting perceptual differences and led us toward a deeper consideration of the interrelations of personality, problem solving, and social cognition. Hemisphericity theorists call our attention to the neurological substrate of information processing and language production. Piaget developed an insightful, non-behaviorist method to study cognitive growth and, more comprehensively than anyone in our time, attempted to articulate the changes in reasoning we see as children develop. And the orality-literacy theorists give us compelling reflection on spoken and written language and encourage us to consider the potential relations between modes of communication and modes of thought. My intention in this essay is not to dismiss these thinkers and theories but to present the difficulties in applying to remedial writers these models of mind. For there is a tendency to accept as fact condensed deductions from them—statements stripped away from the questions, contradictions, and complexities that are central to them. Let me summarize the problems I see with the theories we've been considering.

First, the theories end up levelling rather than elaborating individual differences in cognition. At best, people are placed along slots on a single continuum; at worst they are split into mutually exclusive camps—with one camp clearly having cognitive and social privilege over the other. The complexity of cognition—its astounding glides and its blunderous missteps as well—is narrowed, and the rich variability that exists in any social setting is ignored or reduced. This reductive labelling is going on in composition studies at a time when cognitive researchers in developmental and educational psychology, artificial intelligence, and philosophy are posing more elaborate and domain-specific models of cognition.

Second, and in line with the above, the four theories encourage a drift away from careful, rigorous focus on student writing and on the cognitive processes that seem directly related to it, that reveal themselves as students compose. That is, field dependence-independence, hemisphericity, etc., lead us from a close investigation of the production of written discourse and toward general, wide-ranging processes whose link to writing has, for the most part, been *assumed rather than demonstrated*. Even orality-literacy theory, which certainly concerns language, urges an antagonism between speech and writing that carries with it sweeping judgments about cognition.

The theories also avert or narrow our gaze from the immediate social and linguistic conditions in which the student composes: the rich interplay of purpose, genre, register, textual convention, and institutional expectation (Bartholomae; Bizzell; McCormick). When this textual-institutional context is addressed, it is usually in simplified terms: the faculty—and their discourse—are literate, left-hemispheric, field-independent, etc., and underprepared students are oral, right-hemispheric, and field dependent. I hope my critical surveys have demonstrated the conceptual limits of such labelling.

Third, the theories inadvertently reflect cultural stereotypes that should, themselves, be the subject of our investigation. At least since Plato, we in the West have separated heart from head, and in one powerful manifestation of that split we contrast rational thought with emotional sensibility, intellectual acuity with social awareness—and we often link the analytical vs. holistic opposition to these polarities. (I tried to reveal the confusion inherent in such talk when discussing cognitive style and hemisphericity.) These notions are further influenced by and play into other societal notions about independence and individuality vs. communal and tribal orientations and they domino quickly toward stereotypes about race, class, and gender.

Let me say now that I am not claiming that the research in cognitive style or hemisphericity or any of the other work we surveyed is of necessity racist, sexist, or elitist. The conclusions that can be drawn from the work, however, mesh with—and could have been subtly influenced by—cultural biases that are troubling. This is an important and, I realize, sensitive point. Some assert that student writers coming from particular communities can't reason logically or analytically, that the perceptual processes of these students are more dependent on context than the processes of white, middle-class students, that particular racial or social groups are right-hemispheric, that the student writers we teach from these groups are cognitively egocentric.

A number of recent books have amply demonstrated the way 19th and early 20th century scientific, social scientific, and humanistic assessments of mental capacity and orientation were shaped by that era's racial, gender, and class biases (see, for example, Gilman; Gould; Kamin; and Valenstein). We now find these assessments repellent, but it's important to remember that while some were made by reactionary social propagandists, a number were made as well by thinkers operating with what they saw as rigorous method—and some of those thinkers espoused a liberal social philosophy. This is a powerful illustration of the hidden influences of culture on allegedly objective investigations of mind. We all try to make sense of problematic performance—that's part of a teacher's or a researcher's job—but we must ask ourselves if speculation about cognitive egocentrism and concrete thinking and holistic perception embodies unexamined cultural biases about difference—biases that would be revealed to us if we could adopt other historical and social perspectives.

These summary statements have a number of implications for research.

The leap to theory is a privileged move—it is revered in the academy and allows parsimonious interpretations of the baffling variability of behavior. But a theory, any theory, is no more than a best guess at a given time, simultaneously evocative and flawed. Especially when it comes to judging cognition, we need to be particularly aware of these flaws and limitations, for in our culture judgments about mind carry great weight. A good deal of careful, basic descriptive and definitional work must be done before we embrace a theory, regardless of how compelling it is.

A series of fundamental questions should precede the application of theory: Is the theory formulated in a way that allows application to writing; that is, can it be defined in terms of discourse? Given what we know about writing, how would the theory be expected to manifest itself—i.e., what would it mean textually and dynamically for someone to be a field-dependent writer? What will the theory allow us to explain about writing that we haven't explained before? What will it allow us to do pedagogically that we weren't able to do as well before? Will the theory strip and narrow experience and cognition, or does it promise to open up the histories of students' involvement with writing, their rules, strategies, and assumptions, the invitations and denials that characterized their encounters with print?

Beyond such general questions are more specific guidelines for those of us doing psychological research. Once we undertake an investigation of cognition we must be careful to discuss our findings in terms of the kinds of writing we investigate. Generalizing to other tasks, and particularly to broad cognitive processes, is not warranted without evidence from those other domains. If theories like the four we discussed, but others too (e.g., theories of moral development, social cognition, metacognition, etc.), are appropriated that are built on particular tests, then researchers must thoroughly familiarize themselves with the tests beneath the theories and consult with psychologists who use them. People who are going to administer such tests should take the tests themselves—see what they're like from the inside. My mentor Richard Shavelson also urges researchers to administer the tests to individual students and have them talk about what they're doing, get some sense of how students might interpret or misinterpret the instructions, the various ways they represent the task to themselves, what cognitive processes seem to come into play as the students work with the tests. Furthermore, it must be remembered that the results of testing will be influenced by the degree of familiarity the students have with the tests and by the social situation created in the administration of them. How will these conditions be adjusted for and acknowledged? Finally, the resulting data must be discussed as being specific to the students tested. Generalizing to others must be done with caution.

A special word needs to be said here about comparative studies. If we employ hi-lo designs, expert-novice studies, and the like—which can be powerfully revealing designs—we need to consider our design and our results from historical and sociopolitical perspectives as well as cognitive ones. That is, if class, gender, or race differences emerge—and they certainly could—they should not automatically be assumed to reflect "pure" cognitive differences, but rather effects that might well be conditioned by and interpreted in light of historical, socio-political realities. There is currently a lot of talk about the prospect of forging a social-cognitive orientation to composition research (see, for example, Freedman, Dyson, Flower, and Chafe; Bizzell and Herzberg). One of the exciting results of such an endeavor could be an increased sensitivity to the social forces that shape cognitive activity. I've argued elsewhere for a research framework that intersects the cognitive, affective, and situational dimensions of composing and that involves the systematic combination of multiple methods, particularly ones traditionally thought to be antagonistic. My assumption is that the careful integration of, say, cognitive process-tracing and naturalistic observation methods can both contribute to fresh and generative insight and provide a guard against reductive interpretation (Rose, "Complexity").

Much of this essay has concerned researchers and theoreticians, but at the heart of the discussion is a basic question for any of us working with poor writers: How do we go about judging the thought processes involved with reading and writing when performance is problematic, ineffective, or stunted? If I could compress this essay's investigation down to a single conceptual touchstone, it would be this: Human cognition—even at its most stymied, bungled moments—is rich and varied. It is against this assumption that we should test our theories and research methods and classroom assessments. Do our practices work against classification that encourages single, monolithic explanations of cognitive activity? Do they honor the complexity of interpretive efforts even when those efforts fall short of some desired goal? Do they foster investigation of interaction and protean manifestation rather than investigation of absence: abstraction is absent, consciousness of print is absent, logic is absent? Do they urge reflection on the cultural biases that might be shaping them? We must be vigilant that the systems of intellect we develop or adapt do not ground our students' difficulties in sweeping, essentially one-dimensional perceptual, neurophysiological, psychological, or linguistic processes, systems that drive broad cognitive wedges between those who do well in our schools and those who don't.[5]

NOTES

1. For presentation, qualification, or rebuttal of this orientation see, for example: Ann E. Berthoff, "Is Teaching Still Possible?" *College English* 46 (1984): 743–55; Thomas J. Farrell, "I.Q. and Standard English," *CCC* 34 (1983): 470–85 and the replies to Farrell by

Greenberg, Hartwell, Himley, and Stratton in *CCC* 35 (1984): 455–78; George H. Jensen, "The Reification of the Basic Writer," *Journal of Basic Writing* 5 (1986): 52–64; Andrea Lunsford, "Cognitive Development and the Basic Writer," *College English* 41 (1979): 38–46 and Lunsford, "Cognitive Studies and Teaching Writing," *Perspectives on Research and Scholarship in Composition,* Ed. Ben W. McClelland and Timothy R. Donovan, New York: MLA, (1986): 145–61; Walter J. Ong, "Literacy and Orality in Our Times," *Profession* 79, Ed. Jasper P. Neel, New York: MLA, 1979: 1–7; Lynn Quitman Troyka, "Perspectives on Legacies and Literacy in the 1980s," *CCC* 33 (1982): 252–62 and Troyka, "Defining Basic Writers in Context," *A Sourcebook for Basic Writing Teachers,* Ed. Theresa Enos, New York: Random House, 1987: 2–15; James D. Williams, "Coherence and Cognitive Style," *Written Communication* 2 (1985): 473–91. For illustration of the transfer of this issue to the broader media, see Ellen K. Coughlin, "Literacy: 'Excitement' of New Field Attracts Scholars of Literature," *The Chronicle of Higher Education* 29 (9 Jan. 1985): 1, 10.

    2. For a description of the other tests—the Body Adjustment Test and the rarely used auditory and tactile embedded figures tests—see Witkin, et al.

    3. Witkin later revised his theory, suggesting that the rod and frame test and the embedded figures test were tapping different dimensions of the field dependence-independence construct. This revision, however, gives rise to further problems—see Linn and Kyllonen.

    4. Educators and evaluators often seem locked into a 19th century linear progress conception of the way both societies and individuals appropriate literacy. Graff presents a provocative historical challenge to such notions; here's Vygotsky on individual development: "together with processes of development, forward motion, and appearance of new forms, we can discern processes of curtailment, disappearance, and reverse development of old forms at each step . . . only a naive view of development as a purely evolutionary process. . . can conceal from us the true nature of these processes" (106).

    5. Particular sections of this paper were discussed with or reviewed by specialists who provided a great deal of expert help: Susan Curtiss (neurolinguistics), Richard Leo Enos (classical studies), Sari Gilman (research psychiatry), John R. Hayes, Richard Shavelson, and Catherine Stasz (cognitive and educational psychology), Thomas Huckin (linguistics), Robert Siegler (developmental psychology). David Bartholomae, Linda Flower, Glynda Hull, David Kaufer, and Stephen Witte commented generously on the entire manuscript. The project benefited as well from rich conversation with Mariolina Salvatori and Kathryn Flannery. Versions of the paper were read at Carnegie Mellon, Pitt, Indiana University of Pennsylvania, UCLA, Berkeley, CCCC (Atlanta), Penn State, and UCSD. My thanks for all the ideas generated at those conferences and colloquia. Finally, appreciation is due to Sally Magargee for her research assistance and the Carnegie Mellon Department of English and the Spencer Foundation for their support.

WORKS CITED

Adkins, Arthur W.H. "Orality and Philosophy." Robb 207–27.

Adler, Jonathan. "Abstraction is Uncooperative." *Journal for the Theory of Social Behavior* 14 (1984): 165–81.

Arndt, Stephen, and Dale E. Berger. "Cognitive Mode and Asymmetry in Cerebral Functioning." *Cortex* 14 (1978): 78–86.

Bartholomae, David. "Inventing the University." Rose, *When a Writer Can't Write* 134–65.

Battig, William F. "Within-Individual Differences in 'Cognitive' Processes." *Information Processing and Cognition.* Ed. Robert L. Solso. Hillsdale, NJ: Erlbaum, 1975. 195–228.

Beamon, Karen. "Coordination and Subordination Revisited: Syntactic Complexity in Spoken and Written Narrative Discourse." Tannen, *Coherence in Spoken and Written Discourse* 45–80.

Beaumont, J. Graham. "Methods for Studying Cerebral Hemispheric Function." *Functions of the Right Cerebral Hemisphere.* Ed. A.W. Young. London: Academic Press, 1983. 113–46.

Beaumont, J. Graham, A.W. Young, and I.C. McManus. "Hemisphericity: A Critical Review." *Cognitive Neuropsychology* 2 (1984): 191–212.

Benson, D. Frank, and Eran Zaidel, eds. *The Dual Brain: Hemispheric Specialization in Humans.* New York: Guilford, 1985.

Berthoff, Ann E. "Is Teaching Still Possible?" *College English* 46 (1984): 743–55.

Bizzell, Patricia. "Cognition, Convention, and Certainty: What We Need to Know about Writing." *Pre/Text* 3 (1982): 213–44.

Bizzell, Patricia, and Bruce Herzberg. *The Bedford Bibliography for Teachers of Writing.* Boston: Bedford Books, 1987.

Bogen, Joseph. "The Dual Brain: Some Historical and Methodological Aspects." Benson and Zaidel 27–43.

Bogen, Joseph, et al. "The Other Side of the Brain: The A/P Ratio." *Bulletin of Los Angeles Neurological Society* 37 (1972): 49–61.

Bradshaw, J.L., and N.C. Nettleton. "The Nature of Hemispheric Specialization in Man." *Behavioral and Brain Sciences* 4 (1981): 51–91.

Brainerd, Charles J. "The Stage Question in Cognitive-Developmental Theory." *The Behavioral and Brain Sciences* 2 (1978): 173–81.

Brown, Warren S., James T. Marsh, and Ronald E. Ponsford. "Hemispheric Differences in Event-Related Brain Potentials." Benson and Zaidel 163–79.

Caplan, David. "On the Cerebral Localization of Linguistic Functions: Logical and Empirical Issues Surrounding Deficit Analysis and Functional Localization." *Brain and Language* 14 (1981): 120–37.

Carey, Susan. *Conceptual Change in Childhood.* Cambridge: MIT P, 1985.

Chafe, Wallace L. "Linguistic Differences Produced by Differences in Speaking and Writing." Olson, Torrance, and Hildyard 105–23.

Clanchy, M.T. *From Memory to Written Record: England 1066–1307.* Cambridge: Harvard UP, 1979.

Cole, Michael, and Barbara Means. *Comparative Studies of How People Think.* Cambridge: Harvard UP, 1981.

Cressy, David. "The Environment for Literacy: Accomplishment and Context in Seventeenth-Century England and New England." *Literacy in Historical Perspective.* Ed. Daniel P. Resnick. Washington: Library of Congress, 1983. 23–42.

Cronbach, Lee J. *Essentials of Psychological Testing.* New York: Harper and Row, 1960.

DeRenzi, Ennio. *Disorders of Space Exploration and Cognition.* London: Wiley, 1982.

Donaldson, Margaret. *Children's Minds.* New York: Norton, 1979.

Donchin, Emanuel, Gregory McCarthy, and Marta Kutas. "Electroencephalographic Investigations of Hemispheric Specialization." *Language and Hemispheric Specialization in Man: Cerebral Event-Related Potentials.* Ed. John E. Desmedt. Basel, NY: Karger, 1977. 212–42.

Dumas, Roland, and Arlene Morgan. "EEG Asymmetry as a Function of Occupation, Task and Task Difficulty." *Neuropsychologia* 13 (1975): 214–28.

Efron, Robert. "The Central Auditory System and Issues Related to Hemispheric Specialization." *Assessment of Central Auditory Dysfunction: Foundations and Clinical Correlates*. Ed. Marilyn L. Pinheiro and Frank E. Musiek. Baltimore: Williams and Wilkins, 1985. 143–54.

Ehrlichman, Howard, and Arthur Weinberger. "Lateral Eye Movements and Hemispheric Asymmetry: A Critical Review." *Psychological Bulletin* 85 (1978): 1080–1101.

Elbow, Peter. "The Shifting Relationships Between Speech and Writing." *CCC* 34 (1985): 283–303.

Enos, Richard Leo, and John Ackerman. "*Letteraturizzazione* and Hellenic Rhetoric: An Analysis for Research with Extensions." *Proceedings of 1984 Rhetoric Society of America Conference*. Ed. Charles Kneupper, forthcoming.

Fillmore, Charles J. "On Fluency." *Individual Differences in Language Ability and Language Behavior*. Ed. Charles J. Fillmore, Daniel Kempler, and William S.Y. Wang. New York: Academic Press, 1979. 85–101.

Flavell, John H. *Cognitive Development*. Englewood Cliffs: Prentice-Hall, 1977.

Fodor, Jerry A. *The Modularity of Mind*. Cambridge: MIT P, 1983.

Freedman, Sarah, et al. *Research in Writing: Past, Present, and Future*. Berkeley: Center for the Study of Writing, 1987.

Gardner, Howard. *Frames of Mind*. New York: Basic Books, 1983.

——. *The Mind's New Science*. New York: Basic Books, 1985.

——. "What We Know (and Don't Know) About the Two Halves of the Brain." *Journal of Aesthetic Education* 12 (1978): 113–19.

Gardner, Howard, and Ellen Winner. "Artistry and Aphasia." *Acquired Aphasia*. Ed. Martha Taylor Sarno. New York: Academic Press, 1981. 361–84.

Gelman, Rochelle. "Cognitive Development." *Ann. Rev. Psychol.* (1978): 297–332.

Gevins, A.S., et al. "EEG Patterns During 'Cognitive' Tasks." *Electroencephalography and Clinical Neurophysiology* 47 (1979): 704–10.

Gilman, Sander. *Difference and Pathology*. Ithaca, NY: Cornell UP, 1985.

Ginsburg, Herbert. "Poor Children, African Mathematics, and the Problem of Schooling." *Educational Research Quarterly* 2 (1978): 26–44.

Glaser, Robert. "Education and Thinking: The Role of Knowledge." *American Psychologist* 39 (1984): 93–104.

Goodenow, Jacqueline. "The Nature of Intelligent Behavior: Questions Raised by Cross-Cultural Studies." *The Nature of Intelligence*. Ed. Lauren B. Resnick. Hillsdale, NJ: Erlbaum, 1976. 168–88.

Goody, Jack. *The Domestication of the Savage Mind*. London: Cambridge UP, 1977.

Gould, Stephen Jay. *The Mismeasure of Man*. New York: Norton, 1981.

Graff, Harvey. *The Literacy Myth*. New York: Academic Press, 1979.

——. "Reflections on the History of Literacy: Overview, Critique, and Proposals." *Humanities and Society* 4 (1981): 303–33.

Gruber, Howard E., and J. Jacques Vonèche, eds. *The Essential Piaget*. New York: Basic Books, 1977.

Halliday, M. A. K. "Differences between Spoken and Written Language." *Communication through Reading*. Vol. 2. Ed. Glenda Page, John Elkins, and Barrie O'Connor. Adelaide, SA: Australian Reading Association, 1979. 37–52.

Havelock, Eric. *The Muse Learns to Write*. Cambridge: Harvard UP, 1986.

_____. *Preface to Plato*. Cambridge: Harvard UP, 1963.

Harré, Rom, and Roger Lamb. *The Encyclopedic Dictionary of Psychology*. Cambridge: MIT P, 1983.

Heath, Shirley Brice. "Protean Shapes in Literacy Events: Ever-Shifting Oral and Literate Traditions." *Spoken and Written Language*. Ed. Deborah Tannen. Norwood, NJ: Ablex, 1982. 91–117.

_____. *Ways With Words*. London: Cambridge UP, 1983.

Hillyard, Steve A., and David L. Woods. "Electrophysiological Analysis of Human Brain Function." *Handbook of Behavioral Neurobiology*. Vol. 2. Ed. Michael S. Gazzaniga. New York: Plenum, 1979. 343–78.

Hudson, R.A. *Sociolinguistics*. Cambridge: Cambridge UP, 1986.

Hull, Glynda. "The Editing Process in Writing: A Performance Study of Experts and Novices." Diss. U of Pittsburgh, 1983.

Hunt, Earl. "On the Nature of Intelligence." *Science* 219 (1983): 141–46.

Hunter, Carman St. John, and David Harmon. *Adult Illiteracy in the United States*. New York: McGraw-Hill, 1985.

Inhelder, Barbel, and Jean Piaget. *The Growth of Logical Thinking from Childhood to Adolescence*. Trans. Anne Parsons and Stanley Milgram. New York: Basic Books, 1958.

Jensen, George H. "The Reification of the Basic Writer." *Journal of Basic Writing* 5 (1986): 52–64.

Kamin, Leon J. *The Science and Politics of I.Q.* Hillsdale, NJ: Erlbaum, 1974.

Kuhn, Deanna, Victoria Ho, and Catherine Adams. "Formal Reasoning Among Pre- and Late Adolescents." *Child Development* 50 (1979): 1128–35.

Kurtz, Richard M. "A Conceptual Investigation of Witkin's Notion of Perceptual Style." *Mind* 78 (1969): 522–33.

Latour, Bruno, and Steve Woolgar. *Laboratory Life*. Beverly Hills, CA: Sage, 1979.

Lave, Jean. "Cognitive Consequences of Traditional Apprenticeship Training in West Africa." *Anthropology and Education Quarterly* 8 (1977): 177–80.

LeDoux, Joseph E. "Cerebral Asymmetry and the Integrated Function of the Brain." *Functions of the Right Cerebral Hemisphere*. Ed. Andrew W. Young. London: Academic Press, 1983. 203–16.

Linn, Marcia C., and Patrick Kyllonen. "The Field Dependence-Independence Construct: Some, One, or None." *Journal of Educational Psychology* 73 (1981): 261–73.

Lockridge, Kenneth. *Literacy in Colonial New England*. New York: Norton, 1974.

Margolis, Joseph. "The Emergence of Philosophy." Robb 229–43.

Marrou, H.I. *A History of Education in Antiquity*. Madison, WI: U of Wisconsin P, 1982.

McCormick, Kathleen. *The Cultural Imperatives Underlying Cognitive Acts*. Berkeley: Center for The Study of Writing, 1986.

McKenna, Frank P. "Field Dependence and Personality: A Re-examination." *Social Behavior and Personality* 11 (1983): 51–55.

Messick, Samuel. "Personality Consistencies in Cognition and Creativity." *Individuality in Learning*. Ed. Samuel Messick and Associates. San Francisco: Jossey-Bass, 1976. 4–22.

Ogbu, John U. *Minority Education and Caste*. New York: Academic Press, 1978.

Olson, David R., Nancy Torrance, and Angela Hildyard, eds. *Literacy, Language, and Learning*. New York: Cambridge UP, 1981.

Ong, Walter J. *Orality and Literacy: The Technologizing of the Word*. New York: Methuen, 1982.

Ornstein, Robert E., and David Galin. "Psychological Studies of Consciousness." *Symposium on Consciousness.* Ed. Philip R. Lee et al. New York: Viking, 1976. 53–66.

Oxenham, John. *Literacy: Writing, Reading, and Social Organisation.* London: Routledge and Kegan Paul, 1980.

Perkins, D. N. "General Cognitive Skills: Why Not?" *Thinking and Learning Skills.* Ed. Susan F. Chipman, Judith W. Segal, and Robert Glaser. Hillsdale, NJ: Erlbaum, 1985. 339–63.

Piaget, Jean. "Intellectual Evolution from Adolescence to Adulthood." *Human Development* 15 (1972): 1–12.

Polanyi, Livia. *Telling the American Story: A Structural and Cultural Analysis of Conversational Storytelling.* Norwood, NJ: Ablex, 1985.

Robb, Kevin, ed. *Language and Thought in Early Greek Philosophy.* LaSalle, IL: Monist Library of Philosophy, 1983.

Rogoff, Barbara. *Everyday Cognition.* Cambridge: Harvard UP, 1984.

Rose, Mike. "Complexity, Rigor, Evolving Method, and the Puzzle of Writer's Block: Thoughts on Composing Process Research." Rose, *When a Writer Can't Write* 227–60.

_____, ed. *When a Writer Can't Write: Studies in Writer's Block and Other Composing Process Problems.* New York: Guilford, 1985.

Rugg, Michael D. "Electrophysiological Studies." *Divided Visual Field Studies of Cerebral Organization.* Ed. J. Graham Beaumont. New York: Academic Press, 1982. 129–46.

Scollon, Ron, and Suzanne B. K. Scollon. "Cooking It Up and Boiling It Down: Abstracts in Athabascan Children's Story Retellings." Tannen, *Coherence in Spoken and Written Discourse* 173–97.

Shaughnessy, Mina. *Errors and Expectations.* New York: Oxford UP, 1977.

Siegler, Robert S. "Children's Thinking: The Search For Limits." *The Function of Language and Cognition.* Ed. G.J. Whitehurst and Barry J. Zimmerman. New York: Academic Press, 1979. 83–113.

Sperry, Roger W. "Consciousness, Personal Identity, and the Divided Brain." Benson and Zaidel 11–26.

Tannen, Deborah, ed. *Coherence in Spoken and Written Discourse.* Norwood, NJ: Ablex, 1984.

_____. "A Comparative Analysis of Oral Narrative Strategies: Athenian Greek and American English." *The Pear Stories.* Ed. Wallace Chafe. Norwood, NJ: Ablex, 1980. 51–87.

_____. "Relative Focus on Involvement in Oral and Written Discourse." Olson, Torrance, and Hildyard 124–47.

TenHouten, Warren D. "Social Dominance and Cerebral Hemisphericity: Discriminating Race, Socioeconomic Status, and Sex Groups by Performance on Two Lateralized Tests." *Intern J. Neuroscience* 10 (1980): 223–32.

Toulmin, Stephen. "Epistemology and Developmental Psychology." *Developmental Plasticity.* Ed. Eugene S. Gollin. New York: Academic Press, 1981. 253–67.

Tulkin, S. R., and M. J. Konner. "Alternative Conceptions of Intellectual Functioning." *Human Development* 16 (1973): 33–52.

Valenstein, Elliot S. *Great and Desperate Cures.* New York: Basic Books, 1986.

Vernon, Philip. "The Distinctiveness of Field Independence." *Journal of Personality* 40 (1972): 366–91.

Vygotsky, L. S. *Mind in Society.* Cambridge: Harvard UP, 1978.

Wachtel, Paul L. "Field Dependence and Psychological Differentiation: Reexamination." *Perceptual and Motor Skills* 35 (1972): 174–89.

Whitaker, Harry A., and George A. Ojemann. "Lateralization of Higher Cortical Functions: A Critique." *Evolution and Lateralization of the Brain*. Ed. Stuart Dimond and David Blizard. New York: New York Academy of Science, 1977. 459–73.

Williams, James Dale. "Coherence and Cognitive Style." Diss. U of Southern California, 1983.

Witkin, Herman A. "Psychological Differentiation and Forms of Pathology." *Journal of Abnormal Psychology* 70 (1965): 317–36.

Witkin, Herman A., et al. "Field-Dependent and Field-Independent Cognitive Styles and Their Educational Implications." *Review of Educational Research* 47 (1977): 1–64.

Wittrock, Merlin. "Education and the Cognitive Processes of the Brain." *Education and The Brain*. Ed. Jeanne S. Chall and Allen S. Mirsky. Chicago: U of Chicago P, 1978. 61–102.

Young, Andrew W. "Methodological and Theoretical Bases of Visual Hemifield Studies." *Divided Visual Field Studies of Cerebral Organisation*. Ed. J. Graham Beaumont. New York: Academic Press, 1982. 11–27.

Cognition, Convention, and Certainty

What We Need to Know about Writing

Patricia Bizzell

What do we need to know about writing? Only recently have we needed to ask this question, and the asking has created composition studies. We have needed to ask it because of changing circumstances in the classroom, and our answers will be put to the test there with a speed uncommon in other academic disciplines. The current theoretical debate over how to go about finding these answers, therefore, is not merely an empty exercise. Students' lives will be affected in profound ways.

This profound effect on students is the more to be expected because of the terms in which the "writing problem" has appeared to us—terms that suggest that students' thinking needs remediation as much as their writing. Seeing the problem this way makes it very clear that our teaching task is not only to convey information but also to transform students' whole world view. But if this indeed is our project, we must be aware that it has such scope. Otherwise, we risk burying ethical and political questions under supposedly neutral pedagogical technique. Some of our answers to the question of what we need to know about writing are riskier in this regard than others.

We now see the "writing problem" as a thinking problem primarily because we used to take our students' thinking for granted. We used to assume that students came to us with ideas and we helped them put those ideas into words. We taught style, explaining the formal properties of model essays and evaluating students' products in the light of these models. Some

Previously published in the journal *PRE/TEXT* 3.3 (1982): 213–243. Used by permission of Patricia Bizzell.

students came to us with better ideas than others, but these were simply the brighter or more mature students. All we could do for the duller, more immature students was to hope that exposure to good models might push them along the developmental path.[1]

Over the last twenty years, however, we have encountered in our classrooms more and more students whose ideas seem so ill-considered, by academic standards, that we can no longer see the problem as primarily one of expression. Rather, we feel, "Now I have to teach them to think, too!" And at the same time, students have so much trouble writing Standard English that we are driven away from stylistic considerations back to the basics of grammar and mechanics. Teaching style from model essays has not prepared us to explain or repair these students' deficiencies. The new demands on us as teachers can only be met, it seems, by a reconsideration of the relationship between thought and language. We are pretty much agreed, in other words, that what we need to know about writing has to do with the thinking processes involved in it.

Composition specialists generally agree about some fundamental elements in the development of language and thought. We agree that the normal human individual possesses innate mental capacities to learn a language and to assemble complex conceptual structures. As the individual develops, these capacities are realized in her learning a native tongue and forming thought patterns that organize and interpret experience. The mature exercise of these thought and language capacities takes place in society, in interaction with other individuals, and this interaction modifies the individual's reasoning, speaking, and writing within society. Groups of society members can become accustomed to modifying each other's reasoning and language use in certain ways. Eventually, these familiar ways achieve the status of conventions that bind the group in a discourse community, at work together on some project of interaction with the material world. An individual can belong to more than one discourse community, but her access to the various communities will be unequally conditioned by her social situation.

If composition specialists generally agree about this description, however, we disagree about what part of it is relevant to composition studies. One theoretical camp sees writing as primarily inner-directed, and so is more interested in the structure of language-learning and thinking processes in their earliest state, prior to social influence. The other main theoretical camp sees writing as primarily outer-directed, and so is more interested in the social processes whereby language-learning and thinking capacities are shaped and used in particular communities. In the current debate, each camp seeks to define what we *most* need to know about writing.

Inner-directed theorists seek to discover writing processes that are so fundamental as to be universal. Later elaborations of thinking and language-using should be understood as outgrowths of individual capacities (see Figure 1). Hence, inner-directed theorists are most interested in individual capacities and their earliest interactions with experience (locations #1 and 2, Figure 1). The inner-directed theorists tend to see the kinds of reasoning occurring at all four locations as isomorphic—all the same basic logical structures.[2] They also tend to see differences in language use at different locations as superficial matters of lexical choice; the basic structure of the language cannot change from location to location because this structure is isomorphic with the innate mental structures that enabled one to learn a language, and hence presumably universal and independent of lexical choice. Nevertheless, looking for an argument to justify teaching one form of a language, some inner-directed theorists treat one set of lexical choices as better able than others to make language embody the innate structures.

Figure 1   An inner-directed model of the development of language and thought. Arrows indicate direction of individual's development, beginning with innate capacities and issuing finally in particular instances of use.

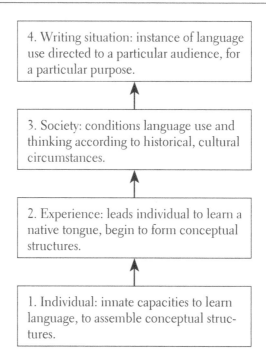

4. Writing situation: instance of language use directed to a particular audience, for a particular purpose.

3. Society: conditions language use and thinking according to historical, cultural circumstances.

2. Experience: leads individual to learn a native tongue, begin to form conceptual structures.

1. Individual: innate capacities to learn language, to assemble conceptual structures.

Insofar as these better choices fall into the patterns of, for example, a "standard" form of a native tongue, they make the standard intellectually superior to other forms.[3]

Inner-directed theorists further claim, in a similar paradox, that the universal, fundamental structures of thought and language can be taught. If our students are unable to have ideas, we should look around locations # 1 and 2 for structural models of the mental processes that are not happening in these students' minds. Once we find these models, we can guide students through the processes until the students' own thought-forming mechanisms "kick on" and they can make concepts on their own. An heuristic procedure is often presented as such a process model.[4] Similarly, if our students are unable to write English, we should look in the same locations for patterns of correct syntax, which we can then ask the students to practice until they internalize the patterns. Sentence-combining exercises offer such pattern practice.[5]

Once students are capable of cognitively sophisticated thinking and writing, they are ready to tackle the problems of a particular writing situation. These problems are usually treated by inner-directed theory as problems of audience analysis. Audience analysis seeks to identify the personal idiosyncracies of readers so that the writer can communicate her message to them in the most persuasive form. The changes made to accommodate an audience, however, are not seen as substantially altering the meaning of the piece of writing because that is based in the underlying structure of thought and language.[6]

In contrast, outer-directed theorists believe that universal, fundamental structures can't be taught; thinking and language use can never occur free of a social context that conditions them (see Figure 2). The outer-directed theorists believe that teaching style from model essays failed not because we were doing the wrong thing but because we weren't aware of what we were doing. Teaching style from model essays, in this view, is teaching the discourse conventions of a particular community — in this case, a community of intellectuals including, but not limited to, academics. But because we were unaware that we were in a discourse community, we taught the conventions as formal structures, as if they were universal patterns of thought and language. What we should do is to teach students that there are such things as discourse conventions.

The outer-directed theorists are sceptical about how we can obtain knowledge of what thinking and language-learning processes are innate. Moreover, they would argue that the individual is already inside a discourse community when she learns a native tongue, since the infant does not learn

Figure 2   An outer-directed model of the development of language and thought. Note that innate capacities have no expression outside discourse communities and that society is made up entirely of discourse communities. Individual has unequal access to different communities. Direction of development is outward from native community.

2. Society: aggregate of discourse communities that all share certain patterns of language-using, thinking conditioned by historical, cultural circumstances.

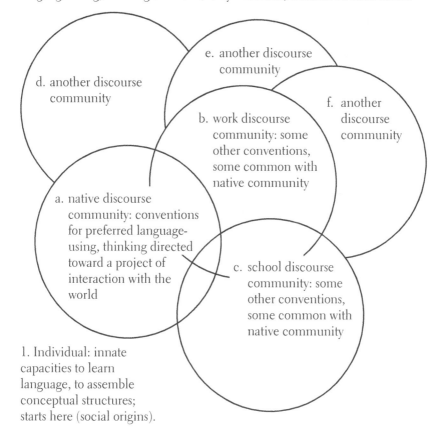

e. another discourse community

d. another discourse community

f. another discourse community

b. work discourse community: some other conventions, some common with native community

a. native discourse community: conventions for preferred language-using, thinking directed toward a project of interaction with the world

c. school discourse community: some other conventions, some common with native community

1. Individual: innate capacities to learn language, to assemble conceptual structures; starts here (social origins).

some generalized form of language but rather the habits of language use in the neighborhood, or the discourse community into which she is born.[7] Since this discourse community already possesses traditional, shared ways of understanding experience, the infant doesn't learn to conceptualize in a social vacuum, either, but is constantly being advised by more mature community members whether her inferences are correct, whether her groupings of experiential data into evidence are significant, and so on.[8] Some outer-directed theorists would go so far as to say that the lines of development of thought and language merge when the native tongue is learned, since one learns to think only by learning a language and one can't have an idea one doesn't have a word for.[9]

Outer-directed theorists would argue that we have no reason to believe, and no convincing way to determine, that our students can't think or use language in complex ways. It's just that they can't think or use language in the ways we want them to. To help them, then, we should be looking for ways to explain discourse conventions. We might find patterns of language use and reasoning that are common to all members of a society, patterns that are part of the set of conventions of every discourse community within the society. Conventions that are common in the society could be used as bridges between different discourse communities—for example, to ease the transition into the academic discourse community for students who come from discourse communities far removed from it.[10]

The staple activity of outer-directed writing instruction will be analysis of the conventions of particular discourse communities (see Figure 2). For example, a major focus of writing-across-the-curriculum programs is to demystify the conventions of the academic discourse community.[11] Discourse analysis goes beyond audience analysis because what is most significant about members of a discourse community is not their personal preferences, prejudices, and so on, but rather the expectations they share by virtue of belonging to that particular community. These expectations are embodied in the discourse conventions, which are in turn conditioned by the community's work. Audience analysis aims to persuade readers that you're right; it is to dress your argument in flattering apparel. Discourse analysis aims to enable you to make that argument, to do intellectual work of significance to the community, and hence, to persuade readers that you are a worthy co-worker.[12]

Answers to what we need to know about writing will have to come from both the inner-directed and the outer-directed theoretical schools if we wish to have a complete picture of the composing process. We need to explain the cognitive and the social factors in writing development, and even more important, the relationship between them. Therefore, we should think of the current debate between the two schools as the kind of fruitful exchange that enlarges knowledge, not as a process that will lead to its own termination, to a theory that silences debate. I would like to show here how one inner-directed theoretical model of writing can be enlarged by an outer-directed critique.

The inner-directed school has been distinguished by its fostering of research on writing that follows scientific methodology, and two of the most important researchers are Linda Flower, a professor of English at Carnegie-Mellon University, and John R. Hayes, a professor of psychology at the same school. They have been conducting research for about six years on what people do when they compose. The goal of this research is to formulate "A Cognitive Process Theory of Writing," according to the title of their recent *College Composition and Communication* essay, under review here.[13] Their work's roots in cognitive psychology can be seen in *Cognitive Processes in Writing*, also reviewed here, the proceedings of a 1978 symposium at Carnegie-Mellon.[14] Flower and Hayes see composing as a kind of problem-solving activity; what interests them are the "invariant" thought processes called into play whenever one is confronted with a writing task. In other words, they assume that although each writing task will have its own environment of purposes and constraints, the mental activity involved in juggling these constraints while moving to accomplish one's purposes does not change from task to task. This problem-solving thought process is the "cognitive process of writing."

In Figure 1, location 2 is approximately where Flower and Hayes would place what they are studying. The cognitive process is triggered by what goes on at location 4 (imposition of a particular writing task); the process may also be shaped by attitudes absorbed at location 3 and modified in the light of success or failure in problem-solving at location 4. Not everyone uses the same cognitive process in writing, some processes are more successful than others, and one's process can be consciously or unconsciously modified. Flower and Hayes seek to describe a model of the most complete and successful composing process they can find through their research.

Protocol analysis is their principle research tool. First, the researcher asks a person (the test subject) to say aloud whatever she is thinking while solving a problem posed by the researcher. For example, Flower and Hayes have asked English teachers to describe what goes through their minds while composing an article describing their jobs for the readers of *Seventeen* magazine. The transcription of what the subject says is the protocol. Next, the researcher scans the protocol looking in the subject's self-description for features predicted by the theory of cognitive activity guiding the research. Flower and Hayes have looked for descriptions of behavior common to current accounts of the writing process, such as "organizing" and "revising." In analyzing the protocol, the researcher must bridge gaps in the protocol caused by the subject's forgetting to mention some of her problem-solving steps. The theory is tested by its ability to bridge these gaps as well as by the appearance in the protocol of features it predicts (Flower and Hayes explain their procedure in "Identifying the Organization of Writing Processes," *Cognitive Processes*, pp. 3–30).

Through their research, Flower and Hayes have been gradually refining a process model of composing (see "Process Theory," p. 370). Its most current version divides the writing situation into three main parts: one, the "task environment," subdivided into "rhetorical problem" and "text produced so far"; two, the "writing process," subdivided into "reviewing" (further subdivided into "revising" and "evaluating"), "translating," and "planning" (further subdivided into "generating," "goal-setting," and "organizing"); and three, the "writer's long-term memory." The task environment is outside the writer, the writing process is inside the writer, and long-term memory can be both inside and outside—that is, in the writer's mind or in books. Task environment and memory are seen as information sources upon which the writer draws while performing the composing activities grouped under "writing process."

This model is hierarchical and recursive rather than sequential in structure; that is, Flower and Hayes do not see the writing process as an invariant order of steps. What is invariant, in their view, is the structural relation of the steps. A writer can "access" memory or task environment, and switch from one composing subprocess to another, at any time while the writing task is being completed; an entity in the model called "monitor" executes these switches. This model does not tell us how to proceed through the composing process, but only that in proceeding, there are certain subprocesses we must include if we want to compose successfully.

Flower and Hayes see this model as resolving current theoretical disagreements about what guides composing. Beginning their "Process Theory" essay with summaries of different but compatible views on composing, Flower and Hayes seem to suggest that while other theorists are like blind men describing an elephant, in the Flower-Hayes model we see the whole beast—or at least we can infer its shape when the porpoise occasionally breaks water, to switch to the animal metaphor Flower and Hayes use (*Cognitive Processes*, pp. 9–10). It is the hierarchical and recursive structure of this model, in Flower and Hayes's view, that makes it superior to other theorists' work and able to control and reconcile other theorists' work.

The Flower-Hayes model may, however, strike many readers as a surprising mix of daunting complexity and disappointing familiarity. When we finally get the new terminology straight in our minds, we find in the model's elaborate cognitive processes just the same writing activities we have been debating about. Consider, for example, the Flower-Hayes model's "monitor," the entity that executes switches between composing subprocesses. On the one hand, the term, borrowed from computer programming, is rather intimidating, especially if we imagine that it names something we didn't know was there before. On the other hand, we find out eventually that "monitor" means simply "the writer's mind making decisions." Borrowing a term from programming masks the question of *why* the writer makes certain decisions. The Flower-Hayes model consistently presents a description of *how* the writing process goes on as if it were capable of answering questions about *why* the writer makes certain choices in certain situations. While it is useful for us to have an overview of the "how," such as the Flower-Hayes model offers, we should not suppose that this will enable us to advise students on difficult questions of practice. To put it another way, if we are going to see students as problem-solvers, we must also see them as problem-solvers situated in discourse communities that guide problem definition and the range of alternative solutions. Outer-directed theory can thus shore up the Flower-Hayes model in two critical areas, planning and translating.

"Translating," according to Flower and Hayes, is "the process of putting ideas into visible language" ("Process Theory," p. 373). They treat written English as a set of containers into which we pour meaning, regardless of how meaning exists before the pouring. The containers may not seem to be in convenient sizes at first—we have to struggle with their "constraints" or "special demands"—but once we internalize these, written language as a factor in the composing process essentially disappears. Writing does not so much contribute to thinking as provide an occasion for thinking—or, more precisely, a substrate upon which thinking can grow. Beyond minor matters of spelling, diction, and so on, we do not have to worry about how students are going to find out about the features of written language because these are already innate.

"Translating," then, remains the emptiest box in the Flower-Hayes model, while "planning" becomes the fullest. During planning, the writer generates and organizes ideas before struggling to put them into words. Language itself is not seen as having a generative force in the planning process, except insofar as it stands as a record of the current progress of the writer's thinking in "text produced so far." Planning processes, therefore, have to be elaborated because they are all the writer has to guide her toward a solution to the particular writing problem. What's missing here is the connection to social context afforded by recognition of the dialectical relationship between thought and language. We can have thoughts for which we have no words, I think, but learning language, though it doesn't exactly teach us to think, teaches us what thoughts matter. To put it another way, we can *know* nothing but what we have words for, if knowledge is what language makes of experience.

Vygotsky has characterized this dialectical relationship of thought and language as the development of "verbal thought." At first, language use and thinking develop separately in the child. But eventually the child comes to understand that language not only names ideas but develops and evaluates them, and then, *"the nature of the* [child's] *development itself changes,* from biological to historical."[15] The child's linguistic and cognitive development culminates in "verbal thought," which "is not a natural, innate form of behavior but is determined by a historical-cultural process and has specific properties and laws that cannot be found in the natural forms of thought and speech" (Vygotsky, p. 51). To illustrate the mature relationship between thought and language, Vygotsky uses situations that are strongly context-bound, such as conversations between lovers or among actors in a play.

Vygotsky's analysis suggests that a model that separates planning and translating will not be fruitful for describing adult language-using because these activities are never separate in adult language-using. There is, to be sure, a basis in the human organism for language-using behavior; Vygotsky calls it "biological," Flower and Hayes call it "cognitive." But while this basis is a legitimate object of study in its own right, even the most complete anatomy of it will not explain adult language-using because, as Vygotsky emphasizes, with the advent of verbal thought the very nature of language-using processes changes. The writing process can only take place after this change occurred. Vygotsky's analysis would suggest, then, not only that we should not separate planning and translating but also that we should understand them as conditioned by social context.

If we accept Vygotsky's analysis as indicating the need to fill in Flower and Hayes's empty "translating" box, then to look for knowledge to fill it, we can turn to sociolinguistics. This discipline seeks to analyze the ways thinking and language-using are conditioned by social context. In studying writing, sociolinguists look for the verbal ties with context. They argue that certain genres, implying certain relations between people, are typical of certain situations. Furthermore, readers do not perceive a text as hanging together logically unless its connections with the social context are as clear as the markers of internal coherence.[16] Therefore, for example, students who struggle to write Standard English need knowledge beyond the rules of grammar, spelling, and so on. They need to know: the habitual attitudes of Standard English users toward this preferred form; the linguistic features that most strongly mark group identity; the conventions that can sometimes be ignored; and so on. Students who do know the rules of Standard English may still seem to academics to be writing "incorrectly" if the students are insensitive to all these other features of language use in the community—then the students are using academic language in unacademic ways.[17]

Composition specialists can learn from sociolinguists to avoid what George Dillon has called the "bottom-to-top" fallacy: the notion that a writer first finds meaning, then puts it into words, then organizes the words into sentences, sentences into paragraphs, etc.[18] Dillon argues, rather, that it is the sense of her whole project that most stimulates a writer's thinking and guides her language use. The discourse gives meaning to the words and not vice versa. For example, such phrases as "it seems to me" and "these results suggest . . ." do not themselves tell us how to interpret such a pattern of qualifying statements. When we encounter these words in a student paper, we are likely to chide the writer for covering up poor research or for being unduly humble. When we encounter the very same words in a scholarly paper, we simply take them to mean that the writer is establishing a properly inquiring persona (see Dillon, p. 91).

Even something as cognitively fundamental as sentence structure takes on meaning from the discourse in which it is deployed. For this reason, for example, revising rules are notoriously unhelpful: they always require further knowledge in order to be applied. We can't "omit needless words" unless we have some additional criteria for "needlessness." We can't even "avoid passive voice" all the time. Passive voice might be preferred by a writer who wants to head her sentence with words that tie it closely to the previous sentence, especially if the kind of discourse she is producing places a high value on markers of internal coherence.[19]

"Putting meaning into words," then, cannot be seen as a mechanical process of finding the right size containers. Instead, with a form of discourse we take on a whole range of possibilities for making meaning. Language-using in social contexts is connected not only to the immediate situation but to the larger society, too, in the form of conventions for construing reality. This relationship between language and world view has prompted M.A.K. Halliday to argue that "the problem of educational failure is not a linguistic problem, if by linguistic we mean a problem of different urban dialects"; at bottom, "it is a semiotic problem, concerned with the different ways in which we have constructed our social reality, and the styles of meaning: we have learned to associate with the various aspects of it."[20] In short, educational problems associated with language use should be understood as difficulties with joining an unfamiliar discourse community.

To look at writing as situated in a discourse community is to blur over the lines between translating and planning in the Flower-Hayes model. Finding words is not a separate process from setting goals. It *is* setting goals, because finding words is always a matter of aligning oneself with a particular discourse community. The community's conventions will include instructions on a preferred form of the native tongue, a specialized vocabulary, a polite technique for establishing persona, and so on. To some extent, the community's conventions can be inferred from analyzing the community's texts. But because the conventions also shape world view, the texts can never be an adequate index of community practice.

Therefore, we should not think of what I am calling a discourse community simply as a group who have decided to abide by certain language-using rules. Rather, we should see the group as an "interpretive community," to use Stanley Fish's term, whose language-using habits are part of a larger pattern of regular interaction with the material world.[21] Because this interaction is always an historical process, changing over time, the community's conventions also change over time. This is not to say that the community's interpretive conventions are arbitrary or that they totally determine individual behavior. They are not arbitrary because they are always conditioned by the on-going work in the community and sanctioned by consensus. At any given time, community members should have no trouble specifying that some kinds of thinking and language-using are obviously appropriate to the community and some are not. Changes in conventions can only define themselves in terms of what is already acceptable (even if such definition means negation of the currently acceptable).

At the same time, some kinds of thinking and language-using are not obviously either appropriate or inappropriate; they are open to debate. An individual who abides by the community's conventions, therefore, can still find areas for initiative—adherence is slavish adherence only for the least productive community members. These "open" areas may be the unsolved problems of the community, experiences that remain anomalous in the community's interpretive scheme, or they may be areas the community has never even considered dealing with. An individual may, however, bring one of these open areas into the range of the community's discourse if her argument for an interpretation of it is sufficiently persuasive in terms the community already understands. As an example of this activity, Mina Shaughnessy has cited Freud's introductory lectures on psychoanalysis.[22]

Producing text within a discourse community, then, cannot take place unless the writer can define her goals in terms of the community's interpretive conventions. Writing is always already writing for some purpose that can only be understood in its community context. Fish has argued not only that the community of literary critics proceeds in this way but furthermore, that the main business of English studies should be to investigate the nature of discourse communities (see Fish, pp. 338–55). It is exactly this sort of analysis that the Flower-Hayes model lacks when trying to explain planning. For Flower and Hayes, "generating" (a subdivision of planning) means finding ideas by using heuristics, not by responding with individual initiative to the community's needs. "Organizing" (another subdivision) means fitting ideas into the range of logical structures available from human thought processes, not finding out what's reasonable in terms of a community's interpretive conventions. In other words, all that's needed for generating and organizing is access to the invariant, universal structures of human cognition (for a critique of this assumption, see Dillon, pp. 50–82).

The weakness of this approach is most apparent in Flower and Hayes's treatment of "goal-setting." They correctly identify goal-setting as the motor of the composing process, its most important element, but in their model they close it off in the most subordinate position (a subdivision of a subdivision of the writing process). In the "Process Theory" essay, Flower and Hayes elaborate their description into "process goals" (directions for the writing process) and "content goals" (directions for affecting the audience), and they also classify goals in terms of levels of abstraction (see "Process Theory," p. 377). Their model's structure cannot order this multifarious account.

Flower and Hayes end the "Process Theory" essay with analysis of a "good" writer's protocol, aimed to explicate the process of goal-setting. The writer is having trouble deciding how to tell *Seventeen* readers about his job as a college English teacher until he decides that many girls think of English as a "tidy" and "prim" subject and that "By God I can change that notion for them." He goes on to frame an introduction that recounts a "crazy skit" his 101 class liked on the first day of school ("Process Theory," pp. 383, 385). Of his "By God" moment of decision, Flower and Hayes say that "he has regenerated and elaborated his top-level goals," and "this consolidation leaves the writer with a new, relatively complex, rhetorically sophisticated working goal, one which encompasses plans for a topic, a persona, and an audience" (p. 383).

Notice the verbs in this explanation: "regenerating" and "elaborating" goals "leave" the writer with regenerated ("new") and elaborated ("complex") goals—which "encompass" what he needs to know to go on writing. The action described here has no force as an explanation not only because it is circular (regeneration causes regeneration), but also because we still don't know where the new goals come from. Flower and Hayes suggest that going through a process simply "leaves" one with the goals, as if the process itself brought them into being. Upon arrival, the goals are found to contain ("encompass") the necessary knowledge—but we still don't know how that knowledge got there.

The *Seventeen* article writer's process of goal-setting, I think, can be better understood if we see it in terms of writing for a discourse community. His initial problem (which seems to be typical of most subjects confronted with this writing task) is to find a way to include these readers in a discourse community for which he is comfortable writing. He places them in the academic discourse community by imagining the girls as students ("they will all have had English," p. 383). Once he has included them in a familiar discourse community, he can find a way to address them that is common in the community: he will argue with them, putting a new interpretation on information they possess in order to correct misconceptions (his "By God" decision). In arguing, he can draw on all the familiar habits of persuasion he has built up in his experience as a teacher (his "crazy skit" decision). He could not have found a way to write this article if he did not have knowledge of a discourse community to draw on.

The Flower-Hayes model does, of course, include a "long-term memory" where such knowledge could be stored, and Flower and Hayes even acknowledge its importance:

> Sometimes a single cue in an assignment, such as "write a persuasive. . . ,"
> can let a writer tap a stored representation of a problem and bring a whole
> raft of writing plans into play. (p. 371)

A "stored representation of a problem" must be a set of directions for producing a certain kind of text—what I have been calling discourse conventions. I would argue that the writer doesn't just tap this representation sometimes but every time a writing task is successfully accomplished. Flower and Hayes give this crucial determinant of text production very off-hand treatment, however. They seem to see writing in response to discourse conventions as response to "semiautomatic plans and goals" that contrast with "goals writers create for a particular paper" (p. 381). Evidently they are seeing discourse conventions simply as rules to be internalized, similar to their treatment of the "constraints" of written English. This reduction of conventions to sets of rules is also suggested by their choice of the limerick as a good example of a "genre" (p. 379).

Hence, although Flower and Hayes acknowledge the existence of discourse conventions, they fail to see conventions' generative power, which is to say that their notion of conventions does not include the interpretive function for which I have been arguing. This neglect of the role of knowledge in composing makes the Flower-Hayes theory particularly insensitive to the problems of poor writers.

> Poor writers will frequently depend on very abstract, undeveloped top-level goals, such as "appeal to a broad range of intellect," even though such goals are much harder to work with than a more operational goal such as "give a brief history of my job." Sondra Perl has seen this phenomenon in the basic writers who kept returning to reread the assignment, searching, it would seem, for ready-made goals, instead of forming their own. Alternatively, poor writers will depend on only very low-level goals, such as finishing a sentence or correctly spelling a word. They will be, as Nancy Sommers's student revisers were, locked in by the myopia in their own goals and criteria. (p. 379)

The implication here seems to be that cognitive deficiency keeps poor writers from forming their own goals, keeps them locked in the myopia of goals appropriate to a much earlier stage of cognitive development. The physical image of poor eyesight is revealing of Flower and Hayes's assumptions about the innate sources of writing problems.

I think these students' difficulties with goal-setting are better understood in terms of their unfamiliarity with the academic discourse community, combined, perhaps, with such limited experience outside their native discourse communities that they are unaware that there is such a thing as a discourse community with conventions to be mastered. What is underdeveloped is their knowledge of the ways experience is constituted and interpreted in the academic discourse community and of the fact that all discourse communities constitute and interpret experience. Basil Bernstein has shown that British working-class students are not cognitively deficient but that, first, their native discourse community's conventions are very different from school conventions, and, second, their lack of a variety of speech partners makes it hard for them to see their problems in school as problems of learning to relate to new speech partners (or an unfamiliar discourse community).[23]

Such students may be unable to set a more operational goal because they do not know the conventions of language-using that define such goals as, for example, a "history." Without such knowledge, they may fall back on goals that worked in the past—perhaps in grammar school where close attention to spelling and grammar was rewarded. Or they may sensibly try to enlarge their knowledge by rereading the assignment, seeking clues to the conventions of this new discourse community or those "ready-made goals" without which no writing gets accomplished. Of course, their search of the assignment may be fruitless if the teacher has not been sufficiently explicit about her expectations. Academics are, perhaps, too ready to assume that such operations as "describe" or "analyze" are self-evident, when in fact they have meanings specific to the academic discourse community and specific to disciplines within that community.

To help poor writers, then, we need to explain that their writing takes place within a community, and to explain what the community's conventions are. Another way of putting this would be to borrow Thomas Kuhn's terminology and explain that "puzzle-solving" writing can go on only under the direction of an established "paradigm" for community activity.[24] As Charles Bazerman's work has shown, the writer within the academic community knows how to relate her text to "the object under study, the literature of the field, the anticipated audience, and the author's own self" via discipline-specific conventions governing "lexicon," "explicit citation and implicit knowledge," "knowledge and attitudes the text assumes that the readers will have," and the "features" of a "public face" (Bazerman, pp. 362–63).

The Flower-Hayes model of writing, then, cannot alone give us a complete picture of the process. We might say that if this model describes the *form* of the composing process, the process cannot go on without the *content* which is knowledge of the conventions of discourse communities. In practice, however, form and content cannot be separated in this way, since discourse conventions shape the goals that drive the writing process. To let the model stand alone as an account of composing is to mask the necessity for the socially situated knowledge without which no writing project gets under way. The problems of letting this model stand alone can be seen in the pedagogy emerging from Flower and Hayes's work. They are inclined to treat the model itself as an heuristic:

> Our model is a model of competent writers. Some writers, though, perhaps to their disadvantage, may fail to use some of the processes. (*Cognitive Processes*, p. 29)

Flower has recently published a textbook that aims to guide students through a complete repertoire of composing strategies.[25]

The difficulty with the textbook's view of writing as problem-solving is that it treats problem-solving as an unfiltered encounter with the underlying structure of reality—"the act of discovering key issues in a problem that often lie hidden under the noisy details of the situation" (p. 21). Having defined a problem, one should: first, "fit it into a category of similar problems"; next, decide on a possible course of action against the problem ("make the problem definition more operational"); "tree" the problem or analyze its parts into a hierarchical structure; "generate alternative solutions"; present a conclusion, which weighs alternatives and acknowledges assumptions and implications of the conclusion (see pp. 21–26). But *first*, how does one define a problem? Although Flower says that "problems are only problems for someone," she doesn't talk about this necessary link between problem definition and interpretive communities (p. 21). Rather, it seems that we will *find* (not make) the problem if we strip away the "noisy details of the situation." I would argue, in contrast, that only the noisy details of the situation can define a problem. To "define" a problem is to interact with the material world according to the conventions of a particular discourse community; these conventions are the only source for categories of similar problems, operational definitions, and alternative solutions, and a conclusion can only be evaluated as "well supported" in terms of a particular community's standards.

I certainly do not mean to suggest that students should not be encouraged to look at reality when they compose—far from it, since I have emphasized the function of writing in doing (intellectual) work in the world. But I do mean to point out that we cannot look at reality in an unfiltered way—"reality" only makes sense when organized by the interpretive conventions of a discourse community. Students often complain that they have nothing to say, whereas "real-world" writers almost never do, precisely because real-world writers are writing for discourse communities in which they know their work can matter, whereas students can see little purpose for their own attempts ("essais") other than to get a grade. For example, Erwin Steinberg has suggested that the superior organization of an electrical engineer's report, as compared to a freshman composition, stems from the engineer's superior knowledge of and experience in a field; what looks like a cognitive difference turns out to have a large social component (see "A Garden of Opportunities and a Thicket of Dangers," *Cognitive Processes*, pp. 163–165). Hence, although Steinberg is sympathetic to the project of finding writing models and heuristics, he cautions, "We must always be careful not to think in terms of a single model, because if we do we'll find one and force everyone to use it—the way English teachers used to require students to make formal outlines before they wrote" (p. 163).

The cognitive psychology approach cuts off writing-as-problem-solving from the context of a discourse community precisely because *one* model is sought (Steinberg's caveat notwithstanding). Discourse communities are tied to historical and cultural circumstances, and hence can only be seen as unenlightening instances of the general theory the cognitive approach seeks: the one model is the universal one. All of the theoretical essays in

Cognitive Processes in Writing seek to find this model. Carl Bereiter offers an account of the stages of development in children's writing processes. Like the Flower-Hayes model, his is recursive—that is, he suggests that children's development includes a certain set of stages but that the order of these stages can be changed. There is, however, a "preferred or 'natural' order of writing development," an order in which the constraints on composing imposed by the necessity of putting thoughts into words are gradually reduced by being "automatized." Bereiter suggests that this order should be adopted in the schools (see "Development in Writing," p. 89).

Collins and Gentner seek to go even further in schematizing their theory as a rule-governed model because they hope to end with a program enabling a computer to compose (see "A Framework for a Cognitive Theory of Writing," pp. 51–52). This would permit the creation of "Writing Land," where computers would guide students through the patterns of the writing process and enhance the students' cognitive activities (see "Framework," pp. 67–70). Computer-assisted composition will help students reduce the constraints imposed by the struggle to put thoughts into words by separating "idea production" and "text production" ("Framework," p. 53). Once the ideas are under control, "the next stage is to impose text structure on the ideas" ("Framework," p. 59).

During text production, Collins and Gentner confidently state, the writer can call on "structural devices, stylistic devices, and content devices"—the term "devices" suggesting rule-governed mechanisms. Yet "unfortunately for the writer, there is no one-to-one correspondence between means and end here"—in other words, no consistency in situation that would permit reliance on rule-governed mechanisms ("Framework," p. 60). Collins and Gentner's analysis frequently bumps up against language's opacity, the contribution to thinking of densely situation-bound meanings embodied in habits of language-using. Because they cannot account for this situational aspect of writing, Collins and Gentner can only define "good writing" as writing that conforms to a set of rules set by some authority (see "Framework," pp. 52–53). This approach leaves them no way to justify the authority's decisions as other than arbitrary, and hence their "rules" turn out to be situation-bound: "Delete extraneous material," "Shorten long paragraphs," and so on ("Framework," p. 65). Such advice is unhelpful to students without other knowledge that enables them to identify the extraneous and over-lengthy, as I noted earlier in my discussion of revising rules.

The fundamental problem with this approach is that it assumes that the rules we can formulate to describe behavior are the same rules that produce the behavior. As attempts to program language-using computers have shown, such structures reveal their lack of explanatory power when applied to an actual situation in which discourse conventions come into play. Programming a computer to use language comes up against a problem of infinite regress of context—or, how do we tell the computer how to tell what's important when things are important only in terms of purposive activity? How can we define, for example, what is "extraneous material," when the quality of being extraneous resides not in the material itself but in its relation to discourse? Or, to use a simpler example, how can we tell the computer when a paragraph is too long except by specifying a range of lines that constitute acceptable lengths? Is there any form of discourse in which 20-line paragraphs are acceptable and 21-line paragraphs are not? As the competence/performance debate in linguistics has suggested, it may be that we cannot have a completely descriptive theory of behavior in widely varying specific situations—that is, we cannot formulate universal rules for context-bound activities. If language-using isn't rule-governed in this sense, however, it still may be regular—that is, we may be able to group situations as likely to share a number of language-using features. But to do this is to describe the conventions of discourse communities.[26]

As I have been arguing, then, both the inner-directed and the outer-directed theoretical schools will have to contribute to a synthesis capable of providing a comprehensive new agenda for composition studies. My critique of Flower and Hayes's work is intended to contribute to such a synthesis, not to delegitimate what they are doing. I do want to raise a serious question, however, about another feature of the inner-directed school, a feature that works against fruitful discussion and synthesis: the quest for certainty. In seeking one universal model of the composing process, inner-directed theorists seek a new set of principles for our discipline that will raise their arguments, as one has put it, "above mere ideology" (Hirsch, p. 4). They seek a kind of certainty they believe is accessible only to science, and their talk of paradigm-shifting invokes Kuhn to announce that our discipline will soon have a scientific basis.[27]

This kind of certainty is presumably analogous to the commonplace elevation of fact over opinion, since it is supposed to end all debate. The inner-directed school therefore has redefined composition research to mean a search for the facts in the real world that prove a theory beyond debate. The Flower-Hayes model claims much prestige from being derived from such supposedly unimpeachable evidence. But its reliance on empirical evidence can be questioned on several grounds. For one thing, protocol analysis is a controversial method even within cognitive psychology because it tends to affect what is being observed (see Gould's remarks, *Cognitive*

Processes, p. 125). Flower and Hayes's work is particularly vulnerable because most of their adult subjects have been English teachers who are familiar with the specialized vocabulary of the theory Flower and Hayes have used to analyze the protocols. Under any circumstances, protocol analysis can lead to "self-fulfilling" prophecy because its assumption that the subject's words mirror her thinking allows the researcher to claim that certain thought processes have occurred if certain words appear in the protocol. Self-fulfilling prophecy is even more likely when test subjects share expert knowledge of these words with the researchers.

The larger point to be made here, however, is that no scientific research, no matter how rigorously it is conducted, possesses the kind of authoritative certainty inner-directed theorists are seeking.[28] It is always desirable, of course, to know more about composing, but it is also necessary to treat this knowledge as provisional, the way scientists treat their findings, if inquiry is not to end. We may wonder, then, why inner-directed theorists are so ready to invest their results with final authority and rush to pedagogical applications. I think it is that certainty appeals to composition specialists these days for various reasons. For one, until recently composition studies was a low-status enclave it was hard to escape; a powerful theory would help us retaliate against the literary critics who dominate English studies. Moreover, such a theory might help us survive what appears to be the long slide of all humanistic disciplines into a low-status enclave. A scientific-sounding theory promises an "accountability" hedge against hard times.

The strongest appeal of certainty, however, is its offer of a solution to our new students' problems that will enable us to undertake their socialization into the academic discourse community without having to consider the ethical and political dimensions of this act. We are reluctant to take up ethical and political questions about what we do because writing teachers have been under a terrific strain. Pressured with increasing asperity by our colleges to prepare students for their other courses, we have also felt anxious in the classroom both when our teaching worked—because we sensed that we were wiping out the students' own culture—and when it didn't—because we were cheating them of a chance to better their situations. Inner-directed pedagogy meets teachers' emotional needs because it can be defended on grounds that are likely to satisfy complaining faculty and administrators, and because its claim to a basis in universals assures us that when we inculcate it, we aren't touching the students' own culture but merely giving them a way around it and up the ladder of success. The corollary is that students for whom the pedagogy doesn't work need no longer be seen as victims of our incompetence but simply as innately inferior.

Invocation of certainty, then, performs the rhetorical function of invocation of the Deity. It guarantees the transcendent authority of values for which we do not need to argue but which we can now apply with the confidence of a "good cause." I would argue, however, that we must understand such a move as the assigning of superhuman authority to a human construction. All knowledge, that is, is of human origin, even scientific knowledge. Indeed, modern philosophy has centered around a critique of scientific knowledge precisely because such knowledge is most likely now to be treated as certain. As Richard Rorty has recently shown, the history of Western philosophy since the Renaissance can be seen as a series of unsuccessful attempts to fight off the admission that such claims for certainty are no longer tenable.[29] There is no way out of confrontation, except among fellow believers, with the necessity of arguing for one's ethical choices.

This confrontation is especially necessary in a pluralistic society such as the United States, in which a heterogeneous school population ensures that pedagogical choices will affect students unequally. Under such circumstances, as Rorty cautions, claims to certainty often express simply a desire for agreement which masks the question of whose interests are being served (see Rorty, p. 335). Teachers' individual ethical choices add up to political consequences, responsibility for which we cannot avoid. We are better off, then, with a disciplinary theory that encourages examination of consequences. For example, inner-directed research might come up with an heuristic that is useful in Basic Writing classes. But if we use it there, we should not imagine that the heuristic allows us to forget who the students are in Basic Writing classes, where they come from, what their prospects are—in short, why these particular students are having educational difficulties.

Ultimately, I am calling for the inspection of what some curriculum theorists have called the "hidden curriculum": the project of initiating students into a particular world view that gives rise to the daily classroom tasks without being consciously examined by teacher or students.[30] If we call what we are teaching "universal" structures or processes, we bury the hidden curriculum even deeper by claiming that our choice of material owes nothing to historical circumstances. To do this is to deny the school's function as an agent of cultural hegemony, or the selective valuation and transmission of world views. The result for students who don't share the school's preferred world views is either failure or deracination. I think we must acknowledge cultural differences in the classroom, even though this means increasing our emotional strain as members of one group trying to mediate contacts among various others.

The kind of pedagogy that would foster responsible inspection of the politically loaded hidden curriculum in composition class is discourse analysis. The exercise of cultural hegemony can be seen as the treatment of one community's discourse conventions as if they simply mirrored reality. To point out that discourse conventions exist would be to politicize the classroom—or rather, to make everyone aware that it is already politicized. World views would become more clearly a matter of conscious commitment, instead of unconscious conformity, if the ways in which they are constituted in discourse communities were analyzed.

This is not to say that we can make the school an ideologically neutral place. The whole force of my argument is that there is no way to *escape* all discourse communities, stand outside them and pronounce judgment. Furthermore, I assent to most of the conventions of the academic discourse community and believe that students from other communities can benefit from learning about them, and learning them. But perhaps we can break up the failure/deracination dilemma for students from communities at a distance from academe. Through discourse analysis we might offer them an understanding of their school difficulties as the problems of a traveler to an unfamiliar country—yet a country in which it is possible to learn the language and the manners and even "go native" while still remembering the land from which one has come.

In his discussion of literary criticism and interpretive communities, Stanley Fish has offered us one set of suggestions for how such ethically and politically conscious education might proceed. Richard Rorty offers another in his vision of philosophy becoming not the arbiter of disciplines but the mediator among them. This "edifying" philosophy will have as its task making us realize that agreement that looks like certainty can occur only "because when a practice has continued long enough the conventions which make it possible—and which permit a consensus on how to divide it into parts—are relatively easy to isolate" (p. 321). Rorty's is not a positivist notion of arbitrary conventions; he sees conventions as the product of communities, situation-bound but also subject to change. Rorty generalizes Kuhn's notions of "normal" and "revolutionary" science to argue that the edifying philosopher's task is to keep reminding us that "normal" discourse is evidently clear and above debate only because we agree about its conventions. Education must begin with normal discourse but should not be limited to it, with its unhelpful distinction between facts and values (see p. 363). For the goal of discovering Truth, Rorty substitutes the goal of continuing conversation, but this will not be a dangerously relativistic goal because always conditioned by and having to answer to an historical framework. Rorty's philosophical community thus resembles Fish's interpretive community.

Finally, then, we should see our answers to the question of what we need to know about writing in the light of a new humanistic synthesis. Philosophy has moved to the position that discourse communities are all we have to rely upon in our quest for certainty. Literary criticism is analyzing how discourse communities function as historically situated interpretive communities. Composition studies should focus upon practice within inter-pretive communities — exactly how conventions work in the world and how they are transmitted. If the work of these disciplines continues to converge, a new synthesis will emerge that revivifies rhetoric as the central discipline of human intellectual endeavor. In view of such a synthesis, the project to make composition studies merely scientific looks obsolete.

I hope that this rhetorical synthesis, because it turns our attention to questions of value and persuasion, will also reawaken us to the collective nature of the whole educational endeavor. There should be no disgrace in discovering that one's work and the understanding that guides it cannot be achieved autonomously. Then the main casualty of our theoretical debate can be the debilitating individualism that adds so much to classroom strain. In other words, let us emphasize not only discourse but also community. I do not mean that we should seek to eliminate the conflicts that arise from our coming from different historical and cultural situations. We should rec-ognize that being so situated is the most important thing we have in common.[31]

NOTES

1. The attitude I'm describing here has been called current-traditionalism, and it still dominates textbooks in the field; see Donald C. Stewart, "Composition Textbooks and the Assault on Tradition," *College Composition and Communication*, 29 (May 1978), pp. 171–76.

2. I am taking this sense of "isomorphic" from Frank D'Angelo, *A Conceptual Theory of Rhetoric* (Cambridge, Mass.: Winthrop, 1975), pp. 16, 26–36.

3. I have in mind here the justification for teaching Standard English advanced in E.D. Hirsch, Jr., *The Philosophy of Composition* (Chicago: Univ. of Chicago Press, 1977).

4. For example, Richard Young has recently characterized his particle-wave-field heuris-tic as based on "universal invariants that underlie all human experience as characteristic of rationality itself"; in "Arts, Crafts, Gifts, and Knacks: Some Disharmonies in the New Rheto-ric," *Visible Language*, 14, no. 4 (1980), 347.

5. For an overview of research on sentence-combining and the arguments for teaching it, see Frank O'Hare, *Sentence Combining: Improving Student Writing without Formal Gram-mar Instruction* (Urbana, Illinois: NCTE, 1973).

6. A new textbook that operates from these principles of audience analysis (and other inner-directed pedagogy) is Janice M. Lauer, Gene Montague, Andrea Lunsford, and Janet Emig, *Four Worlds of Writing* (New York: Harper and Row, 1981).

7. Typically, a discourse community prefers one form of the native tongue, which may be characterized simply by level of formality and specialized vocabulary, or which may be a dialect, or a fully constituted language (in the native tongue's family) with its own grammar rules. The outer-directed theorists thus emphasize "parole" over "langue," to use de Saussure's terms, "performance" over "competence," to use Chomsky's terms. For a good account of such language differences in an American setting, see William Labov, *The Study of Nonstandard English* (1969; revised and enlarged; Urbana, Illinois: NCTE, 1975).

8. See, for example, M.A.K. Halliday, "Language as Social Semiotic," *Language as Social Semiotic* (Baltimore: University Park Press, 1978), pp. 108–26.

9. This attitude has been called the Sapir-Whorf hypothesis, because arguments are advanced for it by linguists Edward Sapir and his pupil, Benjamin Lee Whorf; for a good summary and critique of the Sapir-Whorf hypothesis, see Adam Schaff, *Language and Cognition* (1964; trans. Olgierd Wojtasiewicz, ed. Robert S. Cohen; New York: McGraw-Hill, 1973).

10. This, I think, is the gist of the analysis offered by Mina Shaughnessy, "Beyond the Sentence," *Errors and Expectations* (New York: Oxford Univ. Press, 1977), pp. 226–72.

11. A new textbook that operates from some principles of outer-directed pedagogy is Elaine Maimon, Gerald L. Belcher, Gail W. Hearn, Barbara F. Nodine, and Finbarr W. O'Connor, *Writing in the Arts and Sciences* (Cambridge, Massachusetts: Winthrop, 1981).

12. For an exemplary analysis of academic discourse conventions and how they lead to the accomplishment of the community's work, see Charles Bazerman, "What Written Knowledge Does: Three Examples of Academic Discourse," *Philosophy of the Social Sciences*, 11 (September 1981), pp. 361–87; further references in text.

13. Linda Flower and John R. Hayes, "A Cognitive Process Theory of Writing," *College Composition and Communication*, 32 (December 1981), pp. 365–87; further references in text.

14. Lee W. Gregg and Erwin R. Steinberg, editors, *Cognitive Processes in Writing* (Hillsdale, New Jersey: Lawrence Erlbaum, 1980); further references in text.

15. Lev Vygotsky, *Thought and Language* (1934; rpt. ed. & trans. Eugenia Hanfmann and Gertrude Vakar; Cambridge, Mass.: MIT Press, 1962), p. 51, author's emphasis; further references in text. Vygotsky's pupil A.R. Luria did research among Uzbek peasants which suggests that thought and language interpenetrate to such a degree that perception of optical illusions, for example, changes with cultural experience and level of education; see A.R. Luria, *Cognitive Development* (1974; rpt. trans. Martin Lopez-Morillas and Lynn Solotaroff, ed. Michael Cole; Cambridge, Mass.: Harvard Univ. Press, 1976).

16. See M.A.K. Halliday and Ruqaiya Hasan, *Cohesion in English* (London: Longman, 1976), pp. 19–26.

17. My line of argument here is based on Dell Hymes, "Bilingual Education: Linguistic vs. Sociolinguistic Bases," *Foundations in Sociolinguistics* (Philadelphia: Univ. of Pennsylvania Press, 1974), pp. 119–24; in the same volume, Hymes argues that to uncover the extralinguistic attitudes lending significance to language use, linguists need more contributions from folklorists.

18. George L. Dillon, *Constructing Texts* (Bloomington, Indiana: Indiana Univ. Press, 1981), pp. 1–20; further references in text.

19. A critique of the notion of simplicity-as-clarity has been offered by Richard Lanham, *Style: An Anti-Textbook* (New Haven, Conn.: Yale Univ. Press, 1974). Lanham's later work in composition pedagogy suggests, however, that he is cynical about the position taken in *Style* and not really ready to defend "ornate" language choices outside of special literary circumstances; see Richard Lanham, *Revising Prose* (New York: Scribner, 1979). Dillon, pp. 21–49, is more helpful on understanding the problems with revising rules.

20. Halliday, "Language in Urban Society," p. 163; Halliday suggests that our current difficulties in the composition class may be at least in part a function of the increasing number of students who come from urban areas.

21. See Stanley Fish, *Is There a Text in this Class?* (Cambridge, Mass.: Harvard Univ. Press, 1980), further references in text; the following argument is heavily indebted to Fish's work.

22. Mina Shaughnessy, "Some Needed Research on Writing," *College Composition and Communication*, 27 (December 1977), p. 319.

23. See Basil Bernstein, *Class, Codes and Control* (1971; rpt. New York: Schocken, 1975); and to correct the vulgar error that Bernstein is diagnosing a cognitive deficiency in working-class language, see "The Significance of Bernstein's Work for Sociolinguistic Theory" in Halliday, pp. 101–107. Many dangerous misinterpretations of Bernstein could perhaps have been avoided if he had not chosen to call working-class language-using habits a "restricted code" and middle-class (school-oriented) habits an "elaborated code."

24. The seminal text here is Thomas Kuhn, *The Structure of Scientific Revolutions*, 2d. edition, enlarged (Chicago: Univ. of Chicago Press, 1970). Kuhn is now going so far as to say that "proponents of different theories (or different paradigms, in the broader sense of the term) speak different languages—languages expressing different cognitive commitments, suitable for different worlds"; he announces the study of language's function in theory-making as his current project. See Thomas Kuhn, *The Essential Tension* (Chicago: Univ. of Chicago Press, 1977), pp. 22–23.

25. Linda Flower, *Problem-Solving Strategies for Writing* (New York: Harcourt Brace Jovanovich, 1981); further references in text.

26. In my discussion of Collins and Gentner, I am following the line of argument offered by Hubert L. Dreyfus, *What Computers Can't Do* (New York: Harper and Row, 1972); rpt. 2d. edition, San Francisco: Freeman, 1979). Flower and Hayes's sympathy with the Collins-Gentner approach is suggested not only by the large amount of agreement between the two accounts of composing, but also by the numerous borrowings in the Flower-Hayes model from computer terminology and by Flower and Hayes's suggestion that their model will contribute toward "building a Writer" ("Process Theory," p. 368).

27. For an example of this use of Kuhn, see Maxine Hairston, "The Winds of Change: Thomas Kuhn and the Revolution in the Teaching of Writing," *College Composition and Communication*, 33 (February 1982), pp. 76–88.

28. This argument follows the account of rhetoric's function in the scientific discourse community given by Kuhn in *Structure* and (in a more radical version) by Paul Feyerabend, *Against Method* (1975; rpt. London: Verso, 1978).

29. Richard Rorty, *Philosophy and the Mirror of Nature* (Princeton, NJ: Princeton Univ. Press, 1979); further references in text.

30. On the hidden curriculum and its reproduction of oppressive social power relations, see Michael Apple, *Ideology and Curriculum* (London: Routledge and Kegan Paul, 1979).

31. I would like to thank Bruce Herzberg for the many ideas and the editorial guidance that he has, as usual, contributed to my work.

SECTION THREE

Talking about Writing
in Society

- "Collaborative Learning and the 'Conversation of Mankind'" Kenneth A. Bruffee
- "Reality, Consensus, and Reform in the Rhetoric of Composition Teaching" Greg Myers
- "Consensus and Difference in Collaborative Learning" John Trimbur
- "'Contact Zones' and English Studies" Patricia Bizzell
- "Professing Multiculturalism: The Politics of Style in the Contact Zone" Min-Zhan Lu
- "Beyond the Personal: Theorizing a Politics of Location in Composition Research" Gesa E. Kirsch and Joy S. Ritchie
- "The Public Intellectual, Service Learning, and Activist Research" Ellen Cushman

Positivism has been the dominant paradigm for Western society for four centuries, its premises and assumptions rarely questioned for most of that time. It is no wonder, then, that contemporary composition studies would look to the sciences for explanations for what happens in writing. But anthropological study and various elements of critical theory, beginning in the later 1960s, asked serious questions of positivism, to positivism's search for universal answers, to the very idea that we can think in terms of universals.

Composition studies turned to three lines of inquiry in its search for alternatives to positivism. Comp turned to anthropology's social construction theory and its ethnographic research methodologies. Composition also turned to continental philosophical, psychological, and critical theories of poststructuralism. And composition turned to Stanley Fish's conception of "anti- foundationalism" contained in his 1989 *Doing What Comes Naturally: Change, Rhetoric, and the Practice of Theory in Literary and Legal Studies* (Durham, NC: Duke UP). Anti-foundationalism, poststructuralism, and social construction theory all say there can be no universal truths, no truths free from contextual particularities.

Everything contains reflections, to some degree or other, of the cultural, historical, and political contexts in which inquiry takes place. And to the extent that they are political, they also include points of contact, places where cultures collide and eventually intermingle. These spaces where cultures meet (usually in unequal terms, as matters of conquest and conquered) are what linguist and comparative literature scholar Mary Louise Pratt terms "contact zones," a term which captured the imaginations of those who would turn to the social in composition studies, since "contact zones" captures the cultural, the historical, the political, and the rhetorical. Scientism or positivism, on the other hand, appears inherently flawed in its claiming to transcend the social and the political, thereby failing to make explicit (or even to recognize) the effects of the social and the political in its inquiries.

Collaborative Learning and the "Conversation of Mankind"

KENNETH A. BRUFFEE

There are some signs these days that collaborative learning is of increasing interest to English teachers.[1] Composition teachers seem to be exploring the concept actively. Two years ago the term appeared for the first time in the list of topics suggested by the Executive Committee of the Conference on College Composition and Communication for discussion at the CCCC annual convention. It was eighth or ninth on a list of ten items. Last year it appeared again, first on the list.

Teachers of literature have also begun to talk about collaborative learning, although not always by that name. It is viewed as a way of engaging students more deeply with the text and also as an aspect of professors' engagement with the professional community. At its 1978 convention the Modern Language Association scheduled a multi-session forum entitled "Presence, Knowledge, and Authority in the Teaching of Literature." One of the associated sessions, called "Negotiations of Literary Knowledge," included a discussion of the authority and structure (including the collaborative classroom structure) of "interpretive communities." At the 1983 MLA convention collaborative practices in reestablishing authority and value in literary studies were examined under such rubrics as "Talking to the Academic Community: Conferences as Institutions" and "How Books 11 and 12 of *Paradise Lost* Got to be Valuable" (changes in interpretive attitudes in the community of Miltonists).

Reprinted from *College English* 46.7 (November 1984): 635–52. Used with permission. Readers may find more recent explorations of issues discussed in this article in Kenneth A. Bruffee, *Collaborative Learning: Higher Education, Interdependence, and the Authority of Knowledge* (Baltimore: Johns Hopkins University Press, 2nd edition, 1999).

In both these contexts collaborative learning is discussed sometimes as a process that constitutes fields or disciplines of study and sometimes as a pedagogical tool that "works" in teaching composition and literature. The former discussion, often highly theoretical, usually manages to keep at bay the more troublesome and problematic aspects of collaborative learning. The discussion of classroom practice is less fortunate. What emerges there is that many teachers are unsure about how to use collaborative learning and about when and where, appropriately, it should be used. Many are concerned also that when they try to use collaborative learning in what seem to be effective and appropriate ways, it sometimes quite simply fails.

I sympathize with these experiences. Much the same thing has happened to me. Sometimes collaborative learning works beyond my highest expectations. Sometimes it doesn't work at all. Recently, though, I think I have been more successful. The reason for that increased success seems to be that I know a little more now than I did in the past about the complex ideas that lie behind collaborative learning. This essay is frankly an attempt to encourage other teachers to try collaborative learning and to help them use collaborative learning appropriately and effectively. But it offers no recipes. It is written instead on the assumption that understanding both the history and the complex ideas that underlie collaborative learning can improve its practice and demonstrate its educational value.

The history of collaborative learning as I know it can be briefly sketched. Collaborative learning began to interest American college teachers widely only in the 1980s, but the term was coined and the basic idea first developed in the 1950s and 1960s by a group of British secondary school teachers and by a biologist studying British post-graduate education—specifically, medical education. I myself first encountered the term and some of the ideas implicit in it in Edwin Mason's still interesting but now somewhat dated polemic entitled *Collaborative Learning* (London: Ward Lock Educational Co., 1970), and in Charity James' *Young Lives at Stake: A Reappraisal of Secondary Schools* (London: Collins, 1968). Mason, James, and Leslie Smith, colleagues at Goldsmith's College, University of London, were committed during the Vietnam era to democratizing education and to eliminating from education what were perceived then as socially destructive authoritarian social forms. Collaborative learning as they thought of it emerged from this largely political, topical effort.

The collaborative forms that Mason and his colleagues proposed to establish in education had already been explored and their educational value affirmed, however, by the earlier findings of M. L. J. Abercrombie. Abercrombie's *Anatomy of Judgment* (Harmondsworth: Penguin, 1964) culminated ten years of research on the selection and training of medical students at University College, University of London. The result of her research was to suggest that diagnosis, the art of medical judgment and the key element in successful medical practice, is better learned in small groups of students arriving at diagnoses collaboratively than it is learned by students working individually. Abercrombie began her study by observing the scene that lay people think is most typical of medical education: the group of medical students with a teaching physician gathered around a ward bed to diagnose a patient. She then made a seemingly slight but in outcome enormously important change in the way that scene is usually played out. Instead of asking each individual member of the group of students to diagnose the patient on his or her own, Abercrombie asked the whole group to examine the patient together, discuss the case as a group, and arrive at a consensus, a single diagnosis that they could all agree to. What she found was that students learning diagnosis this way acquired good medical judgment faster than individuals working alone (p. 19).

For American college teachers the roots of collaborative learning lie neither in radical politics nor in research. They lie in the nearly desperate response of harried colleges during the early 1970s to a pressing educational need. A decade ago, faculty and administrators in institutions throughout the country became aware that, increasingly, students entering college had difficulty doing as well in academic studies as their native ability suggested they should be able to do. Of course, some of these students were poorly prepared academically. Many more of them, however, had on paper excellent secondary preparation. The common denominator among both the poorly prepared and the seemingly well-prepared was that, for cultural reasons we may not yet fully understand, all these students seemed to have difficulty adapting to the traditional or "normal" conventions of the college classroom.

One symptom of the difficulty these students had adapting to college life and work was that many refused help when it was offered. The help colleges offered, in the main, were tutoring and counseling programs staffed by graduate students and other professionals. These programs failed because undergraduates refused to use them. Many solutions to this problem were suggested and tried, from mandated programs that forced students to accept help they evidently did not want, to sink-or-swim programs that assumed that students who needed help but didn't seek it out didn't belong in college anyway. One idea that seemed at the time among the most exotic and unlikely (that is, in the jargon of the 60s, among the most "radical") turned out in the event to work rather well. Taking hints about the social organization of learning given by John Bremer, Michael von Moschzisker, and others writing at that time about changes in primary and secondary education, some college faculty members guessed that students were refusing help because the kind of help provided seemed merely an extension of the work, the expectations, and above all the social structure of traditional classroom learning (*The School Without Walls* [New York: Holt, 1971], p. 7). It was traditional classroom learning that seemed to have left these students unprepared in the first place. What they needed, it seemed, was help that was not an extension of but an alternative to traditional classroom teaching.

To provide that alternative some colleges turned to peer tutoring. Through peer tutoring teachers could reach students by organizing them to teach each other. And peer tutoring, it turned out, was just one way of doing that, although perhaps the most readily institutionalized way. Collectively, peer tutoring and similar modes such as peer criticism and classroom group work could be sensibly classified under the convenient term provided by our colleagues in Britain: collaborative learning. What the term meant in practice was a form of indirect teaching in which the teacher sets the problem and organizes students to work it out collaboratively. For example, in one type of collaborative learning, peer criticism (also called peer evaluation), students learn to describe the organizational structure of a peer's paper, paraphrase it, and comment both on what seems well done and what the author might do to improve the work. The teacher then evaluates both the essay and the critical response. In another type of collaborative learning, classroom group work, students in small groups work toward a consensus in response to a task set by the teacher, for example, a question about a play, a poem, or another student's paper. What distinguished collaborative learning in each of its several types from traditional classroom practice was that it did not seem to change what people learned (a supposition that now seems questionable) so much as it changed the social context in which they learned it. Students' work tended to improve when they got help from peers; peers offering help, furthermore, learned from the students they helped and from the activity of helping itself. Collaborative learning, it seemed, harnessed the powerful educative force of peer influence that had been—and largely still is—ignored and hence wasted by traditional forms of education.[2]

More recently, those of us actively interested in collaborative learning have begun to think further about this practical experience. Recent developments in philosophy seem to suggest a conceptual rationale for collaborative learning that yields some unexpected insights into pedagogical practice. A new conception of the nature of knowledge provides direction that we lacked earlier as we muddled through, trying to solve practical problems in practical ways. The better we understand this conceptional rationale, it seems, the more effective our practice of collaborative learning becomes.

In the hope that this experience will prove true for others, the following three sections outline the rationale of collaborative learning as I currently understand it and the relation of that rationale to classroom practice. The final section outlines some as yet not fully worked out implications both of collaborative learning as a practice and of some aspects of its conceptual rationale. Practice and rationale together, I will argue there, have the potential to challenge fairly deeply the theory and practice of traditional classroom teaching.

CONVERSATION AND THE NATURE OF THOUGHT AND KNOWLEDGE

In an important essay on the place of literature in education published some twenty years ago, "The Voice of Poetry in the Conversation of Mankind," Michael Oakeshott argues that what distinguishes human beings from other animals is our ability to participate in unending conversation. "As civilized human beings," Oakeshott writes,

> we are the inheritors, neither of an inquiry about ourselves and the world, nor of an accumulating body of information, but of a conversation, begun in the primeval forests and extended and made more articulate in the course of centuries. It is a conversation which goes on both in public and within each of ourselves. . . . Education, properly speaking, is an initiation into the skill and partnership of this conversation in which we learn to recognize the voices, to distinguish the proper occasions of utterance, and in which we acquire the intellectual and moral habits appropriate to conversation. And it is this conversation which, in the end, gives place and character to every human activity and utterance. (*Rationalism in Politics* [New York: Basic Books, 1962], p. 199)

Oakeshott argues that the human conversation takes place within us as well as among us, and that conversation as it takes place within us is what we call reflective thought. In making this argument he assumes that conversation and reflective thought are related in two ways: causally and functionally. That is, Oakeshott assumes what the work of Lev Vygotsky and others has shown, that reflective thought is public or social conversation internalized (see, for example, Vygotsky, *Mind and Society* [Cambridge, Mass.: Harvard University Press, 1978]). We first experience and learn "the skill and partnership of conversation" in the external arena of direct social exchange with other people. Only then do we learn to displace that "skill and partnership" by playing silently ourselves, in imagination, the parts of all the participants in the conversation. As Clifford Geertz has put it,

> thinking as an overt, public act, involving the purposeful manipulation of objective materials, is probably fundamental to human beings; and thinking as a covert, private act, and without recourse to such materials [is] a derived, though not unuseful, capability. . . . Human thought is consumately social: social in its origins, social in its functions, social in its form, social in its applications.[3]

Since what we experience as reflective thought is related causally to social conversation (we learn one from the other), the two are also related functionally. That is, because thought is internalized conversation, thought and conversation tend to work largely in the same way. Of course, in thought some of the limitations of conversation are absent. Logistics, for example, are no problem at all. I don't have to take the A train or Eastern Airlines flight #221 to get together with myself for a chat. And in thought there are no differences among the participants in preparation, interest, native ability, or spoken vernacular. Each one is just as clever as I can be, or just as dull. On the other hand, in thought some of the less fortunate limitations of conversation may persist. Limitations that may be imposed, for example, by ethnocentrism, inexperience, personal anxiety, economic interests, and paradigmatic inflexibility can constrain my thinking just as they can constrain conversation. If my talk is narrow, superficial, biased, and confined to cliches, my thinking is likely to be so too.

Still, it remains the case that according to this concept of mental activity many of the social forms and conventions of conversation, most of the grammatical, syntactical and rhetorical structures of conversation, and the range, flexibility, impetus, and goals of conversation are the sources of the forms and conventions, structures, impetus, range and flexibility, and the issues of reflective thought.

The relationship I have been drawing here between conversation and thought illuminates the source of the quality, depth, terms, character, and issues of thought. The assumptions underlying my argument differ considerably, however, from the assumptions we ordinarily make about the nature of thought. We ordinarily assume that thought is some sort of given, an "essential attribute" of the human mind. The view that conversation and thought are causally related assumes not that thought is an essential attribute of the human mind but that it is instead an artifact created by social interaction. We can think because we can talk, and we think in ways we have learned to talk. As Stanley Fish has put it, the thoughts we "can think and the mental operations [we] can perform have their source in some or other interpretive community."[4] The range, complexity, and subtlety of our thought, its power, the practical and conceptual uses we can put it to, and the very issues we can address result in large measure directly from the degree to which we have been initiated into what Oakeshott calls the potential "skill and partnership" of human conversation in its public and social form.

To the extent that thought is internalized conversation, then, any effort to understand how we think requires us to understand the nature of conversation; and any effort to understand conversation requires us to understand the nature of community life that generates and maintains conversation. Furthermore, any effort to understand and cultivate in ourselves the kind of thought we value most requires us to understand and cultivate the kinds of community life that establish and maintain conversation that is the origin of that kind of thought. To think well as individuals we must learn to think well collectively—that is, we must learn to converse well. The first steps to learning to think better, therefore, are learning to converse better and learning to establish and maintain the sorts of social context, the sorts of community life, that foster the sorts of conversation members of the community value.

This principle has broad applicability and has implications far beyond those that may be immediately apparent. For example, Thomas Kuhn has argued in *The Structure of Scientific Revolutions*, (2nd ed.: Chicago: University of Chicago Press, 1970) that to understand scientific thought and knowledge we must understand the nature of scientific communities. Scientific knowledge changes not as our "understanding of the world" changes. It changes as scientists organize and reorganize relations among themselves (pp. 209–10). Carrying Kuhn's view and terminology further, Richard Rorty argues in *Philosophy and the Mirror of Nature* (Princeton: Princeton University Press, 1979) that to understand any kind of knowledge we must understand what he calls the social justification of belief. That is, we must understand how knowledge is established and maintained in the "normal discourse" of communities of knowledgeable peers.[5] Stanley Fish completes the argument by saying that these "interpretive communities" are the source of our thought and of the "meanings" we produce through the use and manipulation of symbolic structures, chiefly language. Fish suggests further, reflecting Erving Goffman's conclusion to *The Presentation of Self in Everyday Life* ([New York: Doubleday Anchor, 1959], pp. 252–53), that interpretative communities may also be in large measure the source of what we regard as our very selves (Fish, p. 14). Our feelings and intuitions are as much the product of social relations as our knowledge.

EDUCATIONAL IMPLICATIONS: CONVERSATION, COLLABORATIVE LEARNING, AND "NORMAL DISCOURSE"

The line of argument I have been pursuing has important implications for educators, and especially for those of us who teach English—both literature and composition. If thought is internalized public and social talk, then writing of all kinds is internalized social talk made public and social again. If thought is internalized conversation, then writing is internalized conversation re-externalized.[6]

Like thought, writing is related to conversation in both time and function. Writing is a technologically displaced form of conversation. When we write, having already internalized the "skill and partnership" of conversation, we displace it once more onto the written page. But because thought is already one step away from conversation, the position of writing relative to conversation is more complex than the position of thought relative to conversation. Writing is at once two steps away from conversation and a return to conversation. We converse; we internalize conversation as thought; and then by writing, we re-immerse conversation in its external, social medium.

My ability to write this essay, for example, depends on my ability to talk through with myself the issues I address here. And my ability to talk through an issue with myself derives largely from my ability to converse directly with other people in an immediate social situation. The point is not that the particular thing I write every time must necessarily be something I have talked over with other people first, although I may well often do just that. What I have to say can, of course, originate in thought, and it often does. But my thought itself is conversation as I have learned to internalize it. The point, therefore, is that writing always has its roots deep in the acquired ability to carry on the social symbolic exchange we call conversation.

The inference writing teachers should make from this line of reasoning is that our task must involve engaging students in conversation among themselves at as many points in both the writing and the reading process as possible, and that we should contrive to ensure that students' conversation about what they read and write is similar in as many ways as possible to the way we would like them eventually to read and write. The way they talk with each other determines the way they will think and the way they will write.

To organize students for these purposes is, in as general a way as I can put it, to organize collaborative learning. Collaborative learning provides a social context in which students can experience and practice the kinds of conversation valued by college teachers. The kind of conversation peer tutors engage in with their tutees, for example, can be emotionally involved,

294

intellectually and substantively focused, and personally disinterested. There could be no better source than this of the sort of displaced conversation—writing—valued by college teachers. Similarly, collaborative classroom group work guided by a carefully designed task makes students aware that writing is a social artifact, like the thought that produces it. Writing may seem to be displaced in time and space from the rest of a writer's community of readers and other writers, but in every instance writing is an act, however much displaced, of conversational exchange.

Besides providing a particular kind of conversation, collaborative learning also provides a particular kind of social context for conversation, a particular kind of community—a community of status equals: peers. Students learn the "skill and partnership" of re-externalized conversation, writing, not only in a community that fosters the kind of conversation college teachers value most, but also in a community that approximates the one most students must eventually write for in everyday life, in business, government, and the professions.

It is worthwhile to digress a moment here to establish this last point. In most cases people write in business, government, and the professions mainly to inform and convince other people within the writer's own community, people whose status and assumptions approximate the writer's own.[7] That is, the sort of writing most people do most in their everyday working lives is what Richard Rorty calls "normal discourse." Normal discourse (a term of Rorty's coinage based on Thomas Kuhn's term "normal science") applies to conversation within a community of knowledgeable peers. A community of knowledgeable peers is a group of people who accept, and whose work is guided by, the same paradigms and the same code of values and assumptions. In normal discourse, as Rorty puts it, everyone agrees on the "set of conventions about what counts as a relevant contribution, what counts as a question, what counts as having a good argument for that answer or a good criticism of it." The product of normal discourse is "the sort of statement that can be agreed to be true by all participants whom the other participants count as 'rational'" (p. 320).

The essay I am writing here is an example of normal discourse in this sense. I am writing to members of my own community of knowledgeable peers. My readers and I (I presume) are guided in our work by the same set of conventions about what counts as a relevant contribution, what counts as a question, what counts as having a good argument for that answer or a good criticism of it. I judge my essay finished when I think it conforms to that set of conventions and values. It is within that set of conventions and values that my readers will evaluate the essay, both in terms of its quality and in terms of whether or not it makes sense. Normal discourse is pointed;

it is explanatory and argumentative. Its purpose is to justify belief to the satisfaction of other people within the author's community of knowledgeable peers. Much of what we teach today—or should be teaching—in composition courses is the normal discourse of most academic, professional, and business communities. The rhetoric taught in our composition textbooks comprises—or should comprise—the conventions of normal discourse of those communities.[8]

Teaching normal discourse in its written form is central to a college curriculum, therefore, because the one thing college teachers in most fields commonly want students to acquire, and what teachers in most fields consistently reward students for, is the ability to carry on in speech and writing the normal discourse of the field in question. Normal discourse is what William Perry describes as discourse in the established contexts of knowledge in a field, discourse that makes effective reference to facts as defined within those contexts. In a student who can integrate fact and context together in this way, Perry says, "we recognize a colleague."[9] This is so because to be conversant with the normal discourse in a field of study or endeavor is exactly what we mean by being knowledgeable—that is, knowledge-able—in that field. Not to have mastered the normal discourse of a discipline, no matter how many "facts" or data one may know, is not to be knowledgeable in that discipline. Mastery of a knowledge community's normal discourse is the basic qualification for acceptance into that community.

The kind of writing students find most useful to learn in college, therefore, is not only the kind of writing most appropriate to work in fields of business, government, and the professions. It is also the writing most appropriate to gaining competence in most academic fields that students study in college. What these two kinds of writing have in common is that they are both written within and addressed to a community of status equals: peers. They are both normal discourse.

This point having, I hope, been established, the nature of the particular kind of community that collaborative learning forms becomes clearer. Collaborative learning provides the kind of social context, the kind of community, in which normal discourse occurs: a community of knowledgeable peers. This is one of its main goals: to provide a context in which students can practice and master the normal discourse exercised in established knowledge communities in the academic world and in business, government, and the professions.

But to say this only raises a host of questions. One question is, how can student peers, who are not members of the knowledge communities they hope to enter, who lack the knowledge that constitutes those communities, help other students enter them? The first, more concrete answer to this question is that no student is wholly ignorant and inexperienced. Every student is already a member of several knowledge communities, from canoeing to computers, baseball to ballet. Membership in any one of these communities may not be a resource that will by itself help much directly in learning to organize an essay or explicate a poem. But pooling the resources that a group of peers brings with them to the task may make accessible the normal discourse of the new community they together hope to enter. Students are especially likely to be able to master that discourse collaboratively if their conversation is structured indirectly by the task or problem that a member of that new community (the teacher) has judiciously designed.[10] To the conversation between peer tutors and their tutees in writing, for example, the tutee brings knowledge of the subject to be written about and knowledge of the assignment. The tutor brings sensitivity to the needs and feelings of peers and knowledge of the conventions of discourse and of standard written English. And the conversation is structured in part by the demands of the teacher's assignment and in part by the formal conventions of the communities the teacher represents, the conventions of academic discourse and standard English.

Such conversation among students can break down, of course, if any one of these elements is not present. It can proceed again if the person responsible for providing the missing element, usually but not always the teacher, is flexible enough to adjust his or her contribution accordingly. If, for example, tutees do not bring to the conversation knowledge of the subject and the assignment, then the teacher helps peer tutors see that their most important contribution may be to help tutees begin at the very beginning: how to go about making sufficient acquaintance with the subject matter and how to set out to clarify the assignment. If tutors lack sensitivity to language and to the feelings and needs of their peers, tutees must contribute by making those feelings and needs more clearly evident. If the task or assignment that the teacher has given is unclear or too difficult or too simpleminded to engage students effectively, then the teacher has to revise it. Throughout this process the teacher has to try to help students negotiate the rocks and shoals of social relations that may interfere with their getting on with their work together.

What students do when working collaboratively on their writing is not write or edit or, least of all, read proof. What they do is converse. They talk about the subject and about the assignment. They talk through the writer's understanding of the subject. They converse about their own relationship and, in general, about relationships in an academic or intellectual context between students and teachers. Most of all they converse about and as a part of writing. Similarly, what students do when working collaboratively in small groups in order to read a text with understanding—a poem, a story, or another student's paper—is also to converse. They converse in order to reach consensus in answer to questions the teacher has raised about the text. They converse about and as a part of understanding. In short, they learn, by practicing it in this orderly way, the normal discourse of the academic community.

COLLABORATIVE LEARNING AND THE AUTHORITY OF KNOWLEDGE

The place of conversation in learning, especially in the humanities, is the largest context in which we must see collaborative learning. To say that conversation has a place in learning should not of course seem peculiar to those of us who count ourselves humanists, a category that includes all of us who teach literature and most of us who teach writing. Furthermore, most of us believe that "class discussion" is one of the most effective ways of teaching. The truth, however, is that despite this belief the person who does most of the discussing in most of our discussion classes is the teacher.

This tends to happen because behind our enthusiasm for discussion lies a fundamental distrust of it. The graduate training most of us have enjoyed—or endured—has taught us, in fact, that collaboration and community activity is inappropriate and foreign to work in humanistic disciplines such as English. Humanistic study, we have been led to believe, is a solitary life, and the vitality of the humanities lies in the talents and endeavors of each of us as individuals. What we call discussion is more often than not an adversarial activity pitting individual against individual in an effort to assert what one literary critic has called "will to power over the text," if not over each other. If we look at what we do instead of what we say, we discover that we think of knowledge as something we acquire and wield as individuals relative to each other, not something we generate and maintain in company with and in dependency upon each other.[11]

Only recently have humanists of note, such as Stanley Fish in literary criticism and Richard Rorty in philosophy, begun to take effective steps toward exploring the force and implications of knowledge communities in the humanistic disciplines, and toward redefining the nature of our knowledge as a social artifact. Much of this recent work follows a trail blazed two decades ago by Thomas Kuhn. The historical irony of this course of events lies in the fact that Kuhn developed his notion about the nature of scientific knowledge after first examining the way knowledge is generated, established, and maintained in the humanities and social sciences. For us as humanists to discover in Kuhn and his followers the conceptual rationale of collaborative learning is to see our own chickens come home to roost.

Kuhn's position that even in the "hard" sciences knowledge is a social artifact emerged from his attempt to understand the implications of the increasing indeterminacy of knowledge of all kinds in the twentieth century.[12] To say that knowledge is indeterminate is to say that there is no fixed and certain point of reference, no Arnoldian "touchstone" against which we can measure truth. If there is no such absolute referent, then knowledge must be a thing people make and remake. Knowledge must be a social artifact. But to call knowledge a social artifact, Kuhn argues, is not to say that knowledge is merely relative, that knowledge is what any one of us says it is. Knowledge is maintained and established by communities of knowledgeable peers. It is what together we agree it is, for the time being. Rorty, following Kuhn, argues that communities of knowledgeable peers make knowledge by a process of socially justifying belief. Collaborative learning models this process.

This then is a second and more general answer to the question raised in the preceding section. How can student peers, who are not themselves members of the knowledge communities they hope to enter, help other students to enter those communities? Isn't collaborative learning the blind leading the blind?

It is of course exactly the blind leading the blind if we insist on the Cartesian model of knowledge: that to know is to "see," and that knowledge is information impressed upon the individual mind by some outside source. But if we accept the premise that knowledge is an artifact created by a community of knowledgeable peers constituted by the language of that community, and that learning is a social and not an individual process, then to learn is not to assimilate information and improve our mental eyesight. To learn is to work collaboratively to establish and maintain knowledge among a community of knowledgeable peers through the process that Richard Rorty calls "socially justifying belief." We socially justify belief when we explain to others why one way of understanding how the world hangs together seems to us preferable to other ways of understanding it. We establish knowledge or justify belief collaboratively by challenging each other's biases and presuppositions; by negotiating collectively toward new paradigms of perception, thought, feeling, and expression; and by joining larger, more experienced communities of knowledgeable peers through assenting to those communities' interests, values, language, and paradigms of perception and thought.

If we accept this concept of knowledge and learning even partially and tentatively, it is possible to see collaborative learning as a model of the way that even the most sophisticated scientific knowledge is established and maintained. Knowledge is the product of human beings in a state of continual negotiation or conversation. Education is not a process of assimilating "the truth" but, as Rorty has put it, a process of learning to "take a hand in what is going on" by joining "the conversation of mankind." Collaborative learning is an arena in which students can negotiate their way into that conversation.

COLLABORATIVE LEARNING AND NEW KNOWLEDGE

Seen this way, collaborative learning seems unexceptionable. It is not hard to see it as comfortable, not very surprising, not even very new. In discovering and applying collaborative learning we seem to be, if not exactly reinventing the wheel, certainly rediscovering some of the more obvious implications of that familiar and useful device. Collaborative learning, it seems, is no new thing under the sun. However much we may explore its conceptual ramifications, we must acknowledge the fact that people have always learned from their peers and doggedly persist in doing so whether we professional teachers and educators take a hand in it or not. In Thomas Wolfe's *Look Homeward, Angel* Eugene Gant records how in grammar school he learned to write (in this case, form the words on a page) from his "comrade," learning from a peer what "all instruction failed" to teach him. In business and industry, furthermore, and in professions such as medicine, law, engineering, and architecture—where to work is to learn or fail—collaboration is the norm. All that is new in collaborative learning, it seems, is the systematic application of collaborative principles to that last bastion of hierarchy and individualism, the American college classroom.

This comfortable view, while appropriate, may yet be deceptive. If we follow just a bit further the implications of the rationale for collaborative learning that I have been outlining here, we catch a glimpse of a somewhat startling educational scene. Take, for example, the principle that entering an existing knowledge community involves a process of negotiation. Followed to its logical conclusion this principle implies that education is not a rite of passage in which students passively become initiated into an institution that is monolithic and unchanging. It implies that the means by which students learn to negotiate this entry, collaborative learning, is not merely a better pedagogy, a better way of initiating new members into existing knowledge communities. And it implies that collaborative learning as a classroom practice models more than how knowledge is established and maintained.

The argument pursued here implies, in short, that in the long run collaborative learning models how knowledge is generated, how it changes and grows.

This way of thinking about collaborative learning is somewhat speculative, but it is nevertheless of considerable interest and importance to teachers of English. If, as Rorty suggests, knowledge is a social artifact, if knowledge is belief justified through normal discourse, then the generation of knowledge, what we call "creativity," must also be a social process. It too must involve discourse. But the discourse involved in generating knowledge cannot be normal discourse, since normal discourse maintains knowledge. It is inadequate for generating new knowledge. Knowledge-generating discourse is discourse of quite another kind. It is, to use Rorty's phrase, abnormal discourse.

In contrast to normal discourse, abnormal discourse occurs between coherent communities or within communities when consensus no longer exists with regard to rules, assumptions, goals, values, or mores. Abnormal discourse, Rorty says, "is what happens when someone joins in the discourse who is ignorant of the conventions governing that discourse "or who sets them aside." Whereas normal discourse produces "the sort of statement which can be agreed to be true by all participants whom the other participants count as 'rational,'" "the product of abnormal discourse can be anything from nonsense to intellectual revolution." Unlike the participants in normal discourse who sound "rational" to the others in the community, a person speaking abnormal discourse sounds "either 'kooky' (if he loses his point) or 'revolutionary' (if he gains it)" (pp. 320, 339).

The importance of abnormal discourse to the discussion of collaborative learning is that abnormal discourse serves the function of helping us—immersed as we inevitably are in the everyday normal discourse of our disciplines and professions—to see the provincial nature of normal discourse and of the communities defined by normal discourse. Abnormal discourse sniffs out stale, unproductive knowledge and challenges its authority, that is, the authority of the community which that knowledge constitutes. Its purpose, Rorty says, is to undermine "our reliance upon the knowledge we have gained" through normal discourse. We must occasionally undermine this reliance because normal discourse tends to "block the flow of conversation by presenting [itself] as offering the canonical vocabulary for discussion of a given topic" (pp. 386–387).

Abnormal discourse is therefore necessary to learning. But, ironically, abnormal discourse cannot be directly taught. "There is no discipline that describes" abnormal discourse, Rorty tells us, "any more than there is a discipline devoted to the study of the unpredictable or of 'creativity'" (p. 320).

What we can teach are the tools of normal discourse, that is, both practical rhetoric and rhetorically based modes of literary criticism such as the taxonomy of figures, new-critical analysis, and deconstructive criticism.[13] To leave openings for change, however, we must not teach these tools as universals. We must teach practical rhetoric and critical analysis in such a way that, when necessary, students can turn to abnormal discourse in order to undermine their own and other people's reliance on the canonical conventions and vocabulary of normal discourse. We must teach the use of these tools in such a way that students *can* set them aside, if only momentarily, for the purpose of generating new knowledge, for the purpose, that is, of reconstituting knowledge communities in more satisfactory ways.

It is just here that, as I mentioned at the beginning of this essay, we begin to move beyond our earlier suppositions about what people learn through collaborative learning. Defining knowledge as a social artifact established and maintained through normal discourse challenges the authority of knowledge as we traditionally understand it. But by changing what we usually call the process of learning—the work, the expectations, and the social structure of the traditional classroom—collaborative learning also changes what we usually call the substance of learning. It challenges the authority of knowledge by revealing, as John Trimbur has observed, that authority itself is a social artifact. This revelation and the new awareness that results from it makes authority comprehensible both to us as teachers and to our students. It involves a process of reacculturation. Thus collaborative learning can help students join the established knowledge communities of academic studies, business, and the professions. But it should also help students learn something else. They should learn, Trimbur says, "something about how this social transition takes place, how it involves crises of identity and authority, how students can begin to generate a transitional language to bridge the gap between communities" (private correspondence).

Challenging the traditional authority of knowledge in this way, collaborative learning naturally challenges the traditional basis of the authority of those who teach. Our authority as teachers always derives directly or indirectly from the prevailing conception of the authority of knowledge. In the pre-Cartesian world people tended to believe that the authority of knowledge lodged in one place, the mind of God. In that world teachers derived their authority from their godliness, their nearness to the mind of God. In Cartesian, Mirror-of-Nature epistemology, the authority of knowledge has had three alternative lodgings, each a secular version of the mind of God. We could believe if we chose that the authority of knowledge lodged in some touchstone of value and truth above and beyond ourselves, such as mathematics, creative genius, or the universals of sound reasoning. We could believe that the authority of knowledge lodged in the mind of a person of genius: a Wordsworth, an Einstein, or a Freud. Or we could believe that the authority of knowledge lodged in the nature of the object objectively known: the universe, the human mind, the text of a poem.

Our authority as teachers, accordingly, has had its source in our nearness to one of these secular versions of the mind of God. In the first case we derive our authority from our identification with the "touchstone" of value and truth. Thus, for some of us, mathematicians and poets have, generally speaking, greater authority than, say, sociologists or literary critics. According to the second alternative we derive our authority from intimacy with the greatest minds. Many of us feel that those who have had the good fortune to study with Freud, Faraday, or Faulkner, for example, have greater authority than those who studied with their disciples; or, those who have studied the manuscripts of Joyce's fiction have greater authority than those who merely studied the edited texts. According to the third alternative, we derive our authority as teachers from being in direct touch with the objective world. Most of us feel that those whose knowledge is confirmed by hands-on laboratory experimentation have greater authority than those whose knowledge is based on a synthesis of secondary sources.

Because the concept that knowledge is socially justified belief denies that the authority of knowledge lodges in any of these places, our authority as teachers according to that concept has quite another source as well. Insofar as collaborative learning inducts students into established knowledge communities and teaches them the normal discourse of those communities, we derive our authority as teachers from being certified representatives of the communities of knowledgeable peers that students aspire to join, and that we, as members of our chosen disciplines and also members of the community of the liberally educated public at large, invite and encourage them to join. Teachers are defined in this instance as those members of a knowledge community who accept the responsibility for inducting new members into the community. Without successful teachers the community will die when its current members die, and knowledge as assented to by that community will cease to exist.

Insofar as collaborative learning helps students understand how knowledge is generated through abnormal discourse, however, our authority as teachers derives from another source. It derives from the values of a larger—indeed, the largest possible—community of knowledgeable peers, the community that encompasses all others. The interests of this largest community contradict one of the central interests of local communities such as professional disciplines and fields of study: to maintain established knowledge. The interest of the larger community is to resist this conservative tendency.

Its interest is to bridge gaps among knowledge communities and to open them to change.

The continued vitality of the knowledge communities we value—in particular the community of liberally educated people and its sub-communities, the scholarly and professional disciplines—depends on both these needs being met: to maintain established knowledge and to challenge and change it. As representatives and delegates of a local, disciplinary community, and of the larger community as well, teachers are responsible for the continued vitality of both of the knowledge communities we value. Responsible to both sets of values, therefore, we must perform as conservators *and* agents of change, as custodians of prevailing community values *and* as agents of social transition and reacculturation.

Because by giving students access to the "conversation of mankind," to return to Oakeshott's phrase, collaborative learning can serve both of these seemingly conflicting educational aims at once, it has an especially important role to play in studying and teaching English. It is one way of introducing students to the process by which communities of knowledgeable peers create referential connections between symbolic structures and "reality," that is, by which they establish knowledge and by doing so maintain community growth and coherence. To study adequately any text—student theme or play by Shakespeare—is to study an entire social symbolic process, not just part of it. To study and teach English is to study and teach the social origin, nature, reference, and function of symbolic structures.

The view that knowledge is a social artifact, furthermore, requires a reexamination of our premises as students of English and as teachers. To date, very little work of this sort has been done. One can only guess what might come of a concerted effort on the part of the profession as a whole. The effort might ultimately involve "demystifying" much that we now do as humanists and teachers of the humanities. If we bring to mind, for example, a sampling of important areas of current theoretical thought in and allied to literary criticism, we are likely to find mostly bipolar forms: text and reader, text and writer, symbol and referent, signifier and signified. On the one hand, a critique along the lines I have been following here might involve examining how these theories would differ if they included the third term missing from most of them. How would a psychoanalytically oriented study of metaphor differ, for example, if it acknowledged that psychotherapy is fundamentally a kind of social relationship based on the mutual creation or recreation of symbolic structures by therapist and patient? How would semiotics differ if it acknowledged that all "codes" are symbolic structures constituting language communities and that to understand these codes requires us to examine and understand the complex social symbolic relations among the people who make up language communities? How would practical rhetoric look if we assumed that writer and reader were not adversaries but partners in a common, community-based enterprise? How would it look if we no longer assumed that people write to persuade or to distinguish themselves and their points of view and to enhance their own individuality by gaining the acquiescence of other individuals? How would it look if we assumed instead that people write for the very opposite reason: that people write in order to be accepted, to join, to be regarded as another member of the culture or community that constitutes the writer's audience?

Once we had reexamined in this way how English is studied professionally, we could on the other hand also undertake to reexamine how English is taught as well. If we did that, we might find ourselves taking issue with Stanley Fish's conclusion that to define knowledge as a social artifact generated by interpretive communities has no effect whatsoever on the way we read and teach literature and composition. My argument in this essay suggests, on the contrary, that some changes in our pedagogical attitudes and classroom practices are almost inevitable. These changes would result from integrating our understanding of social symbolic relationships into our teaching—not just into what we teach but also into how we teach it. For example, so long as we think of knowledge as a reflection and synthesis of information about the objective world, then to teach *King Lear* seems to involve providing a "correct" text and rehearsing students in "correct" interpretations of it. "Correct" here means the text and the interpretations that, as Fish puts it, seem "obvious and inescapable" within the knowledge community, within the "institutional or conventional structure," of which we happen to be members (p. 370).

But if we think of knowledge as socially justified belief, then to teach *King Lear* seems to involve creating contexts where students undergo a sort of cultural change. This change would be one in which they loosen ties to the knowledge communities they currently belong to and join another. These two communities would be seen as having quite different sets of values, mores, and goals, and above all quite different languages. To speak in one community of a person asking another to "pray you undo this button" (V, iii) might be merely to tell a mercantile tale, or a prurient one, while in another community such a request could be both a gesture of profound human dignity and a metaphor of the dissolution of a world.

Similarly, so long as we think of learning as reflecting and synthesizing information about the objective world, to teach expository writing is to provide examples, analysis, and exercises in the traditional modes of practical rhetoric—description, narration, comparison-contrast—or examples, analysis, and exercises in the "basic skills" of writing, and to rehearse students in their proper use. But if we think of learning as a social process, the process of socially justifying belief, then to teach expository writing seems to involve something else entirely. It involves demonstrating to students that they know something only when they can explain it in writing to the satisfaction of the community of their knowledgeable peers. To teach this way, in turn, seems to require us to engage students in collaborative work that does not just reinforce the values and skills they begin with, but that promotes a sort of reacculturation.[14]

The argument I have been making here implies, in short, that students and teachers of literature and writing must begin to develop awareness and skill that may seem foreign and irrelevant to our profession at the present time. Organizing collaborative learning effectively requires doing more than throwing students together with their peers with little or no guidance or preparation. To do that is merely to perpetuate, perhaps even aggravate, the many possible negative efforts of peer group influence: conformity, anti-intellectualism, intimidation, and leveling-down of quality. To avoid these pitfalls and to marshal the powerful educational resource of peer group influence requires us to create and maintain a demanding academic environment that makes collaboration—social engagement in intellectual pursuits—a genuine part of students' educational development. And that in turn requires quite new and perhaps more thorough analyses of the elements of our field than we have yet attempted.

NOTES

1. I am indebted for conversation regarding substantive issues raised in this essay to Fellows of the Brooklyn College Institute for Training Peer Tutors and of the Asnuntuck Community College Institute in Collaborative Learning and Peer-Tutor Training, and to Peter Elbow. Both Institutes were supported by grants from the Fund for the Improvement of Postsecondary Education. I am particularly grateful to Peter Hawkes, Harvey Kail, Ronald Maxwell, and John Trimbur for reading the essay in early drafts and for offering suggestions for improvement. The essay is in many ways and at many levels a product of collaborative learning.

2. The educative value of peer group influence is discussed in Theodore M. Newcomb and Everett K. Wilson, eds., *College Peer Groups* (Chicago: Aldine, 1966).

3. *The Interpretation of Cultures* (New York: Basic Books, 1971), pp. 76–77, 360. In addition to "The Growth of Culture and the Evolution of Mind," also relevant in the same volume are "The Impact of the Concept of Man" and "Ideology as a Cultural System," parts four and five.

4. *Is There a Text in This Class?: The Authority of Interpretive Communities* (Cambridge, Mass.: Harvard University Press, 1980), p. 14. Fish develops his argument fully in part 2, pp. 303–371. On the distinction between "interiority" or "inwardness" and "internalization," see Stephen Toulmin, "The Inwardness of Mental Life," *Critical Inquiry*, 6 (1979), 1–16.

5. I have explored some of the larger educational implications of Rorty's argument in "Liberal Education and the Social Justification of Belief," *Liberal Education*, 68 (1982), 95–114.

6. I make a case for this position in "Writing and Reading as Collaborative or Social Acts," in Janice N. Hays, et al, eds., *The Writer's Mind: Writing as a Mode of Thinking* (Urbana, Ill.: National Council of Teachers of English, 1983), pp. 159–169. In the current critical climate the distinction between conversation and speech as sources of writing and thought is important to maintain. Deconstructionist critics such as Paul de Man argue (e.g., in his *Blindness and Insight* [Minneapolis: University of Minnesota Press, 1983]), following Derrida, that writing is not displaced speech but a primary act. This argument defines "writing" in a much broader sense than we are used to, to mean something like "making public" in any manner, including speech. Hence deconstructionist "writing" can be construed as a somewhat static conception of what I am here calling "conversation": a social act. So long as the conversational, hence social, nature of "writing" in the deconstructionist sense remains unrecognized, the aversion of deconstructionist criticism to the primacy of speech as embodying the phenomenological "metaphysics of presence" remains circular. The deconstructionist argument holds that privileging speech "centers" language in persons. But "persons" are fictions. The alternative proposal by deconstruction, however, that writing is "free play," invites centering once again, since the figure of play personifies language. The deconstructionist critique has thus yet to acknowledge sufficiently that language, and its products such as thought and the self, are social artifacts constituted by "interpretive communities."

7. Some writing in business, government, and the professions may of course be like the writing students do in school for teachers, that is, for the sake of practice and evaluation. Certainly some writing in everyday working life is done purely as performance to please superiors in the corporate or department hierarchy, tell them what they already know, and demonstrate to them the writer's proficiency *as* a writer. It may be true, therefore, that learning to write to a person who is not a member of one's own status and knowledge community, that is, to a teacher, has some practical everyday value. But the value of writing of this type is hardly proportionate to the amount of time students normally spend on it.

8. A textbook that acknowledges the normal discourse of academic disciplines and offers ways of learning it in a context of collaborative learning is Elaine Maimon, et al., *Writing in the Arts and Sciences* (Boston: Little Brown, 1981).

9. "Examsmanship and the Liberal Arts," in *Examining in Harvard College: A Collection of Essays by Members of the Harvard Faculty* (Cambridge, Mass.: Harvard University Press, 1963). Quoted from Kenneth A. Bruffee, *A Short Course in Writing* (Boston: Little, Brown, 1980), p. 221.

10. For examples and an explanation of this technique, see my *A Short Course in Writing*, cited above, and "CLTV: Collaborative Learning Television," *Educational Communication and Technology Journal*, 30 (1982), 26–40. Also see Clark Bouton and Russell Y. Garth, eds., *Learning in Groups* (San Francisco: Jossey-Bass, 1983).

11. I discuss the individualistic bias of our current interpretation of the humanistic tradition in "The Structure of Knowledge and the Future of Liberal Education," *Liberal Education*, 67 (1981), 181–185.

12. I trace briefly the history of the growing indeterminacy of knowledge and its relevance to the humanities in "The Structure of Knowledge," cited above.

13. Christopher Norris defines deconstruction somewhat simplistically but usefully for most purposes as "rhetorical questioning" (*Deconstruction: Theory and Practice* [London: Methuen, 1982], p. 21).

14. I suggest some possible curricular implications of the concept of knowledge as socially justified belief in "Liberal Education and the Social Justification of Belief," cited above. See also Clifford Geertz, *Local Knowledge* (New York: Basic Books, 1983), pp. 14–15, 161; Richard M. Rorty, "Hermeneutics, General Studies, and Teaching," *Synergos: Selected Papers from the Synergos Seminars*, George Mason University, 2 (Fall 1982), 1–15; and my "Learning to Live in a World out of Joint: Thomas Kuhn's Message to Humanists Revisited," *Liberal Education*, 70 (1984), 77–81.

Reality, Consensus, and Reform in the Rhetoric of Composition Teaching

GREG MYERS

I would like to raise some political questions about two methods of teaching I use in my writing classes: having small groups of students collaborate on and critique each others' writing, and having case assignments based on some actual writing situation, whether a technical proposal or an anthropology exam. My thinking about these methods is based largely on the detailed and practical suggestions of Peter Elbow and Kenneth Bruffee, and on discussion of their works with other teachers. My means of raising questions will be to compare the writings of Elbow and Bruffee to the work of an earlier writer, Sterling Andrus Leonard (1888–1931), whose Dewey-inspired English education textbook, *English Composition as a Social Problem*, suggested these two teaching methods, which I had considered new, back in 1917. I revive this now-forgotten writer and make these comparisons for two reasons: 1) the distance in time makes it easier for us to see his social context than it is to see the context of Elbow or Bruffee, and 2) the recurrence of these ideas as new ideas suggests that those of us who want to change the way writing is taught tend to overlook the efforts and the lessons of earlier reformers. As Lawrence Cremin says in his history of the progressive movement in education, of which Leonard was a part, "Reform movements are notoriously ahistorical in outlook" (8). Until recently, this ahistoricism has

Reprinted from *College English* 48.2 (February 1986): 154–71. Used with permission.

been characteristic of composition theory, with its reformist attacks on a monolithic tradition.[1]

Leonard's writings are interesting in themselves, even considered apart from their historical importance, and deserve to be rescued from the storage rooms of teachers' college libraries. Besides the comments on collaborative learning and "real" writing that I will be considering, he made a number of other criticisms and suggestions between 1914 and 1930 that could be taken from this year's issues of *College Composition and Communication* or *College English*:

> *On the composing process:* "The ideal of the finished product is absolutely vicious, except as it functions to determine the remote goal." (*English Composition* 190)
>
> *On the development of writing abilities:* "Indeed, growth in the art of writing or speaking may be defined simply as a process of becoming increasingly reader-minded." (*English Composition* 14)
>
> *On freewriting:* "Some may really do best to write first in mad and scrabble haste, for themselves only, and thus clear their thoughts before they attempt to talk or write for anyone else." (*English Composition* 111)
>
> *On the modes:* "Useful as this [classification of the forms of discourse] doubtless is for sorting completed pieces of writing, it does not view the process of writing from the side of the thoughts or ideas the writer has to express and particularly of his purpose in expressing those." ("As to the Forms of Discourse" 202)

He also makes suggestions on invention, on sentence combining, on Piaget's theories, and on the need to avoid petty criticisms of errors and unrealistic, "schoolmastering" standards of usage.[2] But what most interests me is his answer to what he calls "the central problem" of his English education work:

> How, stirred by. . . interesting problems requiring expressing, can the school class be knit into a social group organized for mutual help, and aided to move steadily forward in the arduous way of attaining effective expression? (35).

His emphases on the class as a social group, and on the real basis of writing in "interesting problems" of the students' communities inside and outside the school, anticipate the current interest in what Patricia Bizzell calls "social processes whereby language learning and thinking capacities are shaped and used in particular communities" (215). I will try to show that he also anticipates some of the political dilemmas of present-day reformers.

SOME TERMS: IDEOLOGY, CONSENSUS, AND REALITY

I will be criticizing two sorts of rhetorical appeals that Leonard, and later Elbow and Bruffee, use in arguing for the teaching of writing through groups: an appeal to the authority of consensus, and an appeal to the authority of reality. It may seem perverse to object to appeals that are so common in our field and that are apparently progressive: surely we all see the need to come to reasoned agreement within a community, and to relate our teaching to the real world. To explain why I find these appeals problematic, I need to draw on an indispensible piece of Marxist jargon, the concept of *ideology*. I am not using the word the way it is commonly used to criticize any systematic political belief, as, say, an unsympathetic reader of this article might say my views were distorted by Left wing ideology. I am using it in the sense established by Marx, and modified by twentieth-century Marxists, to describe the whole system of thought and belief that goes with a social and economic system, the thoughts that structure our thinking so deeply that we take them for granted, as the nature of the real world. The concept has been much discussed by Marxists because it helps explain the apparent stability of the capitalist system, despite all its contradictions. It helps explain why people who are oppressed seem to go along with their oppression; the ideology of the oppressive system gives them the structures through which they make sense of their world.[3]

The concept of ideology has been of particular interest to Marxist sociologists of education, who see the school as, at least in part, an institution that adapts ideology to changing economic and social conditions, and produces a new version of ideology for each generation. Schools not only teach academic knowledge; they teach work according to schedule, acceptance of authority, and competition among individuals and between groups. They also help provide a justification for the hierarchies of society, so that, for instance, people accept that manual labor should pay less than mental labor. This process of adapting and carrying on the assumptions of our society is called *reproducing ideology*, by analogy with Marx's description of the reproduction of capital. Recently, radical teachers have asked if school can also be a place where people can resist the reproduction of ideology; they have put less emphasis on the all-embracing power of ideology as a structure, and have focused on the ways students and teachers can break this unthinking acceptance of ideas that support the way things are.[4] Of course, many teachers who are not Marxists agree that the vast differences in our society between rich and poor, black and white, men and women, are bad, and many teachers agree that critical thinking is a good thing. Where Marxist teachers differ from other critics of these injustices is in arguing that the social and economic system that perpetuates the injustices builds a protective structure of ideology that prevents us from thinking critically about it. Thus, what we might think is free and progressive thought may be another way of perpetuating a system we want to change.

I will argue that ideas of *consensus* and *reality*, as they are used by Leonard, though they seem so progressive, are part of the structure of ideology. The construction of a sense of general agreement is as important to the rhetoric of composition teaching as it is to the rhetoric of national politics; look, for instance, at all the articles in this journal asserting a new paradigm in the profession. But if conflict is part of the system, and is necessary to change the system, then consensus, within the system as it is, must mean that some interests have been suppressed or excluded. Similarly, it is common in our profession to show oneself as escaping tired academic forms to enter the real world. But if what we take as reality is always a social construction, then to accept the reality we see now is to accept the structure of illusion our system gives us. Worse, it is to see reality as something natural, outside our control, rather than to see it as something we make in our actions in society.

Since many readers who see the same economic, racial, and sexist injustices I do may not share my conviction that the problems are fundamental and systematic, it may help to use a familiar example from a society all readers will believe is fundamentally and systematically unjust. Huckleberry Finn's thinking is structured by the ideology of a slave-holding society. Though Huck himself does not own any slaves or benefit from this society (recall that he has invested some capital that he found), he hates abolitionists, and he can only think about blacks and whites in the terms he has learned. (Every reader must recall the exchange he has when he tells Aunt Sally the steamboat had blown a cylinder head: "Good gracious! Anybody hurt? — No'm. Killed a nigger. — Well, it's lucky; because sometimes people do get hurt.") But for reasons Huck doesn't entirely understand, and which he would not consider as being in any way political, he is capable of some remarkable acts of resistance to this system: for instance, he makes up elaborate lies on the spur of the moment to keep slave hunters away. There is some chance for change as long as he and others are capable of such resistance. But still he consciously believes in the institution of slavery enough so that he thinks worse of Tom Sawyer, a good boy, for apparently helping free Jim. Huck himself is an agreeable sort who prefers to avoid trouble. Whenever he tries to approach the *consensus* view, to do what he believes is right, he thinks of returning his friend Jim to slavery. Towards the end of the book, he believes he is finally facing *reality* when he admits to himself that in helping Jim escape, he is guilty of stealing property from Jim's owner. Now I am not saying that the social system of present day New York or Texas or Lancashire, where I have been teaching, is like that of ante-bellum Missouri where Huck grows up; what I am saying is that our social system constructs our view of the world as slavery does Huck's, and that the appeals to consensus and to reality may support that ideological view, as they did for Huck.

STERLING LEONARD AND CONSENSUS

I have commented on how current Sterling Leonard's ideas sound today. I would argue that this is because the historical conditions of high school English education in his period, 1900–1930, have some similarities to those in college, and particularly community college, English education in our own time. The high schools then were adapting to a massive influx of immigrants, and to the enrollment of working class students who had previously left school early, if they had attended at all.[5] In a similar way, writing programs like those at the City University of New York have faced the institutional challenge of coping with a group of students who would not previously have attended a university. In both periods, the new students changed the institutions, as well as being changed by them. In both periods, the institutions were responding to the demands of business for a large workforce with a different kind of skills. And in both periods, the teachers of writing were trying to establish their own professional status. A sense of historical conditions can help us see Leonard's progressivism in a social context.

Leonard was a typical reformer of this period, and one could find ideas similar to his in the work of John Dewey, E. L. Thorndike, George Philip Krapp, Fred Newton Scott, C. C. Fries, and I. A. Richards.[6] Leonard worked with all these teachers, in his own schooling at Michigan and Columbia Teachers' College or in his later work as a professor at Wisconsin and a leader of the then new NCTE. But the most important influence on him, and an important influence still on composition theory, was the work of John Dewey. It was from Dewey that Leonard took his central theme—and the theme of most importance to us in trying to criticize his work—the idea of the school as an image of society. For instance, in *The School and Society* (1898), Dewey says, "The great thing to keep in mind, then, regarding the introduction into the school of various forms of active occupation, is that through them the entire spirit of the school is renewed. . . . It gets a chance to become a miniature community, an embryonic society" (15). This quotation refers to both the elements I want to discuss in Leonard's work, the use of the social group of the class, and the emphasis on "real projects," with their reality defined by the analogy to the world outside the school.

Leonard's emphasis on the class as a social group is not just dogmatic Deweyism; he has clearly taught and learned from classes taught this way. In *English Composition as a Social Problem*, for example, he anticipates current ideas in using group work as the basis for "prevision of ideas" (invention), for revision suggestions, and for setting standards of usage. He has practical suggestions to make on teachers' direction of class experimentation (22), on responding (or not responding) to spoken errors (42), on introducing the class to criticism of students' writing (47), on letting the class make up terminology (77), on withholding one's criticisms (97), and on restraining students' carping criticisms of each other: "We must encourage prompt condemnation of guerilla pettifogging whenever we discover signs of it" (164). These passages remind the reader today of the practical advice in Bruffee's *A Short Course in Writing* or Elbow's *Writing Without Teachers*.

But there are passages in which Leonard describes the authority of the classroom group that should make us aware of the dangers of a consensus-based method. Leonard sees his method as furthering the sort of democracy in education promised by Dewey, a democracy he does not see in the traditional classroom. "Our present classrooms are designed chiefly for securing a maximum of order and dispatch. Parliamentary practice is demanded in the custom of addressing the teacher always, and is parodied in the raising of right hands for recognition" (40). Leonard's students have much more to do with each other than this; they are "an interested group of cooperative workers" (65). The danger is that the teacher has merely embodied his or her authority in the more effective guise of class consensus. This guided consensus has a power over individual students that a teacher can not have alone. "What the class may be able, with the help and suggestion of their leader, truly to realize as quite undesirable—cheap or smart or the like—may be quietly branded by the common judgment as unacceptable, and really eliminated" (130). Any teacher who uses group discussions or projects has seen that they can, on occasion, be fierce enforcers of conformity. And Leonard welcomes this enforcement with less worry than we might have. "The erring will be helped sufficiently by a sensation of lowered class temperature, so sharp that even the least sensitive cannot escape it" (149). Leonard does not himself use, but refers to, another teacher's "device . . . of having all children look for such violations [of rules of usage] by any member of the group anywhere and report complete statements and names, and then of deputing committees to write out all such reports on the blackboard each week" (150). Such elaborate machinery might occur to a teacher only during a period of war-time red-baiting hysteria (this was written in 1917), but the tendency to unthinking conformity is always there when consensus is used to set and enforce standards.

The emphasis on the authority of the group that we see in Leonard's textbook is apparent also in his most influential research, his usage studies that attempt to show the differences between formal textbook prescriptions and the language actually used in social transactions. For him the choice is not between correct and incorrect forms, but between the real world of actual usage and the unreal world of school English: "The question appears to turn on whether we wish in these grade and high school years to cultivate excellent homely expressions to fit the daily, informal occasions that we all have to meet most often, or rather a bookish and formal type exclusively" (132). Here he attacks something like what Ken Macrorie calls "Engfish." Leonard does believe that there are some arbitrary rules that must be taught as arbitrary rules. But he believes these rules are very few; thus he is interested in the definition of what the NCTE then called "Minimum Essentials," making a short list of items to be taught by all teachers and consigning the rest of the handbook items to oblivion.

Leonard's authority for the selection of these "essential" items would be actual usage; he has nothing but scorn for the John Simons and Edwin Newmans of his day who would try to impose puristic usage by fiat. "It is easy," he wrote in an early article, "to compile and propagate handbooks of baseless prescriptions; and people will buy them, just as they will buy manuals of etiquette, simply because these announce so many things which 'aren't done' that everyone is convicted of a sin and hastens to remedy the evil. But neither language nor other phases of good manners are settled by these means" ("What About Correct English?" 255). In his Columbia dissertation, *The Doctrine of Correctness in English Usage, 1700–1800*, he traces the origins of many of the handbook rules, and shows they have no basis in the actual usage of any period. This study led to *Current English Usage*, a massive survey to show how little "cultivated usage" supports the handbooks on most disputed items.[7] His views, progressive for the time, had a strong influence on the NCTE's position on usage. But we should note that Leonard's constant appeal to consensus usage assumes the inherent superiority of certain language groups. When he compares grammar books to etiquette books, he assumes, correctly I think, that issues of grammar are debated with such heat because they conceal issues of class, and especially the uneasiness of the middle class about its status. But there is little sense in his usage studies that there might not be just one answer for each item, that different classes or regions or races might have different usages, and that conflicts between these usages reflect other social conflicts. Instead, he carefully chooses certain kinds of respondents, and carefully figures the percentages of respondents approving of each item, and takes the majority vote as the right answer. His authority, he says, is "what various judges have observed about actual use or non-use by cultivated persons" ("Current Definition of Levels in English Usage" 345). But note it is cultivated persons who are to be considered, and experts who are to be the judges. The notion of consensus in usage, while it seems democratic, ignores the conflicts that characterize language change, and leaves the authority of certain types of language unquestioned.

It may seem odd to insist that large social conflicts are behind the use of groups to critique students' papers or the decision on when to use the subjunctive. But Leonard's exercises in democracy can be seen as part of a larger effort to create consensus by eliminating or at least concealing diversity and conflict. This diversity is so well concealed that anyone reading Leonard's articles now, or reading any sampling of articles from the NCTE's *English Journal* of his period, could remain unaware that teachers in many cities would be teaching classes in which most students were foreign born.[8] The only indication of potential conflict would be the way that progressive and traditional educators alike made every class into a civics lesson. If one believes that the society of that time was basically just, and that the treatment of the immigrants and workers, and their children, was just, then the attempt to integrate these newcomers into a consensus view, into the melting pot, was a generous project. But if one reads the history of that period as a history of challenges to a system that promoted great extremes of poverty and wealth, and terrible conditions of living and work, challenges by labor unions, immigrant communities, and new black urban communities, then the attempt by educators to deny the existence of these challenges can be seen as part of a repressive response by the government and corporations. Leonard's Deweyan individualism, though it still sounds progressive to us, strips the student of any identification with class, religion, family, or origins. And these identifications, as we are now coming to see in the controversies over bi-cultural education, can be the beginnings of political action. Deweyan education reassembles these students as units in a classroom group, in which they are conscious only of the demands of a monolithic "society" as enforced by the school and by other students.

LEONARD AND REALITY

It may seem paradoxical, or even perverse, for a radical who keeps referring to the social and economic basis of education to criticize the emphasis on *reality* in the work of Leonard and other progressive educators. Aren't they trying to do, in a practical way, just what I insist on doing in theory? The difference in our views is in how we define reality. For Leonard, what is real is given; we gain knowledge of it through our senses, if we are not deceived by non-empirical assumptions, and we adapt to it as best we can. For a Marxist, reality is not a monolithic thing out there, but a process in society, an ongoing conflict between various groups, which in turn structures that society. People have no simple unmediated perception of reality; the facts we are likely to take as reality are most likely parts of another ideological structure. Think, for example, of the very limited sense "the real world" has had in recent discussion of writing courses—it becomes synonymous with the demands of employers as shown in surveys. By treating the "real world" as the bedrock of our teaching, we perpetuate the idea that reality is something outside us and beyond our efforts to change it.

We have seen that Leonard's rhetorical strategy in his attacks on what he calls "Old Purist Junk" about usage is to compare the formalism of textbooks with the way people use language in the "real world." He makes a similar appeal in replacing the teaching of the modes of discourse with a developmental classification based on the stages a child is supposed to go through in learning the presentation and interpretation of facts. In the earliest assignments a student receives, the student simply reports observations: "All these matters are to be presented as objectively as possible; they are to set forth all the writer's senses have apprehended" ("As to the Forms of Discourse" 202). The purpose of this exercise is to root out merely conventional beliefs, by making the students stick to the facts: "Nothing is of more doubtful value, as an exercise in composition or anything else, than the restatement of fact or interpretation the writer has absorbed but not lived or thought through himself" ("As to the Forms of Discourse" 204). Now I have been attacking just this handing on of uncriticized assumptions. But I disagree with Leonard's belief that the *facts* lie outside these assumptions. If what we think of as facts are determined by our ideological framework, the facts cannot themselves get us beyond that framework.[9] Leonard's textbook says, as do many textbooks today, "The whole art of helping children in writing or speaking, as this study urges it, is based on the idea of showing them how to search out and give not general but specific details" (*English Composition* 105). I too am always asking students for more details. But I am interested in what such details reveal about our assumptions, not in getting beyond assumptions to some external reality.

To take an example, Leonard asks his students to describe a place, and to cut out any statements unsupported by facts. That may lead to a more readable and more academic sounding paper, but it will not tell us what the place is really like. When, for instance, the various students in a basic writing course at Queens College write comparisons of the places they live to the places their parents lived as children, what these places are "really like" is determined by conventional frameworks of progress or nostalgia. What the place is really like might be better understood by comparing all those unsupported generalizations that various people would bring to such a description, comparing, say, the Lower East Side described as oppressive ghetto with the Lower East Side described as warm community, Forest Hills described as success and security with Forest Hills described as silent streets and alienating apartment blocks. No careful attention to the description of stoops or wide lawns will reconcile these descriptions in one objective reality. Both express deeper tensions that go beyond the rhetorical problems set by the assignment.

There is at times an alarming sound to Leonard's enthusiasm for the real world, as there is to his enthusiasm for consensus, that should make us examine our own enthusiasms today. His demand that development in school lead to the world of work and community responsibility, while it frees the school from the empty formalism of lectures, drills, and theme topics, ironically makes it more subservient to ideology. The real world is indistinguishable from the world defined by business publicists: "Meat packers, electric companies, millers, dog breeders, and others have free advertising matter and exhibits which are of the greatest value. Whatever your children want to know is likely to be covered by government or advertising material" ("Composition and Grammar in the Junior High School" 410). Despite the apparent naiveté of this view, Leonard is not by any means a promoter of a narrowly vocational education. Dewey had described the relation between business and education in broad terms.

> Though there should be an organic connection between the school and business life, it is not meant that the school is to prepare the student for any particular business, but that there should be a natural connection of the everyday life of a child with the business environment around him, and that it is the affair of the school to clarify and liberalize this connection, to bring it to consciousness, not by introducing special studies, like commercial geography and arithmetic, but by keeping alive the ordinary bonds of relation. (68)

It is not the connection of business that is in itself disturbing, but the sense of the naturalness and inevitability of this connection as the one way of reaching out to the world outside the school. For Leonard, as for Dewey, to criticize the subordination of education to the needs of business and government is to fail to face reality.

Teachers today are likely to be more skeptical about the uses of advertising. But we still assume the value of making the classroom represent "reality," and we still define this reality in very limited terms which we take uncritically from our economic system. For instance, many of the research studies that seek to define a body of good writing compare the writing of students to that of published writers. Now this makes for some valuable comparisons, but we should note how we just assume, lacking an agreed standard of writing quality, that good writing is writing that can be sold for money. Some editors of composition readers argue, using rhetoric very similar to Leonard's, that this sort of contemporary professional writing is more real than, say, readings taken from the canon of English and American literature. Or other editors of readers argue that the writing of students who have won a national essay contest is more real than the writing of professional magazine writers. All these assertions, whatever the pedagogical value of the materials they propose, beg the question of just how we come to define a real world, and accept that world as something given.

LEONARD AND REFORM

Anyone who has sat through a dull writing class (or has oneself taught a dull class with growing frustration) would recognize Leonard's descriptions of traditional methods of teaching English. He attacks these classes using a rhetoric similar to that of composition reformers today, who present themselves as fighting for more realistic views against the tradition that prevailed before the mid-1960s.[10] Much as I sympathize with the critique given by both periods of reform, I have questions about the way these reformers define themselves against the dubious practices of traditional teachers, who are often at a lower level of the hierarchy of educational prestige. The attack on tradition shifts our focus from the conflicting goals of the school in society to the simpler issue of the competence of individual teachers and the practicality of specific methods.

These questions may be raised most clearly by considering one of Leonard's articles from 1923. "How English Teachers Correct Papers" reports a study in which various groups of student-teachers and teachers were given a list of sentences from both students and famous authors and asked to mark any errors they would require a student to correct (517). Leonard's whole study is something of a trap for the unsuspecting teachers, practically all of whom "fatigued themselves to a point close to insensibility by meticulous correction of a great number of idioms in sentences by De Quincey, Lamb, Pater, Symonds, and authors of similar standing" (517), so that they were too tired to see what Leonard considered actual errors. To complete his attack, Leonard lists "constructive comments" the teachers gave on whole papers they were asked to mark, including "corrections" that made the correct incorrect, "puristic or wholly captious excisions, restatements, arrangements, and additions," and foolish or irrelevant criticisms. Leonard's suggestion that "the wisest teacher proceeds always by way of queries and suggestion, not by dogmatic rules and requirements," is a good one, and has been reiterated recently in articles in the composition journals reporting studies similar to Leonard's.[11] But Leonard's article, like some recent critiques, presents a polemic against dogmatism without either an understanding of its origins, or a model for a new method based on queries and suggestion.

The study shows how much Leonard needs bad teachers to make his argument. I would not deny that there was, and is, a plentiful supply of such teachers to provide examples of arbitrary traditionalism. But I am uneasy with the way the university expert makes them the enemy. He shows how their habits fly in the face of the "reality" revealed by current research, and he judges their judgment against an absolute level of cultivation represented by the writing of "De Quincey, Lamb, Pater, Symonds, and authors of similar standing." I would argue that this kind of top-down reform leads nowhere, because it just reinforces the hierarchy of the teaching profession, reminding teachers that the expertise is somewhere else. Thus in each generation it is the reformers who chair committees, write articles, and edit the journals; by these standards it is the reformers who are the establishment, and the opponents they label traditionalists are the outsiders. And in the 1980s we use the same sort of rhetoric, on the same sort of issues, to the same sort of teachers, to distinguish ourselves from tradition, that the members of that "tradition" used against a previous generation. What is needed to break this circle is more understanding of the conditions under which people teach, and the ideological frameworks within which they think. We should be opposing, not traditional teachers, but a system in which such repressive teaching is, in fact, perfectly appropriate.

I am annoyed with Leonard's rhetoric as a reformer because he assumes authority over other teachers and over students while denying he has it. He assumes authority as trained expert, university professor, empirical researcher, voice of the downtrodden students, bringing enlightenment to normal-school-trained teachers. But he denies his personal authority by saying the students are controlling the classroom, and his curriculum just follows the real world, and his reforms are based on the latest research. If we see that schools can be both places of liberation and places of oppression, then we have to ask how we are using what limited power over people's lives we do have.

CONSENSUS AND REALITY
IN ELBOW AND BRUFFEE

If Leonard were just a forgotten hero of composition theory, like Alexander Bain or Fred Newton Scott, to revive him and then criticize him would be unnecessary and rather unfair. But the example of Leonard can help us criticize the presentation of consensus, reality, and reform in two theorists who carry on the tradition of progressive education, Peter Elbow and Ken Bruffee.

Elbow's *Writing without Teachers* first introduced many of us to the usefulness of groups in the teaching of writing, and gave us some insights into their dynamics. But his more recent book, *Writing with Power*, shifts the emphasis away from the social context, returning to some essential internal power as a way of control of self and others. For Elbow, language may get work done in the social world, and the individual learner may use that social world as a tool to help him or her learn writing, but the system of language is produced by individuals, not by society. It is true that he seems to emphasize the social context of writing and the uses of consensus in his chapters on "Audience" and "Feedback." And he emphasizes the need to make the classroom reflect the world, using terms very much like those of Leonard: "any 'back to basics' movement in the teaching of writing needs to start by ensuring each child the most basic thing of all: a real audience for his written words—an audience that really listens and takes the interchange seriously" (184). This might seem to be a difficult need to satisfy in the composition class, but even in the artificial world of the classroom, "there is always a useful real audience available to whom writing can easily be delivered: other members of the class" (230).

For Elbow, as for Leonard, power over real audiences comes from an immediate connection with reality gained through a breaking down of stifling conventions. Writing with power requires authenticity of expression ("voice") and unmediated realism of perception in which the writer and reader must "see" the object written about (316). The problem with this call for direct experience of reality is that, as with Leonard, one must ask to which reality is one admitted. Elbow, unlike Leonard, acknowledges the existence of fundamentally different views of the world. But he still sees these views as free and individual, not acknowledging the way they are structured by ideology. So in his book, reality is divided between a cold, clear outside and a warm, messy inside. Writing consists of the negotiation between these two sides of the individual. In Elbow's model, the audience is essential to help in revision, but the best words come from deep down inside, from one's voice. Problems are solved in this model by changing the inside; change in the outside, that is, power over others, follows from this success in dealing with oneself. No wonder Elbow ends with a chapter on "Writing and Magic"; magic is the only possible source for such ineffable energies. This relentlessly internal approach to writing is both the book's strength and its weakness. *Writing with Power* consists almost entirely of vivid, often visceral, usually organic metaphors for creation.[12] These metaphors may help us see our processes of writing in new ways, but they also prevent any analysis of the social conditions of our writing. There is no real place in this model for a discourse group that gives one the structures of words one takes for granted.

Elbow has been a powerful writer for reform. Does his insistence that personal authenticity is the source of power apply to his own writing? He refers often to his own internal struggles in writing the book. I would argue, though, that its rhetorical power comes not from these struggles, but from its place in a group of texts. It gives a new metaphorical guise to familiar progressive education concepts, and makes an appeal to individualism that is a commonplace of American rhetoric. It has some affinities with a long line of straight-talking guides to self-improvement. Take, for example, the tone of hip moralism that combines with the traditional moralism of delayed reward in this passage: "If you slip into free-writing for the sake of producing good pieces of writing, then you put a kind of short-run utilitarian pressure on the process, and hinder yourself from getting all the other benefits" (*Writing with Power* 17). Now there is nothing wrong with using the jargon of self-improvement, any more than there is with using Marxist jargon as I do. My point is that both Elbow and I write within discourses developed in social processes, and that his account ignores these processes.

The work of Kenneth Bruffee can help us critique the appeal to reality that Leonard and Elbow make, especially in the recent essays in which Bruffee attempts to establish the theoretical grounds of collaborative learning. But his appeal to consensus is similar to theirs, and I think a lack of analysis of this consensus is the weak point of his theory. We might not see, at first, how different he is from Leonard and Elbow; he says in his textbook *A Short Course in Writing* that he starts with a search for a method of writing that will be *real*. "Peer criticism," he says, "is the most *real* writing students will ever do as students," because the writer has an immediate and actual audience and purpose (115). Similarly, an exercise on reminiscence tells the student, "Just begin at the beginning and tell the whole truth" (3). Where Bruffee differs from Leonard and Elbow begins to be apparent in the next exercise, when he asks the student to retell a "family story" that has become formalized with retelling over time. This exercise suggests, as the personal reminiscence assignment in most textbooks cannot, the degree to which language is given by the social group, in this case the family. The student must try to translate the private language of the family into the language of the classroom, noticing the difference.

For Bruffee, "writing is a communal activity," not just an essence of meaning given by the individual to the community. Instead of tracing language to an original voice inside, Bruffee asks questions to make the reader "see an essay as a 'thing' someone has made, like a table or a chair—something artificially designed, shaped, and put together to serve a purpose" (122). He says his system of peer criticism will enable students to "gain a stronger sense of the degree to which knowledge, like writing itself, is a social phenomenon, and the degree to which the social context in which we learn permeates what we know and how we know it" (116). In his view of knowledge, the group is there from the beginning, defining the terms of thought, and does not simply come in at the end, as an audience.

But while Bruffee shows that reality can be seen as a social construct, he does not give us any way to criticize this construct. Having discovered the role of consensus in the production of knowledge, he takes this consensus as something that just is, rather than a something that might be good or bad. For instance, in his recent essays, he argues for collaborative learning because it is the norm in business, industry, and the professions. This is true enough, but I question whether analogy to these institutions is, in itself, an argument for a teaching method. We need to look at the consensus within these institutions as the result of conflicts, not as a monolith. To decide whether the groups in our classes are introducing students to new communities of discourse, or are confining them in ideological structures, we need a clearer definition than he gives of what these interpretive communities are, and a sense of the historical processes shaping them.

Bruffee defines discourse communities in terms of certain kinds of academic or non-academic knowledge. For instance, he says, "Every student is already a member of several knowledge communities, from canoeing to computers, baseball to ballet" ("Collaborative Learning" 644). Bruffee suggests in another article that social differences are incidental to the process of education and should drop away if the students share an educational goal. "Outside the learning group . . . people may have widely different positions in the management hierarchy of a union or corporation, in the professional or student hierarchy of an educational institution, or in a system of economic or social class. But as collaborative learners all these people are peers. With regard to a course in ethnography or elementary Chinese, the vice-president of a corporation, the janitor, the English professor, the freshman, the society matron, and the shoe salesman must leave their social differences behind" ("CLTV" 38).[13]

This is an attractive and idealistic vision, but it assumes that knowledge is outside the realm of these people's social differences. Look over the list and ask who is most likely to be in a course on ethnography or elementary Chinese? Who, on the other hand, is likely to be in a course on English as a second language or on basic office skills? Who is likely to be in a basic writing course at the City University? To ask such questions is to realize that knowledge is not uniformly distributed in our society, and that it is not all of a piece. If we turn a blind eye to social factors we are likely merely to perpetuate the provision of different kinds of knowledge for the rich and the poor.

Bruffee sometimes includes non-academic knowledge in examples of discourse communities. For instance, he talks in one article about the contribution to the writing group of knowledge gained in office work, or in organizing a household. But what if one considers the knowledge of communities whose interests might be opposed, say the knowledge of social workers and the knowledge of welfare clients, or the knowledge of an accountant and the knowledge of employees in a factory to be closed? Such bodies of knowledge cannot be resolved into a consensus without one side losing something.

How are discourse communities made? Bruffee sees how society furthers thought or hinders it, but he does not see social and economic factors as providing his structures. For him, these factors are unfortunate limitations to our thought and conversation that must be eliminated as much as possible.

> Limitations that may be imposed for example, by ethnocentrism, inexperience, personal anxiety, economic interests, and paradigmatic inflexibility can constrain my thinking just as they can constrain conversation. If my talk is narrow, superficial, biased, and confined to clichés, my thinking is likely to be so too. ("Collaborative Learning" 639)

I would see such limitations as giving the structure to our thought. Ethnocentrism and economic interests are not just unfortunate habits, they are whole systems of ideas that people take for granted and use to make sense of the world. One cannot escape from one's economic interests and ethnic background, but one can try to understand how they shape one's thinking and social actions.

The model Bruffee gives for change in knowledge, adapted from Thomas Kuhn and Richard Rorty, leads us away from such analysis. It attributes the growth of knowledge and change of paradigms to factors internal to the discipline, such as the multiplication of anomalies and the shift of paradigms. The only conflict is between normal science and extraordinary science, or normal discourse and abnormal discourse. An alternative model would be in the work of historians and sociologists of science who see change in terms of social and economic factors.[14] For instance, Bruffee might call his own composition theory a new paradigm, resulting from the new models of Kuhn and Rorty. I might call it an attempt to rationalize theoretically the methods he earlier developed, and I would trace these methods to the institutional need, which he describes in his article, to deal with new kinds of university students. Similarly, I might trace my interest in these questions to my teaching of basic writing at Queens College. Ultimately, I would trace both his thinking and mine to the challenges of Open Admissions at CUNY. And Open Admissions was not the result of a paradigm shift in the philosophy of education; it emerged from the political conflicts of New York City in the 1960s.

Bruffee's recent essay points out that "The view that knowledge is a social artifact . . . requires a reexamination of our premises as students of English and as teachers" ("Collaborative Learning" 650). His suggestions for reform are excellent: he would "demystify" the humanities and the relation of teacher to student by putting them in a social context. But I think he underestimates the difficulty of the reforms he proposes, because he sees the resistance to them as a matter of habit, not of ideology. In *A Short Course*, he describes the problem he is addressing in terms of what he sees as "a conflict between two forces: the docility and dependence created in young people by American schooling and the increasing demand of modern life that human beings be autonomous, flexible, and self-possessed" (vii). But these two forces are not in conflict if we see the interests of employers, rather than "modern life" as the force that makes demands here. Students can be both docile and convinced of their autonomy, freedom of choice, and control of their lives. A school that reproduced this ideological construct would be a successful school.

In his recent article, Bruffee sees some of these dangers clearly enough. He points out the "provincial" nature of what he and Rorty call normal discourse. He also seems to recognize the kinds of possible dangers in the use of collaborative learning that I pointed out in some of Leonard's examples. He refers to the need to avoid "the many possible negative effects of peer group influence: conformity, anti-intellectualism, intimidation, and leveling-down of quality." He would do this by making "collaboration . . . a genuine part of students' educational development" (652). I would do it by emphasizing conflict as well as collaboration. I think he is referring to the same sense of a divided role I have described when he says "we must perform as conservators *and* agents of change, as custodians of prevailing community values *and* as agents of social transition and reacculturation" (650).

LESSONS FOR REFORMERS

I find I have no suggestions for assignments that are as innovative as those of the authors I am criticizing. But that is partly because what I have to suggest is not a method but a stance toward one's teaching. This stance requires a sort of doubleness: an awareness that one's course is part of an ideological structure that keeps people from thinking about their situation, but also a belief that one can resist this structure and help students to criticize it.

The sense of conflict in these three writers is clear enough when they describe their work as teachers. In each case they have a problem with existing institutions; in each case they offer an escape that I don't think works. Leonard, for instance, offers professionalism as an escape from the sense of pointlessness many teachers have: "It becomes clear how different a subject it is coming to be from the sodden, idealless drudgery of themes swoopingly red-inked and at the nearest possible moment thrown into the wastebasket" (193). Escape for him is through attention to the new research in composition in the 1920s ("Research on the Teaching of English"). But research will not change the basic antagonism of student and teacher he describes here.

Elbow, in his advice to students about writing in school, presents powerfully the role and limitations of the teacher:

> Teachers are good for giving criticism because they read papers in piles of 25 or 50. Take that criticism and use it. They are good at making you write when you don't feel like it, simply because they have authority. Instead of resenting this, try appreciating it and internalizing from it what may be the most important skill of all: the ability to write when you are in the wrong mood. They are *not* good at telling you what your writing feels like to a real human being, at taking your words seriously as messages directed to them, at praising you, or perhaps even at noticing you. Get these things elsewhere. (*Writing With Power* 234)

This is excellent advice, but Elbow's solution, that of using the tension between teacher and student, is based on his assumption that there is a world elsewhere of "real human beings." There is, of course, a world outside of school, and he is right to remind us of these other readers and writers. But the kinds of authority embodied in the school are present in the rest of the culture as well. The writer of an engineering proposal, a magazine article, or even a poem, is constrained by structures as powerful as those determining the freshman composition theme. The classroom alienation he takes for granted, in which the teacher processes batches of student raw material, is characteristic, not only of school, but of other institutions in our society. Bruffee traces his own interest in collaborative learning to a similar realization of how alienating his work had become:

> When I began teaching composition, I was still in graduate school. I had large classes, and I did not really know what I was doing. Every class hour seemed to stretch on to eternity. Grading papers took hours and was a dreadful grind. I kept hoping my classes would get smaller and the hour shorter. Instead, my classes got larger and the hour longer. I kept hoping I would learn to grade papers more easily and quickly. That did not happen either. Worst of all, I was not really sure that I was teaching anybody anything. (*Short Course* 184)

All three writers start by considering the drudgery of the work, the enormous numbers of papers, and the opposition of teachers and students. They want a change in the conditions of work, and a system that allows them to teach as well as just evaluate. They make a good case in these passages, whether they realize it or not, that our problems will not be solved just by new methods, or new theories, or new knowledge. We should begin by realizing that our interests are not the same as those of the institutions that employ us, and that the improvement of our work will involve social changes. No amount of merely educational reform will end the alienation described in these passages.

But this is not to say that all attempts at change are foiled by an all-powerful system, and that real change must wait until a revolution. Paul Willis warns other Marxist theorists against such an attitude at the end of *Learning to Labour,* his fine book on ideological reproduction in a British secondary school. He suggests the sort of double role for teachers that I have been arguing for here.

> If we have nothing to say about what to do on Monday morning then everything is yielded to a purist structuralist Marxist tautology: nothing can be done until the basic structures of society are changed but the structures prevent us from making any changes. There is no contradiction in asking practitioners to work on two levels simultaneously—to face immediate

problems in doing 'the best' (so far as they can see it) for their clients whilst appreciating all the time that these very actions may help to produce the structures within which the problems arise. (186)

What this approach means for, say, a basic writing teacher is that one teaches the forms of academic writing, so that students who might not finish four years of college have a better chance of finishing, without assuming that there is anything liberating about these forms or about academic discourse. One teaches job letters to the business communications students who need to get jobs downtown, without teaching that a job downtown is the answer to their problems. I have no specific new ideas for what we should do Monday morning, but I follow with interest those of other radical teachers. In this article, I am asking, not for a new kind of assignment, but for more skepticism about what assignments do to reproduce the structures of our society.

We should keep a similar skepticism about the appeals to reality and consensus in composition theory and research. There have been a number of recent articles calling for a view of writing as a social process.[15] This is a welcome corrective to the individualism of the cognitive psychology models of the 1970s. But we should not let our enthusiasm for this social view lead us to accepting social construction of knowledge as something good in itself. The kind of critique begun in *College English* by Richard Ohmann, Stanley Aronowitz, and others is even more appropriate now that we are seeing writing in a social context. I think these theories will be developed with more sophistication if we draw on critiques developed by such sociologists of education as Apple and Giroux, and on materials provided by historians of education.[16]

Leonard in the 1920s, and Elbow and Bruffee today, have made teachers aware of the need for changes in the way we teach. The work of sociologists and historians of education would help us to remain aware that the changes we propose may finally support an existing consensus and a conception of reality that supports those now in power. Our sense that something is wrong should lead us to criticize our own function in society, as well as our pedagogy. Otherwise, to use a comment of Leonard's from another, entirely different context, "It has less effect than a spoonful of water poured over a flock of ducks" ("Composition and Grammar" 448).

NOTES

1. Some recent historical studies that discuss reform in composition include those by James Berlin (whose book has an extensive bibliography), Michael Halloran, Robert Conners, Wallace Douglas, (whose article appears in a special issue of the *English Journal* devoted to the history of the profession), and Evelyn Wright.

2. See *English Composition as a Social Problem* for references to invention (81), sentence-combining (158), "schoolmastering" (183 and many other references). On Piaget, see "Relating the Teaching of English to Reality" (45).

3. For a discussion of the term, see Raymond Williams, *Keywords*. For a series of reviews of various studies of ideology, see Centre for Contemporary Cultural Studies, *On Ideology*.

4. Several detailed historical and sociological studies along these lines are collected in Michael Apple, ed., *Cultural and Economic Reproduction in Education*. Important earlier articles on ideology in education are collected in the Open University reader, Roger Dale et al., eds., *Schooling and Capitalism: A Sociological Reader*. A recent analysis of educational theories, in clear but rather abstract terms, is Henry Giroux, *Theory and Resistance in Education: A Pedagogy for the Opposition*. Current critical articles on the sociology of education often appear in the journal *Curriculum Inquiry*.

5. See Cremin; David Hogan, "Education and Class Formation: The Peculiarities of Americans," in Apple's collection; and Diane Ravitch's quite readable book on the case of New York City.

6. Biographical information on Leonard is from W. E. Leonard's *DAB* entry. Background to the period is from the books by J. N. Hook and Arthur Applebee, and from Merle Curti's contemporary study. Curti, like me, looks at these ideas from the left, but he considers Dewey's influence entirely progressive. A reviewer of my article recommended the chapter on Leonard by John Brereton in *Traditions of Inquiry* (New York: Oxford UP, 1985). The whole book should be relevant to my topic here, but it was unavailable in Britain as I revised this article.

7. Leonard's study, which he left incomplete at his death, is included in Albert Marckwardt's *Facts About Current English Usage*.

8. On Americanization, see Cremin; Hook; Ravitch; and *English Journal in the 1920s*.

9. See Richard Ohmann, "Use Specific, Definite, Concrete Language."

10. For an example of the rhetoric of composition reform, see Donald Stewart, "Composition Textbooks and the Assault on Tradition," and some of the other articles collected in Gary Tate and Edward P. J. Corbett, eds., *The Writing Teacher's Sourcebook*.

11. Leonard's study is similar to that in Nancy Sommer's recent article, "Responding to Student Writing." Like Leonard, Sommers only gives examples of comments that are badly done. Dan Moshenberg pointed out to me the similarity of Leonard's study to the experiment in poetry criticism I. A. Richards reports in *Practical Criticism*.

12. Those who favor such visceral metaphors should see Lester Faigley's paper, "Peristalsis as Paradigm: From Process to Product."

13. See also two other essays by Bruffee, "The Structure of Knowledge and the Future of Liberal Education," and "Liberal Education and the Social Justification of Belief."

14. A good introduction to the sociology of scientific knowledge is another Open University reader, edited by Barry Barnes and David Edge.

15. See, for example, the very different approaches of Patricia Bizzell, of Bruffee ("Writing and Reading as Collaborative Social Acts"), and of Charles Bazerman ("Scientific Writing as a Social Act"). Bazerman, like Bruffee, has a textbook based on his approach (*The Informed Writer*).

16. For example, one way of seeing how deeply ingrained and uncritical are the psychological categories we use to define basic writers is to read the historical treatment of these categories in Steven Shapin and Barry Barnes, "Head and Hand: Rhetorical Resources in British Pedagogical Writing 1770–1850."

WORKS CITED

Apple, Michael, ed. *Cultural and Economic Reproduction in Education*. London: Routledge, 1982.

Applebee, Arthur. *Tradition and Reform in the Teaching of English*. Urbana: NCTE, 1974.

Aronowitz, Stanley. "Mass Culture and the Eclipse of Reason: The Pedagogical Implications." *College English* 38 (1977): 768–72.

Barnes, Barry, and David Edge, eds. *Science in Context*. Milton Keynes: Open UP, 1982.

Bazerman, Charles. *The Informed Writer*. 2nd ed. Boston: Houghton, 1985.

———. "Scientific Writing as a Social Act." *New Essays in Scientific and Technical Communication*. Ed. Carolyn Miller, et al. Farmingdale, New York: Baywood, 1983. 157–84.

Berlin, James. *Writing Instruction in Nineteenth-Century American Colleges*. Carbondale: Southern Illinois UP Press, 1984.

Bizzell, Patricia. "Cognition, Convention, and Certainty: What We Need to Know About Writing." *Pre/Text* 3 (1982): 213–43.

Bruffee, Kenneth. "CLTV: Collaborative Learning Television." *Educational Communication and Technology Journal* 30 (1982): 26–40.

———. "Collaborative Learning and the 'Conversation of Mankind.'" *College English* 46 (1984): 635–52.

———. "Liberal Education and the Social Justification of Belief." *Liberal Education* 68 (1982): 95–114.

———. *A Short Course in Writing*. 2nd ed. Boston: Winthrop, 1980.

———. "The Structure of Knowledge and the Future of Liberal Education." *Liberal Education* 67 (1981): 177–86.

———. "Writing and Reading as Collaborative Social Acts." *The Writer's Mind*. Ed. Janice Hays. Urbana: NCTE, 1983.

Centre for Contemporary Cultural Studies. *On Ideology*. London: Hutchinson University Library, 1978.

Connors, Robert. "The Rise and Fall of the Modes of Discourse." *College Composition and Communication* 32 (1981): 444–55.

Cremin, Lawrence. *The Transformation of the School*. New York: Vintage, 1961.

Curti, Merle. *The Social Ideas of American Educators*. New York: Scribner's, 1935.

Dale, Roger, et al., eds. *Schooling and Capitalism: A Sociological Reader*. London: Routledge, 1976.

Dewey, John. *The School and Society*. Chicago: U of Chicago P, 1898.

Douglas, Wallace. "Why Know Our History." *English Journal* 68 (1979): 16–21.

Elbow, Peter. *Writing with Power*. New York: Oxford UP, 1982.

———. *Writing without Teachers*. New York: Oxford UP, 1973.

Faigley, Lester. "Peristalsis as Paradigm: From Process to Product." Paper presented at the panel on "Nutrastylistics" at the Conference on College Composition and Communication, Minneapolis, March 1985.

Giroux, Henry. *Theory and Resistance in Education: A Pedagogy for the Opposition*. London: Heinemann Educational Books, 1983.

Halloran, Michael. "Rhetoric in the American College Curriculum: The Decline of Public Discourse." *Pre/Text* 3 (1982): 245–269.

Hook, J. N. *A Long Way Together*. Urbana: NCTE, 1979.

Kantor, Kevin. "Creative Expression in the English Curriculum: An Historical Perspective." *Research in the Teaching of English* 9 (1975): 5–29.

Leonard, Sterling. "As to the Forms of Discourse." *English Journal* 3 (1914): 201–211.

———. "Composition and Grammar in the Junior High School." *The Classroom Teacher* 10 (1927): 309–449.

———. "Current Definition of Levels in English Usage." *English Journal* 16 (1926): 345–59.

———. *The Doctrine of Correctness in English Usage, 1700–1800.* Madison: U of Wisconsin P, 1929.

———. *English Composition as a Social Problem.* Boston: Houghton, 1917.

———. "How English Teachers Correct Papers." *English Journal* 20 (1923): 517–31.

———. "Relating the Teaching of English to Reality." *Nation's Schools* 4 (1929): 45–48.

———. "Research on the Teaching of English." *Journal of Educational Research* 19 (1929): 317–21.

———. "What About Correct English?" *The Teachers Journal and Abstract* 6 (1931): 252–56.

Leonard, W. E. "Sterling Andrus Leonard." *Dictionary of American Biography.* 9: 168–9.

Marckwardt, Albert. *Facts About Current English Usage.* New York: Appleton-Century, 1938.

Ohmann, Richard. *English in America: A Radical View of the Profession.* New York: Oxford UP, 1976.

———. "Use Specific, Definite, Concrete Language." *College English* 41 (1979): 379–89.

Ravitch, Diane. *The Great School Wars: New York City, 1805–1973.* New York: Basic, 1974.

Richards, I. A. *Practical Criticism.* New York: Harcourt, 1929.

Shapin, Steven, and Barry Barnes. "Head and Hand: Rhetorical Resources in British Pedagogical Writing 1770–1850." *Oxford Review of Education* 2 (1976): 235–50.

Sommers, Nancy. "Responding to Student Writing." *College Composition and Communication* 32 (1982): 148–56.

Tate, Gary, and Edward P. J. Corbett, eds. *The Writing Teacher's Sourcebook.* New York: Oxford, 1981.

Williams, Raymond. *Keywords.* London: Oxford UP, 1976.

Willis, Paul. *Learning to Labour: How Working Class Kids Get Working Class Jobs.* Farnborough, England: Saxon, 1977.

Wright, Evelyn. "School English and Public Policy." *College English* 42 (1980): 327–42.

Consensus and Difference in Collaborative Learning

JOHN TRIMBUR

Kenneth A. Bruffee, Harvey S. Wiener, and others have argued that collaborative learning may be distinguished from other forms of group work on the grounds that it organizes students not just to work together on common projects but more important to engage in a process of intellectual negotiation and collective decision-making. The aim of collaborative learning, its advocates hold, is to reach consensus through an expanding conversation. This conversation takes place at a number of levels—first in small discussion groups, next among the groups in a class, then between the class and the teacher, and finally among the class, the teacher, and the wider community of knowledge. In Bruffee's social constructionist pedagogy, the language used to reach consensus acquires greater authority as it acquires greater social weight: the knowledge students put into words counts for more as they test it out, revising and relocating it by taking into account what their peers, the teacher, and voices outside the classroom have to say.

The purpose of this essay is to examine two important criticisms of the politics of collaborative learning in order to explore one of the key terms in collaborative learning, consensus. This seems worth doing because the notion of consensus is one of the most controversial and misunderstood aspects of collaborative learning.

One line of criticism argues that the use of consensus in collaborative learning is an inherently dangerous and potentially totalitarian practice that stifles individual voice and creativity, suppresses differences, and enforces conformity. Thomas S. Johnson, for example, believes that consensus is just

Reprinted from *College English* 51.6 (October 1989): 602–16. Used with permission.

another name for "group think" and conjures images of 1984. Pedro Beade worries that consensus might be used to justify the practices of "a crazy, totalitarian state" (708). These critics of collaborative learning want to rescue the sovereignty and autonomy of the individual from what Johnson calls collaborative learning's "peer indoctrination classes." Underlying these political objections is the sense, as David Foster puts it, that the human mind is "far too mysterious and fascinating" to take the social constructionist route and "ground its utterances" in a "normative social community." According to Foster, collaborative learning is based on an epistemological mistake: Bruffee's "overeager application of the social constructionist label" causes him to overvalue social practices and thus to deny the primacy of individual consciousness in creating knowledge.

A second line of criticism, on the other hand, agrees with Bruffee that things like selves, knowledge, discourse, readers, and writers are indeed socially constructed. What left-wing critics such as Greg Myers do worry about, however, is that Bruffee's social constructionist pedagogy runs the risk of limiting its focus to the internal workings of discourse communities and of overlooking the wider social forces that structure the production of knowledge. To understand the production and validation of knowledge, Myers argues, we need to know not just how knowledge communities operate consensually but how knowledge and its means of production are distributed in an unequal, exclusionary social order and embedded in hierarchical relations of power. Without a critique of the dominant power relations that organize the production of knowledge, left-wing critics hold, the social constructionist rationale for collaborative learning may, unwittingly or not, accommodate its practices to the authority of knowledge it believes it is demystifying.

In this essay I propose to extend the left critique, not to abandon the notion of consensus but to revise it, as a step toward developing a critical practice of collaborative learning. I want to concede that consensus in some of its pedagogical uses may indeed be an accommodation to the workings of normal discourse and function thereby as a component to promote conformity and improve the performance of the system. My point will be, however, that consensus need not inevitably result in accommodation. The politics of consensus depends on the teacher's practice. Consensus, I will argue, can be a powerful instrument for students to generate differences, to identify the systems of authority that organize these differences, and to transform the relations of power that determine who may speak and what counts as a meaningful statement.

Before I outline the critical and transformative projects I believe are implied in collaborative learning, I want to address the fear of conformity in the first line of criticism—the fear that collaborative learning denies differences and threatens individuality. It is important to acknowledge that this fear points to some real problems that arise when students work together in groups—problems such as parochialism, demagoguery, narrow appeals to common sense, an urge to reach noncontroversial consensus without considering alternatives. After all, we cannot realistically expect that collaborative learning will lead students spontaneously to transcend the limits of American culture, its homogenizing force, its engrained suspicion of social and cultural differences, its tendency to reify the other and blame the victim. But if the fear of conformity is a legitimate one, it is not for the reasons the first group of Bruffee's critics gives. Their effort to save the individual from the group is based on an unhelpful and unnecessary polarization of the individual and society.

The limits of these critics' fear of conformity can best be seen, I think, by emphasizing the influence of John Dewey's educational pragmatism on collaborative learning. What Bruffee takes from Dewey is a strong appreciation of the generativity of group life and its promise for classroom teaching. Consensus represents the potentiality of social agency inherent in group life—the capacity for self-organization, cooperation, shared decision-making, and common action. From a pragmatist perspective, the goal of reaching consensus gives the members of a group a stake in collective projects. It does not inhibit individuality, as it does for those who fear consensus will lead to conformity. Rather it enables individuals to participate actively and meaningfully in group life. If anything, it is through the social interaction of shared activity that individuals realize their own power to take control of their situation by collaborating with others.

For Deweyans, the effort to save the individual from the group is at best misguided and at worst reactionary. On one hand, pragmatists see no reason to rescue the individual from "normative communities" because in effect there is nowhere else the individual can be: consciousness is the extension of social experience inward. On the other hand, the desire to escape from "normative communities" and break out of the "prison house of language" by grounding utterances in the generative force of individual consciousness springs from an ideological complex of belief and practice.

Dewey's educational pragmatism recasts the fear that consensus will inevitably lead to conformity as a fear of group life itself. Pedagogies that take the individual as the irreducible, inviolate starting point of education— whether through individualized instruction, cultivation of personal voice, or an emphasis on creativity and self-actualization—inscribe a deeply contradictory ideology of individualism in classroom practice. If these pedagogies seek to liberate the individual, they also simultaneously constitute the student as a social atom, an accounting unit under the teacher's gaze, a record kept by the teacher. The fear of consensus often betrays a fear of peer group influence—a fear that students will keep their own records, work out collective norms, and take action. Rather than the liberation of the individual it claims to be, the fear of "group-think" is implicitly teacher-centered and authoritarian. It prevents a class of students from transforming themselves from an aggregate of individuals into a participatory learning community. The mode of teaching and learning remains what Bruffee calls "authoritarian-individualist": the atomization of students locks them into a one-to-one relation to the teacher, the repository of effective authority in the classroom, and cuts them off from the possibilities of jointly empowering activities carried out in the society of peers. In short, the critique of consensus in the name of individualism is baseless. Consensus does not necessarily violate the individual but instead can enable individuals to empower each other through social activity.

We may now take up the left-wing critique. Here the issue is not the status of the individual but the status of exchange among individuals. We should note, first of all, that Bruffee and his left-wing critics occupy a good deal of common ground concerning the social relationships of intellectual exchange as they are played out in the classroom. For teachers and theorists looking for a critical pedagogy, Bruffee's work has been important because it teaches us to read the classroom and the culture of teaching and learning as a social text.

How we teach, Bruffee suggests, is what we teach. For Bruffee, pedagogy is not a neutral practice of transmitting knowledge from one place to another, from the teacher's head to the students'. The pedagogical project that Bruffee initiated in the early seventies calls into question the dynamics of cultural reproduction in the classroom, a process that normally operates, as it were, behind our backs. What before had seemed commonsensical became in Bruffee's reading of the classroom as a social text a set of historically derived practices—an atomized and authoritarian culture that mystifies the production of knowledge and reproduces hierarchical relations of power and domination. Bruffee's formulation of collaborative learning in the early seventies offers an implicit critique of the culture of the classroom, the sovereignty of the teacher, the reification of knowledge, the atomized authority-dependence of students, and the competitiveness and intellectual hoarding encouraged by the traditional reward system and the wider meritocratic order in higher education.

In his early work, Bruffee sees collaborative learning as part of a wider movement for participatory democracy, shared decision-making, and nonauthoritarian styles of leadership and group life. "In the world which surrounds the classroom," Bruffee says in 1973, "people today are challenging and revising many social and political traditions which have heretofore gone unquestioned"; if education has been resistant to collaboration, "[e]lsewhere, everywhere, collaborative action increasingly pervades our society" ("Collaborative Learning" 634). In Bruffee's account, collaborative learning occurs—along with free universities, grassroots organizing, the consciousness-raising groups of women's liberation, the anti-war movement, and so on—as a moment in the cultural history of the sixties, the name we now give to signify delegitimation of power and the search for alternative forms of social and political life. I think it is not accidental that collaborative learning emerged initially within open admissions programs, as part of a wider response to political pressures from below to extend literacy and access to higher education to black, Hispanic, and working-class people who had formerly been excluded.

From the late seventies to the present, Bruffee has asked what it means to reorganize the social relations in the classroom and how the decentering of authority that takes place in collaborative learning might change the way we talk about the nature of liberal education and the authority of knowledge and its institutions. Bruffee's ongoing efforts to find a language adequate to this task—to theorize collaborative learning as a social constructionist pedagogy—have turned, in the ensuing discussion, into the source of recent left-wing challenges to his work. One of the central issues of contention concerns Bruffee's appropriation of Richard Rorty's notion of conversation.

The term conversation has become a social constructionist code word to talk about knowledge and teaching and learning as social—not cognitive—acts. Knowledge, in this account, is not the result of the confrontation of the individual mind with reality but of the conversation that organizes the available means we have at any given time to talk about reality. Learning, therefore, cannot be understood strictly on cognitive grounds; it means rather joining new communities and taking part in new conversations. Learning, as Rorty puts it, "is a shift in a person's relations with others, not a shift inside the person that now *suits* him to enter new relationships" (*Philosophy* 187). By organizing students to participate in conversation, Bruffee argues, collaborative learning forms transitional communities to help students undergo the stressful and anxiety-inducing process of moving out of their indigenous communities and acquiring fluency in the conversation of liberally educated men and women. For Bruffee, Rorty's notion of conversation provides a rationale for collaborative learning as a process of re-acculturation, of learning to participate in the ongoing discussions of new communities.

This is a powerful rationale because it translates a wider reinterpretation of knowledge taking place in contemporary critical theory to the classroom—and gives us a way to incorporate what Bruffee calls the "social turn" in twentieth-century thought into the theory and practice of teaching. Still, for left-wing teachers and theorists, there is something troubling about Rorty's notion of conversation, something in the metaphor worth unpacking.

For Rorty, the term conversation offers a useful way to talk about the production of knowledge as a social process without reference to metaphysical foundations. Rorty's notion of conversation describes a discourse that has no beginning or end, but no crisis or contradiction, either. Cut loose from metaphysical moorings and transcendental backups, the conversation keeps rolling of its own accord, reproducing itself effortlessly, responsible only to itself, sanctioned by what Rorty sees as the only sanction credible: our loyalty to the conversation and our solidarity with its practices. All we can do is to continue the conversation initiated before we appeared on the scene. "We do not know," Rorty says, "what 'success' would mean except simply 'continuance'" (*Consequences* 172).

In political terms, what Rorty calls "postmodernist bourgeois liberalism" hangs onto the "ideals of the Enlightenment" but gives up the belief in Enlightenment reason. In Rorty's hands, the metaphor of conversation invokes an eighteenth-century vision of freely constituted, discoursing subjects taking part in polite speech, in Enlightenment salons and coffee houses, in the "republic of letters" emerging in the interstices of the absolutist state. To historicize Rorty's metaphor is to disclose what Terry Eagleton calls the "bourgeoisie's dream of freedom": "a society of petty producers whose endlessly available, utterly inexhaustible commodity is discourse itself" (16–17). As Eagleton argues, the "bourgeoisie . . . discovers in discourse an idealized image of its own social relations" (16). Conversation becomes the only truly free market, an ideal discursive space where exchange without domination is possible, where social differences are converted into abstract equalities at the level of speech acts.

Only now, Rorty says, the discourse must operate without the consensus of universal reason that eighteenth-century speakers took to be the normative grounding of their utterances. Given the postmodernist's disbelief in metanarratives of reason and freedom, Rebecca Comay argues, the conversation loses its emancipatory edge and "adapts to the episodic rhythms of commercial culture" (122). If we've traded in the old metaphysical comforts for a cheerful, if ungrounded affirmation of conversation, we do so, Rorty says, so we can "read more, talk more, write more" (*Philosophy* 375). The logic of planned obsolescence drives the conversation as we look for the "new, better, more interesting, more fruitful ways of speaking" (*Philosophy* 360). In a world without foundations, "nobody is so passé as the intellectual czar of the previous generation . . . the man who redescribed all those old descriptions, which, thanks in part to his redescriptions of them, nobody now wants to know anything about" (*Consequences* xl–xli). According to the idealized exchange of a free and open market, conversation keeps circulating in a spectacle of production and consumption. The new becomes old, the fashionable out-of-date, but the conversation itself is inexhaustible. "Evanescent moments in a continuing conversation . . . we keep the conversation going" (*Philosophy* 378).

Stripped of its universalist principles, the conversation turns into an act of assimilation. Unpacked, Rorty's metaphor of conversation offers a version of nonfoundationalism without tears. The consensus that keeps things rolling is no longer based on higher purposes but instead on the recognition that if we cannot discover the truth in any final sense, what we can do is to keep on talking to each other: we can tell stories, give accounts, state reasons, negotiate differences, and so on. The conversation, that is, gives up teleological ends to reaffirm the sociability of intellectual exchange. And if, as Rorty says, the conversation is simply the way we justify our beliefs socially, then we might as well relax, get good at it, and enjoy it.

Of course there are considerable attractions to this view. But there are some problems too. Rorty acknowledges, for example, the tendency of discourse to normalize itself and to block the flow of conversation by posing as a "canonical vocabulary." The conversation, as Rorty starts to acknowledge here, is perpetually materializing itself in institutional forms, alloting the opportunity to speak and arbitrating the terms of discussion. But Rorty, finally, backs away from the full consequences of conversation's normative force. At just the point where we could name the conversation and its underlying consensus as a technology of power and ask how its practices enable and constrain the production of knowledge, privilege and exclude forms of discourse, set its agenda by ignoring or suppressing others. Rorty builds a self-correcting mechanism into the conversation, an invisible hand to keep the discourse circulating and things from going stale. This is abnormal discourse or, as Rorty says, "what happens when someone joins in the discourse who is ignorant of . . . conventions or who sets them aside" (*Philosophy* 320).

Rorty's view of abnormal discourse is, I think, a problematical one. On one hand, it identifies abnormal discourse with a romantic realm of thinking the unthinkable, of solitary voices calling out, of the imagination cutting against the grain. In keeping with this romantic figure of thought, Rorty makes abnormal discourse the activity par excellence not of the group but of the individual—the genius, the rebel, the fool, "some*one* . . . who is ignorant of . . . conventions or sets them aside." This side of abnormal discourse, moreover, resists formulation. There is, Rorty says, "no discipline which describes it, any more than there is a discipline devoted to a study of the unpredictable, or of 'creativity'" (*Philosophy* 320). It is simply "generated by free and leisured conversation . . . as the sparks fly up" (321).

At the same time, though we can't know abnormal discourse on its own terms, we can identify how it functions, but now from a pragmatist perspective, to keep the conversation going. In other words, at just the moment Rorty seems to introduce difference and destabilize the conversation, he turns crisis, conflict, and contradiction into homeostatic gestures whose very expression restabilizes the conversation. What remains, once we've removed universal reason, narratives of emancipation, or "permanent neutral frameworks" as the grounds for adjudicating knowledge claims, is civility, the agreement to keep on talking. The "power of strangeness" in abnormal discourse "to take us out of our old selves" and "to make us into new beings" (*Philosophy* 360) simply reaffirms our solidarity with the conversation.

Left-wing critics are uncomfortable with this position. They want to interrupt the conversation, to denaturalize its workings, and to talk about the way conversation legitimizes itself by its very performance. Left-wing critics worry that Rortyian conversation downplays its own social force and the conflict it generates, the discourses silenced or unheard in the conversation and its representation of itself. They suspect there are other voices to take into account—voices constituted as otherness outside the conversation. For this reason, left-wing critics want to redefine consensus by locating it in the prevailing balance of power, as a marker that sets the boundaries between discourses. As Myers suggests, we need to see consensus in terms of differences and not just of agreements, "as the result of conflicts, not as a monolith" (166). Redefining consensus as a matter of conflict suggests, moreover, that consensus does not so much reconcile differences through rational negotiation. Instead, such a redefinition represents consensus as a strategy that structures differences by organizing them in relation to each other. In this sense, consensus cannot be known without its opposite—without the other voices at the periphery of the conversation.

By looking at consensus in terms of conflict rather than agreement, we get a somewhat different picture of the relationship between normal and abnormal discourse than the one Rorty and Bruffee have offered. Redefining consensus leads us, I think, to abandon the view that abnormal discourse functions as a complement to normal discourse, something which, as Bruffee says, students can turn to from time to time to question business as usual and to keep the conversation going. Instead, abnormal discourse represents the result at any given time of the set of power relations that organizes normal discourse: the acts of permission and prohibition, of incorporation and exclusion that institute the structure and practices of discourse communities. Abnormal discourse is not so much a homeostatic mechanism that keeps the conversation and thereby the community renewed and refreshed. Instead, it refers to dissensus, to marginalized voices, the resistance and contestation both within and outside the conversation, what Roland Barthes calls acratic discourse—the discourses out of power. Abnormal discourse, that is, refers not only to surprises and accidents that emerge when normal discourse reaches a dead end, when, as Wittgenstein puts it, "language goes on holiday." In the account I'm suggesting, it also refers to the relations of power that determine what falls within the current consensus and what is assigned the status of dissent. Abnormal discourse, from this perspective, is neither as romantic nor as pragmatic as Rorty makes it out to be. Rather it offers a way to analyze the strategic moves by which discourse communities legitimize their own conversation by marginalizing others. It becomes a critical term to describe the conflict among discourses and collective wills in the heterogeneous conversation in contemporary public life.

Bruffee argues that such an emphasis on conflict has led his left-wing critics to want to "turn to 'struggle' to force change in 'people's interests'" (Response 714). I would reply that struggle is not something people, left-wing or otherwise, can "turn to" or choose to do. "Struggle," at least the way I understand it, is something we're born into: it's a standard feature of contemporary social existence. We experience "struggle" all the time in everyday life precisely because, as Bruffee points out, we "all belong to many overlapping, mutually inclusive communities." We "experience belonging to each of these communities as both limiting and liberating" (715) in part because we experience the discourses, or what Bruffee calls the "vernacular languages of the communities one belongs to," as a polyphony of voices, an internal conversation traversed by social, cultural, and linguistic differences.

Bruffee uses the term vernacular to call attention to the plurality of voices that constitute our verbal thought. The intersecting vernaculars that we experience contending for our attention and social allegiance, however, are not just plural. They are also organized in hierarchical relations of power. The term vernacular, after all, as Houston Baker reminds us, "signals" on etymological and ideological grounds "'a slave born on his master's estate'" (2). The term vernacular, that is, cannot be understood apart from the relations of domination and subordination it implies. The conversation, in Bakhtin's word, is "heteroglot," a mosaic of vernaculars, the multi-accented idiomatic expression of race, class, and gender differences. The conversation gives voice to the conflicts inherent in an unequal social order and in the asymmetrical relations of power in everyday life.

341

Bruffee worries that "struggle" means interrupting the conversation to "force change in people's interests." Bruffee's worries here betray what seems to me a persistent anxiety in non-foundationalist versions of social constructionist thought about its own radical disclosure: that once we give up extra-historical and universal criteria and reduce the authority of knowledge to a self-legitimizing account of its own practices, we won't have a way to separate persuasion from force, validity claims from plays of power. As Rorty puts it, to "suggest that there is *no* . . . common ground seems to endanger rationality. . . . To question the need for commensuration seems the first step toward a return to a war of 'all against all' " (*Philosophy* 317). In the account I'm suggesting, "struggle" is not a matter of interrupting the conversation to replace consensual validation with force. It refers rather to the relations between the two terms—intellectual negotiation and power—in what we think of as rational argument and public discourse. The term "struggle" is simply a way of shifting rhetorical analysis, as Victor Vitanza has suggested, from Aristotelean persuasion or Burkean identification to an agonistic framework of conflict and difference—to a rhetoric of dissensus.

The choice, as I see it, does not consist of solidarity with a self-explaining conversation or violence. I want to preserve, along with Bruffee and Rorty, the value of civility and consensus. But to do this we will need to rehabilitate the notion of consensus by redefining it in relation to a rhetoric of dissensus. We will need, that is, to look at collaborative learning not merely as a process of consensus-making but more important as a process of identifying differences and locating these differences in relation to each other. The consensus that we ask students to reach in the collaborative classroom will be based not so much on collective agreements as on collective explanations of how people differ, where their differences come from, and whether they can live and work together with these differences.

To think of consensus in terms of dissensus is to challenge a central rationale Bruffee has offered for collaborative learning. Bruffee currently holds that one of the benefits of collaborative learning is that its consensual practices model the normal workings of discourse communities in business, government, the professions, and academia. Myers argues, correctly I think, that Bruffee's use of consensus risks accepting the current production and distribution of knowledge and discourse as unproblematical and given. The limit of Myers' critique, however, is that it concedes Bruffee's claim that consensus is in fact the norm in business, industry, and the professions. In this regard, both Bruffee and Myers seriously underestimate the extent to which the conversations of these discourse communities are regulated not so much by consensual negotiation and shared decision-making as by what

Jürgen Habermas calls a "success orientation" of instrumental control and rational efficiency.

It can be misleading, therefore, to tell students, as social constructionists do, that learning to write means learning to participate in the conversation and consensual practices of various discourse communities. Instead, we need to ask students to explore the rhetoric of dissensus that pervades writing situations. As Susan Wells argues, even such apparently prosaic and "unheroic" tasks as writing manuals for the computer-assisted redesign of an auto body section take place within a complicated network of competing and contradictory interests. In the case of the design manual that Wells cites, the technical writer faces three different audiences. Concerned with the overall operation of a computer system, the first audience of systems programmers may be just as likely to guard their professional knowledge of the system as to collaborate with others. They may, in fact, see the second audience, application programmers responsible for writing programs for specific design tasks, as "enemies" looking for ways to "tweak" or "jiggle" the system to get their work done—and who thereby threaten the overall performance of the system. The third audience of users, on the other hand, needs to know how to operate the system on narrow job-related grounds. But from both the programmers' perspective, this group is an unknown variable, men and women who may be "demonically curious" and want to play with the system, to see how it really works.

By exploring the differential access to knowledge and the relations of power and status that structure this writing situation, Wells says, students can learn not only how technical writers "write for success" by adjusting to multiple audiences. (As it turned out, the technical writer produced a separate manual containing quite different information for each of the audiences.) Students can also learn to articulate a rhetoric of dissensus that will lead them to see that the goal of discourse in this case, as Wells puts it, "is systematic misunderstanding and concealment. . . the total fragmentation and dispersal of knowledge" (256). They can learn, that is, not how consensus is achieved through collaborative negotiation but rather how differences in interest produce conflicts that may in fact block communication and prohibit the development of consensus.

Of course, it is true, as Wells notes, that not all organizations rely upon such a rigid division of labor. Collaboration and consensual decision-making, after all, have become buzz words for "new age" managers and technocrats. Part of the current conventional wisdom about the new information society is that cooperation and collaboration will replace the competitive and individualistic ethos of the entrepreneurial age of industrial capitalism. But finally what collaboration and consensus amount to are not so much new paradigms for a high-tech post-industrial order as new versions of an older industrial psychology adopted to late capitalism—human relations techniques to bolster morale, promote identification with the corporation, legitimize differential access to knowledge and status, and increase productivity. Even in the ostensibly disinterested realm of academics, the production of knowledge is motivated as much by career moves as by consensus, by the efforts of individuals to enhance their credentials and relative position in a field, to build up their fund of cultural capital.

At issue here is not whether collaborative learning reflects more accurately than traditional pedagogies the actual social relations that produce knowledge and make organizations run. Surely it does. But by modeling collaborative learning on the normal workings of discourse communities, Bruffee identifies the authority of knowledge with the prevailing productive apparatus. For social constructionists, this is an uncontroversial point. In one sense, it is the point—that the present configuration of knowledge and its institutions is a social artifact. But in another sense, this line of thought also concedes the authority of knowledge to the professional judgment of experts, to academic specialties and professional training, to the wider meritocratic order of a credentialed society.

If one of the goals of collaborative learning is to replace the traditional hierarchical relations of teaching and learning with the practices of participatory democracy, we must acknowledge that one of the functions of the professions and the modern university has been to specialize and to remove knowledge from public discourse and decision-making, to reduce it to a matter of expertise and technique. By the same token, we must acknowledge that it devalues the notion of consensus to identify it with the current professional monopolies of knowledge. If anything, the prevailing configuration of knowledge and its institutions *prevents* the formation of consensus by shrinking the public sphere and excluding the majority of the population from the conversation.

The effect of Bruffee's use of consensus is to invest a kind of "real world" authority in the discursive practices and tacit understandings that bind the discourse communities of specialists and experts together. It makes the conversation a self-explaining mechanism that legitimizes itself through its performances. "This," we tell students, "is the way we [English teachers, biologists, lawyers, chemical engineers, social workers, whatever] do things around here. There's nothing magical about it. It's just the way we talk to each other." The problem is that invoking the "real world" authority of such consensual practices neutralizes the critical and transformative project of collaborative learning, depoliticizes it, and reduces it to an acculturative technique.

To develop a critical version of collaborative learning, we will need to distinguish between consensus as an acculturative practice that reproduces business as usual and consensus as an oppositional one that challenges the prevailing conditions of production. The point of collaborative learning is not simply to demystify the authority of knowledge by revealing its social character but to transform the productive apparatus, to change the social character of production. In this regard, it will help to cast consensus not as a "real world" practice but as a utopian one.

To draw out the utopian possibilities I believe are implied in collaborative learning, we will need to distinguish between "spurious" and "genuine" consensus, as grounded and problematical as these terms may appear to be. In his theory of "communicative action," Habermas defines "genuine" consensus not as something that actually happens but instead as the counterfactual anticipation that agreement can be reached without coercion or systematic distortion. Consensus, for Habermas, is not, as it is for social constructionists like Bruffee, an empirical account of how discourse communities operate but a critical and normative representation of the conditions necessary for fully realized communication to occur. In Habermas' view, we should represent consensus not as the result at any given time of the prevailing conversation but rather as an aspiration to organize the conversation according to relations of non-domination. The anticipation of consensus, that is, projects what Habermas calls an "ideal speech situation," a utopian discursive space that distributes symmetrically the opportunity to speak, to initiate discourse, to question, to give reasons, to do all those other things necessary to justify knowledge socially. From this perspective, consensus becomes a necessary fiction of reciprocity and mutual recognition, the dream of conversation as perfect dialogue. Understood as a utopian desire, assembled from the partial and fragmentary forms of the current conversation, consensus does not appear as the end or the explanation of the conversation but instead as a means of transforming it.

To cast consensus as a utopian instead of a "real world" practice has a number of implications for the collaborative classroom. For one thing, a utopian representation of consensus offers students a powerful critical instrument to interrogate the conversation—to interrupt it in order to investigate the forces which determine who may speak and what may be said, what inhibits communication and what makes it possible. The normal workings of collaborative learning, as Bruffee describes them, ask students to generate an interpretive response to a literary work or a rhetorical analysis of a piece of writing and then to compare the results to the responses or analyses of their teacher and the community of scholars the teacher represents. The pedagogical goal is to negotiate a common language in the classroom, to draw students into a wider consensus, and to initiate them into the conversation as it is currently organized in the academy. The utopian view of consensus, on the other hand, would abandon this expert-novice model of teaching and learning. Instead consensus would provide students with a critical measure to identify the relations of power in the formation of expert judgment.

Let me give an example here. Collaborative learning in literature classes is often based on the idea that students need to avoid, on the one hand, the objectivism that assumes the meaning is in the text and, on the other, the radical pluralism that assumes we cannot distinguish the merits of one reading from another. Collaborative learning, that is, seeks to locate authority in neither the text nor the reader but in what Stanley Fish calls interpretive communities. From the perspective I am suggesting, however, the identification of collaborative learning with interpretive communities takes for granted the enterprise of interpretation as an end in itself.

In contrast, I think we need to begin collaborative classes by asking why interpretation has become the unquestioned goal of literary studies and what other kinds of readings thereby have been excluded and devalued. We would be interested in the forces which have produced dissensus about how to go about reading a literary text and about what constitutes a literary text in the first place. Students, of course, already know a good deal about all this: they are used to naming Shakespeare and Dickens and Hemingway as literature and disqualifying Stephen King, thrillers, and science fiction. What students have had less opportunity to do is to investigate collectively these implicit hierarchies in terms of the relations of power that organize them. Their literature classes have taught them to segregate kinds of reading but without asking them where these differences come from.

For this reason, we might begin the conversation in literature classes by talking not about how to read a literary text but rather about how the students in the course have been trained to read literature and how their schooled reading differs from the way they read outside of school. By examining these differences, freshmen and sophomores in introductory literature courses, I have found, can begin to examine critically the prevailing representation of literature and the institutional base on which it rests. Students rather quickly will distinguish between literature—which is assigned by teachers and is "good for you"—and the other reading they do—which is "for fun." They explain to each other and to me that literature is filled with "hidden meanings" and that the point of schooled reading is to dig them out, while the reading they do for "fun" produces strong identification with characters and teaches them about "life" or gives them the opportunity to escape from it.

The point of such discussion is not to reach agreement about what properly belongs in the realm of literature and what lies outside of it. Nor is it to abandon the usefulness of schooled reading. Rather what students begin to see is that literature exists as a social category that depends on its relation to non-literature. Students, that is, can begin to sketch the rhetoric of dissensus that structures the dominant representation of what literature is and is not and that produces marked differences in the way they read and experience texts.

Such discussions, moreover, give students permission to elaborate what they already know—namely, that schooled reading for "hidden meanings" reinforces the authority of expert readers and creates professional monopolies of knowledge. By drawing on their own experience as readers in and out of school, students regularly and spontaneously make the same telling point William E. Cain makes in *The Crisis in Criticism* that the institution of literature depends upon the "close reading" of specialist critics. In this regard, one of the most valuable things students bring to a literature class is what we as professional readers have largely forgotten—the imprecise, unanalytical act of non-close reading, the experience of ordinary readers at home, on the subway, or at the beach in the summer, the kind of reading that schooled reading marks as different.

One of the benefits of emphasizing the dissensus that surrounds the act of reading is that it poses consensus not as the goal of the conversation but rather as a critical measure to help students identify the structures of power that inhibit communication among readers (and between teachers and students) by authorizing certain styles of reading while excluding others. What students in introductory literature classes learn, I think, is to overcome the feeling that they don't get the point of literature or that they just like to read "trash." Instead, they learn why readers disagree about what counts as a reading, where the differences they experience as readers come from, and how we might usefully bring these differences into relation to each other. They learn to probe not only the ideology of the institution of literature but also the ideologies of popular reading. Just as they learn how schooled reading constitutes them as students in a complicated relationship to the authority of teachers and the institution of literature, students also learn that the reading they do outside of school is not simply a pastime but more important represents an act of self-formation that organizes their experience and desire in imaginary relations to the popular culture of late capitalism and its construction of race, class, and gender differences.

The revised notion of consensus I am proposing here depends paradoxically on its deferral, not its realization. I am less interested in students achieving consensus (although of course this happens at times) as in their using consensus as a critical instrument to open gaps in the conversation through which differences may emerge. In this regard, the Habermasian representation of consensus as a counterfactual anticipation of fully realized communication offers students a critical tool to identify the structures of power which determine who may speak and what may be said. But more important, this notion of consensus also offers students utopian aspirations to transform the conversation by freeing it from the prevailing constraints on its participants, the manipulations, deceptions, and plays of power. Through a collective investigation of differences, students can begin to imagine ways to change the relations of production and to base the conversation not on consensus but on reciprocity and the mutual recognition of the participants and their differences.

Unlike Habermas, however, I do not believe removing relations of domination and systematic distortion, whether ideological or neurotic, from the conversation is likely to establish the conditions in which consensus will express a "rational will" and "permit what *all* can want" (108). Instead, I want to displace consensus to a horizon which may never be reached. We need to see consensus, I think, not as an agreement that reconciles differences through an ideal conversation but rather as the desire of humans to live and work together with differences. The goal of consensus, it seems to me, ought to be not the unity of generalizable interests but rather what Iris Marion Young calls "an openness to unassimilated otherness" (22). Under the utopian aegis of consensus, students can learn to agree to disagree, not because "everyone has their own opinion," but because justice demands that we recognize the inexhaustibility of difference and that we organize the conditions in which we live and work accordingly.

By organizing students non-hierarchically so that all discursive roles are available to all the participants in a group, collaborative learning can do more than model or represent the normal workings of discourse communities. Students' experience of non-domination in the collaborative classroom can offer them a critical measure to understand the distortions of communication and the plays of power in normal discourse. Replacing the "real world" authority of consensus with a rhetoric of dissensus can lead students to demystify the normal workings of discourse communities. But just as important, a rhetoric of dissensus can lead them to redefine consensus as a utopian project, a dream of difference without domination. The participatory and democratic practices of collaborative learning offer an important instance of what Walter Benjamin, in "The Author as Producer," calls the "exemplary character of production"—the collective effort to "induce other producers to produce" and to "put an improved apparatus at their disposal" (233). In this regard, the exemplary character of production in collaborative learning can release collective energies to turn the means of criticism into a means of transformation, to tap fundamental impulses toward emancipation and justice in the utopian practices of Habermas' "ideal speech situation."

It would be fatuous, of course, to presume that collaborative learning can constitute more than momentarily an alternative to the present asymmetrical relations of power and distribution of knowledge and its means of production. But it can incite desire through common work to resolve, if only symbolically, the contradictions students face because of the prevailing conditions of production—the monopoly of expertise and the impulse to know, the separation of work and play, allegiance to peers and dependence on faculty esteem, the experience of cooperation and the competitiveness of a ranking reward system, the empowering sense of collectivity and the isolating personalization of an individual's fate. A rehabilitated notion of consensus in collaborative learning can provide students with exemplary motives to imagine alternative worlds and transformations of social life and labor. In its deferred and utopian form, consensus offers a way to orchestrate dissensus and to turn the conversation in the collaborative classroom into a heterotopia of voices—a heterogeneity without hierarchy.

WORKS CITED

Baker, Houston A., Jr. *Blues, Ideology, and Afro-American Literature.* Chicago: U of Chicago P, 1984.

Beade, Pedro. Comment. *College English* 49 (1987): 708.

Benjamin, Walter. "The Author as Producer." *Reflections.* Ed. Peter Demetz. New York: Schocken, 1986. 220–38.

Bruffee, Kenneth A. "Collaborative Learning: Some Practical Models." *College English* 34 (1973): 634–43.

_____. Response. *College English* 49 (1987): 711–16.

Cain, William E. *The Crisis in Criticism: Theory, Literature, and Reform in English Studies.* Baltimore: John Hopkins UP, 1984.

Comay, Rebecca. "Interrupting the Conversation: Notes on Rorty." *Telos* 69 (1986): 119–30.

Eagleton, Terry. *The Function of Criticism.* London: Verso, 1984.

Foster, David. Comment. *College English* 49 (1987): 709–11.

Habermas, Jürgen. *Legitimation Crisis.* Trans. Thomas McCarthy. Boston: Beacon, 1975.

Johnson, Thomas S. Comment. *College English* 48 (1986): 76.

Myers, Greg. "Reality, Consensus, and Reform in the Rhetoric of Composition Teaching." *College English* 48 (1986): 154–74.

Rorty, Richard. *The Consequences of Pragmatism.* Minneapolis: U of Minnesota P, 1982.

_____. *Philosophy and the Mirror of Nature.* Princeton: Princeton UP, 1979.

Vitanza, Victor. "Critical Sub/Versions of the History of Philosophical Rhetoric." *Rhetoric Review* 6.1 (1987): 41–66.

Wells, Susan. "Habermas, Communicative Competence, and the Teaching of Technical Discourse." *Theory in the Classroom.* Ed. Cary Nelson. Urbana: U of Illinois P, 1986. 245–69.

Young, Iris Marion. "The Ideal of Community and the Politics of Difference." *Social Theory and Practice* 12.1 (1986): 1–26.

"Contact Zones" and English Studies

PATRICIA BIZZELL

Our Ptolemaic system of literary categories goes creaking and groaning onward, in spite of the widely acknowledged need to overhaul it in response to multiculturalism. This is not to say that there have not been attempts to revise course design in light of new materials and methods. For example, G. Douglas Atkins and Michael L. Johnson's *Writing and Reading Differently* (1985), Susan L. Gabriel and Isaiah Smithson's *Gender in the Classroom* (1990), and James A. Berlin and Michael J. Vivion's *Cultural Studies in the English Classroom* (1992) address the pedagogical consequences of deconstruction, feminist literary theory, and cultural studies, respectively, and also incorporate more diverse literatures. But these attempts to foster innovation in the individual classroom still leave the basic structure of English studies intact.

In Kristin Ross's description of the multicultural world literature and cultural studies program at the University of California at Santa Cruz, she comments indirectly on this problem when she identifies as one stumbling block to the Santa Cruz program the faculty's unwillingness "to depart from their specialized fields" (668). They fended off demands to diversify their course material with plaints like "But I don't have a PhD in South African literature" (668). Ross gives good reasons for forging ahead in spite of such protests, but she doesn't say much about the underlying structure of English studies that still makes us think our scholarship must be organized along national or chronological lines, even though these are inimical to the process of integrating new materials and methods because devised to serve and protect the old ones.

Reprinted from *College English* 56.2 (February 1994): 163–69. Used with permission.

The persistence of the old basic structure can be seen even in an impressive new collection published by the Modern Language Association with the avowed intention of fostering innovation: Stephen Greenblatt and Giles Gunn's *Redrawing the Boundaries: The Transformation of English and American Literary Studies* (1992). Even here, boundaries are not redrawn in fundamentally new ways. Rather, the old, familiar structure of English studies is visible, for instance in chapter divisions that carve literary studies into chronological periods, such as "Seventeenth-Century Studies" (British literature) and "American Literary Studies to the Civil War." Ten such chapters are followed by eleven more, most with the word "Criticism" in the title, implying that here we turn from primary to secondary texts. Yet it is here that we find the most attention to literature by women, gay people, and people of color: separate chapters are devoted, for example, to "Feminist Criticism" and "African American Criticism." Thus other traditional boundaries appear to be reasserted rather than redrawn. Moreover, the field of composition studies appears to remain behind even more impenetrable traditional boundaries. Not only is "Composition Studies" given a separate chapter (in the second set of eleven), but there must be an additional, separate chapter just to explain why composition studies is included in this book at all ("Composition and Literature").

I think we need a radically new system to organize English studies, and I propose that we develop it in response to the materials with which we are now working. Instead of finagling the new literatures and the new pedagogical and critical approaches into our old categories, we should try to find comprehensive new forms that seem to spring from and respond to the new materials. Instead of asking ourselves, for example, "How can I fit Frederick Douglass into my American Renaissance course?" we need to ask, "How should I reconceive my study of literature and composition now that I regard Douglass as an important writer?"

It could be argued that we don't need any new system of categories, that what we should do is simply to knock down the old system and then let everyone do what he or she pleases. This appears to be the approach taken by another recent attempt to chart new courses, the MLA's 1987 English Coalition Conference. Peter Elbow, in his account of this conference, *What Is English?* (1990), tells us there was a "remarkable consensus" at the conference on "the central business of English studies" (17), and it was as follows:

> *Using language* actively in a diversity of ways and settings—that is, not only in the classroom as exercises for teachers but in a range of social settings with various audiences where the language makes a difference.

Reflecting on language use. Turning back and self-consciously reflecting on how one has been using language—examining these processes of talking, listening, writing, and reading.

Trying to ensure that this using and reflecting go on in *conditions of both nourishment and challenge,* that is, conditions where teachers care about students themselves and what they actively learn—not just about skills or scores or grades. (18; emphasis in original)

The tone here, of course, is quite different from that of *Redrawing the Boundaries*—the focus is clearly on pedagogy rather than on the body of scholarly knowledge. I applaud this focus on pedagogy, and I admire the principles laid down above. But I can't help noticing that they appear to have very little to do specifically with the discipline of English studies. To me, they sound like the kind of principles I urge on faculty from all disciplines in my school's writing-across-the-curriculum program. There isn't a course at my school where these principles couldn't be put advantageously into practice. How, then, do they define "the central business of English studies"?

What these principles leave out, as Elbow himself notes, is what people read and write *about* in literary studies. He acknowledges that "you can't make meaning unless you are writing or reading about *something*; . . . practices are always practices *of* a content" (19; emphasis in original). Yet the topic of literary content appeared to be taboo at the conference. As Elbow tells it:

The question of literature was left strikingly moot. Not only was there no consensus, there was a striking avoidance of the issue. It's not that it didn't come up; the question of literature arose recurrently. . . . Yet every time we somehow slid away from the issue into something else. (96, 97)

This sounds to me like repression, not freedom, but I sympathize with the conference members. Small wonder they could not find a way to talk about literature, with the old system of organizing it discredited for lack of inclusiveness and no new system yet accepted. But I am concerned that this kind of avoidance leaves graduate and undergraduate curricula dangerously lacking in guidance—dangerously vulnerable to "cultural literacy" pundits who would shove into the breach the only system still known, namely the old, bad traditional one. Indeed, this threat appeared at the conference itself, and Elbow, although an advocate of composition pedagogies in which each writer is to do pretty much as he or she pleases, was sufficiently troubled by it that he proposes his own list of literary contents for English studies in an appendix.

But exactly how are we to develop a new system of organization from the new materials of study, supposing we agree that this is needed? To do so would seem to require that we make generalizations about the new material—about what, say, might be required to study Asian-American literature adequately—that would be extremely difficult, if not downright presumptuous, to make. I think we need an approach to the diverse world literatures written in English we are now studying that focuses not on their essential nature, whatever that may be, but rather on how they might, not "fit" together exactly, but come into productive dialogue with one another.

I suggest that we address this problem by employing Mary Louise Pratt's concept of the "contact zone":

> I use this term to refer to social spaces where cultures meet, clash, and grapple with each other, often in contexts of highly asymmetrical relations of power, such as colonialism, slavery, or their aftermaths as they are lived out in many parts of the world today. (34)

This concept can aid us both because it emphasizes the conditions of difficulty and struggle under which literatures from different cultures come together (thus forestalling the disrespectful glossing over of differences), and because it gives us a conceptual base for bringing these literatures together, namely, when they occur in or are brought to the same site of struggle or "contact zone."

A "contact zone" is defined primarily in terms of historical circumstances. It is circumscribed in time and space, but with elastic boundaries. Focusing on a contact zone as a way of organizing literary study would mean attempting to include *all* material relevant to the struggles going on there. Pratt's main example of a "contact zone" here is Peru in the late sixteenth and early seventeenth centuries, where she wants to study the interaction among texts by Native Americans (newly discovered by twentieth-century scholars) and the canonical Spanish accounts. I submit that the United States is another such contact zone, or more precisely, a congeries of overlapping contact zones, considered from the first massive immigration of Europeans in the seventeenth century up to the present day. "Multiculturalism" in English studies is a name for our recognition of this condition of living on contested cultural ground, and our desire to represent something of this complexity in our study of literature and literacy.

If we understand that we are teaching in, and about, contact zones, Pratt suggests that we must stop imagining our job to be transmitting a unitary literature and literacy. Under this old model,

The prototypical manifestation of language is generally taken to be the speech of individual adult native speakers face-to-face (as in Saussure's famous diagram) in monolingual, even monodialectal situations—in short, the most homogeneous case, linguistically and socially. The same goes for written communication. (38)

Now, Pratt suggests that we need a new model:

a theory that assumed different things—that argued, for instance, that the most revealing speech situation for understanding language was one involving a gathering of people each of whom spoke two languages and understood a third and held only one language in common with any of the others. (38)

This model treats difference as an asset, not a liability.

Given American diversity, our classrooms are getting to be more like Pratt's new model than the old one. If we respond by "teaching the contact zone," we can foster classrooms where, as in Pratt's experience,

All the students in the class . . . [heard] their culture discussed and objecti-fied in ways that horrified them; all the students saw their roots traced back to legacies of both glory and shame; . . . [but] kinds of marginalization once taken for granted were gone. Virtually every student was having the experience of seeing the world described with him or her in it. (39)

Acknowledging its difficulties, I am suggesting that we need a new system of organization in English studies to make this kind of teaching—and scholar-ship—not only possible, but normative.

In short, I am suggesting that we organize English studies not in terms of literary or chronological periods, nor essentialized racial or gender catego-ries, but rather in terms of historically defined contact zones, moments when different groups within the society contend for the power to interpret what is going on. As suggested above, the chronological, geographical, and generic parameters of any contact zone are defined on the basis of including as much material as possible that is relevant to the issue being contested. Time periods can be short or long, literatures of different groups, languages, or continents can be considered together, all genres are admitted, and so on.

For example, the New England region from about 1600 to about 1800 might be defined as a contact zone in which different groups of Europeans and Native Americans were struggling for the power to say what had hap-pened in their relations with each other. Thus canonical Puritan histories, autobiographies, and captivity narratives would be studied in connection with historical commentaries and memoirs by non-Puritan Europeans (traditionally treated as "minor"), European transcriptions of Native American speeches (problematic but invaluable), and letters, histories, and spiritual autobiographies written by Native Americans in English (unknown in the academy until very recently). The object would not be to represent what the lives of the diverse European immigrant and Native American groups were really like. Rather, the attempt would be to show how each group represented itself imaginatively in relation to the others. We would, in effect, be reading all the texts as brought to the contact zone, for the purpose of communicating across cultural boundaries.

There are several advantages to this approach. First, it provides a rationale for integrating English studies multiculturally. No longer would we be trying to squeeze new material into inappropriate old categories, where its importance could not be adequately appreciated. We would be working with categories that treated multiculturalism as a defining feature, that assumed the richest literary treasures could be found in situations in which different histories, lifeways, and languages are trying to communicate and to deal with the unequal power distribution among them. We would no longer need to ask prejudicial questions, such as whether Frederick Douglass was as "good" on some putative absolute scale of expository value as Henry Thoreau. Rather, we would look at the rhetorical effectiveness of each writer in dealing with the matter in hand, for example, the need to promote civil disobedience in the contact zone created by white and black efforts to define and motivate action in response to slavery in the antebellum U.S.

Second, this approach fully integrates composition and rhetoric into literary studies. Studying texts as they respond to contact zone conditions is studying them rhetorically, studying them as efforts of rhetoric. The historical context provides a way to focus the rhetorical analysis. Moreover, professional and student writing can also be seen as contending in contact zones and experimenting with the textual arts of the contact zone that rhetorical analysis emphasizes. Thus boundaries between "content" (literature) and its traditional inferior, pedagogy (composition), are usefully blurred, as are the distinctions between "high" literature and other kinds of writing, including student writing. Donald McQuade makes a persuasive argument for blurring these boundaries in "Composition and Literature."

At the end of her essay, Pratt calls for the development of what she calls "the pedagogical arts of the contact zone":

> exercises in storytelling and in identifying with the ideas, interests, histories, and attitudes of others; experiments in transculturation and collaborative work and in the arts of critique, parody, and comparison (including

unseemly comparisons between elite and vernacular cultural forms); the redemption of the oral; ways for people to engage with suppressed aspects of history (including their own histories); ways to move *into and out of* rhetorics of authenticity; ground rules for communication across lines of difference and hierarchy that go beyond politeness but maintain mutual respect; a systematic approach to the all-important concept of *cultural mediation.* (40; emphasis in original)

David Bartholomae has recently suggested that we imagine these "arts" translated into exercises in an English class. Imagine, for example, a class in which literature is analyzed for the ways it moves among rhetorics of authenticity, students experiment with attending to suppressed aspects of their own history as part of establishing their writerly personae, and scholarly writing is both shared and opened for parody. Pratt calls this work "cultural mediation"; my phrase for it is "negotiating difference"—studying how various writers in various genres have grappled with the pervasive presence of difference in American life and developed virtues out of necessity. I would include analysis of student writing, for its employment of contact zone rhetorical strategies, and I would include "texts" of all kinds, as required by the contact zones under study—posters, songs, films, videos, and so forth.

Reorganizing literary studies along these lines would mean redesigning courses. For example, at Holy Cross we offer first-year students a choice of either a composition course (a course in the personal essay) or a course that introduces them to literary study by teaching the close reading of works grouped according to genre. Under the new paradigm, there would be no need for two separate courses. The abilities needed both to enter literary studies and to refine one's own writing would be the skills of analyzing and imitating rhetorical arts of the contact zone. Students would learn to critique strategies of negotiating difference in the writing of others and to practice them in their own. So we could offer just one course, writing-intensive but including some reading and analysis of literature (broadly defined).

It would also mean reorganizing graduate study and professional scholarly work in ways I hardly dare to suggest. I suppose that one would no longer become a specialist in American literature, a "Shakespeare man," or a "compositionist." Rather, people's areas of focus would be determined by the kinds of rhetorical problems in which they were interested.

My main object is to get people to work on the project. I have no coherent alternative program to present. But I believe that if we reorganize literary studies in this way, we will be giving a dynamic new direction to our profession. We will be creating disciplinary parameters within which boundaries really can be redrawn to come to terms with the demands of multiculturalism. This new paradigm will stimulate scholarship and give vitally needed guidance to graduate and undergraduate curricula. It might also lead us, in the multicultural literary archives, to stories of hope that can lend us all spiritual sustenance as we renew efforts to make the United States a multicultural democracy. If we are not given to complete the task, neither are we allowed to desist from it.

WORKS CITED

Atkins, G. Douglas, and Michael L. Johnson, eds. *Writing and Reading Differently: Decon-struction and the Teaching of Composition and Literature.* Lawrence: U of Kansas P, 1985.

Bartholomae, David. "The Tidy House: Basic Writing in the American Curriculum." *Journal of Basic Writing* 12 (Spring 1993): 4–21.

Berlin, James A., and Michael J. Vivion, eds. *Cultural Studies in the English Classroom.* Portsmouth, NH: Heinemann-Boynton/Cook, 1992.

Elbow, Peter. *What is English?* New York: MLA, 1990.

Gabriel, Susan L., and Isaiah Smithson, eds. *Gender in the Classroom: Power and Pedagogy.* Urbana: U of Illinois P, 1990.

Greenblatt, Stephen, and Giles Gunn, eds. *Redrawing the Boundaries: The Transformation of English and American Literary Studies.* New York: MLA, 1992.

McQuade, Donald. "Composition and Literature." Greenblatt and Gunn 482–519.

Pratt, Mary Louise. "Arts of the Contact Zone." *Profession 91.* New York: MLA, 1991. 33–40.

Ross, Kristin. "The World Literature and Cultural Studies Program." *Critical Inquiry* 19 (Summer 1993): 666–676.

Professing Multiculturalism
The Politics of Style in the Contact Zone

MIN-ZHAN LU

In her 1991 "Arts of the Contact Zone," Mary Louise Pratt points out that
while colleges and universities have increasingly deployed a rhetoric of
diversity in response to the insistence of non-mainstream groups for fuller
participation, the "import" of "multiculturalism" remains "up for grabs
across the ideological spectrum" (39). I begin with Pratt's reminder because
I want to call attention to the images of "grabbing" and "import." These
depict "multiculturalism" as a construct whose "import"—meanings, implications, and consequences—is available only to those willing to expend the
energy to "grab" it: to search, envision, grasp, articulate, and enact it. And
these images conjure up the act of importing—of bringing in—perspectives
and methods formerly excluded by dominant institutions. I want to articulate one "import" of multiculturalism here by exploring the question of how
to conceive and practice teaching methods which invite a multicultural
approach to style, particularly those styles of student writing which appear to
be ridden with "errors." And I situate this question in the context of English
Studies, a discipline which, on the one hand, has often proclaimed its concern to profess multiculturalism but, on the other hand, has done little to
combat the ghettoization of two of its own cultures, namely composition
teaching and student writing.

My inquiry is motivated by two concerns which I believe I share with a
significant number of composition teachers. The first results from a sense of
division between the ways in which many of us approach style in theory and
in our teaching practices. I have in mind teachers who are aligned in theory

Reprinted from *College Composition and Communication* 45.4 (December 1994): 442–58.
Used with permission.

with a view of composition which contests the separation of form and meaning and which also argues against a conception of "academic discourse" as discrete, fixed, and unified. This alignment, while generating a critical perspective towards traditional methods of teaching style through drills in "correct usage," does not always result in any immediate revision of such methods in classroom practice. Some of us tend to resolve this gap between theory and practice in one of two ways: (1) We set aside a few weeks to teach "usage" or "copyediting" in the traditional way while spending the rest of the term helping students to revise their work on a more conceptual level; or (2) we send students who have "problems" with "usage" to the writing center. Such "resolutions" often leave the teacher frustrated. Because she recognizes the burden on those at the fringe of having to "prove" themselves to those at the center by meeting the standards set by the latter, she cannot but take seriously students' anxiety to master "correct" usage. Nevertheless, she is aware that instead of helping them to overcome such an anxiety, her teaching strategies risk increasing it, as they may reinforce students' sense of the discrepancy between their inability to produce "error-free" prose and their ability to come up with "good ideas," and they may confirm these students' impression that only those who make "errors" need to worry about issues of usage and editing. My second concern has to do with a division many of us feel between our role as composition teachers and the role we play as students, teachers, or scholars in other, supposedly more central areas of English Studies. As our interest in composition teaching, theory, and research evolves, we are increasingly interested in contesting the second-class status of work in composition. At the same time, we are often all too aware that we ourselves are guilty of perpetuating the divisions between composition and other areas of English Studies by approaching the writings of "beginners" or "outsiders" in a manner different from the approach we take to the writings of "experts."

Two stories, both of which took place around the turn of this century, illustrate part of the historical power of that kind of division. The first story comes from Gertrude Stein's *The Autobiography of Alice B. Toklas*. According to Stein, right after she had made arrangements to have her book *Three Lives* printed by Grafton Press of New York, "a very nice American young man" was sent by the press to Paris to check on her:

> You see, [the young man] said slightly hesitant, the director of the Grafton Press is under the impression that perhaps your knowledge of english. But I am an american, said Gertrude Stein indignantly. Yes yes I understand that perfectly now, he said, but perhaps you have not had much experience in writing. I suppose, said [Stein] laughing, you were under the impression

that I was imperfectly educated. He blushed, why no, he said, but you might not have had much experience in writing. Oh yes, she said, oh yes. . . . and you might as well tell [the director] . . . that everything that is written in the manuscript is written with the intention of its being so written and all he has to do is to print it and I will take the responsibility. The young man bowed himself out. (68)

This exchange between an indignant Stein and an embarrassed "young man" reveals some of the criteria used by "educated america" when dealing with an idiosyncratic style. These criteria are (a) the writer's "knowledge of english," which is seen as somehow dependent on whether she is a native speaker, and (b) the writer's "experience in writing," which is seen as related to whether she has been "[im]perfectly educated." Stein, an "American" bearing certification of a "perfect" education from Radcliffe and Johns Hopkins Medical School, knew she had the authority to maintain that everything in her manuscript was "written with the intention of its being so written." Stein's indignation and the embarrassment she elicited from the "young man" suggest that in the early 1900s, ethnic and educational backgrounds were two common denominators for determining whether style represented self-conscious and innovative experimentation or blundering "errors."

The second story took place a few years prior to the Stein event, when the style of another writer, Theodore Dreiser, was also questioned by a publisher to whom he had submitted his first novel, *Sister Carrie*. The rejection letter from Harper faults Dreiser for his "uneven" style which, according to the editors, was "disfigured by . . . colloquialisms" (*Sister Carrie* 519). Existing manuscripts of the book's revision indicate that Dreiser did not defend his style with the kind of authority Stein exhibited. Instead he sought editorial help from his wife Jug and friend Henry because he deemed both to have been better educated than himself. There is evidence in the revised manuscript that Dreiser adopted nearly all of Jug's corrections of grammar and Henry's rewording of his Germanic rhythms and cumulative sentence structures (*Sister Carrie* 580–81). Read in the context of Stein's story, Dreiser's willingness to have all aspects of his style "corrected" might be attributed in part to his acute awareness of the criteria used by "educated america" when dealing with the writing of the son of an impoverished German immigrant with extremely sporadic formal education. The early reception of *Sister Carrie* proves the validity of Dreiser's concern, as even its defenders attributed its "crude" style to his ethnic background and lack of formal education.[1]

Almost a century after these events, more and more English courses are now informed by a view of language as a site of struggle among conflicting discourses with unequal socio-political power. Students in these courses are beginning to approach the style of what they call "real" writers like Stein and Dreiser very differently. Interest in multiculturalism has also shifted the attention of some teachers to writers' success at what Bakhtin calls "dialogically coordinating" a varied and profound "heteroglossia" (295–96). Analysis of style in these classrooms often centers on the politics of the writer's stylistic decisions: (a) mapping the "heteroglossia" on the internal and external scenes of writing, (b) attending to the writer's effort to look at one discourse through the eyes of another, and (c) considering the writer's willingness to resist the centripetal forces of "official" discourses. Viewed from this multicultural perspective on style, the writings of both Dreiser and Stein could be considered in terms of the efforts of each to dialogically coordinate the profound heteroglossia within and outside official "educated" discourses. For readers adopting this perspective, neither Dreiser's ethnic background nor his "imperfect" educational background would be used to dismiss his "uneven" style solely as evidence of "error"—that is, to conclude that his style merely reflects his lack of knowledge or experience in writing. In fact, given the frequency with which writings from what Gloria Anzaldúa has called the "borderlands" are being currently assigned in some English courses and the praise this type of writing receives for its hybridization of "official" discourses, Dreiser's readiness to yield to the authority of the "better educated" now appears conservative—indicating a passive stance towards the hegemony of ethnocentrism and linguistic imperialism. In fact, the publication of the Pennsylvania edition of *Sister Carrie* in 1987 indicates that such a critical view privileging resistance was in operation when the editors decided to delete many of the changes made by the "better educated" Jug and Henry in the hope of preserving the "power and forcefulness" of Dreiser's original prose (*Sister Carrie* 581).

However, Dreiser's reaction still haunts me, especially when I move from teaching students to analyze the idiosyncratic style of "real" writers to helping them to work on their own styles. In my "literature" courses for junior- or senior-level college students or "writing" courses for first-year students, students learn to talk with considerable eloquence about the politics of stylistic decisions made by "real" writers, especially those writing from the borderlands by choice or necessity. Most of the readings I assign for these classes call attention to writers' need and right to contest the unifying force of hegemonic discourses, and thus make Dreiser's submission to the authority of the "better educated" appear dated and passive. Yet the meaning of Dreiser's submissiveness changes for me and most of my students as soon as we move to work on the style of a student writer, especially when we tinker with what we call the writer's "discursive voice"—that is, when dealing with deviations in diction, tone, voice, structure, and so on (which we loosely call the "rhetorical register"), or with punctuation, syntax, sentence structure, and so on (which we refer to as the "grammatical register"). On those occasions, how to sound "right" suddenly becomes a "real" concern for my students: pervasive, immediate, and difficult for me to dismiss. My students' apparent anxiety to reproduce the conventions of "educated" English poses a challenge for my teaching and research. Why is it that in spite of our developing ability to acknowledge the political need and right of "real" writers to experiment with "style," we continue to cling to the belief that such a need and right does not belong to "student writers"? Another way of putting the question would be, why do we assume—as Dreiser did—that until one can prove one's ability to produce "error-free" prose, one has not earned the right to innovative "style"?

Again, I believe Dreiser's account of his own educational experience might shed some light on the question. In *Dawn*, Dreiser writes about his opportunity to attend the University of Indiana, Bloomington for two short terms. A former teacher made arrangements to exempt Dreiser from the preliminary examinations because, Dreiser points out, these exams would have quickly "debarred" him (342). Life as what we might today call an open admissions student at Indiana made Dreiser feel "reduced." He "grieved" at his "inability to grasp . . . such a commonplace as grammar" (378). Even though he knew he was able to apprehend many things and to demonstrate his apprehensions "quite satisfactorily" to himself, he found the curriculum "oppressive," leaving him "mute" with "a feeling of inadequacy" (425). The events surrounding the efforts of Dreiser and Stein to publish their first books indicate that the common approach of the editors, publishers, and critics to their idiosyncratic styles was not coincidental. Dreiser's experience at Indiana, his willingness to have his "uneven" style "corrected," and Stein's quick rebuttal to the "young man" all point to the institutional source of this approach. A common view of "style" as belonging only to those who are beyond "error," and a certain type of college curriculum treating matters of grammar or usage as the prerequisites to higher education, seem mutually reinforcing. It is this belief that pushes students identified as having "problems" to meet such "prerequisites" and assigns teachers trained to deal with such "problems" to the periphery or borderlands of higher education.

Dreiser's memories of Indiana seem symptomatic of the feelings of a significant number of college students I encounter. I have in mind particularly students who seem quick to admit that they are "not good" at writing because they have been identified at some point in their education as needing special—remedial, laboratory, or intensive—instruction in the "basics." Like Dreiser, they are frustrated at their inability to grasp "grammar" because they have been encouraged to view it as "such a commonplace"—something everyone who aspires to become anyone ought to be able to master. And they feel muted and reduced by the curriculum because it does not seem to recognize that they are quite able to grasp subjects other than "grammar" and demonstrate their understanding of such subjects satisfactorily to themselves, if perhaps not in writing to others. It seems to me that one way of helping students to deal with this frustration would be to connect their "difficulties" with the refusal of "real" writers to reproduce the hegemonic conventions of written English. And it seems to me that this will not take place until teachers like myself contest the distinction between "real" and "student" writers and stop treating the idiosyncratic style of the not yet "perfectly educated" solely in terms of "error." One form of contestation could be to apply to student writing the same multicultural approach we have been promoting when analyzing the work of "real" writers. Susan Miller has argued in *Textual Carnivals* that the tendency to treat student writers as "emerging, or as failed, but never as actually responsible 'authors'" has served to maintain the low status of composition studies in its relations to those "outside it, and its self-images and ways of working out its new professionalization" (195–96). An approach to student writing that treats students as real writers would undo such binaries and thus assert the right and ability of writing teachers and students to fully participate in a truly multicultural curriculum.

My aim here is to discuss a teaching method formulated out of my attempt to apply a multicultural approach to student writing: an approach which views the classroom as a potential "contact zone"—which Pratt describes as a space where various cultures "clash, and grapple with each other, often in contexts of highly asymmetrical relations of power" (34). In arguing for a multicultural approach to styles traditionally displaced to the realm of "error," I align my teaching with a tradition in "error" analysis which views even "error-ridden" student writings as texts relevant to critical approaches available to English Studies. I am particularly interested in explicitly foregrounding the category of "resistance" and "change" when helping students to conceptualize the processes of producing and interpreting an idiosyncratic style in students' own writings. In the classroom I envision, the notion of "intention" is presented as the decision of a writer who understands not only the "central role of human agency" but also that such agency is often "enacted under circumstances not of one's choosing" (West 31). I define the writer's attempt to "reproduce" the norms of academic discourses as necessarily involving the re-production—approximating, negotiating, and revising—of these norms. And I do so by asking students to explore the full range of choices and options, including those excluded by the conventions of academic discourses.

These aspects in the classroom I envision inevitably distance it from classrooms influenced by one belief prevalent in ESL courses or courses in "Basic Writing": namely, that a monolingual environment is the most conducive to the learning of "beginners" or "outsiders." This belief overlooks the dialogical nature of students' "inner voices" as well as the multicultural context of students' lives. The classroom I envision also differs from approaches to students' ambivalence towards the effects of education exemplified by Mina Shaughnessy's *Errors and Expectations*. Shaughnessy convincingly shows the relevance to error analysis of a range of feelings common to students likely to be identified as basic writers: their anxiety to "sound academic" and to self-consciously emulate the formal style (194), their low self-esteem as learners and writers, and their sense of ambivalence towards academic discourse. But as I have argued in "Conflict and Struggle," Shaughnessy's goal in acknowledging students' ambivalence is only to help them dissolve it (904–06). Because this ambivalence arises from sources well beyond the classroom—coming from the unequal power relationships pervading the history, culture, and society my students live in—not all students can or even want to get rid of all types of ambivalence. On the contrary, the experiences of writers like Gloria Anzaldúa, bell hooks, and Mike Rose suggest that, appropriately mobilized, a sense of ambivalence might be put to constructive uses in writing.

To foreground the concepts of "resistance" and "change" when analyzing the styles of a student or "real" writer, I ask students to read deviations from the official codes of academic discourses not only in relation to the writer's knowledge of these codes but also in terms of her efforts to negotiate and modify them. Aside from increasing the student's knowledge of and experience in reproducing these official forms, I am most interested in doing three things: (1) enabling students to hear discursive voices which conflict with and struggle against the voices of academic authority; (2) urging them to negotiate a position in response to these colliding voices; and (3) asking them to consider their choice of position in the context of the socio-political power relationships within and among diverse discourses and in the context of their personal life, history, culture, and society.

Because of the tendency in English Studies to ghettoize the culture of composition, I will use some student writing produced in writing courses for first-year students to illustrate how I would actually go about teaching a multicultural approach to style. And I am going to focus on features of writing styles which are commonly displaced to the realm of "error" and thus viewed as peripheral to college English teaching. In using these rather than other types of examples, I hope to illustrate as well the need to view composition as a site which might inform as well as be informed by our effort to profess multiculturalism in other, supposedly more "advanced" and "central" areas of English Studies. David Bartholomae has recently reminded us that there is no need "to import 'multiple cultures' [into the classroom, via anthologies].

They are there, in the classroom, once the institution becomes willing to pay that kind of attention to student writing" (14–15). Such attention, he explains, could produce composition courses in multiculturalism "that worked with the various cultures represented in the practice of its students" (14). My second reason for using these examples is related to the ways in which conflict and struggle have been perceived by teachers specializing in error analysis. These teachers tend to hear arguments foregrounding conflict and struggle in the classroom as sloganeering "the students' right to their own language" in order to eliminate attention to error, or as evidence of a "PC" attack on the "back to basics" movement (see, for example, Traub). The examples I use here, I hope, will demonstrate a way of teaching which neither overlooks the students' potential lack of knowledge and experience in reproducing the dominant codes of academic discourses *nor* dismisses the writer's potential social, political, and linguistic interest in modifying these codes, with emphasis on the word "potential."

When teaching first-year writing classes, I usually introduce the multicultural approach to student writing style around the mid-point of the term, when I feel that students are beginning to apply to their actual practices a view of writing as a process of re-seeing. To present the writer's experimentation with style (including what is generally called "copyediting" or the "correction of error") as an integral part of the revision process, I look for sample student writings with two characteristics. First, I am interested in writings with the kinds of "error" a majority of the class would feel they can easily "spot" and "fix." This type of writing allows me to acknowledge some potential causes of non-conventional styles and effective methods of revising them which are more widely disseminated in traditional writing classrooms and familiar to most students. Second, I look for styles which are also more conducive to my attempt to help the writer to negotiate a new position in relation to the colliding voices active in the scenes of writing.[2]

Following is a handout I have used when teaching first-year composition classes. The two segments on the handout are from the papers one student wrote in response to two assignments, one asking her to discuss an essay, "From a Native Daughter," by Haunani-Kay Trask, and another asking her to comment on the kind of "critical thinking" defined in the "Introduction" to an anthology called *Rereading America*. For the convenience of discussion in this essay, I have added emphasis to the handout:

Segment One:

As a Hawaiian native historian, Trask *can able to* argue for her people. As a Hawaiian native, she was exposed to two totally different viewpoints about her people. She was brought up in Hawaii. During this time, she heard the stories about her people from her parents. Later on she was send to America mainland to pursue higher education, in which she learnt a different stories about her people. Therefore, she understood that the interpretation of land was different between the "haole" and the native. To prove that the "haole" were wrong, she went back to Hawaii and work on the land with other native, so she *can* feel the strong bond with land her people have which the "haole" *could* not feel. The "haole" historians never bother to do so as they were more interested in looking for written evidence. That was why Trask, as a native Hawaiian historian, argued that these "haole" historians were being ignorant and ethnocentric. That is also why Trask suggested the "haole" historians learn the native tongue.

––––––––

Segment Two:

Elements like perceiving things from different perspective, finding and validating each alternative solutions, questioning the unknown and breaking the nutshell of cultural norms are important for developing the ability of "critical thinking." . . . Most of the new universities' students are facing new challenges like staying away from family, peer pressure, culture shock, heavy college work etc. I *can* say that these are the "obstacles" to success. If a student *can able to* approach each situation with different perspectives than the one he brought from high school, I *may* conclude that this particular student has climbed his first step to become a "critical thinker." . . . However, there is one particular obstacle that is really difficult for almost everyone to overcome, that is the cultural rules. From the textbook, I found that cultural rules are deep rooted in our mind and cause us to view things from our respective cultural viewpoint. Even though cultural values lead the way of life of a particular group of people, they blind us as well. I relate to this because I truly believe that the cultural rules of my country, Malaysia, make my life here difficult. In order to achieve a "critical mind," one should try to break from his own cultural rules.

––––––––

"can," verb:

1. to be able to; have the ability, power, or skill to. 2. to know how to. 3. to have the power or means to. 4. to have the right or qualifications to. 5. *may; have permission to. (The Random House Dictionary)*

"able," adjective:

1. having necessary power, skill, resources, or qualifications; qualified; able to lift a trunk; . . . able to vote. *(The Random House Dictionary)*

367

When using this handout, I usually begin by asking students what particularly about the two segments might be said to make the voice of the writer idiosyncratic. My students in both writing and literature classes have been fairly quick in tracing it to the "can able to" structure in the two segments. Then I ask the class to speculate on potential causes of that idiosyncrasy. Students' responses to this question usually go something like this: Here is a "foreign" speaker, a student from Malaysia, trying to use the English idiom "to be able to" and ending up with an "error." So we usually talk a little bit about the difference in grammatical function between the verb "can" and the verb "to be" in relation to the adjective "able." And I describe the writer's own initial interpretation of the cause of this "error": her native language is Chinese. With the help of a tutor, she had realized that the Chinese translation for both "can" and "be able to" is the same. When using the expression "be able to," she would be thinking in Chinese. As a result, she often ended up writing "can able to." I would refer to her own initial reading because I am interested in complicating but not denying the relationship between style and the writer's knowledge of and experience with the conventions of written English. So I try to acknowledge first that exposure to and practice in reproducing the "be able to" structure could be one of the ways to revise these segments.

I then go on to complicate this approach by also calling attention to the relationship between form and meaning. What might be the difference in meaning between "can," "be able to," and "can able to"? Most of the students I have encountered tend to see "can" as interchangeable with "be able to." To them, "can able to" appears redundant, like a double negative. To problematize this reading, I usually call attention to the two dictionary entries included in the handout, especially to definition 5 under "can." Definition 5 opens up a new reading by presenting the word "can" as having one more meaning than "to be able to." Rather than approaching the issue of ability from the perspective of what an individual possesses, definition 5 approaches it from the perspective of the external forces *permitting* something, as in the verb "may."

Most native English speakers among my students tend to argue that in actual usage, only grandmas and schoolteachers make the distinction between "can" and "may." *Everyone* uses "can" and "be able to" interchangeably nowadays. In response, I tell them the writer's position on the issue. She was aware of the distinction—she was the one who first called my attention to definition 5. At this point, a "contact zone" would begin to take shape with three conflicting positions on the meanings of "can" and "able to": the position of a speaker of idiomatic English, the position of the dictionary, and the position of a "foreign" student writer. Since the "foreign" student writer position is here being cast as that of someone lacking knowledge and expertise in formal and idiomatic English and thus the least powerful of the three, I am most interested in furthering the students' existing construction of that position so it is not so easily silenced.

To that end, I pose the question of whether, read in the context of the two segments in the handout, one might argue that the "can" in the two "can able to" structures does not take on the same meaning as the other uses of "can" in the rest of the segments. This line of inquiry usually leads us to compare the meaning of the "can" in the first sentence in Segment One to the two "can's" in the seventh sentence and to the meaning of the "can" in the "can able to" in Segment Two as well as the "can" in the previous sentence or the "may" in the second half of the same sentence. My aim here is to get students to re-construct the voice of the writer by focusing on the various uses of the word "can" in the two segments. When exploring the question, I also try to direct attention to the passive voice (Trask was "brought up in Hawaii" and "send to America mainland to pursue higher education") in the sentences following the statement "Trask can able to argue for her people." I explore with the class how and why this passive voice might be read as indicating that the student writer is approaching Trask's ability from the perspective of the external circumstances of Trask's life—using "can" in the sense of her having the "permission to" become a native Hawaiian historian—as well as from the perspective of her having the qualifications to argue as a historian. The two uses of "can" in sentence seven, however, present Trask's and the "haole" historians' (in)ability to "feel" the Hawaiian's bond with the land as more related to a person's will and attitude rather than to whether each "may"—has the permission to—learn the Hawaiian language or work with the people. ("The 'haole' historians never bother to do so.") Similarly, in the second segment, the "can" in "a student can able to adopt different perspectives," when read in the context of the writer's discussion of the difficulties for "everyone to overcome" the "obstacle" of cultural rules and of her own experience of that difficulty, again foregrounds the role of external conditions and their effect on one's ability to do something. In that sense, this "can" is closer in meaning to the "may" in "I may conclude," a conclusion presented as depending more on the action of someone else than on the ability of the "I" drawing the conclusion. At the same time, this "can" is different from the "can" in the "I can say . . ." since the latter seems to depend on the ability of the speaker to name the situations as "obstacles" rather than on whether or not the speaker has permission to so name them.

In getting the class to enact a "close reading" of the two segments, I aim to shift attention to the relationship between a discursive form, "can able to," and the particular meanings it might be said to create in particular contexts.

As a result, a new question often surfaces: What kind of approach to "ability" is enacted by a speaker of idiomatic English who sees "can" and "be able to" as completely interchangeable in meaning? In exploring this question, students have mentioned popular sayings such as "if there is a will, there is a way"; TV shows such as *Mr. Rogers' Neighborhood* which teach viewers to believe "everyone is special," possessing unique qualities; and various discourses promoting the power of positive thinking. Students begin to perceive the way in which a common treatment of "can" and "to be able to" as interchangeable in meaning might be seen as contributing to a popular American attitude towards the transcendental power of the individual. Once we locate these conflicting approaches to the notion of ability, it becomes clear that the revision or "correction" of the "can able to" in these two segments can no longer take place simply at the level of linguistic form. It must also involve a writer's negotiating a position in relation to value systems with unequal social power in the U.S.: one "popular" and the others "alien," "dated," or "formal" but critical. Once this structural "error" is contextualized in conflicting attitudes towards a belief in the transcendental power of the individual, the issue can no longer be merely one's knowledge of or respect for the authorities of a dictionary English versus colloquial English, or one's competency in a particular language, but also one's alignment with competing discursive positions.

At this point, we will have mapped a contact zone with a range of choices and options both among linguistic forms and among discursive alignments. As we move on to the question of how each of us might revise these two segments, I would make sure that each student further enlarges this contact zone by taking into consideration the specific conditions of her or his life. I would have already introduced my definition of the "conditions of life" in previous assignments and class discussions, a definition that includes a whole range of discursive sites, including those of race, ethnicity, gender, sex, economic class, education, religion, region, recreation, and work. I also encourage each student to think about "life" in terms of the life she has lived in the past, is living in the present, and envisions for the future. Furthermore, I stress that decisions on how to revise should also be related to each student's interpretation(s) of the two texts discussed in the segments. To summarize, the contact zone in which the revision takes place would encompass the collision of at least the following voices: the voice of a "foreign" student writer (as constructed by the class at the beginning of the discussion), the voice(s) of the writer of the two segments (as constructed by the class discussion resulting from a "close reading" of the various uses of "can"), the voice of a dictionary, the voice of a speaker of idiomatic English, the voices important to the specific conditions of each student's life, the voice of a teacher, and the voice emerging from each student's interpretation of the two texts discussed in the two segments.

Since decisions on how to revise the "can able to" structure depend on who is present, the particular ways in which the discussion unfolds, and who is doing the revision, such decisions vary from class to class and student to student. To illustrate the unpredictability of the outcome, let me use two decisions made in two different courses, one by the original writer of the two segments and one by another student whose native language is also Chinese. Like all other students in my class, during the process of a "close reading" of the uses of "can" in these two segments, the original writer encountered a construction of her "voices" which she may not have fully considered before the discussion. Therefore, when revising the two segments, she too had to negotiate with these forms of reading and constructions of voices. Upon reflecting on the conditions of her life, she reviewed the attitude towards "ability" promoted in the particular neighborhood in Malaysia where she grew up. In view of that as well as of her own experience as a daughter (especially her difficulties persuading her parents to let her rather than only their sons go abroad for college), her current difficulty in adjusting to the kind of "critical thinking" promoted in my classroom (which she felt was the direct opposite of what she was told to do in her schooling back home), and her admiration of Trask's courage to "argue for her people," the writer decided to foreground the relationship between individual ability and the conditions in which that ability "may" be realized. With the help of her classmates, she came up with several options. One was to add an "if" clause to a sentence using "be able to." Another was to change "can able to" to "may be able to." One student suggested that she use "can able to" and then tag a sentence to explain her reasoning—her view of "ability." Among the suggestions, the writer picked "may be able to" because, as she put it, it was clearly "grammatically correct" and "says what I want to say." As the term progressed, one of the students in the class used "can able to" playfully in a class discussion, and others caught on. It became a newly coined phrase we shared throughout the term.

However, a Vietnamese American student whose home language is also Chinese took a very different stance towards the hegemonic attitude toward "ability" and for a quite different reason from what led some of my American-born students to identify with the voice of an idiomatic speaker. Using examples from his immigrant community, he argued for the importance of believing in the capacity of the individual. He pointed out that the emphasis on external conditions had made some people in his community fatalistic and afraid to take up the responsibility to make changes. According to him, there is a saying in classic Chinese similar to "if there is a will, there is a way." His parents used it repeatedly when lecturing him. So he was all for using "can" and "be able to" interchangeably to foreground the power of the individual. He hoped more people in his community would adopt this outlook. Accordingly, his revision changed "can able to" to "be able to." At the same time, he also changed the passive voice in the sentences referring to Trask's childhood and education in the first segment to the active voice, arguing that there is enough basis in the essays to sustain that reading.

Given the frequency with which students opt for the voices of academic authority, I used to wonder if this kind of teaching is driven more by my view of language as a site of struggle than by the needs of students eager to internalize and reproduce the conventions of academic discourse. My conclusion is: No, this process of negotiation is particularly meaningful for students anxious to master the codes of academic discourse, especially because their discursive practices are most likely to have to take place in the kind of postmodern capitalist world critics such as Fredric Jameson have characterized. Although the product, their decision to reproduce the code, might remain the same whether it is made with or without a process of negotiation, the activities leading to that decision, and thus its significance, are completely different. Without the negotiation, their choice would be resulting from an attempt to passively absorb and automatically reproduce a predetermined form. In such cases, the student would perceive different discourses, to borrow from Bakhtin, as belonging to different, fixed, and indisputable "chambers" in her consciousness and in society. And she would evaluate her progress by the automatism with which she was able to move in and out of these "chambers." If and when this student experienced some difficulty mastering a particular code, she would view it as a sign of her failure as a learner and writer.

On the other hand, if the student's decision to reproduce a code results from a process of negotiation, then she would have examined the conflict between the codes of Standard English and other discourses. And she would have deliberated not only on the social power of these colliding discourses but also on who she was, is, and aspires to be when making this decision. If the occasion arises in the future when she experiences difficulty in reproducing a particular code, as it very likely will, her reaction may be much more positive and constructive. Learning to work on style in the contact zone is also useful for those students interested in exploring ways of resisting the unifying force of "official" discourse. First, it can help students hear a range of choices and options beyond the confines of their immediate life. Second, negotiating as a group gives them the distance they need but might not have when dealing with their own writing in isolation. Therefore, devoting a few class periods to familiarizing students with this approach to style can be fruitful, especially if students are asked to theorize their action afterwards by reflecting on its strengths and limitations.

Obviously, one of the challenges for such a teaching method is that one can only project but not predict a class discussion on the basis of the chosen sample. In fact, life in the contact zone is by definition dynamic, heterogeneous, and volatile. Bewilderment and suffering as well as revelation and exhilaration are experienced by everyone, teacher and students, at different moments. No one is excluded, no one is safe (Pratt 39). Therefore, learning to become comfortable in making blunders is central to this type of teaching. In fact, there is no better way to teach students the importance of negotiation than by allowing them the opportunity to watch a teacher work her way through a chancy and volatile dialogue. Seemingly simple markers such as skin color, native tongue, ethnic heritage or nationality can neither prescribe nor pre-script the range of voices likely to surface. How to voice and talk to rather than speaking for or about the voices of the "other" within and among cultures is thus not a question which can be resolved prior to or outside of the process of negotiation. Rather, it must remain a concern guiding our action as we take part in it.

Needless to say, this type of teaching would work better when students are also asked to try the same method when analyzing the style of "real" writers so they understand that the "problems" they have with style are shared by all writers. For example, when students in a first-year writing course were reading Trask's essay "From a Native Daughter," I asked them to discuss or write about aspects of her style which seemed to deviate from the style of other historians they had encountered. Several students observed that the paragraphs in Trask's essay are shorter, including a series of one-sentence paragraphs with parallel structures of "And when they wrote . . . they meant . . ." (123–24). Others were struck by the opening of Trask's essay, where she addresses her audience directly and asks that they "greet each other in friendship and love." She tells many more personal stories and uses fewer references for support, and she uses the imagery of a lover to depict the role of language. I urged them to examine these stylistic features in relation to the particular stance Trask seems to have taken towards the conflict between "haole" (white) culture and the native Hawaiian culture. Having approached the writing of a "real" writer from the perspective of the relationship between meaning, form, and social identifications, students are likely to be more motivated in applying this perspective to their own style and its revision.

At the same time, using a student paper to enact a negotiation in the contact zone can create a sense of immediacy and a new level of meaningfulness about abstract concepts discussed or enacted in the assigned readings for students in "literature" and "critical theory" classes. For example, I have used the handout with the "can able to" construction in senior-level critical theory courses when discussing Bakhtin's notion of "internal dialogism," Raymond Williams's concept of "structures of feeling," Cornel West's "prophetic critics and artists of color," and "dense" critiques of colonial discourse by such writers as Edward Said or Homi K. Bhabha. In the process of revising the "can able to" structure in the handout, in actively negotiating conflict in a contact zone, students in literature and cultural critical theory courses can gain a concrete opportunity to test the theories of various critics against their own practice. This type of activity reduces the "alienation" students often experience when asked to "do" theory. Testing theories against their own writing practices can also enable students to become more aware of the specific challenges such theories pose as well as the possibilities they open up for the individual writers committed to practicing these viewpoints. And I have used this method in upper-level literature courses when teaching such "borderland" literature as Sandra Cisneros's short story "Little Miracle, Kept Promises" or *Breaking Bread* by Cornel West and bell hooks. Reading and revising a student text, students can become more sensitive to the ways in which a "real" writer negotiates her way through contending discourses. At the same time, such reading and revision of their own writing allows students to enter into dialogue with "real" writers as "fellow travelers," active learners eager to compare and contrast one another's trials and triumphs.

One reaction to teaching style in the contact zone is fear that it will keep students from wanting to learn the conventions of academic discourse. My experience so far suggests that the unequal sociopolitical power of diverse discourses exerts real pressures on students' stylistic choices. After all, students choose to come to college, the choice of which speaks volumes on that power. The need to write for professors who grade with red pens circling all "errors" is also real for a majority of our students in most classrooms outside English departments. Therefore, although the process of negotiation encourages students to struggle with such unifying forces, it does not and cannot lead them to ignore and forget them. It acknowledges the writer's right and ability to experiment with innovative ways of deploying the codes taught in the classroom. It broadens students' sense of the range of options and choices facing a writer. But it does not choose for the students. Rather, it leaves them to choose in the context of the history, culture, and society in which they live.

NOTES

1. See Anderson, "An Apology for Crudity"; Kazin, *On Native Grounds*; and Mencken, "The Dreiser Bugaboo."

2. For an extended discussion of teaching editing that informs my own, see Horner, "Rethinking," especially pages 188–96.

WORKS CITED

Anderson, Sherwood. "An Apology for Crudity." *The Stature of Theodore Dreiser: A Critical Survey of the Man and His Work.* Ed. Alfred Kazin and Charles Shapiro. Bloomington: Indiana UP, 1965. 81–84.

Anzaldúa, Gloria. *Borderlands/La Frontera: The New Mestiza.* San Francisco: aunt lute, 1987.

Bakhtin, Mikhail. *The Dialogic Imagination.* Ed. Michael Holquist. Trans. Caryl Emerson and Michael Holquist. Austin: U of Texas P, 1981.

Bartholomae, David. "The Tidy House: Basic Writing in the American Curriculum." *Journal of Basic Writing* 12 (1993): 4–21.

Dreiser, Theodore. *Dawn.* New York: Fawcett, 1931.

_____. *Sister Carrie: The Pennsylvania Edition.* Philadelphia: U of Pennsylvania P. 1981.

Horner, Bruce. "Mapping Errors and Expectations for Basic Writing: From the 'Frontier Field' to 'Border Country.'" *English Education* 26 (1994): 29–51.

_____. "Rethinking the 'Sociality' of Error: Teaching Editing as Negotiation." *Rhetoric Review* 11 (1992): 172–99.

Kazin, Alfred. *On Native Grounds: An Interpretation of Modern American Prose Literature.* New York: Harcourt, 1942.

Lu, Min-Zhan. "Conflict and Struggle: The Enemies or Preconditions of Basic Writing?" *College English* 54 (1992): 887–913.

Mencken, H. L. "The Dreiser Bugaboo." *Seven Arts* 2 (1917): 507–17.

Miller, Susan. *Textual Carnivals: The Politics of Composition.* Carbondale: Southern Illinois UP, 1991.

Pratt, Mary Louise. "Arts of the Contact Zone." *Profession* 91 (1991): 33–40.

Shaughnessy, Mina. *Errors and Expectations: A Guide for the Teacher of Basic Writing.* New York: Oxford UP, 1977.

Stein, Gertrude. *The Autobiography of Alice B. Toklas.* New York: Vintage, 1933.

Trask, Haunani-Kay. "From a Native Daughter." *Rereading America: Cultural Contexts for Critical Thinking and Writing.* 2nd ed. Ed. Gary Colombo, Robert Cullen, and Bonnie Lisle. Boston: Bedford, 1989. 118–27.

Traub, James. "P.C. vs. English: Back to Basic." *The New Republic* 8 Feb. 1993: 18–19.

West, Cornel. "The New Cultural Politics of Difference." *Out There: Marginalization and Contemporary Cultures.* Ed. Russel Ferguson, Martha Gever, Trinh T. Minh-Ha, and Cornel West. Cambridge, MA: MIT P, 1990. 19–36.

Acknowledgments: Earlier versions of this paper were delivered at the 1993 CCCC and at the University of Washington. My thanks go to the respondents in the audiences at both occasions. I am also grateful for comments on drafts of this piece from Elizabeth Robertson, Ira Shor, Anne Herrington, and James Seitz. Work on this essay was supported by a grant from the Drake University Center for the Humanities. And I offer special thanks to Bruce Horner for his contributions to the conception and revisions of this essay.

Beyond the Personal

Theorizing a Politics of Location in Composition Research

GESA E. KIRSCH AND JOY S. RITCHIE

In recent years, feminist scholarship has begun to inform much research in composition studies. One particular emphasis has been on admitting the "personal" into our public discourse, on locating ourselves and research participants in our research studies. In what Adrienne Rich calls "a politics of location," theorizing begins with the material, not transcending the personal, but claiming it. The goal is, Rich says in an echo of Hélène Cixous, "to reconnect our thinking and speaking with the body of this particular living human individual, a woman" (213).[1] This new emphasis on the personal, on validating experience as a source of knowledge, raises a number of recurring questions: How does a politics of location inform—and change—research practices? How do we both affirm the importance of "location," and yet understand the limitations of our ability to locate ourselves and others? How do issues of power, gender, race, and class shape a politics of location? What ethical principles are consistent with feminist scholarship and can guide researchers? Although these questions are clearly important in feminist scholarship, they are not merely feminist issues. They mark an important point where feminist theories can inform composition studies. And although we believe women's experiences are an important starting point for research because they have been ignored and omitted in studies of many kinds, we also believe that what can be learned from women's experiences and from

Reprinted from *College Composition and Communication* 46.1 (February 1995): 7–29. Used with permission.

feminist theory has wider implications for composition research; it can become a location for reconsidering what counts as knowledge and for revitalizing research in composition.

In this article, we begin by examining what it means to bring a politics of location to composition research and by foregrounding some of the difficulties of assuming that perspective. We argue that it is not enough to claim the personal and locate ourselves in our scholarship and research. In doing so, we risk creating another set of "master narratives," risk speaking for and essentializing others, and risk being blinded by our own culturally determined world views. Instead, we propose that composition researchers theorize their locations by examining their experiences as reflections of ideology and culture, by reinterpreting their own experiences through the eyes of others, and by recognizing their own split selves, their multiple and often unknowable identities. Further, we propose changes in research practices, such as collaborating with participants in the development of research questions, the interpretation of data at both the descriptive and interpretive levels, and the writing of research reports. Finally, we raise ethical questions that arise from these new research practices. We illustrate our argument with examples drawn from composition, including our own research, but also from scholarship in anthropology, oral history, and sociology. Scholars in those fields have a long history of using ethnomethodological research, have reflected on the role of the personal in research, and have encountered a range of ethical dilemmas.

A POLITICS OF LOCATION
IN FEMINIST RESEARCH

We begin this essay by locating ourselves in this writing, although we recognize that any location is fluid, multiple, and illusive. The impulse to write this article came from a day-long conversation among several women during a workshop on feminism and composition at the 1992 CCCC.[2] These women, though mostly tenured and tenure-tracked and with successful teaching and publication records, were nevertheless frustrated because of the conflicts they experience as feminists in composition living in English departments. The issues we talked about that day suggested that we have been taught to devalue our own experiences as researchers and writers, our relationships with students and other teachers, and our own histories as sources for research and scholarship. As a result, we have often stripped the personal from our writing and research.

As we continued to think about the conflicts women expressed in that group, we began to realize that in part, these conflicts arise from our varied and shifting locations in our discipline, particularly from attempts to hold feminist values and to focus on issues of gender in research, while we still accept the existing epistemologies and methodologies in the field—methodologies that often presuppose objectivity and gender-neutrality. We recognize this tension in our own research. Instead of working to question, resist, and transform traditional research practices, we often find ourselves attempting to live within the contradictions between our feminist beliefs and those traditionally valued in our discipline, even as we write this essay. As we explored these contradictions, we found that many feminists in other disciplines have already begun this work.

We believe researchers in composition must engage in the same kinds of discussions that feminist researchers are having in other disciplines concerning the "politics of location" in research. We hope to advance that discussion by presenting some of the feminist critiques of philosophical, methodological, and ethical assumptions underlying traditional research. In doing so we assert the importance of interrogating the motives for our research and the unspoken power relationships with the "subjects" of our research, considerations we hope will assist us in developing a more ethical approach to research.[3]

If we are to move beyond what Sandra Harding calls an "add women and stir" approach to research (*Feminism* 3), we need to examine just what a politics of location means for research, what are its implications and its limitations. How might we achieve a more problematized politics of location? Rich says that we can no longer utter phrases like "women always. . . ." Instead, she argues: "If we have learned anything in these years of late twentieth-century feminism, it's that that 'always' blots out what we really need to know: When, where, and under what conditions has the statement been true" (214)? But Rich does not suggest that research simply needs to provide the ethnographer's "thick descriptions" of context or to engage in superficial reflexivity. It is not enough to make the facile statements that often occur at the beginning of research articles, to say, "I am a white, middle-class woman from a Midwestern university doing research." She urges women to investigate what has shaped their own perspectives and acknowledge what is contradictory, and perhaps unknowable, in that experience.

In addition to acknowledging our multiple positions, a politics of location must engage us in a rigorous ongoing exploration of *how* we do our research: What assumptions underlie our approaches to research and methodologies? And a politics of location must challenge our conception of *who* we are in our work: How are our conflicting positions, histories, and desires for power implicated in our research questions, methodologies, and conclusions? A politics of location allows us to claim the legitimacy of our experience, but it must be accompanied by a rigorously reflexive examination of ourselves as researchers that is as careful as our observation of the object of our inquiry (Harding, *Whose Science?* 149–50, 161–63). Thus, for example, researchers need to acknowledge the way race (and for most composition scholars this means examining their whiteness), social class, and other circumstances have structured their own thinking and how that, in turn, has shaped their own questions and interpretations. Rich observes: "Marginalized though we have been as women, as white and Western makers of theory, we also marginalize others because our lived experience is thoughtlessly white, because even our 'women's cultures' are rooted in some Western tradition" (219).

Finally, a postmodern feminist perspective leads us to continually question our ability to locate ourselves as researchers and to locate the participants in our research. We need to take into account what psychoanalytic, hermeneutic, and postmodern critics have already shown us about the limitations of our ability to fully understand our own motivations and perspectives. These scholars remind us that we can never fully step outside our culture in order to examine our assumptions, values, and goals. Pretending to do so amounts to what Stanley Fish calls the "theory hope of antifoundationalism" (qtd. in Bizzell 40), the belief that although we reject foundational truth as the basis of knowledge, we can nevertheless use critical analysis to interrogate the historical, political, and social contexts of our knowledge. But, as Fish reminds us, no attempt at analyzing our assumptions is neutral or value-free; it is always a culturally and politically charged activity.

This problematized "politics of location" may seem to make our task impossible; it may make us wonder if we can claim anything for our research. But instead of falling into inaction and despair, we move forward with the awareness that we can only approximate an understanding, noticing the multiple and contradictory positions researchers and participants occupy, complicating and politicizing our investigation, valuing the individual and the local, although we can never hope to understand them fully. We move forward with a willingness to pursue the difficulties inherent in a politics of location accompanied by an equal willingness to be unrelentingly self-reflective.

THE RISK OF ESSENTIALISM

While locating research questions in ourselves and our own experience is vital, it also creates unsettling problems and possibilities for the way we think about knowledge, authority, and power. Feminists have rightly challenged the claims to objectivity in traditional research, arguing that inattention to the researcher's location and subjectivity has led to what Donna Haraway calls the "god trick," researchers' false claims to an ahistorical and universal perspective that has caused gross omissions and erasures in claims of knowledge (qtd. in Harding, *Whose Science?* 153). But feminist theorists have also argued against the uncritical celebration of female experience situated in a fixed or "natural" female identity (Ritchie 255). In fact, it would be dangerous for women, as Teresa Ebert argues, to invest so much in the "local," the individual, the unique, that we forget the global power structures that oppress women (902).

It is not enough, then, to begin locating ourselves and our experiences. In doing so naively, we risk ignoring hierarchies and creating the same unifying and totalizing master narratives that feminist scholars have sought to revise and oppose. More specifically, we risk defining gender biologically rather than recognizing it as a varied set of social relationships. We risk limiting our definitions to a binary of male and female as opposite, inherently different human beings, without seeing the multiple permutations of gendered experience. Jane Flax argues that this will prevent us from adequately asking and answering the questions we need to articulate in order to understand how both men and women are affected by cultural contexts (*Thinking Fragments* 182).

In composition studies we risk making essentializing distinctions about writers: If they are male they must write or think *this* way; if they are female, they must write or think another. New research on gender and writing has made important contributions to composition studies and moved the field from being "gender-blind to [being] gender-sensitive" (Peaden 260), but there remains the tendency to polarize—to essentialize—accounts of gender differences.[4] Don Kraemer suggests that in considering gender and language we look at the "range of social relations they imply" rather than read gender as "one monolithic language" (328). We argue that composition researchers need to resist the drive to generalize about men and women, that we can learn much from studying the multiple ways in which both men and women can express themselves, and that composition teachers need to develop pedagogical practices that encourage students to write in a wide variety of discourse forms, a task that Lillian Bridwell-Bowles has begun to map out successfully in "Discourse and Diversity."

Claiming our experience, then, may be as inadequate for making claims to knowledge as traditional claims from objectivity are. Harding points out that "our experience may lie to us" just as it has lied to male researchers who believed their positions were value-free or universal (*Whose Science?* 286). A number of African American, lesbian, and third world feminists, including bell hooks, have argued that simply privileging our experience may lead us to posit rigid and exclusionary definitions of experience that erase the interlocking structures of race, social class, and heterosexist oppression for men and women ("Feminist Politicization" 107–08). The result is that we create definitions of experience that produce dominant group "common-sense" norms so exclusive that the experience of nonwhite, nondominant people is eliminated, while dominant gender, class, race, and sexuality produce more airtight, fastened down, comprehensive theories. Sidonie Smith observes that feminist researchers "from the dominant culture" can easily appropriate the experiences of others if they are "unselfconscious about the possibility of such cultural appropriation" (401). Consider, for example, the experience that taught one of us (Ritchie) about the problems of cultural appropriation and representation.

Joy Ritchie: As I observed the writing of two women students in an advanced composition class—Manjit Kaur, a Punjabi from Malaysia and BeeTin Choo, a Chinese woman from Singapore—I was struck by the rich and contradictory construction of selfhood in their writing. When I decided to report on their writing, I quickly recognized the political and ethical problems involved in writing *about* them, speaking *for* them, or attempting to represent their experiences. Instead, I invited them to co-author an article, thinking that allowing them to speak for themselves would help me avoid appropriating their writing for my purposes. But I discovered that we still faced many difficult decisions because of the complexity and multiplicity of each of our identities and motivations, most obviously because of our cultural differences, because of the complex power relations between students and professor, and because of the constraints of academic writing. For example, during the time we were writing our essay, after our proposal had been accepted by the editors, BeeTin became increasingly committed to a Christian perspective and was, therefore, uncomfortable with the feminist theoretical framework the other two of us favored. Both women were concerned particularly that their representations of their cultures, written in the relative safety of a classroom, would be misinterpreted by readers and used to solidify existing negative stereotypes of their culture. Whose theory, whose language, whose interpretation, and whose narrative voice would prevail? We had to negotiate these and other questions. I drafted the introduction and conclusion for the essay because I felt some responsibility for ensuring coherence among our three distinct voices, but I struggled, without complete success, to minimize the dominance of my narrative voice.

In a continuing dialogue as we wrote together, I learned more about the way my own cultural context constrained my perspective and often caused me to objectify "others." First, I had to recognize that my assumptions about international students and "Asian women students" led to limited and essentialized understanding of their lives as students, as women, and as writers. BeeTin's silence was not Asian acquiescence to authority; it was a form of resistance. Manjit's exploration of the roles of women in Malaysia and in the United States did not necessarily fit within my western feminist assumptions about women's oppression. I realized that I set apart Manjit and BeeTin as essentialized "others" as I sought to define their voices and to analyze the style, form, and rhetorical features of their writing according to my own training in rhetoric. Although we finished the article, we considered abandoning it at several points because each of us felt at least slightly compromised in the essay that resulted (Ritchie, Kaur, Choo Meyer).

If researchers are to preserve the value of experience as a source of knowledge, they need to locate the experience of others, especially those previously excluded or devalued. But they also need to recognize the impossibility of ever fully understanding another's experiences and to question their motives in gathering, selecting, and presenting those stories. It is important to step back from our own experience, to understand it as a reflection of ideology and culture. But this may not be enough. As Ritchie's work with her students suggests, the tendency to essentialize is only one symptom of what Michelle Fine calls the "knotty entanglement" of self and other (72). As researchers examine more carefully the relationship between themselves and participants, they will need to consider the provocative advice of Trinh Minh-ha: "In writing close to the other of the other, I can only choose to maintain a self-reflexively critical relationship toward the material, a relationship that defines both the subject written and the writing subject undoing the I while asking 'what do I want, wanting to *know* you—or me?'" (76).

Since researchers cannot assume that they understand what is relevant in the lives of others or even what are the important questions to ask, research participants must be invited to articulate research questions, to speak for themselves, to choose the occasions for and forms of representing their experiences. Inevitably, as in Ritchie's work with her students, participants' perspectives will reshape the assumptions and methodologies on which research is based, leading to more collaborative, complex, and "knottily entangled" research practices.

RELATIONSHIP OF THE KNOWER TO THE KNOWN

We have been focusing on the "knower" and her perspective on research. But feminist researchers have another significant and related concern—the "known" and its relationship to the "knower." One of the methodological changes proposed by feminist scholars is to establish more interactive, collaborative, and reciprocal relations between researchers and participants. These changes have come to us from pioneering work of scientists like Barbara McClintock and Evelyn Fox Keller, whose ideas about "objectivity" and the relationship between subject and object of study have complicated feminist research. McClintock's discoveries (documented by Keller) about genetic transposition in maize arose from her unconventional view of the role of the scientist and the relationship of observer and the observed. She no longer thought of the scientist as combative, manipulative, or dominant but rather in a relationship of intimacy and empathy with nature (Keller 117).

As scholars in composition we are uniquely positioned to interact closely with participants since much of our work involves us directly in the lives of students, teachers, and writers as we study their written and oral language. Our research strategies often bring us into lived daily relationships with research participants in ways not possible for biologists or even sociologists. Shirley Brice Heath's *Ways with Words* provides examples of daily lived interactions among research participants and researcher, although she mentions them only occasionally in her narrative: Heath's children played with the children in her study; she transported them in her car; she socialized with them in homes and churches. In the context of her work, Heath's participants became partners in research. Black and white teachers, mill workers, businessmen, and parents whose communities Heath was studying, began themselves to observe and analyze the patterns of language use around them and could therefore begin to formulate questions and initiate change.

One of the assumptions underlying collaboration between researchers and participants is that it will benefit all parties involved in the interaction: Researchers can gather additional insights by getting to know participants in the context of their daily lives, and participants can gain new knowledge about themselves and their lives through the research project. Collaborative research practices often bring about methodological changes as well. One frequently quoted example of methodological innovation resulting from collaborative research is Ann Oakley's interview study of working-class pregnant women. When Oakley encountered women who asked her about prenatal care or other medical information, for example, she found that she could not follow traditional interview procedures: to deflect questions, withhold information, and maintain the role of distanced interviewer. Instead, Oakley decided that she had a moral obligation to assist these women in their quest for information. Consequently, she changed her research methodology in response to research participants: she engaged in dialogue with the women, provided them with information available to her, and helped them get access to prenatal care. Thus, she launched one of the early feminist critiques of social science research methodology. In composition studies, we need to be similarly sensitive to research procedures. Whether we study basic or professional writers, we need to ask participants to collaborate with us, to help us design our research questions, to ask for their feedback, to answer their questions, and to share our knowledge with them.

This formulation of collaborative research still does not go far enough. A feminist politics of location would require the learning about self to be as *reciprocal* as possible—with the researcher also gaining knowledge about her own life or at least reexamining her cultural and gender biases. Sherry Gorelick suggests that "the researcher is transformed in the process of research—influenced and taught by her respondent-participants as she influences them. Theory and practice emerge from their interaction" (469). In composition there are few published accounts in which researchers reflect on the knowledge they gained about themselves and their relations with others due to the research they conducted, and in the few places where such accounts appear, they are often relegated to a preface or epilogue. We suspect this has to do with the format of traditional research reports which do not invite researchers' self-reflections and introspections. But we have anecdotal evidence from colleagues and friends who have discovered that interactive, collaborative research leaves them with a changed understanding of themselves. We have already mentioned one such example: the collaborative writing project Ritchie undertook with two students and the profound questions it raised for her and her position as a white female university professor. Another example emerged in an interview study Kirsch conducted with academic women (*Women Writing the Academy*).

Gesa Kirsch: In my effort to learn more about the concerns of academic women in different disciplines and at different stages of their careers, I invited participants to collaborate with me during various stages of the research: I developed interview questions with the help of women who participated in the study, adding and revising questions in response to initial conversations. I also collaborated with women in the interpretation of interviews. As I began to record and transcribe interviews, I consulted with women about the themes I identified as important in their lives. Thus, I entered into a cycle of conversation whereby both researcher and participants shaped, to some extent, the interpretation of interviews. In many cases, the collaboration between myself and participants was mutually beneficial: the stories women told me transformed my sense of self as writer, as scholar, and as participant in the academic community; women themselves also reported gaining insights into their writing and research processes through the interviews. In some cases, the interviews led to friendships that extended well beyond the duration of my research.

But the cycle of collaboration also had limitations. For example, it was cut short by time constraints I faced as researcher and by participants' interest, availability, and willingness to collaborate with me. I also have to assume that some participants may have felt disappointed, misunderstood, or even manipulated. Although no woman directly expressed this sentiment to me, lack of interest in follow-up conversations and resistance to collaboration suggest that possibility.

Relations between researcher and participants will always retain the potential for misunderstandings, even exploitation—much like other human relationships do. This potential risk, however, should not lead to inaction; rather, researchers can learn to explore sites of conflict for the shifting, multiple, and contradictory positions researchers and participants inevitably occupy and for the ethical questions raised by collaborative research.

ETHICAL QUESTIONS:
ISSUES OF POWER AND COLONIZATION

So far we have argued that a politics of location must begin with researchers who recognize their own subjectivity, who draw on their experiences to formulate research questions even as they recognize the limitations of their perspective, experiences, and understanding. Researchers' reflective and critical stance, however, is only the beginning. They must also investigate the relation between the knower and the known and explore the possibilities of collaboration with participants as they develop research questions, collect data, interpret findings, and write research reports. Finally, they must be open to change themselves, reexamining their own perspective continually as they collaborate with participants and come to recognize how their cultural, ethnic, gendered, and personal histories influence the shape of their research. Ideally, a politics of location enables reciprocal, dialogic, collaborative, and mutually beneficial relations between researchers and participants. However, this "ideal" research scenario often remains just that—an ideal. More often, researchers encounter epistemological, methodological, and—perhaps most troubling—ethical dilemmas. We now turn to ethical issues, such as questions of power and colonization, that scholars are likely to face in the research process.

The work of Michel Foucault and others has allowed us to see how observation, classification, and codification in the discourse of the academy are always exercises of power, sometimes more coercive than others. Issues of power and colonization can become particularly prominent in studies of oppressed or disenfranchised groups, as the example of Daphne Patai's work illustrates. She reflects on her experience of interviewing working-class women in Brazil, many of whom lived in poverty and lacked access to adequate health care and education.

> The dilemma of feminist researchers working on groups less privileged than themselves can be succinctly stated as follows: is it possible—not in theory, but in the actual conditions of the real world today—to write about the oppressed without becoming one of the oppressors? (139)

Patai ultimately answers this question in the negative, arguing that the material, economic, and political conditions that separate privileged feminist researchers from disenfranchised or oppressed women cannot easily be overcome, no matter how emancipatory the research methods are or how much good will the researcher brings to the project. She does not, however, suggest that scholars abandon all research that involves oppressed or disenfranchised people; instead, she suggests that scholars abandon their naiveté and learn to make professional judgments about the context, consequences, and potential benefits and drawbacks of their work.

Other ethical dilemmas can emerge when researchers solicit highly personal information from participants. Judith Stacey, a sociologist, faced an ethical dilemma when she interviewed a fundamentalist Christian woman. This woman revealed that she had been involved in a lesbian relationship before her marriage, but asked Stacey not to disclose that information. Thus, the researcher faced a dilemma:

> What feminist ethical principles could I invoke to guide me here? Principles of respect for research subjects and for a collaborative, egalitarian research relationship demand compliance, but this forced me to collude with the homophobic silencing of lesbian experience, as well as consciously to distort what I considered to be a crucial component of the ethnographic "truth" in my study. Whatever we [the interviewer and interviewee] decided, my ethnography was forced to betray a feminist principle. (114)

At times researchers will find that feminist principles are at odds with ethnographic ones. Feminist principles urge researchers to listen to women's voices, to cooperate with women in the telling of their stories, and to honor their trust. Ethnographic principles, on the other hand, urge researchers to be as accurate, exhaustive, and frank as possible in the process of gathering and presenting information about other people and cultures.

The kinds of ethical dilemmas Patai and Stacey describe also concern composition researchers. While composition research does not necessarily involve "disenfranchised groups," it often concerns groups who have less power and fewer resources than the researchers, such as students, basic writers, K–12 teachers, minorities, and women. Furthermore, composition scholars frequently solicit highly personal information from research participants, much in the same way that writing teachers who assign autobiographical essays can find themselves confronted with details about their students' lives that they never anticipated.[5] Researchers need to consider, for example, the dynamics of the interview situation. Although it may be dishonest to assume the stance of objective, detached interviewer, Sheila Riddell points out that it is equally problematic to position oneself as "just another woman" whose concerns in life are similar to those of the research participant (83–84). Because it creates a false atmosphere of equality and mutuality in which women are often eager to talk, this stance may seem to break down barriers between the researcher and participants, but it may also be manipulative or even coercive, while giving participants a false sense of control. Riddell's interviews with teenaged girls led her to speculate that women may talk more openly in some situations because of their social powerlessness and are thus easily exploited. In a long-term study of English teachers Ritchie faced similar issues.

Joy Ritchie: As my colleague David Wilson and I conducted a study of teachers' developing knowledge of their discipline and its pedagogy, I interviewed Carol Gulyas, one of our participants, several times over a period of four years while she completed her course work and began teaching. Because of the many hours I spent in interviews with her and because of her position as a student in some of our classes and as a research and teaching assistant in our project, we developed a closer relationship with Carol than with other participants, a relationship she described as one of "love and caring." My position of authority, but also our frequent and extended contacts, as well as my position as a woman with similar concerns about children and parents, for example, no doubt caused Carol to be less reserved in revealing connections between her personal life and the development of her voice as a writer, as a teacher, and as a woman. According to Carol, our frequent prompts to reflect on and articulate her learning over several semesters encouraged and deepened her learning. Because Carol was so articulate, self-reflective, and astute in her analyses of herself and her peers, the data she provided, and especially the connection between her personal history and her theoretical learning, were crucial in shaping our conclusions. David and I recognized that our representation of her personal experience in our writing might be a distortion or an appropriation. But because we had been so intrusive in Carol's life, we could not withdraw—nor would we have wanted to—from Carol after the study was over.

We felt more than the usual obligation to become an advocate for Carol in her emerging career, to encourage her to write her own account of her learning, even in counterpoint to our representation of it, and to continue to learn from her as a colleague (Gulyas; Wilson and Ritchie).

A final ethical dilemma we want to discuss concerns anthropologists, oral historians, and composition scholars alike: How can or should researchers respond to participants who do not share the researcher's values, who oppose feminist research goals, or who do not identify with feminist causes? We draw on another example from oral history to illustrate this ethical issue. Sondra Hale, an anthropologist who studies African and Middle Eastern women, reports on the dissonance she experienced in interviews with women who either did not identify themselves as feminists or did not share the researcher's notion of what it means to be a feminist. Hale describes her disappointment with an interview of a Sudanese women's movement leader who ignored Hale's invitation to reflect on her role and position in the movement. Instead, the woman chose to use the interview as an occasion to promote the "party line," to enhance the image of the Sudanese women's movement, even when it meant providing inaccurate information or exaggerating accomplishments. In composition studies, we can face similar dissonances in our interactions with research participants. In the interview study of academic women mentioned above, Kirsch also faced questions of how to interpret women's lives.

Gesa Kirsch: I interviewed a history professor who chose to distance herself from the feminist movement and repeatedly disavowed any interest in, sympathy with, or connections to feminist ideas. Yet she had been a "pioneer" in a field dominated by men and made many comments that were feminist in nature, such as pointing to the discrepancy between her values and those of her male colleagues, describing herself as a woman living in a "foreign" male culture, and expressing an interest in experimenting with forms of writing that went "against the academic grain." How was I to represent her views and comments? Should I use her comments that emphasized dissonance from feminist ideas, or should I offer my feminist reading of her interview? Taking my cues from feminist scholars, I addressed these questions by doing both; I juxtaposed her comments (in extended interview quotes) with my analysis and commentary, thereby giving readers evidence that allowed both perspectives to emerge. Of course, as the writer of the research report, I still retain authority by selecting interview quotes, arranging the text, and drawing on supporting theories.

To some degree, researchers cannot escape a position of power and the potential for appropriating or manipulating information. The point here, however, is not to suggest that scholars ignore or omit data that seem to contradict their views. Rather, the point is to encourage researchers to view dissonances as opportunities to examine deeply held assumptions and to allow multiple voices to emerge in their research studies, an act that will require innovation in writing research reports. (We discuss possibilities for new forms of writing below.) Only in that manner will researchers be able to allow readers to see the conflicting pieces of information they often gather in their work and the potential contradictions inherent in their interpretations.

We are not advocating a relativist approach to research here, however. Instead, we argue that feminist research goals should guide researchers' decisions. Feminist research can be distinguished from other research traditions by its emancipatory goals.[6] Feminist researchers not only set out to study and describe women's lives and experiences, but actively seek to understand and change the conditions of women's social and political realities. Thus, feminist researchers advocate using guiding questions like these for responding to ethical dilemmas: Who benefits from the research/theories? What are the possible outcomes of the research and the possible consequences for research participants? Whose interests are at stake? How and to what extent will the research change social realities for research participants? There are no easy solutions to the range of ethical dilemmas researchers can face. Like Patai, we do not think

> that generic solutions can be found to the dilemmas feminists [and other researchers] face in conducting research, nor do [we] for an instant hold out the hope of devising exact "rules" that will resolve these issues for us. In [our] view, this is impossible because ethical problems do not arise as absolutes requiring "blind justice." (145)

Researchers will face difficult decisions in the research process, but a politics of location requires that researchers interrogate their relations with the people they study and the power they hold over them. Linda Alcoff suggests that "in order to evaluate attempts to speak for others in particular instances, we need to analyze the probable or actual effects of the words on the discursive and material context" (26). At times, researchers will have to refocus their research questions, find additional or different participants, assume roles other than that of participant-observer, leave some data unpublished, or even abandon a research project.

TOWARDS AN ETHICS OF RESEARCH

In the previous section we have raised some of the ethical questions inherent in a feminist politics of location. Although we do not claim to have all the answers, we want to suggest how composition researchers can begin to address these questions. As we have shown, these questions are intertwined with—and highlight the necessity for articulating—ethical concerns. However, as we have attempted earlier in this essay to problematize our understanding of a politics of location, we also need to problematize ethics, informing our view with the vigorous discussion of ethics in which feminists from various disciplines have recently engaged.[7] First we will consider how we might revise our definition of ethics based on caring, collaborative relationships with participants. Next, we suggest changes in research methods and forms of writing to meet these ethical demands, changes that allow multi-vocal, dialogic representations in our research narratives. Finally, we propose a reexamination of the goals and implications of research in a further attempt to examine an ethical stance in our work.

Feminist discussions of ethics call for a fundamental change in the way ethics is conceived. Traditional ethics are based on a fixed set of principles determined through rational means to guide one's approach to all problems. That approach assumes a universal applicability and fails to question beliefs in objectivity and neutrality. It also homogenizes differences in contexts and perspectives and fails to take into account the connection between political and moral questions. In general, feminist philosophers disavow traditional rule-governed ethics based on "universal" principles and on unbending rules, because acting from principle entails acting without experience and context, without a politics of location (e.g., Noddings; Schweickart; Young). An ethic of care often comes to different conclusions than an ethic of principle. Ethical behavior must be guided by natural sentiment or what Noddings calls "caring" within the context of human relationships. Unlike rule-bound ethics, "caring" requires one to place herself in an empathetic relationship in order to understand the other's point of view. For this reason an ethic of care is dependent on the engagement of "the personal"—a particular person of ethical character engaged in the examination of context, motivations, relationships, and responsibility (Tronto, "Beyond Gender" 657–58).

But empathy is not an unproblematic concept. Gregory Clark, paraphrasing Wyschogrod, notes that "an act of empathy is inherently an interpretation that eclipses, at least partially, the full reality of another's difference: it directs me to 'understand' another in my own terms" (66). Feminist critics, while acknowledging the importance of an ethic of care, point out the inherent hierarchies, paternalism, and inequalities even in this "caring" ethical model. Patrocinio Schweickart observes that "an ethic of care is no guarantee against self-deception—a discourse of care can be used to mask exploitative and uncaring conditions" (187). Further, Sarah

Hoagland suggests that Noddings's ethic still posits a one-way relationship rather than a truly reciprocal relationship between the caring and cared-for. Such unidirectional relationships of care, she argues, reinforce oppressive institutions (250–53).

Hoagland's concern seems especially relevant for composition researchers because of the problems inherent in seemingly benevolent but unequal relationships. It suggests that researchers continually interrogate their relations with participants, working toward dialogic, mutually educative, caring relations while at the same time recognizing that the complex power dynamics between researcher and participants can undermine, threaten, or manipulate those relations. Engaging in more collaborative approaches to research can help reduce the distance between researchers and participants. Participants can be brought in as co-researchers; those who have been marginalized can be encouraged to join in posing research questions that matter to them. Not only should participants co-author the questions, they can also work with researchers to negotiate the interpretations of data at both the descriptive and interpretive level. bell hooks is most insistent that white, privileged researchers and writers stop asking disempowered women to tell their stories so that these women can rewrite them in their own language, making their stories their own ("Choosing the Margin" 152). Madeleine Grumet provides further suggestions for reciprocal relationships between researchers and participants.

> So if telling a story requires giving oneself away, then we are obligated to devise a method of receiving stories that mediates the space between the self that tells, the self that told, and the self that listens: a method that returns a story to the teller that is both hers and not hers, that contains her self in good company. (70)

Inevitably caring, reciprocal, collaborative research will lead to complications, but it may also lead to richer, more rigorously examined results. Despite the potential problems of an ethic of care, we prefer, along with Tronto, "a moral theory that can recognize and identify these issues [problems of otherness, privilege, and paternalism] . . . to a moral theory that, because it presumes that all people are equal, is unable even to recognize them" (*Moral Boundaries* 147).

Reciprocal relations also imply that researchers attempt to open themselves to change and learning, to reinterpreting their own lives, and to reinventing their own "otherness" (Harding, *Whose Science?* 217). This means doing more than listening to and becoming more sensitive to the experiences of those who are disenfranchised. It requires researchers to attempt to identify what may be repressed and unconscious in their own experiences, and to claim their own contradictory social and gendered identities. Women can explore their marginality, for example, by considering that a woman scholar is at some level a contradiction in terms, that women in the academy still continue to occupy marginal positions because of their gender (Harding, "Who Knows?" 103). Marginality is not merely determined by sex or skin color; we sometimes make choices that place us in such positions. Men in composition studies, for example, can explore how their work as teachers and scholars often positions them as "other" in English departments that tend to privilege the study of literature and critical theory.[8] African American scholars have theorized the importance of using this perspective to generate new understandings of our discipline (Collins 40–41; hooks, "Choosing the Margin" 149). Collins argues that our own devalued identities can be powerful resources for knowing because the tension that arises from assuming the perspective of "outsiders within" allows us to see what privileged insiders cannot (59). Patricia J. Williams in *The Alchemy of Race and Rights* combines her privileged perspective as a legal scholar and her marginalized personal history as an African American woman to analyze the social and political contexts of such seemingly arcane matters as contract law.[9]

Working from a marginal position also offers the potential for research that moves beyond analyzing gender or race as though they are someone else's problem—not ours. It can lead the more privileged to consider themselves as potential "subjects" of study, and, therefore, reveal more clearly their privileged positions as well as their unacknowledged marginality. In her analysis of self-other relations, Michelle Fine describes the study of one of her students, Nancy Porter. Porter interviewed white "Main Line" women in Philadelphia and revealed how white people's lives are protected from surveillance and how scholars have "sanitized" evidence of the dysfunctional in such privileged lives (73).[10] Historian Minnie Bruce Pratt provides another example of this process. She uses her identity as a white Southerner at the center, but also her identity as a lesbian on the margin, to analyze her understanding of Southern history, to see how her white perspective is challenged by the perspective of African American lives, and by her own "outsider" position as a lesbian. We are not suggesting that scholars engage in self-indulgent privileging of their own stories or that they superimpose their stories on those of others; instead, we suggest that they can place their stories and those of their research participants in dialogue with each other to gain new insights into their own and others' lives. As the women in our discussion group at CCCC acknowledged, because our gender and our position in composition still locates us in a marginal position in many English departments, it gives us one important site from which to see with the perspective of outsiders.

We have already asserted the importance of rigorous self-reflection on the part of the researcher in order to avoid essentializing others and to clarify her own motives, desires, and interests. We also understand that to some extent these will always remain unconscious and unknowable. However, neutrality and objectivity are also myths that mask the power-relations always present in research endeavors. That does not mean that relativism is the only alternative, however. Harding's notion of "strong objectivity" may help us understand how to negotiate this apparent dichotomy between a humanist belief in our ability to represent experience and a paralyzed postmodernist stance that denies the possibility of making any claims or taking action. "Strong objectivity" recognizes the historical, social, culturally situated nature of our motives and values, continually theorizes the impact of those values on our work, and searches for what is being eliminated, distorted, or masked in the process (*Whose Science?* 145–47).[11] As part of this activity we can look at the relationship between our theories and our conclusions. The questions that guide our data collection, the stories we decide to tell or eliminate from our research narratives, the range of conclusions we suppress or include—all are guided by our own positionality and must be acknowledged. This process is difficult because "working from a perspective in which we are trained to want to give a reasoned and connected account, we face live material [such as interviews and ethnographic observations] that is constantly in the process of transformation, that is not organized in the way of academic theories" (Acker, Barry, and Esseveld 149).

In addition to acting from an ethic of care and from the perspective offered by rigorous ongoing scrutiny of our motivations and methods, an ethical stance also suggests that we encode in our research narratives the provisional nature of knowledge that our work generates and the moral dilemmas inherent in research. We need to reconsider our privileging of certain, coherent, and univocal writing and include multiple voices and diverse interpretations in our research narratives, highlighting the ideologies that govern our thinking as well as those that may contradict our own. These "rupturing narratives," as Michelle Fine describes them, "allow us to hear the uppity voices of informants and researchers" (78). Finally, of course, we must be prepared to make the case for new forms of research and writing in our discipline as McCarthy and Fishman and others have begun to do. Traditional research reports, for example, urge writers to come to conclusions and announce their findings. That process demands that researchers make coherent what might be fragmented, and thus that they might sometimes reduce complex phenomena or erase differences for the sake of developing coherent theories.[12]

To avoid such erasing of differences, we need to continue experimenting with new ways of reporting research. In composition, a number of scholars have begun to invent writing that highlights multiple narratives and diverse perspectives. Several examples come to mind: Beverly Clark and Sonja Wiedenhaupt published an article on writers' block that took the form of a dialogue between the researcher and the writer, thereby allowing two distinct voices to tell the story from two different vantage points; Jill Eichhorn, Sara Farris, Karen Hayes, Adriana Hernandez, Susan Jarratt, Karen Powers-Stubbs, and Marian Sciachitano used a symposium to reflect on and theorize their experiences as feminist teachers, writing "both as a collective and in [their] seven different voices" (297); and Susan Miller collaborated and co-authored a study of "academic underlife" with several of her undergraduate students, Worth Anderson, Cynthia Best, Alycia Black, John Hurst, and Brandt Miller.[13] Such innovative writing challenges scholars to find new ways of presenting research, challenges journal editors to develop a greater tolerance for ambiguity and unconventional forms of discourse, and challenges readers to learn new ways of reading and interpreting texts. Fine observes, "When we construct texts collaboratively, self-consciously examining our relations with/for/despite those who have been contained as Others, we move against, we enable resistance to, "Othering" (74). Multivocal reports also disrupt the smooth research narratives we have come to know and expect, highlight rather than suppress the problems of representation in our writing, and expose the multiple, shifting, and contradictory subject positions of researchers and participants.[14]

Finally, a problematized politics of location leads us to research centered in the local and the individual while at the same time acknowledging that research has social consequences in the world. If we work from an ethic of care, we cannot ignore the political and cultural conditions that place us in unequal power relationships with the participants of our research (Hoagland 260). We have seen in the studies of Patai and Oakley and in our own research how deeply implicated issues of power are, in our work. Patti Lather is one of many feminist thinkers who argues strongly that we cannot be satisfied with more research and better data concerning women (or other groups we choose to study). If our research is centered on a politics of location it demands an extra measure of responsibility and accountability on our part. It requires using research as "praxis" to help those who participate with us in research to understand and change their situation, to help those who have been marginalized to speak for themselves. Under these circumstances, it will not be possible to walk away from the research site or those who live in it. Our research instead will need to extend to theory-generating in a self-reflexive and mutually dialogic context to help researchers and participants challenge and change the conditions that keep oppressive structures in place. Only in this extra measure of "care" can our research truly be ethical.

Pursuing the difficulties inherent in a politics of location may lead us beyond some of the frustrations we experience in our work in English departments, because these discussions will inevitably lead us to question our accommodation with the status quo in our discipline, to more seriously question the discipline's traditional ways of asking and answering research questions, to examine the internalized structures, the standard conventions for generating and communicating knowledge in the discipline, and to reshape our agendas for research and action in the field. It will engage us in a rigorous process of analyzing the meaning of the "personal" in our work.

NOTES

1. We frame our article with Adrienne Rich's words realizing that she has been criticized for some of her earlier writing in which she seems to advocate an essentialist position that reinscribes bourgeois individualism and an unproblematic universal feminism. We think her position is an important starting point for discussions of a politics of location, however, because Rich was one of the early theorists attempting to reintroduce the personal in order to challenge the impersonal authority and false universality of interpretive practices that exclude women's writing and women's lives altogether from the academy and other public sites. In the essay we quote, she does acknowledge the social and psychological construction of women's lives and defines "location" as a space in which we move, not as a fixed site. She also foregrounds the tension we want to explore between the degendered, depoliticized subject of post-modernist aesthetics and the universalizing, unified, humanist subject—both positions which can erase the specificity and lived experience of particular women.

2. We realize that our attempt to locate the origins of this article in a single event misrepresents the many origins our work inevitably has. In the first place we had to be motivated to attend the workshop, a motivation we could trace to our reading of feminist literature, to conversations with colleagues and friends, and to our lived everyday experiences as women in the academy and in the culture at large. If we continue this search for origins, we quickly come to realize that questions of location are complex and call for an analysis of the many conflicting layers of reality we experience in our multiple and shifting subject positions.

3. People participating in research studies are traditionally called "subjects." This term, however, is problematic, implying a division if not hierarchy between researchers and subjects, thereby positioning participants as objects of study, not as the complex and contradictory human beings they are. Since we are questioning precisely this division between researchers and subjects, we have chosen to use the terms "research participants" or simply "participants" throughout this article when we are referring to human beings involved in research studies.

4. Heather Brodie Graves, for example, argues that traditional "feminine" and "masculine" traits can be found in writers of both genders; she analyzes the writing of Kenneth Burke for "feminine" traits and that of Julia Kristeva for "masculine" traits to illustrate her point.

5. For discussions of writing teachers faced with highly personal and at times disturbing information in their students' writing, see Carole Deletiner; Cheryl Johnson; Richard E. Miller.

6. For discussions of feminist research goals and methods, see *Beyond Methodology* (Fonow and Cook), *Feminism and Methodology* (Harding), *Feminist Research Methods* (Nielsen), *Feminist Methods in Social Research* (Reinharz).

7. Space does not permit a full discussion of feminist approaches to ethics, particularly an ethic of care. We refer interested readers to discussions in political science (Tronto; Young), in feminist theory and philosophy (Card; Friedman; Hoagland; Houston; Lather; Schweickart), in education and psychology (Fine; Gilligan; Grumet; Noddings; Punch), and in composition studies (Clark; Mortensen and Kirsch).

8. We do not mean to suggest that only scholars who are marginalized can engage in feminist or care-based approaches to research. Rather, we argue for a sense of location that one can actively learn to choose. But we believe that attending to the experiences of marginalized people as well as examining aspects of one's identity that are suppressed are important points of departure for a critical perspective on research.

9. We do not wish to minimize differences among women of different backgrounds, generations, race, class, ethnicity, or other identity-shaping factors. In fact, the position of African American women in the academy is distinctly different from those of white, middle class women and has caused much debate and tension among feminist theorists. We use this example only to suggest that a marginal position can be a source of strength and insight, allowing researchers to formulate new research questions and gain knowledge not readily available to those who occupy more privileged positions.

10. For another revealing study of "whiteness," see *White Women, Race Matters: The Social Construction of Whiteness* by Ruth Frankenberg.

11. Harding's concept of "strong objectivity" is not unproblematic. Flax, for example, argues that it is still based on a notion of "transcendental truth" because it suggests that once we eliminate or reduce gender biases we will have come closer to 'the truth' (Disputed Subjects 141–47). We concur with Flax's critique but find Harding's notion useful as a working concept for researchers trying to assess the ethical dimensions of their work.

12. We recognize the irony of the text we have produced: a relatively univocal, coherent text that argues for experimental, multivocal writing. We have attempted to present multivocality by writing in our individual voices when describing our own research projects and in our collective voice in other sections of this text, but we can imagine more experimental and innovative ways of writing.

13. We list names of all collaborators/authors here to give full credit to the nature of collaborative work; all too often multiple authors disappear in the "et al." convention, a practice that reinforces the dominant single-author model of scholarship.

14. The multivocal texts we advocate are not without risk; besides making new demands on readers, writers, and editors, these texts pose special risks for untenured faculty and graduate students who still have to "prove"—or feel that they still have to prove—their disciplinary membership by using conventional research methods and forms.

WORKS CITED

Acker, Joan, Kate Barry, and Johanna Esseveld. "Objectivity and Truth: Problems in Doing Feminist Research." *Beyond Methodology: Feminist Scholarship as Lived Research.* Ed. Mary Fonow and Judith Cook. Bloomington: Indiana UP, 1991. 133–53.

Alcoff, Linda. "The Problem of Speaking for Others." *Cultural Critique* 20 (1991–92): 5–32.

Anderson, Worth, Cynthia Best, Alycia Black, John Hurst, Brandt Miller, and Susan Miller. "Cross-Curricular Ablex: A Collaborative Report on Ways with Academic Words." *College Composition and Communication* 41 (1990): 11–36.

Bizzell, Patricia. "Foundationalism and Anti-Foundationalism in Composition Studies." *Pre/Text* 7 (1986): 37–56.

Bridwell-Bowles, Lillian. "Discourse and Diversity: Experimental Writing within the Academy." *College Composition and Communication* 43 (1992): 349–68.

Card, Claudia, ed. *Feminist Ethics*. Lawrence: UP of Kansas. 1991.

Clark, Beverly Lyon, and Sonja Wiedenhaupt. "On Blocking and Unblocking Sonja: A Case Study in Two Voices." *College Composition and Communication* 43 (1992): 55–74.

Clark, Gregory. "Rescuing the Discourse of Community." *College Composition and Communication* 45 (1994): 61–74.

Collins, Patricia Hill. "Learning from the Outsider Within: The Sociological Significance of Black Feminist Thought." *(En)Gendering Knowledge: Feminists in Academe.* Ed. Joan Hartman and Ellen Messer-Davidow. Knoxville: U of Tennessee P, 1991. 40–65.

Deletiner, Carole. "Crossing Lines." *College English* 54 (1992): 809–17.

Ebert, Teresa. "The 'Difference' of Postmodern Feminism." *College English* 53 (1991): 886–904.

Eichhorn, Jill, Sara Farris, Karen Hayes, Adriana Hernandez, Susan Jarratt, Karen Powers-Stubbs, and Marian Sciachitano. "A Symposium on Feminist Experiences in the Composition Classroom." *College Composition and Communication* 43 (1992): 297–322.

Fine, Michelle. "Working the Hyphens: Reinventing Self and Other in Qualitative Research." *Handbook of Qualitative Research.* Ed. Norman Denzin and Yvonna Lincoln. Thousand Oaks, CA: Sage, 1994. 70–82.

Flax, Jane. *Thinking Fragments: Psychoanalysis, Feminism, and Postmodernism in the Contemporary West.* Berkeley: U of California P, 1990.

——. *Disputed Subjects: Essays on Psychoanalysis, Politics, and Philosophy.* New York: Routledge, 1993.

Fonow, Mary Margaret, and Judith A. Cook, eds. *Beyond Methodology: Feminist Scholarship as Lived Research.* Bloomington: Indiana UP, 1991.

Frankenberg, Ruth. *White Women, Race Matters: The Social Construction of Whiteness.* Minneapolis: U of Minnesota P, 1993.

Friedman, Marilyn. "Beyond Caring: The De-Moralization of Gender." *Science, Morality, and Feminist Theory.* Ed. Marsha Hanen and Kai Nielsen. Calgary: U of Calgary P, 1987. 87–110.

Gilligan, Carol. *In a Different Voice: Psychological Theory and Women's Development.* Cambridge, MA: Harvard UP, 1982.

Gorelick, Sherry. "Contradictions of Feminist Methodology." *Gender and Society* 4 (1991):459–77.

Graves, Heather Brodie. "Regrinding the Lens of Gender: Problematizing 'Writing as a Woman.'" *Written Communication* 10 (1993):139–63.

Grumet, Madeleine R. "The Politics of Personal Knowledge." *Stories Lives Tell: Narrative and Dialogue in Education.* Ed. Carol Witherell and Nel Noddings. New York: Teachers College P, 1991. 67–77.

Gulyas, Carol. "Reflections on Telling Stories." *English Education* 18 (1994): 189–94.

Hale, Sondra. "Feminist Methods, Process, and Self-Criticism: Interviewing Sudanese Women." *Women's Words: The Feminist Practice of Oral History.* Ed. Sherna Gluck and Daphne Patai. New York: Routledge, 1991. 121–36.

Haraway, Donna. "Situated Knowledges: The Science Question in Feminism and the Privilege of Partial Perspective. *Feminist Studies* 14 (1988): 575–99.

Harding, Sandra, ed. *Feminism and Methodology: Social Science Issues.* Bloomington: Indiana UP, 1987.

———. "Who Knows? Identities and Feminist Epistemology." *(En)Gendering Knowledge: Feminists in Academe.* Ed. Joan Hartman and Ellen Messer-Davidow. Knoxville, TN: U of Tennessee P, 1991. 100–15.

———. *Whose Science? Whose Knowledge? Thinking from Women's Lives.* Ithaca: Cornell UP, 1991.

Heath, Shirley Brice. *Ways with Words: Language, Life, and Work in Communities and Classrooms.* New York: Cambridge UP, 1983.

Hoagland, Sarah Lucia. "Some Thoughts about 'Caring'." *Feminist Ethics.* Ed. Claudia Card. Lawrence: UP of Kansas, 1991. 246–63.

hooks, bell. "Feminist Politicization: A Comment." *Talking Back: Thinking Feminist, Thinking Black.* Boston: South End P, 1985. 105–11.

———. "Choosing the Margin as a Space of Radical Openness." *Yearning: Race, Gender, and Cultural Politics.* Boston: South End P, 1990. 145–54.

Houston, Barbara. "Rescuing Womanly Virtues: Some Dangers of Moral Reclamation." *Science, Morality, and Feminist Theory.* Ed. Marsha Hanen and Kai Nielsen. Calgary: U of Calgary P, 1987. 237–62.

Johnson, Cheryl L. "Participatory Rhetoric and the Teacher as Racial/Gendered Subject." *College English* 56 (1994): 409–19.

Keller, Evelyn Fox. "Dynamic Objectivity: Love, Power, and Knowledge." *Reflections on Gender and Science.* New Haven: Yale UP, 1985. 115–26.

Kirsch, Gesa, E. *Women Writing the Academy: Audience, Authority, and Transformation.* Carbondale: Southern Illinois UP, 1993.

Kraemer, Don J. "Gender and the Autobiographical Essay: A Critical Extension of the Research." *College Composition and Communication* 43 (1992): 323–39.

Lather, Patti. *Getting Smart: Feminist Research and Pedagogy With/In the Postmodern.* New York: Routledge, 1991.

McCarthy, Lucille Parkinson, and Stephen M. Fishman. "A Text for Many Voices: Representing Diversity in Reports of Naturalistic Research." *Ethics and Representation in Qualitative Studies of Literacy.* Ed. Peter Mortensen and Gesa E. Kirsch. Urbana, IL: National Council of Teachers of English, 1996. 155–76.

Miller, Richard E. "Fault Lines in the Contact Zone." *College English* 56 (1994): 389–408.

Minh-ha, Trinh T. *Women, Native, Other: Writing Postcoloniality and Feminism.* Bloomington: Indiana UP, 1989.

Mortensen, Peter, and Gesa Kirsch. "On Authority in the Study of Writing." *College Composition and Communication* 44 (1993): 556–72.

Nielsen, Joyce McCarl, ed. *Feminist Research Methods: Exemplary Readings in the Social Sciences.* San Francisco: Westview, 1990.

Noddings, Nel. *Caring: A Feminine Approach to Ethics and Moral Education.* Berkeley: U of California P, 1984.

Oakley, Ann. "Interviewing Women: A Contradiction in Terms?" *Doing Feminist Research.* Ed. Helen Roberts. New York: Routledge, 1981. 30–61.

Patai, Daphne. "U.S. Academics and Third World Women: Is Ethical Research Possible?" *Women's Words: The Feminist Practice of Oral History.* Ed. Sherna Gluck and Daphne Patai. New York: Routledge, 1991. 137–53.

Peaden, Catherine Hobbs. Rev. of *Gender Issues in the Teaching of English*. Ed. Nancy McCracken and Bruce Appleby. *Journal of Advanced Composition* 13 (1993): 260–63.

Pratt, Minnie Bruce. "Identity: Skin Blood Heart." *Yours in Struggle: Three Feminist Perspectives on Anti-Semitism and Racism*. Ed. Elly Bulkin, Minnie Bruce Pratt, and Barbara Smith. Ithaca, NY: Long Haul P, 1984. 11–63.

Punch, Maurice. "Politics and Ethics in Qualitative Research." *Handbook of Qualitative Research*. Ed. Norman Denzin and Yvonna Lincoln. Thousand Oaks, CA: Sage, 1994. 83–97.

Reinharz, Shulamit. *Feminist Methods in Social Research*. New York: Oxford UP, 1992.

Rich, Adrienne. "Notes on a Politics of Location." *Blood, Bread, and Poetry*. New York: Norton, 1989. 210–31.

Riddell, Sheila. "Exploiting the Exploited? The Ethics of Feminist Educational Research." *The Ethics of Educational Research*. Ed. Robert Burgess. New York: Falmer, 1989. 77–99.

Ritchie, Joy S. "Confronting the Essential Problem: Reconnecting Feminist Theory and Pedagogy." *Journal of Advanced Composition* 10 (1990): 249–71.

Ritchie, Joy S., Manjit Kaur, and Bee Tin Choo Meyer. "Women Students' Autobiographical Writing: The Rhetoric of Discovery and Defiance." *Situated Stories: Valuing Diversity in Composition Research*. Ed. Emily Decker and Kathleen Mary Geissler. Portsmouth, NH: Boynton/Cook Heinemann, 1998. 173–89.

Schweickart, Patrocinio. "In Defense of Femininity: Commentary on Sandra Bartky's Femininity and Domination." *Hypatia* 8 (1993): 178–91.

Smith, Sidonie. "Who's Talking/Who's Talking Back? The Subject of Personal Narrative." *Signs: Journal of Women in Culture and Society* 18 (1993): 392–407.

Stacey, Judith. "Can There Be a Feminist Ethnography?" *Women's Words: The Feminist Practice of Oral History*. Ed. Sherna Gluck and Daphne Patai. New York: Routledge, 1991. 111–19.

Tronto, Joan. "Beyond Gender Difference to a Theory of Care." *Signs: Journal of Women in Culture and Society* 12 (1987): 644–63.

_____. *Moral Boundaries: A Political Argument for an Ethic of Care*. New York: Routledge, 1993.

Williams, Patricia J. *The Alchemy of Race and Rights*. Boston: Harvard UP, 1991.

Wilson, David E., and Joy S. Ritchie. "Resistance, Revision, and Representation: Narrative in Teacher Education." *English Education* 18 (1994): 177–88.

Young, Iris Marion. *Justice and the Politics of Difference*. Princeton: Princeton UP, 1990.

Acknowledgments: We wish to thank colleagues, friends, and CCC reviewers for their comments and encouragement as we developed this essay: Lil Brannon, Robert Brooke, Gregory Clark, Lisa Ede, Elizabeth Flynn, Min-Zhan Lu, and Kate Ronald.

The Public Intellectual, Service Learning, and Activist Research

Ellen Cushman

While I support the good intentions of those who have recently proposed definitions of the public intellectual, I find these definitions problematic in their narrow delineation of the word "public"—they focus on a "public" consisting of middle and upper class policy makers, administrators, and professionals, and, in doing so, omit an important site for uniting knowledge-making and political action: the local community. Canvassing the letters submitted to the October 1997 *PMLA* forum on intellectual work in the twenty-first century, one notices numerous tensions regarding the larger public role of the intellectual:

> New and old intellectuals in the twenty-first century need to try to answer such questions as: "What do people(s) want?" and "What is the meaning of the political?" (Alina Clej; Forum 1123)

> In the next century, the intellectual must be willing to take more risks by choosing exile from confining institutional, theoretical, and discursive formations. (Lawrence Kritzman 1124)

> American intellectuals appear to have entered a period of non-engagement, cherishing their autonomy over engagement and retreating into the ivory tower. (Patrick Saveau 1127)

> If there is a task ahead for the kind of intellectual I have in mind, it lies in the attempt to forge a more secure link between the love of art and human decency. (Steven Greenblatt 1131)

Reprinted from *College English* 61.3 (January 1999): 328–36. Used with permission.

[The modern intellectual's] goal would be to enact in one's research an informed concern with specific questions of public value and policy. (Dominick Lacapra 1134)

A postoccidental intellectual [is] able to think at the intersection of the colonial languages of scholarship and the myriad languages subalternized and banned from cultures of scholarship through five hundred years of colonialism. (Walter Mignolo 1140)

Taken together, these statements indicate a growing pressure for intellectuals to make knowledge that speaks directly to political issues outside of academe's safety zones. This urgency comes in part from administrators and legislators who demand accountability, but it also comes from academics who have grown weary of isolation and specialization and who hope their work might have import for audiences beyond the initiated few. They wonder if knowledge-making can take risks while both cultivating aesthetics and leading to political action. Above all, these quotations reveal the nagging suspicion that academics have yet to realize their full potential in contributing to a more just social order. I believe public intellectuals can indeed contribute to a more just social order, but to do so they have to understand "public" in the broadest sense of the word.

The kind of public intellectuals I have in mind combine their research, teaching, and service efforts in order to address social issues important to community members in under-served neighborhoods. You know these neighborhoods: they're the ones often located close by universities, just beyond the walls and gates, or down the hill, or over the bridge, or past the tracks. The public in these communities isn't usually the one scholars have in mind when they try to define the roles of "public" intellectuals. For example, Pierre Bourdieu recognizes that the intellectual has dual and dueling agendas: "on the one hand, he [*sic*] must belong to an autonomous intellectual world; . . . on the other hand, he must invest the competence and authority he has acquired in the intellectual field in a political action" ("Fourth Lecture" 656). Yet Bourdieu advocates only one kind of political action: "the first objective of intellectuals should be to work collectively in defense of their specific interests and of the means necessary for protecting their own autonomy" (660). Granted, academics must have the secure position that autonomy (typically gained through tenure) provides if the knowledge they make is to be protected from censorship. Yes, academics need to defend their positions, particularly in this socio-economic climate where big business ethics of accountability, total quality management, downsizing, and overuse of part-time labor conspire to erode academics' security within the university. However, the fight for our own autonomy is a limited and self-serving form of political action addressed only to an elite "public" of decision-makers.

Another type of public intellectual, in the limited sense of the word *public*, believes in protecting scholarly autonomy through popularizing intellectual work. Here's Michael Bérubé on this kind of public intellectual: "the future of our ability to produce new knowledges for and about ordinary people—and the availability of education *to* ordinary people—may well depend on how effectively we can . . . make our work intelligible to nonacademics—who then, we hope, will be able to recognize far-right rant about academe for what it is" (176). Going public, turning to mass media, dressing our work in plain garb may help preserve autonomy, may even get intellectuals a moment or two in the media spotlight, but how will this help individuals who have no home, not enough food, or no access to good education? Popularizing scholarship may help solve problems on academe's front lines, but such action does not seem to do democracy any great favors. Popularizing suggests that public intellectuals simply translate their thinking into less specialized terms, then publish in the *New Yorker* or *Academe*. Yet publishing to a greater number of elite audiences works more to bolster our own positions in academe than it does to widen the scope of our civic duties as intellectuals.

Bourdieu and Bérubé belong to the modern ranks of public intellectuals, among whom I might include such currently prominent figures as Henry Louis Gates, Jr., and Stanley Fish. They all share an implied goal of affecting policy and decision-making, and they reach this goal by using their positions of prestige as well as multiple forms of media (newspapers, radio, and television) in order to influence a public beyond the academy, though this public will usually be limited to the educated upper echelons of society. In their dealings with this public, moreover, they typically remain scholars and teachers, offering their superior knowledge to the unenlightened.

When public intellectuals not only reach outside the university, but actually *interact* with the public beyond its walls, they overcome the ivory tower isolation that marks so much current intellectual work. They create knowledge with those whom the knowledge serves. Dovetailing the traditionally separate duties of research, teaching, and service, public intellectuals can use the privilege of their positions to forward the goals of both students and local community members. In doing so, they extend access to the university to a wider community. Academics can reach these goals in two ways: service learning and activist research.

SERVICE LEARNING

To enact citizenship in the larger sense, and to unify the locations of research, teaching, and service, the public intellectual can begin by developing service learning or outreach courses. Service learning asks students (both graduate and undergraduate) to test the merit of what they learn in the university classroom against their experiences as volunteers at local sites such as philanthropic agencies, primary and secondary schools, churches, old-age homes, half-way houses, and shelters. When students enter communities as participant observers, they "begin not as teachers, but as learners in a community setting where the goals and purposes of a 'service' effort are not established beforehand" (Schutz and Gere 145). Students enter the community in a sincere effort to both engage in and observe language use that helps address the topics that are important to community members. When activist fieldwork is a cornerstone of the course, students and community residents can develop reciprocal and dialogic relations with each other; their relationship is a mutually beneficial give-and-take one.

As participant observers, students take fieldnotes that reflect on their experiences with community members and how these experiences relate to the set of readings chosen by the professor. These fieldnotes serve a twofold purpose. First, they offer students a ready supply of examples to analyze in their essays, and second, they become potential source material for the professor. The professors' own notes, video and audio tape recordings, evaluations from the public service organization or area residents, and other literacy artifacts constitute a rich set of materials for knowledge-making. Since the professors also volunteer, teach, and administer the service learning course, they have first-hand familiarity with the important social issues and programmatic needs at the local level, and they tailor the curriculum to fit these. Thus, when activist methods are employed, knowledge-making in outreach courses happens *with* the individuals served. The course must respond to the immediate concerns and longstanding problems of the area in order to remain viable.

In their most limited sense, service learning courses unite in a single mission the traditionally separate duties of research, teaching, and service.

The research contributes

- ♦ to teaching by informing a curriculum that responds to both students' and community members' needs, and
- ♦ to service by indicating emerging problems in the community which the students and curriculum address.

The teaching contributes

- ♦ to research by generating fieldnotes, papers, taped interactions and other materials, and
- ♦ to service by facilitating the community organization's programmatic goals with the volunteer work.

The service contributes

- ♦ to research by addressing political and social issues salient in every-day lived struggles, and
- ♦ to teaching by offering students and professors avenues for testing the utility of previous scholarship in light of community members' daily lives and cultural values.

Because service learning includes an outreach component, the knowledge generated together by the area residents, students, and the professor is exoteric (as opposed to esoteric) and is made in interaction (as opposed to isolation).

Among composition and rhetoric scholars, Bruce Herzberg, Linda Flower, and Aaron Schutz and Anne Ruggles Gere, to name a few, have created community literacy projects which include service learning. Joan Schine has recently discussed elementary and secondary programs in service learning, and Barbara Jacoby addresses the practical and political aspects of developing outreach courses at the university level. Although scholars have begun to develop these outreach initiatives, few have offered a methodology that integrates the civic-minded mission of service learning with the politics of research in local settings.

ACTIVIST RESEARCH

One limitation of service learning courses can be students' perception of themselves as imparting to the poor and undereducated their greater knowledge and skills. Instructors in the service learning course that Anne Ruggles Gere and her colleagues developed noted that "their students often entered seeing themselves as 'liberal saviors,' and that the structure of tutoring had the potential to enhance the students' vision of this 'savior' role" (Schutz and Gere 133). Indeed, if the university representatives understand themselves as coming to the rescue of community residents, students will enact this missionary ideology in their tutoring. Service learning courses can avoid this liberal do-gooder stance when they employ activist research methodologies.

Activist research combines postmodern ethnographic techniques with notions of reciprocity and dialogue to insure reciprocal and mutually beneficial relations among scholars and those with whom knowledge is made. Since a central goal of outreach courses is to make knowledge *with* individuals, scholars need a methodology that avoids the traditional top-down approaches to ethnographic research: "The Bororos of Brazil sink slowly into their collective death, and Lévi-Strauss takes his seat in the French Academy. Even if this injustice disturbs him, the facts remain unchanged. This story is ours as much as his. In this one respect, . . . the intellectuals are still borne on the backs of the common people" (de Certeau 25). Traditional forms of ethnographic fieldwork yield more gains for the intellectual than the community residents. On the other hand, activist ethnographic research insures that, at every level of the ethnographic enterprise—from data collection through interpretation to write-up—the researcher and participants engage in openly negotiated, reciprocal, mutually beneficial relations.

Theories of praxis can be united with notions of emancipatory pedagogy in an effort to create a theoretical framework for activist methodology. Scholars who advocate praxis research find the traditional anthropological method of participant observation unsatisfactory because it has the potential to reproduce an oppressive relationship between the researcher and those studied (Oakley; Lather; Bleich; Porter and Sullivan). Instead of emphasizing observation, research as praxis demands that we actively participate in the community under study (Johannsen; for a thoughtful exploration of the connections between critical ethnography and critical pedagogy, see Lu and Horner). Applied anthropology provides theoretical models for how praxis—loosely definable as ethical action to facilitate social change—enters into the research paradigm, but many scholars still need to do the work of intervention, particularly at the community level.

Praxis research can take emancipatory pedagogy as its model for methods of intervention, since notions of emancipatory pedagogy work with the same types of theoretical underpinnings. Paulo Freire's *Pedagogy of the Oppressed* exemplifies the pragmatic concerns of politically involved teaching aimed at emancipating students. His work teaching illiterate peasants in Latin America has been adapted to American educational needs in schooling institutions (Apple and Weis; Giroux; Luke and Gore; Lankshear and McLaren). Emancipatory teaching can only go so far in instantiating activist research, though, because teachers often apply liberating teaching only in the classroom, and they are hard pressed to create solidarity and dialogue within the institutionalized social structure of American schools. In order to adapt Freire's pedagogy to the United States, we must also practice it outside the academy, where we can often more easily create solidarity. In a conversation with Donaldo Macedo, Freire says: "it is impossible to export pedagogical practices without re-inventing them. Please, tell your fellow American educators not to import me. Ask them to recreate and rewrite my ideas" (Macedo xiv). Our revisions of his pedagogy can be more fully expanded if we move out of the institutionalized setting of classrooms and into our communities. In this way, liberatory teaching can be brought together with praxis research to create the activist research useful to service learning.

Although I have conducted a three-and-a-half year long ethnography of literacy in an inner city (Cushman), Spring 1998 offered me the first opportunity to bridge activist research and service learning through a course called "Social Issues of Literacy." The course links Berkeley undergraduates with the Coronado YMCA in Richmond, a place residents of the East Bay call "the forgotten inner city." Undergraduates read scholarship on literacy, volunteer at the YMCA, write fieldnotes, and then integrate theory and data in case studies. The course has met with initial success in three ways.

First, students immediately saw the tight integration of literacy theory and practice. Their essays revealed careful attention to the scholarship and some rigor in challenging the limitations of these readings against their own observations. One student's paper noted that Scribner and Cole's famous work on Vai literacy showed their limited access to Vai females' literacy practices. Her paper then illustrated two interactions where she noticed how girls were excluded by the boys during storytelling, playing, and writing. She considered methods of participant observation that might invite more of the girls to engage in these activities. At the same time, she conducted informal interviews with the YMCA members in order to understand better how their values for oral and literate language shifted along gender lines. She did this with an eye toward filling gaps in knowledge that she saw in the scholarship on literacy that we read in class.

Second, the outreach course has filled a very real need for the YMCA staff. While this particular YMCA had numerous programs, including African dance, sports, teen pregnancy prevention, and scouting, they needed adults to engage youths in language use that would promote their reading and writing—without reproducing a school atmosphere. As one supervisor told me, "if the undergraduates come in here with too much school-like structure, they could turn the kids off to the reading and writing that they'll need to get ahead in school. So let's create a flexible structure for activities." Her point was subtle; area children hold schoolwork in low esteem, but the adults value the reading and writing needed to succeed in education.

With the supervisor's goals in mind, the undergraduates and I ask the YMCA members what kinds of activities they would like to do and offer a broad range of reading, writing, and artistic events in which they can engage. One ongoing literacy event centers around the creation of personal journals. Shawn, a nine-year-old, told me he wanted his "own journal here [at the YMCA] where I can keep all my stories and things." Together with the undergraduates, the children have produced journals with decorated covers bound with staples or yarn. Inside the journals, they keep their stories, math homework, spelling words, drawings, and letters to the undergraduates and myself. Leafing through a set of completed journals, the YMCA supervisor noted that the children "don't even realize that all the art, math, and writing they're doing in these journals will help them with their schoolwork." At the intersection where university representatives and community members meet, these journals offer a brief illustration of the way in which public intellectuals and community members can work together to identify and ameliorate local-level social issues. In this case, we together found ways to engage in reading and writing that would bridge a problematic split in generational values attached to literacy.

Finally, "Social Issues of Literacy" has met with some success in terms of research: the course has generated numerous literacy artifacts and events which could potentially serve as data for an extended study of community literacy. In exchange for the hours I have invested in curriculum development, site coordination, grant writing, and local research, I have the immediate reward of writing this paper. Thus, at least the initial results indicate that everyone seems to benefit from the service learning and activist research in this project.

However, even with examples of outreach and activist research like this, literary scholars may be hard pressed to see their intellectual work as amenable to service learning courses. To put a finer point on it, can outreach courses help forge a more secure link "between the love of art and human decency" (as Greenblatt put it in the *PMLA* forum), between intellectual work which cultivates aesthetics and work which speaks to common, lived conditions of struggle in the face of vast and deepening social inequalities? If public intellectuals hope to find and generate overlaps between aesthetics and politics, they need to first understand that what they count as art or political choices does not necessarily match what community members count as art or political choices. Because university representatives tend to esteem their own brand of knowledge more than popular forms of knowledge, they deepen the schism between universities and communities. Bourdieu described well the production of legitimate (read specialized, publishable, esoteric, academic) language, which gains material, cultural and symbolic capital by implicitly devaluing nonstandard (read colloquial, vernacular, common, vulgar) language. The educational system, particularly higher education, "contributes significantly to constituting the dominated uses of language as such by consecrating the dominant use as the only legitimate one" through "the devaluation of the common language which results from the very existence of a literary language" (*Language* 60–61). How can public intellectuals link the love of art and human decency if we continue to value university-based knowledge and language more than community-based knowledge and language? Unless the love of art and human decency, as they manifest themselves in university culture, justify themselves against local cultural value systems, academic knowledge-making will remain esoteric, seemingly inapplicable, remote, and elitist.

Public intellectuals challenge the value system of academe by starting with the assumption that all language use and ways of knowing are valuable and worthy of respect. To enact this principle, service learning offers meeting places for community and university values, language, and knowledge to become mutually informative and sustaining, places where greater numbers of people have a say in how knowledge is made, places where area residents, students, and faculty explore works of art, literature, and film to find ways in which these works still resonate with meaning and inform everyday lived struggles. Service learning "mak[es] rhetoric into a social praxis . . . assigning students to effective agency in the ongoing struggle of history" (France 608). Public intellectuals can use service learning as a means to collapse harmful dichotomies that traditional university knowledge espouses: literary/vernacular; high culture/low culture; literature/literacy; objective/subjective; expert/novice. Because these dualities place faculty members in a presumably higher social position, they distance academics from those they hope their knowledge serves—from those their knowledge must serve.

Public intellectuals can use their service, teaching, and research for the benefit of those inside and outside the university. Their knowledge, created with students and community members, can have political implications in contexts beyond the university. Their positions as faculty members can have readily apparent accountability, and their intellectual work can have highly visible impact. In the end, public intellectuals can enact the kind of civic-minded knowledge-making that engages broad audiences in pressing social issues.

WORKS CITED

Apple, Michael, and Lois Weis, eds. *Ideology and Practice in Schooling*. Philadelphia: Temple UP, 1983.

Bérubé, Michael. *Public Access: Literary Theory and American Cultural Politics*. London: Verso, 1994.

Bleich, David. "Ethnography and the Study of Literacy: Prospects for Socially Generous Research." *Into the Field: Sites of Composition Studies*. Ed. Anne Ruggles Gere. New York: MLA, 1993. 176–92.

Bourdieu, Pierre. "Fourth Lecture. Universal Corporatism: The Role of Intellectuals in the Modern World." *Poetics Today* 12.4 (1991): 655–69.

———. *Language and Symbolic Power*. Cambridge: Harvard UP, 1991.

Cushman, Ellen. *The Struggle and the Tools: Oral and Literate Strategies in an Inner City Community*. Albany: SUNY P, 1998.

de Certeau, Michel. *The Practice of Everyday Life*. Berkeley: U of California P, 1984.

Flower, Linda. *The Construction of Negotiated Meaning*. Carbondale: Southern Illinois UP, 1994.

Forum. *PMLA* 112.5 (October 1997): 1121–41.

France, Alan. "Assigning Places: The Function of Introductory Composition as a Cultural Discourse." *College English* 55.6 (1993): 593–609.

Giroux, Henry. *Ideology, Culture, and the Process of Schooling*. Philadelphia: Temple UP, 1981.

Herzberg, Bruce. "Community Service and Critical Teaching." *College Composition and Communication* 45.3 (Oct. 1994): 307–19.

Jacoby, Barbara. *Service-Learning in Higher Education*. San Francisco: Jossey-Bass, 1996.

Johannsen, Agneta. "Applied Anthropology and Post Modernist Ethnography." *Human Organization*. 50.1 (1992): 71–81.

Lankshear, Colin, and Peter McLaren, eds. *Critical Literacy: Politics, Praxis, and the Postmodern*. Albany: SUNY P, 1993.

Lather, Patti. "Research as Praxis." *Harvard Education Review* 56 (1992): 257–77.

Lu, Min-Zhan, and Bruce Horner. "The Problematic of Experience: Redefining Critical Work in Ethnography and Pedagogy." *College English* 60.3 (March 1998): 257–77.

Luke, Carmen, and Jennifer Gore. *Feminism and Critical Pedagogy*. New York: Routledge, 1992.

Macedo, Donaldo. *Literacies of Power: What Americans Are Not Allowed to Know*. Boulder: Westview P, 1994.

Oakley, Anne. "Interviewing Women: A Contradiction in Terms." *Doing Feminist Research*. London: Routledge, 1981. 30–62.

Schine, Joan. *Service Learning*. Chicago: NSSE/U of Chicago P, 1997.

Schutz, Aaron, and Anne Ruggles Gere. "Service Learning and English Studies: Rethinking 'Public' Service." *College English* 60.2 (1998): 129–49.

Sullivan, Pat, and James Porter. *Opening Spaces: Writing Technologies and Critical Research Practices*. Greenwich, CT: Ablex, 1997.

SECTION FOUR

Who We Are, Who We Teach, How We Teach

- "Inventing the University" David Bartholomae
- "When the First Voice You Hear Is Not Your Own" Jacqueline Jones Royster
- "*Memoria* Is a Friend of Ours: On the Discourse of Color" Victor Villanueva
- "Composing as a Woman" Elizabeth A. Flynn
- "Feminism in Composition: Inclusion, Metonymy, and Disruption" Joy Ritchie and Kathleen Boardman
- "Queer: An Impossible Subject for Composition" Jonathan Alexander and Jacqueline Rhodes
- "Rhetorical Sovereignty: What Do American Indians Want from Writing?" Scott Richard Lyons
- "The Myth of Linguistic Homogeneity in U.S. College Composition" Paul Kei Matsuda
- "The Rhetoric of Translingualism" Keith Gilyard
- "How Do We Language So People Stop Killing Each Other, or What Do We Do about White Language Supremacy?" Asao B. Inoue
- "Avoiding the Difference Fixation: Identity Categories, Markers of Difference, and the Teaching of Writing" Stephanie L. Kerschbaum

Once we claim that all knowledge is socially constructed, so that times and places and cultures overlap and intermingle, we are compelled to articulate those times and places and cultures. What is the academic discourse community? Is it as homogeneous as it appears? And if it is, what does that

411

suggest—that there are cultures that are not part of, or at least not recognized by, the academic community? Who comprises the academic community? Who are its students? Each question generates another.

The first answer says, "Let's hear from the members of the community, its teachers and its students." The essay form returns to a central place in the curriculum, narrative discourse, the autobiographical. There was precedent. In the 1930s, Fred Newton Scott of the University of Michigan advocated a writing instruction consisting of the relation between personal experience and the external world, an individual within society, a matter of civic responsibility. Scott's theory would regain popularity in the 1980s, though the curriculum would be associated with the Brazilian pedagogical theorist Paulo Freire rather than Scott, insofar as Freire adds an overtly political impetus to literacy and to writing from what one knows experientially.

When in the early 1970s, the City University of New York opened its doors to any high school graduate wanting admission, the social and the political joined the discussion on the value of narrative and the value of more conventional forms of academic discourse. With open admissions the colleges of the CUNY system were besieged by scores of students who would not have been able to attend college under older admissions policies. These were students—mainly from among the poor and mainly people of color—who believed themselves college material. And their college teachers agreed that these students were otherwise bright—except that the students' reading and writing abilities were so significantly lower than what would be necessary for success in college that, as we have seen, many came to believe that the students were victims of some sort of cognitive shortcoming.

The colleges were baffled. A new range of research was developed to confront and assist these "new" students, nontraditional students, remedial, developmental students. Finally, Mina Shaughnessy coins the term "basic writers," and in the first truly empathetic research work on basic writers, she looks to patterns of error in these students' writing, not cognitive dysfunction. This takes shape as *Errors and Expectations* (New York: Oxford UP, 1977).

But for all its sympathy, there are those who would go a step further, would try to understand the social processes that could relegate such a large number to the trouble-heap, a large number with two essential qualities in common: being poor and not being from the racial or ethnic majority. And in trying to understand, this newer line of scholarship tries to circumvent the reproduction of a school system that has traditionally failed to educate women, the poor, the disabled, or people of color at the same grade of efficiency as others. This gets complicated as rhetorical theory looks to how language is not just the conveyor of knowledge; language is the way knowledge becomes known.

Women show a way. They assert their role within the society at large and within the academy. The central role of women in composition studies makes feminist issues unignorable, with women making up the greater portion of the teaching force, with women playing key roles in developing contemporary composition, with figures like Janet Emig, Mina Shaughnessy, Andrea Lunsford, to name too few. And given American feminism's turn to the autobiographical in its popular and its academic writing, composition's turn to narrative receives further reinforcement.

Others follow suit. In some sense, Richard Rodriguez's *Hunger of Memory* (New York: Bantam, 1983) opens the door, as he writes of his experiences in acquiring abilities in English literacy, the child of Mexican immigrants who becomes a doctoral candidate in British literature. Gloria Anzaldúa publishes *Borderlands/La Frontera* in 1987 (San Francisco: Aunt Lute), crossing ancient native languages as well as Spanish and English, also exploring matters of sexuality as no less important than heritage. Mike Rose, already a known figure in composition studies, writes in *Lives on the Boundary* (New York: Penguin, 1990) of his experiences as a working-class remedial student who eventually succeeds, thanks to some wonderful teachers. A year after Mike Rose's book, Keith Gilyard's *Voices of the Self* (Detroit: Wayne State UP, 1991) is released, the story of an African American growing up in New York. His is a story in multiple genres—autobiography and linguistic analysis of code switching in alternating chapters. Two years later, Victor Villanueva publishes *Bootstraps* (Urbana: NCTE, 1993), a mix of several genres including autobiography, now firmly located within rhetoric and composition studies. In 1994 bell hooks comes out with *Teaching to Transgress* (New York: Routledge).

But what of other "markers of difference," to use the term coined by Stephanie Kerschbaum? What of those whose primary language is not English yet find themselves in purportedly English-only writing classes? Or those whose cultural ways of being are colored by their sexuality, their gender identity, their (dis)ability or neurodiversity? And then again, as Keith Gilyard points out as we explore variations on the prefix "trans" (meaning "on the other side," an interesting prefix in its own right) how do we remain conscious of collectivities rather than the uniqueness of individuals, linguistically matters of idiolect? What began as concerns with "voice," thanks to those like Ken Macrorie, Walker Gibson, Donald Murray, and especially Peter Elbow, emerge in the writings of women, people of color, the multilingual (or "other-lingualed"), queer, and the disabled, the students we teach, the people we are.

Inventing the University

DAVID BARTHOLOMAE

Education may well be, as of right, the instrument whereby every individual, in a society like our own, can gain access to any kind of discourse. But we well know that in its distribution, in what it permits and in what it prevents, it follows the well-trodden battle-lines of social conflict. Every educational system is a political means of maintaining or of modifying the appropriation of discourse, with the knowledge and the powers it carries with it.
> —*Michel Foucault,* The Discourse on Language

. . . the text is the form of the social relationships made visible, palpable, material.
> —*Basil B. Bernstein,* Codes, Modalities and the Process of Cultural Reproduction: A Model

I

Every time a student sits down to write for us, he has to invent the university for the occasion—invent the university, that is, or a branch of it, like history or anthropology or economics or English. The student has to learn to speak our language, to speak as we do, to try on the peculiar ways of knowing, selecting, evaluating, reporting, concluding, and arguing that define the discourse of our community. Or perhaps I should say the *various* discourses of our community, since it is in the nature of a liberal arts education that a student, after the first year or two, must learn to try on a variety of voices and interpretive schemes—to write, for example, as a literary critic one day and as an experimental psychologist the next; to work within fields where the rules governing the presentation of examples or the development of an argument are both distinct and, even to a professional, mysterious.

The student has to appropriate (or be appropriated by) a specialized discourse, and he has to do this as though he were easily and comfortably one with his audience, as though he were a member of the academy or an historian or an anthropologist or an economist; he has to invent the university by assembling and mimicking its language while finding some compromise between idiosyncrasy, a personal history, on the one hand, and the requirements of convention, the history of a discipline, on the other hand. He must learn to speak our language. Or he must dare to speak it or to carry off the bluff, since speaking and writing will most certainly be required long before the skill is "learned." And this, understandably, causes problems.

Let me look quickly at an example. Here is an essay written by a college freshman.

> In the past time I thought that an incident was creative was when I had to make a clay model of the earth, but not of the classical or your everyday model of the earth which consists of the two cores, the mantle and the crust. I thought of these things in a dimension of which it would be unique, but easy to comprehend. Of course, your materials to work with were basic and limited at the same time, but thought help to put this limit into a right attitude or frame of mind to work with the clay.
>
> In the beginning of the clay model, I had to research and learn the different dimensions of the earth (in magnitude, quantity, state of matter, etc.) After this, I learned how to put this into the clay and come up with something different than any other person in my class at the time. In my opinion, color coordination and shape was the key to my creativity of the clay model of the earth.
>
> Creativity is the venture of the mind at work with the mechanics relay to the limbs from the cranium, which stores and triggers this action. It can be a burst of energy released at a precise time a thought is being transmitted. This can cause a frenzy of the human body, but it depends on the characteristics of the individual and how they can relay the message clearly enough through mechanics of the body to us as an observer. Then we must determine if it is creative or a learned process varied by the individuals thought process. Creativity is indeed a tool which has to exist, or our world will not succeed into the future and progress like it should.

I am continually impressed by the patience and goodwill of our students. This student was writing a placement essay during freshman orientation. (The problem set to him was: "Describe a time when you did something you felt to be creative. Then, on the basis of the incident you have described, go on to draw some general conclusions about 'creativity.'") He knew that university faculty would be reading and evaluating his essay, and so he wrote for them.

In some ways it is a remarkable performance. He is trying on the discourse even though he doesn't have the knowledge that would make the discourse more than a routine, a set of conventional rituals and gestures. And he is doing this, I think, even though he *knows* he doesn't have the knowledge that would make the discourse more than a routine. He defines himself as a researcher working systematically, and not as a kid in a high school class: "I thought of these things in a dimension of . . ."; "I had to research and learn the different dimensions of the earth (in magnitude, quantity, state of matter, etc.)." He moves quickly into a specialized language (his approximation of our jargon) and draws both a general, textbook-like conclusion— "Creativity is the venture of the mind at work . . ."—and a resounding peroration—"Creativity is indeed a tool which has to exist, or our world will not succeed into the future and progress like it should." The writer has even picked up the rhythm of our prose with that last "indeed" and with the qualifications and the parenthetical expressions of the opening paragraphs. And through it all he speaks with an impressive air of authority

There is an elaborate but, I will argue, a necessary and enabling fiction at work here as the student dramatizes his experience in a "setting"—the setting required by the discourse—where he can speak to us as a companion, a fellow researcher. As I read the essay, there is only one moment when the fiction is broken, when we are addressed differently. The student says, "Of course, your materials to work with were basic and limited at the same time, but thought help to put this limit into a right attitude or frame of mind to work with the clay." At this point, I think, we become students and he the teacher giving us a lesson (as in, "You take your pencil in your right hand and put your paper in front of you"). This is however, one of the most characteristic slips of basic writers. (I use the term "basic writers" to refer to university students traditionally placed in remedial composition courses.) It is very hard for them to take on the role—the voice, the persona—of an authority whose authority is rooted in scholarship, analysis, or research. They slip, then, into a more immediately available and realizable voice of authority, the voice of a teacher giving a lesson or the voice of a parent lecturing at the dinner table. They offer advice or homilies rather than "academic" conclusions. There is a similar break in the final paragraph, where the conclusion that pushes for a definition ("Creativity is the venture of the mind at work with the mechanics relay to the limbs from the cranium") is replaced by a conclusion that speaks in the voice of an elder ("Creativity is indeed a tool which has to exist, or our world will not succeed into the future and progress like it should").

It is not uncommon, then, to find such breaks in the concluding sections of essays written by basic writers. Here is the concluding section of an essay written by a student about his work as a mechanic. He had been asked to generalize about work after reviewing an on-the-job experience or incident that "stuck in his mind" as somehow significant.

> How could two repairmen miss a leak? Lack of pride? No incentive? Lazy?
> I don't know.

At this point the writer is in a perfect position to speculate, to move from the problem to an analysis of the problem. Here is how the paragraph continues, however (and notice the change in pronoun reference).

> From this point on, I take *my* time, do it right, and don't let customers get under *your* skin. If they have a complaint, tell them to call your boss and he'll be more than glad to handle it. Most important, worry about yourself, and keep a clear eye on everyone, for there's always someone trying to take advantage of you, anytime and anyplace. (Emphasis added)

We get neither a technical discussion nor an "academic" discussion but a Lesson on Life.[1] This is the language he uses to address the general question, "How could two repairmen miss a leak?" The other brand of conclusion, the more academic one, would have required him to speak of his experience in our terms; it would, that is, have required a special vocabulary, a special system of presentation, and an interpretive scheme (or a set of commonplaces) he could have used to identify and talk about the mystery of human error. The writer certainly had access to the range of acceptable commonplaces for such an explanation: "lack of pride," "no incentive," "lazy." Each commonplace would dictate its own set of phrases, examples, and conclusions; and we, his teachers, would know how to write out each argument, just as we know how to write out more specialized arguments of our own. A "commonplace," then, is a culturally or institutionally authorized concept or statement that carries with it its own necessary elaboration. We all use commonplaces to orient ourselves in the world; they provide points of reference and a set of "prearticulated" explanations that are readily available to organize and interpret experience. The phrase, "lack of pride" carries with it its own account of the repairman's error, just as at another point in time a reference to "original sin" would have provided an explanation, or just as in certain university classrooms a reference to "alienation" would enable writers to continue and complete the discussion. While there is a way in which these terms are interchangeable, they are not all permissible: A student in a composition class would most likely be turned away from a discussion of original sin. Commonplaces are the "controlling ideas" of our composition textbooks, textbooks that not only insist on a set form for expository writing but a set view of public life.[2]

When the writer says, "I don't know," then, he is not saying that he has nothing to say. He is saying that he is not in a position to carry on this discussion. And so we are addressed as apprentices rather than as teachers or scholars. In order to speak as a person of status or privilege, the writer can either speak to us in our terms—in the privileged language of university discourse—or, in default (or in defiance) of that, he can speak to us as though we were children, offering us the wisdom of experience.

I think it is possible to say that the language of the "Clay Model" paper has come *through* the writer and not from the writer. The writer has located himself (more precisely, he has located the self that is represented by the "I" on the page) in a context that is finally beyond him, not his own and not available to his immediate procedures for inventing and arranging text. I would not, that is, call this essay an example of "writer-based" prose. I would not say that it is egocentric or that it represents the "interior monologue or a writer thinking and talking to himself" (Flower, 1981, p. 63). It is, rather, the record of a writer who has lost himself in the discourse of his readers. There is a context beyond the intended reader that is not the world but a way of talking about the world, a way of talking that determines the use of examples, the possible conclusions, acceptable commonplaces, and key words for an essay on the construction of a clay model of the earth. This writer has entered the discourse without successfully approximating it.

Linda Flower (1981) has argued that the difficulty inexperienced writers have with writing can be understood as a difficulty in negotiating the transition between "writer-based" and "reader-based" prose. Expert writers, in other words, can better imagine how a reader will respond to a text and can transform or restructure what they have to say around a goal shared with a reader. Teaching students to revise for readers, then, will better prepare them to write initially with a reader in mind. The success of this pedagogy depends on the degree to which a writer can imagine and conform to a reader's goals. The difficulty of this act of imagination and the burden of such conformity are so much at the heart of the problem that a teacher must pause and take stock before offering revision as a solution. A student like the one who wrote the "Clay Model" paper is not so much trapped in a private language as he is shut out from one of the privileged languages of public life, a language he is aware of but cannot control.

II

Our students, I've said, have to appropriate (or be appropriated by) a specialized discourse, and they have to do this as though they were easily or comfortably one with their audience. If you look at the situation this way, suddenly the problem of audience awareness becomes enormously complicated. One of the common assumptions of both composition research and composition teaching is that at some "stage" in the process of composing an essay a writer's ideas or his motives must be tailored to the needs and expectations of his audience. Writers have to "build bridges" between their point of view and the reader's. They have to anticipate and acknowledge the reader's assumptions and biases. They must begin with "common points of departure" before introducing new or controversial arguments. Here is what one of the most popular college textbooks says to students.

> Once you have your purpose clearly in mind, your next task is to define and analyze your audience. A sure sense of your audience—knowing who it is and what assumptions you can reasonably make about it—is crucial to the success of your rhetoric. (Hairston, 1978, p. 107)

It is difficult to imagine, however, how writers can have a purpose before they are located in a discourse, since it is the discourse with its projects and agendas that determines what writers can and will do. The writer who can successfully manipulate an audience (or, to use a less pointed language, the writer who can accommodate her motives to her reader's expectations) is a writer who can both imagine and write from a position of privilege. She must, that is, see herself within a privileged discourse, one that already includes and excludes groups of readers. She must be either equal to or more powerful than those she would address. The writing, then, must somehow transform the political and social relationships between students and teachers.

If my students are going to write for me by knowing who I am—and if this means more than knowing my prejudices, psyching me out—it means knowing what I know; it means having the knowledge of a professor of English. They have, then, to know what I know and how I know what I know (the interpretive schemes that define the way I would work out the problems I set for them); they have to learn to write what I would write or to offer up some approximation of that discourse. The problem of audience awareness, then, is a problem of power and finesse. It cannot be addressed, as it is in most classroom exercises, by giving students privilege and denying the situation of the classroom—usually, that is, by having students write to an outsider, someone excluded from their privileged circle: "Write about 'To His Coy Mistress,' not for your teacher but for the students in your class"; "Describe Pittsburgh to someone who has never been there"; "Explain to a high school senior how best to prepare for college"; "Describe baseball to an Eskimo." Exercises such as these allow students to imagine the needs and goals of a reader, and they bring those needs and goals forward as a dominant constraint in the construction of an essay. And they argue, implicitly, what is generally true about writing—that it is an act of aggression disguised as an act of charity. What these assignments fail to address is the central problem of academic writing, where a student must assume the right of speaking to someone who knows more about baseball or "To His Coy Mistress" than the student does, a reader for whom the general commonplaces and the readily available utterances about a subject are inadequate.

Linda Flower and John Hayes, in an often quoted article (1981), reported on a study of a protocol of an expert writer (an English teacher) writing about his job for readers of *Seventeen* magazine. The key moment for this writer, who seems to have been having trouble getting started, came when he decided that teenage girls read *Seventeen*; that some teenage girls like English because it is tidy ("some of them will have wrong reasons in that English is good because it's tidy—can be a neat tidy little girl"); that some don't like it because it is "prim" and that, "By God, I can change that notion for them." Flower and Hayes's conclusion is that this effort of "exploration and consolidation" gave the writer "a new, relatively complex, rhetorically sophisticated working goal, one which encompasses plans for topic, a persona, and the audience" (p. 383).[3]

Flower and Hayes give us a picture of a writer solving a problem, and the problem as they present it is a cognitive one. It is rooted in the way the writer's knowledge is represented in the writer's mind. The problem resides there, not in the nature of knowledge or in the nature of discourse but in a mental state prior to writing. It is possible, however, to see the problem as (perhaps simultaneously) a problem in the way subjects are located in a field of discourse.

Flower and Hayes divide up the composing process into three distinct activities: "planning or goal-setting," "translating," and "reviewing." The last of these, reviewing (which is further divided into two subprocesses, "evaluating" and "revising"), is particularly powerful, for as a writer continually generates new goals, plans, and text, he is engaging in a process of learning and discovery. Let me quote Flower and Hayes's conclusion at length.

> If one studies the process by which a writer uses a goal to generate ideas, then consolidates those ideas and uses them to revise or regenerate new, more complex goals, one can see this learning process in action. Furthermore, one sees why the process of revising and clarifying goals has such a broad effect, since it is through setting these new goals that the fruits of discovery come back to inform the continuing process of writing. In this instance, some of our most complex and imaginative acts can depend on the elegant simplicity of a few powerful thinking processes. We feel that a cognitive process explanation of discovery, toward which this theory is only a start, will have another special strength. By placing emphasis on the inventive power of the writer, who is able to explore ideas, to develop, act on, test, and regenerate his or her own goals, we are putting an important part of creativity where it belongs—in the hands of the working, thinking writer. (1981, p. 386)

While this conclusion is inspiring, the references to invention and creativity seem to refer to something other than an act of writing—if writing is, finally, words on a page. Flower and Hayes locate the act of writing solely within the mind of the writer. The act of writing, here, has a personal, cognitive history but not a history as a text, as a text that is made possible by prior texts. When located in the perspective afforded by prior texts, writing is seen to exist separate from the writer and his intentions; it is seen in the context of other articles in *Seventeen*, of all articles written for or about women, of all articles written about English teaching, and so on. Reading research has made it possible to say that these prior texts, or a reader's experience with these prior texts, have bearing on how the text is read. Intentions, then, are part of the history of the language itself. I am arguing that these prior texts determine not only how a text like the *Seventeen* article will be read but also how it will be written. Flower and Hayes show us what happens in the writer's mind but not what happens to the writer as his motives are located within our language, a language with its own requirements and agendas, a language that limits what we might say and that makes us write and sound, finally, also like someone else. If you think of other accounts of the composing process—and I'm thinking of accounts as diverse as Richard Rodriguez's *Hunger of Memory* (1983) and Edward Said's *Beginnings* (1975)—you get a very different account of what happens when private motive enters into public discourse, when a personal history becomes a public account. These accounts place the writer in a history that is not of the writer's own invention; and they are chronicles of loss, violence, and compromise.

It is one thing to see the *Seventeen* writer making and revising his plans for a topic, a persona, and an audience; it is another thing to talk about discovery, invention, and creativity. Whatever plans the writer had must finally have been located in language and, it is possible to argue, in a language that is persistently conventional and formulaic. We do not, after all, get to see the *Seventeen* article. We see only the elaborate mental procedures that accompanied the writing of the essay. We see a writer's plans for a persona; we don't see that persona in action. If writing is a process, it is also a product; and it is the product, and not the plan for writing, that locates a writer on the page, that locates him in a text and a style and the codes or conventions that make both of them readable.

Contemporary rhetorical theory has been concerned with the "codes" that constitute discourse (or specialized forms of discourse). These codes determine not only what might be said but also who might be speaking or reading. Barthes (1974), for example, has argued that the moment of writing, where private goals and plans become subject to a public language, is the moment when the writer becomes subject to a language he can neither command nor control. A text, he says, in being written passes through the codes that govern writing and becomes "de-originated," becomes a fragment of something that has always been *already* read, seen, done, experienced" (p. 21). Alongside a text we have always the presence of "off-stage voices," the oversound of all that has been said (e.g., about girls, about English). These voices, the presence of the "already written," stand in defiance of a writer's desire for originality and determine what might be said. A writer does not write (and this is Barthes's famous paradox) but is, himself, written by the languages available to him.

It is possible to see the writer of the *Seventeen* article solving his problem of where to begin by appropriating an available discourse. Perhaps what enabled that writer to write was the moment he located himself as a writer in a familiar field of stereotypes: Readers of *Seventeen* are teenage girls; teenage girls think of English (and English teachers) as "tidy" and "prim," and, "By God, I can change that notion for them." The moment of eureka was not simply a moment of breaking through a cognitive jumble in that individual writer's mind but a moment of breaking into a familiar and established territory—one with insiders and outsiders; one with set phrases, examples, and conclusions.

I'm not offering a criticism of the morals or manners of the teacher who wrote the *Seventeen* article. I think that all writers, in order to write, must imagine for themselves the privilege of being "insiders"—that is, the privilege both of being inside an established and powerful discourse and of being granted a special right to speak. But I think that right to speak is seldom conferred on us—on any of us, teachers or students—by virtue of the fact that we have invented or discovered an original idea. Leading students to believe that they are responsible for something new or original, unless they understand what those words mean with regard to writing, is a dangerous and counterproductive practice. We do have the right to expect students to be active and engaged, but that is a matter of continually and stylistically working against the inevitable presence of conventional language; it is not a matter of inventing a language that is new.

When a student is writing for a teacher, writing becomes more problematic than it was for the *Seventeen* writer (who was writing a version of the "Describe baseball to an Eskimo" exercise). The student, in effect, has to assume privilege without having any. And since students assume privilege by locating themselves within the discourse of a particular community— within a set of specifically acceptable gestures and commonplaces—learning, at least as it is defined in the liberal arts curriculum, becomes more a matter of imitation or parody than a matter of invention and discovery.

To argue that writing problems are also social and political problems is not to break faith with the enterprise of cognitive science. In a recent paper reviewing the tremendous range of research directed at identifying general cognitive skills, David Perkins (in press) has argued that "the higher the level of competence concerned," as in the case of adult learning, "the fewer *general* cognitive control strategies there are." There comes a point, that is, where "field-specific" or "domain-specific" schemata (what I have called "interpretive strategies") become more important than general problem-solving processes. Thinking, learning, writing—all these become bound to the context of a particular discourse. And Perkins concludes:

> Instruction in cognitive control strategies tends to be organized around problem-solving tasks. However, the isolated problem is a creature largely of the classroom. The nonstudent, whether operating in scholarly or more everyday contexts, is likely to find himself or herself involved in what might be called "projects"—which might be anything from writing a novel to designing a shoe to starting a business.

It is interesting to note that Perkins defines the classroom as the place of artificial tasks and, as a consequence, has to place scholarly projects outside the classroom, where they are carried out by the "nonstudent." It is true, I think, that education has failed to involve students in scholarly projects, projects that allow students to act as though they were colleagues in an academic enterprise. Much of the written work that students do is test-taking, report or summary—work that places them outside the official discourse of the academic community, where they are expected to admire and report on what we do, rather than inside that discourse, where they can do its work and participate in a common enterprise.[4] This, however, is a failure of teachers and curriculum designers, who speak of writing as a mode of learning but all too often represent writing as a "tool" to be used by an (hopefully) educated mind.

It could be said, then, that there is a bastard discourse peculiar to the writing most often required of students. Carl Bereiter and Marlene Scardamalia (in press) have written about this discourse (they call it "knowledge-telling"; students who are good at it have learned to cope with academic tasks by developing a "knowledge-telling strategy"), and they have argued that insistence on knowledge-telling discourse undermines educational efforts to extend the variety of discourse schemata available to students.[5] What they actually say is this:

> When we think of knowledge stored in memory we tend these days to think of it as situated in three-dimensional space, with vertical and horizontal connections between sites. Learning is thought to add not only new elements to memory but also new connections, and it is the richness and structure of these connections that would seem . . . to spell the difference between inert and usable knowledge. On this account, the knowledge-telling strategy is educationally faulty because it specifically avoids the forming of connections between previously separated knowledge sites.

It should be clear by now that when I think of "knowledge" I think of it as situated in the discourse that constitutes "knowledge" in a particular discourse community, rather than as situated in mental "knowledge sites." One can remember a discourse, just as one can remember an essay or the movement of a professor's lecture; but this discourse, in effect, also has a memory of its own, its own rich network of structures and connections beyond the deliberate control of any individual imagination.

There is, to be sure, an important distinction to be made between learning history, say, and learning to write as an historian. A student can learn to command and reproduce a set of names, dates, places, and canonical interpretations (to "tell" somebody else's knowledge); but this is not the same thing as learning to "think" (by learning to write) as an historian. The former requires efforts of memory; the latter requires a student to compose a text out of the texts that represent the primary materials of history and in accordance with the texts that define history as an act of report and interpretation.

Let me draw on an example from my own teaching. I don't expect my students to *be* literary critics when they write about *Bleak House*. If a literary critic is a person who wins publication in a professional journal (or if he or she is one who could), the students aren't critics. I do, however, expect my students to be, themselves, invented as literary critics by approximating the language of a literary critic writing about *Bleak House*. My students, then, don't invent the language of literary criticism (they don't, that is, act on their own) but they are, themselves, invented by it. Their papers don't begin with a moment of insight, a "by God" moment that is outside of language. They begin with a moment of appropriation, a moment when they can offer up a sentence that is not theirs as though it were their own. (I can remember when, as a graduate student, I would begin papers by sitting down to write literally in the voice—with the syntax and the key words—of the strongest teacher I had met.)

What I am saying about my students' essays is that they are approximate, not that they are wrong or invalid. They are evidence of a discourse that lies between what I might call the students' primary discourse (what the students might write about *Bleak House* were they not in my class or in any class, and were they not imagining that they were in my class or in any class—if you can imagine any student doing any such thing) and standard, official literary criticism (which is imaginable but impossible to find). The students' essays are evidence of a discourse that lies between these two hypothetical poles. The writing is limited as much by a student's ability to imagine "what might be said" as it is by cognitive control strategies.[6] The act of writing takes the student away from where he is and what he knows and allows him to imagine something else. The approximate discourse, therefore, is evidence of a change, a change that, because we are teachers, we call "development." What our beginning students need to learn is to extend themselves, by successive approximations, into the commonplaces, set phrases, rituals and gestures, habits of mind, tricks of persuasion, obligatory conclusions and necessary connections that determine the "what might be said" and constitute knowledge within the various branches of our academic community.[7]

Pat Bizzell is, I think, one of the most important scholars writing now on "basic writers" (and this is the common name we use for students who are refused unrestrained access to the academic community) and on the special characteristics of academic discourse. In a recent essay, "Cognition, Convention, and Certainty: What We Need to Know about Writing" (1982a), she looks at two schools of composition research and the way they represent the problems that writing poses for writers.[8] For one group, the "inner-directed theorists," the problems are internal, cognitive, rooted in the way the mind represents knowledge to itself. These researchers are concerned with discovering the "universal, fundamental structures of thought and language" and with developing pedagogies to teach or facilitate both basic, general cognitive skills and specific cognitive strategies, or heuristics, directed to serve more specialized needs. Of the second group, the "outer-directed theorists," she says that they are "more interested in the social processes whereby language-learning and thinking capacities are shaped and used in particular communities."

> The staple activity of outer-directed writing instruction will be analysis of the conventions of particular discourse communities. For example, a main focus of writing-across-the-curriculum programs is to demystify the conventions of the academic discourse community. (1982a, p. 218)

The essay offers a detailed analysis of the way the two theoretical camps can best serve the general enterprise of composition research and composition teaching. Its agenda, however, seems to be to counter the influence of the cognitivists and to provide bibliography and encouragement to those interested in the social dimension of language learning.

As far as basic writers are concerned, Bizzell argues that the cognitivists' failure to acknowledge the primary, shaping role of convention in the act of composing makes them "particularly insensitive to the problems of poor writers." She argues that some of those problems, like the problem of establishing and monitoring overall goals for a piece of writing, can be

> better understood in terms of the unfamiliarity with the academic discourse community, combined, perhaps, with such limited experience outside their native discourse communities that they are unaware that there is such a thing as a discourse community with conventions to be mastered. What is underdeveloped is their knowledge both of the ways experience is constituted and interpreted in the academic discourse community and of the fact that all discourse communities constitute and interpret experience. (1982a, p. 230)

One response to the problems of basic writers, then, would be to determine just what the community's conventions are, so that those conventions could be written out, "demystified" and taught in our classrooms. Teachers, as a result, could be more precise and helpful when they ask students to "think," "argue," "describe," or "define." Another response would be to examine the essays written by basic writers—their approximations of academic discourse—to determine more clearly where the problems lie. If we look at their writing, and if we look at it in the context of other student writing, we can better see the points of discord that arise when students try to write their way into the university.

The purpose of the remainder of this chapter will be to examine some of the most striking and characteristic of these problems as they are presented in the expository essays of first-year college students. I will be concerned, then, with university discourse in its most generalized form—as it is represented by introductory courses—and not with the special conventions required by advanced work in the various disciplines. And I will be concerned with the difficult, and often violent accommodations that occur when students locate themselves in a discourse that is not "naturally" or immediately theirs.

III

I have reviewed 500 essays written, as the "Clay Model" essay was, in response to a question used during one of our placement exams at the University of Pittsburgh: "Describe a time when you did something you felt to be creative. Then, on the basis of the incident you have described, go on to draw some general conclusions about "creativity." Some of the essays were written by basic writers (or, more properly, those essays led readers to identify the writers as basic writers); some were written by students who "passed" (who were granted immediate access to the community of writers at the university). As I read these essays, I was looking to determine the stylistic resources that enabled writers to locate themselves within an "academic" discourse. My bias as a reader should be clear by now. I was not looking to see how a writer might represent the skills demanded by a neutral language (a language whose key features were paragraphs, topic sentences, transitions, and the like—features of a clear and orderly mind). I was looking to see what happened when a writer entered into a language to locate himself (a textual self) and his subject; and I was looking to see how, once entered, that language made or unmade the writer.

Here is one essay. Its writer was classified as a basic writer and, since the essay is relatively free of sentence level errors, that decision must have been rooted in some perceived failure of the discourse itself.

> I am very interested in music, and I try to be creative in my interpretation of music. While in highschool, I was a member of a jazz ensemble. The members of the ensemble were given chances to improvise and be creative in various songs. I feel that this was a great experience for me, as well as the other members. I was proud to know that I could use my imagination and feelings to create music other than what was written.
>
> Creativity to me, means being free to express yourself in a way that is unique to you, not having to conform to certain rules and guidelines.

Music is only one of the many areas in which people are given opportunities to show their creativity. Sculpting, carving, building, art, and acting are just a few more areas where people can show their creativity.

Through my music I conveyed feelings and thoughts which were important to me. Music was my means of showing creativity. In whatever form creativity takes, whether it be music, art, or science, it is an important aspect of our lives because it enables us to be individuals.

Notice the key gesture in this essay, one that appears in all but a few of the essays I read. The student defines as his own that which is a commonplace. "Creativity, *to me*, means being free to express yourself in a way that is unique to you, not having to conform to certain rules and guidelines." This act of appropriation constitutes his authority; it constitutes his authority as a writer and not just as a musician (that is, as someone with a story to tell). There were many essays in the set that told only a story—where the writer established his presence as a musician or a skier or someone who painted designs on a van, but not as a person at a remove from that experience interpreting it, treating it as a metaphor for something else (creativity). Unless those stories were long, detailed, and very well told—unless the writer was doing more than saying, "I am a skier" or a musician or a van-painter—those writers were all given low ratings.

Notice also that the writer of the "Jazz" paper locates himself and his experience in relation to the commonplace (creativity is unique expression; it is not having to conform to rules or guidelines) regardless of whether the commonplace is true or not. Anyone who improvises "knows" that improvisation follows rules and guidelines. It is the power of the commonplace—its truth as a recognizable and, the writer believes, as a final statement—that justifies the example and completes the essay. The example, in other words, has value because it stands within the field of the commonplace.[9] It is not the occasion for what one might call an "objective" analysis or a "close" reading. It could also be said that the essay stops with the articulation of the commonplace. The following sections speak only to the power of that statement. The reference to "sculpting, carving, building, art, and acting" attest to the universality of the commonplace (and it attests the writer's nervousness with the status he has appropriated for himself—he is saying, "Now, I'm not the only one here who has done something unique"). The commonplace stands by itself. For this writer, it does not need to be elaborated. By virtue of having written it, he has completed the essay and established the contract by which we may be spoken to as equals: "In whatever form creativity takes, whether it be music, art, or science, it is an important aspect of *our* lives because it enables *us* to be individuals." (For me to break that contract,

429

to argue that *my* life is not represented in that essay, is one way for me to begin as a teacher with that student in that essay.)

All of the papers I read were built around one of three commonplaces: (1) creativity is self-expression, (2) creativity is doing something new or unique, and (3) creativity is using old things in new ways. These are clearly, then, key phrases from the storehouse of things to say about creativity. I've listed them in the order of the students' ratings: A student with the highest rating was more likely to use number three than number one, although each commonplace ran across the range of possible ratings. One could argue that some standard assertions are more powerful than others, but I think the ranking simply represents the power of assertions within our community of readers. Every student was able to offer up an experience that was meant as an example of "creativity"; the lowest range of writers, then, was not represented by students who could not imagine themselves as creative people.[10]

I said that the writer of the "Jazz" paper offered up a commonplace regardless of whether it was true or not; and this, I said, was an instance of the power of a commonplace to determine the meaning of an example. A commonplace determines a system of interpretation that can be used to "place" an example within a standard system of belief. You can see a similar process at work in this essay.

> During the football season, the team was supposed to wear the same type of cleats and the same type socks, I figured that I would change this a little by wearing my white shoes instead of black and to cover up the team socks with a pair of my own white ones. I thought that this looked better than what we were wearing, and I told a few of the other people on the team to change too. They agreed that it did look better and they changed there combination to go along with mine. After the game people came up to us and said that it looked very good the way we wore our socks, and they wanted to know why we changed from the rest of the team.
>
> I feel that creativity comes from when a person lets his imagination come up with ideas and he is not afraid to express them. Once you create something to do it will be original and unique because it came about from your own imagination and if any one else tries to copy it, it won't be the same because you thought of it first from your own ideas.

This is not an elegant paper, but it seems seamless, tidy. If the paper on the clay model of the earth showed an ill fit between the writer and his project, here the discourse seems natural, smooth. You could reproduce this paper and hand it out to a class, and it would take a lot of prompting before the students sensed something fishy and one of the more aggressive ones said something like, "Sure he came up with the idea of wearing white shoes and white socks. Him and Billy 'White-Shoes' Johnson. Come on. He copied the very thing he said was his own idea, 'original and unique.' "

The "I" of this text—the "I" who "figured," "thought," and "felt"—is located in a conventional rhetoric of the self that turns imagination into origination (I made it), that argues an ethic of production (I made it and it is mine), and that argues a tight scheme of intention (I made it because I decided to make it). The rhetoric seems invisible because it is so common. This "I" (the maker) is also located in a version of history that dominates classrooms, the "great man" theory: History is rolling along (the English novel is dominated by a central, intrusive narrative presence; America is in the throes of a Great Depression; during football season the team was supposed to wear the same kind of cleats and socks) until a figure appears, one who can shape history (Henry James, FDR, the writer of the "White Shoes" paper), and everything is changed. In the argument of the "White Shoes" paper, the history goes "I figured . . . I thought . . . I told . . . They agreed . . ." and, as a consequence, "I feel that creativity *comes from when* a person lets his imagination come up with ideas and he is not afraid to express them." The act of appropriation becomes a narrative of courage and conquest. The writer was able to write that story when he was able to imagine himself in that discourse. Getting him out of it will be a difficult matter indeed.

There are ways, I think, that a writer can shape history in the very act of writing it. Some students are able to enter into a discourse but, by stylistic maneuvers, to take possession of it at the same time. They don't originate a discourse, but they locate themselves within it aggressively, self-consciously. Here is another essay on jazz, which for sake of convenience I've shortened. It received a higher rating than the first essay on jazz.

> Jazz has always been thought of as a very original creative field in music. Improvisation, the spontaneous creation of original melodies in a piece of music, makes up a large part of jazz as a musical style. I had the opportunity to be a member of my high school's jazz ensemble for three years, and became an improvisation soloist this year. Throughout the years, I have seen and heard many jazz players, both professional and amateur. The solos performed by these artists were each flavored with that particular individual's style and ideas, along with some of the conventional premises behind improvisation. This particular type of solo work is creative because it is, done on the spur of the moment and blends the performer's ideas with basic guidelines.
>
> I realized my own creative potential when I began soloing. . . .
>
> My solos, just as all the solos generated by others, were original because I combined and shaped other's ideas with mine to create something completely new. Creativity is combining the practical knowledge

and guidelines of a discipline with one's original ideas to bring about a new, original end result, one that is different from everyone else's. Creativity is based on the individual. Two artists can interpret the same scene differently. Each person who creates something does so by bringing out something individual in himself.

The essay is different in some important ways from the first essay on jazz. The writer of the second is more easily able to place himself in the context of an "academic" discussion. The second essay contains an "I" who realized his "creative potential" by soloing; the first contained an "I" who had "a great experience." In the second essay, before the phrase, "I had the opportunity to be a member of my high school's jazz ensemble," there is an introduction that offers a general definition of improvisation and an acknowledgment that other people have thought about jazz and creativity. In fact, throughout the essay the writer offers definitions and counterdefinitions. He is placing himself in the context of what has been said and what might be said. In the first paper, before a similar statement about being a member of a jazz ensemble, there was an introduction that locates jazz solely in the context of this individual's experience: "I am very interested in music." The writer of this first paper was authorized by who he is, a musician, rather than by what he can say about music in the context of what is generally said. The writer of the second essay uses a more specialized vocabulary; he talks about "conventional premises," "creative potential," "musical style," and "practical knowledge." And this is not just a matter of using bigger words, since these terms locate the experience in the context of a recognizable interpretive scheme—on the one hand there is tradition and, on the other, individual talent.

It could be said, then, that this essay is also framed and completed by a commonplace: "Creativity is combining the practical knowledge and guidelines of a discipline with one's original ideas to bring about a new, original end result, one that is different from everyone else's." Here, however, the argument is a more powerful one; and I mean "powerful" in the political sense, since it is an argument that complicates a "naive" assumption (it makes scholarly work possible, in other words), and it does so in terms that come close to those used in current academic debates (over the relation between convention and idiosyncrasy or between rules and creativity). The assertion is almost consumed by the pleas for originality at the end of the sentence; but the point remains that the terms "original" and "different," as they are used at the end of the essay, are problematic, since they must be thought of in the context of "practical knowledge and guidelines of a discipline."

The key distinguishing gesture of this essay, that which makes it "better" than the other, is the way the writer works against a conventional point of view, one that is represented within the essay by conventional phrases that the writer must then work against. In his practice he demonstrates that a writer, and not just a musician, works within "conventional premises." The "I" who comments in this paper (not the "I" of the narrative about a time when he soloed) places himself self-consciously within the context of a conventional discourse about the subject, even as he struggles against the language of that conventional discourse. The opening definition of improvisation, where improvisation is defined as spontaneous creation, is rejected when the writer begins talking about "the conventional premises behind improvisation." The earlier definition is part of the conventional language of those who "have always thought" of jazz as a "very original creative field in music." The paper begins with what "has been said" and then works itself out against the force and logic of what has been said, of what is not only an argument but also a collection of phrases, examples, and definitions.

I had a teacher who once told us that whenever we were stuck for something to say, we should use the following as a "machine" for producing a paper: "While most readers of _____ have said _____, a close and careful reading shows that _____." The writer of the second paper on jazz is using a standard opening gambit, even if it is not announced with flourish. The essay becomes possible when he sets himself against what must become a "naive" assumption—what "most people think." He has defined a closed circle for himself. In fact, you could say that he has laid the ground work for a discipline with its own key terms ("practical knowledge," "disciplinary guidelines," and "original ideas"), with its own agenda and with its own investigative procedures (looking for common features in the work of individual soloists).

The history represented by this student's essay, then, is not the history of a musician and it is not the history of a thought being worked out within an individual mind; it is the history of work being done within and against conventional systems.

In general, as I reviewed essays for this study, I found that the more successful writers set themselves in their essays against what they defined as some more naive way of talking about their subject—against "those who think that . . ."—or against earlier, more naive versions of themselves—"once I thought that. . . ." By trading in one set of commonplaces at the expense of another, they could win themselves status as members of what is taken to be some more privileged group. The ability to imagine privilege enabled writing. Here is one particularly successful essay. Notice the specialized vocabulary, but notice also the way in which the text continually refers to its own language and to the language of others.

> Throughout my life, I have been interested and intrigued by music. My mother has often told me of the times, before I went to school, when I would "conduct" the orchestra on her records. I continued to listen to music and eventually started to play the guitar and the clarinet. Finally, at about the age of twelve, I started to sit down and to try to write songs. Even though my instrumental skills were far from my own high standards, I would spend much of my spare time during the day with a guitar around my neck, trying to produce a piece of music.
>
> Each of these sessions, as I remember them, had a rather set format. I would sit in my bedroom, strumming different combinations of the five or six chords I could play, until I heard a series of which sounded particularly good to me. After this, I set the music to a suitable rhythm, (usually dependent on my mood at the time), and ran through the tune until I could play it fairly easily. Only after this section was complete did I go on to writing lyrics, which generally followed along the lines of the current popular songs on the radio.
>
> At the time of the writing, I felt that my songs were, in themselves, an original creation of my own; that is, I, alone, made them. However, I now see that, in this sense of the word, I was not creative. The songs themselves seem to be an oversimplified form of the music I listened to at the time.
>
> In a more fitting sense, however, I *was* being creative. Since I did not purposely copy my favorite songs, I was, effectively, originating my songs from my own "process of creativity." To achieve my goal, I needed what a composer would call "inspiration" for my piece. In this case the inspiration was the current hit on the radio. Perhaps, with my present point of view, I feel that I used too much "inspiration" in my songs, but, at that time, I did not.
>
> Creativity, therefore, is a process which, in my case, involved a certain series of "small creations" if you like. As well, it is something, the appreciation of which varies with one's point of view, that point of view being set by the person's experience, tastes, and his own personal view of creativity. The less experienced tend to allow for less originality, while the more experienced demand real originality to classify something a "creation." Either way, a term as abstract as this is perfectly correct, and open to interpretation.

This writer is consistently and dramatically conscious of herself forming something to say out of what has been said *and* out of what she has been saying in the act of writing this paper. "Creativity" begins in this paper as "original creation." What she thought was "creativity," however, she now says was imitation; and, as she says, "in a sense of the word" she was not "creative." In another sense, however, she says that she *was* creative, since she didn't purposefully copy the songs but used them as "inspiration."

While the elaborate stylistic display—the pauses, qualifications, and the use of quotation marks—is in part a performance for our benefit, at a more obvious level we as readers are directly addressed in the first sentence of the last paragraph: "Creativity, therefore, is a process which, in my case, involved a certain series of 'small creations' if you like." We are addressed here as adults who can share her perspective on what she has said and who can be expected to understand her terms. If she gets into trouble after this sentence, and I think she does, it is because she doesn't have the courage to generalize from her assertion. Since she has rhetorically separated herself from her younger "self," and since she argues that she has gotten smarter, she assumes that there is some developmental sequence at work here and that, in the world of adults (which must be more complete than the world of children) there must be something like "real creativity." If her world is imperfect (if she can only talk about creation by putting the word in quotation marks), it must be because she is young. When she looks beyond herself to us, she cannot see our work as an extension of her project. She cannot assume that we too will be concerned with the problem of creativity and originality. At least she is not willing to challenge us on those grounds, to generalize her argument, and to argue that even for adults creations are really only "small creations." The sense of privilege that has allowed her to expose her own language cannot be extended to expose ours.

The writing in this piece—that is, the work of the writer within the essay—goes on in spite of, or against, the language that keeps pressing to give another name to her experience as a songwriter and to bring the discussion to closure. (In comparison, think of the quick closure of the "White Shoes" paper.) Its style is difficult, highly qualified. It relies on quotation marks and parody to set off the language and attitudes that belong to the discourse (or the discourses) that it would reject, that it would not take as its own proper location.

David Olson (1981) has argued that the key difference between oral language and written language is that written language separates both the producer and the receiver from the text. For my student writers, this means that they had to learn that what they said (the code) was more important than what they meant (the intention). A writer, in other words, loses his primacy at the moment of writing and must begin to attend to his and his words' conventional, even physical presence on the page. And, Olson says, the writer must learn that his authority is not established through his presence but through his absence—through his ability, that is, to speak as a god-like source beyond the limitations of any particular social or historical moment;

to speak by means of the wisdom of convention, through the oversounds of official or authoritative utterance, as the voice of logic or the voice of the community. He concludes:

> The child's growing competence with this distinctive register of language in which both the meaning and the authority are displaced from the intentions of the speaker and lodged "in the text" may contribute to the similarly specialized and distinctive mode of thought we have come to associate with literacy and formal education. (1918, p. 110)

Olson is writing about children. His generalizations, I think I've shown, can be extended to students writing their way into the academic community. These are educated and literate individuals, to be sure, but they are individuals still outside the peculiar boundaries of the academic community. In the papers I've examined in this chapter, the writers have shown an increasing awareness of the codes (or the competing codes) that operate within a discourse. To speak with authority they have to speak not only in another's voice but through another's code; and they not only have to do this, they have to speak in the voice and through the codes of those of us with power and wisdom; and they not only have to do this, they have to do it before they know what they are doing, before they have a project to participate in, and before, at least in terms of our disciplines, they have anything to say. Our students may be able to enter into a conventional discourse and speak, not as themselves, but through the voice of the community; the university, however, is the place where "common" wisdom is only of negative values — it is something to work against. The movement toward a more specialized discourse begins (or, perhaps, best begins) both when a student can define a position of privilege, a position that sets him against a "common" discourse, and when he or she can work self-consciously, critically, against not only the "common" code but his or her own.

IV

Pat Bizzell, you will recall, argues that the problems of poor writers can be attributed both to their unfamiliarity with the conventions of academic discourse and to their ignorance that there are such things as discourse communities with conventions to be mastered. If the latter is true, I think it is true only in rare cases. All the student writers I've discussed (and, in fact, most of the student writers whose work I've seen) have shown an awareness that something special or something different is required when one writes for an academic classroom. The essays that I have presented in this chapter all, I think, give evidence of writers trying to write their way into a new community. To some degree, however, all of them can be said to be unfamiliar with the conventions of academic discourse.

Problems of convention are both problems of finish and problems of substance. The most substantial academic tasks for students, learning history or sociology or literary criticism, are matters of many courses, much reading and writing, and several years of education. Our students, however, must have a place to begin. They cannot sit through lectures and read textbooks and, as a consequence, write as sociologists or write literary criticism. There must be steps along the way. Some of these steps will be marked by drafts and revisions. Some will be marked by courses, and in an ideal curriculum the preliminary courses would be writing courses, whether housed in an English department or not. For some students, students we call "basic writers," these courses will be in a sense the most basic introduction to the language and methods of academic writing.

Our students, as I've said, must have a place to begin. If the problem of a beginning is the problem of establishing authority, of defining rhetorically or stylistically a position from which one may speak, then the papers I have examined show characteristic student responses to that problem and show levels of approximation or stages in the development of writers who are writing their way into a position of privilege.

As I look over the papers I've discussed, I would arrange them in the following order: the "White Shoes" paper; the first "Jazz" essay; the "Clay Model" paper; the second "Jazz" essay; and, as the most successful paper, the essay on "Composing Songs." The more advanced essays for me, then, are those that are set against the "naive" codes of "everyday" life. (I put the terms "naive" and "everyday" in quotation marks because they are, of course, arbitrary terms.) In the advanced essays one can see a writer claiming an "inside" position of privilege by rejecting the language and commonplaces of a "naive" discourse, the language of "outsiders." The "I" of those essays locates itself against the specialized language of what is presumed to be a more powerful and more privileged community. There are two gestures present then — one imitative and one critical. The writer continually audits and pushes against a language that would render him "like everyone else" and mimics the language and interpretive systems of the privileged community.

At a first level, then, a student might establish his authority by simply stating his own presence within the field of a subject. A student, for example, writes about creativity by telling a story about a time he went skiing. Nothing more. The "I" on the page is a skier, and skiing stands as a representation of a creative act. Neither the skier nor skiing are available for interpretation; they cannot be located in an essay that is not a narrative essay (where skiing might serve metaphorically as an example of, say, a sport where set movements also allow for a personal style). Or a student, as did the one who wrote the "White Shoes" paper, locates a narrative in an unconnected rehearsal of commonplaces about creativity. In both cases, the writers have finessed the requirement to set themselves against the available utterances of the world outside the closed world of the academy. And, again, in the first "Jazz" paper, we have the example of a writer who locates himself within an available commonplace and carries out only rudimentary procedures for elaboration, procedures driven by the commonplace itself and not set against it. Elaboration, in this latter case, is not the opening up of a system but a justification of it.

At a next level I would place student writers who establish their authority by mimicking the rhythm and texture, the "sound," of academic prose, without there being any recognizable interpretive or academic project under way. I'm thinking, here, of the "Clay Model" essay. At an advanced stage, I would place students who establish their authority as *writers*; they claim their authority, not by simply claiming that they are skiers or that they have done something creative, but by placing themselves both within and against a discourse, or within and against competing discourses, and working self-consciously to claim an interpretive project of their own, one that grants them their privilege to speak. This is true, I think, in the case of the second "Jazz" paper and, to a greater degree, in the case of the "Composing Songs" paper.

The levels of development that I've suggested are not marked by corresponding levels in the type or frequency of error, at least not by the type or frequency of sentence-level error. I am arguing, then, that a basic writer is not necessarily a writer who makes a lot of mistakes. In fact, one of the problems with curricula designed to aid basic writers is that they too often begin with the assumption that the key distinguishing feature of a basic writer is the presence of sentence-level error. Students are placed in courses because their placement essays show a high frequency of such errors, and those courses are designed with the goal of making those errors go away. This approach to the problems of the basic writer ignores the degree to which error is less often a constant feature than a marker in the development of a writer. A student who can write a reasonably correct narrative may fall to pieces when faced with a more unfamiliar assignment. More important, however, such courses fail to serve the rest of the curriculum. On every campus there is a significant number of college freshmen who require a course to introduce them to the kinds of writing that are required for a university education. Some of these students can write correct sentences and some cannot; but, as a group, they lack the facility other freshmen possess when they are faced with an academic writing task.

The "White Shoes" essay, for example, shows fewer sentence-level errors than the "Clay Model" paper. This may well be due to the fact that the writer of the "White Shoes" paper stayed well within safe, familiar territory. He kept himself out of trouble by doing what he could easily do. The tortuous syntax of the more advanced papers on my list is a syntax that represents a writer's struggle with a difficult and unfamiliar language, and it is a syntax that can quickly lead an inexperienced writer into trouble. The syntax and punctuation of the "Composing Songs" essay, for example, shows the effort that is required when a writer works against the pressure of conventional discourse. If the prose is inelegant (although I confess I admire those dense sentences) it is still correct. This writer has a command of the linguistic and stylistic resources—the highly embedded sentences, the use of parentheses and quotation marks—required to complete the act of writing. It is easy to imagine the possible pitfalls for a writer working without this facility.

There was no camera trained on the "Clay Model" writer while he was writing, and I have no protocol of what was going through his mind, but it is possible to speculate on the syntactic difficulties of sentences like these: "In the past time I thought that an incident was creative was when I had to make a clay model of the earth, but not of the classical or your everyday model of the earth which consists of the two cores, the mantle and the crust. I thought of these things in a dimension of which it would be unique, but easy to comprehend." The syntactic difficulties appear to be the result of the writer's attempt to use an unusual vocabulary and to extend his sentences beyond the boundaries of what would have been "normal" in his speech or writing. There is reason to believe, that is, that the problem was with *this* kind of sentence, in this context. If the problem of the last sentence is that of holding together the units "I thought," "dimension," "unique" and "easy to comprehend," then the linguistic problem was not a simple matter of sentence construction. I am arguing, then, that such sentences fall apart not because the writer lacked the necessary syntax to glue the pieces together but because he lacked the full statement within which these key words were already operating. While writing, and in the thrust of his need to complete the sentence, he had the key words but not the utterance. (And to recover the utterance, I suspect, he would need to do more than revise the sentence.) The invisible conventions, the prepared phrases remained too distant for the statement to be completed. The writer would have needed to get inside of a discourse that he could in fact only partially imagine. The act of constructing a sentence, then, became something like an act of transcription in which the voice on the tape unexpectedly faded away and became inaudible.

Shaughnessy (1977) speaks of the advanced writer as one who often has a more facile but still incomplete possession of this prior discourse. In the case of the advanced writer, the evidence of a problem is the presence of dissonant, redundant, or imprecise language, as in a sentence such as this: "No education can be *total*, it must be *continuous*."

Such a student, Shaughnessy says, could be said to hear the "melody of formal English" while still unable to make precise or exact distinctions. And, she says,

> the pre-packaging feature of language, the possibility of taking over phrases and whole sentences without much thought about them, threatens the writer now as before. The writer, as we have said, inherits the language out of which he must fabricate his own messages. He is therefore in a constant tangle with the language, obliged to recognize its public, communal nature and yet driven to invent out of this language his own statements. (1977, pp. 207–208)

For the unskilled writer, the problem is different in degree and not in kind. The inexperienced writer is left with a more fragmentary record of the comings and goings of academic discourse. Or, as I said above, he or she often has the key words without the complete statements within which they are already operating.

Let me provide one final example of this kind of syntactic difficulty in another piece of student writing. The writer of this paper seems to be able to sustain a discussion only by continually repeating his first step, producing a litany of strong, general, authoritative assertions that trail quickly into confusion. Notice how the writer seems to stabilize his movement through the paper by returning again and again to recognizable and available commonplace utterances. When he has to move away from them, however, away from the familiar to statements that would extend those utterances, where he, too, must speak, the writing—that is, both the syntax and the structure of the discourse—falls to pieces.

> Many times the times drives a person's life depends on how he uses it. I would like to think about if time is twenty-five hours a day rather than twenty-four hours. Some people think it's the boaring or some people might say it's the pleasure to take one more hour for their life. But I think the time is passing and coming, still we are standing on same position. We should use time as best as we can use about the good way in our life. Everything we do, such as sleep, eat, study, play and doing something for

ourselves. These take the time to do and we could find the individual ability and may process own. It is the important for us and our society. As time going on the world changes therefor we are changing, too. When these situation changes we should follow the suitable case of own. But many times we should decide what's the better way to do so by using time. Sometimes like this kind of situation can cause the success of our lives or ruin. I think every individual of his own thought drive how to use time. These affect are done from environmental causes. So we should work on the better way of our life recognizing the importance of time.

There is a general pattern of disintegration when the writer moves off from standard phrases. This sentence, for example, starts out coherently and then falls apart: "*We should use time as best as we can* use about the good way in our life." The difficulty seems to be one of extending those standard phrases or of connecting them to the main subject reference, "time" (or "the time," a construction that causes many of the problems in the paper). Here is an example of a sentence that shows, in miniature, this problem of connection: "*I think every individual* of his own thought drive how to use *time.*

One of the remarkable things about this paper is that, in spite of all the syntactic confusion, there is the hint of an academic project here. The writer sets out to discuss how to creatively use one's time. The text seems to allude to examples and to stages in an argument, even if in the end it is all pretty incoherent. The gestures of academic authority, however, are clearly present, and present in a form that echoes the procedures in other, more successful papers. The writer sets himself against what "some people think"; he speaks with the air of authority: "But I think. . . . Everything we do. . . . When these situation changes. . . ." And he speaks as though there were a project underway, one where he proposes what he thinks, turns to evidence, and offers a conclusion: "These affect are done from environmental causes. So we should work. . . ." This is the case of a student with the ability to imagine the general outline and rhythm of academic prose but without the ability to carry it out, to complete the sentences. And when he gets lost in the new, in the unknown, in the responsibility of his own commitment to speak, he returns again to the familiar ground of the commonplace.

The challenge to researchers, it seems to me, is to turn their attention again to products, to student writing, since the drama in a student's essay, as he or she struggles with and against the languages of our contemporary life, is as intense and telling as the drama of an essay's mental preparation or physical production. A written text, too, can be a compelling model of the "composing process" once we conceive of a writer as at work within a text and simultaneously, then, within a society, a history, and a culture.

It may very well be that some students will need to learn to crudely mimic the "distinctive register" of academic discourse before they are prepared to actually and legitimately do the work of the discourse, and before they are sophisticated enough with the refinements of tone and gesture to do it with grace or elegance. To say this, however, is to say that our students must be our students. Their initial progress will be marked by their abilities to take on the role of privilege, by their abilities to establish authority. From this point of view, the student who wrote about constructing the clay model of the earth is better prepared for his education than the student who wrote about playing football in white shoes, even though the "White Shoes" paper is relatively error-free and the "Clay Model" paper is not. It will be hard to pry loose the writer of the "White Shoes" paper from the tidy, pat discourse that allows him to dispose of the question of creativity in such a quick and efficient manner. He will have to be convinced that it is better to write sentences he might not so easily control, and he will have to be convinced that it is better to write muddier and more confusing prose (in order that it may sound like ours), and this will be harder than convincing the "Clay Model" writer to continue what he has already begun.

ACKNOWLEDGMENTS

Preparation of this chapter was supported by the Learning Research and Development Center of the University of Pittsburgh, which is supported in part by the National Institute of Education.

NOTES

1. David Olson (1981) has made a similar observation about school-related problems of language learning in younger children. Here is his conclusion: "Hence, depending upon whether children assumed language was primarily suitable for making assertions and conjectures or primarily for making direct or indirect commands, they will either find school texts easy or difficult" (p. 107).

2. For Aristotle, there were both general and specific commonplaces. A speaker, says Aristotle, has a "stock of arguments to which he may turn for a particular need."

> If he knows the *topoi* (regions, places, lines of argument)—and a skilled speaker will know them—he will know where to find what he wants for a special case. The general topics, or *common*places, are regions containing arguments that are common to all branches of knowledge. . . . But there are also special topics (regions, places, *loci*) in which one looks for arguments appertaining to particular branches of knowledge, special sciences, such as ethics or politics. (1932, pp. 154–155)

And, he says, "the topics or places, then, may be indifferently thought of as in the science that is concerned, or in the mind of the speaker." But the question of location is "indifferent" *only* if the mind of the speaker is in line with set opinion, general assumption. For the speaker (or writer) who is not situated so comfortably in the privileged public realm, this is indeed not an indifferent matter at all. If he does not have the commonplace at hand, he will not, in Aristotle's terms, know where to go at all.

3. Pat Bizzell has argued that the *Seventeen* writer's process of goal-setting

> can be better understood if we see it in terms of writing for a discourse community. His initial problem . . . is to find a way to include these readers in a discourse community for which he is comfortable writing. He places them in the academic discourse community by imagining the girls as students. . . . Once he has included them in a familiar discourse community, he can find a way to address them that is common in the community: he will argue with them, putting a new interpretation on information they possess in order to correct misconceptions. (1982a, p. 228)

4. See Bartholomae (1979, 1983) and Rose (1983) for articles on curricula designed to move students into university discourse. The movement to extend writing "across the curriculum" is evidence of a general concern for locating students within the work of the university; see Bizzell (1982a) and Maimon *et al.* (1981). For longer works directed specifically at basic writing, see Ponsot and Deen (1982) and Shaughnessy (1977). For a book describing a course for more advanced students, see Coles (1978).

5. In spite of my misgivings about Bereiter and Scardamalia's interpretation of the cognitive nature of the problem of "inert knowledge," this is an essay I regularly recommend to teachers. It has much to say about the dangers of what seem to be "neutral" forms of classroom discourse and provides, in its final section, a set of recommendations on how a teacher might undo discourse conventions that have become part of the institution of teaching.

6. Stanley Fish (1980) argues that the basis for distinguishing novice from expert readings is the persuasiveness of the discourse used to present and defend a given reading. In particular, see the chapter, "Demonstration vs. Persuasion: Two Models of Critical Activity" (pp. 356–373).

7. Some students, when they come to the university, can do this better than others. When Jonathan Culler says, "the possibility of bringing someone to see that a particular interpretation is a good one assumes shared points of departure and common notions of how to read," he is acknowledging that teaching, at least in English classes, has had to assume that students, to be students, were already to some degree participating in the structures of reading and writing that constitute English studies (quoted in Fish, 1980, p. 366).

Stanley Fish tells us "not to worry" that students will violate our enterprise by offering idiosyncratic readings of standard texts:

> The fear of solipsism, of the imposition by the unconstrained self of its own prejudices, is unfounded because the self does not exist apart from the communal or conventional categories of thought that enable its operations (of thinking, seeing, reading). Once we realize that the conceptions that fill consciousness, including any conception of its own status, are culturally derived, the very notion of an unconstrained self, of a consciousness wholly and dangerously free, becomes incomprehensible. (1980, p. 335)

He, too, is assuming that students, to be students (and not "dangerously free"), must be members in good standing of the community whose immediate head is the English teacher. It is interesting that his parenthetical catalogue of the "operations" of thought, "thinking, seeing, reading," excludes writing, since it is only through written records that we have any real indication of how a student thinks, sees, and reads. (Perhaps "real" is an inappropriate word to use here, since there is certainly a "real" intellectual life that goes on, independent of writing. Let me say that thinking, seeing, and reading are valued in the academic community *only* as they are represented by extended, elaborated written records.) Writing, I presume, is a given for Fish. It is the card of entry into this closed community that constrains and excludes dangerous characters. Students who are excluded from this community are students who do poorly on written placement exams or in freshman composition. They do not, that is, move easily into the privileged discourse of the community, represented by the English literature class.

8. My debt to Bizzell's work should be evident everywhere in this essay. See also Bizzell (1978, 1982b) and Bizzell and Herzberg (1980).

9. Fish says the following about the relationship between student and an object under study:

> we are not to imagine a moment when my students "simply see" a physical configuration of atoms and *then* assign that configuration a significance, according to the situation they happen to be in. To be in the situation (this or any other) is to "see" with the eyes of its interests, its goals, its understood practices, values, and norms, and so to be conferring significance *by* seeing, not after it. The categories of my students' vision are the categories by which they understand themselves to be functioning as students . . . and objects will appear to them in forms related to that way of functioning rather than in some objective or preinterpretive form. (1980, p. 334)

10. I am aware that the papers given the highest rankings offer arguments about creativity and originality similar to my own. If there is a conspiracy here, that is one of the points of my chapter. I should add that my reading of the "content" of basic writers' essays is quite different from Lunsford's (1980).

REFERENCES

Aristotle. (1932). *The rhetoric of Aristotle* (L. Cooper, Trans.) Englewood Cliffs, NJ: Prentice-Hall.

Barthes, R. (1974). *S/Z* (R. Howard, Trans.). New York: Hill & Wang.

Bartholomae, D. (1979). Teaching basic writing: An alternative to basic skills. *Journal of Basic Writing, 2*, 85–109.

Bartholomae, D. (1983). Writing assignments: Where writing begins. In P. Stock (Ed.), *Forum* (pp. 300–312). Montclair, NJ: Boynton/Cook.

Bereiter, C., & Scardamalia, M. (in press). Cognitive coping strategies and the problem of "inert knowledge." In S. S. Chipman, J. W. Segal, & R. Glaser (Eds.), *Thinking and learning skills: Research and open questions* (Vol. 2). Hillsdale, NJ: Erlbaum.

Bizzell, P. (1978). The ethos of academic discourse. *College Composition and Communication, 29*, 351–355.

Bizzell, P. (1982a). Cognition, convention, and certainty: What we need to know about writing. *Pre/text, 3*, 213–244.

Bizzell, P. (1982b). College composition: Initiation into the academic discourse community. *Curriculum Inquiry, 12*, 191–207.

Bizzell, P., & Herzberg, B. (1980). "Inherent" ideology, "universal" history, "empirical" evidence, and "context-free" writing: Some problems with E. D. Hirsch's *The Philosophy of Composition. Modern Language Notes, 95,* 1181–1202.

Coles, W. E., Jr. (1978). *The plural I.* New York: Holt, Rinehart & Winston.

Fish, S. (1980). *Is there a text in this class? The authority of interpretive communities.* Cambridge, MA: Harvard University Press.

Flower, L. S. (1981). Revising writer-based prose. *Journal of Basic Writing, 3,* 62–74.

Flower, L., & Hayes, J. (1981). A cognitive process theory of writing. *College Composition and Communication, 32,* 365–387.

Hairston, M. (1978). *A contemporary rhetoric.* Boston: Houghton Mifflin.

Lunsford, A. A. (1980). The content of basic writers' essays. *College Composition and Communication, 31,* 278–290.

Maimon, E. P., Belcher, G. L., Hearn, G. W., Nodine, B. F., & O'Conner, F. X. (1981). *Writing in the arts and sciences.* Cambridge, MA: Winthrop.

Olson, D. R. (1981). Writing: The divorce of the author from the text. In B. M. Kroll & R. J. Vann (Eds.), *Exploring speaking–writing relationships: Connections and contrasts.* Urbana, IL: National Council of Teachers of English.

Perkins, D. N. (in press). General cognitive skills: Why not? In S. S. Chipman, J. W. Segal, & R. Glaser (Eds.), *Thinking and learning skills: Research and open questions* (Vol. 2). Hillsdale, NJ: Erlbaum.

Ponsot, M., & Deen, R. (1982). *Beat not the poor desk.* Montclair, NJ: Boynton/Cook.

Rodriguez, R. (1983). *Hunger of memory.* New York: Bantam.

Rose, M. (1983). Remedial writing courses: A critique and a proposal. *College English, 45,* 109–128.

Said, E. W. (1975). *Beginnings: Intention and method.* Baltimore: The Johns Hopkins University Press.

Shaughnessy, M. (1977). *Errors and expectations.* New York: Oxford University Press.

When the First Voice You Hear Is Not Your Own

Jacqueline Jones Royster

This essay emerged from my desire to examine closely moments of personal challenge that seem to have import for cross-boundary discourse. These types of moments have constituted an ongoing source of curiosity for me in terms of my own need to understand human difference as a complex reality, a reality that I have found most intriguing within the context of the academic world. From a collectivity of such moments over the years, I have concluded that the most salient point to acknowledge is that "subject" position really is everything.

Using subject position as a terministic screen in cross-boundary discourse permits analysis to operate kaleidoscopically, thereby permitting interpretation to be richly informed by the converging of dialectical perspectives. Subjectivity as a defining value pays attention dynamically to context, ways of knowing, language abilities, and experience, and by doing so it has a consequent potential to deepen, broaden, and enrich our interpretive views in dynamic ways as well. Analytical lenses include the process, results, and impact of negotiating identity, establishing authority, developing strategies for action, carrying forth intent with a particular type of agency, and being compelled by external factors and internal sensibilities to adjust belief and action (or not). In a fundamental way, this enterprise supports the sense of rhetoric, composition, and literacy studies as a field of study that embraces the imperative to understand truths and consequences of language use more fully. This enterprise supports also the imperative to reconsider the beliefs and values which inevitably permit our attitudes and actions in discourse

Reprinted from *College Composition and Communication* 47.1 (February 1996): 29–40. Used with permission.

communities (including colleges, universities, and classrooms) to be systematic, even systemic.

Adopting subjectivity as a defining value, therefore, is instructive. However, the multidimensionality of the instruction also reveals the need for a shift in paradigms, a need that I find especially evident with regard to the notion of "voice," as a central manifestation of subjectivity. My task in this essay, therefore, is threefold. First, I present three scenes which serve as my personal testimony as "subject." These scenes are singular in terms of their being my own stories, but I believe that they are also plural, constituting experiential data that I share with many. My sense of things is that individual stories placed one against another build credibility and offer, as in this case, a litany of evidence from which a call for transformation in theory and practice might rightfully begin. My intent is to suggest that my stories in the company of others demand thoughtful response.

Second, I draw from these scenes a specific direction for transformation, suggesting dimensions of the nature of voicing that remain problematic. My intent is to demonstrate that our critical approaches to voice, again as a central manifestation of subjectivity, are currently skewed toward voice as a spoken or written phenomenon. This intent merges the second task with the third in that I proceed to suggest that theories and practices should be transformed. The call for action in cross-boundary exchange is to refine theory and practice so that they include voicing as a phenomenon that is constructed and expressed visually and orally, *and* as a phenomenon that has import also in being a *thing* heard, perceived, and reconstructed.

SCENE ONE

I have been compelled on too many occasions to count to sit as a well-mannered Other, silently, in a state of tolerance that requires me to be as expressionless as I can manage, while colleagues who occupy a place of entitlement different from my own talk about the history and achievements of people from my ethnic group, or even about their perceptions of our struggles. I have been compelled to listen as they have comfortably claimed the authority to engage in the construction of knowledge and meaning about me and mine, without paying even a passing nod to the fact that sometimes a substantive version of that knowledge might already exist, or to how it might have already been constructed, or to the meanings that might have already been assigned that might make me quite impatient with gaps in their understanding of my community, or to the fact that I, or somebody within my ethnic group, might have an opinion about what they are doing. I have been compelled to listen to speakers, well-meaning though they may think they are, who signal to me rather clearly that subject position is everything. I have come to recognize, however, that when the subject matter is me and the voice is not mine, my sense of order and rightness is disrupted. In metaphoric fashion, these "authorities" let me know, once again, that Columbus has discovered America and claims it now, claims it still for a European crown.

Such scenes bring me to the very edge of a principle that I value deeply as a teacher and a scholar, the principle of the right to inquiry and discovery. When the discovering hits so close to home, however, my response is visceral, not just intellectual, and I am made to look over a precipice. I have found it extremely difficult to allow the voices and experiences of people that I care about deeply to be taken and handled so carelessly and without accountability by strangers.

At the extreme, the African American community, as my personal example, has seen and continues to see its contributions and achievements called into question in grossly negative ways, as in the case of *The Bell Curve*. Such interpretations of who we are as a people open to general interrogation, once again, the innate capacities of "the race" as a whole. As has been the case throughout our history in this country, we are put in jeopardy and on trial in a way that should not exist but does. We are compelled to respond to a rendering of our potential that demands, not that we account for attitudes, actions, and conditions, but that we defend ourselves as human beings. Such interpretations of human potential create a type of discourse that serves as a distraction, as noise that drains off energy and sabotages the work of identifying substantive problems within and across cultural boundaries and the work also of finding solutions that have import, not simply for "a race," but for human beings whose living conditions, values, and preferences vary.

All such close encounters, the extraordinarily insidious ones and the ordinary ones, are definable through the lens of subjectivity, particularly in terms of the power and authority to speak and to make meaning. An analysis of subject position reveals that these interpretations by those outside of the community are not random acts of unkindness. Instead, they embody ways of seeing, knowing, being, and acting that probably suggest as much about the speaker and the context as they do about the targeted subject matter. The advantage with this type of analysis, of course, is that we see the obvious need to contextualize the stranger's perspective among other interpretations and to recognize that an interpretive view is just that—interpretive. A second advantage is that we also see that in our nation's practices these types of interpretations, regardless of how superficial or libelous they may actually be within the context of a more comprehensive view, tend to have considerable consequence in the lives of the targeted group, people in this case whose own voices and perspectives remain still largely under considered and uncredited.

Essentially, though, having a mechanism to see the under considered helps us see the extent to which we add continually to the pile of evidence in this country of cross-cultural misconduct. These types of close encounters that disregard dialectical views are a type of free touching of the powerless by the power-full. This analytical perspective encourages us to acknowledge that marginalized communities are not in a good position to ward off the intrusion of those authorized in mainstream communities to engage in willful action. Historically, such actions have included everything from the displacement of native people from their homelands, to the use of unknowing human subjects in dangerous experiments, to the appropriation and misappropriation of cultural artifacts—art, literature, music, and so on. An insight using the lens of subjectivity, however, is a recognition of the ways in which these moments are indeed moments of violation, perhaps even ultimate violation.

This record of misconduct means that for people like me, on an instinctive level, all outsiders are rightly perceived as suspect. I suspect the genuineness of their interest, the altruism of their actions, and the probability that whatever is being said or done is not to the ultimate benefit and understanding of the people who are subject matter but not subjects. People in the neighborhood where I grew up would say, "Where is their home training?" Imbedded in the question is the idea that when you visit other people's "home places," especially when you have not been invited, you simply can not go tramping around the house like you own the place, no matter how smart you are, or how much imagination you can muster, or how much authority and entitlement outside that home you may be privileged to hold. And you certainly can not go around name calling, saying things like, "You people are intellectually inferior and have a limited capacity to achieve," without taking into account who the family is, what its living has been like, and what its history and achievement have been about.

The concept of "home training" underscores the reality that point of view matters and that we must be trained to respect points of view other than our own. It acknowledges that when we are away from home, we need to know that what we think we see in places that we do not really know very well may not actually be what is there at all. So often, it really is a matter of time, place, resources, and our ability to perceive. Coming to judgment too quickly, drawing on information too narrowly, and saying hurtful, discrediting, dehumanizing things without undisputed proof are not appropriate. Such behavior is not good manners. What comes to mind for me is another saying that I heard constantly when I was growing up, "Do unto others as you would have them do unto you." In this case, we would be implored to draw conclusions about others with care and, when we do draw conclusions, to use the same type of sense and sensibility that we would ideally like for others to use in drawing conclusions about us.

This scene convinces me that what we need in a pressing way in this country and in our very own field is to articulate codes of behavior that can sustain more concretely notions of honor, respect, and good manners across boundaries, with cultural boundaries embodying the need most vividly. Turning the light back onto myself, though, at the same time that my sense of violation may indeed be real, there is the compelling reality that many communities in our nation need to be taken seriously. We all deserve to be taken seriously, which means that critical inquiry and discovery are absolutely necessary. Those of us who love our own communities, we think, most deeply, most uncompromisingly, without reservation for what they are and also are not, must set aside our misgivings about strangers in the interest of the possibility of deeper understanding (and for the more idealistic among us, the possibility of global peace). Those of us who hold these communities close to our hearts, protect them, and embrace them; those who want to preserve the goodness of the minds and souls in them; those who want to preserve consciously, critically, and also lovingly the record of good work within them must take high risk and give over the exclusivity of our rights to know.

It seems to me that the agreement for inquiry and discovery needs to be deliberately reciprocal. All of us, strangers and community members, need to find ways to sustain productivity in what Pratt calls contact zones (199), areas of engagement that in all likelihood will remain contentious. We need to get over our tendencies to be too possessive and to resist locking ourselves into the tunnels of our own visions and direct experience. As community members, we must learn to have new faith in the advantage of sharing. As strangers, we must learn to treat the loved people and places of Others with care and to understand that, when we do not act respectfully and responsibly, we leave ourselves rightly open to wrath. The challenge is not to work with a fear of abuse or a fear of retaliation, however. The challenge is to teach, to engage in research, to write, and to speak with Others with the determination to operate not only with professional and personal integrity, but also with the specific knowledge that communities and their ancestors are watching. If we can set aside our rights to exclusivity in our own home cultures, if we can set aside the tendencies that we all have to think too narrowly, we actually leave open an important possibility. In our nation, we have little idea of the potential that a variety of subjectivities—operating with honor, respect, and reasonable codes of conduct—can bring to critical inquiry or critical problems. What might happen if we treated differences in subject position as critical pieces of the whole, vital to thorough understanding, and central to both problem-finding and problem-solving? This society has not, as yet, really allowed that privilege in a substantial way.

SCENE TWO

As indicated in Scene One, I tend to be enraged at what Tillie Olsen has called the "trespass vision," a vision that comes from intellect and imagination (62), but typically not from lived experience, and sometimes not from the serious study of the subject matter. However, like W. E. B. Du Bois, I've chosen not to be distracted or consumed by my rage at voyeurs, tourists, and trespassers, but to look at what I can do. I see the critical importance of the role of negotiator, someone who can cross boundaries and serve as guide and translator for Others.

In 1903, Du Bois demonstrated this role in *The Souls of Black Folk*. In the "Forethought" of that book, he says: "Leaving, then, the world of the white man, I have stepped within the Veil, raising it that you may view faintly its deeper recesses—the meaning of its religion, the passion of its human sorrow, and the struggle of its greater souls" (1). He sets his rhetorical purpose to be to cross, or at least to straddle, boundaries with the intent of shedding light, a light that has the potential of being useful to people on both sides of the veil. Like Du Bois, I've accepted the idea that what I call my "home place" is a cultural community that exists still quite significantly beyond the confines of a well-insulated community that we call the "mainstream," and that between this world and the one that I call home, systems of insulation impede the vision and narrow the ability to recognize human potential and to understand human history both microscopically and telescopically.

Like Du Bois, I've dedicated myself to raising this veil, to overriding these systems of insulation by raising another voice, my voice in the interest of clarity and accuracy. What I have found too often, however, is that, unlike those who have been entitled to talk about me and mine, when I talk about my own, I face what I call the power and function of deep disbelief, and what Du Bois described as "the sense of always looking at one's self through the eyes of others, of measuring one's soul by the tape of a world that looks on in amused contempt and pity" (5).

An example comes to mind. When I talk about African American women, especially those who were writing non-fiction prose in the nineteenth century, I can expect, even today after so much contemporary scholarship on such writers, to see people who are quite flabbergasted by anything that I share. Reflected on their faces and in their questions and comments, il anyone can manage to speak back to me, is a depth of surprise that is always discomforting. I sense that the surprise, or the silence, if there is little response, does not come from the simple ignorance of unfortunate souls who just happen not to know what I have spent years coming to know. What I suspect is that this type of surprise rather "naturally" emerges in a society that so obviously has the habit of expecting nothing of value, nothing of consequence, nothing of importance, nothing at all positive from its others, so that anything is a surprise; everything is an exception; and nothing of substance can really be claimed as a result.

In identifying this phenomenon, Chandra Talpade Mohanty speaks powerfully about the ways in which this culture co-opts, dissipates, and displaces voices. As demonstrated by my example, one method of absorption that has worked quite well has been essentially rhetorical. In discussing nineteenth century African American women's work, I bring tales of difference and adventure. I bring cultural proofs and instructive examples, all of which invariably must serve as rites of passage to credibility. I also bring the power of story-telling. These tales of adventure in odd places are the transitions by which to historicize and theorize anew with these writers re-inscribed in a rightful place. Such a process respects long-standing practices in African-based cultures of theorizing in narrative form. As Barbara Christian says, we theorize "in the stories we create, in riddles and proverbs, in the play with language, since dynamic rather than fixed ideas seem more to our liking" (336).

The problem is that in order to construct new histories and theories such stories must be perceived not just as "simple stories" to delight and entertain, but as vital layers of a transformative process. A reference point is Langston Hughes and his Simple stories, stories that are a model example of how apparent simplicity has the capacity to unmask truths in ways that are remarkably accessible—through metaphor, analogy, parable, and symbol. However, the problem of articulating new paradigms through stories becomes intractable, if those who are empowered to define impact and consequence decide that the stories are simply stories and if the record of achievement is perceived, as Audre Lorde has said, as "the random droppings of birds" (Foreword xi).

If I take my cue from the life of Ida Wells, and I am bold enough and defiant enough to go beyond the presentation of my stories as juicy tidbits for the delectation of audiences, to actually shift or even subvert a paradigm, I'm much more likely to receive a wide-eyed stare and to have the value and validity of my conceptual position held at a distance, in doubt, and wonderfully absorbed in the silence of appreciation. Through the systems of deep disbelief I become a storyteller, a performer. With such absorptive ability in the systems of interpretation, I have greater difficulty being perceived as a person who theorizes without the mediating voices of those from the inner sanctum, or as a person who might name myself a philosopher, a theorist, a historian who creates paradigms that allow the experiences and the insights of people like me to belong.

What I am compelled to ask when veils seem more like walls is who has the privilege of speaking first? How do we negotiate the privilege of interpretation? When I have tried to fulfill my role as negotiator, I have often walked away knowing that I have spoken, but also knowing, as Anna Julia Cooper knew in 1892, that my voice, like her voice, is still a muted one. I speak, but I can not be heard. Worse, I am heard but I am not believed. Worse yet, I speak but I am not deemed believable. These moments of deep disbelief have helped me to understand much more clearly the wisdom of Audre Lorde when she said: "I have come to believe over and over again that what is most important to me must be spoken, made verbal and shared, even at the risk of having it bruised or misunderstood" (*Sister* 40). Lorde teaches me that, despite whatever frustration and vulnerability I might feel, despite my fear that no one is listening to me or is curious enough to try to understand my voice, it is still better to speak (*Black* 31). I set aside the distractions and permeating noise outside of myself, and I listen, as Howard Thurman recommended, to the sound of the genuine within. I go to a place inside myself and, as Opal Palmer Adisa explains, I listen and learn to "speak without clenching my teeth" (56).

SCENE THREE

There have been occasions when I have indeed been heard and positively received. Even at these times, however, I sometimes can not escape responses that make me most weary. One case in point occurred after a presentation in which I had glossed a scene in a novel that required cultural understanding. When the characters spoke in the scene, I rendered their voices, speaking and explaining, speaking and explaining, trying to translate the experience, to share the sounds of my historical place and to connect those sounds with systems of belief so that deeper understanding of the scene might emerge, and so that those outside of the immediacy of my home culture, the one represented in the novel, might see and understand more and be able to make more useful connections to their own worlds and experiences.

One very well-intentioned response to what I did that day was, "How wonderful it was that you were willing to share with us your 'authentic' voice!" I said, "My 'authentic' voice?" She said, "Oh yes! I've never heard you talk like that, you know, so relaxed. I mean, you're usually great, but, this was really great! You weren't so formal. You didn't have to speak in appropriated academic language. You sounded 'natural.' It was nice to hear you be yourself." I said, "Oh, I see. Yes, I do have a range of voices, and I take quite a bit of pleasure actually in being able to use any of them at will." Not understanding the point that I was trying to make gently, she said, "But this time, it was really you. Thank you."

The conversation continued, but I stopped paying attention. What I didn't feel like saying in a more direct way, a response that my friend surely would have perceived as angry, was that all my voices are authentic, and like bell hooks, I find it "a necessary aspect of self-affirmation not to feel compelled to choose one voice over another, not to claim one as more authentic, but rather to construct social realities that celebrate, acknowledge, and affirm differences, variety" (12). Like hooks, I claim all my voices as my own very much authentic voices, even when it's difficult for others to imagine a person like me having the capacity to do that.

From moments of challenge like this one, I realize that we do not have a paradigm that really allows for what scholars in cultural and postcolonial studies (Anzaldúa, Spivak, Mohanty, Bhabha) have called hybrid people—people who either have the capacity by right of history and development, or who might have created the capacity by right of history and development, to move with dexterity across cultural boundaries, to make themselves comfortable, and to make sense amid the chaos of difference.

As Cornel West points out, most African Americans, for example, dream in English, not in Yoruba, or Hausa, or Wolof. Hybrid people, as demonstrated by the history of Africans in the Western hemisphere, manage a fusion process that allows for survival, certainly. However, it also allows for the development of a peculiar expertise that extends one's range of abilities well beyond ordinary limits, and it supports the opportunity for the development of new and remarkable creative expression, like spirituals, jazz, blues, and what I suspect is happening also with the essay as genre in the hands of African American women. West notes that somebody gave Charlie Parker a saxophone, Miles Davis a trumpet, Hubert Laws a flute, and Les McCann a piano. I suggest that somebody also gave Maria Stewart, Gertrude Mossell, Frances Harper, Alice Walker, Audre Lorde, Toni Morrison, Patricia Williams, June Jordan, bell hooks, Angela Davis and a cadre of other African American women a pencil, a pen, a computer keyboard. In both instances, genius emerges from hybridity, from Africans who, over the course of time and circumstance, have come to dream in English, and I venture to say that all of their voices are authentic.

In sharing these three scenes, I emphasize that there is a pressing need to construct paradigms that permit us to engage in better practices in cross-boundary discourse, whether we are teaching, researching, writing, or talking with Others, whoever those Others happen to be. I would like to emphasize, again, that we look again at "voice" and situate it within a world of symbols, sound, and sense, recognizing that this world operates symphonically. Although the systems of voice production are indeed highly integrated and appear to have singularity in the ways that we come to sound, voicing actually sets in motion multiple systems; prominent among them are systems for speaking but present also are the systems for hearing. We speak within systems that we know significantly through our abilities to negotiate noise and to construct within that noise sense and sensibility.

Several questions come to mind. How can we teach, engage in research, write about, and talk across boundaries *with* others, instead of for, about, and around them? My experiences tell me that we need to do more than just talk and talk back. I believe that in this model we miss a critical moment. We need to talk, yes, and to talk back, yes, but when do we listen? How do we listen? How do we demonstrate that we honor and respect the person talking and what that person is saying, or what the person might say if we valued someone other than ourselves having a turn to speak? How do we translate listening into language and action, into the creation of an appropriate response? How do we really "talk back" rather than talk also? The goal is not, "You talk, I talk." The goal is better practices so that we can exchange perspectives, negotiate meaning, and create understanding with the intent of being in a good position to cooperate, when, like now, cooperation is absolutely necessary.

When I think about this goal, what stands out most is that these questions apply in so much of academic life right now. They certainly apply as we go into classrooms and insist that our students trust us and what we contend is in their best interest. In light of a record in classrooms that seriously questions the range of our abilities to recognize potential, or to appreciate students as non-generic human beings, or to appreciate that they bring with them, always, knowledge, we ask a lot when we ask them to trust. Too often, still, institutionalized equations for placement, positive matriculation, progress, and achievement name, categorize, rank, and file, while our true-to-life students fall between the cracks. I look again to Opal Palmer Adisa for an instructive example. She says:

> Presently, many academics advocate theories which, rather than illuminating the works under scrutiny, obfuscate and problematize these works so that students are rendered speechless. Consequently, the students constantly question what they know, and often, unfortunately, they conclude that they know nothing. (54)

Students may find what we do to be alienating and disheartening. Even when our intentions are quite honorable, silence can descend. Their experiences are not seen, and their voices are not heard. We can find ourselves participating, sometimes consciously, sometimes not, in what Patricia Williams calls "spirit murder" (55). I am reminded in a disconcerting way of a troubling scene from Alex Haley's *Roots.* We engage in practices that say quite insistently to a variety of students in a variety of ways, "Your name is Toby." Why wouldn't students wonder: Who can I trust here? Under what kinds of conditions? When? Why?

In addition to better practices in our classrooms, however, we can also question our ability to talk convincingly with deans, presidents, legislators, and the general public about what we do, how we do it, and why. We have not been conscientious about keeping lines of communication open, and we are now experiencing the consequences of talking primarily to ourselves as we watch funds being cut, programs being eliminated, and national agencies that are vital to our interests being bandied about as if they are post-it notes, randomly stuck on by some ill-informed spendthrift. We must learn to raise a politically active voice with a socially responsible mandate to make a rightful place for education in a country that seems always ready to place the needs of quality education on a sideboard instead of on the table. Seemingly, we have been forever content to let voices other than our own speak authoritatively about our areas of expertise and about us. It is time to speak for ourselves, in our own interests, in the interest of our work, and in the interest of our students.

Better practices are not limited, though, even to these concerns. Of more immediate concern to me this year, given my role as Chair of CCCC, is how to talk across boundaries within our own organization as teachers of English among other teachers of English and language arts from kindergarten through university with interests as varied as those implied by the sections, conferences, and committees of our parent organization, the National Council of Teachers of English (NCTE). Each of the groups within NCTE has its own set of needs, expectations, and concerns, multiplied across the amazing variety of institutional sites across which we work. In times of limited resources and a full slate of critical problems, we must find reasonable ways to negotiate so that we can all thrive reasonably well in the same place.

In our own case, for years now, CCCC has recognized changes in our relationships with NCTE. Since the mid-1980s we have grown exponentially. The field of rhetoric and composition has blossomed and diversified. The climate for higher education has increasingly degenerated, and we have struggled in the midst of change to forge a more satisfying identity and a more positive and productive working relationship with others in NCTE who are facing crises of their own. After 50 years in NCTE, we have grown up, and we have to figure out a new way of being and doing in making sure

457

that we can face our challenges well. We are now in the second year of a concerted effort to engage in a multi-leveled conversation that we hope will leave CCCC well-positioned to face a new century and ongoing challenges. Much, however, depends on the ways in which we talk and listen and talk again in crossing boundaries and creating, or not, the common ground of engagement.

As I look at the lay of this land, I endorse Henry David Thoreau's statement when he said, "Only that day dawns to which we are awake" (267). So my appeal is to urge us all to be awake, awake and listening, awake and operating deliberately on codes of better conduct in the interest of keeping our boundaries fluid, our discourse invigorated with multiple perspectives, and our policies and practices well-tuned toward a clearer respect for human potential and achievement from whatever their source and a clearer understanding that voicing at its best is not just well-spoken but also well-heard.

WORKS CITED

Adisa, Opal Palmer. "I Must Write What I Know So I'll Know That I've Known It All Along." *Sage: A Scholarly Journal on Black Women* 9.2 (1995): 54–57.

Anzaldúa, Gloria. *Borderlands/La Frontera*. San Francisco: Aunt Lute, 1987.

Bhabha, Homi K. *The Location of Culture*. London: Routledge, 1994.

Christian, Barbara. "The Race for Theory." *Cultural Critique* 6 (1987): 335–45.

Cooper, Anna Julia. *A Voice from the South*. New York: Oxford UP, 1988.

Du Bois, W. E. B. *The Souls of Black Folk*. New York: Grammercy, 1994.

Haley, Alex. *Roots*. Garden City: Doubleday, 1976.

Hernstein, Richard J., and Charles Murray. *The Bell Curve: Intelligence and Class Structure in American Life*. New York: Free, 1994.

hooks, bell. *Talking Back: Thinking Feminist, Thinking Black*. Boston: South End, 1989.

Lorde, Audre. *The Black Unicorn*. New York: Norton, 1978.

_____. Foreword. *Wild Women in the Whirlwind*. Ed. Joanne M. Braxton and Andree Nicola McLaughlin. New Brunswick: Rutgers UP, 1990. xi–xiii.

_____. *Sister Outsider*. Freedom: The Crossing Press, 1984.

Mohanty, Chandra Talpade. "On Race and Voice: Challenges for Liberal Education in the 1990s." *Cultural Critique* 14 (Winter 1989–90): 179–208.

_____. "Decolonizing Education: Feminisms and the Politics of Multiculturalism in the 'New' World Order." Ohio State University, Columbus, April 1994.

Olsen, Tillie. *Silences*. New York: Delta, 1978.

Pratt, Mary Louise. "Arts of the Contact Zone." *Profession* 91 (1991): 33–40.

Spivak, Gayatri Chakravorty. *In Other Worlds: Essays in Cultural Politics*. New York: Routledge, 1988.

Thoreau, Henry David. *Walden*. New York: Vintage, 1991.

Thurman, Howard. "The Sound of the Genuine." Spelman College, Atlanta, April 1981.

West, Cornel. "Race Matters." Ohio State U, Columbus, OH, February 1995.

Williams, Patricia. *The Alchemy of Race and Rights*. Cambridge: Harvard UP, 1991.

Memoria Is a Friend of Ours

On the Discourse of Color

VICTOR VILLANUEVA

A memory. Seattle, 1979.

She is a contradiction in stereotypes, not to be pegged. He likes her right off. She wants to go to Belltown, the Denny Regrade, to take photos. He wants to go along. He does, feeling insecure and full of bravado, slipping into the walk of bravado he had perfected as a child in Brooklyn. Stops into a small café at the outskirts of downtown, at the entry to the Regrade. It's a French-style café, the Boulangerie, or some such. To impress her, he speaks French.

"Une tasse de café, s'il vous plaît. Et croissants pour les deux." *Don't laugh. It's how he said it.*

He's an English major, a senior, quite proud of having gotten this far in college. But he's insecure about what this will lead to (since he had only gotten as far as deciding to stay in college till he's finally in over his head). He tells her of a novel he will write someday. His description goes something like this:

> *I've been thinking about a novel about a white Puerto Rican kid who buys into the assimilation myth, hook, line, and sinker. He does all the right things—learns the language, learns how to pronounce "r's" in words like "motherrr" and "waterrr" and how not to trill the "r" when he says "three," and he does well in school. He's even a war hero. Does it all, only to realize that assimilation just can't happen. Yet he can't really be Puerto Rican. So maybe he goes to Puerto Rico to find out who he might have been and what he is tied to. I don't have it all worked out.*

Reprinted from *College English* 67.1 (2004): 9–19. [First published in *Personal Effects: The Social Character of Scholarly Writing*. Ed. Deborah H. Holdstein and David Bleich, Logan: Utah State UP, 2001.] Copyright 2001 by Utah State University Press. Reprinted with permission.

The plot line might not have been worked out, but this was the impulse nevertheless—to keep alive the memory of assimilation denied, a truism turned to myth, to try to hold on to, maybe even to regain, that which had been lost on the road to assimilation.

A reminiscence:

That morning I had spoken with Ceci, my friend the Cuban English profes-sor. Her husband had said something to me over the phone that I had to unravel quickly, immediate translation from my first language to my only language, slipping the Spanish into English to understand. Their baby, I'm told, used to translate into Spanish for her mother when someone spoke in English at home, translated the English into Spanish so that the English professor would understand. Cute.

During that phone conversation, I tried to come up with a familiar Spanish saying about how Cubans and Puerto Ricans are two wings of the same bird. It was there: at the tip of the mind. But I could never. I said it in English. Ceci said it for me in Spanish. Quickly. Then again more slowly. I heard it. I understood it. I recognized it. I still feel unsure that I could pro-duce it. My Spanish is limited to single sentences, never extended stretches of discourse. I can't. At least I don't believe I can. And I listen to salsa and mambo and bomba and plena—the music of my childhood. But I can't dance to it in front of anyone. And phrases from the CDs slip by me, untrans-lated. I am assimilated. I am not.

So I was driving home from some chore or other on the afternoon of the morning I had spoken to Ceci. And in the midst of a left turn I thought: "I'm fifty now, maybe a third of my life left. I wonder if I'll die without ever being fluent in the language that first met my ears." English is the only language I know, really. Yet Spanish is the language of my ear, of my soul. And I try to pass it on to my children. But I'm inadequate.

In some sense, the impulse of the book I had described twenty-one years ago gets worked out in *Bootstraps*, the assimilation myth explicit in the title; the story told then elaborated upon with research and with theory. It's an attempt to play out a kind of Freirean pedagogy: the political explored through the experiential. And it does more. It's

an autobiography with political, theoretical, pedagogical considerations. The story includes ethnographic research. The story includes things tried in classrooms. The story includes speculations on the differences between immigrants and minorities, the class system and language, orality and liter-acy, cultural and critical literacy, Freire, ideology, hegemony, how racism continues and the ways in which racism is allowed to continue despite the profession's best efforts. And in [so doing] the story suggests how we are—all of us—subject to the systemic. This is the personal made public and the public personalized, not for self-glory nor to point fingers, but to suggest how, maybe, to make the exception the rule. (xviii)

I wrote that in 1992. Now some part of that first impulse reasserts itself, fictionalizing, telling the story, reaching back to the heritage that is at risk of passing away quickly. To the kids before my father died last spring:

> *Remember to call your grandpa* abuelo. *He'll like the sound of that, since none of my sister's kids have called him that. If you let him, he'll just watch baseball day and night and not say much. Push him for the stories of Puerto Rico during his childhood. Ask him about catching shrimp with his hands, and the stories of how the neighborhood boys got a Model A Ford, about the revolutionary who hid out in El Yunque, about his time in the Army. Ask about my grandfather, Basilio, and gardening, and working as a groundskeeper and gardener for the university. And ask about* Tío Benito, *the tall farmer, inland, on the coffee hills. "Inland" is important about knowing about being Puerto Rican, about Puerto Rico. I remember when I met him. A tall PR. Man, that was very cool. And he gave me sugar cane from his farm, and a coffee bean, and a lemon that he had cut a hole on the top of. And he told me to chew on the bean, squeeze lemon juice on the tongue, and chew on the cane. I wish I could give you that memory,* mi'jitas.
>
> *Now, Mom is easier. She loves to talk. But she'd rather forget the past. And I don't want the past forgotten, so press her too.*

A poem: Victor Villanueva y Hernándes

Triste lucha la del árbol con espinas	Sad struggle of the tree of thorns
Fuerte ardor que solo a su alma	Fierce feeling covered solely by
se cobija.	your soul
Vano empeño para el ser que vive,	Vain striving for he who lives,
En tratar de comprender su propia vida.	In trying to understand his own life.
Muy dulce es percivir de la noche	So sweet to see your caresses in
sus caricios;	the night
Pero es terrible saber	But so terrible to know
Que más tarde en la madrugada	That later in the light of day
Agonizando todos ellos quedan. . . .	All the agonies remain. . . .
Triste lucha del árbol con espinas	Sad struggle of the tree of thorns
triste lucha la del que ya un	sad struggle of that which is
poquito tarde,	already a little late,
Ni siquiera el más leve	Without even the lightest
suspiro	sigh
su alma alienta.	your soul's breath

Triste e interminable lucha	Sad and interminable struggle
esta que jamás se aleja	that which will never leave
¡Oh, que triste lucha ésta	Oh, how sad this struggle
que a mi pecho	Weighing so on my chest!
Tanto apena!	
¡Triste lucha . . . triste lucha!	Sad struggle . . . sad struggle!
—"En el pasado versa tu presente"	—"In the past turns the present"
19 de enero 1951	19 January 1951

The fiction, the *Bootstraps* retold and fictionalized, would have to begin back then, not quite a generation after the change of hands, when the Spanish colony was handed over to the United States, the changes seen by three generations—*Boricua* to Nuyorican to the middle class of color far removed from the cultural soil of either of the generations, maybe even a wheat field in Eastern Washington. It's important. The memory.

So many have said this so well, that it's hard for me to reiterate without breaking into the academic discourse of cite-and-quote—Adell, JanMohamed and Lloyd, Omi and Winant, Saldívar, San Juan, Singh, Skerrett, and Hogan, Smorkaloff, and the "standards" like Anzaldúa or hooks—all have written about the connections between narratives by people of color and the need to reclaim a memory, memory of an identity in formation and constant reformation, the need to reclaim a memory of an identity as formed through the generations. And I'd say the need to reclaim and retain the memory of the imperial lords, those who have forcibly changed the identities of people of color through colonization.

Nelly, the department's graduate secretary, hands me a flyer for a meeting of the Pacific Islanders' group, inviting me to join the students, staff, and faculty (which includes two department chairs I work with often). We smile at each other. Her cultural ways—Filipina—and mine are so different really— except that we have two out of three imperial lords in common: Spain and the United States. It binds us. Our first imperial lord was there before the world got large, more local: the Japanese and the Caribes. We laugh, while others look and listen on with looks of wondering. It's not their memory.

Memory simply cannot be adequately portrayed in the conventional discourse of the academy.

I am grateful for the acknowledgment of perceptions that academic discourse provides, for the resources the conventions of citation make available, for the ideocentric discourse that displays inductive or deductive lines of reasoning, a way to trace a writer's logical connections.

Academic discourse is cognitively powerful!

But the cognitive alone is insufficient. It can be strong for *logos*. It can be strong for *ethos*. But it is very weak in *pathos*. Academic discourse tries, after all, to reach the Aristotelian ideal of being completely logocentric, though it cannot be freed of the ethical appeal to authority. A demonstration: Agustín Lao, in "Islands at the Crossroads: Puerto Ricanness Traveling between the Translocal Nation and the Global City," writes that

> Puerto Ricans (like other racialized diasporas) function within multiple and ambiguous registers of race and racism. As colonized subjects, all Puerto Ricans are "colored" by colonial discourses. On the other hand, differential processes of racialization can either nominalize Puerto Ricans as "ethnic" and/or allow some light-skinned Puerto Ricans to "pass" as "white." [. . .] A single Puerto Rican "transmigrant" can be classified as *trigueña* on the island, black in Ohio, and Latina in New York. (178–79)

Now consider the rhetorical effect of Professor Lao's assertion (though with qualification) and a couple of stories from this light-skinned Puerto Rican. Both take place during the Summer of 2000:

> *He was picked up at the registration desk of the hotel in Iowa City. The limousine (really a van) driver walks up, a man in his late fifties or early sixties, buzz cut, thick build, surely one more accustomed to hard physical labor, a farmer, one would imagine, given the locale. Says at least the guest is on time, kind of to the person behind the registration desk, kind of to himself, maybe even to the guest. He goes on to say that the last guest he'd picked up had been fifteen minutes late, then didn't pay the fare.*
>
> *Once in the van, the story of the deadbeat develops. It was a family of four, including an infant. No car seat.*
>
> *"I could've had my license pulled, with no car seat for the baby. Then he tries to pay me with a $100 travelers' check, like I carry that kind of money at five in the morning."*
>
> *"Were they foreigners?" assuming the passengers would have overestimated the fluidity of travelers' checks.*
>
> *"Who can know these days. The guy wore a turban. What are you?"*
>
> *Internal soliloquy: He didn't say "rag head," so maybe this is more the condition of the international seaports flowing into the middle of America, the in-migration of the newest immigrants and those new immigrants from the 1930s, a land no longer completely owned by those of Scandinavian and German ancestry. But 1898 and 1917 really should mean something in a situation like this.* [NB: 1898: the U.S. acquisition of Puerto Rico; 1917: US citizenship conferred on all Puerto Ricans]

"*Me? I'm American.*"
"*Coulda fooled me!*"
"*Yeah, well. I'm from New York.*"
The conversation ends. The next passenger turns out to be a black man with a crutch coming out of an upper-middle-class home in the suburbs of Iowa City. Kind of felt sorry for the driver and his comfortable assumptions.

Second story:

It was another one of those receptions produced by the dean of the graduate school. This one was to welcome doctoral fellows in residence. Most were persons of color. I was there as a department chair and as one of the mentors to a couple of the fellows.

The scene: Back porch of the house, clusters of folks with drinks in hand or paper plates with guacamole and chips, talking, smiling, overlooking cows grazing in the valley below and green soft rolling hills nearby, maybe three hundred yards away, where there will soon be wheat blowing beautifully in the wind.

A conversation ensues with one of the fellows, a woman who grew up in the black area of Boston, Roxbury. Listening in is an associate dean, originally from Central Asia, overtly happy to be away from Russian bureaucracy. The conversation turns to race in the wheatland.

VV: "Around here folks don't know if I'm Spanish, Jewish, Italian, from the Middle East, or from South Asia."

Associate Dean: "I would have thought you were Italian."

Roxbury: "I don' know. He looks pretty Portorican to me."

Sure, she knows the hue, she sees the "niggerlips," one of those names I endured as a child, just like Martín.

Martín Espada:

Niggerlips was the high school name
for me.
So called by Douglas
the car mechanic, with green tattoos
on each forearm,
and the choir of round pink faces
that grinned deliciously
from the back row of classrooms,
droned over by teachers
checking attendance too slowly.

Douglas would brag
about cruising his car

near sidewalks of black children
to point an unloaded gun,
to scare niggers
like crows off a tree,
he'd say.

My great-grandfather Luis
was un negrito too,
a shoemaker in the coffee hills
of Puerto Rico, 1900.
The family called him a secret
and kept no photograph.
My father remembers
the childhood white powder
that failed to bleach
his stubborn copper skin,
and the family says
he is still a fly in milk.

So Niggerlips has the mouth
of his great-grandfather,
the song he must have sung
as he pounded the leather and nails,
the heat that courses through copper,
the stubbornness of a fly in milk,
and all you have, Douglas,
is that unloaded gun.

Professor Lao, I would contend, is not quite right. Those of us who are light-skinned don't pass for white; we're just not automatically sorted into the appropriate slot. But more to the point is that Lao's academic discourse (complete with scare quotes and nominalizations) is insufficient, lacks emotional appeal. And though Aristotle thought it not right to sway with emotional appeals, he knew that the greatest impact on listeners is in fact the emotional. The personal here does not negate the need for the academic; it complements, provides an essential element in the rhetorical triangle, an essential element in the intellect—cognition *and* affect. The personal done well is sensorial and intellectual, complete, knowledge known throughout mind and body, even if vicariously.

And for the person of color, it does more. The narrative of the person of color validates. It resonates. It awakens, particularly for those of us who are in institutions where our numbers are few. We know that though we really are Gramsci's exceptions—those who "through 'chance' [. . . have] had opportunities that the thousand others in reality could not or did not have"—our experiences are in no sense unique but are always analogous to other experiences from among those exceptions. So more than narrating the life of one of color so that "one creates this possibility, suggests the process, indicates the opening," in Gramsci's terms (*Selections from Cultural Writings* 132), we remember the results of our having realized the possibility, discovered the process, found the opening, while finding that there is in some sense very little change on the other side. This is what Ellis Cose describes as *The Rage of a Privileged Class*. This is Luis Rodriguez's call, that we'll read below.

Ellis Cose, I've written before ("On Colonies"), explains, mainly by way of anecdote, the reasons African Americans in particular continue to be angry even after having crossed over to the other side. He explains the ways in which little slights continue to display the racism inherent in our society. Those "Dozen Demons" are

1. Inability to fit in.
2. Exclusion from the club.
3. Low expectations.
4. Shattered hopes.
5. Faint praise.
6. Presumption of failure.
7. Coping fatigue.
8. Pigeonholing.
9. Identity troubles.
10. Self-censorship and silence.
11. Mendacity.
12. Guilt by association. (57–68)

I haven't been called a "spic" in many years (except by others of color, perhaps, in fun, I hope). Yet little things happen that betray the underlying racism that affects us all, no matter how appalled by racism we might be. I read Anzaldúa or hooks or the poetry of Espada or Cruz or Esteves or any other writing of color, and I know I haven't become clinically paranoid. I know that I've been poked by one of the demons. Some of the slights signified by Cose are self-imposed, instances of Frantz Fanon's internal colonialism. Some are externally imposed. All can be laid bare through the personal made public.

> There's the story of the academics of color who wrote about the subtle ways in which they find themselves victims of some of Cose's demons—exclusion,

expecting less, presuming failure, pigeonholing as "brown-on-brown" research rather than disinterested research (read: white and classical-empirical). Someone far away reads the essay once published and files suit for slander. The authors had never heard of the person. This is a very funny story to people of color who have heard it—the laughter of verification and white guilt gone awry.

The converse:
"Man, I loved your book [or article or essay]. I could relate. The same things have happened to me," something I've heard time and again wherever I travel. Identity minus troubles among Cose's demons, association guiltless, a new club formed.

Somehow, the spic does remain, despite all the good fortune and accolades, not only from within but from without. While a good academic piece would help me to remember, rich narrative does more for the memory.

And the precedent is old. *Memoria* was the mother of the muses, the most important of the rhetorical offices. Now rhetorics of writing seem to go no further than invention, arrangement, and style; when delivery is still there, it's the matter of "voice." But memory is tied in as well, surely for people of color. It's as if we have accepted Plato's prophecy that literacy would be the downfall of memory, leading only to remembrance. We have to remember Plato, because his writing is significant by virtue of its genre, an attempt at representation of dialogue, of storytelling, of the play. Plato's literacy took shape not as logocentric discourse but as a representation of discourse in action. Though folks like Volosinov have shown that all discourse, written as well as spoken, is dialogic, Plato is maybe the coolest of the philosophers because of the resonance of the dialogue, the possibility for humor, the clear presence of all three points in the rhetorical triangle and the often unspecified dimension which is context. I don't mean to be waxing Platonic, really, only to suggest that there's something to Plato's notion of memory as more than recollection and to his leaning on a written discourse that approximates orality as a means toward arriving at Memory. The narratives of people of color jog our memories as a collective in a scattered world and within an ideology that praises individualism. And this is all the more apparent for the Latino and Latina, whose language contains the assertion of the interconnectedness among identity, memory, and the personal. There is a common saying among Puerto Ricans and Cubans: *Te doy un cuento de mi historia,* literally rendered as "I'll give you a story about my history": me, history and memory, and a story.

A thousand years before the first Europeans arrived on Puerto Rico, the native peoples of the mainland and the lesser Antilles migrated to Puerto

Rico, where they could live in relative peace, able to fish and live off the fresh vegetation—pineapple and varieties of tuber that have no name in English. We don't know the names of the first inhabitants of Puerto Rico. Our history is the history told by the Europeans, who, conferring their values on the land, took the language of the local imperial lords. We only know the names given the first Puerto Ricans by their first colonizers, the first to raid them, the first to enslave them, the ones the Europeans honored by naming the region after them. These first colonizers were the peoples of Carib. And they named the people of that island Arawak and the culture of the Arawak was called Taino. And their island was named Boriquén.

Then came Columbus (or Columbo or Colón. I'm glad we've stopped translating people's names, or I'd have to walk around with the name Conqueror Newton). And then Ponce de León. Then the priests.

And when the slaves of Puerto Rico rebelled, slaves from Africa were brought in, and the Boricuas ran inland, away from the fortressed walls of El Morro, acquiescing to the Spanish yet surreptitiously trading with Dutch and English, French and Italian pirates who would find other ways to enter the island. This subversion became jaibería. So I understand Angel Rama, when he says that it is in the Caribbean that "the plural manifestations of the entire universe insert themselves" (qtd. in Smorkaloff vii). My mother's name is Italian (the line is never lost in the Spanish tradition: my father's mother—Hernándes and my mother becoming María Socorro Cotto de Villanueva, my father was thus Victor Villanueva y Hernándes and me Victor Villanueva y Cotto until we both were Americanized and I became "Jr."). My mother's name: Italian. The memory of that first Italian, whether family or slavemaster (which is how so many of the Tainos got their names, just like the African Americans of the mainland)—lost.

Centuries after the first Europeans later, I am Puerto Rican—a product of the first migrations of Puerto Ricans to New York in the late 1940s, though my mother arrived through what was euphemistically called "indentured servitude," what others called "white slavery," as if somehow more barbaric than the slavery of Africans. And I assimilate. And I don't. But I know how to seem to be—jaibería—and I have the memory—the memory provided by stories told. Memory does hunger. And it's fed through the stories told.

I'm trying to figure this out, somehow: who I am, from where, playing out the mixes within. It isn't a question for me, whether public or private discourses. I am contradictory consciousness. The discourse should reflect that. I am these uneasy mixes of races that make for no race at all yet find themselves victim to racism. The discourse should reflect that. I am an American (in every sense—a boy from Brooklyn, jazz and rock 'n' roll, and from the Americas, with an ancestry dating back before the Europeans), an academic, a person of color—an organically grown traditional intellectual, containing both of Gramsci's intellectual formations, yet not quite his new intellectual. The discourse should reflect that as well. And I am in a wheatfield, attempting to pass on a memory as I attempt to gather one. Personal discourse, the narrative, the auto/biography, helps in that effort, is a necessary adjunct to the academic.

Looking back, we look ahead, and giving ourselves up to the looking back and the looking ahead, knowing the self, and, critically, knowing the self in relation to others, maybe we can be an instrument whereby students can hear the call.

A poem by Luis J. Rodriguez:

The calling came to me
while I languished
in my room, while I
whittled away my youth
in jail cells
and damp *barrio* fields.

It brought me to life,
out of captivity,
in a street-scarred
and tattooed place
I called body.

Until then I waited silently,
a deafening clamor in my head,
but voiceless to all around;
hidden from America's eyes,
a brown boy without a name.

I would sing into a solitary
            tape recorder,
music never to be heard.
I would write my thoughts
in scrambled English;
I would take photos in my mind
            plan out new parks,
            bushy green, concrete free,
            new places to play
            and think.

Waiting.
Then it came.
The calling.
It brought me out of my room.

It forced me to escape
night captors
in street prisons.

It called me to war,
to be writer,
to be scientist
and march with the soldiers
      of change.

It called me from the shadows,
out of the wreckage
of my *barrio*—from among those
who did not exist.

I waited all of 16 years
for this time.

Somehow, unexpected,
I was called.

Memoria calls and pushes us forward. *Memoria* is a friend of ours. We must invite her into our classrooms and into our scholarship.

WORKS CITED

Adell, Sandra. *Double Consciousness/Double Bind: Theoretical Issues in Twentieth-Century Black Literature*. Urbana: U of Illinois P, 1994.

Cose, Ellis. *The Rage of a Privileged Class*. New York: Harper, 1993.

Espada, Martín. "Niggerlips." *Cool Salsa: Bilingual Poems on Growing Up Latino in the United States*. Ed. Lori M. Carlson. New York: Fawcett, 1994. 73–74.

Fanon, Frantz. *Black Skin, White Masks*. Trans. Charles Lam Markmann. New York: Grove, 1967.

Gramsci, Antonio. *Selections from Cultural Writings*. Ed. David Forgacs and Geoffrey Nowell-Smith. Trans. William Boelhower. Cambridge: Harvard UP, 1985.

——. *Selections from the Prison Notebooks*. Ed. and trans. Quintin Hoare and Geoffrey Nowell-Smith. New York: International, 1971.

Grosfoguel, Ramón, Frances Negrón-Muntaner, and Chloé S. Georas. "Beyond Nationalist and Colonialist Discourses: The *Jaiba* Politics of the Puerto-Rican Ethno-Nation," *Puerto Rican Jam: Rethinking Colonialism and Nationalism*. Ed. Frances Negrón-Muntaner and Ramón Grosfoguel. Minneapolis: U of Minnesota P, 1997. 1–36.

JanMohamed, Abdul R., and David Lloyd, eds. *The Nature and Context of Minority Discourse*. New York: Oxford UP, 1990.

Lao, Agustín, "Islands at the Crossroads: Puerto Ricanness Traveling between the Translocal Nation and the Global City." *Puerto Rican Jam: Rethinking Colonialism and Nationalism*. Ed. Frances Negrón-Muntaner and Ramón Grosfoguel. Minneapolis: U of Minnesota P, 1997. 169–88.

Omi, Michael, and Howard Winant. *Racial Formation in the United States: From the 1960s to the 1990s*. New York: Routledge, 1994.

Rodriguez, Luis J. "The Calling." *Cool Salsa: Bilingual Poems on Growing Up Latino in the United States*. Ed. Lori M. Carlson. New York: Fawcett, 1994. 123–24.

Saldívar, Ramón. *Chicano Narrative: The Dialectics of Difference*. Madison: U of Wisconsin P, 1990.

San Juan, E. *Racial Formations/Critical Transformations: Articulations of Power in Ethnic and Racial Studies in the United States*. Atlantic Highlands, NJ: Humanities, 1992.

Singh, Amritjit, Joseph Skerrett, Robert E. Hogan, eds. *Memory, Narrative, and Identity: New Essays in Ethnic American Literature*. Boston: Northeastern UP, 1994.

Smorkaloff, Pamela Maria. *Cuban Writers on and off the Island: Contemporary Narrative Fiction*. New York: Twayne, 1999.

Villanueva, Victor. *Bootstraps: From an American Academic of Color*. Urbana, IL: NCTE, 1993.

——. "On Colonies, Canons, and Ellis Cose's Rage of a Privileged Class." *JAC* 16 (1996): 159–69.

Composing as a Woman

ELIZABETH A. FLYNN

It is not easy to think like a woman in a man's world, in the world of the professions; yet the capacity to do that is a strength which we can try to help our students develop. To think like a woman in a man's world means thinking critically, refusing to accept the givens, making connections between facts and ideas which men have left unconnected. It means remembering that every mind resides in a body; remaining accountable to the female bodies in which we live; constantly retesting given hypotheses against lived experience. It means a constant critique of language, for as Wittgenstein (no feminist) observed, "The limits of my language are the limits of my world." And it means that most difficult thing of all: listening and watching in art and literature, in the social sciences, in all the descriptions we are given of the world, for silences, the absences, the nameless, the unspoken, the encoded—for there we will find the true knowledge of women. And in breaking those silences, naming ourselves, uncovering the hidden, making ourselves present, we begin to define a reality which resonates to us, which affirms our being, which allows the woman teacher and the woman student alike to take ourselves, and each other, seriously: meaning, to begin taking charge of our lives.

—Adrienne Rich, "Taking Women Students Seriously"

The emerging field of composition studies could be described as a feminization of our previous conceptions of how writers write and how writing should be taught.[1] In exploring the nature of the writing process, composition specialists expose the limitations of previous product-oriented approaches by

Reprinted from *College Composition and Communication* 39.4 (December 1988): 423–35. Used with permission.

demystifying the product and in so doing empowering developing writers and readers. Rather than enshrining the text in its final form, they demonstrate that the works produced by established authors are often the result of an extended, frequently enormously frustrating process and that creativity is an activity that results from experience and hard work rather than a mysterious gift reserved for a select few. In a sense, composition specialists replace the figure of the authoritative father with an image of a nurturing mother. Powerfully present in the work of composition researchers and theorists is the ideal of a committed teacher concerned about the growth and maturity of her students who provides feedback on ungraded drafts, reads journals, and attempts to tease out meaning from the seeming incoherence of student language. The field's foremothers come to mind—Janet Emig, Mina Shaughnessy, Ann Berthoff, Win Horner, Maxine Hairston, Shirley Heath, Nancy Martin, Linda Flower, Andrea Lunsford, Sondra Perl, Nancy Sommers, Marion Crowhurst, Lisa Ede. I'll admit the term foremother seems inappropriate as some of these women are still in their thirties and forties—we are speaking here of a very young field. Still, invoking their names suggests that we are also dealing with a field that, from the beginning, has welcomed contributions from women—indeed, has been shaped by women.

The work of male composition researchers and theorists has also contributed significantly to the process of feminization described above. James Britton, for instance, reverses traditional hierarchies by privileging private expression over public transaction, process over product. In arguing that writing for the self is the matrix out of which all forms of writing develop, he valorizes an activity and a mode of expression that have previously been undervalued or invisible, much as feminist literary critics have argued that women's letters and diaries are legitimate literary forms and should be studied and taught alongside more traditional genres. His work has had an enormous impact on the way writing is taught on the elementary and high school levels and in the university, not only in English courses but throughout the curriculum. Writing-Across-the-Curriculum Programs aim to transform pedagogical practices in all disciplines, even those where patriarchal attitudes toward authority are most deeply rooted.

FEMINIST STUDIES
AND COMPOSITION STUDIES

Feminist inquiry and composition studies have much in common. After all, feminist researchers and scholars and composition specialists are usually in the same department and sometimes teach the same courses. Not surprisingly, there have been wonderful moments when feminists have expressed their commitment to the teaching of writing. Florence Howe's essay, "Identity and Expression: A Writing Course for Women," for example, published in *College English* in 1971, describes her use of journals in a writing course designed to empower women. Adrienne Rich's essay, "'When We Dead Awaken': Writing as Re-Vision," politicizes and expands our conception of revision, emphasizing that taking another look at the texts we have generated necessitates revising our cultural assumptions as well.

There have also been wonderful moments when composition specialists have recognized that the marginality of the field of composition studies is linked in important ways to the political marginality of its constituents, many of whom are women who teach part-time. Maxine Hairston, in "Breaking Our Bonds and Reaffirming Our Connections," a slightly revised version of her Chair's address at the 1985 convention of the Conference on College Composition and Communication, draws an analogy between the plight of composition specialists and the plight of many women. For both, their worst problems begin at home and hence are immediate and daily. Both, too, often have complex psychological bonds to the people who frequently are their adversaries (273).

For the most part, though, the fields of feminist studies and composition studies have not engaged each other in a serious or systematic way. The major journals in the field of composition studies do not often include articles addressing feminist issues, and panels on feminism are infrequent at the Conference on College Composition and Communication.[2] As a result, the parallels between feminist studies and composition studies have not been delineated, and the feminist critique that has enriched such diverse fields as linguistics, reading, literary criticism, psychology, sociology, anthropology, religion, and science has had little impact on our models of the composing process or on our understanding of how written language abilities are acquired. We have not examined our research methods or research samples to see if they are androcentric. Nor have we attempted to determine just what it means to compose as a woman.

Feminist research and theory emphasize that males and females differ in their developmental processes and in their interactions with others. They emphasize, as well, that these differences are a result of an imbalance in the social order, of the dominance of men over women. They argue that men have chronicled our historical narratives and defined our fields of inquiry. Women's perspectives have been suppressed, silenced, marginalized, written out of what counts as authoritative knowledge. Difference is erased in a desire to universalize. Men become the standard against which women are judged.

A feminist approach to composition studies would focus on questions of difference and dominance in written language. Do males and females compose differently? Do they acquire language in different ways? Do research methods and research samples in composition studies reflect a male bias? I do not intend to tackle all of these issues. My approach here is a relatively modest one. I will survey recent feminist research on gender differences in social and psychological development, and I will show how this research and theory may be used in examining student writing, thus suggesting directions that a feminist investigation of composition might take.

GENDER DIFFERENCES IN SOCIAL AND PSYCHOLOGICAL DEVELOPMENT

Especially relevant to a feminist consideration of student writing are Nancy Chodorow's *The Reproduction of Mothering*, Carol Gilligan's *In a Different Voice*, and Mary Belenky, Blythe Clinchy, Nancy Goldberger, and Jill Tarule's *Women's Ways of Knowing*. All three books suggest that women and men have different conceptions of self and different modes of interaction with others as a result of their different experiences, especially their early relationship with their primary parent, their mother.

Chodorow's book, published in 1978, is an important examination of what she calls the "psychoanalysis and the sociology of gender," which in turn influenced Gilligan's *In a Different Voice* and Belenky et al.'s *Women's Ways of Knowing*. Chodorow tells us in her preface that her book originated when a feminist group she was affiliated with "wondered what it meant that women parented women." She argues that girls and boys develop different relational capacities and senses of self as a result of growing up in a family in which women mother. Because all children identify first with their mother, a girl's gender and gender role identification processes are continuous with her earliest identifications whereas a boy's are not. The boy gives up, in addition to his oedipal and preoedipal attachment to his mother, his primary identification with her. The more general identification processes for both males and females also follow this pattern. Chodorow says,

> Girls' identification processes, then, are more continuously embedded in and mediated by their ongoing relationship with their mother. They develop through and stress particularistic and affective relationships to others. A boy's identification processes are not likely to be so embedded in or mediated by a real affective relation to his father. At the same time, he tends to deny identification with and relationship to his mother and reject

what he takes to be the feminine world; masculinity is defined as much negatively as positively. Masculine identification processes stress differentiation from others, the denial of affective relation, and categorical universalistic components of the masculine role. Feminine identification processes are relational, whereas masculine identification processes tend to deny relationship. (176)

Carol Gilligan's *In a Different Voice*, published in 1982, builds on Chodorow's findings, focusing especially, though, on differences in the ways in which males and females speak about moral problems. According to Gilligan, women tend to define morality in terms of conflicting responsibilities rather than competing rights, requiring for their resolution a mode of thinking that is contextual and narrative rather than formal and abstract (19). Men, in contrast, equate morality and fairness and tie moral development to the understanding of rights and rules (19). Gilligan uses the metaphors of the web and the ladder to illustrate these distinctions. The web suggests interconnectedness as well as entrapment; the ladder suggests an achievement-orientation as well as individualistic and hierarchical thinking. Gilligan's study aims to correct the inadequacies of Lawrence Kohlberg's delineation of the stages of moral development. Kohlberg's study included only male subjects, and his categories reflect his decidedly male orientation. For him, the highest stages of moral development derive from a reflective understanding of human rights (19).

Belenky, Clinchy, Goldberger, and Tarule, in *Women's Ways of Knowing*, acknowledge their debt to Gilligan, though their main concern is intellectual rather than moral development. Like Gilligan, they recognize that male experience has served as the model in defining processes of intellectual maturation. The mental processes that are involved in considering the abstract and the impersonal have been labeled "thinking" and are attributed primarily to men, while those that deal with the personal and interpersonal fall under the rubric of "emotions" and are largely relegated to women. The particular study they chose to examine and revise is William Perry's *Forms of Intellectual and Ethical Development in the College Years* (1970). While Perry did include some women subjects in his study, only the interviews with men were used in illustrating and validating his scheme of intellectual and ethical development. When Perry assessed women's development on the basis of the categories he developed, the women were found to conform to the patterns he had observed in the male data. Thus, his work reveals what women have in common with men but was poorly designed to uncover those themes that might be more prominent among women. *Women's Ways of Knowing* focuses on "what else women might have to say about the development of their minds and on alternative routes that are sketchy or missing in Perry's version" (9).

Belenky et al. examined the transcripts of interviews with 135 women from a variety of backgrounds and of different ages and generated categories that are suited for describing the stages of women's intellectual development. They found that the quest for self and voice plays a central role in transformations of women's ways of knowing. Silent women have little awareness of their intellectual capacities. They live—selfless and voiceless—at the behest of those around them. External authorities know the truth and are all-powerful. At the positions of received knowledge and procedural knowledge, other voices and external truths prevail. Sense of self is embedded either in external definitions and roles or in identifications with institutions, disciplines, and methods. A sense of authority arises primarily through identification with the power of a group and its agreed-upon ways for knowing. Women at this stage of development have no sense of an authentic or unique voice, little awareness of a centered self. At the position of subjective knowledge, women turn away from others and any external authority. They have not yet acquired a public voice or public authority, though. Finally, women at the phase of constructed knowledge begin an effort to reclaim the self by attempting to integrate knowledge they feel intuitively with knowledge they have learned from others.

STUDENT WRITING

If women and men differ in their relational capacities and in their moral and intellectual development, we would expect to find manifestations of these differences in the student papers we encounter in our first-year composition courses. The student essays I will describe here are narrative descriptions of learning experiences produced in the first of a two-course sequence required of first-year students at Michigan Tech. I've selected the four because they invite commentary from the perspective of the material discussed above. The narratives of the female students are stories of interaction, of connection, or of frustrated connection. The narratives of the male students are stories of achievement, of separation, or of frustrated achievement.

Kim's essay describes a dreamlike experience in which she and her high school girlfriends connected with each other and with nature as a result of a balloon ride they decided to take one summer Sunday afternoon as a way of relieving boredom. From the start, Kim emphasizes communion and tranquility: "It was one of those Sunday afternoons when the sun shines brightly and a soft warm breeze blows gently. A perfect day for a long drive on a country road with my favorite friends." This mood is intensified as they ascend in the balloon: "Higher and higher we went, until the view was over-powering. What once was a warm breeze turned quickly into a cool crisp wind. A feeling of freedom and serenity overtook us as we drifted along slowly." The group felt as if they were "just suspended there on a string, with time non-existent." The experience made them contemplative, and as they drove quietly home, "each one of us collected our thoughts, and to this day we still reminisce about that Sunday afternoon." The experience solidified relationships and led to the formation of a close bond that was renewed every time the day was recollected.

The essay suggests what Chodorow calls relational identification pro-cesses. The members of the group are described as being in harmony with themselves and with the environment. There is no reference to competition or discord. The narrative also suggests a variation on what Belenky et al. call "connected knowing," a form of procedural knowledge that makes possible the most desirable form of knowing, constructed knowledge. Connected knowing is rooted in empathy for others and is intensely personal. Women who are connected knowers are able to detach themselves from the relation-ships and institutions to which they have been subordinated and begin to trust their own intuitions. The women in the narrative were connected doers rather than connected knowers. They went off on their own, left their fami-lies and teachers behind (it was summer vacation, after all), and gave them-selves over to a powerful shared experience. The adventure was, for the most part, a silent one but did lead to satisfying talk.

Kathy also describes an adventure away from home, but hers was far less satisfying, no doubt because it involved considerably more risk. In her narra-tive she makes the point that "foreign countries can be frightening" by focus-ing on a situation in which she and three classmates, two females and a male, found themselves at a train station in Germany separated from the others because they had gotten off to get some refreshments and the train had left without them. She says,

> This left the four of us stranded in an unfamiliar station. Ed was the only person in our group that could speak German fluently, but he still didn't know what to do. Sue got hysterical and Laura tried to calm her down. I stood there stunned. We didn't know what to do.

What they did was turn to Ed, whom Kathy describes as "the smartest one in our group." He told them to get on a train that was on the same track as the original. Kathy realized, though, after talking to some passengers, that they were on the wrong train and urged her classmates to get off. She says,

> I almost panicked. When I convinced the other three we were on the wrong train we opened the doors. As we were getting off, one of the conductors started yelling at us in German. It didn't bother me too much because I couldn't understand what he was saying. One thing about trains in Europe is that they are always on schedule. I think we delayed that train about a minute or two.

In deciding which train to board after getting off the wrong one, they deferred to Ed's judgment once again, but this time they got on the right train. Kathy concludes, "When we got off the train everyone was waiting. It turned out we arrived thirty minutes later than our original train. I was very relieved to see everyone. It was a very frightening experience and I will never forget it."

In focusing on her fears of separation, Kathy reveals her strong need for connection, for affiliation. Her story, like Kim's, emphasizes the importance of relationships, though in a different way. She reveals that she had a strong need to feel part of a group and no desire to rebel, to prove her independence, to differentiate herself from others. This conception of self was a liability as well as a strength in the sense that she became overly dependent on the male authority figure in the group, whom she saw as smarter and more competent than herself. In Belenky et al.'s terms, Kathy acted as if other voices and external truths were more powerful than her own. She did finally speak and act, though, taking it on herself to find out if they were on the right train and ushering the others off when she discovered they were not. She was clearly moving toward the development of an authentic voice and a way of knowing that integrates intuition with authoritative knowledge. After all, she was the real hero of the incident.

The men's narratives stress individuation rather than connection. They are stories of individual achievement or frustrated achievement and conclude by emphasizing separation rather than integration or reintegration into a community. Jim wrote about his "Final Flight," the last cross-country flight required for his pilot's license. That day, everything seemed to go wrong. First, his flight plan had a mistake in it that took $1\frac{1}{2}$ hours to correct. As a result, he left his hometown 2 hours behind schedule. Then the weather deteriorated, forcing him to fly as low as a person can safely fly, with the result that visibility was very poor. He landed safely at his first destination but flew past the second because he was enjoying the view too much. He says,

Then I was off again south bound for Benton Harbor. On the way south along the coast of Lake Michigan the scenery was a beautiful sight. This relieved some of the pressures and made me look forward to the rest of the flight. It was really nice to see the ice flows break away from the shore. While enjoying the view of a power plant on the shore of Lake Michigan I discovered I had flown past the airport.

He finally landed and took off again, but shortly thereafter had to confront darkness, a result of his being behind schedule. He says,

The sky turned totally black by the time I was half-way home. This meant flying in the dark which I had only done once before. Flying in the dark was also illegal for me to do at this time. One thing that made flying at night nice was that you could see lights that were over ninety miles away.

Jim does not emphasize his fear, despite the fact that his situation was more threatening than the one Kathy described, and his reference to his enjoyment of the scenery suggests that his anxiety was not paralyzing or debilitating. At times, his solitary flight was clearly as satisfying as Kim's communal one. When he focuses on the difficulties he encountered, he speaks only of his "problems" and "worries" and concludes that the day turned out to be "long and trying." He sums up his experience as follows: "That day I will long remember for both its significance in my goal in getting my pilot's license and all the problems or worries that it caused me during the long and problem-ridden flight." He emerges the somewhat shaken hero of his adventure; he has achieved his goal in the face of adversity. Significantly, he celebrates his return home by having a bite to eat at McDonald's by himself. His adventure does not end with a union or reunion with others.

Jim's story invites interpretation in the context of Chodorow's claims about male interactional patterns. Chodorow says that the male, in order to feel himself adequately masculine, must distinguish and differentiate himself from others. Jim's adventure was an entirely solitary one. It was also goal-directed—he wanted to obtain his pilot's license and, presumably, prove his competence to himself and others. His narrative calls into question, though, easy equations of abstract reasoning and impersonality with male modes of learning since Jim was clearly as capable as Kim of experiencing moments of exultation, of communion with nature.

Joe's narrative of achievement is actually a story of frustrated achievement, of conflicting attitudes toward an ethic of hard work and sacrifice to achieve a goal. When he was in high school, his father drove him twenty miles to swim practice and twenty miles home every Tuesday through

Friday night between October and March so he could practice for the swim team. He hated this routine and hated the Saturday morning swim meets even more but continued because he thought his parents, especially his father, wanted him to. He says, "I guess it was all for them, the cold work-outs, the evening practices, the weekend meets. I had to keep going for them even though I hated it." Once he realized he was going through his agony for his parents rather than for himself, though, he decided to quit and was surprised to find that his parents supported him. Ultimately, though, he regretted his decision. He says,

> As it turns out now, I wish I had stuck with it. I really had a chance to go somewhere with my talent. I see kids my age who stuck with something for a long time and I envy them for their determination. I wish I had met up to the challenge of sticking with my swimming, because I could have been very good if I would have had their determination.

Joe is motivated to pursue swimming because he thinks his father will be disappointed if he gives it up. His father's presumed hold on him is clearly tenuous, however, because once Joe realizes that he is doing it for him rather than for himself, he quits. Finally, though, it is his gender role identification, his socialization into a male role and a male value system, that allows him to look back on his decision with regret. In college, he has become a competitor, an achiever. He now sees value in the long and pain-ful practices, in a single-minded determination to succeed. The narrative reminds us of Chodorow's point that masculine identification is predomi-nantly a gender role identification rather than identification with a particu-lar parent.

I am hardly claiming that the four narratives are neat illustrations of the feminist positions discussed above. For one thing, those positions are rich in contradiction and complexity and defy easy illustration. For another, the narratives themselves are as often characterized by inconsistency and con-tradiction as by a univocality of theme and tone. Kathy is at once dependent and assertive; Joe can't quite decide if he should have been rebellious or dis-ciplined. Nor am I claiming that what I have found here are characteristic patterns of male and female student writing. I would need a considerably larger and more representative sample to make such a claim hold. I might note, though, that I had little difficulty identifying essays that revealed pat-terns of difference among the twenty-four papers I had to choose from, and I could easily have selected others. Sharon, for instance, described her class trip to Chicago, focusing especially on the relationship she and her classmates were able to establish with her advisor. Diane described "An Unwanted Job" that she seemed unable to quit despite unpleasant working conditions. Mike, like Diane, was dissatisfied with his job, but he expressed his dissatisfaction and was fired. The frightening experience Russ described resulted from his failed attempt to give his car a tune-up; the radiator hose burst, and he found himself in the hospital recovering from third-degree burns. These are stories of relatedness or entanglement; of separation or frustrated achievement.

The description of the student essays is not meant to demonstrate the validity of feminist scholarship but to suggest, instead, that questions raised by feminist researchers and theorists do have a bearing on composition studies and should be pursued. We ought not assume that males and females use language in identical ways or represent the world in a similar fashion. And if their writing strategies and patterns of representation do differ, then ignoring those differences almost certainly means a suppression of women's separate ways of thinking and writing. Our models of the composing process are quite possibly better suited to describing men's ways of composing than to describing women's.[3]

PEDAGOGICAL STRATEGIES

The classroom provides an opportunity for exploring questions about gender differences in language use. Students, I have found, are avid inquirers into their own language processes. An approach I have had success with is to make the question of gender difference in behavior and language use the subject to be investigated in class. In one honors section of first-year English, for instance, course reading included selections from Mary Anne Ferguson's *Images of Women in Literature*, Gilligan's *In a Different Voice*, Alice Walker's *Meridian*, and James Joyce's *A Portrait of the Artist as a Young Man*. Students were also required to keep a reading journal and to submit two formal papers. The first was a description of people they know in order to arrive at generalizations about gender differences in behavior, the second a comparison of some aspect of the Walker and Joyce novels in the light of our class discussions.

During class meetings we shared journal entries, discussed the assigned literature, and self-consciously explored our own reading, writing, and speaking behaviors. In one session, for instance, we shared retellings of Irwin Shaw's "The Girls in Their Summer Dresses," an especially appropriate story since it describes the interaction of a husband and wife as they attempt to deal with the husband's apparently chronic habit of girl-watching. Most of the women were sympathetic to the female protagonist, and several males clearly identified strongly with the male protagonist.

The students reacted favorably to the course. They found Gilligan's book to be challenging, and they enjoyed the heated class discussions. The final journal entry of one of the strongest students in the class, Dorothy, suggests the nature of her development over the ten-week period:

> As this is sort of the wrap-up of what I've learned or how I feel about the class, I'll try to relate this entry to my first one on gender differences.
>
> I'm not so sure that men and women are so similar anymore, as I said in the first entry. The reactions in class especially make me think this. The men were so hostile toward Gilligan's book! I took no offense at it, but then again I'm not a man. I must've even overlooked the parts where she offended the men!
>
> Another thing really bothered me. One day after class, I heard two of the men talking in the hall about how you just have to be really careful about what you say in HU 101H about women, etc. *Why* do they have to be careful?! What did these two *really* want to say? That was pretty disturbing.
>
> However, I do still believe that MTU (or most any college actually) does bring out more similarities than differences. But the differences are still there—I know that.

Dorothy has begun to suspect that males and females read differently, and she has begun to suspect that they talk among themselves differently than they do in mixed company. The reading, writing, and discussing in the course have clearly alerted her to the possibility that gender affects the way in which readers, writers, and speakers use language.

This approach works especially well with honors students. I use somewhat different reading and writing assignments with non-honors students. In one class, for instance, I replaced the Gilligan book with an essay by Dale Spender on conversational patterns in high school classrooms. Students wrote a paper defending or refuting the Spender piece on the basis of their experiences in their own high schools. I have also devised ways of addressing feminist issues in composition courses in which the focus is not explicitly on gender differences. In a course designed to introduce students to fundamentals of research, for instance, students read Marge Piercy's *Woman on the Edge of Time* and did research on questions stimulated by it. They then shared their findings with the entire class in oral presentations. The approach led to wonderful papers on and discussions of the treatment of women in mental institutions, discrimination against minority women, and the ways in which technology can liberate women from oppressive roles.

I return now to my title and to the epigraph that introduces my essay. First, what does it mean to "compose as a woman"? Although the title invokes Jonathan Culler's "Reading as a Woman," a chapter in *On Deconstruction*, I do not mean to suggest by it that I am committed fully to Culler's deconstructive position. Culler maintains that "to read as a woman is to avoid reading as a man, to identify the specific defenses and distortions of male readings and provide correctives" (54). He concludes,

> For a woman to read as a woman is not to repeat an identity or an experience that is given but to play a role she constructs with reference to her identity as a woman, which is also a construct, so that the series can continue: a woman reading as a woman reading as a woman. The noncoincidence reveals an interval, a division within woman or within any reading subject and the "experience" of that subject. (64)

Culler is certainly correct that women often read as men and that they have to be encouraged to defend against this form of alienation. The strategy he suggests is almost entirely reactive, though. To read as a woman is to avoid reading as a man, to be alerted to the pitfalls of men's ways of reading.[4] Rich, too, warns of the dangers of immasculation, of identifying against oneself and learning to think like a man, and she, too, emphasizes the importance of critical activity on the part of the woman student—refusing to accept the givens of our culture, making connections between facts and ideas which men have left unconnected. She is well aware that thinking as a woman involves active construction, the recreation of one's identity. But she also sees value in recovering women's lived experience. In fact, she suggests that women maintain a critical posture in order to get in touch with that experience—to name it, to uncover that which is hidden, to make present that which has been absent. Her approach is active rather than reactive. Women's experience is not entirely a distorted version of male reality, it is not entirely elusive, and it is worthy of recuperation. We must alert our women students to the dangers of immasculation and provide them with a critical perspective. But we must also encourage them to become self-consciously aware of what their experience in the world has been and how this experience is related to the politics of gender. Then we must encourage our women students to write from the power of that experience.

NOTES

1. I received invaluable feedback on drafts of this essay from Carol Berkenkotter, Art Young, Marilyn Cooper, John Willinsky, Diane Shoos, John Flynn, Richard Gebhardt, and three anonymous *CCC* reviewers.

2. The 1988 Conference on College Composition and Communication was a notable exception. It had a record number of panels on feminist or gender-related issues and a number of sessions devoted to political concerns. I should add, too, that an exception to the generalization that feminist studies and composition studies have not confronted each other is Cynthia Caywood and Gillian Overing's very useful anthology, *Teaching Writing: Pedagogy, Gender, and Equity.* In their introduction to the book, Caywood and Overing note the striking parallels between writing theory and feminist theory. They conclude, "[T]he process model, insofar as it facilitates and legitimizes the fullest expression of the individual voice, is compatible with the feminist re-visioning of hierarchy, if not essential to it" (xiv). Pamela Annas, in her essay, "Silences: Feminist Language Research and the Teaching of Writing," describes a course she teaches at the University of Massachusetts at Boston, entitled "Writing as Women." In the course, she focuses on the question of silence—"what kinds of silence there are; the voices inside you that tell you to be quiet, the voices outside you that drown you out or politely dismiss what you say or do not understand you, the silence inside you that avoids saying anything important even to yourself, internal and external forms of censorship, and the stress that it produces" (3–4). Carol A. Stanger in "The Sexual Politics of the One-to-One Tutorial Approach and Collaborative Learning" argues that the one-to-one tutorial is essentially hierarchical and hence a male mode of teaching whereas collaborative learning is female and relational rather than hierarchical. She uses Gilligan's images of the ladder and the web to illustrate her point. Elisabeth Daeumer and Sandra Runzo suggest that the teaching of writing is comparable to the activity of mothering in that it is a form of "women's work." Mothers socialize young children to insure that they become acceptable citizens, and teachers' work, like the work of mothers, is usually devalued (45–46).

3. It should be clear by now that my optimistic claim at the outset of the essay that the field of composition studies has feminized our conception of written communication needs qualification. I have already mentioned that the field has developed, for the most part, independent of feminist studies and as a result has not explored written communication in the context of women's special needs and problems. Also, feminist inquiry is beginning to reveal that work in cognate fields that have influenced the development of composition studies is androcentric. For an exploration of the androcentrism of theories of the reading process see Patrocinio P. Schweickart, "Reading Ourselves: Toward a Feminist Theory of Reading."

4. Elaine Showalter, in "Reading as a Woman: Jonathan Culler and the Deconstruction of Feminist Criticism," argues that "Culler's deconstructionist priorities lead him to overstate the essentialist dilemma of defining the *woman* reader, when in most cases what is intended and implied is a *feminist* reader" (126).

WORKS CITED

Annas, Pamela J. "Silences: Feminist Language Research and the Teaching of Writing." *Teaching Writing: Pedagogy, Gender, and Equity.* Ed. Cynthia L. Caywood and Gillian R. Overing. Albany: State U of New York P, 1987. 3–17.

Belenky, Mary Field, et al. *Women's Ways of Knowing: The Development of Self, Voice, and Mind.* New York: Basic Books, 1986.

Britton, James, et al. *The Development of Writing Abilities (11–18).* London: Macmillan Education, 1975.

Caywood, Cynthia L., and Gillian R. Overing. Introduction. *Teaching Writing: Pedagogy, Gender, and Equity.* Ed. Cynthia L. Caywood and Gillian R. Overing. Albany: State U of New York P, 1987. xi–xvi.

Chodorow, Nancy. *The Reproduction of Mothering: Psychoanalysis and the Sociology of Gender.* Berkeley: U of California P, 1978.

Culler, Jonathan. *On Deconstruction: Theory and Criticism after Structuralism.* Ithaca: Cornell UP, 1982.

Daeumer, Elisabeth, and Sandra Runzo. "Transforming the Composition Classroom." *Teaching Writing: Pedagogy, Gender, and Equity.* Ed. Cynthia L. Caywood and Gillian R. Overing. Albany: State U of New York P, 1987. 45–62.

Gilligan, Carol. *In a Different Voice: Psychological Theory and Women's Development.* Cambridge: Harvard UP, 1982.

Hairston, Maxine. "Breaking Our Bonds and Reaffirming Our Connections." *College Composition and Communication* 36 (October 1985): 272–82.

Howe, Florence. "Identity and Expression: A Writing Course for Women." *College English* 32 (May 1971): 863–71. Rpt. in Howe, *Myths of Coeducation: Selected Essays, 1964–1983.* Bloomington: Indiana UP, 1984. 28–37.

Kohlberg, Lawrence. "Moral Stages and Moralization: The Cognitive-Development Approach." *Moral Development and Behavior.* Ed. T. Lickona. New York: Holt, 1976. 31–53.

Perry, William G. *Forms of Intellectual and Ethical Development in the College Years.* New York: Holt, Rinehart & Winston, 1970.

Rich, Adrienne. "Taking Women Students Seriously." *On Lies, Secrets, and Silence: Selected Prose, 1966–1978.* New York: W.W. Norton, 1979. 237–45.

_____. "'When We Dead Awaken': Writing as Re-Vision." *On Lies, Secrets, and Silence: Selected Prose, 1966–1978.* New York: W.W. Norton, 1979. 33–49.

Schweickart, Patrocinio P. "Reading Ourselves: Toward a Feminist Theory of Reading." *Gender and Reading: Essays on Readers, Texts and Contexts.* Ed. Elizabeth A. Flynn and Patrocinio P. Schweickart. Baltimore: Johns Hopkins UP, 1986. 31–62.

Showalter, Elaine. "Reading as a Woman: Jonathan Culler and the Deconstruction of Feminist Criticism." *Men and Feminism.* Ed. Alice Jardine and Paul Smith. New York: Methuen, 1987. 123–27.

Stanger, Carol A. "The Sexual Politics of the One-to-One Tutorial Approach and Collaborative Learning." *Teaching Writing: Pedagogy, Gender, and Equity.* Ed. Cynthia L. Caywood and Gillian R. Overing. Albany: State U of New York P, 1987. 31–44.

Feminism in Composition

Inclusion, Metonymy, and Disruption

Joy Ritchie and Kathleen Boardman

At a time when composition is engaged in clarifying its theoretical, political, and pedagogical histories, it is appropriate to construct a story of feminism's involvement in the disciplinary conversations. Despite the recent burgeoning of feminist perspectives in our discipline, it is not easy to delineate how feminism has functioned over the past three decades to shape and critique our understandings of the gendered nature of writing, teaching, and institutions. Although some accounts suggest that feminism, until recently, has been absent or at least late-blooming in the field, we find a more complex relationship in our rereading of essays and books in composition written from a feminist perspective—in particular, the many accounts of personal experience in the field written by feminists and by women since the 1970s. In this essay we look, and look again, at the few articles and notes that appeared in *CCC*, *College English*, and *English Journal* in the early 1970s. We also focus on feminist retrospective accounts—re-visions of composition written since the mid-1980s.

In writing this brief critical historical survey, we have found ourselves working from various impulses. First, we want to document and celebrate the vitality of feminism in composition, from its early manifestations in the small scattering of essays published in the 1970s (some of them frequently cited, others forgotten) to the explosion of feminist theory and well-documented feminist practice of the last decade. We wish to point out that much early feminist work in composition is not documented in our official publications,

Reprinted from *College Composition and Communication* 50.4 (June 1999): 585–606. Used with permission.

having occurred in informal conversations, in classrooms, and in committee meetings. At the same time, we want to suggest ways to examine and theorize experiential accounts—both published and unpublished—of feminism in composition. We must also consider seriously the causes and consequences of the delay in feminism's emergence in the published forums of our discipline and the extent to which feminism, despite its recent vitality, has remained contained or marginalized in composition. Finally, we hope to speculate on the positive and negative potential of inclusive, metonymic, and disruptive strategies for feminism's contribution to composition's narratives.

In the past decade, feminists have been visibly active in our discipline. They have examined the subjectivity of the gendered student and the position of women writers in the profession. Questioning assumptions about genre, form, and style, they have provided an impetus to seek alternative writing practices. Feminist perspectives have produced analyses of the gendered nature of the classroom, the feminization of English teaching, the working conditions for female teachers, and the implications of feminist theory for scholarship. Feminist scholars like Andrea Lunsford and Cheryl Glenn have begun rewriting the rhetorical tradition by reclaiming, refiguring, and regendering "Rhetorica." They are also critiquing earlier constructions of history and scholarship in composition. And from a different direction, scholars are drawing upon feminist, African American, lesbian, Native American, and class-based examinations of difference in order to complicate definitions of diversity within composition. Two recent essay collections, Susan Jarratt and Lynn Worsham's *Feminism and Composition Studies: In Other Words*, and Louise Phelps and Janet Emig's *Feminine Principles and Women's Experience in American Composition and Rhetoric*, especially highlight the strength of feminism(s) in composition and show how important feminism has been in shaping women's definitions of themselves, their work, and their commitment to pursuing questions of equity in the field.

Yet in the 1970s, while the work of composition as an emerging discipline was occurring right next door to, down the hall from, or in the basement under the work of feminist linguists and literary scholars, composition's official published discussions were largely silent on issues of gender. There is little explicit evidence of systematic theorizing about gender from the 1950s to the late 1980s. As late as 1988, Elizabeth Flynn could write, "For the most part . . . the fields of feminist studies and composition studies have not engaged each other in a serious or systematic way" (425). Indeed, when we began this study, we framed it as a paradox: prior to the mid-1980s, feminism seemed absent from composition but present among compositionists. From those early investigations we pulled one useful reminder: that the connections of composition and feminism have not been an inevitable result of the presence of so many women in the field. But subsequent conversations with a number of longtime teachers and scholars, who spoke to us about their own feminist beliefs and activities in composition dating back to the 1960s, reminded us that the near-absence of feminism from our publications does not constitute absence from the field.

The absence-presence binary also did not help us explain our own history as feminists in composition. As secondary English teachers, teaching women's literature and applying our feminist perspectives to high school courses in the 1970s, we moved into graduate courses and tenure track jobs in composition in the late 1980s and 1990s. Reflecting on our own experience, we recognized that much of the creative feminist energy in composition's history is not visible in the publications we searched: it appeared in informal conversations, in basement classrooms, and in committees on which women served. This energy might be viewed as ephemeral, yet we can testify, along with others, that it created solidarity among women, influenced students and colleagues, and helped form an epistemology on which later feminist work could grow. Sharon Crowley reminds us further that composition allowed and acknowledged women's participation in teaching and scholarship before many other disciplines began to do so—as we see from the important work of Josephine Miles, Winifred Horner, Ann Berthoff, Janet Emig and others. Still, Theresa Enos' collection of anecdotes from women in the field over the last several decades cautions us that the job conditions and security for many of these practitioners were terrible.

Crowley's and Enos' different perspectives point again to a history of women and feminism in composition that cannot be constructed in a tidy narrative. In the documents and accounts we have read and heard, we find three overlapping tropes that shed light on the roles feminism has played in composition and in the strategies women have used to gain a place in its conversations: (1) Following the pattern of developing feminist thought in the 1970s and 1980s, many early feminist accounts in composition sought *inclusion* and equality for women. (2) More recent accounts like those of Louise Phelps and Janet Emig posit feminism as a "subterranean" unspoken presence (xv), and Susan Jarratt and Laura Brady suggest the *metonymy* or contiguity of feminism and composition. (3) Also developing during this time has been what feminist postmodernists define as *disruption* and critique of hegemonic narratives—resistance, interruption, and finally redirection of composition's business as usual.

While it's tempting to posit this as a linear, evolutionary set of tropes—that women have grown out of and into as we've matured theoretically—we find it too restrictive to do so. These narratives coexist and have multiple functions, often depending on the historical or theoretical context in which they are read. For example, some early attempts at inclusion, based on experiential accounts, function also as disruptive narratives, and a number of very recent accounts might be characterized as primarily metonymic narratives. Furthermore, each of these tropes has both advantages and disadvantages for feminism in composition: for example, a narrative aimed at *including* women may also function to *contain* feminism within narrow boundaries. We also emphasize that we are not interested in categorizing narratives (and narrators) as "inclusionist," "disruptionist," and so on. Rather we hope to tease out the tropes, show how these narratives can be reread in multiple ways, and suggest how each one enacts one or more epistemological positions with respect to women's experience, identity, and difference.

As we reread for these rhetorical strategies, we find that the conceptions of experience in each of these sets of narratives also require examination. Most of the feminist writing in composition is grounded in accounts of personal experience. For example, many women have told powerful stories of their first recognition of their marginality in a field they had previously thought of as theirs. We must beware of reading these moving accounts too transparently and untheoretically. In her essay "Experience," Joan W. Scott offers a useful caution:

> When experience is taken as the origin of knowledge, the vision of the individual subject (the person who had the experience or the historian who recounts it) becomes the bedrock of evidence upon which explanation is built. Questions about the constructed nature of experience, about how subjects are constituted as different in the first place, about how one's vision is structured—about language (or discourse) and history—are left aside. (25)

Scott reminds us that narratives of experience should be encountered not as uncontested truth but as catalysts for further analysis of the conditions that shape experience.

We want to be clear about our view of experience: we are not dismissing such accounts but only suggesting ways to read and listen to them. The problem is not that these narratives are personal or that they are experiential, but that they are often untheorized. In understanding both the value and the limitations of feminist uses of experience in our field, we have found the work of Scott and of Rosemary Hennessy particularly useful. Both address "experience" as a construct and show ways to continue to value women's experiences as sources of knowledge; but they also suggest ways to theorize experience to make it a more critical rhetorical tool. Scott advises us to keep in mind that "experience is at once always already an interpretation and is in need of inter-pretation. What counts as experience is neither self-evident nor straightfor-ward; it is always contested, always therefore political" (37). Hennessy views experience as a critical tool for examining the values and ideologies used to construct women's experiences, but she adds an important qualification for ensuring that women's experience is not narrowly read. Any critical theoriz-ing of women's experience must be undertaken in the context of a continual "re-contextualization of the relationship between personal and group history and political priorities" (Minnie Bruce Pratt, qtd. in Hennessy 99) and in relation to the "counterhegemonic discourses" of others (99). We have found that by attending to certain feminist tropes in our discipline, we can not only begin to tease out the relationships between composition and feminism, but also gain a better sense of the important dialectical relationships between experience and theory.

ADDING WOMEN: NARRATIVES AIMED AT INCLUSION

Correcting the long absence of women from intellectual and political land-scapes, inserting women's perspectives into contexts dominated by patriar-chy, and giving women equal status with men have constituted one of the central feminist projects—that of *inclusion.* This effort to add women has been criticized retrospectively as ineffective because it arises from Enlight-enment conceptions of individual autonomy and the unquestioned "truth" of individual experience. Discussions of inclusion of women *as* women may reinforce essentialist or biological definitions of gender, and they often neglect to theorize the discourses that keep women and minorities margin-alized. Most critically, many attempts to include women in the conversa-tions of the field have in fact added only white, middle-class, heterosexual women. Despite these criticisms, we need to reread these attempts from their cultural context and for their first steps toward gender awareness. As Suzanne Clark reminds us, "feminists challenging a certain kind of femi-nism in composition represent a luxury: women now have a sufficient num-ber to play out [their] anxieties of influence" (94). Our analyses need to take into account cultural and historical contexts out of which women were working that made these assumptions viable at the time.

Some of the first published evidence of the initiative to add women to the conversation came in NCTE publications aimed primarily at secondary teachers. The March 1972 *English Journal* printed "The Undiscovered," Robert A. Bennett's NCTE presidential address of the previous November.

In highlighting "the undiscovered human resources of our professional organization" (352), Bennett includes girls and women among "those peoples of American society who have not yet been allowed to make their fullest contribution":

> The talents of the great number of women teachers who are today still non-members of the Council or who are inactive in Council affairs, provide another undiscovered resource. As a professional organization, we must reach out to these women and encourage them . . . to become full partners in our common effort. (353)

After urging the organization to examine wage and promotion policies, document discriminatory practices, and work for recognition of women in curriculum and pedagogy, Bennett declares, "NCTE must take a stand for recognition of the contribution of women to society and to our profession. We have not done it. Let's get at it" (353).

Two months later, *English Journal* carried a short "Open Letter from Janet Emig, Chairwoman, NCTE Committee on the Role and Image of Women," asking the membership to nominate committee members and to send information about any "instances of discrimination against women in the profession, either in the form of a brief narrative or, if you are the woman involved, as a signed or as an anonymous case history" (710). A direct result of NCTE's new commitment to include women, Emig's committee was soliciting stories that would potentially disrupt business-as-usual in the profession, (a practice that Theresa Enos repeated more than 20 years later for *Gender Roles and Faculty Lives in Rhetoric and Composition*). The CCCC Committee on the Status of Women also continues to solicit narratives, in various forums, in order to ascertain more clearly the status of women in the field.

While a review of CCC from the late 1960s through the late 1980s uncovers few essays or other documents that would indicate a gendered feminist consciousness in composition, two landmark special issues of *College English*, in 1971 and 1972, report on the newly formed MLA Commission on the Status of Women in the Profession and document courses designed by feminists in English to reshape the curriculum from the standpoint of women students. The narratives in these special issues set the pattern for the impulse a decade or more later in composition to add women to its perspectives. Arising from the writers' own consciousness-raising experiences, the narratives articulate the potential for student and teacher subjectivities that are not neutral or universal but uniquely influenced by the textual, social, and political context of gender. Florence Howe's impassioned 1971 essay, in which she inserts her own personal account of discrimination, reports the inequities in women's status she uncovered as chair of the MLA commission. In addition to these first attempts to address women's low status in the profession, Howe and Elaine Showalter both illustrate their efforts to rectify the lack of women's texts and perspectives in English courses. Showalter describes her newly organized course, "The Educated Woman in Literature," in practical terms, and Howe presents a writing course she designed to help women alter their self-image "from centuries of *belief* in their inferiority, as well as from male-dominated and controlled institutions" (863). A second special issue of *College English* (October 1972) contains important essays concerning women's inclusion in the discipline of English, among them Tillie Olsen's "Women Who Are Writers in Our Century: One Out of Twelve" and Adrienne Rich's "When We Dead Awaken: Writing as Re-vision." Each of these essays seeks to insert women—their perspectives, their writing, their lived experiences—into a discipline from which they had been excluded.

In "Taking Women Students Seriously," her important 1978 essay emphasizing the necessity of including women's perspectives in education, Adrienne Rich described how the experience of changing from one teaching context to another allowed her to translate the critical questions she asked as a writing instructor of minority students into parallel questions she needed to ask about women students:

> How does a woman gain a sense of her *self* in a system . . . which devalues work done by women, denies the importance of female experience, and is physically violent toward women? . . . How do we, as women, teach women students a canon of literature which has consistently excluded or depreciated female experience? (239)

These early essays set a pattern for subsequent inclusive questions that women in composition began asking. Beginning by describing their own consciousness-raising experiences in their essays, the writers moved on to document the concrete changes in teaching and critical perspectives they advocated. What are women's experiences in classrooms, in institutions? How do women use language? How are women writers different from male writers? Questions like these included women in ways that had not been possible in a "gender-blind" field of composition; they set the stage for writers in the 1980s like Pamela Annas and Elizabeth Flynn to engage them further in work that again sought women's inclusion in the field and sparked feminist discussions for a newer generation of women.[1]

In the late 70s, the trope of inclusion appeared in essays applying feminist language research to composition by investigating claims made by

Robin Lakoff in her 1975 *Language and Woman's Place*—that women, by using a ladylike middle-class language, contributed to their own oppression. Lakoff's argument reflected the "dominance" approach to women's language use that was prominent among feminists of the 70s: attributing gender differences in language mainly to social oppression of women. Joan Bolker's 1979 *College English* article, "Teaching Griselda to Write," is a practitioner's account of her experience struggling with the absence of voice and authority in the work of "good-girl" student writers. The many citations of this short article in the past 19 years suggest that it has resonated with feminists in composition. In 1978, two articles examining women's "different" style appeared in CCC. In "The Feminine Style: Theory and Fact," Mary P. Hiatt discusses her study of the stylistic features of women's and men's writing. She reports "clear evidence of a feminine style . . . [that] is in fact rather different from the common assumptions about it" (226). Contrary to Lakoff's generalizations about women's oral language, women's written style, according to Hiatt, has "no excesses of length or complexity or emotion" (226). In "Women in a Double-Bind: Hazards of the Argumentative Edge," Sheila Ortiz Taylor draws composition instructors' attention to the "invisible, though real, disadvantage" that women students face in writing courses because "both the methods and the goals of such classes are alien to them" (385). She argues that the competitive, impersonal style of traditional argument alienates women; she urges instructors to validate "conversational tone, dramatic technique, and intimate reader involvement" (389).

Among the first composition articles to train the spotlight on women's language experiences, these essays highlight deficiency. (Ironically, as in Lakoff's book, an essentialized "woman" is both *included* and *found lacking*.) Bolker, Taylor, and Hiatt respond differently to the idea that women students must have special problems because a feminine style represents deficiency. Taylor uses the language of victimization to describe the woman student: "She must feel that something is wrong with her, a self-destructive disapproval common enough in women. . . . of course, much of the damage has been done by the time our students reach us. They have been taught a special language" (385). But Taylor adds that a feminine style of argument is only "deficient" because society has refused to validate it. Bolker believes that with more self-esteem and voice, the good girl can be a contender in the arena of the dominant discourse. Hiatt implies that readers need to be more discerning about the gender differences they *think* they see. None of these articles is heavily theorized; with the possible exception of Hiatt's, they arise from and return directly to classroom experience. Because they do not attend closely to larger systemic issues of power and discourse, these studies also make it possible for feminist concerns to be contained, encapsulated, or dismissed as "women's issues." Yet essays like these deserve credit for challenging the field's gender-blindness by insisting that women be included in narratives of classroom writing practices. They have contributed to a sense of intuitive connection between composition and those who ask, at least implicitly, "What difference might it make if the student (or teacher) is female?"

MAKING INTUITIVE CONNECTIONS: NARRATIVES OF METONYMIC RELATIONSHIP

In their introduction to *Teaching Writing: Pedagogy, Gender, and Equity*, one of the first books to connect writing and feminism in composition, Cynthia Caywood and Gillian Overing say that despite the absence of explicit discussion, they had experienced as practitioners an "intuitive understanding" of a "fundamental connection" between feminism and revisionist writing theory. While highlighting an absence of attention to gender, they also posit a more complicated reading of this absence by pointing to the nearly parallel lives of composition and feminist theory. According to this story, the two have run for years in the same direction, along close trajectories; to bring the fields together it is necessary only to notice the shared goals and common directions, and to make connections more visible and explicit. Caywood and Overing ask, "At what point did our parallel interests in feminism and revisionist writing theory converge?" (xi). More recently Susan Jarratt, Laura Brady, Janet Emig, and Louise Phelps have suggested that the boundaries have been permeable between feminist work in literary studies, the social sciences, and composition. This resonates with our own sense, as practitioners in the 70s, that boundaries between feminism and composition were often marked by unarticulated overlaps and crossovers. This permeability may have been partly the result of the interdisciplinary nature of composition, which drew for its theoretical substance from linguistics, cognitive and developmental psychology, and literary criticism. But while this intuitive connection may have created alliances among women in composition and feminists in other fields, it may also have delayed the emergence of feminist theory and continued its marginalization in the field.

Various factors account for the intuitive sense of connection that many of us have experienced and narrated. First, emerging pedagogical theories spoke a language that resonated with feminism's concerns of the time: coming to voice and consciousness, illuminating experience and its relationship to individual identity, playing the believing game rather than the doubting game, collaborating rather than competing, subverting hierarchy in the classroom. These watchwords characterized composition's link to liberal political and social agendas shared by feminist scholars in other disciplines and aimed at challenging established traditions, epistemologies, and practices of the academy.[2] Sharon Crowley explicitly connects Dewey's progressivism with Janet Emig's development of "process pedagogies," arguing that this link between progressivism and process pedagogies was vitally important in reconceptualizing composition "as an art rather than a course," and "because its theorists discovered a way to talk about student writing that authorized teachers to think of themselves as researchers" (17). This reconceptualization resonated for feminists theoretically and politically.

Secondly, at that time many women in the profession were doing double-duty as composition and literature teachers. Among the *College English* authors represented in the special issues we have pointed out, Florence Howe taught composition and wrote about how her course focused on women, and Adrienne Rich taught writing with Mina Shaughnessy in the SEEK program at CCNY. Many feminist composition instructors, coming from literary critical backgrounds, continued reading in their fields and appropriating whatever feminist approaches seemed useful—much as compositionists of the 80s and 90s have appropriated the work of Belenky, Clinchy, Goldberger, and Tarule and poststructuralist feminists.

The material conditions surrounding women in composition have also contributed to a felt sense of the feminist connections to our work. Composition was and still is constructed as women's work, and the majority of workers were women; many of us teaching writing or working on composition degrees during the 70s and 80s were newly arrived from secondary teaching. Surrounded by colleagues with similar career patterns, we entered conversations that enacted an interplay between our lives and our professional work. The drawbacks of the "feminization" of the field were not theorized until several years later.

Finally, as the field developed in the 1970s, although journal editors and the professional hierarchy were primarily male, the names of women were also moving into prominent places: Mina Shaughnessy, Janet Emig, Ann Berthoff, Sondra Perl, Anne Gere, Lillian Bridwell-Bowles, and others were writing many of the important articles and books we studied. Many feminists refer with appreciation to the "foremothers," first for their presence as models, and secondly for their ideas which, though not articulated in terms of gender, are often read, in retrospect, as consistent with feminist practice. In many cases, these ideas have to do with nurturing, collaboration, revisioning, and decentering.

Some retrospective accounts use theory to make the composition-feminism connections less intuitive, more explicit. Turning from foremothers to "midwives," Carolyn Ericksen Hill uses feminist theory to read composition history through the gendering of practices, of theories, and of the field itself.[3] She reads the label "midwives" back onto male composition theorists active in the 60s and early 70s: Peter Elbow, Ken Macrorie, John Schultz, and William Coles, Jr. Without necessarily claiming them as feminists, she can, with the aid of postmodern theory, gender their approach as feminine and place their work in a certain feminist context: they helped "birth" the experiential self. The expressivist/nurturing feminist connection has often been made in passing, but Hill's label "midwives" claims these key composition figures for feminist theorizing—and also marginalizes them. In the 1990s, Hill argues, these four "expressivist" figures have been pushed to the edge of a newly theorized and professionalized field; their gender-blindness and humanistic model of the autonomous self have had to make way for gender difference and shifting subject positions, powerful constructs for feminist analysis. Hill sees in the compartmentalization—rather than dynamic rereading—of the four men's so-called expressivism a parallel with the "othering" of "woman," and of feminism, that continues to occur.

The rereading of "foremothers"—or even "midwives"—as feminist precursors may also be problematic if it ignores context and complexity, as we see from a few examples of foremothers who resist labeling. In the late 1970s, Ann Berthoff roundly rejected the gendering of logic and the either/ or-ism of all discussions of women's ways of knowing; she reaffirmed this rejection at the 1998 CCCC convention. Still, the foremother figures can both exemplify and disrupt the notion of the feminization of the field. As fore*mothers* they are both marginalized and typically characterized as nurturers. But insofar as they are envisioned as *fore*mothers, as founders, they are not feminized but rather constructed in a traditionally masculine position.

Evidence that stories of connection continue to resonate with us may be found in Jan Zlotnik Schmidt's introduction to *Women/Writing/Teaching*, a 1998 collection of essays by women writers and teachers. Schmidt emphasizes the importance of women's experience in making writing-teaching connections and expresses her hope that readers will also "explore their own life stories, their development of selfhood, their multiple identities as writers, teachers, and writing teachers" (xii). Retrospective narratives that create foremothers, midwives, connections, and nurturing community in composition's history foreground the double potential of the metonymic relationship between feminism and composition. This intuitive connection helps to create a sense of solidarity and vitality. But it may also reinforce the very structures that keep feminist perspectives contained in a separate, benign category rather than giving feminist analysis a central place, or at least keeping it insistently, vocally disruptive of the discipline's metanarratives. For example, some feminist practitioners have told powerful stories about replacing hierarchical, agonistic classroom environments with decentered, nurturing classrooms based on an ethic of care. But, as Eileen Schell argues, "femin*in*ist pedagogy, although compelling, may reinforce rather than critique or transform patriarchal structures by reinscribing what Magda Lewis calls the 'woman as caretaker ideology'" ("The Cost" 74, our italics).

Granting feminism's intuitive connections with a discipline that challenged current-traditional conceptions of language and introduced new decentered writing pedagogies, it is also important to recognize that some feminist agendas were more likely to disrupt than to aid composition's early progress toward full disciplinary status. Composition needed to build institutional legitimacy in the traditional academy; a fundamental feminist goal was to disrupt rather than extend patriarchal discourses and their assumptions about knowledge. Composition sought a single theory of the writing process and the writing subject; feminist theorists challenged notions of a singular universal concept of truth. The trope of metonymy may have difficulty expanding to cover some of these adversarial relationships.

FEMINIST DISRUPTIONS

Composition has many narratives of feminist disruption which emphasize neither inclusion nor intuitive connection but rather represent some form of feminism (newly experienced or theorized) reaching back to reread and even reconfigure past experience and practice. We see increasing numbers of current feminists drawing on postmodern theories to analyze and critique the basic "process" narratives of composition's first 20 years, to raise questions about difference(s), and to critique disciplinary practices and structures that have shaped composition. Disruption is often linked to postmodern theories of power, discourse, and ideology rather than to consciousness-raising sessions, discussions of pedagogy, or attempts to create equitable and inclusive conditions for women. In order to intervene significantly in power structures that keep women subordinate, feminists investigate and uncover the contradictions in those dominant structures. The feminist narratives we have reread remind us, however, that efforts at inclusion, connection, and disruption often work synthetically rather than as adversaries or as unequal partners. As Theresa Enos says, her book's "most powerful use of 'data' is the narrative, in the stories that help us define our places in academia so that we can better trace our future" (1).

The explicit recognition of composition's lack of attention to women's material lives has led women in anger, frustration, and recognition to tell the stories of their coming to awareness. A classic feminist narrative of the early 70s is the story of a "good girl," silenced by her compulsion to please, whose recognition of her oppression releases an anger strong enough to overcome politeness and fear; thus she finds both her voice and an agenda for change. The consciousness-raising sessions of the late 60s and early 70s provided a model for this narrative, as did the two special women's issues of *College English*, 1971–72, that we have mentioned. In "When We Dead Awaken," Rich told her own story of frustration at the demands that she be good at all the roles women were supposed to play, while Howe, after narrating how she had acquiesced in years of inequitable treatment, wrote, "Eighteen months as commission Chairwoman [of the MLA Commission on the Status of Women] has eroded that wry smile. I feel now a growing anger as I come to realize that . . . I am not alone in my state" (849).

Many of today's feminist accounts of the 60s and 70s follow a similar pattern. Lynn Z. Bloom's essay, "Teaching College English as a Woman" (1992), is a scathing look at the bad old days in college English, when a woman in the field—whether student or teacher—would be exploited if she did not get angry and speak up. Bloom recalls a conversion experience when, as a part-time composition instructor, she finally was able to obtain office space: in a basement room full of desks, on the floor under the stairs, next to the kitty litter. Surveying these wretched conditions, she told herself, "If I ever agree to do this again, I deserve what I get" (821). Separated by more than 20 years, Bloom's and Howe's angry accounts illustrate what we might call individual, liberal disruption: the idea that once a woman sees clearly, her life is changed, and she is thus empowered to become effectively active for change and reform. These accounts show the "revisioning" that feminist thinking has enabled individual women to do. We read these accounts as disruptive because in addition to realizing that the liberal Enlightenment agenda hasn't included *her*, each of these women also recognizes that she must take action to disrupt and change the structures that have kept her subordinate.

Other women who are currently doing feminist work in composition studies have provided similar testimonies of naive compliance, oppressed silence, eventual recognition, and new outspokenness.[4] That we now have so many such narratives may mean that women in composition today are finally in a position to claim the authority of the autobiographical; it may also mean that, largely due to feminist efforts, the conventions of scholarly discourse have expanded to include the personal narrative as a way of situating oneself in one's scholarship. But perhaps the personal testimony remains an effective—and still necessary—tool of disruption. Many of these stories are disruptive because they expose "the pattern of well-rewarded, male supervision of under-rewarded, female workers" that has existed in composition and "is entrenched in our whole culture" (Enos vii). The disruption that is so central to the consciousness-raising narrative itself also highlights gaps in our reading of our past and of business as usual. Rereading the consciousness-raising essays that have recurred in composition over the past 25 years can show us more sites where women have been silent but where feminists want to rupture that silence.

Many narratives deal with experiences in teaching and department politics, but a 1993 retrospective account by Nancy McCracken, Lois Green, and Claudia Greenwood tells how they acquiesced as researchers to a field characterized by "a persistent silence on the subject of gender" in its "landmark research studies on writing development and writing processes" (352). Now writing collaboratively, they return to studies of teacher responses to student writing that they had published earlier (and separately), reinterpreting those studies in terms of gender differences. These authors emphasize that until the late 80s the climate in composition studies had made it difficult to notice or report gender differences in empirical studies: "None of us went looking for gender differences. When the data began to speak of gender, we dared not listen" (356). They recount their worries about being accused of biological determinism, about seeming to exclude men, about appearing unprofessional, and about calling attention to themselves as women. Now, they say, they feel empowered not only to note gender difference but to insist on it. Theirs is not a story of breaking silence by themselves. Instead, the current "research environment in which it is both important and safe to study the interplay between students' gender and their development as writers" (354) has made it possible to revise their findings. Their story is not about singular heroism but about collaboration, in a network of mutual support, in a research/scholarly environment that has made discursive structures more visible. Their story is not about going solo against a hostile discipline but about rereading the field and their own complicity. Their reading disrupts, among other things, their *own* research, by requiring that they return to it and revise it.

Some of the early disruptive narratives we have mentioned are reformist, and they may even be read as attempts at inclusion as well as disruption. Another form of disruptive narrative is less grounded in the impulse for individual disruption and change, but seeks wider consideration of difference. Such critiques often create conflict and may evoke more resistance because they demand changes in institutional and epistemological structures that

502

conflict with composition's continuing need to establish legitimacy. They support the emergence of different perspectives rather than suppressing them. In these accounts difference is expanded from the single male/female binary to differences, taking into account multiple inflections of social class, sexual orientation, and race. For example, Harriet Malinowitz's study of lesbian and gay students in writing classes and Shirley Wilson Logan's writing on the confluence of race and gender in composition both attempt to expand our understanding of what differences can mean in composition classrooms. They articulate the connections among differences as well as show the privileging or erasure of some categories by others. Writing out of her own experience as a Chinese student speaking several languages, Min-Zhan Lu has drawn upon third-world and minority feminisms as well as other cultural theorists to disrupt composition teachers' view of the conflicts students face in negotiating the political, linguistic, and rhetorical "borderlands" between home and school. She reopens a debate about the processes of acculturation and accommodation at work in writing classrooms, particularly those that serve minority and immigrant students. In doing so, she rereads the work of Mina Shaughnessy, Thomas Farrell, Kenneth Bruffee, and others in light of current contexts in order to critique the wider public debates about literacy and to highlight the cultural conflicts and necessary resistances of today's students on the margins.

At times these disruptions can create tension and anger even among feminists, highlighting the way feminism itself is shaped by and embedded in existing hierarchical discourses. This conflict may seem to undermine any sense of solidarity that existed when feminism appeared in a more intuitive rather than carefully articulated and scrutinized form. But in fact, such conflict may produce one of feminism's most important benefits—the proliferation of differences. Nedra Reynolds argues: "Feminists daring to criticize other feminists have opened up spaces for analyzing difference; they interrupted the discourses of feminism in the singular to make possible feminism in the plural" (66). Other disruptive narratives of difference are only now emerging and await further exploration. Constructs like Gloria Anzaldúa's *mestiza*, Trinh T. Minh-ha's subject-in-the-making, Donna Haraway's cyborg, and Judith Butler's performer of gender extend postmodern notions of difference in disruptive directions with their advocacy of multiplicity, fluidity, hybridity, and indeterminacy.

Feminists in composition in the past decade have used postmodern theories to reread the feminization and the femin*in*ization of composition as problematic and to seek to revise institutional frameworks. The preponderance of women in composition has not led inevitably to the triumph of feminist interests and values in the field. For example, Susan Miller tells the story of the "sad women in the basement" and describes feminization as the "female coding" of the "ideologically constructed identity for the teacher of composition" (123); it involves constructing composition as "women's work." Feminization refers to the gendering of the entire field of composition and of various activities that have taken place within it (nonhierarchical pedagogy, the writing process movement, "romantic" philosophies, nurturing of writers). For Miller, feminization points to the devaluation of the composition instructor, and the subordination of composition to literature, throughout the history of the field. For Rhonda Grego and Nancy Thompson, compositionists "still reside within our gendered roles," but we are not limited to a traditional "wifely" role because the field has lately been "developing terms and methods through which to name our work at least to ourselves, if not yet fully to the ruling apparatus of the academic system" (68). In *Gypsy Academics and Mother Teachers*, Eileen Schell combines materialist feminist and postmodern perspectives, labor and institutional history, and the personal narratives of women nontenure-track teachers to analyze the gendered division of labor in composition and to critique femin*i*nization — the coopting of the "ethic of care." She also provides strategies for coalition-building and tangible plans of action for reconceptualizing women's positions and reshaping institutional structures. Feminization narratives like these work disruptively in two directions: their analysis foregrounds the political position of composition within institutional structures, but it also highlights tensions within women's roles and interests in composition.

Finally, disruptive narratives in composition have begun to analyze the established narratives of the discipline and the agency of students and teachers constructed by those narratives. They explore the ideologies underlying the discourses where composition has been situated, including those espoused by feminists, to underscore the contradictions and dangers that those create for women as well as for the field in general. An early example is Susan Jarratt's rereading of Peter Elbow's work and of the tendency in feminism and expressivism to suppress conflict and promote consensus.[5] She argues that such a stance fails to arm women students and teachers with the tools to confront the power relations inherent in their positions. An important recent example of disruption is Nedra Reynolds' rereading of several major narratives in the field. Reynolds emphasizes that interruption — talking back, forcibly breaking into the prevailing discourse of a field — is a way to create agency: "Agency is not simply about finding one's own voice but also about intervening in discourses of the everyday [this would include personal experience narratives] and cultivating rhetorical tactics that make interruption and resistance an important part of any conversation" (59). She points out the tendency of "some of the most important voices in composition today . . . to ignore work in feminism that might complement or complicate their ideas" (66). She not only "interrupts" some of the major cultural studies theorists but also analyzes the conceptions of subjectivity and agency in the work of James Berlin, John Trimbur, and Lester Faigley. She criticizes the dominant narrative's tendency to compartmentalize interrupters and disrupters as "rude women," thereby denying them agency. As part of the evidence for her argument, she tells stories about a cultural studies conference where bell hooks and other women participants analyzed the "terror" of the typical "white supremacist hierarchy" (65). Reynolds urges women to develop strategies for interrupting dominant discourses in composition and challenges them to offer their students the means to resist rigid forms of discourse.

CONCLUSION: IN EXCESS

These three different but also converging narratives of feminism suggest a rich tradition of feminist thought and activity in composition: pushing for admission, working intuitively alongside, and interrupting the conversation. We believe these three tropes may help us read and revise feminism's evolving place in the narratives of composition; they provide useful insight for feminists about existing tensions in the relationship of theory to experience and practice; and they point to strategies feminists may seek to promote or avoid in the future.

In composition's last three decades, the impulse has been toward legitimation, theory-building, and consolidation. The disruption and the assertion of difference that feminists and others represent have come slowly and with struggle; they have been delayed and even suppressed by the need to build a more unified disciplinary discourse. In several recent metanarratives that assess where composition has come from and where it is going, we find traces of these three lines of feminist thought that may help us see where feminism might most usefully lead composition and where they might go together. These recent commentaries demonstrate that tropes of inclusion and metonymic connection still define feminism's relationship to the field.

In *Fragments of Rationality*, Lester Faigley practices inclusion as he credits feminism for its efforts to theorize a postmodern subject with agency; he also cites the contributions of feminists in foregrounding important pedagogical and political questions. James Berlin's *Rhetorics, Poetics, Cultures* does not mention feminism, but this book, like Faigley's, does cite several postmodern feminists' efforts to theorize subjectivity and difference. In Joseph Harris' *A Teaching Subject: Composition Since 1966*, the connections

between women practitioners, feminism, and "the teaching subject" are neither articulated nor connected; they remain an unspoken presence. Like Berlin, Sharon Crowley argues in *Composition in the University* that despite its
progress over the past 30 years, composition has remained a conservative discipline, still trapped in current-traditionalism, still shackled to the service
role of Freshman English, and still bound to the limitations of humanism in
English departments. Unlike Berlin, she looks to feminist thought for its disruptive power, as one of several theoretical perspectives that might help dis-
lodge composition from narrow disciplinary confines.

The representation of feminist perspectives in these recent commentaries suggests that in the future these relationships will persist—with unspoken alliances between feminist thought and composition, and inclusive
reliance on postmodern feminism(s) where they advance the general argument. But it is to the disruptive strategy, framed in dialogue with inclusivity
and metonymy, that we return. It is tempting to see disruption as the newest
and best hope for feminism and to privilege theorizing as the most worthwhile activity for feminism and composition. But it's also clear that different
emphases may be more effective as rhetorical contexts shift and historical
moments change. While efforts at inclusion suffer from the limitations
we've outlined, and untheorized or unarticulated practices also create risks
of marginalization and erasure, disruptive strategies, by themselves, also
have limitations. The history of feminism suggests that it is necessary to do
more than interrupt a disciplinary conversation. Disruption may be only
temporary, and as Reynolds and others point out, it's easy to push disrupters
to the sidelines, to stop listening to them and to marginalize them once
again. In addition, the task of disruption requires rhetorical skill. Those who
interrupt may gain momentary attention, but those who can't sustain the
conversation, hold up the argument, or tell an absorbing story will soon
drop—or be dropped—from the discussion.

Certainly feminists in composition have provided the field with models
for persuasive and beautiful writing that tells and disrupts stories of experience. (Lynn Worsham's "After Words: A Choice of Words Remains" is a
recent example.) If theorizing and disruption are detached from lived experience and material history, they may remain irrelevant. And if disruption only
fractures and doesn't again create connection, a sense of an even tentatively
inclusive agenda, it will lack the vital energy and supportive alliances to sustain its own taxing work. Over the last 30 years, feminists have demonstrated
that critique and disruption are never finished and that coalition-building
and collaboration are vital for change.

Our rereading of 30 years of feminist writing suggests that in both early
and more recent work, feminism has been most challenging and disruptive

and also provided a sense of alliance and inclusion when it has maintained a dialogical relationship between theory and experience. Despite its short history, feminist work in composition can certainly provide many revitalizing demonstrations of this dialogical relationship as one of its contributions to academic feminism. Virtually all the feminist work we've reviewed and see emerging has, at least in part, claimed, interpreted, and revised accounts of experience and history: the personal history of one's life as a woman, the practice of the teacher, or the experience of the scholar. As Suzanne Clark points out, narratives of experience theorized become possible sites of agency: "At the same time that stories of personal experience invoke and recite determinant categories of identity . . . such stories also produce an excess not easily retrofitted as the norm" (98). Rather than dismissing stories of experience, Clark suggests that we look at them for what is "excessive," that is, for parts of the narrative that do not fit our current explanations: "What refuses, despite the sometimes daunting applications of straitjacket pseudo-sciences, to be contained?" (98). One of feminism's most potentially powerful tools is the deployment of what is excessive, what is other. Difference, "otherness," disrupts, as Rosemary Hennessy argues, because the "gaps, contradictions, *aporias*" that otherness creates force dominant perspectives into crisis management to "seal over or manage the contradictions. . . . But they also serve as the inaugural space for critique" (92).

Many gaps remain for feminists to explore in composition and in its relationship to English and the broader culture. Although researchers have now examined from a feminist perspective the status of women in composition and the feminized status of composition within English studies, many women still teach composition in the "basement," and the wider institutional, economic, and cultural conditions continue to create barriers against improving their status. Although women and men in our field have considered how class, gender, and race may shape their pedagogy, we have not thoroughly come to terms with students' or teachers' gendered, classed, or raced position in the academy—or the continuing failure to provide a viable education for many minority students or encouragement for minority colleagues in our field. Although various critics have highlighted the gender blindness of liberatory and critical pedagogies, we have not thoroughly considered how such theories and pedagogies stop short of realizing their goals where women students, minorities, and gay and lesbian students are concerned. Although we have a body of metacommentary on research methodologies and ethical representation of research subjects, we have only begun to explore effective ways to connect our research to wider public concerns and debates about literacy.

Our own interest in diversity and multiplicity makes us curious about the possible uses of "excess" as a trope for feminists in composition of the present and future. Already we are exploring feminist or "diverse discourses," which are in excess of what a singular linear argument requires. We are pushing for notions and accounts of agency that exceed limited ideas of the determined subject. Might the re-visionary stories of the next generation refer to greedy visions of *more* as well as angry recognitions of *lack*? Can we envision narratives of a disruptive practice that overflows as well as challenges? Excess might be proposed as inclusion with a difference: uncontained and without limits.

At this time when composition is reviewing its past and seeking to chart new directions, a glance beyond the academy suggests that political and economic conditions will create continuing intellectual and practical "straitjackets" in composition's next 50 years. The energy of feminists will be vital to the disruption of restrictive theory and practice. This energy will be important for sustaining coalitions for change; it is our best hope for inclusion and proliferation of difference, multiplicity, and uncontainable excess.

NOTES

1. In two recent collections of essays on composition, Villanueva's *Cross-Talk in Comp Theory*, and Bloom, Daiker, and White's *Composition in the Twenty-First Century*, the only essay specifically from a feminist perspective is Flynn's 1988 "Composing as a Woman." The frequent inclusion of this essay suggests the impact it has had; the fact that it is the only one included suggests that, in some venues at least, it has been used to contain feminism at the same time.

2. For example, the February 1970 issue of *CCC* contains articles by Donald Murray and by William Coles articulating many of the crucial progressive assumptions emerging in composition: the value of individual students' writing as an articulation of agency and selfhood rather than merely as an object of diagnosis and correction. The *CCC* journals of that year also contain several proposals for alternative freshman English courses for minority students, and the October 1972 issue contains the CCCC Executive Committee's Resolution, "The Student's Right to His Own Language." Although they remain steadfastly gender-blind, essays like these attest to the profession's increasing attempts in the late 60s and 70s to redefine writing and writing instruction. These disciplinary calls for cultural diversity in the curriculum and for the students' rights to their own language caused a great deal of ferment in the profession and foregrounded issues of difference, yet they still did not open a discursive space for women to speak as women writers and teachers or to consider the gendered implications of Coles' goal for writing: "to allow the student to put himself together" (28).

3. Belenky, Clinchy, Goldberger, and Tarule are noted for their use of "midwife" in their discussion of educators who promote constructed knowledge. But the term was applied to writing instructors much earlier. In 1970, Stephen Judy wrote in *English Journal* (which he was later to edit): "We need to discard the structure of the composition teacher as one who passes on knowledge about writing, makes assignments, and corrects errors on themes. A more appropriate role can be described as that of coach or catalyst, or one that I prefer, that of midwife: one who assists in the process of bringing something forth but does not participate in the process himself" (217). This passage suggests possibilities for metonymy; the

masculine pronoun may simply illustrate composition's gender-blindness, but it may also be a trace of the gender-shifting that Hill does twenty years later. Judy adds, "It would be difficult for a midwife to do *her* job adequately if the expectant mother knew she were going to be graded on the results" (217, italics ours).

4. Wendy Bishop, Lillian Bridwell-Bowles, Louise Phelps, and Nancy Sommers are just a few of the women who have written personal narratives that practice and reflect on disruption of a status quo. Jacqueline Jones Royster writes, "I have been compelled on too many occasions to count to sit as a well-mannered Other" (30). Theresa Enos' *Gender Roles and Faculty Lives in Rhetoric and Composition* contains a number of anonymous stories from women in composition, along with her narrative of her own experience as an "academically battered woman" (ix). Gesa Kirsch's interviews with women in various academic disciplines explore their interpretations of their experiences as writers and raise "questions of gender and language, women's participation in public discourse, and women's 'ways of writing'" (xvii). A new collection, *Women/Writing/Teaching*, edited by Jan Zlotnik Schmidt presents ten previously published and ten new essays by women that examine their personal experiences as writers and teachers.

5. We could cite numerous other examples: Patricia Sullivan's rereading of Stephen North's *The Making of Knowledge in Composition;* Nancy Welch's use of feminist theory and her own experience to reread Lacan and other theorists and to disrupt composition's conceptualization of revision; and the important work of increasing numbers of feminists rereading and regendering the rhetorical tradition from Aspasia to Ida B. Wells, from Gertrude Buck to Toni Morrison.

WORKS CITED

Annas, Pamela J. "Style as Politics: A Feminist Approach to the Teaching of Writing." *College English* 47 (1985): 360–71.

Belenky, Mary Field, Blythe McVicker Clinchy, Nancy Rule Goldberger, and Jill Mattuck Tarule. *Women's Ways of Knowing: The Development of Self, Voice, and Mind.* New York: Basic, 1986.

Bennett, Robert A. "NCTE Presidential Address: The Undiscovered." *English Journal* 61 (1972): 351–57.

Berlin, James. *Rhetorics, Poetics, and Cultures: Refiguring College English Studies.* Urbana: NCTE, 1996.

Berthoff, Ann E. "Rhetoric as Hermeneutic." *CCC* 42 (1991): 279–87.

Bishop, Wendy. "Learning Our Own Ways to Situate Composition and Feminist Studies in the English Department." *Journal of Advanced Composition* 10 (1990): 339–55.

Bloom, Lynn Z. "Teaching College English as a Woman." *College English* 54 (1992): 818–25.

Bloom, Lynn Z., Donald A. Daiker, and Edward M. White, eds. *Composition in the Twenty-First Century: Crisis and Change.* Carbondale: Southern Illinois UP, 1996.

Bolker, Joan. "Teaching Griselda to Write." *College English* 40 (1979): 906–08.

Brady, Laura. "The Reproduction of Othering." Jarratt and Worsham 21–44.

Bridwell-Bowles, Lillian. "Freedom, Form, Function: Varieties of Academic Discourse." *CCC* 46 (1995): 46–61.

Caywood, Cynthia, and Gillian Overing, eds. *Teaching Writing: Pedagogy, Gender, and Equity.* Albany: State U of New York P, 1987.

Clark, Suzanne. "Argument and Composition." Jarratt and Worsham 94–99.

Coles, William, Jr. "The Sense of Nonsense as a Design for Sequential Writing Assignments." *CCC* 21 (1970): 27–34.

Crowley, Sharon. *Composition in the University: Historical and Polemical Essays.* Pittsburgh Series in Composition, Literacy, and Culture. Pittsburgh: U of Pittsburgh P, 1998.

Enos, Theresa. *Gender Roles and Faculty Lives in Rhetoric and Composition.* Carbondale: Southern Illinois UP, 1996.

Faigley, Lester. *Fragments of Rationality: Postmodernity and the Subject of Composition.* Pittsburgh Series in Composition, Literacy, and Culture. Pittsburgh, U of Pittsburgh P, 1992.

Flynn, Elizabeth A. "Composing as a Woman." *CCC* 39 (1988) : 423–35.

Fontaine, Sheryl I., and Susan Hunter, eds. *Writing Ourselves into the Story: Unheard Voices from Composition Studies.* Carbondale: Southern Illinois UP, 1993. 1–17.

Grego, Rhonda, and Nancy Thompson. "Repositioning Remediation: Renegotiating Composition's Work in the Academy." *CCC* 47 (1996): 62–84.

Harris, Joseph. *A Teaching Subject: Composition Since 1966.* Upper Saddle River: Prentice, 1997.

Hennessy, Rosemary. *Materialist Feminism and the Politics of Discourse.* Thinking Gender Series. New York: Routledge, 1992.

Hiatt, Mary P. "The Feminine Style: Theory and Fact." *CCC* 29 (1978): 222–26.

Hill, Carolyn Ericksen. *Writing from the Margins: Power and Pedagogy for Teachers of Composition.* New York: Oxford UP, 1990.

Howe, Florence. "A Report on Women and the Profession." *College English* 32 (1971): 847–54.

——. "Identity and Expression: A Writing Course for Women." *College English* 32 (1971): 863–71.

Jarratt, Susan C. "Feminism and Composition: The Case for Conflict." *Contending with Words: Composition and Rhetoric in a Postmodern Age.* Ed. Patricia Harkin and John Schilb. New York: MLA, 1991. 105–23.

Jarratt, Susan C.,and Lynn Worsham, eds. *Feminism and Composition Studies: In Other Words.* New York: MLA, 1998.

Judy, Stephen. "The Search for Structures in the Teaching of Composition." *English Journal* 59 (1970): 213–18.

Kirsch, Gesa E. *Women Writing the Academy: Audience, Authority, and Transformation.* Studies in Writing and Rhetoric. Carbondale: Southern Illinois UP, 1992.

Kirsch, Gesa E., and Patricia A. Sullivan, eds. *Methods and Methodology in Composition Research.* Carbondale: Southern Illinois UP, 1992.

Lakoff, Robin. *Language and Woman's Place.* New York: Harper, 1975.

Logan, Shirley W., ed. *With Pen and Voice: The Rhetoric of Nineteenth Century African-American Women.* Carbondale: Southern Illinois UP, 1995.

Lu, Min-Zhan. "Conflict and Struggle: The Enemies or Preconditions of Basic Writing?" *College English* 54 (1992): 887–913.

——. "From Silence to Words: Writing as Struggle." Perl 165–76.

Malinowitz, Harriet. *Textual Orientations: Lesbian and Gay Students and the Making of Discourse Communities.* Portsmouth: Boynton, Heinemann, 1995.

McCracken, Nancy, Lois Green, and Claudia Greenwood. "Gender in Composition Research: A Strange Silence." Fontaine and Hunter 352–73.

Miller, Susan. *Textual Carnivals: The Politics of Composition.* Carbondale: Southern Illinois UP, 1991.

Murray, Donald M. "The Interior View: One Writer's Philosophy of Composition." *CCC* 21 (1970): 21–26.

Olsen, Tillie. "Women Who Are Writers in Our Century: One Out of Twelve." *College English* 34 (1972): 6–17.

"Open Letter from Janet Emig, Chairwoman, NCTE Committee on the Role and Image of Women." *English Journal* 61 (1972): 710.

Perl, Sondra, ed. *Landmark Essays on Writing Process.* Landmark Essays Series 7. Davis: Hermagoras, 1994.

Phelps, Louise W. "Becoming a Warrior: Lessons of the Feminist Workplace." Phelps and Emig 289–339.

Phelps, Louise W., and Janet Emig, eds. *Feminine Principles and Women's Experience in American Composition and Rhetoric.* Pittsburgh Series in Composition, Literacy, and Culture. Pittsburgh: U of Pittsburgh P, 1995.

Reynolds, Nedra. "Interrupting Our Way to Agency: Feminist Cultural Studies and Composition." Jarratt and Worsham 58–73.

Rich, Adrienne. "When We Dead Awaken: Writing as Re-vision." *College English* 34 (1972): 18–25.

——. "Taking Women Students Seriously." *On Lies, Secrets, and Silence: Selected Prose 1966–1978.* New York: Norton, 1979. 237–45.

Royster, Jacqueline Jones. "When the First Voice You Hear Is Not Your Own." *CCC* 47 (1996): 29–40.

Schell, Eileen. *Gypsy Academics and Mother- Teachers: Gender, Contingent Labor, and Writing Instruction.* Portsmouth: Boynton, 1998.

——. "The Costs of Caring: 'Feminism' and Contingent Women Workers in Composition Studies." Jarratt and Worsham 74–93.

Schmidt, Jan Zlotnik, ed. *Women/Writing/ Teaching.* Albany: State U of New York P, 1998.

Scott, Joan. "Experience." *Feminists Theorize the Political.* Ed. Judith Butler and Joan W. Scott. New York: Routledge, 1992. 22–40.

Showalter, Elaine. "Women and the Literary Curriculum." *College English* 32 (1971): 855–62.

Sommers, Nancy. "Between the Drafts." Perl 217–24.

Sullivan, Patricia A. "Feminism and Methodology." Kirsch and Sullivan 37–61.

Taylor, Sheila Ortiz. "Women in a Double- Bind: Hazards of the Argumentative Edge." *CCC* 29 (1978): 385–89.

"The Students' Right to Their Own Language." *CCC* 25 Special Issue (1974): 1–32.

The Secretary's Report of Executive Committee. "The Student's Right to His Own Language." *CCC* 21 (1970): 319–28.

Villanueva Jr., Victor, ed. *Cross-Talk in Comp Theory.* Urbana: NCTE, 1997.

Welch, Nancy. *Getting Restless: Rethinking Revision in Writing Instruction.* Portsmouth: Boynton, 1997.

Worsham, Lynn. "After Words: A Choice of Words Remains." Jarratt and Worsham 329–56.

Queer: An Impossible Subject for Composition

JONATHAN ALEXANDER AND JACQUELINE RHODES

If I say that now, writing now, are too many people who have no concept of art as energy, of art as space, I think you will follow me. I think you will realise that if fiction is to have any future in the technological dream/nightmare of the twenty-first century, it needs, more than ever, to remember itself as imaginative, innovative, Other. To do this the writer must reclaim lineage and language.

—Jeannette Winterson

1

What makes a subject possible? What conditions, presuppositions, and investments must necessarily prefigure the emergence of any subject as a possible field of knowledge, even of knowability? And conversely, what makes some subjects *impossible*—either illegible in the lexicon of the knowing or impoverished in the economy of the knowable?

2

This *essai* offers a series of gestures toward the known and the unknowable, the currently possible and the potentially impossible. We juxtapose and

First published in *JAC* 31.1-2 (2011): 177–206. Reprinted with permission of the authors.

improvise to enact and embody both the possibility of speaking queerly to composition and the impossibility of composing queerness. We critique and suggest. We *queer* and refuse to be contained by the methodology of queering. We understand that this may not be understandable. We embrace and fail to embrace the excess of such a queer[ed/ing] knowing.

3

Queerness has long been one of composition's *difficult* subjects. Scholarship about the intersections among queerness, literacy, and writing instruction remains relatively sparse and under-read, while textbooks that attempt to incorporate LGBT themes and readings usually reprint the "usual suspects," such as highly binarized debates about gay marriage. Queer compositionists have certainly contributed important essays that prod us to think critically about the importance of LGBT content in our writing curricula, to be attentive to the particular literacy and instructional concerns of LGBT students, and even to consider the potential implications of queer theory for the teaching of writing. However, while comparable work in feminist thinking, critical pedagogies, and postmodernity in general have created significant movements within the field of rhetoric and composition studies, queerness and queer theory have not, despite their significant contributions "across the hall"—that is, to *literary* study. Alexander and David Wallace point out that the "queer turn" never actually happened, despite the work of several scholars over several decades (318-19).

We might catch a sense of the (unfortunate) inefficacy of queer compositionists' work by taking stock, if just briefly, of the principal movements within it. Harriet Malinowitz's 1995 book, *Textual Orientations: Lesbian and Gay Students and the Making of Discourse Communities*, argued importantly for taking stock of lesbians and gays and their literacy practices, while Jonathan Alexander and Michelle Gibson argued in their special cluster of *JAC* that "Queer theory moves us beyond the multicultural task of accepting and validating identity and moves us toward the more difficult process of understanding how identity, even the most intimate perceptions of self, arise out of a complex matrix of shifting social power" (3). In the same issue of *JAC*, Connie Monson and Jacqueline Rhodes specified the kind of rhetorical work that queer theory might accomplish: "Queer theory can offer crucial insight into the constructions of subjectivity, desire, and literacy already operative within the institutional site of the composition classroom, providing a place from which to critique and transform those constructions" (79).

Throughout such work—whether inviting (or imploring that) comp/ rhet scholars and pedagogues pay attention to LG (and BT) students in the writing classroom or suggesting that queer theory has uses for re-visioning our teaching of composition—a repeated refrain can be heard in all of this work: the call to bring the insights of the queer from the margins of experience to the center of composition, perhaps even to the center of the composing process as it is figured and taught in the composition classroom. As Malinowitz put it, "The sort of pedagogy I am proposing would entail thinking about the ways margins produce not only abject outsiderhood but also profoundly unique ways of self-defining, knowing, and acting; and about how, though people usually want to leave the margins, they *do* want to be able to bring with them the sharp vision that comes from living with friction and contradiction"(252).

We question, though, the usefulness of leaving the margins. We question what, if anything, queerness has to say to composition, as currently configured and taught in the majority of U.S. classrooms. And while we applaud the work of "queer compositionists," having occupied that scholarly and pedagogical site ourselves, we have now come to believe that queerness is not simply one of composition's difficult subjects.

Queerness is one of composition's *impossible* subjects.

4

A number of interrelated knowledge/power complexes make queerness impossible in composition. First, and perhaps easiest: the juxtaposition of sex and schooling forms a theoretically compelling yet politically dangerous (institutionally suicidal?) site. Sex, especially non-normative sexual relations, is never "appropriate" in the classroom. It disturbs our composure. The parallel tongues of school and sex can only exist if they promise not to touch.

This promise delivers a great irony to a field heavily invested in language, rhetoric, "doing things with words"—for what is more persuasive than sex? What is more rhetorical than sex? For dyed-in-the-wool Aristotelians, we might offer an examination of artistic proofs (and more importantly, *inartistic* proofs) involved in the rhetorical situation of sexual desire; for the acolytes of Burke, we could propose a pentadic look at sex (the act, the agent, the actor, the scene, the purpose). Indeed, for the "posties," we might remind them of what they've written about text and desire, and the anticipation with which we come to a text in order to read it. If we look to Lacan, and the idea of lack, we approach a text as we approach a new lover. If it's an assigned text, it's an assigned lover, it's an arranged marriage. It's somebody we don't particularly want to fuck, and yet we know we must, if we're to succeed in some other endeavor. And so we consume the text, the lover, not for its own purposes but to *get at* something else. Thus, sexuality, like discourse, works as a system for accomplishing the not-here; what we have is the idea of *rhetoric as displacement*, a ratcheting-up of the queer distance between signifier/act and idea.

Sex: do it in the appropriate place, with the appropriate people (please note the wide ways in which you determine "appropriate," in this case heeding the rhetorical situation of your own erection). The notion of the "appropriate" or the "decorous," from classical rhetoric: think of how this regulates desire—doesn't it beg for rhetorical analysis? But what are the appropriate objects/subjects of desire, and when can we *speak* them? When can we speak *about* them? The persuasive and rhetorical powers of sex are rarely, if ever, considered proper subjects of the composition classroom. Even less proper are the queer subjects themselves that cast into relief the persuasive and rhetorical power of normalizing heterosexuality.

Second, and speaking of queerness, the ways in which queerness is typically represented renders it unrepresentable. Queerness becomes a series of tropes or clichés that elide its differences from normative heterosexuality. In the process, we never realize the potential critical agency of a fully represented queerness; queerness becomes yet another subject position that must be given glancing acknowledgement in the growing multicultural pantheon, another diversity "charm" on the bracelet. Hence, the nod in composition texts to the "coming out" story or the fight of queers for the right to be married. In both cases, queerness marks just another surface difference (since we're all the same on the inside, after all), a difference that only ever has relevance when positioned against the normative (since queers really want to be married and settle down, just like the straights). Such formulations erase the critical difference of queerness.

But third, and most importantly, we contend that queerness is essentially about impossibility and excess. In our current socio-cultural and political context, queerness is the gesture of the unrepresentable, the call for a space of impossibility, the insistence that not everything be *composed*. Granted, we see gays and lesbians, even transsexuals and some bisexuals, identified and represented in a variety of mass media, some of which finds its way periodically into composition classrooms. But for us, queerness is most attractive-theoretically, personally, and politically—in its potential illegibility, its inability to be reductively represented, its disruptive potential. In a word, its impossibility. In another word, its excess.

Judith Butler writes, "If the identity we say we are cannot possibly capture us and marks immediately an excess and opacity that falls outside the categories of identity, then any effort 'to give an account of oneself' will have to fail in order to approach being true" (42). At many different moments, queerness appears (or emerges or erupts) to trouble normalcy, legitimacy, signification. It doesn't fit. It skews the realities we construct for ourselves. It bends and detours realities constructed *for us* that try to induce a heteronormative sense of stability and progress through the replication of particular kinds of people in particular kinds of families.

5

Queerness exceeds the composed self.

6

Sara Ahmed argues in *Queer Phenomenology*:

> To follow a line is to become invested in that line, and also to be committed to "where" it will take us. We do not stay apart from the lines we follow, even if we take the line as a strategy, which we hope to keep apart from our identity. And yet, there are different kinds of investment and commitment. For some, following certain straight lines might be lived as a pledge of allegiance on moral and political grounds to "what" that line leads to. But for others, certain lines might be followed because of a lack of resources to support a life of deviation, because of commitments they have already made, or because the experience of disorientation is simply too shattering to endure. (176)

And,

> In calling for a politics that involves disorientation, which registers that disorientation shatters our involvement in a world, it is important not to make disorientation an obligation or a responsibility for those who identify as queer. It is not up to queers to disorientate straights, just as it is not up to bodies of color to do the work of antiracism, although of course disorientation might still happen and we do "do" this work. Disorientation, then, would not be a politics of the will but an effect of how we do politics, which in turn is shaped by the prior matter of simply how we live. (177)

7

With Foucault in mind here—the idea that the experience of the self is "an attempt to determine what one can and cannot do with one's available freedom" (*Ethics* 276)—and with this other sense that such attempts often come upon us suddenly, physically, without deliberation, we ask: What is the place of *this* self, the physical, anxious, sometimes shamefaced, sometimes turned-on (sometimes all at once) self? What is the place of this self in contemporary composition and rhetoric?

8

Eurythmics, "Sweet Dreams" (1983):

> Sweet dreams are made of this
> Who am I to disagree?
> Travel the world and the seven seas
> Everybody's looking for something
> Some of them want to use you
> Some of them want to get used by you
> Some of them want to abuse you
> Some of them want to be abused

9

In the past, when we have talked about "queer composition," we have focused on the importance of embracing sexuality as a topic in composition courses, of the potential critiques that queer theory offers of entrenched narratives of heteronormativity, and of challenging our discipline to think about what true inclusivity might mean and be. Now, it seems more important to see how queerness challenges the very subject of composition, of what it means to compose, of what it means to *be composed*.

Queerness has the potential to stretch our sense of not only what *can* be composed, but *how* it can be composed. If queerness means more than just one more static representation of "diversity," containable in its knowability, then it must *move* in multiple directions at once, embracing multi-modality, multi-genre texts, and even, when available or perhaps necessary, multi-media. We understand the importance of authoring "composed" essays; we don't deny the very real and material need to help students develop the kinds of compositions—the kind of composure—that make them legible in the marketplace, not just of ideas but of hard currency. But we want also to make room for the kinds of writing-and the kinds of subjects—that challenge such composure, that offer rich, capacious, and (yes) excessive ways of thinking and writing.

Queerness pushes hard at composition. It insists that we look at what is *not* composed—but more importantly, it insists that we heed what *refuses* to be composed. Put another way, if queerness is the excess of sexual identities, the part that exceeds easy and knowable encapsulation in identity, then it is also the excess of composition, of stories, narratives, arguments, and texts that are easily, knowingly "composed."

Cross-Eyed [Jonathan]

I am cross-eyed. And my crossed-eye (sometimes the right, sometimes the left, depending on which I am favoring at the moment) is perhaps my most visible physical characteristic-besides my whiteness and my maleness. People often wonder if I'm looking at them when we speak. Opticians express surprise that I spend so much time reading. Some students seem particularly non-plussed.

"Who are you talking to?"

"I'm talking to you, but I'm looking at all of you."

Bentham and Foucault's panopticon is thus reborn in my classrooms.

But for all of its social salience, only one person not associated with optometry—a seventeen year old high school student "shadowing" me as part of a senior class project on careers—has ever mentioned it directly.

"What's wrong with your eye?"

"I'm cross-eyed."

"Why don't you fix it?"

If the first question didn't give me pause, the candor of the second forced me to focus a bit on why I had not undergone surgery to correct the "problem." After a moment, I offered three reasons.

First, the cost of the operation, considered purely cosmetic, would not be covered by my insurance, and I can think of better ways to spend three thousand dollars. Second, the crossed-eye serves a "screening" function: if an individual dismisses me (for friendship, as a serious scholar, as an intelligent person, when cruising) because of this physical oddity, then I know that s/he is probably too superficial for my tastes. Third, I enjoy the willful queerness of having a crossed-eye, especially since such could be "fixed" and bring me closer to "normal" looking.

Interestingly, no one else has ever talked about it—to my face. In fact, when I've mentioned it myself in an off-hand, casual sort of way, the visible discomfort I produce takes me somewhat by surprise, as though I were speaking the unspeakable, focusing on that which would give most people a headache. I am pointing out, in fact, how out of focus I am. I am willfully not normal. And that makes people—even my tolerant, accepting, open-minded, and sometimes provocatively liberal colleagues—squirm.

Return to the high school student. I didn't mention that he was a gay high school student, who picked me especially because he wanted to "shadow" a gay professor, since that is what he would be if he decided to become a higher educator. It struck me, that of all people, he is the one who should point out the obvious. But, on further thought, I wasn't surprised at all. For, being a late adolescent, he was highly conscious of what does and does not fit in. His gayness only raised that awareness to a higher degree. And he was surprised that I, an openly queer man, would not try better to fit in, to erase as many differences as possible between me and the "normals." After all, in verbally marking myself as queer, I had already stepped outside the boundaries of the normal and accepted; we aggravate the issue with a physical marker of abnormality.

And that is exactly why I have liked it. In fact, my crossed-eye(s) exist(s) in an interesting metonymic relationship to my sense of queerness, queer identity, and social placement vis-a-vis that queer identity. It/They is/are a small but salient feature/figure that announces simultaneously a peculiar way of seeing the world and a peculiar way of being seen by the world.

But in my delight is the seed of a misgiving, my own potential de-composition as a subject. I wonder what it would be like not to be crossed-eyed-not, I think, out of any nascent desire to be or appear "normal," but because, after a certain point, my crossed eyed appearance is normal. I wonder what it would be like to be other than I am. Not normal. But other, continually other. This is the queer moment: the desire to be other than what one is—and the movement toward that otherness.

10

Multiculturally inflected pedagogies have resulted, if unintentionally, in the containment of queerness, in the trimming of excess that robs queerness of its potential critical power. The "coming out" story, for instance, typifies the kind of narrative of queerness frequently found in composition readers that offers us a contained, controlled, and composed experience of queerness—one designed to promote sympathy. But such narratives also promote an understanding of *a very specific kind of queerness*, one that is not angry, not critical, and ultimately not aware of the very real differences, the real *critical* differences, among people in a pluralistic society. Such unknowing containment curtails critique of the kinds of systems that position people as possible (or impossible) subjects. As Rhodes writes,

I must remain the *material or embodied* queer, for even as we move away from identity politics and toward performative notions of gender and sexual identity, LGBT folk still face the "real world" consequences of queer identity within the academy. It is a wonderful thing to practice queer theory—even to get your first-year students to explore performativity and gender construction—but it is another thing entirely to wonder if you're going to get the shit kicked out of you for being a "queer" when you walk out to the parking lot at night.

The narratives of inclusion that undergird the multicultural classroom compose differences as units of exchange—to be truly multicultural, we must have a certain multicultural "k" factor, as it were, and so we increase that factor by trading one essay by bell hooks for another by Ana Castillo (a 1:1 factor), one by E.M. Forster for another by Gloria Naylor (a+1 gain). Composition of these differences depends on balance, on even-handed ness, on seeming neutrality. To "compose oneself' in the current system means to accept this structure, this classroom, this multiculturalism—it requires the participants not only to accept the idea of difference, but the idea of difference as a neutral genre (*gender* [Eng.]= *genre* [Fr.], among other things). Composition, then, relies on a particular stance toward difference.

To be queer in such a system seems doubly impossible, for queerness relies on notions of excess and distinctly discomposed bodies for its critical purchase. Queerness is a disruption in the service of nothing, pure in its joyful enraged body, sexed-up and inappropriate. To "compose onself," to subjugate the flesh to the will, is to shove oneself back in the closet, to ignore the eminently persuasive call of one's erection.

11

Donna Haraway, "'Gender' for a Marxist Dictionary: The Sexual Politics of a Word":

Keyword
Gender (English), *Geschlecht* (German), *Genre* (French), *Genera* (Spanish)
[T]he root of the English, French, and Spanish words is the Latin verb, *generare*, to beget, and the Latin stem *gener-*, race or kind. . . . The substantives "Geschlect," "gender," "genre," and "genero" refer to the notion of sort, kind, and class. In English, "gender" has been used in this "generic" sense continuously since at least the fourteenth century. In French, Gennan, Spanish, and English, words for "gender" refer to grammatical and literary categories. The modem English and Gennan words, "gender" and "Geschlecht" adhere closely to concepts of sex, sexuality, sexual difference, generation, engendering, and so on, while the

French and Spanish seem not to carry those meanings as readily "Gender" is at the heart of constructions and classifications of systems of difference. Complex differentiation and merging oftenns for "sex" and "gender" are part of the political history of the words . . . The shared categorical racial and sexual meanings of gender point to the interwoven modern histories of colonial, racist, and sexual oppressions in systems of bodily production and inscription and their consequent liberatory and oppositional discourses. (129–30)

Available Freedom:
The Teacher's Body, Part I [Jackie]

I came out in 1984. I was almost 19, finishing my first year of college at a liberal arts university in a western state. In that state in 1984, sexual contact between members of the same sex was considered a felony—"deviant sexual conduct"— punishable by five years in jail, a $10,000 fine, or both. There was only one gay bar in the entire state, somewhere in the outer reaches of interstate travel. In the university town where I lived, there was a small, local organization that had its office above an old second-run movie theater down town. It sponsored two or three dances a year, and hundreds of lesbian and gay folk came from around the state to socialize. We had only begun to hear about a "gay cancer" that was hitting the big U.S. cities.

In 1999, when I started my job at my current university, AIDS had claimed over 12 million lives around the world. We had been "not asking" and "not telling" for six years. I had domestic partner benefits. Everyone knew about Ellen DeGeneres. Queer Nation, ACT UP, and the Lesbian Avengers had waxed and waned. It was a year before Vermont legally recognized civil unions. It was a year after Matthew Shepard had been murdered in Wyoming. Now, in the eleven years since I became a lesbian professor rather than a lesbian student, there have been nearly 10,000 hate crimes in the U.S. based on sexual orientation. Our campus has been besieged mightily by the College Republicans, who discovered that they can blame anything (rising student fees, most recently) on the LGBT population and, mostly, get away with it.

I don't bring up this personal background to win victimization points for the queer team, but rather to point to sex, violence, and punishment as very real, material considerations that structure part of our "available freedom." To deny or sidestep these material considerations means to leave out a crucial part of the construction of identity within rhetoric.

12

Composition has a long history of accommodation, of steadily bringing many different voices together to tell the story of literacy and of literate citizenship. We speak of "creating a space," of helping others "find a voice." To a great extent, this work has served us well; now, however, we need to explore the possibility that some spaces simply do not overlap, that some voices cannot be heard together. Grappling with the incommensurable spaces in composition allows us to approach our work not only with greater subtlety and sophistication, but with a greater understanding of the complexities—and impossibilities—inherent in any democratic project that wants to make a space for different voices, different views.

Robert McRuer, in *Crip Theory: Cultural Signs of Queerness and Disability*, comes closest to articulating our dis-ease with composition's call to composure. In a chapter addressing composition pedagogy and its failure to account and make room for critical pedagogies addressing issues of disability and queerness, McRuer argues how,

> Despite the best efforts of many individual composition theorists and instructors, and despite a decades-long conversation about process and revision, composition in the corporate university remains a practice that is focused on a fetishized final product, whether it is the final paper, the final grade, or the student body with measurable skills. (151)

For McRuer, our current institutions of higher learning (the "corporate university") privilege marketable skills and figure composition as "servicing" not only other disciplines but to corporate interests wanting students and potential employees with particular kinds of skill sets. In the process, as he puts it, "[t]he call to produce orderly and efficient writing/docile subjects thus takes on a heightened urgency in our particular moment" (154).

This argument works the metaphoric slippage between the "fetishized final products" of the composition course and the "docile subjects" that are called to produce such texts. For McRuer, the call to compose is the call to be composed. As such, the un-composed subjects—be they the subjects of written compositions or the subjects composing those compositions—must discipline themselves to fit the needs and demands of a skills-driven pedagogical (and ultimately corporate) economy. McRuer points to queer and disabled discourses, topics, and bodies that do not fit normative expectations for what "good workers" (or "good writers") should look like, how they should behave, or what they should do with their bodies; underneath those expectations is the desire that we all contribute to the maintenance of the corporate status quo. Queers and the disabled, and the disabled queer, are not always "docile bodies," and they frequently challenge normalizing discourses—in work, in play, in learning, in relation to one another, and in intimate encounters.

McRuer questions our field's call to composure: "How, then, to acknowledge and affirm the experiences we draw from multiple academic and non-academic communities where compositing (in all senses of the word) is clearly an unruly, disorderly cultural practice? Can composition theory work against the simplistic formulation of that which is proper, orderly, and harmonious?" (147). To address such questions, McRuer recounts his experiences in teaching writing-intensive courses that pick up queer and disabled subjects as objects of critical inquiry. Forwarding the concept of "de-composition" and the use of "alternative corporealities," he describes the movement into his writing classroom of "[d]iverse and perverse erotic proclivities (decidedly not the homogenous and domesticated married identity . . .), multiple genders, and various disabilities," which critically questioned normative assumptions of bodies, identities, and relationality (165); pedagogically, such "de-composition" is inimical to "'nuts and bolts' approaches that somehow streamline the process of composition instruction through manuals, teaching 'strategies' exchanged like recipes," and rather foregrounds an "*ongoing attentiveness* to how a given composition class will intersect with local or national issues" (165–66).

McRuer's goal, as he puts it, is to "position queer theory and disability studies at the center of composition theory," and while we applaud both the attempt and his reconceptualization of his composition courses, we are less sanguine about the attempted disruption of composition practices by claiming queer theory or disability studies—the margin—as the center of composition. Such moves seem more rhetorical than material in their gestures. That is, we can claim to *move* composition by *re-centering* it on theories of the margins, but our sense is that what is ultimately moved is the "subject" or "topic" into a classroom that in turn disciplines it into a docile body.

While we cannot claim to know, for instance, exactly what transpired in McRuer's classes, we are struck by the lack of writing samples *from "decomposed" students* in his chapter. Where, in other words, are the material effects of de-composition? What is the "product" of de-composition? Perhaps a withholding of such texts is designed to trouble our desire to see a "product," but it nonetheless leaves us wondering what such texts might look like.

13

Winterson: "I wanted to create an imaginative reality sufficiently at odds with our daily reality to startle us out of it" ("Work" 188).

14

We *are* here, and we *are* queer, and while our presence in the field of rhetoric and composition has, at times, been variously ignored, tolerated, and occasionally (if rarely) somewhat celebrated, we have resisted the field's disciplining. That is, we have been and remain somewhat outside the fold of rhetoric and composition, launching salvos through periodic articles and the all-too-rare book or journal collection.

We refuse the gesture of bemoaning that outsider status. Instead, we *celebrate* it. We have come to realize that what might make queer composition actually work is the uncomfortable fit, the awkward alignment that doesn't quite cohere. You offer us an identity, a category with expectations, and we try on a different gender's clothes. You ask for guidelines about treating LGBT students, and we turn away to go dancing. You want to publish our articles, and we talk about bodies, fucking. You try to figure out a place for us at your table, and we spit in your plate.

Are you confused? We were, admittedly. We started to forget the power of the queer, and the necessity of queering rhetorical practices to make—not just *room*—but *trouble* for rhetoric and composition. Our field asks, consistently, for the right answer, for the best practices, for the way to do things to satisfy different "stakeholders." And while we acknowledge the usefulness of best practices, of constructive paradigms, we also just as equally demand acknowledgment of the kinds of practices that *disrupt*, that *disturb*, that show us our logic and our reason coming apart at the seams in the groping toward articulation of something all-together Other, not yet spoken, but often *felt*.

15

The work of Foucault stands, controversially but compellingly, as a call to trace out the genealogies of knowledge—and knowledge as *power*—that shape our conception of our bodies and desires, that call forth certain desires for praise and others for censure, and that in the process construct our deep sense of subjectivity. If Foucault is correct in his assertion that, since the late nineteenth century at least, sex and subjectivity are nearly synonymous, then the desiring body is the workshop of identity, the site of the creation of particular kinds of being, and the making impossible of other kinds of being. As many queer theorists and scholars of sexuality have maintained, the disciplining of desire into straight and gay identities has become one of the most powerful ways in which we now "know" who we are, expressing and articulating senses of self that seems so intimately personal but that is clearly constructed socially in the creation and dissemination of categories of sexual behavior that become, seemingly retroactively, indices of deep-seated being. Put another way, the terrain of organized sexualities (gay/straight, even male/ female) is mapped onto the potentially plural domain of desiring bodies, creating the story of our identities in the process.

But the queer is not always so subject to disciplining, so willingly abject. Foucault's work in the history of sexuality begins with the sexologists, who, in their convoluted classifications systems detailing the diversity of erotic practice, actually laid the groundwork for some of our most basic identity divisions along the lines of sexual practice, internalized as identity/desire. But many sexologists (with the exception of those like Havelock Ellis) sought classifications not to applaud the diversity of erotic experience, but to discipline it. And in the internalization of desire as identity—what you want to fuck is more than what you want to do; it is what you *are*—we see the emergence of both sanctioned and pathological identities. An increasingly psychologized culture invites you to monitor your own desires in relation to the "norm," and the panopticon of social control becomes one with the creation of the modern soul. The normative organizes, at the level of the individual, what kinds of bodies and desires should be reproduced—notably, hetero-normative bodies and desires.

Indeed, Foucault knew that the emergence of norms always bore within it the possibility of resistance, of counter-claims. And just as sexologists, psychologists, and psychiatrists would pathologize non-normative erotic practices and desires, so those who found themselves called "sick" began questioning their label, querying the story that the medical professionals were telling about their lives. While it took nearly a hundred years, from the end of the nineteenth century until the early 1970s for the medical establishment to de-pathologize homosexuality (at least officially), the presence of the queer consistently disrupted the normative, existing as the bit that wouldn't fit into hetero-normative matrices of identity, self-knowledge, and social power.

We argue that the point of the queer is to disrupt stability, to call into question the ways in which we are all called to compose ourselves. And as a movement of disruption, it is often difficult to track, to catch, to *identify*.

Gays and lesbians are often positioned in relation to the normative, often as those seeking a place at the table—and many gays and lesbians *are* seeking that place. But in our lives as a gay man and as a lesbian, we have encountered numerous instances in which our queerness most certainly does *not* fit in, where it marks us as separate, as possessing and possessed by a subjectivity that is often incommensurably other.

Those are often our most delicious moments—and the most critically insightful and revealing. We are not like the straights, and we believe that any writing pedagogy, any effective composition pedagogy that seeks to grapple successfully with queerness must first acknowledge that irremedial, incommensurable, delectable *difference*.

16

What is the place of the sexual selves, the somatic bodies, in rhetoric and composition? We are most comfortable with discussions of identity that are accessible to analytic language-that is, we like to talk about things that can be talked about. The feedback loop inherent in this system necessarily elides considerations of the body, of sex, of queerness. We want to gesture toward a history of usable practices—perhaps à la Geoff Sire in *Composition as a Happening*—that risk a *lack* of composure. We wish to cultivate textual practices that risk a bit of discomfort in order to air different insights, different knowledges, different bodies, different ways of being. We see this work as not just the (re)claiming of lost voices, but of cultivating useful *rhetorical practices* that might still find a place for critical work today. We seek *queer* rhetorical practices—practices that recognize the necessity sometimes of saying "No," of saying "Fuck, no," of offering an impassioned, embodied, and visceral reaction to the practices of normalization that limit not just freedom, but the *imagination* of possibility, of potential.

17

Laurie Anderson, "Language is a Virus" (1986):

> Well I was talking to a friend
> And I was saying: I wanted you
> And I was looking for you
> But I couldn't find you
> I couldn't find you
> And he said: Hey!

Are you talking to me?
Or are you just practicing
For one of those performances of yours?
Huh?
Language! It's a virus!
Language! It's a virus!

18

To a great extent, queerness and its subjects are asked to make themselves known in a classroom, either through the overt narrative of the coming-out story or through adherence to or deviation from certain tropes of "homonormative" life—gay marriage, homophobia, AIDS. Drawing on Levinasian ideas of othering, Judith Butler argues that this sort of demand for knowledge constitutes a type of "ethical violence," in which we ask for a sort of completely coherent self-identity even as we recognize in ourselves our own incoherence. That is, as she writes in *Giving an Account of Oneself*:

> In a sense, the ethical stance consists in asking the question "Who are you?" and continuing to ask it without any expectation of a full or final answer. The other to whom I pose this question will not be captured by any answer that might arrive to satisfy it. So if there is, in the question, a desire for recognition, this desire will be under an obligation to keep itself alive as desire and not to resolve itself. . . . To revise recognition as an ethical project, we will need to see it as, in principle, unsatisfiable. (43)

19

We are one of composition's impossible subjects.

20

Susan Miller concludes her *Norton Anthology of Composition Studies* with Russel Durst's review article, "Writing at the Postsecondary Level," which broadly surveys recent trends and potential future directions of our field. Durst concludes by asserting that "the field presently finds itself in something of a rut." Specifically, Durst argues that composition "lacks a defining feature of powerful orthodoxy *within* composition studies to work against, such as current-traditional teaching or the cognitive emphasis. And in the past, it has been the idea of working against an oppressive status quo that most strongly motivated composition scholars to develop exciting new interpretations and approaches" (1677). Durst is both right and wrong. He's right in his very *felt* sense that resisting and working against a status quo is generative. Right on. But he's wrong in his sense that there is no prevailing status quo.

We are not going to argue that the heteronorm is the status quo of composition studies—though it is. Our argument is broader, our resistance deeper. We *do* feel a status quo at work in our field—the status quo of the *composed* text, of the drive toward polished writing, of using even the messy genres of digitally enabled communication for the generation of finished texts.

21

In asking students to create well-articulated, organized, and coherent texts, we ask them to compose themselves—to order their ideas, their presentation, their texts. The free-form creativity of brainstorming and prewriting must eventually give way to the composed text that presents its arguments in a hopefully complex but nonetheless rational, straightforward manner. Excess, often characterized as the extraneous, the "off topic," must be trimmed to produce shapely texts.

22

But what about that excess?

23

Ceci n'est pas un auteur composé.

24

Let us return to McRuer's provocative questions, which inaugurate his chapter: "How, then, to acknowledge and affirm the experiences we draw from multiple academic and non-academic communities where compositing (in all senses of the word) is clearly an unruly, disorderly cultural practice? Can composition theory work against the simplistic formulation of that which is proper, orderly, and harmonious?" (147). In answer to the first question, we believe that "acknowledging and affirming the experiences" of the other may necessarily result in a process of *disciplining* that other. In other words, when the "other" becomes a subject of composition—whether a queered other, a raced other, a disabled other—it is called to compose itself. Its unruliness, its disorder are articulated in composed products, most often the "coming-out" narrative or a literacy narrative, recounting how one came to know oneself and understand one's "otherness" in relation to others. But isn't this the work of the composition classroom: to make articulate and ordered the subjects under scrutiny? As such, to address the second question, the answer is *no*. No, composition theory may not be able to "work against the simplistic formulation of that which is proper, orderly, and harmonious." To do so would be to engage in work that is *not* composition. Such work is *impossible* for composition.

25

Again, Ahmed:

> The straight body is not simply in a "neutral" position: or if it is the neutral position, then this alignment is only an effect of the repetition of past gestures, which give the body its contours and the "impression" of its skin. The body emerges from this history of doing, which is also a history of not doing, of paths not taken, which also involves the loss, impossible to know or to even register, of what might have followed from such paths. As such, the body is directed as a condition of its arrival, as a direction that gives the body its line. And yet we can still ask, what happens if the orientation of the body is not restored? What happens when disorientation cannot simply be overcome by the "force" of the vertical? What do we do, if disorientation itself becomes worldly or becomes what is given? (159)

Queer composition is impossible; the excess and disorientation of one disrupts the containment of the other.

26

Such impossibility, such disorientation, lays the ground for a new kind of writing instruction, *a new kind of writing*. In grappling with impossibility, with the hard realization that some subjects *cannot* be known, with the understanding that certain realms of experience are incommensurable and hence *not* open to mutual understanding, we encounter radical alterity and the need to ground communicative exchange—and ethical responsibility toward one another—in ways that do not assume commonality, similarity, or identity.

A queer tradition of texts suggests to us that we need excess in order to produce texts that perform complicated critical work. Sometimes that excess is in the affective domain, as in the difficult emotions produced by texts—emotions that readers do not always know what to do with or know how to contain. But excess also exists textually as written movements and gestures that defy intellectual containability, that transgress our sense of what is knowable. Such moves also perform important critical work in asking us to think other, or at least to acknowledge movement, possibility, and being outside of the normative.

27

What might it mean, then, to "compose queerly," even as we recognize the potential impossibility of such? Works by Kathy Acker, Dennis Cooper, and Gloria Anzaldúa are part of a queer tradition that shows us how excess challenges normative understandings of being, subjectivity, and possibility. Such difficult texts reveal the call to composure as an ideological, disciplining gesture that delimits, in Foucault's words, our sense of available freedom. Transgressive literary texts have played an increasingly important role in the life of the contemporary queer and feminist imaginations, especially as such literature foregrounds the ways in which queers of many stripes resist dominating, normalizing, and homophobic narratives about their lives and loves. Acker, Cooper, Gary Indiana, Anzaldúa, Winterson, and others often portray characters engaging in acts of transgressive resistance—in acts that simultaneously resist the restrictive and impoverished identities that we are called to compose for ourselves and for re-presentation to others. Further, resistance to such identities transgresses the dichotomies, binarisms, and boundaries that attempt to order identity, culture, and social interaction along delimiting lines of patriarchal and heterosexist ideologies. As such, these authors' works provide much-needed imaginative models and sources of inspiration for carving queer spaces, identities, and lives out of an often-hostile social, political, and cultural matrix.

But, as Winterson notes in a refrain repeated throughout her most recent collection of experimental fiction, *The World and Other Places*, "What you risk shows what you value." While acts of transgression have often been figured (particularly by literary and queer theorists) as acts of resistance, it is important to note that they are also acts of assertion, performances of the transgressors' investments and values both against and within the social matrix he or she is transgressing. Thus, transgression never simply resists or negates; it also inevitably, if unconsciously, asserts.

Put another way, the negating and reverse discourses of transgression produce their own reverse discourses—but this time, they are discourses of assertion, personal investment, and value. The recognition of such values is significant, especially since it offers queers the opportunity to begin configuring their lives in modes not necessarily tied to the binarisms and constraints of *identity* in the hetero-normative world. Further, a productive discussion of "queer values" provides queers a possible entrance into and grounding within the various discourses of values currently circulating in our culture. And, finally, a consideration of values inevitably leads to the possibility of articulating a queer ethics, which may be useful in moving the discussion of rights for queers away from the constraints and limitations of identity models—as well as provide more opportunities for strategic discourse with other groups seeking to enhance their experience of freedom in our society.

28

What we might ask is what the field of composition looks like given the impossibility of narrative "closure" of queer difference.

29

Available Freedom:
The Teacher's Body, Part II [Jackie]

Who taught me the composition of the lesbian body? I learned from my first lovers, each of whom was a decade older than me. I was fortunate to come out into a community of actively feminist lesbians who wanted to enculturate me: books, music, history, and tall tales. This sort of composition takes place over time, with a great deal of emotional investment, a particular mix of private instruction into the peculiar public space of lesbian community.

This sort of composition, of course, points to the crux of the problem with institutionalized queerness. Where does our private sexuality intersect with our public performance of it?

A good deal of what is fascinating about the "savage other" is its existence as our alter ego, as an idealized abstraction of what lurks beneath our veneer of civilization. It is crucial to remember this point, for it is the queer subject's own "savageness" in the classroom that both licenses her to speak (by giving inside/knowledge) and makes her suspect. The automatic and presumptive sexualizing/fetishizing of the queer body constructs us as Other, destabilizes our Be-ing, forces an intimacy with anyone in our orbit. The body of the queer becomes the "public sphere" of the multicultural classroom, mediating private self and state authority (as expressed in the narratives of inclusion underlying multicultural classrooms).

It is alarming to realize that one's body is not one's own, particularly if one is in a context (the classroom) in which "bodies" and "passions" and "emotions" are not supposed to exist at all. To be "embodied" by others and then filled with meaning is disconcerting, and it is threatening. How are we to "compose ourselves" in such a system? Such composition comes at unacknowledged personal cost—moral, social, religious, sometimes legal cost. Sometimes it comes at great physical cost. Is it worth it? Maybe. There's not a right answer to that question.

30

We seek to carve out—even in nonfoundational, always—already questioning ways—honorable, lucid, even *real* places for our students and us to engage in the life of the mind—and of the body.

31

Ultimately, our view demands that we embrace the incommensurability of bodily self and representation at the same time as we acknowledge the importance of lived experience to the formation of an ethical stance. We want to clarify up front, however, that our sense of sexuality and ethics does not cover "appropriate" sexual behavior or sexual manners, but instead draws on a close examination of the discourses surrounding the sexual self. What behaviors, what subjectivities, what possibilities, and what impossibilities are created through the intersections of sex and text? It is with this view in mind that we attempt to perform in this book our own queer encounters—as sexed, sexual, and queer beings—with a variety of texts.

32

Imaginary Syllabus

COURSE:ENGLISH 101
INSTRUCTOR: YOU & ME & OTHERS
REQUIRED TEXTS: *Blood and Guts in High School* by Kathy Acker

ABOUT THIS COURSE: "Some things are better left unsaid, but they still turn me inside out . . . turning inside out . . . turning inside out." —Annie Lennox, "Why?"

ASSIGNMENTS: Compose your own *Blood and Guts in High School.* You may include drawings, passages in a foreign language, puzzles, comics, autobiographical narrative, instructions, poetry. Articulate the impossibility of your possibility. Plagiarize but acknowledge your plagiarism. Reflect rhetorically.

DAILY SCHEDULE: Read, write, think—daily.

33

Certainly, we understand some of the potential critiques that our approach will encounter among those in our field. Having both worked as writing program administrators, we know what it is like to be confronted with an overwhelming glut of composition agendas, ideologies, and practices— all clamoring for attention, trying to snag our gaze, if only for a second. Questions posed to us by faculty, graduate teaching assistants, and adjuncts are varied, often evoking complex issues and debates: Is it okay if I teach literature in my comp class? How would I use an ethnographic approach to writing instruction? To what extent must I consider visual literacies and rhetorics in my courses? How do I use technology to teach writing? Do I *have* to use technology to teach writing? Do you favor expressivist, social-epistemic, post-process, or current traditionalist pedagogies?

Inevitably, questions about what we *should* do, about specific skills we *should* focus on, about what particular direction our instruction *should* take, both excite and stymie the conversation. We debate vigorously but reach no consensus. And, at the end of such sessions, our mental inboxes are full. In so many ways, we have benefited from and appreciate our field's diversity of approaches to writing instruction a diversity that matches the wealth, depth, and multi-dimensionality of writing itself.

34

This is not your docile body speaking.

35

Teaching involves making choices—what texts to teach, what assignments to give, what writerly values to promote, what pedagogical methods to deploy. Inevitably, in making choices, we ignore any number of pedagogical and scholarly possibilities so that we can get down to business, to do the work that needs to be done, to teach students to write in the best ways we know how. We see an energy, a vitality in composing queerly that is productive of text and critique. We want our students to compose with that energy and that vitality.

36

We seduce you.

37

We desire a composition that does not always call us to be composed. We cannot deny the efficacy of teaching students usable, even marketable skills. But we deny a composition that makes no room for the critically uncomposable and that fails to understand itself as fundamentally inhospitable to the de-compositions of queerness. Acknowledging this inhospitability, this incommensurability, inaugurates a discussion that may put composition and queerness into an impossible but nonetheless productive dialogue.

38

What is queer eomposition, then? It is valuing works that unsettle us, and inviting students to unsettle us with their own formal, stylistic, and content-rich experimentations and improvisations. It is valuing free form work. It is embracing a capaciousness of style. It is a willingness to break with logic, reason, the logos. It is recognizing the logic of the impossible.

We value the forgotten genres: poetry, manifestos, graffiti, leaflets, erotica. We value spontaneity. We value ephemera. We value the erotics of writing. We value anger and being pissed off. We value queer love and queer rage and the articulation of such as a necessarily messy and disruptive politics. We value the possibly impossible.

39

Kathy Acker: "What this society does is marginalize artists. 'Oh, artists, they have nothing to do with politics.' So the experimental—it's a way of saying things. I hate this way of saying things. I want to say 'fuck, shit, prick.' That's my way of talking, that's my way of saying 'I hate you'" (Friedman 21).

40

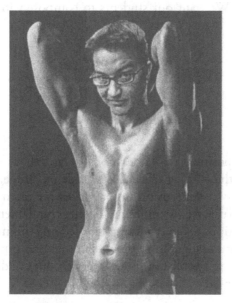

Ceci n'est pas un auteur composé.

41

"Queers Read This: I Hate Straights" was a leaflet distributed in 1990 at a New York Pride March. In it, the anonymous authors advocated a forceful approach in which queers should be proud of their sexuality and their "sexualness"—and settle for nothing less than an acknowledgment of that sexuality. While not as "anti-straight"as the title might suggest, the tone is aggressive:

The next time some straight person comes down on you for being angry, tell them that until things change, you don't need any more evidence that the world turns at your expense. You don't need to see only hetero couples grocery shopping on your TV . . . You don't want any more baby pictures shoved in your face until you can have or keep your own. No more weddings, showers, anniversaries, please, unless they are our own brothers and sisters celebrating. And tell them not to dismiss you by saying "You have rights," "You have privileges," "You are overreacting," or "You have a victim's mentality." Tell them "Go away from me, until you change." Go away and try on a world without the brave, strong queers that are its backbone, that are its guts and brains and souls. Go tell them go away until they have spent a month walking hand in hand in public with someone of the same sex. After they survive that, then you'll hear what they have to say about queer anger.

Otherwise, tell them to shut up and listen. (148)

What we value about this passage as a potential reading is its emphasis on the incommensurable, on the spaces in our understanding of one another that either get overlooked in multicultural awareness or that are too difficult to grapple with because they allude to such radical differences in experience— and that are, hence, ignored. Granted, such readings may be polarizing for some students, even somewhat threatening. But we are increasingly convinced that part of our work as compositionists is to work with students on writing that *is* threatening, that fundamentally questions what we believe or hold to be true. Writing *is* often unsettling. And while "I Hate Straights" is a kind of writing we don't often encourage in our classrooms, we wonder how avoiding it, even in the name of promoting tolerance, may be hampering our students' appreciation for both writing *and* for an ethical understanding that acknowledges precisely where our ability to understand ends.

42

Shut up and listen.

43

TO READ: Kathy Acker, *Blood and Guts in High School*; Patrick Califia-Rice, *Speaking Sex to Power*; Jonathan Ned Katz, *The Invention of Heterosexuality*; Alison Bechdel, *Fun Home* and *Dykes to Watch Out For*; Michael Warner, *The Trouble with Normal*; David Halperin, *Saint Foucault*; Gloria Anzaldúa, *La Frontera/Borderlands*; Michel Foucault, *Ethics: Subjectivity and Truth*.

44

A conclusion, at this point, would be impossible.

University of California
Irvine, California

California State University
San Bernardino, California

WORKS CITED

Acker, Kathy. *Blood and Guts in High School*. New York: Grove, 1978.

Alexander, Jonathan, and David Wallace. "The Queer Turn in Composition Studies: Reviewing and Assessing an Emerging Scholarship." *College Composition and Communication* 61 (2009): 300–20.

Alexander, Jonathan, and Michelle Gibson. "Queer Composition(s): Queer Theory in the Writing Classroom." *JAC* 24 (2004): 1–22.

Ahmed, Sara. *Queer Phenomenology: Orientations, Objects, Others*. Durham: Duke UP, 2006.

Anderson, Laurie. "Language Is a Virus." *Home of the Brave*. Warner, 1986.

Anzaldúa, Gloria. *Borderlands/La Frontera: The New Mestiza*. 3rd ed. San Francisco: Aunt Lute, 2007.

Bechdel, Alison. *Fun Home: A Family Tragicomic*. Boston: Mariner, 2006.

Butler, Judith. *Giving an Account of Oneself*. New York: Fordham UP, 2005.

Califia-Rice, Patrick. *Speaking Sex to Power. The Politics of Queer Sex*. San Francisco: Cleis, 2002.

Durst, Russel K. "Writing at the Postsecondary Level." *The Norton Book of Composition Studies*. Ed. Susan Miller. New York: Norton, 2009.

Eurythmics. "Sweet Dreams." *Sweet Dreams (Are Made of This)*. RCA, 1983.

Foucault, Michel. *Ethics: Subjectivity and Truth*. Vol. I. *Essential Works of Foucault*. Ed. P. Rabinow. New York: New P, 1997.

———. *The History of Sexuality*, Vol. I: *An Introduction*. Trans. R. Hurley. London: Penguin, 1990.

Friedman, Ellen G. "A Conversation with Kathy Acker." *Review of Contemporary Fiction* 9 (1989): 12–22.

Halperin, David M. *Saint Foucault: Towards a Gay Hagiography*. New York: Oxford UP, 1995.

Haraway, Donna J. "'Gender' for a Marxist Dictionary: The Sexual Politics of a Word." *Simians, Cyborgs, and Women: The Reinvention of Nature*. London: Free, 1991. 127–48.

Katz, Jonathan Ned. *The Invention of Heterosexuality*. New York: Dutton, I 995.

Lennox, Annie. "Why?" *Diva*. Arista, 1992. CD.

Malinowitz, Harriet. *Textual Orientations: Lesbian and Gay Students and the Making of Discourse Communities*. Portsmouth: Heinemann, 1995.

McRuer, Robert. *Crip Theory: Cultural Signs of Queerness and Disability*. New York: New York UP, 2006.

Miller, Richard E. "Fault Lines in the Contact Zone: Assessing Homophobic Student Writing." *Lesbian and Gay Studies and the Teaching of English*. Ed. William J. Spurlin. Urbana: NCTE, 2000. 234–52.

Monson, Connie L., and Jacqueline Rhodes. "Risking Queer: Pedagogy, Perfonnativity, and Desire in Writing Classrooms." *JAC* 24 (2004): 79–92.

"Queers Read This: I Hate Straights." New York Gay Pride March, 1990.

Rhodes, Jacqueline. Introduction. *Sexualities, Technologies, and literacies: Metonymy and Material Online*. Spec. issue, *Computers and Composition Online*. Fall 2003/Spring 2004.

Sire, Geoffrey. *Composition as a Happening*. Logan: Utah State UP, 2002.

Warner, Michael. *The Trouble with Normal: Sex Politics and the Ethics of Queer Life*. Cambridge: Harvard UP, 1999.

Winterson, Jeannette. "A Work of My Own." *Art Objects: Essays on Ecstasy and Effrontery*. New York: Vintage, 1995. 165–92.

———. *The World and Other Places: Stories*. New York: Vintage, 2000.

Rhetorical Sovereignty: What Do American Indians Want from Writing?

Scott Richard Lyons

After years of colonization, oppression, and resistance, American Indians are making clear what they want from the heretofore compromised technology of writing. Rhetorical sovereignty, a people's control of its meaning, is found in sites legal, aesthetic, and pedagogical, and composition studies can both contribute to and learn from this work.

> *Now, brothers and sisters . . . the white man has his ways. Oh gracious me, he has his ways. He talks about the Word. He talks through it and around it. He builds upon it with syllables, with prefixes and suffixes and hyphens and accents. He adds and subtracts and divides and multiplies the Word. And in all of this he subtracts the Truth. And, brothers and sisters, you have come to live in the white man's world. Now the white man deals in words, and he deals easily, with grace and sleight of hand. And in his presence, here on his own ground, you are as children, mere babes in the woods.*
>
> —N. Scott Momaday (*House*, 93–94)

> *A student asked, "Can Essential Nature be destroyed?"*
> *Coyote said, "Yes, it can."*
> *The student asked, "How can Essential Nature be destroyed?"*
> *Coyote said, "With an eraser."*
> —Robert Aitken

Reprinted from *College Composition and Communication* 51.3 (February 2000): 447–468. Used with permission.

In *My People the Sioux,* Luther Standing Bear recounts the moment when he and other children arrived at the Carlisle Indian School and received for the first time the European implements of writing. "Although we were yet wearing our Indian clothes," Standing Bear writes, "we were marched into a school room, where we were each given a pencil and slate. We were seated at single desks. We soon discovered that the pencils made marks on the slate" (*Sioux* 136). Pulling their blankets over their heads to conceal both slate and the marks they would make upon them, a child's act of modesty, the children's first impulse was to draw scenes from their recently departed home life—"a man on a pony chasing a buffalo, or a boy shooting birds in a tree, or it might be one of our Indian games"—and when finished, "we dropped our blankets down on the seat and marched up to the teacher with our slates to show what we had drawn" (*Sioux* 136). Picture these children withdrawing into their blankets with a curious new technology, concealing their texts from each other and the teacher until just the right moment, then emerging from their blankets proud and eager to share the fruits of their labor. They were, at least until this point, the same children, and the marks they made were earnest representations of their lives. Shortly thereafter, however, this same technology would be used to change them:

> One day when we came to school there was a lot of writing on one of the blackboards. We did not know what it meant, but our interpreter came into the room and said, 'Do you see all these marks on the blackboard? Well, each word is a white man's name. They are going to give each one of you one of these names by which you will hereafter be known.' None of the names were read or explained to us, so of course we did not know the sound or meaning of any of them. (*Sioux* 136–37)

These arbitrary, meaningless names were selected by students who were given a pointer by the teacher; the chosen name was then written on cloth and sewed on the back of each student's shirt. Standing Bear recalls how the first boy to choose a name looked back at the others "as much as to say . . . 'Is it right for me to take a white man's name?'" (*Sioux* 137). But Standing Bear himself "took the pointer and acted as if I were about to touch an enemy" (*Sioux* 137), counting coup on the text, so to speak, and probably eliciting laughter in support of his mock bravery from the other kids. "Soon we all had names of white men sewed on our backs" (*Sioux* 137).

That laughter, which is not in Standing Bear's book but remains my guess, my desire, would nonetheless be short-lived, as is known by anyone familiar with the boarding school story. As David Wallace Adams tells it in *Education for Extinction,* this tale "constitutes yet another deplorable episode in the long and tragic history of Indian-white relations"— specifically, the development of education designed to promote "the eradication of all traces of tribal identity and culture, replacing them with the commonplace knowledge and values of white civilization" (336, 335). This forced replacement of one identity for another, a cultural violence enabled in part through acts of physical violence, was in so many ways located at the scene of writing. More horrific than most scenes of writing, however, the boarding school stands out as the ultimate symbol of white domination, even genocide, through assimilation in the American Indian experience. And although Standing Bear and others would recall multiple forms of Indian resistance, from torching schools to running away to counting coup on the Western text, the duplicitous interrelationships between writing, violence, and colonization developed during the nineteenth-century—not only in the boarding schools but at the signings of hundreds of treaties, most of which were dishonored by whites—would set into motion a persistent distrust of the written word in English, one that resonates in homes and schools and courts of law still today. If our respect for the Word remains resolute, our faith in the written word is compromised at best.

What do Indians want from writing? Certainly something other than the names of white men sewn to our backs. And for its part, resistance to assimilation through the acts of writing should entail something more than counting coup on the text (or for that matter, torching the school). I suggest that our highest hopes for literacy at this point rest upon a vision we might name *rhetorical sovereignty.* Sovereignty, of course, has long been a contested term in Native discourse, and its shifting meanings over time attest to an ongoing struggle between Americans and the hundreds of Indian nations that occupy this land. Our claims to sovereignty entail much more than arguments for tax-exempt status or the right to build and operate casinos; they are nothing less than our attempt to survive and flourish as a people. Sovereignty is the guiding story in our pursuit of self-determination, the general strategy by which we aim to best recover our losses from the ravages of colonization: our lands, our languages, our cultures, our self-respect. For indigenous people everywhere, sovereignty is an ideal principle, the beacon by which we seek the paths to agency and power and community renewal. Attacks on sovereignty are attacks on what it enables us to pursue; the pursuit of sovereignty is an attempt to revive not our past, but our possibilities. Rhetorical sovereignty is the inherent right and ability of *peoples* to determine their own communicative needs and desires in this pursuit, to decide for themselves the goals, modes, styles, and languages of public discourse. Placing the scene of writing squarely back into the particular contingency of the Indian rhetorical situation, rhetorical sovereignty requires of writing teachers more than a renewed commitment to listening and learning; it also requires a radical rethinking of how and what we teach as the written word at all levels of schooling, from preschool to graduate curricula and beyond. In what follows, I hope to sketch out some preliminary notes toward the praxis that is rhetorical sovereignty. I begin with a discussion of the concept of sovereignty, followed by a dialogue between the fields of composition and rhetoric and Native American studies, concluding with some very general recommendations for expanding our canons and curricula. My argument is motivated in part by my sense of being haunted by that little boy's backward glance to those other Indian children: *Is it right for me to take a white man's name?*

SOVEREIGNTY IS (ALSO) RHETORICAL

Sovereignty, as I generally use and understand the term, denotes the right of a people to conduct its own affairs, in its own place, in its own way. The concept of sovereignty originated in feudal Europe, and as a term it arrived to the English language by way of France; *souverain* signified a ruler accountable to no one save himself or God (Duchacek 47). Early modern European monarchs employed the language of sovereignty to secure their grip on state power in the face of a threatening nobility and papacy. A declaration of one's right to rule, a monarch's claim to sovereignty "stood as a ringing assertion of absolute political authority at home, one that could imply designs on territory abroad" (Fowler and Bunck 5). As modern nations and states underwent their various forms of development, the concept was consistently deployed to address not only domestic authority at home but a state's relative independence *from* and *among* other states; thus, sovereignty came to mean something systemic and relational. A sovereign's power was generally a force understood in relation to other sovereigns in the emerging international scene; hence, "a sovereign was to respect the sovereignty of its peers" (Fowler and Bunck 6). As political institutions continued to develop under modernity, the meanings of sovereignty changed with them, signifying such matters as the right to make and enforce laws, notions of political legitimacy and international recognition, and national self-determination. While the meanings of sovereignty have shifted and continue to shift over time, the concept has nonetheless carried with it a sense of locatable and recognizable power. In fact, the location of power has depended upon the crucial act of recognition—and vice versa.

From the early moments of first contact on this continent, the construction of Indian and non-Indian senses of sovereignty was a contested and contradictory process. It was also a rhetorical one. Although there is no possible way to describe its many and complicated logics in necessary detail here, we can see that for at least two centuries following Columbus, "European states were compelled to recognize and engage Indian nations as political actors in their diplomatic activities" (Berman 128). They did this in large part through making treaties with Indian nations, a process that created a relationship between groups of "an international rather than internal character," even in sites of severe colonizing activity (Berman 129). This acknowledged sense of Indian national sovereignty was so strong among European states that it actually became a means of legitimizing European claims to new world resources; a territorial dispute between the English and the Dutch, say, might be settled by one side producing a treaty with the sovereign nation who actually owned the land (Berman 132). After the American Revolution, the United States maintained the practice of treaty-making with Indian nations begun by European powers, and "from the beginning of its political existence, recognized a measure of autonomy in the Indian bands and tribes" (Prucha, *Treaties* 2). During the years 1778–1868, the U.S. signed and ratified some 367 treaties with Indian nations, all of which presumed a sense of sovereignty on the part of Indian groups. About two-thirds of those treaties were land deals, and as Prucha points out, "cession of Indian lands . . . was an indication of Indian sovereignty over those lands, and the recognition by the United States of Indian ownership to the lands remaining strengthened the concept" (*Treaties* 4). You can't give up what you don't own, after all; nor can you buy what's already yours.

However, the Americans would gradually assume a dominant stance in Indian-white relations, leading to an erosion of Native sovereignty that Prucha credits to overwhelming American military strength, growing Indian economic dependence on white goods, and treaty provisions that left stipulations to be carried out by Congress (Prucha, *Treaties* 6–7). After the American Revolution, it wasn't long before the nation-to-nation stance Indians and their interlocutors had operated from was simultaneously attacked and affirmed in a couple of landmark U.S. Supreme Court cases concerning the Cherokee of Georgia facing removal in the early nineteenth century. In *Cherokee Nation v. Georgia* (1831), Chief Justice John Marshall's famous pronouncement of the Cherokees as a "domestic dependent nation" constituted the United States' first major, unilateral reinterpretation of Indian sovereignty, one further tinkered with a year later by the same court in *Worcester v. Georgia* (1832). In the former opinion, Marshall deemed the Cherokees limited in their claim to sovereignty, seeing them as a nation not-quite-foreign, but suggested nonetheless that the Cherokees still formed "a distinct political society, separated by others, capable of managing its own affairs and governing itself" (Prucha, *Documents* 58). This somewhat glaring contradiction was explained in the latter decision, where Marshall opined that "Indian nations had always been considered as distinct, independent political communities, retaining their original natural rights, as the undisputed possessors of the soil, from time immemorial, *with the single exception* imposed by irresistible power" (Prucha, *Documents* 60; emphasis mine). In other words, while recognizing Indian sovereignty in terms we can fairly describe as eternal and absolute, the Supreme Court's decisions on the Cherokee cases ultimately caved in to what would become a persistent, uniquely American, and wholly imperialist notion of recognition-from-above. The United States could limit Cherokee sovereignty simply because it could, and it could because it is the United States. American exceptionalism won the day, thanks to its "irresistible power," and while U.S. plenary power wouldn't become fully articulated in a legal sense until *United States v. Kagama* in 1886, it found its rhetorical groundwork laid solidly in the Cherokee cases of the 1830s.

In a sense, these cases exemplify what we might call rhetorical imperialism: the ability of dominant powers to assert control of others by setting the terms of debate. These terms are often definitional—that is, they *identify* the parties discussed by describing them in certain ways. Take, for example, Marshall's rather self-reflective analysis of the language of sovereignty in his *Worcester v. Georgia* opinion:

> . . . 'treaty' and 'nation' are words of our own language, selected in our diplomatic and legislative proceedings . . . having each a definite and well-understood meaning. We have applied them to Indians, as we have applied them to the other nations of the earth. They are applied to all in the same sense. (Prucha, *Documents* 60)

In short, Indians are defined here as fellow nations requiring treaties. Yet in *Cherokee Nation v. Georgia*, Marshall wrote that "the term foreign nation" *wasn't* quite applicable to Indian nations, suggesting instead that the Cherokee Nation's "relation to the United States resembles that of a ward to his guardian." This was because Indians—"savages" newly arrived on "civilization's" fresh path—were "in a state of pupilage" (Prucha, *Documents* 59). More than an agonistic legal contest over sovereign rights, the language of this decision shows Indian people being completely redefined by their interlocutors: a ward or pupil—that is, a child—is quite a different animal than a fellow nation in the community of sovereigns. As the exercise of rhetorical imperialism, Marshall's metaphors effectively paved the way for the United States to assume a position of political *paternalism* over Indian nations that has thrived up to this very day—chalk one up for the "Great White Father." The lesson here seems obvious: namely, he who sets the terms sets the limits. And likewise the rewriting of Indian sovereignty would continue over time. As Prucha points out, the word "tribe" increasingly came to replace "nation" in treaties, substituting one highly ideological European word for another, and with the Abolition of Treaty-Making Act of 1871, a powerful little rider tacked on to an Indian appropriations bill that formally ended the practice of treaty-making, "treaties" henceforth came to be called "agreements" by the authoring Americans (Prucha, *Treaties* 4, 211–13). From "sovereign" to "ward," from "nation" to "tribe," and from "treaty" to "agreement," the erosion of Indian national sovereignty can be credited in part to a rhetorically imperialist use of writing by white powers, and from that point on, much of the discourse on tribal sovereignty has nit-picked, albeit powerfully, around terms and definitions.

None of this stopped Indian exercises of sovereignty—it just threw things into different modes and sites of contest, for instance, that of language and representation. Not to downplay the tremendous cost to Indian people these struggles for sovereignty have entailed, but I want to point out that the dominant stance achieved by the Americans must continue to be seen as merely that—dominant, not omnipotent—which is far from saying all things are said and done. Indian nations still possess, and are still recognized to possess, varying and constantly shifting degrees of sovereignty. While hegemonic versions of the American Indian story implying the obverse continue to be told in schools, scholarship, and popular culture—generally in the past tense—discourses of resistance and renewal have never ceased in Indian country, and these marginalized narratives of the continuing struggle for Indian sovereignty are making themselves more and more visible in public representations and talk. It's worthwhile to note how so much of this struggle—from treaties to court cases to the growing popularity of Native American literature—has taken place at what we might call the colonized scene of writing: a site of contact-zone rhetoric in its fullest sense. One way of approaching this site is to find in American legal, political, and cultural written discourses recurrent, yet ambivalent, assaults on Native sovereignty answered by recurrent, yet subordinate, defenses and redefinitions of the same by Indians. These textual exchanges are eminently rhetorical: arguments motivated by highly ideological conflations and intertwinings of motives, beliefs, and assumptions that do not lend themselves to a sense of consensually-derived conclusions. One reason for this is certainly due to power imbalances between whites and Indians, but another seems owing to truly salient differences in cultural understandings of what it means to be political human beings. That is, I want to suggest that the rhetorics of sovereignty advanced by both Indian and non-Indian people often claim to be talking about the same thing, when actually they differ considerably.

For example, for Western powers after the Enlightenment, the meaning of sovereignty became contingent upon freshly formed conceptions of the modern nation-state and new bourgeois ideologies of the individual. The former was a legal-political understanding of the right to popular self-governance freed from the shackles of older forms of monarchical sovereignty, the latter a new subjectivity enjoyed and defended by the bourgeoisie. Both were generated from a desire to develop and protect the idea of private property. In this context, for a thinker like Kant, sovereignty became essentially procedural, the exercise of reason and public critique generated by the bourgeoisie who as "the people" construct the nation-state through the act of making coercive laws, and subsequently as "sovereign" coerce through them as a *nation* and are coerced by them as *individuals* ("Metaphysics" 142). Sovereignty for Kant was a largely technical process of communicative rationality ultimately designed to benefit and control solitary monads; hence, the nation-state became something of an instrument. Sovereignty rested primarily with the "public," itself constituted by the communicating mass of wholly "private" individuals acting out of self-interest (Kant, "Enlightenment" 55–7; see also Habermas). The dialectic of private and public constituted the business of the nation-state, even while resting upon a series of exclusions (for example, of gender, race, and class) that belied its utopian claims to equality, as public sphere theorists have demonstrated (see Fraser; Ryan). But ultimately, for the young United States of the Enlightenment, sovereignty was exercised through the communicative procedures developed and maintained by individuals who, through reason, would form the public and run the nation-state (Eley).

By contrast, Indians who entered into treaties as nations are better understood as representing themselves as a *people:*

> The idea of the people is primarily a religious conception, and with most American Indian tribes it begins somewhere in the primordial mists. In that time the people were gathered together but did not yet see themselves as a distinct people. A holy man had a dream or a vision; quasi-mythological figures of cosmic importance revealed themselves, or in some other manner the people were instructed. They were given ceremonies and rituals that enabled them to find their place on the continent. (Deloria and Lytle 8)

A people is a group of human beings united together by history, language, culture, or some combination therein—a community joined in union for a common purpose: the survival and flourishing of the people itself. It has always been from an understanding of themselves as a people that Indian groups have constructed themselves as a nation. In *The Power of Identity,* Manuel Castells defines nations as "cultural communes constructed in people's minds and collective memory by the sharing of history and political projects," adding a political dimension to a sense of peoplehood (51). In his analysis, nations, with or without states, tend to be organized around the sensual cultural material of peoples—for example, language—and the First Nations were and are no exception (Castells 31). "Indians had a good idea of nationhood," Deloria and Lytle write, defining the exercise of nationhood as "decision-making that is free and uninhibited within the community" and suggesting it was always conducted out of regard for the survival and flourishing of the people (8, 13). In that sense, the making of political decisions by Indian people hasn't been the work of a nation-state so much as that of a *nation-people.* The sovereignty of individuals and the privileging of procedure are less important in the logic of a nation-people, which takes as its supreme charge the sovereignty of the group through a privileging of its traditions and culture and continuity.

One example of a nation-people might be found in the system of Cherokee towns prior to their formal and essentially forced incorporation as a nation-state in the early nineteenth century, itself a desperate political maneuver in the face of impending removal. Some sixty in all, traditional Cherokee towns in Georgia were generally decentralized but loosely linked through language and kinship, each village ultimately retaining its own sense of independence (Champagne 25). As both people and nation, "the Cherokees found unity in an overarching principle that governed their behavior in both domestic and foreign affairs." Namely, "Cherokees believed that human beings had the responsibility for maintaining cosmic order by respecting categories and maintaining boundaries" (Perdue 56). These categories and boundaries were often derived from mythological understandings of their culture but were also open to democratic contest in council houses (Champagne 29). This was no nation of individuals, nor one reducible to procedure; rather, the Cherokees found their national identity and interests in the concept of the people. Reason, deployed regularly and at will in council-house decision making, did not militate against their understandings of themselves as a group; nor was reason contingent upon a sense of privacy. Rather, reason and rationality were deployed always with an idealistic eye toward the betterment of the people, including but not limited to the individuals which constituted it, through the practices of tradition and culture.

Another, more cosmopolitan example of a nation-people is the Haudenosaunee, or Iroquois League, which was actually a consciously constructed confederation of *different* peoples based upon the principle of peaceful coexistence. As Onandaga leader and professor Oren Lyons tells it, "Haudenosaunee political organization demonstrated that a form of participatory democracy was possible on a fairly large geographic scale," and what's striking in his account is how democratic procedures were constructed into a "primordial" myth that spoke to and of multiple cultures (32). Linked by the story of the Peacemaker and the practice of respectful communication, the Haudenosaunee were—and remain—a *multicultural* nation-people (34–42). "Since the beginning of our memory," Lyons writes, "this distinctiveness has been seen as a foundation for mutual respect; and we have therefore always honored the fundamental right of peoples and their societies to be different" (42). Here, too, the traditions of the people coexisted with the exercise of a communal, communicative rationality:

> Indian decision-making processes at the local level required the free input of information and advice for these processes to work at all. Any proposal brought to the Haudenosaunee was carried to each of the nations, where it was discussed either in clan or general meetings; the sentiments of the nation were then carried by the principal chiefs to the confederate council . . . and the chiefs had the authority to negotiate details of a proposed agreement according to their own judgment and in line with political reality. (Lyons 32)

Thus conceived, Haudenosaunee sovereignty is probably best understood as the right of a people to exist and enter into agreements with other peoples for the sole purpose of promoting, not suppressing, local cultures and traditions, even while united by a common political project—in this case, the noble goal of peace between peoples.

In the context of the colonized scene of writing, the distinction between a nation-state and a nation-people might get at the root of why Indians and non-Indians tend to view things like treaties so differently even today. "In almost every treaty," Deloria and Lytle write, "the concern of the Indians was the preservation of the people": that is, the successful perpetuation of life, land rights, community, and cultural practice (8). Sovereignty in this regard is concerned not only with political procedures or individual rights but with a whole way of life. Non-Indian reductions of Indian claims to sovereignty as arguments for "self-governance"—that is, for a degree of local financial and political control modeled after western governmental systems—obscures this holistic people-oriented emphasis. "Self-government is not an Indian idea," write Deloria and Lytle. "It originates in the minds of non-Indians who have reduced the traditional ways to dust" (15). Self-governance is certainly the work of a state but not necessarily that of a people; a people requires something more. However, while self-governance alone may not constitute the whole part and parcel of sovereignty, it nonetheless remains a crucial component. "I believe that the future of our nations is singularly dependent upon our ability to self-govern," writes Robert B. Porter. "If we can do this, then all of our other problems—the loss of language and culture, the need for economic stability, and the preservation of tribal sovereignty—can then be addressed and, hopefully, resolved" (73). What we might need, then, is an understanding of the twin pillars of sovereignty: the power to self-govern and the affirmation of peoplehood. For without self-governance, especially in America, the people fragment into a destructive and chaotic individualism, and without the people, there is no one left to govern and simply nothing left to protect.

And so it has been with both self-governance and the people in mind that Indians have been advancing new rhetorics of sovereignty—both to themselves and to outside powers—and some of these have found their way into the academy. In *We Talk, You Listen,* Deloria explicitly addresses the concept in a chapter entitled "Power, Sovereignty, and Freedom." Suggesting that "few members of racial minority groups have realized that inherent in their peculiar experience on this continent is hidden the basic recognition of their power and sovereignty," Deloria argues for action at the group level to replace legal claims for self-determination "since power cannot be given and accepted" (115); rather, it must be first asserted and then recognized. As Robert Warrior points out, Deloria's is a "process-centered definition of sovereignty," one contingent upon the renewal of groups at the community level (91). From this reading of Deloria, Warrior has advanced his own concept of "intellectual sovereignty," a process devoted to community renewal through the paying of attention to the American Indian intellectual tradition, one he lays out in the form of a materialist history (1–3). While I question the end game of a project promoting Indian intellectuals studying Indian intellectuals, Warrior's work still has much to offer in a mainstream academic culture still obsessed with canonicity. Warrior has been praised for this work by Elizabeth Cook-Lynn, who finds most other critics, including some Natives, afraid to take on the nationalist implications of sovereignty in their critical theory and work (90–91). Cook-Lynn also criticizes mainstream multiculturalism, which she argues "has not and will not cast much light on the centuries-long struggle for sovereignty faced by the people" because it remains "in conflict with the concept of American Indian sovereignty, since it emphasizes matters of spirituality and culture" divorced from national recognition (91). Mainstream multiculturalism is not sovereignty *per se* because it abstracts its sense of culture from the people and from the land, and while it may indeed affirm the rightful and creative existence of Indian cultures and peoples among others, it tends not to discuss that other pillar of sovereignty: self-government. Mainstream multiculturalism may focus on the *people* but typically not the *nation* and thus isn't necessarily the practice or honoring of Indian sovereignty.

In all three of these thinkers, the rhetoric of sovereignty takes on a decidedly nationalistic cast, but while they all advocate focusing on action at the community level, none of them can adequately be described as purely separatist. Rather, in explicit opposition to this, Warrior calls for Indians to "withdraw without becoming separatists, being willing to reach out for the contradictions within our experience and open ourselves to the pain and the joy of others" (124). Rather than representing an enclave, sovereignty here is the ability to assert oneself renewed—in the presence of others. It is a people's right to rebuild, its demand to exist and present its gifts to the world. Also key to these thinkers' rhetorics of sovereignty is an adamant refusal to disassociate culture, identity, and power from the *land*, and it is precisely this commitment to place that makes the concept of rhetorical sovereignty an empowering device for all forms of community. While most Indians have a special relationship with the land in the form of an actual land base (reservations), this relationship is made truly meaningful by a consistent cultural refusal to interact with that land as private property or purely exploitable resource. Land, culture, and community are inseparable in Indian country, which might explain Native resistance to such policies as the Dawes Allotment Act of a century ago, which tried to transform Indians into bourgeois whites by making them property-holding farmers. This cultural resistance has consistently been made in objection to the way such policies divide Indian communities and disrupt traditional culture with radically individualist ideologies, and whenever I see community activists of whatever stripe—Black, Hmong, working-class, etc.—making arguments on behalf of "our community" in the face of apparently naked economic self-interest, I think those, too, are claims to sovereignty made by different groups. But most important, as voices of the people, scholars like Deloria, Warrior, and Cook-Lynn are asserting themselves as members of sovereign Indian nations, deploying power and seeking recognition at the colonized scene of writing.

I have gone on (and perhaps on and on) about the concept of sovereignty because I think it is not well understood by most non-Indian scholars and teachers. I also think the idea has something to offer the discourses of multiculturalism and critical race theory, or to anyone who sides with the oppressed or who works for community renewal, because of its applicability to the many contested sites (and actual places) of power in multiple senses: legal, cultural, intellectual, material, and so on. Sovereignty is a concept that has a history of contest, shifting meanings, and culturally specific rhetorics. A reclamation of sovereignty by any group remains, as Deloria argues above, a recognition of that group's power—a recognition made by both self and other. It is not something "new" or, worse, something "given" by dominant groups, and for the sake of the people, we might all do well to contemplate what that might mean.

RHETORICAL SOVEREIGNTY AT THE C & R RANCH

All of which brings me back to where I started: what do American Indians want from writing? At stake in this discussion are the peoples defined by the writing itself; thus one important tenet of rhetorical sovereignty would be to allow Indians to have some say about the nature of their textual representations. The best way to honor this creed would be to have Indian people themselves do the writing, but it might also be recognized that some representations are better than others, whoever the author. On that note, a quick perusal through the composition and rhetoric literature of the past few years shows a growing interest in American Indians and a general concern for including Native knowledges and voices in classrooms and curricula that should be commended. But some of this work hinders rhetorical sovereignty by presenting readers with Indian stereotypes, cultural appropriation, and a virtual absence of discourse on sovereignty and the status of Indian nations—that is, with a kind of rhetorical imperialism. Sometimes this writing has been done with all the best of intentions, but on that note it might be good to recall that Chief Justice Marshall, the original architect of limited sovereignty for Indians, was generally considered a very pro-Indian thinker in his day—to Indian-hating President Andrew Jackson's continual dismay—even as Marshall was busy composing the foundational documents for American imperialist control over tribes. So without getting into where good intentions sometimes lead, let me say for now that some of our most prominent work on Indians is not yet part of the solution.

Take, for example, the recent publication of George Kennedy's *Comparative Rhetoric: An Historical and Cross-Cultural Introduction.* Kennedy, who has taught me so much in his books about classical Greek and Roman rhetoric and who I continue to honor as a great scholar of those subjects, has now seen fit to locate rhetoric in nature and to place its history on a developmental, essentially evolutionary, model, the entire scheme of which seems to be based upon Western stereotypes of the Other. Divided into two sections, the oral and the literate, the study begins with an investigation of the rhetoric of animals, including bird calls, and works its way "up" through the language of "oral" indigenous people, then through the literacy of Egyptians, Chinese, Indians (from India) to its grand finale in the civilizations of Greece and Rome. In that order, African Americans are not even mentioned, which Kermit Campbell might have criticized more strongly in his mainly positive review of the "pioneering" work (174). It's worth noting that this evolutionary study actually works backwards in time; most of Kennedy's examples of "North American Indian Rhetoric" (Chapter 5), for example, are taken from the nineteenth century, a particularly devastating yet rhetorically profuse time for most Native people. Why Kennedy didn't acknowledge the overwhelming proliferation of *writing* by Native people during that century—not the least of which can be found in the many tribal newspapers of those years, for instance, in the bilingual *Cherokee Phoenix* of the 1820s—probably owes itself to the deeply ingrained stereotypes of Indians as 1) essentially oral creatures, and 2) existing only in an imagined savage past. Both of those persistent stereotypes are examined together in *Forked Tongues: Speech, Writing, and Representation in North American Indian Texts* by David Murray, who points out that in communicative exchanges between Indians and whites, "the cultural translation is all one-way, and the penalty to the subordinate group for not adapting to the demands of the dominant group is to cease to exist" (6). Thus, the logic Kennedy employs in his study might lead some to the conclusion that a writing Indian is no Indian at all.

In addition to the effect of making questions of sovereignty a moot point, Kennedy's erasure of real Indians serves other agendas as well. Finding in "early human language" a "connecting link" between the rhetoric of animals and that of oral (but not literate) humans, Kennedy has basically provided a theory of the Missing Link located within the speech of the people (2). The result is a quiet assumption that Indians are something less than human, if something more than animals. I don't know how else to take his comparison of red deer stags and "Eskimos" (by which I think he means Inuit):

> In a previous chapter I described the rhetoric of red deer stags in seeking rights to mate with females—vocal encounters, stalking, and fights with their horns if one animal does not give way. A similar sequence has characterized Eskimo quarrels over women: insults, threatening gestures, and fights in the form of butting or wrestling contests. (77)

And here I thought all that butting and wrestling was something we did for fun. What Inuit *women* might have to say about this characterization of their dating life notwithstanding, I have to ask if this is really where we want to go in the study of comparative rhetorics. Cultural evolutionism, a nineteenth-century phenomenon associated with early anthropologists like Lewis Henry Morgan (who studied "the vanishing Indian"), has long been used to justify an ideology of savagery-barbarism-civilization, which in turn has always operated to the detriment of Indian peoples (see Berkhofer, 49–61). To locate Indian rhetoric at an early point on the Great Chain of Speaking not only ignores *this* kind of speech for a claim about *that* kind, the results of which may be dehumanizing, but by implication also suggests that today's Indian peoples are probably not real anymore. I suppose Kennedy wanted to find oral eloquence and the like among Indian cultures, but through his desire, and his acceptance and perpetuation of stereotypes, he seems to have lost sight of actually existing indigenous people and has uncharacteristically misplaced rhetoric.

The oral-literate binary—which I apparently (and mistakenly) had thought dismantled by now—also lurks ominously in Bruce Ballenger's "Methods of Memory: On Native American Storytelling." Ballenger appropriates what he calls an "'Indian way' of remembering" to make sense of his own life and writing, "methods" he locates in Native oral traditions (790; 792–3). Of course, his access to this oral tradition is enabled completely through the reading of Native *writers,* but never mind: the point of the article, it seems to me, is to grab and make use of what even Ballenger admits does not belong to him with the express purpose of "creat[ing] the 'whole story' of myself'" (795). In other words, the "Indian way" serves as a kind of supplemental technology to aid and abet the construction of Ballenger's self as a sovereign, unique individual: a highly literate white man with all the benefits and privileges therein. "It is always the 'I'—not the 'we'—that concerns me most," Ballenger writes, adding that what distinguishes him from real Indians is his motivation for "self-expression" (795). Not unlike Tonto, then, the Indian is there for the taking as a kind of helper and teacher in the white man's quest to Know Thyself. Since Ballenger's essay on Native American storytelling isn't about Native Americans at all, but rather about what Ballenger apparently feels free to *take* from Natives, we must find in this writing the logic of cultural imperialism. Wendy Rose has argued that by "appropriating indigenous cultures and distorting them for its own purposes . . . the dominant society can neatly eclipse every aspect of contemporary native reality, from land rights to issues of religious freedom" (404). Indeed, Ballenger's own expansive familiarity with Indian writers did not lead him to discuss any of the issues facing the people today (and which are often represented in the novels he reads); on the contrary, he seems to accept things as they are. One particularly troubling moment for me was his discussion of place in Native literature; after making the solid claim that Indians "tend to see the land as something with a presence"—fair enough—Ballenger goes on to recall his times on the shores of Lake Michigan, formerly and in some cases still Anishinabe country, remembered by him "with a kind of reverence" as, in his word, "unpeopled" (798). The actual history of peopling and unpeopling on those shores would be a worthwhile thing to investigate.

Ballenger's essay is perhaps a sensitive one to criticize because it is interspersed with some painful recollections of his childhood. But I have some painful recollections of my own, as many Native people do. Right now I'm thinking of my two young Ojibwe cousins who committed suicide in the same year—one in his early twenties, the other barely approaching his teens—two deaths that might be attributed to a kind of self-hatred experienced by many Indian youths today who find themselves trapped in colonial wreckage: poverty, violence, a racist dominant culture that hates and excludes them. Consider the findings of a recent study on American Indian crime produced by the Justice Department which found that "American Indians are victims of violent crime at a rate of more than double that of the rest of the population" ("American"). In seven out of ten of those episodes, the offender is non-Indian. The report also stated that the number of American Indians per capita in state and federal prisons is some thirty-eight percent above the national average; the rate in local jails is four times the national average. The arrest rate for alcohol-related offenses is more than twice the rate for the total population ("American"). Or consider the fact that "Native people endure the poorest quality of life in this country," because of which "1,000 more Native men, women, and children die each year than would be expected if they were living in the same conditions as white America." (This, remember, out of a total population of only 1.5 million.) "If these same conditions existed throughout the total population of our country, 150,000 more American people would die *each year*" (Charleston 17; emphasis in original). Nobody ever wants to appropriate stuff like that.

Rhetorical sovereignty, however, compels us to face it. It is always the "we"—not the "I"—that concerns me most, and my particular motivation is the pursuit of social justice. Or let's simply call it sanity in an age of unchecked American imperialism, rampant consumer capitalism on an unprecedented global scale, haphazard and unsustainable depletions and abuses of natural resources, naked European and American aggression around the globe, racism, sexism, homophobia, and the ever-widening gap between rich and poor in America and everywhere. In contexts such as these, there are very good reasons to fight for indigenous rights. Indigenous people, who in some senses are now forming a global movement (seen, for example, in growing international indigenous support for the Zapatista movement in Chiapas), may constitute the world's most adamant refusal of current expansions of global capitalism and imperialism that plague so many and benefit so few. As groups like Greenpeace have argued:

> Native people's homelands encompass many of the planet's last tracts of wilderness—ecosystems that shelter millions of endangered species, buffer the global climate, and regulate hydrological cycles. Even without considering questions of human rights and the intrinsic value of cultures, indigenous survival is a matter of crucial importance. We in the world's dominant cultures simply can not sustain the Earth's ecological health without the help of the world's endangered cultures. (qtd. in Owens 233)

However, the people themselves are among those endangered species. Brazil alone has lost something like 90 tribes this century, and over half of all remaining 6,000 indigenous languages worldwide will become extinct in the next (Owens 233). Unless the people can prevent that from happening.

Composition and rhetoric certainly isn't going to stop it, although we can do some things that might have us play a more meaningful role—which brings me back yet again to the question: what do Indians want from writing? So far, I hope to have identified a few things Indians generally do *not* want from writing: stereotypes, cultural appropriation, exclusion, ignorance, irrelevance, rhetorical imperialism. The people want sovereignty, and in the context of the colonized scene of writing, rhetorical sovereignty. As the inherent right and ability of peoples to determine their own communicative needs and desires in the pursuit of self-determination, rhetorical sovereignty requires above all the presence of an Indian voice, speaking or writing in an ongoing context of colonization and setting at least some of the terms of debate. Ideally, that voice would often employ a Native language. "Language, in particular, helps to decolonize the mind," writes the Hawaiian nationalist Haunani-Kay Trask. "Thinking in one's own cultural referents leads to conceptualizing in one's own world view which, in turn, leads to disagreement with and eventual opposition to the dominant ideology" (54). The crucial subject of Native language in literacy research cannot be taken up here, except perhaps to say *nindozhibii'igemin*. But while it's hard to predict what that Indian voice would say in our many and varied classrooms—most of them Indian-free, some located at tribal colleges, others constituting dynamic contact-zones of their own—I can point to scholarly work in a couple of sites that might help us orient our commitment to rhetorical sovereignty and imagine new practices.

One location of rhetorical sovereignty that should be of interest to rhetoricians is the Tribal Law and Government Center, based at the University of Kansas Law School and directed by Seneca legal scholar (and former Attorney General of the Seneca Nation) Robert B. Porter. Focusing its energies on the study and development of tribal law (which is not the same thing as federal Indian law but rather the law of sovereign Indian nations), the Center sponsors the Indian Law Institute each summer for tribal officials, a yearly conference, and a specialization in tribal law within the law program. Of particular interest for our purposes, the Center has been sponsoring annual rearguments of some of the most powerful federal legal decisions in the history of Indian sovereignty, for example, *Cherokee Nation v. Georgia* and *Lone Wolf v. Hitchcock*. Under the auspices of the "Supreme Court of the American Indian Nations," these retrials are conducted by a distinguished array of Indian and non-Indian lawyers and judges, and the briefs they produce are published alongside the original opinions and briefs and are available for study and teaching (Ayana, Guhin, Yazzie). Critical pedagogues, contact-zone theorists, and post/anti-colonial rhetoricians might take note of these powerful Indian countersentences to colonialism; after all, these reargued indigenous responses to legal and political history constitute an ongoing and dynamic practice of rhetorical sovereignty, and we could teach them.

Another key site of rhetorical sovereignty is the report produced by the Indian Nations At Risk Task Force (INARTF), "Toward True Native Education: A Treaty of 1992," which was commissioned by the Department of Education in 1990. INARTF was a 14-member committee established by U.S. Secretary of Education Lauro Cavazos and directed by Choctaw education professor, G. Mike Charleston. With two exceptions it was an Indian committee, and the document they produced is a classic example of the exercise of rhetorical sovereignty. First, as its title suggests, the report announces itself as a *treaty,* one designed to put an end to the "secret war" (also referred to as a "cold war") waged against indigenous peoples (Charleston 15–16). Distinguishing the metaphor of war from other more dominant ones in liberal and educational discourse—for example, the idea of an Indian "plight" and the notion of a "tug-of-war" between cultures—the report justifies the war metaphor on two accounts. First, this "war is over the continued existence of tribal societies of American Indians and Alaska Natives"; that is, at issue isn't so much the curing of Indian ills or celebration of diversity but rather a recognition of Indian sovereignty. Second, war is *stopped* by treaties between mutually recognized sovereign entities (16). The "Treaty of 1992," then, offers an educational theory inseparable from a recognition of sovereignty and a plea to stop the violence as well. Arguing that "school has become the weapon of choice for non-Native societies" to attack tribal sovereignty in all of its manifestations, the report distinguishes three types of Indian education. *Pseudo Native education* is "a process that diligently attempts to teach Native students the standard American curriculum needed to assimilate into American society" (19–20). *Quasi Native education* is "an education that sincerely attempts to make American education more culturally relevant and supportive of Native students and Native communities" through the teaching of Native cultural trinkets like "legends, history, and Native words" (27). *True Native education* rejects any "division between school climate and culture and . . . community climate and culture," replacing hierarchical models of curricula and pedagogy with a concerted community effort, envisioned by the committee as a circle (40, 31). What true Native education calls for in the final analysis is nothing less than the formal institutionalization of rhetorical sovereignty.

This rethought education remains insistent upon dialogue, land, and the continuation of the people, so we should all consider the implications of another metaphor in the INARTF report: the "new Ghost Dance."

Invoking the first Ghost Dance movement of a century ago, a prophetic religious movement praying for the return of Indian power (answered by whites with the brutal slaughter of Chief Big Foot's band of Lakota at the Wounded Knee massacre of 1890), the Treaty of 1992 insists that the "new Ghost Dance calls Native *and* non-Native people to join together and take action." For non-Native participants, the new Ghost Dance "requires a major change in their behaviors, attitudes, and values"; for Natives, much of the work will be decolonization of the mind and self (28). Educators "need to teach the reasons for the hundreds of treaties and agreements between the various tribes and the United States" and promote "a basic understanding, respect, and appreciation for American Indian and Alaskan Native cultures" to all students (29). Altogether, this approach would work for "a revival of tribal life and the return of harmony among all relations of creation" (28). I can think of no better document than this to help us begin the work of rhetorical sovereignty in our field and start answering the question of what Indians want from writing. The metaphors of the INARTF report—treaty, war, Ghost Dance—are carefully chosen signifiers that aim to cast into full relief the fault lines of Indian-white interaction in America, and the report should be read as an extended hand, not a fist, in the very serious pursuit of a people's sovereignty. How will we respond?

I suggest we begin by prioritizing the study of American Indian rhetoric—and the rhetoric of the Indian—in our graduate curricula and writing programs, focusing on the history of both secret and not-so-secret wars in the contact-zone. We should be teaching the treaties and federal Indian laws as rhetorical texts themselves, situating our work within both historical and contemporary contexts. We should also study the ideologies of Indianness and Manifest Destiny that have governed it all. No student should encounter a Native American text without having learned something about Indian peoples' historical and ongoing struggles for sovereignty, and teachers of Native students in particular should create a space for those kinds of discussions. This work would continually examine one's relationship to Indian sovereignty, as well as expand our canons and current knowledge in ways that would hopefully make them more relevant to and reflective of actual populations on this land. On that note, I also think this site should be read and taught not in separation from other groups, but alongside the histories, rhetorics, and struggles of African-Americans and other "racial" or ethnic groups, women, sexual minorities, the disabled, and still others, locating history and writing instruction in the powerful context of American rhetorical struggle.

Ideally, this work should focus on local and community levels in hopes of lending support to the work already being done there. "There" is sometimes difficult to locate, I realize, but every university and school exists in a place, on a land, with a history and a community of struggle: every place has its peoples. For example, the Cincinnati-Tristate region where I went to graduate school, and which sometimes struck me as the most Indian-free zone I had ever seen, actually boasts a Native population of 2,365 people ("American"). Who are they, what is their history, and what are they facing now? Some of them are certainly homeless, and so their history might be read in the context of a current struggle. In that place, on that land, members of the local arts community have proposed moving the Drop-Inn Center, the area's largest homeless shelter, away from a gentrifying neighborhood so arts patrons won't have to look at the poor and despondent on their way to the concert (Knight 1). Considering geographer Neil Smith's contention that gentrifying inner-city neighborhoods like this one (Over-the-Rhine) constitute "the new frontier"—the site of increasing white "settlement" to the displacement of the "savages" who live there—it's perfectly reasonable to conclude that the Cincinnati controversy is nothing less than another debate over *removal*. What could be more teachable than this in the pursuit of sovereignty?

Ethnographers and service-learning theorists have already begun the valuable work of theorizing community-based pedagogy, but my hopes are also pinned on classroom theories oriented toward the formation of *publics*. Susan Wells has provided our best thinking so far toward these ends, arguing for and theorizing writing instruction geared toward "public literate action" (334). Wells would rethink publicly-oriented writing classrooms in four different ways: 1) as a version of the public sphere, 2) as a site for the study of public discourse, 3) as a place to produce student writing that might actually enter public space, and 4) as a location for the examination of how academic discourses and disciplinary knowledges intervene in the public (338–39). Read alongside the INARTF recommendations in the context of rhetorical sovereignty, her proposals sound vital to me, for sovereignty has always been on some level a public pursuit of recognition. A focus on American Indian publics is especially appropriate now in the fresh wake of two rather substantial Indian victories in the public, both of which have everything to do with literacy and rhetoric, reading and writing and arguing. The first is the April 1999 Supreme Court upholding of the 1837 Chippewa Treaty in Minnesota that guarantees my own people the right to hunt and fish on ceded lands (*Minnesota v. Mille Lacs Band*). The second is the federal

Trademark Trial and Appeal Board's disrecognition of the Washington Redskins trademark, a move that could cost that organization millions of dollars in lost (because unprotected) revenues and, hence, provides a financial incentive to change the name (Rich 3). These victories were won by Native people who learned how to fight battles in both court and the culture-at-large, who knew how to read and write the legal system, interrogate and challenge cultural semiotics, generate public opinion, form publics, and create solidarity with others. That behind each of these victories were contests over the acts of reading and writing is obvious; what needs to be underscored is that both are also victories of rhetorical sovereignty. Both initiatives arose from the grassroots, each in their own way fought over questions of land and identity, and the ultimate outcome of both was an honoring of "a whole way of life," another productive step in the perpetuation of the people. Shouldn't the teaching of (American Indian) rhetoric be geared toward these kinds of outcomes?

That's what I want from writing. My particular desire asks a lot, I know, from teachers and students and readers and writers and texts. It wants to read history through a contemporary lens and continually beckon forth the public. It asks everyone, especially teachers, to think carefully about their positions, locations, and alignments: the differences and connections between sovereignty and solidarity. It wishes to reinscribe the land and reread the people; it cries for revision. However, without some turn in the current assault on affirmative action, I suspect all talk on rhetorical sovereignty will likely happen away from the university. Luther Standing Bear, writing in the 1930s, knew as much in his push for rhetorical sovereignty in American schools. "The Indian," he wrote, "should become his own historian, giving his account of the race—fewer and fewer accounts of the wars and more of statecraft, legends, languages, oratory, and philosophical conceptions" (*Eagle* 254). What did Standing Bear, formerly that little boy who once counted coup on the classroom text, want from writing? "No longer should the Indian be dehumanized in order to make material for lurid and cheap fiction to embellish street-stands," he *wrote*. "Rather, a fair and correct history of the native American should be incorporated in the curriculum of the public school" (*Eagle* 254).

Is it right for me to take a white man's name? The answer, it would seem, has always been no. But that refusal has never meant giving up or going away; rather, a No over there can sometimes enable Yes over here. The ability to speak both—indeed, to speak at all—is the right and the theory and the practice and the poetry of rhetorical sovereignty. *Ningiigid, nindinawe:* I speak, I speak like the people with whom I live.

WORKS CITED

Adams, David Wallace. *Education for Extinction: American Indians and the Boarding School Experience, 1875–1928.* Lawrence: U of Kansas P, 1995.

Aitken, Robert. "Essential Nature." *Coyote's Journal.* Eds. James Koller, "Gogisgi" Carroll Arnett, Steve Nemirow, and Peter Blue Cloud. Berkeley: Wingbow, 1982. 47.

"American Indians' Victim Rate Double Norm." *Cincinnati Enquirer* 15 Feb. 1999: A3.

Ayana, James. "Brief of Lone Wolf, Principal Chief of the Kiowas, to the Supreme Court of the American Indian Nations." *The Kansas Journal of Law and Public Policy* 7.1 (Winter 1997): 117–45.

Ballenger, Bruce. "Methods of Memory: On Native American Storytelling." *College English* 59 (1997): 789–800.

Berkhofer, Robert F., Jr. *The White Man's Indian: Images of the American Indian from Columbus to the Present.* New York: Vintage, 1978.

Berman, Howard R. "Perspectives on American Indian Sovereignty and International Law, 1600–1776." *Exiled in the Land of the Free: Democracy, Indian Nations, and the U.S. Constitution.* Eds. Chief Oren Lyons and John Mohawk. Santa Fe: Clear Light Publishers, 1992. 125–88.

Calhoun, Craig, ed. *Habermas and the Public Sphere.* Cambridge: MIT P, 1994.

Campbell, Kermit. "Rev. of *Comparative Rhetoric: An Historical and Cross-Cultural Introduction,* by George A. Kennedy." *Rhetoric Review* 17 (1998): 170–74.

Castells, Manuel. *The Power of Identity.* Oxford: Blackwell, 1997.

Champagne, Duane. *Social Order and Political Change: Constitutional Governments among the Cherokee, the Choctaw, the Chickasaw, and the Creek.* Stanford: Stanford UP, 1992.

Charleston, G. Mike. "Toward True Native Education: A Treaty of 1992. Final Report of the Indian Nations At Risk Task Force." *Journal of American Indian Education* 33.2 (1994): 7–56.

Cherokee Nation v. Georgia, 30 U.S. 1. U.S. Supreme Court. 1831.

Cook-Lynn, Elizabeth. "The American Indian Fiction Writers: Cosmopolitanism, Nationalism, the Third World, and First Nation Sovereignty." *Why I Can't Read Wallace Stegner and Other Essays: A Tribal Voice.* Madison: U of Wisconsin P, 1996. 78–98.

Deloria, Vine, Jr. *We Talk, You Listen: New Tribes, New Turf.* New York: Macmillan, 1970.

Deloria, Vine, Jr., and Clifford M. Lytle. *The Nations Within: The Past and Future of American Indian Sovereignty.* Austin: U of Texas P, 1984.

Duchacek, Ivo D. *Nations and Men: International Politics Today.* New York: Holt, Rinehart and Winston, 1966.

Eley, Geoff. "Nations, Publics, and Political Cultures: Placing Habermas in the Nineteenth Century." Calhoun 289–339.

Fowler, Michael Ross, and Julie Marie Bunck. *Law, Power, and the Sovereign State: The Evolution and Application of the Concept of Sovereignty.* University Park: Pennsylvania State UP, 1995.

Fraser, Nancy. "Rethinking the Public Sphere: A Contribution to the Critique of Actually Existing Democracy." Calhoun 109–42.

Guhin, John P. "Brief of Ethan A. Hitchcock, Secretary of the Interior, to the Supreme Court of the American Indian Nations." *The Kansas Journal of Law and Public Policy* 7.1 (Winter 1997): 146–69.

Habermas, Jurgen. *The Structural Transformation of the Public Sphere: An Inquiry into a Category of Bourgeois Society.* Trans. Thomas Burger. Cambridge: MIT P, 1989.

Kant, Immanuel. "An Answer to the Question: 'What is Enlightenment?'" *Political Writings.* 2nd Eng. ed. Ed. Hans Reiss. Trans. H. B. Nisbet. Cambridge: Cambridge UP, 1991. 54–60.

———. "*The Metaphysics of Morals:* Introduction to the Theory of Right." *Political Writings.* 2nd Eng. ed. Ed. Hans Reiss. Trans. H. B. Nisbet. Cambridge: Cambridge UP, 1991. 131–75.

Kennedy, George A. *Comparative Rhetoric: An Historical and Cross-Cultural Introduction.* New York: Oxford UP, 1998.

Knight, Susan. "New Arts Center Proposal Pits the Rich against the Poor." *Streetvibes, The Tri-State's Homeless Grapevine.* March 1999:1–3.

Lone Wolf v. Hitchcock. 187 U.S. 553. U.S. Supreme Court. 1903.

Lyons, Oren. "The American Indian in the Past." *Exiled in the Land of the Free: Democracy, Indian Nations, and the U.S. Constitution.* Eds. Chief Oren Lyons and John Mohawk. Santa Fe: Clear Light Publishers, 1992. 13–42.

Minnesota v. Mille Lacs Band of Chippewa Indians, 97 U.S. 1337. U.S. Supreme Court. 1999.

Momaday, N. Scott. *House Made of Dawn.* New York: Harper, 1989.

Murray, David. *Forked Tongues: Speech, Writing, and Representation in North American Indian Texts.* Bloomington: Indiana UP, 1991.

Owens, Louis. *Mixedblood Messages: Literature, Film, Family, Place.* Norman: U of Oklahoma P, 1998.

Perdue, Theda. *The Cherokee Removal: A Brief History with Documents.* New York: Bedford, 1995.

Porter, Robert B. "Strengthening Tribal Sovereignty through Government Reform: What Are the Issues?" *The Kansas Journal of Law and Public Policy* 7.1 (Winter 1997): 72–105.

Prucha, Francis Paul. *American Indian Treaties: The History of a Political Anomaly.* Berkeley: U of California P, 1994.

———, ed. *Documents of United States Indian Policy.* 2nd ed. Lincoln: U of Nebraska P, 1990.

Rich, Sue. "'Redskins' and 'Indian Red' No More." *The Circle: Native American News and Arts.* Apr. 1999: 3.

Rose, Wendy. "The Great Pretenders: Further Reflections on Whiteshamanism." *The State of Native America: Genocide, Colonization, Resistance.* Ed. M. Annette Jaimes. Boston: South End, 1992. 403–22.

Ryan, Mary. "Gender and Public Access: Women's Politics in Nineteenth-Century America." Calhoun 259–88.

Smith, Neil. *The New Urban Frontier: Gentrification and the Revanchist City.* New York: Routledge, 1996.

Standing Bear, Luther. *Land of the Spotted Eagle.* Boston: Houghton Mifflin, 1933.

———. *My People the Sioux.* Lincoln: U of Nebraska P, 1975.

Trask, Haunani-Kay. *From a Native Daughter: Colonialism and Sovereignty in Hawai'i.* Monroe, GA: Common Courage, 1993.

Warrior, Robert Allen. *Tribal Secrets: Recovering American Indian Intellectual Traditions.* Minneapolis: U of Minnesota P, 1995.

Wells, Susan. "Rogue Cops and Health Care: What Do We Want from Public Writing?" *College Composition and Communication* 47 (1996): 325–41.

Worcester v. Georgia, 31 U.S. 515, 562. U.S. Supreme Court. 1832.

Yazzie, Robert. "Opinion: Cherokee Nation v. Georgia." *The Kansas Journal of Law and Public Policy* 7.1 (Winter 1997): 159–73.

The Myth of Linguistic Homogeneity in U.S. College Composition

Paul Kei Matsuda

In "English Only and U.S. College Composition," Bruce Horner and John Trimbur identify the tacit policy of unidirectional English monolingualism, which makes moving students toward the dominant variety of English the only conceivable way of dealing with language issues in composition instruction. This policy of unidirectional monolingualism is an important concept to critique because it accounts for the relative lack of attention to multilingualism in composition scholarship. Yet it does not seem to explain why second-language issues have not become a central concern in composition studies. After all, if U.S. composition had accepted the policy of unidirectional monolingualism, *all* composition teachers would have been expected to learn how to teach the dominant variety of English to students who come from different language backgrounds. This has not been the case. While Geneva Smitherman and Victor Villanueva argue that coursework on language issues (though certainly not a monolingualist approach) should be part of every English teacher's professional preparation (4), relatively few graduate programs in composition studies offer courses on those issues, and even fewer require such courses. As a result, the vast majority of U.S. college composition programs remain unprepared for second-language writers who enroll

Reprinted from *College English* 68.6 (July 2006): 637–651. Used with permission.

in the mainstream composition courses. To account for this situation, I want to take Horner and Trimbur's argument a step further and suggest that the dominant discourse of U.S. college composition not only has accepted English Only as an ideal but it already assumes the state of English-only, in which students are native English speakers by default.

That second-language writing has not yet become a central concern in composition studies seems paradoxical given the historical origin of U.S. college composition as a way of "containing" language differences and sealing them off from the rest of U.S. higher education. Robert J. Connors has suggested that U.S. composition arose in response to perceived language differences—texts written by ostensibly some of the brightest native English speakers that included numerous errors in "[p]unctuation, capitalization, spelling, [and] syntax" (*Composition* 128). Susan Miller also points out that college composition "has provided a continuing way to separate the unpredestined from those who belong [. . .] by encouraging them to leave school, or more vaguely, by convincing large numbers of *native speakers* and otherwise accomplished *citizens* that they are 'not good at English'" (74; emphasis added). To a large extent, however, issues that prompted the rise of the composition requirement are weak forms of language differences that affect native speakers of English—matters of convention and style as well as performance errors that arise from factors such as unfamiliar tasks, topics, audiences, or genres. While U.S. composition has maintained its ambivalent relationship with those weak forms of language differences, it has been responding to the presence of stronger forms of language differences—differences that affect students who did not grow up speaking privileged varieties of English—not by adjusting its pedagogical practices systematically at the level of the entire field but by relegating the responsibility of working with those differences to second-language specialists (Matsuda, "Composition"; Shuck).

I am not trying to imply that there has not been *any* effort to address second-language issues in composition studies. I recognize that a growing number of writing teachers who face those issues in their classes on a daily basis have developed, often on their own initiative, additional expertise in issues related to language differences. What I want to call into question is why the issue of language difference has not become a central concern for *everyone* who is involved in composition instruction, research, assessment, and administration. I argue that the lack of "a profession-wide response" (Valdés 128) to the presence of strong forms of language differences in U.S. composition stems from what I call the myth of linguistic homogeneity—the tacit and widespread acceptance of the dominant image of composition students as native speakers of a privileged variety of English. To show how the myth of linguistic homogeneity came into being, I examine the early history of various attempts at linguistic containment, which created a condition that makes it seem acceptable to dismiss language differences. My intention is not to argue against all forms of linguistic containment. Rather, I want to problematize its long-term implication—the perpetuation of the myth of linguistic homogeneity—which has in turn kept U.S. composition from fully recognizing the presence of second-language writers who do not fit the dominant image of college students.

THE IMAGE OF COLLEGE STUDENTS AND THE MYTH OF LINGUISTIC HOMOGENEITY

Behind any pedagogy is an image of prototypical students—the teacher's imagined audience. This image embodies a set of assumptions about who the students are, where they come from, where they are going, what they already know, what they need to know, and how best to teach them. It is not necessarily the concrete image of any individual student but an abstraction that comes from continual encounters with the dominant student population in local institutional settings as well as the dominant disciplinary discourses. Images of students are not monolithic; just as teachers incorporate pedagogical practices from various and even conflicting perspectives, their images of students are multiple and complex, reflecting local institutional arrangements as well as the teaching philosophies and worldviews of individual teachers. Although there is no such thing as a generalized college composition student, overlaps in various teachers' images of students constitute a dominant image—a set of socially shared generalizations. Those generalizations in turn warrant the link between abstract disciplinary practices and concrete classroom practices.

Having a certain image of students is not problematic in itself; images of students are inevitable and even necessary. Without those images, discussing pedagogical issues across institutions would be impossible. An image of students becomes problematic when it inaccurately represents the actual student population in the classroom to the extent that it inhibits the teacher's ability to recognize and address the presence of differences. Just as the assumption of whiteness as the colorless norm has rendered some students of color invisible in the discourse of composition studies (Prendergast 51), theoretical practices that do not recognize and challenge other inaccurate images reinforce the marginal status of those students by rendering them invisible in the professional discourse. At the same time, pedagogical practices based on an inaccurate image of students continue to alienate students who do not fit the image.

One of the persisting elements of the dominant image of students in English studies is the assumption that students are by default native speakers of a privileged variety of English from the United States. Although the image of students as native speakers of privileged varieties of English is seldom articulated or defended—an indication that English-only is already taken for granted—it does surface from time to time in the work of those who are otherwise knowledgeable about issues of language and difference. A prime example is Patrick Hartwell's "Grammar, Grammars, and the Teaching of Grammar," a widely known critique of grammar instruction in the composition classroom. In his analysis of a grammar exercise, he writes that "[t]he rule, however valuable it may be for non-native speakers, is, for the most part, simply unusable for native speakers of the language" (116). While this is a reasonable claim, to argue against certain pedagogical strategies based on their relevance to native speakers seems to imply the assumption of the native-English-speaker norm. Hartwell also claims that "[n]ative speakers of English, regardless of dialect, show tacit mastery of the conventions of Standard English" (123), which seems to trivialize important structural differences between privileged varieties of U.S. English and many other domestic and international varieties of English.

Language issues are also inextricably tied to the goal of college composition, which is to help students become "better writers." Although definitions of what constitutes a better writer may vary, implicit in most teachers' definitions of "writing well" is the ability to produce English that is unmarked in the eyes of teachers who are custodians of privileged varieties of English or, in more socially situated pedagogies, of an audience of native English speakers who would judge the writer's credibility or even intelligence on the basis of grammaticality. (As a practicing writing teacher, I do not claim to be immune to this charge.) Since any form of writing assessment—holistic, multiple-trait, or portfolio assessment—explicitly or implicitly includes language as one of the criteria, writing teachers regularly and inevitably engage in what Bonny Norton and Sue Starfield have termed "covert language assessment" (292). As they point out, this practice is not problematic in itself, especially if language issues are deliberately and explicitly included in the assessment criteria *and* if students are receiving adequate instruction on language issues. In many composition classrooms, however, language issues beyond simple "grammar" correction are not addressed extensively even when the assessment of student texts is based at least partly on students' proficiency in the privileged variety of English. As Connors has pointed out, "the sentence [. . .] as an element of composition pedagogy is hardly mentioned today outside of textbooks" ("Erasure" 97), and has become a "half-hidden and seldom-discussed classroom practice on the level of, say, vocabulary quizzes" (120). It is not unusual for teachers who are overwhelmed by the presence of language differences to tell students simply to "proofread more carefully" or to "go to the writing center"; those who are not native speakers of dominant varieties of English are thus being held accountable for what is not being taught. The current practice might be appropriate if all students could reasonably be expected to come to the composition classroom having already internalized a privileged variety of English—its grammar and the rhetorical practices associated with it. Such an expectation, however, does not accurately reflect the student population in today's college composition classrooms. In the 2003–04 academic year, there were 572,509 international students in U.S. colleges (Institute of International Education, *Open Doors 2004*), most of whom came from countries where English is not the dominant language. Although the number has declined slightly in recent years, international students are not likely to disappear from U.S. higher education any time soon. In fact, many institutions continue to recruit international students— because they bring foreign capital (at an out-of-state rate), increase visible ethnic diversity (which, unlike linguistic diversity, is highly valued), and enhance the international reputation of the institutions—even as they reduce or eliminate instructional support programs designed to help those students succeed (Dadak; Kubota and Abels). In addition, there is a growing number of resident second-language writers who are permanent residents or citizens of the United States. Linda Harklau, Meryl Siegal, and Kay M. Losey estimate that there are at least 150,000 to 225,000 active learners of English graduating from U.S. high schools each year (2–3). These figures do not include an overwhelmingly large number of functional bilinguals—students who have a high level of proficiency in both English and another language spoken at home (Valdés)—or native speakers of traditionally underprivileged varieties of English, including what has come to be known as world Englishes. The myth of linguistic homogeneity—the assumption that college students are by default native speakers of a privileged variety of English—is seriously out of sync with the sociolinguistic reality of today's U.S. higher education as well as of U.S. society at large. This discrepancy is especially problematic considering the status of first-year composition as the only course that is required of virtually all college students in a country where, according to a 2000 U.S. Census, "more than one in six people five years of age and older reported speaking a language other than English at home" (Bayley 269).

THE POLICY OF LINGUISTIC CONTAINMENT IN U.S. COLLEGE COMPOSITION

The perpetuation of the myth of linguistic homogeneity in U.S. college composition has been facilitated by the concomitant policy of linguistic containment that has kept language differences invisible in the required composition course and in the discourse of composition studies. Since its beginning in the late nineteenth century at Harvard and elsewhere, the first-year composition course has been a site of linguistic containment, quarantining from the rest of higher education students who have not yet been socialized into the dominant linguistic practices (Miller 74). While institutions have used the composition course as a site of linguistic containment for non-native speakers of privileged varieties of English, institutions have found ways to exclude more substantive forms of language differences even from the composition course by enacting several strategies for linguistic containment. The first and most obvious strategy is to exclude language differences from entering higher education altogether by filtering them out in the admission process. Another common strategy, especially when the number of students from unprivileged language backgrounds is relatively small, is to ignore language issues, attributing any difficulties to individual students' inadequate academic preparation. Even when language differences are recognized by the teacher, those differences are often contained by sending students to the writing center, where students encounter peer tutors who are even less likely to be prepared to work with language differences than are composition teachers (Trimbur 27–28).

The policy of containment is enacted most strongly through the placement procedure, which is unique to composition programs in the sense that students do not normally have the option of choosing a second-language section—perhaps with the exception of speech communication courses. The all-too-common practice of using language proficiency tests for composition placement (Crusan 20) is a clear indication that the policy of linguistic containment is at work. Even when direct assessment of writing is used for placement, the use of holistic scoring may lead raters to give disproportionate weight to language differences because "a text is so internally complex (e.g., highly developed but fraught with grammatical errors) that it requires more than a single number to capture its strengths and weaknesses" (Hamp-Lyons 760). Based on placement test results, many students are placed in noncredit "remedial" courses where they are expected to erase the traces of their language differences before they are allowed to enroll in the required composition course. In other cases, students are placed—sometimes after their initial placement in mainstream composition courses—in a separate track of composition courses for nonnative English speakers that can satisfy the composition requirement. These courses, though sometimes costly to students, provide useful language support for them and are necessary for many students who will be entering the composition course as well as courses in other disciplines where the myth of linguistic homogeneity prevails. At the same time, these placement practices also reify the myth by making it seem as if language differences can be effectively removed from mainstream composition courses.

In the remainder of this essay, I examine the emergence of the myth of linguistic homogeneity and the concomitant policy of linguistic containment in the late nineteenth and the early twentieth centuries— the formative years of U.S. college composition. U.S. higher education during this period is marked by several influxes of international students, many of whom came from countries where English was not the dominant language. Each of these influxes was met not by attempts to reform composition pedagogy but by efforts to contain language differences— efforts that continue even today. I focus on developments before the 1960s because it was the period when a number of significant changes took place. Although English had long been part of U.S. higher education, the English language began to take the center stage in the late nineteenth century through the use of English composition as part of the college entrance exam (Brereton 9) and through the creation of the English composition course that tacitly endorsed the policy of unidirectional monolingualism (Horner and Trimbur 596–97). It was also during this period that language differences in the composition classroom became an issue because of the presence of a growing number of international students, and many of the placement options for second-language writers were created (Matsuda and Silva; Silva). My focus is on international students because, until the latter half of the twentieth century, resident students from underprivileged language backgrounds were systematically excluded from higher education altogether (Matsuda, "Basic" 69–72).

WAVES OF INTERNATIONAL STUDENTS AND THE POLICY OF CONTAINMENT

The image of U.S. college students as native speakers of more or less similar, privileged varieties of English had already been firmly established by the mid-nineteenth century. Although the larger U.S. society had always been multilingual (Bayley 269), language differences were generally excluded from English-dominated higher education of the nineteenth century. The assumption of the native-English-speaker norm was, at least on the surface, more or less accurate in the mid-nineteenth century, when access to college education was restricted to students from certain ethnic, gender, religious, socioeconomic, and linguistic backgrounds. As David Russell notes, U.S. colleges before the end of the Civil War were "by modern standards extraordinarily homogeneous, guaranteeing a linguistic common ground" (35). While U.S. higher education began to shift from exclusive, elitist establishment to more inclusive vehicle for mass education during the latter half of the nineteenth century, the traditional image of college students remained unchallenged for the most part. Although the creation of what have come to be known as historically black colleges had provided African American students access to higher education since the early nineteenth century, they did not affect the dominant image because they were physically segregated from the rest of the college student population. In fact, those colleges served as the sites of containment—ethnic as well as linguistic. The Morrill Act, first passed in 1862 and then extended in 1890, gave rise to land-grant institutions across the nation that made college education open to women as well as to students from a wider variety of socioeconomic groups. Yet, native speakers of nonprivileged varieties of English did not enter higher education in large numbers because the ability to speak privileged varieties of English was often equated with racialized views of the speaker's intelligence.

One of the major institutional initiatives that contributed to the exclusion of language differences was the creation of the entrance exam—first instituted at Harvard in 1874 and then quickly and widely adopted by other institutions. The entrance exam at Harvard was motivated in part by "a growing awareness of the importance of linguistic class distinctions in the United States" (Connors, *Composition* 128).

Harvard course catalogs during this period indicate that the entrance exam at Harvard included "reading English aloud" or writing with "[c]orrect [. . .] spelling, punctuation, grammar, and expression" (qtd. in Brereton 34). Miller also points out that "forms of this examination became the most powerful instrument for discriminating among students in higher education" (63), effectively excluding students who did not fit the dominant linguistic profile. Even in the nineteenth century, however, the assumption of linguistic homogeneity in higher education was not entirely accurate, and it moved farther and farther away from the sociolinguistic reality of U.S. higher education. One group of students who brought significant language differences were international students who entered U.S. higher education through different admission processes and therefore were not subject to linguistic filtering (Matsuda, "Basic" 71–72).

The history of international ESL students in U.S. higher education goes at least as far back as 1784, when Yale hosted a student from Latin America; in the mid-1800s, students from China and Japan also attended Yale and Amherst College (King 11). The first sizable influx of international students came in the latter half of the nineteenth century, when U.S. higher education began to attract an increasing number of students from other countries as it developed research universities modeled after German institutions. Most of these international students were from Asian countries that were "undergoing modernization with the help of knowledge acquired from Western countries" (Bennett, Passin, and McKnight 26). During the late nineteenth century, European students also came to U.S. higher education "not so much seeking an education that was not available to them at home, as out of a desire to see America, the 'country of the future'" (Institute of International Education, 1955 *Handbook*, 6).

In the late nineteenth century, when many of the international students were sponsored by their governments, language preparation was generally considered to be the responsibility of individual students or their sponsoring governments, and

U.S. colleges and universities usually provided little or no institutional support for international students' cultural and linguistic adjustments. For instance, students from China and Japan, most of whom were sponsored by their respective governments, usually received language instruction before coming to the United States. In many cases, however, their language preparation was less than adequate by the standard of U.S. institutions, and they were sent to preparatory schools, where they were "placed in classes with the youngest children" (Schwantes 194). The Japanese government continued to send students to U.S. colleges; however, they were selected by a rigid examination, and their progress was monitored by a supervisor sent by the Japanese government (Institute of International Education, 1955 *Handbook,* 4). By the 1880s, the practice of holding the sponsoring government responsible for providing language preparation became difficult to sustain as the number of government-sponsored students declined, giving way to an increasing number of privately funded students (Bennett, Passin, and McKnight 32).

The second influx came in the early part of the twentieth century, when internationally known research institutions began to attract a growing number of international students, most from countries where English was not the dominant language. Although in 1911 there were only 3,645 international students in U.S. higher education, the number began to grow rapidly after the conclusion of World War I (1914–18). This change was due partly to European students' dissatisfaction "with their own traditions of education" as well as Asian students' need for "new foundations for modern systems of education" (Kandel 39). Another factor that contributed to the growth was the national interest of the United States. The U.S. government's growing concern with post-WWI international relations—especially with European nations—prompted the establishment in 1919 of the Institute of International Education (IIE) with support from the Carnegie Endowment for International Peace. The IIE was successful in "stimulat[ing] interest in student exchange, [and] encouraging public and private groups to sponsor international students" (Institute of International Education, 1955 *Handbook,* 7). By 1920, the number of international students had reached 6,163 and was continuing to increase (Institute of International Education, 1961 *Handbook,* 230). In 1930, U.S. colleges and universities reported the presence of 9,961 international students (Darian 105).

The growing presence of international students from non-English-dominant countries became an issue among hosting institutions. Some educators recognized the problem of the traditional pedagogy based on the dominant image of students. Isaac Leon Kandel, for example, wrote that international students did not benefit as much from the instruction not because of their lack of ability but because "courses were organized primarily with the American student, familiar with American ideals, aims, history, and social and political background, in mind" (50). The solution, however, was not to challenge the dominant image but to contain issues of linguistic and cultural differences by providing additional instruction—

an approach that might have seemed reasonable when the number of international students was relatively small. To provide linguistic support for those who did not fit the traditional image of college students, institutions began to develop special English-language courses. According to a 1923 survey of four hundred institutions, all but two institutions stated that they had "provision for special language help by official courses or by voluntary conversation classes" (Parson 155). Although it continued to be "a common rule to refuse admission to students who are unable to speak and read English," about 50 percent of institutions offered "special courses for backward students" (155).

In 1911, Joseph Raleigh Nelson in the Engineering College at the University of Michigan created the first English courses specifically designed for international students (Klinger 1845–47), followed by Teachers College of Columbia University, which created special courses for matriculated international students in 1923 (Kandel 54). Harvard University created its first English courses for international students in 1927, and George Washington University and Cornell University followed suit in 1931 (Allen 307; Darian 77). While there were some exceptions—such as the program at Michigan, which continued for several decades—many of these early programs were ad hoc in nature. The initial innovation at Harvard ceased to exist after a while and, by the 1940s, second-language writers at Harvard had come to be mainstreamed into "regular" sections of composition courses with additional help from individual tutoring services (Gibian 157). At George Washington, the separate section of composition "used the same materials as the sections for Americans and [. . .] was conducted by the same teacher"; however, "none of the English instructors really desired to teach that group," and this program was later found to be unsuccessful (Rogers 394). The courses at Columbia, which allowed students to enroll simultaneously in college-level courses, were also found to be ineffective in containing language differences (Kandel 54). Other institutions, especially where the number of international students was relatively small, dealt with language differences "by a process of scattering foreigners through different courses, so that they must mingle freely with others, rather than segregating them for group study in classes where they may persist in using their own language" (Parson 155).

Following the announcement of the Good Neighbor Policy in 1933, the State Department began to bring international students from Latin America to provide them with scientific and technical training, a development that led to the creation, in 1941, of the English Language

Institute (ELI) at the University of Michigan. As an intensive program, it separated students from the college-level courses for a period of several months while they focused on developing their English language proficiency. Although the program was initially intended for Spanish-speaking graduate students from Latin America, it later broadened its scope to include undergraduate students and students from other language backgrounds. The Michigan ELI provided a model for intensive English programs throughout the United States and in many other countries, paving the way for the next wave of ESL courses, which were created after World War II (Matsuda, "Composition" 701–06).

Although the number of international students had declined somewhat during the Depression and World War II, the conclusion of the war brought another influx of international students. The international student population surged from less than 8,000 in 1945 to 10,341 in 1946 (Darian 105), when the United States replaced Germany as the most popular destination for international students. The number doubled in the next two years and, by 1949, there were 26,759 international students (Institute of International Education, 1949 *Handbook,* 7, 14). To contain the language differences these students brought with them, an increasing number of institutions—including those that had relatively small but steady enrollments of international students—began to create separate English courses and programs on a permanent basis (Schueler 309). In 1949, Harvard once again created a special non-credit course for small groups of students from Europe, providing a preparation for the required composition course (Gibian 157). At about the same time, Queens College developed a multilevel intensive English language program with its own teaching and testing materials (Schueler 312–14). Tulane University also created a noncredit English course for second-language writers. Sumner Ives reported that all nonnative English speakers at Tulane, unless "individually excused," were required to enroll in a special English course for nonnative speakers before taking the required English course. This program was unique in that the status of the course was determined after the beginning of the semester. Based on a reading test during the orientation, the teacher would decide whether each student should move to a "regular section" or remain in the remedial course. When most of the remaining students had limited English proficiency, the course was taught as a remedial English language course, using the materials developed by the ELI at Michigan. The course became credit-bearing when a large number of students had reached advanced English proficiency, and the textbooks for regular sections of composition courses were used (Ives 142–43).

The number of ESL writing courses continued to grow. In 1953, according to Harold B. Allen, about 150 institutions reported the existence of English-as-a-second-language programs for international students; by 1969, the number had nearly doubled. In addition, 114 institutions reported that they offered summer programs for international students (Allen 308). Initially, many of those courses were offered on a noncredit basis as preparation for a regular English requirement. These courses focused not only on writing but also on reading and oral communication skills. Noncredit English courses for nonnative speakers offered at many institutions adopted the textbook series developed by the ELI at Michigan, and intensive language courses modeled after Michigan's ELI also became widespread, providing systematic instruction before second-language writers were allowed to enroll in regular college-level courses.

Yet a semester or two of extra language instruction was often not enough to help students fit the dominant image—after all, learning a second language is a time-consuming process, especially for adult learners—and they continued to bring language differences to college composition courses. For this reason, institutions began to develop a separate track of required composition courses for second-language writers—courses that were designed to keep language differences out of the required composition course. In 1954, Michigan's Department of English Language and Literature in the College of Literature, Science, and Art created one of the first credit-bearing ESL composition courses that paralleled the sections of English courses for native speakers of English (Klinger 1849). The University of Washington followed suit with a three-credit composition course for second-language writers, which emphasized purposeful cross-cultural communication with an audience rather than the language drills or linguistic analyses commonly used in intensive language programs at the time (Marquardt 31).

EMBRACING LANGUAGE DIFFERENCES AS THE NEW NORM

The assumption of linguistic homogeneity, which was more or less accurate in U.S. higher education institutions of the mid-nineteenth century, became increasingly inaccurate as linguistic diversity grew over the last two centuries. Yet the growing presence of international students did not lead to a fundamental reconsideration of the dominant image of students in the composition classroom. It was not because the separate placement practices were able to eliminate language differences. For a number of reasons, none of these programs was able to contain language differences completely: because language learning is a time-consuming process; because students often come with a wide range of English-language proficiency levels; and because developing placement procedures that can account for language differences is not an easy task. As Ives wrote, "neither a frankly non-credit course for all, nor [NNES students'] segregation into separate but parallel courses, nor their distribution throughout the regular courses is completely satisfactory" (142). Instead, the dominant image of students remained unchallenged because the policy of containment kept language differences in the composition classroom from reaching a critical mass, thus creating the false impression that all language differences could and should be addressed elsewhere. In other words, the policy of unidirectional monolingualism was enacted not so much through pedagogical practices in the main-stream composition course as through delegation of students to remedial or parallel courses that were designed to keep language differences from entering the composition course in the first place.

The policy of containment and the continuing dominance of the myth of linguistic homogeneity have serious implications not only for international second-language writers but also for resident second-language writers as well as for native speakers of unprivileged varieties of English. Many institutions place students into basic writing classes without distinguishing writing issues and language issues partly because underlying language differences are not easily discernible by observing student texts that seem, at least on the surface, strikingly similar to one another (Matsuda, "Basic" 74). As a result, basic writing courses often enroll many second-language writers—both international and resident—although many basic writing courses, like the credit-bearing composition courses, are designed primarily for U.S. citizens who are native speakers of a variety of English (68).

By pointing out the problem of the policy of containment, however, I do not mean to suggest that these placement practices be abandoned. On the contrary, many students do need and even prefer these placement options. As George Braine suggests, many—though certainly not all—second-language writers prefer second-language sections of composition, where they feel more comfortable and where they are more likely to succeed. To deny these support programs would be to further marginalize nonnative speakers of English in institutions of higher education where the myth of linguistic homogeneity will likely continue to inform the curriculum as well as many teachers' attitude toward language differences. Instead, composition teachers need to resist the popular conclusion that follows the policy of containment—that the college composition classroom can be a monolingual space. To work effectively with the student population in the twenty-first century, all composition teachers need to reimagine the composition classroom as the multilingual space that it is, where the presence of language differences is the default.[1]

NOTE

1. I am grateful to Min-Zhan Lu, Bruce Horner, Dwight Atkinson, and Christina Ortmeier-Hooper for their helpful and constructive comments on earlier versions of this essay.

WORKS CITED

Allen, Harold B. "English as a Second Language." *Current Trends in Linguistics: Linguistics in North America.* Vol. 10. Ed. Thomas A. Sebeok. The Hague: Mouton, 1973. 295–320.

Bayley, Robert. "Linguistic Diversity and English Language Acquisition." *Language in the USA: Themes for the Twenty-First Century.* Ed. Edward Finegan and John R. Rickford. Cambridge: Cambridge UP, 2004. 268–86.

Bennett, John W., Herbert Passin, and Robert K. McKnight. *In Search of Identity: The Japanese Overseas Scholar in America and Japan.* Minneapolis: U of Minnesota P, 1958.

Braine, George. "ESL Students in First-Year Writing Courses: ESL versus Mainstream Classes." *Journal of Second Language Writing* 5 (1996): 91–107.

Brereton, John C. *The Origins of Composition Studies in the American College, 1875–1925: A Documentary History.* Pittsburgh: U of Pittsburgh P, 1995.

Connors, Robert J. *Composition-Rhetoric: Backgrounds, Theory, and Pedagogy.* Pittsburgh: U of Pittsburgh P, 1997.

———. "The Erasure of the Sentence." *CCC* 52 (2000): 96–128.

Crusan, Deborah. "An Assessment of ESL Writing Placement Assessment." *Assessing Writing* 8 (2002): 17–30.

Dadak, Angela. "No ESL Allowed: A Case of One College Writing Program's Practices." *Politics of Second Language Writing: In Search of the Promised Land.* Ed. Paul Kei Matsuda, Christina Ortmeier-Hooper, and Xiaoye You. West Lafayette, IN: Parlor, forthcoming.

Darian, Stephen G. *English as a Foreign Language: History, Development and Methods of Teaching.* Norman: U of Oklahoma P, 1972.

Gibian, George. "College English for Foreign Students." *College English* 13 (1951): 157–60.

Hamp-Lyons, Liz. "Rating Nonnative Writing: The Trouble with Holistic Scoring." *TESOL Quarterly* 29 (1995): 759–62.

Harklau, Linda, Meryl Siegal, and Kay M. Losey. "Linguistically Diverse Students and College Writing: What Is Equitable and Appropriate?" *Generation 1.5 Meets College Composition: Issues in the Teaching of Writing to U.S.-Educated Learners of ESL*. Ed. Linda Harklau, Kay M. Losey, and Meryl Siegal. Mahwah, NJ: Erlbaum, 1999. 1–14.

Hartwell, Patrick. "Grammar, Grammars, and the Teaching of Grammar." *College English* 47 (1985): 105–27.

Horner, Bruce, and John Trimbur. "English Only and U.S. College Composition." *CCC* 53 (2002): 594–630.

Institute of International Education. *Handbook on International Study: A Guide for Foreign Students and for U.S. Students on Study Abroad*. New York: Institute of International Education, 1955.

———. *Handbook on International Study: For Foreign Nationals*. New York: Institute of International Education, 1961.

———. *Open Doors 2004*. New York: Institute of International Education, 2005. Ives, Sumner. "Help for the Foreign Student." *CCC* 4 (1953): 141–44.

Kandel, Isaac Leon. *United States Activities in International Cultural Relations*. Washington, DC: American Council on Education, 1945.

King, Henry H. "Outline History of Student Migrations." *The Foreign Students in America*. Ed. W. Reginald Wheeler, Henry H. King, and Alexander B. Davidson. New York: Association, 1925. 3–38.

Klinger, Robert B. "The International Center." *The University of Michigan: An Encyclopedic Survey in Four Volumes*. Vol. 4. Ed. Walter A. Donnelly. Ann Arbor: U of Michigan P, 1958. 1843–49.

Kubota, Ryuko, and Kimberly Abels. "Improving Institutional ESL/EAP Support for International Students: Seeking the Promised Land." *Politics of Second Language Writing: In Search of the Promised Land*. Ed. Paul Kei Matsuda, Christina Ortmeier-Hooper, and Xiaoye You. West Lafayette, IN: Parlor, forthcoming.

Marquardt, William F. "Composition in English as a Second Language: Cross Cultural Communication." *CCC* 17 (1966): 29–33.

Matsuda, Paul Kei. "Composition Studies and ESL Writing: A Disciplinary Division of Labor." *CCC* 50 (1999): 699–721.

———. "Basic Writing and Second Language Writers: Toward an Inclusive Definition." *Journal of Basic Writing* 22 (2003): 67–89.

Matsuda, Paul Kei, and Tony Silva. "Cross-Cultural Composition: Mediated Integration of U.S. and International Students." *Composition Studies* 27 (1999): 15–30.

Miller, Susan. *Textual Carnivals: The Politics of Composition*. Carbondale: Southern Illinois UP, 1991.

Norton, Bonny, and Sue Starfield. "Covert Language Assessment in Academic Writing." *Language Testing* 14 (1997): 278–94.

Parson, A. B. "The Foreign Student and the American College." *The Foreign Students in America*. Ed. W. Reginald Wheeler, Henry H. King, and Alexander B. Davidson. New York: Association, 1925. 149–74.

Prendergast, Catherine. "Race: The Absent Presence in Composition Studies." *CCC* 50 (1998): 36–53. Rogers, Gretchen L. "Freshman English for Foreigners." *School and Society* 61 (1945): 394–96.

Russell, David. *Writing in the Academic Disciplines: A Curricular History*. 2nd ed. Carbondale: Southern Illinois UP, 2002.

Schueler, Herbert. "English for Foreign Students." *Journal of Higher Education* 20 (1949): 309–16.

Schwantes, Robert S. *Japanese and Americans: A Century of Cultural Relations.* New York: Harper and Brothers and the Council on Foreign Relations, 1955.

Shuck, Gail. "Combating Monolingualism: A Novice Administrator's Challenge." *WPA: Writing Program Administration* (forthcoming).

Silva, Tony. "An Examination of Writing Program Administrator's Options for the Placement of ESL Students in First Year Writing Classes." *Writing Program Administration* 18.1/2 (1994): 37–43.

Smitherman, Geneva, and Victor Villanueva. Introduction. *Language Diversity in the Classroom: From Intention to Practice.* Ed. Smitherman and Villanueva. Carbondale: Southern Illinois UP, 2003.

Trimbur, John. "Peer Tutoring: A Contradiction in Terms?" *Writing Center Journal* 7.2 (1987): 21–28.

Valdés, Guadalupe. "Bilingual Minorities and Language Issues in Writing: Toward Profession-wide Response to a New Challenge." *Written Communication* 9 (1992): 85–136.

The Rhetoric of Translingualism

Keith Gilyard

The arc of moral composition studies is long, King might say, but it bends toward translingualism.[1] I would agree insofar as the term *translingualism* galvanizes the multidimensional repudiation of monolingual curriculums and yields praxis informed by an understanding that language and language standards are situational, political, arbitrary, and palimpsestic. If, as Vygotsky indicates, a "word is a microcosm of human consciousness" (153), then it is also a microcosm of human history. Every utterance contains tracings of migration, mixing, negotiation, or conquest. Stories have been programmed into our languages just as they have been stamped into our genes. Moreover, translingualism incorporates the view that all language users, or *languagers*, are perpetually producing and experimenting with multiple varieties of language. Thus, translingualists grasp that the institutional enactment of language standards is repressive in some cases and restrictive in all.

Yet I imagine that proponents of translingualism will still have to grapple with the question of how much language prescriptiveness they are comfortable with—lest they assert "none at all" and, as they work in political arenas in which they assess students, seem to evade politics, the last thing a self-respecting translingualist wants to be caught doing. It also appears to me that continual revisiting and reworking of several other concepts of language and difference are necessary to forge a stronger narrative about translingualism. In addition to talk about student language rights, I am concerned on this occasion with the flattening of language differences, the notion of language as an abstraction, the danger of translingualism becoming an alienating theory for some scholars of color, and deeper study of powerfully translanguaging students.

Reprinted from *College English* 78.3 (January 2016): 284–289. Used with permission.

As is evident from reading essays such as John Trimbur's discussion in this issue of the 1974 CCCC "Students' Right to Their Own Language" (SRTOL), the resolution remains a touchstone in composition studies for progressive language campaigns. But as I have suggested elsewhere, the language rights of ethnic assemblages, most prominently African Americans, were the issue and not the language rights of students conceived as individuals (Gilyard 95). No vision was expressed claiming, for example, "my own idiosyncratic thing" as a language that should be honored in schools. Rather, a particular political problem, the harsh penalizing of students who were firmly tethered linguistically to an institutionally discredited heritage, was being addressed. The representative students at the heart of the students' right work of earlier decades were not the idealized ones at the heart of the present translingualist conception. The latter students are more shifting and unpredictable, heterogeneous and fluid, as we all are. They are not the minority others numerically but are the majority not-others occupying the default position, the norm, and are being hindered, at the very least, by gatekeepers. They are less the repressed indigenous ethnics overdetermined by dialect and more the polyglot products of contemporary global dispersion.

None of this depiction is objectionable. A good cause needs a good symbol. I advocate, however, that this symbol needs to be highlighted more and needs its specific hardships detailed. Perhaps numerous accounts in this vein exist of which I am unaware. That would be no surprise. My current impression, though, is that the translanguaging subject generally comes off in the scholarly literature as a sort of linguistic everyperson, which makes it hard to see the suffering and the political imperative as clearly as in the heyday of SRTOL. In other words, if translanguaging is the unqualified norm, then by definition it is something that all students, including high achievers, perform. So what problem is there to address? If the answer is that every translanguaging student, regardless of educational success, could stand to be better educated with respect to the inner workings of the discourses and power dynamics that impact their lives, then the project of translingualism is indistinguishable from other species of critical pedagogy. But it should be. The material fallout of the encounter of so-called unsuccessful or disabled students with institutional language power is always a matter of urgency. So what is the case for action expressed in terms that make translingualism as forwarded by its adherents indispensable? I won't detail a case here; one is implicit throughout this symposium, particularly in the writing of Ellen Cushman. I'll simply opine that the best argument for translingualism as a paradigm dramatizes negative power-linguistic formations and aligns translingualism firmly with the progressive "rights" framing of several of the language scholars mentioned by Trimbur, people such as James Sledd, Geneva Smitherman, and Victor Villanueva.

Of course, standards are the flip side of rights. What play inside class is a *my thing, my t'ing, my thang, mi cosa* student and other similar students supposed to get? I say, whatever it takes to allow them to negotiate the structures of schooling. I construct the totally self-referential student as an extreme to illustrate a point. In actuality, I have never met a college student who did not wish to expand his or her verbal repertoire. The key is to allow the experimentation that will facilitate such a process and remove barriers such as high-stakes testing and noncredit so-called remedial classes. I also, in answer to the second of Juan Guerra's queries (228), see value in explicit discussions of translingualism, though the only wisdom I hold about likely consequences is that anything with respect to student perspective can happen. After thirty-five years in the classroom, I have to emphasize that word—*anything*. (My response to Guerra's first question is that I would not expect students to mimic any specific strategy, so-called code-meshing or not, and that rhetorical astuteness is always the aim relative to emergent *and* standardized language, standardizing also being a process of emergence.)

Related to the issues of students' language rights and institutional standards is the tendency to flatten language differences in some theorizing about translingualism. Translingualists are clear about the fact that we all differ as language users from each other and in relation to a perceived standard. Often elided, however, is the recognition that we don't all differ from said standard in the same way. Given that context matters, a concept that is a key component of translingual analysis, one would always want to be careful not to level difference this way. A person purportedly two pounds overweight does not have the same relationship to a standard of trimness as a person considered two hundred pounds overweight. And not all translingual writers are stigmatized in the same manner. A possible consequence of positing a sameness of difference is that needed academic allies could read such a maneuver as a devaluing of the historical and unresolved struggles of groups that have been traditionally underrepresented in the academy and suffer disproportionately in relation to it. Now, I don't claim that "sameness of difference" is the explicit mantra of any particular translingualist, but I do believe that, in some spaces of surplus meaning beyond explicit statement, such declaration is "heard." Obviously, a scholar such as Anis Bawarshi is correct to assert, "We are always translingual." We all do negotiate language differences within networks of power, and so on. This is a liberating premise that illustrates the arbitrariness of "correctness." But to be an attractive alternative to the widest range of folks invested in combating pernicious language instruction—in some cases the linguistics of white supremacy, to make it plain—translingualism has to be sure to promote analyses of language, diversity, and power that steer clear of any formulation that might be interpreted as a sameness-of-difference model.

Translingualists also may want to reconsider how firmly to link themselves to talk that languages are really abstractions (see Lu and Horner). The idea seems to me a peculiar spin on the old competence-performance construct, the questions of what a language user knows intuitively and what a language user performs. I maintain that people do *have* language competences and do, in fact, have languages. The head of an unlit match is not the subsequent flame, but it is not an abstraction. Particular language competences, not the easiest mechanisms to study, residing as they do in regions of the brain, make possible particular language performances, though competences themselves are an inadequate explanation of actual performances. Nonetheless, when I am around a group of people who speak a language foreign to me, it amounts to nothing to counsel myself that language is really an abstraction and that those speakers don't really have that language that I don't comprehend. All are agreed that performed language has material force; *translingualism* can be encoded as a print symposium, for example. Each of the language elements that lead to such an outcome is real.

I understand the translingualist focus on performance. It is easy to see performance as a site of transformation. Performance can destabilize responses tied to fixed categories and can potentially undermine harmful standards. Moreover, I could comfortably concede the point about language abstraction to the likes of Louis-Jean Calvet if I didn't fear that a totalizing embrace of performance could make competence seem a less worthy enterprise of study. Much of the progressive language argument since the 1960s has stood on the cataloging of competences, on explaining the logic of language varieties spoken and written by so-called ethnic minorities. More of that kind of work would be a valuable complement to theorizing about performance. In addition, an anchor in competence could save translingualism from going down the same path as some deconstruction efforts regarding race. In certain corners, people have devoted more time and energy to talking about how unreal race is, how socially constructed and performative it is, than to addressing the damage of racism.

By remaining wary of a sameness-of-difference model, soft-pedaling the language-as-abstraction trope, supporting work on language competence, and fronting language-rights discourse, translingualism avoids becoming off-putting to scholars of color in the manner that post-modernist and poststructuralist theory were in the 1980s and 1990s. At least that is a conclusion that some scholars of color have expressed to me. When such scholars and their academic constituencies were claiming empowering, though somewhat static, identities and attempting to come on center, as it were, the preference to valorize theories of fluidity and decentering reigned supreme in English departments, conferences, and publishing outlets. I recall serving on a search committee charged with locating a *theory* person. Given institutional politics, the job announcement contained the obligatory phrase about being particularly interested in minority applicants. I shared with committee members that minorities were heavily disposed to challenge theory. I learned more about the challenge to minorities in that search. A couple of dozen were included among the several hundred applicants. None made the initial cut.

This anecdote is both wistful and cautionary. I imagine that at some point, if not already, job ads will express preference for someone who identifies with translingualism. How expansively is that field of study to be construed?

One of the strongest moves that translingualists can make is to document students' efforts. We need the stories of struggle, as I have suggested, and those should include tales of triumph. I think of this in connection to Trimbur's discussion in this issue of the implementation of open admissions at the City University of New York (CUNY) and the formation of basic writing as a field (220–22). His contribution doubles, he asserts, as a brief prehistory of translingualism, and he emphasizes the role played by pioneering instructors such as the valiant Mina Shaughnessy, who, at City College, a unit of CUNY, sensibly and sensitively taught students who were strangers to the academy and inexperienced in handling all of its relevant discourses. Trimbur also sketches the student strike at City College in the spring of 1969, led by the Black and Puerto Rican Student Community (BPRSM) in association with sympathizers such as the left-wing W. E. B. Du Bois Club, which pushed university officials beyond a gradualist, tokenist pace and forced their hands on open admissions. The administration planned a modest open-admissions experiment for 1975. The students forced a massive one in 1970, an event that signaled to some historians the most impressive civil rights victory in the history of higher education (see Biondi 114). By 1975, five times as many Black and Puerto Rican students attended CUNY than was the case in 1969. However, the favorable result at City College was not narrowly ethnic in either conception or outcome. It was radical and broad. Student leaders working across ethnic lines—Asian-American student participation was crucial as well—conceived of access to higher education as a right of the working class, indeed a right of citizenship. Overall enrollments in CUNY rose dramatically as did the percentage of New York City high school graduates who attended college (134-35).

I surmise that an interesting task for translingualists would be to write histories of the translanguagers who organized at City College and other places. The tribulations of Shaughnessy's students have been well recorded in composition studies. What about the language output of the protestors at City College such as Sekou Sundiata and Louis Reyes Rivera, who wrote manifestoes, issued circulars, and composed memorandums? Rivera was a co-founder of *The Paper*, the first periodical run by Puerto Rican and African-American students at the college. An examination of that publication and other documents would generate a fuller portrait of student life at City College during the open-admissions era and perhaps point to models for radical, translingual engagement in ways that Shaughnessy's work, for all of her good intentions, does not.

Ultimately, the translingualist project will not be denied. It needs rhetorical refinement and may at some point require another name. But its rejection of the monolingual paradigm is certainly the way forward.

NOTE

1. On August 16, 1967, in Atlanta, Martin Luther King, Jr. delivered before the Southern Christian Leadership Conference a speech titled "Where Do We Go From Here?" In that context, he proclaimed, echoing Theodore Parker, "The arc of the moral universe is long, but it bends toward justice."

WORKS CITED

Bawarshi, Anis. "Beyond the Genre Fixation: A Translingual Perspective on Genre." *College English* 78.3 (2016): 243–49. Print.

Biondi, Martha. *The Black Revolution on Campus*. Berkeley: U of California P, 2012. Print.

Calvet, Louis-Jean. *Pour une* écologie *des langues du monde*. Plon, 1999. Trans. Andrew Brown, *Towards an Ecology of World Languages*. London: Polity, 2006. Print.

Cushman, Ellen. "Translingual and Decolonial Approaches to Meaning Making." *College English* 78.3 (2016): 234–42. Print.

Gilyard, Keith. True to the Language Game: African American Discourse, Cultural Politics, and Pedagogy. New York: Routledge, 2011. Print.

Guerra, Juan C. "Cultivating a Rhetorical Sensibility in the Translingual Writing Classroom." *College English* 78.3 (2016): 228–33. Print.

Lu, Min-Zhan, and Bruce Horner. "Introduction: Translingual Work." *College English* 78.3 (2016): 207–18. Print.

Trimbur, John. "Translingualism and Close Reading." *College English* 78.3 (2016): 219–27. Print.

Vygotsky, Lev. *Thought and Language*. Trans. Eugenia Hanfmann and Gertrude Vakor. Cambridge: The M.I.T. Press, 1962. Print.

How Do We Language So People Stop Killing Each Other, or What Do We Do about White Language Supremacy?

Asao B. Inoue

To open, I humbly make a land acknowledgment. I would like to recognize and acknowledge the indigenous people of this land: the Lenni Lenape, Shawnee, and Hodinöhšönih—the six Nations, that is, the Mohawk, Oneida, Onondaga, Seneca, Cayuga and Tuscarora. We are gathered today on Jö:deogë', an Onödowa'ga or Senaca word for Pittsburgh or "between two rivers": the Welhik Hane and Mënaonkihëla. These are the Lenape words for the Allegheny and Monongahela rivers, which translate to the "best flowing river of the hills" and "where the banks cave in and erode." While a land acknowledgment is not enough, it is an important social justice and decolonial practice that promotes indigenous visibility and a reminder that we are on settled indigenous land. Let this land acknowledgment be an opening for all of us to contemplate a way to join in decolonial and indigenous movements for sovereignty and self-determination. Lastly, I am grateful to Melissa Borgia-Askey and Sandy Gajehsoh Dowdy for valuable etymological and pronunciation help. Also, I thank Andrea Riley Mukavetz and the American Indian Caucus for helping me with this land acknowledgment, and providing the convention with similar language for everyone to use in their sessions this year.

Reprinted from *College Composition and Communication* 71.2 (December 2019): 352–369. Used with permission.

Now, I must prepare everyone for what I'm about to say. The message I offer comes from a deep sense of love and compassion for everyone who makes the sacrifices it takes to teach writing and rhetoric in our world today. I know you are good people. And because I love you, I will be honest with you, and it may hurt. But I promise you, it hurts not because I've done something wrong, but because I'm exposing your racial wounds. These wounds are the precursors to the killing referenced in my title. I also ask many of you to be patient as I first address my colleagues of color, but the fact that I must ask for your patience to do this is evidence of the White supremacy that even we, conscientious teachers of writing, are saturated in. My colleagues of color, I wink and nod. We will break the steel cage of White supremacy, of White racial bias, of the many bars, like the physical bars of the jails and prisons that house the 2.3 million US inmates, 67 percent of which are our brothers and sisters of color, yet we make up only about 37 percent of the US population ("Who's in Prison"; "Incarceration"). I know, I don't need to tell you this. You know it. With Black men being jailed at rates five times that of their White peers, and Latinos at twice the rate of Whites, it's likely that some of us know friends or family members who have had physical cages placed around them. We academics of color in this room have many things in common with the US prison population, one being the steel cage of racism.

The cages are also figurative, but no less real in their effects. Michelle Alexander recounts Iris Marion Young's metaphor for oppression, applying it to the racism that causes such incarceration rates (Alexander 179). Among many other injustices, I add to this list the way we judge, assess, give feedback to, and grade writing by students of color in our classrooms. Yes, the ways we judge language form some of the steel bars around our students and ourselves—we too maintain White supremacy, even as we fight against it in other ways. We ain't just internally colonized, we're internally jailed. As Alexander reminds us, and we likely feel each day, the overdetermined nature of racism explains why we can change or eliminate one unfair thing in a system, or school, or classroom—such as our curriculum or our bodies' presence—yet still find that our students of color struggle and fail—even when we are there to help them, showing them that others like them have made it. We hold up the flag of opportunity and say, "Please, don't give up. Follow me!"

But we in this room made it despite the system, not because of it, yet we are part of the system now. We are the exceptions that prove the rule, as Victor Villanueva has reminded us (personal communication; *Bootstraps* xvii). We are contradictions. Again, my colleagues of color, I don't need to tell you this. You live it, but sometimes we have to remind ourselves of the magnitude of shit—that we are not oppressed alone. We need to commiserate together here in this place because often we may be alone at our home institutions. We need to lament together. Of course, I commiserate with you today in the presence of White people, so there are other reasons I remind us of the steel cage of racism. We should lament together. It builds coalitions among the variously oppressed, such as our LGBTQIA colleagues, many of whom are White.

The metaphor of the cage of racism reminds me of the famous "iron cage" metaphor coined by Max Weber in 1905. The term in German he used was, *stalhartes Gehäuse*, which was translated into English as "iron cage" but has also been translated as "shell as hard as steel" (Weber 120–21). What Weber was describing was the way in which capitalist societies, particularly in the US with its strong Protestantism, created conditions in which people self-govern their actions and beliefs, even their desires, through overdetermined structures in the market economy. This is due to the fact that no matter what you as an individual believe or do, you always are implicated and circulate in market economies that dictate the nature of the cage around you (Weber 12)—that is, dictate your own self-governance, your boundaries and desires. You are always beholden to the market. The market I call your attention to today is the market of White language preferences in schools, although it is also not hard to find the connections between it and the flows of capital.

I am overly simplifying Weber, but I call his ideas to your attention, my colleagues of color, because many White folks wish to make the racist problems we experience, such as prison and educational racism, and the White bias of those systems, as about something else, about mostly economics, laziness, or bad values. But these are interconnected and intersectional dimensions. In fact, Ronald Takaki calls on Weber's "iron cage" metaphor to highlight both the steel cage of racism and of what he terms "republicanism" (ix), which is another way to say American Whiteness. Even we academics and teachers of color are trapped in cages of such American Whiteness.

And if we are going talk about cages and racism, we should remember the first published instance of cages of racism. In Paul Laurence Dunbar's 1899 poem "Sympathy," the bird sees the bright sun, the grass, the stream, but it cannot fly. It is caged, beating bloody wings against the bars, singing, not "of joy or glee," but "a plea." The poem's narrator, perhaps Dunbar himself, ends: "I know why the caged bird sings!" While they are both speaking of the Black experience in the US, Maya Angelou's famous poem, inspired by Dunbar's, explains the context for the cage of racism that we, all people of color, feel around us all the time but not in the same ways. That context is White bias, or Takaki's cage of republicanism, only Angelou's Whiteness is that which is not in the cage. It is the market that makes up Weber's *stalhartes Gehäuse*, his "shell as hard as steel." Angelou's poem states: "The free bird thinks of another breeze . . . And the fat worms waiting on a dawn-bright lawn / and he names the sky his own" (Angelou). Who has been allowed to name people, places, things, the processes of writing and revision, theories of rhetoric? Who has named your sky? Who has named your writing, my friends? Who has named your pedagogies? Who has named your ways of judging language, my colleagues of color?

Angelou ends the poem with "The caged bird sings / with a fearful trill / of things unknown / but longed for still . . . for the caged bird / sings of freedom." "A fearful trill" that is "longed for still" that is "freedom." What does it mean for you, my colleagues of color, to sing your freedom in your classrooms, your scholarship, your pedagogies? Is it the freedom from the White naming that is such a thick part of our disciplines' histories? Is it freedom from the White habits of language that cover us all—is it freedom from White language supremacy?

Again, I know, many of you are also doing this work, speaking these truths. I have heard and seen you do so. I have seen White people around you smile at your words, then not take them, turn and go on in their White world, a world that rewards their silence and hesitation. I thank you, my brothers and sisters of color. And I stand up here today asking everyone to listen, to see, to know you as you are, to stop *saying shit* about injustice while doing *jack shit* about it. We are all needed in this project, this fight, this work, these labors. But because most in the room, in our disciplines, are White, I have to speak to them too, many of whom sit on their hands, with love in their hearts, but stillness in their bodies.

Let us have tough compassion for our White colleagues. They don't have the years of anti-White language supremacy training we do. They've been paid off too many times to even recognize the bribes. Many even think they *earned* the bribes they take. It is their wages, or as David Roediger says, it is the "wages of whiteness." They've never lived in the same worlds we have. And it ain't all their fault. But finding fault ain't the point. Change is. Revolution. Reconciliation. Redemption. My colleagues of color, I hope I offer you fuel, words of charcoal and fire to go back to your schools and institutions and make things burn—melt the steel bars of racism and White language supremacy in your places. So please know, I'm speaking *with* you, my colleagues of color. You are with me. You too are speaking, have spoken. Now, let me ask the White folks in the room a question. When I addressed only my colleagues of color just a minute ago, how did you feel? How did it make you feel in your skin to be excluded? How did it feel to be talked *about* and not talked *to*, to be the object of the discussion and not the subject? How does it feel to be the problem?[1] How does it make you feel to be the one in the way of progress, no matter what you have said or what your agendas are, how hard you worked, or how sincere you are? It's unfair, isn't it? You are good people. And yet you are the problem, but you don't want to be. Think about that for a minute. You can be a problem even when you try not to be. Sit and lament in your discomfort and its sources. Search. If our goal is a more socially just world, we don't need more good people. We need good changes, good structures, and good work that make good changes, structures, and people.

Are you uncomfortable yet? Do you feel misunderstood? Are you thinking, he's not talking about me—he's speaking of those other White folks, the less conscious ones. Are you thinking: I know, he ain't talking about me. I'm so woke, I use the word *woke*. But I am talking about all of you. No White person escapes it. And because I am often racially ambiguous, I cannot exclude myself either. In the right light, I can be White—even if I don't get all the privileges that *habitus*, or that set of dispositions, is meant to confer in our society. So, I'm not going to tell you that you are going to be alright. I'm not going to say that you—you White folks in this room—are the special ones. You thinking you're special is the problem. It always has been, because you, and White people just like you who came before you, have had most of the power, decided most of the things, built the steel cage of White language supremacy that we exist in today, both in and outside of the academy—and likely, many of you didn't know you did it. You just thought you were doing language work, doing teaching, doing good work, judging students and their languages in conscientious and kind ways, helping them, preparing them, giving them what was good for them. Just as it is unfair that in our world most indigenous, Latinx, and Black Americans will never get the chance to do what we do, to be teachers, or professors, or researchers, or something else that taps their own potentials because of the racist steel bars set around them, it is equally unfair that you perpetuate racism and White language supremacy not just through your words and actions, but through your body in a place like this or in your classrooms, despite your better intentions. Let me repeat that to compassionately urge you to

595

sit in some discomfort: White people can perpetuate White supremacy by being present. You can perpetuate White language supremacy through the presence of your bodies in places like this.

That feels unfair to say so bluntly, doesn't it? You perpetuate White language supremacy in your classrooms because you are White and stand in front of students, as many White teachers have before you, judging, assessing, grading, professing on the same kinds of language standards, standards that came from your group of people. It's the truth. It ain't fair, but it's the truth. Your body perpetuates racism, just as Black bodies attract unwarranted police aggression by being Black. Neither dynamic is preferred, neither is right, but that's the shit—the steel cage—we're in. The sooner we can accept this fact, the sooner we can get to cutting the bars.

Now, I'm not saying you need to leave. Far from it. We need you, my White colleagues. This is the elephant in the room. It's big and white and obscures everyone's view. And we all need to see it in order to see around it. And it gets in the way of understanding our practices of language as a weapon that we use against our students.

What does any of this have to do with answering the question: How do we language so people stop killing each other? I'm trying to set up the problem of the conditions of White language supremacy, not just in our society and schools, but in our own minds, in our habits of mind, in our dispositions, our bodies, our *habitus*, in the discursive, bodily, and performative ways we use and judge language (Bourdieu; Inoue, *Antiracist* 42–43). This means many of us can acknowledge White language supremacy as the status quo in our classrooms and society, but not see all of it, and so perpetuate it. I'm trying to explain the conditions in our classrooms that cause your judgments to be weaponized as a White teacher, or even a teacher of color who must take on a White racial *habitus* to have the job you have. It takes conditions of White language supremacy to make our judgments about logic, clarity, organization, and conventions a hand grenade, with the pin pulled. All we have to do is give them to another and let go of the hammer. These judgments, these standards, seem like they're just about language, just about communication, just about preparation for the future, just about good critical thinking and communicating. Here's a hint: When we start qualifying our ideas with the word *just*, we are trying to convince ourselves of the lies we are telling. We are trying to convince ourselves of a diminished sense of the power and significance of rhetoric, of words, of language.

So, back to my title. It comes from Mary Rose O'Reilley's invocation of Ihab Hassan's question.[2] Hassan was an Arab American literary theorist, born in Egypt, which I believe made his asking of the question quite real, not figurative or imaginative. O'Reilley's short 1989 article in which she offers the question is a kind of rumination on her teaching life to that point, which began in the 1960s. So how do we language so people stop killing each other? The practices of languaging are fundamentally practices of judging. What is reading rhetorically or considering the rhetorical situation for a writer or speaker, if not a series of judgments? In a world of police brutality against Black and Brown people in the US, of border walls and regressive and harmful immigration policies that traumatize and separate children from parents, of increasing violence against Muslims and LGBTQIA, of women losing their rights to control their own bodies, of overt White supremacy on US streets, of mass shootings in schools, of the conscious poisoning of Black and Brown people's communities, of a complete disregard for indigenous people's rights to their lands and cultures, of blatant refusals to be compassionate to the hundreds of thousands of refugees around the world, where do we really think this violence, discord, and killing starts? What are the natures of the ecologies in which some people find it necessary to oppress or kill others who are different from them, who identify or think or speak or worship or love differently than them? All of these decisions are made by judging others by our own standards and inevitably finding others wanting, deficient. People who judge in these ways lack practices of problematizing their own existential situations and lack experience sitting in the discomfort that problematizing brings. They lack an ability to sit with paradox, guilt, pain, and blame and make something else out of it all.

Again, let me compassionately urge you to sit in discomfort: If you use a single standard to grade your students' languaging, you engage in racism. You actively promote White language supremacy, which is the handmaiden to White bias in the world, the kind that kills Black men on the streets by the hands of the police through profiling and good ol' fashion prejudice.

So, how do we, English and literacy teachers, judge language so people stop killing each other? I have argued that labor-based grading contracts explicitly address in writing classrooms the problem of grading locally diverse students (*Antiracist; Labor-Based*), the paradox of teachers who are by necessity steeped in a White racial *habitus*, steeped in white language bias, while many of their students are not—a White racial *habitus* that if you are White you cannot fully see, hear, or feel (the social world has trained you not to), yet it is the source of your privileges, likely part of the reason you are in front of the class in the first place. If we can confront such paradoxes in our judgments of language, in our *habitus*, then maybe some of the killing may stop. But first, we have to painfully reconcile our habits of judgment, and that means painfully reconciling the paradox between ourselves and our actions. As Bourdieu's term *habitus* makes clear, one's judgment is not simply one's own individual judgment of something. It is never simply an individual practice. It is consubstantial, interconnected, to the social world we live in.

As many of you know, in Freire's *Pedagogy of the Oppressed*, problem-posing education moves through a process of listening to the community outside of the classroom, identifying problems or issues, and then dialoguing with student participants using codes, or cultural artifacts that embody language, such as media, newspapers, articles, TV shows, movies, plays, and so forth that represent many sides of the problem or issue (Shor 38), that reveal the problem as paradoxes. From these codes, participants again listen carefully to them in order to describe what they see, hear, and feel, offering their own experiences that relate to those codes, questioning the codes, and, of course, moving to articulate things to do as a response (Shor 39; Brown 40–41). This means that problem posing is an ongoing process of interrogating the paradox of judgment, how we see, hear, or feel, how we language the world into existence, how we are simultaneously right and wrong, and how that languaging makes and unmakes us simultaneously.

Put another way: Our personal choices and judgments of our students are both personal and a part of larger social and disciplinary structures that also form the boundaries within which we act and judge. Raymond Williams describes this dynamic as simultaneously a "setting of limits" and an "exertion of pressures" in a particular direction (87). So part of being a woke writing teacher, then, is a constant posing of problems about my own existential writing assessment situation, a continual articulating of paradoxes in my judgment that complicate how I make judgments, how I read and make meaning of the symbols my students give me and that I give back to them, how White language supremacy places limits and pressures on me, despite my efforts to counter such things, just as they do my students. So to see such paradoxes in how we judge is to see through the natural, or to see things that are natural as paradoxes, thus not natural at all, but contrived by determined systems and choices (Villanueva, *Bootstraps* 54). And in our classrooms, journals, committee rooms, and writing standards, what do you think the natural is? What have you left unquestioned about your ways of judging language or students? Do you think that White racial *habitus*, the historical White language biases in our disciplines and lives, have affected these places, or the building of something such as the "Framework for Success in Postsecondary Writing"? Or your own pedagogies? Or your own ways of judging student writing, what you see, and can see, as clear, effective, and compelling? Do you think you're special, immune to the biases?

Let's look at one sacred cow in our discipline, "Framework for Success in Postsecondary Writing." What do you think the habit of mind that the Framework calls "metacognition" (5) is and looks like in students in your classroom? How do you evaluate it or grade it? Where did you get your ideas? Think of two or three writers or texts that have markers of such a habit of mind, perhaps ones you might show as examples of such a practice. Where did those writers and texts get their habits from, their dispositions to do this exemplary work? How might you characterize those writers or their texts' performative, bodily, and discursive dispositions? Did they magically escape the White biases in their worlds or educations? Were they the exceptions? Are they special?

What I like about the Framework is its de-emphasis on hierarchy and ranking performances that would fall within any given habit of mind. But is that how departments and programs use the Framework? Do they use it to dismantle hierarchies within student social formations? Or is it just a pedagogy and not an assessment philosophy, not a philosophy that structures the way you judge and grade writing in your classrooms, the way you dole out opportunity? Do you still have a standard next to the Framework? Is the Framework being used as a method to get students to write White, but not used to attend to an ever-widening universe of reflective discourses? But White language supremacy has crafted the Framework in more insidious ways. This makes the framework's presence still dangerous if we don't see it for what it is. As I'm sure most of you know, we live in a deeply segregated society. The *Washington Post*'s May 10, 2018, story shows maps from demographic data, illustrating just how segregated by race we are. Here's the city we are currently in.[3] The red dots are White residents, the blue are Black residents. The downtown area where the three rivers converge is a White center of commerce and tourism, the business district, the heart of a White supremacy. That's where we are, the place where they make the steel bars. Let's not forget that. And when you go to dinner tonight, or as you move from session to session, notice who serves you. Who picks up after you, or fills water containers in this White center? How are we not in this "steel city" in a steel cage of White supremacy?

So the twenty-three good, smart members of the team that created the Framework were mostly White and were produced by such a segregated society. Let me dramatize this for you. Here's the Framework's task force.

Where do you think these folks learned their languaging? Who do you think most or all of their friends were in school? What schools do you think they went to? Now, I don't know the answers to these questions for these individuals, but I do know the patterns in the US, which they cannot escape. If you're White, you kick it with White people. If you're Black, you kick it with other Black people, but you may work with White people. It may seem melodramatic to show all these White faces when I could have just told you that eighteen or nineteen of the members of the Framework's task force were White. It may appear that I'm pointing fingers at individuals unnecessarily. Calling out people for things they do not control. If you think that, you are missing the point. You are feeling your White fragility.

I ask you compassionately: notice your own White fragility. The point is the inevitable and embodied Whiteness. It can be very visceral, thick in the air, for us people of color. I need you to feel how Whiteness in good-hearted, smart people, like these folks, who do great work, can fill a room with their Whiteness to the point that the one or two people of color in the room can feel suffocated. I want you to feel how a good group of folks like this can silence the few bodies of color in the room, never examine their own White habits of judgment, and then canonize those White habits as simply habits of everyone's mind. I want you to see how this steel bar is installed in the cage of White language supremacy that imprisons us all.

But there's more. White language supremacy also looks like this. The four authors of the article in *College English* (Peggy O'Neill, Linda Adler-Kassner, Anne M. Hall, and Cathy Fleischer) that explains the process and the Framework were all White women. To the leaders of the task force's credit, who are the authors of this article, they point to a place one can find all the task force members and their bios, a website.[4] The paradox in this is that O'Neill, Adler-Kassner, Hall, and Fleischer do not control their Whiteness. But they do control how they deploy it, how they make it visible, and the privileges of leadership it conveys to them. This is not to say they have not worked hard, or deserve credit for their work, or even that the work they did isn't good work. It is to say that problematizing their own Whiteness should reveal this kind of painful paradox: that good work, done by conscientious White people, can still kill people of color by codifying White language supremacy. The presence of their White bodies perpetuates historical racial injustices. Damned if they do, damned if they don't. There are no easy ways out of the steel cage of White language supremacy.

How do we check this in our lives? One key practice in problematizing is *deep listening*—it anchors everything in the process. We cannot problem-pose without deep listening. Krista Ratcliffe named a similar cross-cultural practice, "rhetorical listening" (26), as a response to Jacqueline Jones Royster's CCCC Chair's address. Royster asks us: "How do we listen," how do we do more than "talk back," how do we exchange, negotiate, and collaboratively create perspectives, meaning, and understanding (38)? Ratcliffe offers a way that centers on acknowledging Whiteness and listening deeply to others, or "consciously standing under discourses that surround us and others . . . letting [them] wash over, through, and around us and then letting them lie there to inform our politics and ethics" (28). These listening practices are important, but let's not forget that Ratcliffe is a critical, White academic who realizes *she* must listen likely because that is not the habit of language most White academics practice, particularly White males. The "we" and "us" is White teachers and academics. The other side to this practice is the body of color talking, being heard by the White listener—Royster being listened to by Ratcliffe.

Ten years after O'Reilley wrote the article from which I derived my title, she revisited her teaching in *Radical Presence: Teaching as Contemplative Practice*. In that book, she describes the practices of deep listening in her classroom, concluding that "[o]ne can, I think, listen someone into existence, encourage a stronger self to emerge or a new talent to flourish" (21). It's attractive, isn't it? But wait. Doesn't it reenact a whitely stance of control and agency? Who's doing the making here? *The teacher listens* her students into existence? It's Pygmalion all over again. It's the Whitely Rex Harrison languaging Audrey Hepburn into existence when we know, ain't nothin' wrong with Audrey but Rex's judgments. This isn't quite what Royster had in mind, I think.

Thich Nhat Hanh, the Vietnamese monk and long-time social justice activist, bases most of his teachings about peace on a kind of deep listening, or as I prefer to think of it, a *deep and mindful attending* to the other in our presence. This reveals "listening" as limited, as it is only an auditory metaphor. Attending is more holistic and embodied. Hanh reminds us that every person has a "suchness" that can be understood and attended to, on the other's terms. He explains, "If we want to live in peace and happiness with a person, we have to see the suchness of that person" (68). We have to understand others without trying to control or change them. In fact, love and understanding, or deep attending, are the same for Hanh, and to practice it, one must ask the other for help. We cannot do it alone. I am taken particularly by his suggested practice. Hanh says, "sit close to the one you love, hold his or her hand, and ask, 'do I understand you enough? Or am

I making you suffer? Please tell me so that I can learn to love you properly'" (80). Imagine this kind of assessment practice in your classrooms with your students. Assessment might be a problem-posing process that continually attends to questions such as: "Do I understand you enough? Am I making you suffer? Please help me to read your languaging properly."

What strikes me about deep attending is its compassion and its potential for growing the patience in all of us that is needed when we confront students who are different from us, who do not look or sound or come from the same places as we do. Deep attending also opens space for those of us who have only been listening but would like to speak, and be heard. I'm sure all of us would say that we listen or attend to our students carefully. But Royster asks all of us:

> [W]hen do we listen? How do we listen? How do we demonstrate that we honor and respect the person talking and what that person is saying, or what the person might say if we valued someone other than ourselves having a turn to speak? How do we translate listening into language and action, into the creation of an appropriate response? How do we really "talk back" rather than talk also? The goal is not, "You talk, I talk." The goal is better practices so that we can exchange perspectives, negotiate meaning, and create understanding with the intent of being in a good position to cooperate, when, like now, cooperation is absolutely necessary. (38)

I reiterate and reframe Royster's questions: *How* are you attending, exactly? What are the markers of your compassionate attending? How is your attending a practice of judgment that your students can notice? How is it a practice that recognizes their existence without overly controlling them?

I hope you can hear the structural in what I'm asking. How do we language so people stop killing each other?

Part of my answer is that some must be silent, leave enough space between utterances, so that problematizing can happen. I'm not saying we have to change our perspectives, soften our hearts. Our hearts are not the problem. In fact, I'm actually saying the opposite, that we cannot change our biases in judging so easily, and that your perspectives that you've cultivated over your lifetime are not the key to making a more just society, classroom, pedagogy, or grading practice. The key is changing the structures, cutting the steel bars, altering the ecology, in which your biases function in your classrooms and communities. I'm saying, we must change the way power moves through White racial biases, through standards of English that make White language supremacy. We must stop justifying White standards of writing as a necessary evil. Evil in any form is never necessary. We must stop saying that we have to teach this dominant English because it's what students need to succeed tomorrow. They only need it because we keep teaching it!

***

I'd like to end with a parable.

You are tired and starving, on the verge of death, needing any kind of sustenance, walking on a road in a land of plenty. You've been walking for weeks. You come upon a house, with a lush garden next to it, full of fruits and vegetables. You knock on the door. A man answers, and you beg, "Please, can you help me? I'm dying. I need some food, anything you can spare. Please, help me. I'll tend your garden if you'll share the food with me."

Now, the man has lived in this house his whole life. He inherited it and the beautiful garden from his parents. In fact, he made it bigger and more fruitful. He worked hard at it and in it. He has so much now that he sells the excess. His house has become bigger. The man has lived his entire life with this beautiful, fruitful garden, tending it carefully, working hard in it. It is his, even though one cannot really own earth, or its products. Who can really own earth? It was here before the man and will be here after he is dead. But the illusion of possession is there because the garden has always been there for him, always served him, and he has watered it with the language of possession. *This is my garden*, he says. I tend this garden of mine. I own this garden. I have worked this garden. It grows for me. Its bounty is mine. So when you come to his door, and ask for his food, he feels uncomfortable— he's never really had to share. In fact, he kinda feels that sharing may not help you. How will you know the benefits of laboring in your own garden? Charity won't get you your own garden, will it? So he says, "I'm sorry. I really do understand how hungry you are, how tired, how much you need food to live right now, but I don't feel comfortable giving you my food. I've never done that before. I want to help you *in the right way*, and that takes time for me to know. It will take time, so please, come back tomorrow, and maybe then I'll be ready to share my food."

What a sense of blind privilege it is to tell a starving person at your doorstep, in your house of plenty, in a land of abundance, that you just don't *yet* feel comfortable enough to share your food. It isn't just that in the parable the man's privilege allows him to make a decision based on his own selfish sense of comfort, his selfish sense of readiness, or that he feels he knows the best timetable for helping the other in his midst. The deeper, more galling problem here is that his comfort comes at the cost of your pain. The deeper problem is that you, the starving person at the doorstep, cannot wait—you are fucking starving! And the man with plenty asks you from his privileged position to wait, come back tomorrow. Please, my comfort and readiness to give, he implicitly says, is more important than your safety or health.

Now, my fable isn't meant to offer a lesson in helping others, or being compassionate—although one could hear those lessons. It is meant to be an allegory for how we make decisions as writing and literacy teachers, particularly about classroom grading and assessment practices, about how we use a particular dominant, White standard. It is about our decisions to continue to reinforce White language supremacy in our classrooms that give many of us power over students, while we tell our students how much right they have to their languages, how much we care and embrace the diversity of languages that they bring and use, yet we tacitly contradict these messages by asking them to wait just a bit longer for us to feel comfortable enough to change our classroom practices, to change the way standards work against them, despite the linguistic truths we know about the communicative effectiveness of all languages.

We delude ourselves by saying that it's what others less enlightened than us will judge their languaging on, so we must use these dominant standards today, thinking that our soft words and kind eyes and good intentions will salve the pain and harm and erasure that the use of a single, universal standard inflicts. We act as if we have no power whatsoever in changing such language judgment practices—we, language teachers and researchers, have no power with language?

Our decisions NOT to build more radical, antiracist, and anti-White language supremacist assessment ecologies in our classrooms often are based on our own selfish sense of comfort, selfish sense of not being ready to share our gardens. I cannot tell you how many times I've heard writing teachers, ones who are conscientious, critical, and experienced, say to me, "I'm just not ready . . . I don't feel comfortable yet, maybe next semester." What a blind sense of privilege! What a lack of compassion—if compassion is more than feeling empathy, but a doing of something, a suffering *with* others. What a lack of asking the deep attending and problematizing question: Am I causing you to suffer? Many of your students of color, your students who do not embody enough of the White habits of language that make up your standards, stand at your classroom doors and die for your comfort, die as they wait for you to be ready.

I realize that it may sound as if I'm being overly dramatic and using a flawed metaphor. Our students of color, for instance, are not linguistically starving. We need nothing given to us to be effective language users. We already are and always have been. We are Eliza Doolittle speaking well. Food is not a metaphor for language in my parable. It is a metaphor for power. People of color have never controlled the standards in schools or disciplines. Standards of English have never come from us, unless we allowed ourselves to be colonized—and let's not fool ourselves, all teachers of color are colonized to some degree. Even for those who resist that colonizing, being colonized is how you get to be teachers of color, that's why *color* is added to the term. It's a shitty compromise to make, to sacrifice some bit of your body, to cut out a part of your tongue, to let some of your soul wink out of existence, in order to live, prosper, or make change in the world for those who come after you.

So, don't get hung up on the nuances of the allegory. Food in the story is not language. It is power, the power to judge and make or control standards. The point is a Marxian one. Who owns the means of opportunity production in the classroom? We all may hate it, but most of us are still required to give grades, and those are the keys to opportunity. Just because our students of color are linguistically rich does not mean that by default those riches can be exchanged in your classroom economies if the economy is not set up to accept those riches. Some of your students may be starving with pockets and purses full of useless coins in the bustling market of your classrooms, because you don't accept their money, even though you tell them how valuable it is. Hold on to it, you say. It's your identity, your heritage. But everywhere we go, those heritage coins ain't worth shit in the White economies of the academy and marketplace. So, you tell them, you gotta exchange that currency, code-switch. But we tell you, I don't have access to the money changer, and he charges interest that I cannot afford—there is value lost in the exchange. And you say, try anyway.

Am I being overly dramatic with this parable, with this talk? Are your students really dying in front of you? Do we students, teachers, and academics of color really cut out a fleshy chunk of our tongues just to have the pleasure of pretending to be the equal of Whites in the academy? Do the vast majority of you do harm by using a single standard of English to assess and grade in your classrooms, all the while patting yourselves on the backs for how much good you are doing, how much you're helping your poor students of color? Does your dominant, White set of linguistic habits of language kill people? Is your body in the places you circulate part of the problem of White language supremacy? This is the problematizing we must all do.

Thank you and peace to you.

NOTES

1. W. E. B. Du Bois opens *The Souls of Black Folk* with: "Between me and the other world there is ever an unasked question: unasked by some through feelings of delicacy; by others through the difficulty of rightly framing it. To the real question, How does it feel to be a problem?" (1–2).

2. O'Reilley recalls Hassan's question this way: "Is it possible to teach English so that people stop killing each other?" ("Exterminate" 143).

3. On the web page of the article, a reader can enter any city in the US and see a map of its demographics. Because the map is in color, it is not reproducible in this journal, but one can see such a map on the *Washington Post's* article page (https://wapo.st/2KyC4jA?tid=ss_tw).

4. The Framework's task force members and their biographies are listed on the CWPA Website at http://wpacouncil.org/framework/taskforce.

WORKS CITED

Alexander, Michelle. *The New Jim Crow: Mass Incarceration in the Age of Colorblindness*. New Press, 2012.

Angelou, Maya. "Caged Bird." *Poetry Foundation*, 1983, https://www.poetryfoundation.org/poems/48989/caged-bird. Accessed 25 Aug. 2018.

Bourdieu, Pierre. *Distinction: A Social Critique of the Judgement of Taste*. Harvard UP, 1984.

Brown, Philip Melvin. "An Examination of Freire's Problem-Posing Pedagogy: The Experiences of Three Middle School Teachers Implementing Theory into Practice." Diss., U of Georgia, 2013.

Du Bois, W. E. B. *The Souls of Black Folk*. 1903. Bantam Books, 1989.

Dunbar, Paul Laurence. "Sympathy." 1899. *Poets.org*. Accessed 25 Aug. 2018.

"Framework for Success in Postsecondary Writing." Council of Writing Program Administrators, National Council of Teachers of English, and the National Writing Project, 2011. http://wpacouncil.org/framework.

Freire, Paulo. *Pedagogy of the Oppressed*. 30th anniversary ed., translated by Myra Bergman Ramos, Continuum, 2000.

Hanh, Thich Nhat. *Peace Is Every Step: The Path of Mindfulness in Everyday Life*. Bantam, 1991.

"Incarceration." The Sentencing Project, 2017. https://www.sentencingproject.org/issues/incarceration/. Accessed 28 Aug 2018.

Inoue, Asao B. *Antiracist Writing Assessment Ecologies: Teaching and Assessing Writing for a Socially Just Future*. WAC Clearinghouse and Parlor P, 2015.

———. *Labor-Based Grading Contracts: Building Equity and Inclusion in the Compassionate Writing Classroom*. WAC Clearinghouse and UP of Colorado, 2019.

O'Neill, Peggy, et al. "Creating the 'Framework for Success in Postsecondary Writing." *College English*, vol. 74, no. 6, 2012, pp. 520–24.

O'Reilley, Mary Rose. "'Exterminate . . . the Brutes'—And Other Things That Go Wrong In Student-Centered Teaching." *College English*, vol. 51, no. 2, 1989, pp. 142–46.

———. *Radical Presence: Teaching as Contemplative Practice*. Boynton/ Cook, 1998. Ratcliffe, Krista. *Rhetorical Listening: Identification, Gender, and Whiteness*. Southern Illinois UP, 2005.

Roediger, David. *The Wages of Whiteness: Race and the Making of the American Working Class*. Rev. ed., Verso, 1991.

Royster, Jacqueline Jones. "When the First Voice You Hear Is Not Your Own." *College Composition and Communication*, vol. 47, no. 1, 1996, pp. 29–40.

Shor, Ira. *Empowering Education: Critical Teaching for Social Change*. U of Chicago P, 1992.

Takaki, Ronald. *Iron Cages: Race and Culture in 19th-Century America*. Rev. ed., Oxford UP, 2000.

Villanueva, Victor, Jr. *Bootstraps: From an American Academic of Color*. National

———. Email message. Received 10 Dec. 2018.

Weber, Max. *The Protestant Ethic and the "Spirit" of Capitalism and Other Writings*. 1905. Penguin Books, 2002.

"Who's in Prison in America." Open-Invest, 21 Feb. 2018. https://www.openinvest.co/blog/statistics-prison-america/. Accessed 28 Aug. 2018.

Williams, Aaron, and Armand Emamdjomeh. "America Is More Diverse than Ever—But Still Segregated." *Washington Post*, 2 May 2018. https://wapo.st/2KyC4jA?tid=ss_tw. Accessed 10 May 2018.

Williams, Raymond. *Marxism and Literature*. Oxford UP, 1977.

Avoiding the Difference Fixation
Identity Categories, Markers of Difference, and the Teaching of Writing

STEPHANIE L. KERSCHBAUM

In order to show difference as a dynamic, relational, and emergent construct, this article introduces "markers of difference," rhetorical cues that signal the presence of difference between one or more interlocutors, and suggests practical means by which teachers can engage this concept to improve their teaching practice.

When I was about a year old, my parents noticed that I did not react to loud noises, so they sat me in my high chair, stood behind me, and banged on some pots and pans. I didn't so much as flinch. In that moment, their interpretation of me as "a really laid-back baby" became "She's deaf, and that's why she doesn't get upset when Johnny yells or the dog barks." That re-categorization created new ways for them to make sense of my behavior: it is not that my parents didn't connect with me prior to learning that I have a profound hearing loss in both ears, but that the frame through which they made sense of me changed. Similarly, my own relationship to my disability has shifted, and continues to shift, over time and across contexts. Deafness does not exist for me as some concrete fact of my life with an

Reprinted from *College Composition and Communication* 63.4 (June 2012): 616–644. Used with permission.

absolute meaning that I can readily define for readers here and now in this article. Deafness takes on different meanings in a variety of institutional and social contexts, mediated through human relationships and technologies of all kinds. My deafness is very different from my friend Tom's deafness, and the two of us experience deafness very differently than does my grandmother. Yet even these comparisons are flawed because none of the three of us has an entirely stable "sort" of deafness whose meaning transcends the particular interactional contexts in which we find ourselves. Although I can describe to *College Composition and Communication* readers my deafness, explain ways that Tom, myself, and my grandmother embody different kinds of deafness, and portray some of the ways that each of us addresses our deafness in our daily lives, such explanations are only partial and passing because deafness, like any other identity category, is to be understood both through the contexts in which we communicate and act *and* by our embodiments of it. This discussion of deafness illustrates a conundrum that exists across studies of difference in writing research: even as scholars of difference frame identity as, in Helen Fox's words, "multiple, or layered, or ever changing" (256), there is little understanding of how such understandings are constructed and negotiated on a moment-by-moment basis. In other words, how is knowledge about groups (e.g., deaf people) brought to bear on interactions with individual people affiliated with those groups (such as myself, Tom, or my grandmother)? Or, considered from another direction, how does knowledge gleaned through interaction with me, Tom, or my grandmother contribute to a collective awareness about deaf people? These questions point to concerns about essentialism and determinism as well as about how individual identities intersect with broader cultural categories. As Fox notes, descriptions of cultural groups are often seen as "'traditional' or unchanging, rather than as systems that blend and shift in response to pressures from the environment and their own members' ingenuity" (259). Such framing of cultural groups in relatively static terms highlights one of the challenges faced by contemporary writing studies scholars: that of using discourses about difference to attend simultaneously to broad group characteristics and to instability within categories. To address this issue, many writing researchers have described their own complex relationships to language, identity, and knowledge (e.g., hooks; Okawa; Villanueva; Young). However, writing teachers—particularly those new to teaching—frequently express anxiety about how to bring this nuance and richness into their classroom practices. In order to more fully respond to questions about how awareness of broad categories of identity matter when someone stands in front of a classroom or talks one-on-one with a student or responds to an email, what is needed is a flexible means for examining and re-examining the interplay between identity categories and the communicative performances in which those categories become meaningful.

These questions have long been central to examinations of difference and diversity and their implications for writing pedagogy. This work ranges broadly, as some researchers perform close studies of individual writers or groups of writers in order to help teachers understand the work these writers are doing (e.g., Cushman; Dunn; Lieber; Morris; Sohn) while other scholars build intersectional analyses of how particular category memberships are complexly articulated within writers' lives and discourses (e.g., Alexander; Fernheimer; LeCourt, *Identity* and "Performing"; Royster). In yet another vein of research, scholars examine the means by which individuals communicate across linguistic and cultural differences inside and outside of the classroom (e.g., Flower; Flower, Long, and Higgins; Glazier; Lyons). Taken together, this research on writers, populations, groups, and discourses offers sensitive, nuanced, and detailed portraits of difference. However, despite the many contributions made by this body of scholarship, it still presents some difficulties for teachers working to develop classroom environments sensitive to the ever-changing terrain of difference. The scholarship on difference described here urges teachers to develop deep knowledge bases about the writers they are likely to encounter in two primary ways: by becoming more aware of differences that have received little attention and by developing new insights on familiar differences. But at the same time that this research focuses teachers' attention in particular ways, new points of analysis and inquiry are always emerging as significant. How is attention to new points of difference cultivated against a backdrop of traditional identity categories? Discourses of difference that fix individual writers or groups of writers in time and space can frustrate, rather than enable, the development of pedagogical resources that attend simultaneously to broad conceptual categories *and* to the highly individual encounters that occur within writing classrooms on a daily basis.

In this essay, my aim is to show how a specific focus on interactionally emergent and rhetorically negotiated elements of a communicative situation can enrich the study of difference in composition research. I develop this argument by first identifying two strategies used by writing researchers when forwarding new understandings of difference. I then demonstrate that these strategies take categories as a central unit of analysis and interpretation. This overemphasis on categories, I argue, leads to the problem of fixing difference in order to study it. Thus, the phrase *fixing difference* here refers both to the process of treating difference as a stable thing or property that can be identified and fixed in place as well as to attempts to fix, that is, improve, the way difference is understood. To move away from this difference fixation, I build on writing scholarship that takes as a central focus the articulation of change and argue that teachers and researchers should orient to difference as rhetorically negotiated through a process named here as *marking difference*. When marking difference rhetors and audiences alike display and respond to markers of difference, those rhetorical cues that signal the presence of difference between two or more participants. To illustrate this perspective on difference, I then analyze a brief encounter between two students performing peer review in a first-year writing classroom, showing that even in the smallest moments of communication markers of difference make visible the dynamism, relationality, and emergence of difference. Attention to marking in conjunction with more familiar and often unconscious categorization processes can help teachers and researchers mediate between broad conceptual tools for talking about difference and the unique qualities of individual moments of interaction.

Perspectives on difference that focus on categories as a means for identifying and unpacking difference exhibit an impulse toward fixity that can constrain their usefulness for negotiating the shifting terrain of difference in writing classrooms. This fixity is visible in two strategies for addressing difference and diversity: taxonomizing difference and redefining categories. In taxonomizing difference, writing researchers seek to develop more precise language for identifying types of writers and students. Through these careful classification schemes, scholars work to avoid over-simplistic portrayals of students by attending to intersections among various identity categories both within individuals (e.g., De and Gregory) and between groups (e.g., Gonsalves) or by offering more precise definitions of the categories used to identify writers (e.g., Valdes; Harklau, Losey, and Siegal). Scholarship in this vein urges teachers to attend to a constellation of details about a student in order to consider that student not solely as, say, white, or German American, or deaf, but as the embodiment of a complex set of identifications that must be considered together, rather than independent from one another. The strength of such approaches is that they broaden the range of interpretive possibilities. Rather than allowing any given classification to determine a teacher's assessment of a student, the rich confluence of multiple factors holds open more potential directions for an interaction. However, in its emphasis on categorical means for identifying students, taxonomizing difference focuses teachers' attention from the outset on particular identity categories, and this focusing can make it difficult for teachers to identify other relevant, but not-already-taxonomized, factors that influence a communicative situation.

A second strategy reflected in writing studies research alongside considerations of intersecting categories is that of redefining categories. Within this approach, scholars complicate traditional understandings of categorical identifications such as race, ethnicity, gender, socioeconomic class, disability, and religion, as well as of categories developed within writing studies (e.g., ESL writers, basic writers). The categorical redefinitions performed by this scholarship, such as in Christina Ortmeier-Hooper's "English May Be My Second Language, but I'm not ESL," have helped us resist essentialism by showing the nuance and variety within any given grouping of writers. Yet, the central means offered to instructors for developing their own teaching and being responsive to their students is that of performing such categorical redefinition themselves by identifying categories of students and drawing on research and personal experience to continually reshape them. It is important for teachers to avoid reifying categories of students, but practices of categorical redefinition can also have the unfortunate consequence of maintaining attention to categories that may or may not be central to a given classroom interaction. The challenge lies in the inability of a stable set of fixed labels circulating within composition studies to adequately account for and describe the changes that are always occurring.

Both taxonomizing difference and redefining categories have enhanced teaching with and across differences, but they tend toward fixity by freezing particular subjects, details, and interpretations within the research literature. Yet, this scholarship, which creates a more precise language for difference and offers nuanced portrayals of various identity categories, is not motivated by a desire to freeze differences in time and space, but instead, by a desire to open up new interpretive ground and broaden the range of potential meanings available within categorical frames. Indeed, writing researchers have taken numerous approaches to documenting ongoing transformations of meaning, in many cases influenced by ethnographic research methods and methodologies (Lillis) and an explosion of writing research looking at writing in context (Juzwik et al.). Key to these efforts is increased attention to flexibility and change. In *Rhetorical Listening*, for example, Krista Ratcliffe challenges the logic of whiteness, which she defines as "a trope that fosters stasis by resisting and denying differences" (114), by urging readers to employ a variety of means of rhetorical listening to resist such fixity. Such listening is always situational, she notes, always in the moment. This emphasis on situatedness is also evident in performance-based analyses that focus on how individuals artfully use particular resources at particular times for particular audiences in order to create specific identities (Gonçalves). Other writing scholars use revision as a trope for understanding the creation and recreation of identity through writing (Herrington and Curtis; Jung; Lee; Young). In literacy studies, researchers such as Suzanne Rumsey and Gail Hawisher and Cynthia Selfe have examined how multimodal forms of literacy (quilting and online social networks) reveal identity building and literacy transmission as unpredictable and dynamic processes. Finally, some scholars have begun to incorporate *time* as a dimension for interpreting classroom activity in order to describe identity construction as an ongoing process occurring across different time scales (see Lemke) in classrooms and through writing (Wortham, *Learning*; Burgess and Ivanič).

Despite the acknowledgments made within this research about continual change, resistance, and transformation through language, there remains a gap in writing studies with regard to the resources made available for writing teachers wishing to address difference. What means does the scholarship offer for doing this work without reducing unique, individual interactions to a broad category or a particular representation in the research literature? These reductions happen in spite of teachers' best efforts and are in many ways part of human behavior and sense making. As sociologist and gender theorist Cecilia Ridgeway explains in *Framed by Gender*, "social relations are situations in which people form a sense of who they are in the situation and, therefore, how they should behave, by considering themselves in relation to whom they assume others are in that situation" (6–7). But what details people notice, and consequently use, to define themselves and others are affected by a wide variety of factors, from personal and professional experiences to academic learning. This perspective is reinforced by anthropologist Renato Rosaldo as he notes that "[a]ll interpretations are provisional; they are made by positioned subjects *who are prepared to know certain things and not others*" (8, emphasis added). A few examples from our scholarly literature can help illustrate the danger of presuming understanding as well as the challenges of keeping meaning indeterminate. In *Authoring*, Janis and Richard Haswell describe the results of a study in which they asked sixty-four readers to respond to two student texts, provide suggestions for revision, and discuss their impressions of the students' gender. They found that the respondents drew upon broad gender stereotypes to interpret these texts and offer suggestions for revision. Haswell and Haswell's results dovetail with Ridgeway's work on the persistence of gender inequality. Ridgeway shows how individuals negotiate new situations by framing them with cultural beliefs—that is, stereotypes—about gender that consequently reinforce these beliefs and maintain gender inequality.

Identifying categories and using shared cultural beliefs to interpret those categories is not the only way student writing and experiences are fixed in time and space, however. A second problematic strategy is that of over-identification. Educational researchers Mary Louise Gomez, Anne Burda Walker, and Michelle L. Page describe processes of over-identification that occurred between student teachers and their students. The student teachers articulated connections between themselves and their students, but in making these connections they also ignored significant differences between themselves and their students. Recognizing a similar phenomenon in her own work with working-class students, Donna LeCourt acknowledges how hard it is to avoid assuming or presuming to "know" her students ("Performing"), a question Julie Lindquist takes up at length in "What's the Trouble with Knowing Students? Only Time Will Tell." These are key challenges faced by teachers and researchers who pay close attention to difference.

The current focus on difference in writing studies has prepared teachers to attend to particular details and has reinforced the need to continually become aware of new ones—that is, to hold open interpretations rather than presume understanding—but it has not yet fully articulated *how* such new interpretations might be built. The remainder of this article, then, suggests a new approach to difference in which teachers and researchers can practice a kind of attention to difference that cultivates awareness of new details, provides opportunity to interpret and re-interpret those details, and contextualizes them within specific moments of writing, teaching, and learning. This perspective complements processes of category identification and offers a means for mediating between category recognition and individual interaction.

FROM FIXING TO MARKING: READING DIFFERENCE INTERACTIONALLY

Categorical identification is integral to the human sense-making processes, but recognizing any given identity category (or categories) does not necessarily enable an understanding of what that identification means.

In some cases, categorical recognition can constrain individuals' openness to various interpretive possibilities. In other words, identifying that I am deaf, am female, grew up in suburban Ohio, and wear glasses does not translate neatly into a pedagogical or interactional course of action. Moreover, knowledge about what it means to be deaf, for example, is frequently challenged by people who simultaneously fit and do not fit stereotypical or broadly circulating notions of deafness. To address this gap between categorical knowledge and interactional processes, composition studies needs a way of considering difference in the classroom that enables attention to the ways that differences take shape within and through the interactions that surround writing. From such a perspective, difference, rather than being presentable through categories and remaining relatively inert across time and space, is dynamic, relational, and emergent. Composition research cannot approach the study of difference by cataloguing or even predicting all the potential differences that might affect any given situation or set of writers and audiences. So we must learn to act—to listen, as Katherine Schultz and Krista Ratcliffe have argued—as difference itself takes shape when people learn and write in a wide variety of social contexts.

To demonstrate how such an orientation to difference might be built, I perform two closely related theoretical and empirical analyses. First, I draw on the ethical scholarship of Mikhail Bakhtin to articulate an orientation to difference as dynamic, emergent, and relational—three qualities that are not always well represented in talk about difference in writing research. Within that theoretical lens, I develop the concept of markers of difference, contextually embedded rhetorical cues that signal the presence of difference between one or more interlocutors, and suggest that markers of difference can bridge the conceptual gap between knowledge about difference and interactional involvement with difference. Second, I analyze a brief conversation between two students performing peer review in a first-year writing classroom to demonstrate markers of difference in action. A marker-based orientation to difference is crucial for contemporary writing research because when we write and read, we wrestle with not just texts, but with selves. To read and respond to others involves making sense of the locations individuals occupy in relation to others, and doing such work requires a way of asking and answering questions about how people are different from one another and what those differences mean.

In contrast to understanding difference as a thing or object that can be named or described, I define difference as a relation between two individuals that is predicated upon their separateness from one another, or what Bakhtin refers to as noncoincidence in being. This relation is signaled by the display and uptake of markers of difference. Difference-as-relation drives communicative efforts because it is part of a continual interplay between identification and differentiation. This interplay reveals the lived experience of difference as highly dynamic. Categories rarely capture that dynamism because categorical coherence lies in the ability to move across contexts. In addition, categories tend to suppress attention to the agency expressed by individual actors as they display and respond to difference. Thus, I want to shift some emphasis away from the categories and move toward understanding how categories take on meaning within interactions. Marking difference is a rhetorical lens—rhetorical because it emphasizes the relationship between speaker/writer and audience as well as the situated nature of all communicative activity—that acknowledges the important role that identity categories play in interaction. At the same time, markers of difference underscore attention to difference as it is performed during the moment-to-moment vicissitudes of communication.

Because they foreground individual responsibility and the uniqueness of each act of communication, Bakhtin's early ethical writings in *Toward a Philosophy of the Act* and *Art and Answerability* are important to this understanding of difference. What Bakhtin calls the "once-occurrent event of Being" (*Toward* 2) can be understood in terms of the singularity of each rhetorical situation. No two individuals will ever have the same relation to one another as they do to any other individual, and no situation will be exactly like any other current, past, or future situation. Bakhtin's work also foregrounds individual activity, which he describes as "participatory" and "responsible." Individuals have a responsibility, he argues, to make the most of every moment. To accept this responsibility is to maintain an openness to the Other, to keep possibilities open rather than to close them off.

Bakhtin's conceptions of "the once-occurrent event of being" and of responsibility to the Other in communication highlight difference as dynamic, relational, and emergent. Difference is dynamic because meanings shift from moment to moment and are continually evolving. To return to the example of my deafness, when I encounter a student who doesn't realize I'm deaf and asks me about my accent, I am positioned very differently than I am by a student who does realize that I'm deaf and who asks me if I know sign language. In both cases it may be the sound of my voice that marks me as different to these students, but each one takes up that marker in different ways and puts me in a different position to respond.

In turn, as the conversations progress, the first student comes to realize that I'm not a foreigner and that I am deaf (shifting the meaning of the different-sounding voice), and the second student comes to realize that I may embody qualities that differentiate me from their expectations about deaf people. I, in my turn, choose to display particular cues in response— explaining that I'm deaf to the first student and saying aloud, "Yes, I do," to the second while not signing anything—in an attempt to assert to them my own identity claims. In interaction, then, what any one marker means for individual identity and interactional possibility is always shifting. Markers point to that dynamism by highlighting how individuals can deploy different markers to challenge or modify previous ones.

While it is true that categorical definitions and associations change over time, the categories themselves do not reflect the subtle moment-by-moment changes in individuals' impressions of one another that occur in interaction. This is what Bakhtin describes as the "unfinishedness" of being. He writes, "I have to be, for myself, someone who is axiologically yet-to-be, someone who does not coincide with his already existing makeup" (*Art* 13). Every semester when I meet students for the first time, even though this situation is a very familiar one, at the same time, no one semester beginning is identical to other semesters. I confess to once upon a time feeling a secret thrill when students would comment that at first they didn't even realize I was deaf. Now, however, I always assert my deafness. I have learned—from repeated encounters of this sort—my preferred way of managing the situation. I am not the same person I was when I felt that excitement at "passing," and I never seem to answer questions about my deafness the same way twice. I am always yet-to-be, always moving toward a new position or awareness, using different tools and resources for managing my identity in these situations.

In being yet-to-be, individuals are never coincident even with themselves. They do not remain in the same place, they do not carry or display the same differences, and what those differences are and what they mean is always shifting. Part of the reason differences are always shifting is because difference is relational. No two individuals have the same relation to one another, and difference cannot be considered in isolation: it inherently implies a comparison. I am not different by virtue of my deafness any more than a hearing person is "different" because he or she can hear. I am different from other deaf people, and I am different from people who can hear. While many aspects of self and other cannot be fully articulated (or even apprehended by individuals themselves), it is with markers of difference that people create, display, and respond to changes in self and other and the perceived relations between them. To acknowledge individuals' yet-to-be-ness is to maintain an openness to one's own and others' identities and to refuse to take identity markers as fixed.

Following from these principles of dynamism and relationality, difference is emergent. It does not exist outside of the interactional moment but, rather, takes shape as individuals make choices about what to reveal about themselves, what to notice or comment upon—or to not notice or comment upon. In order to communicate across difference, people must always be looking to learn what more they do not know about the Other; they must avoid presuming they can know the Other as a totalized and whole consciousness. It is insulting, for example, when students who have taken basic sign language classes try to sign to me instead of speaking, assuming that sign language is the best way to communicate with me simply because I am deaf. To presume to know me is to close off interactional possibilities rather than to hold them open. Bakhtin describes the assumption of wholeness in terms of moments where people step outside of themselves and enter into ("consummate") the Other (*Art*). But just as students cannot literally enter into my mind and "know" me, total consummation can never occur because it would violate the uniqueness of every moment of being. Indeed, this uniqueness is such that people are never even coincident with themselves: I am always yet-to-be, I am always coming to know who I am. I cannot know every aspect of even my own identity and self. As Bakhtin writes, one's life "finds no rest within itself and never coincides with its given presently existing makeup" (*Art* 15).

Because markers are fleeting, often existing only in a single moment, they demand sensitivity to each moment. The ephemerality of markers helps balance the persistence of categories, which sometimes seem to freeze people in time and space. Difference is not "out there" waiting to be found and identified but is always coming-to-be through the here-and-now of interaction. In the moment of interaction, engaging difference is part of a situated activity during which individuals, both consciously and subconsciously, display markers of difference in order to distinguish between themselves and others. When people decide to use a particular marker, that decision is cast against already-existing ideas of how Others may respond to that marker, and interlocutors choose the markers they hope will best accomplish their interactional and relational goals.

In processes of coming to know the Other and coming to know the self, the relationality of difference comes into sharpest focus: it is only through interaction with others that people are able to apprehend themselves. This awareness, subsequently, shapes their consciousness of the markers to which others are orienting and how they take on meaning. This process is akin to what Bakhtin described as "evaluat[ing] our exterior not for ourselves, but *for* others *through* others" (*Art* 33, emphasis in original). Identities are always in flux, always "yet-to-be," so they are never fully known or knowable entities, and knowledge about self comes only through encounters with others. Encountering others in the here and now gives individuals insight into their own selves. When I meet students who ask about my accent, I am reminded that I sound "different" from many nondeaf speakers when I talk, in a way that I am not when speaking with people who are already familiar with my speaking voice. By situating my own understanding against that of others, I am able to make predictions about how the markers I display will be taken up and responded to. While I cannot completely alter my speaking voice to adapt to a particular situation, many times I do make a concerted effort to address any challenges that may be posed by my voice when I anticipate that someone will have difficulty understanding me. Taken together, these three elements—dynamism, relationality, and emergence—constitute a rhetorical presentation of difference in their emphasis on how individuals call attention to—or suppress—difference as well as how they respond to differences displayed by others.

At this point, it will be helpful to distinguish my use of the word *marker* from another common use: to refer to objects or modes that are marked, such as a marked case in linguistics. The marked case is stressed and set apart from unmarked or otherwise un-emphasized cases. For example, when Ruth Frankenberg talks about whiteness as "a set of cultural practices that are usually unmarked and unnamed" and describes the task of her book as that of "exploring, mapping, and examining the terrain of whiteness" (1), she argues that there are salient features of whiteness that can be identified ("marked") even though they are not currently named and discussed. In this context, people may describe practices of "marking difference" that locate difference against an unstated norm, such as when someone might say that my deafness marks me as different. I do not use the term *marker* in this way. To evoke my deafness as a difference, it must be considered relationally—how does my not hearing (of a particular form) make me different from a specific interlocutor? Is this difference taken up by either participant? And if so, how does this marker of difference—whatever it is that cues my deafness or my interlocutor's relationship to my deafness—become salient for each of us?

Thus, in opposition to the way a categorical orientation presumes the significance of a broad label for interactional possibility, these markers show difference as shaped through interaction. For something to be a marker of difference, it must be taken up in a communicative encounter. On its own, a marker has no stable meaning. This is one reason that markers of difference are so deeply rhetorical: they require involvement between a speaker/writer and an audience, and they must be located in their rhetorical context. Markers are used to point to and articulate difference, and some markers are readily engaged while other intended markers may be ignored, suppressed, or disregarded. Category labels can also be used as markers—names with which people mark themselves as, say, members of a particular group.[1] I do this when I describe myself as "deaf " (and, sometimes, as "profoundly deaf," although this more specialized term is only meaningful for particular audiences). It is a rhetorical choice: I do not say "hard-of-hearing" or "partially deaf " or "hearing-aid-wearer," although these terms are used by other people in talking about me. In this way people use categorical terms to mark others as well as assert their own identity claims. Markers of difference provide a mechanism for realizing the ephemerality of difference in interaction while also attending to the categorical representations and signifiers that influence what gets noticed and how meaning gets made.

COMMENTS ON A COMMA:
A MARKER BASED MICRO ANALYSIS

Moving from the theoretical to the empirical, this section shows how an analysis focusing on markers of difference might proceed. While the preceding discussion drew from general examples of some ways that I negotiate my deafness, I turn here to an excerpt of conversation in which differences in authority emerge between two students through their talk. The distinction between these two examples of marking difference is significant. The former is a set of anecdotal reflections on conscious and purposeful ways that I negotiate language and environment to accomplish communicative goals, while the latter, an examination of recorded classroom discourse, reveals a subtle process of marking difference in an immediate communicative moment. Because marking difference is so intimately tied to the display and recognition of identities, it is an important means by which individuals gauge their willingness (or unwillingness) to engage with another person. Consequently, attention to everyday talk of the sort displayed below is an important resource for teachers as they reflect upon the ways that they and their students build relations with and respond to others within the classroom environment. Before moving into this discussion, I review some background on the study design that informed the data generation and analysis to expose how categorical orientations to difference are deeply embedded within research paradigms.

The design of the study presented here incorporates two central research questions: "How are differences engaged by students in the writing classroom?" and "What role does writing play in the engagement of difference?" When the proposal for this study was under institutional review, feedback from reviewers frequently requested further information on the kinds of differences under investigation—gender, race, class, or the like. Ironically, the mere asking of this question revealed how entrenched the notion of difference as thing-existing-outside-of-the-moment-of-interaction was. Instead of identifying particular differences at the outset, the study focused on what differences became relevant for participants as well as how they became relevant. I expected the study would uncover interactions around difference that spoke to broader categories, such as conversations about race, ethnicity, and gender, or encounters that directly or indirectly invoked identity-related issues, particularly because all of the students in this writing class were also enrolled in a sociology course focused on racial issues in the United States, and because the course was part of one of Midwestern University's major diversity initiatives.[2] However, attention to difference between students rarely involved references to categorical identity signifiers. Students in this writing classroom almost never talked about their own or others' race, ethnicity, gender, disability, or socioeconomic class affiliations. What they did do is work hard to position themselves alongside one another and to construct identities that would be considered persuasive and interesting to others. Similar identity work is performed by teachers crafting their teacherly identities within the classroom. The conversation analyzed below is an everyday occurrence of identity work in which two women each attempt to establish their own interpretive authority by displaying markers of difference that distinguish one's authority from the other's.

At this point, revisiting the difficulty of using categorical description as an entry into analyses of this sort will reinforce the differences between these approaches. A categorical approach might begin by describing the three women—Blia, Lindsey, and Choua—noting that each woman is a first-semester student at the university. It might also use category terms circulating within this particular institutional context to note that Blia and Choua are Southeast Asian American and Lindsey is white. In description of this sort, readers are called upon to notice the women's ages, their gender, and their race-ethnic identifications. Such noticing is heavily influenced by context. There are innumerable other ways these women could have been described. For example, one reader of this essay noted that at universities in the Southwest, a student might choose to self-identify as "Anglo" rather than "white." Or, readers might be asked to notice each student's declared major, or their hometown, or even hair color or clothing style. Yet, even when such descriptions acknowledge that no one can know from the outset what information will be most important for understanding conversation, a key assumption motivating this analytic approach is that "relevant" descriptive information is necessary to contextualize a particular situation or setting. But no matter how detailed or attentive the teacher or analyst is, any noticing presumes the relevance of a particular set of category identifications to the conversation and is limited to what the teacher/analyst is already aware of as potentially significant. As such, these noticings can reveal more about the teacher/analyst's positionality (Rosaldo), rather than about how individuals in this context are orienting to one another. Reading difference through categories—looking for specific identity markers in order to place people into one category or another—can prevent an analyst or teacher from attending to less apparent differences. It can also prevent them from picking up on what participants themselves may be orienting to in an interaction; what may be evident to one person is not necessarily meaningful to another. Now, I am in no way suggesting that teachers and researchers should ignore how race, ethnicity, age, and gender affect these women's talk. I am also not suggesting—impossible as this would be—that people avoid categorical observation altogether. What I am saying, though, is that until we look at how these women are interacting with one another we cannot presume to know how any particular identity categories or their intersections are influencing how Blia, Lindsey, and Choua are identifying themselves. No descriptions of these women, no matter how rich, can determine or fully account for the differences between them that are brought to bear on the here and now of their peer review work. While some might argue that categorical description is a predictor rather than a determinant of individual positions, understanding categories as predictive is useful only insofar as teachers and researchers have tools for revisiting or revising the meanings attributed to categories. Markers of difference address this gap because the repeated noticing of particular markers or styles of marking can cultivate complex articulations of difference that bring life to relatively inert identity categories. In this way, markers of difference help build reflexivity between teachers and researchers' categorical awareness and the meanings that are ascribed to those categories.

Table 1 provides an overview of questions made available to us by categorical and marker-based orientations to difference. These questions reinforce ways that analyses of difference are shaped by underlying orientations to difference. The analysis below focuses on the second set of questions, emphasizing a perspective that works from participants' communicative work within the interactional moment and seeks to understand how their rhetorical choices respond to, constitute, and direct that moment.

Table 1. Questions for Categorical- and Marker-Based Analyses of Difference

Categorical Lens	Markers of Difference
• What differences are present in the classroom? • What categories do individuals belong to? • What categories can be ascribed to particular individuals? • What can we learn about the individuals in the classroom? • What information about the self is being communicated in talk?	• How do individuals position themselves alongside others? • How are individuals positioned by others? • How do individuals acknowledge similarities and differences between themselves and others? • What differences are made salient through classroom interactions? • How are students and teachers learning with others in the classroom?

Having emphasized an analytic approach that focuses on interactional activity for what it can reveal about participants' orientations to one another, I now examine a short conversational exchange that took place during a peer review session. This particular excerpt was chosen for several reasons. Thus far to illustrate processes of marking difference, I have primarily drawn on anecdotal examples taken from my personal experiences negotiating my deafness in a variety of teaching situations. This sort of anecdotal reflection forms a significant part of my teaching practice (a point to which I return below), but not all of the differences significant to my interactions with others are as easily recognized and articulated as my deafness. Moreover, because I am attuned to my deafness being an influential element of my discourse with others, I sometimes fail to recognize other differences that are marked and engaged in those exchanges. With the analysis of this excerpt, then, I aim to show one way that differences take shape through interaction and to encourage greater attention to the nuances and subtleties of individual classroom discourse.

The snippet of talk analyzed here was taken from Blia, Choua, and Lindsey's conversation about one sentence in Choua's draft. The full discussion of this sentence took up nearly one hundred lines of transcript and was the women's longest sustained conversation about a single element of any of their papers.[3] In the ten-line excerpt from this conversation reproduced below, Blia and Choua address Blia's peer review suggestion that Choua add a comma to her sentence, and they engage in a series of affiliative and dis-affiliative moves that enact a complex relationship between them.[4] Details provided within the transcript, such as when Blia and Choua's talk overlapped as well as the volume at which particular words are spoken, provide important clues for considering where and how markers of difference emerge,[5] and they open space for future attention to how markers of difference can be identified in individuals' talk and interaction. The transcript picks up just as Blia reads part of Choua's sentence aloud ("but in the dictionary") and points to her written suggestion that Choua add a comma after the words "dictionary definition" in her essay draft. Choua, rather than simply accepting the suggestion, challenges it, saying "<u>but</u> they don't need commas" (181). The four subsequent conversational turns develop this initial disagreement.

180. BLIA: but in the dictionary [(???)
181. CHOUA: [<u>but</u> they don't need commas
                            because didn't we learn over the summer tha::t
182.   you only put commas when you're separating a fragment
                            of two sentences on either side (1.3)
183. BLIA: u::m: I've been taught differently (1.0)
184.   if you're um (0.8)
185. CHOUA: I was taught <u>here::</u>
186.   s[o::
187. BLIA: [oh
188. CHOUA: that's::
189.   but it doesn't matter:: I don't care (2.5)

In lines 181–82, Choua rejects Blia's suggestion, saying, "<u>but</u> they don't need commas." She then attempts to mitigate that disagreement by inviting Blia to share in her assessment: "because didn't we learn over the summer tha::t" (182). While Choua's "we" initially seems to reference a shared learning experience, Blia's response rejects that identification, as she tells Choua, "I've been taught differently" (183). In this turn, Blia's first-person singular pronoun "I" stands in contrast to Choua's use of "we." When Blia asserts her "I", she privileges her own learning over Choua's. Blia also does not respond to Choua's understanding of the rules of comma use, nor does she affirm the position of knowledge Choua attempts to establish. Instead, Blia displays two markers of difference—the words "I" and "differently"—to distinguish herself from Choua (they have not shared a learning experience), as well as to differentiate between what the two women have learned. Choua then pushes back by offering additional information via another marker of difference to re-establish a knowledgeable stance: "I was taught <u>here::</u>" (185), suggesting that place of learning is significant in considering what weight should be accorded to the women's knowledge about punctuation.

The moment Choua asserts the validity of her learning experience "<u>here::</u>" is an especially significant one in terms of the display of markers of difference in this interaction. With this utterance, Choua responds to two previously displayed markers: (a) Blia's verb "taught" and (b) Blia's assertion of having been taught "differently." To the first, Choua's shift from "didn't we learn" (182) to "I was taught" (185) follows Blia's invocation of authority and enables a direct comparison between having been taught here as opposed to somewhere else. To the second, Choua highlights the difference between here and differently. With this marker, Choua resituates the discussion in terms of where she has gained her knowledge. This shifts the difference being marked from authority of person (teacher versus student) to authority of place (proximity versus distance). In other words, Choua's claim is not just about having been taught something (which she and Blia have both experienced), but about the heightened authority that her having been taught might carry in relation to Blia's. Learning *here*, at Midwestern University, Choua might be arguing, has greater influence than some other, more remote learning experience. Blia does not take up this element of Choua's claim, however, and the topic is dropped when Choua abruptly says, "but it doesn't matter:: I don't care" (189). The women do not revisit the comma topic in the remainder of their peer review conversation.

The markers of difference used in this conversation range widely. In just six conversational turns, Blia and Choua have displayed markers that draw on past experiences with writing instruction, positioning cues, explicit differentiation from one another, and punctuation rules as the two women identify themselves in particular ways. It is important to note that the markers displayed and interpreted by Blia and Choua are framed not only by the immediate peer review context in which the conversation is happening but also by broader sociopolitical contexts that motivate and guide the interpretations they each make of the unfolding discourse. Take another look at Choua's utterance "I was taught <u>here::</u> / s[o::" (185–86) and Blia's subsequent response, "[oh" (187). When Choua makes her claim of having been taught "<u>here::</u>," she evokes an orientation to rules of punctuation that are socially situated and contingent on place or situation. Unlike Choua, Blia may not see punctuation rules as negotiable depending on context. This is one small way that broader sociocultural frameworks, including past experiences with schooling and authority figures, as well as cultural narratives about different types of people intersect with and influence the discourse that takes place within the classroom.

Blia and Choua's peer conversation reveals complex dynamics of disagreement and consensus and shows one way that differences in perception can become material for negotiation among individuals. Such talk exposes some of the power relations that are operating within students' interactions with one another. This episode in particular underscores the stakes involved for students when they share their writing and talk about it with one another: they run the risk of being misunderstood and the risk of being positioned in undesirable ways by others—positions that they may not always be able to directly influence or change. These are not minor concerns for college students negotiating complicated and unfamiliar social environments; nor are they minor concerns for teachers establishing their subject positions in front of a classroom.

IMPLICATIONS OF A MARKER-BASED PERSPECTIVE FOR WRITING TEACHING

How can attention to markers of difference help teachers foster productive classroom environments and teach more effectively? Before entering a specific discussion of ways that markers of difference can enhance teaching and peer review practices, however, it will be useful to re-emphasize the distinction between markers of difference and identity markers more generally. Markers of difference are always situated, negotiable, and part of individual interactions. They are also framed by and interpreted within broader sociopolitical contexts. Markers of difference differ from identity markers because markers of difference do not refer to qualities that characterize particular identities, such as the way skin color may mark a person's racial or ethnic identity or the way clothing choices and hair styles may mark a person's gender, socioeconomic status, or sexuality. Identity markers of this sort *are* important to interaction, as disability theorist Tobin Siebers has pointed out, because they contribute to the identifiability of difference. Identifiability refers not simply to the existence of difference but to the representations and meanings attached to those differences (Siebers 17). As Siebers notes, not all differences are identifiable. Earlier in this essay, for example, I mentioned that I wear glasses. However, "glasses wearing," unlike "hearing-aid wearing," is not a difference often remarked upon or, as Siebers puts it, identified as difference, even between people who do not wear glasses and people who do.

Moreover, that a particular difference is identified (gender, for example, is almost always identified in individual interaction) does not in and of itself mean that that difference will be rhetorically engaged or negotiated as a marker of difference in the interaction. Thus, markers of difference do not provide cross-contextual understanding of the meaning associated with any particular identity marker. As a marker of difference, my hearing aids do not have a stable signification outside of an interactional context. So even as my past experiences with making my deafness perceptible affect whether I decide to get neon green or tan hearing aids, there is no dictionary of markers of deafness that I can pull out to understand whether, and how, my hearing aids will become salient in any given interaction. Yet, at the same time that I argue for the contextual and situated nature of markers of difference, markers of difference do inform individuals' awareness of broader cultural categories. Prior experiences of negotiating markers of difference alongside recurring cultural narratives provide material with which people draw more general conclusions about deafness and deaf people.

Given this distinction between the dynamic, relational, and emergent markers that signal individuals' uptake of difference and the general markers that point to identity categories, we can then consider how markers of difference can improve the work of peer review and teaching writing. Such markers can help teachers resist initial or simplistic generalizations and enable the re-examination of texts and interactions for what people choose to highlight or foreground about themselves and others. In forwarding the set of recommendations detailed below, this concept of marking difference is put in conversation with professional discourses about teaching and learning, specifically the "Framework for Success in Postsecondary Writing" (FSPW) developed by the Council of Writing Program Administrators (CWPA), the National Council of Teachers of English (NCTE), and the National Writing Project (NWP). The FSPW puts forth eight "habits of mind" crucial for students' success in writing. These eight habits of mind are also deeply applicable to the work of learning how to teach writing. In the recommendations for paying attention to markers of difference in teaching practice below, I highlight three of these habits of mind: increased *openness* to new information and interpretations; *flexibility* in reinterpreting and re-appropriating classroom discourses and artifacts; and heightened *metacognition* in reflecting upon specific moments of writing, teaching, and learning.

To show how these habits of mind can be cultivated through attention to markers of difference, the remainder of this section suggests practical ways that teachers can attend to markers of difference in their everyday work. Teachers and students use markers of difference to assert their identities and interpretations and to make sense of relationships being established between themselves and others. In the classroom discussed in this article, these identities and self- and other interpretations were prominent during several recurring interactional practices: telling narratives, agreeing and disagreeing with others, and withdrawing from or dismissing a topic. Consequently, these particular dynamics merit special attention from teachers as they consider how markers of difference influence and shape the negotiations that they and their students undertake with one another. I briefly describe each of these dynamics and then turn to specific strategies for attending to the markers of difference displayed therein. Sharing stories is an interactional practice that has received a great deal of attention across several fields of study, most notably in education and sociolinguistics. Elsewhere, I analyze how students exchange narratives in order to solicit details about others and to shore up particular self-identifications. Students' narratives were crafted to highlight particular markers of difference, and students often artfully paralleled markers in their own narratives with those deployed in others' tellings (Kerschbaum). Teachers' narratives display similar elements of creativity. Educational anthropologist Stanton Wortham shows how "participant-examples," a specific type of teacher-narrative in which teachers create hypothetical stories about students in the classroom to illustrate classroom concepts, provide insight into the ways that teachers identify students (*Acting; Narratives*). In another vein of research on teachers' stories, educational researchers Lesley Rex and colleagues analyze teachers' pedagogical stories for what models they offer students for success and achievement in the classroom. In these ways, narratives provide rich sources of information regarding how individuals characterize others. In reflecting upon these stories, teachers might ask: What traits, features, and qualities are described or highlighted? How are characters in the narratives portrayed? What plotlines do these characters follow, and what kinds of action or activity are available to them? In what ways are selves and others implicated in these narratives?

Two other interactional patterns—agreeing and disagreeing and withdrawing from or dismissing topics—played a significant role in student and teacher talk. The conversational excerpt from Blia and Choua's peer review session displays both of these dynamics. Blia and Choua actively disagree on the placement of a comma, and Choua ends the topic by withdrawing from it, downplaying the importance of coming to a consensus. Withdrawals of this sort were not uncommon in students' peer review talk. When students disagreed, their reaction was often to agree to disagree or to dismiss the topic. These avoidances and dismissals warrant closer examination: What precipitates someone's decision to drop a topic and avoid further discussion? What markers of difference emerge as individuals collaboratively address issues of topic relevance and importance? These questions are significant not just for what they reveal about what teachers and students deem worthy of discussion, but also for what they suggest regarding topics up for negotiation. Similarly, when individuals express agreement or disagreement, what markers of difference signal to them interpretations that allow them to stake their positions and construct them through discourse?

In turning to specific ways that teachers can attend to these three interactional patterns through the lens of marking difference, this section focuses on how teachers can make more explicit the work that markers of difference do in the course of their everyday practices. In many ways these suggestions are already a part of teachers' careful reflection upon their teaching, but the emphasis here is on developing a heightened sensitivity to the differences already part of everyday discourse as well as to those that others may be bringing to new awareness. Perhaps the most central means for teachers to begin this work is to consider their own teacher identity. They might ask themselves, "How would I characterize myself as a teacher? What choices do I make in presenting this teacher identity to my students?" Examples of this sort of metacognitive reflection have been published in a variety of locations. For instance, Lad Tobin, Deshae Lott, Christina Russell MacDonald, and Mark Mossman each describe their own conscious negotiations in displaying particular teacher roles and identities in their classrooms. This work entails the display of markers of difference that are taken up in a variety of ways by students, and that are rhetorically negotiated and emergent within different classroom settings. Teachers can look across these reflections to consider what kinds of things are chosen in order to signal particular teacher identities as well as to identify how students and other participants have responded to these cues. A second approach for "noticing patterns of noticing" accomplished with markers of difference entails turning the lens away from self-portrayals to other portrayals, asking, How would I characterize my class (or an individual student)? In reflecting on those questions, teachers would attend to the traits, features, or characteristics that are remarked upon, asking further, "What elements are highlighted, and which ones are downplayed or not addressed?" To access the dynamism and change that invariably occur in perception over the course of an academic term or over the course of a teaching career, teachers could perform these activities several times and reflect each time on the features, traits, elements, and practices that are foregrounded and backgrounded in different characterizations. Considered across time, different patterns of observation will emerge, and these patterns will point to both what Rosaldo describes as the analyst/teacher's own positionality and preparedness to notice certain things as well as to the observable cues signaled by those participating in the co-construction of classroom discourse, activity, and writing. For such reflections to be most productive, teachers need to maintain an openness to new and alternate possibilities as they revisit their observations.

Alongside attention to descriptions of self and others, a third strategy is to document the use of participant examples in classroom discourse. In reflecting on classroom practices, or while designing lesson plans, teachers might ask themselves, "Which examples do I (will I) leave abstract, in hypothetical space, and which examples do I (will I) make concrete by invoking specific students to illustrate them? Which students do I (will I) call upon in crafting these examples and why?" It is through such reflection that teachers can become critically aware of how they are mobilizing resources within the classroom, including references to artifacts that they and their students bring with them to class (books, writing implements, computer screens, coffee mugs, clothing) as well as spatial relationships (proximity and distance) to actualize these examples and develop student learning. These reflections can encourage greater flexibility in teachers' appropriation of instructional resources. There are many ways of performing these reflections. I like to annotate my daily lesson plans after each class meeting. Others, such as literacy scholar Morris Young, who shares some of his reflections on teaching in the final chapter of *Minor Re/Visions*, might keep a running journal related to their teaching. In these journals teachers might record feelings, emotions, responses, observations, or even tell stories that offer clues to how they construct classrooms, describe teaching selves, and identify salient classroom elements.

A fourth strategy for tracing the deployment of markers of difference in teaching is to consider responses to student writing. Texts are sites upon which differences are enacted, and these differences become perceptible in both student-to-student feedback (as seen in students' peer review marks on classmates' essays *and* in the talk about those comments) as well as in teacher-student feedback. When are comments made? Why? What kinds?

What changes are suggested or implied by these marks? What cues signal differences between the reader's and the writer's perspective? These marks are more than just suggestions for change; they also indicate a reader's stance toward the text and the potential space created for future versions of that text.

A fifth and final recommendation emerging from attention to Blia and Choua's conversation is that of developing a means for recording and revisiting actual moments of classroom discourse. While anecdotal recall and other reflective tools are essential for encouraging metacognition, there is also rich potential in looking at what is actually happening during classroom discussion. In Blia and Choua's writing classroom, for instance, their teacher might look across the peer review conversations for the interactional patterns described above. Key to reexamining classroom performance is the consideration of what new details and differences teachers might become more attuned to. What can students' own talk reveal about the dynamics of difference in classroom spaces? In order to do this work, teachers might take advantage of the technology resources on their campus to make video or audio recordings that can later be revisited.

CONCLUSION: MARKING THE WAY FROM HERE

These teaching methods reinforce two central goals of using markers of difference in teaching writing. First, markers of difference build from the ground up an understanding of differences that are relevant to individuals involved in an interaction. Second, markers of difference enable reflexivity between familiar categories that are already part of conscious identifications and the everyday interactions in which these categories take on greater complexity, resonance, and nuance. Thus, markers of difference are a resource for coming to know others, work that writing scholars have long advocated, even while acknowledging that there are many challenges to cultivating such knowledge. The major contribution that markers of difference make to this conversation is that they resist the impulse to reduce getting to know students to filling out beginning-of-the-semester questionnaires, or to the use of demographic surveys to describe general types of students likely to be found at a particular college or university. Markers of difference answer the question of how demographic knowledge takes on salience by insisting on locating these characteristics and observations within contexts of use, thus providing a valuable pedagogical resource for teachers aiming to cultivate such sensitivity in their everyday teaching practices.

ACKNOWLEDGMENTS

I am deeply grateful to Melissa Ianetta, whose insight and critical acumen has been invaluable. Thanks, too, to Michael McCamley, Steve Bernhardt, Christine Cucciarre, and Margaret Price for their feedback on early drafts of this work. To Peter Elbow and members of the 2009 UMass Summer Institute—Donna Strickland, Bonnie Sunstein, David Fleming, Asao Inoue, Tom Newkirk, Carmen Kynard, and Hephzibah Roskelly—thank you for the fellowship and generosity you showed in responding to my work-in-progress. And finally, my utmost gratitude to Kathleen Yancey, Robert Brooke, Sue Hum, and Nancy Barron for their comments, which helped me construct a stronger version of this manuscript.

NOTES

1. See, for example, DeFina and West and Fenstermaker for insightful analyses of how individuals use categories in talk to name identities and constitute them interactionally.

2. The school's name as well as participants' names are pseudonyms, and all identifying details have been masked to preserve anonymity.

3. A "line" of a transcript consists of what is spoken between breaths or pauses.

4. Markers of difference take on a variety of forms and can emerge through word choice, emphasis, volume, as well as other verbal cues for signaling meaning. For this reason, I provide a fairly detailed transcript, including information about when students paused or when their talk overlapped or interrupted one another, as illustrated with square brackets indicating the point of overlap/interruption. Considered across time and contexts, the detail in this transcript is designed to enable attention to as many potential markers of difference as possible. Other valuable sources of meaning making not transcribed here include gestures (Wolfe; Godbee) and gaze (Everts), both of which could contribute to interpretations of how students signal and reinforce particular interpretations and cues.

5. In this transcript, pauses longer than half a second are measured in seconds and indicated by a number within parentheses at the end of the line. A left square bracket indicates overlapping talk. An underline indicates words spoken at a higher volume relative to adjacent talk, colons are used to indicate extended sounds, and inaudible words are represented with three question marks within parentheses.

WORKS CITED

Alexander, Jonathan. *Literacy, Sexuality, Pedagogy: Theory and Practice for Composition Studies.* Logan: Utah State UP, 2008. Print.

Bakhtin, Mikhail. *Art and Answerability: Early Philosophical Essays by M. M. Bakhtin.* Trans. Vadim Liapunov. Austin: U of Texas P, 1990. Print.

———. *Toward a Philosophy of the Act.* Trans. Vadim Liapunov. Austin: U of Texas P, 1993. Print.

Burgess, Amy, and Roz Ivanic̆. "Writing and Being Written: Issues of Identity across Timescales." *Written Communication* 27.2 (2010): 228–55. Print.

Cushman, Ellen. "Toward a Rhetoric of Self-Representation: Identity Politics in Indian Country and Rhetoric and Composition." *College Composition and Communication* 60.2 (2008): 321–65. Print.

De, Esha Niyogi, and Donna Uthus Gregory. "Decolonizing the Classroom." *Writing in Multicultural Settings*. Ed. Carol Severino, Juan Guerra, and Johnella Butler. New York: MLA, 1997. 118–32. Print.

De Fina, Anna. *Identity in Narrative: A Study of Immigrant Discourse*. Philadelphia: John Benjamins, 2003. Print.

Dunn, Patricia. *Learning Re-Abled: The Learning Disability Controversy and Composition Studies*. Portsmouth: Boynton/Cook, 1995. WAC Clearinghouse. Web. 27 Mar. 2011.

Everts, Elisa. "Modalities of Turn-Taking in Blind/Sighted Interaction: Better to Be Seen and Not Heard?" In *Discourse and Technology: Multimodal Discourse Analysis*. Ed. Philip LeVine and Ron Scollon. Washington: Georgetown UP, 2004. 128–45. Print.

Fernheimer, Janice. "Black Jewish Identity Conflict: A Divided Universal Audience and the Impact of Dissociative Disruption." *Rhetoric Society Quarterly* 39.1 (2009): 46–72. Print.

Flower, Linda. "Talking across Difference: Intercultural Rhetoric and the Search for Situated Knowledge." *College Composition and Communication* 55.1 (2003): 38–68. Print.

Flower, Linda, Elenore Long, and Lorraine Higgins. *Learning to Rival: A Literate Practice for Intercultural Inquiry*. Mahwah: Lawrence Erlbaum, 2000. Print.

Fox, Helen. Afterword. In *Social Change in Diverse Teaching Contexts*. Ed. Nancy G. Barron, Nancy Grimm, and Sybille Gruber. New York: Peter Lang, 2006. 251–66. Print.

"Framework for Success in Postsecondary Writing." Council of Writing Program Administrators, National Council of Teachers of English, and National Writing Project. Jan. 2011. Web. 15 Sept. 2011.

Frankenberg, Ruth. *White Women, Race Matters: The Social Construction of Whiteness*. Minneapolis: U of Minnesota P, 1993. Print.

Glazier, Jocelyn. "Developing Cultural Fluency: Arab and Jewish Students Engaging in One Another's Company." *Harvard Educational Review* 73.2 (2003): 141–63. Print.

Godbee, Beth. "'We're in This Together': Illustrating Potentials for Social Change in Talk about Writing." Unpublished manuscript. Print.

Gomez, Mary Louise, Anne Burda Walker, and Michelle L. Page. "Personal Experience as a Guide to Teaching." *Teaching and Teacher Education* 16 (2000): 731–47. Print.

Gonçalves, Zan Meyer. *Sexuality and the Politics of Ethos*. Carbondale: Southern Illinois UP, 2005. Print.

Gonsalves, Lisa. "Making Connections: Addressing the Pitfalls of White Faculty/ Black Male Student Communication." *College Composition and Communication* 53.3 (2000): 435–65. Print.

Harklau, Linda, Kay Losey, and Meryl Siegal, eds. *Generation 1.5 Meets College Composition: Issues in the Teaching of Writing to U.S.-Educated Learners of ESL*. Mahwah: Lawrence Erlbaum, 1999. Print.

Haswell, Janis, and Richard Haswell. *Authoring: An Essay for the English Profession on Potentiality and Singularity*. Logan: Utah State UP, 2010. Print.

Hawisher, Gail, and Cynthia Selfe, with Yi-Huey Guo and Lu Liu. "Globalization and Agency: Designing and Redesigning the Literacies of Cyberspace." *College English* 68.6 (2006): 619–36. Print.

Herrington, Anne, and Marcia Curtis. *Persons in Process: Four Stories of Writing and Personal Development in College*. Urbana: NCTE, 2000. Print.

hooks, bell. *Talking Back: Thinking Feminist, Thinking Black*. Boston: South End, 1989. Print.

Jung, Julie. *Revisionary Rhetoric, Feminist Pedagogy, and Multigenre Texts*. Carbondale: Southern Illinois UP, 2005. Print.

Juzwik, Mary, Svjetlana Curcic, Kimberly Wolbers, Kathleen D. Moxley, Lisa M. Dimling, and Rebecca K. Shankland. "Writing into the 21st Century: An Overview of Research on Writing, 1999 to 2004." *Written Communication* 26.4 (2006): 451–76. Print.

Kerschbaum, Stephanie. "Classroom Narratives and Ethical Responsibility: How Markers of Difference Can Inform Teaching." *Narrative Discourse Analysis for Teacher Educators.* Ed. Lesley Rex and Mary M. Juzwik. Cresskill: Hampton P, 2011. 77–104. Print.

LeCourt, Donna. *Identity Matters: Schooling the Student Body in Academic Discourse.* Albany: State U of New York P, 2004. Print.

——. "Performing Working-Class Identity in Composition: Toward a Pedagogy of Textual Practice." *College English* 69.1 (2006): 30–51. Print.

Lee, Amy. *Composing Critical Pedagogies: Teaching Writing as Revision.* Urbana: NCTE, 2000. Print.

Lemke, Jay. "Across the Scales of Time: Artifacts, Activities, and Meanings in Ecosocial Systems." *Mind, Culture, and Activity* 7.4 (2000): 273–90. Web. 4 Apr. 2011.

Lieber, Andrea. "A Virtual *Viebershul:* Blogging and the Blurring of Public and Private among Orthodox Jewish Women." *College English* 72.6 (2010): 621–37. Print.

Lillis, Theresa. "Ethnography as Method, Methodology, and 'Deep Theorizing': Closing the Gap between Text and Context in Academic Writing Research." *Written Communication* 25.3 (2008): 353–88. Print.

Lindquist, Julie. "What's the Trouble with Knowing Students? Only Time Will Tell." *Pedagogy: Critical Approaches to Teaching Literature, Language, Composition, and Culture* 10.1 (2009): 175–287. Web. 15 Jan. 2010.

Lorr, Deshae. "Going to Class with (Going to Clash with?) the Disabled Person: Educators, Students, and Their Spoken and Unspoken Negotiations." In *Embodied Rhetorics: Disability in Language and Culture.* Ed. James C. Wilson and Cynthia Lewiecki-Wilson. Carbondale: Southern Illinois UP, 2001. 135–53. Print.

Lyons, Scott. "Rhetorical Sovereignty: What Do American Indians Want from Writing?" *College Composition and Communication* 51.3 (2000): 447–68. Print.

MacDonald, Christina Russell. "Imagining Our Teaching Selves." In *Teaching Writing: Landmarks and Horizons.* Ed. Christina Russell MacDonald and Robert L. MacDonald. Carbondale: Southern Illinois UP, 2002. 171–83. Print.

Morris, Amanda Lynch. "Native American Stand-Up Comedy: Epideictic Strategies in the Contact Zone." *Rhetoric Review* 30.1 (2011): 37–53. Print.

Mossman, Mark. "Visible Disability in the College Classroom." *College English* 64.6 (2002): 645–59. Print.

Okawa, Gail. "'Resurfacing Roots': Developing a Pedagogy of Language Awareness from Two Views." In *Language Diversity in the Classroom: From Intention to Practice.* Ed. Geneva Smitherman and Victor Villanueva. Carbondale: Southern Illinois UP, 2003. 109–33. Print.

Ortmeier-Hooper, Christina. "English May Be My Second Language, but I'm Not 'ESL.'" *College Composition and Communication* 59.3 (2008): 389–419. Print.

Ratcliffe, Krista. *Rhetorical Listening: Identification, Gender, Whiteness.* Carbondale: Southern Illinois UP, 2005. Print.

Rex, Lesley, Timothy Murnen, Jack Hobbs, and David McEachen. "Teachers' Pedagogical Stories and the Shaping of Classroom Participation: 'The Dancer' and 'Graveyard Shift at the 7-11.'" *American Educational Research Journal* 39.3 (2002): 765–96. Print.

Ridgeway, Cecilia. *Framed by Gender: How Gender Inequality Persists in the Modern World.* New York: Oxford UP, 2011. Print.

Rosaldo, Renato. *Culture and Truth: The Remaking of Social Analysis.* Boston: Beacon P, 1989. Print.

Royster, Jacqueline Jones. *Traces of a Stream: Literacy and Social Change among African American Women.* Pittsburgh: U of Pittsburgh P, 2000. Print.

Rumsey, Suzanne. "Heritage Literacy: Adoption, Adaptation, and Alienation of Multimodal Literacy Tools." *College Composition and Communication* 60.3 (2009): 573–86. Print.

Schultz, Katherine. *Listening: A Framework for Teaching across Differences.* New York: Teachers College P, 2003. Print.

Siebers, Tobin. *Disability Theory.* Ann Arbor: U of Michigan P, 2008. Print.

Sohn, Kathleen Kelleher. "Whistlin' and Crowin' Women of Appalachia." *College Composition and Communication* 54 (2003): 423–52. Print.

Tobin, Lad. "Self-Disclosure as a Strategic Teaching Tool: What I Do—and Don't— Tell My Students." *College English* 73.2 (2010): 196–206. Print.

Valdes, Guadalupe. "Bilingual Minorities and Language Issues in Writing." *Written Communication* 9.1 (1992): 85–136. Print.

Villanueva, Victor. *Bootstraps: From an American Academic of Color.* Urbana: NCTE, 1993. Print.

West, Candace, and Sarah Fenstermaker. "Accountability in Action: The Accomplishment of Gender, Race, and Class in a Meeting of the University of California Board of Regents." *Discourse and Society* 13.4 (2002): 537–63. Web. 13 May 2010.

Wolfe, Joanna. "Gesture and Collaborative Planning: A Case Study of a Student Writing Group." *Written Communication* 22.3 (2005): 298–332. Print.

Wortham, Stanton. *Acting Out Participant Examples in the Classroom.* Philadelphia: John Benjamins, 1994. Print.

———. *Learning Identity: The Joint Emergence of Social Identification and Academic Learning.* New York: Cambridge UP, 2006. Print.

———. *Narratives in Action.* New York: Teachers College P, 2001. Print.

Young, Morris. *Minor Re/Visions: Asian American Literacy Narratives as a Rhetoric of Citizenship.* Carbondale: Southern Illinois UP, 2004. Print.

Section Five

Virtual Talk

Composing beyond the Word

- "The Politics of the Interface: Power and Its Exercise in Electronic Contact Zones" Cynthia L. Selfe and Richard J. Selfe, Jr.
- "Blinded by the Letter: Why Are We Using Literacy as a Metaphor for Everything Else?" Anne Frances Wysocki and Johndan Johnson-Eilola
- "Made Not Only in Words: Composition in a New Key" Kathleen Blake Yancey
- "Lessons from History: Teaching with Technology in 100 Years of *English Journal*" Ben McCorkle and Jason Palmeri
- "Oakland, the Word, and the Divide: How We All Missed the Moment" Adam J. Banks
- "A Multimodal Task-Based Framework for Composing" Jody Shipka
- "Response to Cynthia L. Selfe's 'The Movement of Air, the Breath of Meaning: Aurality and Multimodal Composing'" Doug Hesse
- "Response to Doug Hesse" Cynthia L. Selfe
- "Race, Rhetoric, and Technology: A Case Study of Decolonial Technical Communication Theory, Methodology, and Pedagogy" Angela M. Haas

The inclusion of computer technology in composition classrooms forced a renewed attention on pedagogical form and content. To address this seemingly radical shift, a new journal came into the profession in 1985, the former newsletter *Computers and Composition*. It marked the beginning of discussions about what would be termed *computer-assisted writing*, and that would eventually become an integral part of all that we do. Scholars like Gail Hawisher explored the impact of moving from typewriters to word processors. Others, like Richard Lanham, explored how new electronic media redefined the word itself, which now was comprised of text, sight, and sound, and was no longer even necessarily linear. This new mode of discourse, hypertext, became the topic of discussion about new methods of reading, writing, and knowing.

Those embracing new technologies, generally those with the resources to acquire them (the "material access" as Banks describes it), turned to synchronous and asynchronous online communication such as MUDs (multi-user domains), MOOs (multi-user domains, object oriented), listservs, and message boards to hold classroom discussions. These spaces generated a wealth of scholarship on such questions as student ethics, subjectivity, and teacher authority. Such conversations continued as universities implemented classroom-management systems. The design of these digital spaces—even early graphical-user interfaces, as Selfe and Selfe remind us—are deeply ideological and come with their own set of assumptions about who are students are and how they *should* compose.

Similar lines of inquiry to those seen in hypertext theory and practice, as well the visual composing happening in early online spaces like MOOs, are echoed in multimodal theory and practices. In 1994, a group of literacy scholars met in New London, New Hampshire, to develop a pedagogy that would "account for the burgeoning variety of text forms associated with information and multimedia technologies." Composition's multimodal turn, which happened in the early 2000s, was heavily influenced by the New London Group's pedagogy of multiliteracies, one that involves students in the production and analysis of visual, linguistic, aural, spatial, and gestural literacies.

While multimodality was treated as a new turn, one ushered in by technological advances that required us to engage in composing beyond the linguistic, folks like McCorkle and Palmeri argue there is nothing particularly *new* about it. In addition, Jody Shipka suggests that multimodality and digitality are not synonymous. And when we take into account all of the ways we and our students produce and consume communication, is it even our job as compositionists to teach modes beyond the linguistic? The exchange between Selfe and Hesse, prompted by Selfe's "The Movement of Air, the Breath of Meaning," provides us with questions for reflection.

Given this is a "Comp Theory" anthology, it may seem curious we are ending with an essay ostensibly about technical communication. Yet, the questions Haas raises, the arguments she makes about making visible the relationships between race, rhetoric, and technology studies, and the classroom examples she provides, offer a model for doing decolonial work. For as Haas reminds us, "even in the most progressive spaces and places, the colonial rhetorical detritus of racism and ethnocentrism remains" (306). What we teach and how we teach it cultures us into ways of being in the world.

The Politics of the Interface

Power and Its Exercise in Electronic Contact Zones

CYNTHIA L. SELFE AND RICHARD J. SELFE, JR.

Over a casual lunch at a recent professional conference, Trent Batson, a professor at Gallaudet University, told us a story that made us think about borders and
their effects. He had been visiting Mexico on a short day trip in the company of
an academic colleague who taught at Mt. Holyoke but had been born in India.
On the way back into the United States, these colleagues entered two separate
lines at the stations marking the official re-entry point to this country. Border
guards, observing the darker skin of the one colleague stopped him—as they
did all people who, in Batson's words, "looked vaguely Mexican." The Indian
colleague, having lived and worked in this country for a number of years, had
made the mistake of thinking that this border, this country, was an open one.
He carried only a photocopy of the green card that identified him as a "resident
alien," rather than the card itself, as required by United States law.

Given these relatively unexceptional circumstances, what followed
seemed significant to us—the Indian-born colleague was detained by officials and eventually fined—even though he carried additional materials
identifying him as a professor at Holyoke. Batson was not stopped or questioned. He was also not allowed to accompany his friend, who was taken to
an office by the border guards where he was detained for half an hour. Batson was allowed to watch the proceedings through a window, to gaze on the
administration and application of American law.

On the surface of the story, no real harm was done: the detainment was
short term, the fine minimal, the laws for resident aliens clear. But for us, as

Reprinted from *College Composition and Communication* 45.4 (December 1994): 480–504.
Used with permission.

citizens of the United States, the telling of this story had a chilling effect. We were ashamed not only about the assumptions that the border guards seem to have made but also of the cultural values that the story revealed. As Midwesterners who live relatively far from the border in question, we were taken aback by the story—by the guards' reactions, by the feelings these reactions suggest about Mexican nationals, and by the treatment that people of color receive every day in our own country. We should not, of course, have been surprised at all. It is at the geopolitical borders of countries that the formations of social power, normally hidden, are laid embarrassingly bare—where power in its rawest form is exercised.

If at the time of this story's original telling we didn't like what it made us think about our country, it was not until we had reflected more closely on the incident that we began to unpack the various ways in which it seemed meaningful and bothersome to us—in general, for our own professional lives as teachers and, in specific, for the more specialized instructional work that we do in computer-supported writing and learning environments. The longer we thought about it, the more we realized that the borders represented in this story, the values built into them and constituted continually by them, were—and are—present in our own classrooms as well. These borders are represented and reproduced in so many commonplace ways, at so many levels, that they frequently remain invisible to us. One place in which such borders remain quite visible, we realized, is in the computers that we, and many other teachers of English, use within classrooms. When re-considering this story in light of our own experiences, we began to see how teachers of English who use computers are often involved in establishing and maintaining borders themselves—whether or not they acknowledge or support such a project—and, thus, in contributing to a larger cultural system of differential power that has resulted in the systematic domination and marginalization of certain groups of students, including among them: women, non-whites, and individuals who speak languages other than English.

This article represents our further thinking about these realizations. In it, we begin the task of describing some of the political and ideological boundary lands associated with computer interfaces that we—and many other teachers of composition—now use in our classrooms. We also talk about the ways in which these borders are at least partly constructed along ideological axes that represent dominant tendencies in our culture, about the ways in which the borders evident in computer interfaces can be mapped as complex political landscapes, about the ways in which the borders can serve to prevent the circulation of individuals for political purposes, and about the ways in which teachers and students can learn to see and alter such borders in productive ways. At the end of the paper, we talk about tactics that teachers can use to enact a radical pedagogy of electronic borders and borderlands.

As a way into this examination, we look at computer interfaces as linguistic contact zones, in Mary Louise Pratt's words, "social spaces where cultures meet, clash, and grapple with each other, often in contexts of highly asymmetrical relations of power, such as colonialism, slavery, or their aftermaths as they are lived out in many parts of the world today" (34). Within this context, we talk about computer interfaces as maps that enact—among other things—the gestures and deeds of colonialism, continuously and with a great deal of success. This is not to claim, of course, that the *only* educational effects computers have is one of re-producing oppression or colonial mentalities. Indeed, from the work of computers and composition specialists, it is clear that computers, like other complex technologies, are articulated in many ways with a range of existing cultural forces and with a variety of projects in our educational system, projects that run the gamut from liberatory to oppressive. However, because recent scholarship on computers has tended to focus in overoptimistic ways on the positive contributions that technology can make to English composition classrooms, our goal in this piece is to sketch the outlines of an alternative vision for teachers, one that might encourage them to adopt a more critical and reflective approach to their use of computers.[1] Such a picture provides a necessary balance, we believe. An overly optimistic vision of technology is not only reductive, and, thus, inaccurate, it is also dangerous in that it renders less visible the negative contributions of technology that may work potently and effectively against critically reflective habits and efforts of good teachers and students. Our goal is to help teachers identify some of the effects of domination and colonialism associated with computer use so that they can establish a new discursive territory within which to understand the relationships between technology and education.

COMPUTERS AS LEARNING ENVIRONMENTS: HISTORY AND MOTIVATION

For the last decade, English composition teachers have been using computers in classrooms to create electronic forums—on local-area networks (LANs) and wide-area networks (WANs)—within which writers and readers can create, exchange, and comment on texts. These spaces, it has been noted, have the potential for supporting student-centered learning and discursive practices that can be different from, and—some claim—more engaging and democratic than those occurring within traditional classroom settings.[2] Such a vision is all the more tantalizing given our recognition that the education taking place in traditional classrooms—despite our best intentions—contributes, in part, to a continuing cultural tendency to marginalize and oppress groups of people due to their race, gender, or ethnic background. Gomez, for example, citing Wheelock and Dorman, compares the 12% dropout rate for white students to the 17% rate for African American students, 18% for Hispanic students, and 29.2% for Native American students (319–20). Giroux notes that "in many urban cities the dropout rate for nonwhite children exceeds 60% (with New York City at 70%)" (111). As teachers of English, we recognize, in other words, that we work in an educational system that instructs students about oppression and inequity, by example, even as we strive to erase such lessons from the official curriculum. This situation and these figures, as June Jordan notes, are all the more dramatic in light of the fact that only 15% of the entrants into the American workforce will be white males by the year 2000 and that some states like California will have 61% non-white students in their populations by the year 2010 (22). And as Mary Louise Gomez further reminds us, most schools can expect 30–40% of their student population to come from a non-English language background by the end of this decade (319).

This continuing pattern has encouraged many teachers of English to turn to—among other things—computer-supported writing environments as places within which they and students can try to enact educational practices that are more democratic and less systematically oppressive: for example, student-centered, on-line discussion groups in which individuals discover their own motivations for using language; on-line conferences in which students' race, gender, age, and sexual preference may not figure in the same ways that they do in more conventional face-to-face settings; collaborative groups in which students learn to negotiate discursive power. To create and maintain these communities—to defend their use and value—we have often used what Hawisher and Selfe have identified as an overly positive "rhetoric of technology" (55) that portrays computer-supported forums—among ourselves, to administrators, to students—as democratic spaces, what Mary Louise Pratt might call "linguistic utopias"(48) within which cues of gender, race, and socioeconomic status are minimized; students speak without interruption; and marginalized individuals can acquire more central voices. And if this rhetoric is helpful in that it describes what we *want* to happen—and sometimes, to some extent, *does* happen—in our classrooms, it is also dangerous. Through its use, we legitimate the status quo of computer use and, as Hawisher and Selfe note, "de-legitimate critique"(53)—thus allowing ourselves to think erroneously that the use of computers and networks provides discursive landscapes that are, in Mary Louise Pratt's words, "the same for all players" (38).

The rhetoric of technology obscures the fact that, within our current educational system—even though computers are associated with the potential for great reform—they are not necessarily serving democratic ends. Computer interfaces, for example, are *also* sites within which the ideological and material legacies of racism, sexism, and colonialism are continuously written and re-written along with more positive cultural legacies.[3] Perhaps the most salient evidence for this claim lies in the different uses to which computers are put in minority classrooms and majority classrooms. Sheingold, Martin, and Endreweit, for example, note that in schools with large minority enrollments computers are used primarily to provide basic skills instruction delivered by drill-and-practice software. . . . In contrast, computer use in majority schools is characterized by its emphasis on the use of computers as tools to develop higher order literary and cognitive skills as objects of study (e.g., instruction focused on computer literacy and programming" (89). Charles Piller, in a recent article in *MacWorld*, notes that minority populations and lower socioeconomic populations are America's growing "technological underclass" (218) and, thus, that these students are the least likely to gain skills during their public schooling experience that will serve them well in a world increasingly dependent on technology.

The recognition of this situation, for many computer-using teachers of English, is not possible without a great deal of pain. It demands our realization that—while we, as individual English teachers, may very strongly support democratic reform, broad involvement, or egalitarian education, and while our teaching and computer use may be aimed toward these ends—we are also simultaneously participating in a cultural project that, at some level and to some degree, seems to support racist, sexist, and colonial attitudes. This is true even as our profession broadly supports more productive and progressive forms of educational action. If we hope to get English composition teachers to recognize how our use of computers achieves both great good and great evil—often at the same time, as Joseph Weizenbaum points out—we have to educate them to be technology *critics* as well as technology users. This recognition requires that composition teachers acquire the intellectual habits of reflecting on and discussing the cultural and ideological characteristics of technology—and the implications of these characteristics—in educational contexts. With such a realization, we maintain, English composition teachers can begin to exert an increasingly active influence on the cultural project of technology design.

MAPPING THE INTERFACE OF COMPUTERS AS EDUCATIONAL SPACE

The project that we have described is not a simple one, nor is it one that we can describe fully here. We can, however, provide an extended example of the agenda we want to pursue by focusing in particular ways on computer *interfaces*, those primary representations of computer systems or programs that show up on screens used by both teachers and students. Within the virtual space represented by these interfaces, and elsewhere within computer systems, the values of our culture—ideological, political, economic, educational—are mapped both implicitly and explicitly, constituting a complex set of material relations among culture, technology, and technology users. In effect, interfaces are cultural maps of computer systems, and as Denis Wood points out, such maps are never ideologically innocent or inert. Like other maps that Wood mentions—the medieval *mappaemundi* that offer a Christian-centered vision of the 13th century world or the Mercater projection that provides a Euro-centric view of the Earth's geography in the 20th century—the maps of computer interfaces order the virtual world according to a certain set of historical and social values that make up our culture. The users of maps, as a result, read cultural information just as surely as they read geographical information—through a coherent set of stereotyped images that the creators of maps offer as "direct testimony" (Berger 69) of the world, of social formations and socially organized tendencies, of a culture's historical development (Wood 145). The enhanced power of maps, growing out of their long association with the projects of science and geography, resides in the fact that they purport to represent fact—the world, a particular space—as it is in reality, while they naturalize the political and ideological interests of their authors (Wood 2).

Given this background, we can better understand why it is important to identify the cultural information passed along in the maps of computer interfaces—especially because this information can serve to reproduce, on numerous discursive levels and through a complex set of conservative forces, the asymmetrical power relations that, in part, have shaped the educational system we labor within and that students are exposed to. What is mapped in computer interfaces—just as what is mapped in other social and cultural artifacts such as our educational system—is both "ownership" and opportunity (Wood 21). In this sense, we maintain, the "ferocious" (Wood 25) effectiveness of computer interfaces as maps is established as much by what they do *not* show about American culture as by what they *do*. Primary computer interfaces do not, for example, provide direct evidence of different cultures and races that make up the American social complex, nor do they show much evidence of different linguistic groups or groups of differing economic status. It is only when we recognize these gestures of omission for what they are, as interested versions of reality, that we can begin to examine the naturalizing functions of computer interfaces and, as educators, break the frame to extend the discursive horizon (Laclau and Mouffe 19) of the landscape we have created and that, in turn, creates us and the students in our classes.

Once we recognize these functions, we also begin to understand the ideological gesture of the interface's map as a "flawed, partial, incomplete" (Wood 26) and interested vision of reality, at least partly constructed from the perspective of, and for the benefit of, dominant forces in our culture. In particular—given that these technologies have grown out of the predominately male, white, middle-class, professional cultures associated with the military-industrial complex—the virtual reality of computer interfaces represents, in part and to a visible degree, a tendency to value monoculturalism, capitalism, and phallologic thinking, and does so, more importantly, to the exclusion of other perspectives. Grounded in these values, computer interfaces, we maintain, enact small but continuous gestures of domination and colonialism. To examine these claims, we have to turn directly to examples that illustrate the ways in which such maps "name, marginalize, and define difference as the devalued Other" (Giroux 33)—not in a totalizing fashion but through many subtly potent gestures enacted continuously and naturalized as parts of technological systems. Such examples are not difficult to come by if we examine the borderland of the interface from the perspective of non-dominant groups in our culture.

Interfaces as Maps of Capitalism and Class Privilege

In general, computer interfaces present reality as framed in the perspective of modern capitalism, thus, orienting technology along an existing axis of class privilege. The graphically intuitive Macintosh interface provides a good example of this orientation. That interface, and the software applications commonly represented within it, map the virtual world as a *desktop*—constructing virtual reality, by association, in terms of corporate culture and the values of professionalism. This reality is constituted by and for white middle- and upper-class users to replicate a world that they know and feel comfortable within. The objects represented within this world are those familiar primarily to the white-collar inhabitants of that corporate culture: manila folders, files, documents, telephones, fax machines, clocks and watches, and desk calendars. We can grasp the power of this ideological orientation—and thus sense its implications—by shifting our perspective to what it does *not* include, what it leaves unstated. The interface does not, for example, represent the world in terms of a kitchen counter top, a mechanic's workbench, or a fast-food restaurant—each of which would constitute the virtual world in different terms according to the values and orientations of, respectively, women in the home, skilled laborers, or the rapidly increasing numbers of employees in the fast-food industry.

Built into computer interfaces are also a series of semiotic messages that support this alignment along the axes of class, race, and gender. The white pointer hand, for example, ubiquitous in the Macintosh primary interface, is one such gesture, as are the menu items of the Appleshare server tray and hand, calculator, the moving van (for the font DA mover), the suitcase, and the desk calendar. Others images—those included in the HyperCard interface commercial clip art collections, and in the Apple systems documentation—include a preponderance of white people and icons of middle- and upper-class white culture and professional, office-oriented computer use. These images signal—to users of color, to users who come from a non-English language background, to users from low socio-economic backgrounds—that entering the virtual worlds of interfaces also means, at least in part and at some level, entering a world constituted around the lives and values of white, male, middle- and upper-class professionals. Users of color, users from non-English language background, users from a low socio-economic class who view this map of reality, submit—if only partially and momentarily—to an interested version of reality represented in terms of both language and image.

When users recognize the corporate orientation of the interface, they also begin to understand more about how computers as a technology are ideologically associated with capitalism. Computer interfaces, for example, can serve to reproduce a value on the commodification of information. On the Macintosh desktop, for instance, the raw material of information is gathered in databases and files, stored in folders and on hard drives, accumulated within artificially expanded memory spaces, and finally manipulated and written in the form of documents that acquire their own authority and value within a capitalist economy.

All of these information products—following the prevailing model of text-as-commodity established in what Jay D. Bolter calls the "late age of print" (1)—are "owned" by an author who can protect work with a "password" and accord "privileges" to readers according to the relationship and involvement she would like them to have with a text. This commodification of information is also played out at additional levels within computer interfaces. Through interfaces, for example, students now learn to access and depend on sources like BITNET or Internet, library systems in other states, and information bases around the world for the information they need.

These electronic spaces—which are subject to increasing legislation and control—are at the same time becoming more expensive and more rigidly aligned along the related axes of class privilege and capitalism. The refinement and use of packet charging technologies, for example, and the increasing exploitation of large-scale commercial networks that appeal to the public will continue to support such an alignment. Recent figures published in a recent *New York Times* article indicate that commercial public networks such as Prodigy and Compuserve charge approximately $50 for starter kits on their systems, between $8 and $15 for basic use each month, and some additional per-message or per-minute charges as well. The capital stake that commercial groups have in promoting these electronic systems to citizens is not a small one: Information-as-commodity is big business—approximately 3.4 million people subscribe to commercial networks at the rates we have mentioned (Grimes 13–15).

Interfaces as Maps of Discursive Privilege

The orientation of the interface along the axis of class privilege is made increasingly systematic by the application of related discursive constraints. Primary interfaces, for example, also generally serve to reproduce the privileged position of Standard English as the language of choice or default, and, in this way, contribute to the tendency to ignore, or even erase, the cultures of non-English language background speakers in this country. Although the global expansion of technology is exerting an increasingly strong influence on the computer industry—and thus interfaces in other languages are becoming more common—these influences are resisted at many levels and in many ways, and this resistance is represented vividly in the maps of computer interfaces. A more particular example of this orientation exists in most word-processing programs—those tools we present students with so that they can "express" themselves in the language of our choosing. Many such programs commercially distributed in this country present their menued items only in English, despite the fact that, as Mary Louise Gomez reminds us, most schools can expect 30–40% of their student population to come from a non-English language background by the end of the decade (319). Those word-processing programs that *do* present an alternative-language interface market their non-English language background products separately, adding additional cost; or market them only in other countries, making them difficult to obtain especially with education discounts; or retain the privileged position of English simply by default. WordPerfect 5.1 for the IBM, for instance, which presents English menus as the default interface, does allow users to operate in other languages—among them three versions of English

(Australian, Great Britain, and United States) and only one of Spanish, in addition to Catalan (*WordPerfect for DOS* 325). To write or edit in another language, users must go to a "Layout" pull-down menu and then select—with some irony, we hope—the item labeled "Other" (324). As the manual for WordPerfect notes, moreover, the thesaurus and spell checkers accompanying the regular WordPerfect package come only in English. One can order versions of this thesaurus and spell checker in other languages, but they come at an additional cost. The telephone number which one uses to place such an order, the *Reference* manual notes, further, is "not toll-free" (326).

This decision to use English as a default language—articulated, as we have pointed out, with the custom of identifying non-English language background speakers as a marginalized "Other" and the socio-economic forces that limit access to software in other languages—clearly has important implications for our educational system, for teachers and for students. In schools, this default position means that students from other races and cultures who hope to use the computer as a tool for empowerment must—at some level—submit to the colonial power of language and adopt English as their primary means of communication, even if this submission is only partial or momentary. Few schools and few teachers can find a realistic perspective from which to resist the tendential forces associated with this default to English as a standard. Certainly, those schools that may most need fully functional bi- and tri-lingual interfaces are the *least* likely to have the monies available to purchase additional packages. This characteristic focus of interfaces on Standard English is further supported and exacerbated by the fact that style and grammar packages are generally based on an overly narrow—and erroneous—vision of "correct" language use and spelling checkers that exert a continuously normative influence (LeBlanc) within the setting of colonial discourse. Both kinds of software can serve to de-value linguistic diversity and inscribe nonstandard language users as Other within the interface, the classroom, the educational system, and the culture.

We got an idea of just how powerful and evenly dispersed this cultural inscription is—how systematically it operates—when we attended the 1992 convention of the National Council of Teachers of English. At that gathering, a software company demonstrated a word-processing package designed to present a bilingual (Spanish/English) interface. The package was available in a low-cost, school-edition package for approximately $300 and in a site-license, networkable version for approximately $1500. As the package's literature pointed out, users could employ a pull-down menu system to select the Spanish mode—where all menus, dialog boxes, help, and messages appear in Spanish. When we tested the software in the Spanish mode, however, we found the keystroke options did not change correspondingly to the same language. In fact those options, which depend, for the most part on mnemonic aids—apple-D for "delete"—remain keyed to the English words even when the corresponding Spanish menu items—"eliminar," for example—start with different letters. A student using this program, then, should she want to use the keystroke options, might be able to write in Spanish, but would have to think at some level in English.

This value on English as the privileged language of computer interfaces—and the effects of the design decisions that support this system—are certainly not limited to the United States. For example, a recent international gathering on computer-based instruction (Teleteaching '93) sponsored by the International Federation for Information Processing and focused on the use of computers for global distance education projects, required all sessions and discussions to be conducted in English—even though the conference was held in Norway and many representatives from non-English speaking countries were in attendance. This decision, presented to participants as a necessary convenience, recognized the extent to which Americans have influenced computer design, computer use, and computer applications over the past decade, and the fact that English has been, during this same period, the world language of science and technology. The language of computers has thus become English by default: The majority of standard interfaces are English, much of the documentation for these interfaces and the machines they operate on is in English, and the systems that currently support global computing networks rely on English as a standard exchange language. At the conference in question, several presenters from non-English speaking countries, for instance, noted that the educational conversations and projects they set up for French, German, Russian, or Slovakian students were conducted in English because these exchanges relied on the ability to link computers and systems through a common exchange standard called American Standard Code for Information Interchange (ASCII) that does not adequately support languages other than English. ASCII—because it was originally based on a 7-bit code—can handle, as Charles Petzold points out, only "26 lowercase letters, 26 uppercase letters, 10 numbers, and 33 symbols and punctuation marks" unless it is extended by 8-bit byte computer systems that allow it to handle 128 additional characters. Even with these additional characters, ASCII's alphabetic limitations preclude the full and adequate representation of Greek, Hebrew, Cyrillic, and Han characters (374–75).

In a recent article about Unicode—a proposed international replacement for ASCII—Petzold explores some of the implications of relying solely on ASCII:

There's a big problem with ASCII and that problem is indicated by the first word of the acronym. ASCII is truly an *American* standard, but there's a whole wide world outside our borders where ASCII is simply inadequate. It isn't even good enough for countries that share our language, for where is the British pound sign in ASCII? . . . ASCII . . . is not only inadequate for the written languages of much of the world, but also for many people who live right in my own neighborhood. . . . We simply can't be so parochial as to foster a system as exclusive and limiting as ASCII. The personal computing revolution is quickly encompassing much of the world, and it's totally absurd that the dominant standard is based solely on English as it is spoken in the U.S. (375)

Although this limitation may not represent a large problem to academic professionals, such a limited system makes global computer communications unnecessarily difficult for student learners who speak languages other than English. What remains most interesting about this situation—especially given that teachers, scholars, and computer designers generally acknowledge the limitations of ASCII—is that the change to a more broadly accommodating system has been so slow, even though the technological means for representing other alphabetic systems (e.g., the memory, the programming mechanics, the computer hardware) have been available for some time now. To change ASCII, however, is to work against a complex set of tendential forces encouraging inertia—because changing ASCII means changing existing software, hardware, documentation, and programming approaches. It also requires that individuals and groups in the computer industry abandon English as the *natural* language of, the natural standard for, computer technology. Such changes do not happen easily or quickly.

Interfaces as Maps of Rationalism and Logocentric Privilege

If the map of the interface is oriented simultaneously along the axes of class, race, and cultural privilege, it is also aligned with the values of rationality, hierarchy, and logocentrism characteristic of Western patriarchal cultures. IBM's DOS environment, for example, is fundamentally dependent on an hierarchical representation of knowledge, a perspective characteristically—while not exclusively—associated with patriarchal cultures and rationalistic traditions of making meaning. This way of representing knowledge within computer environments, although not essentially limiting or exclusive by itself, becomes so when linked to a positivist value on rationality and logic as *foundational* ways of knowing that function to exclude other ways of knowing, such as association, intuition, or bricolage. This validation of positivism, rationality, hierarchy, and logic as the only authorized contexts for "knowing" and representing knowledge continues to inform—and limit—many formal aspects of computer programming and technology design. As Winograd and Flores note, the current rationalistic framework that informs the design of computers and their interfaces is "based on a misinterpretation of the nature of human cognition and language," one that provides "only impoverished possibilities for modeling and enlarging the scope of human understanding" (78). As a result, these authors continue, "We are now witnessing a major breakdown in the design of computer technology—a breakdown that reveals the rationalistically oriented background of discourse within which our current understanding [of technology] is embedded" (78–79). A similar case has been made by Ted Nelson, a pioneer in the design of hypertext interfaces, who has referred to the conceptual structure of hierarchical file systems as an "enormous barrier" to creative thinking. Nelson has characterized the effects of such systems as both "oppressive and devastating." The "tyranny" of hierarchical systems, Nelson contends, "imposes intricate, fixed pathways that we must commit to memory" and "forbid acting on inspiration." He adds, further, that such systems cause programmers to "oversimplify" their representation of data and the uses of such data within computer interfaces (83–84).

As Sherry Turkle and Seymour Papert point out, this conventional validation of—and dependence on—hierarchy, rationality, and logic is all the more potent because it is operative at all levels of computer interface design and programming. Computer programmers are educated to solve problems using hierarchical approaches to problem solving and to represent relationships in programs abstractly, within a strict syntactical system of linear propositional logic. This "formal, propositional" way of constructing knowledge (129) has come to constitute a "canonical style" (133) for programmers who are solving problems and representing information, a privileged way of relating ideas one to the other that has become "literally synonymous with knowledge" (129) in computer science. So synonymous has this way of thinking become with knowledge, in fact, that computer scientists have come to see propositional thinking not as *one* way of knowing, but as the *only* way of knowing. It has become equated with "formal" and "logical" thinking, and given "a privileged status" (133) within computer science.

Recently, however, increasing numbers of computer specialists have begun to identify the limitations inherent in relying on hierarchical approaches and data representations—in dealing with learners who have varying levels and kinds of visualization skills, in training programmers to apply epistemologically diverse approaches to programming problems, and in representing non-hierarchically organized information structures like *wicked* or *fuzzy* problems (complex problems with no definitive formulations or solutions), and in coping with natural language input.[4]

Several programming paradigms have been suggested as alternatives and supplements to hierarchical representations of knowledge, such as object-oriented programming systems (OOPS) and iconic interfaces that represent knowledge, concepts, or programs through small pictures, called *objects* or *icons*. Such methods of programming and designing computer interfaces, some computer designers contend, can support alternative approaches to constructing meaning—though "bricolage," for example, a term that Turkle and Papert (135) use in reference to the work of Claude Levi-Strauss. Bricolage, as Turkle and Papert employ the term, refers to the construction of meaning through the arrangement and rearrangement of concrete, well-known materials, often in an intuitive rather than logical manner. Bricoleurs get to know a subject by interacting with it physically, by manipulating materials, or symbols, or icons in rich associative patterns, by arranging and re-arranging them constantly until they fit together in a satisfying or meaningful way. Bricoleurs reason "from within" (144) to come to an understanding of a problem through a direct "physical path of access" (145) rather than reasoning with the help of a traditionally validated pattern of logical representation that depends on objective distancing.

Turkle and Papert contend that allowing for bricolage as a way of representing knowledge will encourage an "epistemological pluralism" within the "computer culture" (153) that might especially benefit individuals who feel "more comfortable with a relational, interactive, active, and connected approach to objects" (150). In particular, Turkle and Papert link bricolage with approaches to problem solving that are culturally determined and articulated with gender. Drawing on the work of Carol Gilligan, Evelyn Fox Keller, and Sandra Harding and Merrill Hintikka, these authors suggest that women, in particular, might benefit from conceptual frameworks that would support bricolage, but not exclude rationalistically determined approaches such as hierarchical representations. It could be a mistake, however, as Judith Butler points out, to see gender itself in such fixed terms or to consider the continual construction and re-constructions of gender identities as other than complex, momentary, and contradictory "intersections" (3) of cultural and political forces. As played out realistically within the maps of computer interfaces, Turkle and Papert's suggestions prove more problematic. The Macintosh interface, for instance, allows for both bricolage and rationalistically determined representations of hierarchy—that is, documents, folders, and text nodes can be arranged and re-arranged according to alternative relations of space, time, association, and intuition *or* according to more traditional logical relations of hierarchy and classification. As we have tried to indicate, however, the alignment of these cultural maps along the articulated axes of capitalism, class, gender, and race creates a set of tendential forces that continues to value approaches associated primarily with dominant ideological positions.

Given the characteristics of the interface as a linguistic contact zone, our uses of computers in English classrooms certainly seem capable of supporting what Henry Giroux calls "imperialist master narratives" (57) of colonial dominance, even as they make the promise of technological liberation and progress. Students who want to use computers are continually confronted with these grand narratives which foreground a value on middle-class, corporate culture; capitalism and the commodification of information; Standard English; and rationalistic ways of representing knowledge. These values simultaneously do violence to and encourage the rejection of the languages of different races and the values of non-dominant cultural and gender groups. When students from these groups enter the linguistic borderlands of the interface, in other words, they often learn that they must abandon their own culture or gender and acknowledge the dominance of other groups. As Pratt and Said, among others, note, such individuals are forced, at some level, into "simultaneously identifying with dominant groups" and disassociating themselves from the colonial values of these groups (Pratt 59, citing Moreau).

This is, as we see it, one of the ways in which educators use computers—albeit unconsciously—to enact what Elspeth Stuckey calls "the violence of literacy." Each time we ask students from a marginalized cultural group to use computers, we ask them—require them—to learn a system of literacy that "distance[s] them from the ways of equality" (94). When we connect the regularly dispersed violence of literacy education to the use of computers, as technology critics like C. Paul Olson and Andrew Feenberg point out, we get more than the sum of the parts. We get, indeed, a master narrative that resonates all too successfully with modernist myths of technological progress: Civilization and reason, as manifested in an increasingly literate people, are supported in their historical evolution by continual improvements of industry and science. If teachers hear this resonance, we think they understand the need to identify and correct the tone.

WHAT TO DO?

Scholars who use technology and educators who teach with technology will, no doubt, find it difficult to study the maps of computer interfaces in a critical light to identify the many layers of culture and ideology they represent. As Denis Wood suggests, the greatest difficulty of all comes when we understand that we must locate ourselves in relation to the map. At this point, we end up asking ourselves where we stand in this colonial landscape, how we have cast our own multiple subjective positions within the territory that we have created and examined. Are we the cartographers who compose the map in our own cultural image—as white-collar professionals, many of us white or privileged? Are we members of a dominant group that profits from the map's reproductive function—as official representatives of an educational system and, in the case of many institutions of higher learning, the State? In part, of course, we do (already and always, as they say) stand in these places, but we can also—by revealing the partial and flawed nature of the map, by acknowledging our own role in composing the map—claim other vantage places as well. In particular, we can take with increasing seriousness the role of serving as technology critics when we use computers in the classroom and when we work with other teachers to integrate technology within these learning spaces. As Elspeth Stuckey, in *The Violence of Literacy*, says of literacy education in general—when we finally get around to "seeing" how a system supports repression, we can also find ways to alter the nature of our involvement in it:

> A system takes a lot of trouble. A system must be devised and implemented. To be sure, much of its design is tacit, its implementation an extension of usual modes of comfortable life. That is why uncomfortable people can often change a system. They can see it. (126)

So what do we do as educators and as the teachers of teachers? In our own classrooms, the continuing process has to be centered on a continuing foregrounding of the problems we have sketched out here, which leads us to suggest some related strategies for re-drawing the territory of the interface with students. To begin, however, we have to learn to recognize—and teach students to recognize—the interface as an interested and partial map of our culture and as a linguistic contact zone that reveals power differentials. We need to teach students and ourselves to recognize computer interfaces as non-innocent physical borders (between the regular world and the virtual world), cultural borders (between the haves and the have-nots), and linguistic borders. These borders we need to recognize as cultural formations "historically constructed and socially organized within rules and regulations that limit and enable particular identities, individual capacities, and social forms" (Giroux 30). We also need to teach students and ourselves useful strategies of crossing—and demystifying—these borders. It is important to understand that we continually re-map and renegotiate borders in our lives.

One of the ways to come to this understanding is through working with students and computer specialists to re-design/re-imagine/re-create interfaces that attempt to avoid disabling and devaluing non-white, non-English language background students, and women. Our goal in creating these new interfaces should be to help rewrite the relationships between the center and the margins of our culture and, in Henry Giroux's words, "extend rather than erase the possibility for enabling human agency" (27) among currently marginalized and oppressed groups represented within the culture and the educational system. Although it is important to recognize—given the strong tendential forces of our cultural and the regularly dispersed nature of ideological systems—that any progress we make toward these goals will be partial, temporary, and contradictory, there are a few practices (what de Certeau might call *tactics*) that could help us enact a border pedagogy in computer-supported writing environments. We would like to spend the last part of this article identifying a few of these practical approaches that might be of use in composition programs at the college and university level.

Becoming Technology Critics as Well as Technology Users

One tactic for responding to the interested nature of computer interfaces has to do with encouraging a general level of critical awareness about technology issues on the part of both pre-service and in-service teachers. Currently, most teachers of composition studies at the collegiate level are educated to deal with technology not as critics but as users—if, indeed, they are educated to deal with it at all. Few programs that educate college-level teachers of composition, for example, require students to take coursework in technology studies. If they are lucky, new faculty or graduate teaching assistants at an institution may be introduced—during an orientation for instructors or during a graduate course in teaching composition—to a computer facility that they can use for their teaching. Often, these introductions accomplish nothing more than exposing teachers to one or more software programs available for use in the classroom, and allowing time for some minimal hands-on practice with the software. Few composition programs or English departments, however, make a systematic effort to provide parallel instruction on technology issues as they touch on educational projects—stressing readings and discussions on technology criticism, or on the growing body of scholarship and research associated with computers and composition studies.[5] As a result, teachers of composition—and prospective teachers of composition—may learn to use technology, but not to think carefully about the implications of its use within their own classrooms.

Influencing this situation is an additional set of forces that encourage relatively conservative teaching strategies in connection with technology and relatively little room for reflection on these strategies. Given the costs

involved in computing, most composition programs and English departments must depend on access to generic *computing* environments rather
than facilities designed specifically to provide computer-supported *writers'*
environments. Such generic facilities, because they are administered and
maintained by computer specialists rather than teachers of English, foreground an emphasis on the machine and its use rather than on a critical
approach to teaching composition with computer support. Characteristic of
these facilities, often located in interior rooms or basements, are rows of
numbered machines arranged to look very much like traditional classrooms
and often networked so that they can be controlled from a single teacher's
workstation at the front of the room. In such settings, and often armed with
very little preparation or training, teachers of composition also have little
encouragement to make changes in conventionally influenced teaching
approaches they observe in regular classrooms, as Klem and Moran note
(5–22). In such an environment, for example, it may become difficult to
have students working in flexible groupings, to avoid a teacher-centered
classroom, or to provide students room to take some charge of their own
learning.

Operating within these parameters, it is recognizably difficult to educate
teachers of composition as technology critics and to inculcate the intellectual habit of reflecting critically on the effects that technology might have
within composition classrooms. Writing program administrators and individual teachers can, however, take some steps toward this goal by making
sure that their programs—whether pre-service or in-service—are spending at
least as much time educating teachers about important technology issues
(access to technology, design of technology, ideologies associated with technology) as they are on training them to use technology. Among the efforts
that might be undertaken by teachers and program administrators in support
of this goal are collecting and circulating articles and books that provide critical as well as optimistic visions of technology, setting up research groups
and teaching observations to encourage reflective teaching habits in computer-supported writing facilities, encouraging faculty to participate in
e-mail lists that discuss technology issues as they are manifested in English
composition classrooms, and sponsoring talks by informed scholars who
examine technology issues from critical perspectives.[6]

Contributing to Technology Design

A second tactic for addressing the interested nature of computer interfaces is
more narrowly and specifically focused on the efforts of those faculty who
are computers and composition specialists. Given the embryonic state of

this field and the traditional educational reward structures within which computers and composition specialists must function to earn tenure, promotion, and professional recognition, these colleagues have focused most of their efforts during the past fifteen years on identifying, exploring, and testing pedagogical uses of available computer technologies—suggesting, for example, effective ways to integrate the use of word-processing packages, on-line conferences, or idea generation packages into the teaching of English composition classes.[7] Less effort, therefore, has been available to invest in software design efforts—which can be costly in terms of resources and professional advancement, as LeBlanc points out—and almost no involvement has been encouraged in the design of primary interfaces. Without such an involvement by humanist scholars and teachers—especially those individuals who are familiar with language and learning theory, who understand issues raised by technology studies and cultural studies—interface design will continue to be dominated primarily by computer scientists and will lack perspectives that could be contributed by humanist scholars.

Fortunately, avenues for involvement in software design efforts are becoming more accessible. Computers and composition specialists who find the penalties associated with the effort to design specific software packages to be overly costly in terms of tenure, promotion, and advancement, can also influence software design through collective professional action aimed at general technology design efforts. Professional organizations such as the Alliance for Computers in Writing,[8] International Federation of Information Processing, and even the National Council of Teachers of English (through committees like the Instruction Technology Committee, and the CCCC Committee on Computers) currently influence the design of software through various formal and informal strategies of collective action: by identifying groups of teachers and professional educators who can engage directly in conversations with software manufacturers and vendors, by charging committees to take on the task of making systematic suggestions to these manufacturers after consulting with reflective computer-using teachers, by identifying outstanding efforts in software design, by publishing papers and reviews that include critical examinations of design implications in the classroom, and by identifying the kinds of products that are limited in their classroom usefulness. Many of these committees and organizations also hold ongoing discussions of computer issues of interest to teachers of composition on the Internet. Within these forums—which often are global in their participation and include a mix of computer scientists, educators, software designers, and content specialists—computers and composition specialists can encourage discussions that focus on interfaces, language issues, cultural reproduction, learning theories, and critical theories of language use. Through these conversations, computers and composition specialists can contribute to an increasingly critical awareness of technology issues on the part of individuals involved directly in the design of technology. Such conversations—if they can serve to extend and transform the existing intellectual and political terrain for various groups of people—could have, in Laclau and Mouffe's words, a "profound subversive power" (155).

Re-Conceiving the Map of the Interface

A third suggestion for addressing the interested map of reality offered by computer interfaces is to involve composition teachers and students in composition classes in an ongoing project to revise interfaces as *texts*. The purpose of these map-making sessions would be to come up with ideas for changing the interface to reflect a range of cultural, linguistic, and ideological perspectives. Faculty who specialize in computers and composition studies can serve as key resource people in this effort, although the goal is to involve *all* computer-using teachers and students in conceptualizing alternative maps of computer interfaces. The outcome of such sessions should not be to redesign interfaces in a technical sense, but rather to reconceive of them according to the experiences of a broad range of writers and teachers of writing: identifying desirable features generally unavailable in primary interfaces (a light pen for writing in the margins of documents, or a highlighter for color coding related documents), suggesting ways of customizing interfaces for the needs of various writers and readers (adding a read-aloud option for writers who want to hear how their texts sound), or imagining productive metaphors around which interfaces can be built (mechanics' workbenches, kitchen countertops, garages). In these sessions—to further reduce the focus on technical expertise—teachers and students can represent their interface re-revision ideas either through prose descriptions or pencil-and-pen drawings.

For those faculty and teachers who are more adventurous in terms of technology, some relatively simple computer-based tools already exist that could support these projects at a level accessible to non-specialists. Teachers and students can use the computer-based drawing and illustration packages they are already familiar with, for example, to create representations of re-designed interface screens to which they add new features. In addition, software designers for the Macintosh have already published scores of alternative icons and images that can be used by English composition teachers, and students, to customize primary computer interfaces. Matrix Communication Associates of Pittsburgh, for instance, is now marketing a package of African American computer graphics and has plans to market graphics packages that more adequately represent other ethnic groups as well (Creedy). With such packages, faculty and graduate students who have very little familiarity with computers can illustrate how they would like to incorporate various features into primary interfaces—creating icons for bulletin boards, on-line conferences, multiple user dimensions, or other student-centered learning spaces that they would like to include in an interface. It is possible that the representations identified by writing teachers and students can later be used by software and hardware design specialists as the basis for more technical projects that might actually produce working versions of alternative interfaces.

To support these conceptual redesign efforts, computers and composition specialists can also work with both teachers and students to assemble expanded libraries of images that appeal to writers of different ages, races, sexual preferences, classes, and lifestyles. These icons should be chosen to resonate with a range of different cultural and ideological positions—delicatessens and 7-Elevens, babies and rocking chairs, rosetta stones and piñatas, apartment buildings and subway maps, powwow dances and storytellers— which can be used to customize systems for different groups of writers. The goal in identifying these images and icons, in Henry Giroux's words, would be to help students and teachers focus on the act of crossing borders "moving in and out of borders constructed around coordinates of difference and power," learning and negotiating "the shifting parameters of place, identity, history, and power" (136). This project may help us and students to see that the interests represented within maps are "neither singular nor simple" (Wood 94) and that interests concealed in one map, one representation of a culture, can be revealed and foregrounded in another.

TOWARD A CRITICAL READING OF INTERFACES

For both teachers and students, Giroux notes, the project of eliminating oppression based on class, race, and gender involves "an ongoing contest within every aspect of daily life," a continual project of mapping and remapping the educational, political, and ideological spaces we want to occupy." He continues, "no tradition should ever be seen as received in this project" (155–56). In this sense, English teachers cannot be content to understand the maps of computer interfaces as simple, uncomplicated spaces. Rather, we need to prepare ourselves and the students with whom we work to map these virtual spaces as sites of "multiple and heterogeneous borders where different histories, languages, experiences, and voices intermingle amidst diverse relations of power and privilege" (Giroux 169). At the

661

same time, it is prudent to acknowledge the complications and contradictions inherent in such work. As Winograd and Flores point out, our continuing efforts toward revealing the interested nature of computer interfaces will, in part, contribute to concealment because "as carriers of a tradition, we cannot be objective observers of it." This realization, however, cannot provide an excuse for inaction. We must also, as these authors note, take on the responsibility of continuing to "work towards unconcealment . . . and let our awareness guide our actions in creating and applying technology" (179).

ACKNOWLEDGMENTS

We owe a great deal of gratitude to colleagues who helped us work through the ideas in this article. The generosity and intellectual contributions of Marilyn Cooper, Jim Sosnoski, and Joe Janangelo are evident in the best aspects of this paper.

NOTES

1. For more critical discussions of the overly optimistic rhetoric associated with computer use in composition classrooms, see Faigley's description of a synchronous network conversation (*Fragments* 163–99), Barton's discussion of the dominant discourses associated with technology ("Interpreting the Discourses of Technology"), Hawisher and Selfe's exploration of teachers' claims about computer use ("The Rhetoric of Technology"), and Romano's discussion of bias in on-line conversations ("The Egalitarianism Narrative").

2. Readers who want to explore the potential of electronic forums on WANs or LANs may want to consult: Barker and Kemp's "Network Theory"; Bruce, Peyton, and Batson's *Networked Classrooms*; Cooper and Selfe's "Computer Conferences"; Eldred's "Computers, Composition and the Social View"; Faigley's "Subverting the Electronic Notebook"; Handa's *Computers and Community*; Kiesler, Siegel, and McGuire's "Social Psychological Aspects"; and Spitzer's "Computer Conferencing."

3. Discussions of the ways in which racism, sexism, and power relationships related to colonialism are enacted in connection with technology use can be found in Gomez's "The Equitable Teaching of Composition," Hawisher and Selfe's "Rhetoric of Technology," Jessup's "Feminism and Computers," and LeBlanc's "Competing Ideologies."

4. For descriptions of the challenges associated with wicked problems and fuzzy logic, readers may want to refer to: Ambler, Burnett, and Zimmerman; Kurzweil; Seagull and Walker; Turkle and Papert; and Winograd and Flores.

5. For criticism related to technology, we recommend the works of Feenberg, Kramare, Olson, Ohmann.

6. Several such lists exist for teachers of composition. Megabyte University (MBU), for instance, focuses on issues surrounding the use of computers in writing-intensive classrooms and BreadNet serves to connect English teachers who have attended Breadloaf seminars. To obtain information on Megabyte University, contact Fred Kemp, the founder of MBU, at Texas Tech University (YKFOK@TTACS1.TTU.EDU). To obtain additional information about BreadNet, contact Bill Wright (BWRIGHT@TMN.COM). The National Council of Teachers of English is currently engaged in designing a computer network that will connect teachers of English across the country. For additional information on NCTENet, contact

Tharon Howard, Chair of the NCTE Instructional Technology Committee, at Clemson University (THARON@HUBCAP.CLEMSON.EDU).

7. The advent of computers and composition studies is typically dated from 1975, when Ellen Nold's *CCC* article, "Fear and Trembling," gave voice to the concerns English composition teachers had about technology (and thus gave impetus to focused work in this area), or from 1979, when Hugh Burns published the first dissertation that systematically examined the effects of computer-assisted instruction on student writers' invention efforts. The first fully assembled microcomputer, the Apple II, marketed in 1976, provided the actual technological means of introducing computers into composition classrooms in a meaningful way. These machines provided composition teachers with word-processing systems that were far easier to teach and far less difficult to use than the clumsy line-editors offered on mainframe computers in the seventies.

8. The Alliance for Computers in Writing is a national coalition of teachers, publishers, professional organizations, and educational institutions interested in promoting the effective use of computers in English composition classrooms. For more information on the Alliance for Computers and Writing, contact Trent Batson, Gallaudet University (TWBATSON@ GALLUA.BITNET).

WORKS CITED

Ambler, Allen L., Margaret M. Burnett, and Betsy A. Zimmerman. "Operational versus Definitional: A Perspective on Programming Paradigms." *Computer* (September 1992): 28–43.

Barker, Thomas T., and Fred O. Kemp. "Network Theory: A Postmodern Pedagogy for the Writing Classroom." *Computers and Community: Teaching Composition in the Twenty-First Century.* Ed. Carolyn Handa. Portsmouth, NH: Boynton 1–27.

Barton, Ellen. "Interpreting the Discourses of Technology." *Literacy and Computers: The Complications of Teaching and Learning on Technology.* Ed. Cynthia L. Selfe and Susan Hilligoss. New York: MLA, 1994. 56–75.

Batson, Trent. "The ENFI Project: A Networked Classroom Approach to Writing Instruction." *Academic Computing* (February/March 1988): 32–33, 55–56.

Berger, John. *Ways of Seeing.* New York: Penguin Books, 1972.

Bolter, Jay D. *Writing Space: The Computer, Hypertext, and the History of Writing.* Hillsdale, NJ: Erlbaum, 1991.

Bruce, Bertram, Joy Freeft Peyton, and Trent Batson. *Network-Based Classrooms: Promises and Realities.* New York: Cambridge UP, 1993.

Burns, Hugh. "Stimulating Rhetorical Invention through Computer-Assisted Instruction." Diss. U of Texas at Austin, 1979.

Butler, Judith. *Gender Trouble: Feminism and the Subversion of Identity.* New York: Routledge, 1990.

Cooper, Marilyn M., and Cynthia L. Selfe. "Computer Conferences and Learning: Authority, Resistance, and Internally Persuasive Discourse." *College English* 52 (1990): 847–69.

Creedy, Steve. "Local Firm's African-American Computer Graphics Fill Void." *Pittsburgh Post Gazette* 23 August 1993: B8.

de Certeau, Michel. *The Practice of Everyday Life.* Trans. Steven Randall. Berkeley: U of California P, 1984.

Deleuze, Gilles, and Félix Guattari. A *Thousand Plateaus: Capitalism and Schizophrenia.* Trans. Brian Massumi. Minneapolis, MN: U of Minnesota P, 1987.

Eldred, Janet C. "Computers, Composition, and the Social View." *Critical Perspectives on Computers and Composition Studies.* Ed. Gail E. Hawisher and Cynthia L. Selfe. New York: Teachers College P, 1989. 201–18.

Faigley, Lester. "Subverting the Electronic Notebook: Teaching Writing Using Networked Computers." *The Writing Teacher as Researcher: Essays in the Theory and Practice of Class-Based Research.* Ed. Donald A. Daiker and Max Morenberg. Portsmouth, NH: Boynton, 1990. 290–311.

Faigley, Lester. *Fragments of Rationality: Postmodernity and the Subject of Composition.* Pittsburgh: U of Pittsburgh P, 1992.

Feenberg, Andrew. *Critical Theory of Technology.* New York: Oxford UP, 1991.

Flores, Mary J. "Computer Conferencing: Composing a Feminist Community of Writers." *Computers and Community: Teaching Composition in the Twenty-First Century.* Ed. Carolyn Handa. Portsmouth, NH: Boynton, 1990. 106–17.

Foucault, Michel. "Space, Knowledge, and Power." *The Foucault Reader.* Ed. Paul Rabinow. New York: Pantheon, 1984. 239–56.

Gilligan, Carol. *In a Different Voice: Psychological Theory and Women's Development.* Cambridge, MA: Harvard UP, 1982.

Giroux, Henry A. *Border Crossings: Cultural Workers and the Politics of Education.* New York: Routledge, 1992.

Gomez, Mary L. "The Equitable Teaching of Composition." *Evolving Perspectives on Computers and Composition Studies.* Ed. Gail E. Hawisher and Cynthia L. Selfe. Urbana, IL: NCTE, 1991. 318–35.

Grimes, William. "Computer as a Cultural Tool." *New York Times* 1 December 1992: C 13–15.

Handa, Carolyn, ed. *Computers and Community: Teaching Composition in the Twenty-First Century.* Portsmouth, NH: Boynton, 1990.

Harding, Sandra, and Merrill B. Hintikka, eds. *Discovering Reality: Feminist Perspectives on Epistemology, Metaphysics, Methodology, and Philosophy of Science.* London: Reidel, 1983.

Hawisher, Gail E., and Cynthia L. Selfe. "Voices in College Classrooms: The Dynamics of Electronic Discussion." *The Quarterly* 14 (Summer 1992): 24–28, 32.

——. "The Rhetoric of Technology and the Electronic Writing Class." *CCC* 42 (1991): 55–65.

——. "Tradition and Change in Computer-Supported Writing Environments." *Theoretical and Critical Perspectives on Teacher Change.* Ed. P. Kahaney, J. Janangelo, and L. A. M. Perry. Norwood, NJ: Ablex, 1993. 155–86.

Janangelo, Joseph. "Technopower and Technoppression: Some Abuses of Power and Control in Computer-Assisted Writing Environments." *Computers and Composition* 9 (November 1991): 47–64.

Jessup, Emily. "Feminism and Computers in Composition Instruction." *Evolving Perspectives on Computers and Composition Studies: Questions for the 1990s.* Ed. Gail E. Hawisher and Cynthia L. Selfe. Urbana, IL: 1991. 336–55.

Jordan, June. *ON CALL: Political Essays.* Boston, MA: South End 1985.

——. "Toward a Manifest New Destiny." *The Progressive* (February 1992): 18, 23.

Keller, Evelyn F. *Reflections on Gender and Science.* New Haven: Yale UP, 1985.

Kiesler, Sara, Jane Siegel, and Timothy W. McGuire. "Social Psychological Aspects of Computer-Mediated Communication." *American Psychologist* 39 (1984): 1123–34.

Klem, Elizabeth, and Charles Moran. "Teachers in a Strange LANd: Learning to Teach in a Networked Writing Classroom." *Computers and Composition* 9 (August 1992): 5–22.

Kramare, Cheris, ed. *Technology and Women's Voices: Keeping in Touch.* New York: Routledge, 1988.

Kremers, Marshall. "Adams Sherman Hill Meets ENFI: An Inquiry and a Retrospective." *Computers and Composition* 5 (August 1988): 69–77.

Kurzweil, Raymond. *The Age of Intelligent Machines.* Cambridge, MA: MIT P, 1990.

Laclau, Ernesto, and Chantel Mouffe. *Hegemony and Socialist Strategy: Towards a Radical Democratic Politics.* London: Verso, 1985.

LeBlanc, Paul. "Competing Ideologies in Software Design for Computer-Aided Composition." *Computers and Composition* 7 (April 1990): 8–19.

Moreau, N. B. "Education, Ideology, and Class/Sex Identity." *Language and Power.* Ed. Cheris Kramarae. Beverly Hills, CA: Sage, 1984. 43–61.

Nelson, Theodor H. "The Tyranny of the File." *Datamation* 15 December 1986: 83–86.

Nold, Ellen. "Fear and Trembling: A Humanist Approaches the Computer." *CCC* 26 (1975): 269–273.

Ohmann, Richard. "Literacy, Technology, and Monopoly Capitalism." *College English* 47 (1985): 675–689.

Olson, C. Paul. "Who Computes?" *Critical Pedagogy and Cultural Power.* Ed. David Livingstone. South Hadley, MA: Berglii, 1987. 179–204

Petzold, Charles. "Move Over, ASCII! Unicode Is Here." *PC Magazine* 12 (26 October 1993): 374–376.

Piller, Charles. "Separate Realities: The Creation of the Technological Underclass in America's Public Schools." *MacWorld* (September 1992): 218–30.

Pratt, Mary Louise. "Linguistic Utopias." *The Linguistics of Writing.* Ed. Nigel Fabb et al. Manchester: Manchester UP, 1987. 48–66.

———. "Arts of the Contact Zone." *Profession* 91(1991): 33–40.

Romano Susan. "The Egalitarianism Narrative: Whose Story? Which Yardstick?" *Computers and Composition* 10 (August 1993): 5–28.

Said, Edward. "Reflections on Exile." *Out There: Marginalization and Contemporary Cultures.* Ed. Russell Fergeson, Martha Gever, Trinh T. Minh-ha, and Cornell West. Cambridge, MA: MIT P, 1990. 357–68.

Seagull, J. F., and N. Walker. "The Effects of Hierarchical Structure and Visualization on Computerized Information Retrieval." *International Journal of Human-Computer Interaction* 4 (1992): 369–485.

Selfe, Cynthia L. "English Teachers and the Humanization of Computers: Networking Communities of Readers and Writers." *On Literacy and Its Teaching: Issues in English Education.* Ed. Gail E. Hawisher and Anna O. Soter. Albany, NY: State U of New York P, 1990. 190–205.

———. "Technology in the English Classroom: Computers through the Lens of Feminist Theory." *Computers and Community: Teaching Composition in the Twenty-First Century.* Ed. Carolyn Handa. Portsmouth, NH: Boynton, 1990. 118–39.

Selfe, Cynthia L., and Paul R. Meyer. "Testing Claims for On-Line Conferences." *Written Communication* 8 (1991): 163–92.

Sheingold, Karen, L. M. Martin, and M. W. Endreweit. "Preparing Urban Teachers for the Technological Future." *Mirrors of Minds: Patterns of Experience in Educational Computing.* Ed. Roy D. Pea and Karen Sheingold. Norwood, NJ: Ablex, 1987. 67–85.

Spitzer, Michael. "Computer Conferencing: An Emerging Technology." *Critical Perspectives in Computers and Composition Instruction.* Ed. Gail E. Hawisher and Cynthia L. Selfe. New York: Teachers College P, 1989. 187–200.

Springer, Claudia. "The Pleasure of the Interface." *Screen* 32 (1991): 303–23.

Stuckey, Elspeth. *The Violence of Literacy.* Portsmouth, NH: Boynton, 1991.

Turkle, Sherry, and Seymour Papert. "Epistomological Pluralism: Styles and Voices within the Computer Culture." *Signs* 16 (1990): 128–57.

Virilio, Paul. *Speed and Politics: An Essay on Dromology.* Trans. Mark Polizzotti. New York: Semiotext(e), 1987.

Weizenbaum, Joseph. "Not without Us: A Challenge to Computer Professionals to Use Their Power to Bring the Present Insanity to a Halt." *Fellowship* (October/ November 1986): 8–10.

Wheelock, Ann, and Gail Dorman. *Before It's Too Late.* Boston, MA: Massachusetts Advocacy Commission, 1989.

Winograd, Terry, and Fernando Flores. *Understanding Computers and Cognition: A New Foundation for Design.* Reading, MA: Addison, 1986.

Wood, Denis. *The Power of Maps.* New York: Guilford, 1992.

WordPerfect for DOS: Reference for IBM Personal Computers and PC Networks, 1989.

Blinded by the Letter

Why Are We Using Literacy as a Metaphor for Everything Else?

Anne Frances Wysocki and Johndan Johnson-Eilola

Too easily does "literacy" slip off our tongues, we think, and get put next to other terms: visual literacy, computer literacy, video literacy, media literacy, multimedia literacy, television literacy, technological literacy. Too much is hidden by "literacy," we think, too much packed into those letters—too much that we are wrong to bring with us, implicitly or no.

So:

Our first question in this essay: *what are we likely to carry with us when we ask that our relationship with all technologies should be like that we have with the technology of printed words?* ʰAsking questions helps build knowledge.

Our second question: *what other possibilities might we use for expressing our relationships with and within technologies?*

> "Examining titles in the ERIC database for 1980–94, inclusive, indicates that educators felt moved to discuss almost two hundred different kinds of literacy during those fifteen years; that is, two hundred different kinds of modified literacy as opposed to plain, unmodified literacy." This is from Dianne G. Kanawati's article, "How Can I Be Literate: Counting the Ways," where the author found, among the 197 total references in the ERIC database, Cash-culture Literacy, Christian Literacy, Discipline Literacy, Risk Literacy, Somatic Literacy, Water Literacy, Competitive Literacy, and Post-Literacy.

Reprinted from *Passions, Pedagogies, and 21st Century Technologies*. Ed. Gail E. Hawisher and Cynthia L. Selfe. Logan: Utah State UP and Urbana, IL: NCTE, 1999. 349–368. Copyright 1999 by Utah State University Press. Reprinted with permission.

FIRST

There are two bundles we carry with us when we ask that our relationship with all technologies should be like that we have with printed words. There is, first, a bundle of stories we have accumulated about what literacy is and does; second, there is our regard for the object to which we relate within literacy.

THE BUNDLE OF STORIES

"Of course you can learn how to read. Do you want to try?"

—Ransom Stoddard (James Stewart) to Hallie (Vera Miles),
his future wife, in *The Man Who Shot Liberty Valance*

At almost the ending of *The Man Who Shot Liberty Valance*, Ransom Stoddard and his wife Hallie are returning by train to Washington D.C. for what he says will be his last term as senator. He has recently finished recounting how he, a lawyer opposed to guns, helped bring law—and order—and statehood—and "book learning"—to the open territory around Shinbone (an unidentified territory in the U.S. West).

Hallie looks out the train window and says to Ransom, "It was once a wilderness. Now it's a garden."

In an earlier scene in a makeshift schoolroom (with "Education is the basis of law and order" written on the blackboard at the front), Ransom asks Pompey, a man of middle years and a student in the class, to talk about "the basic law of the land." Pompey, who works for Tom Donovan (John Wayne), starts to talk, with hesitant pauses in his sentences but with pride, about the Constitution; Jimmy Stewart corrects him: Pompey means the Declaration of Independence. Pompey starts again: "We hold these truths to be, uh, self-evident, that . . ."

He stops. Ransom finishes for him, ". . . all men are created equal." "I knew that, Mr. Ranse," says Pompey, "but I just plumb forgot it."

The room is disrupted by Tom entering to tell of how the cattlemen—who are fighting statehood because it will close off the free range—will bring violence down upon the townspeople and farmers who want a state. But, of course, eventually, Jimmy Stewart's gentle and learned ways help tame the area into statehood.

b

February 13, 1996

President Clinton announced today his intent to nominate Mary D. Green to the National Institute for Literacy Board...

The National Institute for Literacy was created to assist in upgrading the workforce, reducing welfare dependency, raising the standard of literacy and creating safer communities.

(http://www.ed.gov./PressRelease/02-1996/whpr24.html)

c

People who read, according to our reading of McLuhan, do nothing; they are helpless as the words they read pass through their eyes to shape them:

> ... print causes nationalism and not tribalism; and print causes price systems and markets such as cannot exist without print. (50)

> ... the assumption of homogeneous repeatability derived from the printed page, when extended to all the other concerns of life, led gradually to all those forms of production and social organization from which the Western world derives many satisfactions and nearly all of its characteristic traits. (144)

> ... the mere accustomation to repetitive, lineal patterns of the printed page strongly disposed people to transfer such approaches to all kinds of problems. (151)

> And quantification means the translation of non-visual relations and realities into visual terms, a procedure inherent in the phonetic alphabet. (161)

Or, as Walter J. Ong puts it in *Orality and Literacy*, literacy fulfils our destiny:

> . . . without writing, human consciousness cannot achieve its fuller potentials, cannot produce other beautiful and powerful creations. . . . Literacy . . . is absolutely necessary for the development not only of science but also of history, philosophy, explicative understanding of literature and of any art, and indeed for the explanation of language (including oral speech) itself. (15)

X X X

It is thus a large but not unruly bundle that comes with "literacy": John Wayne, Jimmy Stewart, the taming of the U.S. west, democracy, an upgraded workforce, less welfare dependency, our forms of production and social organization, science, and philosophy. The various descriptions and quotations above (a small selection from many possible) argue that if we acquire the basic skills of reading and writing—if we are literate—we have, or will have, all the goods the stories bundle together, no matter who or where or when we are.

"We think," writes Glynda Hull, "of reading and writing as generic, the intellectual equivalent of all-purpose flour, and we assume that, once mastered, these skills can and will be used in any context for any purpose, and that they are ideologically neutral and value-free" (34).

When we speak of "technological literacy," then, or of "computer literacy" or of "[fill-in-the-blank] literacy," we probably mean that we wish to give others some basic, neutral, context-less set of skills whose acquisition will bring the bearer economic and social goods and privileges. Aimée Dore says as much in an article titled "What Constitutes Literacy in a Culture with Diverse and Changing Means of Communication?":

> . . . most people in education and communication are comfortable using the term "literacy" for [describing a relation to print, visual objects, television, and computer] because the various literacies have in common the image of people able to use symbol systems and the media or technologies in which they are instantiated in order to express themselves and to communicate with others, to do so effectively, and to do so in socially desirable ways. (145)

The same belief in a discrete set of basic skills shows itself in a recent White House document.

AMERICA'S TECHNOLOGY LITERACY CHALLENGE

February 15, 1996

"In our schools, every classroom in America must be connected to the information superhighway with computers and good software and well-trained teachers. . . . I ask Congress to support this education technology initiative so that we can make sure this national partnership succeeds." President Clinton, State of the Union, January 23, 1996

NATIONAL MISSION TO MAKE EVERY YOUNG PERSON TECH-NOLOGICALLY LITERATE: The President has launched a national mission to make all children technologically literate by the dawn of the 21st century, equipped with communication, math, science, and critical thinking skills essential to prepare them for the Information Age. He challenges the private sector, schools, teachers, parents, students, community groups, state and local governments, and the federal government, to meet this goal by building four pillars that will:

1. Provide all teachers the training and support they need to help students learn through computers and the information superhighway;

2. Develop effective and engaging software and on-line learning resources as an integral part of the school curriculum;

3. Provide access to modern computers for all teachers and students;

4. Connect every school and classroom in America to the information superhighway.

But—and (unfortunately) of course—this notion of discrete skills is only a partial view of "literacy." The bundle of meanings and implications that comes with this word is, we argue alongside many other writers, much denser and messier.

In "Arts of the Contact Zone," Mary Louise Pratt describes a 1200 page manuscript, dated 1613, discovered in Copenhagen in 1908:

Written in a mixture of Quechua and ungrammatical, expressive Spanish, the manuscript was a letter addressed by an unknown but apparently literate Andean to King Phillip III of Spain. . . .

The second half of the epistle . . . combines a description of colonial society in the Andean region with a passionate denunciation of Spanish exploitation and abuse. (34–35)

But:

No one, it appeared, had ever bothered to read it or figured out how. (34)

In *The Man Who Shot Liberty Valance*, reading and writing don't get Pompey (an African-American man) or Hallie (the white wife) or the Mexican children in Ransom's classroom or their parents the right to vote in the move towards statehood; that privilege is reserved for the white men in the movie—some of whom cannot read and write. In the non-film reality of our present time, becoming literate in English does not help a young Navajo woman feel that she has a real place in Anglo culture, as Anne DiPardo describes, nor does it help the Native Alaskans or African-Americans about whom Lisa Delpit writes feel that they really belong as students in graduate programs or as teachers in U.S. schools. Hull provides a catalogue of writers who warn that U.S. supremacy in business will be eroded by illiteracy in the workforce, but then Hull describes the experiences of two African-American women whose "failure" at a job (processing checks for a bank) was due not to their lack of literacy skills but to day care and transportation and economic problems unacknowledged by their employers.

In spite of the stories we quoted above, literacy alone—some set of basic skills—is not what improves people's lives.

Both Harvey J. Graff, in the early 1980s, and Ruth Finnegan, in the early 1990s, use "literacy myth" to name the belief that literacy will bring us everything the stories above promise; according to Finnegan,

> This story has been around for a long time. It reflects popular and still widely held assumptions: that literacy is a good thing, both the sign and the cause of progress, and that without it we and others would still be in the dark ages. Although it is under attack from a number of directions, this view is still in many circles the conventional wisdom and has played a large part in the rhetoric—and to some extent, therefore—in the practice of educationalists and "development" experts. (32)

Brian Street argues that the idea of such an autonomous literacy, whose acquisition necessarily causes progress, has played a part in the practice of

national and international literacy programs; using programs in Iran, Great Britain, and Mozambique as examples, he argues that such programs—which claim to bring economic growth by giving people a simple neutral skill—ignore and override and irrevocably change the lives and culture of those who are made literate: "[T]hese grandiose claims for 'academic' literacy," he writes, "are merely those of a small elite attempting to maintain positions of power and influence by attributing universality and neutrality to their own cultural conventions" (224).

In *The Violence of Literacy*, Elspeth Stuckey's words are equally strong for those who believe that literacy is or can be neutral:

> In the United States we live the mythology of a classless society. . . . In a society bound by such a mythology, our views about literacy are our views about political economy and social opportunity. . . . Far from engineering freedom, our current approaches to literacy corroborate other social practices that prevent freedom and limit opportunity. (vii)

And:

> We must take responsibility for the racism throughout schooling, the racism leveled most brutally and effectively in children's earliest years of schooling by literacy whose achievements can be seen in the loss of a third or more poor students by schooling's end. (122)

Or, as Finnegan puts it:

> The myth can be seen as playing an essential ideological function for the governing social, political, or educational order, whether manifested by earlier imperial expansion or by current national or international inequalities. So, when people might want, for example, houses or jobs or economic reform, they are instead given literacy programs. (41)

When we speak then of "literacy" as though it were a basic, neutral, contextless set of skills, the word keeps us hoping—in the face of lives and arguments to the contrary—that there could be an easy cure for economic and social and political pain, that only a lack of literacy keeps people poor or oppressed.

And when we believe this—that poverty and oppression result from a lack of a simple, neutral set of skills—we have trouble understanding why everyone and anyone can't acquire the skills: there must be something wrong with someone who can't correctly learn what most of us acquired easily, in our early years in home or school. Delpit describes classrooms where students and teachers have cultural and grammatical differences, with the teachers then judging their students' "actions, words, intellects, families, and communities as inadequate at best, as collections of pathologies at worst" (xiv). According to Stanley Aronowitz, Walter Lippman and John Dewey argued for the importance of education and literacy because they thought that "lacking education the 'people' are inherently incapable of governing themselves" (298) When people aren't literate — when under this conception of literacy they are not economically secure or part of the culture of the rest of us — it is because of some (inherent?) failure of theirs. We ask them, by using a conception of literacy that allows us to ask them, to blame themselves. We overlook, if not forget, the economic and social and political structures that work to keep people in their places.

> If "literacy" is a deceptive promise of basic skills that on their own will fix someone's life, why do we wish to use this term when we speak of the relationship we desire for our students and others to have with newer technologies?

2

THE SECOND BUNDLE: THE OBJECTS WE ADDRESS THROUGH THE RELATION OF LITERACY

a

> The paged book became the physical embodiment, the incarnation, of the text it contained. (Bolter 86)

b

> . . . if, in an era of uncertain values, we want to keep alive respect for ideas and knowledge, it is important to give books a form that encourages respect. (Levarie 306)

d

Prepare a narrative of all which has held it.

Prepare a narrative of all which has held it.

Prepare a narrative of prepare a narrative of all which has held it.

Out of the whole.

Out of the whole wide world I chose it.

Out of the whole wide world I chose it. (Stein 253)

X X X X

The other day, in *Dear Abby*, this was part of the opening letter:

> An ongoing cycle of illiteracy haunts children on the edges of poverty. When teachers ask their students to bring a favorite book to class to share, these children show up with an advertisement or a coupon book because they have no books at home.
>
> Abby, please help these children learn to love books and reading.
> (*Daily Mining Gazette*, Houghton, MI, 11/19/96)

As we have argued above, we believe that "literacy" is presented as a necessary and sufficient set of skills for entree to the good life when it is really a diversion from social and political situations. We do not, however, deny that reading and writing can be a useful set of skills amongst all the skills and practices and behaviors and attributes we all need in order to flourish in our present culture . . .
> . . . *but why should anyone love books—the objects—in and of themselves?*

In "Literacy and the Colonization of Memory," Walter D. Mignolo argues that when the Spaniards colonized the area we now call Mexico, they were so steeped in book culture that they believed the Mexica had no sense of history—because the Mexica recorded their pasts in paintings rather than in words in books—and hence that the Mexica "lacked intelligence and humanity" (96).

> (For a more detailed description of this meeting between the Inca and the Spanish—and more about how this incident hinging on a [the?] book can be tied to other consequences of literacy, see Diamond 68–81.)

Constance Classen, in *Worlds of Sense: Exploring the Senses in History and Across Cultures*, describes an incident in the Spanish colonization of the Inca, whose cosmology relied on hearing:

... the Spanish priest accompanying the expedition gave a brief summary of Christian doctrine, denounced Inca religion as invented by the Devil, and demanded that Atahualpa become the vassal of the Holy Roman Emperor. While giving his address the priest held a book, either the Bible or a breviary, in one hand. Atahualpa, deeply offended by this speech, . . . demanded of the priest by what authority he made these claims. The friar held up the book to him. Atahualpa examined it, but as it said nothing to him he dropped it to the ground. This rejection of the essence of European civilization was the excuse the Spanish needed to begin their massacre. (110)

This attachment to books as essence hasn't changed in the hundreds of years following that massacre; witness Sven Birkerts' words from *The Gutenberg Elegies: The Fate of Reading in an Electronic Age*:

I stare at the textual field on my friend's [computer] screen and I am unpersuaded. Indeed, this glimpse of the future—if it is the future—has me clinging all the more tightly to my books, the very idea of them. If I ever took them for granted, I do no longer. I now see each one as a portable enclosure, a place I can repair to release the private, unsocialized, dreaming self. A book is a solitude, privacy; it is a way of holding the self apart from the crush of the outer world. Hypertext—at least the spirit of hypertext, which I see as the spirit of the times—promises to deliver me from the "liberating domination" of the author. It promises to spring me from the univocal linearity which is precisely the constraint that fills me with a sense of possibility as I read my way across fixed acres of print. (164)

Birkerts' attachment to books is more self-conscious than the Spanish friar's, perhaps, but it is nonetheless just as closed off to other forms of expression that might offer other senses of possibility. For both men, dream and value and self and culture and world seem to be fully enclosed within literacy, objectified in—and not separable from—the book.

Birkerts' words call to our minds Habermas, who wrote that a necessary (but not sufficient) step in the development of a critical public in the 18th century was that men read to themselves: in the privacy of their reading they developed a sense of individuated self, a self that could hold a position in the public sphere (45–56). Robert Romanyshyn puts an earlier date to the book's relation to this individuation:

Linear perspective vision was a fifteenth-century artistic invention for representing three dimensional depth on the two-dimensional canvas. It was a geometrization of vision which began as an invention and became a convention, a cultural habit of mind. . . . At approximately the same time that Alberti's procedures [for perspective] are mapping the world as a geometric grid, laying it out in linear fashion, the book will be introduced and mass-produced. The linearity of the geometric world will find its counterpart in the linear literacy of the book, where line by line, sentence by sentence, the chronological structures of the book will mirror the sequential, ordered, linear structure of time in the sciences. In addition, the interiorization of individual subjectivity within the room of consciousness will find apt expression in the private act of reading and in silence, unlike the manuscript consciousness of the Middle Ages, where reading was done aloud. (349–351)

The exact date of this interiorization of a self is not important to our words here; rather, what we wish to call attention to is how writers like McLuhan and Ong, and Birkerts accept that books—once they have somehow acquired the form we now take for granted, small enough for us to hold and carry about, and containing texts that encourage us to see continuity stretching like words linearly over the time of many pages—ask us to think of ourselves as selves. These writers' words are like commands—or interpellations—hailing us to see our selves and the possibilities of our world delimited between the covers of the book; Ivan Illich and Barry Sanders put it the following way in *ABC: The Alphabetization of the Popular Mind:*

> The idea of a self that continues to glimmer in thought or memory, occasionally retrieved and examined in the light of day, cannot exist without the text. Where there is no alphabet, there can be neither memory conceived as a storehouse nor the "I" as its appointed watchman. With the alphabet both text and self became possible, but only slowly, and they became the social construct on which we found all our perceptions as literate people. (72)

Here are other descriptions (several possibilities from among many) of our relationship with books, and of how that relationship is to shape us:

> Ramus was entirely right in his insistence on the supremacy of the new printed book in the classroom. For only there could the homogenizing effects of the new medium be given heavy stress in young lives. Students processed by print technology in this way would be able to translate every kind of problem and experience into the new visual kind of lineal order. (McLuhan 146)

> What is written has a disembodied existence; knowledge is no longer contained within human bodies but exists separately from them. In a literate society, therefore, knowledge—and by extension, the cosmos—is devitalized,

> de-personalized, and reified. The literate world is a silent, still world, one in which the primary means of gaining knowledge is by looking and reflecting. . . . (Classen 110)

> . . . print is a singularly impersonal medium. Lay preachers and teachers who addressed congregations from afar [through texts] often seemed to speak with a more authoritative voice than those who could be heard and seen within a given community. (Eisenstein 148)

To the book, then, the writers we have quoted attribute our sense of self, our memories, our possibilities, the specific linear forms of analysis we use, our attitude towards knowledge, our belief in the authority of certain kinds of knowledge, our sense of the world.

What has been encompassed by the book, then, is the second (but still not unruly) bundle we promised in our beginning. If the first bundle that comes with "literacy" is the promise of social, political, and economic improvement, it is because the second bundle is the book, which covers

who we are and what we might be and the institutions in which we act. If the Spanish friar had not thought this, if he had not acted out of a notion of "literacy" so tied to the singular object of the book, there would have been no massacre.

What else might we be—or be open to—if we did not see ourselves and our world so defined in books?

Y

When we discuss "technological literacy" or "computer literacy" or "[fill in the blank] literacy," we cannot pull "literacy" away from the two bundles of meanings and implications we have described. We may argue that we want to use "literacy" because it is a handy shortcut for covering a wide range of skills and procedures and practices; we may argue, "That's not what we meant at all; we really meant something broader, more open." But we are still using "literacy," which, unless we deny our histories, comes to us in the bundles we have just begun to unpack.

And our unpacking allows us now to offer up a response to the question that titles our work here: why are we using literacy as a metaphor for everything else? If we have unpacked "literacy" at all adequately, we hope we can now argue that "literacy" gets put behind "technological" or "computer" because "literacy" is already used to encompass everything we think worthy of our consideration: the term automatically upgrades its prefix. If "literacy" is already closely tied to our sense of how the world was colonized and settled and tamed, if "literacy" is already (deceptively) tied to political and social and economic improvement, if "literacy" already is the boundary of our sense of who we are, then why not apply the notion to newer technologies?

But. When we speak of the relationship we hope to establish—for ourselves and for our students—with newer technologies, do we want to carry forward all these particular attachments and meanings and possibilities?

Do we want to speak in the context of a set of practices and beliefs those with decision-making powers use to cultivate, to settle, to tame those without—so that those without remain without and blame themselves? When we say or write "technological literacy" how can we not expect others to hear, even if only partially, that we believe there is some minimum set of technological skills everyone should have—and that it is their own fault if they do not have them? And that it is therefore their own fault if they are not successful and mainstream? How can we not expect others to hear that this literacy constitutes not only a necessary but a sufficient condition for attaining The Good Life?

Do we want to use a word that contains within it a relation to a singular object that we use to narrow our sense of who we are and what we are capable of? Do we want to continue a relationship that is externalized, linear, private, visual, static, and authoritative? When we say, "computer literacy," for example, what part of this relationship to the book are we asking ourselves or our students to establish with, within, and through computers?

> Why aren't we instead working to come up with other terms and understandings—other more complex expressions—of our relationship with and within technologies?

SECOND

SO: WHAT OTHER POSSIBILITIES MIGHT WE USE FOR EXPRESSING OUR RELATIONSHIPS WITH TECHNOLOGIES?

In what follows (in only visually linear form) we analyze and reconstruct new approaches to communication that prioritize ways of knowing other than those dependent on "literacy."

There are two bundles in our writing here as well, but they are far from neat and tidy bundles, and we must pull them together rather than unpack them. These bundles unravel even as we write and revise and as you (and you and you) read: first we will offer an interpretation of what it might mean to think of literacy under postmodernism; second, we will begin to shift terms, suggesting other ways to think of literacy that begin moving away from the baggage outlined in the bundles above. And rather than simplifying any of the issues we have unbundled in the first section of our writing, the sorts of "literacy" we are about to discuss (we will abandon the term eventually) complicate, question, challenge, and make contingent.

LITERACY IN SPACE

Chia suspected that her mother's perception of time differed from her own in radical and mysterious ways. Not just in the way that a month, to Chia's mother, was not a very long time, but in the way that her mother's "now" was such a narrow and literal thing. News-governed, Chia believed. Cable-fed. A present honed to whatever very instant of a helicopter traffic report.

Chia's "now" was digital, effortlessly elastic, instant recall supported by global systems she'd never have to bother comprehending.

(The requisite William Gibson quotation, 13–14)

Having everything on-line is fantastic. Now as soon as a transfer is completed, it's there! You can really look up what you need. If someone calls, you know exactly what's going on. Sometimes you are looking for a part of a case that someone else has. You used to have to go looking for it, and maybe you wouldn't find it. Now you can see where it is without getting up from your seat. It's all right there at my fingertips. (Clerk in Stock and Bond Transfer Department in a recently computerized insurance underwriter, quoted in Zuboff 157–158).

The great obsession of the nineteenth century was, as we know, history: with its themes of development and of suspension, of crisis and cycle, themes of the ever-accumulating past, with its great preponderance of dead men and the menacing glaciation of the world. The nineteenth century found its

680

essential mythological resources in the second principle of thermodynamics. The present epoch will perhaps be above all the epoch of space. We are in the epoch of simultaneity: we are in the epoch of juxtaposition, the epoch of the near and far, of the side-by-side, of the dispersed. We are at a moment, I believe, when our experience of the world is less that of a long life developing through time than that of a network that connects points and intersects with its own skein. One could perhaps say that certain ideological conflicts animating present-day polemics oppose the pious descendents of time and the determined inhabitants of space. (Foucault 22)

Begin here, in a linear flow of text that suggests a flow of time, by imagining what literacy might be if we conceived it primarily as a spatial relation to information.

Although literacy has long been bound up with spaces (consider the geopolitical stories in the bundles we discussed above/earlier, for example), literacy changes profoundly if we choose to prioritize space over time. This shift has been frequently described by others with the term "postmodernism," although that term has become so complex and contradictory—so rich—that we use it to gesture generally rather than to point accurately; we are not here to argue whether the "postmodern condition" is indeed the one in which we find ourselves, but rather to use the thinking of different writers identified with postmodernism to lay out some possible relations with and within communication technologies.

> I believe the most striking emblem of this new mode of thinking relationships can be found in the work of Nam June Paik, whose stacked or scattered television screens, positioned at intervals within lush vegetation, or winking down at us from a ceiling of strange new video stars, recapitulate over and over again prearranged sequences or loops of images which return at dyssynchronous moments on various screens. The older aesthetic is then practiced by viewers, who, bewildered by this discontinuous variety, decided to concentrate on a single screen, as though the relatively worthless image sequence to be followed there had some organic value in its own right. The postmodernist viewer, however, is called upon to do the impossible, namely, to see all the screens at once, in their radical and random difference. . . . (Jameson 31).

How is it that we are able to see all the screens at once? Prioritizing space over time—and so looking away from time and also then from history—removes origins, futures, and progress: we see "all the screens"—all the information—all at once. In a spatially organized understanding of communication and knowledge, past and future can only merely be other locations in space. We are left with a sort of spread-out and flat simultaneity through which we travel.

> On a flat world, it is difficult to build an argument or to move directly from one point to the next because surfaces can be very slippery. Glissage or sliding is the preferred mode of transport. (Hebdige 170)

This "simultaneity" could be a way of thinking about how we have wired our communications and our "working knowledge" to new technologies. The speed with which we can move amongst screens of information—their visual, near instantaneous presence to us all at once—suggests that it is possible to describe information not as something we send from place to place, in books or on paper, over time, but as something we move (and hence think) within. Where "intertextuality" has long been understood at a conceptual level—text citing text citing text in an unseen network of reference—we now have conditions that allow it the possibility of it being material, visible and navigable, writable and readable, on our computer screens. "Literacy"—if we describe it as some set of skills that allows us to work with the information structures of our time—then becomes the ability to move in the new-technology spaces of information, the ability to make the instantaneous connections between informational objects that allow us to see them all at once.

> As long as the game is not a game of perfect information, the advantage will be with the player who has knowledge and can obtain information. By definition, this is the case with the student in a learning situation. But in games of perfect information, the best performativity cannot consist in obtaining additional information in this way. It comes rather from arranging the data in a new way, which is what constitutes a "move" properly speaking. This new arrangement is usually achieved by connecting together series of data that were previously held to be independent. This capacity to articulate what used to be separate can be called imagination. Speed is one of its properties. (Lyotard 52)

But seeing information (and hence "literacy") in that way plays itself back on how we conceive of the space we are creating by and within new communication technologies. The speed of our imaginations—our ability to make instantaneous connections—relies on the construction of information spaces that can be navigated so quickly that space seems compressed for us. With new communication technologies, we want to be able to—we feel we can—move from one end of space to another nearly instantaneously; we can bring any set of places—any set of things—together into one.

In one way of looking, then, this is not just about privileging space over time, but about time and space collapsing into each other . . . and if we can work as though time does not ration out what we can do, then we can work as though space doesn't either: with new communication technologies, space, like information, can become less something we experience and more something we simply work with/in, making creative connections and reconnections.

For flatness is corrosive and infectious. Who, after all, is Paul Virilio anyway? The name sounds as if it belongs to a B movie actor, a member of *Frankie Goes to Hollywood*, a contestant in a body-building competition. I know that "he" writes books but does such a person actually exist? In the land of the gentrified cut-up, as in the place of dreams, anything imaginable can happen, anything at all. The permutations are unlimited: high / low / folk culture; pop music / opera; street fashion / haute couture; journalism / science fiction / critical theory; advertising / critical theory / haute couture. . . . With the sudden loss of gravity, the lines that hold the terms apart waver and collapse. (Hebdige 161)

In this way of looking, the collapse of our experience of "technological" space can also correspond to a collapse of "real" space. Two steps are at work here: first, physically distant locations are wired up, so that it seems the one with whom I am communicating is just on the other side of the screen; second, the possibility that virtual spaces are collapsible leads to the idea that real spaces are likewise. This may sound like faulty logic, but, instead, the shift is straightforward: if communication is real, then the spaces in which it occurs are also real.

But what are we, then, in this space of all spaces all at once and no temporal flow? Under the sense of literacy we unpacked in the earlier/previous part of this writing, we rely on our ability to construct ourselves at some nexus between past and future, to have faith in the present as the point where past and future meet like (exactly like) a reader progressing through a linear text, uniting what has gone before with what is now and with what will come.

[P]ersonal identity is itself the effect of a certain temporal unification of past and future with one's present. . . . If we are unable to unify the past, present, and future of the sentence, we are similarly unable to unify the past, present, and future of our own biographical experience or psychic life. (Jameson 27)

When everything is all at once, what do we do?

Long ago, there must have been a golden age of harmony between heaven and earth. High was high; low was low; inside was in; and outside was out. But now we have money. Now, everything is out of balance. They say, "Time is money." But they got it all wrong: Time is the absence of money. (Wenders.)

The shift towards privileging space over time—what so many say is a hallmark of now—can have a frightening and dangerous result: the shift towards postmodernism acts in a radical unbinding of history from subjectivity. The unbinding can become so overpowering that it colonizes subjectivities and tears them apart; with no guarantees of either a stable past or a connected future, it is impossible to believe in the unity of a single, stable subject—the subject of our previous discussions of literacy.

But the unbinding can also be understood as opening up room for another view of ourselves: in understanding the implications of a postmodern worldview, we open ourselves to the possibility of remaking cultural meanings and identities. The connotations of literacy, as we discussed it in the first sections of our writing, suggest a process of mechanical and passive individual reception: the book gives us who we are, the book sets the limits for who we allow into the realms of privilege. If we understand communication not as discrete bundles of stuff that are held together in some unified space, that exist linearly through time, and that we pass along, but as instead different possible constructed relations between information that is spread out all before us, then . . . living becomes movement among (and within) sign systems.

Data Warehouse. *noun* 1: a process that collects data from various applications in an organization's operational systems, integrates the information into a logical model of business subject areas, stores it in a manner accessible to decision makers and delivers it to them through report-writing and query tools. The goal is to put standardized and comparable corporate information into employees' hands, enabling an enterprisewide view of the business. (McWilliams DW/ 2)

Symbolic analysts solve, identify, and broker problems by manipulating symbols. They simplify reality into abstract images that can be rearranged, juggled, experimented with, communicated to other specialists, and then, eventually, transformed back into reality. The manipulations are done with analytic tools, sharpened by experience. (Reich 178)

Here is the possibility of understanding our relation to our communication technologies as not being one through which we are passively, mechanically shaped. There is the possibility of seeing ourselves as not just moving through information, but of us moving through it and making and changing conscious constructions of it as we go. This is not about handing books to children or high-school dropouts or the underdeveloped, and hoping that they will pick up enough skills to be able to lose themselves in reading (and so to come back with different selves that better fit a dominant culture); it is instead about how we all might understand ourselves as active participants in how information gets "rearranged, juggled, experimented with" to make the reality of different cultures. This involves, of course, understanding our selves within the making and changing.

And this involves, then, not just thinking that we should pass along discrete sets of skills to others—or pretending that those discrete sets of skills are all that it takes to have a different life. There are certainly skills needed for connecting and reconnecting information—but the relationships to communication technologies we are describing now and here ask, in necessary addition, for a shared and discussed, ongoing, reconception of the space and time we use together and in which we find (and can construct) information and ourselves.

This reconception is thus not about handing down skills to others who are not where we are, but about figuring out how we all are where we are, and about how we all participate in making these spaces and the various selves we find here.

ARTICULATING LITERACY

So what else? We hope to have made it clear by now that our questions never have simple, bounded answers. No single term—such as "literacy"—can support the weight of the shifting, contingent activities we have been describing.

There are many possibilities—other than literacy, other than postmodernism—for how we might conceive our relationships with communication technologies (and no single correct answer). We can work from Stuart Hall's term "articulation" to suggest something else yet again.

> In England, the term [articulation] has a nice double meaning because "articulate" means to utter, to speak forth, to be articulate. It carries that sense of language-ing, of expressing, etc. But we also speak of an "articulated" lorry (truck): a lorry where the front (cab) and the back (trailer) can, but need not necessarily, be connected to one another. The two parts are connected to each other, but through a specific linkage, that can be broken. An articulation is thus the form of the connection that can make a unity of two different elements, under certain conditions. It is a linkage which is not necessary, determined, absolute and essential for all time. You have to ask, under what circumstances can a connection be forged or made? (Hall 53)

Under this understanding of relationships, then, we could describe literacy not as a monolithic term but as a cloud of sometimes contradictory nexus points among different positions. Literacy can be seen as not a skill but a process of situating and resituating representations in social spaces.

> So the so-called "unity" of a discourse is really an articulation of different, distinct elements which can be re-articulated in different ways because they have no necessary "belongingness." The "unity" which matters is a linkage between that articulated discourse and the social forces with which it can, under certain historical conditions, but need not necessarily, be connected. Thus, a theory of articulation is both a way of understanding how ideological elements come, under certain conditions, to cohere together within a discourse, and a way of asking how they do or do not become articulated, at specific conjunctures, to certain political subjects. Let me put that the other way: a theory of articulation asks how an ideology discovers its subject rather than how the subject thinks the necessary and inevitable thoughts which belong to it; it enables us to think how an ideology empowers people, enabling them to begin to make some sense or intelligibility of their historical situation, without reducing those forms of intelligibility to their socioeconomic or class location or social position. (Hall 53)

With the notion of connection, in articulation, comes the notion of potential disconnection. Literacy here shifts away from receiving a self to the necessary act of continual remaking, of understanding the "unity" of an object (social, political, intellectual) and simultaneously seeing that that unity is contingent, supported by the efforts of the writer/reader and the cultures in which they live.

> With and through articulation, we engage the concrete in order to change it, that is, to rearticulate it. To understand theory and method in this way shifts perspective from the acquisition or application of an epistemology to the creative process of articulating, of thinking of relations and connections as how we come to know and as creating what we know. Articulation is, then, not just a thing (not just connections) but a process of creating connections, much in the same way that hegemony is not domination but the process of creating and maintaining consensus or of co-ordinating interests. (Slack 114)

Articulation is only one among many ways of re-presenting literacy. Jim Collins, paralleling Jameson's discussions, offers an "architectural" model as one possibility:

> Appropriation is not simply an anti-Romantic stance opposed to the mythology of pure genius; this shift also involves profound changes in regard to the mutability of both information and the forms of cultural authority which govern (or used to govern) its circulation. To appropriate is to take control over that which originated elsewhere for semiotic/ideological purposes. . . .

> The determination to take possession . . . does not signify the denial of cultural authority but, rather, the refusal to grant cultural *sovereignity* to any institution, as it counters one sort of authority with another. (Collins 92–93)

Still other possible terms abound: Deleuze and Guattari describe the rhizomic nature of the nomad; Pratt offers linguistic contact zones; Giroux constructs border spaces; Anzaldua occupies borderlands. With such new bundles, we suggest new ways of relating to technologies (including texts) and to each other: both a process and a structure bound up (literally and figuratively) with social change.

BUT . . .

None of these terms exhausts new possibilities for "literacy," but only suggests productive ways of questioning our current positions, of unpacking old bundles and remaking new ones. Unpack ours and make your own.

A NOTE ON THE ILLUSTRATIONS

The drawings of people with books (and the one illustration of a woman with a television) come from a collection of clip art produced by the Volk Corporation and the Harry Volk Jr. Art Studio, both in Pleasantville, NJ, from 1959 through 1968. In the various small books of clip art from which these illustrations come, all the people are white and clearly middle class; there are many illustrations of women and children holding books; if men have printed matter in their hands, it is account books or newspapers—unless they are shown reading to their families (as one illustration here shows).

REFERENCES

Birkerts, Sven. 1994. *The Gutenberg Elegies*. New York: Ballantine.

Bolter, Jay David. 1991. *Writing Space: The Computer, Hypertext, and the History of Writing*. Hillsdale, NJ: Erlbaum.

Clinton, William J. 1998. Remarks at Technology '98 Conference. *Federal Document Clearing House Political Transcripts*. 26 Feb.

Eisenstein, Elizabeth L. 1979. *The Printing Press as an Agent of Change*. Cambridge: Cambridge UP.

Habermas, Jürgen. 1990. *Moral Consciousness and Communicative Action*, trans. Christian Lenhardt and Shierry Weber Nicholsen. Cambridge, MA: The MIT P.

Jameson, Fredric. 1991. *Postmodernism, Or, the Cultural Logic of Late Capitalism*. Durham, NC: Duke UP.

Lyotard, Jean-François. 1988. *The Differend: Phrases in Dispute*, trans. Georges Van Den Abbeele. Minneapolis: U of Minnesota P.

Ong, Walter J. 1982. *Orality and Literacy*. New York: Methuen.

Street, Brian V. 1984. *Literacy in Theory and Practice*. Cambridge: Cambridge UP.

Stuckey, J. Elspeth. 1991. *The Violence of Literacy*. Portsmouth, NH: Boynton/Cook.

Zuboff, Shoshana. 1988. *In the Age of the New Machine: The Future of Work and Power*. New York: Basic Books.

Made Not Only in Words

Composition in a New Key

KATHLEEN BLAKE YANCEY

Words strain,

Crack and sometimes break, under the burden,

Under the tension, slip, slide, perish,

Decay with imprecision, will not stay in place,

Will not stay still.

Sometimes, you know, you have a moment.

For us, this is one such moment. In coming together at CCCC, we leave our institutional sites of work; we gather together—we quite literally convene—at a not-quite-ephemeral site of disciplinary and professional work.

At this opening session in particular, inhabited with the echoes of those who came before and anticipating the voices of those who will follow—we pause and we commence.

We have a moment.

I come to this podium this morning fully conscious of the rather daunting responsibility attached to this occasion— a responsibility heightened by what my distinguished predecessors have said in their Chair's Addresses.

—Anne Ruggles Gere 1994

Reprinted from *College Composition and Communication* 56.2 (December 2004): 297–328. Used with permission. Due to space constraints, material originally set as sidebars is now set as centered, italic text within two lines.

These moments: they aren't all alike, nor are they equal. And how we value them is in part a function of how we understand them, how we connect them to other moments, how we anticipate the moments to come. For compositionists, of this time and of this place, this moment—this moment *right* now—is like none other.

Never before has the proliferation of writings outside the academy so counterpointed the compositions inside. Never before have the technologies of writing contributed so quickly to the creation of new genres. The consequence of these two factors is the creation of a writing public that, in development and in linkage to technology, parallels the development of a reading public in the 19th century. And these parallels, they raise good questions, suggest ways that literacy is created across spaces, across time.

On March 22, 2004, I delivered the "Chair's Address." This talk was twenty-six pages, more or less, double-spaced, and composed in Garamond 12. While I talked, two synchronized PowerPoint slide shows ran independently, one to my right, another to my left. Together, the two slide shows included eighty-four slides.[1] There was one spotlight on me; otherwise, the theatre was dark, lit only by that spot and the slide shows. Oddly, I found myself "delivering" the Chair's Address to an audience I could not see. As Chris Farris pointed out to me later, given this setting, the talk was more dramatic performance than address.

Or: what genre was I invoking?

Literacy today is in the midst of a tectonic change. Even inside of school, never before have writing and composing generated such diversity in definition. What do our references to writing mean? Do they mean print only? That's definitely what writing is if we look at national assessments, assuming that the assessment includes writing at all and is not strictly a test of grammar and usage. According to these assessments—an alphabet soup of assessments, the SAT, the NEAP, the ACT—writing IS "words on paper," composed on the page with

a pen or pencil by students who write words on paper, yes—but who *also* compose words and images and create audio files on Web logs (blogs), in word processors, with video editors and Web editors and in e-mail and on presentation software and in instant messaging and on listservs and on bulletin boards—and no doubt in whatever genre will emerge in the next ten minutes.[2]

Note that no one is *making* anyone *do* any of this writing. Don't you wish that the energy and motivation that students bring to some of these other genres they would bring to our assignments? How is it that what we teach and what we test can be so different from what our students know as

But the main insight I have about my own literacy history is that none of the important or meaningful writing I have ever produced happened as a result of a writing assignment given in a classroom.

—Lillian Bridwell Bowles 1995

writing? What *is* writing, really? It includes print: that seems obvious. But: Does it include writing for the screen? How visual is it? Is it the ability to move textual resources among spaces, as suggested by Johndan Johnson-Eilola? Is composing, as James Porter suggests, not only about medium but also specifically about technology? Suppose I said that basically writing is interfacing? What does that add to our definition of writing? What about the circulation of writing, and the relationship of writing to the various modes of delivery?

In planning this address—what some called a script, others a transcript—I designed a multi-genred and mediated text that would embody and illustrate the claims of the talk. To accomplish this aim, I developed "stock" of two kinds. I collected verbal material, based on readings, some of my own writings, and some of my students' work. Concurrently, I collected images, again from my own work, photographs from places I knew, and images from the public domain. Collecting these different materials and putting them in dialogue with each other was a key part of this composing process.

And what do these questions mean with respect to another kind of delivery, the curricular and pedagogical delivery of college composition, in classroom to seminar room to online chat room to studio?

Collectively, these questions sound a moment for composition in a new key.

To explain what I mean by this more fully, I'll detail what this moment is, and why and how it matters for us, and what it is that we might want to do about it in a talk I have subtitled Composition in Four Quartets.

QUARTET ONE

In my beginning is my end.

We have a moment.

In some ways our moment is like that in 19th-century Britain when a new reading public composed of middle- and working-class peoples came into being. Technology played a major role in this creation: with a new steam printing press and cheaper paper, reading material became more accessible. There were political and economic reasons as well. Economic changes of the 19th century came in the context of a globalization connected to travel, adventure, colonialism, and a massive demographic shift from farm to city changing the material conditions of work and life.[3] Economically, what has been called the Industrial Age promoted a "rising" middle class, indeed a bourgeoisie, that had the funds to buy print reading material and the leisure in which to read it and that began to have some political rights—and to press for more. From the perspective of literature, the genre receiving the most attention was the novel, which is said to have encouraged readers and in some ways to have created them. As important for our purposes, these novels were often *published in another form first*, typically in serial installments that the public read monthly. In other words, the emergence of this reading public co-occurred with the emergence of a multiply genred and distributed novel. All of Dickens's novels, for instance, were so published, "generally in monthly parts." And the readers were more than consumers; they helped shape the development of the text-in-process. Put differently, the "fluctuations of public demand" influenced the ways that Dickens and other novelists developed future episodes. The British novels of the 19th century were from the very beginning developed and distributed in multiple genres made possible by a new technology, the novelist writing in the context of and for very specific readers who, in turn, provided responses influencing the development of the text in question.

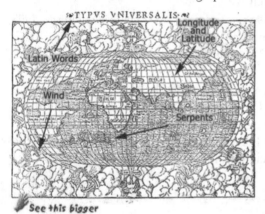

See this bigger

The images, in other words, did not simply punctuate a written text; together words and images were (and are) the materials of composition.[4]

> *The Chair's Address is, of course, one genre, what Mike Palmquist has called a "call to action" genre. In medium, this address was plural— delivered simultaneously through the human voice and through the PowerPoint slides, both in relation to and also mediated by the twenty-six pages of written text.[5] In response to some requests for the script, I created a version of it in the spirit of an executive summary. Another version is being developed for CCC Online; its logic is different still. And then there is the text you are reading now, which includes a limited number of slides (reproduced) that are arranged anew. This "Chair's Address" also includes new images and new verbal text—like the meta-text you are reading now.*
>
> *All of which leads me to ask: how many compositions are in this text?*

People read together, sometimes in "reading circles," sites of domestic engagement, but also in public places. Technological constraints—bad lighting, eyesight overstrained by working conditions[6] —encouraged such communal readings, since in this setting no single pair of eyes was overly strained. People also gathered frequently to hear authors read their own works in staged readings. For these 19th-century novels, the patterns of circulation thus included both oral and written forums. Or: new forms of writing—the serials, the newspapers, the triple-decker Victorian novel— encouraged new reading publics who read for new purposes.

And all of this happened outside of school.

Today, we are witnessing a parallel creation, that of a *writing* public made plural, and as in the case of the development of a reading public, it's taking place largely outside of school—and this in an age of universal education. Moreover, unlike what

> *Modern physics long since made us learn that the world out there has more space than stuff anyway, and it is in the spaces that we find relationships.*
>
> *—Richard Lloyd Jones 1978*

happens in our classes, *no one is forcing this public to write.* There are no As here, no Dean's lists, no writing teacher to keep tabs on you. Whatever the exchange value may be for these writers—and there are millions of them, here and around the world—it's certainly not grades. Rather, the writing seems to operate in an economy driven by use value. The context for this writing public, expanded anew, is cause for concern and optimism. On the one hand, a loss in jobs in this country caused (it is said) by globalization is connected to a rise in corporate profits detailed in one accounting report after another, and we are assured by those in Washington that such job loss is actually *good* for us. As one commentator on NPR put it in early March, we've moved from just-in-time jobs to just-in-time people. Such an approach to labor is not news to those of us in composition: we apparently got there first. On the other hand, those committed to another vision of globalization see in it the chance for a (newfound) cooperation and communication among peoples, one with potential to transform the world and its peoples positively. At best, it could help foster a world peace never known before. At least, as we have seen over the course of the last year, it is (finally) more difficult to conduct any war in secret.

It's worth asking what the principles of all these compositions are. Pages have interfaces, although like much that is ubiquitous, we don't attend to such interfaces as we might. The fact that you have one interface governing the entire text, however, does provide a frame. What is the frame for (and thus the theory governing) a composition in multiple parts? For that matter, how does this text—with call outs, palimpsest notes, and images—cohere?

And:
How do we create such a text?
How do we read it?
How do we value it?

Not least, how will we teach it?

Like 19th-century readers creating their own social contexts for reading in reading circles, writers in the 21st century self-organize into what seem to be overlapping technologically driven writing circles, what we might call a series of newly imagined communities, communities that cross borders of all kinds—nation state, class, gender, ethnicity. Composers gather in Internet chat rooms; they participate in listservs dedicated to both the ridiculous and the sublime; they mobilize for health concerns, for political causes, for research, and for travel advice. Indeed, for Howard Dean's candidacy we saw the first blog for a presidential candidate. Many of the Internet texts are multiply genred and purposed: MoveOn.com sends e-mails, collects money, and hosts a Web site simultaneously. Flash mobs gather for minutes-long social outings; political flash mobs gather for purposes of political reform. And I repeat: like the members of the newly developed reading public, the members of the writing public have learned—in this case, to write, to think together, to organize, and to act within these forums—largely without instruction and, more

Because we are essentially in partnership with the wider community attempting to share meaningfully in the working out of a community responsibility, we must be in communication with the other parts of the community.

—Vivian Davis 1979

to the point here, largely without *our* instruction. They need neither self-assessment nor our assessment: they have a rhetorical situation, a purpose, a potentially worldwide audience, a choice of technology and medium—and they write.

The literacies that composers engage in today are multiple. They include print literacy practices (like spelling) that URL's require; they include visual literacy; they include network literacy. As important, these literacies are textured and in relationship to each other. Perhaps most important, these literacies are social in a way that school literacy all too often only pretends to be.

Some of these new Internet genres—e-mail, instant messaging, and so on—divide along lines based in age and in formal schooling. Faculty—the school insiders—use e-mail daily, considering it essential to academic and personal life. In contrast, students use instant messaging at least as often, and unlike most of us, they *like* it. Faculty see blogs—if they see them at all—as (yet) another site for learning, typically in school; students see blogs as a means of organizing social action, a place for geographically far-flung friends to gather, a site for poets and musicians to plan a jam. But our

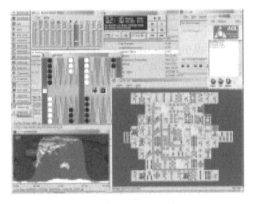

experiences are the same in one key way: most faculty and students alike *all have learned these genres on our own, outside of school.* Given *this* extracurricular writing curriculum and its success, I have to wonder out loud if in some pretty important ways and within the relatively short space of not quite ten years, we may already have become anachronistic.

Of course, as Anne Gere demonstrated in her own Chair's Address, writing has always been embedded in an extra-curriculum. Public institutions now design for such a curriculum, bringing together what computer game designer Frank Lantz calls a convergence of digital and physical space. Examples include new public libraries, especially those in Salt Lake City and in Seattle. In their designs, both architectural and curricular, these institutions overlap and interplay "domestic spaces" (like Seattle's "living room" inside the library), "conventional" library spaces, and electronic spaces.[7]

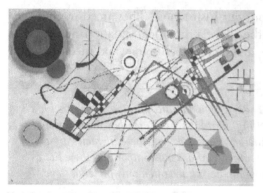

Kandinsky, Composition VII

Some disturbing data suggests that traditional English departments already are. According to the list of departmental administrators published in the PMLA, over the last twenty years, we have seen a decline in the number of departments called English of about 30%. Let me state this more dramatically: of the number of English departments whose administrators were included on the list in 1985, about one in three has disappeared. Why? They may have simply stopped being represented for any number of reasons: a shortage of funds, a transfer of the listing elsewhere. Naturally, this statistic doesn't mean that English is disappearing as an institutional unit. Most obviously, it means that fewer units calling themselves English are listed in the PMLA. And when plotted against another trend line—the *increase* of units called something other than English, like departments of communication and divisions of humanities—it seems more plausible that *something* reductionist in nature is happening to English departments generally. They are being consolidated into other units or disappearing.[8] Another data point tells the same story: according to the Association of Departments of English (ADE), if English departments were graduating English majors at the same rate graduated in 1966, we would congratulate 100,000 students this year. Instead, we will offer English degrees to half that number—50,000.[9] And these data points may well explain why the number of tenure-line jobs in English continues its now altogether-too-familiar decline (which makes the continuing increase in tenure-line jobs in rhetoric and composition all the more remarkable). Of course, for many of us, this may be a moot point. We may not be housed in English departments ourselves, and most of us don't teach courses in the major because the major continues to be defined as *territorias literati*, a point to which I will return. Still, enough of us do reside in English to understand that as English goes, so may we.

Although interpretations of data around the status of English departments vary, here something in English studies is clearly underway. The data points I report plot one trend line, a line that in its downward direction contrasts with the upward swing of the plot line for rhetoric and composition. In the midst of this moment, a new discourse that repositions English and humanities is emerging. The latest evidence: As I write this, literary scholar Helen Vendler, in her NEH Jefferson Address, has attempted an English-centric redefinition of the humanities that excludes both history and philosophy.

These shifts: are they minor tremors signifying routine academic seismic activity that makes the world more stable? Alternatively, are they tremors occurring along the fault lines of tectonic plates that will in the not-too-distant future change the very topography of higher education?

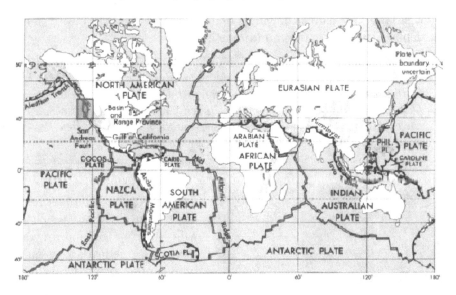

These questions assume greater significance as evidence of other tremors within higher education make themselves felt. In the last two decades, we've seen a shift in the way the country views higher education. According to a 2004 edition of *U.S. News & World Report* (Shea), beginning in the Reagan era, the U.S.

Composition is a part of a higher education and the persistent problems in composition are tied to larger issues in the world, in our country, in higher education generally and in each academic institution specifically.

—Miriam Chaplin 1988

began moving away from the view that college is good for the *country*, a view that enfranchises all of us, and began shifting toward the view that higher education is good for the *individual*. Given this shift, perhaps it makes a perverse kind of sense that even though more than half of college students work, they still graduate with debt exceeding $15,000. During this same period, public institutions became state-supported institutions, then state-assisted schools, then state-affiliated schools, and now state-located schools. States haven't abandoned support of education: rather, they have redirected the revenue streams away from the institutions and toward the consumers, the students. In other words, historically, public funds went to public institutions; today, in many states, including mine, they go directly to the students—chiefly through scholarships titled Hope or Freedom, which one economist has likened to vouchers for K–12. And the worst-case scenario has already been proposed in Colorado: take all funding for public institutions and distribute it not to them but directly to students.[10] Educationally, in the words of Robert Putnam, we are increasingly bowling alone, and apart from the damage it will do to the individual schools, I worry about the damage it will do to the country as a commons.

Additional evidence of our unwillingness, as members of a commons, to support higher education is abundant. Again, as I write this, President Bush's plan to maintain the level of funding for Pell Grants goes almost unchallenged. Given that tuition costs have risen and the number of eligible students has likewise risen, what this means is less support for students.

Relevant to literacy specifically, we can record other tremors, specifically those associated with the screen, and in that focus, they return us to questions around what it means to write. Further, I'd suggest that they constitute a serious challenge to us. As articulated by Elizabeth Daley, dean of the University of Southern California School of Television & Cinema, this view of literacy makes a clear distinction—both in practice and in institutional home—between print literacy and screen literacy. Linking what happens outside of school to what we might do inside, Daley observes that both in metaphorical analogy and in use, the screen has become ubiquitous. "Metaphors from the screen have become common in our daily conversation," she says ("Expanding" 34). Think about these everyday terms: close up, flash back, frame, cut to the chase, segue. Our daily communicative, social, and intellectual practices are screen-permeated. Further, her argument is that *the screen is the language of the vernacular*, that if we do not include it in the school curriculum, we will become as irrelevant as faculty professing in Latin. "No longer," she declares, "can students be considered truly educated by mastering reading and writing alone. The ability to negotiate through life by combining words with pictures with audio and video to express thoughts will be the mark of the educated student" ("Speaking"). Specifically, she proposes that the literacy of the screen, which she says *parallels* oral literacy and print literacy, become a *third* literacy required of all undergraduates. Not surprisingly, she believes such literacy should be taught not in composition classrooms but in media studies programs. Not least, Daley argues that education needs to get in step with life practices and should endeavor to assist students to negotiate through life.

Part of what's at issue with screen literacy is how it too enables the making of stories, a common question we ask of literary texts, a common question we ask of students and of ourselves. As Daley suggests, the screen is very much part of the thinking around narrative. In reviewing 21 Grams, for instance, film critic Roger Ebert brings the issue into relief (perhaps ironically?) when he says: "Imagining how heartbreaking the conclusion would have been if we had arrived at it in the ordinary way by starting at the beginning, I felt as if an unnecessary screen of technique had been placed between the story and the audience."

What do these conceptions of reading and writing publics, these tremors in the world and in higher education and in English have to do with composition?

QUARTET TWO

A people without history
Is not redeemed from time, for history is a pattern
Of timeless moments.

We have a moment.

What we make of this moment is contextualized by our own history as a discipline. Many have noted the role that first-year composition played in the formation of CCCC: it was our raison d'etre—and a worthy cause. We focused then on the gatekeeping

Someone has estimated that there are at least nine thousand of us teaching in college courses in composition and communication.

—*John Gerber 1950*

moment, the moment when students enter college and in particular on that transition moment between high school and college. It's worth considering, however, how this gatekeeping situation has changed in the last fifty-five years.

Early in the decade when CCCC was formed, in 1949, only 30% of students graduated from high school; only 20% of high school graduates even began college, typically at four-year liberal arts institutions; and fewer than 6% graduated. Today, depending on your source, about 89% of students graduate from high school, and some 65% begin college ("America's"). In other words, at various times—in high school in AP classes and dual-enrollment classes, just after high school, years after completing high school—many students—indeed most students—do begin college.[11]

It's almost impossible to know how many students finish high school. Some finish after four years; some finish after another year or two in an alternative setting; some finish through the GED program. And it is so that some don't finish at all. Where they don't finish, typically in urban settings and in impoverished states, life is harder all the way around. Still, if we in college could graduate the same percentage of students as our colleagues in high school do, we'd nearly triple our graduation rate.

But what happens? They don't finish: only 28% of Americans complete four years of college. It looks bleaker as you go to certain categories: 17% of African Americans have college degrees, 10.6% of Latinos, even fewer Native Americans (Wright). Still, too often we define ourselves as that first-year course. Suppose that if instead of focusing on the gatekeeping year, we saw composition education as a *gateway*? Suppose that we enlarged our focus to include *both* moments, gatekeeping and gateway? And further suppose, to paraphrase Elizabeth Daley, that we designed a curriculum in composition that prepared students to become members of the writing public and to negotiate life. How might that alter what we think and what we do?

Such an agenda is consistent with data that account for successful college experiences. Richard Light, for instance, demonstrates that one of the key factors students and alumni cite in studies of how college can work well is writing. The National Survey of Student Engagement—in both two- and

700

four-year school versions—sounds the same note. We know that writing makes a difference—both at the gatekeeping moment and as students progress through the gateway.

Of course, in this moment in composition's history, I'm making certain assumptions about writing that as a disciplinary community, we are still ambivalent about. What should be the future shape of composition? Questioning the role of technology in composition programs—shall we teach print, digital, composition, communication, or all of the above?—continues to confound us. Do we want to confine our efforts to print literacy only—or, alternatively, to print literacy predominately? Given a dearth of

resources—from hardware to professional development, from student access to what Gail Hawisher calls the bandwidth digital divide—many of us continue to focus on print. Given a concern that postmodernism and infobits could undermine a sustained rational discourse that is fundamental to democracy, many of us vote for the known that is, not, coincidentally, what our colleagues expect us to deliver in the composition classroom: the print of CCCC—coherence, clarity, consistency, and (not least) correctness.

In the Portraits of Composition Research Study, respondents spoke in chorus about the move to digital texts. Nearly all respondents expect students to submit texts composed in a word processor; nearly half of the respondents respond to student texts via e-mail. But very few—less than 30%—use a course management system.[12]

At the same time, when reviewed, our own practices suggest that we have already committed to a theory of communication that is both/and: print and digital. Given the way we *produce* print—sooner or later inside a word processor—we are digital already, at least in process. Given the course management systems like Blackboard and WebCT, we have committed to the screen for administrative purposes at least. Given the oral communication context of peer review, our teaching requires that students participate in mixed communicative modes. Given the digital portfolios coming into their own, even the move by CCCC to provide LCD's and Internet connects to panelists upon request and for free, we teachers and students seem to have moved already—to communication modes assuming digital literacy. And

thinking about our own presentations here: when we consider how these presentations will morph into other talks, into articles for print and online journals, into books, indeed into our classrooms, it becomes pretty clear that we *already* inhabit a model of communication practices incorporating multiple genres related to each other, those multiple genres remediated across contexts of time and space, linked one to the next, circulating across and around rhetorical situations both inside and outside school.

This is composition—*and* this is the *content* of composition.

That composition has a content at all—other than process—is a radical claim. The CCCCs was founded with a concern about what the content of first-year composition should be, and it is a concern that continues to energize us even today.

If we cannot go home again to the days when print was the sole medium, what will the new curricular home for composition look like?

QUARTET THREE

Words, after speech, reach
Into the silence. Only by the form, the pattern,
Can words or music reach
The stillness, as a Chinese jar still
Moves perpetually in its stillness.

We have a moment.

At this moment, we need to focus on three changes: Develop a new curriculum; revisit and revise our writing-across-the-curriculum efforts; and develop a major in composition and rhetoric.[13]

Since the limits of time and space preclude my detailing all three, I will focus on the first, developing *a new curriculum for the 21st century*, a curriculum that carries forward the best of what we have created to date, that brings together the writing outside of school and that inside. This composition is located in a new vocabulary, a new set of practices, and a new set of outcomes; it will focus our research in new and provocative ways; it has as its goal the creation of

> *To accept rhetoric and composition . . . as legitimate parts of the graduate curriculum is not a sign of dissolution, dispersion, and decomposition. It is, rather a sign that we are regaining our composure, taking composure to mean composition in all of its senses.*
>
> *—Frank D'Angelo 1980*

thoughtful, informed, technologically adept writing publics. This goal entails the other two: extending this new composition curriculum horizontally throughout the academy and extending it vertically through our own major. In other words, it is past time that we fill the glaringly empty spot between first-year composition and graduate education with a composition major.

And in the time and space that's left, I want to sketch briefly what this new curriculum might look like.

To begin thinking about a revised curriculum for composition, we might note the most significant change that has occurred in composition over the last thirty years: the process movement. Although not everyone agrees that the process movement radically altered the teaching of composition (see Crowley; Matsuda), most do think that process—as we defined it in the research of scholars like Janet Emig and Linda Flower and as brought into the classroom by teachers like us—did revolutionize the teaching of writing. We had a new vocabulary, some of it—like invention—ancient, some of it—writing process and rewriting and freewriting—new. We developed pedagogy anew: peer review, redrafting, portfolio assessment. But nothing stays still, and process approaches have given way to other emphases. Recently, we have seen several approaches seeking to update that work, some on the left in the form of cultural studies and post-process; some more interested in psychological approaches like those located in felt sense; others more interested in the connections composition can forge with like-minded educational initiatives such as service learning and first-year experience programs.

Erika Lindemann's work on the bibliographic categories that organize and construct composition reveals the role that process both has and has not played in the discipline. Lindemann notes that while in the 1986 CCCC Bibliography process was included in three of twelve categories (or 25%), it is completely absent in the 2001 MLA successor to the Cs bibliography.

What's interesting is that regardless of the changes that are advocated as we attempt to create a post-process compositional curriculum, most (not all but most) attempt this without questioning or altering the late-20th-century basis of composition. To put the point directly, composition in this school context, and in direct contrast to the *world* context, remains chiefly focused on the writer qua writer, sequestered from the means of production. Our model of teaching composing, as generous, varied, and flexible as it is in terms of aims and as innovative as it is in terms of pedagogy—and it is all of these—(still) embodies the narrow and the singular in its emphasis on a primary and single human relationship: the writer in relation to the teacher. In contrast to the reading public nearly two centuries ago, the "real" reading public of school is solitary, the teacher whose reading consists of print text delivered on the teacher's desk. In contrast to the development of a writing public, the classroom writer is not a member of a collaborative group with a common project linked to the world at large and delivered in multiple genres and media, but a singular person writing over and over again—to the teacher.

What no one, including writing teachers, foresaw twenty years ago was the extent to which the creation of wealth would be divorced from labor and redistributed, leaving the United States the most economically polarized among industrialized nations, with the divide between rich and poor continuing to widen.

—Lester Faigley 1997

John Trimbur calls our school model of writing the in loco parentis model: we are the parents who in our practices continue to infantilize our students as we focus their gaze and their energy and their reflection on the moments of creation, on process. I tend to think of it in another, complementary way, as a remediated tutorial model of writing. In other words, it seems to me that in all our efforts to improve the teaching of composition—to reduce class size, for instance, to conference with students, to respond vociferously to each student paper, and to understand that in our students' eyes we are the respondent who matters—we seek to approximate the one-to-one tutorial model. Quite apart from the fact that such an effort is doomed—about a hundred years ago, Edwin Hopkins asked if we could teach composition under the current conditions,[14] which conditions then are the same conditions we work in today, and immediately answered, "NO"—I have to wonder why we want to work this way, wonder why *this* is the neo-Platonic mode to which we continuously aspire. Not that the process model is bad, I hasten to add: students do engage with each other, often do write to the world, and frequently do develop elaborated processes—all to the good. But if we believe that writing is social, shouldn't the system of circulation—the paths that the writing takes—extend beyond and around the single path from student to teacher?

I am interested in the terms we use to constitute our subject, the terms we take for granted and the degree to which we take them for granted. Today I'll stick to the three terms of our name, composition, communication, conference. These terms are our legacy; we must not betray those who have given them to us. They are also our problem, our burden, since they resist reflection and change.

—David Bartholomae 1989

More to the point, the list of what students aren't asked to do in the current model—and what they might—is long:

♦ consider the issue of intertextual circulation: how what they are composing relates or compares to "real world" genres;

♦ consider what the best medium and the best delivery for such a communication might be and then create and share those different communication pieces in those different media, to different audiences;

♦ think explicitly about what they might "transfer" from one medium to the next: what moves forward, what gets left out, what gets added—and what they have learned about composing in this transfer process;

♦ consider how to transfer what they have learned in one site and how that could or could not transfer to another, be that site on campus or off;[15]

♦ think about how these practices help prepare them to become members of a writing public.

A Boston skyline, the old juxtaposed with the new, old and new interfaced. An architectural intertextuality.

What I'm proposing is that we move to a new model of composing where students are explicitly asked to engage in these considerations, to engage in these activities, to develop as members of a writing public. Such a model of composition is located in three key expressions:

Circulation of composition

Canons of rhetoric

Deicity of technology

Let me begin with circulation: although they are related, I will here outline and exemplify two kinds: (1) the circulation of texts generally, and (2) the circulation of a student's own work within an educational culture. Texts circulate: they move across contexts, between media, across time. Writers compose in the context of other writers and thinkers and speakers. They imitate them directly and indirectly; they quote them, write in direct reference to them, paraphrase them, and frame their own work in these contexts. This circulation is the one, perhaps, with which we are most familiar: we often talk about it as intertextuality, as a conversation that we invite students to join. The conversation, of course, occurs through genres and is really many conversations, with texts circulating in multiple, interrelated ways.

Conceptually, composition itself is in circulation. From music and art, it carries an aesthetic dimension. From chemistry and architecture, it carries an interest in materials. Pedagogically, borrowing from Joe Janangelo and Pablo Picasso, I have talked elsewhere about students as "ongoing compositions." We see such humans-as-compositions in any collected work, summarized minimally in a resume or vita; developed and illustrated more fully and reflectively in a portfolio. Regardless of whether we see such composing or not, it is always in play. In the context of compositionists as professionals, we compose ourselves, both individually, in the words of Elizabeth Flynn, and as participants of a community, in the words of Andrea Lunsford's Chair's Address.

What I am calling circulation can go by other names: Charles Bazerman and David Russell, for instance, call it activity theory, but basically it's the same point: As they explain,

> Writing is alive when it is being written, read, remembered, contemplated, followed—when it is part of human activity. . . . The signs on the page serve to mediate between people, activate their thoughts, direct their attention, coordinate their actions, provide the means of relationship. It is in the context of their activities that people consider texts and give meaning to texts. And it is in the organization of activities that people find the needs, stances, interactions, tasks that orient their attention toward texts they write and read. So to study text production, text reception, text meaning, text value apart from their animating activities is to miss the core of text's being.

So: circulation.

With the help of David Russell and Arturo Yañez, let me put a classroom face on what this might look like in terms of curriculum. They tell the story of a student caught in an all-too-familiar dilemma. Beth, the student, is an aspiring journalist convinced of the integrity and objectivity of reportorial accounting; moreover, she believes that good writing is good writing is good writing, regardless of the discipline. Which means, of course, that good writing is the writing she understands and practices. The problem: she's enrolled in an Irish literature class that she needs for graduation, a class where good writing—located in interpretation and exercise of judgment—looks very different. To her, this historical writing feels inexact and duplicitous; and it makes history, which she has understood as an exercise in "Just the facts, ma'am"—as completely alien. What activity theory adds to this mix is a means of making sense of these seemingly disparate texts and ways of knowing.

> Professional historians . . . critically examine and interpret (and reinterpret) primary documents according to the methods (rules, norms) of history. They argue and debate to persuade other experts. And when enough experts (or the enough powerful experts) arrive at consensus, that consensus is put into textbooks for high school students and generally perceived as "fact." And, perhaps, that consensus is eventually put into popular history books, of the kind that journalists review and the rest of us Big Picture People sometimes read—to find the "facts" of history. (Russell and Yañez)

Who writes the "first draft" of history can change, of course, as can patterns of circulation. Concerns around such issues are not merely academic, as is clear in the following New York Times *commentary on the relationship between genres and the roles they are currently playing in this historical moment: "The sudden outpouring of inside details in books about the Bush administration is all the more remarkable because of the administration's previous success at controlling the flow of information to the press about its workings. It is a phenomenon that is creating an unusual reversal in which books—the musty vessels traditionally used to convey patient reflection into the archives—are superceding newspapers as the first draft of history, leaving the press corps to cover the books themselves as news."*

Thinking in terms of circulation, in other words, enables students to understand the epistemology, the conventions, and the integrity of different fields and their genres. Using that as a point of departure allows students to complete the task *and* move closer to the big picture of writing. Trimbur makes an analogous point in outlining a curricular approach where students in health sciences understand how different genres even within the same field function epistemologically: research genres to make scientific knowledge; public health articles deriving from the research genres both diluting and distributing it, each according to its own logic and conventions. His purpose?

> I want students to see that the shift in register and genre between a journal article and a news report amounts to a shift in modality—the relative credibility and authoritativeness invested in written statements—that marks

journal articles as 'original' contributions and news reports as secondary and derivative. (213)

Media themselves provide another example of circulation. As Jay Bolter and Richard Grusin explain in *Remediation*, and as McLuhan suggested before that, nearly every medium is re/mediated on another

> *We look at the present through a rear-view mirror. We march backwards into the future.*
>
> —*Marshall McLuhan 1964*

medium. In other words, consciously or otherwise, we create the new in the context of the old and based on the model of the old. Television is commonly understood to be remediated on film, for example, and the Web is commonly understood to be remediated on print. Remediation can be back-ended as well, as we see in the most recent CNN interface on TV, which is quite explicitly remediated on the Web. The new, then, repeats what came

before, while at the same time remaking that which it models. This isn't a new phenomenon, however, as we remember from the development of that 19th-century novel, which appeared in multiple genres and media: serials, triple-deckers, performances. Fast forward to the 21st century: imagine that in composition classes students, like Victorian novelists before them, focus on remediating their own texts. Beginning with a handout or one pager, they define a key term of the course and revise that on the basis of class response; in addition, they move the material of that handout to a five-slide Power-Point show presented to the class and itself

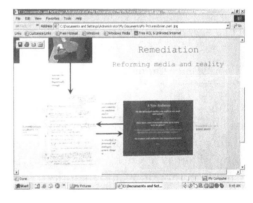

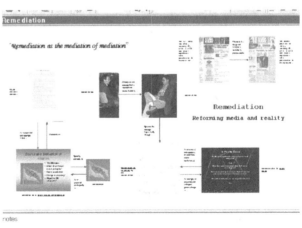

revised. Suppose that they move this material to a poster, then to a presentation, then to a conventional written text. For the conventional written text, they brainstorm in class and on a blog, thinking individually and communally about which of these tasks "counts" as writing—and why. As they move from medium to medium, they consider what they move forward, what they leave out, what they add, and for each of these write a reflection in which they consider how the medium itself shapes what they create. The class culminates with text in which they write a reflective theory about what writing is and how it is influenced or shaped or determined by media and technology. Located in the rhetoric of purpose, audience, genre, this model of circulation is particularly oriented to medium and technology; it permits a student, as Brian Morrison does here, to define composition as "the thoughtful gathering, construction, or reconstruction of a literate act in any given media."

Speaking of Remediation . . .

Have you heard Sheryl Crow's version of Rod Stewart's "The First Cut Is the Deepest"?

Or how about Moulin Rouge?

These three related approaches: all oriented to the circulation of texts, to genre, to media, and to ways that writing gets made, both individually and culturally. As important, all three of these approaches, in their analysis of textual relationships and contexts, in their theories and examples of how writing works, and in their situating the student as a maker of knowledge, map the content for new composition. And if you are saying, but I can't do all this in first-year composition, I'm going to reply, "Exactly." First-year composition is a place to begin; carrying this forward is the work of the major in composition and rhetoric.

What is the relationship between and among remediating texts, carrying forward materials, finding new sources, and representing and inventing a self?

One thing that is clear to me as I compose this text for the page is that this remediation feels less like a small morphing of a text from one medium to another than it does like creating a new text. And it's not mere perception: this composition is longer by over 2,000 words, most of which comment on, extend, and complicate the earlier voiced text.

A second kind of circulation, occurring within the bounds of school and often within the classroom, has to do with the variety of academic texts that students create, with the places in which those texts are created and distributed, and with how *this circulation* contributes to student development in writing. We have some fine research in this sense of circulation that accounts for students moving forward in their writing: research conducted by Lee Ann Carroll, Nancy Sommers and Laura Saltz, Marilyn Sternglass, Richard Haswell, and Elizabeth Chiseri-Strater. Typically, such studies focus on how and what students "transfer" from one site to another; Anne Beaufort's study asks the same question but applied to the site of work. And often we ask students to engage in this activity themselves: in their reflections, students account for the progress (or not) of their texts; of what they have learned in the construction of such texts; in their portfolios—be they digital or print—students comment and demonstrate the circulation of the course.

A vignette composed by Paul Prior and Jody Shipka shows us another way to think about circulation that focused exclusively on a single text.

> A psychology professor reports to us that when she is revising an article for publication she works at home and does the family laundry. She sets the buzzer on the dryer so that approximately every 45 minutes to an hour she is pulled away from the text to tend the laundry downstairs. As she empties the dryer, sorts and folds, reloads, her mind wanders a bit and she begins to recall things she wanted to do with the text, begins to think of new questions or ideas, things that she had not been recalling or thinking of as she focused on the text when she was upstairs minutes before. She perceives this break from the text, this opportunity to reflect, as a very productive part of the process.

What Prior and Shipka point out, of course, is that this text is produced through two activity systems: the domestic and the disciplinary.[16] They raise provocative questions about the role the buzzer plays in the drafting process, about the spaces created here for reflection, about the role reflection plays in composing.

This too is circulation; this too is composition.

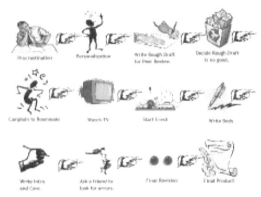

A map of his writing process by first-year writer Josh Reynolds.

Bill Watterson, the creator of Calvin and Hobbes, *talks about how circulation of another kind can influence the development of a creator, in this case of a cartoonist. He notes, "The challenge of any cartoonist is not just to duplicate the achievements of the past, but to build on them as well" (9–10).*

He argues it is thus necessary for the cartoonist to have access to earlier cartoons, through their collection and republication—in book form.[17]

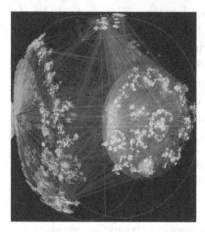

As I move into the second expression, the canons of rhetoric—invention, arrangement, style, memory, and delivery—I'm aware that these are hardly new. I wonder about how we understand them, however. Like others before me, I would note that we have separated delivery and memory from invention, arrangement, and style in ways that are counterproductive. Let me further say that too often we treat them as discrete entities when in fact they are interrelated. Let me share with you an image. Don't ask me why, but I have always understood each canon as sitting on a rhetorical shelf, as though a freshly laundered cotton blanket in a laundry closet. I take one canon down—my favorite, if truth be told, is invention—use it, then put it neatly back on the shelf. But as my options for delivering texts have widened—from the page to the screen to the networked screen and then back to the page anew—I've begun to see the canons not as discrete entities like those blankets on shelves but, rather, as related to each other in much the same way as the elements of Burke's pentad are related: the canons interact, and through that interaction they contribute to new exigencies for invention, arrangement, representation, and identity. Or: they change what is possible.

It's instructive to attempt to map the relationship between and among the canons. As I continue to explore delivery—of text, of instruction, of public extracurricula—delivery seems at the heart of the relationship, but I can see how at other times, other canons take that place.

The revolution, if there is one, is the social one of interconnectivity.

—James Porter 2003

Richard Lanham, of course, has argued that with the addition of the digital to the set of media in which we compose, delivery takes on a critical role, and I think that's so. But much more specifically, what a shift in the means of delivery does is bring invention and arrangement into a new relationship with each other. The writer of the page has fundamentally different opportunities than the creator of a hypertext. Anne Wysocki is right about the interface of the page—that is, it has one, and it's worth paying attention to—but even so, as we read the pages of an article, we typically do so line by line, left to right, as you do now: page one before page two. This is the fixed default arrangement. The writer *invented* through such a text is a function of that arrangement. In other words, you can only invent inside what an arrangement permits—and different media permit different arrangements. By contrast, the creator of a hypertext can create a text that, like the page, moves forward. In addition, however, hypertext composers can create other arrangements, almost as in three rather than two dimensions. You can move horizontally, right branching; you can then left branch. The writer invented in a medium permitting these arrangements is quite different—a difference of kind, not degree.

We used to have a stable definition of composing and of the author. These have changed. The freedom to invent, to arrange multiply, can be a wonderful thing. It can also evoke anxiety, somewhat akin to discovering that the tectonic plates underlying the continents are not stable but, in fact, are shifting constantly.

The tectonic plate theory of continental drift was "discovered" in 1965. Rohman and Wlecke's stage-model of writing was "discovered" a year earlier; Rohman's CCC article detailing prewriting was published the year following, in 1965.

Given my own teaching and research interests, I see such differences, particularly in portfolios. In a print portfolio, remediated on a book, the arrangement is singular. In a digital portfolio, remediated on a gallery, the arrangements are plural. And the students invented in each are quite different. In a print portfolio, the tendency is to tell a single story, one with a single claim and an accumulating body of evidence. In arrangement, a digital portfolio—again, by contrast—is multiple, is defined by links. Because you can link externally as well as internally and because those links are material, you have more contexts you can link to, more strata you can layer, more

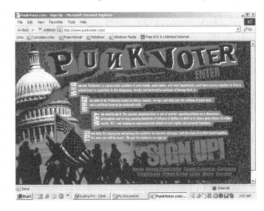

"you" to invent, more invention to represent. In sum, the potential of arrangement is a function of delivery, and *what and how you arrange*—which becomes a function of the medium you choose—*is who you invent*.[18] Moreover, I suspect that as multiple means of delivery become more routinized, we will understand *each* of the canons differently, and we will understand and be able to map their interrelationships.

My third and final expression is the deicity of technology. *Deixis*, linguistically, refers to words like *now* and *then*, words whose "meanings change quickly depending on the time or space in which they are uttered" (Leu et al.) or read. The word *Now* when I wrote this text is one time; as I read the word *Now* in San Antonio was a second time; and now, when this talk is published in *CCC* and who knows how many people do (or do not!) read *this* Chair's Address, it will be many, many other times. Literacy is deictic. The speed of technological change has affected literacy, as we know. The particular claim that D. J. Leu, C. K. Kinzer, J. Coiro, and D. Cammack (among others) have made is this: "technological change happens so rapidly that the changes to literacy are limited not by technology but rather by our ability to adapt and acquire the new literacies that emerge." Deixis, they say, "is a defining quality of the new literacies of the Internet" and other information communication technologies.

Leu and his colleagues note how our working in a context of deixis changes the way we teach. No longer, they say, can we speak from the podium with the expertise of old. Instead, faculty and students will consider questions and use various technologies to help address them, with the faculty member guiding the work, and in some cases learning along with the students. In composition, we need to learn how to read and write e-texts—synthesizing, questioning, evaluating, and importing from them—databases and catalogues, hyper-texts and archives, Web essays and portfolios.

And this means we all need to learn more about how to use images and sources, how to document them appropriately, how to create our own.

According to Leu and his coauthors, there are three sources for this deictic nature of literacy:

1. transformations of literacy because of technological change,
2. the use of increasingly efficient technologies of communication that rapidly spread new literacies, and
3. envisionments of new literacy potentials within new technologies.

Although deixis might be a new term to many of us, the first two claims are familiar. As we saw in the case of the 19th-century reader, technology changes literacy: that's the kind of trans-

> *By paying critical attention to lessons about* technology, *we can re-learn important lessons about* literacy.
>
> —*Cindy Selfe 1999*

formation we are seeing now with regard to writers. Technology, of course, has always been ubiquitous: as Dennis Baron points out, a pencil is a technology. At the same time, however, *this* digital, networked technology continuously promotes itself and new literacies—through the marketing efforts of the corporations that develop these technologies; through open source and shareware and freeware; through our ability to download new programs and formats that are essentially new engines for a literacy no one can quite predict. The dissemination of this potential capacity is built into this model of technology. Given its worldwide distribution and its democratization of authorship, that's new.

The third source—what Leu calls "envisionments of new literacy potentials within new technologies"—is provocative. Here is what he is referring to: the ability of someone to take a given technology and find a use for it that may be at odds with its design. The example he provides is this. Suppose that you are writing an e-mail but decide to compose the e-mail inside a word processor, which is a different (if related) technology. In this scenario,

> a word processor can be transformed into a tool for composing e-mail messages, a purpose for which it was not designed, but a function it fills admirably. This potential only comes to life when a person envisions a new function for a technology and *enacts this envisionment*. In essence, we can say that she envisioned how to repurpose a technology for a new and different function. Envisionments such as this happen regularly as individuals encounter new problems and seek solutions in new and creative uses of existing technologies. (Leu et al.)

Envisionment is a practice most of us engage in, typically without thinking about it as such. Teachers use a spreadsheet for grading purposes. A colleague uses a spreadsheet for a digital portfolio template for her class of 120 students. Elementary teachers use PowerPoint for reluctant writers. High school teachers use textboxes for peer review and links for research hypercards. College teachers invite blocked writers to draft in an e-mail program.

A modest proposal: one outcome for all writers is the ability to use many kinds of technologies for their intended purposes and for other purposes, as needed and as imagined.

Or: writers use technology rhetorically.

Writing, by its very nature, encourages abstraction, and in the shuttling process from the past to the present, from the particular to the general, from the concrete to the abstract, we seek relationships and find meaning.

—*William Irmscher 1979*

And let me provide another example. For the last several years, I have worked with graduate students in architecture, and one of their practices is meeting monthly to talk about how their projects and theses are developing. Now, given that it's architecture, they do more than talk: they *show*—in pinups on the walls, in a one-page handout, and in a set of PowerPoint slides. Something that grabbed my attention almost immediately was how those slides were being used: not for *presentation* of a finished idea, as the design of them would have it—and as the name, presentation software, suggests—but, rather, for a different purpose: for exploration, in fact as a new space for drafting ideas. Since then, in several different classes, I've used PowerPoint in just this way, as a site for a rough draft, shared with a real audience. Or: envisionment. What other technologies might be re-envisioned and to what effects? What envisionments have students already created that we don't know about? And how do we build this ability—envisioning—into our curriculum?

This new composition includes rhetoric and is about literacy. New composition includes the literacy of print: it adds on to it and brings the notions of practice and activity and circulation and media and screen and networking to our conceptions of process. It will require a new expertise of us as it does of our students. And ultimately, new composition may require a new site for learning for all of us.

QUARTET FOUR

Time present and time past
Are both perhaps present in time future,
And time future contained in time past.

We have a moment.

In her study *Institutionalizing Literacy*, Mary Trachsel makes the argument that when we separate an activity related to curriculum from it, faculty lose control over curriculum to the detriment of students and faculty alike. Trachsel, of course, is speaking of assessment, and how historically it has been cleaved from curriculum, particularly at the gatekeeping moment when students enter college— and she cites the SAT as evidence of the claim. I would make the same observation about technology. If we continue to partition it off as just something technical, or outside the parameters governing composing, or limit it to the screen of the course management system, or think of it in terms of the bells and whistles and templates of the Power-Point screen, students in our classes learn only to *fill up* those templates and *fill in* those electric boxes—which, in their ability to invite intellectual work, are the moral equivalent of the dots on a multiple choice test. Students will not compose and create, making use of all the means of persuasion and all the possible resources thereto; rather, they will complete someone else's software package; they will be the invention of that package.

These spaces—the intertextual, overlapping curricular spaces—between school and the public, including print and screen, are still ours to study, to examine, to work in, and to claim. They are the province of first-year composition but are not limited to it. This curricular change includes renewed attention to WAC. It includes a new major in whatever site: English department, writing studies department, rhetorical studies program. The institutional site is less important than the major itself, which can begin to secure our position in the academy while it makes space for the writing that students do on their own, now, without us.

> *It is time to speak for ourselves, in our own interests, in the interest of our own work, and in the interest of our students.*
>
> *— Jacqueline Jones Royster 1996*

The metaphors we use to describe also construct. The metaphor of tectonic change, particularly when used in the context of the changes of the 19th century, can help us understand how pervasive our current challenges are, how necessary our efforts to adapt.

So this talk: yes, it's about change. Change, as we saw in the 19th century, and as we see now, can be very difficult, can be unnerving. I used the

717

metaphor of tremors intentionally. A little more than twenty years ago we talked about "winds of change" (Hairston); today the changes are those of tremors. These are *structural* changes—global, educational, technological. Like seismic tremors, these signal a re-formation in process, and because we exist on the borders of our own tectonic plates—rhetoric, composition and communication, process, activity, service and social justice—we are at the very center of those tremors.

Perhaps the most important of the plates on which we stand is advocacy, especially at this moment. As the Dixie Chicks point out, voting is an excellent means of self-expression. In helping create writing publics, we also foster the development of citizens who vote, of citizens whose civic literacy is global in its sensibility and its communicative potential, and whose commitment to humanity is characterized by consistency and generosity as well as the ability to write for purposes that are unconstrained and audiences that are nearly unlimited.

It's an ambitious agenda I laid before you in San Antonio and that I lay before you in these pages today, but yes, this is made not only in words: composition in a new key.

ACKNOWLEDGMENTS

Gracious thanks to the CCCC audience in San Antonio and to those who helped me before I arrived there: Kristi and Shawn Apostel, Michael Crawford, Will Dickert, Teddi Fishman, Morgan Gresham, Doug Hesse, Martin Jacobi, Brian Morrison, Michael Neal, Josh Reynolds, Summer Smith Taylor, and Irwin Weiser. For special help in the selection and placement of images and in the overall design of this text, many thanks to Marilyn Cooper.

Thanks also to the following for permission to reprint. Lines from "Burnt Norton" on pages 297, 308 and 320 from *Four Quartets* by T.S. Eliot, copyright 1936 by Harcourt, Inc., and renewed 1964 by T.S. Eliot, reprinted by permission of the publisher. A line from "East Coker" on page 299 from *Four Quartets* by T.S. Eliot, copyright 1940 by T.S. Eliot and renewed 1968 by Esmc Valerie Eliot, reprinted by permission of Harcourt, Inc. Lines from "Little Gidding" on page 305 from *Four Quartets* by T.S. Eliot 1942 and renewed 1970 by Esmc Valerie Eliot, reprinted by permission of Harcourt, Inc. *Composition VII* by Wassily Kandinsky on page 303, copyright 2004 Artists Rights Society (ARS), New York/ADAGP, Paris, reprinted by permission.

NOTES

1. The slides were arranged so that duplicates showed up simultaneously at various points in the presentation: two screens showed the same slide. Also, as the performance progressed, some slides were repeated, in part to provide some contour to the performance, in part to provide some coherence. I attempt to explain the logic of this composition in *Composition in a New Key*, forthcoming.

2. In the 1980's, compositionists were excited about the role that process was playing—in our teaching, in the assessment of student work, in our own research. Given the disparity between the out-of-school, often digitally composed genres that students currently work in and the form that current assessments are taking—even the much ballyhooed new SAT "writing test" includes a component on grammar and usage that is allowed *more* time than the pencil-and-paper draft portion—Marshall McLuhan's point about marching backwards into the future sounds all too true. For a compelling analysis of the disjunction between what we teach and what is being assessed, see Miles McCrimmon, "High School Writing Practices in the Age of Standards: Implications for College Composition."

3. The relationship between and among technology, literacy practices, nation states, and centralized control is considerably more complicated than I can pursue here. For an analysis that focuses on the materiality of literacy practices and technology, see Lester Faigley's *Material Literacy and Visual Design*; for a discussion that emphasizes the centralization of the nation state as related to literacy and technology, see Ronald Deibert's *Parchment, Printing, and Hypermedia: Communication in World Order Transformation* and Deborah Brandt's *Literacy in American Lives*.

4. Digital compositions include other materials as well: audio files, for instance. For a discussion of such materials in the context of remediation and composition, see Scott Halbritter.

5. The talk I delivered was not precisely the same as the written text. For historical purposes, CCCC videotapes the talk, and what seemed obvious to me at the time is so in retrospect: the two "talks" differ.

6. How various technologies—from technology producing light to that associated with various printing presses—interact to influence the development of literacy (and whose needs this literacy serves) is a (another) question worth pursuing.

7. You don't have to be present to see them: online, you can see the home pages for the Seattle Public Library and the Salt Lake City Library. For a fuller discussion of the lessons regarding these spaces that libraries have to teach us, see Yancey, "Episodes in the Spaces of the Plural Commons."

8. The idea that English departments are being consolidated into other units was first drawn to my attention by Tina Good, at Suffolk County Community College, who has conducted a study of the SUNY system, verifying the claim in that context.

9. As David Lawrence, the executive director of the Association of Departments of English (ADE), has pointed out to me, there's no reason to regard the number of majors from 1966 as the ideal or the norm, and it is the case that English majors still rank in the top ten of all majors (calculated based on a U.S. government database). Point taken. Still, this seems small comfort to me (as a member of an English department) when I remember that more students go to college and graduate today, in 2004, than did in 1966, so the numbers for the English major, it seems to me, ought to grow, not hold steady. In a population that is increasing, maintaining constitutes a decline, as the numbers attest. One reply to such a view, as explained in the *ADE* report "The Undergraduate English Major," is to put the numbers in

larger historical perspective. In this case, that entails the observation that the "semicaptive" audience of majors that English used to have—that is, women—are now choosing to major in other fields, especially biology, psychology, and business, which given our interest in gender equity is a good thing. *Of course.* Still, the trend lines—number of majors, number of tenure-line hires, number of English departments—plot a narrative that those of us who are aligned with English should not ignore.

10. On May 10, 2004, the Colorado legislature passed this bill, which provides funding vouchers to all college students in the state to be applied to all kinds of postsecondary institutions, including private schools. The implications of this bill are widespread: for an early analysis, see Chris Kampfe and Kyle Endres.

11. As this list indicates, a number of so-called college classes are actually *delivered* in high school: what does this say about college composition? With several others, I attempt to answer this question: see Yancey, *Delivering College Composition: The Fifth Canon,* Heinemann 2004.

12. The respondents included more than 1,800 faculty members from forty-eight states, split about 40/60 between two-year and four-year faculty. In terms of faculty status, 17% identified as graduate students and 23% as adjunct faculty. For a fuller description and analysis of the results, see Yancey et al., "Portraits of Composition: How Writing Gets Taught in the Early Twenty-First Century."

13. The idea for a major in rhetoric and composition is not new. Keith Miller was kind enough to point me toward the George Tade, Gary Tate, and Jim Corder article in *CCC,* "For Sale, Lease, or Rent: A Curriculum for an Undergraduate Program in Rhetoric." And some 25 years later, Robert Connors makes the philosophical argument in his Afterword to *Coming of Age.*

14. For a full account of the influence of Edwin Hopkins, see the article by John Heyda and Randall Popken.

15. As I look over the list of items here, the key word seems to be transfer: from composing site to composing site, from classroom to classroom, from one experience to the next. As I have suggested elsewhere, Donald Schon's notion of "reflective transfer" is crucial to this development. See Yancey, *Reflection in the Writing Classroom.*

16. The activity systems mapped by Paul Prior and Jody Shipka parallel the spaces architects are designing into various kinds of buildings: both conceive of human activity organized into multiple overlapping spaces. Another way to theorize composition of the 21st century is through the overlapping curricular, activity, and physical spaces where it occurs now and where it might occur. In this construct, the circulation of composition takes yet another definition.

17. Bill Watterson has several books that in their commentary on processes, media, and transfer are models for the observation, analysis, and insight we often find in portfolio reflections.

18. For a fuller account of both kinds of portfolios, see Yancey, "Postmodernism, Palimpsest, and Portfolios: Theoretical Issues in the Representation of Student Work" and *Teaching Literature as Reflective Practice,* especially chapter five.

WORKS CITED

ADE. "Report of the Undergraduate English Major." Report of the 2001–2002 ADE Ad Hoc Committee on the English Major. *ADE* (Fall/Winter 2003): 68–91.

"America's Fortunes." Atlantic Online (January/February 2004) 21 Mar 04 <http:www. theatlantic.com/cgi-bin/send.cgi?pae=http%3A//www.the atlantic.com/issues>.

Baron, Dennis. "From Pencils to Pixels." *Passions, Pedagogies, and 21st Century Technologies*. Ed. Gail Hawisher and Cynthia Selfe. Logan: Utah State UP, 1999. 15–34.

Bartholomae, David. "Freshman English, Composition, and CCCC." *College Communication and Composition* 40.1 (1989): 38–50.

Bazerman, Charles, and David Russell, eds. *Writing Selves, Writing Societies: Research from Activity Perspectives*. Fort Collins, CO: The WAC Clearinghouse and Mind, Culture, and Activity. 1 June 2004 <http://wac.colostate.edu/books/selves_societies/intro.cfm>.

Beaufort, Anne. *Writing in the Real World: Making the Transition from School to Work*. New York: Teachers College P, 1999.

Bolter, Jay David, and Richard Grusin. *Remediation: Understanding New Media*. Cambridge: MIT P, 2000.

Brandt, Deborah. *Literacy in American Lives*. New York: Cambridge UP, 2001.

Bridwell-Bowles, Lillian. "Freedom, Form, Function: Varieties of Academic Discourse." *College Communication and Composition* 46.1 (1995): 46–61.

Carroll, Lee Ann. *Rehearsing New Roles: How College Students Develop as Writers*. Carbondale: Southern Illinois UP, 2002.

Chaplin, Miriam T. "Issues, Perspectives, and Possibilities." *College Composition and Communication* 39.1 (1988): 52–62.

Chiseri-Strater, Elizabeth. *Academic Literacies: The Public and Private Discourse of University Students*. Portsmouth, NH: Boynton/Cook, 1991.

Connors, Robert. Afterword. *Coming of Age: The Advanced Writing Curriculum*. Ed. Linda K. Shamoon, Rebecca Moore Howard, Sandra Jamieson, and Robert A. Schwegler. Portsmouth, NH: Boynton/Cook, 2000. 143–49.

Crowley, Sharon. *Composition in the University: Historical and Polemical Essays*. Pittsburgh: U of Pittsburgh, 1998.

D'Angelo, Frank. "Regaining Our Composure." *College Composition and Communication* 31.4 (1980): 420–26.

Daley, Elizabeth. "Expanding the Concept of Literacy." *Educause Review* 38.2 (2003): 33–40.

———. "Speaking the Languages of Literacy." Speech, University of Michigan, April 2003. 9 Aug. 04 <http://web.si. umich.edu/news/news-detail.cfm? NewsItemID=350>.

Davis, Vivian I. "Our Excellence: Where Do We Grow from Here?" *College Composition and Communication* 30.1 (1979): 26–31.

Deibert, Ronald. *Parchment, Printing, and Hypermedia: Communication in World Order Transformation*. New York: Columbia UP, 1997.

Ebert, Roger. Review of *21 Grams*. *Chicago Sun Times* (2003) 1 June 2004 <http://www. suntimes.com/ebert/ebert_reviews/2003/11/112606.html>.

Emig, Janet. *The Composing Processes of Twelfth Graders*. Urbana, IL: NCTE, 1971.

Faigley, Lester. "Literacy after the Revolution." *College Composition and Communication* 48.1 (1997): 30–43.

———. "Material Literacy and Visual Design." In *Rhetorical Bodies: Toward a Material Rhetoric*. Ed. Jack Selzer and Sharon Crowley. Madison: U of Wisconsin P, 1999. 171–201.

Flower, Linda, and John Hayes. "A Cognitive Process Theory of Writing." *College Composition and Communication* 32.4 (1981): 365–87.

Flynn, Elizabeth. "Composing as a Woman." *College Composition and Communication* 39.4 (1988): 423–35.

Gerber, John C. "The Conference on College Composition and Communication." *College Composition and Communication* 1.1 (1950): 12.

Gere, Anne Ruggles. "Kitchen Tables and Rented Rooms: The Extracurriculum of Composition." *College Composition and Communication* 45.1 (1994): 75–92.

Good, Tina. Personal discussion, 25 April 2003.

Hairston, Maxine. "The Winds of Change: Thomas Kuhn and the Revolution in the Teaching of Writing." *College Composition and Communication* 33.1: 76–88.

Halbritter, Scott. "Sound Arguments: Aural Rhetoric in Multimedia Composition." PhD diss. University of North Carolina, 2004.

Haswell, Richard. *Gaining Ground in College: Tales of Development and Interpretation.* Dallas, TX: Southern Methodist UP, 1991.

Hawisher, Gail. Personal discussion. Feb 2004.

Heyda, John. "Industrial-Strength Composition and the Impact of Load on Teaching." *More Than 100 Years of Solitude: WPA Work before 1976.* Ed. Barbara L'Eppateur and Lisa Mastrangelo. Forthcoming.

Hopkins, Edwin. "Can Good English Composition Be Done under the Current Conditions?" *English Journal* 1 (1912): 1–8.

Irmscher, William F. "Writing as a Way of Learning and Developing." *College Composition and Communication* 30.3 (1979): 240–44.

Johnson-Eilola, Johndan. "Writing about Writing." Speech, Computers and Writing Town Hall Meeting, 2002, Illinois State University.

Jones, Richard Lloyd. "A View from the Center." *College Composition and Communication* 29.1 (1978): 24–29.

Kampfe, Chris, and Kyle Endres. "Vouchers to Change the Way Higher Ed is Funded." *The Rocky Mountain Collegian.* 10 May 2004. <http://www.collegian.com/vnews/display.v/ART/2004/05/07/409b21d2bfdee?in_archive=1>.

Lanham, Richard. *The Electronic Word: Democracy, Technology, and the Arts.* Chicago: U of Chicago P, 1993.

Lawrence, David. E-mail to author. April 2004.

Leu, D. J., C. K. Kinzer, J. Coiro, and D. Cammack. "Toward a Theory of New Literacies Emerging from the Internet and Other ICT." *Theoretical Models and Processes of Reading.* 5th ed. Ed. R. Ruddel and Norman Unrau. D. E. International Reading Association, 2004. 4 Aug. 2004 (Preprint version) <http://www.readingonline.org/newliteracies/leu>.

Light, Richard J. *Making the Most of College: Students Speak Their Minds.* Cambridge: Harvard UP, 2001.

Lindemann, Erika. "Early Bibliographic Work in Composition Studies." *Profession* (2002): 151–58.

Lunsford, Andrea. "Composing Ourselves: Politics, Commitment, and the Teaching of Writing." *College Composition and Communication* 41.1 (1990): 71–82.

McCrimmon, Miles. "High School Writing Practices in the Age of Standards: Implications for College Composition." Forthcoming.

McLuhan, Marshall. *Understanding Media: The Extensions of Man.* 1964. Cambridge: MIT P, 1994.

Matsuda, Paul. "Process and Post Process: A Discursive History." *Journal of Second Language Writing* 12 (2003): 65–83.

Palmquist, Michael. "Review: Made Not Only in Words: Composition in a New Key." 15 April 2004. *Across the Disciplines* at the WAC Clearinghouse. 1 June 2004 <http://wac. colostate.edu/atd/reviews/cccc2004/viewmessage.cfm?messageid =61>.

Popken, Randall. "Edwin Hopkins and the Costly Labor of Composition Teaching." *College Composition and Communication* 55.4 (2004): 618–42.

Porter, James. "Why Technology Matters to Writing: A Cyberwriter's Tale." *Computers and Composition* 20.3 (2003): 375–94.

Prior, Paul, and Jody Shipka. "Chronotopic Laminations: Tracing the Contours of Literate Activity." *Writing Selves, Writing Societies: Research from Activity Perspectives.* Ed. Charles Bazerman and David Russell. Fort Collins, CO: The WAC Clearinghouse, and Mind, Culture, and Activity, 180–238. 1 June 2004 <http://wac.colostate.edu/books/ selves_ societies/prior>.

Putnam, Robert. *Bowling Alone.* New York: Simon and Schuster, 2000.

Reynolds, Josh. "Writing Process Map." *My English Portfolio.* 1 June 2004 <http://people. clemson.edu/~jsreyno/Process. htm>.

Rohman, D. Gordon. "Prewriting: The Stage of Discovery in the Writing Process." *College Composition and Communication* 16.2 (1965): 106–12.

Rohman, D. Gordon, and Albert O. Wlecke. "Pre-Writing: The Construction and Applications of Models for Concept Formation in Writing." Cooperative Research Project No. 2174. USOE: Washington, DC.

Royster, Jacqueline Jones. "When the First Voice You Hear Is Not Your Own." *College Composition and Communication* 47.1 (1996): 29–40.

Russell, David, and Arturo Yañez. "Big Picture People Rarely Become Historians: Genre Systems and the Contradictions of General Education." *Writing Selves, Writing Societies: Research from Activity Perspectives.* Ed. Charles Bazerman and David Russell. Fort Collins, CO: The WAC Clearinghouse, and Mind, Culture, and Activity. 1 June 2004 <http://wac.colostate.edu/books/selves_societies/russell>.

Selfe, Cynthia L. "Technology and Literacy: A Story about the Perils of Not Paying Attention." *College Composition and Communication* 50.3 (1999): 411–36.

Shea, Rachel Hartigan. "How We Got Here." *U.S. News and World Report,* 9 Aug 2004: 70–73.

Sommers, Nancy, and Laura Saltz. "The Novice as Expert: Writing the Freshman Year." *College Composition and Communication* 56.1 (2004): 124–49.

Sternglass, Marilyn. *Time to Know Them: A Longitudinal Study of Writing and Learning at the College Level.* Mahwah, NJ: Lawrence Erlbaum Associates, 1997.

Tade, George, Gary Tate, and Jim Corder. "For Sale, Lease, or Rent: A Curriculum for an Undergraduate Program in Rhetoric." *College Composition and Communication* 26.1 (1975): 20–24.

Trachsel, Mary. *Institutionalizing Literacy: The Historical Role of College Entrance Examinations in English.* Carbondale: Southern Illinois UP, 1992.

Trimbur, John. "Composition and the Circulation of Writing." *College Composition and Communication* 52.2 (2000): 188–219.

Vendler, Helen. "The Ocean, the Bird, and the Scholar." NEH Jefferson Address, 6 May 2004. 9 Aug. 04 <http://www.neh. gov/whoweare/vendler/lecture.html>.

Watterson, Bill. *Sunday Pages 1985–1995: An Exhibition Catalogue.* Kansas City, MO: Andrews McMeel Publishing, 2000.

Wright, John ed. *New York Times 2004 Almanac*. New York: Penguin, 2003.

Wysocki, Anne, and Julia Jasken. "What Should Be an Unforgettable Face." *Computers and Composition* 21.1 (2004): 29–49.

Yancey, Kathleen Blake. "Episodes in the Spaces of the Plural Commons: Curriculum, Administration, and Design of Composition in the 21st Century." Speech, Writing Program Administration, Delaware, 14 July 2004.

———. "Postmodernism, Palimpsest, and Portfolios: Theoretical Issues in the Representation of Student Work." *College Composition and Communication* 55.4 (2004): 738–61.

———. *Reflection in the Writing Classroom*. Logan: Utah State UP, 1998.

———. *Teaching Literature as Reflective Practice*. Urbana, IL: NCTE, 2004.

Yancey, Kathleen Blake, Teddi Fishman, Morgan Gresham, Michael Neal, and Summer Smith Taylor. "Portraits of Composition: How Postsecondary Writing Gets Taught in the Early Twenty-First Century." Forthcoming.

Lessons from History
Teaching with Technology in
100 Years of English Journal

Ben McCorkle and Jason Palmeri

This article investigates 100 years of articles in **English Journal** *(1912–2012) that focus on teaching with or about communication technologies and media.*

If you've been reading the pages of *English Journal* recently, you've seen many calls for teachers to move beyond print literacy to engage students in composing and analyzing the emerging media of our time: digital videos (Ranker; Staples), podcasts (Goodson and Skillen), video games (Adams; Jolley), and Facebook (Kitsis), to name but a few. Faced with these steady calls to keep up with new media developments, we English teachers often find ourselves longing for a simpler time when books reigned supreme and "English was English." Yet, if we look back at the past 100 years of *English Journal*, we can remind ourselves that English teachers have long been adapting their curricula and methods to incorporate the visual and auditory media of their time. As is often the case, the past we romanticize doesn't always look the way we imagine it.

In 1931, for example, Ruth Batten recounted her struggle with a group of seemingly "stupid and lazy" students who refused to write conventional essays until she hit upon the idea of asking them to collaboratively produce a radio program for broadcast to a real audience; once the students were composing in a new media form that was personally meaningful to them, Batten noted

Reprinted from *English Journal* 105.6 (July 2016): 18–24. Used with permission.

with delight that they took agency for their learning and drafted high-quality scripts (160). In 1937, Louise G. Whitehead reported that students in her class greatly enjoyed making a film adaptation of *David Copperfield*, finding that they developed a richer, more engaged appreciation of the book as a result. Based on this experience, Whitehead argued that English teachers are now living "in a visual age" and must adapt their methods to keep up with the times (317). Although many *English Journal* authors in the 1930s were enthusiastic about teaching film and radio in the English class, numerous authors warily emphasized the need for English teachers to carefully guide students' media use. Indeed, one author, Joseph Mersand, highlighted the importance of judicious selection of radio programs by recounting the case of a Toledo junior high student who "shot his principal under the inspiration of radio programs to which he was listening" (469). One imagines that if Mr. Mersand were writing today, he might be decrying the pernicious effects of violent video games, while Ms. Whitehead might be engaging students in using iMovie to create video versions of books on the Common Core reading list. As English teachers confront the challenges of the contemporary digital moment, we contend that there are many lessons to be learned from both the inspiring innovations and the limiting pitfalls of past English teachers' approaches to teaching "new" media.

Recently, the two of us set out to explore issues of *English Journal* from 1912 to 2012, specifically looking for articles that involved the introduction of "new" technologies of communication in the English classroom. We eventually discovered and systematically coded 787 articles about new communication media in *English Journal*. We located articles about new media in all but two years of the journal's history (it appears that authors in 1920 and 1921 were uniquely traditionalist).

Through this research, we've come to realize that the oft-heralded golden age when English was just limited to print books never really existed—or if it did, it was very long ago.

METHODS, OR, HOW WE FOUND THESE ARTICLES AND MADE SENSE OF THEM

Although some scholars have drawn on the *English Journal* archive to write histories of technological approaches to teaching English (Hicks et al.; Jones; Palmeri; White), these histories rely on close readings of a small number of articles. By contrast, our approach uses a method called "distant reading" (Moretti; Mueller) that can enable us to gain a more expansive understanding of how English teachers have engaged with technology over time. More directly, our research approach has been inspired by Mark Faust and Mark Dressman's insightful analytic coding of 93 years of *English Journal* articles about poetry. Adapting Faust and Dressman's approach for gathering and analyzing data, we reviewed titles for all articles from 100 years of *English Journal*, selecting those that explicitly mentioned media or technology in the title while also reviewing articles with ambiguous titles that might allude to our subject. At the outset, we developed a coding scheme for analyzing what kinds of technology the articles discussed, what arguments the authors made about technology, and what instructional goals informed their uses of technology.

Early in the process, we initially refined our coding scheme by reading and coding the same sample years, afterward discussing how we arrived at certain decisions and developing a shared understanding of our coding criteria. We then read and coded alternate years, periodically reviewing and conferring about each other's coding. What follows are graphical representations of five of the key lessons we learned from our time investigating the *English Journal* archives.

LESSON ONE: ENGLISH HAS ALWAYS BEEN ABOUT MORE THAN BOOKS

When we look back at the history of *English Journal*, we can see that the field has long engaged with types and forms of media beyond the print book.

As we explored this 100-year span, we coded 117 articles about audio media (radio, phonographs, audio tape recorders, etc.), 311 articles about

Figure 1. Number of Articles by Type of Media

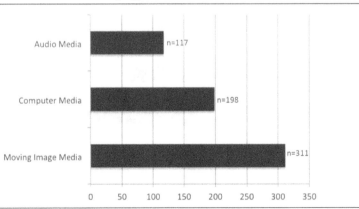

moving image media (film, television, and video), and 198 articles about computer media (PCs, word processors, laptops). As early as 1913, English teachers were adapting their pedagogy to the new medium of silent film, striving, as Robert W. Neal so bitingly put it, to make "the devil useful." In the 1930s alone, *English Journal* featured 28 articles about teaching with radio and 32 about teaching with film. Starting in the early 1980s, the computer emerged as a sustained presence in the journal. Yet despite this large body of work on media pedagogy, English teachers too often continue to be stereotyped as conservative traditionalists committed solely to musty books and antique inkwells. We hope that our historical recovery work can help us challenge these narrow misconceptions about what our field entails, and help empower teachers to think of novel ways of integrating media-based assignments into their classrooms.

LESSON TWO: "NEW MEDIA" HAVE LONG BEEN CONNECTED TO STUDENT ENGAGEMENT

When we began this project, we imagined we would find many denunciations of how new media were harming traditional reading and writing, or "alphabetic literacy," as we term it. Surprisingly, we found only 53 articles (approximately 6.7 percent) that emphasized the harmful effects of new media on students' reading and writing, while we found 461 articles (approximately 59 percent) that explicitly emphasized how working with new media could improve students' alphabetic literacy. In particular, teachers valued new media because

Figure 2. Common Arguments/Attitudes Concerning New Media

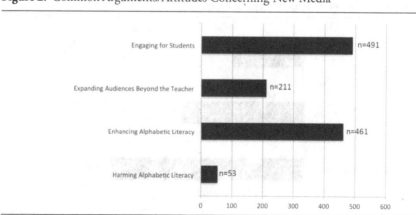

they viewed them as more engaging for students (491 articles). Whether they were having students listen to Shakespeare on the radio (Carney) or make their own film adaptations of the poem "Lady of the Lake" (Hodge), *English Journal* authors regularly asserted that new media could be a tool to reinvigorate student engagement with print texts. In addition to seeing new media as a boon for the teaching of reading, teachers also emphasized how media assignments could motivate student writing by enabling them to compose for audiences beyond the classroom—whether it be writing and performing radio news broadcasts (Tyler) or circulating writing to peers via a computer network (Holvig).

Although an aversion to print reading is often seen as a problem unique to the digital generation, it turns out that teachers have been worrying about students' supposedly waning interest in books for more than 100 years. And, throughout the past century, English teachers have been harnessing students' interest in new media as a way to enhance their engagement with print texts. So when you find yourself asking students to perform a *Romeo and Juliet* scene on digital video or to create a persuasive audio public service announcement, you can take comfort that you are part of a long tradition of English teachers who've been adapting their pedagogies to students' "new media" interests. And, when you find yourself worrying that the novel is going to die a death by a thousand text messages, it is important to recognize that new media need not be a threat to old media in a zero-sum game; rather, English teachers can help students draw connections among—and take pleasure in—multiple media forms interacting with one another.

LESSON THREE: THERE IS A LONG HISTORY OF MEDIA PRODUCTION AS PART OF ENGLISH TEACHING

English teachers have long been engaging students in *producing* media texts as well as analyzing them. Our coding scheme distinguished between whether an article emphasized media production or reception primarily. For example, an article on teaching students to view a film or read a website would be coded as reception, whereas students making a film or composing a website would be classified as production; in some cases, we classified an activity as media production if students were making something like a radio or TV broadcast even if they were not using professional tools. For example, students performing a radio play script while sitting behind a curtain would count as production (Cothrin), as would students creating an actual radio program for live broadcast (Tyler).

We had initially anticipated that reception would far outpace production as a pedagogical goal, largely owing to factors such as limited access to technology, steep learning curves, or curricuar guidelines favoring the development of traditional literacy skills. We were surprised, however, to discover the degree to which teachers designed assignments that involved composing with new media. In fact, aside from a few sporadic years, we find that production has otherwise enjoyed a nearcontinuous place in our history of teaching with new media, even at times outpacing reception. While English teachers who experiment with new media today often must defend against the charge that they are departing from their traditional area of expertise, this history can empower us to demonstrate that our field has a substantial tradition of teaching media production—in other words, we have long recognized that students will best be able to critically analyze media if they gain experience making it.

Figure 3. Production vs. Reception

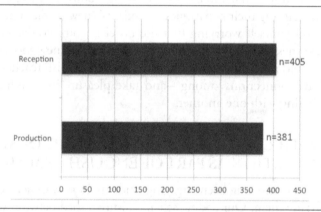

LESSON FOUR: MOMENTS WHEN MEDIA ARE "NEW" PRESENT OPPORTUNITIES FOR INNOVATION

Emerging media forms often open up spaces to experiment in the classroom, especially in the early stages. We found that radio and film production were heavily foregrounded in the 1930s when these media were relatively new, but as the century progressed, teachers increasingly positioned radio and film primarily as texts for analysis. There was a smaller uptick in moving image production in the 1970s and 1980s, when new and more inexpensive film and video cameras came on the scene, but we still have not seen a return to the audio and visual production heyday of the 1930s (although, as we discuss in the following section, the computer is increasingly becoming a tool for this type of production in the classroom). This history reminds us that those moments when media are *new* present opportunities for innovation—opportunities for productively rethinking what the work of the English class entails. But, as media become more familiar and pervasive, there is a risk that we will forget these innovative media production pedagogies and return to positioning students solely as media consumers. In our current moment of great technological change, we have a unique chance to rethink what it means to teach English, but our challenge will be to sustain these curricular changes over the long haul, resisting the forces of conservatism that seek to "force the new media to do the work of the old" (McLuhan and Fiore 81).

Figure 4. Common Arguments/Attitudes Concerning New Media

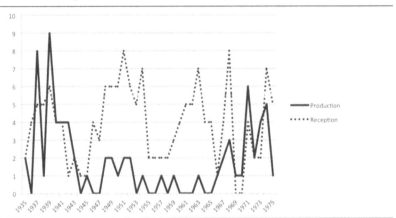

LESSON FIVE: THE COMPUTER
HAS BEEN A GAME CHANGER

After some initial excitement in the 1960s about how computers might become tools for grading (Daigon) or teaching literature (Stowe and Maggio), *English Journal* turned away from computers until the early 1980s, when compact word processors and personal computers began to proliferate. From this point on, English teachers emphasized the computer as a tool for student-centered production: out of 198 total articles focusing on the computer, 151 emphasized production, while only 46 emphasized reception (one lone article, which offered advice on buying a microcomputer, did not exhibit an obvious pedagogical emphasis). In particular, teachers embraced computers as a tool for writing instruction. Although there was some talk of using computers to help students with grammar (Shuman), many of the computer articles emphasized process-based writing activities such as inventing ideas, peer response, revision, and distributing to audiences (Hawisher; Holvig; Kinkead; Lake). In this way, we can see that the computer (alongside writing process research) contributed to a powerful shift in the field, placing student writing at the center of the English course.

Figure 5. Computer Media Articles by Year

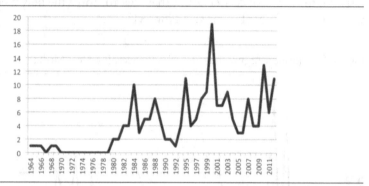

Because early personal computers had relatively limited image and audio editing capacity, the focus has largely been on composing alphabetic texts. It was only in recent years that teachers began thinking of the computer as a device for teaching multimodal composing (e.g., visually enhanced websites, podcasts, videos). Whereas initial bursts of interest in film and radio production waned relatively quickly, the computer has been positioned as a key production device in English classrooms for more than 30 years, with a growing emphasis on students composing visual and audio texts that extend beyond the classroom. One distinguishing characteristic of the computer as a production technology is that it facilitates composing in a *variety* of forms (graphics, audio, video, and various combinations) that were previously confined to specialized technologies. We expect that the computer will have staying power in the field going forward as computing technologies increasingly become integrated into many kinds of mobile devices. We must remember that computer access has been and continues to be unequally distributed among schools and students (Banks; Selfe); while the computer certainly has been a game changer on the pages of *English Journal*, we as a field still need to fight for societal changes that can enable all students across diverse contexts to employ computers as tools for reaching public audiences.

LEARNING FROM THE PAST, REMAKING THE FUTURE

When looking for inspiration for incorporating new media in our classrooms, we need not just turn to scholarship published in the past few years. Teachers considering using podcasts in class might turn back to the rich history of radio pedagogy—especially revisiting articles in the 1930s demonstrating that audio production can be a powerful form of civic engagement for students (Cullimore). Teachers considering a digital storytelling project might look back at work in the 1970s about video documentary production as a way to engage students in social action (Cromer). We find throughout the history of *English Journal* many examples of methods that engage students in composing new media, not just analyzing it; it is our position that teachers who work with new media will best serve their students by promoting media production in addition to reception as a way to foster responsible and engaged models of digital citizenry.

Along with providing inspiration, this history also can warn us of pitfalls to avoid. Over the years in *English Journal*, we've seen too many teachers unnecessarily restricting student media use to viewing or listening to adaptations of canonical literature without considering how fully engaging with media could lead to a more expansive vision of English pedagogy. When we look back at past ways that teachers limited the transformative potential of new media, we can be reminded of the importance of embracing our current new media moment as an opportunity to collaborate with students in remaking our pedagogies. The benefit of hindsight can also importantly remind us of the need to be humble about our claims about how new media are transforming young students. Where radio was once seen as a scary promoter of violence (Mersand), today's teachers often try to get their students to listen to NPR rather than play violent video games. And while English teachers in the 1950s worried that their students were more influenced by television than books (Rugg), some of that generation of students have grown up to become the stereotypical grandparents trying to convince their grandchildren to put down the mobile phone and pick up a book. When we remember the long history of cultural fears about how new media would replace traditional reading and writing, we can avoid reductively viewing students as "digital natives" (Palfrey and Gasser) wholly different from the generations that have gone before. Instead, we can work with students to develop innovative ways of combining print and new media literacy learning.

Drawing on this history can also help advocates of technology-enhanced instruction challenge the persistent stereotype that English has always been a print-centered discipline. By educating stakeholders (administrators, teachers, students, parents, legislators) on English studies' centurylong relationship with technology, advocates can help create a culture of support and sustainability that ensures greater understanding and acceptance of technology-based instruction for the future. When English teachers are represented in popular media, we are too often still positioned as dated, book-loving frumps. While our article is one step toward challenging this representation, we encourage fellow teachers to employ today's new media to create and circulate more complex pictures of the exciting work that English teachers and students do with audio, visual, and multimodal composing in our classrooms.

To this end, we are currently developing a more in-depth analysis of our findings in an interactive digital format for online publication in the near future, so please follow us on Twitter for updates at @illiac and @jasonpalmeri.

WORKS CITED

Adams, Megan Glover. "Engaging 21st-Century Adolescents: Video Games in the Reading Classroom." *English Journal* 98.6 (2009): 56–59. Print.

Banks, Adam. *Race, Rhetoric, and Technology: Searching for Higher Ground.* Mahwah: Erlbaum, 2006. Print.

Batten, Ruth. "A Radio Contract in English." *English Journal* 20.2 (1931): 158–60. Print.

Carney, Elizabeth. "Experiencing Shakespeare through the Radio Theater Party." *English Journal* 27.2 (1938): 133–36. Print.

Cothrin, Lola. "Advertisements and Radio Plays with Plan for Supervised Study." *English Journal* 24.2 (1935): 133–34. Print.

Cromer, Nancy. "Multi-Media: Making a Videotape: A Group Experience." *English Journal* 65.5 (1976): 94–95. Print.

Cullimore, Catherine. "A Radio Workshop Club." *English Journal* 37.6 (1948): 318–20. Print.

Daigon, Arthur. "Computer Grading of English Composition." *English Journal* 55.1 (1966): 46–52. Print.

Faust, Mark, and Mark Dressman. "The Other Tradition: Populist Perspectives on Teaching Poetry, as Published in *English Journal*, 1912–2005." *English Education* 41.2 (2009): 114–34. Print.

Goodson, Lori Atkins, and Matt Skillen. "Small-Town Perspectives, Big-Time Motivation: Composing and Producing Place-Based Podcasts." *English Journal* 100.1 (2010): 53–57. Print.

Hawisher, Gail E. "The Computer Daybook: A Multifaceted Tool." *English Journal* 77.3 (1988): 71–73. Print.

Hicks, Troy, Carl Young, Sara Kajder, and Bud Hunt. "Same as It Ever Was: Enacting the Promise of Teaching, Writing, and New Media." *English Journal* 101.3 (2012): 68–74. Print.

Hodge, Mary Ruth. "Making a Motion Picture of 'The Lady of the Lake.'" *English Journal* 27.5 (1938): 388–95. Print.

Holvig, Kenneth C. "Computers in the Classroom: Jamming the Phone Lines: Pencils, Notebooks, and Modems." *English Journal* 78.8 (1989): 68–70. Print. Jolley, Kristie. "Video Games to Reading: Reaching Out to Reluctant Readers." *English Journal* 97.4 (2008): 81–86. Print.

Jones, Joseph. "'Making the Devil Useful': Audio-Visual Aids for Teaching Writing." *On the Blunt Edge: Technology in Composition's History and Pedagogy.* Ed. Shane Borrowman. Anderson: Parlor, 2012. 85–97. Print.

Kinkead, Joyce. "Wired: Computer Networks in the English Classroom." *English Journal* 77.7 (1988): 39–41. Print.

Kitsis, Stacy. "The Facebook Generation: Homework as Social Networking." *English Journal* 98.2 (2008): 30–36. Print.

Lake, Dan. "Computers in the Classroom: Moving Words." *English Journal* 77.1 (1988): 83–85. Print.

McLuhan, Marshall, and Quentin Fiore. *The Medium Is the Message: An Inventory of Effects.* New York: Bantam, 1967. Print.

Mersand, Joseph. "Radio Makes Readers." *English Journal* 27.6 (1938): 469–75. Print.

Moretti, Franco. *Distant Reading.* London: Verso, 2013. Print.

Mueller, Derek. "Grasping Rhetoric and Composition by Its Long Tail: What Graphs Can Tell Us about the Field's Changing Shape." *College Composition and Communication* 64.1 (2012): 195–223. Print.

Neal, Robert W. "Making the Devil Useful." *English Journal* 2.10 (1913): 658–60. Print.

Palfrey, John, and Urs Gasser. *Born Digital: Understanding the First Generation of Digital Natives.* New York: Basic, 2010. Print.

Palmeri, Jason. *Remixing Composition: A History of Multimodal Writing Pedagogy.* Carbondale: Southern Illinois UP, 2012. Print.

Ranker, Jason. "A New Perspective on Inquiry: A Case Study of Digital Video Production." *English Journal* 97.1 (2007): 77–82. Print.

Rugg, Martin. "A Reading Beachhead against TV." *English Journal* 43.9 (1954): 521–22. Print.

Selfe, Cynthia. *Technology and Literacy in the 21st Century: The Importance of Paying Attention.* Carbondale: Southern Illinois UP, 1999. Print.

Shuman, R. Baird. "A Dozen Ways for English Teachers to Use Microcomputers." *English Journal* 74.6 (1985): 37–39. Print.

Staples, Jeanine. "Innovative Writing Instruction: 'Does My iMovie Suck?': Assessing Teacher Candidates' Digital Composition Processes." *English Journal* 99.5 (2010): 95–99. Print.

Stowe, Richard A., and Andrew J. Maggio. "Language and Poetry in Sight and Sound." *English Journal* 54.5 (1965): 410–13. Print.

Tyler, I. Keith. "Recent Developments in Radio Education." *English Journal* 28.3 (1939): 193–99. Print.

White, Gene. "From Magic Lanterns to Microcomputers: The Evolution of the Visual Aid in the English Classroom." *English Journal* 73.3 (1984): 59–62. Print.

Whitehead, Louise G. "The Motion Picture as a Medium of Class Instruction." *English Journal* 26.4 (1937): 315–17. Print.

Oakland, the Word, and the Divide

How We All Missed the Moment

ADAM J. BANKS

I once thought I could never imagine what it would have been like to be among the newly freed slaves after the shock of it all when the word finally came down, after the Juneteenth celebrations, after the pained attempts to locate lost family and loved ones, when the difficult work of reconstruction sat there waiting to be done. Same thing with those who helped to build Black lives and opportunities anew after the decades long struggle of African American leftists, moderates, liberals, and conservatives resulted in the temporary victories of the Civil Rights and Voting Rights Acts. It all seemed so basic when I learned bits of the histories of those moments: how could we not have gotten further? How could the rare coalescence of a national political will to change and legislation attempting to make that will some kind of reality not result in more tangible progress? How could Washington and DuBois still be debating what should have been obvious more than 30 years after emancipation? How could activists be left with such shambles of an education system 50 years after *Brown v. Board* when Blackfolk were infected with a euphoria that had them chanting "free by 63!"?

Why is it that we end up in this endless cycle when we learn about Black freedom struggle? Over and over and over again, victory, then inertia, then contentiousness then the sickening feeling that such history making

Reprinted from *Race, Rhetoric, and Technology: Searching for Higher Ground* by Adam J. Banks (Mahwah, NJ: Lawrence Erlbaum and Urbana, IL: NCTE, 2006). Used by permission.

victories made little difference in the long run? As an undergraduate with all of the idealism of 18- and 20-year-olds everywhere and all of the certitude that things were so clear and so easy, none of this made sense. The crack epidemic making shambles of my family and neighborhood at the exact same time Dr. King's birthday was being recognized as a national holiday? Surely the Negroes in whatever parallel universe might be watching us were shaking their heads as I was. Then I saw, on a much smaller scale, admittedly, how these travesties take place: the Digital Divide and Oakland. What happened (and didn't happen) with the alignment of these two national discussions in rhetoric and composition's theorizing and teaching, showed me what happens when Black warriors get caught on the wrong end of time warps being forced yet again to defend Black humanity, and when both well meaning and reactionary elements of the mainstream refuse to change. This is partially out of their insistence on subjecting that very humanity to debate and partially out of a blindness to the grounds on which we're all forced to live out our collective humanity, shifting rapidly while forcing that very, very old debate, in a nation where seemingly promising legislation or policy turned out to be nearly bankrupt.

This is exactly what happened in the late 1990s—the Department of Commerce introduced the Digital Divide as a concept to acknowledge the systematic differences in technology access that African Americans, other racial minorities and those in rural areas experienced and attempted policy initiatives that members of the Clinton administration thought would help to erase those gaps. Although what seemed to be a promising bit of political will emerged for educators to address problems of technology access in their schools, colleges, and universities, this issue failed to even make it onto academics' collective radar, with few exceptions. And a major part of why educators all over the country, at all levels, missed it, is because of their inability to avoid, yet again, the debate over Black humanity—in this case, educability in standardized English, because of the Oakland controversy.

Rhetoric and composition, as well as the technology sector in American society, have functioned very much in the same way as the legal system (that I examine in chapter four), in that each rests on a history that has branded African Americans as utter outsiders, unworthy of full, equitable, and just access because they are non-technological, unable to learn Standard English, in essence, non-citizens. Because of the persistence of these constructions, access to technologies and the discursive practices that determine power relations in our society, the Digital Divide, and the larger history of African Americans, is essentially a rhetorical problem. And because African American exclusions from the educational system that determines access to employment (and therefore the technologies that undergird the American economy) are so rooted in the specter of the Ebonics speaker and writer, the rhetorical problems that dominate understandings of race in our discipline are technological problems.

The history of these constructions extends back into Enlightenment notions of race and forward into the present. Neither rhetoric and composition nor the technology sector have found ways to discuss their continued exclusions of Black people, both continuing to define the rhetor and the technology user as White by default. This longstanding theoretical blind spot is especially pronounced in a field like English Studies, where race, technology, and questions of access are all addressed, sometimes even energetically, but where the connections between them are almost never explored. This chapter is an exploration of that odd silence as it has been carried out in the major journals and some other writings in composition and technical communication over the last 10 years, as well as in the development of African American rhetoric since it entered the university as an area of study. I examine this problem of representation by looking at the flashpoint where the Digital Divide and the Oakland controversy collided, and I argue that while there are staggering silences on the connections between these issues, silences that were made even more profound by the missed opportunities that national conversations about the Digital Divide provided, the twin sites of composition and technical communication are especially productive sites from which to address problems of technological access. African American rhetorical study can help bridge those sites, end those silences, and bring new theoretical tools to bear on the conversations about the relationships between technologies, literacies, and discourses that English Studies more broadly has plunged itself into.

RACE AND TECHNOLOGY ACCESS DURING THE GREAT EBONICS DEBATE

It might seem entirely irrelevant to some, but I'm fascinated with the fact that during the period of what is often called the greatest advance in technology in the last 100 years—and what many still like to suggest is the most important communication technology to emerge since the printing press—the nation and English departments throughout were mired helplessly in yet another Ebonics debate we'd already been through decades ago.

I'm still fascinated with the simultaneity of these events, nearly 10 years later, for many reasons: I wonder why the Oakland School Board's claim on federal resources for educating Black children caused such a furor two decades after the Ann Arbor trial, 30 years after the CCCC "Students'

739

Right" document, and almost 50 years after the Brown decision; why, almost to a person, Black "leaders" and advocates sounded just like White conservatives (and still do, given the despair and rage in Bill Cosby's recent rants about Black children not wanting to learn Standard English and their parents not caring enough to ensure that they do); and why assumptions about the supposed inferiority of African American varieties of English that have been dismantled consistently by Black and White linguists alike over the last several decades still hold such force, especially with language teachers and professionals. The most important reason I'm still fascinated with the connection between these events is because of what wasn't happening during that debate: serious, thoughtful discussion about race and the problem of access to computers, the Internet, and information technologies.

Although African American engineers and science professionals, and even some mainstream policymakers, have long understood the importance of equal access to these technologies, writing and communication teachers of all races have been mostly silent on the subject. If, however, the most important characteristic of computers and the Internet is their role as communication technologies—if, as Jay David Bolter and many others have argued, these tools have begun a revolution in communication more significant than any other in the 500 years since Gutenberg's printing press—the results for African Americans, who have consistently and often systematically been denied access to these technologies, will be catastrophic.

This said, English departments (specifically rhetoric and composition and technical communication programs) have been staggeringly silent about the problematic relationship between race and technology access that became crystallized in the term "Digital Divide." This silence is a peculiar one, given the facts that composition as a field owes its existence in many ways to the project of making equal access to higher education real, and has worked diligently, if not always effectively, at important points in its history to address the role of race in those struggles, especially as that struggle has been made manifest in scholars' and practitioners' longstanding debates about Ebonics. The silence is even more stark if one really considers technology access to be a rhetorical problem, because if it is, technical communication and rhetoric and composition more broadly are the intellectual spaces within English Studies, and maybe even the university as a whole, that have the potential to do the most to address it. I use the rest of this chapter to examine that silence over the last decade as it echoes throughout journals and books published in composition and technical communication, as well as in African American rhetoric, to show just how little has been said, offer an assessment of those attempts scholars have made, and identify places where we can speak across the divides inside our own discipline that maintain the severity of the Digital Divide that remains so pervasive. The point of this rehearsal of the work that has been done is not to castigate individual scholars or the allegiances that exist within our discipline. Rather, it is to show the opportunity we all missed but can still grasp, in adding depth to the shallow treatment technology access received when it finally did attract the attention of policymakers in the Clinton and Bush administrations; to show just how promising extended dialogue across our own disciplinary lines could be in making real progress in improving technology access for African Americans and all Americans, in making inquiry into technological issues a real part of the intellectual work of rhetoric and composition; and possibly—if genuine dialogue across those disciplinary silences ever begins—reshape the futures of rhetoric/composition, technical communication, and African American rhetorics.

During the last ten years since the Digital Divide and broader technology access issues emerged in the national conversation, not a single article in the three major technical communication journals, *Technical Communication, Technical Communication Quarterly,* and the *Journal of Technical Writing and Communication,* addresses the Divide or any technology access issue, although all of these journals frequently take up questions of the promises and perils of computers and the Internet. No article in *Technical Communication* addresses any issue related to race and technology—in fact, no article in the journal takes up the question of race at all—in spite of a significant presence of African-American and Latino/a engineers (because engineering and science students are the major audience for many technical communication programs and courses) in the workplace. When "cultural" issues are raised, the subject is broached in the service of global capitalism, focused on international students, employees, or clients. International in these cases often means those from Arab, Asian, or European countries. *Technical Communication Quarterly* manages a grudging nod in the direction of Black people with Heather Brodie Graves and Robert Graves' contribution on the need for cultural sensitivity in technical editing, "Masters, Slaves, and Infant Mortality." The *Journal of Technical Writing and Communication* continues the silence on access, but includes two articles on African Americans and communication: a study of Ebonics that purports to examine student attitudes toward the language variety by "translating" a Jesse Jackson speech into Ebonics. This article says nothing about the specific features of African American varieties of English their translation used, however, or why their version focused on the features it did. The authors of the second article present it as "a descriptive study of the Black communication style by African Americans within an organization." This 1997 article, "A Descriptive Study of the Use of the Black Communication

Style by African Americans within an Organization," by Vonnie Corsini and Christine Fagliasso, ends with the familiar call for an awareness of cultural differences.

Composition hasn't done much better. The discipline's major journal, *College Composition and Communication,* has published very few articles on technology access and writing instruction: Cynthia Selfe's 1997 chair's address to the annual conference, "Technology and Literacy: A Story about the Perils of Not Paying Attention," and "The Politics of the Interface: Power and Its Exercise in Electronic Contact Zones," a 1994 article by Cindy and Richard Selfe demonstrating that computer and other technology interfaces can uphold the very exclusions many thought they would eradicate. The good news is that their work has helped to push composition in a more progressive direction than technical communication, one that acknowledges the political and social forces at work in the development and use of any technology—and acknowledges racism as one of those forces. Unfortunately, that's about it.

How is it that the convergence of race and technology in the problem of differentiated access is ignored, evaded, or elided in a discipline that has long struggled with issues of race and access, and one that sees its work as teaching students and professionals to become critical users of technologies? How is it that the ways African Americans and other people of color use digital technologies are entirely neglected even in the few conversations that do take place? This discursive divide occurs in part because both areas have simply been slow to make the connection. Charles Moran calls scholars to this theoretical nexus in his essay "Access: The 'A' Word in Technology Studies," arguing that composition has to carefully, thoughtfully engage problems of race, gender, and wealth differences and what their resulting problems of access portend for teaching, research, and writing. This article appears in 1999, almost 2 decades after the emergence of the journal, *Computers and Composition,* and almost 5 years since the Department of Commerce's landmark Digital Divide reports, with Moran acknowledging that his work represents first steps for this kind of inquiry: "most of us simply do not deal with the relationship between wealth and access. I think of some of the major texts in our field . . . none of which raises the question of access in a substantial way" (p. 210). Moran continues, with a reflection on the institutional side of this neglect, "I would add to this list too, university alumni magazines and public relations documents that boast of their institution's technology without mentioning the fact that it is available only to a privileged few" (p. 210), and adds that scholarly anthologies in composition are complicit as well. Moran's critique of university public relations organs might seem trivial compared with the curricular and infrastructure work that does not happen, or universities' policy failures and their inability to reach out to communities and school districts that are desperate for their leadership and support, but his point is that institutional chest thumping to reach out to those who have been privileged while those failures remain is hypocritical, especially when many such guides and newsletters and magazines often find women and people of color to pose for token pictures to tout their commitments to "diversity."

James Porter does important work to clear out space for issues of access in the discipline in his book *Rhetorical Ethics and Internetworked Writing* that starts to take into account social and pedagogical issues, even if the book seems, at first glance, not to directly address how race and ethnicity might affect the definition of access he offers. Porter notes that access "may well be the number one ethical issue for internetworked writing" (p. 102), citing a need for scholars to move beyond the focus of most conversations about technology and access on the "haves" and find ways to genuinely include the "have nots." Cynthia Selfe also calls attention to the importance of access, and explores the importance of race in that conversation in her book-length treatment, *Technology and Literacy in the Twenty-First Century: The Importance of Paying Attention:*

> But if the project to expand technological literacy has been justified as a means of achieving positive social change and new opportunity, to date it has failed to yield the significant positive social progress or productive changes that many people have come to hope for. Indeed, the American school system as a whole, and in the culture that this system reflects, computers continue to be distributed differentially along the related axes of race and socioeconomic status, and this distribution contributes to ongoing patterns of racism and to the continuation of poverty. It is a fact, for instance, that schools primarily serving students of color and poor students continue to have access to fewer computers than do schools primarily serving affluent students or White students. And it is a fact that schools primarily serving students of color and poor students continue to have less access to the Internet, to multimedia equipment, to CD ROM equipment, to local-area networks, and to videodisk technology than do schools primarily serving more affluent and White students. (p. 6)

Selfe tells a truth we're loath to admit when we have to think about systemic exclusions: they *still* exist, and they're *still* tied to race. Selfe's project as she outlines it in this part of her book is significant not just because it begins to explore race and technology access. She also uses the book to examine the social and political implications that are involved in, but often hidden in, conversations about technologies by looking at the Clinton administration's

"Technology Literacy Challenge." What appeared to be a positive agenda by President Clinton, with its stated goals of "wiring every school in America," posed the danger, according to Selfe, of merely providing technology producers with the perfect market for their products: passive consumers dependent on those technologies, but unable to effect any meaningful change in the lives of those who have been marginalized.

Meaningful access to any technology involves political power and literacies: "in a formulation that literacy educators will feel most keenly, the project to expand technological literacy implicates literacy and illiteracy—in their officially defined forms—in the continued reproduction of poverty and racism. And it implicates teachers as well" (p. 7). That implication has become much more explicit in the years since Clinton's departure from office, because even those policies, with all their attendant dangers that Selfe points out, have been completely reversed. So not only did the Department of Commerce remove all of the "Falling through the Net" reports from its Web sites immediately upon the arrival of the new administration and reduce the Divide to a case of class envy (as I'll detail later), but the Department of Education stole and cruelly used the Children Defense Fund's "No Child Left Behind" slogan to sell policies that cut funding for schools that needed it most and identified thousands of schools serving poorer students and students of color as irrevocably "failing." But the subtitle of Selfe's book shows us just how much work remains for all of us in composition, computers and writing, and technical communication: "The Importance of Paying Attention." Both Selfe and Moran note that the field has not paid attention as of the turn of the century, imploring the field to finally catch up and take things digital and access to them seriously.

While race, and especially the connections between race and technology access, serve as what Catherine Prendergrast would call the "absent presence in composition," conveniently contained within easy labels that prevent action on an anti-racist agenda (like tolerance, multiculturalism, and diversity, to take those in common parlance these days) (p. 36), the silence is not all-engulfing, as small numbers have begun to pay attention. There is important work being done with, and in response to, Selfe and Porter, even if that work still amounts to rumors and rumblings where strength and passion are needed.

Moran and Selfe, in an article published in *English Journal*, geared primarily to K–12 English and Language Arts teachers, "Teaching English Across the Technology/Wealth Gap," continue their call for teachers to place the Digital Divide at the center of research, teaching, and activism for writing specialists, and acknowledge the critical role race places in access to digital technologies. They also press on to identify important problems for those who take up the challenge. Selfe and Moran argue in the article that embracing technology uncritically can not only contribute to worsening the wealth gap and power differences between people of color and Whites, but also make teachers the best allies a global capitalist society could hope for:

> Advocates for technology often have an agenda that has nothing to do with our students' learning. If one is a politician or academic administrator in this decade, it is almost mandatory to call for technology in our schools, not because of any proven link between technology and learning—there really is no consistent evidence of such a link, especially in language arts and literacy studies—but because technology is seen as a quick and cheap fix for the perceived problems in our educational system. Anything associated with technology has a special glow these days. We note this in regard to the extraordinary bubble in technology stocks that is helping to drive the stock market. . . . In language arts and English classrooms, we need to recognize that we can no longer simply educate students to become technology users—and consumers on autopilot—without helping them learn how to understand technology issues from socially and politically informed perspectives . . . [otherwise] we may, without realizing it, be contributing to the education of citizens who are habituated to technology but who have little critical awareness about, or understanding of, the complex relationships among humans and machines and the cultural contexts within which the two interact. (pp. 48, 52)

An investigation into the conditions of technology access and its relationship to education by the *Baltimore Sun* shows just how serious the problem is. Even when there is decent material access to computers, software, and internet connections, educators, students, and parents are still often hoodwinked, bamboozled, run amok, led astray, as Malcolm would put it. The fact that the grounds of officially sanctioned literacies are always changing, while students and schools in Black, Brown, and poor school districts are continually labeled as needing remediation as they navigate the seismic shifts in those grounds, in the high-stakes version of my electronic games parable in the prologue, leads to a collective desperation by parents, educators, and students themselves. Caught between the rock of political invective labeling them as failures and the hard place of magic pill solutions sold to them by technology companies, families and schools often make huge investments in technologies and still never escape the cycle.

The *Baltimore Sun* series "Poor Schools, Rich Targets" shows the devastation the convergence of forces Selfe calls us to attend: the Prince George's County, Maryland, school district, in response to the pressure of being designated a school in need of improvement under reporting standards included in the No Child Left Behind Act, held trials for an Algebra software package it might purchase. According to the article, this package, named "Plato," costs on average about $60,000 per school. Huge investments like these are not abnormal. Camden, New Jersey's school district, with 19,000 students, paid almost $11 million in site licenses to Compass Learning and a suite of educational video games from Lightspan. These programs are typically of the skill/drill/kill variety, and often only offer remediation. Compositionists can only wonder what happened to all of the intellectual struggle they waged over the last fifty years to move writing instruction beyond such a narrow focus, especially in schools and districts that have habitually reserved such instruction for poor students and students of color while children in Camden are stuck in labs working on grammar baseball games:

> One girl who was working on a punctuation drill was told to insert a comma in the appropriate place in the following sentence: "Robots will teach science in high school trade schools and kindergarten." The girl stared at the screen, which was illustrated with a picture of a robot, and then moved the mouse to place the comma between "school" and "trade." The screen lit up: She was right! Then it gave her another sentence to test the same skill: "The robots of 2019 will be able to see feel and have a better understanding of the world." Staring at the screen, the girl moved to add the comma to the correct spot again. (MacGillis, *Baltimore Sun*, 2004)

This is what Camden paid $11 million for, and the site licenses are only good for 3 years, after which time, of course, new versions will have been released costing even more. Administrators often feel that the expense is the only choice they have—a more justifiable use of funds than spending it on recruiting and paying signing bonuses to stronger teachers they often feel will not remain with the districts for any significant length of time.

Given these problems, Selfe and Moran articulate an agenda based on activism for equitable access across racial and economic lines, but for an access that is critically informed. This is the most important point for me, when we consider the ways Black students are continually dumbed down by skills-only curricula, whether in the name of "raising standards" which usually results in remediation and those same exclusions based on Black students not being prepared enough for whatever the new dominant understanding of literacy is in place at a given time. Technology issues must be as much the work of writing and communication teachers and scholars as writing and communication are, and we must find ways to build students' and teachers' digital literacies in the current environment of poorly funded schools and racialized education politics.

Toward the end of making the Digital Divide a central issue in curricula and pushing professional organizations to take public stands on technology policy issues, Selfe and Moran call on teachers to find ways to use any and all tools available in the project to expand access now. They suggest that given the expense of cutting-edge technologies and the fact that there is always some new cutting-edge software package or hardware tool being sold as the next great answer, the job of promoting digital literacies and writing abilities might often be best accomplished with lower-end tools (p. 52). Regardless of whether one pursues this strategy or not, the most important change in perspective for writing teachers is that they must make sure clearly articulated pedagogical goals drive all technology decisions so that purchases, training, and planning related to technology implementation remains relevant to the learning, social, political, and economic needs of those we hope to serve.

So a theoretical framework for initial action is in place in the field, if the voices offering it remain isolated ones. Jeffrey Grabill makes gestures toward filling an important void in computers and writing scholarship with his 1998 *Computers and Composition* article, "Utopic Visions, the Technopoor, and Public Access: Writing Technologies in a Community Literacy Program." This void is the need to engage some of the nascent policy/political/theoretical commitments in studies of how issues of access are played out in specific learning and teaching sites. Grabill's work is significant not only because it is concerned with access, but also because he argues that it is time for computers and writing specialists to take their work outside the composition classroom, to consider how "our understanding of how people write with computers will change because work in nonschool settings will alter inquiries and the knowledge produced" (p. 311). Grabill's understanding of access is built on Porter's definition (infrastructure, literacies, acceptance) and Porter's argument that access—who gets the resources, where they get access, what the environments will look like, and who will make decisions on all of these questions—is the key ethical issue that must drive all of our conversations about technologies and their relationship to written communication (p. 301). The Adult Basic Education program that Grabill studies serves primarily White women, but it clears valuable theoretical ground for composition and computers and writing faculty interested in community technology issues, and could link up in important ways with work on African American literacies outside the classroom as Elaine Richardson (2003) and Beverly Moss (2003) take it up in their respective books, *African American Literacies* and *A Community Text Arises*.

A few other pieces, mainly Susan Romano's (1993) "The Egalitarianism Narrative: Whose Story? Whose Yardstick?" and Kristine Blair's "Literacy, Dialogue, and Difference," advocate the use of computer-mediated communication technologies in the writing classroom, and attempt to disrupt simplistic assumptions that computers will magically create equal, democratic environments—moves that speak back in important ways to technology theorists like William Mitchell, whose *City of Bits* offers an architecture and urban planning model for the development of cyberspace with no consideration of the relationship between the racist histories of those professions and those who employ them and live and flee from the spaces they have designed and planned. Romano's and Blair's studies foreground valuable questions of Hispanic identity online, but are not overtly concerned with access.

One piece that does directly examine the connections between race and technology access as they affect African Americans is Elaine Richardson's "African American Women Instructors: In a Net." In her case study of three Black female writing instructors, Richardson works to show the political forces involved in their decisions to become more technologically literate, and to employ digital tools in their teaching. Richardson acknowledges the importance of technology access from the outset, but notes that women of color, because of the positions they often occupy as untenured or contingent faculty, do not have the luxury of adopting critical positions on technological issues or "opting out" based on their critiques that other members of the academy, and particularly English departments, tend to have. This constraint, when combined with obstacles that hinder these three instructors from gaining meaningful access (increased teaching loads, graduate study, publishing requirements, family and other responsibilities), can make access, even when it is achieved, highly problematic. Richardson's study helps shed light on the complexities of access, showing that it certainly includes all of the elements of Porter's initial definition, but also extends beyond materials, skills, and community acceptance. The burden of access is not only the responsibility of those seeking it, but is a systemic burden as well.

Although many African American scholars and teachers are concerned about how new technologies might open up possibilities for resistance to racism and participation in American society on their own terms, the pressing need for these writers has often been to address the perception that African Americans just don't "do" science and technology. In "Computers on Campus: The Black-White Technology Gap," a *Journal of Blacks in Higher Education* article published in 1993, Terese Kreuzer quotes Richard Goldsby, an African American teaching Biology at Amherst College at the time: "They aren't likely to be hackers or computer nerds. Computers are not part of Black culture" (p. 93). A jarring comment, even if made 12 years ago, but one repeated many times in different ways in the scholarship on African Americans and science and technology. In another *JBHE* article, "Will Blacks in Higher Education Be Detoured off the Information

Superhighway," Raymond Slater recognizes the difficult selling job in store for those who care about access:

> Black kids are not going to have the access to computers or online informa-
> tion services. We need to turn educators on to this problem. We are not
> sure how it's going to be done, but if it doesn't happen the technology gap
> between the races is going to widen. It's already wide, but it's going to get
> worse. (1999, p. 98)

Lois Powell (1990) begins an article in the *Journal of Negro Education* with the heading "The Black Scientist, a Rare Species." Some claim that there is no real problem with access to science and technology fields, but as recently as 2000, the National Action Council for Minorities in Engineer-ing (NACME), a consortium of fellowship programs, faculty, foundation members, and National Science Foundation representatives working to solve this problem, published *Access Denied: Race, Ethnicity, and the Scien-tific Enterprise*, examining the systemic factors limiting the participation of people of color in the sciences, engineering, and mathematics.

Knowledge of the systemic barriers that Black people have faced in the sciences and technology doesn't help much here. Goldsby's comment still echoes: "computers are not part of Black culture." However laced with the same kinds of self-defeating stereotypes about Black people that undergirded the Ebonics debate, Goldsby's concern points to the perception that the sci-ences and technology have never been central to African American strug-gles against racism and for equal participation in American society. Almost 25 years ago, Herman and Barbara Young (1977), in "Science and Black Studies," urged Black Studies programs to make study of the sciences a more central part of their curricula: "most Black studies programs have been con-centrated in the fields of humanities, history, and the social sciences. They have neglected one area of special significance in achieving their objectives, which is the contributions of Black men to the fields of science" (p. 381). They argue that African Americans have a long history of achievement in the sciences, and that more focus on those achievements would help meet all of Black Studies' major disciplinary goals, including "provid[ing] alterna-tive ideologies for social change" (p. 380).

A quarter of a century later, few African American Studies programs have answered the call. Abdul Alkalimat, African American Studies director at the University of Toledo, is one of those who has, however, by explicitly linking technology to inquiry in African American Studies. In addition to creating eBlack, the online presence of Toledo's Africana Studies program, and in Alkalimat's words, the "virtualization of the Black experience," he uses the current moment's conversations about technology to keep reflections about what African Americans can and should do with technolog(ies) grounded in past struggle.

As he argues in an article published on cy.Rev (www.cyRev.com), "Technological Revolution and Prospects for African American Liberation in the 21st Century" (2001a), the relationship between technological change and the economic, social, cultural, and political struggle of African American people is the missing link in the "history of African American history." Technological advances that improved the mechanization of the cotton and auto industries bring this relationship into relief for Alkalimat: "[c]otton and auto, as the leading sectors of the US economy—19th century agricultural and 20th century industrial production—helped to structure more than 150 years of African American labor. It has been this economic structure of how agriculture and industry have utilized African American labor that has set the stage for all of African American history." The perfection of the cotton gin provides the quintessential example of this relationship between technology innovation and African American struggle in Alkalimat's analysis, as it is the creation of the cotton gin that made cotton King and slavery even more profitable than it had been by the 1800s.

What makes this relationship important for the study of African American rhetoric is the fact that not only did these technological changes structure the conditions in which African American people lived, but they influenced the environments in which they organized to resist those conditions. Just as the cotton gin mechanized the cleaning of cotton and created incredible demands for slave labor, Alkalimat notes, the mechanical cotton picker made sharecroppers obsolete, and was thus another important factor in what is commonly known as the "second great migration" of African Americans to the North (those migrating from the South after 1940) and led to conditions becoming favorable for the Civil Rights movement to emerge. He shows a similar pattern of high demand for African American labor being created, and then obliterated by technological change in the automobile industry, and points to the staggering unemployment statistics for African American men in the 1980s and 1990s in northern cities as evidence.

One need not agree with the breadth of Alkalimat's claim that "the most profound historical changes are linked to changes in technology" to take from his analysis an understanding that there are important connections between technological history in the United States and African American struggle. An important part of this connection is the relationship between communication technologies and rhetorical production. It is this relationship that I want to point to, as a way of extending Alkalimat's argument and making it relevant for African American rhetorical study.

Advances in communication technologies do not simply amount to minor changes in the medium. All technologies come packaged with a set of politics: if those technologies are not inherently political, the conditions in which they are created and in which they circulate into a society are political and influence their uses in that society (Winner, 1986), and those politics can profoundly change the spaces in which messages are created, received, and used. The potential of the changes in these spaces can be staggering when considered in light of the communicative possibilities they can either open up or shut down. One's ability to understand and operate within those changed spaces determines whether her or his linguistic dexterity is even relevant—as any faculty member who has been flamed (translation: dissed) on an e-mail listserv will be happy to explain.

Radio provides a better example: what it represents as a communication space and its potential as a medium for both entertainment and activism are not only dependent on the transmission of sound through amplified or frequency modulations or the broadcasting power that determines a radio station's reach. The politics of the Federal Communications Commission's decision to expand the numbers of stations individual companies can own in a particular market has turned a local medium into a national one and had effects ranging as wide a spectrum as wholesale changes in programming formats and the near elimination of the Disc Jockey as a relevant figure in the life of a community, beyond making paid advertising appearances for those businesses who can afford them. These effects produce both rhetorical problems and opportunities, as the Tom Joyner Morning Show demonstrates. Sophisticated rhetors and technology users must be aware not only of the politics that come packaged with technologies, but also of the responses they both enable and limit.

African Americans' ability to make the move from "ideology to information," and to take African American experience into new technological spaces, to digitize African American history, struggle, and celebration, is important not only to survival for Alkalimat. It is also a move that offers possibilities that did not exist before: "[w]hile ideological struggle has persisted the information revolution has undercut the material conditions for ideological ignorance. The information revolution has increased our capacity to produce, store, distribute, and consume all texts—written, oral, and visual" (Alkalimat, 2001b). eBlack, as a model of what is possible when African American Studies, traditions, and struggle are digitized, is currently comprised of 5 programs or parts:

- ♦ Professional connection and discourse: eBlack edits and manages H Afro-Am, a listserv designed to connect faculty and graduate students in professional conversations in and about African American Studies. In the 3 years of its existence, it has attracted 1,000 members, and allows conversations that might never happen between scholars and students across wide geographic distances.

♦ Curriculum development through distance education: eBlack is developing a Pan-African studies program via the Internet, using distance education.

♦ Community Service: eBlack works to create websites for local churches in the Toledo area, and teach church members to create and maintain websites.

♦ Continuing Struggle, the African American Radical Congress: eBlack used the web to convene African American activists to "reinvigorate African American radicalism." Alkalimat notes that although many of the activists involved were skeptical about whether cyberspace could be an important site of struggle, organizing in this way not only allowed participants to document their work in spaces they could control, but that also prevented "factionalism and a hardening of ideological lines."

♦ Research Web site on Malcolm X: Alkalimat sees the web as an opportunity to combat the exclusions that are inherent in those institutions that have developed major archives of the papers of African Americans, like the Schomburg Center and many university libraries. The potential cyberspace provides for digitizing African American history can not only open up access to important figures like Malcolm X, but help to recover lost voices as well, including African American women, who Alkalimat notes, have been all but ignored by major archives.

What is important about Alkalimat's work with eBlack is not just that the histories and work of African American leaders, activists, and organization can be put online, but that cyberspace can transform that work because it is a space that, for all of the barriers to access that exist now, can allow more direct control of one's message than other media. As the Internet is currently constructed, a person who has a connection can view any site she wishes (that is not password protected, of course). Those with messages to share can target them directly to people they want to reach, unhindered by a television network's assumptions about African American people, or the limited range of AM radio or Cable television public access channels, for example. And it is far easier to own the means of production than it is a television station, radio station, newspaper, or magazine. So the possibilities for individual activists and rhetors are impressive, but they are just as bright for students and scholars of African American rhetoric.

Imagine, for example, if as a result of eBlack's work with churches in the Toledo area, or of any effort in any town, that twenty years from now, 2 or 5 or 10 churches in that area have Web sites that have archived all of their pastors' sermons (either in print, audio, video, or some combination of forms) over that 20 year period, with examples of church bulletins, directories, activities, and newsletters as well. One of the most studied forms in African American rhetoric, the sermon becomes much easier to study thoroughly, because many of the five challenges to offering rhetorical criticism of sermons that Lyndrey Niles identifies can be greatly minimized:

- Most African American sermons were not and are not prepared in manuscript form.
- Most African American sermons through the centuries were not and are not tape-recorded during delivery.
- Some preachers are reluctant to release copies for criticism.
- Because most African American sermons are in dialogue form, manuscripts may not satisfactorily represent what actually took place in the church.
- Sermons in the African American tradition were not written to be read. Much of the real impact, therefore, is lost unless the critic knows how the words would have sounded, and can picture the delivery in his or her mind as he or she reads the manuscript.

As I noted earlier and Niles' problems show, African American rhetoric has always been multimedia, has always been about body and voice and image, even when they only set the stage for language. Even within a definition of African American rhetoric as being about the word, careful considerations of how current technologies can extend its study will provide a much richer body of work for rhetorical criticism and analysis.

This connection is not just about the politics of a particular writing, speaking, or designing space, nor is it just about the benefits that can exist for students and scholars of rhetoric. Technologies shape all five of the classical canons of Rhetoric, and greatly affect the rhetorical situation, however one might define the concept. Whether the technology involved is a soapbox, a megaphone, printing press, typewriter, telegraph, microphone, television, radio, or Web site, the tools available affect the means available because of how they configure relationships between rhetors and their potential audiences.

Black intellectuals have always been concerned with improving African American participation in the sciences and technology, and to the degree that the humanities and social sciences are privileged, that emerges from the specific nature of the intellectual underpinnings of Western racism. Henry Louis Gates, Jr. and Nellie McKay (1997) look directly at this privileging of the humanities, offering some understanding of why literary production has had such a central role in African American struggle against racism for more than 200 years: "African American slaves, remarkably, sought to write themselves out of slavery by mastering the Anglo-American belletristic tradition" in ways "that both talked `Black' and, through its unrelenting indictment of the institution of slavery, talked back" (pp. xxvii, xxviii). Literature—and literacies—hold this important place for several reasons, Gates and McKay contend. Black inferiority was a dominant theme in Enlightenment philosophy and science, as they show through extensive quotations from Immanuel Kant, David Hume, and Thomas Jefferson. Many people already know the story of Enlightenment justifications of racism, but the assumptions that Black people had "no ingenious manufacturers amongst them, no arts, no sciences" (p. xxx) was accompanied by a draconian body of public laws, making two forms of literacy punishable by law: the mastery of letters and the mastery of the drum" (p. xxix). Gates' introduction to *Race, Writing, and Difference* quotes a passage from Hume that makes these assumptions explicit:

> I am apt to suspect the negroes, and in general all the other species of men (for there are four or five different kinds) to be naturally inferior to the Whites. There never was a civilized nation of any other complexion than White, nor even any individual eminent either in action or speculation. No ingenious manufacturers amongst them, no arts, no sciences . . . . Such a uniform and constant difference could not happen, in so many countries and ages, if nature had not made an original distinction betwixt these breeds of men. Not to mention our colonies, there are negroe slaves dispersed all over Europe, of which none ever discovered any symptoms of ingenuity . . . . In Jamaica indeed they talk of one negroe as a man of parts and learning [Francis Williams, the Cambridge-educated poet who wrote verse in Latin]; but 'tis likely he is admired for very slender accomplishments, like a parrot, who speaks a few words plainly. (1986, p. 10)

Given this legal and intellectual history, it becomes easy to read African Americans' commitment to literacy as a technological commitment and all of the means they have employed toward achieving literacy as technological mastery.

This connection between Black language and literary traditions and political struggle becomes even more explicit in Larry Neal's manifesto defining the Black Arts Movement. It is the Black Arts Movement that "is the aesthetic and spiritual sister of the Black Power concept" (p. 122). While the Black Arts Movement articulated goals for literary production that were very different from those of Phillis Wheatley or writers in the Harlem Renaissance, the larger purpose remained the same—to undermine Western racism based in pseudo science by using literature to talk back by talking Black, as

> writing, many philosophers argued in the Enlightenment, stood alone among the fine arts as the most salient repository of "genius," the visible sign of reason itself. In this subordinate role, however, writing, although secondary to reason, was nevertheless the medium of reason's expression. We know reason by its representations (Gates and McKay, 1997, p. xxx).

The fact that this literacy and literary activity was always engaged in a relationship with scientific and technological discourse cannot be overstated. V. P. Franklin and Bettye Collier-Thomas show this relationship in their reflection on Carter G. Woodson's (1969) work in founding the *Journal of Negro History.* They note that Woodson made it clear that this was to be "a quarterly scientific magazine" committed to publishing scholarly research and documents on the history and cultures of Africa and the peoples of African descent around the world. Woodson understood that publishing these articles and collecting these materials was the only way "that the Negro could escape the awful fate of becoming a negligible factor in the thought of the world." The activities pursued by the members of the Association for the Study of Negro Life and History (ASNLH) would "enable scientifically trained men and women to produce treatises based on the whole truth." V. P. Franklin used the life writings of African American literary artists and political leaders to demonstrate that "race vindication" was a major activity for Black intellectuals from the 19th century. African American preachers, professors, publishers, and other highly educated professionals put their intellect and training in service to the race to deconstruct the discursive structures erected in science, medicine, the law, and historical discourse to uphold the mental and cultural inferiority of African peoples (p. 1).

In other words, the chasm between literary and cultural production on one hand and scientific and technological pursuits on the other is not a part of the Black intellectual tradition, at least for one of the greatest intellectuals of that tradition, Dr. Carter G. Woodson. But just as dangerous as assumptions that Black people are not technologically inclined, is the assumption that race is, and should be, irrelevant online.

The case I make throughout this book for an African American digital rhetoric probably seems contrary to some. It might even seem odd to attempt to argue that the entire African American rhetorical tradition can and should be read with a focus on the importance of technologies and African Americans' access to them. After all, the story of African American rhetoric to this point has been primarily understood as being about mastery of "the word," written and especially oral, throughout our history. Examples of this focus on speeches and essays abound, from foundational texts defining the scope of Black rhetorical study to articles analyzing specific rhetorical performances, regardless of the disciplinary homes (English Studies or Speech and Communication) of their authors. The titles of some of the major works in the field demonstrate this focus: Alice Moore Dunbar Nelson's (2000) *Masterpieces of Negro Eloquence*, Arthur Smith's (now Molefi Asante) *Voice of Black Revolution*, Philip Foner's (1975) anthology *Voice of Black America*, Foner and Branham's (1998) follow-up edition *Lift Every Voice*, Geneva Smitherman's (1986) trailblazing theoretical work *Talkin and Testifyin: The Language of Black America* and Gerald Early's (1992) collection on the African American essay *Speech and Power: The Afro American Essays and Its Cultural Contents from Polemics to Pulpit* are but a few examples. This is not to say that individual scholars in African American rhetoric have not discussed technology issues, but rather that traditions of Black mastery of spoken and written language and their use of it in collective struggle remains the frame that organizes the field.

Using such a frame works, obviously, for many reasons—not only because of its congruence with the events of that history from Frederick Douglass' ability to trick White playmates into teaching him to read when it was illegal for him to learn, to Ida B. Wells' crusading uses of argument in "A Red Record" to condemn state-supported terror and lynchings of Black people, to Barack Obama's celebrated 2004 speech at the Democratic National Convention (a speech far more worthy of note for its poetic delivery than for any new Black progressive agenda, as it offered none)—but because it allows a relatively coherent view of that history. Because African American history has been so much about anti-racist struggle, because that struggle has been so consistently about making the argument for equal and meaningful participation in the nation, and because our greatest victories often emerge from the linguistic and argumentative brilliance of activists, poets, teachers, grassroots organizers, preachers, politicians, essayists, and musicians, it makes sense to organize that study around the spoken and written word.

It also allows for a somewhat stable narrative. One can link the power and commitment of Stevie Wonder's music to the development of Malcolm X's political voice and his ability to simultaneously take the best elements of the African American homiletic tradition and turn that tradition on its head. Carol Mosely Braun's fly signifyin on Jesse Helms in formal legislative debate (Crenshaw, 1997) can be connected to innumerable unnamed people across historical eras and social, political, and economic circumstances based on their use of argument to pursue a collective agenda on behalf of African American people, whether that agenda be one of resistance and revolution (Smith) or access to some notion of "the good life" (Golden & Rieke). Just as important, the word as the organizing trope of African American rhetorical study provides scholars and students with a ground on which to offer that narrative unshaken by the rapid changes that occur in communication media. It doesn't matter whether we talk about poetry that had to be authenticated by 18 of Boston's "most prominent citizens" because it could not be conceived that it was written by an African American person, as in the case of Phillis Wheatley, or the multimedia connectivity of Tom Joyner's attempts to get African American folks to "party with a purpose," the same analytical tools allow for conversations about all African American rhetorical production.

This promise of analytical stability across rhetorical situations and across communication media is a tempting one. So tempting, in fact, that to claim that technologies can be just as important a concept as the word is to take on a challenge, and might even seem to border on the heretical. Technology issues seem to be entirely unconnected to the making of arguments, and everyone knows how troubling African American relationships with technologies have been. But that's just the argument I want to make. Alongside our understanding of the centrality of language to African American rhetorical production, a parallel examination of how African American rhetors have used and manipulated communication technologies can foster both access and transformation.

As strenuously as I follow Abdul Alkalimat's lead, arguing that African American rhetoric has always been about technology issues, and that study in African American rhetoric should be opened up to examine more carefully those writing, designing, and performative acts that are acknowledged (but not appreciated as rhetorical in nature), I also argue that these other acts and texts need to be included *with*, not instead of, oratory. I believe, with Philip Foner and Branham, editors of *Lift Every Voice*, that even now, with all of our technologies, oratory is still the genre of public engagement—the genre where the work any group of people commit to begins. As important as the Internet, books, magazines, journals, songs, dances, nightclubs, church services, and many other spaces are, it's still the sermon, the conference, the convention, the political speech, where the people make their commitments known. This is even more the case in African American communities, where Black people place an even greater emphasis on one's speaking ability, as those who are seen as African American public intellectuals themselves would have to attest. Had Cornel West never written any of the 20 books he has written, or written 20 more, his influence in African American communities would still depend to a large extent on his ability to "make it plain, reb," and make whatever knowledge he has translate at the podium. That said, work in African American rhetoric has to involve examining the technology issues involved in oratory at least as much as opening up Black rhetorical traditions to visual, electronic, and design issues.

Beth Kolko shows what is possible when scholars across this discursive divide do pay attention to each other, however. She argues that the history of racialized exclusions and their attendant assumptions of utter Black difference and irrelevance are programmed right into the interface of online environments like MOOs and MUDs—writing spaces similar to chats that accounted for much of the initial popularity of "cyberspace." Her essay, "Erasing @race: Going White in the (Inter)face," questions how race as a category has been elided in such media through various design choices, and it further investigates how the construction of "raceless" interfaces affects the communicative possibilities of virtual worlds (p. 214). This elision is a hallmark not only of the MOO and MUD environments with which Kolko is concerned—"the history of online communities demonstrates a dropping-out of marked race within cyberspace" (p. 214).

Kolko builds on the work of Richard and Cynthia Selfe (1994) with her examination of the interface as a raced yet e-raced space. This problem is important, in her words, because

> what this line of inquiry seems to represent is a growing awareness that technology interfaces carry the power to prescribe representative norms and patterns, constructing a self-replicating and exclusionary category of "ideal" user, one that, in some very particular instances of cyberspace, is a definitively White user. (p. 218)

This is a very different conclusion about racelessness in online spaces than that reached by many theorists caught up in the initial technological rapture, who frequently assumed that cyberspace as raceless space would mean that race, gender, and economic class would no longer matter and would usher in new, equal, and thoroughly democratic worlds—both online and off.

Elaine Richardson and Samantha Blackmon are among very few African Americans in Rhetoric and Composition who address these issues. Their work, along with that of individuals like Kolko, Richard and Cynthia Selfe, James Porter, Jeff Grabill, and Johndan Johnson-Eilola, is important for several reasons. It takes technology access seriously as an intellectual and activist project for Rhetoric and Composition and Technical Communication instruction; it acknowledges directly the connections that exist between gender, class, and racism rather than attempting to reduce the Digital Divide to an outbreak of class envy, as has current FCC Chair (and son of U.S. Secretary of State, Colin Powell) Michael Powell; and it offers glimpses into an agenda for addressing the Digital Divide that goes beyond the mere existence of hardware and software to the quality of that hardware and software and Internet connections, technological literacies, and critical understandings of technology that are needed to gain meaningful access to any technology. Unfortunately, the fact that I can name the individuals who have attended to these concerns and review the work done to address them in the space of a decade has kept the Digital Divide firmly in place for Blackfolk and in the academy. In fact, we are guilty of exacerbating its persistence when, for a brief moment from 1995 to 2001, there existed some amount of political will to do something about it, even if the Clinton administration's efforts to address the Digital Divide seemed based on a definition that amounts to the same access African American children have to public education or Black Floridians to the franchise: a vaguely articulated right to be in the same space *if* one navigates all the other barriers that prevent that presence. An examination of Clinton's policy initiatives on technology access and some of the shortsighted (sometimes well-intentioned, sometimes not) debates about whether a Divide even exists and how important it might be will begin to show one of the many ways technology access is a rhetorical problem and the need for our critical focus on it.

While one reason for the persistence of the Digital Divide is the reduction of African Americans to the level of people who have neither language, rhetoric, nor technology, another reason is the level of contest that exists around the term, especially when it is connected to race. Thus, the Digital Divide involves both contest and silence: debate over whether there is a Divide at all, waged by politicians, foundations, and business interests now; debate over whether race is a factor in whatever problems in technology access might exist; and concern that the use of a term like *Digital Divide* represents African Americans unfairly and does more to further the erasure of Black people by continuing to cast them as the utter outsider. These debates all carry assumptions about what constitutes access to computers, the Internet, or any digital technology that, even when guided by the best of intentions, threaten disaster if not addressed. This danger exists because those assumptions will guide legal, corporate, and educational policies that can trap Black people into roles as passive consumers of technologies rather than producers and partners, and worse, lead to continued electronic invisibility and economic, educational, and political injustice.

While African Americans have often at least implicitly understood technological issues as central to Black advancement, public recognition of race as a factor affecting access to digital technologies is a recent phenomenon, and largely due to the work of Larry Irving and many others on "Falling through the Net," the series of U.S. Department of Commerce reports that introduced the term *Digital Divide* to the lexicon in 1995. "Falling through the Net," in all four of its versions, acknowledged race as a factor just as important as education, income level, and geography in determining who is and is not able to obtain technology access. The first of the four reports, subtitled "A Survey of the Haves and Have Nots in Rural and Urban America," published in July 1995, examined access to the NII or National Information Infrastructure, by measuring the rates of telephone, computer, and modem "penetration" (i.e., the numbers of people who had telephones, computers, and computer modems in their homes). The major findings of the report were that education, age, and residence either in rural areas or central cities were important factors determining access to the Internet, but that race was just as crucial. Rural and city African Americans had the lowest rates of computer ownership, but the few who were online were significant in how they used the tools. Those African Americans were more likely than many other groups to use the Net to look for jobs, to take classes online, and access government reports. The policy recommendations of "Falling through the Net" focused on connectivity: to develop more specific profiles of those who had telephones, computers and modems, and to provide assistance, primarily through an interim tactic of supporting community access providers like libraries and public schools. The fundamental assumption of the first report was the concept of universal access—that every household that wanted to connect to the National Information Infrastructure should, and ultimately, would be able to do so.

Three years later, the Department of Commerce and NTIA released a revision of the report, "Falling through the Net II: New Data on the Digital Divide." The focus of this revision was primarily in providing a clearer look at the patterns that emerged from the first study, using 48,000 door-to-door surveys completed by the Census Bureau in 1997. In other words, the goals were to be able to better aggregate and disaggregate the data about who was connected and who was not, and to gauge the degree to which the patterns presented in the first report held or changed. The NTIA found that even with significant growth in computer ownership and Internet connectivity, the gap between numbers of African Americans who had access and the broader population *increased* between 1994 and 1997 (a difference of 21.2%

in computer ownership rates in 1997 as opposed to a 16.4% difference in 1994). Further, as ubiquitous as telephone usage seemed to be for many during the 1980s and 1990s, there were still large gaps in telephone penetration across racial lines. Data collected for this report revealed that Whites were more than twice as likely to own a computer as Black people (40% vs. 19%) and almost three times more likely to be connected to the Net from home (21.2% vs. 7.7%). The policy recommendations in the second report remained the same; namely that more needed to be done to get people connected to the Internet, and that public access points would be an important means for providing that access. Again, the focus was on computer, telephone, and modem ownership as constituting access, and the report failed to engage the implications of Black, Latino/a and Native American people being disproportionately forced to share access in cramped public spaces while others worked in the comfort of home, with the leisure of learning skills and nuances of how the technologies worked. This assumption that mere physical proximity to a technology or ownership of the products is all there is to access is a troubling one that still dominates many studies on technology access.

The next of the reports, released in 1999 and subtitled "Defining the Digital Divide," concludes by acknowledging the likely persistence of the Divide, and begins to offer data on computer and Internet usage in schools and libraries. The connections that some of us now take for granted between technologies, literacies, and education thanks to Cindy Selfe's book emerge here, as this version of the report warns the nation that it will be impossible to eliminate race as a problem in American society without addressing technology and information access. The report noted that economic survival would soon be tied to information access, and recommended policies and strategies aimed at filling the gaps that still existed in computer ownership and Internet connectivity, including lower prices, lease arrangements, and free computers, but took what amounts to a laissez-faire, free-markets-solve-most-problems pass given to those in the technology sector, arguing that increasing price competition between companies trying to gain market share would do much to minimize many of these gaps. This version of the report made references to issues of the relevance of technologies in peoples' lives and content (such as software and documentation), but these references were brief and did more to skip over these problems than address them. The report called for outreach that would "let them know why they should care—how new technologies can open new opportunities for them and their children." To use an old missionary metaphor, salvation was only possible if the heathen saw the error in their ways and converted while government and business could continue to operate as usual.

The final version of the report, published in October 2000, sounds like a reelection campaign speech, proclaiming mission accomplished. It reported major progress among all groups, based on the same notion of connectivity (computer, telephone, and modem ownership) as the only important elements determining one's overall access, although it also considered computer use in public places as the third version did. The final report accounted more fully for how those with access used the Net, with information broken down into categories recognizing work, research, shopping, personal, and entertainment uses. Again, access is still defined as mere connectivity: not as literacies and community acceptance, as Porter argued for; not as critical awareness or change in the lives of individuals or communities, as African American rhetors have always argued for.

Other studies were undertaken to pursue some of the questions sparked by the "Falling through the Net" series. Two of the more widely cited of these reports were Donna Hoffman and Thomas Novak's "Bridging the Digital Divide: The Impact of Race on Computer Access and Internet Use" and the Pew Internet and American Life Project's "African Americans and the Internet," both also released in 2000. While the Hoffman and Novak report acknowledges significant differences in access to the Internet by race, that access is also still defined by the access = connectivity model: questions focused on whether and how one used the Internet (in the last week, in the last 6 months),and whether that use took place at home or work, or at other locations. What is important about the Hoffman and Novak study is that, as the later NTIA reports do, it controls for education and income and shows that the Digital Divide is significantly connected to race. The conclusions from their work were that more African Americans were online than previously thought, and that African Americans need multiple points of access because home computer ownership rates are so different across racial lines.

The Pew report looked more at how African Americans used the Net than on questions of connectivity. Tracking a sample of 12,571 adults—2,087 of them African American—for 6 months, the study concluded that African Americans are more likely to have looked for job information, religious information, music, video, and audio clips, and more likely to have looked for places to live online than the general population. The Pew study, however, interpreted all of its results solely by comparison with the uses to which White Americans put computers and the Internet, repeating the erasure Beth Kolko argued is a fundamental characteristic of technology decision makers, making Whites' uses of these tools a technological default, rather than viewing the results through a lens focused on African Americans' needs, experiences, and histories with the technologies. The major result of the Pew study was that the Divide, in their view, was narrowing, and this conclusion has generated much conversation about whether or not people need to continue to view the Digital Divide as an "African American" problem.

Regardless of the problems in definition of access operative in the initial "Falling through the Net" studies, however, Larry Irving, its principal author, was very clear about trying to call the nation's attention to it as a problem of the legacy of racial exclusions in this country (no matter how muted the language might seem), calling it not only a major economic issue for Black people, but a Civil Rights issue as well. The reports on the Divide were used to support policies throughout President Clinton's administration that had universal access for all Americans as their stated goal. The potential these policies offered educators, even with all of their flaws in defining access as mere connectivity, was short-lived, however, because the concept of a Digital Divide that was deeply rooted in the stubbornness of racial exclusions came under attack from several quarters. Some politicians and public figures attacked the notion that such a phenomenon as a systematic Divide in technology access even existed, while others argued that its determining factor was class, and therefore, irrelevant, since, after all, class differences will always exist. Finally, even some Blackfolk committed to digital progress for African Americans grew weary of what seemed to be the same old, same old: more definitions of Black people as behind, and intentional silence about the technological innovation that has always been there, obscured by the story of a Divide.

In widely reported comments from his first press conference as the new chair of the Federal Communications Commission, Michael Powell maliciously reduced the Digital Divide to a toy fetish, announcing for all, from the beginning, that the Bush administration wasn't havin it, saying, "I think there's a Mercedes Divide. I'd like to have one, but I can't afford one." He continued, "I don't mean to be completely flip about this . . . but it shouldn't be used to justify the notion of essentially the socialization of the deployment of the infrastructure," a contention completely contradicting the "Falling through the Net" reports' tepid strategies of wiring schools and libraries and its mild, responsibility-evading conclusions that the marketplace would eliminate any problems in access that remained. Of course, under Powell's leadership, the FCC would later mandate that televisions makers equip sets with high-definition technology rather than allowing free market forces that Republicans and Democrats alike often tout to allow consumers to decide whether they wanted such changes, a kind of "socialism" for Sony and Magnavox and other television makers, but such ironies did not matter when the FCC made the later decision. Intervention on behalf of technology producers to force innovation, force the obsolescence of millions of perfectly good television sets in the next decade was more important than intervention to help African Americans, American Indians, Latino/Hispanic peoples, and poor Whites in urban and rural areas achieve anything resembling "basic" access to the National Information Infrastructure. After referring to the "so-called Digital Divide," Powell added in the same press conference, "I think the term sometimes is dangerous in that it suggests that the minute there's a new and innovative technology in the market, there's a divide unless it is equitably distributed among every part of the society." And in what became the ultimate sign of disrespect, given the FCC's later policy decisions, he added, "You know what? It's going to be the wealthier people who have the largess to go out and buy $4,000 high-definition TVs first. Does that mean there's an HDTV divide? No." Now, of course, no political leader, corporate executive, researcher, or teacher has ever argued that Mercedes Benz cars or HDTVs will be necessary for people to gain employment or participate in democracy, as politicians and legions of academics, community leaders and others have about computer-related communication technologies. However, this point was clearly irrelevant to Powell, who was content to dismiss all of these concerns and the nation's racist past and present as just the latest case of economic playa-hatin.

Not everyone challenging the concept of the Digital Divide or the racial element of the Divide are as polemical, political, or maliciously short-sighted as Chairman Powell was in his attempt to deflate the entire concept of the Information Superhighway (as the NII was called) to a high-end import car and a form of television the public still hasn't decided it wants to adopt yet, despite the FCC's activism on its behalf. Some African Americans in the technology industry have made moves to re-center conversations about the Divide away from race and toward class as the major factor. Barry Cooper and David Ellington are among those technology professionals. A Salon.com (Rawlinson, 1999) article quotes Cooper, the CEO of BlackVoices.com, as saying that "people have legitimate concerns, but if [there] is a divide, it is economic." Ellington, founder and CEO of NetNoir.com, concurs: "I don't feel there is much of a divide anymore. The Internet is becoming relevant in our lives as a result of e-mail and chat sites, and African Americans are going online in droves." In these cases, the same understanding of access as mere connectivity and usage, the same assumptions that drove the major early studies of the Divide, were being used to dismantle the concept.

A collection of Black academics known as AfroGeeks also have serious problems with the persistence of the Divide as a trope, calling attention to the serious gaps in access that Black people continue to face. The group presents its motto as "from technophobia to technophilia" and is far more concerned with the ways discussions about the Digital Divide have "erased" the contributions of technology innovators. The group's home on the web, http://www.afrogeeks.com, hosted on the University of California at Santa Barbara server, announces boldly:

> In recent years, African Americans, especially, have been portrayed as poster children for the digital divide discourse. Though rarely represented as full participants in the information technology revolution, Black people are among the earliest adopters and comprise some of the most ardent and innovative users of IT. It is too often widespread ignorance of African Diasporic people's long history of technology adoption that limits fair and fiscally sound IT investments, policies and opportunities for Black communities locally and globally. Such racially aligned politics of investment create a self-fulfilling prophesy or circular logic wherein the lack of equitable access to technology in Black communities produces a corresponding lack of technology literacy and competencies.
>
> Thus, necessary high-tech investments are not made in such under-served communities because many consider it fiscally irresponsible, which, in turn, perpetuates this vicious cycle. Despite such formidable odds, Black people continue to break out of this cycle of socially constructed technological determinism. It is this way that African Disaporic people's many successes within new media and information technologies are too often overshadowed by the significant inequalities in technology access.

In other words, "you ignorant niggas is keeping me from getting mine, with all that noise about the access you ain't got." This seems like a harsh assessment of an argument that clearly speaks some truth, but the assessment is just for several reasons. The Digital Divide is not the equivalent of national "why Johnny can't read" campaigns that brand Black people illiterate in the service of continued American racism, but rather, was deployed by Black technology innovators in the Clinton administration (namely Irving and William Kennard, the FCC chair who preceded Michael Powell), community organizations, academics like Abdul Alkalimat, and activists in order to call attention to systemic inequalities—the same inequalities that the Afro-Geeks acknowledge in their rant. Moreover, their embrace of technologies is unequivocal, lumping those with any critical consciousness about the ills they could cause or exacerbate as Luddites and technophobes who are part of the problem by announcing that the transition must be from phobia to philia. More worrisome than either of these issues, however, is the fact that they see their erasure as the *result of* the struggle for equitable access rather than part of the larger problem of the Divide, reflecting the same crabs-in-the-barrel mentality, the same scorn for Black people who have been systematically denied the educations and digital literacies they enjoy that were the worst excesses of turn of the 20th-century uplift ideology.

Although there are no absolute unities and many middle and upper-middle class Blackfolk will not have the same commitments as those who still struggle against systematic exclusion, middle class invisibility and the utter exclusion of working and poor Black people from the technologies, politics, and economies of mainstream American life still emerge from the same history of racism rather than problems we might have with each other. Rhetors like Marcus Garvey preached this incessantly, appealing for unity as we fight the issues that affect us rather than attacking each other over superficial differences. Unfortunately, these appeals for unity came out as bitter attacks on those Garvey saw as Black liberals imitating Whites, but the spirit of his argument beyond the rancor in his need to write himself into the discourse remain. In "An Exposé of the Caste System Among Negroes," Garvey (1923) writes, "unfortunately, there is a disposition on the part of a certain element of our people in America, the West Indies, and Africa, to hold themselves up as the 'better class' or 'privileged' group" (p. 268). Garvey saw this developing caste as rooted in class, which at that point in time often meant skin complexion. Rather than skin politics, the issue here is digital politics, where the AfroGeeks charge that it is Black technology activists and their allies, rather than larger systems of racism, that have denied them due recognition for their achievements.

I want to temper the charge just a bit at this point, because I do not believe the group intends to target Black activists as they do. It seems they misread the Digital Divide and the work toward equitable access it sparked as yet another in the long line of efforts I detailed earlier in the chapter, identifying Black students as Ebonics students needing remediation, and Black technology users and potential users as digital illiterates needing remediation. But to confuse Larry Irving and William Kennard for Rod Paige and Michael Powell is every bit as disingenuous—especially because the AfroGeeks are academics—as some of Garvey's well-known charges that W. E. B. DuBois worked against Black interests. By identifying "Digital Divide discourse" as the problem denying them their respect, the AfroGeeks risk the problem of seeming to try to write themselves into the larger digital discourse at the expense of young people and adults who can't eat or get decent jobs in an education system that has never yet answered the essential challenge of the *Brown vs. Board* case and verdict from 50 years ago.

DEFINING ACCESS—AND A NEW VISION FOR AFRICAN AMERICAN RHETORIC

Fortunately, not all African American technology professionals view the Divide as Powell, Ellington, and Cooper do, nor do they all argue that we must stop talking about the Divide. And, in spite of the numerous debates that mark this territory, there is hope that those concerned with equal technology access for Black people can make that argument and demand that long traditions of Black technology innovation can be recognized. More sophisticated approaches to these debates can point us to higher ground, to more nuanced understandings of exactly what constitutes access, and a vision of what African American rhetoric might look like in this digital age. Let me begin this section with another version of the call I've issued:

> What is usually missing in our celebrations of African American history is a focus on how technological change contributes to the structural basis of African American history. . . . The entire sweep of African American history needs to be examined on the basis that technological change creates the main structural context for the grand historical narrative of enslavement and the subsequent freedom struggle. (Alkalimat, 2001a)

And one possible response, given the context of the Digital Divide we find ourselves in:

> The folks promoting this nonsense—I call them "tricknologists"—are the high tech equivalent of the three card monty dealers you see on street corners. You know the game: they get you to follow one card, and all the while the real action is somewhere else. Well, that's exactly what the New Age tricknologists are doing with the Digital Divide debate. The trick is simple: the first step is to narrow the definition of the Divide, by saying that computer ownership and Internet usage are how we measure minority participation in the new, high-tech economy. In fact, all these statistics prove is that minorities are closing the gap in becoming consumers of technology, not in being producers or equal partners. . . . Saying that the Digital Divide is closing because minorities have greater access to computers is like saying minorities have a stake in the automobile industry because they drive cars, or that they are Bill Gates because they own Microsoft Office 2000. (Taborn, 2001, p. 8)

You won't find too many engineers in African American rhetoric anthologies, but Tyrone Taborn, as publisher of *U.S. Black Engineer: Information Technology*, is obviously grounded in the tradition. His magazine is billed as "the African American community's technology magazine," continuing in the history of periodicals committed to advocacy for African American people. As is clear in the previous quote, taken from the February 2001 "Community Awareness" issue, Taborn understands technology as one of the major battlegrounds for African American struggle in this era of post–Civil Rights retrenchment. More than just an intriguing rhetorical performance

767

in its own right, with its comparison of technology decision makers with everyday slicksters, Taborn's article shines a spotlight on the connections that have always existed between communication technologies, questions of access, and the African American rhetorical tradition. These connections can allow a new look at that tradition and how scholars might engage it in a new century, toward the combined ends of full participation in American society and the preservation and celebration of African American identity.

The history of African American rhetoric is, in many ways, one of individuals and collectives of writers, speakers, visual artists, and designers mastering, manipulating, and working around available technologies, even when access to them had been denied the masses of Black people. Through concentrating on this connection between communication technologies and rhetorical production, by looking forward to African American futures to look back through traditions of struggle, African American rhetorical scholars can not only offer far richer analyses of those speeches and writings considered to be within the tradition, but can also open those traditions up beyond just the word and show it has always been multimedia, using *all* the available means in resisting racism and pursuing justice and equal access on behalf of African American people.

Taborn helps us to understand that the AfroGeeks are partially right, but that Larry Irving and William Kennard are as well, as is Abdul Alkalimat in his work over the last decade. We must complicate access, and use our understanding of it to look forward, imagining Black futures, then back through African American rhetorical traditions and legacies of struggle, understanding histories to be created in the service of the futures we want.

What exactly, then, constitutes technology access, and how can it, whatever it is, sustain new visions of African American rhetoric, and rhetoric and composition, more broadly? Before moving to that central point, I want to reiterate that this current context of technology access—of the Digital Divide and its connection to America's larger racial ravine—is an especially productive one in which to offer a new look forward to a new conception of African American rhetoric. This is because the Divide itself is a rhetorical problem at least as much as it is a technical or material one, and because technology issues have always functioned as a metaphor for imagining collective Black futures. As a field that has always had to address issues of access either directly or indirectly, African American rhetoric becomes central to both broader rhetorical and digital theory. And study at this important intersection of issues can continue the work of transforming the nation by eliminating that Divide, by addressing the real effects of technological exclusions, just as those rhetors we study always have. There are: the continual removal of Black labor from the workforce, inadequate health care, a legal system that operates on the presumption of Black guilt, a continual White flight into and out of urban centers, voting systems that conveniently do not work in major elections, and computer and information industries that operate comfortably under the assumption that Black people are non-technological while they spend billions of dollars to recruit, train, and develop temporary talent from overseas—when companies don't just send the jobs themselves overseas. All of this is at least possible—if technological issues make it onto our maps of the field, and if we end the silences that have prevented composition, computers and writing, and other elements of English Studies from taking Black intellectual traditions seriously.

A technological reading of African American rhetorical history offers at least three benefits beyond the obvious one of a more thorough appreciation of Black contributions to, challenges to, and even transformations of, the nation:

♦ A richer set of tools for analyzing those speeches and texts that have always been considered part of the tradition;

♦ A wider set of texts, images, sounds, and issues to address, and

♦ A chance to develop the arguments and policies that will end the Digital Divide and challenge the nation to accept responsibility for the exclusions programmed into its technologies rather than continue to assume that technologies are neutral and that there is nothing systematic about the differences in American life that remain tied significantly to race.

Attempting a useful definition of meaningful access is a difficult task, but all of the partial answers that have emerged throughout this chapter show that it is possible: Porter's call for literacies and community acceptance in addition to the black boxes that dominate the Digital Divide reports; equal distribution of the black boxes themselves; the Selfes' and Charles Moran's call for critical awareness of the roles technologies play so that we avoid becoming passive consumers; even the AfroGeeks' insistence that we eliminate the centuries-old constructions of Black people as utterly illiterate and therefore unworthy of participation in the society and the technologies that govern it. All of these can contribute to an understanding of access that goes beyond the material and move us closer to the transformative ideals that unify Black rhetorical traditions.

One of the difficulties in defining access lies in the stubbornness of common understandings of technologies as merely the instruments people use to extend their power and comfort. Technologies also include the systems of knowledge we must acquire to use any particular tool and the networks of information, economic, and power relations that enable that tool's use. An example might help clarify this point. Law enforcement is a technological system for protecting the persons and property in a society, as well as the desired patterns of relations between them. Regardless of the availability of individual tools to police in their work (guns, nightsticks, pepper spray, hands, feet, squad car computers, dashboard video cameras) and the wide range of force those tools represent, young Black and Latino men (and increasingly, women) are killed, injured, arrested, charged, and convicted at higher rates than other groups of people in this country.

Observers from different academic disciplines would offer very different explanations for why these patterns endure, why as a nation we were not horrified enough by the cases of Amadou Diallo and Abner Louima to demand fundamental change in policing, although we were (I use *we* sarcastically here) angry enough to press for changes to the judicial system in the aftermath of the Simpson verdict. I have no desire to take up those disagreements here. My point is simply this: any decision about how police use the tools and force they have is largely a result of what they have been taught about when and how to use them and the mandates police forces are given that construct crime and criminals in particular ways. Because of these literacies and processes and encoded forms of knowledge, one will almost always hear a defense of officers being within the law or policy of using the "maximum allowable force" in answering a brutality complaint rather than being expected to use the minimum force necessary to subdue a suspect.

The Clinton administration efforts I've cited throughout this chapter to "wire every school in America" in the mid to late 1990s offer another example. Many technologists and educators argued passionately that computers and the Internet connections in schools would be the great equalizer in American education. Ensuring that all students had networked computers in their schools would not only avail them of information that had never been distributed equally in their land-based schools, but would make their teachers better and motivate students to learn. For all of the passion that went into creating programs and writing grants to install hardware, software, and connections in schools, no mechanisms were in place to ask how the new computers would be used. Few resources existed for school systems to teach either students or faculty how to even use these tools, much less integrate them into anti-racist democratic teaching agendas. Few considered the difference that anywhere from a 5 to a 25 year head start would make for teachers, students, and parents who had already been indoctrinated into digital culture, and more importantly, had been made comfortable enough with computers and the Net to take advantage and ownership of the technologies. And when people did begin to consider these issues in the last few years, almost no African Americans were present where the decisions were being made, either in technology companies, policy think tanks, university faculties, consulting companies, vendors, IST or technical writing faculties, or the policies, documentation, content, interfaces and environments, or training efforts any of them created.

The problem with the Digital Divide as a concept for addressing systematic differences in access to digital technologies is that it came to signify mere material access to computers and the Internet, and failed to hold anyone responsible for creating even the narrow material conditions it prescribed. Beyond the tools themselves, meaningful access requires users, individually and collectively, to be able to use, critique, resist, design, and change technologies in ways that are relevant to their lives and needs, rather than those of the corporations that hope to sell them. Let me sketch what I believe is a more effective matrix for understanding technology access and then conclude with some reflections on what this changed understanding might mean for writing instruction—the work of composition, computers and writing, technical communication, and African American rhetoric.

Of course, one has to own or be near places that will allow him or her to use computers, software, Internet connections, and other communication technologies when needed. The "Falling through the Net" reports, along with many other studies, brought this need to our attention. I call this *material access*, and meaningful access begins with equality in the material conditions that drive technology use or nonuse. To really play out the implications of this statement would mean that there can be no real digital equality without fundamental transformations of the economic relations in our nation. But even that "revolution" alone would not be enough.

For material access to have any effect on people's lives or on their participation in the society, they must also have the knowledge and skills necessary to use those tools effectively, or what I'll label as *functional access*. I use this term because, just like functional literacy, it is insufficient for economic or political power or for many kinds of participation in the nation's social or cultural structures. Porter's call for us to understand access as involving the skills and knowledge necessary to benefit from technologies is partially a call for this kind of access.

Porter also notes that people must actually embrace the technologies involved, that there must be a level of community awareness and acceptance in order for those technologies to mean anything. Beyond the tools themselves and the knowledge and skills necessary for their effective use, people must actually use them; they must have *experiential access*, or an access that makes the tools a relevant part of their lives. In addition to discerning relevance in the technologies, people must have some involvement in the spaces where technologies are created, designed, and planned and where policies and regulations are written. They must be present in the processes by which technologies come to mean what they mean for us. This notion of experiential access is a kind of fusion of Porter's understanding of access and Taborn's insistence that access also includes power in the creation and shaping of our technologies.

Richard and Cynthia Selfe's work, along with that of Charles Moran, show us that not even these layers of access, alone, are enough. Members of a particular community must also develop understandings of the benefits and problems of any technology well enough to be able to critique, resist, and avoid them when necessary as well as using them when necessary. School districts must know when the wonderful sales pitches of computer companies—and maybe even their donations—won't work for their budgets, curricula, and strategic plans. I term this ability *critical access*. Let me offer what might seem to be a simplistic non-technological example here. Just as we make decisions about what foods are healthy for us or not healthy for us, or which ones fit our bodies' needs at a particular time when at a supermarket or restaurant, any group of people must know how to be intelligent users and producers of technology if access is to mean more than mere ownership of or proximity to random bits of plastic and metal.

Supermarket savings cards provide a more relevant—and seemingly ubiquitous—technological example. These cards, offered by large supermarket chains, are used to track consumer purchases. These chains then use, sell, and trade this information with many other corporations in order to create demographic profiles of communities and make decisions on whether to expand or withhold products and services to them, just as credit card companies and other corporations do. Oscar Gandy describes the potential for racism in the ways corporations gather and use this information in his article "It's Discrimination, Stupid!" Given the obvious value and use of this information and the way supermarkets virtually force consumers to sign up for these cards with pricing strategies that make any product savings dependent on one's ownership of a savings card, and given the pricing disparities that often exist in grocery stores that major chains operate in inner cities, African Americans and many other groups of people face important decisions about whether or not they should own or use these cards, and if they do, under what terms. Just as Operation Breadbasket organized consumer education and boycotts in the 1970s to encourage Black consumers to withhold their business from companies that did not hire Black people, it is past time for African Americans to engage in targeted and mass protests and boycotts of supermarkets, science and technology departments in universities, and corporations in the technology sector that fail to recruit, hire,

772

or promote African Americans and members of other underrepresented groups while they spend billions of dollars on myriad programs (including the H1B visa program) to recruit technical talent from overseas.

The understanding of access I take here echoes the language of literacies that has become common even in non-academic circles, and is informed by Stuart Selber and Johndan Johnson-Eilola's (2001) framework of "thinking, doing, and teaching" that they argue can provide the multidimensional basis that instruction in technical communication needs to better prepare its students for the complexities involved in the technologies with which they will live and work (p. 4). It is also one that locates technology as a site and means for African Americans' continued efforts to "carve out free spaces in oppressive locations such as the classroom, the streets, the airwaves" (p. 16), as Elaine Richardson documents as the purpose of other Black literate practices. In other words, technology is both one of those sites of struggle and a possible means of liberation, something we can not only survive but transform in our own interests.

This taxonomy of access that I have begun to piece together—to quilt—from the patches of others' definitions and debates is best thought of rhetorically as taking place along the related axes of critique, use, and design. The larger project of making access meaningful for African Americans and other marginalized groups must combine participation, resistance, and the re-creation, the reimagining of technological systems, artifacts, processes, and the economic, power, and social relations that are embedded within them. Table 1 begins to establish the relations between the items on my list and the traditions of critique, use, and design that often govern explorations at the intersection of rhetoric and technology. The questions I include within it represent only the merest of beginnings, but include issues I address later in the book as well as concerns taken up by others like Tyrone Taborn, Cynthia Selfe, James Porter, and others.

It bears repeating at this point that computers, the Internet, and other technologies included in the Digital Divide are only a part of the larger racial ravine—the complex of technological divides that have always operated in American history, and have always been used to maintain exclusions connected to race. The ways racial exclusions are built into our technologies and into our society operate to continue and even ensure those exclusions while allowing individual members of that society to avoid responsibility for that exclusion. This helps to explain why the computer industry—the only major American industry to truly emerge in the aftermath of the Civil Rights and Black Power movements—remains the most segregated in the American workforce. At the same time individual companies continue to congratulate themselves for having inclusive advertising

Table 1

Critique	Use	Design
What are the patterns of computer and technology ownership by race? How are those patterns overdetermined by present patterns of racial exclusion?	How does the distribution of a technology affect how people use it (material access)?	How can the aesthetics and functions of technological artifacts and interfaces be made more culturally relevant?
Where do African Americans use computers, and how do the policies and assumptions about education at work in those spaces affect the uses that are available to them (material access, critical access, functional access, experiential access)?	What cultural retentions do African Americans and other people of color bring to the technologies they use? What relationships exist between these retentions and the acquisition of digital literacies (functional access)?	How can the cultural relevance of design questions like this affect the degree to which users embrace technologies and take ownership of them (experiential access)?
What economic and policy factors influence those patterns (material access)?	How can technical communication address race and culture more effectively in areas like the writing and design of documentation and policy (functional access, experiential access)?	What specific visual and design traditions can African Americans bring to technology design?
What tools do activists, scholars, teachers, users have available to interrupt and intervene in closed technological systems (critical access)?	How can educators avoid being swindled by technology companies eager to manipulate their desperation? How can they make better spending decisions with the limited resources they have? What pedagogical aims direct technology spending choices (functional access, critical access)?	How can African Americans counter the design processes and practices of technology firms that have rigorously excluded them (critical access)?
	How does one decide when to promote low-tech solutions to specific users' and learners' needs (critical access, material access)?	

campaigns or for funding individual "minority" science and engineering programs or offering occasional grants and "legacy" (translation, 2nd, 3rd generation or older) machines and stripped down education versions of software programs in order to foster brand loyalty.

Ownership of computers and other digital technologies, knowledge of their uses, participation in their processes, and even critique of their failings are not enough either, however. The way of looking at race and technologies, and of a meaningful technology access, goes further: to transformation. This kind of look at race and technology posits that our nation is a construct, or system, maybe even a technological system, and the Constitution, federal, state, and local laws, are part of the code that runs it. Social spaces like schools, cities, the workplace, and the court system are all interfaces where people use that system. African American struggle as reflected in its rhetorical traditions was always an attempt to both change the interfaces of that system and fundamentally change the codes that determine how the system works. My exploration of technology issues in African American rhetoric, then, is intended to document the ways Black people have hacked or jacked access to *and* transformed the technologies of American life to serve the needs of Black people and all its citizens. My goal here is not merely to encourage long-denied appreciation of these traditions of struggle, but to enable new (as well as ever present but unrecognized) strategies and tactics for pursuing African American freedom in this recalcitrant racial moment.

African American rhetoric has been about all of this and more; Black people have continually worked for a *transformative access* to all of the technologies that make up American life. By transformative access, I mean that African Americans have always argued for a genuine inclusion in technologies and the networks of power that help determine what they become, but never merely for the sake of inclusion. African American rhetorical practices call attention to the ways that the interfaces of American life, be they public facilities, education, employment, transportation, the legal system, or computer technologies, have always been bound up in contests over language, and have always been rhetorical—about the use of persuasion, in these cases, toward demonstrably tangible ends.

One might argue, that at best, the United States has adopted what we can call a "user-friendly" racism in the aftermath of Black freedom struggles of the middle and late 20th century: a language of tolerance and facile efforts to make individual interfaces more accessible (such as public facilities and education) in a system that remains fundamentally unchanged, and in constant contest over even those minimal efforts. Just as Civil Rights struggle was about far more than the right to sit next to White people at lunch counters or in schools, technological struggle in this century must be about much more than merely owning or being near computers or any other technological tool. The question is not about how many of our schools are wired, but rather, as Martin King put it in one of his final speeches, "Remaining Awake through a Great Revolution," the problem of how "through our technological and scientific genius, we have made of this world a neighborhood and yet, we have not had the ethical commitment to make of it a brotherhood . . . [we live with the] unhappy truth that racism is a way of life . . . spoken and unspoken, acknowledged and denied, subtle and not so subtle" (1991, p. 270). King's point in this speech, which I take up in more detail in the next chapter, is that the racism in our society infects our technologies just as it infects our media, our schools, our politics, our economy, and that the technologies themselves must be transformed. What does this transformative ideal look like? What set of attitudes, commitments, and goals might enable one to pursue this kind of transformation?

REFERENCES

AfroGeeks. Retrieved from http://research.ucsb.edu/cbs/projects/afrogeeks.html. Accessed October 15, 2004.

Alkalimat, A. (2001a). Technological revolution and prospects for Black liberation in the 21st century. *cy.rev.* World Wide Web. Accessed June 13, 2001 from http://www.cyrev.net.

Alkalimat, A. (2001b). eBlack: A 21st century challenge. *eBlackStudies.* World Wide Web. Accessed June 13, 2001 from http://eblackstudies.net/eblack.html.

Asante, M. K. (1969). *Rhetoric of Black revolution.* Boston: Allyn & Bacon.

Blair, K. (1998). Literacy, dialogue, and difference in the "electronic contact zone." *Computers and Composition, 15,* 317–329.

Bolter, J. D. (1991). *Writing space: The computer, hypertext, and the history of writing.* Hillsdale, NJ: Lawrence Erlbaum Associates.

Corsini, V., & Fogliasso, C. (1997). A descriptive study of the use of the Black communication style by African-Americans within an organization. *Journal of Technical Writing and Communication, 27*(1), 33–47.

Crenshaw, C. (1997). Resisting Whiteness' rhetorical silence. *Western Journal of Communication, 61*(3), 253–278.

Dunbar-Nelson, A. M. (2000). *Masterpieces of Negro eloquence.* Mineola, NY: Dover Publications.

Early, G. (Ed.). (1992). *Speech and power: The African-American essay and its cultural contents from polemics to pulpit: Vol. 1.* Hopewell, NJ: The Ecco Press.

Falling through the Net: A survey of the "have nots" in rural and urban America. NTIA July 1995 http://www.ntia.doc.gov/ntiahome/fallingthru.html.

Falling through the Net II: New data on the Digital Divide. NTIA July 1998 http://www.ntia.doc.gov/ntiahome/net2/.

Falling through the Net III: Defining the Digital Divide. NTIA July 1999 http://www.ntia.doc.gov/ntiahome/fttn99/contents.html.

Falling through the Net IV: Toward digital inclusion. NTIA July 2000 http://www.ntia.doc.gov/ntiahome/fttn00/contents00.html.

Foner, P. S. (1975). *Voice of Black America*. New York: Capricorn Books.

Foner, P. S., & Branham, R. J. (Eds.). (1998). *Lift every voice*. Tuscaloosa: University of Alabama Press.

Franklin, V. P., & Collier-Thomas, B. (1990). Biography, race vindication, and African American intellectuals: Introductory essay. *Journal of Negro History*, 81(1), 1–16.

Gandy, O. (1995). It's discrimination, stupid! In J. Brook & I. Boal (Eds.), *Resisting the virtual life: The culture and politics of information* (pp. 35–47). San Francisco: City Lights.

Garvey, M. (1923). An exposé of the caste system among Negroes. In M. Marable & L. Mullings (Eds.), *Let nobody turn us around: Voices of reform, resistance, and renewal*. Lanham, MD: Rowan and Littlefield.

Gates, H. L. (1986). *Race, writing, and difference*. Chicago: University of Chicago.

Gates, H., & McKay, N. (1997). *The Norton anthology of African American literature* (pp. xxxvii–xli). New York: W. W. Norton & Company.

Grabill, J. T. (1998). Utopic visions, the technopoor, and public access: Writing technologies in a community literacy program. *Computers and Composition*, 15, 297–315.

Hoffman, D., & Novak, T. (1998). *Bridging the Digital Divide: The impact of race on computer access and computer use*. Accessed December 5, 2001 from wwww2000.ogsm. vanderbilt.edu/papers/race/science.html.

King, M. L. (1991). Remaining awake through a great revolution. In M. Washington (Ed.), *Testament of hope: The essential writings and speeches of Martin Luther King, Jr.* (pp. 197–201). San Francisco: Harper.

Kolko, B. E. (2000). Erasing @race: Going White in the (inter)face. In B. E. Kolko, L. Makamura, & G. B. Rodman (Eds.), *Race in cyberspace* (pp. 213–232). New York: Routledge.

Kreuzer, T. (1993). Computers on campus: The Black-White technology gap. *Journal of Blacks in Higher Education*, 12(4), 88–95.

MacGillis, A. (2004, September 19–25). Poor schools, rich targets. Retrieved October 15, 2004 from the *Baltimore Sun* http://www.baltimoresun.com/nationworld/balte. software21sep21,1,1793980.story?ctrack=1&cstet=true.

Mitchell, W. J. (1995). *City of bits: Space, place, and the infobahn*. Cambridge, MA: Massachusetts Institute of Technology Press.

Moran, C. (1999). Access: The a-word in technology studies. In G. E. Hawisher & C. L. Selfe (Eds.), *Passions, pedagogies, and 21st century technologies* (pp. 205–220). Logan, UT: Utah State University Press and Urbana, IL: National Council of Teachers of English.

Moran, C., & Selfe, C. L. (1999). Teaching English across the technology/wealth gap. *English Journal*, 88(6), 48–55.

Moss, B. (2003). *A community text arises: A literate text and a literacy tradition in African American churches*. Creskill, NJ: Hampton Press.

Neal, L. (1999). The Black aesthetic. In H. A. Ervin (Ed.), *African American literary criticism* (pp. 122–128). New York: Twayne.

Porter, J. E. (1998). *Rhetorical ethics and internetworked writing*. Greenwich, CT: Albex.

Powell, L. (1990). Factors associated with the underrepresentation of African Americans in mathematics and science. *Journal of Negro Education*, 59(3), 292–298.

Prendergrast, C. (1998). Race: The present absence in composition studies. *College Composition and Communication*, 50(1), 36–53.

Rawlinson, R. (1999). Can Robert Johnson bring more Blacks online? Accessed December 1, 2001 from http://archive.salon.com/tech/feature/1999/10/06/bet_johnson/print.html.

Richardson, E. (1997). African American women instructors: In a net. *Computers and Composition*, 14(2), 279–287.

Richardson, E. (2003). *African American literacies.* London: Routledge.

Romano, S. (1993). The egalitarianism narrative: Whose story? Whose yardstick? *Computers and Composition, 10*(3), 7–28.

Selber, S., & Johnson-Eilola, J. (2001). Sketching a framework for graduate education in technical communication. *Technical Communication Quarterly, 10,* 403–437.

Selfe, C. L. (1999). *Technology and literacy in the twenty-first century: The importance of paying attention.* Carbondale, IL: Southern Illinois University Press.

Slater, R. (1994). Will Blacks in higher education be detoured off the information superhighway? *Journal of Blacks in Higher Education, 3,* 96–99.

Smitherman, G. (1986). *Talkin and testifyin: The language of Black America.* Detroit, MI: Wayne State University Press.

Taborn, T. (2001). The art of Tricknology. *U.S. Black engineer: Information technology.* Baltimore, MD: Career Communication Group.

Winner, L. (1986). *The whale and the reactor: A search for limits in an age of high technology.* Chicago: University of Chicago.

Woodson, C. G. (1969). *Negro orators and their orations.* New York: Russell & Russell.

Young, H. A., & Young, B. H. (1977). Science and Black studies. *Journal of Negro Education, 46*(4), 380–387.

A Multimodal Task-Based Framework for Composing

Jody Shipka

This essay presents a task-based multimodal framework for composing grounded in theories of multiple media and goal formation. By examining the way two students negotiated the complex communicative tasks presented them in class, the essay underscores the benefits associated with asking students to attend to the various motives, activities, tools, and environments that occasion, support, and complicate the production of academic as well as everyday texts.

> *Never before has the proliferation of writings outside the academy so counterpointed the compositions inside.*
> —Kathleen Yancey, in her 2004 CCCC Chair's Address

> *By privileging composing as the main site of instruction, the teaching of writing has taken up what Karl Marx calls a "onesided" view of production, and thereby has largely erased the cycle that links the production, distribution, exchange, and consumption of writing.*
> —John Trimbur

In her 2002 article, "From Analysis to Design: Visual Communication in the Teaching of Writing," Diana George argues that "the terms of debate typical in our discussions of visual literacy and the teaching of writing have limited the kinds of assignments we might imagine for composition" (14–15).

Reprinted from *College Composition and Communication* 57.2 (December 2005): 277–306. Used with permission.

Maintaining that "current discussions of visual communication and writing instruction have only tapped the surface of possibilities for the role of visual communication in the composition class" (12), George invites readers to consider how a new configuration of verbal/visual relationships that involves "more than image analysis, image-as-prompt, or image-as-dumbed-down-language" (32) might affect the work students engage in in the composition classroom. While George insists that students do not necessarily have a more sophisticated understanding and command of visual literacy than their instructors do, the highly sophisticated sampling of visual arguments featured at the start of her piece effectively underscores a point she goes on to make, namely, that "our students have a much richer imagination for what we might accomplish with the visual than our journals have yet to address" (12).

While discussions of visual communication provide one point of entry for rethinking the course's semiotic and productive potentials, they also raise the question of whether discussing visual/verbal literacies and the production of visual arguments is *all* we might do. At a time when many within composition studies have begun questioning the field's "single, exclusive and intensive focus on written language" (Kress 85), and its exclusion of the wide variety of sign systems and technologies students routinely engage, we might also begin asking how the purposeful uptake, transformation, incorporation, combination, juxtaposition, and *even three-dimensional layering* of words and visuals—as well as textures, sounds, scents, and even tastes—provide us with still other ways of imagining the work students might produce for the composition course. Given the field's strong tendency to "equate the activity of composing with writing itself," thereby missing "the complex delivery systems through which writing circulates" (Trimbur 190, see also Welch and Yancey), we need to do *more* than simply expand the media and communicative contexts in which students work. Increasing the range of semiotic resources with which students are allowed to work will not, *in and of itself*, lead to a greater awareness of the ways systems of delivery, reception, and circulation shape (and take shape from) the means and modes of production. Instead, I argue, composition courses present students with the opportunity to begin structuring the occasions for, as well as the reception and delivery of, the work they produce.[1]

The past seven years have afforded me opportunities to begin exploring this wider field of possibilities in the courses I teach. The following examples of student work are offered with the intent of initiating new conversations about the ways students' uptakes of a much wider, richer repertoire of semiotic resources, coupled with their efforts to purposefully structure the delivery and reception of that work, afford new ways of thinking, acting, and working within and beyond the space of the first-year composition classroom.

Figure 1. Lindsay's portfolio

So how's this for a complex multimodal rhetorical event? The day portfolios were due, Lindsay Freeberg[2] arranged to have a large blue bag containing eleven numbered gift boxes delivered to my office along with a card addressed "To whom it may concern" (Fig. 1).

The left side of the card functioned as the table of contents, listing which pieces of Lindsay's work would be found inside which boxes, while the right side contained a set of explicit instructions for receiving and recirculating that work. In keeping with the context of gift-giving that Lindsay had established, her semester's worth of work had been repurposed as a collection of valuable "tokens." Lindsay wrote:

Dear Receiver of Tokens,

Hi, my name is Lindsay Freeberg. You're probably wondering what the heck is going on and why you have a bag filled with numbered boxes. I'm sorry to say that this isn't a present just for you, it's for everyone, but I'll get back to that later [. . .]. All right, back to how these tokens are for everyone. You're probably wondering how everyone is going to see this. Well, here's what you have to do. Read everything, but don't just read it quickly, let is [*sic*] soak in for awhile and read it again. Sign the card somewhere, comment if you want to. If there isn't any more room, add pages to the card. Now, think of someone. Got them? Good. Secretly give the bag to them as I gave it to you. All I ask you to do is keep this going.

Or this? After completing a task that requires students to research the history of a word using the online version of the *Oxford English Dictionary,* Prakas Itarut turned in a manila envelope containing an unmarked floppy disk and a typed, text-only treatment of the word "scare." At the top of this text the following message appeared:

To get a true experience of what I am about to tell you, please read this paper at night and follow the directions exactly as it is told.

There is a disk included with this paper.

Please insert it into a PC that is equipped with sound. Now open this paper in Microsoft Word.

By now, you should be reading this message on a computer screen. If you haven't done what I mentioned above, please do so now.

Had I been brave enough to set aside the typed text and experience the remaining portions of the piece in the way Prakas recommended, the first thing I would have encountered in the on-screen version was a sampling of the various meanings and uses of the word "scare" that Prakas had excerpted from the *OED*. I would also have encountered the option to "click here," which, in turn, would have taken me to a file on the disk containing the *OED*'s full entry for "scare." Following this, I would have found another set of instructions prompting me to execute the "MC Program" file contained on the floppy. I would have then been prompted to return to the *OED* file, where I would have found five scary tales that I had been asked to read "slowly" and "if possible" out loud. Had I paced my out-loud reading of the tales as Prakas hoped I would, I would have been in the middle of the following passage when the MC Program triggered for the first time, replacing Prakas's text with the ghostly image of a woman's face while the computer issued a scream:

> Scare: To frighten, terrify.
> **C. 1256** Ancient Thai people—there is a belief that there is such a thing as a ghost/ spiritual power in the world we live in today. Ghost in this sense is usually misrepresented. It is not an ugly monster in a Halloween party or a cute Casper. It can be so simple as just another person. Imagine yourselves alone in a bathroom at night looking in the mirror and [you] see another person behind you [. . .]

Provided that I had been brave enough to set aside the hard-copy version of the tales and experience Prakas's reenvisioning of the *OED* in the way he intended (I was not), I would have found instructions for deactivating the MC Program in this final "frightening" tale:

> **C. 2001** MC Program—An English teacher executed the MC Program which was created to stimulate [*sic*] the true experience of the definition of this word. Luckily, she was smart enough to either restart the computer or hit ctrl-alt-delete to end the MC Program.

Suspecting that his instructor would *not* be brave enough to experience the piece in the way he intended, he knew that many of his classmates would be. To this end, Prakas asked permission to post a link for a Web-based version of the piece on the course Web site, where he dared classmates to experience his terrifying treatment of the *OED*.

And finally: After receiving a task entitled "A History of 'This' Space,"[3] Maggie Christiano considered conducting a small-scale, survey-based study of people living in public versus private university housing as a way of determining if there were connections between where students lived and how well they might be adjusting to their first semester in college. Engineered, in part, as a way of providing students with the opportunity of telling future readers something about who they were and what they did, valued, feared, enjoyed, etc., at a specific point in their college careers, the task presented Maggie with an opportunity to explore a question that concerned her at the time the task was assigned: How, or more specifically *how well*, might a group of first-semester college students be adjusting to living away from home? Admitting that she was so homesick for the first month of her college career that she had entertained the idea of dropping out, Maggie wanted to know if her classmates were adjusting more quickly to their post-high-school lives. Stressing that part of the appeal of the survey-based study had to do with allowing her to satisfy the task requirements without spending much time with other students with whom she suspected she had little in common, Maggie's plans for the history changed after a class session during which her classmates began talking about where they were from, where they had gone to high school, and so on. While the conversation had little to do with being homesick, the session significantly altered Maggie's feelings about her classmates as well as her involvement in the class. Deciding to jettison the dorm life study, she began a new, time-intensive history, one that still allowed her to focus on the idea of home while serving as a "tribute" to the class.

Maggie began collecting data for her history by asking her classmates to identify the place that they called home and to briefly describe the place itself and/or their feelings about that place. She then began the process of researching her classmates' hometowns online, both in hopes of learning something about those hometowns and of finding a Web site that she could later repurpose based on the information her classmates had provided her with. If, for instance, a classmate described his hometown as "famous for its big mall and many health clubs," Maggie would look for a Web site for a store in that mall or for a health club in town. After successfully pairing each member of the class with a hometown Web site, Maggie gave her classmates a word related to the Web site that she planned to use (e.g., the word might be "shoe" or "sock" if the Web site was for a shoe store, as it was in my case) and asked them to write a paragraph or two about that word, jotting down anything that came to mind. At this time, Maggie also requested that each of her classmates bring in an object representing the word so that she could take a picture of each person with his or her object. Maggie's contribution to the history consisted of a twenty-five-page collection of cleverly repurposed Web pages in which Maggie had strategically inserted her classmates' "with-object" photos and portions of their writings into the saved "original" version of the Web sites (see Fig. 2).

Accompanying the collection was a taped news special that Maggie scripted and then filmed over fall break. The video features Maggie in a series of "live, late-breaking Rhetoric 105 news reports," the majority of which had been filmed while Maggie stood in front of the specific hometown locations featured in the repurposed collection of Web pages.

Cognizant that the student work featured above may seem strange, especially when the norm for student work is equated with linear, argumentative, thesis-driven print texts that are passed forward in class and geared primarily, if not exclusively, to an audience of one (the instructor), I would suggest that the rhetorical, material, methodological, and technological choices students made while engineering these complex rhetorical events merit serious and sustained attention. Based on the kind, quality, and scope of work I have witnessed students producing for the past seven years, I am moved to argue, with George's claim in mind, that students have a much richer imagination for what might be accomplished in the course than our journals *have yet even begun to imagine,* let alone to address.[4]

In this essay, I look to theories of goal-oriented activity as a way of reconceptualizing production, delivery, and reception in the composition classroom. To illustrate some of the implications of the multimodal, task-based approach to composing I will be describing here, I also present two examples of students working to negotiate the complex communicative tasks that they undertook in my class. Taken together, these accounts suggest that, when called upon to set their own goals and to structure the production, delivery, and reception of the work they accomplish in the course, students can: (1) demonstrate an enhanced awareness of the affordances provided by the variety of media they employ in service of those goals; (2) successfully engineer ways of contextualizing, structuring, and realizing the production, representation, distribution, delivery, and reception of their work; and (3) become better equipped to negotiate the range of communicative contexts they find themselves encountering both in and outside of school.

Figure 2. One of Maggie's repurposed hometown Web pages

Home   About Us   Products   Hiking   Privacy/Security   Contact Us

Red Wing Shoe Store, Champaign, IL. Home of 4.0 Jody Shipka

All Products ▼

Pudding Shoe

Toll-Free
1-888-217-1234

Smart Hikers Love SmartWool Pudding Shoe™ Socks!

If you were worried about sticky feet, worry no more. SmartWool Pudding Shoe™ is here to rescue you. They are lined with comfortable rubber and wool. There is a good reason these socks have earned product excellence awards from the pudding lovers' press. They are another product of the talented Jody Shipka. Everything she produces is "A" work.

This is our **home base** and "Shaky and Mabel" location. We offer the full range of Red Wing Shoe Company brands, as well as Superfeet and SmartWool™ Socks. We have a friendly, knowledgeable staff waiting to get you fit in the right shoes or boots. We have a bright, modern store with a convenient location in Central Illinois. Visit us if you are in the area. Click here for a map to the store.

There are very few shoe stores that offer the level of service and fitting expertise that we do. We will measure **both** your feet and help you select the shoes or boots that suit your needs. Did you know that most people have different size feet? What do you do? The key to comfort is to buy the size to fit your larger foot. We have the expertise to fit our customers for all-day comfort and make the necessary adjustments for fit.

Here we have Jody Shipka, one our fully-trained and pleasant shoe-fitters showing off her newest "grade A" work. She has designed a new model for Red Wing. It is called the Pudding Shoe. The theory behind the pudding shoe is that say you are walking along and you get a yearning for pudding. Well all you have to do is take your shoe off and Presto: a snack pack is waiting for you right there.
The pudding shoes come in all sizes and colors. Our most popular color is "Leopard on the Prowl." Other colors include "Pretty in Pink," "Kooky Orange," and many others.

Store Hours:
Mon. Wed. Fri. Email to set up appt.
Tue. Th. 10-11 AM and 1215-2 PM
Saturday Closed
Sunday Closed

Tel. 217-244-1462
Fax 217-333-4321

Address:
608 South Wright Street.
Urbana, IL. 61801

Back to Top

FROM WRITING ASSIGNMENTS TO COMMUNICATIVE TASKS: ENGINEERING COMPLEX RHETORICAL EVENTS

Robert Connors called it the "inescapable question" and one that composition instructors must address prior to committing to the kinds of assignments they will provide for students: "Should [one] emphasize honest, personal writing? stress academic, argumentative, or practical subjects? or try somehow to create a balance between these discourse aims?" (296). That this question is a crucial one is evidenced by the tremendous amount of scholarship devoted to providing practitioners with strategies for offering students opportunities to engage with course materials that are, at once, personally and socially relevant and intellectually rigorous. As inquiry-based approaches to composing were increasingly offered as a way of bridging the distance between personal and academic discourse aims, practitioners were also cautioned about the ways that overly prescriptive assignments might actually militate against intellectual "mystery" (Davis and Shadle 441) and perpetuate instead a mechanical fill-in-the-blanks or "cookbook" (Bridwell-Bowles 56) approach to composing. In other words, by providing students with what the cognitive anthropologist Edwin Hutchins would call solution procedure "strips"—relatively stable and seemingly linear sequences of steps that are offered as a means of leading people through the successful accomplishment of a given task (294), overly prescriptive assignments afforded students the possibility of bypassing the inquiry phase as they searched for the "implicit clues that reveal what really counts and what can be ignored in completing a particular assignment" (Nelson 413). Consider, for instance, the way the following hypothetical assignment prompt, one derived from many I have seen, forecloses inquiry by signaling the specific ways students are to successfully accomplish the task:

> Choose three of the five essays listed below and compose a four to five-page argumentative typewritten essay in response to those essays. Double space your text, use a 12-point standard font and 1-inch margins all around, and make sure your thesis statement is clear, arguable, and underlined; make sure the piece is structured logically and that your work is carefully proofread.

Here, the *scope* and *purpose* of the work are already established for the student: a four to five-page argumentative essay in which the student demonstrates his or her ability to use outside sources as the basis of an argument. The *methods, materials,* and *technologies* he or she is expected to employ are also predetermined: reading and critically engaging the assigned texts, using at least three of these as the basis for a logically structured linear argumentative essay, the use of paper plus some device that produces print text, etc. Equally problematic is the way the prompt suggests a logic of composing that proceeds in an orderly, top-down manner: the student first chooses the essays he or she would like to work with; then composes an argumentative, thesis-driven essay; then proofreads the essay; and last, marking the end of the composing process, underlines the thesis statement. More troubling still, the prompt says nothing about the ways in which, or the specific conditions under which, students' work will be collected and assessed. In fact, to imagine the last line of the assignment reading "Once the paper is finished, you will pass this forward in class, and the instructor will read it, respond to it, and then provide you with a grade," could seem silly, a way of stating the obvious. After all, what else might one possibly imagine doing?

In pointing out the limitations of this kind of assignment, I am not suggesting that the work students produce for a course should be free from adhering to the standards associated with a specific communicative practice or genre. I am also not suggesting that the classroom become an intellectual free-for-all where assignments, due dates, and any expectation of student accountability is jettisoned as they become free to write when, how, or even *if* they want to. I am suggesting that assignments that predetermine goals and narrowly limit the materials, methodologies, and technologies that students employ in service of those goals while ignoring the "complex delivery systems through which writing circulates" (Trimbur 190), perpetuate arhetorical, mechanical, one sided views of production.

As an alternative, I propose a goal-directed multimodal task-based framework for composing that I have been developing in classes since 1997. Based in part on Walter Doyle's definition of academic tasks, the framework is geared toward increasing students' rhetorical, material, and methodological flexibility by requiring them to determine the purposes and contexts of the work they produce. Importantly, students working within this framework also assume responsibility for generating the solution procedure strips, or what I prefer to think of as the more dynamic and flexible "action sequences" (Hutchins 293), that will guide them through the successful accomplishment of each assigned task. In Maggie's case, for instance, the hometown history involved the creation of the following steps or *complex action sequences:* (1) collecting various kinds of data from classmates; (2) researching and later repurposing hometown Web sites; (3) scripting the "live" news reports; (4) devising a way of representing those hometown locations she could not actually travel to; (5) recruiting the help of a camera person; (6) traveling to the hometown locations; (7) filming the reports; (8) transferring that footage to VHS tape for ease of viewing; (9) composing the introduction to the piece and instructions for using the piece; and (10) ordering and binding the collection of repurposed Web pages. By refusing to hand students a list of nonnegotiable steps that must be accomplished in order to satisfy a specific course objective, the framework asks students to consider how fairly simple, straightforward, and relatively familiar communicative objectives might be accomplished in any number of ways, depending upon how they decide to *contextualize, frame,* or *situate* their response to those objectives.

Take, for instance, an objective often associated with first-year composition programs, asking students to use course readings or outside sources as the basis for an argument. Rather than requiring students to produce a thesis driven, linear print essay that is, more often than not, intended for the instructor alone, students approach this objective by contextualizing it in ways that are of interest or importance to them. They decide *how, why, where,* and even *when* that argument based on specific readings will be experienced by its recipient(s). Following these decisions, they begin generating the complex action sequences leading to the realization of their final product(s). For Prakas, a desire to underscore the point that the *OED* database provided "poor connection[s] between the word and the actual meaning" served as the catalyst for the steps leading to the creation of the piece's on-screen component. More specifically, Prakas's inclusion of the tales and his appropriation of the MC program was his attempt to "rewrite" the database, providing those who experienced the onscreen version with what he believed was a truer sense of the word. At the end of his piece, Prakas explicitly states that his reenvisioning of *OED* data was crafted, in part, as a teaching tool and, in part, as a prototype for a "truer," or more interactive, version of the *OED*:

> Hopefully if you followed the direction [*sic*] exactly as I told you, by now you should know the true meaning of the word "scare." For the benefit of those people who are starting to learn English (I used to be one myself), it will be very interesting to see a dictionary in the future that uses a similar method as I did above to describe definitions of words.

Instructors working within this framework are still responsible for designing tasks in accordance with course goals and objectives. Yet, again, rather than predetermining the specific materials and methodologies that students employ in service of those goals, tasks are structured in ways that ask *students* to assume responsibility for attending to the following:

- the *product(s)* they will formulate in response to a given task—this might take the form of a printed text, a performance, a handmade or repurposed object, *or, should students choose to engineer a multipart rhetorical event, any combination thereof*
- the *operations, processes,* or *methodologies* that will be (or could be) employed in generating that product—depending on what students aim to achieve, this might involve collecting data from texts, conducting surveys, interviews or experiments, sewing, searching online, woodworking, filming, recording, shopping, staging rehearsals, etc.
- the *resources, materials,* and *technologies* that will be (or could be) employed in the generation of that product—again, depending on what they aim to achieve this could involve, paper, wood, libraries, computers, needle and thread, stores, food, music, glue, tape, etc.
- the specific *conditions* in, under, or with which the final product will be experienced—this involves determining or otherwise structuring the delivery, reception, and/or circulation of their final product. (Adapted from Doyle 161)

Importantly, upon completing each task provided to them over the course of a semester, students are required to compose a highly detailed written account of their work, something that my students typically refer to as the "heads-up" statement. While the specific issues they are asked to attend to in these statements change depending on the task assigned, students must always account for the specific goals they aimed to achieve with their work and then specifically address how the rhetorical, material, methodological, and technological choices they made contributed to the realization of their goals.

To better understand the role these detailed accounts of goals and choices play in a multimodal, task-based framework, it may be helpful to compare them to the practice of asking students to underline their thesis statement prior to handing in a completed essay. Just as asking students to underline a thesis statement before turning in a linear, thesis-driven essay has served the purpose of reminding students of the importance of having a thesis statement (and preferably one that was arguable, clearly stated, and compelling enough to be used as a device for structuring the content of their essay), asking students to produce an account of their goals and choices reminds them of the importance of *assessing rhetorical contexts, setting goals,* and *making purposeful choices.* More important, requiring students to produce these statements underscores the importance of being able to speak to goals and choices in a way that highlights *how, when, why,* and *for whom* those goals and choices afford and constrain different potentials for knowing, acting, and interacting.

As a way of concretely illustrating what these statements look and sound like, I offer the following heads-up statement, which accompanied a student's response to an intensive research-based task that was assigned midsemester and that required students to examine the way a person, place, thing, idea, etc., was represented in a wide variety of sources.[5] The student whose heads-up statement appears below chose to focus on the way her sources represented a 1950s version of womanhood. The final product was housed inside a DVD case for the film *Mona Lisa Smile,* within which the bulk of the author's research was contained in a thick "chapter" booklet. The student was asked to articulate her goals for the piece and to identify the main point(s) she was attempting to make with this piece. She was then asked to account for how the various choices she had made allowed her to accomplish her goals. The student wrote:

1. My goals for this piece were to reflect the data through my representation of the data [in keeping with the ways] the sources themselves were presented to society. Many of my sources came from different forms of media and therefore I wanted to present my analysis of the sources in the form of a media source. I wanted the reader/viewer to experience the intake of information like women in the fifties did when presented with media from that era. The argument that I make in this piece is that media from the 1950s impact the dreams of women in that day. I argue that the media has messages behind it that influence women to choose the life of being a housewife. I believe that the media was a strong force in that day and women were highly impressionable by the media. The sources that I have chosen for this project are either artifacts of media in the fifties or they are articles from today and they discuss the impact of media on women in that day.

2. [My] Choices and Reasons:
   Why presented inside the cover of the movie *Mona Lisa Smile?*
   I chose to present my data inside the movie because not only was this movie the main inspiration for my topic but also I wanted the viewer/reader to be able to experience what I learned from the movie.

Why presented in a booklet? I formatted my data and reflection into this booklet because I wanted it to look like a little booklet that comes with some movies that tells about the summary and reviews of the movie. I also wanted this booklet to aid the viewer as they watch the film. I wanted them to have background knowledge about the issues discussed in the movie so they can have a better understanding.

Why is the first section labeled with the title "summary"? I titled the first section "summary" because movie reviews always start out with a brief summary of the film. In this case it is a brief summary of my topic and the sources as well as an overview of the film. I wanted this booklet to look like a guide to the movie.

Why is the following section labeled with "scene selection" and subtitled with "chapters"? The section is titled "scene selection" because often with movies on DVD they give a list of the different scenes you can select to watch. I found this to be appropriate because the reader can choose which information they want to read, which analyses they want to look at. The subtitles of "chapter" are appropriate because movies will often title the different scenes by chapters. I chose to title the sections with "chapter" because each section talks about a different type of media and my analysis of its impact on the dream of women in the fifties.

Why is the next section of the booklet titled "reviews"? This section is titled "reviews" because I wanted to stay with the movie review aspect. The phrases in the review are my analysis of the movie as a source. They are also my concluding thoughts on the topic. This seemed to suit since a movie review discusses the movie much like how my comments analyze the movie as a source.

Why is the last section titled "credits"? [B]ecause the credits of a movie give appreciation to all the people behind the scenes of the movie. This section is my works cited page. This seemed appropriate because it gives recognition to all the sources that were a part of my analysis about my topic.

Why did I choose the sources that I did? I chose my sources to come from actual forms of media in the fifties because I wanted to look at and analyze the real source. Some of my sources are pieces that reflect on a certain media. I chose to use them as a few of my sources because I wanted to look at how they inform today's public of the issues. These sources also helped to aid my analysis of the primary sources and my discussion of the topic.

Knowing that they will be expected to produce these highly detailed accounts discourages students from generating rushed and thoughtless responses to tasks. Almost without exception, statements that contain unclear or generalized statements of goals and vague explanations of the choices made in support of those goals introduce work that has not been afforded the time or effort the task required. Consider, for example, the difference between the heads-up statement offered above and the following:[6]

> My goal was to *kind of try* to convince *a lot of people* that *a lot of things* about *society today* are *unjust.* I did this by interviewing *a lot of random people* and finding *a bunch* of sources that agreed with me and disagreed with me. I basically decided to type all my information and then I decided to put it inside an old social studies textbook that I still had from high school. (My italics)

In addition to dissuading students from starting a task at the last minute, the statements provide instructors with ways of navigating and assessing student work. Instead of spending time trying to determine exactly how or why students might have engaged in a particular task the way they did, the statements allow instructors to frame their response to students' work in increasingly efficient, purposeful, and constructive ways by focusing on the specific goals and choices students have selected and shared with the instructor.[7]

A multimodal task-based framework not only requires that students work hard, but, related to this, *differently,* and it does so by foregrounding the complex processes associated with goal formation and attainment. Activity theorist A. N. Leont'ev[8] argues that these crucial processes are too often overlooked "under laboratory conditions or in pedagogical experiments" where the subject is offered a "prepared" goal (62). Following Hegel in insisting that an individual "cannot define the goal of his action until he has acted," Leont'ev maintains that the "selection and conscious perceptions of goals are by no means automatic or instantaneous acts. Rather, they are a relatively long process of *testing goals through action* and, so to speak, fleshing them out" (62).

Precisely because this multimodal task-based framework refuses to provide students with prepared goals, students learn by doing. For students who have grown accustomed to instructors telling them exactly what they need to do, this way of working can be time-consuming and frustrating, especially when the students discover potentials for enriching their work that may require them to set aside the work they have already begun and return to an earlier stage in the production process. However time-consuming this process of "testing goals through action" may be for some, those who have experienced this form of deep revision have reported that they no longer equate revision with proofreading. Rather, revision has become *re-vision*: A demanding process that involves both the potential and the willingness to reimagine the goals, contexts, and consequences associated with their work.

This is not to say that only those students who opt to jettison their original work in favor of creating something more complex have benefited from this enriched sense of revision. Even those who make the smallest adjustments to their work begin demonstrating a more nuanced understanding of *as well as a greater appreciation for* the productive tension that often exists between knowledge and action, an understanding that often leads to greater communicative flexibility insofar as they begin recognizing that

> [k]nowledge as organized for a particular task can never be sufficiently detailed, sufficiently precise, to anticipate exactly the conditions or results of actions. Action is never totally controlled by the actor but influenced by the vagaries of the physical and social world. Thus, in any given instance, knowledge is continually being refined, enriched, or completely revised by experience. (Keller and Keller 127)

This is also not to say that students offered prompts like the one mentioned earlier ("Choose three of the five essays listed below . . . "), would not come to both recognize and appreciate the complex ways that knowledge and action "are each open to alteration by the other as behavior proceeds" (Keller and Keller 125). I would argue, however, that a multimodal task-based framework—precisely because it demands that students both think and act more flexibly as they assume responsibility for determining *what* needs to be done along with *how* it might possibly be achieved—positions them in the thick of things, and in so doing, foregrounds these complex issues in ways that more prescriptive prompts may not.

A multimodal task-based orientation requires a great deal from students, to be sure. Making the shift from highly prescriptive assignments to multimodal tasks is challenging for students unaccustomed to thinking about and accounting for the work they are trying to achieve in academic spaces. Even those eager to assume more responsibility for their work and/ or to explore various materials, methodologies, and technologies often find the tasks more challenging than they had first anticipated. Still, I would argue, making the shift to these more open-ended, complexly mediated tasks is both worthwhile and necessary, especially at a time when many (see, especially, Chiseri-Strater; Geisler; George; Hocks; Sirc; and Welch) have underscored the importance of establishing an atmosphere in which students are able to prove that, beyond being critically minded consumers of existing knowledge, they are also extremely capable, critically minded producers of new knowledge.

ENACTING A MULTIMODAL TASK-BASED FRAMEWORK

To provide readers with a better sense of how this framework has been enacted in the classroom, I examine the way two students enrolled in my spring 2004 section of Rhetoric 105, a university first-year composition course, negotiated a task called "the *OED*." Assigned during the fourth week of the semester, it requires students to use the online version of the *Oxford English Dictionary*, a source many students find boring and frustrating, to research the etymology of any word they choose. Designed, in part, to prepare students for the extensive research project assigned later in the semester, this task requires that the data students find in the *OED* make up at least three-fourths of their response. Geared also toward increasing students' rhetorical and material flexibility, the task requires that students generate at least three tentative (paragraph-long) plans for representing the data they have collected, before attending the in-class workshop held a week and a half after the task is assigned. For example, a student who researched the word "find" came to the workshop with one plan for a scavenger hunt, another for an online game, and yet another for an article in a magazine aimed at people devoted to the *OED*. During the workshop sessions, students address what they consider the specific affordances associated with each of their plans while soliciting feedback from their peers.

Before examining the ways Karen Rust and Mike Ragano negotiated this task, it is important to say that the student work featured here both is, and is not, representative of the work students typically produce for the class. In focusing specifically on Rust's and Ragano's work, I do not mean to imply that students routinely gravitate toward choices that involve engineering complex tests or producing videos. As the sampling of work featured at the start of this piece suggests, when students are called upon to set their own goals and to explore the variety of ways those goals might be accomplished, the work they produce tends to defy any easy attempt to categorize by quality or kind. What *is* representative about these pieces has to do with the critical engagement and rhetorical flexibility their producers demonstrated throughout the process of accomplishing them, the sophisticated ways they were able to attend to the twinned questions of *what* they sought to do and *why*, and how, in the process of negotiating a task-based multimodal approach to composing, they began forging important connections between the classroom and other lived spaces.[9]

ACCOUNTS OF PRODUCTION, DELIVERY, AND RECEPTION

Before the semester began, Karen Rust assumed, as did many of her peers, that the course was going to be the "typical English class," where students would be expected to read assigned texts and produce responses to those texts "presented in the typical five-paragraph essay format." While her experience in this class was in keeping with her idea of typical to the extent that students were expected to read and respond to a series of assigned texts, Karen had not been expecting that the course would "force [her] to build upon [her] past skills and former approaches to writing." Admitting that she was extremely frustrated for the first part of the semester, Karen, an architecture major, saw her *OED* project, the "Mirror IQ Test," as her opportunity to articulate that frustration through a piece that was intentionally designed to make the "participant feel the same way [Karen] did in finding an idea to fulfill the assignments [she] was given." Her heads-up statement provides a strikingly rich set of goals for how her complex treatment of the word "mirror" should affect its recipient:

> The point behind the creation of the mirror IQ test is that I wanted to inform the participant of the definitions and uses of the word mirror along with demonstrating my frustration during the research for the test itself. It took me almost two and a half weeks before I could even figure out what to do for the assignment and I was becoming extremely frustrated in the process [. . .]. I wanted the participant to feel the pressure of completing the test in a given amount of time much like how I felt pressure trying to complete the assignment in the amount of time I had.

The "Mirror IQ Test" came inside a 9-by-12-inch manila envelope that was addressed to the instructor. Karen's university address appeared in the top left corner. A plastic bag containing nine mirrors was stapled to the front of the envelope. Inside the envelope was a typed sheet of paper entitled "Setting Description and Instructions," a stapled four-page, single-spaced copy of the test printed entirely in reverse (a technique often referred to as "mirror-writing"), a duplicate copy of the test that was printed "normally," an answer key for the test, and a two-page single-spaced heads-up statement for the piece.

Although the instructions and setting description did little in terms of showcasing her *OED* data, Karen said that both were crucial in terms of helping her situate the piece by simulating a high-stakes timed testing atmosphere similar to what she had experienced while taking tests like the SAT and the ACT. Karen hoped the setting description, in particular, would work to exacerbate whatever anxiety the recipient[10] might have been experiencing at the prospect of having to complete the test in the thirty minutes allotted:

> Imagine you are sitting in an empty classroom with just one desk in the center and a ticking clock in the background. The room is drafty and cold with very dim light. It is eight o'clock [and] the score from this test will determine your future by deciding which school you will be accepted to. You tried to study for the test but your friends, your parents, and your annoying siblings continually distracted you [. . .]. You ended up only studying for an hour before you fell asleep, and now you are only half awake to take the exam.
>
> [. . .] When you dig out your pencil the tip is broken. You search for a pencil sharpener but there isn't one in the room so you have to ask the proctor for another one. They hand you a stubby pencil with no eraser and tell you to sit down because the exam is starting.

The setting description also provided Karen with the opportunity to write herself into the piece by cataloging some of the "distractions and annoyances" she encountered while working on this task. Here Karen alludes to the distractions of dorm life, fatigue, and feelings of being ill-prepared and alone, feelings that may have stemmed from the in-class workshop that left Karen concerned that many of her classmates had devised more solid plans for the OED than she had been able to. Yet instead of explicitly stating that the problems were ones *she* experienced while composing this test, her use of the second person allowed her to distance herself from those experiences. Frustration, stress, anxiety, and ill-preparedness were no longer associated with the position Karen was able to assume here as the creator and administrator of this test. Rather, they belonged to whoever was unfortunate enough to have to take the test.

The test itself comprised *OED* data that Karen had arranged in four sections: multiple choice, fill-in-the-blank, matching, and identifying correct spellings of "mirror." Cognizant that any other attempts to explicitly

796

foreground the anxiety, frustration, or intellectual impotence that she experienced while composing the piece might compromise the authority of the test as well as her authority as student-turned-expert-test-creator, every choice Karen made while engineering the test needed to leave the recipient with little doubt that he or she had not only been able to successfully *take on* the specific challenges associated with the task, but that she had been able *to take them over* as well.

After creating a master copy of the test in her word-processing program, Karen began adjusting that copy, alternating the types and sizes of the fonts. Following this, she began the process of reversing the entire document in image-editing software (Fig. 4). In addition to "increasing the difficulty and confusion" one would experience while taking the test, Karen said the manipulation of the word-processed document provided her with a very specific way of "reflecting" the difficulty she had trying to decipher some of the older (less-familiar) portions of the *OED* entry she had been working with.

For someone invested in doing everything possible to ensure that the test taker would fail to complete the test in the time allotted, Karen's decision to provide the test taker with a packet of mirrors was not indicative of either a slip-up on her part or of her willingness to level the playing field by providing resources for navigating the complex text. In fact, Karen said that most of the mirrors included in the kit had been specifically chosen for having features

Figure 4. An excerpt from "Mirror IQ Test"

Part III

Below is a list of **objects** or **terms** that contain or use mirrors. Match the object with its definition. Each match is worth 2 points.

(For questions 14-21 use mirror 7)

14. **Mirror ball** _____
15. *Mirror carp* _____
16. **Mirror dory** _____
17. Mirror drum _____
18. Mirror fugue _____
19. Mirror galvanometer _____
20. MIRROR LENS _____
21. Mirror lock-up _____

a. a sensitive galvanometer in which the from a reading is indicated by a beam of light reflected mirror attached to the magnetic coil which responds to the current.

b. an ornamental variety of the common carp, artificially bred, which has a series of enlarged scales along the middle of each side.

c. a scanning device, first used in early television transmitters and receivers, consisting of a rotating drum having its curved surface covered with a number of equally spaced plane mirrors, the number of mirrors determining the number of scanning lines.

---

that would make it almost impossible for anyone to see or read much of anything with them. Some were concave, some convex, and almost all of them were made of a substance that precluded them from reflecting anything at all. One mirror in particular, while it had been large enough and of a decent-enough quality to have provided an adequate reflection of the test, was covered in black tape so that only a small portion of the middle of the mirror was left to reflect anything. In her heads-up statement Karen wrote that she chose to tape the mirror to "briefly hit a point" that she wanted to make with the piece, namely, "that when we look into mirrors we only look at a small part of the whole. We tend to focus on our nose or our lips instead of stepping back and looking at all of it together."

By creating an environment that required the test taker to employ media (i.e., the mirrors) not typically associated with test taking, Karen seems to be suggesting that *just because* one is given permission to take up a variety of media does not necessarily make a task any easier. In fact, in addition to altering one's perspective on what composing practices might potentially require and afford (much as Karen's collection of mirrors works to suggest), the increase in media often makes the business of composing (or in Karen's case, of test making and taking) that much more challenging, as there is often, quite literally, infinitely more stuff for students to handle.

Mike Ragano, a business major, also admitted that the tasks had been a source of frustration for him, stressing that it often took a good deal of time, effort, and thought to come up with ideas for responding to each new task. Upon receiving the OED task description, however, Mike felt he had lucked out, as he knew exactly what he hoped to do:

> I choose the word "power" because it has a great deal of meaning to me. I love war movies that talk about military and political power and I love to weight lift which is about muscular power [. . . ;] it is also an older word and I was confident that I could find a lot of research on it in the *OED*. [. . .] I wanted to do a fun movie. I felt that a lot of the work that I had done in the class was time consuming and I felt that a movie would be an easy and fun change of pace. I thought that I could make power seem fun and interesting.

While deciding on a word, purpose, and method of representation before looking through several sets of *OED* data is fairly unusual—more often than not, students will have to switch words a few times before settling on one they can use—accomplishing the task would not prove especially easy for Mike. His heads-up statement continues: "After thinking more about how I might actually accomplish my goal and after spending countless hours staring at the *OED,* I realized that there was nothing amusing or fun about it. I couldn't think of a single way to portray the information as funny."

Mike's treatment of the word "power" took the form of a "public access type" show that attempted to "mimic" a program Mike recalled seeing years before. In his heads-up statement Mike explained: "The [gardening] show was very boring and it upset me that the host could be so passionate about such a boring subject. I decided to use this genre to bore my watcher." In choosing to burn "Interpretations of the *OED*" on CD, Mike was also able to structure viewers' reception of his work in ways that aligned with the specific forms of physical and intellectual "punishment" he felt he had to endure while sitting in front of the computer looking for usable *OED* data online.

"Interpretations" was shot in black and white, Mike's way of ensuring that the episode would "bore the socks off " the viewer. At the start of the episode, we meet "Russ" (the host of the show and someone not enrolled in the course), a man with shoulder-length hair, who is dressed in a tweed sports coat and seated in a chair positioned against a very plain background. On Russ's lap was a copy of Mike's rhetoric course packet, which Mike had repurposed in hopes of making it appear that Russ was actually reading from a volume of the *OED.* Inside the spiral-bound packet was a script containing various spellings and uses of the word *power.*

After welcoming viewers to the show and promising them an "intimate evening" spent "delving into the word 'power' and all it has to offer," Russ makes a reference to Mr. Rogers, removes his shoes, and settles into his chair. Following this, Russ begins holding up what Mike's script calls "signs" (i.e., pieces of paper) containing different spellings of the word "power." Russ displays and spells aloud twelve "signs" in all, including: poer, poeir, pouwer, pouwere, pouoir, pouer, pouere, poweer, pouar, powar, pover, and finally, the one Russ refers to as "our good old trusty stand-by companion, p-o-w-e-r." For Mike, the decision to have Russ read each spelling aloud *and with ever-increasing enthusiasm* was intended as a way of "really getting his message across" by making the episode "drag on and on with unnecessary long [and boring] parts." Interestingly enough, this (two minutes plus) portion of the piece seems to have had a reverse effect on audiences insofar as the 130-plus viewers who have viewed the episode have suggested that the spelling segment is quite funny.

If Russ's portions of the video allowed Mike to both *purposefully* and *playfully* represent the data he collected from the *OED* and to illustrate the powerfully numbing experience of sitting alone in his dorm room searching the *OED* database, the three commercials interspersed throughout the video are suggestive of another form of power Mike had to negotiate while composing his piece—the power of friendship, video games, good movies, and food. Put otherwise, the power of extracurricular diversions.

In his heads-up statement Mike explained that the colorful, loud, and cluttered space that served as backdrop for the commercials was offered as a contrast to the "horribly furnished room with little visual stimulation" in which Russ and the *OED* were positioned. As a way of providing a tighter link between Russ's portion of the piece and the commercials, Mike made the problem of trying to find the time and desire to complete his OED task the central focus of the commercials. Two of the "visually stimulating" commercials began with roughly the same shot, one that featured Mike sitting alone in his dorm room in front of the computer with his copy of the rhetoric course packet in his lap. Within minutes, friends began entering the room offering him "fun and interesting distractions" from doing his work. As Russ's appearances as the obedient and passionate student-scholar of the *OED* in the black-and-white segments of the video were meant to suggest, the student Mike portrays in the commercials ultimately gives in to the power of these other distractions and places his rhetoric to the side. Despite making promises to the contrary at the end of each commercial, Mike continues to procrastinate, and so fails to complete the task himself.

Or does he? It may be important to note here that "Interpretations" gave Mike the opportunity to revisit an issue he had begun addressing in his earlier work, namely that of trying to reconcile the distractions posed by extracurricular interests and practices with those posed by curricular ones. While the piece as a whole worked to suggest that Mike (the commercial persona) found a way of reconciling this problem by having Russ tend to his curricular distractions, thereby freeing commercial-Mike to tend to the extracurricular ones, the processes that Mike (as a Rhetoric 105 student) employed while producing the video suggest that he did, after all, find ways to both productively and *simultaneously* manage both forms of distraction. Explaining that he had "some really great people at his dorm" who had previously volunteered to assist him with work he had been producing for the course, Mike said he approached the *OED* task with the thought of taking people up on their offers. By "subcontracting" various parts of the project to other people (i.e., while Mike would conduct the research, compose the script, and take on most of the directing, he put his friends in charge of filming and editing the video, designing the two sets, and deciding who would play the various supporting roles in the piece), Mike said he was able to approach the task feeling less like its sole author or creator and more like a project manager whose primary concern had to do with organizing and overseeing the various resources and talents each member of the team brought to the project. In this way, Mike felt that his way of approaching the task resonated with his long-term career goals (to work in business/management) in ways that working alone on the piece would not have afforded.

TERMS, CONDITIONS, CONCLUSIONS

In "Quartet Three" of her 2004 CCCC Chair's Address, Kathleen Blake Yancey calls for the development of an activity-based multimodal curriculum for the twenty-first century, one that allows us to carry forward the "best of what we have created to date" (16) as we continue forging purposeful connections among the literate activities that students encounter both within and beyond the space of the classroom proper. The task-based multimodal framework offered here represents, I suggest, one way of responding to Yancey's call. It highlights what students might accomplish when they are provided with opportunities: (1) to set their own goals for the work they engage in in the course; (2) to draw upon a wider range of communicative resources than courses have typically allowed; (3) to speak to the ways the various choices they have made serve, alter, or complicate those goals; and (4) to attend to the various ways in which communicative texts and events shape, and take shape from, the contexts and media in which they are produced and received.

In keeping with Anne Wysocki's definition of new-media texts, the complex work students produce within this framework need not be digital but might be made, or as I prefer to put it, *purposefully engineered,* out of anything (15) or, should students be interested in producing multipart rhetorical events, out of *any number or combinations of things:* print texts, digital media, live or videotaped performances, old photographs, "intact" objects, repurposed (i.e., transformed or remediated) objects, etc. "Rather than taking talk and writing as [its] starting point," as composition courses have tended to do, the framework I have proposed here privileges innovative choosing by treating all modes, materials, and methodologies "as equally significant for meaning and communication, potentially so at least" (Jewitt and Kress 4). While the framework still requires that students produce a substantial amount of writing for the course, the fact that they are drawing upon multiple semiotic resources as they compose work suggests that students are doing something that is at once *more and other than* writing (i.e., placing and arranging words on a page or screen). I would argue that students who are called upon to choose among and later to order, align, and/or transform the various resources they find at hand tend to work in ways that more closely resemble the ways choreographers or engineers do. To return to an example offered at the start of this piece, Lindsay's portfolio involved a trip to the store (importantly, not having a car, Lindsay said her shopping options were limited to those stores along the bus line) where she selected and purchased the gift boxes, a gift bag, ribbon, and the greeting card that she later repurposed. To successfully pull off the event, Lindsay also needed to arrange for a method of delivering the piece, to compose the specific instructions for experiencing, and later recirculating her semester's worth of work, and, of course, to arrange the various word-processed texts and repurposed objects (a CD, a gameboard, etc.) contained within the gift boxes. For Mike Ragano, "Interpretations of the *OED*" involved not only the production of a script based on his *OED* data, but also, with this, the complex orchestration of those bodies (i.e., their energy, time, talent, access to, and experience with technology) who had earlier volunteered to assist Mike in the production of work for the course. Following Wysocki, I would stress that what is most important about this complexly engineered work "is that whoever produces the text and whoever consumes it understands—because the text asks them to, in one way or another—that the various materialities of the text contribute to how it, like its producers and consumers, is read and understood" (15).

When students are called upon to work within a multimodal task-based framework, questions associated with materiality and the delivery, reception, and circulation of texts, objects, and events are no longer viewed as separate from or incidental to the means and methods of production, but as integral parts of invention and production processes. Again, for Lindsay, the goal of regiving her semester's work determined the specific choices she made to realize this action: from where she shopped and how she got there to what she bought and how she transformed the gift card, as well as the specific ways she chose to represent, and later dictate the circulation of her semester's work. Similarly, most of the choices that Prakas, Maggie, Karen, and Mike made while engineering their events were predicated upon the understanding, if not the *hope*, that their work would be experienced by specific, not to mention *multiple*, audiences—the instructor, peers, future readers, etc.—in very specific ways.

Convinced as I am of the richness, intelligence, and sophistication of the work I have witnessed students producing over the years, I admit that as I began exploring the various ways I might present this framework along with the students' accounts of the work they produced I kept returning to a point Yancey makes in her address, namely that the development of a new curriculum for composition will likely involve "a new vocabulary, a new set of practices, and a new set of outcomes" (16). As the framework proposed here involves new terms (vocabularies), conditions (practices), and conclusions (outcomes/ products), I wondered if the terms I was using, the practices students were engaging in, and the work they had produced for the class might strike some as strange and too little in keeping with "the best of what we have created to date." While cognizant that the complexly engineered work featured here might not resemble the student work many have grown accustomed to assigning and responding to, I wanted to conclude by underscoring the ways I see this framework working to achieve more familiar goals.

First, students working within this framework are still writing, conducting research, and responding to complex social texts, including ones they have engineered, ones engineered by their peers, and others that they encounter in curricular and extracurricular domains. Second, in keeping with the "WPA Outcomes Statement for First-Year Composition" adopted in April 2000, students working with this framework are extensively and deeply involved in

- Focusing on a purpose
- Responding to the needs of different audiences
- Responding appropriately to different kinds of rhetorical situations
- Using conventions of format and structure appropriate to the rhetorical situation
- Adopting appropriate voice, tone, and level of formality
- Understanding how genres shape reading and writing
- Writing in several genres
- Integrating their own ideas with those of others
- Understanding the relationships among language, knowledge, and power
- Understanding the collaborative and social aspects of writing processes
- Using a variety of technologies to address a range of audiences
- Learning common formats for different kinds of texts
- Controlling such surface features as syntax, grammar, punctuation, and spelling (Council 520–22)

Finally, students are still "doing" process and learning about revision. However, I would maintain that what students come to understand about potentials for processes, *processing,* and revision is far richer and more complex when practiced within this kind of goal-directed multimodal task-based framework. When students come to understand process and revision as concepts that both shape, and take shape from, the specific goals, objectives, and tools *with which,* as well as the specific environments *in which,* they interact while composing, they stand a far better chance of appreciating how processes and revision also play an integral role in the continual (re) development of genres, practices, belief systems, institutions, subjectivities, and histories. And, of course, in the ongoing (re)development of lives.

ACKNOWLEDGMENTS

I thank Lindsay Freeberg, Prakas Itarut, Maggie Christiano, Karen Rust, and Michael Ragano for allowing me to share their work with others. I would also like to thank Judith Briggs, Paul Prior, Janine Solberg, and, most especially, Sarah MacDonald for the helpful comments and suggestions they offered on earlier versions of this manuscript.

NOTES

1. This essay was inspired by a presentation Sarah MacDonald and I gave at the 2004 Allerton Articulation Conference in Monticello, Illinois. After arranging the work produced by eight of our students in "audio-equipped stations" throughout the room, we provided participants with headsets that they could plug into the tape players located near the students' work. Participants could then listen to the students' voices as they addressed: (1) the goals they had been trying to achieve with their work and (2) the specific rhetorical and material choices they made in service of those goals.

2. With the written permission of each of the students included in this piece, I am using real names. Students were also offered the option of pseudonyms.

3. Inspired by the dearth of information on students' lived experience with or in composition classrooms, this task allows students the opportunity to tell others something about who they were or what they did at a specific point in their college careers. Students are encouraged to begin the task by *defining* the specific "space(s)" their history will represent. Following this, students are asked to *decide* what it is about that space they would like to represent for others. Students are asked to determine the *methodology* (or methodologies) they will employ while collecting data and the *means* by which they will represent their findings. At the end of the year, those contributions that allow it are copied, bound, and distributed to class members. Students are also asked whether I may donate a copy of their contribution to the Student Life Archive on campus.

4. This point is echoed by Kathleen Blake Yancey in her 2004 CCCC Chair's Address, "Made Not Only in Words: Composition in a New Key," in which she calls for the development of an activity-based, multimodal curriculum for the new century. As part of the "ambitious agenda" Yancey begins outlining here, students would be afforded opportunities to consider what the "best medium and best delivery" for their work might be and to "create and share those different communication pieces in those different media, to different audiences."

5. Depending upon what students have chosen to research, sources have included academic texts, Web sites, popular fiction, advice manuals, textbooks, children's books, film, art, bumper

stickers, print newspapers and magazines, toys, candles, jewelry, and other objects. From a pedagogical point of view, the broader objective associated with this task is inviting students to think beyond the two-sided or procon research papers that many have reported composing in high school classes and to think about how an issue, object, or argument is represented, complicated, or perpetuated in a wide variety of sources. Thus emphasis is placed not on what *the student* thinks about an issue so much as on what the student thinks about *the ways that issue* (person, place, thing) is represented in a wide variety of sources. Students are asked to pay special attention to the kind and quality of work their sources do and to base their responses to the task on their attempt to account for how those sources accomplish the work students see them doing. Students are encouraged to consider how access to and use of a source might contribute to its persuasiveness, value, and power, or lack thereof.

6. The statement of goals and choices offered here is not one that a student actually composed for the course but loosely modeled upon some of the less comprehensive statements I have received over the years. With this said, I tend to see statements of this kind only at the start of the semester as students are adjusting to what the framework specifically requires of them.

7. Should students choose to engineer final products whose complexity may preclude the instructor from experiencing that work precisely as the student intended, the statements serve an additional purpose in allowing students the opportunity of describing or even enacting what the instructor might have actually experienced had he or she been able to experience the work as it was intended to be experienced.

8. In her 2004 Chair's Address, Yancey also pointed to the value of activity theory for reconceptualizing the work of first-year composition. To see various uses of activity theory in studies of writing, see Charles Bazerman and David Russell's online collection, *Writing Selves, Writing Societies: Research from Activity Perspectives.*

9. For discussions on the importance of connecting work done in the classroom with other lived spaces, see, for example, Bridwell-Bowles; Chiseri-Strater; Davis and Shadle; Durst; Harris; Latterell; Prior and Shipka; and Sirc.

10. The choice to use "recipient" to indicate audience issues here is deliberate. Within the context of the Rhetoric 105 classroom proper I am, of course, a primary recipient of the students' work. However, depending upon how a student chooses to frame response to a task, the potential audience for that work may, *and almost without exception does,* include other recipients, both real (classmates, friends, family members, etc.) and imagined/potential. In Karen's case, the envelope was addressed to me but the language of the test itself (i.e., test-taking "participants") points toward a wider potential audience. For many students, the challenge often becomes one of dealing with these double, triple, or even quadruple contextualizing moves. More baldly stated, students will always be cognizant of my role as (or in) an audience. At the same time, they must make their work resonate in whatever other contexts, genres, or activity systems their work maps onto the activity of "doing tasks for Rhetoric 105." This mapping or complex layering of contexts is nicely illustrated by Prakas's work, where the instructor, his classmates, and those just beginning to learn English are included as potential audiences for this work. The same could be said for Maggie's or Lindsay's work, where the issue of audience extends well beyond the space of one particular college composition classroom.

WORKS CITED

Bazerman, Charles, and David Russell, eds. *Writing Selves, Writing Societies: Research from Activity Perspectives.* Fort Collins, CO: WAC Clearinghouse, 2003. 14 Aug. 2005 http://wac.colo state.edu/ books/selves_societies.

Bridwell-Bowles, Lillian. "Freedom, Form, Function." *CCC* 46.1 (Feb. 1995): 46–61.

Chiseri-Strater, Elizabeth. *Academic Literacies: The Public and Private Discourse of University Students.* Portsmouth, NH: Heinemann, 1991.

Connors, Robert J. *Composition-Rhetoric: Backgrounds, Theory, and Pedagogy.* Pittsburgh: U of Pittsburgh P, 1997.

Council of Writing Program Administrators. "WPA Outcomes Statement for First-Year Composition." *The Writing Program Administrator's Resource.* Ed. Stuart C. Brown and Theresa Enos. Mahwah, NJ: Erlbaum, 2002. 519–22.

Davis, Robert, and Mark Shadle. "'Building a Mystery': Alternative Research Writing and the Academic Act of Seeking." *CCC* 51.3 (Feb. 2000): 417–46.

Doyle, Walter. "Academic Work." *Review of Educational Research* 53.2 (Summer 1983): 159–99.

Durst, Russel K. *Collision Course: Conflict, Negotiation, and Learning in College Composition.* Urbana, IL: NCTE, 1999.

Geisler, Cheryl. "Writing and Learning at Cross Purposes in the Academy." *Reconceiving Writing, Rethinking Writing Instruction.* Ed. Joseph Petraglia. Mahwah, NJ: Erlbaum, 1995. 101–20.

George, Diana. "From Analysis to Design: Visual Communication in the Teaching of Writing." *CCC* 45.1 (Sept. 2002): 11–39.

Harris, Joseph. *A Teaching Subject: Composition since 1966.* Pittsburgh: U of Pittsburgh P, 1997.

Hocks, Mary E. "Understanding Visual Rhetoric in Digital Writing Environments." *CCC* 54.4 (June 2003): 629–56.

Hutchins, Edwin. *Cognition in the Wild.* Cambridge, MA: MIT P, 1995.

Jewitt, Carey, and Gunther Kress. Introduction. *Multimodal Literacy.* Ed. Carey Jewitt and Gunther Kress. New York: Lang, 2003. 1–18.

Keller, Charles, and Janet Dixon Keller. "Thinking and Acting with Iron." *Understanding Practice: Perspectives on Activity and Context.* Ed. Seth Chaiklin and Jean Lave. Cambridge: Cambridge UP, 1993. 125–43.

Kress, Gunther. "'English at the Crossroads: Rethinking Curricula of Communication in the Context of the Turn to the Visual." *Passions, Pedagogies, and 21st Century Technologies.* Ed. Gail E. Hawisher and Cynthia L. Selfe. Logan: Utah State UP, 1999. 66–88.

Latterell, Catherine G. "Reexperiencing the Ordinary: Mapping Technology's Impact on Everyday Life." *Practice in Context: Situating the Work of Writing Teachers.* Ed. Cindy Moore and Peggy O'Neill. Urbana, IL: NCTE, 2002. 12–21.

Leont'ev, A. N. "The Problem of Activity in Psychology." *The Concept of Activity in Soviet Psychology.* Ed. James V. Wertsch. Armonk, NY: Sharpe, 1981. 37–71.

Nelson, Jennie. "Reading Classrooms as Text: Exploring Student Writers' Interpretive Practices." *CCC* 46.3 (Oct. 1995): 411–29.

Prior, Paul, and Jody Shipka. "Chronotopic Laminations: Tracing the Contours of Literate Activity." Bazerman and Russell 180–238.

Sirc, Geoffrey. *English Composition as a Happening.* Logan: Utah State UP, 2002.

Trimbur, John. "Composition and the Circulation of Writing." *CCC* 52.2 (Dec. 2000): 188–219.

Welch, Kathleen. *Electric Rhetoric: Classical Rhetoric, Oralism, and a New Literacy.* Cambridge, MA: MIT P, 1999.

Wysocki, Anne Frances. "Opening New Media to Writing: Openings and Justifications." *Writing New Media: Theory and Applications for Expanding the Teaching of Composition.* Ed. Anne Frances Wysocki, Johndan JohnsonEilola, Cynthia L. Selfe, and Geoffrey Sirc. Logan: Utah State UP, 2004. 1–41.

Yancey, Kathleen Blake. "Made Not Only in Words: Composition in a New Key." 2004 CCCC Chair's Address. *CCC* 56.2 (Dec. 2004): 297–328.

P. 810

Writing is basically the main
~~subject,~~ topic while rhetoric 為 are the sub-topics.
                      band
              composition

Both of the definitions are important
and considered equal. (p. 810)

Essentially, he's saying that composition
and rhetoric needs to be taught in every
English class as they are just as important
as any other subject in English.

In order to make her point, Selfe
uses the word aurality which is a
complex word that relates to
    hearing.

Response to Cynthia L. Selfe's "The Movement of Air, the Breath of Meaning: Aurality and Multimodal Composing"

Doug Hesse

Editor's Note: Doug Hesse has written a commentary on "The Movement of Air, the Breath of Meaning: Aurality and Multimodal Composing" by Cynthia L. Selfe, which appeared in *College Composition and Communication* 60.4 (June 2009) 616–63. Cynthia then responds to Doug's remarks. The full text of the original article is available at the *CCC* website: www.nc te.org/cccc/ccc.

[handwritten annotation: Aurality is ~~then~~ relating to hearing.]

Cindy Selfe makes a compelling argument that compositionists should embrace aurality as an aspect of our classrooms. She sketches the deep history of speaking and listening in composition course forebears; suggests writing's privilege is a historical manifestation of class, race, and gender interests; and cites the increasingly prominent (even dominant) role that aural and visual modes play in contemporary communication, especially in popular spheres and especially among current students. Her work is careful and alluring. Teaching as she would have us teach is not only inviting but also consonant with national calls for expanded views of literacy and textuality, such as NCTE's policy brief on *21st Century Literacies*. And yet (you knew

Reprinted from *College Composition and Communication* 61.3 (February 2010): 602–605. Used with permission.

[handwritten: Even though she seemed good, Selfe seemed to focus more on small picture stuff.]

the "yet" was coming), it begs two questions. In raising them, I'm not saying that Selfe is wrong but, rather, that there are large prior issues that we need to sort.

Question 1: Is the curricular space that our field inhabits "rhetoric/composing" or is it "writing/composing?" Without tracing the debate over whether contemporary composition was born of rhetoric or parented by something else, I'll simply note that "rhetoric" is a more capacious territory. A course in rhetoric, understood in the term's current breadth, admits to "the available means of persuasion" any and all possible modes of delivery, paragraph to pixel to pantomime, with rhetorical situation determining the best fit. Writing describes a subset of rhetoric: those productions whose mode of delivery is written language. In composition-as-rhetoric, a wordless cartoon or a minor-key melody may be an acceptable target discourse. In composition-as-writing, they would not (though an intermingling of word and image in some fuzzy ratio and relationship would).

I make this observation not to elevate one definition over the other. Indeed, my point is ultimately that the profession needs to have this out, at a high conceptual level rather than an accretive lower one. We need to do this with the full participation of all stakeholders in composition courses, especially if they're required. I'll offer a *reductio ad absurdum* analogy. If I am teaching a studio course in "watercolor" but devote substantial instruction to casting bronzes, I'll have to defend my curriculum more than if I were teaching a course in "making art." Or, even more extremely, if I'm to teach German but, noting the world's economic drift (not to mention sheer numbers), I decide instead to teach Chinese, I shouldn't be surprised if some stakeholders object.

Now, I see Cindy's aim in this article as nothing short of calling for an expansive redefinition (she would see it as a reclamation) of composition as rhetoric. I'm persuadable but pragmatic. I just think we need to be forthright and open about the terms of that work, all the way from how we name courses to how we specify the artifacts and genres students produce in them. There are political as well as philosophical implications. The political issues include curricular turf and institutional sanction. As many have noted, the term "composition" is enjoying a surprising and welcome resurrection from its entombment as first-year comp. If we're going to use it as the umbrella for a wider host of textual practices than academic writing or public argument, then we ought to be clear in our catalogs and to our colleagues that we're shifting the definition.

Question 2: Whose interests should the composition class serve? Historically we've shuttled between three of them: those of the academy, those of the workplace, and those of the polis, with an occasional fourth and fifth: those of the individual, including in social relationships, and those of discourse, especially in aesthetic production. As long as language was deemed factorable into discrete skills, arts, or operations, it didn't much matter which interests were privileged. Any one was a path to any other. We could just give students tools: vocabulary, sentence, paragraph; invention, revision, editing; font, hanging indent, track change; link, crop, fade. However, it's hard to be so sanguine, in the aftermath of genre and activity theory, that any tool neatly transfers to any sphere or purpose. Perhaps the best we can do is tour students through the taxonomy of roles, audiences, situations, affordances, constraints, and rhetoricity: a tall order for a course or two.

Selfe's perspective on interests is especially fresh—and, as a result, complex. After acknowledging that "writing will continue to be a hallmark of educated citizens in the United States for some time to come," she goes further:

> I *do* want to argue that teachers of composition need to pay attention to, and come to value, the *multiple* ways in which students compose and communicate meaning, the exciting hybrid, multimodal texts they create—in both nondigital and digital environments—to meet their own needs in a changing world. We need to better understand the importance that students attach to composing, exchanging, and interpreting new and different kinds of texts that help them make sense of their experiences and lives—songs and lyrics, videos, written essays illustrated with images, personal Web pages that include sound clips. We need to learn from their motivated efforts to communicate with each other, for themselves and for others, often in resistance to the world we have created for them. We need to respect the rhetorical sovereignty of young people from different backgrounds, communities, colors, and cultures, to observe and understand the rhetorical choices they are making, and to offer them new ways of making meaning, new choices, new ways of accomplishing their goals. (642)

I'll set aside empirical questions of how many students actually are composing (as opposed to consuming) in what kinds of modes and media (a recent Pew study, for example, reports that 11 percent of teens have a website and 27 percent a blog, with 65 percent using social networking sites; see Lenhart). I want instead to focus on the clash between the rhetorical choices young people are making and the rhetorical choices they are not making (and, to be fair, neither are vast swaths of the general population), the goals they set, the goals they don't.

The tension between the "rhetorical sovereignty" of individuals and the expectations of the work and civic realms in which they might participate has both pragmatic and philosophical dimensions. The clash is nothing new; in educational theory, it tracks through Dewey, Emerson, the German romantics, and so on. At stake is how composing for the self-sponsored and largely ludic purposes that Selfe aptly celebrates might connect to purposes and environments that are, instead, obliged and sanctioned. The hope seems that student engagement will make them responsive to our "offer" (which, I assume, they can decline) of "new ways of making meaning," ways that I trust can include writing extended connective prose.

The question of whose interests the course ought to serve ultimately is an ethical one. Part of it involves "what's good for the student"—but the student as worker, citizen, friend, soul? Part of it is "what's good for the various cultures and subcultures" in which decisions are made, resources distributed, and ideas championed. As I'm writing, national health care reform is generating huge volumes of rhetorical activity; I long for more reasoned and developed rationales than the glib sound and image bites proffered from all angles. Critics will rightly cite that alphabetic and essayistic literacy hasn't yet created social equality or economic justice, let alone happiness, so what's to lose in expanding compositional modes? Fair point. I simply submit that there are ethical as well as rhetorical dimensions to the affordances and constraints of modes and media, and that education has long tempered "what works" or "what's interesting" with "what should be."

My purpose is to temper Selfe's thoughtful argument, because the practices it advocates entail more than some supplemental tweak of current courses. At stake are fundamental boundaries of our curricular landscape and our sense of its stakeholders, interests, and purposes. Like many readers of her article, I'm inclined to make a place for the aurality in my own teaching even as I ponder whether I'm overstepping or sidestepping professional roles that best serve student and social interests.

Temper - person's state of mind

WORKS CITED

Lenhart, Amanda. "Teens and Social Media: An Overview." Pew Internet: Pew Internet and American Life Project. 10 Apr. 2009. Web. 12 Aug. 2009.

21st Century Literacies. Urbana: NCTE, 2008. Web. 17 Aug. 2009.

In this case, temper means to act as a balance\neutralizer.

Response to Doug Hesse

Cynthia L. Selfe

Doug Hesse's thoughtful response to "The Movement of Air" gets right to the heart of the profession's favorite questions about integrating digital and multimodal assignments into composition classes: "What is the proper subject matter for composition classes?" (often asked, "Is the composition classroom *really* the right place to teach video production/audio editing?" or "Why should I teach audio or video composing when I don't even have enough time to teach writing?") and "Whose interests are we serving with composition curricula?" (also asked, "Do we really need to teach students how to compose YouTube videos?")

Let's start with the first question, "What is the proper subject matter for composition classes?" As Hesse articulates the question, "Is the curricular space that our field inhabits "rhetoric/composing" or is it "writing/composing?" Here, I'll throw down publicly as an adherent of rhetoric/composing as the more capacious choice; to me, it suggests an openness to multiple modalities of rhetorical expression. In this admission, however, I refuse to leave "writing" out of the equation. As I said in my *CCC* article, "my argument is not *either / or*, but *both / and*" (641).

For me, the inclusion of multiple modes of rhetorical expression represents a simple acknowledgment that a literacy education focused solely on *writing* will produce citizens with an overly narrow and exclusionary understanding of the world and the variety of audiences who will read and respond to their work. In the twenty-first century, we live in an increasingly globalized world where people speak different languages, come from different cultures, learn and make meaning in different media contexts

Reprinted from *College Composition and Communication* 61.3 (February 2010): 606–610. Used with permission.

and with different expressive modalities. In such an environment, although writing retains a privileged position, literate citizens, increasingly, need to make use of *all* semiotic channels to communicate effectively among different groups and for different purposes. To educate students appropriately and responsibly for this world, I try to design my composition classes as places where students *begin the complex process* of learning how to make use of all sorts of design resources (New London Group)— spoken and written words, still and moving images, sounds and music, among them—to communicate in rhetorically effective ways.

This approach doesn't mean that students will learn the *advanced* skills they might encounter in more specialized creative writing classes, technical communication classes, photography classes, digital audio or digital video production classes, or art classes. Instead, they'll learn how to go through a set of basic rhetorical processes: analyzing the rhetorical context and purposes for communication tasks, thinking about audiences and their needs, conducting research on related communications and how others have addressed similar tasks; deploying rhetorical strategies of invention, organization, arrangement, and delivery; composing drafts that address particular rhetorical contexts by combining modes of expression, responding to critically informed feedback on their own rhetorical communications, and offering feedback to other communicators on their own drafts. For me, these rhetorically informed activities *are the proper content for composition classes*.

Because writing continues to occupy a privileged position in the world (and because I am particularly tied to writing as a mode of expression), I involve students in *lots* of reading and writing tasks. But I also recognize that some of the students with whom I work and some of the audiences with whom these students are communicating—some visual artists; scientists; individuals in deaf and hard-of-hearing communities; musicians; some individuals who are blind or have limited sight; some individuals from other cultures or who speak English as a second, third, or fourth language; some individuals who have different learning styles, among many, many others—may, on occasion, find it useful to acquire information and to compose it not only through writing alone, but also through photographs, charts, graphs, still and moving images, and aural elements as well. Indeed, many audiences benefit from *several* semiotic systems to make sense of communications in certain rhetorical contexts. So, I want students to think about such people and to compose communications that might convey meaning appropriately and effectively to various groups and individuals.

Theoretically, I locate my educational theory on these matters in the concept of "civic pluralism," as a goal for education in a globalized world. address some of the problems that face the human race. Within this context, I understand written words, photographs, video and audio clips, drawings, and animations as valuable cultural resources that can be combined to compose texts that communicate meaning in a variety of rhetorically effective ways for a variety of audiences.

Pragmatically, of course, I can only teach so much in any one course, so I try to teach some basic rhetorical processes for analyzing and composing meaning that can serve students well in a range of communicative situations, with a range of audiences, and for a range of purposes. We write lots, but we also compose in different modalities as well—and we try to compare the effectiveness with which each one of us assembles and deploys different semiotic resources to communicate in the context of each task.

The second thoughtful question that Hesse raises is, "Whose interests are we serving with composition curricula?" Here, Hesse points out the key "tension between the 'rhetorical sovereignty' of individuals and the expectations of the work and civic realms in which they might participate," between "self-sponsored" and "obliged and sanctioned" forms and modes of composing. We can't, in short, simply let students use the composing modalities they prefer; rather, we are also obliged to teach them how to compose with modalities that may be unfamiliar and difficult but expected of educated citizens and within workplaces. On this point, we agree: one goal of education is to broaden students' thinking and abilities, to add to their composing repertoires, rather than to limit them artificially. I might, in fact, go farther with this point, suggesting that faculty in rhetoric and composition should serve as role models in this regard, showing students that they, too, are willing to learn new ways of composing, to expand their own skills and abilities beyond the alphabetic by practicing with different modalities of expression that may be unfamiliar and difficult but increasingly expected and valuable in different twenty-firstcentury rhetorical contexts both in and out of the academy.

There is one more important point I'd like to make about Doug Hesse's response. In discussing the ethical responsibilities of composition teachers, Hesse gives the example of the current health care debate and confesses that he longs for "more reasoned and developed rationales." On this point, we agree. We part ways, however, when Hesse equates "more reasoned and developed rationales" with the *written word*, and less reasoned "glib" reasoning with "sound[s] and image[s]." This last move comes too close, for me, to reinscribing a mistaken and problematic dichotomy between word and image; in this dichotomy, alphabetic writing is aligned with high art, seriousness, intellectual understanding, and rigorous exploration while images and aural forms of expression are aligned with low art, vernacular understanding, frivolity, and entertainment. The work of scholars like John Berger, Diana George, and William Costanzo, among many others, argues that such distinctions are both mistaken and inaccurate. So it is not surprising that I don't buy this part of Hesse's argument. Indeed, I consider it indicative of our profession's single-minded focus on the alphabetic, a focus that can sometimes blind us to other ways of knowing and making meaning. This point can be made on a practical level as well. I can certainly identify what seem like glib print essays on health care that I, personally, believe fail to contribute productively to an understanding of complex health care issues. And, conversely, there are texts in other forms—video, audio, image—that I, personally, find well reasoned, well documented, carefully thought out, and informative. Of course, the reverse is also true—there are well-reasoned, extended printed reports that contribute to our understanding of the health care crisis, and there are many multimodal accounts that are glib and fatuous.

My point is that no one medium or modality—certainly not writing—has a corner on reason, thoughtfulness, effectiveness, *or* glibness. Personally, I think that the complex constellations of problems associated with our health care crisis will not be addressed or understood through printed reports or essays alone. Rather, the individuals and groups who need to come together to address health care will require multiple semiotic channels and multiple modes of expression to share their various perspectives; exchange information and insights; understand what each other is getting at; figure out what is at stake for various groups; and invent new ways of thinking about healthy populations, lifestyles, and medical care.

Doug Hesse and I both believe that there are important "ethical as well as rhetorical dimensions" to the exploration of the "affordances and constraints of modes and media" and that the stakes in discussing the role of multimodality in composition classes focus our attention on the "boundaries of our curricular landscape and our sense of its stakeholders, interests, and purposes." From my own ethical perspective, I have found it increasingly difficult to understand why we think writing is the *only* rhetorical tool composition specialists should teach or deploy, and why we have come to believe that "writing is not simply *one* way of knowing" but, rather "*the* way" (Dunn 15). I wonder if this overly narrow focus on the printed word isn't an artifact of our own education, our own historical worldview, our own personal investment in print and its products. Similarly, I wonder why the multimodal texts that we and students now so frequently encounter in the world shouldn't inform some of the rhetorically based reading and composing activities we take up within our classes.

WORKS CITED

Berger, John. *Ways of Seeing*. London: Penguin, 1972. Print.

Cope, Bill, and Mary Kalantzis, eds. *Multiliteracies: Literacy Learning and the Design of Social Futures*. London: Routledge, 2000. Print.

Costanzo, William. "Film as Composition." *College Composition and Communication*. 37.1 (1986): 79–86. Print.

Dunn, Patricia A. *Learning Re-Abled: The Learning Disability Controversy and Composition Studies*. Portsmouth: Boynton/Cook, 1995.

George, Diana. "From Analysis to Design: Visual Communication in the Teaching of Writing." *College Composition and Communication* 54.1 (2002): 11–39.

Race, Rhetoric, and Technology
A Case Study of Decolonial Technical Communication Theory, Methodology, and Pedagogy

Angela M. Haas

This article engages disciplinary (and interdisciplinary) conversations at the intersections of race, rhetoric, technology, and technical communication and offers a case study of curriculum development that supports disciplinary inquiry at these complex interstices. Specifically, informed by a decolonial framework, this article discusses the status of cultural and critical race studies in technical communication scholarship; tentative definitions of race, rhetoric, and technology; the cultural usability research conducted and located accountability in the process of designing a graduate course that studies rhetorics of race and technology; and the implications of this inquiry for the discipline, field, and practices of technical communication.

This is a hypertext—part informal report on my work toward listening to theory, building a course, and selecting the right tools for the job; part status report on where the discipline is at in its work at the interstices of race and technical communication studies; part disciplinary, curricular, and pedagogical praxis; part lesson plan for examining the ongoing legacies of imperialism in the Americas on and in our disciplinary work; part memoir of

First published in *Journal of Business and Technical Communication* 26.3 (2012): 277–310.
Copyright © 2012 by Angela M. Haas. Reprinted by permission of SAGE Publications..

a pretenure faculty trying to pay her fine graduate training forward and make her work usable and useful for her students and herself.

The first graduate seminar I taught at Illinois State University (ISU) was a topics course in technology in English Studies that I named race, rhetoric, and technology after the book that inspired it, Banks's (2006) *Race, Rhetoric, and Technology*. The course itself and the intellectual work therein would certainly have been more enriched by the recent conversations about race and ethnicity emerging in the discipline today (Banks, 2011; Ding, 2009; Savage & Mattson, 2011; Savage & Matveeva, 2011; Williams, 2010), but little scholarship concerning race existed in our field when I designed the course in 2009. Thus, I had to piece together a curriculum I could believe in by weaving together the scant threads of inquiry on race, rhetoric, and technology in our field with some of the existing strands in cultural, critical race, rhetorical, and feminist studies. Collectively, this interdisciplinary inquiry provided me and my students with multiple places to stand in the field at connected but different intellectual intersections.

This article maps out these intellectual locations by tracing conversations at the intersections of race, rhetoric, technology, and technical communication studies that informed this graduate course. Although these conversations transpired before, during, and after I taught this graduate course, I situate them primarily within the context of this graduate course so as to demonstrate how place matters. Despite this localization, I also situate this case study within larger discussions of race, ethnicity, and culture in technical communication and computers and composition studies. To be sure, this article offers a literature review on the status of race studies in technical communication scholarship and pedagogy and the tentative definitions of race, rhetoric, and technology from which I operate and that informed the course design. Further, I describe the course-design process—from prototype to delivery—including cultural usability research; my decolonial and located accountability approach to employing theories, methodologies, and pedagogies in my curricula; as well as some of my missteps along the way. Moreover, I provide disciplinary and pedagogical implications of this inquiry by discussing multiple intellectual openings for further study at the intersections of race, rhetoric, and technology and calling for future work on issues of race and ethnicity in technical communication research, pedagogy, and practice. Ultimately, this article demonstrates how race and place matter to technical communication research, scholarship, curriculum design, and pedagogy. In fact, they are key to what can be imagined, what gets imagined, and who imagines in our profession.

INTERDISCIPLINARY WORK IN
RACE + RHETORIC + TECHNOLOGY

This story of disciplinary work at the intersections of race, rhetoric, and technology studies is likely an untraditional one, so I worry about its reception. To explain, I did not enter the field of technical communication in a conventional way. Disenchanted by my 2½ years of secondary teaching experience, I started looking for another job to carry me until I could go on to graduate school. I ultimately applied for and was offered a new technical writing position at the factory where my mom worked for more than 20 years. I took the job but was not excited about it for a number of reasons. For one, I took the job not because I chose it but because I was fleeing my other job. But most important, as a mixed-race, working-class, first-generation college graduate, I never wanted to work in a factory like my parents and grandparents did. That is one of the reasons I went to college, after all.

In sum, I had technical writing experience long before I had course work in it—doing technical communication work at three different jobs at three different-sized factories that all were within the automotive industry. But I was not trained in the discipline of technical communication until 10 years later. And that academic training differed from my lived, embodied field experiences as a trained technical communicator for an industry doing rhetorical, technical, and technological work. Thus, I bring to this story of the discipline—perhaps more aptly understood as a story from the periphery of the discipline—a subjectivity that has steered me toward the borderlands of inquiry in computers and composition and in technical communication, looking for where either or both intersect with cultural studies so that I could recognize myself in what I read at times and so that I might have a place to stand in the discipline as I did in the workplace.

At the time, I designed the race, rhetoric, and technology course in spring 2009 and taught it in fall 2009, a growing concern with cultural studies was emerging within technical communication scholarship. Although several scholars were concerned with the cultural influences and effects of technical communication practices prior to the late 1990s (Flynn, 1997; Herndl, 1993; Katz, 1992, 1993; Slack, Miller, & Doak, 1993), Longo (1998) explicitly made the case for technical communication scholarship that is grounded in cultural studies inquiry so that we might more fully account for the ways in which "struggles for knowledge legitimation . . . are influenced by [larger cultural] institutional, political, economic, and/or social relationships, pressures, and tensions" (p. 61).

821

Thankfully, many in the field responded to Longo's call, which resulted in a growing number of case studies of international and cross-cultural technical communication (Barnum & Huilin, 2006), international and intercultural rhetorics of professional communication (St. Germaine-Madison, 2006; Thatcher, 2000, 2006), postcolonial technical communication (Jeyaraj, 2004), race and regulatory writing (Williams, 2006), disability studies and technical communication (Palmeri, 2006), and health and risk communication in cultural and community contexts (Bowdon, 2004; Sauer, 2003; Scott, 2003)—to name just a few strands of inquiry and some of the scholars engaging with them. Further, in 2006, Scott and Longo's special issue of *Technical Communication Quarterly* provided the field with a critical collection of essays that simultaneously evidence, justify, and call for the field's move toward making the "cultural turn." And Scott, Longo, and Wills (2006) edited the pivotal collection *Critical Power Tools: Technical Communication and Cultural Studies* that

> testifies and responds to the field's need for more research and teaching approaches that historicize technical communication's roles in hegemonic power relations—approaches that are openly critical of nonegalitarian, unethical practices and subject positions, that promote values other than conformity, efficiency, and effectiveness, and that account for technical communication's broader cultural conditions, circulation, and effects. (p. 1)

The intellectual work of these scholars makes evident that cultural studies approaches to technical communication research, practice, and pedagogy can guide and support us in creating more culturally responsive and responsible texts that accommodate their users.

Despite this promise of cultural studies work in technical communication, only a few scholars within our field are doing work specifically and explicitly at the intersections of race, ethnicity, rhetoric, and technology studies. Thus, while I did use some of the aforementioned work—as well as cultural theory (de Certeau, 1984; Foucault, 1972; Spurr, 1993)—to frame the course, we focused our inquiry around the work of scholars in technical communication who specifically work at the intersections of race, rhetoric, technology, and technical communication. Specifically, we studied Sun's (2006) theory of cultural usability and case study of Chinese cell phone users; Banks's (2006) critique of the "whitinizing" of media, theory of transformative access, and historiographical case studies of AfricanAmerican traditions of technology and design (e.g., slave quilts, black architecture, urban planning); and Johnson,

Pimentel, and Pimentel's (2008) critical race framework that demonstrated the normalization of whiteness in early technical documents on New Mexico.[1] Collectively, this work helped me, my students, and the discipline to consider more deeply how race affects the ways in which technologies and documents are designed and used, how national and political values can inspire users to transform the work of technologies beyond their designed intent, and how non-Western cultures use and produce with Western and non-Western technologies differently than Westerners do. Perhaps in this increasingly global marketplace that supposedly values user-centered design, such research might remind us that all our users are not reflections of ourselves.

Unfortunately, this work was not enough to build a graduate course on, so I looked to scholars in computers and composition inquiry, as well as cultural and communication studies, in order to facilitate rich discussions about race, rhetoric, and technology in technical communication studies. Thus, the work that I used to build on that foundational research included, but was not limited to, the following texts[2]: Ebo's (1998) cultural critique of race, class, and gender on the Internet; Gómez Peña's (1996) work on the "Chicano Interneta"; Kolko, Nakamura, and Rodman's (2000) edited collection that interrogates race in cyberspace; Nelson, Tu, and Hines's (2001) compilation of case studies that explore the relationships between race and technology and how people of color use technologies in their everyday lives; Bray's (1997) gynotechnics theoretical framework and historiography of Chinese women's technological innovation in imperial China; Fernandez, Wilding, and Wright's (2003) edited collection that interrogates the intersections of discourses on race, technology, and cyberfeminisms; Monroe's (2004) cross-examination of the digital divide in relation to race, writing, and technology in the classroom; Nakamura's (2007) investigation of digital racial formations and networked media images of user's racialized bodies; and Wilson and Stewart's (2008) edited collection of case studies of technological and design practices of global indigenous communities.

Although our inquiry can clearly benefit from these studies, I think that the discipline of technical communication is on the verge of reciprocating by contributing to the interdisciplinary work transpiring at the intersections of race, rhetoric, and technology. To do so, I suggest that we begin a more visible discussion about how the relationship between the three can and should affect technical communication inquiry and practices. In the next section, I attempt to do just that.

DEFINING RACE, RHETORIC, AND TECHNOLOGY

Now that I have better situated this article in relation to the field, in this section, I contextualize the inquiry that transpired in and thus informed this graduate course and invite technical communication scholars and practitioners to contribute further to the conversation. Specifically, I provide the epistemological and decolonial framework for my understanding of race, rhetoric, and technology and acknowledge that this framework and the corresponding reading choices prescribed certain understandings for students enrolled in the course. My definitions are dynamic, rather than static, because they are open to revision as I continue to learn from the overlaps with and divergences from other definitions to which colleagues in the field may subscribe. Therefore, in the spirit of rhetoric, I offer these definitions as openings to future conversations in our field, not definitive answers, so that our uniquely situated field might further contribute to disciplinary, interdisciplinary, and everyday understandings of race, rhetoric, and technology.

Defining Race

To begin, my understandings of race are heavily influenced by critical race theory. Given this, I assign readings that engage technical communication students with critical rhetorics and histories of race, ethnicity, and racism that critique the limitations of the notion that race is genetic or biological. For one, race is a rhetorical construct, but it is not only rhetorical. As language and literacy scholar Gilyard (2004) explained, "race, constructed or not, is real in its effects" (p. ix). It is a real lived, social, political, embodied experience that affects everyone, directly or indirectly, on an everyday basis. According to anthropologist and African American studies scholar Smedley (2007), race

> *does indeed exist* and should be viewed not as something biologically tangible and existing in the outside world that has to be discovered, described, and defined, but as a cultural creation, a product of human invention very much like fairies, leprechauns, banshees, ghosts, and werewolves. (p. 5)

From its first persistent usage in reference to humans in the 18th century, race was and is one way of perceiving, interpreting, and dealing with difference— sustained by the ideological model of dividing and categorizing separate, exclusive groups that are conceived and perceived as inherently unequal human populations. Thus, Smedley's (2007) work helps us to understand that race is not only rhetorical but a systematic worldview used to justify conflict and competition—and ultimately racism. Despite that race is a rhetorical construct not only informed by, but representative of, a worldview, rhetorics of race operate within U.S. culture in specific ways. Smedley (2007) explained that

> race signifies rigidity and permanence of position and status within a ranking order that is based on what is believed to be the unalterable reality of innate biological differences. Ethnicity is conditional, temporal, even volitional, and not amenable to biology or biological processes. (p. 34)

Thus, despite that rhetorics of ethnicity may be more etymologically and culturally accurate when engaging issues of ethnic difference, rhetorics of race are highly prevalent in public discourse and are thus useful in engaging others in critical discussions of race. As Gilyard (2004) put it, "given how saturated with conceptions of race our society is, . . . utilizing the semantic term race is unavoidable if one is truly interested in communicating with large numbers of people not only to contest racial reasoning but also to contest, in a concrete way, racial hierarchies" (p. ix).

Race scientists argue that although humans are 99.9 percent alike genetically, the remaining 0.1 percent difference is highly significant. But Smedley (2007) countered that no research into this slight biological difference can help us to understand the phenomenon of race in U.S. society; only the domain of sociocultural studies can. To facilitate student engagement with this domain, some of the readings that I assigned in the first few weeks of the semester included selections from Smedley's work, rhetoric and composition scholar Villanueva's (1999) article "On the Rhetoric and Precedents of Racism," selections from legal scholar E. N. Gates's (1997) edited collection of critical race theory, H. L. Gates's (1986) edited collection on the relationships between race, writing, and difference, and Johnson et al.'s (2008) study of the rhetorics of whiteness and racism in early technical communication about New Mexico.

Collectively, these texts offer readers highly complex and historically situated rhetorical, social, and ideological understandings of race. But Johnson et al.'s (2008) work brings these conversations to technical communication studies. To be sure, they use a critical race and whiteness theoretical framework—informed by an understanding that "race is a social construction that is neither stable nor objective" (p. 213)—to determine the various ways in which whiteness emerges in these early technical documents vis-à-vis "color blindness (refusal to see color), selective attribution (specific application of race), whitewashing (the removal of race for whites), and privileged language (the valuation of one knowledge or ideology over another)" (p. 215).

More so than many scholars realize, engaging in conversations of critical race theory can work toward more culturally responsible understandings of how race and ethnicity influence technical communication theories, methodologies, pedagogies, and practices. We often like to believe that technical communication, like legal writing, is written objectively and is void of culture, thus making it more accessible. But just as legal scholar Williams (1991) demonstrated that legal writing is indeed not void of culture but is instead saturated in white male culture, I argue that technical communication also has a history of ignoring the ways in which our work is saturated with white male culture—which has real effects related to privilege and oppression on the lives and work of designers, writers, editors, and audiences of technical communication. Race is the marked Other; when unmarked and unnamed, it goes unnoticed. Critical race theory helps us to understand that all writing is subjective and influenced by our race as well as other intersecting identities, such as ethnicity, nationality, class, gender, generation, sexuality, ability and disability, and religion and spirituality.

Thus, critical race theory also helps us to engage in important discussions on whiteness as part of the larger complex conversation of race. Whiteness often goes underexamined, as many in U.S. society think that only people of color have a racial identity. Take, for instance, Arizona's ban on ethnic studies (Arizona's Revised Statutes, 2010). The ban does not include the study of British literature (or other European literature) even though it is also an ethnic study. It focuses only on banning the study of particular (read *Other*) ethnicities, such as Latino, Chicano, and America-Indian histories and literatures. Further, the ethnic hair section of the cosmetics in grocery and beauty supply stories signifies a particular (read *Other*) ethnic hair when in reality all hair is ethnic. As cultural critic Fusco put it, "racial identities are not only black, Latino, Asian, Native American, and so on; they are also white. To ignore white ethnicity is to redouble its hegemony by naturalising it. Without specifically addressing white ethnicity, there can be no critical evaluation of the construction of the other" (cited in hooks, 1990b, p. 171).

Given this necessity to address white ethnicity and the accepted view of technical communicators as public intellectuals, my class also engaged in discussions of whiteness by reading Roediger's (1997) critique that social construction approaches to understanding race "work" intellectually but that this understanding is not enough. Arguing that we need clearer political directions and subsequent actions for matters of race and class, he offered one direction for this action, an attack on whiteness with a "central focus on exposing how whiteness is used to make whites settle for hopelessness in politics and misery in everyday life"—as well as to justify feelings of "community-lessness" among those who make destructive claims of "reverse racism" rather than productive injunctions of "reverse racism (now)!" (pp. 16–17). This work helps to situate whiteness as a racial construct too, but one that also must be interrogated. As many critical race theorists make clear, critiquing racism often proves to be limited and shallow without integrating a deep critique of whiteness.

Finally, as part of this critique of whiteness, we should closely examine the growing misperception that we are living in a post-race society. I posit that so many white people want to believe that the United States is postrace precisely because of the lie of whiteness and the problems therein. Roediger (2007) discussed some of these problems:

> There is an American culture, but it is thoroughly "mulatto." . . . If there is a Southern culture, it is still more thoroughly mulatto than the broader American one. There are Irish American songs, Italian neighborhoods, Slavic American traditions, German American villages, and so on. But such specific ethnic cultures always stand in danger of being swallowed by the lie of whiteness. Whiteness describes, from Little Big Horn to Simi Valley, not a culture but precisely the absence of culture. It is empty and therefore terrifying to attempt to build an identity based on what one isn't and whom one can hold back. (p. 13)

Once people give up their own ethnic cultures, they are less likely to advocate for the sustainability of others' cultures. The belief in a post-race society is also a convenient way of absolving citizens of the responsibility for knowing the history of race relations in this nation, the ways in which the legacies of colonialism and racism still play out today, and the ways in which we are both survivors of and complicit in the legacies of both. To promote this knowledge, the aforementioned readings were supplemented with statistics from surveys of people of color, including how regularly they incur racist incidents, and popular news articles about race-based incidents in the news at the time (fall 2009), such as the arrest of Harvard professor Henry Louis Gates by Sergeant James Crowley of the Cambridge Police Department when Gates attempted to enter his own home, the accusations that Supreme Court justice Sonia Sotomayor was biased and a racist (based on her acknowledging that she is woman of Latina lineage), and a Philadelphia swim club's exclusion of a summer-camp class full of black children (fearing that the children would "change the complexion" of the pool)—to name just a few. Reading stories of everyday racism may help students from all backgrounds to realize that racism still persists and is further compounded by the burden placed on people of color to be the only ones who recognize that—and they affirm the stories of students whose lives have been controlled by and bodies have been marked by racism.

In sum, the course reading and the dialogue it fosters provide a scaffold for critical discussions about race, rhetoric, and technology. Ultimately, I promote a critical approach to talking about race in the discipline, workplace, classroom, and society because it opens up critical conversations about all races and complicates our understandings of race, ethnicity, multiculturalism, whiteness, diversity, racism, ethnocentrism, and post-race. Further, this critical race approach is intersectional in its understandings of race and as it relates to ethnicity, nationality, class, gender, generation, sexuality, ability and disability, and religion and spirituality. A critical race approach maps and reads these representational and relational dynamics—in any media or mode—and is concerned with cultural histories and material bodies. It is critical in service of social justice. As Gilyard (2004) elucidated, "critical ethnicity [and race] is a search for the elements in various ethnic narratives that have the most political potential in a push for a more humane society, and it represents an impulse to share the fruits of that search with our students" (p. ix).

Defining Rhetoric

Given that conversations about rhetoric have been widespread in the field of technical communication, this section will be brief. Further, all but one of the students in the course had some training in rhetoric, but I nonetheless provided students with my decolonial approach to rhetoric and assigned some required and recommended readings on rhetoric. To be clear, I understand *rhetoric* as the negotiation of cultural information—and its historical, social, economic, and political influences—to affect social action (persuade). I also believe that every culture has its own rhetorical roots, traditions, and practices. Although sometimes forgotten, rhetoric seeks engagement with and participation in effective and responsible civic discourse. Rhetoric is a techné, or art of knowing—a revealing, an opening up. Atwill (1998) offered several characteristics of techne:

1. A techné is never a static normative body of knowledge. It may be described as a dynamis (or power), transferable guides and strategies, a cunningly conceived plan—even a trick or trap. This knowledge is stable enough to be taught and transferred but flexible enough to be adapted to particular situations and purposes.
2. A techné resists identification with a normative subject. The subjects identified with techné are often in a state of flux or transformation . . . .
3. Techné marks a domain of intervention and invention. (p. 48)

In sum, rhetoric is always already cultural. It takes into account that subjectivity and knowledge are interrelated. Despite that rhetoric relies on stabilizing this knowledge in order to represent it to others, that knowledge can only be fixed momentarily and tentatively because dynamic social, historical, cultural, political, and economic factors continue to influence its production—and what individuals can know and the knowledge that rhetoric can represent is limited. Thus, rhetoric is a result, a precursor, and a limit to productive knowledge making.

Rhetoric ties to race and to technology in two common ways: (a) Rhetoric has historically worked to prescribe, limit, categorize, and define both race and technology, and (b) rhetoric has historically worked to upend prescribed, limited, categorized, and defined notions of race and technology, thereby opening up new discussions about race and technology. Thus, rhetoric can both reinscribe traditional notions of race and technology and revise them in ways that reveal or support new understandings.

In essence, for decolonial ideologies to emerge, new rhetorics must be spoken, written, or otherwise delivered into existence. Even in the most progressive spaces and places, the colonial rhetorical detritus[3] of racism and ethnocentrism remains, and if these worldviews and rhetorics go unchallenged, they will continue to influence who and what we think of when we consider issues of race and technological literacy and expertise. Thus, I challenge myself, the discipline, my colleagues, and my students to consider how the language we use might serve to redress the long standing legacies of colonialism and imperialism, particularly in the rhetoric that we choose to employ to represent our work and the work of others. Thus, in my graduate course we read several online resources that provide general overviews of rhetoric and rhetorical studies in conjunction with Villanueva's (1999) work on the rhetorics and precedents of racism and selections from Spurr's (1993) heuristic for recognizing and interrogating the rhetorics of empire.

Defining Technology

My understanding of technology is informed by cultural and rhetorical theories as together these theories interrogate how inequalities of power are produced, maintained, and transformed through culture and its rhetorics. If employed not just for analysis but also for the redressing of these inequalities, these theories can facilitate broader, more flexible, and more historically situated definitions of technology and intercultural considerations of technological theories and practices: definitions that reflect a larger history of technological design and use by people of color and that in turn rupture widely held theoretical and political assumptions and racial stereotypes about technological expertise.

Increasingly, computers and composition and technical communication inquiry recognizes technologies not as transparent things but as cultural artifacts imbued with histories and values that shape the ways in which people see themselves and others in relation to technology. In fact, disciplinary scholarship within the last five years demonstrates a trend in concern for the relationships between rhetoric, technology, and culture (Alexander & Banks, 2004; Banks, 2006, 2011; Blackmon, 2002, 2007; Haas, 2005; Monroe, 2004). Thus, technology is both integral to culture and always already cultural. Just as the rhetoric we compose can never be objective, neither can the technologies we design. Technologies are not neutral or objective—nor are the ways that we use them. It takes just one short discussion of the slave branding iron and the technologies of the eugenics movement to make this clear to technical communication students.

Similarly, just as rhetoric is a techné, so too is technology. People tend to conflate new media with definitions of technology, heralding as technologies only the emerging ones and relegating to tools or crafts the older and more ubiquitous technologies. This rhetorical privileging of new over old is reminiscent of the colonial high and low art debates and thus works to obscure, if not erase, diverse traditions of technological use, production, and expertise. Thus, I position technology as a techné in light of this colonial conflict of connotation. Ross (2005) traced the rhetorical roots of technology, reporting that in the early 17th century, "'technology' was used to describe a systematic treatment, for example, a study of the arts, especially the useful or mechanical arts" and that in the mid-19th century, "its chief use pertained to industrial crafts. These applied skills and techniques were identified with manufacture and trade" (p. 342). Not long after this time, the investment in scientific research—as well as a number of other cultural, capitalist, political influences—eroded the distinction between science and technology and increased the distinctions and hierarchies between arts, crafts, tools, machines, and technologies.

What communication scholars Slack and Wise (2005) found most curious about these historical definitions is that they "treat technology as an application, capability, manner of doing, and specialized aspect, but not as a thing.' In contrast, "when technology is referred to in popular discourse [today], . . . it is almost always as things (tractors, pacemakers, computers, and so on)." Further, Slack and Wise provided examples of typical dictionary definitions that situate the most common meaning of *technology* as "things that are useful; that is, as things that have . . . some 'practical application.' So technology is, at least in terms of its most popular usage, a constructed and useful thing" (p. 95).

This definition of technology as a thing has its affordances and limits. For one, it allows us to position a technology as something discrete and isolatable from culture—and thus observable and knowable. But as Slack and Wise (2005) demonstrated, "the formulation of technology as things that are useful deflects vision toward the tool-like use of these things, and away from the work or role of these things beyond matters of usefulness" (p. 97). Thus, rhetoric and cultural studies help us to better theorize the interdependent relationships between living and nonliving actors as well as the rhetorical and cultural work that technologies do in our everyday lives (in the discipline, our classrooms, popular media, workplaces, and beyond).

Given all that, it is critical that we interrogate the tension between technology as things, technology as work, and technology in relation to multiple and diverse actors when we grapple with the technicalities of technology. Elizabeth Grosz suggested that "technology is that which ensures and continually refines the ongoing negotiations between bodies and things, that deepening investment of the one, the body, in the other, the thing" (as cited in Slack & Wise, 2005, p. 97). Further, using a cultural and rhetorical theory—specifically a study of the rhetorics of empire (Spurr, 1993) and Slack and Wise's *Culture þ Technology*—we can interrogate Western paradigms and rhetorics of progress, convenience, and control as they pertain to our understanding of technology and who we consider technologically literate or advanced. Ultimately, this interrogation can help us to think through technologies and our relationships to them as rhetorical and technological assemblages and articulations.

Through this interrogation, we can imagine broader definitions of technology in more responsible ways—historically and culturally—than we can with contemporary fixations on new media. A critical step toward this broader understanding is to closely study the relationships between older and newer media. Haas (1999) posited that "the relationship between old and new technologies is complex and often fraught in practice, and it is one that deserves a rich theoretical accounting . . . [that goes] beyond oversimplified, bifurcated models of technological development." To critique these models—the *simple replacement model*, "which assumes that old and new technologies are clearly differentiated from one another, both theoretically and in practice, and that new technologies simply replace older, obsolete technologies," and the *straightforward progress model*, "a new-is-better view in which new technologies are more advanced and therefore more efficient, more powerful, or both" (p. 210)—Haas observed and reported on three case studies of relationships between old and new technologies. Ultimately, her study evidences that the relationship realities in three different workplaces fall short of the standard, oversimplified explanations of the relationship between literacy and old and new technologies—and that there is much to learn from older media in order to imagine more useful and usable technologies and workplaces in the future.

I suggest that we would be in a better position to engage in rich theoretical accountings of the relationships between old and new technologies if we included diverse and underrepresented histories of technological use, production, and expertise in our disciplinary conversations. In ways that bring to technical communication what Powell (2002) called for in rhetoric and composition studies, we must "gather up the strands from our multiple participations . . . name them as relatives and take them home" (p. 19). For example, in an earlier article (Haas, 2007), I composed a hypertextual, decolonial, historiographical narrative that simultaneously recovered traditional histories of hypertext and digital rhetoric from the shadows of new media and engaged a "new," underrepresented history of American Indian hypertextual and digital rhetorical work. To do so, I positioned wampum belts, a beaded belt that signifies alliances, as a technology. Further, in cultural anthropologist Bray's (1997) historiography of Chinese women's technological innovation in imperial China, she developed a new theoretical framework for technology studies, *gynotechnics*, "a technical system that produces ideas about women, and therefore about a gender system and about hierarchical relations in general." In doing so, Bray contextualized her study within three technological sites that are "particularly important in giving shape and meaning to the lives of women in late imperial China: the building of houses, the weaving of cloth, and the producing of children" (p. 4). Finally, in a cultural usability case study, Sun (2006) demonstrated the centrality of culture and ethnicity to localization practices.

In addition to these studies of technological use along racial and gender lines are other studies that help us to better historicize how certain technologies have been unequally delegated and prescribed along gender, ethnic, class, and ability lines—and how technologies prescribe identities— in conjunction with our disciplinary studies on technical communication in a variety of contemporary and historical workplaces and living spaces. For example, Slack and Wise (2005) offered a case study of the bridges over the parkways on Long Island, which were designed and built with amazingly low overpasses (with only 9 feet of clearance in some places) that prevented those who drive trucks or ride busses from accessing Long Island. According to Robert Caro, the biographer of Robert Moses, the architect who designed these bridges—as well as many other major public works in New York from the 1920s through the 1970s— Moses deliberately designed the overpasses "to hinder poor people and blacks, not only from using the parkways, but also from accessing Jones Beach, a park Moses designed. In this case, the task delegated to the technology was in part that of racial and class discrimination" (as cited in Slack & Wise, 2005, p. 158). Thus, technology is not just what does the work, it is the work—and that work relies on an ongoing relationship between bodies and things. It is precisely this understanding that informs my article (Haas, 2007) that situates wampum belts (used by many tribes indigenous to the United States) as hypertextual—and the race, rhetoric, and technology course design. Specifically, this course aims to rupture racial stereotypes and widely held theoretical and political assumptions by providing case studies on certain culturally situated technological practices of a specific race, using a broader, more flexible, and more historically situated definition of technology and considerations of technological theories and practices. The case studies thus reflect a larger history of technological design and use by people of color and other underrepresented populations.

Summary: Assemblages of Race, Rhetoric, and Technology

Although many may understand rhetorics on race and technology as texts about technology that are composed by and for people of color, we must remember that race is a colonial rhetorical by-product that seeks to erase diversity in ethnicity, including the diversity in the ethnicity of European Americans here in the United States. Thus, such rhetorics are concerned with discursive forms, strategies, and tactics of particular ethnic and technological assemblages and the rhetorical work therein. As technical communication scholars, teachers, practitioners, public intellectuals, and activists, we should be concerned with how these assemblages are constructed and represented in technical communication theories, methodologies, pedagogies, and practices. In fact, I posit that we have an ethical obligation to do so. Engaging critical race theories—and other complementary cultural theories—can help us to foster deeper understandings of the ways in which the relationships between race, rhetoric, and technology have complex implications for all areas of our field, from user-centered research, risk communication, regulatory writing, and legal literacies to information architecture, digital and visual rhetoric, medical rhetoric, scientific rhetoric, workplace writing, globalization and localization, community informatics, curricular programs, pedagogy, and more. The sections that follow are my humble offerings to thinking through just a few of the possible implications and results of this type of inquiry, of using critical race theory and decolonial pedagogy for the sake of extending those theories and building new ones that are usable and useful for the field of technical communication, as broadly understood.

SPRING 2009: DESIGNING RACE, RHETORIC, AND TECHNOLOGY

I originally designed this course for the fall 2007–spring 2008 job-market cycle, and I circulated an abbreviated syllabus for it at every face-to-face interview. So my technical communication colleagues knew that I wanted to teach the course from the moment they hired me in 2008, and they supported me in this endeavor. Given that two years had passed since the initial design and that I now had a specific audience instead of an imagined one, revisions were necessary. Thus, I conducted an informal cultural usability study on the prototype of the curriculum design. To do so, I engaged the work of cultural usability scholars (Suchman, 2000; Sun, 2006) to help me to critically and reflexively review and revise my initial curriculum design so that it might simultaneously appeal to a localized population of ISU graduate students and meet my intellectual and curricular goals—and to account for any scholarship at the intersections of race, rhetoric, and technology that emerged during those two years.

Although Suchman's (2000) critical sensibility to design was tied to technologies, it can and should inform curriculum design as well. She promoted the paradigm shift of design from nowhere to views from somewhere by engaging in what she called "located accountability," which is

> precisely the fact that our vision of the world is a vision from somewhere—
> that it's based in an embodied, and therefore partial, perspective—that makes

us personally responsible for it. The only possibility for the creation of effective technologies, from this perspective, is through collective knowledge of the particular and multiple locations of their production and use. (n.p.)

This approach to design both relieves me of the responsibility to possibly cover all things related to race, rhetoric, and technology for all possible students and expects me to be transparent about and accountable for how my positionality and subjectivities influence my course-design decisions.

Given my investment in located accountability, then, I must confess that I had little more than one semester's experience in this new institutional and geographic location before the deadline for course descriptions and thus had limited experience with "locating [myself] within the extended networks of working relations" that constituted the pedagogical system from which I was working, which is required of located accountability in any technical system. As Suchman (2000) put it, "Working relations are understood as sociomaterial connections that sustain the visible and invisible work required to construct coherent technologies and put them into use" (n.p.). Applied to curricular and pedagogical systems, then, working relations are the relational and sociomaterial connections required to design usable and useful curriculum. Although I was confident about programmatic buy-in, I had limited experience with a small pool of potential target users of my course before revising and promoting the design prototype. So I began my informal, discount cultural usability research with my primary target users: graduate students in English Studies.[4]

Primary Target Users: ISU Graduate Students

A better understanding of my primary target users, ISU graduate students, and their expectations depends on a better understanding of the institutional context in which the faculty, students, and staff operate as well. Briefly, the Technology in English Studies graduate course serves as one of eight course options for the technical writing and new media studies area of the master's in professional writing and rhetorics degree program, but it is not required for any degree completion. Therefore, I had to design this course to appeal to graduate students across all areas of English studies and perhaps even outside the Department of English in order to persuade students to enroll in this course and ensure that the course would *make*, or be viable. I spoke with and e-mailed the graduate students I knew in the department, pitched the course title and brief abstract, and then asked them about their interest and concerns. Only two students at that time seemed interested in race studies and the course, and one was finished with his course work. I assumed that he would decide not to enroll in the course, but after speaking with me, he decided to audit the course and write a chapter of his dissertation for it. So at that point, I had two students signed up for the course, both interested in technical communication: one student in the first year of her PhD who was interested in transnational feminism and technology studies, the other a PhD candidate interested in studying the localization of the sexual-pharmaceutical instructions in Ghana. I became concerned that the course would not make, so as I and the two loyal students grew more excited about the course, I went to my secondary target users: the graduate director and my colleagues in the rhetoric, composition, and technical communication caucus.

I asked each colleague who had much more experience with my primary target users to try to give the course some good press and recruit some potential students for the course. Confiding to a few of them that I worried that the course title might be too progressive for the primarily moderate, Midwestern, Euro-American audience served by the Department of English, I asked whether I should change the course title to cultural rhetorics and technology. Two colleagues conveyed that they supported me and the course and thought I should stand behind my course as is. A senior colleague, however, advised me to accommodate a more diverse cultural studies and interdisciplinary approach to designing the course but to keep the title of the course as is. He was convinced that if I changed the title, the course would sound less "racy" and "edgy." Although I thought that perhaps the course should sound less race based in order to appeal to a broader audience with less experience in critically engaging in discussions about race, the context of our conversation made it evident that he meant that the change in the title would make the course sound less exciting and exotic.

Although I was initially troubled by this senior colleague's advice and whether I should follow it, I deeply wanted to teach the course. I needed this course for me and my students. I know what reading Banks's (2006) *Race, Rhetoric, and Technology* meant to me when I first read it midway through my PhD. I recognized the possibility in that book: a possible space for race and technology studies in rhetoric and composition and technical communication studies—room for my work. So I revised the course. I made room in it for my students' work. I wanted them to recognize themselves in some of the readings. (Many white students who attend ISU do not recognize themselves as part of one or more ethnic groups. They see people of color as belonging to races, not white people.) To do so, I changed the course description to further appeal to a broader English studies audience, and I employed rhetoric that signified a broader cultural studies approach to the course rather than my original focus on decolonial and critical race theories. Despite making these changes to the curb appeal of the course, I kept the infrastructure predominantly the same, with the exception of paring down a few of the required chapters in the texts and adding some cultural theory and Jenkins's (2008) *Convergence Culture*.[5]

I then followed my colleague's additional advice to send the revised course description to the caucus and graduate director to ask them to distribute it widely. This is the description of the course that circulated:

> Race, Rhetoric, & Technology. Drawing on rhetorical, cultural, and critical race theories, this course interrogates the complex relationships between cultures, rhetorics, and technologies in an effort to migrate away from studies of a monolithic technological culture and toward studies of specific, multiple and varied cultures of technological expertise. Specifically, we will study the everyday technological theories and practices of specific, culturally-situated communities and the intersectionality of those practices with race, ethnicity, nationality, class, gender, generation, sexuality, (dis)ability, and religion. Further, in response to Western obsessions with new media, we will examine rhetorics that employ broader, more flexible, and more historically situated definitions of technology and considerations of technological theories and practices that allow us to develop a deeper understanding of the relationships between older and newer technologies. Ultimately, this course serves a response to calls from cultural rhetoric scholars like Villanueva, Royster, Gilyard, Powell, Lyons, Ming Mao, Monberg, and Young to decolonize the Western rhetorical canon and epistemology, from computers & writing scholars Selfe & Selfe (1994) for writing faculty who teach with technology to be more cognizant of the colonial constructs that we may inadvertently reinscribe in our classrooms, and from technical communication scholars Scott & Longo (2006) for our discipline to make a cultural turn and to retheorize our theories and practices as assemblages of "contested, localized, conjunctural knowledges" that must be put into dialogue. Further, our inquiry in this class will contribute to intellectual trends over the last decade that recognize technology not as transparent things but as cultural artifacts imbued with histories and values—histories and values that shape the ways in which people see themselves and others in relation to technology.

Before course-cutting time, nine students were enrolled: the original two technical communication graduate students, a PhD student in rhetoric and composition, three masters students in the professional writing and rhetorics sequence, a masters student in the visual culture program (in the art history department), a high school teacher needing graduate credits for state licensure, and an at-large graduate student who just returned to school that semester. I needed five students to remain enrolled through the first week of classes in the fall.

Secondary Target User: The Professor

In complying with located accountability, I am making transparent that I am justifying some of the changes to you, my dear reader, and to myself by expressing my desire to make room in the course for my students' work. But as a mixed-race, German American/Eastern Cherokee, working-class, first-generation college graduate, decolonial feminist, I also wanted room for my work. And there were books that I thought they needed to read, but I also wanted to read them in order to be able to engage in smart dialogue with others interested in culture, power, media and technology, technical communication, and public and private rhetorics and to further my own research. My primary goals for the graduate course Race, Rhetoric, and Technology, then, were to

- build and gain facility with a variety of theories and methodologies that will assist us in the critical study of the complex relationship between rhetoric, race, and technology
- interrogate how ethnicity, nationality, class, gender, generation, sexuality, ability and disability, and religion and spirituality intersect with race within specific cultural sites of technological expertise
- examine how and why systems of power and rhetorics from those in power have historically shaped how we regard specific cultures in relation to their technological expertise—or lack thereof—and privilege new media over old media
- consider how globalization affects local technological economies and practices
- investigate local and grassroots tactics of resistance to systems and rhetorics from or of power
- study specific cultural sites of technological theories and practices and the texts and discourses from and about those cultures
- encourage responsible and intellectual engagement with the technological traditions of Other cultures (instead of merely consuming them)

- position as ethical action deeper engagements with non-Western and nonpatriarchal cultural technological histories, discourses, and literatures
- facilitate knowledge work worthy of scholarly presentation or publication
- promote such intellectual work as social justice work within our disciplines and the world around us

To support these goals, I had specific texts in mind, some that I had read before, and some that I just wanted to read—and though I have not specified which texts were which, I have already mentioned the primary texts that I engaged in this course.

Also, I am invested in and thus deploy a decolonial feminist methodology in my course designs and a decolonial pedagogy in how I teach those courses, including this one. In brief, *decolonial* methodologies and pedagogies serve to (a) redress colonial influences on perceptions of people, literacy, language, culture, and community and the relationships therein and (b) support the coexistence of cultures, languages, literacies, memories, histories, places, and spaces—and encourage respectful and reciprocal dialogue between and across them. As part of this pedagogy, I interrogate how colonialism and imperialism have informed our understandings of race, rhetoric, and technology, including, but not limited to, how we have historically been informed about race via technology and technical communication and which races have been considered technically and technologically superior and inferior—and why. Thus, my pedagogical and curricular approach both builds on and extends feminist scholarship on technical communication and Grobman's (1999) call to employ multicultural perspectives in our pedagogy in order to transform our classrooms to contact zones.

Finally, as part of this decolonial methodology and pedagogy, I decided that—in spite of my prior lack of success in both maintaining and assigning blogs—I should maintain a class blog, with students maintaining their own individual blogs so that others in the discipline might read, engage with, and learn from the inquiry of our online learning community. I also thought that the class's digital intellectual work would help to inform others in the public sphere about colonial influences on the agency of specific racialized populations in relation to technology, thereby decolonizing our habits of mind and corresponding rhetorics as they pertain to race and technology relations. As Suchman (2000) put it, "Our interventions in identities and relations of technology production are part of a larger enterprise of disrupting and remaking the social world" (n.p.).

FALL 2009: TEACHING RACE, RHETORIC, AND TECHNOLOGY

All nine students showed up on the first day. The high school teacher dropped out after the first night of the course. The at-large student dropped out during week 3, after deciding that he was not ready to come back to school. I advised another student to drop the course after week 6 because the student had made back-to-back, borderline racist and sexist verbal attacks toward me and a fellow student, the only student of color in the class. The attacks occurred during the latter student's class facilitation on international localization, glocalization, and globalization practices of technology transfers in general and subsequent presentation on the globalization of the sexual-pharmaceutical industry and its impacts on Ghana (i.e., how the lack of localized documentation accompanying sexual-enhancement drugs hinders medical and community literacies in Ghana and thus puts the lives of many Ghanians at risk). This left six students in the course.

The primary deliverables required in the course, in addition to regular attendance and contributions to the knowledge production of our learning community, included the following:

- *Weekly critical responses.* Students were expected to post 500- to 1,000-word responses to their blogs on a weekly basis. These were to briefly summarize the main ideas of the reading or readings for that week and then analyze some dimension of the author's argument (e.g., rhetoric, evidence, logic, implications). They did not need to be elegant, just engaging. (I posit that when students diligently and critically think through the readings prior to class, they engage in better classroom discussions and make more thoughtful connections between the readings and their own research, teaching, and professional trajectories.)

- *Class presentation.* Each student was charged with leading a 20- to 30-minute class discussion based on the readings for one week, their interpretations of the readings, their peers' interpretations, and their positions on a critical issue related to or raised by the readings. They were to prepare discussion questions and provide some sort of visual supplement (e.g., handouts, PowerPoint presentations).

- *Course project.* Each student was expected to engage in a semester-long project related to their interest in the everyday technological theories and practices that transpire in a specific, culturally situated community. Several required deliverables were related to this culminating course project:

- meeting with the professor regarding project ideas
- project proposal (500 to 1,000 words) with attached tentative bibliography
- review: MAs were required to submit an amazon.com or other specific online review of a text related to the culture or community studied; PhDs were required to write a book review for a journal and highly encouraged to submit it for publication consideration
- annotated bibliography: a summary and analysis of no less than eight sources, with an introduction that points to relevant themes, trends, controversies, etc., that will inform the course project
- proposal to present the research project at a professional or scholarly conference
- project: PhD students were required to write a research-based seminar paper (that can serve as a conference presentation or be submitted as a scholarly article); MA students had the option of writing a seminar paper, designing a curriculum unit, or writing a white paper or a popular article
- presentation of project to the class

The course readings and discussions centered on highly theoretical work that informed and supported research-based projects that were not pedagogical in nature.

Their research-based projects provided students with an opportunity for both critical inquiry and professionalization practices, from learning the genres of conference proposals, review essays, seminar papers, and the like to researching and sustaining a theoretical discussion and case study of technological expertise, many of which are of publication quality. Here is a summary of the students' projects:

- Through the lens of de Certeau's theories of production, one PhD student interested in transnational feminisms in technical communication studies examined how reproductive technologies are prescribed for and poached by Chinese and Euro-American women.
- Using a few case studies of Massively Multiplayer Online Role-Playing Games (MMORPGs), an MA student interested in

game design merged decolonial and poststructuralist theories to analyze how virtual world building in MMORPGs parallels and diverges from face-to-face nation building in the classification and surveillance of players.

- A part-time MA student and full-time public relations and communication specialist for university marketing interested in game design employed Spurr's (1993) rhetorical tropes of empire to examine representations and performances of gender in a few popular video games produced in Japan.

- A part-time MA student and full-time technical communicator for a local yet large international corporate headquarters theorized the best practices for universities and corporations to engage in intellectual alliances and collaborative relationships with local communities to build community technology centers.

- An MA student in visual culture analyzed artists who have aligned themselves with and emerged within street art culture and how this culture has appropriated and invented their own way of seeing and critiquing the world with visual designs, codes, languages, and technologies.

- A PhD student interested in globalization and the localization of technologies worked toward building a decolonial theory and methodology for his dissertation project, which studies the rhetoric and cultural usability of the writing, transfer, translation, distribution, and circulation of information products related to the use of aphrodisiacs and sexual-enhancement drugs in Ghana and, thus, the impact of these information products on the cultural efficacy of the drugs.

Despite the tension caused by the student whom I asked to withdraw from the course, an unexpected conversation in which the only two people of color in the classroom had to convince a Euro-American male that racism still in fact exists, and my abandonment of the course blog almost midsemester (after week 7 out of 16), these projects demonstrate that some progressive and productive inquiry transpired in this course, inquiry that has the potential to make social justice happen in corporate, academic, and community workplaces.

In fact, one student (Frost, 2010) published her review essay with *Computers and Composition*. The student working on the dissertation successfully defended and secured a tenure-track position in an international technical communication program. Both of the two MA students interested in game studies and working toward their professional writing and rhetorics degrees graduated, and one presented his work from this class at the 2010 Computers and Writing conference. Both are still hoping to work as technical writers or game designers in the gaming industry, and one even published the review of an MMORPG game written for the class on a high-profile online gaming site. The other MA in professional writing and rhetorics also graduated, and she completed the capstone project by revising the project completed for this course and developing the best practices for building and sustaining culturally responsible and respectful corporate–academic partnerships. All but one of the students in the course situated race and ethnicity as at least one of the intersecting cultural frameworks, if not the primary framework for their project.

IMPLICATIONS

According to Gilyard (2004), "the most important question relative to ethnicity and curriculum is what conceptions of ethnicity (and the race conversation) can we circulate that best contribute to social justice efforts" (p. vii). I suggest that the interdisciplinary, decolonial critical race research, curriculum design, and pedagogy offered here provide the field with several openings for further considering how to broach conversations about design and technology theory from and about scholars and users who are people of color—and from other underrepresented populations—in technical communication studies. I offer this work in conjunction with Johnson et al.'s (2008) and Banks's (2006) work so that the discipline may understand how

> racism is enforced and maintained through our technologies and the assumptions we design and program into them—and into our uses of them. Without systematic study of our relationships with technologies and technological issues, we remain subject to those technologies and the larger patterns of racism and racial exclusion that still govern American society. (Banks, 2006, p. 10)

As such, our discipline has an ethical imperative to respond, as public intellectuals, advocates for users, and disciplinary workers in a diverse field of scholars and practitioners.

To begin, although cultural studies work in technical communication may support work at the intellectual interstices of race, rhetoric, and technology, it may not do so directly. To explain, I made concessions in the write-up of my course description to allow for a broader understanding of cultural studies. I justified making these concessions because I wanted to allow for an intersectional approach to identity that understands race as interdependent and interrelational with gender, class, ability and disability, sexual orientation, nationality, generation, religion, and more. But just because a broader understanding of cultural studies can allow for this intersectional approach, it does not require it. Thus, we must make critical race theory a central and visible framework for research and analysis because some students will opt out if we let them, as was the case with one of my students.

But remaining vigilant to this centrality is difficult when we weigh the institutional pressures and policies for graduate-course enrollment and curriculum design and the research interests of graduate students versus professors' goals for community-knowledge work—and the concession that is easy to make is that some cultural consideration is better than none in our discipline and classrooms. Nonetheless, I tried to make clear in this article that further inquiry into the institutional contexts within which courses are designed, named, and delivered is needed in both our local places and our professional spaces. For example, this case study demonstrates that there are varying understandings of what it means and might look like to make technical communication curriculum more enticing and race conscious. Perhaps located accountability can serve as a usable and useful framework for interrogating and reflecting on these aspects of curriculum design within institutional, cultural, professional, personal, global, and local contexts for courses that address issues of race and ethnicity in technical communication theory, research, pedagogy, and practice.

Further, many of us who value critical race theory and decolonial methodologies but are not in the position to offer an entire course on race, rhetoric, and technology may wonder about the value and sustainability of this framework in other technical communication courses. Although I cannot demonstrate the centrality of critical race theory to every course assignment, we can make it visible nonetheless. For example, in all of my technical communication courses, we begin with a low-stakes cultural identity map assignment, in which students brainstorm a list of their cultural affiliations—including race, ethnicity, class, gender, nationality, abilities, sexuality, religion, and others—and then visually map out the cultural influences to signify the weight of and relationships between and across each cultural influence. They then compose a reflection memo where they specify the visual rhetorical and cultural strategies that they employed and how these cultural influences may affect their perceptions of and interactions with people, texts, and technologies from other cultures. In both introductory and advanced technical communication courses, I have assigned an informal report on a cultural and technological artifact analysis, in which students research a non-Western technology (or a technology typically understood as outside of dominant, hegemonic Western culture) or a technology that is at least 100 years old and answer the following research questions: How is this communication technology articulated, used, produced, reproduced, or distributed in this specific cultural context? And how do these practices differ from dominant practices? But these are only a couple of suggestions out of dozens of possible curricular approaches.

Unfortunately, making critical race theory central to our inquiry can be uncomfortable for professors and students, depending on their socioeconomical, geographical, racial, gendered, political—and otherwise embodied—location. Regardless of their ethnic backgrounds, professors are always already held up for scrutiny as to their motivations for teaching ethnic texts, whether it be white liberal guilt, the anger of a professor of color, or some other rhetorical trope used to justify resistance to radical pedagogies, social justice pedagogies, or pedagogies of the oppressed. We should expect at least some resistance, even if minimal, and prepare for these moments, if possible.

Located accountability can assist us in this preparation, as we should make our curricular and pedagogical goals as well as the theories and methodologies underpinning those goals, transparent to our students from the start of the semester. But this transparency approach to preparing us and informing our students has its limits. For example, I followed this suggestion, yet I still had to negotiate student hostility toward my curriculum and others who flourished in it. Thus, located accountability should also include thinking through a pedagogical policy that provides students in our classes, those resistant and those engaged, with the rules for engagement in critical race studies: a professionalism and respect policy that prepares and protects both students and professors.[6] Those of us who teach in ways that challenge privilege and power should expect resistance but not disrespectful behavior. Thus, on the first day of every class, I explain that while I do not support an intellectually safe space in my class, I do expect that we engage in ways that support a physically and emotionally safe space for all members of our learning community. Thus, we all have responsibility and accountability for collectively and collaboratively creating that space.

hooks (1990a) reminded pedagogues how to go about meeting our responsibilities in this endeavor. She claimed that "we must engage decolonization as a critical practice if we are to have meaningful chances of survival even as we must simultaneously cope with the loss of political grounding which made radical activism more possible" (p. 513). We must call "attention to those shared sensibilities which cross boundaries of class, gender, race, etc. that could be fertile ground for the construction of empathy—ties that would promote recognition of common commitments, and serve as a base for solidarity and coalition" (p. 514). Such constructions of empathy open up our imaginings of all people and things as interactors, capable of productive and meaningful culturally situated knowledge work.

Thus, like Johnson (1998), I call for alliances between all designers and users of technologies and the discipline, alliances that result in technologies or information products that are collaboratively "created through a process of 'give and take' that places users on a par with the developers and the system itself: a space within which users and developers can learn to value each other's knowledge and accept the responsibilities of technological design and development in new, shared ways" (p. 33). This approach to engaging diverse interactors strives to dismantle the historically hierarchical relationship between designer and user and intervene with one of equal cooperation. It strives to rebuild a disciplinary foundation that is usable, useful, and dynamic in local contexts, one that listens to the cultural and critical race rhetorics of use that—because of power relations, certain languages, statements, and discursive formations—were once silent in the writing of design, technology, and usability theories.

Among other areas of inquiry important to technical communication studies, employing a decolonial, critical race framework in our research, pedagogy, and other technical communication workplace practices will rupture dominant notions of what it means to be—and who gets to be considered—technical or technologically advanced. What is considered technical to one population might not be considered technical to another. Categories such as beginner, advanced beginner, competent, semitechnical, and highly technical shift depending on the user's level of access to and interaction with a given technological product or document. Tiers of technological literacy collapse when broadening our understanding of technology in relation to these shifting categories of expertise. Finally, this framework also pushes user-centered design theorists and practitioners to interrogate the extent to which all designers imagine users that mirror themselves—and calls into question the extent to which designers are capable of imagining users different from themselves. I posit that decolonial, critical race theories, methodologies, and pedagogies have the potential to help us imagine that we are capable and that doing so will generate responsible and productive ways of imagining a diversity of users of and participants in our discipline and other technical communication workplaces.

ACKNOWLEDGMENTS

I write this article with deep appreciation of many. First, thank you to Miriam Williams and Octavio Pimentel for your work on this special issue and for supporting my work—and to the two anonymous peer reviewers for your helpful feedback on an earlier version of this article. Further, I am grateful for my dear friend and colleague Julie Jung and your sage advice on revising this piece—and for being interested in my work. Finally, thanks to Jeff Grabill for providing me with inspiration and guidance during the formative stages of this research project.

DECLARATION OF CONFLICTING INTERESTS

The author declared no potential conflicts of interest with respect to the research, authorship, and/or publication of this article.

FUNDING

The author received no financial support for the research, authorship, and/or publication of this article.

NOTES

1. At the time I taught this course, I wish I would have known about Williams's (2006) discourse analysis of—and rhetorical and historical contexts for— postbellum regulatory writing and its influence on the inherent mistrust African Americans have of government regulations and the government officials who write them. But I did teach Williams's (2010) work in my spring 2011 graduate topics course Cultural Studies in Technical Communication.

2. I assigned some of these texts in full; from others, I assigned select chapters.

3. Thanks to my dear friend and colleague Chris De Santis for introducing me to the word *detritus* and its context as it pertains to spider remains or debris.

4. Although I now name this research cultural usability, it did not transpire in a traditional way. I discovered topics and readings that graduate students were interested in—and projects they would benefit from—by researching the course and how it had been taught and received in the past; engaging in informal conversations with graduate students, graduate faculty, and the graduate director about graduate-student needs related to this course; and learning the majors of the students enrolled in the course. I plan to conduct a formal cultural usability study inspired and informed by this research in a future course-design project.

5. The book order had to be submitted in spring 2009, so I decided which texts to include knowing only the two students enrolled in the course. But later I adjusted some of the article readings to supplement the texts after I learned the majors of the other students, which were indicated in the online system that allows faculty to know which students enroll in their courses.

6. My working course policy on professionalism and respect reads as follows: As students, technical communicators, and community members in this course, you are expected to conduct yourself in a professional and respectful manner and to be aware of how your words and actions impact those around you. Each of us should feel free to express our thoughts and opinions openly, without fear of penalty, as long as we do so in a courteous way. Although we may not always agree with one another and may challenge each other to think about rhetoric, technical communication, writing, societies, cultures, races, and technologies in new ways, I expect you to treat every person in this class as a valuable and respected member. Thus, no harsh tones, hateful language, or disrespectful behavior of any kind will be tolerated. Furthermore, refrain from speaking, whispering, sleeping, playing on the computer, programming your cell phone, or engaging in other disrespectful behavior while someone else has the floor. When you enter the classroom, you should be engaged with the class—so turn off your cell phone and MP3 player, and tune into the class! If you engage in any unprofessional and/or disrespectful behavior, your project and/or semester grades will be penalized, or you may be asked to drop or withdraw from the course.

REFERENCES

Alexander, J., & Banks, W. P. (2004). Sexualities, technologies, and the teaching of writing: A critical overview. *Computers and Composition, 21*, 273–293.

Arizona's Revised Statutes, AZ HB 2281, 49th Leg., 2nd Sess. (2010).

Atwill, J. M. (1998). *Rhetoric reclaimed: Aristotle and the liberal arts tradition.* Ithaca, NY: Cornell University Press.

Banks, A. (2006). *Race, rhetoric, and technology: Searching for higher ground.* Mahwah, NJ: Erlbaum.

———. (2011). *Digital griots: African American rhetoric in a multimedia age.* Carbondale, Southern Illinois University Press.

Barnum, C. A., & Huilin, L. (2006). Chinese and American technical communication: A cross-cultural comparison of differences. *Technical Communication, 53*, 143–166.

Blackmon, S. (2002). "But I'm just white"; Or, how "Other" pedagogies can benefit all students. In B. Huot & P. Takayoshi (Eds.), *Teaching writing with computers* (pp. 92–102). Boston, MA: Houghton Mifflin.

———. (2007). (Cyber) conspiracy theories? African-American students in the computerized writing environment. In P. Takayoshi & P. Sullivan (Eds.), *Labor, writing technologies, and the shaping of composition in the academy* (pp. 153–166). Cresskill, NJ: Hampton Press.

Bowdon, M. (2004). Technical communication and the role of the public intellectual: A community HIV-prevention case study. *Technical Communication Quarterly, 13*, 325–340.

Bray, F. (1997). *Technology and gender: Fabrics of power in late imperial China.*

Berkeley, University of California Press.

De Certeau, M. (1984). *The practice of everyday life.* Trans. S. F. Rendall. Berkely, University of California Press.

Ding, H. (2009). Rhetorics of alternative media in an emerging epidemic: SARS, censorship, and extra-institutional risk communication. *Technical Communication Quarterly, 18*, 327–350.

Ebo, B. (Ed.). (1998). *Cyberghetto or cybertopia? Race, class and gender on the Internet.* Westport, CT: Praeger.

Fernandez, M., Wilding, F., & Wright, M. M. (Eds.). (2003). *Domain errors! Cyberfeminist Practices (a subRosa project).* Brooklyn, NY: Autonomedia.

Flynn, E. A. (1997). Emergent feminist technical communication. *Technical Communication Quarterly, 6,* 313–320.

Foucault, M. (1972). *The archaeology of knowledge & the discourse on language* (Trans. A. M. Sheridan Smith). New York, NY: Pantheon.

Frost, E. (2010). Book review of Francesca Bray's technology and gender: Fabrics of power in late imperial China. *Computers and Composition, 27,* 324–327.

Gates, E. N. (Ed.). (1997). *Racial classification and history.* New York, NY: Routledge.

Gates, H. L. (Ed.). (1986). *"Race," writing, and difference.* Chicago, IL: University of Chicago Press.

Gilyard, K. (2004). Preface. In K. Gilyard & V. Nunley (Eds), *Rhetoric and ethnicity* (pp. v–x). Portsmouth, NH: Boynton/Cook.

Gómez Peña, G. (1996). The virtual barrio @ the other frontier (or the Chicano Interneta). In L. H. Leeson (Ed.), *Clicking in: Hot links to a digital culture* (pp. 173–182). Seattle, WA: Bay Press.

Grobman, L. (1999). Beyond internationalization: Multicultural education in the professional writing contact zone. *Journal of Business and Technical Communication, 13,* 427–448.

Haas, A. M. (2005). Making online spaces more native to American Indians: A digital diversity recommendation. *Computers and Composition Online.* Retrieved from http://www.bgsu.edu/cconline/Haas/index.htm

———. (2007). Wampum as hypertext: An American Indian intellectual tradition of multimedia theory and practice. *Studies in American Indian Literatures, 19,* 77–100.

Haas, C. (1999). On the relationship between old and new technologies. *Computers & Composition, 16,* 209–228.

Herndl, C. (1993). Teaching discourse and reproducing culture: A critique of research and pedagogy in professional and non-academic writing. *College Composition and Communication, 44,* 349–363.

hooks, b. (1990a). Postmodern blackness. *Postmodern culture* 1 *(1),* pp. 510–518. Retrieved March 15, 2011, from the Project MUSE database.

———. (1990b). Representing whiteness: Seeing wings of desire. In *Yearning: Race, gender, and cultural politics* (pp. 165–172). Boston, MA: South End Press.

Jenkins, H. (2008). *Convergence culture: Where old and new media collide.* New York, New York University Press.

Jeyaraj, J. (2004). Liminality and othering: The issue of rhetorical authority in technical discourse. *Journal of Business and Technical Communication, 18,* 9–38.

Johnson, J. R., Pimentel, O., & Pimentel, C. (2008). Writing new Mexico white: A critical analysis of early representations of new Mexico in technical writing. *Journal of Business and Technical Communication, 22,* 211–236.

Johnson, R. R. (1998). *User-centered technology: A rhetorical theory for computers and other mundane artifacts.* Albany, NY: SUNY Press.

Katz, S. B. (1992). The ethic of expediency: Classical rhetoric, technology, and the Holocaust. *College English, 54,* 225–275.

———. (1993). Aristotle's rhetoric, Hitler's program, and the ideological problem of praxis, power, and professional discourse. *Journal of Business and Technical Communication, 7,* 37–62.

Kolko, B., Nakamura, L., & Rodman, G. (Eds.). (2000). *Race in cyberspace*. New York, NY: Routledge.

Longo, B. (1998). An approach for applying cultural study theory to technical writing research. *Technical Communication Quarterly, 7*, 53–73.

Monroe, B. J. (2004). *Crossing the digital divide: Race, writing, and technology in the classroom*. New York, NY: Teachers College Press.

Nakamura, L. (2007). *Digitizing race: Visual cultures of the Internet*. Minneapolis University of Minnesota Press.

Nelson, A., Tu, T. L. N., & Hines, A. H. (Eds.). (2001). *Technicolor: Race, technology, and everyday life*. New York, NY: New York University Press.

Palmeri, J. (2006). Disability studies, cultural analysis, and the critical practice of technical communication pedagogy. *Technical Communication Quarterly, 15*, 49–65.

Powell, M. (2002). Listening to ghosts: An alternative (non) argument. In C. Schroeder, H. Fox, & P. Bizzell (Eds.), *ALT DIS: Alternative discourses for the academy* (pp. 11–22). Portsmouth, NH: Boynton/Cook-Heinemann.

Roediger, D. R. (1997). Introduction: From the social construction of race to the abolition of whiteness. In E. N. Gates (Ed.), *Racial classification and history* (pp. 345–363). New York, NY: Routledge.

Ross, A. (2005). Technology. In T. Bennett, L. Grossburg & M. Morris (Eds.), *New keywords: A revised vocabulary of culture and society*. Malden, MA: Blackwell.

Sauer, B. (2003). *The rhetoric of risk*. Mahwah, NJ: Erlbaum.

Savage, G., & Mattson, K. (2011). Perspectives on diversity in technical communication programs. *Programmatic Perspectives, 3*, 5–57.

Savage, G., & Matveeva, N. (2011). Seeking inter-racial collaborations in program design: A report on a study of technical and scientific communication programs in historically black colleges and universities (HBCUs) and tribal colleges and universities (TCUs) in the United States. *Programmatic Perspectives, 3*, 58–85.

Scott, J. B. (2003). *Risky rhetoric: AIDS and the cultural practices of HIV testing*. Carbondale, Southern Illinois University Press.

Scott, J. B., & Longo, B. (2006). Guest editors' introduction: Making the cultural turn. *Technical Communication Quarterly, 15*, 3–7.

Scott, J. B., Longo, B., & Wills, K. V. (Eds.). (2006). *Critical power tools: Technical communication and cultural studies*. New York, NY: SUNY Press.

Selfe, C. L., & Selfe, R. J., Jr. (1994). The politics of the interface: Power and its exercise in electronic contact zones. *CCC, 45*, 480–504.

Slack, J. D., Miller, D. J., & Doak, J. (1993). The technical communicator as author: Meaning, power, authority. *Journal of Business and Technical Communication, 7*, 12–36.

Slack, J. D., & Wise, J. M. (2005). *Culture þ technology: A primer*. New York, NY: Lang.

Smedley, A. (2007). *Race in North America: Origin and evolution of a worldview* (3rd ed.). Boulder, CO: Westview Press.

Spurr, D. (1993). *The rhetoric of empire: Colonial discourse in journalism, travel writing, and imperial administration*. Durham, NY: Duke University Press.

St. Germaine-Madison, N. (2006). Instructions, visuals, and the English-speaking bias of technical communication. *Technical Communication Quarterly, 53*, 184–194.

Suchman, L. (2000). Located accountabilities in technology production. *Cultural usability: Towards a critical design sensibility*. Retrieved from http://www. mlab.uiah.fi/culturalusability/papers/Suchman_paper.html

Sun, H. (2006). The triumph of users: Achieving cultural usability goals with user localization. *Technical Communication Quarterly, 15,* 457–481.

Thatcher, B. L. (2000). Writing policies and procedures in a U.S./South American context. *Technical Communication Quarterly, 9,* 365–399.

———. (2006). Intercultural rhetoric, technology transfer, and writing in U.S.– Mexico border maquilas. *Technical Communication Quarterly, 15,* 385–405.

Villanueva, V. (1999). On the rhetoric and precedents of racism. *CCC, 50,* 645–661.

Williams, M. F. (2006). Tracing W. E. B. Dubois' "color line" in government regulations. *Journal of Technical Writing and Communication, 36,* 141–165.

———. (2010). *From black codes to recodification: Removing the veil from regulatory writing.* Amityville, NY: Baywood.

Williams, P. J. (1991). *The alchemy of race and rights: Diary of a law professor.* Cambridge, MA: Harvard University Press.

Wilson, P., & Stewart, M. (Eds.). (2008). *Global indigenous media: Cultures, poetics, and politics.* Durham, NC: Duke University Press.

A List of Resources

Adler-Kassner, Linda, and Elizabeth Wardle. *Naming What We Know: Threshold Concepts of Writing Studies.* UP of Colorado, 2015.

Anzaldúa, Gloria. *Borderlands/La Frontera.* Aunt Lute Books, 1999.

Applebee, Arthur N. *Tradition and Reform in the Teaching of English: A History.* NCTE, 1974.

Aristotle. *The Rhetoric and the Poetics of Aristotle.* Translated by W. Rhys Roberts and Ingram Bywater, Random House, 1954.

Arola, Kristin L. "Composing as Culturing: An American Indian Approach to Digital Ethics." *Handbook of Writing, Literacies, and Education in Digital Cultures,* edited by Kathy Mills et al., Routledge, 2018, pp. 275–84.

Ayash, Nancy Bou. *Toward Translingual Realities in Composition: (Re)Working Local Language Representations and Practices.* UP of Colorado, 2019.

Bain, Alexander. *English Composition and Rhetoric: A Manual.* Longmans, 1877.

Baker-Bell, April. *Linguistic Justice: Black Language, Literacy, Identity, and Pedagogy.* NCTE and Routledge, 2020.

Baker-Bell, April, et al. "This Ain't Another Statement! This Is a DEMAND for Black Linguistic Justice!" Conference on College Composition & Communication, July 2020, https://cccc.ncte.org/cccc/ demand-for-black-linguistic-justice?fbclid=IwAR305_0URSbMIR5OV p0h Lmm9osWbt20nGNf7H9IgqNkts8hNs_-tzpFmkDw.

Ball, Arnetha F., and Ted Lardner. *African American Literacies Unleashed: Vernacular English and the Composition Classroom.* Southern Illinois UP, 2005.

Banks, Adam J. *Race, Rhetoric, and Technology: Searching for Higher Ground.* NCTE and Erlbaum, 2006.

Bartholomae, David, and Anthony Petrosky. *Facts, Artifacts, and Counterfacts: Theory and Method for a Reading and Writing Course.* Heinemann, 1986.

———, editors. *Ways of Reading: An Anthology for Writers.* 4th ed., Bedford/ St. Martin's, 1996.

Belanoff, Pat, and Marcia Dickson, editors. *Portfolios: Process and Product.* Heinemann, 1991.

Benson, Thomas W., and Michael H. Prosser, editors. *Readings in Classical Rhetoric.* Allyn and Bacon, 1969.

Berlin, James A. *Rhetoric and Reality: Writing Instruction in American Colleges, 1900–1985.* Southern Illinois UP, 1987.

———. *Rhetorics, Poetics, and Cultures: Refiguring College English Studies.* NCTE, 1996.

———. *Writing Instruction in Nineteenth-Century American Colleges.* Southern Illinois UP, 1984.

Bizzell, Patricia. *Academic Discourse and Critical Consciousness.* U of Pittsburgh P, 1992.

Blair, Kristine, and Pamela Takayoshi, editors. *Feminist Cyberscapes: Mapping Gendered Academic Spaces.* Ablex, 1999.

Britton, James, et al. *The Development of Writing Abilities (11–18).* Macmillan, 1975.

Brody, Miriam. *Manly Writing: Gender, Rhetoric, and the Rise of Composition.* Southern Illinois UP, 1993.

Canagarajah, Suresh. *Transnational Literacy Autobiographies as Translingual Writing.* Routledge, 2020.

CCCC Committee on Globalization of Postsecondary Writing Instruction and Research. "CCCC Statement on Globalization in Writing Studies Pedagogy and Research." *College Composition and Communication,* vol. 70, no. 4, 2019, pp. 681–90.

Condon, Frankie, and Vershawn Ashanti Young, editors. *Performing Antiracist Pedagogy in Rhetoric, Writing, and Communication.* The WAC Clearinghouse; UP of Colorado, 2017.

Cooper, Charles R., and Lee Odell, editors. *Evaluating Writing: Describing, Measuring, Judging.* NCTE, 1977.

Corbett, Edward P. J. *Classical Rhetoric for the Modern Student.* 3rd ed., Oxford UP, 1990.

Craig, Collin. "Courting the Abject: A Taxonomy of Black Queer Rhetoric." *College English,* vol. 79, no. 6, 2017, pp. 619–39, www.jstor.org/ stable/44805944.

Crowley, Sharon. *Ancient Rhetorics for Contemporary Students.* Macmillan, 1994.

———. *The Methodical Memory: Invention in Current-Traditional Rhetoric.* Southern Illinois UP, 1990.

Daiker, Donald A., et al. *The Writer's Options: College Sentence Combining.* Harper and Row, 1979.

Dolmage, Jay Timothy. *Academic Ableism: Disability and Higher Education.* U of Michigan P, 2017.

Elbow, Peter. *What Is English?* Modern Language Association, 1990.

———. *Writing with Power: Techniques for Mastering the Writing Process.* Oxford UP, 1981.

———. *Writing without Teachers.* Oxford UP, 1973.

Emig, Janet. *The Composing Processes of Twelfth Graders.* NCTE, 1971.

Enos, Theresa, editor. *A Sourcebook for Basic Writing Teachers.* Random House, 1987.

Faigley, Lester. *Fragments of Rationality: Postmodernity and the Subject of Composition.* U of Pittsburgh P, 1992.

Faris, Michael J., et al., editors. *Amplifying Soundwriting Pedagogies: Integrating Sound into Rhetoric and Writing.* The WAC Clearinghouse; UP of Colorado, 2022.

Flower, Linda. *The Construction of Negotiated Meaning: A Social Cognitive Theory of Writing.* Southern Illinois UP, 1994.

Fowler, Shelli B., and Victor Villanueva, editors. *Included in English Studies: Learning Climates That Cultivate Racial and Ethnic Diversity.* American Association for Higher Education, 2002.

Freire, Paulo. *Cultural Action for Freedom.* Harvard Educational Review, 1970.

———. *Pedagogy of the Oppressed.* Translated by Myra Bergman Ramos, Herder and Herder, 1970.

Freire, Paulo, and Donaldo Macedo. *Literacy: Reading the Word and the World.* Bergin & Garvey, 1987.

Gere, Anne Ruggles. *Writing Groups: History, Theory, and Implications.* Southern Illinois UP, 1987.

Gibson, W. Walker. *Tough, Sweet & Stuffy: An Essay on Modern American Prose Styles.* Indiana UP, 1966.

Gilyard, Keith, editor. *Race, Rhetoric, and Composition.* Boynton/Cook, 1999.

———. *Voices of the Self: A Study of Language Competence.* Wayne State UP, 1991.

Golden, James L., and Edward P. J. Corbett. *The Rhetoric of Blair, Campbell, and Whately.* Holt, Rinehart and Winston, 1968.

Gonzales, Laura. *Sites of Translation: What Multilinguals Can Teach Us about Digital Writing and Rhetoric.* University of Michigan Press, 2018.

Gramsci, Antonio. *Selections from Cultural Writings,* edited by David Forgacs and Geoffrey Nowell-Smith. Translated by William Boelhower, Harvard UP, 1985.

———. *Selections from the Prison Notebooks,* edited by Quintin Hoare and Geoffrey Nowell Smith. International Publishers, 1971.

Graves, Richard L., editor. *Rhetoric and Composition: A Sourcebook for Teachers and Writers.* 2nd ed., Boynton/Cook, 1984.

Hassel, Holly, and Cassandra Phillips. *Materiality and Writing Studies: Aligning Labor, Scholarship, and Teaching.* NCTE, 2022.

Havelock, Eric A. *Preface to Plato.* Harvard UP, 1963.

Hawisher, Gail E., and Cynthia L. Selfe, editors. *Global Literacies and the World-Wide Web.* Routledge, 2000.

Heath, Shirley Brice. *Ways with Words: Language, Life, and Work in Communities and Classrooms.* Cambridge UP, 1983.

hooks, bell. *Teaching to Transgress: Education as the Practice of Freedom.* Routledge, 1994.

Horner, Bruce, and Min-Zhan Lu. *Representing the "Other": Basic Writers and the Teaching of Basic Writing.* NCTE, 1999.

Inoue, Asao B. *Antiracist Writing Assessment Ecologies: Tending and Assessing Writing for a Socially Just Future.* Parlor Press, 2015.

Irmscher, William. *Teaching Expository Writing.* Holt, Rinehart and Winston, 1979.

Jarratt, Susan C. *Rereading the Sophists: Classical Rhetoric Refigured.* Southern Illinois UP, 1991.

Kells, Michelle Hall, and Valerie Balester, editors. *Attending to the Margins: Writing, Researching, and Teaching on the Front Lines.* Boynton/Cook, 1999.

Kennedy, George. *Classical Rhetoric and Its Christian and Secular Tradition from Ancient to Modern Times.* 2nd ed., U of North Carolina P, 1999.

Kent, Thomas, editor. *Post-Process Theory: Beyond the Writing-Process Paradigm.* Southern Illinois UP, 1999.

Kerschbaum, Stephanie L. *Toward a New Rhetoric of Difference.* NCTE, 2014.

King, Lisa Michelle, et al., editors. *Survivance, Sovereignty, and Story: Teaching American Indian Rhetorics.* Utah State UP, 2015.

Kolko, Beth E., et al., editors. *Race in Cyberspace.* Routledge, 2000.

Kynard, Carmen. "Teaching While Black: Witnessing and Countering Disciplinary Whiteness, Racial Violence, and University Race-Management." *Literacy in Composition Studies,* vol. 3, no. 1, 2015, pp. 1–20.

———. *Vernacular Insurrections: Race, Black Protest, and the New Century in Composition-Literacies Studies.* SUNY Press, 2013.

Lessig, Lawrence. *Remix: Making Art and Commerce Thrive in the Hybrid Economy.* Penguin, 2008.

Lindemann, Erika. *A Rhetoric for Writing Teachers.* 4th ed., Oxford UP, 2001.

Locke, John. *An Essay Concerning Human Understanding,* edited by Peter H. Nidditch, Clarendon Press, 1975.

Macrorie, Ken. *The I-Search Paper.* Boynton/Cook, 1988.

———. *Uptaught.* Hayden, 1970.

Marrou, H. I. *A History of Education in Antiquity.* Sheed and Ward, 1956.

Martinez, Aja Y. *Counterstory: The Rhetoric and Writing of Critical Race Theory.* NCTE, 2020.

Mathieu, Paula. *Tactics of Hope: The Public Turn in English Composition.* Boynton/Cook, 2005.

Matsen, Patricia P., et al., editors. *Readings from Classical Rhetoric.* Southern Illinois UP, 1990.

Matsuda, Paul Kei, et al., editors. *Professionalizing Second Language Writing.* Parlor Press, 2017.

Mellon, John C. *Transformational Sentence-Combining: A Method for Enhancing the Development of Syntactic Fluency in English Composition.* NCTE, 1969.

Miller, Susan, editor. *The Norton Book of Composition Studies.* W. W. Norton, 2009.

Moffett, James. *Teaching the Universe of Discourse.* Houghton Mifflin, 1983.

Moss, Beverly. "Where Would We Be? Legacies, Roll Calls, and the Teaching of Writing in HBCUs." *Composition Studies,* vol. 49, no. 1, 2021, pp. 144–48.

Murphy, James J., editor. *Rhetoric in the Middle Ages: A History of Rhetorical Theory from St. Augustine to the Renaissance.* U of California P, 1974.

———, editor. *The Rhetorical Tradition and Modern Writing.* Modern Language Association, 1982.

———. *A Short History of Writing Instruction: From Ancient Greece to Twentieth-Century America.* Hermagoras, 1990.

Murray, Donald. *A Writer Teaches Writing.* Houghton Mifflin, 1968.

Nelson, Cary, and Lawrence Grossberg, editors. *Marxism and the Interpretation of Culture.* U of Illinois P, 1988.

Ohmann, Richard M. *English in America: A Radical View of the Profession.* Oxford UP, 1976.

Ong, Walter J. *Orality and Literacy: The Technologizing of the Word.* Methuen, 1982.

Perryman-Clark, Staci M., and Collin L. Craig, editors. *Black Perspectives in Writing Program Administration: From the Margins to the Center.* NCTE, 2019.

Piaget, Jean. *The Language and Thought of the Child.* Translated by Marjorie Gabain, World Publishing, 1971.

Plato. *Phaedrus.* Translated by R. Hackforth. Cambridge UP, 1952.

Plemons, Anna. *Beyond Progress in the Prison Classroom: Options and Opportunities.* NCTE, 2019.

Powell, Malea. "Rhetorics of Survivance: How American Indians Use Writing." *College Composition and Communication,* vol. 53, no. 3, 2002, pp. 396–434.

Powell, Malea, et al. "Our Story Begins Here: Constellating Cultural Rhetorics." *enculturation: A Journal of Rhetoric, Writing, and Culture,* no. 18, 2014.

Price, Margaret. *Mad at School: Rhetorics of Mental Disability and Academic Life.* U of Michigan P, 2011.

Pritchard, Eric Darnell. *Fashioning Lives: Black Queers and the Politics of Literacy.* Southern Illinois UP, 2016.

Quintilian. *On the Teaching of Speaking and Writing,* edited by James J. Murphy, Southern Illinois UP, 1987.

Reynolds, Nedra. *Geographies of Writing: Inhabiting Places and Encountering Difference.* Southern Illinois UP, 2004.

Rhodes, Jacqueline, and Jonathan Alexander, editors. *The Routledge Handbook of Queer Rhetoric.* Routledge, 2022.

Rose, Mike. *Lives on the Boundary: A Moving Account of the Struggles and Achievements of America's Educationally Underprepared.* Penguin, 1989.

Rose, Shirley K., and Irwin Weiser, editors. *The Internationalization of US Writing Programs.* Utah State UP, 2018.

Royster, Jacqueline Jones, and Gesa E. Kirsch. *Feminist Rhetorical Practices: New Horizons for Rhetoric, Composition, and Literacy Studies.* Southern Illinois UP, 2012.

Ruiz, Iris D., and Raúl Sánchez, editors. *Decolonizing Rhetoric and Composition Studies: New Latinx Keywords for Theory and Pedagogy.* Palgrave Macmillan, 2016.

Sano-Franchini, Jennifer, et al., editors. *Building a Community, Having a Home: A History of the Conference on College Composition and Communication Asian/Asian American Caucus.* Parlor Press, 2017.

Schroeder, Christopher, et al., editors. *ALT DIS: Alternative Discourses and the Academy.* Boynton/Cook, 2002.

Scott, Tony. *Dangerous Writing: Understanding the Political Economy of Composition.* Utah State UP, 2009.

Scribner, Silvia, and Michael Cole. *The Psychology of Literacy.* Harvard UP, 1981.

Shaughnessy, Mina. *Errors and Expectations: A Guide for the Teacher of Basic Writing.* Oxford UP, 1977.

Shipka, Jody. *Toward a Composition Made Whole.* U of Pittsburgh P, 2011.

Shor, Ira, and Paulo Freire. *A Pedagogy for Liberation: Dialogues on Transforming Education.* Bergin & Garvey, 1987.

Smitherman, Geneva. *Talkin and Testifyin: The Language of Black America.* Wayne State UP, 1986.

Swearingen, C. Jan. *Rhetoric and Irony: Western Literacy and Western Lies.* Oxford UP, 1991.

Tate, Gary, editor. *Teaching Composition: Twelve Bibliographical Essays.* Rev. ed., Texas Christian UP, 1987.

Tate, Gary, and Edward P. J. Corbett, editors. *The Writing Teacher's Sourcebook.* 2nd ed., Oxford UP, 1988.

Villanueva, Victor, Jr. *Bootstraps: From an American Academic of Color.* NCTE, 1993.

Vygotsky, Lev. *Thought and Language.* Translated by Eugenia Hanfmann and Gertrude Vakar, MIT Press, 1962.

Yagelski, Robert P. *Literacy Matters: Writing and Reading the Social Self.* Teachers College Press, 2000.

Young, Morris. *Minor Re/Visions: Asian American Literacy Narratives as a Rhetoric of Citizenship.* Southern Illinois UP, 2004.

Young, Richard E., et al. *Rhetoric: Discovery and Change.* Harcourt, Brace & World, 1970.

Index

Editors

Kristin L. Arola is the Karen L. Gillmor Endowed Associate Professor of Professional and Public Writing and also serves as the interim director of the American Indian and Indigenous Studies Program at Michigan State University. Her research and teaching are rooted in Ojibwe community practices, histories, and futures. Specifically, she looks to how Indigenous knowledge systems can help reimagine decision making, problem solving, and research practices.

Victor Villanueva is Regents Professor Emeritus, a former director of comp, director of a university-wide writing program, director of an American Studies program, English department chair (twice!), former editor of the Studies in Writing and Rhetoric monograph series of the Conference on College Composition and Communication, former head of that organization, its Exemplar, Rhetorician of the Year, and other honors—especially the honor of having worked with so many undergraduate and graduate students. His work always concerns the rhetorics of racism.

This book was typeset in 11/13 Adobe Garamond Pro by Barbara Frazier.
Typefaces used on the cover and spine were Electra and Gill Sans.
The book was printed on 50-lb. white, offset paper.